Computer Dictionary

and

Handbook

Computer Dictionary and Handbook

by

Charles J. Sippl

and

Roger J. Sippl

Howard W. Sams & Co., Inc.

4300 WEST 62ND ST. INDIANAPOLIS, INDIANA 46268 USA

Indianapolis, Indiana 46268

THIRD EDITION
SECOND PRINTING—1980

International Standard Book Number: 0-672-21632-9
Library of Congress Catalog Card Number: 79-67133

Printed in the United States of America.

Preface

Because personal computers are now cost-effective and require only a few hours of training, more and more systems are being used in homes and businesses. As a result, they are reaching users who are totally uninitiated in the use of computers. These users, especially those in the business community, need to learn exactly what the move to microelectronics is all about. As they search for answers, they are perplexed by the jargon used in the computer industry, and they discover that they must quickly educate themselves in computer language. They must study and master at least the basics because it is becoming very unbusinesslike, and even unfashionable, to ask exactly what is a 64K RAM, a semiconductor, or a bubble memory.

When the first computer is installed in a business, not only are the owners and managers of the business apprehensive, but also the majority of the office and administrative personnel are suspicious and even frightened by the changes that take place. Management must help these people with a calm and knowledgeable approach to explaining what is happening. Therefore, they must know something about the "mysterious" computer jargon.

Filling the need for this information is the purpose of this book. In addition to the definitions of terms, of equal value are the appendixes, which serve as a "state-of-the-art" guide section that provides a focus on the most essential elements of computer concepts that we all must review from time to time.

This is a "browsing" dictionary. It is a tutorial book that does not try to be brief. Many definitions and explanations are long and are designed to be so. Users of this book can easily and leisurely browse through the main and supplemental entries of an "area," such as "data base," to learn significant detail about the products, procedures, problems, and proliferating applications. While we have included many definitions related to the technologies, the art of programming, the basics of electronics, and the essential internal components of systems, we have limited them to as few as possible and kept them as clear and "unconfusing" as the literature makes them. Hundreds of product manuals, applications notes, inventor explanations, manufacturer descriptions, seminar notes, and conference proceedings (reprints of speeches, product reports, system descriptions, and so on) make up the base from which the definitions were analyzed and reviewed.

THE MOVE TOWARD DISTRIBUTED DATA PROCESSING

Cost containment in accounting, sales promotion and development, resource allocation, and labor expense is just one of the reasons for implementing small computer systems. Many banks, hospitals, educational institutions, large businesses, and other institutions are turning to smaller computers instead of large computers to reduce costs. With these much simpler and more effective systems, costs are identified more quickly, response to processed information is more rapid and accurate, and better planning is achieved because more "what-if" calculations can be made quickly and easily. Many low-cost flexible systems provide a quality environment that also demonstrates time savings and efficiencies. Office environments that accommodate the new collaborations between people and computers have a great effect on productivity.

Many managers who were formerly uninitiated with respect to computers have used their desktop systems to become "information experts" very quickly. They have eliminated barriers that existed between people and computers. They have not been required to learn the intricacies of the machine, the protocols, and the process of fine-honing programs. Instead they have become more able to concentrate on problems and solutions because the facts and files are instantly available, often in easy-to-analyze graphic form. The computer has been applied to the storage, search, and presentation of information; users can now respond more conveniently, confidently, and accurately to data, using the judgmental and intuitive capabilities only they and not computers possess. A new class of "knowledge workers" has arrived on the business scene. The below $10,000 microcomputer systems that rent for less than $350 a month (about a quarter of the overall cost of the average office worker's salary, "extras," and equipment) are finally doing what users want. Users no longer are forced to do "what the computer demands." The new low-cost microcomputer systems are designed to be "friendly" because most "speak" to practically any office worker in understandable "languages."

Some of the computers offered to small and very small businesses are, in effect, intelligent assistants offering techniques that lead and prompt users to find the information they need, to complete the job, or to follow the procedures required by management. Operators use specifically designed keys and "HELP" commands; they call up "menus" of available information, touching the screen or keying in responses as indicated. Many systems use voice input and output to achieve immediate response in the most often used applications. Automatic "speller programs" detect and correct the inevitable spelling errors. Procedural errors are reported immediately in English, and protected (unerasable) formats are displayed for easy fill-in. Good systems do not interfere with the way people work naturally. "Windowing" on some systems allows segments of several files to be displayed on a single screen simultaneously. Highlights, blinking, underline, movable cursors (position indicators), and easy horizontal or vertical scrolling allow movement of information on and off the screen or segments of the screen.

All this and more make computer systems convenient and powerful, and quickly useful to inexperienced managers and "knowledge workers." No programming is necessary by the operator. By simply typing a number or letter, or with a light pen or finger (with touch-sensitive screens) pointed appropriately, the menu can be made to provide multiple colors, character sizes, and type fonts; bring forth graphs and charts; draw lines; edit sentences; and bring forth even more detailed menus for special-subject data-base investigation. This is why we offer special sections in several appendixes on terminals, graphics, and data-base systems.

Low-cost desktop problem-solving computers put the power to defeat the "business-breaker," administrative overhead, where it is needed most, at the fingertips of knowledgeable users. A typical system is a compact package with the ingredients for interactive computing: a resident, LSI, ROM-based operating system; a large user memory; tape cartridge storage; crt; user-definable keyboard; multiple and selectable i/o variety; and low-cost thermal or letter-quality printer and optional plotter and crt-face copier. Many will add other options, such as voice output synthesizers, voice input recognition systems, light pens and touch-sensitive screens, etc.

The typical system just described begs for explanations, requires experienced analysis, and is fraught with dangers of technological obsolescence. This dictionary will help. LSI and ROM are fully explained in the definitions section. An operating system is a difficult topic often best left to design engineers, expert programmers, and hobby computerists; it is the demonstrated performance that counts. A "large user memory" can be something of personal choice among a wide variety of devices—magnetic disk systems (double-sided, double density, miniaturized floppy or fixed types, and so on), optical or videodisc systems with bit capacities of hundreds of billions, bubbles, CCDs, and on and on. Cathode-ray-tubes (crt's) are only one type (though the major one) of terminal, but the variety and special advantages and attributes of terminals fill books and catalogs. Input-output devices and printers or other hard-copy devices can be chosen to enhance system operation, but without care in selection they can become obsolete either before or as they are purchased.

Business people want solutions, not more problems; they want easy, smooth information storage, retrieval, and processing systems that anyone can use. They do not want complex components of a system that only expensive systems analysts and lead programmers can operate, control, and maintain. The appendix sections of this book can aid significantly in this regard, and the definition entries, particularly the depth and range of them, can help a user avoid being strangled in an office by unfriendly and unfathomable systems that won't be flexible, expandable, or easily operated. Computer systems are needed to survive in this highly complex, fiercely competitive business world. Users can afford them, and increase efficiency and profitability by using them. But, beware! Develop the knowledge now to make correct choices, to question vendor's claims intelligently, to understand demonstrations of the capabilities of competitive systems, and to make the right choices among numerous high-technology alternatives. Learn the language!

In the appendixes, we develop knowledge needed for proper software selection. Most users of small and very small business computer systems become overly concerned about software. They hear and read about packaged software, custom software, software availability on ROM cartridges, disks, cassettes, striped cards, videodiscs, and so on. They know they can create their own software or amend and adapt tried and tested programs; they can buy programs from stores, manufacturers, special software houses, through catalogs, and from competitors, associations, friends, and neighbors. Within two years after the introduction of the Radio Shack TRS-80 computer for under $600, one firm compiled a catalog (*TRS-80 Software Source*) that contained more than 4000 listings of TRS-80 software that was available from 250 vendors. The software availability problem, if there is one, is vastly overstated.

PERSONAL COMPUTERS

The packaging of more and more capabilities for logic processing, device control, information storage, communications simplicities, and intelligent decision-making onto tiny large-scale integration (LSI) and very large-scale integration (VLSI) chips at constantly dropping prices has amazed everyone both inside and outside the industry. Distributed systems using the computers based on these "cheap chips" have proved more reliable and economical by far than former standard computers and minicomputers. No computer component has decreased in price more dramatically than microprocessors and programmable memory elements. It is now almost standard to place microcomputers close to the activity using them, but this greatly increases the amount of information that must be communicated between systems and to and from outside data bases. Data bases in the form of viewdata, teletext, and other similar two-way, interactive systems will spur the sales of small computers.

Personal computers can be defined as low-cost, small (often portable), personally controllable "turnkey" (plug-and-go) microprocessor-based stored-program ease-of-use systems that accept wide ranges of peripheral memory and input-output equipment. Practically anyone can buy or rent them and use them with a minimum of training. There are endless types of applications. One list includes 5000 distinct applications of computers, and the range increases as more and more people discover ever more uses, write more programs, and find more devices and systems to control.

INTEGRATED INFORMATION SYSTEMS

In a great many offices, word-processing systems, as significantly more than typewriter replacements, have preceded office data-processing equipment. Word processing is much more than "the production of syntactic text that may be retrieved and amended." It is informative to take a glance at a description of one of the more popular word processing systems. One system built around two stand-alone devices, each controlled by a microcomputer, offers partial-page and dual-page display; printers linked to microprocessors via fiber-optic cables (light-wave communication); and 300-bit-per-second modems with RS232, Telex, and TWX communications options. They are program loadable via diskette and offer word processing (text editing) software in addition to packages that include forms, math, and sort programs. Added communications processors with separate software programs provide asynchronous communication to similarly equipped devices and data processing equipment and/or communications to Telex, TWX, and other networks. Transactions can be handled in a background mode while word processing operations are conducted on-screen. Scroll is unlimited, displays can be split into two pages for merging or processing two documents simultaneously; printing is bidirectional with optical sensors to identify top edge, left edge, and skew of paper and indicate which print wheel is in use. Printers are linked to processors via fiber-optic cable; the optical links may be used to attach shared disk drives to several machines and to printers up to a kilometer away.

It is obvious that those businesses or professional offices that purchase word processing (WP) equipment must do so with almost immediate upgrades to data processing in mind. These systems have wide ranges of expandability options that also include electronic mail. "Intelligent, communicating copiers" are becoming integral parts of such systems, offering graphics, high-speed image printing, and instant long-distance communication. Some have objectives to eliminate paper, or at least to make a start in that direction. Users have calculated that improving office efficiency by 5% increases "bottom-line" profitability by 30%. Linking WP equipment to data-processing equipment and large data bases and communicating with automated copier/printers seems like such a "natural thing" that most of the latest equipment systems offerings point in this direction. How fast these mergers take place depends on how simply it can be done. Again, look to the use of a multitude of $5 to $15 microprocessors embedded within the equipment—accepting, processing, controlling, and being programmable, too, all at reasonable costs while eliminating large numbers of mechanical devices and fixed (and expensive) electronics in each device.

Every manager, in order to be in the loop, must have a desktop computer. Some executives are reported to have two and even three desktop computers in their offices, each with specific capabilities for WP, data processing, communications (data-base retrieval), and special graphics hard-copy production. Users cannot simply tack on a computer-oriented applications package to a WP system and vice-versa; there is the significant technical problem of creating the ability to have access to the same files and to allow programmability to be available to word processing as well as data processing. "Bandage" approaches simply will not work.

We end this introduction with this observation: clearly, technology is far ahead of the users. Systems are capable of doing more things than users are able to put into practice. The prices and the efficiencies are so attractive that users are starting to understand and want these systems; and, they will learn how to use, control, and expand them despite the challenges. They will do this with education, and books such as this can play an important part in that pursuit.

CHARLES J. SIPPL
ROGER J. SIPPL

Acknowledgments

The authors wish to express their thanks and appreciation to practically every major firm in the computer industry for their willingness to cooperate in supplying information necessary for the completion of this text. Some individuals and firms were especially generous in supplying manuals, photographs, and other miscellaneous materials for the first edition. We welcome the opportunity to list some of their names: R. P. (Bud) Hurst, Robert F. Korinke, and R. S. Cecil, all of IBM; Don Sanden and Henry Lee of GE; Michael Frawley and H. R. Wise of NCR; Harold Clark of the Union Bank of Los Angeles; C. H. Simmons and W. M. Aamoth of UNIVAC; Henry J. Meier, Jr., of Burroughs; Robert G. Strayton of Honeywell; Thomas I. Bradshaw of RCA; Richard F. Musson and Jerry Murphy of Digital Equipment Co.; Thomas Buchholz of Control Data Corporation; Clyde C. Ball of Philco. Some of our academic colleagues who were of particular assistance are Dr. Herbert Stone, California State College at Long Beach; Dr. Donald Moore, California State College at Los Angeles; Dr. Taylor Meloan, University of Southern California; Dr. Harold Somers and Dr. William Allen, University of California, Los Angeles; and Thomas Badger and Marion Shapiro, University of California Extension.

About the Authors

Charles J. Sippl is a writer, educator, and consultant to the computer, communications, and solar-control-systems industries. He is the author of the article "Computers" for the *Encyclopaedia Britannica* and more than a dozen dictionaries and professional books. He obtained his Bachelor of Science degree from the University of Wisconsin and his Master of Arts degree from the University of Miami (Florida). His work toward a PhD degree was accomplished at the University of California at Berkeley and Los Angeles. He has taught computer and management science courses at several California universities and has offered seminars and lectures to financial analysts and military procurement officers throughout the United States.

Roger J. Sippl is a computer science graduate of the University of California at Berkeley. He is a consultant in medical computer systems technology as well as a course developer, teacher, and seminar leader. He is coauthor with his father of two books. He has been a software development project leader and continues with his specialty of data-base management system software.

How To Use This Book

In the dictionary entries, all terms of more than one word have been alphabetized as though they were one word. For example, "demand fetching" appears between "demand" and "demand paging." Abbreviations are alphabetized as though they were words; for example, LFU appears between "lexicon" and "librarian" instead of at the beginning of the L section.

For ease in locating terms, the first and last entries on each page appear as catch words at the top of the page.

Extensive cross-referencing has been used as an aid in locating terms you might look for in more than one place. For example, there are entries for both "self-checking code" and "code, self-checking."

Contents

A

ABA — Abbreviation for American Bankers Association.

abacus — A device for performing calculations by sliding beads or counters along rods. An early (3000 B.C.) form of biquinary calculator.

ABA number — A coding number assigned to banks by the American Bankers Association to assist in check clearing.

ABEND, unrecoverable — An error condition that results in abnormal termination of a program, in contrast with recoverable ABEND.

abort — A procedure to terminate execution of a program when an irrecoverable error, mistake, or malfunction occurs.

abort timer, communication — A device designed to monitor dial-up (DDD) modems continuously for receipt of data traffic. If, after a call is established, data is not received within a preset (adjustable) time, the abort timer will disconnect (hang up) the call, making the modem available for additional users.

abrasiveness — The quality or characteristic of being able to abrade, scratch, or wear away a material. An important factor in optical character recognition where damage to the read screen may affect the reading process detrimentally and cause a large reject rate.

absolute address — 1. An actual location in storage of a particular unit of data; address that the control unit can interpret directly. 2. The label assigned by the engineer to a particular storage area in the computer. 3. A pattern of characters that identifies a unique storage location or device without further modification. (Synonymous with machine address.)

absolute addressing — A method of signaling or addressing which has the address part of an instruction as the actual address to be specified, and in which the address part is called the absolute address.

absolute assembler — A specific type of assembly-language program designed to produce binary programs containing only absolute addresses and address references.

absolute code — *See* code, absolute.

absolute coding — Coding in which instructions are written in the basic machine language; i.e., coding using absolute operators and addresses. Coding that does not require processing before it can be understood by the computer.

absolute error — The magnitude of the error disregarding the algebraic sign, or if a vectorial error, disregarding its direction.

absolute instruction — *See* instruction, absolute.

absolute language — *Same as* machine language.

absolute loader — A specific loader routine designed to load programs and associated data in the absolute address format and into the system memory for execution.

absolute value — A particular quantity, the magnitude of which is known by the computer, but the algebraic sign is not relevant.

abstract — 1. A short form or summary of a document. 2. To shorten or summarize a document.

abstracting, automatic — Searching for the criteria by which human beings judge what should be abstracted from a document, as programmed.

abstracting service — An organization that provides summary information or documents in a given subject field.

abstract symbol — *See* symbol, abstract.

A-bus — The primary internal source bus in the ALU of many microcomputers.

ACC — Abbreviation for accumulator.

acceleration period — The period of time in which a card reader and/or punch physically move(s) the card into a position where the data can be read.

acceleration time — The time between the interpretation of instructions to read or write on tape, and the transfer of information to or from the tape into storage, or from storage into tape, as the case may be. (Synonymous with start time.)

access — Concerns the process of obtaining data from or placing data in storage.

access-address, second-level — *Same as* address, indirect.

access, arbitrary — *See* arbitrary access.

access coding, minimal — The reference to programming which is done in order to locate the data in such a manner as to reduce the access time and minimize the amount of time required to transfer words from auxiliary storage to main memory.

access, direct — A memory device which allows the particular address to be accessed in a manner independent of the location of that address; thus, the items stored in the memory can be addressed or accessed in the same amount of time for each location. Consequently, access by a program is not dependent upon the previously accessed position.

access, disk — *See* disk access.

access, immediate — Pertaining to the ability to directly obtain data from, or place data in, a storage device or register without serial delay due to other units of data, and usually in a relatively short period of time.

access, instantaneous — *Same as* access, immediate.

access method — The software link between the program and the data that must be transferred in and out of memory by the program. It is defined by both the physical and logical file structures and the properties of the programming languages and operating systems involved. Examples of access methods are serial access, virtual sequential access method (VSAM), indexed or keyed sequential access method (ISAM or KSAM), and hierarchical indexed sequential access method.

access mode — In COBOL, a technique that is used to obtain a specific logic record from, or place a specific logic record into, a file assigned to a mass-storage device.

access, multiple — Reference to a system from which output or input can be received or dispatched from more than one location.

access, parallel — The process of obtaining information from storage or placing information in storage, where the time required for such access is dependent on the simultaneous transfer of all elements of a word from a given storage location. (Synonymous with simultaneous access.)

access, queried — Referencing to an automatic sequencing of the transfer of data among the peripherals under the control of the program.

access, random — 1. Pertains to the process of obtaining information from or placing information in storage, where the time required for such access is independent of the location of the information most recently obtained or placed in storage. 2. Pertaining to a device in which random access, as defined in definition 1, can be achieved without effective penalty in time.

access, remote batch — Remote access to information and remote access for information are the keys that have pushed data communications to its position of growth and controversy at the present time. The time-sharing concept in its broadest definition also includes message switching, data acquisition, intercomputer communication, data bank, and the transfer and servicing of large amounts of lower-priority and lower cost "stacked-job" processing.

access scan — A procedure for receiving data from the files by searching each data item until the desired one is obtained.

access, sequential — *See* sequential-access storage.

access, serial — Pertains to the process of obtaining information from or placing information in storage, where the time required for such access is dependent on the necessity for waiting while nondesired storage locations are processed in turn.

access, simultaneous — *See* access, parallel.

access storage devices, direct — Units of computer equipment which have capabilities of direct and rapid access to storage.

access storage, immediate access — *See* storage, immediate access.

access time — 1. The time interval between the instant at which information is called for from storage and the instant at which delivery is completed, i.e., the read time. 2. The time interval between the instant at which data are ready for storage and the instant at which storage is completed, i.e., the write time.

access time, reading — *See* reading access time.

access time, storage, zero — *See* storage, zero-access.

access time, tape — The time during tape playback between the moment information is called for and the moment it is delivered.

access, zero — The capability of a device to transfer data in or out of a location without undue delays, i.e., due to other units of data. The transfer occurs in a parallel fashion or simultaneously and not serially.

accounting — Some executive systems include an accounting function which maintains an accurate and equitable record of machine-time usage. This information, logged on an appropriate output unit, is available to the user for his own purposes.

accounting checks — Accuracy controls on input data that are based on such accounting principles as control totals, cross totals, or hash totals.

accumulator — A part of the logical-arithmetic unit of a computer. It may be used for intermediate storage, to form algebraic sums, or for other intermediate operations. *See* register.

accumulator jump instruction — An instruction that tells the computer to leave the established program sequence at or after the time the accumulator has reached a certain status.

accumulator register — That part of the arithmetic unit in which the results of an operation remain, and into which numbers are brought from storage, and from which numbers may be taken for storage.

accumulator, running — A memory device which has been programmed so as to make the next item of data retrieved the one that was put in most recently. This method of retrieval is also called the push-down list.

accumulator shift instruction — A computer instruction that causes the contents of a register to be displaced by some specific number of digit positions left or right.

accuracy — Freedom from error. Accuracy contrasts with precision; e.g., a four-place table, correctly computed, is accurate; a six-place table containing an error is more precise, but not more accurate.

accuracy-control system — A system of error detection and control.

ac dump — The intentional, accidental, or conditional removal of all alternating current or power from a system or component. An ac dump usually results in the removal of all power, since direct current is usually supplied through a rectifier or converter.

ac erasing — To erase magnetic recording material by using a device that is powered with alternating current.

acetate base — Magnetic tapes that have a transparent backing of cellulose acetate film.

ACIA — Abbreviation for Asynchronous Communications Interface Adapter. An ACIA provides the data formatting and control to interface serial asynchronous data communications information to bus organized systems. The bus interface of some systems includes select, enable, read/write, interrupt, and bus interface logic to allow data transfer over various bidirectional data buses. In many systems, data transmission is accomplished in the serial mode; many MPUs have bus systems that operate in the parallel mode. By performing parallel-to-serial and serial-to-parallel conversions, the ACIA provides the means for communications between the MPU and peripheral equipment such as modems, TTYs, crt terminals, keyboard/printers, and other equipment requiring an asynchronous data format.

ACK/NAK transmission — When an error-detecting scheme is used, some means must be provided for retransmission of the block in error. The receiver may signal the sender with an acknowledgment (ACK) of error-free receipt or a negative acknowledgment (NAK) of error detection. To allow for lost messages, the sender usually retransmits upon receipt of an NAK or when a specified time has elapsed without receipt of an ACK. This is one form of automatic repeat request (ARQ).

ACM — Abbreviation for Association for Computing Machinery.

A-conversion — A FORTRAN instruction to transmit alphanumeric data to and from variables in storage.

acoustic coupler — A device that provides an interface between a printer or display terminal and a standard commercial telephone line through a standard telephone handset. The handset fits into two rubber muffs mounted in a small enclosure. The interface often is entirely acoustic, with one muff containing a speaker and the other a microphone. The acoustic coupler circuitry generally converts EIA-level digital signals from the terminal transmitter to frequency shift keyed (fsk) tones to drive the speaker. It also converts fsk tones from the microphone to EIA-level digital signals to drive the terminal receiver.

acoustic delay line — A device using regenerated shock waves in a conducting medium (for example, mercury) for storing information.

acoustic memory — Computer memory that uses a sonic delay line.

acoustic modem — Any of various types of modulator-demodulator devices that convert electrical signals to telephone tones and back again. The conversion occurs through acoustic coupling (placing speakers near the phone) or direct coupling to the line. Most modems use the RS-232C interface standard.

acquisition, data — *See* data acquisition.

acquisition system, data — *See* data-acquisition system.

acronym — A word formed from the first letter or letters of the words in a name, term, or phrase; e.g., SAGE from Semi-Automatic Ground Environment, and ALGOL from ALGOrithmic Language.

ac signaling — The use of alternating-current signals or tones to accomplish transmission of information and/or control signals.

action cycle — Refers to the complete operation performed on data. Includes basic steps of origination, input, manipulation, output, and storage.

action line — That line of the raster which is used during the active period when a cathode-ray storage tube is operating in a serial mode.

action period — *See* period, action.

action spot — In a cathode-ray tube, the spot of the raster on the face of the tube used to store the digit or character.

activate key (button) — *See* button, initiate.

active element — A circuit or device that receives energy from a source other than the main input signal.

active file — A file which is being used and to which entries or references are made on a current basis.

active master file — A master file containing items which are relatively active as contrasted to static or reference items.

active master item — The most active items on a master file measured by usage of the data.

activity — 1. A term to indicate that a record in a master file is used, altered, or referred to. 2. A measure of the changes made concerning the use of files of data; e.g., the part of the file or the number of records.

activity level — The value taken by a structural variable in an intermediate or final solution to a programming problem.

activity ratio — When a file is processed, the ratio of the number of records that have activity to the total number of records in that file.

actual address — *See* address, actual.

actual instruction — *See* instruction, effective.

actual time — *Same as* time, real.

actuating signal — A particular input pulse in the control circuity of computers.

ACU — Automatic Calling Unit. Any of various dialing devices supplied by communications carriers or available for purchase elsewhere that permit business machines and computers to dial calls automatically over the communications network.

acyclic feeding — A system employed by character readers in character recognition which senses the trailing edge of the preceding document and triggers automatically the feeding of the following document. This system allows character recognition of varying sized documents.

A/D analog-digital converter — Circuit used to convert information in analog form into digital form, e.g., in digital voltmeters and other devices.

ADAPSO — An association of United States and Canadian data processing service organizations that includes a software development and marketing group.

adapter, channel — A device that permits connections between various data channels of differing equipment. Most devices permit data transfer at the rate of the slower channel.

adapter unit, display — *See* display adapter unit.

adapting — This concerns the ability of a system to change its performance characteristics in response to its environment.

adapting, self — The ability of a computer system to change its performance characteristics in response to its environment.

adaptive channel allocation — A method of multiplexing in which the information capacities of channels are not predetermined but are assigned on demand.

adaptive control action — Various types of control actions by which automatic means are used to change the type and/or influence of control parameters in such a way as to improve the performance of the control system.

ADC — Analog-to-Digital Converter. A device or circuit that changes input analog voltages to their equivalent digital (binary or binary-coded decimal) values for acceptance by the memory of a digital processor.

ADCCP — Advanced Data Communication Control Procedures.

ADCON (address constant) — A value or expression used to calculate the real or virtual storage addresses.

A/D converter — An A/D converter performs the operations of quantizing and coding a signal in a finite amount of time that depends on the resolution of the converter and the particular conversion method used. The speed of conversion required in a particular situation depends on the time variation of the signal to be converted and the amount of resolution required. The time required to make a measurement or conversion is generally called the aperture time.

add, Boolean — Same as OR in set theory. *Same as* OR gate, positive.

addend — The number or quantity to be added to another number or quantity (augend) to produce the result (sum).

adder — A device that forms as an output, the sum of two or more numbers presented as inputs. Often no data retention feature is included; i.e., the output signal remains only as long as the input signals are present.

adder, analog — An amplifier (analog computer) with output voltage which is the weighted sum of the input voltages. The heights correspond to the positional significance of a given numbering system and would be proportional to the conductances of the circuit elements in the input leads.

adder, digital — *See* digital adder.

add-in memories — Various types of memories are available to expand internal memory. Two semiconductor types are in general use—bipolar and MOS (metal-oxide-silicon). Of the two types, bipolar can be faster but is higher in cost. It consumes more power and, therefore, dissipates more heat. MOS memories are more compact, and their speed is sufficient for most applications.

addition — In data processing, that function of combining quantities according to various circuitry designs, specific machine rules regarding changes in values, and types of carryover operations.

additional character — A character that is neither a letter nor a number, but that is usually a punctuation mark, %, *, #; i.e., a member of a specialized alphabet. Specific meanings are assigned to this character to use it to convey special information.

addition, destructive — The sum appears in the location previously occupied by the augend which is thus lost. The addend remains in its original location.

addition item — An item that is to be added at a specific place to an already established file. Addition master item would be the proper term if file is a master file.

addition, nondestructive — The first operand placed in the arithmetic register is the augend, the next operand is the addend, and the sum replaces the augend and thus becomes the augend for a subsequent addition.

addition record — A record that results in the creation of a new record in the master file that is being updated.

addition, serial — A special addition procedure in which the corresponding digit pairs of the numbers added are processed individually beginning with the low-order digits. Carries, in general, are propagated as they occur.

addition table — The area of main storage that holds a table of numbers to be used during the table-scan concept of addition.

addition, zero access — Similar to immediate access. Addition is performed by adding a number to one already stored in an accumulator, and the sum is formed in the same accumulator. The sum is thus available for the next operation, and no access time is involved for the addend or the sum storage.

add, logical — A Boolean algebra operation on two binary numbers. The result is one if either one or both numbers are a one; if both digits are zero, then the result is zero.

add operation — An add instruction in which the result is the sum, and the result is usually apparent in the storage location previously occupied by one of the operands.

address — 1. A label, name, or number identifying a register, location, or unit where information is stored. 2. The operand part of an instruction. 3. In communications, the coded representation of the destination of a message. 4. To call a specific piece of information from the memory or to put it in the memory.

addressable-pollable terminal — A terminal is addressable when it has its own unique identifier. All data sent to the terminal must be preceded by their addresses. Pollable means that the terminal responds to status inquiries from the computer. Each terminal in the system is queried by the computer in succession. The ability of the terminal to respond to the poll and to identify itself makes it pollable.

addressable register — A temporary storage location with a fixed location and address number.

address, absolute — An address that indicates the exact storage location where the referenced operand is to be found or stored in the actual machine-code address numbering system. (Synonymous with specific address, and related to absolute code.)

address, actual — The real or designed address built into the computer by the manufacturer as a storage location or register. Adjacent addresses usually have adjacent numbers. It is the specific or machine address that is used particularly in diagnosing machine faults.

address alignment — Most computers offer more efficient manipulation of character data when certain alignments are observed. Alignment is related both to the way data is addressed by the machine instructions and by the way data is transferred from the memory to the processor. On word machines, this transfer is usually done word by word, whereas on byte machines it is done one byte at a time, two bytes at a time (starting with even address), or four bytes at a time on the fastest machines (starting with addresses divisible by 8). These four options then correspond to no alignment, half-word alignment, full-word alignment, and double-word alignment, respectively.

address, arithmetic — A technique of assembly language which appends an address modifier, consisting of a sign and from one to four decimal digits, to a symbolic tag in order to designate a memory location address location which relates to the location represented by the tag. *See* relative address.

address, base — 1. A number that appears as an address in a computer instruction, but which serves as the base, index, initial or starting point for subsequent addresses to be modified. (Synonymous with presumptive address and reference address.) 2. A number used in symbolic coding in conjunction with a relative address.

address, binary-coded — An address which is expressed in binary form—sometimes lacking the absolute or machine address.

address bus — A unidirectional bus over which appears digital information that identifies either a particular memory location or a particular i/o device.

address, calculated — An address most often generated or developed by machine instructions contained in the program which uses the address. This address may be determined as a result of some program or process and it may depend upon some condition or set of criteria.

address, checking file program — A program to check addresses, when macros instruct to write on the file, to see that the program is not writing on the wrong area.

address code, single — *See* code, single-address.

address code, zero — *See* code, zero address.

address comparator — A device used to verify that the correct address is being read. The comparison is made between the address being read and the specified address.

address computation — A computation that produces or modifies the address portion of an instruction.

address, constant — *See* address, base.

address conversion — The translation of the symbolic addresses or relative addresses into absolute addresses by using the computer and an assembly program or by manual means.

address, counter program register — *Same as* address, program counter.

address, direct — An address that indicates the location where the referenced operand is to be found or stored with no reference to an index register or B-box (Synonymous with first-level address.)

address, direct reference — A virtual address that is not modified by indirect addressing, but may be modified by indexing.

address, double — *Same as* address, indirect.

address, dummy — An artificial address used for illustration or instruction purposes.

addressed location, specific — To aid in random access, data may be directly stored and retrieved from a specific addressed location without the need for a sequential search as is necessary with magnetic tape.

addressed location, specified — *Same as* addressed location, specific.

addressed memory — Memory sections containing each individual register.

address effective — 1. A modified address. 2. The address actually considered to be used in a particular execution of a computer instruction. 3. An address obtained by the combination of the contents of a specific index register with the address of an instruction.

address, effective virtual — The virtual address value after only indirect addressing and/or indexing modifications have been accomplished, but before memory mapping is performed.

addresses of address — Programming technique used mainly with subroutines.

address field — The specific portion of a computer word that contains either the address of the operand or the information necessary to derive that address.

address field, disk — On some systems, an address field contains the track and sector addresses for the sector that follows. One type consists of four bytes of address information followed by two bytes of cyclic redundancy check (CRC).

address, first-level — *Same as* address, direct.

address, floating — Formerly, an address written in such a way that it could easily be converted to a machine address by indexing, assembly, or by some other means.

address format — The arrangement of the address parts of an instruction. The expression "plus-one" is frequently used to indicate that one of the addresses specifies the location of the next instruction to be executed, such as one plus one, two plus one, three plus one, four plus one.

address, four — A method of specifying the location of operands and instructions; the storage location of the two operands and the storage location of the results of the operation are cited, and the storage location of the next instruction to be executed is also cited.

address, four plus one — An arrangement of the address parts of an instruction. The use of "plus" is to indicate that one of the addresses states or specifies the location of the next instruction to be executed, such as, one "plus" one, two "plus" one, etc.

address, functional instruction — *See* address instruction, functional.

address, generated — *Same as* address, calculated.

address, immediate — An instruction address in which the address part of the instruction is the operand. (Synonymous with zero-level address.)

address, indexed — An address that is to be modified or has been modified by an index register or similar device. (Synonymous with variable address.)

address, indirect — 1. An address that specifies a storage location whose content is either an indirect address or another indirect address. 2. A single instruction address that is at once the address of another address. The second address is the specific address of the data to be processed. This is classified as single-level indirect addressing. But, the second address could also be indirect, which is then second-level indirect addressing. This same process could develop third, fourth, fifth, and other levels of indirect addressing.

address, indirect reference — A reference address in an instruction that contains a 1 in bit position 0; the virtual address of the location that contains the direct address. If indirect addressing is called for by an instruction, the reference address field is used to access a word location that contains the direct reference address; this then replaces the indirect reference address and is used as an operand address value. Indirect addressing is limited to one level and is performed prior to indexing (some computers).

addressing — Any memory location can be addressed in any one of three formats: direct, indirect, or indexed addressing. The use of binary addressing eliminates the necessity of complex machine-language coding schemes to represent memory addresses in expanded configurations. Index-register usage is by no means restricted; indexed addressing is possible in all instruction formats. In addition, indexed addressing is simplified by a convenient loop-control technique that automatically increments and tests index register contents.

addressing, common data bus — In some systems, during execution, instructions and data defined in a program are stored into and loaded from specific memory locations, the accumulator, or selected registers. Because in some microprocessors the memory (read/write and read-only) and peripherals are on a common data bus, any instruction used to address memory may be used to address peripherals.

addressing, deferred — Preferred term for indirect addressing in which the address part specifies a location containing an address, and which in turn specifies a location containing an address, etc., until the specified location address is eventually found. A preset or conditioned number of iterations is set by a termination indicator.

addressing, direct — A procedure for specifically citing an operand in the instruction by the operand's location in storage. The direct address is the number representing the storage location.

addressing, disk file — The operation that locates information on a random access file.

addressing, file pockets — In a random file, a small area or pocket in which one or more records are kept. This is an economical method of holding a small number of records.

addressing, fixed-position — Permits selective updating of tape information, as in magnetic disk or drum storage devices. Units as small as a single computer word may be stored or recorded on tape without disturbing adjacent information. Data blocks are numbered and completely addressable. Interrecord gaps are eliminated, thereby increasing tape-storage capacity.

addressing, hash — A calculation of the approximate address of a record in a file by some semi-empirical function.

addressing, immediate — A particular system of specifying the locations of operands and instructions in the same storage location, i.e., at the same address. This is contrasted with normal addressing in which the instruction word is stored at one address or location and contains the addresses of other locations in which the operands are stored.

addressing, implied — *Same as* addressing, repetitive.

addressing, indexed — An addressing mode in which the address part of an instruction is modified by the contents in an auxiliary (index) register during the execution of that instruction.

addressing, indirect — 1. A method of computer cross reference in which one memory location indicates where the correct address of the main fact can be found. 2. Any level of addressing other than the first level of direct addressing. 3. Translation of symbolic instructions into machine-language instructions on a computer other than that for which the program was written.

addressing level — A determination of the number of steps of indirect address which have been applied to a particular program. First level is direct addressing, i.e., the address part of the instruction word has the address of the operand in storage. In second level addressing (indirect), the address part of the instruction word gives the storage location where the address of the operand may be found.

addressing, multilevel — *Same as* address, indirect.

addressing, one-ahead — *Same as* addressing, repetitive.

addressing, real-time — *Same as* addressing, immediate.

addressing, relative — A procedure or method of addressing in which the absolute address is obtained by means of the address modification, either simulated or actual, and is performed by the addition of a given number to the address part of an instruction, i.e., the address part of the presumptive instruction is known as the relative address.

addressing, repetitive — A specific method of addressing for some computers which have a variable instruction format. Instructions which have a zero address instruction format, for example, refer again automatically to the location affected by the last instruction executed.

addressing, self-relative — In relative addressing, the number added corresponds to the address of the instruction under consideration.

addressing, specific — A procedure or method of addressing in which the address part of an instruction is the actual address to be specified, i.e., the address part is known as the specific address or the absolute address.

addressing, stepped — *See* addressing, repetitive.

addressing, symbolic — The procedure for using alphabetic or alphanumeric labels to specify various storage locations for particular programs; i.e., before program execution, the symbolic address is converted to an absolute address.

addressing, three-level — Instruction words contain the address which specifies the storage location of the address which, in turn, has the address of the storage location which contains the address of the operand, i.e., three references to storage locations for obtaining the desired operand.

addressing, two-level — A procedure for addressing in which the instruction word changes addresses designating the storage locations where the addresses of the operands are to be found. If two references in storage locations need to be obtained, this will use an indirect address and a second level address.

addressing types — Many microcomputers have ten or more memory addressing modes that address all words, bytes, and individual bits, sometimes in a full range of 64K words of memory. Some are: direct, direct indexed, indirect, indirect indexed, program relative, program relative indirect, base relative, base relative indexed, base relative indirect, base relative indirect/indexed, and literal.

addressing, virtual — *Same as* addressing, immediate.

addressing, zero-level — *Same as* addressing, immediate.

address, instruction — The address of the storage location where the instruction word is stored. The next instruction to be performed is determined by the control program of the instruction addresses, and the machine control automatically refers to these addresses sequentially unless otherwise directed to skip or branch, or directed by other schemes.

address instruction, functional — An instruction that has no particular operation part since the operation is specified by the address parts, i.e., some two addresses which are specified might designate storage locations having contents which are always added.

address instruction, immediate — A specific instruction which contains the value of the operand in its address part rather than the address of the operand. It is used most often for incrementing a count by a fixed amount, or masking a partial-word field of data, or for testing a special character for identical characteristics with the immediate character in the instruction.

address instruction, operational — *Same as* address instruction, functional.

address instruction, three — *Same as* address, three.

address instruction, three-plus-one — *Same as* address, four.

address instruction, two-plus-one — *Same as* address, three.

addressless instruction format — A particular instruction format which contains no address part, used either when no address is required, or when the address is in some way implicit.

address, machine — An absolute, direct, unindexed address expressed as such, or resulting after indexing and other processing has been completed.

address marks, disk — Special address marks are obtained by coding specific combinations of data and clock bits. On some disks, the special combinations of data and clock bits can be decoded as any binary pattern to trigger recognition of an index address mark or an ID address mark, or a deleted address mark.

address, microprocessor — The addressing capacity of a microprocessor is a function of the number of address lines maintained by the processor. The most common address size is 65,536 memory locations and is referred to as 64K or 65K words or bytes of memory, where K stands for 1024. It takes 16 bits of address information to address 64K. For a 16-bit machine, this is a natural size. For an 8-bit processor, two bytes are used to give the 16-bit address. Some 8-bit processors address only 4K, 8K, or 16K. The 4-bit processors usually have limited addressing capability, perhaps 1K to 4K bytes. The addressing capacity of a microcomputer often defines both the number of memory locations and the number of input/output (i/o) devices accessible, since many of the microprocessors access i/o devices directly via memory addresses.

address modes, microprocessor — Processor addressing modes include sequential, forward, or backward addressing, address indexing, indirect addressing, 16-bit word addressing, 8-bit byte addressing, and stack addressing. Variable-length instruction formatting allows a minimum number of words to be used for each addressing mode. The result is efficient use of program storage space.

address modification — 1. The process of changing the address part of a machine instruction by means of coded instruction. 2. A change in the address portion of an instruction or command such that, if the routine containing the instruction or command is repeated, the computer will go to a new address or location for data or instructions. *See* address computation.

address, multiple — A type of instruction that specifies the addresses of two or more items which may be the addresses of locations of inputs or outputs of the calculating unit, or the addresses of locations of instructions for the control unit. The term multiaddress is also used in characterizing computers, e.g., two-, three-, or four-address machines. (Synonymous with multiaddress.)

address, Nth-level — An indirect address which might be second level, third level addresses, etc., that specify addresses of desired operands.

address one — *Same as* single address.

address, one-level — *Same as* direct address.

address, one plus one — An instruction system having the property that each complete instruction includes an operation and two addresses, one for the location of a register in the storage containing the item to be operated upon, and one for the location containing the next instruction.

address, operand — In indirect addressing, the address of the instruction refers to a location whose content is not the operand but rather the address of the operand. The address of the operand is called the indirect address, usually signaled as an indirect address by the presence of an extra flag bit.

address, operand effective — An address obtained at the time of execution by the computer to give the actual operand address.

address, P — Location to which the program branches, or to which data is transposed (certain equipment).

address, page — The eight high-order bits of a virtual address or an actual address, which represent a page of memory (some computers).

address part — The part of an instruction word that defines the address of a register or locations.

address, presumptive — *See* address, base.

address, program counter — A register in which the address of the current instruction is recorded.

address, Q — A source location in internal storage of some types of equipment, from which data is transferred.

address, quadruple — *Same as* address, four.

address, real-time — *Same as* address, immediate.

address, reference — A number that appears as an address in a computer instruction, but which serves as the base, index, initial or starting point for subsequent addresses to be modified. (Synonymous with presumptive address.)

address, regional — A specific address usually set within a series of consecutive addresses, such as in the A region of consecutive addresses.

address register — A register in which an address is stored.

address, register field — The portion of an instruction word that contains a register address.

address, relative — A label used to identify a word in a routine or subroutine with respect to its position in that routine or subroutine. Relative addresses are translated into absolute addresses by the addition of some specific "reference" address, usually that at which the first word of the routine is stored; e.g., if a relative-address instruction specified an address N, and the address of the first word of the routine is K, then the absolute address is N + K.

address, result — That address into which the results of an arithmetic process are transferred.

address, second-level — *Same as* address, indirect.

address, single — A system of machine instructions in which each complete instruction explicitly describes one operation and involves one storage location. (Related to one-address instruction.)

address, single-level — *Same as* direct address.

address size — The maximum number of binary digits in an instruction used in directly addressing memory.

address source, instruction — *Same as* address instruction, functional.

address, specific — An address that indicates the exact storage location where the referenced operand is to be found or stored in the actual machine-code address numbering system. (Related to absolute code.)

address storage, display lights — The various indicator lights on the control panel that specify the bit pattern in a selected address.

address, symbolic — 1. A label chosen to identify a particular word, function, or other information in a routine, independent of the location of the information within the routine; floating address. 2. A label, alphabetic or alphameric, used to specify a storage location in the context of a particular program. Often, programs are first written using symbolic addresses in some convenient code which is then translated into absolute addresses by an assembly program.

address, synthetic — *Same as* address, calculated.

address system, one-over-one — A machine-language system that uses two addresses; one of these may be a reference for data.

address, third-level — In an indirect or multilevel addressing system, the third address sought in the attempt to arrive at the location of an operand. The machine interprets the contents of the first two storage locations as addresses rather than as operands.

address, three — A method of specifying the location of operands and instruction in which the storage location of the two operands and the storage location of the results of the operations are cited, and in which the location or address of the next instruction to be executed is also to be specified, e.g., addend, augend, and sum addresses all specified in one instruction word.

address, three-plus-one — *Same as* address, four.

address, triple — *Same as* address, three.

address, two — An instruction that includes an operation and specifies the location of an operand and the result of the operation.

address, two-level — *Same as* address, indirect.

address, variable — An address that is to be modified or has been modified by an index register or similar device.

address, virtual — *Same as* address, immediate.

address, zero-level — An instruction address in which the address part of the instruction is the operand.

add, special — This is similar to double-precision addition in that it concerns addition of numbers having twice as many digits as the particular computer register is capable of containing.

add-subtract time — The time required to perform an addition or subtraction, exclusive of the time required to obtain the quantities from storage and put the sum or difference back in storage.

add time — *See* time, add.

add to storage — The process which immediately enters the final sum of the accumulator into the computer memory.

add without carry gate — *Same as* gate, exclusive OR.

A/D Interface — Several firms offer a "building block" subsystem useful for implementation of the analog-to-digital conversion (ADC) function. The devices permit the construction of high performance ADCs at a fraction of the cost of comparable modular units. With this subsystem, the critical analog processing is done on the monolithic chip, and the less critical digital system of counters and gates is left for the system designer to implement.

ADIS — Abbreviation for A Data Interchange System.

adjacency — 1. Relates to character recognition and printing conditions. Reference lines designate spacing between two consecutive characters. 2. A condition in character recognition in which two consecutive characters, either printed or handwritten, are closer than the specified distance.

adjacent channel — A channel whose frequency band is adjacent to that of the reference channel.

adjacent-channel interference — Such interference or "noise" occurs when two modulated carrier channels are situated or placed too close together in frequency so that one or both sidebands extend from one channel into the other.

adjacent-channel selectivity — Receivers have characteristics which govern their ability to reject signals or channels adjacent to that of the desired signals.

adjustment, character — The address adjustment in which the literal used to modify the address has reference to a specific given number or group of characters.

administrative data processing — An expression usually meaning business data processing such as the recording, classifying, or summarizing of transactions, activities, events, etc. Usually of a financial nature, or the collection, retrieval, or control of such items.

admissible mark — *See* mark, admissible.

ADP (Automatic Data Processing) — 1. Pertaining to equipment such as EAM (Electronic Accounting Machines) and EDP (Electronic Data Processing) equipment units or systems. 2. Data processing performed by a system of electronic or electrical machines so interconnected and interacting as to reduce to a minimum the need for human assistance or intervention.

ADPE — Abbreviation for Automatic Data Processing Equipment.

ADPS — Abbreviation for Automatic Data Processing System.

AFIPS — Abbreviation for American Federation of Information Processing Societies, an association of American data processing groups formerly called AFID.

agenda — The set of control-language statements used to prescribe a solution path or run procedures; an ordered list of the major operations constituting a procedure for a solution or computer run. (This usage corresponds roughly to the ordinary "agenda" for a meeting.)

A ignore B gate, negative — *See* gate, B ignore A negative.

A implies B gate — *Same as* gate, B OR-NOT A.

A implies B gate, negative — *Same as* gate, A AND-NOT B.

alarm — A signal, by display or audio device, which signifies that an error has occurred, or an emergency condition exists that is interfering or could interfere with the proper execution or completion of a program.

alarm, audible — This is an audio signal which indicates that a predetermined condition has been met or detected, that a malfunction has occurred in the equipment, or that a program error or a problem condition exists.

alarm display — A visual display signal such as on a crt or radar screen which would alert the operator to conditions which require attention.

alarm-repeated transmission — An audible alarm which sounds after three successive failures to transmit (or receive) a line.

alertor — A device to watch the man who watches the machine. The alertor consists of a small box connected to a large floor pad laced with wires. Any movement on the pad keeps the box content. But, should there be no movement from the operator during a suspicious interval of time, the alertor concludes he is either inattentive or napping, and sounds an alarm.

algebra, Boolean — *See* Boolean algebra.

algebraic expression — A statement expressed in various symbols, signs, and abbreviations following mathematical rules and syntax to designate variables, constants, functions, and rules.

algebraic language — *See* language, algebraic.

Algebraic Language, International — *See* Language, International Algebraic.

ALGOL — 1. ALGOrithmic Language. An arithmetic language by which numerical procedures may be precisely presented to a computer in a standard form. The language is intended not only as a means of directly presenting any numerical procedure to any suitable computer for which a compiler exists, but also as a means of communicating numerical procedures among individuals. The language itself is a result of international cooperation to obtain a standardized algorithmic language. The International Algebraic Language is the forerunner of ALGOL. 2. ALGebraic Oriented Language (some authors). The international procedural language.

ALGOL 10 — A FORTRAN-like programming language that offers the scientific advantages of FORTRAN and advanced algorithmic processing capabilities. Used mainly on time-sharing systems. (Digital Equipment Corp.)

ALGOL 68 — Much like ALGOL 10, this version of the language offers input-/output facilities more prone for the batch environment. Used mainly on batch systems, although it is also used on some select time-sharing systems. (IBM.)

algorithm — A defined process or set of rules that leads and assures development of a desired output from a given input. A sequence of formulas and/or algebraic/logical steps to calculate or determine a given task; processing rules.

algorithm convergence — An algorithm is said to converge if it is certain to yield its solution in a finite number of steps. It is a much stronger requirement than the mathematical convergence of the sequence of obtained function values.

algorithmic — Pertaining to a constructive calculating process usually assumed to lead to the solution of a problem in a finite number of steps.

algorithmic language — *Same as* ALGOL.

algorithmic routine — That specific routine which directs the computer in a program to solve a problem in a finite or specified number of steps, but not relying on a trial and error procedure. The solution and solution method are exact and must always reach the specific answer.

algorithm, programming — A programming algorithm is a rule which is often applied to solve a commonly encountered problem. Such an algorithm specifies the rules by which data is to be processed in a design to meet the objective of the program. Thus, it is a method, rule, or procedure used to design a solution for a particular problem or class of problems.

algorithm, scheduling — A set of rules that is included in the scheduling routine of the executive program. The scheduling algorithm determines the length of a user's quantum and the frequency with which this quantum is repeated.

algorithm translation — Various sets of rules, specific methods, or procedures used to obtain translations from one language to various others. Often this is done by the computer using computational methods to solve the algorithm.

alias — 1. A label which is an alternate for something of the same type for which it is being used. Various primary or secondary names are used in computer slang such as red tape, GIGO, kludge, etc., which may be aliases for the basic or primary term. 2. Alternate entry point where program execution is allowed to begin.

A-light — A control panel light which monitors the A-register and signals parity check errors.

aligned words, microcomputer — In some systems, instructions are always addressed as 16-bit words. Words and instructions are aligned; that is, the leftmost byte of a word or instruction word has an even-numbered address. Words are aligned to avoid the time penalty resulting from successive fetches of the high and low byte of a word spanning the alignment boundary. Aligned words improve access speed and permit the doubling of the relative ranges of many instructions.

alignment — The process of adjusting components of a system for proper interrelationship. The term is applied especially to the synchronization of components in a system.

allocate — To assign storage locations to the main routines and subroutines, thereby fixing the absolute values of any symbolic address.

allocate storage — The assignment of specific storage areas for exact purposes, such as holding Input/Output data, constants, specific routines, scratchpad storage, stored routines, priority or executive instructions, housekeeping, or end programs.

allocation — The assignment of blocks of data to specified blocks of storage.

allocation, dynamic-storage — Each time a subroutine is called using this feature, the unique storage area for that subroutine is assigned to the first storage available. Thus, all subroutines called on the same level will share the same storage area. This results in a significant storage saving in many cases. In addition, a recursive subroutine call is possible because a new storage area is assigned each time a subroutine is entered. This feature, together with in-line symbolic coding, provides real-time capability.

allocation of hardware resources, time-sharing — *See* time-sharing allocation of hardware resources.

allocation, resource — A program which integrates the allocation of resources (men, machines, materials, money, and space) with scheduling, by time period, of project activities.

allocation, storage — The process of reserving blocks of storage to specified blocks of information.

allotting — A process of selection in which the objects are given assignments before the actual selecting procedure is initiated.

alpha — 1. The first letter of the Greek alphabet and, thus, a symbol representing first. 2. An abbreviation for Alphanumeric. 3. A feature of representation of data in alphabetical characters in contrast to numerical.

alphabet — A specific kind of character set excluding numerals, i.e., the character set most frequently used in a natural language.

alphabetic — Using only letters of the alphabet and the special characters of period, comma, asterisk, and others.

alphabetic addressing — The procedure for using alphabetic or alphanumeric labels to specify various storage locations for particular programs; i.e., before program execution, the alphabetic address is converted to an absolute address.

alphabetic code — A system of alphabetic abbreviations used in preparing information for input to a machine; e.g., Boston, New York, Philadelphia, and Washington may in alphabetical coding be reported as BS, NY, PH, WA. (Contrasted with numeric code.)

alphabetic-numeric — The characters that include letters of the alphabet, numerals, and other symbols, such as punctuation or mathematical symbols.

alphabetic string — A string or group of characters all of which are letters. A string is a one dimensional array of characters, letters, etc., ordered by references to the relations between adjacent numbers.

alphabetic word — A specific word entirely of characters of an alphabet or special signs and symbols.

alphameric — A contraction of alphanumeric and alphabetic-numeric.

alphameric characters — A generic term for numeric digits, alphabetic characters, and special characters.

alphameric code — *Same as* code, alphanumeric.

alphanumeric — A contraction of alphabetic-numeric.

alphanumerical — A coding system capable of representing alphabetical characters and other symbols as well as numbers.

alphanumeric character set — Special character set of letters and digits and other special characters including especially punctuation marks.

alphanumeric instruction — The name given to instructions that can be used equally well with alphabetic or numeric kinds of data.

alphanumeric reader — An optical character recognition device that automatically reads and transmits typewritten messages.

altering — An operation for inserting, deleting, or changing information.

altering errors — Internal, machine-generated errors resulting from incorrect data transfer within the machine.

alter mode — A program condition that permits changing or updating data in storage.

alternate optima — Distinct solutions to the same optimization problem.

alternate routing — A communications term relating to the assignment of other communications paths to a particular destination if the primary path has become unavailable.

alternation gate — *Same as* gate, OR.

alternative denial gate — *Same as* gate, NAND.

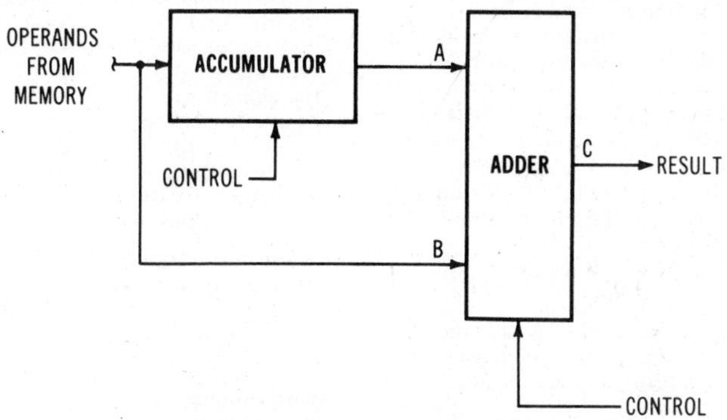

ALU—arithmetic and logical unit (one type).

ALU—Arithmetic and Logical Unit — The portion of the hardware of a computer in which arithmetic and logical operations are performed. The arithmetic unit generally consists of an accumulator, some special registers for the storage of operands and results, supplemented by shifting and sequencing circuitry for implementing multiplication, division, and other desired operations.

ambiguity — Having more than one meaning or interpretation. In computer processing, ambiguity is often the result of changes of state in various systems.

ambiguity error — A gross error, usually transient, occurring in the reading of digits of numbers and imprecise synchronism which causes changes in different digit positions, such as in analog-to-digital conversion. Guard signals can aid in avoiding such errors.

AMBIT — A programming language for algebraic symbol manipulation.

American Federation of Information Processing Societies (AFIPS) — Headquarters: Montvale, N.J. An organization of computer-related societies. Its members include: The Association for Computer Machinery; The Institute of Electrical and Electronics Engineers Computer Group; Simulation Councils, Inc.; American Society for Information Science. Its affiliates include: American Institute of Certified Public Accountants; American Statistical Association; Association for Computational Linguistics; Society for Industrial and Applied Mathematics; Society for Information Display; Association of Data Processing Services Organizations.

American National Standards Institute (ANSI) — This organization organizes committees formed of computer users, manufacturers, etc., to develop and publish industry standards, e.g., ANSI FORTRAN, ANSI Standard Code for Periodical Identification, etc. Previous names: American Standards Association (ASA) and United States of America Standards Institute (USASI).

American Standard Code for Information Interchange (ASCII) — Usually pronounced "Askee." A standard data-transmission code that was introduced to achieve compatibility between data devices. It consists of 7 information bits and 1 parity bit for error-checking purposes, thus allowing 128 code combinations. If the eighth bit is not used for parity, 256 code combinations are possible.

American Standards Association — A former name of the American National Standards Institute.

amplifier — A unidirectional device which is capable of putting out an enlargement of the waveform of the electric current, voltage, or power that is supplied to the input.

amplifier, computing — This amplifier combines functions of amplification and performance of operations. Computing amplifiers are often summing amplifiers, analog adders, or sign reversing amplifiers.

amplifier, differential — This amplifier has two signal-input channels and one signal output channel, which have characteristics such as instantaneous output signals which are directly proportional to the difference between the instantaneous values of the input signals.

amplifier, differentiating — An amplifier, infrequently used in analog computers, whose output voltage is proportional to the derivative of the input voltage with respect to time.

amplifier, direct-coupled — *Same as* amplifier, direct-current.

amplifier, direct-current — A specific analog computer amplifier which uses resistors for coupling signals in and out of the active elements, i.e., a vacuum tube or transistor. It is then capable of amplifying input signal currents despite how slowly the input signals might vary in time.

amplifier, drift-corrected — A specific "direct-coupled" analog computer amplifier which reduces or stops drift; i.e., the output voltage does not change in value without a corresponding change in input signal voltage.

amplifier, operational — *Same as* amplifier, computing.

amplifier, see-saw — *Same as* amplifier, sign-reversing.

amplifier, sign-reversing — A specific analog computer amplifier which has output voltage equal to the input voltage but opposite in sign.

amplifier, valve control — Some systems have integrating amplifiers which accept analog signals from time-sharing valve output modules, provide memory and conditioning for the signal, and generate control output signals.

amplitude, pulse — The maximum instantaneous value of a pulse.

analog — The representation of numerical quantities by means of physical variables, e.g., translation, rotation, voltage, or resistance. (Contrasted with digital.)

analog adder — Also known as a summer in analog representation; a unit with two or more input variables and one output variable which is equal to the sum, or a specific weighted sum, of the input variables.

analog assignment of variables — Consists of deciding which quantities on the computer will represent which variables in the problem. The user must know the mathematical laws controlling the variables in the problem as well as the laws controlling the currents, voltages, and reactances in the computer. He then matches those quantities which are analogous to each other; that is, quantities which obey the same mathematical laws. For example, water pressure can be analogous to voltage, while water flow can be analogous to current.

analog back-up — A designed alternate method of process control most often used by conventional analog instruments in the event of a failure in the computer system.

analog channel — A channel on which the information transmitted can take any value between the defined limits of the channel.

analog computer — *See* computer, analog.

analog data — *See* data, analog.

analog device — A mechanism that represents numbers by physical quantities, e.g., by lengths, as in a slide rule, or by voltages or currents, as in a differential analyzer or a computer of the analog type.

analog divider — A unit with two input variables and one output variable which is proportional to the quotient of the input variables, provided that all the variables are within the operating range of the unit. An analog multiplier unit can be used in the feedback path of an operational amplifier to perform division. These two units combined become an analog divider.

analog input — Units feature modular packaged equipment used to convert voltage or current signals into digital values. The modules used to accomplish the conversions include analog-to-digital converters, multiplexors, amplifiers, and other signal conditioning equipment.

analog input expander — This unit allows a complete analog input system to be configured around the data-adapter unit.

analog input module — In some systems, devices that convert analog input signals from process instrumentation into a digit code for transmission to the computer.

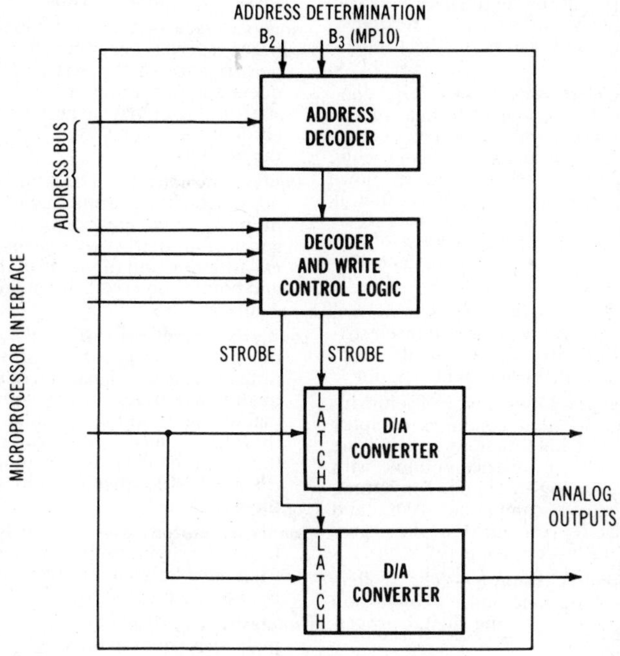

Analog-to-digital LSI (example).

analog multiplier — A unit that generates analog products from two or more input signals. The output variable is proportional to the product of the input variables.

analog network — A circuit or circuits that represent(s) physical variables in such a manner as to permit the expression and solution of mathematical relationships between the variables, or to permit the solution directly by electric or electronic means.

analog output — As opposed to digital output, the amplitude is continuously proportionate to the stimulus, the proportionality being limited by the resolution of the device.

analog processor-controller (P-C) — The processor-controller (P-C) can be used for editing, supervisory control, direct control, or data analysis. A control and data path provides for the attachment of the system where more powerful supervision is required. For example, the system may be used to integrate the commercial aspects of an application with the controlling operations exercised by an analog computer. Some multiprocessor system capabilities enable the handling of real-time applications of any size or complexity.

analog representation — A representation that does not have discrete values but is continuously variable.

analog simulation — Use of an electrical system to represent a physical system. The actual system and the electrical model are analogous in that the variables that demonstrate their characteristics are described by relations that are mathematically equivalent. The actual system has thus been simulated because of the similarity of operation of the electrical model and the physical system. This capability of the analog computer is of great value in performing scientific research or engineering design calculations because it permits an insight into the relationship between the mathematical equations and the response of the physical system. Once the electrical model is completed, well-controlled experiments can be performed quickly, inexpensively, and with great flexibility to predict the behavior of the primary physical system.

analog-to-digital conversion — The conversion of analog signals from a voltage level to digital information is accomplished by an analog-to-digital converter (ADC). Such converters, however, are complex enough so that if multiple sources of analog signals are to be converted, they share the use of one ADC. The switching is accomplished by a multiplexer.

analog-to-digital converter — A device that changes physical motion or electrical voltage into digital factors; e.g., turns of a shaft into a number input.

analog-to-digital LSI — A type of semiconductor device that combines complex linear and digital functions on the same chip. One-chip microcomputers with onboard analog-to-digital converters, microprocessor-compatible ADs, and codecs are representative of these products. (Illustration, page 17.)

analog-to-digital sensing — The collection of analog data and its conversion for presentation to the digital processor-controller.

analysis — The methodological investigation of a problem by a consistent procedure, and its separation into related units for further detailed study.

analysis block — A relocatable part of the computer storage in which program testing or statistical data are stored which can later be utilized to analyze the performance of the system. During program testing there may be an analysis block for each transaction in the system, and when the transaction leaves the system this block is dumped into a file or tape.

analysis, contour — *See* contour analysis.

analysis, file — The examination, study, and resolution of file characteristics to determine similarities, number and type of redundancies, and to check labeling and listing of documents which affect data elements contained in files.

analysis, logic — The delineation or determination of the specific steps required to produce the desired computer output or derive the intelligence information from the given or ascertained input data or model. Such logic studies are completed for many computer processes, programs, or runs.

analysis mode — A mode of operation in which special programs monitor the performance of the system for subsequent analysis. Program testing data or statistical data may be automatically recording when the system is running in the analysis mode.

analysis, numerical — The study of methods of obtaining useful quantitative solutions to mathematical problems, regardless of whether an analytic solution exists or not, and the study of the errors and bounds on errors in obtaining such solutions.

analysis, operations — The use of scientific method procedures to solve operational problems. Management thus uses quantitative bases for developing optimal decisions and predictions. Some of these procedures are: linear programming, probability information, game theory, PERT, queuing, and statistical theory.

analysis, procedure — The analysis of a business activity to determine precisely what must be accomplished, and how it is to be accomplished.

analysis, statistical — One of the four main techniques of operations research. Data gathering, arranging, sorting, sequencing, and evaluating are all common statistical analyses. Three other techniques are linear programming, queuing theory, and simulation. Statistical analysis combines mathematical techniques and computer technology to handle a wide range of business and scientific problems wherever large amounts of information or data must be evaluated and analyzed.

analysis, systems — The examination of an activity, procedure, method, technique, or a business to determine what must be accomplished and how the necessary operations may best be accomplished.

analyst — An individual who is skilled and trained to define problems and to analyze, develop, and express algorithms for their solution, especially algorithms that may be resolved and implemented by a computer.

analyst, systems — A person who designs information-handling procedures which incorporate computer processing. The systems analyst is usually highly skilled in defining problems and developing algorithms for their solution.

analytical engine — The name Charles Babbage gave to one of his primitive computer devices. Conceived in 1833, the analytical engine was the first general-purpose automatic digital computer. It embodied all the fundamental principles of the modern digital computer. It was theoretically capable of executing any mathematical operation; it stored sequences of instructions in memory, and it was to use punched cards modeled after those used in the Jacquard loom as mass memory for storage of mathematical tables. Babbage's concept of the analytical engine is one of the truly great intellectual achievements of all time.

analytic relationship — The relationship that exists between concepts and corresponding terms, by virtue of their definition and inherent scope of meaning.

analyzer, differential — A computer (usually analog) designed and used primarily for solving many types of differential equations.

analyzer, logic — Logic analyzers take a digital picture of the data presented on several parallel data-bus lines, and store it in a semiconductor memory for later analysis. When the input levels rise or fall through preset input thresholds, the data is recognized as ones or zeros and stored in memory cells. Memory contents can be accessed later and converted to oscilloscope displays for convenient analysis.

analyzer, logic test — These instruments do for the analysis of complex digital equipment what the oscilloscope does for real-time signal analysis by providing views of multiple channels of sequential data, even if the data are nonrecurring, providing true simultaneous acquisition of multiple data channels, and providing data sequence displays that occur before a trigger.

analyzer, network — An analog device designed primarily for simulating electrical networks. (Synonymous with network calculator.)

ancillary equipment — *Same as* equipment, peripheral.

AND — 1. A logical operator that has the property that if P is a statement and Q is a statement, then P AND Q are true if both statements are true, false if either is false or both are false. Truth is normally expressed by the value 1, falsity by 0. The AND operator is often represented by a centered dot (P·Q), by no sign (PQ), by an inverted "u" or logical product symbol (P∩Q), or by the letter "X" or multiplication symbol (P×Q). Note that the letters AND are capitalized to differentiate between the logical operator and the word *and* in common usage. 2. The logical operation which makes use of the AND operator or logical product.

AND circuit — *Same as* gate, AND.

AND gate — *See* gate, AND.

AND gate, positive — *Same as* gate, AND.

AND-NOT gate — *Same as* gate, A AND-NOT B or gate, B AND-NOT A.

AND operator — *See* AND.

AND unit — *Same as* gate, AND.

anglicize — Usually means to translate from programming language to English phrases, i.e., to state the precise meaning of various coded statements in exact and understandable language.

annex memory — Small memory unit used as a go-between for the input and output units and the main memory. Better known as a buffer.

annex storage — *Same as* associative storage.

annotate — To include explanations or descriptions of portions of programs; to add information or data to clarify relations, significance, or priorities.

annotation — Added descriptive comments or explanatory notes.

ANSI FORTRAN IV (Standard X3.9-1968) — This is a FORTRAN used by many firms with extensions for in-line assembly language, bit and byte arrays, logical expressions, rational expressions, labeled and unlabeled COMMON, encode/decode statements, free format i/o, and subscripts of any legal integer expression.

ANSI standards — American National Standards Institute standards are widely used by US firms as guides, although they are often modified. Data-processing standards from ANSI range from the definition of ASCII to the determination of over-all datacom system performance. Many have been adopted by the US Government, are called FIPS (Federal Information-Processing Standards), and are mandatory for the Department of Defense.

ANSI Subcommittee X3S3 — Within the American National Standards Institute (ANSI), under Sectional Committee X3 on Computers and Information Processing, Subcommittee X3S3 is responsible for defining the characteristics of digital data generating and receiving systems that function with communication systems and for developing and recommending standards for data communications. Five task groups have been established under X3S3. Task Group X3S33 is responsible for standardizing data communication formats. Its twofold scope of activities is to define formats for data communication of bits within characters and of characters within a hierarchy of groups, and to outline functional control requirements and procedures for data systems other than those required for control of a data link.

answer back — A transmission from the receiving business machine in response to a request from the transmitting machine, e.g., the business machine acknowledges that it is ready to accept or has received data.

answer, inquiry (remote) — *See* inquiry answer (remote).

anticipation mode — A visual means of representing binary information. One binary digit is represented by a line, and the binary digit in the opposite state is represented by the absence of a line.

anticipatory staging — The movement of blocks of storage between disk and main memory in anticipation of their being needed by running programs. This is to be contrasted with demand staging.

anticoincidence gate — *Same as* gate, exclusive OR.

anti-setoff powder — *See* powder, anti-setoff.

any-sequence queue — A collection of items in the system which are waiting for the attention of the processor. The any-sequence queue is organized so that items may be removed from the collection without regard to the sequence in which they entered it.

A OR-NOT B gate — *See* gate, A OR-NOT B.

aperture time — The time required to make a measurement or conversion with an A/D converter. Aperture time can be considered to be a time uncertainty or amplitude uncertainty. The aperture and amplitude uncertainty are related by the time rate of change of the signal.

APL language — A programming language developed by Iverson. An unusually extensive set of operators and data structures are used to implement what is considered by many to be the most flexible, powerful, and concise algorithmic/procedural language in existence. Primarily used from conversational terminals, its applicability to "production" job processing is limited, but its value for educational and investigative work is great.

application — The system or problem to which a computer is applied. Reference is often made to an application as being either of the computational type, wherein arithmetic computations predominate, or of the data-processing type, wherein data-handling operations predominate.

application, inquiry — *See* inquiry application.

application package — A series of interrelated routines and subroutines designed to perform a specific task.

application, real time — *See* real-time application.

application, slave — A fail-safe or backup system (application) whereby a slave or second computer performs the same steps of the same programs so that if the master computer fails or malfunctions, the slave computer continues without a deterioration of operations. Various space or urgent real-time applications require this double-precision or double safety feature.

applications, processor-controller — *See* processor-controller applications.

applications programs — Mathematical routines, including sine, cosine, tangent, arc sine, square root, natural logarithms, and exponential functions.

applications study — The detailed process of determining a system or set of procedures for using a computer for definite functions or operations, and establishing specifications to be used as a base for the selection of equipment suitable to the specific needs.

application, standby — An application in which two or more computers are tied together as a part of a single over-all system, and which, as in the case of an inquiry application, stand ready for immediate activation and appropriate action.

approach, brute-force — To try to undertake with existing equipment the mass of problems that do not use precise computations or logical manipulation (as accounting problems and scientific problems do).

approach, heuristic — An approach that encourages further experimentation and investigation. An intuitive trial-and-error method of attacking a problem as opposed to the algorithmic method.

approach, systems — A systems approach pertains to looking at the overall situation rather than the narrow implications of the task at hand, particularly looking for interrelationships between the task at hand and other functions which relate to it.

APT (Automatically Programmed Tools) — A system for the computer-assisted programming of numerically controlled machine tools, flame cutters, drafting machines, and similar equipment.

arbitrary access — Equal access time to all memory locations, independent of the location of the previous memory reference. *See* random access.

area, clear — *Same as* band, clear.

area, constant — A part of storage designated to store the invariable quantities required for processing.

area, fixed — The area on a disk where data files or image programs may be stored and protected.

area, input — A section of internal storage of a computer reserved for the receiving and processing of input information.

area, input/output — *Same as* storage, working.

area, instruction — A part of storage allocated to receive and store the group of instructions to be executed.

area, output — A section of internal storage reserved for storing data which are to be transferred out of the computer.

area search — The examination of a large group of documents to select those that pertain to one group, such as one category, class, etc.

areas in storage — The assignment of characters, fields, or words in processor storage in order to complete program editing, printing, read-in, punching, constants, write-out, and other procedures.

areas, overflow, file — *See* overflow areas, file.

area, storage — *See* storage area.

area, working — *See* storage, working.

a-register — *See* register, arithmetic.

argument — 1. The known reference factor necessary to find the desired item (function) in a table. 2. A variable upon whose value the value of a function depends. The arguments of a function are listed in parentheses after the function name, whenever that function is used. The computations specified by the function definition occur using the variables specified as arguments.

argument addresses — Some systems offer a single instruction to resolve any number of argument addresses, storing the results in the stack for use by the subroutines needed. Depending on addressing mode, these instructions run 4 to 10 times faster than equivalent software routines. This is especially significant in programs with frequent parameter transfers (such as FORTRAN or data collection with scaling and conversion).

argument transfer instructions — Some systems offer argument transfer instructions that facilitate the movement of arguments (or parameters) from a program to a subroutine. The full addressing power of larger architecture is applied to these functions; base relative, indexed, and indirect argument addresses are passed to subroutines and resolved by these instructions, often to 16-bit absolute addresses for fast argument accessing.

arithmetic address — Specific locations which are used for the results of computations.

arithmetical operation — An operation completed according to arithmetical rules; i.e., the operands are the addend and augend and the result is the sum.

arithmetic and logic unit, ALU microcomputers — That CPU chip logic which actually executes the operations requested by an input command is called the arithmetic and logic unit (ALU), since in every case some combination of arithmetic and/or logical operations is required. A part of CPU chip logic, the control unit, decodes the instruction (stored in the instruction register) in order to enable the required ALU logic, and thus implement the arithmetic and/or logical operations required by the instruction.

arithmetic check — A verification of arithmetic computation, e.g., multiplying 4 by 2 to check against the product obtained by multiplying 2 by 4.

arithmetic expression — An expression containing any combination of data-names, numeric literals, and named constants, joined by one or more arithmetic operators in such a way that the expression as a whole can be reduced to a single numeric value.

arithmetic, external — Operations performed outside of the computer itself as by peripheral or ancillary units but which may or may not become part of the total problem or program on an interrupt basis.

arithmetic, floating-decimal — A method of calculation which automatically accounts for the location of the radix point. This is usually accomplished by handling the number as a signed mantissa times the radix raised to an integral exponent; e.g., the decimal number $+88.3$ might be written as $+.883\times10^2$; the binary number $-.0011$ as $-.11\times2^{-2}$.

arithmetic, floating point operation — *See* floating-point arithmetic (operation).

arithmetic instruction — The operator part of this instruction specifies an arithmetic operation: add, subtract, multiply, divide, powers, or square-root. Not a logical operation such as logic sum, logic multiply, or compare.

arithmetic, internal — The computations performed by the arithmetic unit of a computer.

arithmetic, multiple — A procedure for performing arithmetic on a digital computer in which several parts of one or more numbers are used in arithmetic operations which yield several results.

arithmetic, multiprecision — A form of arithmetic similar to double precision arithmetic except that two or more words may be used to represent each number.

arithmetic operation — Any of the fundamental operations of arithmetic, e.g., the binary operations of addition, subtraction, multiplication, and division, and the binary operations of negation and absolute value.

arithmetic operation, binary — Digital computer operations such as add and subtract performed with operands with output results in binary notation.

arithmetic organ — *Same as* arithmetic section.

arithmetic, parallel — A process in which simultaneous operations are performed on all digits of a number and in which partial sums and numbers are formed or shifted.

arithmetic, partial — *See* arithmetic, multiple.

arithmetic product — A result developed as two numbers are multiplied as, in decimal notation, $6\times10=60$. In data processing, the product is the result of performing the logic AND operation.

arithmetic registers, microprocessors — Arithmetic (or ALU) registers are those on which arithmetic and logic functions can be performed; the register can be a source or destination of operands for the operation. Registers that can supply but not receive operands for the ALU are not considered arithmetic registers by many evaluators.

arithmetic section — The portion of the hardware of a computer in which arithmetic and logical operations are performed. The arithmetic unit generally consists of an accumulator, some special registers for the storage of operands and results, and shifting and sequencing circuitry for implementing multiplication, division, and other desired operations. (Synonymous with ALU.)

arithmetic, serial — An operation in which each number is divided into digits to be operated upon singly, usually in the adder-subtracter or a comparator. The same number of addition operations are required as there are binary digits in the operands; a simpler and slower operation than parallel arithmetic.

arithmetic shift — A shift of digits to the left or right within a fixed framework in order to multiply or divide by a power of the given number base equivalent to the number of positions shifted.

arithmetic unit — *See* arithmetic section.

arm, disk (moving) — *See* disk, moving arm.

armed interrupt — *See* interrupt, armed.

ARPANET — A large packet-switched network developed by the Department of Defense in 1969.

ARQ — Automatic request for repeat. An automatic system which provides error correction by utilizing a constant ratio code and a closed loop to request retransmission of mutilated characters as indicated by receipt of nonconstant ratio characters.

ARQ, continuous — Automatic request for repeat (ARQ) in continuous mode has the transmitter sending one block after another without stopping. The receiver and transmitter retain individual counts of the blocks outstanding and provide buffer storage to retain those blocks. Only when an erroneous block is detected does the receiver tell the transmitter to resend that block and all subsequent in-transit, but unacknowledged blocks.

array — A series of items arranged in a meaningful pattern.

array, cell — A set of elements arranged in a meaningful pattern so that rows and columns form a matrix. Specific data can be identified by naming specific cells in the matrix by row and column.

array, closed — An array that can only be extended if the newly added elements do not alter the value of the entire array.

array, data — A representation of data in the form of signs or symbols recorded on tape, cards, etc.

array pitch — *See* pitch, row.

array processors — Various 32-bit programmable floating-point array processors are available for use with 16- and 32-bit minicomputers. These coprocessors reduce the time to do strings of iterative arithmetic by several orders of magnitude.

artificial cognition — The optical sensing of a displayed character in which the machine or equipment selects from its memory the shape of the character that is closest to the character being displayed.

artificial intelligence — 1. Research and study in methods for the development of a machine that can improve its own operations. The development or capability of a machine that can proceed or perform functions that are normally concerned with human intelligence, as learning, adapting, reasoning, self-correction, automatic improvement. 2. The study of computer and related techniques to supplement the intellectual capabilities of man. As man has invented and used tools to increase his physical powers, he now is beginning to use artificial intelligence to increase his mental powers. In a more restricted sense, the study of techniques for more effective use of digital computers by improved programming techniques.

artificial language — A language specifically designed for ease of communication in a particular area of endeavor, but one that is not yet natural to that area. This is contrasted with a natural language which has evolved through long usage.

artificial perception — *See* artificial cognition.

ARU — Audio-Response Unit. A device designed to connect a computer system to a telephone to provide voice response to inquiries made.

ascending sort — A sort in which the final sequence of records is such that successive keys compare greater than, less than, or equal to.

ASCII — American Standard Code for Information Interchange. A standard 8-bit information code used with most computers and data terminals. It may be used in the parallel mode (all bits present simultaneously on separate lines) or the serial mode (one bit at a time on a single line). Most systems do not use the eighth bit of the code, and it is, therefore, assumed to be a logic one at all times. Some systems, however, use the eighth bit for parity or error testing. The remaining seven bits provide a total of 128 possible characters. Of these, one group of 32 is reserved for the upper-case alphabet and a few punctuation marks. Another group of 32 is used for numbers, spacing, and additional punctuation symbols. Rarely used punctuation marks and a lower-case alphabet are assigned a third group of 32. Finally, the last 32 combinations are assigned as machine or control commands. This group is not actually printed but is provided to handle hardware operations such as line feed (LF) or carriage return (CR).

ASIS — Abbreviation for American Society for Information Science, formerly American Documentation Institute.

ASLIB — Abbreviation for Association of Special Libraries and Information Bureaus.

ASR — Automatic Send-Receive set. A combination teletypewriter, transmitter, and receiver with transmission capability from either keyboard or paper tape. Most often used in half-duplex circuit.

assemble — 1. To prepare an object language program from a symbolic language program by substituting machine operation codes for symbolic operation codes and absolute or relocatable addresses for symbolic addresses. 2. To integrate subroutines (supplied, selected, or generated) into the main routine, by adapting or changing relative and symbolic addresses to absolute form or incorporating, or placing in storage.

assembler — A computer program that operates on symbolic input data to produce from such data machine instructions by carrying out such functions as: translation of symbolic-operation codes into computer-operating instructions, assigning locations in storage for successive instructions, or computation of absolute addresses from symbolic addresses. An assembler generally translates input symbolic codes into machine instructions, item for item, and produces as an output the same number of instructions or constants that were defined in the input symbolic codes.

assembler directive commands — Assembler directive commands provide the programmer with the ability to generate data words and values based on specific conditions at assembly time. The instruction operation codes are assigned mnemonics which describe the hardware function of each instruction.

assembler directives — The symbolic assembler directives control or direct the assembly processor just as operation codes control or direct the central computer. These directives are represented by mnemonics.

assembler, macro — Some macroassemblers bring high level language features to assembly language programming. Macroinstructions translate a single multiargument source line into a sequence of machine instructions. These macros can be accumulated in easily used libraries that eliminate repetition. Expanded expression evaluation, on some systems, allows the use of FORTRAN-like expressions with machine language efficiency. Extensive listing control directives generate self-documenting programs with a minimum of programmer effort on these systems.

assembler, microcomputer — Programs written in assembly language are translated by an assembler program into executable machine programs. The assembly process is basically one of converting symbolic instructions into binary machine instructions for machine instructions and data, and performing auxiliary functions necessary to produce an executable machine program.

assembler, one-to-one — A straightforward translating program which generally produces only one instruction in the object language for each instruction in the source language.

assembler operators — *See* assembler program.

assembler program — The assembler is an assembly program for a symbolic-coding language. It is composed of simple, brief expressions that provide rapid translation from symbolic to machine-language relocatable-object coding for the computer. The assembly language includes a variety of operators which allow the fabrication of desired fields based on information generated at assembly time. The instruction-operation codes are assigned mnemonics which describe the hardware function of each instruction. Assembler-directive commands provide the programmer with the ability to generate data words and values based on specific conditions at assembly time.

assembler, relocatable — A specific program that acts as an ordinary assembler to translate object code from assembly language source code with memory locations specified as displacements from a relative origin or as external references. This type of assembler facilitates the running of programs in any memory area.

assembler, resident — An assembler that runs on the machine for which it generates code. Used most often for developing software. It eliminates the need for another computer system or a time-sharing service, which is needed for most cross assemblers.

assembler, reverse — A program that generates a complete symbol table, places equate statements at the beginning of the newly created source program, and inserts labels at appropriate locations throughout the program. The source program can be listed on the terminal or printer and stored on disk as a source program. The new source file may then be edited, relocated, and reassembled as desired. A typical program is available on paper tape, cassette, or diskette.

assembler, symbolic — The symbolic assembler lets the programmer code instructions in a symbolic language. The assembler allows mnemomic symbols to be used for instruction codes and addresses. Constant and variable storage registers can be automatically assigned. The assembler produces a binary object tape and lists a symbol with memory allocations and useful diagnostic messages.

assembler, two-pass — An assembler which requires scanning of the source program twice. The first pass constructs a symbol table, and the second pass does the translation.

assembling — The process of composing or integrating instructions into subroutines or main routines for acceptance and use by computing units.

assembling a program — The preparation of a program for actual execution by a computer. Generally refers to the process of converting mnemonic representations used by programmers to actual binary patterns used by a CPU.

assembly — The translation of a source program written in a symbolic language into an object or target program in a machine language.

assembly control, IF statement — This feature allows for bypassing sections of an object program at assembly time under control of external indications.

assembly-control statements — Statements that instruct the assembly program in the performance of a wide variety of functions related to creating an object program.

assembly language — A machine-oriented language for programming, such as ARGUS or EASY, which belongs to an assembly program or system.

assembly language coding — Assembly languages are used to avoid coding directly into machine code; mnemonics are used for both the command instructions and the operands, and it is usually not necessary to label the address for every instruction. In an instruction such as, ADD Y, Y is a mnemonic for a location. Assembly programs generate in a one-to-one fashion a set of machine-coded instructions as contrasted to a complier, or macro language, wherein one compiler instruction can generate many machine instructions, i.e., such as FORTAN, COBOL, etc.

assembly-language output — A symbolic assembly-language listing of the binary object program output of the compiler. The listing contains the symbolic instructions equivalent to the binary code output from the compiler. This assembly-language output listing is useful as a debugging aid. By including certain pseudo-operations codes in in-line assembly language, the assembly-language output can be assembled by the assembler. This allows modification of programs at the assembly-language level.

assembly language processor — A language processor that accepts words, statements, and phrases to produce machine instructions. It is more than an assembly program because it has compiler powers. The macroassembler permits segmentation of a large program so that portions may be tested separately. It also provides extensive program analysis to aid in debugging.

assembly line balancing — A specialized program allowing production control management to plan the most efficient and profitable man-work element relationship in an assembly line operation.

assembly list — A printed list which is the by-product of an assembly procedure. It lists in logical-instruction sequence all details of a routine, showing the coded and symbolic notation next to the actual notations established by the assembly procedure. This listing is highly useful in the debugging of routines.

assembly-output language — In some systems, an optional symbolic assembly language that lists the object code output from a high-level language compiler. This can be very helpful for users as a debugging tool because it can show exact machine code in a readable format.

assembly program — *See* assembly routine.

assembly routine — A computer program that operates on symbolic input data to produce from such data machine instructions by carrying out such functions as: translation of symbolic-operation codes into computer-operating instructions; assigning locations in storage for successive instructions; or computation of absolute addresses from symbolic addresses. An assembler generally translates input symbolic codes into machine instructions item for item, and produces as output the same number of instructions or constants which were defined in the input symbolic codes. (Synonymous with assembly program, and related to compiler.)

assembly, selective — A procedure in which run tapes contain a specific program selected by the programmer from both an input deck of new programs and a tape file of previously processed symbolic programs.

assembly, symbolic — The first level of language described for a class of processor programs.

assembly system — 1. An automatic system (software) that includes a language and machine-language programs. Such supplementary programs perform such programming functions as checkout, updating, and others. 2. An assembly system comprises two elements, a symbolic language and an assembly program, that translate source programs written in the symbolic language into machine language.

assembly, system, symbolic — A program system developed in two parts; a symbolic-language program, and a computer program (processor). The processor translates a source program developed in symbolic language to a machine object program.

assembly testing — The testing of a group of functionally related programs to determine whether or not the group operates according to specifications. The programs may be related in that they have access to common data, occupy high-speed storage simultaneously, operate under common program control, or perform an integrated task.

assembly unit — 1. A device that performs the function of associating and joining several parts or piecing together a program. 2. A portion of a program that is capable of being assembled into a larger whole program.

assertion — Relates to flow charting as a presumption or anticipation of a condition or some content concerning the data design, program, or processing.

assignment, facilities (Executive) — The assignment of memory and external facilities to meet the requirements which are defined symbolically in a job program selected for initiation. Executive maintains a list of all allocatable facilities which is updated to reflect release of facilities by programs during, or at termination of, a run.

Association for Computer Machinery (ACM) — A professional and technical society whose publications, conferences and activities are designed to help advance the art, specifically as regards machinery and system design, language and program development, and other related activities. It is a member of the American Federation of Information Processing Societies (AFIPS).

Association of Data Processing Service Organizations (ADAPSO) — An association of US and Canadian data-processing service organizations.

associative indexing — A study following two approaches—the automatic generation of word association maps based on lists of words from the text, and representations based on the number of times words appear in the text.

associative memories — With associative-memory capability, high-speed memory searches within computers are based on content or subject matter rather than being limited to locating data through specified "addresses."

associative storage — A type of storage in which storage locations are identified by their contents, not by names or positions. Synonymous with content-addressed storage.

assumed decimal point — The point within a numeric item at which the decimal point is assumed to be located. When a numeric item is to be used within a computer, the location of the assumed decimal point is considered to be at the right, unless otherwise specified in the appropriate record description entry. It will not occupy an actual space in storage, but it will be used by the computer to align the value properly for calculation.

asterisk protection — The insertion of a series of asterisks on the left of the most significant digit. This scheme is commonly used in check protection systems.

asynchronous — A mode of computer operation in which performance of the next command is started by a signal that the previous command has been completed. Contrast with synchronous, characterized by a fixed time cycle for the execution of operations.

asynchronous computer — A computer in which the performance of each operation starts as a result of a signal either that the previous operation has been completed, or that the parts of the computer required for the next operation are now available. (Contrasted with synchronous computer.)

asynchronous device — A unit which has an operating speed not related to any particular frequency of the system to which it is connected.

asynchronous machine — A machine which has an operating speed not related to any fixed or specific frequency of the system. Since no fixed period or interval signals the next event, it may begin at the end of a prior one, without regard to the time it might take.

asynchronous operation — The method of processing in which one operation is completed before the next operation is initiated.

asynchronous operator — *See* asynchronous.

asynchronous signaling — Codes used in signaling, in which characters provide their own start and stop indicators.

asynchronous transmission — A method of transmitting data in which each transmitted character is preceded by a start bit and followed by a stop bit, thus permitting the interval between characters to vary. Asynchronous transmission is advantageous when transmission is irregular (such as that initiated by a keyboard operator's typing speed). It is also inexpensive due to the simple interface logic and circuitry required. Synchronous transmission, on the other hand, makes better use of the transmission facility by eliminating the start and stop bits on each character. Furthermore, synchronous data is suitable for multilevel modulation which combines two or four bits in one signal element (baud). Synchronous modems offer higher transmission speeds, but are more expensive because they require precisely synchronized clock and data.

asynchronous working — *See* asynchronous.

asyndetic — 1. Omitting conjunctions or connectives. 2. Pertaining to a catalog without cross references.

ATE — Automatic Test Equipment

atomic symbols — *See* symbols, atomic.

ATS — Abbreviation for Administrative Terminal System.

attached processing — An approach to computer system architecture in which an arbitrary number of compact, inexpensive computers are linked together to form a large-scale computing facility. Some of these computers handle data file management and retrieval, while others execute applications programs. Individual computer processors are relieved from the burden of performing many different tasks simultaneously.

attached support processor (ASP) — The utilization of multiple computers, usually two, connected via channel-to-channel adaptors, to increase the efficiency in processing many short duration jobs.

attended operation — In data set applications, individuals are required at both stations to establish the connection and transfer the data sets from talk (voice) mode to data mode.

attention device — A device programmed to indicate a new display on a screen of lasting displays by some different shapes, sizes, or light intensity, or by making older displays smaller, dimmer, or of another shape.

attenuate — To reduce the amplitude of an action or signal.

attenuation — Reduction of energy of an action or signal. Measurement may be made as units, decibels, or percentages.

attribute — A subdividing descriptor of an entity. Whereas entities are the items about which information is kept, the attributes of the entities are the particular characteristics of interest. In data bases, entities are tracked by records of a particular record type, and the attributes of the entities are recorded by the data in the record fields.

audible alarm — *See* alarm, audible.

audio — Frequencies that can be heard by the human ear (usually 15 to 20,000 hertz).

audio-cassette record interface — A device that allows virtually unlimited memory storage for data or software. Operates by modulating audio frequencies in the record mode. Demodulates recorded data in playback mode.

audio response — A form of output that uses verbal replies to inquiries. The computer can be programmed to seek answers to inquiries made on a time-shared on-line system and then to utilize a special audio response unit which elicits the appropriate prerecorded response to the inquiry. Of course, inquiries must be of the nature for which the audio response has been prepared. In demand deposit account lookup, for example, the teller dials the computer's special number and then enters an identity code, customer account number, and an inquiry code telling the computer what to look up. The computer then immediately relays the customer's balance back to the teller in the form of a spoken message from the audio response system. This is an actual human voice composed of selected words that are retrieved from a prestored vocabulary and sent over phone lines.

audio-response unit — A device that can link a computer system to a telephone network to provide voice responses to inquiries made from telephone-type terminals. The audio response is composed from a vocabulary prerecorded in a digitally coded voice on a disk storage device.

audiotape storage unit — A unit capable of storing computer programs and/or data on ordinary audio cassette tape; audio tones are used to represent binary data.

audit — The operations developed to corroborate the evidence as regards authenticity and validity of the data that are introduced into the data-processing problem or system.

audit-in-depth — Detailed examination of all manipulations performed on a single transaction or piece of information.

auditing — Source data, methodology, and report conclusions and sums are checked for accuracy and validity as well as credibility in the auditing process through the use of studied techniques and information sources.

audit program — A program designed to enable use of the computer as an auditing tool.

audit trail — The trail or path left by a transaction when it is processed. The trail begins with the original documents, transactions entries, and posting of records and is complete with the report. Validity tests of records are achieved by this method. An audit trail must be incorporated into every procedure; provision for it should be made early so that it becomes an integral part. In creating an audit trail it is necessary to provide: (A) Transaction documentation which is detailed enough to permit the association of any one record with its original source document. (B) A system of accounting controls which provides that all transactions have been processed and that accounting records are in balance. (C) Documentation from which any transaction can be recreated and its processing continued, should that transaction be misplaced or destroyed at some point in the procedure.

augend — The number or quantity to which another number or quantity (addend) is added to produce the result (sum).

augment — To increase a quantity in order to bring it to its full value.

augmenter — The quantity added to another to bring it to its full value. An augmenter is usually positive; however, when "added," a negative quantity is also called an augmenter.

autoabstract — A collection of words selected from a document, arranged in a meaningful order, commonly by an automatic or machine method.

auto bypass — A capability that permits continuous operation of downstream terminals when another terminal in the daisy chain is powered down.

autocode — Use of the computer itself to develop the machine-coded program from macrocodes, i.e., the conversion of symbolic codes for operations and addresses.

autocoder — An IBM programming language.

autodecrement mode — In some systems, this mode is useful for processing data in a list in the reverse direction. The contents of the selected general register are decremented and then used as the address of the operand. The choices of these features (post increment, predecrement) on some systems are designed to facilitate hardware/software stack operations.

autoincrement mode — In some systems, this mode provides for automatic stepping of a pointer through sequential elements of a table of operands. It assumes the contents of the selected general register to be the address of the operand. Contents of the registers, on these systems, are stepped to address the next sequential location. The autoincrement mode is useful for array processing and stack processing. It will access an element of a table or it may be used for a variety of purposes.

auto-indexed addressing — An addressing mode that results in the contents of an index register being automatically altered by some specified amount each time such an instruction is actually executed.

auto-man — A type of locking switch which indicates and controls methods of operation, such as automatic or manual.

automata theory — The development of theory which relates the study of principles of operations and applications of automatic devices to various behaviorist concepts and theories.

automated data medium — *Same as* data, machine readable.

automatic abstracting — Searching for the criteria by which human beings judge what should be abstracted from a document, as programmed.

automatically programmed tools (APT) — APT is a system for the computer-assisted programming of numerically controlled machine tools, flame cutters, drafting machines, and similar equipment.

automatic carriage — A device on a printer that moves continuous-form paper under machine control.

automatic character generation — In addition to automatic line generation, the display hardware can display characters specified by 6-bit codes. Each character is displayed in an average of 15 μsec (some systems).

automatic check — A provision constructed in hardware for verifying the accuracy of information transmitted, manipulated, or stored by any unit or device in a computer. (Synonymous with built-in check, built-in automatic check, hardware check, and related to program check.)

automatic checking — Processors are constructed and designed for verification of information transmitted, computed, or stored. The procedure is complete when all processes in the machine are automatically checked, or else the check is considered a partial verification. Partial checking concerns either the number and proportion of the processes that are checked, or the number and proportion of the machine units that are assigned to checking.

automatic check interrupts — *See* interrupts, automatic check.

automatic checkout systems — *See* checkout systems, automatic.

automatic code — A code that allows a machine to translate or convert a symbolic language into a machine language for automatic machine or computer operations.

automatic coding — A technique by which a machine translates a routine written in a synthetic language into coded machine instructions; e.g., assembling is automatic coding.

automatic coding language — A technique, device, or language, such that the computer is assisted in doing part of the coding task.

automatic corrections — *See* correction, automatic error.

automatic data medium — *See* data, machine readable.

automatic data processing (ADP) — Data processing performed by a system of electronic or electrical machines so interconnected and interacting as to reduce to a minimum the need for human assistance or intervention.

automatic data-processing system — *See* automatic data processing.

automatic data-switching center — A data-switching center which senses contents of messages and relays such information without human handling or intervention. Same as automatic message switching.

automatic dictionary — The component of a language-translating machine that will provide a word-for-word substitution from one language to another. In automatic searching systems, the automatic dictionary is the component that substitutes codes for words or phrases during the encoding operation. (Related to machine translation.)

automatic electronic data-switching center — A communications center designed for relaying digitized information by automatic electronic means.

automatic error correction — A technique, usually requiring the use of special codes and/or automatic retransmission, that detects and corrects errors occurring in transmission. The degree of correction depends upon coding and equipment configuration.

automatic error detection — The program itself, or the program embedded in a more complicated system, is usually designed to detect its own errors, print them out with the cause, and, if so designed, take steps to correct them.

automatic exchange — An exchange in which communication between subscribers is effected without the intervention of operators, and is completed by means of devices and equipment set in operation by the originating subscriber's instrument.

automatic gain control (AGC) — An amplifier circuit designed to provide output levels for computer crt terminals within a specific limited range no matter what the input levels are.

automatic hold — In an analog computer, attainment of the hold condition automatically through amplitude comparison of a problem variable, or through an overload condition.

automatic interrupt — An automatic program-controlled interrupt system that causes a hardware jump to a predetermined location. There are five types of interrupt: (1) input/output, (2) programmer error, (3) machine error, (4) supervisor call, and (5) external (for example, timer turned to negative value, alert button on console, external lines from another processor). There is further subdivision under the five types. Unwanted interrupts, such as an anticipated overflow, can be "masked out" (some computers).

automatic loader — A loader program implemented in a special ROM (read-only memory) that allows loading of binary paper tapes or the first record or sector of a mass storage device. The program is equivalent to a bootstrap loader plus a binary loader. When an automatic loader is installed, it is seldom necessary to key in a bootstrap program to load the binary loader.

automatic message — Incoming messages are automatically directed to one or more outgoing circuits, according to intelligence contained in the message.

automatic message-switching center — A center in which messages are automatically routed according to information in them.

automatic plotting — *See* plotting, automatic.

automatic program interrupt — The ability of computers to put "first things first"; abandon one operation, temporarily, when a priority operation arises, do that one, and go on from there. The interruption is caused by a specific predetermined condition.

automatic programming — The method or technique whereby the computer itself is used to transform or translate programming from a language or form that is easy for a human being to produce, into a language that is efficient for the computer to carry out. Examples of automatic programming are compiling, assembling, and interpretive routines.

automatic programming language — A device, technique, or language which permits the computer to aid in doing part of the coding and programming.

automatic ragged-right justification — Text in memory is automatically ragged-right justified. Text is wrapped around the right-hand margin such that the last character of a word may be at the margin setting, but not exceed it.

automatic recovery program — *See* program, automatic recovery.

automatic routine — A routine that is executed independently of manual operations, but only if certain conditions occur within a program or record, or during some other process.

automatic send-receive — *See* ASR.

automatic sequencing — The ability of equipment to put information in order or in a connected series without human intervention.

automatic sequential operation — To develop a series or family of solutions from a set of equations, various initial conditions are recalculated with other parameters.

automatic stop — An automatic halting of a computer processing operation as the result of an error detected by built-in checking devices.

automatic switchover — An operating system which has a stand-by machine that is capable of detecting when the on-line machine is faulty and once this determination is made, to switch this operation to itself.

automatic tape transmitter — *See* tape transmitter, automatic.

automatic transaction recorder — Routines or systems are developed for recording several facts about each transaction with minimum manual input; e.g., worker and job identification are picked up from plates or individual cards, start-stop times are checked by clock notations, completions are developed by recording dials at inquiry stations throughout plants. This data capture method is used in mechanical payroll systems using badge readers and a digital clock for capturing employee working hours.

automation — The generalized term used to convey the dedicated use or exploitation of automatic machines or devices designed to control various processes, such as machine tools, routine office procedures, accounting, and several thousand other applications.

automation, source-data — The many methods of recording information in coded forms on paper tapes, punched cards, or tags that can be used over and over again to produce many other records without rewriting. (Synonymous with SDA.)

automaton — A machine designed to simulate the operations of living things, or to respond automatically to predesigned programs, stimuli, or signals. An automatic or self-acting or reacting system, often with capability to form logic decisions on the basis of programmed criteria, guides, or rules of its designers. Some automatons mimic living organisms and are responsive to environmental conditions.

automonitor — 1. To instruct an automatic computer to make a record of its information-handling operations. 2. A program or routine for the purpose stated in definition 1.

automonitor routine — A particular executive program or routine which develops a selective record of a computer's execution of another program to be completed.

automotive computer — A microcomputer installed in an automobile and used to monitor such quantities as speed, distance, fuel flow, time, battery voltage, and coolant temperature. In one type of system, a fuel management system indicates instantaneous and average fuel consumption, fuel used and remaining, and distance and time until empty; a crystal clock provides time, elapsed time, trip time, stopwatch, and alarm; and a cruise control accelerates the vehicle to any preselected speed, can be instructed to adjust to the flow of traffic, and incorporates a resume control.

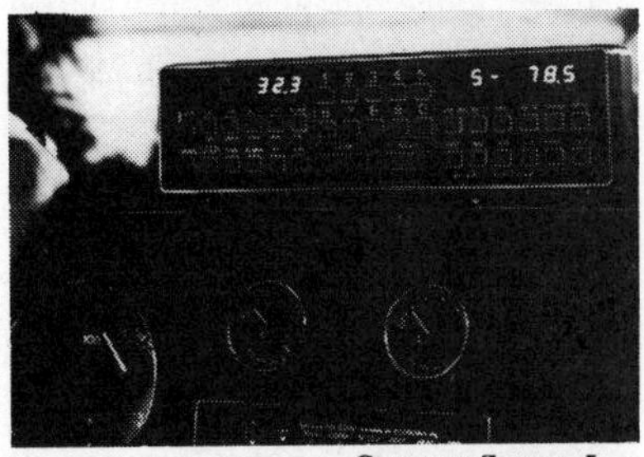

Courtesy Zemco, Inc.

Automotive computer.

autonomous devices — Some computer systems consist of processors, memories, and input/output devices. Since each device is autonomous (no device is dependent upon another for its timing), a system configuration can include memory modules of different speeds, processors of different types sharing the same memory modules, and standard or unique input/output devices.

autonomous working — The initiation and execution of a part of a computer or automation system independent and separate from other operations being performed on other parts of the system. The independent set of operations on various data are themselves often only monitored.

autopiler — A specific automatic compiler.

autopolling — Pertaining to a party-line type circuit with equipment that provides for automatic transmission from station to station by predetermined programming or arrangement.

auxiliary console — A console other than the main console.

auxiliary equipment — The peripheral equipment or devices which may or may not be in direct communication with the central processing unit of a computer.

auxiliary operation — An operation performed by equipment not under continuous control of the central processing unit.

auxiliary routine — A routine designed to assist in the operation of the computer, and in debugging other routines.

auxiliary storage — *Same as* storage, external.

availability — The ratio or percent of the time, during a certain period, that a piece of equipment is operating correctly, to the total time in that period. Also called operating ratio.

available machine time — The elapsed time when a computer is in operating condition, whether or not it is in use.

available storage list — *Same as* storage list, uncommitted.

average calculating operation — *See* calculating operation, average.

average-edge line — An imaginary line, in optical character recognition, that traces and smoothes the form of the printed or hand-written character to better convey the intended form.

average, moving — An average performed on data in which some of the values are more heavily valued than others.

average operation time — *See* operation time, average.

average random access time — The average time required to reach a specific point (or item of data) at an address chosen at random when the unit starts from an address which has also been selected at random. For i/o devices, the average random access time is generally equal to the worst case access time divided by two.

average transmission rate — *Same as* data transfer rate, average.

awaiting repair time — The interval of time from when the operator reports a fault or failure until the time when the engineer or maintenance man starts to repair the unit. If no fault is found, this time interval is called operating delay.

axis, reference — A line that is fixed or permanent—either horizontal or vertical—that is used as a reference for character design specification, location, and shape, for optical character recognition purposes.

B

Babbage, Charles — The British mathematician (1792–1871) whose "analytical engine" anticipated the automatic digital computer by more than a century. Babbage was also interested in the fields of geology, archeology, and astronomy, besides being an early exponent of the science of operations research. After working on several earlier calculating machines, Babbage conceived of his analytical engine in 1833 and devoted the rest of his life to its development. It was the first general-purpose automatic digital computer, was theoretically capable of executing any mathematical operation, could store sequences of instructions in memory, and used punched cards as mass memory for storage of mathematical tables. Unfortunately, Babbage's ideas were developed in a world without sophisticated electronic devices, so most of his work was scorned by his contemporaries. Nevertheless, Babbage's concept of the analytical engine ranks with the greatest intellectual achievements of all time.

background — In time-sharing and multiprogramming, the lower-priority work done by the computer when real-time, conversational, high-priority, or quick-response programs are inactive.

background processing — Work which has a low priority and is handled by the computer when higher priority or real-time entries are not occurring. Batch processing such as inventory control, payroll, housekeeping, etc., are often treated as background processing but can be interrupted on orders from terminals or inquiries from other units.

background program — A program that is not time-dependent. This program is of a lower priority than the foreground or main program and is at halt or standby while the main program runs.

background noise — 1. Extra bits or words that must be ignored or removed from the data at the time the data is used. 2. Errors introduced into the data in a system, especially one or more characteristics of any entity such as voltage, current, and data. 3. Loosely, any disturbance tending to interfere with the normal operation of a device or system.

background reflectance — *See* reflectance, background.

backing storage — *Same as* storage, external.

backplane — Connector blocks and wiring units constituting most or all of the interconnecting circuits of a system. For example, the printed circuit modules of a personal computer make up the system and are mounted by plugging into the backplane.

backspace — To move one unit in the reverse or backward direction as opposed to moving one unit in the forward direction, e.g., to move back one record or file on an i/o device.

backspace character — *See* character, backspace.

backspace key — That specific push button which causes a selected tape unit to backspace one record.

back-up — Relates to on-site or remote equipment which is designed and available to complete the operation or redo the operation in the event of primary equipment failure.

back-up copy — A copy preserved, usually on a different medium, as protection from destruction of original data or processed information.

back-up system — Such systems combine several sophisticated error detection and correction techniques which spot and correct equipment and transmission errors.

Backus-naur form — *Same as* Backus normal form.

Backus normal form (BNF) — A formal language structure for syntax parsing used in design of ALGOL-60.

backward-forward counter — A counter having both an add and subtract input, and capable of counting in either an increasing or a decreasing direction.

backward read — *See* read, backward.

badge reader — A device which senses data from a card or badge inserted into it. For example, an on-line controlled door entry can be achieved by inserting a badge into a terminal and transmitting the badge number to a computer. The computer checks this number against a particular listing and, if the number is found, sends a data message to the terminal causing the terminal to activate a customer-provided circuit that releases the door lock.

balanced circuits — Circuits that are terminated by a network whose impedance balances the impedance of the line so that the return losses are infinite.

balanced error — An error relating to a range which has a balance of zero, or a mean value of zero. A measure of balance in which the range of errors are equally probable, i.e., the highest and lowest values in the range are equal in value but have opposite signs.

balanced sorting — A technique used in a sort program to merge strings of sequenced data. The power of the merge is equal to T/2.

balancing error — A specific error which in effect balances or offsets another error, i.e., two offsetting errors of equal values or same numbers of opposite signs could exist and would be most difficult to detect or correct because the various check totals would agree or compare favorably.

band — 1. A group of tracks on a magnetic disk or on a magnetic drum. 2. In communications, the frequency spectrum between two defined limits.

band, clear — For documents to be used in optical character recognition, certain areas must be kept clear of ink or marks. The clear band is used by the OCR equipment and must be free of unrelated printing.

B AND-NOT A gate — *See* gate, B AND-NOT A.

bandwidth — The difference between the limiting frequencies of a continuous frequency band. Also, the range of frequencies within which performance falls within specified limits with regard to specific characteristics.

bank deposits, automatic — Individuals may arrange with some banks to have their paychecks, Social Security checks, military pay, or other regular income credited automatically to their accounts.

Courtesy Burroughs Corp.

Bank teller machine.

UPC

MSI

Bar codes.

The depositor in most cases receives a notice of deposit, but the actual transfer of funds is done by means of magnetic tape, which carries information from one computer to another.

bank POS terminals — Terminals in stores which are tied, through a network of computers and communications gear, to an account in a bank computer. When the customer presents his plastic card to the clerk, and so authorizes payment, the system makes sure the customer has sufficient funds on deposit, then immediately transfers the amount of the purchase from the customer's account to that of the store. POS is an abbreviation for point of sale.

bank teller machines, cash dispensing — Automatic machines that pay out cash when a customer inserts a plastic card and enters a personal identification number on a keyboard. The machines are connected to a host computer; they may be available at remote locations at all hours; and they may also offer such other services as making deposits and transferring funds between savings and checking accounts.

banner word — The first word in a file record.

bar code — Coding of consumer or other products by marking packages or labels with combinations of bars of varying thicknesses to represent characters and numerals. The various codes, Universal Product Code (UPC) and others, are designed to be read by optical wands or stationary in-counter readers.

bar-code optical scanner — *See* optical scanner, bar-code.

bar, fixed type — A type bar on a printer that cannot be removed by an operator. Therefore, the printer unit has a fixed alphabet.

bar, interchangeable type — A printer type bar which can be removed by the operator to change from one alphabet to another.

bar printer — *See* printer, bar.

bar, type — *See* printer type bar.

base — *See* number, base.

base address — 1. A number that appears as an address in a computer instruction, but which serves as the base, index, initial, or starting point for subsequent addresses to be modified. (Synonymous with presumptive address and reference address.) 2. A number used in symbolic coding in conjunction with a relative address.

baseband — The frequency band occupied by information signals before they are combined with a carrier in the modulation process.

baseband transmission — Direct transmission of pulses over short distances (50 feet to 10 miles) using privately owned cable or common-carrier wire pairs. Longer-distance communication must use modulated carriers.

base, data — The set of data or information from which conclusions can be drawn. This is the set of data that is internally accessible to the computer and on which the computer performs operations.

base notation — *See* notation, base.

base notation, mixed — A method of expressing a quantity by using two or more characters, where each character is of a different radix.

base number — *See* number, base.

base register — *Same as* index register.

BASIC — Beginner's All-purpose Symbolic Instruction Code. A procedure-level computer language that is well-suited for time-sharing. BASIC, developed at Dartmouth College, is probably one of the easiest computer programming languages to learn and master. These attributes have allowed BASIC to be instrumental in the spread of time-sharing to businesses that are not within the computer industry.

basic code — *Same as* code, absolute.

basic coding — *See* absolute coding.

BASIC graphic extensions — BASIC graphic extensions offer important BASIC extensions, including: special graphic primitives, file system data access; matrices for graphic manipulation; string functions for text handling; and high-level interrupts to access the processor whenever users need it.

BASIC immediate execution mode — A feature that allows the user to examine, modify, and control sections of the running program that have been stopped at selected points. This is an aid in program debugging. A single statement or a small part of a program can be executed immediately after being input.

basic linkage — A linkage that is used repeatedly in one routine, program, or system and that follows the same set of rules each time. *See* linkage.

BASIC, multiuser — Multiuser BASIC is a fast incremental compiler developed for use as a conversational programming language. It provides on-line time-shared access to the microcomputer. Several users simultaneously can develop programs, enter and retrieve data, examine files, and communicate.

basic telecommunications access method — An access method that permits read/write communications with remote devices. Abbreviated BTAM.

BASIC, Tiny — A language designed to require only a small amount of memory and to be easy for children to learn and use. To this end, an Interpretive Language (IL) was developed. The IL is a language within a language. It forms the framework or skeleton on which Tiny BASIC is built. One feature of writing in IL is that programs can be more easily rewritten for different microprocessors.

batch — A group of records or documents considered as a single unit for the purpose of processing.

batch data processing — *See* batch processing.

batch entry mode, terminal — Many terminals may be operated in what is commonly referred to as a batch-entry mode. This means that the operator may form the message within the terminal, perform editing as required, and send the entire text to the computer when satisfied the message is correct. This method of message formation is in contrast to a character mode, in which a character is immediately transmitted to the computer as it is generated from the keyboard.

batching with a control total — In batching with a control total, some data field that is common to all items or documents is accumulated for the control total which then becomes the basis for balancing operations during processing. The control field may be an amount, a quantity, an item code, an account number, etc.

batch input reader — This is used to effect direct assignment of a sequential input device to a sequence of serially executed programs.

batch input spooler — This is used to effect spooled input from a sequential input device to a sequence of programs which may execute in parallel.

batch output spooler — This is used to effect spooled output to a sequential output device.

batch process — A sequential-processing procedure that uses an accumulation or group of units; this is in contrast to online processing, during which each unit of data or information is processed immediately at the time of presentation to the top of the processing sequence.

batch processing — A systems approach to processing where a number of similar input items are grouped for processing during the same machine run.

batch processing, real-time — *See* real-time batch processing.

batch, remote — The method of entering jobs for the computer to perform through a remote terminal as opposed to normal batch processing, where inputting the job must take place in the computer center.

batch ticket — A control document that summarizes the control totals and identifies the appropriate group of source documents.

batch total — 1. The sum of certain quantities, pertaining to batches of unit records, used to verify accuracy of operations on a particular batch of records; e.g., in a payroll calculation, the batches might be departments, and batch totals could be number of employees in the department, total hours worked in the department, total pay for the department. Batches, however, may be arbitrary, such as orders received from 9 am to 11 am on a certain day. 2. Each or any of a number of sums that can be calculated from a series of records which are intended to serve as aids to check the accuracy of computer operations.

batch transaction files — Transactions accumulated as a batch ready for processing against the master file.

batch transmission, RFT systems — Transmission in which forms stored with released for transmission status code are automatically batch transmitted to the central site computer upon receipt of the next computer poll. Optionally, on some systems, batches may be held until completed and released in a group of multiple batches.

baud — A technical term, originally used to express the capabilities of a telegraph transmission facility in terms of "modulation rate per unit of time . . ." For practical purposes, it is now used interchangeably with "bits per second" as the unit of measure of data flow. It was derived from the name Baudot, after whom the Baudot Code was named. Example: If the duration of audit is 20 milliseconds, the modulation rate is 50 bauds.

baud rate — The transmission rate, which is in effect synonymous with signal events (usually bits) per second. It is used as a measure of serial data flow between computers and/or communication equipment or devices.

bauds, data transmission — The measure of the speed of a transmission. A baud is equal to one signal element per second.

B-box — *Same as* index register.

B-bus — The second source bus to the ALU in many 2- or 3-bus microcomputers.

BCD (Binary Coded Decimal) — A numerical representation in which decimal digits are represented by binary numerals. The most common binary code is the 8–4–2–1. In binary coded decimal the number 14 would be 0001 0100.

BCD coding — A system of representing decimal equivalents by a series of four binary digits.

BCO (Binary Coded Octal) — In this system, binary numbers are used to represent octal digits of an octal number. In the common 4–2–1 octal code 101 equals octal 5.

BCP messages — Byte Control Protocol messages. These messages are transmitted in units called blocks. The components of a transmission block include several parts. The *header* field contains auxiliary information that identifies the address of the message destination or source, the job number (if any), the type of message (data or control), the control action, and a positive or negative acknowledgment to ensure error-free reception of a previous message or messages. Control actions are used to reset or initialize a secondary station, to acknowledge good or bad reception of blocks, to inquire why a response or acknowledgment has not occurred within a specific time period, or to abort a transfer sequence.

BCS — British Computer Society.

beam storage — Storage units which use one or more beams of electrons or light to gain access to individual storage cells for operation. Most often, cathode ray tube storage.

beat — 1. One of the fundamental states of the control unit of a computer or the duration of such a state. A beat might be designed to set up a correct circuit to perform a function, and execution of it might be the next beat. The duration might be a single word period. 2. A time measurement for a given computer word to pass a given point as in serial storage delay-lines. All of the bits of a word must pass through the input control gate; the beat is then the sum of all the bit times.

begin — A procedure delimiter in the ALGOL language.

beginning-of-information marker (BIM) — A reflective spot on the back of a magnetic tape, 10 feet from the physical beginning of the tape, which is sensed photoelectrically to indicate the point on tape at which recording may begin.

beginning of tape control — *See* beginning of information marker (BIM).

beginning of tape marker — *See* beginning of information marker (BIM).

beginning tape label — A description which appears at the beginning of a tape describing the content of the tape.

Bell data jack — A device through which modems may connect directly to the telephone network instead of through a data access arrangement (DAA), which formerly was rented from the phone companies.

benchmark — A point of reference from which measurements can be made.

benchmark problem — 1. A problem to evaluate the performance of computers relative to each other. 2. A routine used to determine the speed performance of a computer. One method is to use one-tenth of the time required to perform nine complete additions and one complete multiplication. A complete addition or a complete multiplication time includes the time required to procure two operands from storage, perform the operation and store the result, and the time required to select and execute the required number of instructions to do this.

benchmark routine — A set of routines or problems which will help determine the performance of a given piece of equipment.

benchmark tests — Various tests for assisting in measurement of product performance under typical conditions of use. Typically, a program or group of programs can run on several computers for purposes of comparing speed, throughput, ease of conversion, special timing programs, etc.

B EXCEPT A gate — *Same as* gate, B AND-NOT A.

bias — 1. The departure from a reference value of the average of a set of values. 2. An unbalanced range of error, i.e., having an average error that is not zero. 3. An operating voltage applied to elements of a transistor or vacuum tube to set the operating characteristics.

bias check — A means of testing circuits for incipient or intermittent failures developed by varying the voltages applied to the circuit. Such marginal or bias checks are helpful prior to extended run periods.

bias distortion — 1. Bias distortion or bias of start-stop teletypewriter signals is the uniform shifting of the beginning of all marking pulses from their proper positions in relation to the beginning of the start pulse. 2. Distortion affecting a two-condition (or binary) modulation (or restitution), in which all the significant intervals corresponding to one of the two significant conditions have longer or shorter durations than the corresponding theoretical durations.

biased exponent — *See* exponent, biased.

bias, internal (teletypewriter) — The bias, either marking or spacing, that may occur within a start-stop teletypewriter receiving mechanism, and which will have the same effect on the margins of operation as a bias which is external to the receiver.

bias, marking — A bias distortion which lengthens the marking impulse by advancing the mark-to-space transition.

bias, ordering — 1. A check on the exactness of the order of alphabetic words or numerals. 2. A unique characteristic of a sequence which keeps it away from or toward a needed, designed, or desired order. In consequence, some degree of effort is required to achieve the desired order other than would normally be expected, say, from a random distribution.

bias, spacing — A bias distortion which lengthens the spacing impulse by delaying the space-to-mark transition.

bias test — *See* bias check.

bias testing — *See* testing, marginal.

bibliography — 1. A list of documents pertaining to a given subject or author. 2. An annotated catalog of documents.

biconditional gate — *Same as* gate, exclusive NOR.

biconditional statement — A logic condition that exists when two conditions are either both true or both false; a logical AND or NAND gate.

bidirectional — Pertaining to a type of bus structure in which a single conductor is used to transmit data or signals in either direction between a peripheral device and a central processor or memory.

bidirectional data bus — A data bus in which digital information can be transferred in either direction. With reference to some microcomputers, the bidirectional data path by which data is transferred between the microprocessor chip, memory, and i/o devices.

bidirectional flow — Flow that can extend over the same flow lines in either direction as in flowcharting by being represented by a single flowline.

bidirectional operation — An operation in which reading, writing, and searching may be conducted in either direction, thus saving time and providing easy access to stored information.

bifurcation — A logic condition where only two states are possible. This is the basic logic pattern of binary digital computers.

B ignore A gate — *See* gate, B ignore A.

B ignore A gate, negative — *See* gate, B ignore A negative.

billibit — One billion bits. *Same as* kilomegabit.

billicycle — One billion cycles.

billisecond — *Same as* nanosecond.

BIM — *See* beginning of information marker.

B implies A gate, negative — *Same as* gate, B AND-NOT A.

binary — 1. A numbering system based on 2's rather than 10's which uses only the digits 0 and 1 when written. 2. A characteristic, property, or condition in which there are but two possible alternatives; e.g., the binary number system using 2 as its base and using only the digits zero (0) and one (1). *See* number system.

binary arithmetical operation — An arithmetical operation with operands and results represented in binary notation.

binary arithmetic operation — *See* arithmetic operation, binary.

binary baud rate — Binary speed through a serial interface is traditionally defined as the number of signal elements per second. When each element is one bit, the baud rate equals the number of bits per second.

binary card — *See* card, binary.

binary cell — A cell of one binary digit capacity.

binary chain — A series of binary circuits existing in one of two possible states and so arranged that each circuit can affect or modify the condition of the circuit following it.

binary code — A coding system in which the encoding of any data is done through the use of bits, i.e., 0 or 1.

binary code, cyclic — *Same as* code, cyclic.

binary-coded address — *See* address, binary-coded.

binary-coded character — One element of a notation system representing alphameric characters such as decimal digits, alphabetic letters, and punctuation marks, by a predetermined configuration of consecutive binary digits.

binary-coded decimal (BCD) — Pertaining to a decimal notation in which the individual decimal digits are each represented by a binary code group; i.e., in the 8–4–2–1 coded decimal notation, the number twenty-three is represented as 0010 0011. In pure binary notation, twenty-three is represented by 10111.

binary-coded decimal notation — A method of representing each figure in a decimal number by a four-figured binary number.

binary-coded decimal number — A number usually consisting of successive groups of figures, in which each group of four figures is a binary number that represents, but does not necessarily equal arithmetically, a particular figure in an associated decimal number; e.g., if the three rightmost figures of a decimal number are 262, the three rightmost figure groups of the binary coded decimal number might be 0010, 0110, and 0010.

binary-coded decimal representation (BCD) — A system of representing decimal numbers. Each decimal digit is represented by a combination of four binary digits (bits), as follows:

Binary	*Decimal*	*Binary*	*Decimal*
0000	0	0101	5
0001	1	0110	6
0010	2	0111	7
0011	3	1000	8
0100	4	1001	9

binary-coded digit — One element of a notation system for representing a decimal digit by a fixed number of binary positions.

binary code, dense — Particular binary coding system which uses all possible binary representations and positions. The binary-coded-decimal notation does not use 6 of the 16 possible patterns and thus, in effect, wastes computing space.

binary-coded octal — A coding system in which binary numbers are used to represent the octal digits of an octal number.

binary counter — 1. A counter that counts according to the binary number system. 2. A counter capable of assuming one of two stable states.

binary digit — A numeral in the binary scale of notation. This digit may be zero (0), or one (1). It may be equivalent to an on or off condition, a yes, or a no. Often abbreviated to "bit." Computers use this kind of number internally. Follow the table below by progressing geometrically per column right to left, and add the column values where one appears, i.e., 7 is 1, 2, 4, 0, right to left.

	Column Values
	8 4 2 1
0 is	0 0 0 0
1 is	0 0 0 1
2 is	0 0 1 0
3 is	0 0 1 1
4 is	0 1 0 0
5 is	0 1 0 1
6 is	0 1 1 0
7 is	0 1 1 1
8 is	1 0 0 0
9 is	1 0 0 1

binary digits, equivalent — A comparison to establish an equivalency of the number of binary digit places which are necessary to represent a given number in another radix, such as decimal (10). Decimal, octal, binary-coded-decimal, and straight binary are expressed with the same values but each requires a different number of digit places for the same values.

binary element — An element of data which may assume either of two values or states, i.e., 0, 1 or +, −.

binary incremental representation — In this type of incremental representation, the value of an increment is limited to one of the two values plus one or minus one for each quantum step. The maximum positive rate of change is represented as a continuous string of plus ones, and the maximum negative rate of change is a continuous string of minus ones.

binary logic — Digital logic elements which operate with two distinct states. The two states are variously called true and false, high and low, on and off, or 1 and 0. In computers they are represented by two different voltage levels. The level which is more positive (or less negative) than the other is called the high level, the other the low level. If the true (1) level is the most positive voltage, such logic is referred to as positive true or positive logic.

binary mode — Operations using basic machine arithmetic may use binary mode, i.e., the number system with a base 2, allowing only the digits 0 and 1, in contrast to the decimal system of base 10 with digits, 0, 1, 2 . . . . . 9.

binary normal — *Same as* binary.

binary notation — *See* number, binary.

binary number — A number, usually consisting of more than one figure, representing a sum in which the individual quantity represented by each figure is based on a radix of two. The figures used are 0 and 1.

binary number system — *See* binary number.

binary numeral — The binary representation of a number; e.g., 0101 is the binary numeral and "V" is the roman numeral of the number of fingers on one hand.

binary operation — An operation which depends on the applications and the strict adherence to the rules of Boolean algebra, i.e., any operation in which the operands and results take either one of two values or states such as logic operations on single bits.

binary, ordinary — *See* binary.

binary pair — A circuit which has two states, each requiring an appropriate trigger for excitation and transition from one state to the other.

binary point — That point in a binary number which separates the integral from the fractional part. It is analogous to the decimal point for a decimal number.

binary, pure — *Same as* binary.

binary, reflected — A code using the binary 0 and 1, and so constructed that each successive code is derived from its predecessor by inverting only one bit. Reflected binary is a particular form of gray code.

binary scale (or numbering system) — A numbering system having a radix (base) of two. Thus, only two symbols (0 and 1) are needed.

binary search — A search in which a set of items is divided into two parts, where one part is rejected, and the process is repeated on the accepted part until the item with the desired property is found. (Synonymous with dichotomizing search.)

binary signaling — A communications mode in which information is passed by the presence and absence, or plus and minus variations, of one parameter of the signaling medium only.

binary, straight — *Same as* binary.

binary synchronous communications — Abbreviated BSC. A line control procedure for communicating. It can be expressed in several data codes: 8-bit EBCDIC, 7-bit USASCII, or 6-bit transcode. The only requirements are that the code should include the required line control characters and that these characters should be used according to specified rules.

binary table search, data-base — A binary search table is an ordered listing; the search technique is to compare first on the midpoint of the table, and then on the midpoint of the half containing the desired argument. The table is successively halved until the proper entry is found. The half containing the desired argument can be identified because the table is in ordered sequence.

binary-to-decimal conversion — Conversion of a binary number to the equivalent decimal number, i.e., a base two number to a base ten number.

binary variable — A variable which assumes values in a set containing exactly two elements, often symbolized as 0 and 1. This is often confused with double-value variable; e.g., $y = \pm\sqrt{x}$. (Synonymous with two-state variable.)

binary-weighted error-detection system — This system is based upon the concept of assigning binary-one values to all marking pulses or each code combination.

binary zero — Contrasted to the only other binary representation, 1, the binary zero represents the lack of magnitude, and is represented as the presence or absence of a punched hole in a card or tape, a metallic spot, a current or lack of current, etc.

bin, tape — A magnetic tape storage device with movable read/record heads or fixed heads for each loop. The heads and loops can move to particular or selected locations on a tape, thus providing more rapid access time than for plain serial reels of tape which must be rewound.

bionics — The application of knowledge gained from the analysis of living systems to the creation of hardware that will perform functions in a manner analogous to the more sophisticated functions of the living system.

biosensor — A mechanism for detecting and transmitting biological data from an organism in a way which permits display or storage of results.

bipolar (unipolar) — When a logical "true" input is represented by an electrical voltage polarity opposite to that representing a logical "false" input, the signal is defined as bipolar. If both "true" and "false" inputs are represented by the same electrical voltage polarity, the signal is defined as unipolar.

biquinary — A two-part representation of a decimal digit consisting of a binary portion with values of 0 or 5, and a quinary portion with values of 0 through 4; e.g., the number 7 is coded as 12 which implies 5 and 2.

biquinary code — *See* code, biquinary.

biquinary number — *See* number, biquinary.

biquinary system — *See* code, biquinary.

bistable — Pertaining to devices capable of assuming either one of two stable states.

bistable latch — A standard flip-flop which can be enabled to store a logical 1 or a logical 0. In basic use, one bistable latch device is commonly used in memory and register circuits for the storage of each bit.

bisync — Bisynchronous transmission, or IBM Bisync, is a set of conventions used by IBM for controlling synchronous transmission. These conventions are rules and procedures for controlling the message format and line protocol. The set of conventions adopted for structuring a single transmitted block of data is called the message format. These conventions specify what data link control characters can be used for starting and ending a message. They also specify the type of error checking to be performed, which bytes are included and which are excluded in the check, and the methods for utilizing the data link escape character.

bit — 1. A binary digit; hence, a unit of data in binary notation. In the binary numbering system, only two marks (0 and 1) are used. Each of these marks is called a binary digit. 2. A single pulse in a group of pulses. 3. A unit of information capacity of a storage device. The capacity in bits is the logarithm to the base two of the number of possible states of the device. (Related to storage capacity.)

bit bumming — The process of trying to squeeze the required software into the minimum amount of memory in a microcomputer system.

bit, check — A binary check digit; often a parity bit. (Related to parity check and self-checking number.)

bit combination — *Same as* bit pattern.

bit density — A measure of the number of bits recorded per unit of length or area.

bit, flag — A specific information bit that indicates a type or form of demarcation that has been reached. This may be carry, overflow, etc. Generally the flag bit refers to special conditions, such as various types of interrupts.

bit, guard — A bit which indicates whether a main or disk memory word or group of words is to be filed.

bit, information — In data communication, bits which are genuine data source bits and not those used for error control or checking procedures.

bit instructions — Instructions that test, set, or reset any bit in memory and may be used for setting flags and for monitoring and controlling on-off functions such as switches, relays, valves, and indicators.

bit location — A storage position on a record capable of storing one bit.

bit parallel — Pertaining to a specific method of simultaneous movement or transmission over separate wires of all bits in a contiguous set of bits.

bit, parity — A check bit that indicates whether the total number of binary "1" digits in a character or word (excluding the parity bit) is odd or even. If a "1" parity bit indicates an odd number of "1" digits, then a "0" bit indicates an even number of them. If the total number of "1" bits, including the parity bit, is always even, the system is called an even-parity system. In an odd-parity system, the total number of "1" bits, including the parity bit, is always odd.

bit pattern — A combination of N binary digits to represent 2 to the N possible choices; e.g., a 3-bit pattern represents 8 possible combinations.

bit, presence — An individual sentinel bit which appears in the descriptor to indicate that information which is being referenced is in the high-speed storage area.

bit rate — The rate at which binary digits, or pulses representing them, pass a given point on a communications line or channel. (Clarified by baud and channel capacity.)

bit-rate generators — Devices that provide the reference frequencies required by serial interfaces (TTY, UART, cassette, modem).

bit serial — Pertaining to a method of sequentially moving or transferring a contiguous set of bits one at a time over a single wire, according to a fixed sequence.

bit, serial-by — *See* serial-by-bit.

bit, sign — A binary digit used as a sign draft.

bit significance — The presence or absence of a bit in a certain location of an instruction word which designates the instruction to be of certain type, for example, zero vs. one-address instruction.

bits, information — Bits that are generated by the data source and which are not used for error-control by the data-transmission system.

bit site — A location on magnetic recording media where a bit of information is stored.

bit-slice microprocessor architecture — The basic architecture of a multiple bit-slice processor can be split into three major blocks: the bit slices, the controller, and the control store. The ALU (arithmetic-logic unit) and the MAR (memory address register) are usually combined into a single circuit referred to as a bit slice. Typically, bit-slice chips are 2 bits or 4 bits wide. Bit slices can be cascaded to create word lengths tailored to the application. For example, if an application requires a 14-bit word, seven 2-bit slices can be cascaded together.

bits, punctuation — The use of a variable-length data format requires that there be a method of indicating the actual length of a unit of information. This requirement is fulfilled by two punctuation bits associated with each memory location. These bits can constitute a word mark—used to define the length of a field; an item mark—used to define the length of an item; or a record mark—used to define the length of a record.

bits, service — Such overhead bits which are not check bits, as, for example, request for repetition, numbering sequence, others.

bits, string of — It is most common and conventional to add a string of bits at the end of a block, in magnetic tapes, to allow a parity check in the columns of the entire block or record.

bit, stop — The last element of a character designed for asynchronous serial transmission that defines the character space immediately to the left of the most significant character in accumulator storage.

bit stream — This is a term used regularly in conjunction with transmission methods in which character separation is accomplished by the terminal equipment, and the bits are transmitted over the circuit in a consecutive line of bits.

bit stream transmission — The method of transmitting characters at fixed time intervals. No stop and start elements are used, and the bits making up the characters follow each other without pause.

bit string — A one-dimensional array of bits ordered by reference to the relations between adjacent numbers.

black box — A generic term used to describe an unspecified device which performs a special function or in which known inputs produce known outputs in a fixed relationship (computer).

blank — 1. A regimented place of storage where data may be stored, e.g., a location in a storage medium. (Synonymous with space.) 2. A character on a printer used to indicate an output space in which nothing is printed. 3. A condition of "no information at all" in a given column of a punched card or in a given location in a perforated tape. In the case of tape, the feed hole is perforated but no intelligence is perforated into the same vertical column. In some cases, however, processing equipment may be programmed to recognize a blank and perform certain functions as with other codes.

blank character — Any character or characters used to produce a character space on an output medium.

blank deleter — A device that eliminates the receiving of blanks in perforated paper tape.

blank instruction — *See* instruction, dummy.

blank, switching — A specific range of values in which the incoming signal can be altered without also changing the outgoing response. (Synonymous with dead band and dead zone.)

blank-transmission test — This feature allows the checking of any data field for all blank positions. As a computer control, it can be used to prevent the destruction of existing records in storage, indicate when the last item from a spread card has been processed, skip calculation if a rate or factor field is blank, etc.

blast — The release of various specified areas or blocks of either main or auxiliary storage no longer needed by an operational program. This type program will execute a blast macroinstruction which causes the control program to return the address of the area blasted to its list of storage available for use by future operational programs.

bleed, ink — *See* ink bleed

blind (unblind) — The selective controlling of a transmission printer or reperforator. Example: used to prevent prices from typing on a receiving teletypewriter.

B-line — *Same as* index register.

blinking cursor — The cursor is sometimes designed to blink at 1 to 6 Hz to attract the operator's attention. Its controls can lie in hardware or software, and include home (top left position on the screen), left (one character to the left), right (one character to the right), up (one row up), down (one row down), and return (left position on the next lower row) functions. Variations are numerous, however.

block — 1. A collection or group of words, records, or characters which are handled as a single unit. In real-time systems, blocks are used to describe input-/output or working storage areas in main storage. A file storage block is often called a "physical record." 2. The set of locations or tape positions in which a block of words, as defined above, is stored or recorded. 3. A circuit assemblage which functions as a unit, e.g., a circuit building block of standard design, and the logic block in a sequential circuit.

block access, data-base — Block access relates to the grouping of records into physical blocks during the mapping of a file onto a storage medium. Blocks represent the physical view of data. For those programs that do not require system support of logical access to records, it is possible to read and write physical blocks.

block, analysis — A relocatable part of the computer storage in which program testing or statistical data are stored which can later be used to analyze the performance of the system. During program testing there may be an analysis block for each transaction in the system, and when the transaction leaves the system this block is dumped into a file or tape.

block check characters — Abbreviated BCC. Line control procedures include the generation, transmission, and testing of check bits. These check bits, often called block check characters, make up the trailer field of the transmission block. They are generated by a checking algorithm that is usually applied to the information field of a block.

block, control — A storage location which contains information in condensed, formalized form necessary for the control of a task, function, or operation.

block, data-set control — *See* data-set control block.

block diagram — 1. A sequential, graphic representation of operations of the various computer machines through the use of symbols which represent functional steps rather than the physical structural details. The block diagram is usually the gross or macro diagram for the entire integrated system or large application areas. Flowcharts then provide the specific detail of various operations. 2. A graphical representation of the hardware in a computer system. The primary purpose of a block diagram is to indicate the paths, along with information and-/or control flows, between the various parts of a computer system. It should not be confused with the term flowchart.

block, entry — *See* entry block.

blockette — A subdivision of a group of consecutive machine words transferred as a unit, particularly with reference to input and output.

block, event control — A unique information (control) block designed to control status of operations which are waiting for an act or special signal to happen; i.e., processing may be halted until one or more events occur. Usually a WAIT macroinstruction is involved.

block gap — The space and/or distance between particular blocks of data or instructions on a tape or other storage medium left blank in order to separate blocks of data. Insertion of such blanks by programmers or by automatic means is to fix block lengths. Tapes can be stopped, for example, or they can be brought up to standard speed again, within such gaps.

block gaps, cassette — Placement of data onto the recordable region of a cassette tape is organized into units called files. Adjacent files are separated by file gaps, which are generated under software control. Each file consists of one or more blocks separated by block gaps. Block gaps are generated automatically. Each block consists of one or more bytes of data and two cyclic redundancy check (CRC) bytes. Under program control, the CRC bytes are appended when a block is written and checked when a block is read.

block ignore character — *See* character, block ignore.

blocking — To efficiently decrease the number of starts and stops; a combining of two or more items or groups of items.

blocking data, ANSI — It is usually convenient to organize data on tape into words, blocks, and files. Tapes are gapped periodically for this purpose, which permits reading equipment to stop off data as well as to frame or reference the serial data stream. The standard ANSI format is a block-oriented system in which data is recorded in phase encoding with 72 characters per block and space in the block for control characters (line feed and carriage return, etc.) and a preamble and postamble. Each block is separated by at least 6 inches of gap which frames the data.

blocking factor — The limit of the data records which can be contained in a given block on tape.

block, input — 1. A section of internal storage of a computer reserved for the receiving and processing of input information. (Synonymous with input area.) 2. An input buffer. 3. A block of computer words considered as a unit and intended or destined to be transferred from an external source or storage medium to the internal storage of the computer.

block length — The total number of records, words, or characters contained in one block.

block loading — A technique for program loading in which the control sections of the program or program segment are loaded into adjacent positions in the main memory.

blockmark — A storage-indicator mark which indicates the end of a block of data that would be written on tape for a processor that handles variable-length blocks on tape.

block, message reference — The storage areas and working storage set aside by the system when more than one message is being processed in parallel by the system. This message reference block is associated with that message so long as it registers in the computer for processing.

block, order — 1. A group of computer words or a record being transferred out of the equipment. 2. A section of storage reserved to handle such outputs.

block, output — 1. A block of computer words considered as a unit and intended or destined to be transferred from an internal storage medium to an external destination. 2. A section of internal storage reserved for storing data which are to be transferred out of the computer. (Synonymous with output area.) 3. A block used as an output buffer.

block parity system — A system of using an additional bit to a block of information to detect single-bit errors in the whole block.

block record — A specific storage area of fixed size which usually contains a main memory or file storage, organized into standard blocks to allow more flexibility in storage allocation and control.

blocks — Records are transferred to and from magnetic tapes in the form of blocks (sometimes called physical records). A block (physical record) may contain one or more records (logical). Records may be reduced to blocks on tape to reduce the acceleration and deceleration time.

block sort — A sort of one or more of the most significant characters of a key to serve as a means of making workable sized groups from a large volume of records to be sorted.

block splitting — *See* cellular splitting.

block, standby — A location always set aside in storage for communication with buffers in order to make more efficient use of such buffers.

block, storage — A portion or section of storage usually within a storage area. A storage block is considered a single element for holding a specific or fixed number of words.

block structure — A technique allowing program segmentation into blocks of information or subroutines of a total program.

block, table — A distinct portion or subset of a table of data or instructions, usually specifically identified for more convenient access.

block transfer — The conveyance of a group of consecutive words from one place to another.

block, variable — In a variable block the number of characters in the block is determined by the programmer (usually between some practical limits).

blue ribbon program — *Same as* program, star.

BNF — Abbreviation for Backus normal form.

board — An electrical panel which can be altered with the addition or deletion of external wiring. Also known as a plugboard, panel, or wire board.

board, control — *Same as* control panel.

board, plotting — The flat surface unit of a plotter; that part of a plotting machine or unit on which plots, curves, or displays of lines, diagrams, symbols, etc., are transferred or transformed. The plotting board is the output section of the total plotter machine displaying the results of the plotter's manipulation of analog or digital data, usually for human use.

board, plug — *See* plugboard computer.

board, problem — *See* plugboard computer.

board, wiring — *See* plugboard computer.

book — A particular large segment of memory most often used in virtual memory addressing.

book, documentation — All the material needed to document a computer application, including problem statement, flowcharts, coding, and operating instructions.

bookkeeping operation — *Same as* housekeeping.

book, run — Material needed to code document a computer application, including problem statement, flowcharts, coding, and operating instructions.

Boolean — Pertaining to the algebra developed by George Boole.

Boolean add — *Same as* gate, OR.

Boolean algebra — An algebra named for George Boole. This algebra is similar in form to ordinary algebra, but with classes, propositions, one-of-circuit elements, etc., for variables rather than data values. It includes the operators AND, OR, NOT, EXCEPT, IF, THEN.

Boolean calculus — Boolean algebra modified to include time. Thus, such additional operators as after, while, happen, delay, before, etc., are provided. It is concerned with binary-state changes with time (triggers, delay lines).

Boolean complement — *Same as* gate, NOT.

Boolean connective — A symbol between two operands or before the operands. Such symbols are for exclusion, conjunction, nonequivalence, disjunction, etc.

Boolean logic — A mathematical analysis of logic. Applications of Boolean logic include information retrieval and circuit-switching designs.

Boolean operation — A logic or math manipulation, association, or operation which uses or applies the rules of Boolean algebra. The operands, states, or results assume either one of two values, conditions, or states when determined or evaluated as to which of such two states is in being or to be assumed, by either of the two variables or expressions, such as on/off; go/no-go, zero-/one; etc.

Boolean operation, binary — A specific Boolean operation on two operands, the result of which depends upon both of them. The results from each of four possible combinations of values p and q form a truth table, or Boolean operation table.

Boolean operation, dyadic — An operation in Boolean algebra performed on or with two operands and in which the result is dependent upon both of them. Operations on or with two operands are usually represented with connective symbols written between them. . . . as "union" or other Boolean connectives.

Such connective operands or operations are most often related to Boolean truth tables.

Boolean operation, monadic — An operation performed on one operand.

Boolean operation table — A table which shows the value of the results from each of four possible combinations of values p and q. This is synonymous with truth table, but Boolean operation table is the preferred use in electronic data processing procedures.

Boolean variable — The use of two-valued Boolean algebra to assume either one of the only two values possible. Examples: true or false; on or off; open or closed. Basically, all digital computers use the two-state or two-variable Boolean algebra in construction and operation.

bootleg program — *See* program, bootleg.

bootstrap — 1. A technique or device designed to bring itself into a desired state by means of its own action. For example, a machine routine whose first few instructions are sufficient to bring the rest of itself into the computer from an input device. This usually involves either the manual entering of a few instructions, or the use of a special key on the console. 2. A brief developer subroutine which, while in storage, controls the computer to read in other data such as a loading routine, after control has been transferred to it.

bootstrap input program — Very popular programs which have simple preset computer operations to facilitate information or program input reading and which also contain instructions to be read until the program is assembled or executed; i.e., one instruction pulls other preset instructions.

bootstrap loader — A subroutine which is usually automatic and built into the hardware of the computer, which is capable of initiating the reading of another subroutine whose first instructions are designed to bring in the rest of the subroutine and thus initiate the total program schedule.

bootstrap loading routine — *See* loading routine (bootstrap).

bootstrap memory — The bootstrap memory is a time-saving device built into the main computer. One consists of sixteen 30-bit words of wired storage. It is programmed (wired) to fit the specialized needs of various computer users. The program and words in the bootstrap memory cannot be altered by the computer but can be manually changed when necessary. The purpose of the bootstrap memory is to provide for the automatic reading of new programs into the computer, with protection against erasing its vital instructions (some computers).

bootstrapping, communication line — Some of the computing systems at the end of lines for which the line-control procedure is used will have their software loaded and the system restarted via the communications line. This starting up of an inoperative system is called "bootstrapping." The bootstrap procedure can be part of the line control procedure or it can be embedded in the text field.

bootstrap routine, tape — Some load tapes have, as the first block, a bootstrap routine which serves to bring in the remainder of the resident and various other parts of the system. The bootstrap routines also provide a simple card load routine, a panic dump, and a method of patching the resident system prior to writing it to drum.

BOP messages — Abbreviation for Bit Oriented Protocol messages. They are transmitted in frames, and all messages adhere to one standard frame format.

bore — Inside diameter of the hub on a tape reel.

B OR-NOT A gate — *See* gate, B OR-NOT A.

borrow — An arithmetically negative carry. It occurs in direct subtraction by raising the low order digit of the minuend by one unit of the next higher order digit; e.g., when subtracting 67 from 92, a tens digit is borrowed from the 9, to raise the 2 to a factor of 12; the 7 of 67 is then subtracted from the 12 to yield 5 as the units digit of the difference; the 6 is then subtracted from 8, or 9 − 1, yielding 2 as the tens digit of the difference.

BOT, cartridge — Abbreviation for Beginning Of Tape. The point to which a cartridge tape is rewound.

bound — The upper or lower limit of values that can be permitted.

boundary, byte — In an IBM 360 system, any core address within the computer.

boundary, character — 1. A real or imaginary rectangle which serves as a boundary, in character recognition, between consecutive characters or successive lines on a source document. 2. A character recognition term indicating the largest rectangle with a side parallel to the reference edge of the document. Each of the sides of this rectangle is tangent to the printed outline of a particular character.

boundary register — A special register used in a multiprogrammed system to designate the upper and lower addresses of each user's program block in the main memory.

bound, tape — *Same as* tape limited.

box — In a programming flow chart, a logical unit of computer programming surrounded by a rectangle and treated as a unit.

box, B- — *See* index register.

box, decision — The symbol used in flowcharting to indicate a choice or branching in the information-processing path.

box, loop — A specific register used as an index register but only to modify instructions immediately prior to their execution. For example, a number or symbol is addended to an instruction as the last step before the instruction is executed and the instruction is thus modified, but without changing the instruction as it is stored in memory.

box, stunt — A device used in teleprinters to perform nonreadout functions such as carriage return, line feed, ring signal bell, answer cdc's and tsc's, etc.

box, universal button — *See* button box, universal.

bps — Abbreviation for Bits Per Second. In serial transmission, the instantaneous bit speed with which a device or channel transmits a character.

BPS — Abbreviation for basic programming support. BPS card and BPS tape systems are the two simplest and smallest operating systems available for main-line IBM System 360 computers.

branch — 1. To depart from the normal sequence of executing instruction in a computer. (Synonymous with jump.) 2. A machine instruction that can cause a departure as in definition 1. (Synonymous with transfer.) 3. A sequence of instructions that is executed as a result of a decision instruction. 4. The selection of one, two, or more possible paths in the flow of control based on some criterion. The instructions which mechanize this concept are sometimes called branch instructions; however, the terms transfer of control and jump are more widely used.

branch calling — *Same as* calling sequence.

branch, computed — A common example is the GO TO $N_1N_2N_3 \ldots N_1$. Branching occurs to N_1, depending on the computed current value of 1. Assigned branches of the form GO TO 1, where 1 is an assigned address, may also be available.

branch, conditional — An instruction which is interpreted as an unconditional transfer if a specified condition or set of conditions is satisfied. If the condition is not satisfied, the instruction causes the computer to proceed in its normal sequence of control. A conditional transfer also includes the testing of the condition.

branch group instruction — Instruction including the conditional and unconditional jump instructions, subroutine call instructions for maintaining the stack, and internal control flags.

branching — A computer operation, similar to switching, where a selection is made between two or more possible courses of action depending upon some related fact or condition.

branch instruction — An instruction to a computer that enables the programmer to instruct the computer to choose between alternative suprograms, depending upon the conditions determined by the computer during the execution of the program. (Synonymous with transfer instruction.)

branch instruction conditions — The decision-making instruction which, on appropriate conditions, forces a new address into the program counter (PC). The conditions may be a zero result, overflow on add, an external flag raised, and hundreds more. One of two alternate program segments in the memory is chosen, depending upon the results obtained.

branch instruction test — Most such instructions are of the testing type; i.e., if some arithmetic relation is satisfied, such as X being greater than A or less than A, then a jump or branch will occur to some specified instruction, where X is usually the contents of a machine register.

branch-on indicator — *See* indicator, branch-on.

branch-on switch setting — Branching is often designed by the use of certain memory locations or index registers to set the value of the switches. The presetting of a switch may cause the program to branch to the appropriate one of N points, where N is the number of possible switch settings.

branchpoint — A point in a routine where one of two or more choices is selected under control of the routine.

branch, unconditional — An instruction which switches the sequence of control to some specified location. (Synonymous with unconditional jump, and unconditional transfer of control.)

breadboard — Developmental or prototype version of a circuit. Solderless sockets and bus strips in modular form are often used to create expandable matrices for placement of ICs, capacitors, resistors, and so forth for computer systems.

breadboard, intelligent — A unit designed for the development of discrete logic, i/o interfacing, memory systems, and microcomputer circuits. It is often supplied as a complete integrated package; the console connects directly to the microcomputer, allowing circuits to be implemented in hardware and transferred to software in a step-by-step manner. Hardware-software tradeoffs can be studied and circuit designs tested extensively since the computer and breadboard communicate via the programmable parallel i/o board of the computer.

break — To break, in a communication circuit, the receiver user interrupts the sending user and takes control of the circuit. The term is used especially in connection with half-duplex telegraph circuits and two-way telephone circuits equipped with voice-operated devices.

break key — On some systems, a device that forces an interrupt of incoming messages when used with half-duplex systems. The transmission line is held low as long as the key is depressed. The key is included for compatibility with half-duplex systems.

breakpoint — 1. A point in a program as specified by an instruction, instruction digit, or other condition, where the program may be interrupted by external intervention or by a monitor routine. 2. A point in a computer program at which conditional interruption, to permit visual check, printing out, or other analyzing, may occur. Breakpoints are usually used in debugging operations.

breakpoint card, development systems — In some systems, the breakpoint card monitors the system bus and halts execution of a user's program if a user-specified transaction occurs. The user may specify that a break should occur on any combination of the following transactions on some systems: read, memory write, i/o port read, i/o port write. In addition, the user may specify that the selected transactions have specified addresses or data bus bit patterns.

breakpoint, conditional — A breakpoint at which the routine may be continued as coded if desired conditions are satisfied.

breakpoint instruction — 1. An instruction which will cause a computer to stop or to transfer control in some standard fashion to a supervisory routine that can monitor the progress of the interrupted program. 2. An instruction which, if some specified switch is set, will cause the computer to stop or take other special action.

breakpoint instruction, conditional — A conditional jump instruction, which if some specified switch is set, will cause the computer to stop, after which either the routine may be continued as coded, or a jump may be forced.

breakpoint switch — A manually operated switch which controls conditional operation at breakpoints; it is used primarily in debugging.

breakpoint symbol — A symbol which may be optionally included in an instruction, as an indication, tag, or flag, to designate it as a breakpoint.

break, sequence (sorting) — That point in a file between the end of one string and the start of another.

break, string — The point at which a sort can find no more records with sufficiently high control keys to fit on the current output string.

breakthrough — An interruption in the intended character stroke in optical character recognition.

break, transcription — A flowchart symbol or device that shows the relation between two files. The symbol is directional and suggests the flow of information from one file to the file that is affected by the information. The operation symbol should be on the history lines of the file that is affected.

B-register — *Same as* index register.

bridge, central-office — Like the data sets and lines, the central-office bridges are supplied and installed by the telephone company. A bridge, located in the telephone company central office, combines lines from several offices into one line to provide optimum transaction loads for each line going to the processing center. Up to nine offices can be combined into one line, with a corresponding reduction in line and data set costs.

brightness — The average reflectance of paper, in character recognition, measured in relation to a standard surface.

broadband — Also called wideband. Pertaining to a channel with a bandwidth greater than voice-grade channels, characterized by speeds of 10,000 to 50,000 bps.

broadcast — Some control stations have the ability to broadcast messages simultaneously to all stations on a circuit. This is accomplished by using a call which is common to all stations.

Brussels classification — *See* universal decimal classification.

brute-force approach — To try to undertake with existing equipment the mass of problems that do not use precise computation or logical manipulations (as accounting problems and scientific problems do).

BSAM — Abbreviation for Basic Sequential Access Method, a data-base system.

BSC — Abbreviation for Binary Synchronous Communications. A uniform discipline, using a defined set of control characters and control character sequences, for synchronized transmission of binary coded data between stations in a data communications system. Also called BISYNC.

In BSC systems, transmission is half-duplex. The line must be turned around twice between each block (once for the acknowledgment sequence and once for the data block). All the fields are delimited by control characters, and acknowledgments are handled by separate control sequences. There is an acknowledgment sequence required for each block. BSC supports both point-to-point and multipoint lines.

An important BSC protocol characteristic is its ability to detect transmission errors and to retransmit data until it has been received correctly. If it is necessary to send every one of the EBCDIC character set's 256 codes, the transparency feature—which allows control characters to be used as data characters—must be specified for both the communications control unit (CCU) and the RJE terminal.

B-store — *Same as* index register.

BTAM — Abbreviation for Basic Telecommunications Access Method. A method used to control the transfer of data between main storage and local or remote terminals. BTAM provides the applications program with macroinstructions for using the capabilities of the devices supported. BTAM supports binary synchronous as well as start/stop communication.

BTP — Abbreviation for Batch Transfer Program. Data transfers for some local and remote terminals are controlled by a batch transfer program, which can accommodate more than one terminal. Data transfer is supported under VTAM (virtual telecommunications access method). In addition to its regular functions, BTP allows for the addition of user-written routines for modifying or deleting records.

bubble memory — A memory device based on magnetic bubbles, which are tiny cylinders of magnetic material "floating" in a film of magnetic material. The bubbles are polarized in the opposite direction from the rest of the material. Methods have been developed for creating and destroying bubbles and for moving them around. The presence or absence of bubbles can represent digital information, and this information can be manipulated by moving the bubbles. Metal paths are laid on top of the bubble chip in loops, and bubbles are switched about the chips like trains on tracks. (Although the bubbles move, the magnetic material does not, so there are no moving parts.) Magnetic bubble memory has advantages over conventional electromagnetic storage devices in terms of its electronic reliability, high access speed, smaller size, and reduced weight and power consumption.

bubble sort — A sorting technique which exchanges a pair of numbers if they are out of order.

bucket — 1. A slang expression used to indicate some portion of storage specifically reserved for accumulating data, or totals; e.g., "throw it in bucket #1" is a possible expression. Commonly used in initial planning. 2. A general term for a specific reference in storage, e.g., a section of storage, the location of a word, a storage cell, etc.

buffer — 1. The auxiliary data-storage device which holds data temporarily and which may also perform other functions in conjunction with various input/output machines. 2. A storage device used to compensate for a difference in rate of flow of data, or time of occurrence of events when transmitting data from one device to another. 3. A logical OR circuit. 4. An isolating component designed to eliminate the reaction of a driven circuit on the circuits driving it, e.g., a buffer amplifier. 5. A device used to supply additional drive capability.

buffer amplifier — An amplifier designed to isolate a preceding circuit from the effects of a following circuit.

buffered input/output channels — *See* input/output section, buffered.

buffered input/output section — *See* input-/output section, buffered.

buffered keyboard printers — Keyboard printers that include some type of buffering from the line as opposed to those that transmit directly to the line when a key is depressed.

buffer gate — *Same as* gate, OR.

buffering exchange — A technique for input/output buffering which prevents or avoids the internal movement of data. Buffers are either filled, empty, or actively in use, by an input/output device. Exchange buffering relates to distinct areas set aside for work and for buffering.

buffer, input/output — Permits data-word transfers to and from memory to proceed without main program attention. May be programmed so that when input/output transfer is complete, the computer generates an internal interrupt.

buffer output — A buffer developed to receive and store data being transmitted into a computer, and which usually includes instructions.

buffer register — A temporary storage register in a CPU or peripheral device capable of receiving or transmitting data at different i/o rates. Data buffer registers are generally positioned between the computer and slower system components, allowing data to flow at the computer's i/o rate.

buffer register, output — *See* register, output buffer.

buffer size, display — The minimum and maximum number of words reserved for display units and used, with automatic refreshing, to present a flicker-free picture.

buffer storage — 1. Any device that temporarily stores information during a transfer of information. 2. Secondary storage used exclusively for assembly and transfer of data between internal and external storage. 3. A synchronizing element between two different forms of storage, usually between internal and external.

buffer storage area — A temporary storage area for data. This may be a single word of storage (such as in an output port latch holding data until the output device has accepted it). A buffer area in main memory can range from a single location to a large block.

buffer storage locations — A set of locations used to compensate for a difference in rate of flow of data, or time of occurrence of events, when transmitting data from one device to another.

buffer, terminal — The buffer in an electronic terminal is a memory that can store enough bits to represent at least one character. Larger buffers store a word, a line, or a whole message.

bug — 1. Any mechanical, electrical or electronic defect that interferes with, or "bugs up" the operation of the computer. It can also be a defect in the coding of the program. (If you're diffident about using this word, call it a malfunction.) 2. A mistake in the design of a routine or a computer, or a malfunction.

bug monitors, communications — Data communications monitors used to spot problems in systems hardware and software, and detail errors caused by software bugs, equipment malfunction, or line troubles.

bug patches — As bugs are uncovered in a program, patches can be inserted and documented in order to fix the mistakes. When a number of patches have been made, they should be incorporated into the source program and the program should be reassembled. This ensures a well-documented program.

building block principle — A system that permits the addition of other equipment units to form a larger system. Also called modularity.

built-in checks (automatic) — Built-in checks should be taken advantage of and not duplicated by wired, programmed, or manual controls. They function as a result of internal machine circuitry and are, therefore, performed automatically. Some of these checks are common to all machines. For example, all machines have checks which stop the machine for a timing error, a blown fuse, or an operation that is impossible or in conflict with another. Computers utilize input/output checks, instruction checks, and parity checks. The input check ensures that all data is read and coded correctly into machine language; the output check ensures that the output characters are correctly set up for punching and printing. The instruction check permits the execution of only those instructions having a valid operation code and instruction format. The parity check verifies each character in the computer on the basis of an odd or even bit configuration. To ensure accuracy in disk-storage write operations, internal circuitry automatically compares the written record against the one from which it was written, or requires that a compare instruction doing this be executed before another disk-storage operation. In magnetic-tape operations, each character and each channel within a record must pass a validity check for an odd or even number of bits; the system determines whether the bit count is odd or even.

built-in controls — Various error-checking techniques built into EDP equipment by the manufacturer.

built-in storage — *See* storage, internal.

built-in tracing structure — *See* tracing structure, built-in.

bulk eraser — A device which erases or destroys the magnetic information on a reel of tape without removing the tape from the reel.

bulk storage — Storage of large-volume capacity used to supplement the high-speed storage which can be made addressable, such as disks and drums, or remain nonaddressable with magnetic tapes. Other names for this type of storage are external or secondary storage.

bulk testing — *See* testing, saturation.

bureau, service — *See* service bureau.

burn in — A specific phase of component testing in which very early mortality or failures are discovered or screened out by running the circuit for a specified length of time, typically 168 hours.

burst — The separation of sheets of a continuous form.

burst, error — A data transmission technique using a specified number of correct bits interspersed with designed error bits. The last erroneous bit in a burst and the first erronous bit in the successive burst are separated by the specified number of correct bits. The group of bits in which two successive erroneous bits are always separated by less than a specific number of correct bits.

burst mode — A mode of communications between the processor and i/o devices. When a signal from an i/o device operating through the multiplexer channel indicates burst mode, the receiving unit continues to fetch bits until the unit is finished.

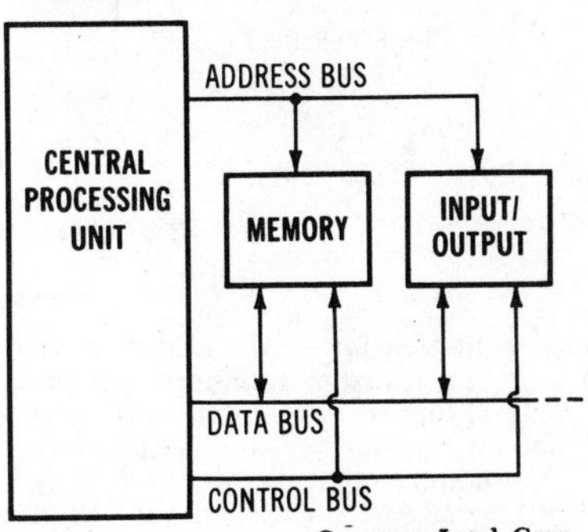

Courtesy Intel Corp.

Buses.

bus — 1. A circuit over which data or power is transmitted. Often one which acts as a common connection among a number of locations. (Synonymous with trunk.) 2. A path over which information is transferred, from any of several sources to any of several destinations.

bus address register — A register, used in some systems, that contains the last noninstruction fetch bus address for various destination modes.

bus, check — *See* check bus.

bus cycles — Generally, each processor instruction requires one or more bus cycles. The first operation required is one that fetches an instruction from the location addressed by the program counter. If no further operands are referenced in memory or an i/o device, no additional bus cycles are required for an instruction execution. If memory or a device is referenced, however, on most systems, one or more additional bus cycles are required.

bus, data — Most computers communicate internally through the use of a data bus. Most are bidirectional, e.g., capable of transferring data to and from the CPU and storage and peripheral devices.

bus, digit-transfer — An electrical path used to transfer numbers (electrical pulses) that represent data and instructions to various registers and counters. On-off and similar transfer lines or control signals are not considered to be digit-transfer buses.

bus drivers, output — All major output signals from the standard computer used in programmed and data-break information transfers are power amplified by bus-driver modules to allow them to drive a very heavy circuit load.

bus error traps — Bus error traps are time-out errors in some systems, i.e., attempts to reference addresses on the bus that have made no response within a certain length of time. In general, these are caused by attempts to reference nonexistent memory or attempts to reference nonexistent peripheral devices. Bus error traps cause processor traps through a specific trap vector address.

bus family — A group of signals considered together. For example, an address bus consists of all the signals needed to define any of the possible memory or i/o locations in the system, a data bus handles all communication of instructions and data, and a control bus is used by the CPU to direct the actions of the other elements in the system.

bus hub — A location on the control panel which permits several entries or exits of pulse signals.

business application — Close groupings of related activities for treatment as specific units; e.g., inventory-control processes, order and sales entries, customer-credit reports and accounting, automated purchasing models, and others may be treated as units for conversion to electronic data processing and operating systems.

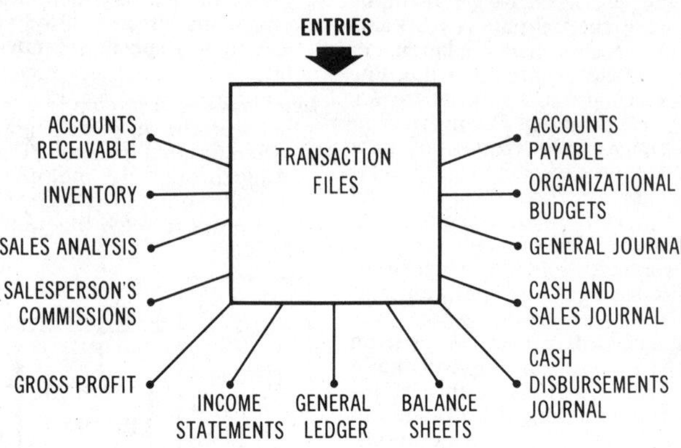

Business application.

business-data processing — The almost boundless variety of commercial applications from actual transactions (in contrast to problem solutions). Such processes involve and concern file processing, manipulations, and reporting, plus planning procedures for operating or quality control, capital, and project budgeting.

business-graphics components — Devices used in combining alphanumeric and graphic information to enable visualization of data for business applications.

Devices include crt displays, pen plotters, laser plotters, ink-jet plotters, and plasma displays.

busing, daisy chain — A procedure of propagating signals along a bus. Devices not requesting a daisy-chained signal respond by passing the signal on. The first device requesting the signal responds to it by performing an action and breaks the daisy-chained signal continuity. This scheme permits assignment of device priorities based on the electrical position of the device along the bus.

bus lines, i/o — Parallel lines and control logic are referred to collectively as the i/o bus. They transfer information between microprocessor and i/o devices. The bus contains three types of lines: data, device address, and command. Data lines consist either of one bidirectional set or two unidirectional sets. In the latter case, one set is used exclusively for inputting of data to the CPU and the other for outputting of data. In most cases the width of the bus (number of lines) equals the word length of the microprocessor. Device-address lines are used to identify i/o devices. The theoretical maximum number of available address lines changes significantly from one microprocessor to another. Command lines allow a peripheral to indicate to the CPU that it has finished its previous operation and is ready for another transfer end.

bus loading — The amount of current drain, resistance, capacitance, or other electronic parameters that may affect the characteristics or driving requirements of an electronic pathway in a circuit that supplies a number of devices.

bus, LSI-11 — A specific type of bus developed as a link between processor and peripheral elements of the system. The LSI-11 bus comprises 38 bidirectional signal lines, along which addresses, data, and control signals are sent. Some signals contain time-multiplexed information. Communication between devices on the bus is asynchronous. A master/slave relationship exists between two devices on the bus throughout any transaction between them. At any time, one device (the "bus master") controls the bus; this master device initiates the bus transaction. Data may be transferred either to or from the master device. Arbitration between devices (i.e., which one becomes bus master at a given time) is decided by the processor.

bus master — The device controlling the current bus transaction in a system that has a bus structure in which control of data transfers on the bus is shared between the CPU and associated peripheral devices.

bus, microcomputer — In the case of microcomputers, at least three types of buses are used. One consists of the lines that carry signals between chips in a microprocessor system. A second is the so-called functional bus, such as the general-purpose interface bus (IEEE standard 488-1975 and ANSI standard MC 1.1-1975) that transfers signals to and from peripheral control devices, whether those devices are attached to computers or not. A third type concerns address lines to memory, shared data lines, and the control signals that link the system cards together. This is also the world that raises many key questions. There are key differences between the MULTIBUS and the S-100 bus, and it is not possible to plug an S-100 compatible peripheral into an LSI-11 bus. It is too late to adopt one standard.

bus multiplexing — A method of conveying both address and data words (or bytes) over the same bus. For example, in one system, during a programmed data transfer, the processor first asserts an address on the bus for a fixed time. After the address time has been completed, the processor executes the programmed input or output data transfer; the actual data transfer is asynchronous and requires a reply from the addressed device. Bus synchronization and control signals provide this function.

bus polling protocol — In some systems the bus protocol allows for a vectored interrupt by the device. Hence, device polling is not required in interrupt processing routines. This results in a considerable savings in processing time when many devices requiring interrupt service are interfaced along the bus. When an interrupting device receives an interrupt grant signal, the device passes to the processor an interrupt vector. The vector points to two addresses which contain a new processor status word and the starting address of the interrupt service routine for the particular device.

bus priority structure — Since many buses are used by processors and i/o devices, there is a priority structure to determine which device gets control of the bus. Often every device on the bus which is capable of becoming bus master is assigned a priority according to its position along the bus. When two devices which are capable of becoming a bus master request use of the bus simultaneously, the device with the higher priority position will receive control.

bus slave — The device currently receiving or transmitting data from or to the bus master in a system that has a bus structure in which control of data transfers on the bus is shared between the CPU and associated peripheral devices.

bust — The malperformance of a programmer or machine operator.

bus wire — A group of wires that allows the memory, the CPU, and the i/o devices to exchange words.

button, activate — *Same as* button, initiate.

button box, universal — A coined term for a set of push buttons whose functions are determined by the computer program.

button, emergency — Some units contain a button which, when depressed, is designed to prevent further destruction or malady in the event of a current failure, or when the operator knows no other corrective act.

button, initiate — A control panel switch which causes the first step of a subroutine or sequence of programmed steps to be started to perform the cycling or movement of operations.

button, intervention — *Same as* button, emergency.

button, panic — *See* button, emergency.

buttons, function — The small typewriter-key–like buttons found on many specialized input/output terminals which are used to query the system or have it perform certain operations. For example, on the remote-inquiry terminal used in a stock quotation system, a three letter combination identifies any stock, and by punching the right function button, earnings, sales, dividends, volume, etc., can be displayed.

button, start — *Same as* button, initiate.

bypass procedure — A procedure used to get the most vital information into the main computer when the line control computer fails. The few direct control lines into the main computer are frequently switched to maximize different terminal input. Teleprinters, paper tape punches, telephones, etc., are used to provide bypass.

byproduct — Data in some form developed without additional effort from a device whose basic purpose is to perform some other operation.

byte — 1. A generic term to indicate a measureable portion of consecutive binary digits, e.g., an 8-bit or 16-bit byte. 2. A sequence of adjacent binary digits operated upon as a unit and usually shorter than a word.

byte, effective — The byte actually accessed in an operation on a single byte or byte string.

byte, effective location — The actual storage location pointed to by the effective virtual address of a byte addressing instruction.

byte, hexadecimal — While two hexadecimal digits can be used to specify a byte, the byte is usually a group of eight bits carried as a unit. Hexadecimal number systems use 0, 1, 2, 3, 4, 5, 6, 7, 8, 9, A, B, C, D, E, and F to represent all possible values of a 4-bit digit.

byte instructions — In some systems, the design includes a full complement of instructions that manipulate byte operands. Then, since all addressing is byte-oriented, byte manipulation addressing is straightforward. Byte instructions with autoincrement or autodecrement direct addressing cause the specified register to be modified by one to point to the next byte of data. Byte operations in register mode access the low-order byte of the specified register. These provisions enable the processor to perform as either a word or byte processor.

byte manipulation — The ability to manipulate, as individual instructions, groups of bits such as characters. A byte is considered to be eight bits in most cases, and forms either one character or two numerals.

byte multiplexing — A process in which time slots on a channel are delegated to individual slow input/output devices so that bytes from one after another can be interlaced on the channel to or from main memory.

C

C — A somewhat structured high-level programming language designed to optimize run time, size, and efficiency. It was developed as the systems programming language of the UNIX operating system on the PDP 11/70 minicomputer from Digital Equipment Corp.

cable — Assembly of one or more conductors within an enveloping protection sheath so constructed as to permit the use of conductors separately or in groups.

cable, coaxial — Coaxial cable consists of a central conductor, an outer conductive braid, and a protective coating.

cable, combination — A cable that has conductors grouped in combinations, such as pairs and quads.

cable, composite — In communications use, a composite cable is one in which conductors of different gauges or types are combined under one sheath.

cable, duplex — A type of cable constructed of two insulated stranded conductors twisted together. They may or may not share a common insulating covering.

cable, flat — *See* cable, tape.

cable, paired — A particular cable in which all of the conductors are arranged in the form of twisted pairs, none of which are arranged with others to form quads.

cables noise — When digital equipments are cabled together, care must be taken to minimize crosstalk between the individual conductors in the cables. Because of the fast rise and fall times characteristic of digital signals, these individual conductors can often generate significant amounts of noise.

cable, tape — A cable containing flat metallic ribbon conductors, all lying side by side in the same plane and imbedded in a material which insulates and binds them together.

cable termination — Matching of the characteristic impedance of the wire with the impedance of the receiver and transmitter. As a pulse is sent to the other end, the energy of the pulse is dissipated by the termination of the wire. If the wire is not terminated properly, a reflection of the pulse will travel back to the source, and a condition called ringing will occur.

cache — A buffer type of high-speed memory that is filled at medium speed from main memory, often with instructions and programs. Higher operating speeds can be achieved with those items found in cache memory; if not found, a new segment is loaded.

cache memory "hit" — Since the cache memory contains copies of portions of main memory, its effectiveness is based on the percentage of time that the data to be fetched can be transferred from the high-speed cache, as opposed to other, lower-speed memories. A "hit" occurs if the data is found in cache. A "miss" occurs if the data is not found in cache, and must be fetched from main memory.

cache memory look ahead — The principle of program locality states that programs have a tendency to make most accesses in the neighborhood of locations accessed in the recent past. Programs typically excute instructions in straight lines or small loops, with the next few accesses likely to be a few words ahead of or behind the current location. Stacks grow and shrink from one end, with the next few accesses near the current top. Data elements are often scanned through sequentially. The cache uses these behavioral characteristics by bringing in extra words on each access to main memory (look ahead) and keeping copies of recently used words (look behind).

CAD — Computer-Aided Design. The capability of a computer to be used for automated industrial, statistical, biological, etc., design through visual devices.

CAD/CAM systems — Computer-Aided Design and Computer-Aided Manufacturing systems. These systems usually include a cathode ray tube display, keyboard, plotter, and one or more graphic input devices. These elements comprise a user work station that is linked to peripherals such as readers, printers, tape and disk drives, and a microcomputer base. CAD/CAM systems can help design parts and machinery, generate schematics, diagram complex wiring arrangements and printed circuit boards, create accurate artwork on glass or film, calculate manufacturing specifications, list parts, and furnish bills of materials.

CAI — Abbreviation for Computer-Aided Instruction. An educational concept that places the student in a conversational mode with a computer that has a preprogrammed study plan. The programmed course selects the next topic or phase of study according to previous responses from the student, allowing each student to progress at a pace directly related to his learning capability.

calculated address — *See* address, calculated.

calculating, card-programmed — Card-programmed calculating uses many connected or separate machines. That is, an accounting machine reads from punched cards the various factors for calculating, and the codes instruct the machines about calculations to be made, thus involving multiple steps of data processing.

calculating operation, average — An indication of the calculating speed of the computer determined by taking the mean time for nine additions and one multiplication.

calculating operation, representative — *Same as* calculating operation, average.

calculating time, representative — *See* time, representative-computing.

calculator — A particular device for performing arithmetic, usually requiring frequent manual intervention. Generally, a device or machine used to carry out logical and arithmetic digital calculations of any type.

calculator chip — A chip containing a microprocessor that has a built-in microprogram to solve arithmetic functions.

calculator, network — An analog device designed primarily for simulating electrical networks.

calculator pad, terminal — With programmability in the controller, some terminals can perform computations on accumulated data locally, rather than having to send all raw data to the host computer. Typical examples of such computations are price extensions from unit prices and quantities, quantity discounts, and tax amounts. With such local computations, the terminal can then prepare an invoice locally.

calculator structure — The present calculator can be defined as a small, highly specialized computer. The memory structure consists of both a fixed and a variable memory. The fixed portion, a read-only memory (ROM), provides a system control program called firmware —meaning nonchangeable instructions. This contrasts with general-purpose computers programmed by software, and random-logic systems that use hard-wired circuitry.

calculus, Boolean — An extension of Boolean algebra which includes other variables, such as time, step functions, changes of state, delay.

calculus of variations — A specific calculus which relates to the maxima/minima theory of definite integrals. The integrands are functions of dependent variables, independent variables, and their derivatives.

calibrated instrumentation — Instrumentation in which have been ascertained, usually by comparison with a standard, the locations at which scale/chart graduations should be placed to correspond to a series of values of the quantity that the instrument is to measure, receive, or transmit.

call — The branching or transfer of control to a specified closed subroutine.

call direction code — Abbreviated CDC. An identifying call, usually of two letters, which is transmitted to an outlying receiver and which automatically turns on its printer (selective calling).

call in — To transfer control of a digital computer temporarily from a main routine to a subroutine which is inserted in the sequence of calculating operations to fulfill a subsidiary purpose.

calling branch — *Same as* calling sequence.

calling, selective — This is a form of a teletypewriter communications system. A particular loop may include several machines, but with selective calling, only the machine selected will respond. The device that controls the individual machines in response to a selective call (CDC) is called a stunt box.

calling sequence — A basic set of instructions used to begin or initialize or to transfer control to a subroutine, but usually to complete the return of control after the execution of a subroutine is finished.

call instruction — A type of instruction that diverts program execution to a new area in memory (sequence of directives) and yet allows eventual return to the original sequence of directives.

call number — A group of characters identifying a subroutine and containing: (a) information concerning parameters to be inserted in the subroutine, (b) information to be used in generating the subroutine, or (c) information related to the operands.

call, program — A request by various user application programs for operating system (OS) or executive service. Such a call results in control being passed from the user program to the monitor or executive module of the overall operating system.

calls, subroutine — *See* subroutine calls.

call word — *See* word, call.

CAM — Abbreviation for Content Addressable Memory. A type of associative memory addressed by the contents or meaning rather than memory position or location.

CAMAC — The IEEE-583 instrument interface standard. It is an in-depth specification used for general interfacing of instruments in the nuclear industry, often preferred over the IEEE-488 standard.

Cambridge Polish — Used in the LISP language, the Polish operators = and × are allowed to have more than two operands.

CAM devices — Abbreviation for Content Addressable Memory devices. R/W RAMs with an access mechanism that retrieves the addresses of data which match an attribute presented to the inputs. Most are programmed by writing into the array via a separate addressing and control path.

camp-on — A special method for holding a call for a line that is in use, and signaling when it becomes free.

cancel character — A specific control character designed to indicate that the data with which it is associated is erroneous or is to be disregarded.

CANCL status word — This status word indicates that the remote computing system has deleted some information.

canned software — Also called packages. Generalized programs that are prewritten and debugged and are designed to perform one or more general functions. Business functions include accounts receivable, accounts payable, general ledger, payroll, or inventory control.

canonical — A regular, standard, or simplified form of an expression or schema. For example, any Boolean expression can be transformed into a canonical sum of products or canonical product of sums.

canonical schema — A model of a data base which represents the inherent informational nature of the data and the relationships between the parts of the data base. Hence, this description is independent of individual applications and software or hardware mechanisms which are employed in representing and using the data.

capacity — 1. The total quantity of data that a part of a computer can hold or handle. 2. The capability of a specific system to store data, accept transactions, process data, and generate reports.

capacity, channel — The maximum possible information-transmission rate through a channel at a specified error rate. The channel capacity may be measured in bits per second or bauds.

capacity, circuit — The number of communications channels which can be handled by a given circuit simultaneously.

capacity, output — The number of loads that can be driven by the output of a circuit.

capacity, processing — Often the maximum limitation of places of a number that can be processed at any one time.

capacity, register — The number of digits, characters, or bits that a register can store.

capstan — The rotating shaft on a magnetic-tape handling unit which is used to impart uniform motion to the magnetic tape when engaged.

card — 1. The paperboard material formed in uniform size and shape which is punched or marked in various arrays to be sensed electronically or visually by brushes or feelers or by photoelectric pickup. The standard card is 7⅜ inches long by 3¼ inches wide and contains 80 columns and 12 punch positions. 2. An internal plug-in unit for printed-circuit wiring and components.

card, binary — The fundamental punched card containing binary numerals representing numbers, characters, or control symbols in columns and rows.

card cage, microcomputer — The structure that contains the circuit cards in a microcomputer system. A typical unit is of rugged construction and fits the industry standard 19-inch cabinetry occupying 7 RETMA increments (12.25 inches). Some units come with mother boards and can accommodate 20 printed circuit boards. The bus structure is often the standard 100-pin bus of the personal computers (S-100), for which a variety of cards are available from many manufacturers.

card cage, standard — A supporting structure that generally holds up to nine printed circuit cards and can be mounted in a number of different enclosures at various angles. In one system, this card cage features the use of a printed-circuit backplane that allows the computer to communicate with any of many PC boards. It also allows the wire-wrapping of special features to the computer.

card code — The combinations of punched holes which represent characters (letters, digits, etc.) in a punched card.

card code, OCR-A — The standard marking approved by the National Retail Merchants Association (NRMA).

card column — One of the vertical lines of punching positions on a punched card.

card, CPU — For many applications, the most economical way of including computer capability in a product is via the standard expansion of a CPU chip into a computer card. For example, every microcomputer CPU chip must operate in conjunction with a memory module and must have CPU-to-memory interface logic; if the CPU communicates with standard peripheral devices (e.g., a disk unit or line printer), the computer card will supply the necessary interface between the CPU chip and peripheral device controller.

card cycle — The time required to read or punch a card.

card data recorder — Various card data recorders punch, verify, print, and interpret cards. Some units are designed to skip columns not requiring interpreting, interpret numeric portions only, or print leading zeros under program control. On some units, cards can be verified immediately after they have been punched.

card, Hollerith — A common name for the standard punched card, 3¼ by 7⅜ inches, usually divided into 80 columns of punch hole sites. A combination of punches in a column zone (and field) can represent letters, digits, or symbols. The card was named in honor of Dr. Herman Hollerith, who invented it in 1889.

card image — 1. A representation in storage of the holes punched in a card, in such a manner that the holes are represented by one binary digit and the unpunched spaces are represented by the other binary digit. 2. In machine language, a duplication of the data contained in a punch card.

card, magnetic — A card, usually with a rectangular flat surface, of any material coated with a magnetic substance on which data is recorded, such that it can be read by an automatic device.

card mag stripe reader — A device for reading mag-stripe ID cards.

card, printed-circuit — A card, usually of laminate or resinous material of the insulating type, which is used for the mounting of an electrical circuit. Together the base and circuit make up the card.

card reader — A device which senses and translates into internal form the holes in punched cards.

card reader, mark sense — A device that reads tab cards marked with soft lead pencil, and lets the user enter programs and numerical data into the computer. Also, programs can be written off-line without the computer.

card row — One of the horizontal lines of punching positions on a punched card.

card verifying — A means of checking the accuracy of key punching. It is a duplication check. A second operator verifies the original punching by depressing the keys of a verifier while reading the same source data. The machine compares the key depressed with the hole already punched in the card.

caret — A symbol (an inverted v) used to indicate the location of an insertion.

carriage — A control mechanism for a typewriter or other listing device that can automatically control the feeding, spacing, skipping, and ejecting of paper or preprinted forms.

carrier, data — The selected medium used to transport or carry data or information. Examples are punched cards, magnetic tapes, and punched paper tapes.

carriers, value-added — A class of communications common carrier authorized to lease raw communication trunks from the transmission carriers, augment these facilities with computerized switching, and provide enhanced or "value-added" communications services. Some are now employing a technology called packet switching to provide value-added data communications services. Packet switching is a communications technology, but it has its roots in the computer field rather than in the communications field, for it was developed by computer users in order to better meet their communication requirements.

carry — 1. A signal, or expression, produced as a result of an arithmetic operation on one digit place of two or more numbers expressed in positional notation and transferred to the next higher place for processing there. 2. A signal or expression, as defined in (1) above, which arises in adding, when the sum of two digits in the same digit place equals or exceeds the base of the number system in use. If a carry into a digit place will result in a carry out of the same digit place, and if the normal adding circuit is bypassed when generating this new carry, it is called a high-speed carry, or standing-on-nines carry. If the normal adding circuit is used in such a case, the carry is called a cascaded carry. If a carry resulting from the addition of carries is not allowed to propagate, e.g., when forming the partial product in one step of a multiplication process, the process is called a partial carry. If it is allowed to propagate, the process is called a complete carry. If a carry generated in the most significant digit place is sent directly to the least significant place, e.g., when adding two negative numbers using nine complements, that carry is called an end-around carry. (Synonymous with cascaded carry, complete carry, end-around carry, high-speed carry, and partial carry.) 3. A signal or expression in direct subtraction, as defined in (1) above, which arises when the difference between the digits is less than zero. Such a carry is frequently called a borrow. (Related to borrow.) 4. The action of forwarding a carry. 5. The command directing a carry to be forwarded.

carry, cascaded — *See* cascaded carry.

carry, complete — A carry which is allowed to propagate.

carry, end-around — A carry from the most significant digit place to the least significant place.

carry flag — An indicator that signals when a register overflow or underflow condition occurs during mathematical operations with an accumulator. It is sometimes also considered as a one cell extension of an accumulator during selected operations such as the execution of "rotate" instructions.

carry/link bit — On some systems, this bit is set if a carry from the most significant bit occurs during an add, a complement-and-add, or a decimal-add instruction. The bit is also included in the shift right with link and the rotate right with link instructions.

carry look-ahead — A circuit that in effect predicts the final carry from propagate and generate signals supplied by partial adders. It is used to speed up significantly binary addition by eliminating the carry propagation (or ripple) delay.

carry, partial — The technique in parallel addition wherein some or all of the carries are stored temporarily instead of being allowed to propagate immediately.

Cartesian coordinates, digitizing system — Some systems have the ability to define completely the axis system of the work. This allows for rotated, nonorthogonal axis definition with a step-wise linear approximation of nonlinear scales. Some larger systems allow definition of 32 Y axes and 2 X axes. This allows multiple scalings for multitrace strip charts, such as well logs, to be defined. Or a data classification technique may be defined (for example, map contours on layer 1, boundaries on layer 2, etc.).

cartridge recorder, ANSI standard — The ANSI standard for cartridge recorders specifies that blocks of data be bracketed by known bit patterns. First comes a 16-bit preamble, followed by a data block of up to 2048 eight-bit bytes. A 16-bit cyclic-redundancy check and a 16-bit postamble follow the data block. The preamble has 15 0s followed by a 1. Preambles establish timing for reading data when the tape moves forward. The postamble, a 1 followed by 15 0s, sets the timing for reading data in reverse. Note that for both directions of tape travel, data are preceded by a string of

15 0s and a 1. This pattern can be used to locate data in a deskewing register.

CAS — Abbreviation for Column Address Strobe.

cascade control — An automatic control system in which various control units are linked in sequence, each control unit regulating the operation of the next control unit in line.

cascaded carry — 1. A carry using the normal adding circuit rather than any special or high-speed circuit. 2. In parallel addition, a carry process in which the addition of two numerals results in a sum numeral and a carry numeral which are in turn added together, this process being repeated until no new carries are generated.

split-package items automatically and provides discount capability and a refund key.

cassette — A self-contained package of reel-to-reel blank or recorded film, magnetic tape, or electronically embossable vinyl tape for recording of sound or computer input signals, which is continuous and self-rewinding. Similar to a cartridge, but of slightly different design.

cassette bootstrap loader — A typical cassette bootstrap loader automatically locates the top of memory and relocates itself to the top of memory, enabling program loading from memory location zero. During the process of locating the top of memory, a full memory test is

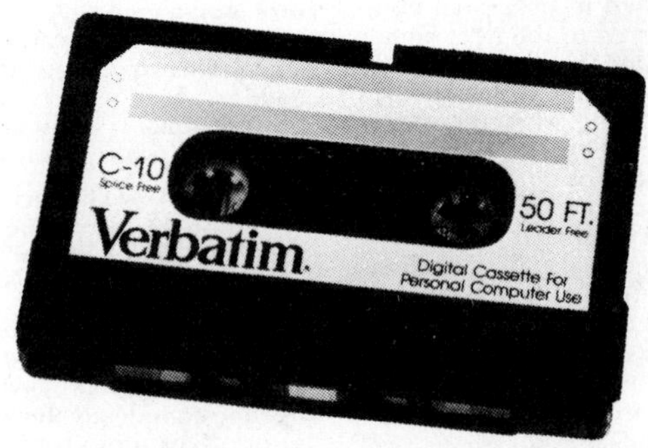

Courtesy Verbatim Corp.

Cassette.

cascade merging — A technique used in a sort program to merge strings of sequenced data and performed a T—1 on part of the data, T/2 on parts of the data, and so on. Strings of sequenced data are distributed in a Fibonacci series on the work tapes preceding each merge. The effective power of the merge varies between T—1 and T/2.

case, test — *See* test case.

cash register, electronic — A cash register with electronic computational and record-keeping capabilities. A typical unit prints a locked-in detail tape that reports the date, consecutive number, item count, clerk, function, and department for each transaction. The receipt carries this information as well as a programmable store name and other messages. This unit calculates multiples of identically priced items and prices of

made every time the load button is pressed.

cassette buffer, ANSI protocol — The cassette buffer writes, reads, rewinds, and does limited editing under microprocessor control at the operator's command. In the ANSI protocol, messages are automatically segmented by the buffer into blocks of 256 or fewer characters, with each block assigned a number sequentially for easy detection of missing blocks.

cassette, digital — A typical digital cassette holds at least 282 feet of 0.15-inch tape. Differences between digital and most audio cassettes include an ANSI locating notch, reusable write-enable tabs, pullout-proof leaders, and holes at the beginning and end of the tape. The recording qualities of the two types also differ. A flat belt provides built-in direct drive and tensioning for the 0.25-inch-wide recording tape in a 3M-type cartridge. Internal guides align the tape.

cassette recorder, microcomputer-based — Any of numerous digital cassette recorders programmed to log data from any user-specified instrument in formats readable by almost any type of terminal or cassette. One type is standard with custom cabling for interfacing to the data sampling instrument.

cassette tape data organization — Generally in cassette systems, data is recorded on tape in a single bit-serial track. Since there is no prerecorded timing or format tract (such as in other major magnetic tape systems), data must be sequentially recorded and retrieved as in conventional tape systems.

cassette tape transport system — The mechanism that moves the cassette tape during recording and playback. The tape transport is the central item that each of the other major components interfaces. It must also accurately position the tape with respect to the head and move the tape at a constant speed. This requires electronic circuitry to control tape motion, record and/or amplify the data signals, and format the data, when necessary.

casting-out-nines check — *See* check, casting-out-nines.

catalog — 1. A list of items with descriptive data, usually arranged so that a specific kind of information can be readily located. 2. To assign a representative label for a document according to a definite set of rules.

catalog, union — Often meant to merge a compiled list of the contents of two or more tape libraries.

catastrophic failure — *See* failure, catastrophic.

category — 1. A natural classification. 2. A logical grouping of associated documents.

category, display — *See* display catagory.

catena — A chain, a series, especially a connected series.

catenate — *See* concatenate.

cathode-ray tube — 1. An electronic vacuum tube containing a screen on which information may be stored by means of a multigrid modulated beam of electrons from the thermionic emitter; storage is effected by means of charged or uncharged spots. 2. A vacuum tube in which a beam of electrons can be focused to a small point on a luminescent screen and can be varied in position and intensity to form a pattern.

cathode-ray tube memories — Memories in which photosensitive surfaces are used as a target upon which an electron beam reads and writes information. These surfaces are incorporated into a cathode ray tube (crt), and circuitry for addressing the photosensitive surface is used to control the crt electron beam.

CCD storage — Storage based on charge-coupled devices (CCDs). CCDs, like RAMs, are volatile storage devices. Also, a read function from a CCD does not destroy data. This nondestructive read of the CCD tends to simplify its required i/o electronics as compared to control electronics necessary for magnetic core arrays. CCDs, however, are not random access; they are serial storage devices similar in function to the traditional delay line. Effectively operating as an extensive shift register, the CCD must cycle data through a read point (or points) in order to access the desired stored information. Compared to disk and drum, CCD memories are more reliable and easier to maintain. Power dissipation per bit is lower for CCD than for any other major memory technology, simplifying the corresponding cooling requirements; size and weight are also low.

CCITT — (Comité Consultatif International Télégraphique et Téléphonique). The International Telegraph and Telephone Consultative Committee, an international organization concerned with devising and proposing recommendations for international telecommunications.

CCITT interface — A United Nations communications standard considered mandatory in Europe and other continents. It is very closely akin to the American EIA Standard RS-232 B or C, which has been accepted as an interface requirement between data processing and terminal or data communication equipment by American manufacturers of data-transmission and business equipment.

CCITT X.21 protocols — A character-controlled protocol for call establishment and a bit-oriented protocol for data transfer. X.21 has gained popularity because of its single five-pin DTE-to-DCE interface for level I. Its level II implementation can be facilitated by a multiprotocol DLC chip.

CDC — Abbreviation for Call Direction Code. An identifying call, usually two letters, which is transmitted to an outlying receiver and automatically turns on its printer (selective calling).

Ceefax — A system by which data is transmitted on tv picture lines in the vertical blanking interval, which are not ordinarily visible. The data cannot be accessed by unauthorized users because a special decoder is needed. Data is transmitted in the 17th, 18th, 330th, and 331st lines in the British system in an NRZ (nonreturn to zero) format. The receiving system must provide its own clock because NRZ has no built-in clock signal.

cell — A location specified by all or part of the address and possessed of the faculty of store. Specific terms such as column, field, location, and block are preferable when appropriate.

cell, binary — A one-bit register or bit position.

cell, disturbed — A magnetic cell which has received one or more partial drive pulses in the opposite sense since it was set or reset.

cell, magnetic — A binary storage cell in which the two values of one binary digit are represented by different patterns of magnetism, and in which means of setting and sensing the contents are stationary with respect to the magnetic material.

cells, dedicated trap — *See* trap, dedicated cells.

cellular splitting — A technique for accommodating additional information in a system that allocates storage in units of cells. When information must be added to a full cell, the cell is split into two half-full cells. The new information is added to one of these new cells. *Same as* block splitting.

center, automatic-switching — Communications center designed specifically for relaying digitized data by automatic electronic methods.

center, data-processing — A computer installation providing data-processing service for others, sometimes called customers, on a reimbursable or nonreimbursable basis.

center, data switching — *See* switching center.

center, EDP — Electronic data processing center, a complete complex including one or more computers.

centerline, stroke — Printed character specification drawings and a line used to designate the position and shape of the locus of character stroke midpoints.

center, relay — A system in which data transmissions between stations on different circuits within a network are accomplished by routing the data through a central point. (Synonymous with message switching center.)

center, store-and-forward switching — A message-switching center in which the message accepted from the sender, whenever he offers it, is held in a physical store and forwarded to the receiver, whenever he is able to accept it.

center, switching — A location in which incoming data from one circuit is transferred to the proper outgoing circuit.

central character, font-change — *Same as* character, font change.

central computer, input/output — Communication between the central computer and the peripheral units of some computer systems may be performed over all input/output channels. Each of the several channels allows bidirectional transfers of data and control signals between the central computer and the peripheral devices.

central control panel — *See* control panel.

central control unit — *See* central processing unit.

central file, on-line — *See* file, on-line (central).

centralized control — In a computer, the control of all processing by a single operational unit.

centralized data processing — Data processing performed at a single, central location on data obtained from several geographical locations or managerial levels. Decentralized data processing involves processing at various managerial levels or geographical points throughout the organization.

centralized input/output coordination, time sharing — *See* time sharing, centralized input/output coordination.

central office exchange — The place where a communication common carrier locates the equipment which interconnects subscribers and circuits.

central processing element (bit slices) — Each central processing element (CPE) represents a 2-bit or 4-bit slice through the data-processing section of a computer. In some systems, several CPEs may be arrayed in parallel to form a processor of any desired word length. The microprocessor, which together with the microprogram memory controls the step-by-step operation of the processor, is itself a powerful microprogrammed state sequencer.

central processing unit — Abbreviated CPU. The unit of a computing system that contains the circuits that control and perform the execution of instructions.

central processing, unit loop — The main routine or a control program and that which is associated with the control of the internal status of the processing unit, in contrast to those control programs of routines developed with terminals and file storage input-output.

central processing unit, microcomputer — The CPU is the primary functioning unit of any computer system. Its basic architecture consists of storage elements called registers, computational circuits designated as the arithmetic-logic unit (ALU), the control block, and input-output ports. A microprocessor built with LSI technology often contains a CPU on a single chip. Because such a chip has limited storage space, memory implementation is added in modular fashion on associated chips. Most microcomputers consist of a CPU chip and others for memory and i/o.

central processor — *See* central processing unit.

central processor organization — The computer can be divided into three main sections: arithmetic and control, input/output, and memory. The arithmetic and control section carries out the directives of the program. The calculations, routing of information, and control of the other sections occurs in this part of the central processor. All information going in and coming out of the central processor is handled by the input/output section. It also controls the operation of all peripheral equipment. The memory section is the heart of the central processor; it provides temporary storage for data and instructions. Because of its importance, the total cycle time of the memory is the main determining factor in the overall speed of the processor.

central scanning loop — A loop of instructions which determines which task is to be performed next. After each item of work is completed, control is transferred to the central scanning loop which searches for processing requests in order to determine the next item to be processed. The computer may cycle idly in the central scanning loop if no item requires its attention, or it may go into a wait state which is interrupted if the need arises. The central scanning loop is the nucleus of a set of supervisory programs.

central terminal unit — Abbreviated CTU. This unit supervises communication between the teller consoles and the processing center. It receives incoming messages at random intervals, stores them until the central processor is ready to process them, and returns the processed replies to the teller consoles which originated the transactions (bank application).

cerdip — Abbreviation for Ceramic Dual In-line Package.

certified tape — Computer tape that is machine checked on all tracks throughout each roll and is certified by the supplier to have less than a specific total number of errors or to have zero errors.

certifier, tape — A peripheral device or unit designed to locate defects in magnetic tape before use, such as oxide emissions, unevenness, bubbles, etc.

CF — *See* control footing.

CH — *See* control heading.

chain — 1. Any series of items linked together. 2. Pertaining to a routine consisting of segments which are run through the computer in tandem, only one segment being within the computer at any one time and each segment using the output from the previous program as its input.

chain additions program — An instruction set that will permit new records to be added to a file.

chain, binary — A series of flip-flops (binary circuits) which exist in either one of two states, but each circuit can affect or change the following circuit.

chain code — An arrangement in a cyclic sequence of some or all of the possible different N-bit words, in which adjacent words are linked by the relationship that each word is derived from its neighbor by displacing the bits one digit position to the left or right, dropping the leading bit, and inserting a bit at the end. The value of the inserted bit needs only to meet the requirement that a word must not recur before the cycle is complete; e.g., 000 001 010 011 111 100 000. . . .

chained file — A computer file arranged so that each data item or key in a record in the chain has the address of another record with the same data or key. To retrieve all data that contains the given key, only the first address need be found, since the next address is adjacent to it, and that one is adjacent to the next, etc.

chained list — A list of items, each of which contains an identifier for the next item in a particular order, but such order does not have any particular relation to the order in which the items are stored.

chained record — Physical records, located randomly in main or auxiliary memory modules, that are linked or chained by means of a control field in each record which contains the address of the next record in the series or chain. Long and complete waiting lists or files can be connected or chained in this way.

chaining — 1. A system of storing records in which each record belongs to a list or group of records, and has a linking field for tracing the chain. 2. The capability of an object program to call another object program for execution after its own execution has been performed.

chaining, command — The execution of a sequence of i/o commands in a command list, under control of an IOP, on one or more logical records.

chaining, data — The gathering (or scattering) of information within one physical record, from (or to) more than one region of memory, by means of successive i/o commands.

chaining search — A particular search key is chosen, and when a search of an interconnected set is made whose key matches the search key, the content of the address includes the key matching the search key. It also contains either the item itself or the location of the item sought—or another address is sought and found in the content, the process being repeated until either the item is found or the chain is terminated.

chain links — 1. Various series of linked data items. 2. In sequential processing, successive program segments, each of which relies on the previous segment for its input.

chain maintenance program — An instruction set that will permit the deletion of records from a file.

chain printer — *See* printer, chain.

chain printing principle — The printing of a full line in a single print cycle. Data, representing the columns, is abstracted serially by character, parallel by bit from the buffer and then compared to the chain position counter. When coincidence takes place, the appropriate hammer is energized. When the number of energized hammers in a line equals the number of printable characters loaded into the buffer (not including blanks), the print cycle is terminated, and the printer advances the paper. The printer then becomes ready to accept the next line of data. This "adaptive control" technique allows the printer to move to the next line as soon as the buffer is empty, instead of continuing to read the blank spaces that constitute the rest of the line.

chain reaction — The initiation of multiple levels of address modification with few instructions.

chain search — A search key is used and is transformed to bring out an initial address. If the contents of the initial address contain the key matching the search key, the contents contain the sum or other information sought. If unsuccessful, another address is found in the contents, and the process is repeated until the item is found or the chain ends. Thus, a chain search operates in a file of unordered but related or interconnected data.

changeable storage — *See* storage, changeable.

change, control — *See* control change.

change dump — A print-out or output recording of the contents of all storage locations in which a change has been made since the previous change dump.

change file — A list of transactions processed against the master file.

change record — A record which results in

changing of some of the information in the corresponding master file record.

changes, pending — Occurrences of various types have prevented successful processing of transactions such as: program errors, records deleted from files, data mistakes, "frozen" accounts, and others. Such deviations from the normal require hold-ups or delays pending decisions resulting in changes.

change, step — The change from one value to another in a single increment in negligible time.

change tape — A paper tape or magnetic tape carrying information that is to be used to update filed information. This filed information is often on a master tape. (Synonymous with transaction tape.)

channel — 1. A path along which signals can be sent, e.g., data channel, output channel. 2. The portion of a storage medium that is accessible to a given reading station, e.g., track, band. 3. A unit which controls the operation of one or more i/o units. 4. One or more parallel tracks treated as a unit. 5. In a circulating storage, a channel is one recirculating path containing a fixed number of words stored serially by word. (Synonymous with band.)

channel adapter — A device which permits the connection between data channels of differing equipment. The device allows data transfer at the rate of the slower channel.

channel, analog — A channel on which the information transmitted can take any value between the limits defined by the channel. Voice channels are analog channels.

channel, broad-band — A channel capable of providing data-communication rates higher than those of voice-band channels. It also provides higher reliability. Current facilities can provide transmission rates up to several million bits per second.

channel capacity — The maximum possible information-transmission rate through a channel at a specified error rate. The channel capacity may be measured in bits per second or bauds.

channel, Class-D — The Class-D channel can be used to transmit punched paper tape at approximately 240 words per minute, depending upon the code element (5-, 6-, 7-, or 8-level code) employed. It could also be used to transmit 80-column punched cards at the rate of 10 to 11 per minute.

channel, Class-E — The Class-E data channel is capable of transmission rates up to 1200 baud. The channel will also accept polar-pulse input conforming to EIA standards, and will deliver signals at the destination having the same characteristics.

channel controllers — Units which allow several central elements in the computer to share, in a changing manner, a pool of millions of characters of main memory that can be partitioned into numerous (at least 8) different memories.

channel, data — The bidirectional data path between the i/o devices and the main memory in a digital computer that permits one or more i/o operations to take place concurrently with computation.

channel, dedicated — A specific channel that has been reserved or committed or set aside for a very specific use or application.

channel, DMA — The direct memory access (DMA) channel capability permits faster data transfer speeds. The basic approach is to bypass the registers and provide direct access to the memory bus. Another significant feature included in some of these is a vectored interrupt capability. The number of separate interrupt lines accommodated typically is four or more. These newer designs have been referred to as the second generation in microprocessors. Second generation features include: separate address and data bus lines, multiple address modes (e.g., direct, indirect, relative, and indexed), more instructions, more versatile register stack operation, vectored interrupts, direct memory access, standard RAM and ROM.

channel, duplex — A channel providing simultaneous transmission in both directions.

channel, four-wire — A two-way circuit where the signals simultaneously follow separate and distinct paths, in opposite directions, in the transmission medium.

channel, half-duplex — A channel capable of transmitting and receiving signals, but in only one direction at a time.

channel, information — The transmission and intervening equipment involved in the transfer of information in a given direction between two terminals. An information channel includes the modulator and demodulator and any error-control equipment irrespective of its location, as well as the backward channel, when provided.

channel, information (transfer) — The functional connection between the source and the sink data terminal equipments. It includes the circuit and the associated data communications equipments. Also, the assembly of data communications and circuits including a reverse channel if it exists.

channel, input — The channel which first brings in or introduces signals or data to a computing device.

channel, input/output — A specific channel which permits simultaneous communications, and independently so, between various storage units or any of the various input or output units. Such a channel is the control channel for most peripheral devices and quite often performs various checks on data transfers such as validity checks, etc.

channel, i/o — A bidirectional data path between the i/o devices and the main memory in a digital calculator that permits one or more i/o operations to happen concurrently with computation.

channel, narrow-band — A channel with data-communication capabilities up to 300 bits per second.

channel, output — That particular or dedicated channel reserved for removal or carrying of data from a peripheral device.

channel reliability — The percentage of time that the channel meets the arbitrary standards established by the user.

channel scheduler — A program whose function is to see that a list of requests for input/output operations are executed in a desirable sequence. The channel scheduler program sequentially initiates the next operation on the list after it has completed one operation on a channel.

channel, selector — The selector channel is designed primarily for such devices as tape units and disk files. When the selector channel is directed to make connection with one input or output unit, all other units on that channel are locked out until the first unit is released. The selector channel is capable of handling high-speed units overlapped with processing, so that a stream of data can be fed to storage while the processing unit is performing arithmetic or logic operations for another phase of the program.

channel, simplex — A channel which permits transmission in one direction only.

channels, paper tape — *See* tape channels, paper.

channels, read/write — The degree of peripheral simultaneity in any computer system depends on the number of read/write channels in the system. A read/write channel is a bidirectional data path across an interface between the main memory and a peripheral device. Whenever an input/output operation is to be performed, a programmer-assigned read/write channel completes the path between the required peripheral device and the main memory.

channels, tape, punched-paper — The parallel tracks along the length of the tape.

channel status routine (BSY) — BSY (busy) is called by drivers to determine the status of a channel. A driver cannot use a channel until the channel is free. When BSY is called, it retains control until the channel is free. The status of each channel available to the system is contained in the channel status table (CST). This table contains one entry for each channel. Each time a driver is called, it waits for the necessary channel to be free. When an input/output operation is initiated, the driver sets the channel status at busy. Upon completion of the interrupt, the channel status is set at not busy.

channel switching — *Same as* input/output switching.

channel synchronizer — The channel synchronizer provides the proper interface between the central computer and the peripheral equipment. Other control functions of the channel synchronizer include: primary interpreting of the function words; searching by comparison of an identifier with data read from a peripheral unit; and providing the central computer with peripheral-unit status information.

channel, time-derived — Any of the channels obtained by time-division multiplexing of a channel.

channel-to-channel connection — A device for rapid data transfer between two computers. A channel adapter is available that permits the connection between any two channels on any two systems. Data is transferred at the rate of the slower channel. *See* direct control connection.

channel, voice-band — A communications channel having an effective bandwidth of up to 3000 hertz. Equipment is available from the carriers and independent suppliers for data transmission at speeds up to 9600 bits per second.

channel, voice-grade — *See* channel, voice-band.

channel waiting queue — The group of items in the system needing the attention of the channel scheduler program which executes the items in queue in a desirable sequence.

channel, wideband common carrier — Wideband channels are facilities that the common carriers provide for transferring data at speeds up to the 1 million baud region. The availability of these facilities depends on what equipment the common carrier has in the subscriber's geographic area. There are many modems available for use with common carrier facilities, many of which are supplied by the common carriers.

chapter — Programs are often divided into self-contained parts, most often called segments or sections, and often times chapters, in order to be able to execute the program without maintaining it in its entirety in the internal storage medium at any one time. Other program divisions are pages, paragraphs, books.

character — 1. One symbol of a set of elementary symbols such as those corresponding to the keys on a typewriter. The symbols usually include the decimal digits 0 through 9, the letters A through Z, punctuation marks, operation symbols, and any other single symbols which a computer may read, store, or write. 2. The electrical, magnetic, or mechanical profile used to represent a character in a computer, and its various storage and peripheral devices. A character may be represented by a group of other elementary marks, such as bits or pulses.

character, additional — *Same as* character, special.

character adjustment — The address adjustment in which the literal used to modify the address has reference to a specific given number or group of characters.

character, alphameric — A generic term for numeric digits, alphabetic characters, and special characters.

character, backspace — One which creates action of the printing mechanism without printing. The backspace character causes a spacing backwards of one character width.

character, binary-coded — An element of notation which represents alphanumeric characters as decimal digits, letters, and symbols by a set configuration of consecutive binary digits.

character, blank — A specific character designed and used to separate groups of characters. In some computers an actual symbol such as * is used to signify a blank, and thus assurance is positive that a blank space did not develop from machine malfunction or keypunch operator error.

character, block ignore — One of the many control characters which indicates that an error in data preparation or transmission has occurred and certain predetermined amounts of data should be ignored. In some particular cases the amount to be ignored is a partial block of characters back to the most recently occurring block mark.

character boundary — A real or imaginary rectangle which serves as a boundary, in character recognition, between consecutive characters or successive lines on a source document.

character, check — *See* check character.

character checking, inadmissible — Numerous internal checks continually monitor the accuracy of the system and guard against incipient malfunction. Typical are the parity and inadmissible characters check; an automatic read-back of magnetic tape and magnetic cards as the information is being recorded. The electronic tests which precede each use of magnetic tape or magnetic cards ensure that the operator has not set switches improperly.

character, code — A particular arrangement of code elements used in a code to represent a single value or symbol.

character, coded — A character represented by a specific code.

character, coded extension — A distinct character designed to indicate that succeeding characters are to be interpreted using a different code.

character code, forbidden — In the binary coding of characters, a bit code which indicates an error in coding.

character, command — Characters, when used as code elements, can initiate, modify, or stop a control operation. Characters may be used, for example, to control the carriage return, etc., on various devices or control the devices themselves.

character, control — *See* character, command.

character crowding — The effect of reducing the time interval between subsequent characters read from tape, caused by a combination of mechanical skew, gap scatter, jitter, amplitude variation, etc. Also called packing.

character, device control — A specific control character to switch devices on or off, usually in telecommunications systems, but also used with other data processing equipment.

character edge — In optical character recognition, there is an imaginary edge which runs along the optical discontinuity between the printed area and the unprinted area of a printed symbol or character. The optical discontinuity is observed by a change in the reflectivity along this imaginary line which is transverse to the character edge.

character element — 1. A basic information element as transmitted, printed, displayed, etc., or used to control communications, when used as a code. 2. Groups of bits, pulses, etc., occurring in a time period normally representing that for a character or symbolic representation.

character emitter — An electromechanical device which emits a timed pulse or group of pulses in some code.

character, end-of-message — Some programmers use specific characters or groups of characters such as OUT, ROGER, EOM to indicate the end of a message.

character, erase — A character which most often represents a character to be ignored or signifies that the preceding or following item is to be ignored as prescribed by some fixed convention of the machine or as programmed. It may signify that some particular action is to be prevented, or it may signify an erase or destroy action on a tape or disk.

character, error — One of the control characters used to indicate that an error in data preparation or transmission has occurred. It also usually signifies that a certain predetermined amount of coming or recently transmitted data should be ignored.

character, escape — A control character which serves to assign, either temporarily or permanently, various new or different meanings to specific coded representations. Examples are: locking-shift characters, nonlocking shift characters, shift-out or shift-in characters, font-change characters, etc. Thus, escape characters permit a limited code to represent a wide range of characters since it assigns more than one meaning to each character representation.

character fill — 1. A procedure of storing the same character or symbol in storage locations, in a group of storage locations, or even in a complete storage unit of a computer. 2. To replace all data in a particular storage device in a group of locations by bringing all the cells to a prescribed or desired state.

character, font-change — A control character which causes the next character to determine which type font is to be used until the next font-change character comes up.

character, forbidden — *Same as* character, illegal.

character, format — A specific control character used to control a key printer. This character does not print but may cause backspacing, tabulating, new lines, etc.

character format memory — Memory storing technique of storing one character in each addressable location.

character, form-feed — The character which controls the printer or demands action of the printer, in this case to feed forms.

character, functional — *See* character, command.

character generation, automatic — *See* automatic character generation.

character graphics — A process by which pictures may be programmed. One typewriter-style keyboard has a graphic key and graphic symbols engraved on the key tops for use in the same manner as shifting for upper case on a typewriter. The graphic symbols may be used as though they were text when the graphic and shift-lock keys are depressed.

character, ignore — *See* ignore.

character, ignore block — The character which indicates that an error in data preparation or transmission has occurred and certain predetermined amounts of coming or recently transmitted data should be ignored. In this particular case, the amount to be ignored is a partial block of characters back to the most recently occurring block mark.

character, illegal — A character or combination of bits which is not accepted as a valid representation by the machine design or by a specific routine. Illegal characters are commonly detected and used as an indication of machine malfunction.

character, improper — *Same as* character, illegal.

character, instruction — *See* character, command.

characteristic — The integral part of a logarithm; the exponent of a normalized number.

characteristic distortion — 1. A fixed distortion which results in either shortened or lengthened impulses. It generally does not change in degree from day to day. 2. Distortions caused by transients which, as a result of the modulation, are present in the transmission channel and depend on its transmission qualities.

characteristic overflow — A situation developed in floating-point arithmetic if an attempt is made to develop a characteristic greater than a specified number.

characteristics, noise — *See* noise characteristics.

characteristic underflow — A situation developed in floating-point arithmetic if an attempt is made to develop a characteristic less than a specified number.

character, layout — A specific control character used to control a printer. This character does not print but may cause back-spacing, tabulating, new lines, etc.

character, least significant — The character in the rightmost position in a number or word.

character, locking shift — A common control character which causes all characters which follow to shift to a different character set until the shift character representative of that set is met, whereupon reversion is then made to the original character set. A shiftout character makes the change, while the shift-in character changes the character set back to the original. This action is somewhat analagous to shifting to capital letters on a typewriter by pressing the lock and shift keys.

character misregistration — The improper state of appearance of a character, in character recognition, with respect to a real or imaginary horizontal base line in a character reader.

character, most significant — The character in the leftmost position in a number or word.

character, new-line — A particular functional character which controls or demands action of the printer, in this case, a new line.

character, nonlocking shift — A special control character which causes one (sometimes more) characters following to shift to that of another total set of characters, for example, to caps or italics. Similar to a nonlocking shift key on a typewriter.

character, numeric — *Same as* digit.

character, operational — *See* character, command.

character outline — The graphic pattern formed by the stroke edges of a handwritten or printed character in character recognition.

character, pad — Character introduced to use up time while a function (usually mechanical) is being accomplished, e.g., carriage return, form eject, etc.

character, paper throw — A character which controls or demands action of the printer; in this case a paper throw.

character pitch — *See* pitch, character.

character, print control — A specific control character used to affect printing operations such as feeding, spacing, font selection.

character, protection — A character selected by the programmer or built into the machine which replaces a zero which has been suppressed to avoid error or false statements. Such characters are usually symbols, such as an ampersand or an asterisk.

character reader — A specialized device which can convert data represented in one of the type fonts or scripts read by human beings directly into machine language. Such a reader may operate optically; or if the characters are printed in magnetic ink, the device may operate magnetically or optically.

character recognition — The computer process of reading, identifying, and encoding a printed character.

character, redundant — A character specifically added to a group of characters to ensure conformity with certain rules which can be used to detect computer malfunction.

character, separating — One of the control characters designed to set out various hierarchies in data structures, i.e., to separate the parts or units. For example, SP might mean space between words, while S1 might mean spaces between sentences, S2 space between paragraphs, S4 space between pages, etc. Other separating characters might indicate parenthetical or bracketed matter in context or mathematics.

character, serial by — *See* serial-by-bit.

character set — An agreed set of representations, called characters, from which selections are made to denote and distinguish data. Each character differs from all others, and the total number of characters in a given set is fixed; e.g., a set may include the numerals 0 to 9, the letters A to Z, punctuation marks, and a blank or space.

character, shift-in — *See* character, locking shift.

character, shift-out (SO) — A code extension character that can be used by itself to substitute another character set for the standard character set, usually to access additional graphic characters.

characters, idle — Control characters interchanged by a synchronized transmitter and receiver to maintain synchronization during nondata periods.

character size — The number of binary digits in a single character in the storage device.

character skew — A form of character misregistration, in character recognition, such that the image to be recognized appears in a skewed condition with respect to a real or imaginary horizontal base line.

characters, machine readable — The symbols (printed, typed, or written) that can be interpreted by both people and optical character recognition equipment.

character-spacing reference line — An optical character recognition term related to a vertical line used to determine the horizontal spacing of characters. It may equally divide the distance between the sides of a character boundary or it may coincide with the centerline of a vertical stroke.

character, special — A character which is neither a numeral nor a letter but may be a symbol, such as /,*/$,=, or ?.

characters, polling — A set of characters designed to be peculiar to a terminal and the polling operation. Response to these characters indicates to the computer whether or not the terminal has a message to send.

character, start of heading — A single character or set of characters communicated by a polled terminal, indicating to other stations on the line that the data to follow specifies the addresses of stations on the line that are to receive the answering message.

character, start of text — A specific control character designed to terminate and separate a heading and mark the beginning of the actual text.

character string — A sequence or group of connected characters, connected by codes, key words, or other programming or associative techniques.

character stroke — Optical character recognition (OCR) lines, points, arcs, and other marks are often used as parts or portions of graphic characters. Even the dot over the letter i or the cross of a t is a stroke.

character style — In optical character recognition (OCR), a distinctive construction, with no restriction as to size, that is common to a group of characters. Different sizes of a given character style are proportional in all respects.

character subset — A smaller set of certain characters from a larger or universal set, all with specified common features. If all men is one set, tall men would be a subset, both sets being men and the subset being a smaller group with the common characteristic.

character, sync — A character transmitted to establish character synchronization in synchronous communication. When the receiving station recognizes the sync character, the receiving station is said to be synchronized with the transmitting station, and communication can begin.

character, tabulation — A specific character which controls the printer or demands action. In this case a tabulation character to begin tabulation.

character transfer rate — The speed at which data may be read from or written to the unit, exclusive of seek or latency delays.

character, transmission control — Some characters may be interspersed with regular data characters, but in effect are so designed or coded to control an operation such as recording, interpreting, transferring, or some type of processing. A character controlling transmission is one of these types.

charge coupled device memories — The basic charge coupled device (CCD), a type of analog shift register, is a semiconductor device in which an applied electrical field induces potential minima for signal charge packets at storage sites at or near the surface of the semiconductor material. Varying the applied electric field shifts the potential minima to adjacent storage sites, transferring the signal charge in a controlled manner within the semiconductor substrate from storage site to adjacent storage site in serial fashion. Appropriate manipulation of the imposed electrical field recirculates, stores, or delays the signal charges in their movement through the substrate. Thus, electrical signal charges, representing information, can be generated (read in), translated (moved or shifted), and retrieved (read out).

charge, storage — *See* storage charge.

chart, detail — A flowchart in minute detail of a sequence of operations. (The symbols of the detail chart usually denote an individual step or computer operation.) A detail chart is more detailed than a logic chart, usually reflects the particular computer characteristics and instructions, and facilitates the actual coding of the program in the manner intended by the programmer preparing the chart.

chart, grid — A representation of the relations between inputs, files, and outputs in matrix form.

chart, logic — A flowchart of a program or portions of a program showing the major logical steps intended to solve a problem. The symbols of the logic chart usually denote routines and subroutines and should represent the computer run in terms of highlights and control points. The level of detail in a particular logic chart may vary from one run to another and from one program to another, depending on the requirements of the program, and at the prerogative of the person preparing the chart.

chart, plugboard — A diagrammatic chart showing where plugs or wires are to be inserted into a plugboard. Other information displayed relates to placement and setting of switches, digit emitters, and other specific uses of the plugboard.

chart, process — *Same as* flowchart.

chart, run — A flowchart of one or more computer runs in terms of input and output.

chart, spacing — A form for developing a layout and spacing or general design of printed output, as well as the preparation of the carriage control tape.

chart, system — A symbolic representation of the main data flows and operations indigenous to an information-handling procedure.

chart, Veitch — A table or chart which shows all the information contained in a truth table. It displays columns and rows headed with the combinations of variables in Gray code groupings, and sequences in straight binary number sequence.

chassis assembly — A structure that provides mounting locations for the processor, power supply, and peripheral interface cards. The chassis assembly is often designed using a printed circuit backplane for all interconnecting wiring.

check — 1. A means of verifying the accuracy of data transmitted, manipulated, or stored by any unit or device in a computer. 2. A process of partial or complete testing of the correctness of machine operations, the existence of certain prescribed conditions within the computer, or the correctness of the results produced by a program. A check of any of these conditions may be made automatically by the equipment or may be programmed.

check, accounting — An accuracy control on input data that is based on an accounting principle such as control totals.

check, arithmetic — A check which uses mathematical identities or other properties, occasionally with some degree of discrepancy being acceptable, e.g., checking multiplication by verifying that A×B=B×A.

check, automatic — A provision constructed in hardware for verifying the accuracy of information transmitted, manipulated, or stored by any unit or device in a computer. (Synonymous with built-in check, built-in automatic check, hardware check.)

check, bias — *See* bias check.

check bit — A binary check digit; often a parity bit. (Related to parity check, and self-checking number.)

check, built-in — A provision constructed in hardware for verifying the accuracy of information transmitted, manipulated, or stored by any unit or device in a computer.

check, built-in automatic — A provision constructed in hardware for verifying the accuracy of information transmitted, manipulated, or stored by any unit or device in a computer.

check bus — Relates to a set or group of parallel lines for transmission of data to a particular checking device or unit such as a check register, a parity checker, or a comparator.

check, casting-out-nines — A check devised for arithmetic operations by using the remainder obtained from the operand and dividing by nine, performing the same operation on the remainders as are performed on the operands. The remainder can be obtained by dividing by nine or by adding the digits. The remainders of both should be the same.

check character — One or more characters carried in such a fashion that if a single error occurs (excluding compensating errors) a check will fail, and the error will be reported.

check code — To isolate and remove mistakes from a routine.

check, consistency — A process for verifying that a piece of data is consistent with the rules prescribed for its handling.

check, copy — *See* check, transfer.

check, diagnostic — A specific check used to locate a malfunction in a computer.

check digit — *See* digit, check.

check digit, parity — If a check bit is added to a string or if its complement is added, it is called a parity bit. If the check bit is appended, it is called an even parity check. If the complement is added, the string contains an odd number of ones, and the check is called an odd parity check.

check digit, sum — A check digit produced by a sum check.

check, dump — A check which usually consists of adding all the digits during dumping, and verifying the sum when retransferring.

check, duplication — A check which requires that the results of two independent performances, either concurrently on duplicate equipment or at different times on the same equipment, of the same operation be identical.

check, echo — A check of accuracy of transmission in which the information which was transmitted to an output device is returned to the information source and compared with the original information, to ensure accuracy of output.

check, even-odd — *See* check digit, parity.

check, even parity — One or more redundant digits in the word as a self-checking or error-detecting code to detect malfunctions of equipment in data-transfer operations. (Related to forbidden-combination check and parity check.)

check, false code — *See* check, forbidden-combination.

check, forbidden-combination — A check, usually automatic, that tests for the occurrence of a nonpermissible code expression. A self-checking code or error-detecting code uses code expressions such that one or more errors in a code expression produces a forbidden combination. A parity check makes use of a self-checking code employing binary digits in which the total number of 1's or 0's in each permissible code expression is always even or always odd. A check may be made either for even parity or odd parity. A redundancy check employs a self-checking code that makes use of redundant digits called check digits. Some of the various names that have been applied to this type of check are forbidden-pulse combination, unused order, improper instruction, unallowable digits, improper command, false code, forbidden digit, nonexistent code, and unused code.

check, forbidden-digit — *Same as* check, forbidden-combination.

check, hardware — A provision constructed in hardware for verifying the accuracy of information transmitted, manipulated, or stored by any unit or device in a computer. (Synonymous with built-in check, built-in automatic check.)

check, illegal-command — *See* check, forbidden-combination.

check, improper-command — *See* check, forbidden-combination.

check indicator — A device which displays or announces that an error has been made or that a failure has occurred.

check-indicator instruction — An instruction which directs a signal device that is turned on to call the operator's attention to the fact that there is some discrepancy in the instruction now in use.

check indicator, overflow — *See* indicator, overflow check.

check indicator, sign — *See* indicator, sign check.

checking and recovery error — Parity is computed or checked on all references to central store. If a parity error occurs, the computer will interrupt to the proper location, an alarm will sound, and the appropriate fault lights will be flashed on the operator's console. For all real-time applications, the system will attempt to recover. Once the computer has satisfactorily recovered, the system will continue normal operation.

checking, automatic — Numerous internal checks continually monitor the accuracy of the system and guard against incipient malfunction. Typical are the parity and inadmissible-character check, automatic readback of magnetic tape and magnetic cards as the information is being recorded, the electronic tests which precede each use of magnetic tape or magnetic cards to ensure that the operator has not inadvertently set switches improperly. These internal automatic tests are supplemented by the instructions which may be programmed to ensure proper setup of certain units prior to their use. Console switches are designed to protect against inadvertent or improper use, and interlocks are provided on peripheral units to guard against operator error.

checking characters, inadmissible (automatic) — *See* character checking, inadmissible.

checking code, error — *See* code, error checking.

checking loop — A method of checking the accuracy of transmission of data in which the received data are returned to the sending end for comparison with the original data, which are stored there for this purpose.

checking, module — *Same as* module testing.

checking program — A specific type of diagnostic (error-discovering) program which examines programs or data for the most obvious mistakes.

checking, redundant — The specific use of added or extra digits or bits in order to diagnose, detect, or cause errors which can arise as a result of unwarranted dropping or gaining of digits or bits.

checking, sequence — *See* sequence checking.

check, instruction — *See* check, forbidden-combination.

check light — A control panel indicator light which indicates parity errors or arithmetic overflow conditions.

check, limit — A type of check on the input for the purpose of ensuring that only valid codes or transaction types are permitted. If, for instance, there are only four transaction types, the limit check will reveal an error situation if a transaction other than the four is encountered. A limit check will detect transportation errors as in the case where an 83 was mistakenly input as a 38. In such a case, the 38 would show up as an error.

check, longitudinal — An even or odd parity check at fixed intervals during data transmission.

check, machine — This is a functional check to determine the proper operating characteristics of equipment to ensure that all instructions are being properly decoded and arithmetic operations are being performed properly. The use of check or parity bits to determine proper operation of storage units.

check, marginal — A preventive maintenance procedure in which certain operating conditions are varied about their normal values in order to detect and locate incipient defective units; e.g., supply voltage or frequency may be varied. (Synonymous with marginal test and high-low bias test, and related to check.)

check, mathematical — *Same as* check, arithmetic.

check, modulo-N — 1. A check that makes use of a check number that is equal to the remainder of the desired number when divided by N; e.g., in a modulo-4 check, the check number will be 0, 1, 2, or 3, and the remainder of A when divided by 4 must equal the reported check number B; otherwise, an equipment malfunction has occurred. 2. A method of verification by congruences, e.g., casting out nines. (Related to self-checking number.)

check, nonexistence code — *See* check, forbidden-combination.

check number — A number composed of one or more digits and used to detect equipment malfunctions in data-transfer operations. If a check number consists of only one digit, it is synonymous with check digit.

check, odd-even — *See* check digit, parity.

check, odd parity — *See* check digit, parity.

checkout — A general term used to describe a set of routines developed to provide the programmer with a complete evaluation of his program under operating conditions. Checkout routines are provided by most manufacturers of equipment.

checkout, program — A standard run of a program on a computer to determine if all designs and results of a program are as anticipated.

checkout routine — Any of various routines to aid programmers in the debugging of their routines. Some typical routines are storage, printout, and device printout.

checkout systems, automatic — Static and dynamic tests on components and subsystems of aircraft and submarine simulators, aircraft weapons complexes, missiles, etc., require automatic test facilities. Checkout of each element yields an evaluation of the overall system operation and provides data fundamental to the logical troubleshooting of defective systems and components.

check, overflow — *See* overflow check.

check, page — A procedure for controlling the accuracy of data by verifying that the value of a piece of data falls between certain pre-established maximum and minimum values.

check, parity — *See* parity check.

check, parity, longitudinal (communications) — *See* parity check, longitudinal (communications).

checkpoint — In a machine run, a point in time at which processing is momentarily halted to make a magnetic tape record of the condition of all the variables of the machine run, such as the position of input and output tapes and a copy of working storage. Checkpoints are used in conjunction with a restart routine to minimize reprocessing time occasioned by functional failures.

checkpoint and restart procedures — Checkpoint and restart procedures, which are techniques associated with computers, make it possible, in the event of an error or interruption, to continue processing from the last checkpoint rather than from the beginning of the run. These techniques are included in applications which require many hours of processing time, since heavy machine scheduling and deadlines generally do not permit a complete rerun. To establish checkpoints, processing intervals are determined, each being based upon a certain number of items, transactions, or records processed. At each interval or checkpoint, the stored program identifies input and output records and then records them along with the contents of important storage areas such as counters and registers; at the same time, accuracy of processing up to that point is established. Restart procedures are the means by which processing is continued after an error or interruption. Each set of restart procedures includes the necessary operator and stored-program instructions for (1) locating the last checkpoint, (2) reading the machine for reprocessing, and (3) entering the main routine at that point.

checkpoint routine — A series of instructions that generate information for further verification.

checkpoint sorting — Also, restart point. The point at which a restart (or rerun) can be initiated. Memory, registers, and the position of tapes are recorded at this point.

check problem — A problem chosen to determine whether the computer or a program is operating correctly.

check, program — The technique for observing program errors and malfunction through the use of sample data about which there are known results.

check, programmed — 1. A system of determining the correct program and machine functioning either by running a sample problem with similar programming and known answer, including mathematical or logical checks such as comparing A times B with B times A, and usually where reliance is placed on a high probability of correctness rather than built-in error-detection circuits, or by building a checking system into the actual program being run and utilized for checking during the actual running of the problem. 2. A procedure for checking which is specifically designed to be an integral part of the total program.

check, range — A procedure for controlling the accuracy of data by verifying that the value of a piece of data falls between certain pre-established maximum and minimum values.

check, read-back — *Same as* check, echo.

check, read/write — An accuracy check on reading, writing, sensing, and punching, by comparing what has been written, usually by running the originals and the newly printed or punched cards through a comparator to check for errors.

check, redundancy — A specific or automatic check which is based on the systematic insertion of components or characters developed especially for checking purposes. (Related to parity check.)

check, redundant — A check which makes use of redundant characters. (Related to parity check, and forbidden-combination check.)

check register — A register used to temporarily store information where it may be checked with the result of a succeeding transfer of this information.

check reset key — A push button that acknowledges an error and resets the error detection mechanism indicated by the check light. This is required to restart a program after an error has been discovered in batch mode.

check, residue — *Same as* check, modulo-N.

check, routine — *Same as* check, programmed.

check, selection — A check, usually automatic, to verify that the correct register or other device has been selected in the performance of an instruction.

check, sequence — A data-processing operation designed to check the sequence of the items in a file assumed to be already in sequence.

check sign indicator — An error-checking device, indicating no sign or improper signing of a field used for arithmetic processes. The machine can, upon interrogation, be made to stop or enter into a correction routine.

check solution — A solution to a problem obtained by independent means to verify a computer solution.

checks, photocell light — Checks performed on data read from cards passing through a card reader.

check, static — An equipment setup check performed by comparing measurements taken in the reset mode or hold mode for a single value of the independent variable, and including initial rates of change, with the results received from some alternative method of computation. This type of check reveals the static errors and often reveals the instantaneous values of dynamic errors.

check sum — The sum used in a summation check.

check, summation — A check in which groups of digits are summed, usually without regard for overflow, and that sum checked against a previously computed sum to verify that no digits have been changed since the last summation.

check symbol — A symbol for representation of a check sum, which is normally attached or appended to the original string and is copied along with it. Such a check on copying is usually completed by recomputing and then matching this sum with the original sum.

check, system — A check on the overall performance of the system, usually not made by built-in computer check circuits, e.g., control totals, hash totals, and record counts.

check total — One of a number of totals or sums which can be correlated in some procedure or manner as a check for consistency of reconciliation in a set of calculations.

check, transfer — A check which verifies that information is transferred correctly from one place to another. It is usually done by comparing each character with a copy of the same character transferred at a different time or by a different route.

check, transmission longitudinal — An even or odd parity check at fixed intervals during data transmission.

check, transverse — A system of error control based on the check that some preset rules for the formation of characters are observed.

check trunk — A set or group of parallel lines for transmission of data to a particular checking device or unit such as a check register, a parity checker, or a comparator.

check, twin — A continuous duplication check achieved by duplication of hardware and automatic comparison.

check, unallowable code — *See* check, forbidden-combination.

check, unallowable instruction — *See* check, forbidden-combination.

check, validity — A check based upon known limits or upon given information or computer results; e.g., a calendar month will not be numbered greater than 12, and a week does not have more than 168 hours.

check word — A machine word is often used to represent a check symbol, and this is appended and printed to the block, thus signifying the check.

chip — An integrated circuit or integration of many circuits on a wafer slice, most often of silicon, which contains these circuits.

chip architecture — Functionally, the microprocessor chip includes the arithmetic logic unit (ALU), the general-purpose registers, and the control-bus structure. The architecture is to some degree dependent on the partitioning of

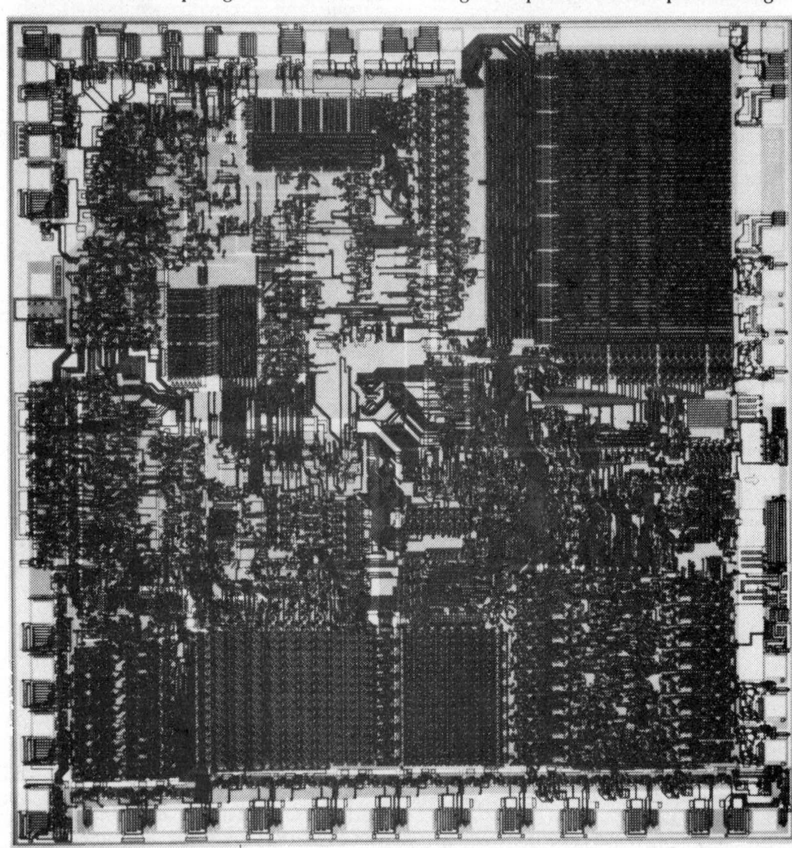

Courtesy Intel Corp.

Chip architecture (8086 16-bit microprocessor chip).

the processor between one or more chips, the number of contacts each chip has, the chip size, the off-chip memory, and i/o bus structure.

chip carrier — A plug-in type of device for mounting LSI chips on circuit boards. They may be used for protecting the chip from the thermal shock of soldering; avoiding board damage arising from the difficulty of removing ICs with many leads; minimizing chip damage from static charges or leakage current during handling or soldering; easing prototyping, design changes, programming and field repairs, and testing; and lowering inventory costs, because chips are cheaper to stock than whole boards. There are no leads to be bent, straightened, or cut. Sockets for electrical test and burn-in are available for many of the carrier designs.

chip, circuit — In a microprocessor, a single device composed of transistors, diodes, and other components as interconnected by various chemical processes. It usually has been cut from a larger wafer, usually of silicon.

chip, communications — To ensure that the receiving end understands the transmitted data, line-protocol chips often are employed. For telecommunications, chips like LSI tone-receivers, codecs and filters, and subscriber line-interface circuits are available for signaling, voice /PCM processing, and interfacing to local control nodes, respectively. In addition, RAMs can help boost data-handling efficiency through schemes like time-division multiplexing.

chip, i/o — To complete their microcomputer product line, each manufacturer tries to offer a complete set of i/o interface chips; i/o chips are implemented in MOS or bipolar technologies depending on the requirements. Those designed to fit a particular device to a microprocessor save the designer-programmer time in development and reduce the overall number of chips in the microcomputer. The next step was to make these interface chips parameter selectable so that several models of one kind of peripheral can be handled by one chip.

chip LSI technology — The large-scale integration (LSI) technology used to build microprocessor chips primarily centers around metal oxide semiconductor (MOS) devices. Chip densities on MOS devices range from 500 to 10,000 transistors per chip. The size of a chip typically ranges from 0.15 inch square to 0.25 inch square. The chips are mounted into dual in-line packages (DIPs), which typically have 18,24, or 40 pins for mounting on a printed circuit card. The p-channel MOS (PMOS) was the predominant technology for the calculator chips and most of the 4-bit and 8-bit processors. The PMOS 8-bit microprocessors with especially good design are still sometimes competitive with the newer NMOS 8-bit chips.

chip, memory — The memory section of a microcomputer usually accounts for a major portion of the chips. All three kinds of memory are used. Random access memory (RAM) chips are used primarily for variable data and scratch pad. Read-only (ROM) chips are used to store instruction sequences. Programmable Read-Only Memory (PROM) chips are used for quickly tailoring the general-purpose microcomputers for specific applications. RAMs are expensive compared to ROMs, but the data in the ROMs must be stored at the time they are created, so there is a production delay associated with them as well as a "programming" cost. PROM chips, some of which can be erased by ultraviolet light and reprogrammed, are used in place of ROMs when small quantities are involved.

chip microprocessor — The so-called "computer on a chip"; the LSI circuits, residing on a single silicon chip, capable of performing the essential functions of a computer CPU.

chip processes — The processes involved in producing integrated circuits. Different service firms specialize in each: circuit design and layout, mask making, wafer fabrication, assembly, and test. The IC designer normally works with a logic diagram. Since system design and partitioning can be critical, the design house usually works closely with customer engineers. Many design services use sophisticated computer-aided design (CAD) systems.

chip register architecture — The arrangement of registers on a chip, including the number and function of on-chip registers, the type and depth of the stack register, interrupt capability, and the direct-memory-access feature. Essentially, the only register a processor needs is an accumulator. However, the accumulator must have access to memory, and an instruction set should permit immediate addressing and data manipulation between the memory and the accumulator. If indirect addressing is available, even special indexing registers can be imitated by using memory locations as registers. The advantage of using on-chip registers instead of memory space is that the instructions are faster and the bits required are fewer.

chip select — Various LSI chips normally have one or several chip selects. The CS line is used to select one chip among many. When selected, the chip examines the rest of its pins, in particular the address bus which specifies a location/register within the chip. Multiple chip-selects are used to eliminate the use of external decoders, but result in a higher pin count.

CICS — Abbreviation for Customer Information Control System. CICS provides an interface between the operating system access methods and applications programs to allow remote or local display terminal interaction with the data base in the central processor. Different versions include time management facilities and support for bisync, dial-up, PL 1 support, and expanded data-base control items such as file browsing and dynamic file open and close.

CIM — Abbreviation for Computer Input Microfilm. The CIM process involves scanning an image on microfilm, converting the digital representation to computer language, and arranging the information in memory, such as magnetic tape. The imagery to be scanned can be charts, graphs, plans, drawings, pictures, digital marks, or alphanumeric characters. The basic purpose of CIM is to place information that is on microfilm into a computer in order to manipulate the data. Updating can be done by combining with new data or deleting or rearranging the old data. Automatic interpretation of information is also possible. The medium (microfilm) is easier to handle than paper. It is also possible to have higher accuracy when working with transmitted light rather than reflected light.

CIOCS — Abbreviation for Communication Input/Output Control System.

circuit — 1. A system of conductors and related electrical elements through which electrical current flows. 2. A communications link between two or more points.

circuit, AND — *See* AND circuit.

circuit, balanced — A circuit terminated by a network whose impedance losses are infinite.

circuit, bistable — A circuit which has two states, each requiring an appropriate trigger for excitation and transition from one state to the other.

circuit, bus — Usually a group of circuits that provide a communication path between two or more devices, such as between a central processor, memory, and peripherals.

circuit, bus driver — A circuit designed to amplify a bus data or control signal sufficiently to assure valid receipt of that signal at the destination.

circuit capacity — The number of communications channels that can be handled by a given circuit at the same time.

circuit, clear-to-send — *See* clear-to-send circuit.

circuit, coincidence — *Same as* gate, AND.

circuit, computer — Circuits used in the construction of digital computers. They include storage circuits, triggering circuits, gating circuits, inverting circuits, and timing circuits. In addition, there may be other circuits used in smaller quantities, such as power amplifiers for driving heavier loads, indicators, output devices, and amplifiers for receiving signals from external devices, as well as oscillators for obtaining the clock frequency.

circuit dropout — The momentary interruption of a transmission because of the complete failure of a circuit.

circuit, equality — A device whose output signal represents one only when signals representing identical n-bit numbers are applied to both its inputs.

circuit, integrated (IC) — One of several logic circuits, gates, and flip-flops which are etched on single crystals, ceramics, or other semiconductor materials and designed to use geometric etching and conductive ink or chemical deposition techniques all within a hermetically sealed chip. Some chips with many resistors and transistors are extremely tiny; others are in effect "sandwiches" of individual chips.

circuit, logic — One of certain circuits used to perform logical functions. The functions are AND, NAND, OR, NOR and Exclusive OR. The output of these circuits is dependent on the state (1 or 0) of the inputs.

circuit, monostable — A circuit which has one stable state and one unstable state, and which undergoes a complete cycle of change in response to a single triggering excitation.

circuit, nanosecond — Computer logic circuits, or other electronic circuits, which have gradient pulse rise or fall times measured in billionths of a second or less. A nanosecond is 1 billionth of a second.

circuit, NOT — *Same as* gate, NOT.

circuit, OR — *See* gate, OR.

circuit, received-data — Signals on this circuit are originated by the receiving-signal converter, in response to signals received over the communication media. This circuit is not required for send-only messages. In half-duplex service, the receiving-signal converter shall hold marking condition on the received-data circuit when the remote data has its send-request circuit in the "off" condition. Optionally, in half-duplex service, the received-data circuit may be used to monitor transmitted signals, e.g., for local copy.

circuit reliability — The percentage of time the circuit meets arbitrary standards set by the user.

circuitry, arithmetic — High-speed arithmetic unit which provides fixed and floating-point operations in one computer.

circuits, control — The circuits which cause the computer to carry out the instructions in proper sequence, and which can control by permitting only the coded conditions to continue or function.

circuit, send-request — Signals on this circuit are originated in the data-terminal equipment to select whether the signal converter is to be conditioned to transmit or to receive. For half-duplex service, when the signal on the send-request circuit is switched to the "on" condition, the signal converter switches to the transmit condition, without regard to any signals that may be received from the communications facility. When this signal is switched to the "off" condition, the signal converter switches to the receive condition, without regard to any signals on the transmitted-data circuit. Data-terminal equipment intended for use with send-only service holds the send-request circuit in the "on" condition at all times. Data-terminal equipment intended for use with receive-only service holds the send-request circuit in the "off" condition at all times. This circuit is not required for full-duplex service.

circuit shift — *See* shift, circular.

circuit, side — One of two physical circuits in a phantom group.

circuit, single — A telegraph circuit capable of nonsimultaneous two-way communications.

circuits, instruction control — *Same as* circuits, control.

circuits, priority — The priority circuits of the control unit grant memory access to the various units of the system in a sequence that enables each input/output device and system running time to be used most efficiently. The priority circuits receive, store, and grant requests for access to memory made by the input/output synchronizers and the central processor. When simultaneous requests are made, the priority circuits select the synchronizer that is to be granted memory access according to the relative data-transfer rate of the input/output device controlled by each synchronizer. A synchronizer that controls a unit with a relatively slow transfer rate, such as the card-punch unit, requires access to memory less often than a synchronizer that controls a unit with a relatively fast transfer rate, such as a tape unit; thus, the card-punch unit synchronizer has a lower priority than the tape-unit synchronizer. The central processor has the lowest priority, since delaying a central-processor request for memory access will not disrupt the execution cycle or cause loss of information (some systems).

circuit switching — A system in which stations on different circuits within a network are joined by connecting the two circuits together.

circuit switching delays — Two aspects of a circuit switch network that contribute to delay are the time spent waiting for an available channel and the time required for the carrying of signaling messages. The aspect of a packet switch network considered with respect to its delaying effect is the spread of time gaps between packets in a message as they pass through the network.

circuit tester — A typical circuit-tester system employs a digital processor and storage media to supply programmed test instructions, translate product error data, and perform arithmetic computations. The test system can also communicate with a remotely located "host" computer.

circuit, transmitted-data — Signals on this circuit are originated by the data-terminal equipment for transmission on the data-communication channel. This circuit is not required for receive-only service.

circuit, tributary — A circuit which connects an individual drop, or drops, to a switching center.

circuit, trunk — A circuit which connects two switching centers.

circuit, voice-grade — A circuit suitable for the transmission of speech, digital or analog data, or facsimile, and generally with a frequency range of about 300–3000 Hz.

circular file — An organization for highly volatile files. New records that are added replace the oldest records.

circular shift — *See* shift, circular.

citation — A reference statement relating to other sources of data or special notes concerning the data on punched cards.

citation index — An index or reference list of documents mentioned in a specific document or document set.

class — 1. A set of individuals, documents, data, etc., with similar characteristics. 2. A subdivision of a category.

Class-D channel — A transmission circuit which can transmit punched paper tape at the rate of 240 words per minute, or punch card data at the rate of approximately 10 cards (80 columns) per minute.

Class-E channel — A data transmission circuit which can transmit data at the rate of 1200 bits per second.

classification — An arrangement of data in classes or groups. This is required to produce summary reports.

classification, concept — A particular type of classification for retrieving information from storage units based on specific concepts or images. Concepts may be identified by a word or a group of words, but they define the concept, and when concepts are assigned to documents they are then identified during searches.

classify — To arrange data into classes or groups according to a definite plan or method.

clause — A part of a statement in COBOL. It may describe structures, give initial values to items, or redefine data defined by a previous clause.

clear — An activity to place one or more storage locations into a prescribed state, usually zero or the space character. Contrast with set.

clear area — Any area to be kept free, by designation, of printing or any markings in character recognition.

clear band — In optical character recognition (OCR), a specified area that is to be kept free of printing or any other markings not related to machine reading.

clear-to-send circuit — Signals on this circuit are originated in the signal converter. For send-only and full-duplex service, the signal converter holds the clear-to-send circuit in the "on" condition at all times. This circuit is not required for receive-only service. For half-duplex service, when the send-request signal is switched to the "on" condition, the clear-to-send circuit is switched to the "on" condition after a time delay sufficient to effect the reversal of direction of transmission equipment. When the send-request circuit is switched back to the "off" condition, the clear-to-send circuit is switched back to the "off" condition.

clock — A time-keeping, pulse-counting, frequency-measuring, or synchronizing device within a computer system. Such clocks are of various types, as: real-time clock, which measures the past or used time in the same analogous scale as external events it will be used to describe; a master clock, which is the source of pulses required for computer operation; programmable clock, whose time values are transmitted into a clock register and which may be accessed as determined by clock instructions in the program.

clock, control — The electronic clock usually contained in the hardware which times the instruction sets, and times the flow and manipulation of the data.

clock counter — A memory location that records the progress of real time, or its approximation, by accumulating counts produced by a (clock) count pulse interrupt.

clock, master — *See* master clock.

clock pulse — *See* pulse, clock.

clock rate — The time rate at which pulses are emitted from the clock. The clock rate determines the rate at which logical or arithmetic gating is performed with a synchronous computer.

clock, real-time — A clock which indicates the passage of actual time, in contrast to a fictitious time set up by the computer program.

clock, real-time (time-sharing) — *See* time sharing, real-time clock.

clock signal — A fundamental repetitive signal which times or controls most operations in electronic data processing equipment.

clock slips — Relative shifts of the system clock with respect to data in synchronous systems. Clock slips can cause modems to lose synchronization.

clock system — The timing system that is used to cycle the computer through the various states required during operation. Systems may require only a single clock or several of them. One of the most popular CPUs requires four.

clock system, bit-slice microprocessor single-phase — In a single-phase clock system, one clock and its inverse are used to drive all circuits, with the sequencer triggered on one edge of the waveform and the bit slice triggered on the opposite edge.

clock system, bit-slice microprocessor two-phase — A two-phase clock (two separate clock signals generated from a common source) can be used if each phase is fed to different elements to speed processing. Clocking can be optimized for individual sections better in a multiphase system, since each duty cycle can be separately adjusted.

clock system, microcomputer — A microprocessor-based clock system can generate a time base entirely in software. In one design, a 12-hour clock, 4-year calendar, and 12-hour elapsed-time indicator are implemented and displayed on a 3½-hour clock, and the other two timing functions are displayed for a predetermined time upon demand. The microprocessor includes a dedicated direct-memory-access (DMA) pointer on-chip, which is used to generate timing functions with accuracies limited only by the crystal-clock oscillator tolerance.

clock time measurements — For a hardware design, timing can be done by external logic, in which a clock signal interrupts the microprocessor and updates a counter at a fixed time interval. For a software design, the microprocessor performs timing by monitoring its instruction flow, since each section of the program executes within a specific time.

clock, time of day — Records time in hours, minutes, seconds, over 24-hour range and sends time to central processor upon command.

clock track — A specific track upon which a desired pattern of digits has been recorded and thus provides a clock signal.

closed array — An array which cannot be extended at either end.

closed loop — 1. A group of instructions which are repeated indefinitely. 2. Pertaining to a system with feedback type of control, such that the output is used to modify the input.

closed-loop system — A system in which the computer controls an external program or process without human intervention. An example of a closed-loop process-control system would be the computer connected directly to instrumentation through a digital-to-analog converter to complete the feedback loop. The computer could then take control directly to the process by setting controllers and activating switches, valves, etc.

close-down, disorderly — A system stoppage due to an equipment error wherein it is impossible to do an orderly close-down. Special precautions are necessary to prevent the loss of messages and duplication in record updating.

close-down, orderly — The stopping of the system in a way that ensures an orderly restart and no destruction of messages. When a system is forced to stop, an orderly close-down provides that all records are updated that should be updated and that no records are erroneously updated again when the restart is made. Furthermore, all incoming and outgoing transmissions are completed, with a message sent to the terminals which notifies the operators of the close-down.

closed routine — A routine which is not inserted as a block of instructions within a main routine, but is entered by basic linkage from the main routine.

closed shop — 1. A computing installation at which all computer programming, coding, and operating functions are performed by members of a regular computing group. 2. The operation of a computer facility where programming service to the user is the responsibility of a group of specialists, thereby effectively separating the phase of task formulation from that of computer implementation. The programmers are not allowed in the computer room to run or oversee the running of their programs. (Contrasted with open shop.)

closed subroutine — *See* subroutine, closed.

clustering — In indexing, the grouping of elements within a table caused by equal hash indices. Hash index is the initial estimate of the location of an entry within a table.

CML — Abbreviation for Current Mode Logic.

CNC — Abbreviation for Computer Numerical Control. A system for computer control of machine tools such as lathes and milling machines.

CNC tool management — Some CNC systems provide automatic random tool selection, cutter diameter compensation, tool length storage, and tool length trim to increase tool utilization and machine productivity for machining centers. In one system, tool numbers up to 8 digits in length may be entered into the control. This enables direct input via tape of tool part numbers rather than pocket location. Tape or keyboard entry at setup coordinates tool part number and pocket storage location as well as its unique diameter and length values, and override of spindle speed or feed rate if desired.

coalesce — The act of combining two or more files into one.

COBOL — Acronym for COmmon Business Oriented Language. This is a common procedural language designed for commercial data processing as developed and defined by a national committee of computer manufacturers and users. It is a specific language by which business-data processing procedure may be precisely described in a standard form. The language is intended not only as a means for directly presenting any business program to any suitable computer for which a compiler exists, but also as a means of communicating such procedures among individuals.

COBOL, data division — The data division describes the data to be processed by the object program. It contains a file section which describes the files used. There may be a working storage section which allocates memory space for the storage of intermediate results.

COBOL, environment division — The environment division describes the computer on which the source program is to be compiled, the computer on which the object program is to be executed, and the relationship between data files and input/output media. The configuration section contains three paragraphs which deal with the overall specifications of the computer involved and equates actual hardware names with mnemonic names supplied by the programmer. The input/output section consists of two paragraphs which identify each file and specify input/output techniques, respectively.

COBOL, identification division — Identifies the source program and provides optional documentation information.

COBOL language — The English-language statements of COBOL provide a relatively machine-independent method of expressing a business-oriented problem to the computer. Commonly used nouns, verbs, and the connectives are used in the procedural portion of a COBOL program to construct easily understood sentences. The excellent documentation provided by COBOL—problem definition as well as a method of solution—enables more than one programmer to work on a particular problem with minimal duplication of effort.

COBOL library — A COBOL library processor is available to store and retrieve data and procedure division descriptions, and it provides dynamic dumps of specified data areas to facilitate program checkout.

COBOL, procedure division — The procedure division describes the procedures to be used in processing the data described in the data division; it contains all the necessary steps to solve a given problem. Procedures are written as sentences that are combined to form named paragraphs. Likewise, paragraphs may be combined to form sections. Paragraph and section names are assigned by the programmer so that control may be transferred from one section or paragraph to another.

COBOL segmentation — COBOL programs can be segmented by use of priority numbers on procedural sections.

COBOL word — A word given a preassigned meaning in COBOL language, including both optional and key words that must be used in their prescribed context; also called "reserve words." The standard list of COBOL reserved words is supplemented by a manufacturer's list for each machine with a COBOL compiler.

Codabar code — *See* bar codes (illustration).

CODASYL — Acronym for COnference for DAta SYstems Languages. A group, created by the Department of Defense, computer users, and manufacturers, which has specified a number of manufacturer-independent, application-independent software tools designed to form the basis of data-base management. The programming language COBOL is a product of this committee.

code — 1. A system of symbols for representing data or instructions in a computer or a tabulating machine. 2. To translate the program for the solution of a problem on a given computer into a sequence of machine language or pseudoinstructions and addresses acceptable to that computer. (Related to encode.)

code, absolute — A code using absolute addresses and absolute operation codes, i.e., a code which indicates the exact location where the referenced operand is to be found or stored. (Synonymous with one-level code and specific code, and related to absolute address.)

code, access control — Used in conjunction with the memory map option, which determines whether or not a CPU operating in the slave mode may read from, obtain instructions from, or write into a given page of virtual addresses.

code, alphabetic — A system of alphabetic abbreviations used in preparing information for input into a machine; e.g., Boston, New York, Philadelphia, and Washington may be reported in alphabetical coding as BS, NY, PH, WA. (Contrasted with numeric code.)

code, alphanumeric — The code of the set of characters used, i.e., both letters and digits.

code, augmented operation — A particular code which is further defined or limited by information found in another position of an instruction, i.e., an instruction word but one which has addresses considered as the operation code.

code, automatic — A code which allows a machine to translate or convert a symbolic language into a machine language for automatic machine or computer operations.

code, basic — *Same as* code, absolute.

code, binary — A coding system in which the encoding of any data is done through the use of bits, i.e., 0 or 1.

code, biquinary — A two-part code in which each decimal digit is represented by the sum of the two parts, one of which has the value of decimal zero or five, and the other the values zero through four. The abacus and soroban both use biquinary codes. An example follows.

Decimal	*Biquinary*	*Interpretation*
0	0 000	0+0
1	0 001	0+1
2	0 010	0+2
3	0 011	0+3
4	0 100	0+4
5	1 000	5+0
6	1 001	5+1
7	1 010	5+2
8	1 011	5+3
9	1 100	5+4

codec — Acronym for COder-DECoder.

code, card — The combinations of punched holes which represent characters (letters, digits, etc.) in a punched card.

code chain — An arrangement in a cyclic sequence of some or all of the possible different N-bit words, in which adjacent words are linked by the relation that each word is derived from its neighbors by displacing the bits one digit position to the left or right, dropping the leading bit, and inserting a bit at the end. The value of the inserting bit needs only to meet the requirement that a word must not recur before the cycle is complete, e.g., 000 001 010 101 011 111 110 100 000 . . . .

code, character — A particular arrangement of code elements used in a code to represent a single value or symbol.

code character, extension — A distinct character designed to indicate that succeeding characters are to be interpreted using a different code.

code check — To isolate and remove mistakes from a routine.

code check, false — *See* check, forbidden-combination.

code-checking time — The time spent checking out a problem on the machine, making sure that the problem is set up correctly, and that the code is correct.

code, command — *See* code, operation.

code, computer — 1. A system of combinations of binary digits used by a given computer. (Synonymous with machine code.) 2. A repertoire of instructions.

code, computer instruction — An instruction code designed for specific computers.

code, constant ratio — A code in which all characters are represented by combinations having a fixed ratio of ones to zeros.

code conversion — A process for changing the bit groupings for characters in one code into the corresponding character bit groupings for a second code.

code converter — A device that automatically changes an input code to another output code.

code, cyclic — A binary code in which sequential numbers are represented by expressions which are the same, except in one place, and in that place differ by one unit. Thus, in going from one decimal digit to the next sequential digit, only one binary digit changes its value. (Synonymous with Gray code.)

Decimal	*Binary*	*Gray*
0	000	000
1	001	001
2	010	011
3	011	010
4	100	110
5	101	111

code data — Sets of symbols which are used to represent various data items for data elements on a one-for-one basis. A single number or symbol might represent a particular week or month.

code, data conversion — The translation of alphanumeric data into a form acceptable to the computer. This is usually done by the computer during the input of the data.

code, data link — A number of different coding schemes are used to represent characters in data communications systems. The codes differ primarily in the number of bits used to represent characters and the particular patterns of bits which correspond to the characters. Characters are divided into graphic characters, representing a symbol, and control characters which are used to control a terminal, a computer function, or communications.

coded character — *See* character, coded.

coded decimal — Describing a form of notation by which each decimal digit separately is expressed in some other number system; e.g., in the 8–4–2–1 coded decimal notation, the number twelve is represented as 0001 0010, for 1 and 2, whereas in pure or straight binary notation it is represented as 1100. Other coded decimal notations used are the 5–4–2–1, the excess three, and the 2–3–2–1 codes.

coded decimal notation — A method of representing each figure in a decimal number by a character or group of characters.

code, dense binary — A code in which all possible states of the binary code are used.

code, dictionary — An alphabetical arrangement of English words and terms, associated with their code representations. (Related to reverse-code dictionary.)

code, direct — A code which specifies the use of actual computer command and address configurations.

code-directing character — One or several routing indicators at the start of a message that determine message destination.

coded program — A program which has been expressed in the code or language of a specific machine or programming system.

coded stop — A stop instruction built into the routine.

code element — The elemental unit from which a code is constructed; e.g., Baudot code is a binary representation of the alphabet and numerals in which a grouping, presence, or absence of five elements expresses the code information.

code, end-of-loop — Loops are terminated by letting the cards run out and restarting the machine, or by using preset values in cards or tapes, or by testing on branches or values in counters, etc. When certain columns, never used for data, are reserved for end of loop codes, loop endings are preprogrammed. Such codes terminate loops when counters reach preset values, causing branching to occur.

code error — Illegal control code on a binary card.

code, error-checking — A designed code for either detecting or correcting errors in the information as represented and used particularly in transmission or storage of data in computers. Various types of check bits are the main components of such codes.

code, error-correcting — A code in which each telegraph data signal conforms to rules on construction, so that departures from this construction in the received signal can be automatically detected, and which permits the automatic correction, at the receive terminal, of some or all of the errors. Such codes require more signal elements than are necessary to convey the basic information.

code, error-detecting — A code in which errors produce forbidden combinations. A single error-detecting code produces a forbidden combination if a digit gains or loses a single bit. A double error-detecting code produces a forbidden combination if a digit gains or loses either one or two bits and so forth. (Synonymous with self-checking code, and related to self-checking number.)

code, excess-three — A binary-coded decimal code in which each digit is represented by the binary equivalent of that number plus three. For example, the decimal digits 0, 1, 9, are represented as 0011, 0100, 1100, respectively.

code extension character — A distinct character designed to indicate that succeeding characters are to be interpreted using a different code.

code, false — *See* character, illegal.

code, forbidden — *Same as* code, illegal.

code, forbidden-character — *Same as* code, illegal.

code, four-address — *See* address, four.

code, gray — *See* code, cyclic.

code, group — A form of minimum-distance code in which a valid representation comprises a set of digits (data) just sufficient to identify and distinguish the representation, and a set of check digits arranged to give the required minimum signal distance between any two valid representations.

code, Hamming — One of the error-correction code systems in use today, named after the inventor.

code, Hollerith — An alphanumeric punched-card code invented by Dr. Herman Hollerith in 1889. The top three positions in a column are called "zone" punches (12, 11, and 0 or Y, X, and 0, from the top downward) and are combined with the remaining punches, or digit punches (1 through 9), to represent alphabetic, numeric, and special characters. For example, A is a combination of a Y (12) punch and a 1 punch; L is a combination of an X (11) punch and a 3 punch, etc.

code, identifying — A code placed in perforated tape or punched cards to identify the contents therein, or their origin.

code, illegal — A code character or symbol which appears to be the proper element but really is not a true member of the defined alphabet or specific language. If forbidden patterns, characters, or symbols present themselves, they are judged to be mistakes or the results of malfunctions.

code, improper — *Same as* code, illegal.

code inhibit — A function that provides lockout of particular unwanted or nonmeaningful sets of codes, under such conditions as shift or external control. Or the inhibit can activate some keys, when desired, as the screen erase.

code, instruction — An artificial language for describing or expressing the instructions which can be carried out by a digital computer. In automatically sequenced computers, the instruction code is used when describing or expressing sequences of instructions, and each instruction word usually contains a part specifying the operation to be performed and one or more addresses which identify a particular location in storage. Sometimes an address part of an instruction is not intended to specify a location in storage, but is used for some other purpose.

code, interpretive — A routine which decodes and immediately executes instructions written as pseudocodes. This is contrasted with a compiler which decodes the pseudocodes into a machine-language routine to be executed at a later time. The essential characteristic of an interpretive routine is that a particular pseudocode operation must be decoded each time it is executed.

code, machine — The absolute numbers, names, or symbols assigned by the machine designer to any part of the machine.

code, machine instruction — *Same as* code, instruction.

code, machine-language — 1. A system of combinations of binary digits used by a given computer. (Synonymous with computer code.) 2. A repertoire of instructions.

code, MICR — In magnetic ink character recognition, the special code consists of a set of 10 numeric symbols and four special symbols standardized as Font E-13B developed for the American Bankers Association. The characters are visually readable through the use of magnetic sensing heads in various types of magnetic ink recognition equipment. The special symbols mentioned above are amount, dash, transit number, and on us.

code, minimum-access — A system of coding which minimizes the effect of delays for transfer of data or instructions between storage and other machine components. (Related to optimum code, minimum-latency code, and minimum-access coding.)

code, minimum-latency — *See* code, minimum-access.

code, mnemonic — An instruction code using conventional abbreviations instead of numeric codes in order to facilitate easy recognition. Examples: MLT for multiply, SUB for subtract, instead of "12."

code, m out of n — A form of fixed weight binary code in which m of the n digits are always in the same state.

code, multiple-address — An instruction code in which an instruction word can specify more than one address to be used during the operation. In a typical instruction of a four-address code, the addresses specify the location of two operands, the location at which the results are to be stored, and the location of the next instruction in the sequence. In a typical three-address code, the fourth address specifying the location of the next instructions is dispensed with; the instructions are taken from storage in a preassigned order. In a typical two-address code, the addresses may specify the locations of the operands. The results may be placed at one of the addresses, or the destination of the results may be specified by another instruction.

code, N-ary — A code employing N distinguishable types of code elements.

code, nonexistent — *See* character, illegal.

code, nonexistent check — *See* check, forbidden-combination.

code, nonprint (NP code) — The third case of a teleprinter, in which functions may be performed and signals passed through without printing or spacing taking place. The nonprint code is the function code which triggers this condition.

code, numeric — A system of numerical abbreviations used in the preparation of information for input into a machine; i.e., all information is reduced to numerical quantities.

code, object — The code produced by a compiler or special assembler which can be executed on the target computer.

code, one-address — *See* instruction, one-address.

code, one-level — *See* code, absolute.

code, operation — 1. A combination of bits specifying an absolute machine-language operator, or the symbolic representation of the machine-language operator. 2. That part of an instruction that designates the operation of arithmetic, logic, or transfer to be performed.

code, operation field — The portion of an instruction word that contains the operation code.

code, optimum — A computer code which is particularly efficient with regard to a particular aspect, e.g., minimum time of execution, minimum or efficient use of storage space, and minimum coding time. (Related to minimum-access code.)

code, order — *See* code, operation.

code, own — A code developed and made a part of a standard routine to extend or change the routine to accomplish specific jobs or tasks.

code, pulse — A code in which sets of pulses have been assigned particular meanings.

coder/decoder chips — Integrated circuits that convert voice to digital form and back in PCM and delta-modulation systems.

code, redundant — A code using more signal elements than necessary to represent the intrinsic information; used for checking purposes.

code, relative — A code in which all addresses are specified or written with respect to an arbitrarily selected position, or in which all addresses are represented symbolically in a computable form.

code repertory — *Same as* code, instruction.

code, reproduction — Function codes in a master tape which are carried through the data-processing operations and also appear in the product tape.

code, self-checking — A code in which errors produce forbidden combinations. A single-error detecting code produces a forbidden combination if a digit gains or loses a single bit. A double-error detecting code produces a forbidden combination if a digit gains or loses either one or two bits, and so forth. (Related to self-checking number.)

code, self-complementing — A memory system in which the complement of the numbering system used equals the complement of the decimal equivalent.

code, self-demarcating — A code in which the symbols are so arranged and selected that the generation of false combinations by interaction of segments from two successive codes is prevented.

code set — A complete or closed set or group representation defined as a code, such as a group of three-letter sets for codes of various military or government bureaus.

codes, function — Codes which appear in tape or cards to operate machine functions, such as carriage return, space, shift, tabulate, etc.

code, short — A system of instructions that causes an automaton to behave as if it were another, specified automaton.

code, single-address — An instruction which contains the location of the data and the operation or sequence of operations to be performed on this data.

codes, instruction operation — The instruction operation codes are assigned mnemonics which describe the hardware function of each instruction. Assembler directive commands provide the programmer with the ability to generate data words and values based on specific conditions at assembly time.

code, skeletal — The framework of a routine which is completed by a generalized routine using input parameters.

code, skip — A functional code which instructs the machine to skip certain predetermined fields.

codes, mnemonic operation — The writing of operation codes in a symbolic notation which is easier to remember than the actual operation codes of the machine. This code must be converted to actual operation codes before execution, which is done as part of any assembly, interpretive, or compiling routine.

code, specific — *See* code, absolute.

code, symbolic — A code that expresses programs in source language, i.e., by referring to storage locations and machine operations by symbolic names and addresses which are independent of their hardware-determined names and addresses.

code, ternary — A code in which only three states are considered.

code, three-address — *See* address, three.

code track — A track of a paper tape other than the feed track.

code, two-out-of-five — A system of encoding the decimal digits zero, one, . . . 9, where each digit is represented by binary digits of which 2 are zeros and 3 are ones or vice versa.

code, unitary — A code having only one digit; the number of times it is repeated determines the quantity it represents.

code, unused — *See* character, illegal.

code, zero address — An instruction code which contains no instruction code for the next address.

coding — 1. The act of preparing in code or pseudocode a list of the successive computer operations required to solve a specific problem. 2. The ordered list, in computer code or pseudocode, of the successive computer operations for solving a specific problem.

coding, alphabetic — A system of abbreviation used in preparing information for input into a computer such that the information is reported in the form of letters, e.g., New York as NY, carriage return as CN, etc.

coding, assembly language — Assembly languages are used to avoid coding directly into machine code; mnemonics are used for both the command instructions and the operands, and it is usually not necessary to label the address for every instruction. In an instruction such as ADD Y, Y is a mnemonic for a location. Assembly programs generate in a one-to-one fashion a set of machine-coded instructions as contrasted to a compiler, or macro language, wherein one compiler instruction can generate many machine instructions, i.e., such as FORTRAN, COBOL, etc.

coding, automatic — Any technique in which a computer is used to help bridge the gap between some "easiest" form, intellectually and manually, of describing the steps to be followed in solving a given problem and some "most efficient" final coding of the same problem for a given computer; two basic forms are compilation routines and interpretation routines.

coding, ECD — A system of representing decimal equivalents by a series of four binary digits.

coding, fixed-form — Specific coding instructions with a fixed field assigned to particular labels, operations codes, and operand parts of the instruction.

coding, forced — *Same as* programming, minimum access.

coding format, symbolic — In writing instructions using the assembly language, the programmer is primarily concerned with three fields; a label field, an operation field, and an operand field. It is possible to relate the symbolic coding to its associated flowchart, if desired, by appending comments to each instruction line or program segment.

coding, in-line — A portion of coding which is stored in the main path of a routine. *See* open subroutine.

coding line — A single command or instruction for a computer to solve.

coding, machine — This coding uses the machine order code, which is directly interpreted by the instruction register. For a decimal machine, an example of a code might be 600141 1100, which would be the order to put the contents of location 141 into the upper arithmetic accumulator and then go to location 1100 to get the next instruction, whereas in a binary machine, an example of an order code might be 0000100000000000020, which might be interpreted as adding the contents of memory location 20 (in binary) to the arithmetic accumulator.

coding, machine language — Coding in the form in which instructions are executed by the computer.

coding, minimum-access — The process of developing or applying a minimum-access code. (Related to optimum code and minimum-latency code.)

coding, minimum delay — *Same as* programming, minimum access.

coding, minimum latency — *Same as* programming, minimum access.

coding, nonnumeric — Pertaining to the various nonnumeric abbreviations used to prepare information for input to computers. Closely akin to mnemonic coding.

coding, numeric — A system of abbreviation used in preparation of information for machine acceptance by reducing all information to numerical quantities; in contrast to alphabetic coding.

coding, optimum — The preparation of a programming routine with a view toward optimizing or idealizing the specific situation.

coding, out-of-line — A portion of coding which is stored away from the main path of a routine. *See* subroutine, closed.

coding, own (sorting) — Special coding provided by the programmer, which is integrated with sort/merge coding.

coding, relative — Coding in which all addresses refer to an arbitrarily selected position, or in which all addresses are represented symbolically.

coding sheet — A form upon which computer instructions are written prior to being punched into cards.

coding, specific — Coding in which all addresses refer to particular registers and locations.

coding, straight-line — *See* straight-line code.

coding, symbolic — *See* symbolic coding.

coding tools — Tools and techniques to simplify the phase of microcomputer design generally called coding. The basic tools available are: assemblers, editors, loaders, compilers, and microprogramming. In addition, hardware or software simulators are available for program testing and error locating.

coefficient — A number or factor put before and multiplying another.

coefficient, floating-point — That specific part of a floating-point number or representation that expresses the number of times that the number base with exponent is to be multiplied, i.e., the number 5.06 in the number 5.06×10^{18} is the floating-point coefficient. This means it will be expanded by 10^{18}.

coefficient matrix — The matrix of left-hand side coefficients in a system of linear equations. It is to be distinguished from the matrix obtained by appending the right-hand side, which is called the "augmented matrix" of the system. It may be thought of as including a full set of logical vectors to convert inequality constraints to equations. In the case of the modified simplex array, it also contains the objective function coefficients.

coefficient scale — *Same as* scale factor.

cognition, artificial — The optical sensing of a displayed character in which the machine or equipment selects from memory the shape of the character that is closest to the character being displayed.

cognition, machine — Certain machines have the capability to sense optically a displayed character and to select from a given repertory of characters the specific character which is nearest in shape to the character which is displayed. The various shapes of characters are based on statistical norms, and if different shapes arise, new characters join the repertory. This suggests a type of artificial learning because perception and interpretation are based on experience.

coincidence circuit — *Same as* gate, AND.

coincidence error — The difference in time for switching of different integrators to the compute mode or the hold mode.

coincidence gate — *Same as* gate, AND.

coincident-current selection — The selection of a magnetic core, for reading or writing, by the simultaneous application of two or more currents.

collate programs and tape sort — Generalized programs that adapt themselves, as directed by programmer-specified parameters, to operate in a particular configuration to sort and collate data into a particular format.

collating sequence — A sequence of characters as arranged in the order of their relative precedence. The collating sequence of a particular computer is determined as part of its design; each character acceptable to the computer has a preassigned place in this sequence. A collating sequence is used primarily in comparing operations.

collation sequence — The sequence in which the characters acceptable to a computer are ordered.

collection, data — The act of bringing data from one or more points to a central point. May be in-plant or out-plant.

collection, factory data — *See* data collection stations.

collection stations, data — *See* data collection stations.

collision — As regards indexing, two elements with the same hash index. A hash index is the initial estimate of the location of an entry within a table.

colon — 1. A delimiter indicating a pause, break, or stop. 2. The symbol used to separate items in the colon classification system. 3. One of the character or digit positions in a positional-notation representation of a unit of information; columns are usually numbered from right to left column, zero being the rightmost column if there is no point, or the column immediately to the left of the point if there is one.

color — In optical character recognition (OCR), the spectral appearance of the image dependent upon the spectral reflectance of the image. The spectral response of the observer and the spectral composition of incident light.

column — 1. A character or digit position in a positional-information format, particularly one in which characters appear in rows, and the rows are placed one above another, e.g., the rightmost column in a five decimal place table, or in a list of data. 2. A character or digit position in a physical device, such as punch card or a register, corresponding to a position in a written table or list, e.g., the rightmost place in a register, or the third column in an eighty-column punch card.

COM — As with many acronyms, there may be various interpretations of what the letters stand for. COM is generally defined as Computer Output Microfilm, Computer Output Microfilmer, or Computer Output Microform. Occasionally the letters may also stand for Computer Onto Microfilm, Computer Output on Microfilm, Computer Output Microfiche, or Computer Onto Microfiche. CIM generally means Computer Input Microfilm, or Computer Input from Microfilm.

combination bit — *Same as* bit pattern.

combination, forbidden — *Same as* character, illegal.

combination hub — An electrical jack connection which will emit or receive electrical impulses on a control panel.

combined read/write head — A particular magnetic head which is used to read and to write.

combiner — A functional block which groups several inputs which are separated by space to form a single output.

COM/computer application — A blend of microfilm and computer technology. COM and high-speed microfilm retrieval equipment have been adapted to such tasks as accounts receivable, accounts payable, invoice processing, apparel fabrics, consumer products, traffic department, bill of lading activity for all departments, medical and personnel records files, and purchasing. In each case, speed is increased and file space decreased.

COM indexing — The means by which the information on a microfiche is retrieved. There are several indexing techniques available today. These include: corner indexing, column indexing, master-file indexing, and cross-reference indexing.

command — 1. An electronic pulse, signal, or set of signals to start, stop, or continue some operation. It is incorrect to use command as a synonym for instruction. 2. The portion of an instruction word which specifies the operation to be performed.

command chaining — The execution of a sequence of i/o commands in a command list, under control of an IOP, on one or more logical records.

command character — *See* character, command.

command check, illegal — *Same as* check, forbidden-combination.

command check, improper — *Same as* check, forbidden-combination.

command check, unused — *See* check, forbidden-combination.

command code — *See* code, operation.

command control program — A program that handles all commands addressed to the system from the user consoles. These commands would include requests to log in or out, a request to use the edit program, requests to have a program placed on the run queue, requests to load a program, etc.

command decoder — The command decoder preprocesses commands from the user console. This program is used to convert parameters, etc., before the command is sent to the program for which the command is intended.

command double word — A double word that contains detailed information concerning a portion of an input/output operation.

command functions — Instructions used by the central processor to govern the circuitry to carry out some particular action.

command, illegal — *See* character, illegal.

command language — *See* language, command.

command list — A sequence of steps, generated by the CPU, pertaining to the performance of an i/o operation.

command mode time sharing — *See* time sharing, command mode.

command pointer — A specific multiple-bit register that indicates the memory location being accessed in the control store (microprogram store).

commands, system (time sharing) — *See* time sharing system commands.

command, transfer — *See* transfer command.

command, unused — *See* character, illegal.

comment — An expression which explains or identifies a particular step in a routine, but which has no effect on the operation of the computer in performing the instructions for the routine.

common assembler directive — *See* assembler directive commands.

common business oriented language — *See* COBOL.

common carrier telecommunications — Telecommunications provided by an administration or private operating agency and intended mainly, in a public correspondence service, for the transmission, emission, or reception of signs, signals, written images and sounds or intelligence of a nature by wire, radio, optical, or other electromagnetic systems between specific points subject to appropriate remuneration. Common carrier telecommunications may include several branches, e.g., telegraph service, telephone service, data transmission service, etc.

common error — The maximum size of common was not specified in the first loaded program.

common field — A field accessible to two or more routines.

common hub — A common connection such as a ground voltage that provides this voltage to other circuits that are connected.

common language — A language or macro code which can be read or written by many different machines or by various groups of users.

common language, OCR — *See* language, common (OCR).

common machine language — A machine-sensible information representation which is common to a related group of data-processing machines.

communality — That proportion of one correlated variance held in common with other measures in the same set.

communication — The process of transferring information in the various media from one point, person, or device to another.

communication channel — Voice, mail, messenger, telephone, telegraph, microwave, teletype, and other media are available for transmitting business data over short or very great distances; e.g. a Telpak or microwave channel is a communication channel with data-transmission rates up to 100,000 characters per second.

communication, data — The transmission of data from one point to another.

communication data systems — Real-time systems that interface between teletypewriter stations and the computer. These are ideal for multiuser computer time-sharing, message-switching systems, and data-collection processing systems. A variety of systems are available for half-duplex and full-duplex operation with 64 stations and up.

communication link — The physical means of connecting one location to another for the purpose of transmitting and receiving information.

communication, real-time processing — To close the gap in time between the actual transaction and its recognition by the processing system, a basic concept has been devised—real-time processing. A real-time system is a combined data processing and communications system which involves the direct communication of transaction data between remote locations and a central computer, via communication lines, and allows the data to be processed while the business transaction is actually taking place. A real-time system may be thought of as a communications-oriented data-processing system which is capable of performing batch-processing functions while concurrently processing inquiries or messages, and generating responses in a time interval directly related to the operational requirements of the system.

communications and inquiry systems — Systems are now provided for diversified on-site and long-distance inquiry and data-communications networks. Centralized records and data-processing operations can be tied in with information sources at remote locations, and will provide instant on-line response to interrogations and data from a large number of inquiry stations. Communication networks may include up to 5985 standard teletypewriter stations and up to 120 electric-typewriter stations (some computers).

communications, audio — *See* audio-response unit.

communications buffer — In a computer communications network, a buffer is a storage device used to compensate for a difference in the rate of flow of data received and transmitted along the numerous communication lines converging on the data processing center. The communications buffer orders information from many operators and controls the information so it can be processed by the computer without confusion. The buffer has memory and control circuitry of its own for storing incoming messages that the computer is not ready to process and storing outgoing messages which have to be delayed because of busy lines.

communications channels — Paths for transmitting signals. They are typically obtained from the common carrier; channels may access the public switched telephone network or may be obtained on a leased private-line basis.

communications codes — ASCII is one of the most often used and accepted codes. Special characters are set aside for the purpose of communications control. These control functions include synchronization, message heading, and control. Of the other existing codes, the more widely used ones are: EBCDIC, extended binary coded decimal interchange code; the 5-bit Baudot code found in old teleprinter equipment; the four of eight code; the IBM punched-card Hollerith code; the BCD, binary coded decimal, code; and the 6-bit transcode. EBCDIC is an 8-level code similar to ASCII except that while ASCII uses its eighth level for parity bits, EBCDIC uses it for information bits, thereby extending the range of characters to 256.

communications control character — A specific character which designates the operation to be performed by some peripheral device. As with other characters, it is represented by a pattern of printed binary digits or holes in tapes or cards. Its execution usually causes control changes on printers, for example, back space, skip line, or rewind on tapes. Other types of characters relate to EOM, such as end-of-message, etc.

communications controller, multiprotocol — Abbreviated MPCC. The MPCC is used for synchronous transmission in which characters are transmitted as a contiguous bit stream with the transmitter and receiver synchronized by a bit rate clock. It performs a variety of protocol handling functions, including zero insertion and deletion, flag/abort generation and detection, CRC generation and checking, and secondary address comparison.

communications device, input/output — Any subscriber (user) equipment which introduces data into or extracts data from a data-communications system.

communications, executive — *See* executive communications.

communications interface — *See* interface, communications.

communications monitors — Computer operating systems specifically designed for handling communications. Their functions essentially parallel those of a local-mode operating system except that lines, rather than devices, are the managed entities.

communication software — Sets of software for monitoring communication activities include the following routines: Interrupt—Upon a program interrupt, this routine directs data transfer between the communication control unit and the central processor and then returns control to the main program; Message Queuing—Controls the order in which messages are stored, processed, and transmitted; Error Control—Corrects errors in messages received from other communication stations.

communications processing — The transmission of data to the central computer for processing from a remote terminal as opposed to a terminal connected directly to the central computer.

Communications Satellite Corporation — COMSAT, the US representative in the 85-member INTELSAT Organization, provides technical and operational services for the global system under a management services contract with INTELSAT. Traffic on the system is coordinated through an Operations Center located at COMSAT Headquarters in Washington, DC.

communications system — A computer system which handles on-line, real-time applications. A typical communications system would consist of the following: a teletypewriter, visual display, or audio answer-back device connected to an ordinary telephone line through a communication multiplexor, a device which converts the keyed-in characters to electronic pulses for transmission over the telephone line. An interface device in the computer center translates these pulses into binary code and delivers the character to computer storage. After receipt of the entire message, the central computer searches or stores the requested information and sends back the appropriate response.

Important elements of any communications system are the modems (MODulator/DEModulator) which connect the communications multiplexor from the remote output to the interface device in the computer center. On the transmission end, the modulator converts the signals or pulses to the right codes and readies them for transmission over a communication line. On the receiving end, a demodulator reconverts the signals for communication to the computer via the computer interface device.

communications systems, standard — Half-duplex transmission connects A to B over a two-wire channel. One end can send while the other receives, and the stations can reverse roles. Duplex transmission over nonswitched four-wire circuits allows simultaneous transmission and reception. In nonswitched multipoint transmission, several secondary stations share one duplex channel. The primary station polls its tributaries. Point-to-point switched systems establish a new transmitter-to-receiver path for each call.

compacting, storage — *See* storage compacting.

compaction — A series of techniques used for the reduction of space, bandwidth, cost, transmission, generating time, and the storage of data. These techniques are designed to eliminate repetition, remove irrelevances, and employ special coding techniques.

compaction, curve fitting — A specific method of data compaction developed by substituting analytical expressions for data to be stored or transmitted. An example is the breaking of curves into straight line segments, and then transmitting only the slope, intercept, and acceptable range for each line segment.

compaction, curve-pattern — *See* compaction, curve-fitting.

compaction, data — *See* data compaction.

compaction, floating-point — Data compaction which uses exponents to specify the scale or range, such as to set the decimal point of a number, or set of numbers. In this system, each number is expressed as a coefficient which is to be multiplied by a power of ten to express the actual magnitude. An example is the number 32,760,000, which can be expressed as 3276×10^4, or 3276 (4).

compaction, frequency-analysis — A form of data compaction using specific coded expressions to represent a number of different frequencies of different magnitudes to express, compare, or indicate a curve or geometric configuration. Only identifiable coefficients might be necessary to compare and thus transmit a whole series of fundamental frequencies.

compaction, incremental — A procedure for data compaction using only the initial value and all subsequent changes in storage for transmission. A saving in time and space is achieved when only the changes at specific intervals are transmitted or processed.

compaction of file records — The reduction of space required for records by compressing or compacting the records by means of specialized coding and formating under a programmed routine. A balance, though, must be maintained in a system between processing time and main storage, and the reduction of file size and channel utilization.

compaction, slope-keypoint — A data compaction procedure using statements of specific points of departure. Direction or slope of departure is transmitted until the deviation from a prescribed condition exceeds a specified value, and, at that point, a new slope or keypoint is signaled.

compander — A device, for use on a telephone channel, designed to improve the voice and cross-talk performance. The input is effectively compressed for transmission and then expanded to near original form at the receiving end. A compander may distort some types of data signals.

companion keyboard — An auxiliary keyboard device which is usually located remotely from the main unit.

comparand — A word or number used for a comparison to another word or number.

comparator — 1. A device for comparing two different transcriptions of the same information to verify the accuracy of transcription, storage, arithmetic operation, or other processes, in which a signal is given dependent on some relation between two items; i.e., one item is larger than, smaller than, or equal to the other. 2. A circuit that compares two signals and indicates agreement or disagreement; a signal may be given indicating whether they are equal or unequal.

comparator-sorter — A unit of punch card equipment which has the capability of sorting and selecting particular cards, sequence checking them, and making comparisons between stored data and these new items.

comparator, tape — A machine which automatically compares two tapes which are expected to be identical. The comparison is row by row, and the machine shops when a discrepancy occurs.

compare — To determine whether a particular quantity is higher, equal to, or lower than another quantity, or to determine whether one piece of data is exactly like another.

compare and print — A specified number of records from each of two tapes are compared, record for record, with all nonidentical records printed in either alphanumeric or octal mode.

compare facility — The ability of a machine to execute set instructions depending upon the outcome of various possible combinations.

compare instruction — An instruction that compares (subtracts) the value in one register against the value in another, and sets the status of various flags according to the results of the comparison operation.

comparison — The act of comparing and, usually, acting on the result of the comparison. The common forms are comparison of two numbers for identity, comparison of two numbers for relative magnitude, and comparison of two signs, plus or minus.

comparison, logic — *See* comparator.

comparison, logical — The operation concerned with the determination of similarity or dissimilarity of two items; e.g., if A and B are alike, the result shall be "1" or yes, if A and B are not alike or equal, the result shall be "zero" or no, signifying "not alike."

comparison-of-pairs sorting — The comparison of the keys in two records and placement of the higher value ahead of the smaller value for descending sequences.

comparison testing — Real-time comparison between the actual output responses of the device under test and those of a known-good reference device when the same input stimulus patterns are applied to both devices in parallel.

compatibility — The quality of an instruction to be translatable or executable on more than one class of computer.

compatibility, equipment — The characteristic of computers by which one computer may accept and process data prepared by another computer without conversion or code modification.

compatibility, firmware — Compatibility among data processing systems facilitates execution or conversion of existing programs, data interchange, and the implementation of compilers having equivalent execution-time semantics. Compatibility can be achieved via the basic hardware design or by (software or firmware) interpretation. Firmware, or microprogramming, has attracted attention in this context as promising hardware-like compatibility with software-like implementation techniques.

compatibility objectives — Compatibility relates to the transfer of programs or data from one system to another. Typically, objectives are: direct execution of programs originally written for another system (this implies complete instruction and data type compatibility), facilitating data interchange with another system (this implies compatible data types and a common code set, but does not require compatible instruction formats, register structures, and the like), easing conversion of assembly language programs (this calls for similar instruction formats and register concepts but does not necessarily imply a precise copy of any aspect of the earlier system), and facilitating the implementation of compilers having identical execution-time semantics (this would require common data types and instructions providing identical results for operations on such data).

compatibility, program — A distinctive feature of programming aids is that they and the object programs which they produce are operationally compatible with one another. This property enables the operating system to draw all elements into an integrated whole. Object programs produced by program preparation aids (other than conversion programs), as well as programs from the software library itself, may all be intermixed on run tapes and processed by the program loading, updating, and selection. Complete program and data compatibility is a built-in feature of many processors. A single machine language is used with all models, enabling the user to run a program written for any smaller system on any larger system. Programs for a minimum computer model, for example, can also run on any other larger processor, usually with a considerable gain in performance because of faster cycle times and increased peripheral simultaneity.

compatibility, systems — In complex systems applications, modules are often completely compatible electrically, logically, and mechanically with other systems components, which include digital computers, a complete line of input/output devices, and analog interface equipment.

compatibility test — Specific tests run to check acceptability of both software and hardware as a system.

compatible — That particular characteristic of a device, program, etc., which makes it acceptable to a computer or another device, i.e., a suitable tape width, similarity of operating speeds, etc.

compatible hardware — Components, peripheral equipment, or other devices which can be used on more than one system with little or no adjustment.

compatible software — Languages which can be used on more than one computer system.

compendium — An abbreviated summary of the essentials of a subject.

compilation, program — *See* program compilation.

compilation time — The time during which a source language is compiled (translated) as opposed to the time during which the program is actually being run (execution time).

compile — To produce a machine-language routine from a routine written in source language by selecting appropriate subroutines from a subroutine library, as directed by the instructions or other symbols of the original routine, supplying the linkage which combines the subroutines into a workable routine, and translating the subroutines and linkage into machine language. The compiled routine is then ready to be loaded into storage and run; i.e., the compiler does not usually run the routine it produces.

compiler — A computer program more powerful than an assembler. In addition to its translating function which is generally the same process as that used in an assembler, it is able to replace certain items of input with series of instructions, usually called subroutines. Thus, where an assembler translates item for item and produces as output the same number of instructions or constants which were put into it, a compiler will do more than this. The program which results from compiling is a translated and expanded version of the original. (Synonymous with compiling routine, and related to assembler.)

compiler, beginner's algebraic symbolic interpretive — *See* BASIC.

compiler, COBOL — The compiler is completely modularized into relocatable elements and is handled as any program in the system, thus providing for easy expandabality and maintenance. Likewise, the COBOL processor produces as its output relocatable binary elements stored on the drum or mass storage, which are indistinguishable from other elements in the system. Other outputs from the compiler include extensive diagnostic messages, source-language listings, machine-language listings, and special cross-reference listings of name definitions and their references. The machine-language listing consists of side-by-side procedure division statements and the corresponding generated symbolic machine code.

compiler-compiler — A machine-independent language which generates compilers for any specific machine.

compiler diagnostics — The compiler diagnostics are of four categories: Precautionary; print warning message and continue compilation. Correctable; try to correct the error, print explanatory message and continue compilation. Uncorrectable; if intent of programmer cannot be determined, print a diagnostic message, reject the clause or statement, and continue compilation. Catastrophic; when so many errors have occurred that no more useful diagnostic information can be produced, terminate the compilation.

compile routine — *See* routine, compile.

compiling duration — The time necessary to translate one computer program into an acceptable language for another computer, or to transform or translate to an assembly program, and often to generating and diagnostic programs.

compiling phase — The time used to translate one computer program into another equivalent program in an acceptable assembly, structure, and language.

compiling program — A translating program designed to transform, to assemble, or to structure programs expressed in other languages into same or equivalent programs expressed in terms of the particular computer language for which a particular machine was designed. Compiling programs or compilers most often include assemblers (or programs) as well as diagnostic and generating programs within them. The computer which is using the compiling program or compiler is called the source computer or compiling computer, and the computer in which the program is used or is to be used is called the object computer or target computer. The occasion or run of compilation or translation is called the compiling phase, while the use of the newly translated program is the run. Time to translate is compile duration.

compiling routine — A computer program more powerful than an assembler. In addition to its translating function which is generally the same process as that used in an assembler, it is able to replace certain items of input with series of instructions, usually called subroutines. Thus, where an assembler translates item for item, and produces as output the same number of instructions or constants which were put into it, a compiler will do more than this. The program which results from compiling is a translated and expanded version of the original. (Related to assembler.)

complement — A quantity expressed to the base N, which is derived from a given quantity by a particular rule; frequently used to represent the negative of the given quantity. A complement on N is obtained by subtracting each digit of the given quantity from N−1, adding unity to the least significant digit, and performing all resulting carrys; e.g., and two's complement of binary 11010 is 00110; the tens complement of decimal 456 is 544. A complement on N−1 is obtained by subtracting each digit of the given quantity from N−1; e.g., the ones complement of binary 11010 is 00101; the nines complement of decimal 456 is 543. (Synonymous with radix-minus-1 complement and radix complement.)

complementary operations — In any Boolean operation, a complementary operation is the negation of the result of the first or original operation. In computing, it is represented when zero is substituted for 1 and 1 is substituted for zero in the tabulated values for r for the first or original operation.

complementary operator — An operator whose results are the NOT of a given operator, i.e., NOR or NAND.

complementation, Boolean — *Same as* gate, NOT.

complement, Boolean — *Same as* gate, NOT.

complement, diminished — Radix minus one complement.

complementer — A device which is designed to reverse a signal, state, or condition into its opposite or, in some cases, alternate.

complement instruction — A built-in feature designed to provide a number of instructions for each programmed instruction.

complement, nines — A decimal system in which each decimal digit in the subtrahend is first subtracted from 9.

complement, noughts — Radix complement.

complement, ones — A numeral in binary which is derived from another binary number when it is the result of a change in the sense of every digit, i.e., the sum of a number and its ones complement is a number of all 1 bits. A number 110, 101, 100, 011 when added to its ones complement, 001, 010, 011, 100 has a sum of 111, 111, 111, 111.

complement on N — An expression meant to make a determination of the radix complement.

complement on N−1 — An expression meant to make a determination of the radix-minus-one complement.

complement, radix — *See* complement.

complement, radix-minus one — *See* complement.

complement, tens — The radix complement of a numeral whose radix is ten. The tens complement is obtained by subtracting each digit of a number from 9, and adding 1 to the least significant digit of the resultant number. For example, the tens complement of 2456 is 7544.

complement, true — *Same as* complement.

complement, twos — For binary numbers, a value derived by subtracting an original number from the base number (or a power of the base number). For decimal numbers, the equivalent of the twos complement would be the tens complement.

complement, zero — *Same as* complement, radix.

complete carry — When a carry resulting from the addition of carries is not allowed to propagate it is called a partial carry. When it is allowed to propagate it is called a complete carry.

complete instruction — A specific instruction which takes in a complete computer operation including the execution of that operation.

completeness — The contrast to programs that are incomplete due to transfers to nonexistent statement numbers, improper DO nesting, illegal transfer into the range of a DO loop, etc.

completeness errors — *See* errors, completeness.

completeness errors, remote-computing system — *See* errors, completeness (remote-computing system).

complete operation — An operation that includes obtaining the instruction, obtaining all operands from storage, performing the operation, and returning the results to storage.

complete routine — A routine that does not require modification before it is used. Such routines are usually in company or manufacturer libraries.

component — A basic part. An element.

component derating — To ensure reliable system operation under extremely adverse conditions and with limit-value components, components used in circuit modules are derated far below manufacturers' specification.

component, solid-state — A component whose operation depends on the control of electric or magnetic phenomena in solids, e.g., a transistor, crystal diode, or ferrite.

composition errors — Errors that are detected as soon as the user enters the offending statement. He may immediately substitute a correct statement.

composition file — The filing of records within a storage unit.

composition (remote computing system) errors — *See* errors, composition (remote computing system).

compound condition — A number of simple logic conditions such as AND, NOT, or OR logic gates that can be combined to form compound logic operations.

compound logical element — Computer circuitry which provides an output resulting from multiple inputs.

compression, data — Techniques that save storage space by eliminating gaps, empty fields, redundancies, or unnecessary data to shorten the length of records or blocks.

compression, digit — *See* digit compression.

compression, zero — That process which eliminates the storage of insignificant leading zeros. For clarification, *see* zero suppression.

COM processing — The conversion of information created by a computer in digital form to an analog signal that modifies an energy source exposing a microimage on film. The film can be in roll form, either 16 mm or 35 mm, or 105 mm as microfiche; it can also be 35-mm chips, either as separate units or in aperture cards.

computation, address — A computation that produces or modifies the address portion of an instruction.

computational stability — That particular degree to which a computational process remains valid and reliable when subjected to various conditions which tend to produce errors, mistakes, or malfunctions.

computation, implicit — Computation using a self-nulling principle in which, for example, the variable sought first is assumed to exist, after which a synthetic variable is produced according to an equation and compared with a corresponding known variable and the difference between the synthetic and the known variable driven to zero by correcting the assumed variable. Although the term applies to most analog circuits, even a single operational amplifier, it is restricted usually to computation performed by the following circuits. 1. Circuits in which a function is generated at the output of a single high-gain dc amplifier in the feedback path. 2. Circuits in which combinations of computing elements are interconnected in closed loops to satisfy implicit equations. 3. Circuits in which linear or nonlinear differential equations yield the solutions to a system of algebraic or transcendental equations in the steady state.

computed branch — *See* branch, computed.

compute limited — A restriction in computing equipment limiting the output because operations are delayed awaiting completion of a computation operation.

computer — A device capable of accepting information, applying prescribed processes to the information, and supplying the results of these processes. It usually consists of input and output devices, storage, arithmetic and logical units, and a control unit.

computer administrative records — These records provide the source of statistics that tell how the computer use is distributed—that is, by department, by programmer, by time, and by application.

computer-aided design — A system by means of which engineers create a design and see the proposed product in front of them on a graphics screen or in a computer printout. With the computer, the proposed product can be analyzed for stress, vibration, heat, and other factors, and checked against government and industry standards.

computer-aided dispatch — Abbreviated CAD. A system in which an alphanumeric keyboard and crt terminals replace hand-written incident cards and a conveyer belt in radio dispatching operations.

computer-aided instruction (CAI) — An educational concept which places the student in a conversational mode with a computer which has a preprogrammed study plan. The programmed course selects the next topic or phase of study according to previous responses from the student, allowing each student to progress at a pace directly related to his learning capability.

computer, analog — A computer which represents variables by physical analogies. Thus, any computer that solves problems by translating physical conditions such as flow, temperature, pressure, angular position, or voltage into related mechanical or electrical quantities, and uses mechanical or electrical equivalent circuits as an analog for the physical phenomenon being investigated. In general, it is a computer which uses an analog for each variable and produces analogs as output. Thus, an analog computer measures continuously, whereas a digital computer counts discretely. (Related to data-processing machine.)

computer animation — Use of computer techniques in the production of animated motion pictures. In sound films, 24 frames must be displayed every second. Thus a normal animation requires thousands of drawings. The speed of the computer can save the time required to draw the many pictures animation demands. Also, a computer can quickly generate perspective drawings of objects. Perspective, the reduction in size of objects as they move away from the viewer, gives pictures three-dimensional realism. Many cartoons do not use perspective drawings because of the time required to draw them. With the aid of computers, this realism in animation is easily achieved. Computers also can produce the effects of wide-angle or telescopic lenses, and they can simulate lighting from any angle.

computer-assisted instruction — Abbreviated CAI. Applications in which a computing system is used to assist in the instruction of students. The application usually involves a dialog between the student and a computer program that informs him of his mistakes as he makes them.

computer, asynchronous — A computer in which the performance of each operation starts as a result of a signal that the previous operation has been completed, or that the parts of the computer required for the next operation are now available. (Contrasted with synchronous computer.)

computer, automatic — A computer which performs long sequences of operations without human intervention.

computer cartography — A science that utilizes computer-generated maps to portray relationships among massive amounts of data. In essence, computer maps translate pages of statistics into pictures, allowing data that would otherwise take days or weeks to relate and comprehend to be understood in a matter of minutes. The concept has applications in such areas as corporate planning, forestry, energy, law enforcement, city and regional planning, banking, marketing, environmental management, instruction, health planning, research, site selection, agriculture, and politics.

computer center — *See* EDP center.

computer circuits — Circuits used in the construction of digital computers. They include storage circuits, triggering circuits, gating circuits, inverting circuits, and timing circuits. In addition, there may be other circuits used in smaller quantities, such as power amplifiers for driving heavier loads, indicators, output devices, and amplifiers for receiving signals from external devices, as well as oscillators for obtaining the clock frequency.

computer code — 1. A system of combinations of binary digits used by a given computer. (Synonymous with machine code.) 2. A repertoire of instructions.

computer configuration — The particular set of equipment so connected to form a single computer center or system for various computer runs.

it is a stored-program digital computer capable of performing sequences of internally stored instructions, as opposed to calculators, such as card programmed calculators, on which the sequence is impressed manually. (Related to data-processing machine.)

computer, first generation — Refers to the technological era of development of the computer when the vacuum tube was the main electronic element. First generation equipment was predominantly manufactured in the years 1953–1960 and included the Univac I, IBM 704, RCA Bizmac, and the Honeywell D-1000. The second generation of computer equipment began in about 1959 and was characterized by the utilization of transistors instead of vacuum tubes.

Computer console. Courtesy Burroughs Corp.

computer console — A part of a computer used for communication between operator or maintenance engineer and the computer.

computer, control — *See* control computer.

computer-dependent language — *See* language, machine oriented.

computer, digital — A computer which processes information represented by combinations of discrete or discontinuous data, as compared with an analog computer for continuous data. More specifically, it is a device for performing sequences of arithmetic and logical operations, not only on data, but also on its own program. Still more specifically,

The third generation of computer equipment began in about 1964 and featured microcircuits or miniaturization of components. There is not yet a clear consensus as to the definition of a fourth generation of equipment.

computer generated map — A map constructed through mathematical projections with the aid of a computer. The process begins with sets of geographical coordinates which define the boundaries of the areas to be mapped. These coordinates are manipulated with appropriate mathematical procedures to convert the geographical data to map coordinates, and these final numeric figures are used to draw the maps. In practice, accurate maps require defining tens of thousands, hundreds of thousands, or even millions of reference points. Not only can the mathematical mapping computations be carried out on the microcomputer, but with a suitable graphics device various maps can be drawn in final form.

computer graphics — Items such as digitizers, displays, computer software, printers, plotters, microfilm apparatus, light pens, and other similar peripheral devices. Such systems can generally be divided into three main sections, all tied to the computer: the input, editing, and output stages.

computer, host — *See* host computer.

computer, hybrid — A computer designed to perform both analog and digital computing for distinct or special purposes. Many are used in automated production.

computer image processing — The objectives of computer-assisted image processing fall into three categories: the removal of known image degradations, a procedure known as "image restoration"; the exaggeration of obscure details, or "image enhancement"; and the location and mensuration of specific details, a process called "information extraction."

computer-independent language — A programming language which is not a computer language, but one which requires translation or compiling to any one of a variety of computer languages. The language which is a particular language of that machine or one which has compilers for translating to its own machine language.

computer installation — A single computer configuration, facility, center, or system consisting of one or more mainframes and endless potential combinations of peripheral, communications, input/output, and other types of support devices.

computer instruction — A machine instruction for a specific computer.

computer instruction code — An instruction code designed for specific computers, i.e., the machine language.

computer instruction set — A particular set of computer instructions which usually require no compiling and work directly to and within the computer.

computer interface types — Methods for transferring data into or out of a computer. They include programmed i/o, direct memory access (DMA), and interrupt data transfer. In programmed i/o, the computer controls data transfer independently of the data acquisition peripheral, and transfer occurs on a single-word basis. This interface finds few uses because the computer becomes delayed while waiting for slow devices. DMA interfaces allow block transfer of data into or out of memory at high speed, limited only by memory cycle time, and are commonly used for data transfer to and from mass storage devices. During interrupt data transfer, the peripheral interrupts the program when it is ready to transfer or receive data. Low- and medium-speed devices including many data acquisition subsystems often use this type of interface.

computerized numerical control — Abbreviated CNC. A numerical control system for which a dedicated, stored program computer is used to perform some or all of the basic numerical control functions.

computerized operations research — *See* operations research, computerized.

computer language — A programming procedure or language in which instructions are computer instructions only. A machine language as contrasted to a problem-oriented language, which must be compiled to a computer language before a machine can use it directly.

computer language symbols (standard) — Prescribed graphical shapes used to represent special meanings or functions in any computer program.

computer, large scale — Large scale computers provide, in conjunction with high level languages and operating systems, extremely complex and powerful programmable logic to attack complex problems which require highly centralized computing power. Examples, CDC 7600, CRAY I, AMDAHL 470, ILLIAC IV and others. Some are HMS machines that operate at speeds of 100 million instructions per second.

computer learning — That process by which computers modify programs according to their own memory or experience, i.e., changes of logic paths, parameter values.

computer limited — A specific condition of a computer in which the time required for computation exceeds the time required for some other type of operation such as card or tape reading and punching. This happens quite frequently with computers that perform scientific types of calculations, and especially if computers permit concurrent reading, computing, writing, etc. If the computing time is less than that required for other operations, then the computer might be limited by other procedures, i.e., input-output limited, etc.

plish computer networking. These consist of (1) the user communication interface, (2) the communications subnetwork, and (3) facilities for the network control function.

computer operation — 1. The electronic action resulting from an instruction. In general, it is a computer manipulation required to secure results. 2. One of many designed or predetermined operations which are built-in or performed directly, i.e., jump, subtract.

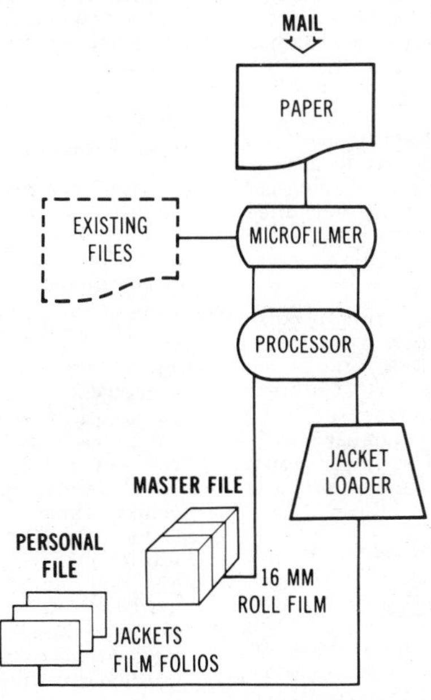

Computer-output microfilm.

computer logic — The logical operations of the computer, consisting generally of five operations—add, subtract, multiply, divide, and compare. This simple processing logic is enough to allow the computer to accomplish the majority of its tasks when properly programmed.

computer, master/slave — *See* master/-slave system.

computer network — A configuration of two or more computers linked to share information and resources. A computer having the capability to participate in a network is called a node. Three types of facilities in addition to the host computer are generally required to accom-

computer operation, multiple — *See* multiple-computer operation.

computer operations manager — *See* manager, operations.

computer-oriented language — A related term for a programming language requiring a low degree of translation. Such programs usually run very efficiently on a related computer but require very extensive translation or compiling on another variety of computer.

computer-output microfilm (COM) — A microfilm printer that will take output directly from the computer, thus substituting for line printer or tape output.

computer program — A plan or routine or

set of instructions for solving a problem on a computer, as contrasted with such terms as fiscal program, military program, and development program.

computer programming language — The machine language that the computer was designed to understand. This is contrasted with compiler systems such as FORTRAN or COBOL.

computer, remote — A system which has four principal components: a central processor, a communications linkage, a terminal device, and a user. These components interact in some environment to carry out a task.

computer run — *See* run.

computer, satellite — A processor connected locally or remotely to a larger central processor, and performing certain processing tasks, sometimes independent of the central processor, sometimes subordinate to the central processor.

computer science — The entire spectrum of theoretical and applied disciplines connected with the development and application of computers. Contributions have come mostly from such fields as mathematics, logic, language analysis, programming, computer design, systems engineering, and information systems.

computer, second generation — A computer belonging to the era of technological development when the transistor replaced vacuum tubes. Machines using transistors occupy much less space, operate faster, require less maintenance, and are more reliable. The second generation computer was prominent in the years 1959–1964 and included the IBM 1401, the Honeywell 800, the RCA 501, and the Remington Rand Solid-State 80.

computer-sensitive language — *See* language, computer-sensitive.

computer, sensor-based — A type of computer designed and programmed to receive real-time data (analog or digital) from transducers, sensors, and other data sources that monitor a physical process. The computer may also generate signals to elements that control the process. For example, the computer might receive data from a gauge or flowmeter, compare the data with a predetermined standard, and then produce a signal that operates a relay, valve, or other control mechanism.

computer service organization — An organization that provides either personnel or total systems planning, operation, and other related support for customers. The national organization is ADAPSO (Association of DAta Processing Service Organizations).

computer, slave — A fail-safe or backup system (application), whereby a slave or second computer performs the steps of the same program so that if the master computer fails or malfunctions, the slave computer continues without a deterioration of operations.

computer store — *See* storage.

computer, synchronous — A calculating device in which the performance of any operation does not start as a result of a signal that the previous operation has been completed. The performance of all operations is controlled with equally spaced signals from a master clock.

computer systems, distributed — The arrangement of computers within an organization in which the organization's computer-complex has many separate computing facilities all working in a cooperative manner, rather than the conventional single computer at a single location. Versatility of a computer system is often increased if small computers in geographically dispersed branches are used for simple tasks and a powerful central computer is available for larger tasks. Frequently an organization's central files are stored at the central computing facility, with the geographically dispersed smaller computers calling on the central files when they need them. Such an arrangement lessens the load on the central computer and reduces both the volume and cost of data transmission.

computer word — *See* word, computer.

computing — A generic term for all mathematical and logical operations carried out according to precise rules of procedure.

computing amplifier — This amplifier combines functions of amplification and performance of operations. Computing amplifiers are often summing amplifiers, analog adders, or sign reversing amplifiers. Most are used in analog computing systems.

computing element — A computer component that performs the mathematical operations required for problem solution.

computing machinery — Systems of equipment capable of processing data in accordance with the design of the devices and the programming and instructions of the total system. Such systems usually consist of interconnected input/output, storage, communications, and other specific-purpose units.

computing, multiaccess — This implies that more than one identical input/output terminal may be directly used with the system; usually they are remote, such as teletypewriter or other typewriter-like units.

computing systems, remote consistency errors — *See* errors, consistency (remote-computing system).

COMSAT — Communications Satellite Corporation. COMSAT is the privately owned US corporation formed in February 1963 to carry out a mandate of the Congress under the Communications Satellite Act of 1962. The Act directed COMSAT to establish a global commercial communications satellite system in cooperation with other countries as quickly as practical. COMSAT derives most of its revenues from the satellite services it provides to the US communications common carriers serving the public between the US and foreign points.

concatenate — To unite in a series; to link together; to chain.

concatenated data set — A data set temporarily formed by uniting the data contained in several independent data sets in a specific sequence.

concatenated key — A series of characters, which constitute more than one field, that may be used to search for records or sort data according to a hierarchy of fields.

concentration, data — Generally, a collection of data at an intermediate point from several low- and medium-speed lines for retransmission across high-speed lines.

concentrator — A device used in data communications to multiplex numerous low-speed communications lines onto a single high-speed communications line.

concept coordination — A term used to describe the basic principles of various punched-card and mechanized information-retrieval systems which involve the multidimensional analysis of information and coordinate retrieval. In concept coordination, independently assigned concepts are used to characterize the subject contents of documents, and the latter are identified during searching by means of either such assigned concepts or a combination of the same.

conceptual modeling — A method of making a model to fit the results of a biological experiment, then conducting another experiment to find out whether the model is right or wrong. The models are created continuously, and are tested and changed in a cycles manner. The physical sciences have developed through the years in this way, but there has been little use of the approach in biology, mainly because the kind of mathematics that developed is not well suited to biology. But now computers can get around this problem, and the important technique of conceptual modeling is beginning to be used in biology.

conceptual schema — The overall logical (as opposed to physical) structure of a data base.

concordance — An alphabetic list of words and phrases appearing in a document, with an indication of the place where those words and phrases appear.

concordance program — In some systems, a program that reads a free-form assembler source input and produces an alphabetized cross-reference listing of all symbols and their references, by line number.

concordant — A specific type or arrangement of information or data into fixed or harmonious locations on particular documents.

concurrency, executive-system — The executive system is a multiprogramming control system with the capabilities of running (scheduling, loading, executing) one or more programs based on store and peripheral availability and requirements. The system provides for the sequential execution of data-dependent jobs while allowing job sequences to be run in parallel with other unrelated sequenced jobs or unsequenced jobs. Job schedules may be entered as far in advance as necessary with provision to allow late-entered jobs to be selected in advance of previously submitted lower-priority jobs. The executive system controls all input/output and interrupt handling as well as providing automatic loading, facility assignments, dynamic timesharing between jobs, terminal actions, and job time accounting records. The executive system's ability to maximize the utilization of the internal speeds of the computer by timesharing both internal and external storage with many programs, its ability to dynamically assign facilities (central store, magnetic tapes, etc.) to new jobs as they become available, and its complete control of the entire system assures efficiency in total system throughput.

concurrency mode — By themselves, some systems can operate only with the protocol for which they were built, or that they can emulate through their modification. But when two units are connected together, one with batch capability and one with data entry and inquiry features, then either type of terminal can function with either protocol, in an operating mode called concurrency. The desired protocol is selected simply by flipping a switch on the keyboard of either terminal. Since these protocols are used for various applications, a single terminal may take the place of several.

concurrency, operations (real-time) — The great point is that the real-time system is at no moment necessarily committed to real time operations or to batch processing operations exclusively. Both may proceed concurrently and several kinds of each may proceed concurrently under the control of an internally stored executive program. But the real-time operations always have priority, and the system will assign its facilities as these priorities require, relinquishing them to other activities, such as engineering calculations or normal business processing tasks, as soon as they are no longer needed to keep pace with real-time events.

In this way, maximum use may be made of the components of any desired configuration of the real-time system; and the advantages of its enormous storage capacity, speed, flexibility, and communications capabilities may be obtained at a low cost per unit of work accomplished. Experience indicates that the real-time system will quite probably outperform by a wide margin any other system of its kind in a wide range of applications.

concurrency, real time — Real-time is a mode of operation in which data, necessary to the control and/or execution of a transaction, can be processed in time for the transaction to be affected by the results of the processing. Real-time processing is most usually identified with great speed, but speed is relative. The essence of real time is concurrency . . . simultaneity. Real-time is the ultimate refinement in the integration of data-processing with communications. Real-time eliminates slow information-gathering procedures, dated reporting techniques, and lax communications; ensures that facts within the system are as timely as a prevailing situation, as current as the decisions which they must support. Real-time provides answers when answers are needed, delivers data instantly whenever the need for that data arises. Incoming information is edited, updated, and made available on demand at every level of responsibility. Imminent departures from established standards are automatically detected and management notified in time for action.

concurrent — The occurrence of two or more events within the same time period, i.e., two computers or programs operating simultaneously.

concurrent i/o — Pertaining to terminals that are capable of performing i/o tasks such as communications to the host computer, printing, and file management without halting ongoing data entry operation.

concurrent operating control — Operating systems provide the ability for several programs to share the computer at the same time. Concurrent operations include job processing while performing inquiry of peripheral utility operations, time sharing, and multiprogramming. For example, in the operation mode, a teleprocessing application (servicing terminals) can be under way concurrently with both stacked-job batch processing and peripheral utility-type operations.

concurrent operation — This term is used to refer to various methods in electronic data processing in which multiple instructions or operations of different instructions are executed simultaneously. Concurrent operation refers to computers working as contrasted to computer programming. This concept is one of the basic tenets of time-sharing, priority processing, etc.

concurrent processing — The operation of a computer which has some or all of the program for more than one run stored simultaneously in its memory, and which executes these programs concurrently by time-shared control. *See* multiprogramming.

concurrent processing, peripheral — *See* peripheral processing, concurrent.

concurrent real-time processing — To close the gap in time between the actual transaction and its recognition by the processing system, a new concept has been devised, real-time processing. A real-time system is a combined data-processing and communications system which involves the direct communication of transaction data between remote locations and a central computer, via communication lines, and allows the data to be processed while the business transaction is actually taking place. A real-time system may be thought of as a communications-oriented data-processing system which is capable of performing batch-processing functions while concurrently processing inquiries or messages, and generating responses in a time interval directly related to the operational requirements of the system.

concurrent working — This term is used to refer to various methods in electronic data processing in which multiple instructions or operations of different instructions are executed simultaneously. Concurrent working refers to computer operation as contrasted to computer programming. This concept is one of the basic tenets of time-sharing, priority processing, etc.

condition — In the COBOL system one of a set of specified values that a data item can assume; the status of a switch as specified in the special-names paragraph of the environment division; a simple conditional expression. *See* conditional expression.

conditional — Subject to various constraints, i.e., the result of a comparison made during the program or subject to human intervention.

conditional branch — *See* branch, conditional.

conditional breakpoint — A breakpoint at which the routine may be continued as coded if desired conditions are satisfied.

conditional-breakpoint instruction — A conditional-jump instruction which, if some specified switch is set or situation exists, will cause the computer to stop, after which either the routine may be continued as coded, or a jump may be forced.

conditional dump — *See* branch, conditional.

conditional expression — In the COBOL language, an expression which has the particular characteristic that, taken as a whole, it may be either true or false, in accordance with the rules.

conditional instructions — A group of instructions that can take more than one course of action (go to different memory locations) based on the condition of a status flag at the time a particular type of conditional instruction is executed.

conditional jump — An instruction to a computer that will cause the proper one of two (or more) addresses to be used in obtaining the next instruction, depending on some property of one or more numerical expressions of other conditions. Also referred to as conditional transfer of control.

conditional macroexpansion — *See* macroexpansion, conditional.

conditional transfer — *See* branch, conditional.

conditional transfer instruction — *See* branch, conditional.

conditional transfer of control — *Same as* branch.

condition, compound — A number of simple logic conditions such as AND, NOT, or logic gates that can be combined to form compound logic operations.

condition, entry — A necessary and specified requirement, in computer programming, that must be met before a subroutine can be entered; for example, the use of a counter.

conditioning, signal — To process the form or mode of a signal so as to make it intelligible to, or compatible with, a given device, including such manipulation as pulse shaping, pulse clipping, digitizing, and linearizing.

condition, initial — The value of a variable at the start of computation.

condition name — In a source language, programmers often tentatively or conditionally assign names to one or more possible values or ranges of values, which any particular item might represent. An item called month may have values 1 through 12 and may be referred to by such condition names as January, March, etc.

conditions — Expressions that, when taken as a whole, may assume one of a number of states. In programming it is the result of a test, e.g., greater than, less than, overflow, negative, etc.

confidence level — A degree of probability and/or of certainty that can be expressed as a percentage.

confidence unit — *Same as* gate, AND.

configuration — A group of machines that are interconnected and are programmed to operate as a system.

configuration, computer — The particular set of equipment so connected to form a single computer center or system for various computer runs.

conjunction — The logical operation which makes use of the AND operator or logical product. The conjunction of two variables, or expressions, may be written as A·B, A^B, A∩B, or just plain AB. These may also be described as an intersection when using Venn diagrams. (Clarified by AND; gate, AND; and contrasted with disjunction.)

conjunction gate — *Same as* gate, AND.

conjunctive search — A search defined in terms of a logical product, i.e., conjunctive form, in contrast to a disjunctive form, or logical sum.

connecting cable — The cable used to transfer electrical impulses between two pieces of equipment.

connection, channel-to-channel — A device for rapid data transfer between two computers. A channel adapter is available that permits connection between any two channels on any two systems. Data is transferred at the rate of the slower channel.

connective — Related to Boolean algebra, it is that specific symbol which signifies the operation to be performed, i.e., in computing, usually between the operands.

connective, logical — Most logical connectives are Boolean operators, such as AND, OR, etc. Particular words which make new statements from given conditional statements; the calculation of the truth or falsity of new statements plus the logical meaning of the connective, such as AND, OR, NEITHER, NOR. Truth tables are of considerable aid in showing the equivalence of the logical connectives.

connective word — A COBOL reserved term to denote the presence of a qualifier. It may also be used to form a compound condition.

connector — 1. A symbol to represent the junction of two consecutive lines of flow on a flowchart or block diagram. 2. An operator to indicate the relationship between two parts of a logical statement. 3. In a flowchart, the means of representing the convergence of more than one flow line into one, or the divergence of one flow line into more than one. It may also represent a break in a single flow line for continuation in another area.

connector, fixed — Used in flowcharting to indicate that only the result indicator can exist after a process completion.

connector, flowchart — The symbol representing the junction of two consecutive lines of flow on a flowchart, block diagram, or logic diagram.

connector, multiple — A connector to indicate the merging of several lines of flow into one line, or the dispersal of one line of flow into several lines.

connector, variable — 1. A flowchart symbol representing a sequence connection which is not fixed, but which can be varied by the flowchart procedure itself. 2. The device which inserts instructions in a program corresponding to selection of paths appearing in a flowchart. 3. The computer instructions which cause a logical chain to take one of several alternative paths. (Synonymous with N-way switch and programmed switch.)

connect time — The amount of time that elapses while the user of a remote terminal is connected to a time-shared system. Connect time is usually measured by the duration between sign-on and sign-off.

consistency (remote-computing system)

errors — *See* errors, consistency (remote computing system).

consistent unit — A specific unit which contrasts from a linear unit in which all input and output variables are represented in the same way, for example, by voltages only.

console — The unit of a computer where the control keys and certain special devices are located. This unit may contain the start key, stop key, power key, sense switches, etc., as well as lights which display the information located in certain registers. It may be used to control the machine manually; correct errors; determine the status of machine circuits, registers, and counters; determine the contents of storage; and manually revise the contents of storage.

console, auxiliary — As contrasted to main consoles, some computers or units have additional banks of controls, displays, switches, and other devices for operator manipulation or visual access to operations.

console debugging — *See* debugging, console.

console, duplex — A switchover console connecting two or more computers and used to govern which computer is to be on-line.

console, utility control — A computer console that is primarily used to control utility and maintenance programs.

constant(s) — 1. The quantities or messages that will be present in the machine and available as data for the program, and which usually are not subject to change with time. 2. A character or group of characters usually representing a value, key or standard, used by the computer to identify, locate, measure, or test in order to make a decision.

constant address — *See* address, base.

constant area — A part of storage designated to store the invariable quantities required for processing.

constant, figurative — One of several constants which have been prenamed and predefined in a COBOL processor so that they can be written in the program without having to be described in the data division.

constant instruction — An instruction not intended to be executed as an instruction, written in the form of a constant. (Related to dummy instruction.)

constants (FORTRAN) — When used in computations, a constant is any number that does not change from one execution of the program to the next. It appears in its actual numerical form in the statement. For example, in the following statement, 3 is a constant since it appears in actual numerical form:

```
J = 3*K
```

Two types of constants may be written: integer constants and real constants (characterized by being written with a decimal point). The rules for writing each of these constants are given in various manuals.

constants, integer (FORTRAN) — An integer constant is written without a decimal point, using the decimal digits 0, 1, . . . 9. A preceding + or − sign is optional. An unsigned integer constant is assumed to be positive.

constants, real (FORTRAN) — A real constant is written with a decimal point, using the decimal digits 0, 1, . . . 9. A preceding + or − sign is optional. An unsigned real constant is assumed to be positive. An integer exponent preceded by an E may follow a real constant. The exponent may have a preceding + or − sign. An unsigned exponent is assumed to be positive.

constants, system — System constants are permanent locations contained in the monitor. These locations contain data used by system programs. Some contain data that may be used by object programs.

constant storage — A part of storage designated to store the invariable quantities required for processing.

constant words — Descriptive data that is fixed and does not generally appear as an element of input.

constraint — An equation or inequality relating the variables in an optimization problem. A feasible (primal) solution must satisfy all the constraints including column-type restrictions (bounds, nonnegativity, etc.)

constraint matrix — In linear programming, the augmented matrix of the constraint equations; it is the matrix formed by the coefficient columns, or left-hand sides, and the column of constants.

contact interface — A type of connecting arrangement between a data set and business machine in which data and control signals are interchanged through contact closures. These contact closures are similar to the operation of switches and relays.

content — Data, characters, words, or other units which are held specifically addressable in some storage unit are said to be its content.

content-addressable memory — A memory where the storage locations are identified by their contents rather than their addresses. Enables faster interrogation to retrieve a particular element.

content addressable parallel processor — Abbreviated CAPP. One type of content addressable memory is called REM (recognition memory). It differs from conventional memory by eliminating serial searching. An item may be accessed simply by being named. REM can be written into and read from like ordinary memory, but has parallel processing functions, including six types of recognize and multiwrite. The recognition operations replace serial searching, while multiwrite allows the processor to write into multiple locations with a single instruction. Individual bit masking may be applied to all of the operations, including ordinary (location accessed) read and write. A data processing system with these functions is known as a content addressable parallel processor.

content-addressed storage — *See* storage, content-addressed.

contention — A condition on a multipoint communication channel when two or more locations try to transmit at the same time. If the channel is not free, the requesting terminal will have to queue. The queue of contention is solved either on a first come first served basis or by a prearranged sequence.

contents — The information stored in any storage medium. Quite prevalently, the symbol () is used to indicate "the contents of"; (A) indicates the contents of register A; (T_2) may indicate the contents of the tape on input/output unit two, etc.

context — The words or data directly before and after a word that influence its meaning.

contiguous — Adjacent or adjoining.

contingency interrupt — The program is interrupted if any of the following events occur at the operator's console: the operator requests use of the keyboard to type in information; a character has been typed in or out; a type-in has been completed; or the operator requests a program stop.

Contingency interrupt also occurs if an arithmetic operation resulted in an overflow, an invalid operation code was specified, or the clock was addressed after clock power was removed.

continue, FORTRAN — A statement which does not generate machine code. It is useful as the last statement in a DO loop.

continuity check — A check made of the information bearer channel or channels in a connection to verify that an information path exists.

continuous forms — Any source information, for character recognition, that is contained in reel form such as cash-register receipts.

continuous processing — The technique of constantly processing input items. This is sometimes referred to as on-line or real-time processing and is contrasted to batch processing.

continuous stationary readers — The special class of character readers for optical character recognition, which process only forms of predefined dimensions such as a tally roll of recorded cash-register receipts.

continuous systems modeling program — A digital simulated analog system.

contour analysis — A reading technique, in optical character recognition, which uses a roving spot of light to trace the outline of a character by bouncing around the edges. This system is usually used for handwritten material because of the nonstandardized appearance of the input. The result of the contour tracing is compared to a complete character set within a library in an attempt to determine which character has been traced.

contrast — *See* reflectance, background.

control — 1. The part of a digital computer or processor which determines the execution and interpretation of instructions in proper sequence, including the decoding of each instruction and the application of the proper signals to the arithmetic unit and other registers in accordance with the decoded information. 2. Frequently, it is one or more of the components in any mechanism responsible for interpreting and carrying out manually initiated directions.

Sometimes it is called manual control. 3. In some business applications, a mathematical check. 4. In programming, instructions which determine conditional jumps are often referred to as control instructions, and the time sequence of execution of instructions is called the flow of control.

control accuracy — Degree of correspondence between the controlled variable and the ideal value.

control, beginning of tape — *See* beginning-of-information marker.

control block — A storage location which contains information in condensed, formalized form necessary for the control of a task, function, operation, or quantity of information.

control block, event — A unique information (control) block designed to control status of operations which are waiting for an entry or special signal, i.e., processing may be halted until one or more events occur. Usually a WAIT macroinstruction is involved.

control board — *See* control panel.

control bus — A set of control lines (paths), usually from 10 to 100, with a function to carry the synchronization and control information necessary to the computer system. Such signals might be interrupt, hold, acknowledge, read, write, etc.

control, cascade — An automatic-control system in which various control units are linked in sequence, each control unit regulating the operation of the next control unit in line.

control center, program — This feature directs and controls the computer through all phases of its operation. Each program control center may contain programs for four or more separate applications. It obsoletes externally attached control bars and other single job programming devices.

control, centralized — The control of all processing by a single operational unit.

control change — When the last of items is to be added, for example, and the computing function is then changed by the program to sorting or printing, a control change has occurred. Such functional changes in cards are represented by changes in the control field.

control change, minor — When control changes of different levels of significance are used, they can be given distinguishing titles such as a minor control change, then intermediate, or next major—to establish a hierarchy related to the importance of the data.

control character — A character whose occurrence in a particular context initiates, modifies, or stops a control function. A control character may be recorded for use in a subsequent action. A control character is not a graphic character, but may have a graphic representation in some circumstances.

control character, device — *See* character, device control.

control character, print — *See* character, print control.

control character, separating — One of a set of control characters used to delimit hierarchic units of data. The first separating character in a hierarchy might be used between words, paragraphs, or for nested brackets, etc.

control circuits — The circuits which cause the computer to carry out the instructions in proper sequence.

control circuits, instruction — *Same as* control circuits.

control clock — The electronic clock, usually contained in the hardware, which times the instruction sets and the flow of and manipulation of the data.

control, closed loop — *See* closed loop.

control codes, terminal — Between a video terminal and a computer system, information flows in the form of special codes. A good part of that information concerns the letters, numbers, and symbols that make up the main contents of a company's business files, management reports, etc. Codes for these characters are quite standard; terminal manufacturers use the same character codes as do the computer manufacturers. However, in addition to character codes, another important kind of information also flows between the computer and the terminal in the form of control codes that instruct just how the text is to be handled. For example, control codes might instruct the display to "move to the next line" or to "tab to column 35." Each system manufacturer chooses its own control code versions and imbeds those codes in the programs that operate the computer and perform business tasks.

control, command, program — *See* command control program.

control computer — A computer which, by means of inputs from and outputs to a process, directly controls the operation of elements in that process.

control, concurrent operating — See concurrent operating control.

control, concurrent-operations — An operating system, like the executive, provides the ability for several programs to share the computer at the same time. Concurrent operations and control include job processing while performing inquiry or peripheral utility operations, time sharing, and multiprogramming. For example, in this operation mode, a teleprocessing application (servicing terminals) can be under way concurrently with both stacked-job batch processing and peripheral utility-type operations.

control counter — The device which contains or retains the address of the next instruction word.

control data — *See* data, control.

control, data-initiated — *See* data-initiated control.

control devices, communications — Communication lines and data devices can be attached directly to the system channel via a control unit that performs character assembly and transmission control. The control unit may be either the data-adapter unit or the transmission control.

control, direct — When one unit of peripheral equipment is under the control of another unit without human intervention, the controlling unit is then on-line to the second unit, which is under direct control of the first. If human intervention is necessary, the controlling unit is said to be off-line to the second, but the controlling unit has indirect control over the second unit while an operator acts as the link in the control sequence.

control, dynamic — Operating a digital computer in such a manner that the computer can alter the instructions as the computation proceeds, or during the sequence in which the instructions are executed, or both.

control equipment, remote — *See* equipment, remote-control.

control, executive system — Primary control of the executive system is by control information fed to the system by one or more input devices which may be either on-line or at various remote sites. This control information is similar in nature to present control-card operations, but allows additional flexibility and standardization.

control, feedback — A type of system control obtained when a portion of the output signal is operated on and fed back to the input in order to obtain a desired effect.

control flags, message — Flags that indicate whether the information being transmitted is a data or control-only message or whether it is the first, intermediate, or last block of a message.

control, flow — *See* flow control.

control footing — A summary or total at the end of a control group or for various control groups, i.e., a minor total.

control, format — Controlling the arrangement of data in an individual medium.

control function — An operation to control a device, i.e., the starting or stopping of a carriage, or a font change, rewind, or transmission reading.

control heading — A title or short definition of a control group of records which appear in front of each such group.

control, indirect — When one peripheral unit controls another through various types of electronic ties, but a human is part of the chain of control with necessary intervention, the first unit is said to be in indirect control of the second.

control, input/output real-time — *See* input/output, real time control.

control, input/output (unit) — There are several portions of control that direct interactions between the processing unit and input and output equipment. One control is written to control actions with tape, card, and printer equipment. A second control is specifically designed for random processing of records stored on direct-access devices. It is a separate control in order to minimize seek times.

control instructions — The instructions in this category are used to manipulate data within the main memory and the control memory, to prepare main memory storage areas for the processing of data fields, and to control the sequential selection and interpretation of instructions in the stored program.

control instruction transfer — *Same as* instruction transfer.

control, intermittent — A control system in which a controlled variable is monitored periodically, an intermittent correcting signal thus being supplied to the controller.

control, job flow — Job flow control includes: input/output transition between jobs and job segments, unit assignments, initial loading and initialization when the computer is first turned on; control between jobs; and control over the type of operation made, ranging from simple stacked jobs through teleprocessing systems performing concurrent operations.

control, job-processing — The job-processing control is the portion of the control program which starts job operations, assigns input/output units, and performs functions needed to proceed from one job to another.

control keys, keyboard — On most crt terminals, control keys move and control the cursor, switch the terminal from one application to another, switch the communication disciplines, and cause the performance of other functions.

controlled machine tools, numerically — *See* APT.

controlled variable — A quantity, condition, or part of a system which is subject to manipulation, regulation, or control by computer.

controller — A module or specific device which operates automatically to regulate a controlled variable or system.

controller, channel — A device that provides an independent data path to storage and assures multiprocessor systems maximum availability, allowing each processing unit to have access to every channel in the system.

controller, floating — A controller in which the rate of change of the output is a continuous or piecewise continuous function of the actuating error signal.

controller, program — That unit in a central processor controlling the execution of the computer instructions and their sequence of operations.

controller, programmable — A solid-state device that can be used to control the operations and processes of industrial and process equipment. Conventional control systems function through the medium of electromechanical relays which initiate control operations by routing the flow of electric current in prescribed ways. The programmable controller, on the other hand, initiates control actions (turning a motor on or off, opening or closing a valve) according to programmed instructions that tell it how to respond to specific conditions in the controlled machine.

control line — The randomly or sequentially timed cycle control that tells each terminal in a reel when to start transmitting. A method of communication line and terminal control.

controlling elements, forward — Those elements in the control system which change a variable in response to the actuating signal.

controlling system — Usually refers to a feedback control system; i.e., that portion which compares functions of a directly controlled variable and a set point and adjusts a manipulated variable as a function of the difference. It includes the reference input elements, summing point, forward and final controlling elements, as well as feedback elements (including sensing element).

control logic — The sequence of steps or events necessary to perform a particular function. Each step or event is defined to be either a single arithmetic or a single Boolean expression.

control logic and interrupts — *See* interrupts and control logic.

control, manual — The direction of a computer by means of manually operated switches.

control, master — 1. An application-oriented routine usually applied to the highest level of a subroutine hierarchy. 2. A computer program to control operation of the system, designed to reduce the amount of intervention required of the operator. Master control schedules programs to be processed, initiates segments of programs, controls input/output traffic, informs operator and verifies his actions, and performs corrective action on program errors or system malfunction.

control-message display — A device which shows in plain language form a particular sequence of events. The sequence of events represents events that have occurred in the past, events presently taking place, and/or events that will take place in the future.

control-message error, illegal — *See* error, illegal control-message.

control messages — Messages used to determine who transmits or receives, to acknowledge good or bad reception of blocks, or to abort transfer sequences. Such procedures are usually called handshaking procedures. Some of these procedures are recovery procedures. Acknowledgement information gives good or bad status with respect to messages sent in the opposite direction. Such information is part of the error recovery procedure, and this field is often called the response field.

control, minor — The least significant or lowest category of report grouping of basic detail.

control mode — The state that all terminals on a line must be in to allow line discipline, line control, or terminal selection to occur. When all terminals on a line are in the control mode, characters on the line are viewed as control characters performing line discipline, that is, polling or addressing.

control module, interface — *Same as* compiler, COBOL.

control nondata i/o operations — Processes which relate to input/output operations as differentiated or exclusive of data manipulation, such as tape rewinding.

control number — This is the quantity or number (value) which must be the result of a process or problem in order to prove the accuracy of the process or problem.

control, numeric — That field of computer activity which centers around the control of machine tools by mechanical devices, e.g., a computer can control assembly-line tools for machining.

control, numerical — Descriptive of systems in which digital computers are used for the control of operations, particularly of automatic machines, e.g., drilling or boring machines, wherein the operation control is applied at discrete points in the operation or process. (Contrasted with process control, in which control is applied continuously.)

control, operating (concurrent) — Operating systems provide the ability for several programs to share the computer at the same time. Concurrent operations include job processing while performing inquiry or peripheral utility operations, time sharing, and multiprogramming. For example, in the operation mode, a teleprocessing application, servicing terminals can be under way concurrently with both stacked-job batch processing and peripheral utility-type operations.

control output module — A device in some systems that stores commands and translates them into signals which can be used for control purposes. Some can generate digital outputs to control on-off devices or to pulse set-point stations. Others can generate analog outputs—voltage or current—to operate valves and other process control devices.

control panel — 1. An interconnection device, usually removable, which employs removable wires to control the operation of computing equipment. It is used on punch-card machines to carry out functions which are under control of the user. On computers it is used primarily to control input and output functions. 2. A device or component of some data-processing machines, which permits the expression of instructions in a semifixed computer program by the insertion of pins, plugs, or wires into sockets, or hubs in the device, in a pattern to represent instructions, and thus making electrical interconnections which may be sensed by the data-processing machine. (Synonymous with plugboard and related to pinboard.) 3. A part of a computer console that contains manual controls.

control panel, maintenance — A panel of indicator lights and switches on which are displayed a particular sequence of routines, and from which repairmen can determine changes to execute.

control panel, operator's — *See* operator's control panel.

control panel, operator's request — A panel consisting of indicator lights and switches by which an operator can request the computer to perform particular functions.

control panel or console — Two methods of operator control are provided in conjunction with the control unit: a control panel, or an operator's console. Either method provides a visual indication of the status of the entire system and permits manual intervention in the system's operation. The control panel contains various control switches by which the operator can start and stop the machine and can load and interrogate both main and control memory locations. "Sense" switches may be used in conjunction with programmed instructions to stop processing or to select predetermined program paths, thereby increasing the flexibility of a program.

control panel, programming — A panel consisting of indicator lights and switches by which a programmer can enter or change routines in the computer.

control pen — *See* light pen.

control print character — A specific control character used to affect printing operations such as feeding, spacing, font selection.

control printing — A list of the control group for purposes of identification without the list of the detail records.

control, process — Descriptive of systems in which computers, most frequently analog computers, are used for the automatic regulation of operations or processes. Typical are operations in the production of chemicals wherein the operation control is applied continuously, and adjustments to regulate the operation are directed by the computer to keep the value of a controlled variable constant. (Contrasted with numerical control.)

control, production — As applied by computers, a data acquisition system from the floor of a production line or process for the speedup and simplification of the flow of production information for management.

control program — A sequence of instructions which prescribe the series of steps to be taken by a system, a computer, or any other device.

control program, command — A program to handle all commands addressed to the system from the user consoles. These commands would include requests to log in or out, a request to use the edit program, requests to have a program placed on the run queue, requests to load a program, etc.

control program, master — *Same as* program, master control.

control program (microprocessor) — A specific designed sequence of instructions that guides the CPU through the various operations otherwise programmed. Most often this program is permanently stored in ROM memory where it can be accessed but not erased by the CPU during operations.

control program types — Most control programs contain many routines that would otherwise have to be put into each individual program. Such routines include those for handling error conditions, interruptions from the console, or interruptions from a communications terminal. There are also routines for handling input and output equipment. Because these routines are prewritten, the programmer is saved a good deal of effort, and the likelihood of programming errors is reduced.

control, proportional — A method of control in which the intensity of action varies linearly as the condition being regulated deviates from the prescribed condition.

control, real-time input/output — *See* real-time control, input/output.

control register — *See* register, control.

control register, sequence — *See* register, sequence control.

control routine — A primary routine that controls loading and relocation of routines and in some cases makes use of instructions which are known to the general programmer. Effectively, control routines are part of the machine itself (synonymous with monitor routine, supervisory routine, and supervisory program).

control routine, resident — A special routine that is in effect part of the machine and that controls the loading and relocation of other routines, often employing instructions not available to the user, i.e., protected by the manufacturer.

control schedule, record — A type of master record or schedule designating all activities involved regarding disposition of business records, i.e., transfers, retention, etc.

control section — The primary sequence of instructions or data within a program that can be transferred from outside the program segment in which it is contained. The control section can be deleted or replaced with a control section from other program segments. Microprocessors are changing the structure and procedure of many such devices and systems.

control section, input/output — *See* input-/output control section.

control, selection — The control device that assists the instruction control unit in performing the selection of instructions to be executed.

control sequence — The normal order of selection of instructions for execution. In some computers, one of the addresses in each instruction specifies the control sequence. In most other computers, the sequence is consecutive except where a transfer occurs.

control sequence, processing — *See* processing control sequence.

control, sequential — A mode of computer operation in which instructions are executed in consecutive order by ascending or descending addresses of storage locations, unless otherwise specified by a jump.

control, serial number — Messages are controlled by assigning a number at the time of origination and adding additional numbers as the message passes through specific points.

controls, executive program — The program execution controls determine relative priority of programs that are ready to run, and load other programs into storage. They handle the allocation and protection of main storage blocks, the interval timer, error diagnostic routines, and checkpoint procedures.

control signals — Various control signals are provided to control and to ensure the orderly flow of information words between the central computer and the peripheral subsystems. These signals do not transmit data, but are used to command and to identify the transfer of information words at the proper times and in the proper sequence. These control signals travel over the control lines of the input/output channel. A listing of these control signals and their respective functions is provided.

controls, peripheral — Peripheral controls regulate the transfer of data between the central processor and peripheral devices. Specifically, they reconcile the mechanical speeds of the peripheral devices with the electronic speed of the central processor, and minimize the interruption of central-processor activity due to peripheral data transfers.

control state (display) — All modes can specify that the display enter the control state in which 12-bit words are decoded as instructions to change display parameters, change mode, or change the address of access to the computer memory (some systems).

control statement, job — Individual statements used to direct an operating system in its functions, as contrasted to information needed to process a job but not intended directly for the operating system itself.

control statements — 1. Statements used to direct the flow of the program, either causing specific transfers or making transfers dependent upon meeting certain specified conditions. 2. Instructions which convey control information to the processor, but do not develop machine-language instructions, i.e., symbolic statements.

control statements, assembly — *See* assembly-control statements.

control station — A switching network station directing operations such as polling, averting, recovering, selecting.

control store, bit-slice machine — A memory circuit designed to hold the sequence of commands that determines operations of the sequential state operation (machine). It is often referred to as the microprogram store.

control supervisor — A control system furnishing data to a centralized location, allowing the operator to supervise or monitor the controlling of a process, operation, or calculation.

control, supervisory — A control system which furnishes intelligence, usually to a centralized location, to be used by an operator to supervise the control of a process or operation.

control switch, operation — *See* switch, operation-control.

control, symbiont — *See* symbiont control.

control system — A system of the closed-loop type in which the computer is used to govern external processes.

control system and data acquisition — *See* data acquisition and control system.

control system, concurrent — This environment allows for the concurrent operation of many programs; it allows the system to react immediately to the inquiries, requests, and demands of many different users at local and remote stations; it allows for the stringent demands of real-time applications; it is able to store, file, retrieve, and protect large blocks of data; and it makes optimum use of all available hardware facilities, while minimizing job turn-around time.

Only through central control of all activities can this environment of the combined hardware and software systems be fully established and maintained to satisfy the requirements of all applications; this responsibility for efficient, flexible, centralized control is borne by the executive system. The executive system controls and coordinates the functions of this complex internal environment, and by presenting a relatively simple interface to the programmer, allows him to use the system easily, while relieving him of concern for the internal interaction between his program and other coexistent programs.

control system, real-time — *See* real-time control system.

control systems, internal — Programmed controls built into the system to govern the flow of computer operations.

control tape — A paper or plastic tape used to control the carriage operation of some printing output devices. Also called carriage tape.

control tape mechanism — That part of the printer which controls the printing carriage to permit desired and designed hard copy printout, i.e., the specific device which reads paper tape containing particular instructions for controlling the carriage operations.

control tape sequence — *See* tape, program.

control total — A sum of numbers in a specified record field of a batch of records determined repetitiously during the processing operation, so that any discrepancy from the control indicates an error. A control total often has some significance in itself, but may not, as, for example, when a control total is determined as the sum of identification numbers of records. (Related to hash total.)

control, traffic — A method of optimizing the flow of work through a factory by means of a computer.

control, transfer — To copy, exchange, read, record, store, transmit, transport, or write data.

control transfer instruction — *See* branch.

control transfer instruction, conditioned — *See* branch, conditional.

control, transfer of — *See* branch.

control, trap settings — Trap settings control which interrupt signals will be allowed to interrupt a program in process. If a trap is armed, then the associated interrupt conditions will be permitted to interrupt the main program when they occur. A trap that has not been armed, or has been disarmed, inhibits the occurrence of interrupt signals.

control, unconditional transfer of — *See* branch, unconditional.

control unit — 1. A portion of the hardware of an automatic digital computer that directs sequence of operations, interprets coded instructions, and initiates proper commands to computer circuits to execute instructions. 2. An auxiliary component of a computer located behind the "mainframe" and other component equipment such as tape units, printers and card readers, for the purpose of controlling these components.

control unit, central — *Same as* central processing unit.

control unit, common — This unit is that portion of the terminal whose primary function is to control and coordinate the flow of data between the data device(s) and the communication facility.

control unit, data communications — *See* data communications control unit.

control unit, input/output — *See* input/output control unit.

control unit, peripheral — An intermediary control device which links a peripheral unit to the central processor, or in the case of off-line operation, to another peripheral unit.

control word — 1. A word, usually the first or last of a record, or first or last word of a block, that carries indicative information for the following words, records, or blocks. 2. A word which is used to transmit processing information from the control program to the operational programs, or between operational programs. Most systems normally contain the several significant fields within the record.

conventional equipment — That equipment which is generally considered to be part of the computer system but which is not specifically part of the computer itself. Various card handling devices, tape handlers, and disk units, if not built into the mainframe or wired in, would be conventional equipment; e.g., a teletypewriter device.

conventions — Standard and accepted procedures in programs and systems analysis. The abbreviations, symbols, and their meanings as developed for particular systems and programs.

convergence, algorithm — An algorithm is said to converge if it is certain to yield its solution in a finite number of steps. It is a much stronger requirement than the mathematical convergence of the sequence of obtained function values.

conversational — Pertaining to a mode of processing that involves step-by-step interaction between the user and a computer.

conversational compilers, time sharing — *See* time sharing, conversational compilers.

conversational guidance — User/computer communications in a conversational or dialog mode, where the user takes some action and the system responds. The system then requests a specific category of input or takes other action, and the user again responds. In this alternating stimulus-response mode, the system can and should provide guidance to the user on the form and content of the user response.

conversational guidance, time sharing — *See* time sharing, conversational guidance.

conversational language — A language utilizing a near-English character set which facilitates communication between the computer and the user. For example, BASIC is one of the more commonly used conversational languages.

conversational mode — 1. This mode of operation means that real-time man-machine communications are maintained. In this mode the system is used exclusively for servicing remote terminals. 2. The term given to the man-machine communicating technique that is the great dream of the future. This permits the user to "talk" to the machine locally instead of operating with the present restriction of having to tell the machine precisely what it is to do.

conversational mode operation — In this mode the system is used exclusively for servicing remote terminals. Real-time man-machine communications are maintained.

conversational processing — The user is said to be communicating with the system in a "conversational" manner when each statement he enters through the terminal is processed (translated, verified, and, if desired, executed) immediately. The system then sends a reply to the terminal. The information contained in the reply varies. For example, it might be a message indicating that the previous statement contained an error. Operations in the conversational manner must be in either of two possible modes: the program mode or the command mode.

conversational programming — A technique used in instructing the computer to perform its operations, whereby common vocabulary can be utilized by the user to describe his procedures most accurately. If a statement cannot be understood by the computer, it asks the user for a clarified instruction. This conversational procedure continues until the user has selected the series of statements in the proper sequence which will solve his problem. Conversational programming saves the user the inconvenience of having to study other programming languages extensively before he can solve his problem.

conversational time sharing — The simultaneous utilization of a computer system by multiple users at remote locations, each being equipped with a remote terminal. The user and the computer usually communicate by way of a higher-level, easy-to-learn computer language.

conversion — 1. The process of changing information from one form of representation to another, such as from the language of one type of machine to that of another, or from magnetic tape to the printed page. (Synonymous with data conversion.) 2. The process of changing from one data-processing method to another, or from one type of equipment to another, e.g., conversion from punch-card equipment to magnetic-tape equipment.

conversion, A — A FORTRAN instruction to transmit alphanumeric to and from variables in storage.

conversion, binary to decimal — The process of converting a number written to the base of two to the equivalent number written to the base of ten.

conversion, code — A process for changing the bit groupings for characters in one code into the corresponding character bit groupings for a second code.

conversion, data — The process of changing information from one form of representation to another, such as from the language of one type of machine to that of another, or from magnetic tape to the printed page.

conversion, data code — The translation of alphanumeric data into a form acceptable to the computer. This is usually done by the computer during the input of the data.

conversion, decimal to binary — The process of converting a number written to the base of ten, or decimal, into the equivalent number written to the base of two, or binary.

conversion device — A particular device or piece of peripheral equipment which converts data from one form into another form or medium, but without changing the data, content, or information.

conversion equipment — The equipment that is capable of transposing or transcribing the information from one type of data-processing medium to render it acceptable as input to another type of processing medium.

conversion F — One of the three types of format specifications in FORTRAN. F-conversion is used to convert floating-point data for input/output operation.

conversion, file — The transformation of parts of customer account records, employee records, and the like from their original documents into magnetic files by the computer.

conversion mode — Communication between a terminal and the computer, in which each entry from the terminal elicits a response from the computer and vice versa.

conversion programs — These programs enable users of several competitive systems to take advantage of the superior throughput and cost performance characteristics of computers without incurring prohibitive programming costs.

conversion program, symbolic — *See* symbolic conversion program.

conversion routine — A flexible and generalized program which can be used by a programmer to change the presentation of data from one form to another such as from card to disk.

conversion time — The length of time required to read out all the digits in a given coded word.

convert — 1. To change numerical information from one number base to another. 2. To transfer information from one recorded medium to another.

converter — An interface to transform information from one form to another.

converter, card-to-tape — A device which converts information directly from punched cards to punched or magnetic tape.

converter, language — *See* language converter.

converter, tape-to-tape — *See* tape-to-tape converter.

converter, (telegraphy) — A telegraph repeater in which the input and output signals are formed according to the same code, but not according to the same type of electrical modulation.

converting — Transferring data from one form to a different form.

convex programming — *See* programming, convex.

cooperation index — *See* index, cooperation.

cooperative installation — An agreement by a group of users to band together and install a single computer to service all of them. The advantages are that they can afford a larger computer, have access to more capability, and achieve maximum economy and maximum service. The disadvantages are those associated with having many masters with differing priorities.

coordinate indexing — A system of indexing individual documents by descriptors of equal rank, so that a library can be searched for a combination of one or more descriptors.

coordinate paper — Marginally punched, continuous-form graph paper normally used for printout on an XY plotter.

coordinate retrieval — *Same as* concept coordination.

coordinate storage — *See* storage, coordinate.

coordination, concept — *See* concept coordination.

copy — To reproduce information in a

new location replacing whatever was previously stored there and leaving the source of the information unchanged.

copy check — *See* check transfer.

copy, hard — A printed copy of machine output, e.g., printed reports, listings, documents, and summaries.

cordless plugs — On patchcords, if connectors do not include a flexible portion, they are termed cordless plugs.

core — A configuration of magnetic material that is placed in a spatial relationship to current-carrying conductors, and whose magnetic properties are essential to its use. It is used to concentrate an induced magnetic field as in a transformer, induction coil, or armature, to retain a magnetic polarization for the purpose of storing data, or for its nonlinear properties as in a logic element. It may be made of such material as iron, iron oxide, or ferrite, and in such shapes as wires, tapes, toroids, or thin film.

correcting signal — In synchronous systems, a special signal that may be sent recurrently for correction of data.

correction — A quantity (equal in absolute value to the error) added to a calculated or observed value to obtain the true value.

correction, automatic — *See* error correction, automatic.

correction, automatic error — A technique, usually requiring the use of special codes and/or automatic retransmission, which detects and corrects errors occurring in transmission. The degree of correction depends upon coding and equipment configuration.

correction, error (transmission) — *Same as* error correction, automatic.

correction program — A particular routine that is designed to be used in or after a computer failure, malfunction, or program or operator error and that thereby reconstitutes the routine being executed before the error or malfunction and from the most recent or closest rerun point.

corrective maintenance — *See* maintenance, corrective.

corrective routine, error — A series of computer instructions programmed to correct a detected error.

correlation, fact — *See* fact correlation.

correlative indexing — *Same as* coordinate indexing.

count — The consecutive or successive increase or decrease of a common cumulative total of the number of times an event appears, e.g., the count of the number of iterations already completed or which remain to be completed.

counter — 1. A device for storing a number and allowing the number to be increased or decreased as directed by the instructions needed. An adding wheel or device. 2. A device, such as a register or storage location, used to represent the number of occurrences of an event.

counter, binary — 1. A counter which counts according to the binary number system. 2. A counter capable of assuming one of two stable states.

counter, control — *Same as* register, control.

counter, cycle — *See* cycle counter.

counter, decade — A counter which counts to ten in one column, or place of a decimal number, or one which counts to nine and resets to zero at the next count.

counter, decrement — A counter in which the numerical contents are reduced on each count. A decrement of one is usually assumed unless specified otherwise.

counter, delay — In the central unit of some computers, a counter that can temporarily delay a program long enough for the completion of an operation.

counter, forward-backward — A counter having both an add and subtract input, so that it is capable of counting in either an increasing or a decreasing direction.

counter inhibit — The bit, in the program status double-word, that indicates whether (if one) or not (if zero) all (clock) count zero interrupts are inhibited.

counter, instructions — *Same as* register, control.

counter, locations — *Same as* register, control.

counter, modulo-N — A counter which in a recurring sequence counts through N states and then repeats. For example, a modulo-6 counter stores 0,1,2,3,4,5,0,-1,2,3,4,5 . . . in sequence as it counts.

counter operation — A counter is a digital device consisting of flip-flops connected so that it counts the number of pulses it receives on its input. The count is provided as a binary number output. A counter has a maximum count, depending on its size, called a modulus, or just mod. For example, a mod-8 counter can count up to seven, and on the eighth input it resets itself back to a count of zero. When it resets, it also provides an output pulse which could be counted by another counter. Thus a counter divides an input frequency by its modulus. The mod-8 counter, for example, would provide an output pulse every eight input pulses, so if its input frequency were 1000 pulses per second, the output would have only 125 pulses per second.

counter, origin — The circuitry which develops the location of the start of the next instruction by adding the instruction word length to the initial value and to the running total after each instruction.

counter, printing — The printing counter of the magnetic tape terminal advances by one for each tape block transmitted or received. At the end of transmission, the total number of tape blocks for the run is printed automatically. During a run, upon the detection of an error block when receiving, the number of that tape block is printed.

counter, program — *Same as* register control.

counter, program-address — A register in which the address of the current instruction is recorded. (Synonymous with instruction counter.)

counter, repeat — The repeat counter is used to control repeated operations, such as block transfer and repeated search commands. To execute a repeated instruction "k" times, the repeat counter must be loaded with "k" prior to the execution of the instruction. A repeated sequence may be suspended to process an interrupt, with circuitry providing for the completion of the repeated sequence after the interrupt has been processed.

counter, reversible — When the number stored in a counter is capable of being increased or decreased according to the value of various types of control signals, the counter is termed reversible.

counter, ring — A loop of bistable elements interconnected so that one and only one is in a specified state at any given time and such that, as input signals are counted, the position of the element in the specified state moves in an ordered sequence around the loop.

counter, sequence — *Same as* register, sequence control.

counter, step — A counter used in the arithmetical unit to count the steps in multiplication, division, and shift operation.

counter, subsequence — A specific type of instruction counter designed to step through or count microoperations, i.e., part of larger operations.

count modulo-N — When a number stored in a counter reverts to zero in the counting sequence after reaching a maximum value of (N−1), the counter is said to count modulo-N.

count zero interrupt — An interrupt level that is triggered when an associated (clock) counter pulse interrupt has produced a zero result in a clock counter.

coupled computers — An installation in which computers are joined to carry out special applications such as two computers operating in parallel and used as a check on one another, or when they are coupled or joined so that the off-line computer is programmed to watch the on-line computer and, if needed, switch operation to itself.

coupler, acoustic — A device that converts electrical signals into audio signals, enabling data to be transmitted over the public telephone network via a conventional telephone handset.

coupling, cross-talk — *See* talk, cross.

CPM — Abbreviation for Cards Per Minute.

CP/M — Abbreviation for Control Program/Microcomputer.

CPP — Abbreviation for Card-Punching Printer.

cps — Abbreviation for both "characters per second" and "cycles per second."

CPU — Central Processing Unit. The central processor of the computer system. It contains the main storage, arithmetic unit, and special register groups.

CPU card — An assembly consisting of a CPU chip and the extra logic elements required to provide the ability to transmit data between the CPU chip pins and external devices, a clock that generates timing signals used by the CPU chip, and the means for knowing where data is to be read and where data must be sent.

CPU chip — A CPU chip may be visualized as one universal chip which performs the functions of numerous individual chips. The CPU chip requires two sets of input signals to generate one set of output signals. The input and output signals correspond to the chip inputs and outputs. The instruction signals tell the CPU chips which individual logic chip to emulate. In order for the versatility of a CPU chip to be useful, it must emulate logic equivalents to more than one chip.

CPU elements — The principal elements of the central processing unit (CPU) control the interpretation and execution of instructions. Generally they include the ALU, timing and control, accumulator, scratch-pad memory, program counter (PC) and address stack, instruction register and decode, parallel data and i/o bus, and memory and i/o control.

CPU expander — A unit designed to permit a user to run several types of software on a single system without modifying the software. Some of the first units contained 8080, Z-80, and 6800 chips on the same board, with four PIAs for control and several multiplexers and demultiplexers.

CPU handshaking — The interaction between the CPU and various peripheral devices. For example, a printer might have some logic to designate when it is ready for a new character, or the CPU can act upon several status conditions of all ranges of signals from i/o devices.

CPU slices — CPU slices are generally 2- or 4-bit parts of a CPU. Users must define an instruction set and the architecture which executes that instruction set, then develop the interface between that architecture and the memory containing the control program and the i/o system which connects into devices, and then provide a system package.

CPU time — The actual computational time necessary to process a set of instructions in the arithmetic and logic units of the computer.

crash — A breakdown, i.e., an event in which a system becomes inoperative or lost in a loop, or is blocked, most often due to a hardware failure or software malfunction. For example, in a disk system, a head crash concerns an accidental impact of the read-write head on the disk surface. Each peripheral has its specific type of crash.

credit-card reader — A microprocessor-based card reader for credit authorization and security applications. It can read the magnetic stripe imbedded in most major credit cards.

crippled leap-frog test — A variation of the leap-frog test, modified so that it repeats its tests from a single set of storage locations rather than a changing set of locations.

criteria, sequencing (sorting) — The field in a record which determines, or is used for determining, the sequence of records in a file.

criterion — A value used for testing, comparing, or judging, e.g., in determining whether a condition is plus or minus, true or false; also, a rule or test for making a decision in a computer or by humans.

criterion, cycle — *See* cycle criterion.

critical path — The longest time path in a project which has to be done as quickly as possible. Because the overall time required to complete the project cannot be less than that required along the critical path, it requires the most careful monitoring. Any delay along this path causes the project to be delayed, while minor delays along noncritical paths do not. *See* PERT network.

Critical Path Method (CPM) — The XDS, CPM package offers a flexible tool for computer users requiring a project scheduling and process evaluation system. The XDS, CPM package has the following features: optimum schedules can be developed, including total project duration and cost constraints; process can be monitored throughout the project, with critical paths flagged for attention downstream; change and current status information can be incorporated easily without total rescheduling; calendar data, including holiday effects, are automatically reported. (XDS)

critical path scheduling — A monitoring system that continuously checks progress in programming needs of an operating system to report and prevent slippage. Reports generated by this monitoring of computer programming needs in which jobs to be done are sorted will indicate the most critical items on the critical path of the computer.

CROM — Abbreviation for Control Read Only Memory. A specific ROM that has been designed and microprogrammed to decode control logic. It is a major component of several types of microprocessors.

cross assembler — A program run on one computer for the purpose of translating instructions for a different computer.

crossbar — A type of common control switching system using the crossbar or coordinate switch. Crossbar switching systems are ideally suited to data switching due to their low-noise characteristic, and they can be equipped for Touch-Tone dialing.

cross-channel switching — This optional feature permits direct program access to attached input/output devices through two channels.

crosscheck — To check the computing by two different methods.

cross compiling/assembling — A method in which an existing minicomputer, large computer, or time-sharing service can be used to write and debug what will become a microcomputer program. The advantage is that the designer has access to all of the conventional peripherals, and the object code he or she produces on them can, in the final stage, be loaded into the microcomputer system.

crossfire — Interference from one telegraph circuit to another telegraph circuit or into telephone circuits.

crossfoot — 1. The addition of several horizontal fields of information from cards or across a document. 2. To add several horizontal fields of numeric information, usually for checking or totaling purposes. 3. The process whereby numbers in different fields of the same punch card are added or subtracted and the result punched into another field of the same card. Or, a check in which totals secured by one method in a given problem are compared with totals obtained by another method. The totals should be equal if no error has been made.

crossfooting — Crossfooting is the addition and/or subtraction of factors in a horizontal spread to prove processing accuracy. It can be used on a payroll register to prove that the final totals of net pay and deductions equal the final total earnings; this provides control on report preparation as well as calculating and card-punching operations. In posting transactions to records that are stored in a computer (e.g., accounts receivable), crossfooting is used to prove the accuracy of posting either as each transaction is posted, or collectively at the end of the run, or both.

cross-program — A specific program in software development in which a program for computer X resides (executes) on computer Y. Used for tests, program development, simulations, etc.

cross-sectional testing — A series of tests to get a representative sampling of system performance. These tests are usually one-pass tests such as an acceptance test.

cross software — Software that lets users develop programs for a target computer on a host computer.

cross tracking — A crosslike array of bright dots on the display, used for locating points and lines or for drawing curves.

cross-validation — The verification of results by replicating an experiment under independent conditions.

crowding, character — The reduction of the time or space interval on magnetic tape between characters.

crt — Abbreviation for Cathode-Ray Tube.

crt, beam-penetration — There are two types of color crt's—monochrome and full color. Monochrome crt's rely on color phosphors, and more than one color is possible on a crt screen by layering phosphors. Different colors appear one at a time, depending on anode potential—how far the electron beam penetrates the phosphor layers. This technique for producing color is called beam penetration.

crt function key — A key on a crt terminal that, when depressed, transmits a signal to the computer which can be equated to a prestored typewriter message of many strokes. Special consoles of various types have been developed for particular users. Examples are airline agent's sets, badge readers, and stockbroker's inquiry consoles.

crt highlighting — A display capability used for distinguishing between variable data and protected data such as field labels or error messages. This can be done by blinking, underlining, or varying the intensity of the characters.

crt inquiry display — Information is placed into the computer through the alphanu-

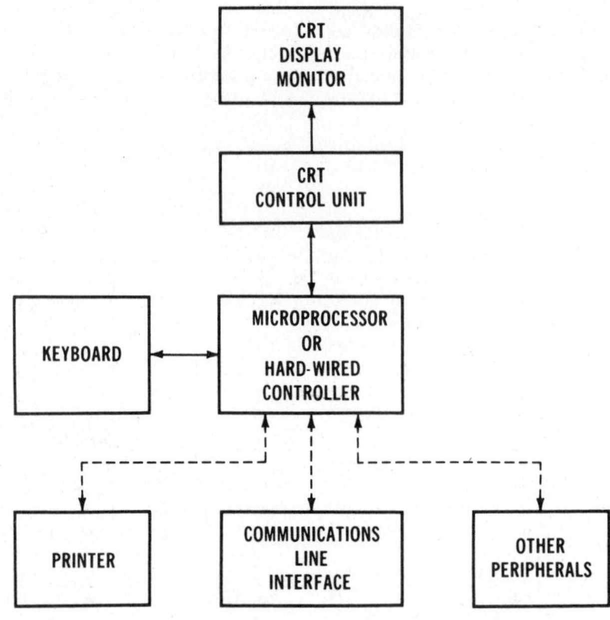

Crt terminal.

meric keyboard and is simultaneously displayed on its crt. The unit then displays a reply to the inquiry on its screen.

crt loader/monitor — A system by which each contact in the control circuit is displayed on a crt as entered from the keyboard, providing immediate verification of the program and permitting editing and correction. Entire memory programs can be stored on magnetic-tape cassettes or punched tape for use in verification, dumping and reloading, or programming other controllers.

crt, raster scan — A display in which the screen is scanned line by line and the information on the screen is refreshed 60 times per second. Storage terminals, on the other hand, require no refreshing; a storage-tube unit retains its image until the entire screen is cleared or portions of the display are altered with a light pen.

crt storage — *See* storage, electrostatic.

crt terminal — The basic crt terminal consists of a display monitor, a control unit, a controller, and a keyboard. A printer, the communications interface, and other peripherals can also be added.

crt terminal, intelligent — A crt terminal that is equivalent functionally to a minicomputer, although not as powerful as one. A fully intelligent terminal has a programmable i/o capability and acts more as a data collection and manipulation facility than a mere input device to the host. It can be used to execute comparatively complex editing functions, such as table look-up, character checking, data extension, and input accumulation.

cryogenic element — Various high speed circuits which use the superconductivity characteristics of materials operating at or near absolute zero temperatures.

cryogenic memory — *Same as* cryogenic storage.

cryogenics — The study and use of devices utilizing properties of materials near absolute zero in temperature. At these temperatures large current changes can be obtained from relatively small magnetic-field changes.

cryogenic storage — This type of storage depends for its operation on the properties of specific materials, which can become superconductive when their temperatures fall below certain very low temperatures. Since superconductors have zero resistance, they have the ability to maintain or store a current permanently.

cryostat — A device that uses evaporative and condensing cycles to achieve extremely low temperatures and is often used to liquify gases.

cryotron — A device utilizing properties assumed by metals at near absolute zero temperature so that large current changes can be obtained by relatively small magnetic-field changes.

CSL — Abbreviation for Computer Sensitive Language.

CTC — Abbreviation for Conditional Transfer of Control.

cue — An instruction, address, or miscellaneous statement containing a key used to initiate entry into a closed subroutine at a specified entry point.

cumulative indexing — *See* indexing, cumulative.

current-instruction register — The control section register that contains the instruction currently being executed after it is brought to the control section from memory. Also called instruction register.

current time — *See* time, real.

cursor — A position indicator employed in a display on a video terminal to indicate a character to be corrected or a position in which data is to be entered. On some terminals, the cursor can be moved around freely, but usually the movements are more restricted. Typical cursors include a line under the character at hand, a nondestructive blinking white block, and a white block on which an existing character on the screen is reversed. Typical cursor keyboard commands are up, down, left, right, home, and return left to next line on new line command. With the up, down, left, and right keys, there is usually a repeating feature for rapid long-distance cursor movement. When cursor control keys are not enough, other interactive control devices are sometimes available as options. These include a joystick, a light pen, a trackball, and a set of thumbwheel controls. These techniques are most useful on graphic terminals.

curve — The graphical representation of the relationship between two variables (line, points, bar graphs, histograms).

curve fitting — *See* compaction, curve fitting.

curve follower — A peripheral unit which reads data that is represented in graphs.

curve-pattern compaction — *See* compaction, curve fitting.

customer engineering section — Those pieces or sections of equipment which remain unavailable to programmers or operators but which are intended for exclusive use, maintenance, or operations by the engineers employed by the equipment manufacturer.

custom IC — An integrated circuit manufactured to a specific customer's design and specifications. Most often, high development costs restrict custom chips to users of very large volumes in order to write that cost off over many devices. Games, appliances, and so on are often controlled by custom chips.

custom software — Programs designed specifically to meet one user's particular requirements.

CUTS — Acronym for Cassette User Tape System.

cyberculture — A composite word derived from cybernetics and culture.

cybernetics — The field of technology involved in the comparative study of the control and intracommunication of information-handling machines and nervous systems of animals and man in order to understand and improve communication.

cycle — 1. A self-contained series of instructions in which the last instruction can modify and repeat itself until a terminal condition is reached. The productive instructions in the loop generally manipulate the operands, while bookkeeping instructions modify the productive instructions and keep count of the number of repetitions. A loop may contain any number of conditions for termination. The equivalent of a loop can be achieved by the technique of straight-line coding, whereby the repetition of productive and bookkeeping operations is accomplished by explicitly writing the instructions for each repetition. 2. A nonarithmetic shift in which digits dropped off at one end of a word are returned at the other end in circular fashion, e.g., cycle left and cycle right. 3. An occurrence, phenomenon, or interval of space or time that recurs regularly and in the same sequence, e.g., the interval required for completion of one operation in a repetitive sequence of operations. 4. To repeat a set of operations a prescribed number of times including, when required, supplying necessary address changes by arithmetical processes or by means of a hardware device, such as a cycle counter, B-box, or index register.

cycle availability — That specific time period during which stored information can be read.

cycle count — The increase or decrease of the cycle index by a unit or by an arbitrary integer.

cycle counter — The accumulator or counter of a cycle index.

cycle criterion — 1. The number of times a cycle is to be repeated. 2. The register in which that number is stored.

cycled interrupt — The change, by sequence or specific operation cycle of control, to the next or specific function in a predetermined manner or order.

cycle, execution — That portion of a machine cycle during which the actual execution of the instruction takes place. Some operations need a large number of these cycles to complete the operation, and the normal instruction/operation alteration will be held up during this time.

cycle, grandfather — The period during which magnetic-tape records are retained before reusing, so that records can be reconstructed in the event of loss of information stored on a magnetic tape.

cycle, in action — The complete operation performed on data. Includes basic steps of origination, input, manipulation, output, and storage.

cycle index — The number of times a cycle has been executed, or the difference or negative of the difference between the number that has been executed and the number of repetitions desired.

cycle, instruction — The steps involved in the processing of an instruction.

cycle, intermediate — An unconditional branch instruction may address itself, i.e., a branch command is called, executed, and a cycle is set up, which may be used for stopping a machine.

cycle, machine — The shortest period of time, in the operation of a digital computer, for a sequence of events to repeat itself.

cycle, major — 1. The maximum access time of a recirculating serial storage element. 2. A number of minor cycles.

cycle, memory — 1. The process of reading and restoring information in main memory. 2. The time required to complete this process.

cycle, minor — The time interval between the appearance of corresponding parts of successive words in a storage device which provides serial access to storage positions.

cycle, null — The time necessary to cycle through a program without introducing data. This establishes the lower bound for program processing time.

cycle reset — The return of a cycle index to its initial or some preselected condition.

cycle, search — The sequence of events or time interval needed for the occurrence of a fixed number of events required to complete a single search operation, such as carrying out a comparison.

cycle shift — Removal of the digits of a number (or characters of a word) from one end of a number or word and their insertion, in the same sequence, at the other end.

cycle stealing — A condition in which the processor allows the direct memory access controller to take control of the system bus while the processor is doing internal work.

cycle-stealing data acquisition — *See* data acquisition, cycle-stealing.

cycle, storage — A periodic sequence of events occurring when information is transferred to or from the storage device of a computer. Storing, sensing, and regeneration form parts of the storage sequence.

cycle time — The interval between the call for, and the delivery of, information from a storage unit or device.

cycle time, processor — The computer can be divided into three main sections: arithmetic and control, input/output, and memory. The arithmetic and control section carries out the directives of the program. The calculations, routing of information, and control of other sections occur in this part of the central processor. All information going in and out of the central processor is handled by the i/o section. It also controls the operation of all peripheral equipment. The memory section is the heart of the central processor; it provides temporary storage for data and instructions. Because of its importance, the total cycle time of the memory is the main determining factor in the overall speed of the processor.

cycle time, storage (in microseconds) — For main storage, the total time to read and restore one storage word. For disk or other random storage, the total time for one revolution.

cycle, work — The time necessary for a sequence of events, steps, or operations required for tasks.

cyclic code — *See* code, cyclic.

cyclic code (permuted) — *Same as* code, cyclic.

cyclic feeding — A system used by character recognition readers, in which each individual input document is issued to the document transport at a predetermined and constant rate.

cyclic redundancy check — Abbreviated CRC. A polynomial division of the bit stream by a CRC polynomial. The dividend polynomial is initially preset to 0, and the 1s and 0s of the data stream become the coefficients of the dividend polynomial. The division uses subtraction modulo 2 (no carries), and the remainder is transmitted as the error check field. The receiving station compares the transmitted remainder with its own computed remainder, and an equal condition indicates that no error has occurred. The polynomial value depends on the protocol and code set being used.

cyclic shift — *See* shift, circular.

cyclic storage — *Same as* storage, circulating.

cycling, tape — An updating procedure which creates a new tape file.

cylinder — For disk units with multiple read-write heads, all of the data tracks under the read-write heads can be accessed without mechanical movement of the heads. If each disk surface has one read-write head, the tracks under them can be thought of as a cylinder consisting of one track from each disk.

cylinder concept — The concept that data on all tracks above and below the one currently being used is available by merely switching read/write heads. Allows access to large amounts of information with no extra movement of the access device.

D

DAB — Abbreviation for display assignment bits, and for display attention bits.

dagger operation — *Same as* gate, NAND.

daisy chain — Refers to a specific method of propagating signals along a bus. This method is often used in applications in which devices not requesting a daisy-chained signal respond by passing a signal on. In practice, the first device requesting the signal responds to it by performing an action and breaks the daisy-chained signal continuity. The daisy-chain scheme permits assignment of device priorities based on the electrical position of the device along the bus (some systems).

daisy-chain bus — A daisy-chain bus is very similar to the party line, except that the connections are made in serial fashion. Each unit can modify the signal before passing it on to the next device. This approach is used mainly for signals related to interrupts or polling circuits. Whenever a device requires service, it blocks the signal. A priority is thus established, since the devices that are closest to the microprocessor usually have the first chance to request service.

daisy-chain device priority — On some systems, device priority is determined by the position of the module in the computer backplane. A signal passes through each module in turn forming a "daisy chain" through them. The closer a module is to the processor, the higher its hardware priority in the daisy chain. The priority chaining scheme requires that there be no empty slots between modules, as this would break the chain.

daisy-chaining terminal — Daisy-chaining is generally the same as multidropping, except that often no modems are used;

however, the terminals share the same data link. The data link comes from the computer, goes to the first terminal, comes out of the first terminal and on to the second terminal, etc. All terminals share the same data link and the same computer port.

DAS — Abbreviation for digital-analog simulator.

DASD (direct access storage devices) — *See* storage, direct access.

data — 1. A general term used to denote any or all facts, numbers, letters and symbols that refer to or describe an object, idea, condition, situation, or other factors. It connotes basic elements of information which can be processed or produced by a computer. Sometimes data are considered to be expressible only in numerical form, but information is not so limited. (Related to information.) 2. Plural of the term datum. Collectively used to designate alphabetic or numeric material serving as a basis of discussion.

data above voice (DAV) — A transmission system which carries digital data on a portion of the microwave radio spectrum above the frequency used for voice transmission.

data acquisition — Process data are acquired by the data acquisition (DA) system, converted into digital information, and printed to provide: (a) operating records for accounting and supervisory purposes, or (b) a record of experimental data.

data acquisition and control system (DAC) — The system is designed to handle a wide variety of real-time applications, process control, and high-speed data acquisition. Each system is individually tailored with modular building blocks that are easily integrated to meet specific system requirements. A large family of real-time process input/output (i/o) devices is included, such as analog input, analog output, contact sense, and contact operate, as well as data processing i/o units, such as magnetic tape, disk storage, line printer, graph plotter, card, and paper tape input and output. Data are received and transmitted on either a high-speed cycle-steal basis or under program control, depending on the intrinsic data rate of the i/o device.

data acquisition, cycle-stealing — The display receives data and control words from the memory unit via the data-break channel. The data-break channel is a high-speed, direct-access channel that passes words to the program in execution.

data-acquisition system — A system designed to gather data from multiple remote locations at a certain computing facility.

data-adapter unit (communications) — The data-adapter unit greatly expands the input/output capabilities of the system. It provides direct connection of a variety of remote and local external devices to a system. These devices include the data-collection system, the data-communication system, process-communication system, telegraph terminals, telemetry terminals, and control and data-acquisition equipment.

data administrator — A high ranking member of management responsible for future information needs. The data administrator is not responsible for the design or maintenance of any particular data base, but is more concerned with the purity and quality as well as the value of the information as a corporate resource.

data, analog — The physical representation of information so that the representation bears an exact relationship to the original information. The electrical signals on a telephone channel are an analog-data representation of the original voice.

data array — A representation of data in the form of signs and symbols as recorded on tape, cards, etc.

data bank — A collection of data pertaining to a given subject or application. Many data banks are organized by and manipulated through data base management systems, but this is not necessarily the true use.

data base — A typical data base is a vast and continuously updated file of information, abstracts, or references on a particular subject or subjects. On-line data bases are designed so that by using subject headings, key words, key phrases, or authors, users can quickly and economically search for, sort, analyze and print out data on their terminal.

data base administrator — An individual who is in charge of controlling the content, design, and use of one or more data bases to avoid uncontrolled redundancies and to enhance development.

Programmers and analysts access this person to request new or different informational content in the data base. The data base administrator coordinates the needs and modifies the logical and/or physical structure of the data base to achieve the highest overall efficiency. This person reports to the data administrator who is responsible for all of the company's informational corporate resources.

data base components — The basic components to be dealt with include: data entities, data attributes, logical relationships, documentation, data modeling, data events and functions, access paths and response requirements, and administration analysis.

data base control — A data base is a multifile, logically unified data structure created, loaded and maintained by a data management system. A more specific and highly organized and defined structure than a data bank.

data base hierarchy — On some systems the hierarchy of data structures is divided into segments, records, fields, and so on. On one type the data structure consists of records divided into segments which are divided into fields. A unique alphanumeric name (symbolic name) is assigned to each field, and a field may be further subdivided by defining it more than once within a single file definition, e.g., 4-byte field can be divided into two 2-byte subfields, each with a different name. Each segment is assigned key items at the definition time, indicating those fields which define the segment to its parent segment, on these systems.

data base language — A typical data base language (DBL) is much like COBOL in that it is structured and higher level, but is designed for a multitasking interactive data base environment. One type of DBL is comprised of two sections: a variable section which defines task constants and working storage; and a procedure section with 88 instructions that cover the full range required for operation of a business system. These include normal procedure statement plus procedure control, program to program communication, and utilities.

data base management — A systematic approach to storing, updating, and retrieval of information stored as data items, usually in the form of records in a file, where many users, or even many remote installations, will use common data banks.

data base management and reporting, time sharing — *See* time sharing, data base management and reporting.

data base management system — A software product that controls a data structure containing interrelated data stored so as to optimize accessibility, control redundancy, and offer multiple views of the data to multiple application programs. Data base management systems also implement data independence to varying degrees. Utilities, multiprogramming capabilities and the sophistication of the data dictionary vary with different products and vendors.

data base storage structures, access — Storage structures include: direct, indirect, and those with symbolic pointers. Other types are flat, sorted, and chained files. Methods of access include: sequential (physical, logical, indexed), direct (random, indexed, inverted list, secondary index), and indirect (via parent, sibling, descendant).

data, biased — A distribution of records in a file which is nonrandom with respect to the sequencing or sorting criteria. Biased data affects sorting time, depending on the technique used during the first pass on the data.

data buffer — *Same as* buffer.

data buffer register — Refers to a temporary storage register in a CPU or a peripheral device capable of receiving or transmitting data at different i/o rates. Data buffer registers are most often positioned between the computer and slower system components, allowing data to flow at the computer's established input-output rate.

data bus components — A typical system data bus is composed of three signal buses. An example is a data bus that consists of 16 bidirectional data lines. The timing bus provides the basic system clocks as well as address and data strobes which indicate when data is valid on the bus. The control bus provides a priority system for bus access, signals to indicate whether the current transaction is a read or write from memory or a peripheral, an extended cycle signal, and a response line to indicate that a peripheral device has accepted an order sent over the system bus.

data capture, direct — A technique employed in cash registers or on sales slips whereby customer account numbers, the amount of the purchase, and other information are automatically recorded, read by an optical reading device, and sent to the computer to be processed. Its use permits the generation of more timely and accurate transaction data.

data capture, POS — A method employed by point-of-sales terminals whereby customer account numbers, the amount of the purchase, and other information are automatically recorded, and sent to the computer to be processed.

data capture, speech synthesis — Any method of using speech as a direct form of data input.

data carrier — The selected medium used to transport or carry (communicate) data or information. Punched cards, magnetic tapes, and punched paper tapes are examples. Most often data is easily transported independently of the devices used in reading or interpreting such data or information.

data cell — The smallest unit of data which cannot be further subdivided such as a magnetic bit.

data chaining — The gathering (or scattering) of information within one physical record, from (or to) more than one region of memory, by means of successive i/o commands.

data channel — The bidirectional data path between the i/o devices and the main memory in a digital computer that permits one or more i/o operations to happen concurrently with computation.

data channel multiplexer — The multiplexer option expands the data-break facilities of the computer to allow large numbers of input/output devices to transfer data directly with the main memory, via the memory buffer register. Simultaneous data-break requests are serviced by the multiplexer according to prewired priority.

data chip (microprocessor chip set) — The data chip, in some systems, contains the data paths, logic, arithmetic logic unit (ALU), processor status bits, and registers. On some systems, registers include general registers and an instruction register. The user's program has access to all registers and processor status (PS) bits. In some microprocessor chip sets, all instructions enter this chip via the bus. Data and addresses to and from this type microprocessor are also transferred to and from the processor over the bus.

data circuit, transmitted — Signals on this circuit are originated by the data terminal equipment for transmission on the data communication channel. This circuit is not required for receive-only service.

data-code conversion — The translation of alphanumeric data into a form acceptable to the computer. This is usually done by the computer itself during the input of the data.

data code, numeric — A digital code used to represent numerals and some special characters.

data collection — The act of bringing data from one or more points to a central point.

data collection and analysis — Process data are collected by the P-C (processor-controller) for mathematical analysis. Current performance figures are compared with those obtained in the past, and the results are printed for process analysis and management evaluation.

data collection, factory — *See* data collection stations.

data collection stations — Devices installed on production floors which allow a company to collect detailed data about the time employees have worked on each job, for payroll purposes. When an employee starts or stops work on a job, he punches in or out at the nearest data collection station. His employee number, the job number, and the time are recorded on a punched paper tape in the machine to form computer-readable records of employee time by job.

data-collection system — This system gathers manufacturing information from electronic in-plant reporting stations and transmits it directly to the computer. The information is processed as it is received. Reports can be produced which indicate, for example, job cost or machine utilization. Information can enter the processor in several ways, including punched card, plastic badge, keyboard, or data cartridge. The latter logs production data on a pocket-sized recording device that the employee maintains at his work station.

data communication — The transmission of the representation of information from one point to another.

data communications basic system types — Various different basic classes include: telephone line, satellite, packet switching, microwave, distributed data base, distributed processing, transaction driven, data staging, memory queuing/disk queuing, message switching, and others.

data communications buffer — Enables addressable hard copy printers to operate at different speeds independently of communications line speeds.

data communications control unit — The unit that scans the central terminal unit buffers for messages, and transfers them to the central processor.

data communications equipment — The data communication process generally requires at least five elements: a transmitter or source of information; a message; a binary serial interface; a communication channel or link; and a receiver of transmitted information. A data communications interface is often needed to make the binary serial data compatible with the communication channel.

data communications hardware/software — Basic hardware and software are the building blocks of data communications. Hardware elements (terminals, modems, multiplexers) are described in terms of their functions and how they relate to each other. Software is introduced in the process of defining codes, data and control characters, parity, baud rate, synchronous/asynchronous, digital/analog, half/full/duplex and other transmission concepts.

data communications protocol — A typical data communications protocol is an agreement between computers (or their peripherals) that establishes and terminates a connection; identifies the sending and receiving stations; assures message integrity; and accommodates text, programs, control characters and differentiates among the three.

data communications structure — A typical data-com system sets up according to three main hardware sections, each holding a pair of computers or terminals, one transmitting, the other receiving; binary serial interfaces, also called data-terminal equipment (DTE); data-com interfaces, also called data-circuit terminating equipment (DCE).

data-communication station — A data station is an all-purpose remote communication terminal which can be used for a broad range of applications involving direct, on-line data transmission to and from the company. Branch offices, warehouses, remote reporting locations throughout a plant, or any other company outpost can communicate directly with a centrally located computer via the data station. When not being used for actual on-line transmission (remote mode), the data station can be used offline (local mode) for activities such as data preparation and editing.

data compaction — A series of techniques used for the reduction of space, bandwidth, cost, transmission, generating time, and the storage of data. These techniques are designed for the elimination of repetition, removal of irrelevancies, and employment of special coding techniques.

data compression — *See* data compaction.

data concentration formatting — Formatting of data is an aspect of information concentration. ASCII formatting of raw data for remote transmission to a host is one example. The numerical data can be packed into four bits per digit (a nibble) and two digits per byte. With this type of packing, memory usage is very efficient. Systems that process hexadecimal information make extensive use of packed data formats. Typical applications for data concentration occur in line concentration for POS (point of sale) terminal devices, multiterminal key-to-tape and key-to-disk systems, and scientific data accumulators.

data concentrator — One type allows a single modem to support multiple remote devices. Combinations include hardcopy printer, video displays, TTY. Operating on a contention basis, i/o's are on a first-come or selective basis.

data concentrator, remote — In a representative network, the remote data concentrator (RDC) helps reduce line costs by accepting messages from many terminals via slow-speed lines and transmitting them to the host processor via a single high-speed synchronous line. Buffering of data from the low-speed lines smooths out communications to the host. In many cases traffic loads will necessitate several RDC-host lines.

data connector — A device which permits

connection of customer-owned modems or data sets to the regular telephone network. It limits the power applied to the line and provides network control and signaling functions.

data, control — The items of data which are used to identify, select, execute or modify another routine, record, file, operation or data value.

data delay — 1. The measured time concerned in the delay or waiting period for information before another process would be performed. 2. A delay attributable to some contingency within the data itself.

data description — An entry in the data division of a COBOL program describing the characteristics of a data item in terms of level, name, length, and alphanumeric content.

data description language — A language for describing the named data components of a data base and the relationships between the data components. The DDL also specifies the sorting and searching fields. A description written in the DDL is subsequently compiled into data base file structures which will accommodate the loading of data. The description of the data base that is successfully compiled and loaded with data becomes the operational data base scheme.

data descriptors — A data descriptor, as its name implies, describes data (i.e., a data area) by pointing to one or more contiguous data locations. Consequently, a particular data descriptor may be concerned with many memory locations. More than this, however, a data descriptor is also concerned with the presence, in core, of the data it describes. This is necessarily so particularly because of the data-overlay capabilities of the computer. A descriptor is concerned with many aspects of storage. These aspects are indicated by various bits in the descriptor.

data design — A particular layout or format of computer storage or machine storage allocation, i.e., for input and output. Often related to flowcharts and diagrams to define procedures and practices for problem solution.

data dictionary — A data dictionary is a repository of information about the definition, structure, and usage of data. It does not contain the actual data itself. In effect, the data dictionary contains the name of each data type (element), its definition (size and type), where and how it is used, and its relationship to other data.

data dictionary, integrated — This is a data dictionary that is functionally involved in accesses to the data base. Value limits and data types that are recorded in nonintegrated dictionaries require that programmers take the responsibility for coding the integrity checks into the applications programs. An integrated data dictionary performs the required checking automatically and disallows illegal modifications, thus functionally enforcing the data definitions it contains. This also increases the independence between the data and the software that manipulates it, thus lowering software maintenance costs and time.

data, digital — Information represented by a code consisting of a sequence of discrete elements, i.e., a zero or a one.

data division — A division of a COBOL program describing the characteristics of data (files, records, and data elements). Data division describes the data to be processed by the object program. It contains a file section which describes the files used. There may be a working storage section which allocates memory space for the storage of intermediate results.

data element — 1. A group of characters that specify an item at or near the basic level. An elementary item, e.g., "hour" —contains no subordinate item. A group item, e.g., "date," which consists of day, month, and year—contains items that may be used separately and therefore treated as elementary items. 2. A specific item of information appearing in a set of data; e.g., in the following set of data, each item is a data element: the quantity of a supply item issued, a unit rate, an amount, and the balance of stock items on hand. 3. The smallest unit of information to which reference is made, such as customer code, invoice number, unit price, etc.

data, end of — The signal that is read or generated when the final record of a file has been read or written.

data entry — The writing, reading, or posting to a coding form or to a terminal or processing medium, of information or instructions. A datum or item which is usually entered on one line, a single entity of processing.

data entry terminals — Usually data entry terminals are simple, single-function systems, often prepackaged and preprogrammed. They are easy to install but hard to tailor to a specific application, and difficult to upgrade. Data entry systems, on the other hand, are easy to upgrade because they usually support a comprehensive line of add-on memories, communications interfaces, i/o devices, and data storage peripherals.

data entry terminal system — Most data entry terminal systems use minicomputers and microcomputers and have the capability to accept data from a display terminal and either store it on a diskette or transmit it to the host computer. The host stores the messages or prints them directly on the printer. The micro or mini supports data storage and i/o peripherals so users can add terminals, mass storage, i/o devices and peripherals needed to do the job without converting application software

data error — A deviation from correctness in data, usually an error, which occurred prior to processing the data.

data evaluation — The examination and analysis of data to make an assessment of its inherent meaning, probable accuracy, relevancy, and relation to given situations or context.

data-exchange system — The fundamental operation of the data-exchange system is to accept data from a number of input channels, sort the data according to priority and destination, perform any necessary translation functions, and retransmit the data as output channels become available. Concurrently, the system may perform a variety of housekeeping chores, such as checking for errors, maintaining message logs or maps, and keeping track of the source and number of messages that flow through the system.

data field — An area located in the main memory which contains a data record.

data files — Aggregations of data sets for definite usage. The file may contain one or more different data sets. A permanent data file is one in which the data is perpetually subject to being updated, e.g., a name and address file. A working data file is a temporary accumulation of data sets which is destroyed after the data has been transferred to another form.

data files, working — *See* data files.

data flowchart — A flowchart showing the path of the data step by step in a problem solution or through a system.

data format — Rules and procedures that describe the way data is held in a file or record, whether in character form, as binary numbers, etc.

data-formatting statements — These statements instruct the assembly program to set up constants and reserved memory areas and to punctuate memory to indicate field boundaries.

data frames — Data frames are written on some tapes at a density of either 200 or 556 bits per inch. Data block length is not specified. When the end of a block is reached and no more data is transmitted, the tape comes to a stop. After the last block in the file (related group of blocks), the end-of file sentinel (tapemark) is written to indicate the termination of the file (some systems).

data gathering — *Same as* data collection.

data handling — 1. The production of records and reports. 2. The performance of those data-processing chores common to most users such as sorting, input-/output operation, and report generation.

data-handling system — 1. A system of automatic and semiautomatic devices used in the collection, transmission, reception, and storage of information in digital form. 2. A system in which data is sorted, decoded or stored in a particular form; related to data reduction.

data hierarchy — Structuring data into the subsets within a set, such as bit, byte, character, word, block, record, file, and bank.

data independence — A quality of a database environment that allows changing the logical or physical structure of a data base without changing the applications software that manipulates it. Data independence can be implemented on many levels. The physical implementation, arrangement and proximity of the data on storage media, may be changeable without altering the logical view expected by programs. Further independence is demonstrated by systems that allow the logical view of the data to be changed without requiring changes to programs that do not use that data.

data-initiated control — Jobs can be initiated and run automatically, according to preset rules, upon receipt of a signal or message from an external source using data. For example, in a teleprocessing application, jobs are performed upon receipt of messages from remote terminals. Data from a remote terminal can initiate loading of a program from the library; the program then processes the data and makes appropriate response to the originating terminal. Messages can be logged and queued on a secondary device, routed, and transmitted to other terminals. Inquiry by name, account number, or other key data can initiate a search of files stored in the system, find the requested information, and respond to the requester.

data input — 1. Any data upon which one or more of the basic processing functions are to be performed, such as coding, sorting, computing, summarizing, and reporting, recording, and communication. 2. Data ready for processing and on the input channel of an input device such as an optical reader, card reader, logic element or gate.

data input/output register, single-chip system — On some systems, the data input/output register is not accessible to the programmer. It is used for temporary storage of all input/output data received via or transmitted over the 8-bit bidirectional data bus during the data-transfer interval of each input/output cycle.

data input—voice answerback (DIVA) — A communications system in which a user sends input to a computer using a data terminal which may be a Touch-Tone telephone and receives a voice answerback (output) from the computer which may be either actual recorded or synthesized human voice.

data interchange code — A variation of the ASCII code, this is primarily different from ASCII in that some printing characters are replaced by nonprinting control characters, and the parity is specified to be odd. This code is now readily adaptable to computer-to-computer communications.

data in voice (DIV) — The type of transmission in which digital data displaces voice circuits in a microwave channel.

data item — Sometimes called a datum. A specific member of a data set denoted by a data element; for instance Monday, the name of a specific member of the set of the days of a week. The week is the data element, Monday the data item, and 05 could be the data code.

data layout — 1. A predetermined arrangement of characters, fields, lines, punctuation, page numbers, etc. 2. A defined arrangement of words, totals, characters, stubs, headings, etc., for a desired clear presentation of data or print-output, such as a financial record.

data level — A rank or reference number used to indicate to a compiling program the position of data in a particular hierarchy.

data link — Equipment which permits the transmission of information in data format.

data link control — A data link control (DLC), sometimes called line discipline or first level protocol, is a set of rules that are followed by interconnected computers or terminals in order to ensure the orderly transfer of information. The basic functions of a DLC are to:

1. Establish and terminate a connection between two stations.
2. Assure message integrity through error detection, requests for retransmission, and positive or negative acknowledgments.
3. Identify sender and receiver through polling or selection.
4. Handle special control functions such as requests for status, station reset, reset acknowledge, start, start acknowledge, and disconnect.

Higher level protocols are responsible for functions such as message buffering, code conversion, recognizing and reporting faulty conditions in terminals or lines, communication with the host mainframe, and management of the communication network.

data link control types — Data link control (DLC) can be classified into byte control protocols (BCPs) and bit oriented protocols (BOPs). In BCPs, a defined set of communication control characters effects the orderly operation of the data link. These control characters are part of an information code set, such as ASCII or EBCDIC. The code set also consists of graphic characters (alphanumeric, $, ., etc.) and peripheral device control characters (LF, CR, BS, etc.). BCP messages are transmitted in blocks which are composed of a header or control field, a body or text field, and trailer or error checking field.

data link, multipoint — For multipoint operation (often called multidrop), one station in the network is always designated as the control or primary station. The remaining stations are designated as tributary or secondary stations. The control station controls all transmissions within the multipoint data link, which is normally established over leased (nonswitched) lines. This is called a centralized multipoint operation. The control station initiates all transmissions by selecting or polling a secondary station. Any transmission over the data link is between the designated primary station and one of the secondary stations. The other stations in the network are in a passive monitoring mode. Multipoint channels may be full-duplex or half-duplex. Frequently, only a primary station on a multipoint channel will operate full-duplex while the secondary stations are half-duplex. This is known as multi-multipoint operation.

data link, switched network — On a switched network, the data link is disconnected after the two stations complete their transmissions. A new data link is created for each subsequent transmission by standard dialing procedures (manual or automatic). The new data link may be established with any other station in the network. Information flow is in one direction at a time (half-duplex) on the switched network.

data location — *See* location.

data logging equipment — Equipment ranging from the simple devices which provide only visual readout, to systems which include a microcomputer or minicomputer and all of their available peripherals. In general, the number of inputs which can be accommodated is independent of the complexity of the equipment: all equipment can handle any number of inputs desired. This excludes the large computer-based systems, since they are principally closed-loop process control systems, not data logging systems.

data, machine readable — Being able to be sensed or read by a specific device, i.e., information on tapes, cards, drums, disks, etc., that is capable of being read by a machine.

data management programming system — A system of programs designed to provide a human operator with the capability for querying, augmenting, and manipulating large computer-stored data bases in a natural language.

data manipulation — The performance of those data-processing chores common to most users, such as sorting, input-/output operations, and report generation.

data manipulation language (DML) — One type of DML is a language which the programmer uses to communicate between the application program and the data base. DML is not a complete language by itself, but relies on a host language to furnish a framework and to provide the procedural capabilities required to manipulate data in primary storage. Comprehensive safeguards and analytical capabilities within DML assure proper processing. Diagnostic messages indicate the successful execution of a function, or the status in the case of an unsuccessful execution. For example, DML will indicate that a duplicate record already exists if the user attempts to add such a duplicate record to the data base.

data, mass — An amount of data too great to store in the central processing unit (CPU) at any given time, usually stored in a mass data auxiliary unit.

data, master — A set of data which is altered infrequently and supplies basic data for processing operations. The data content of a master file. Examples include: names, badge numbers, or pay rate in personnel data, or stock numbers, stock descriptions, or units of measure in stock-control data.

datamation — A shortened term for automatic data processing; taken from data and automation.

data, mechanized — The device or material which is used to convey data to a sensing device or unit, i.e., punched cards, tapes.

data media — *See* continuous forms.

data medium — The selected medium used to transport or carry (communicate) data or information. Punched cards, magnetic tapes, and punched paper tapes—and lately portable disks —are examples, most often easily transported independently of the devices used in reading or interpreting such data or information.

data medium, automated — *See* data, machine readable.

data medium, parallel — A medium for recording or entering data and also an input/output medium for computers such as cards, tapes, paper, and disks.

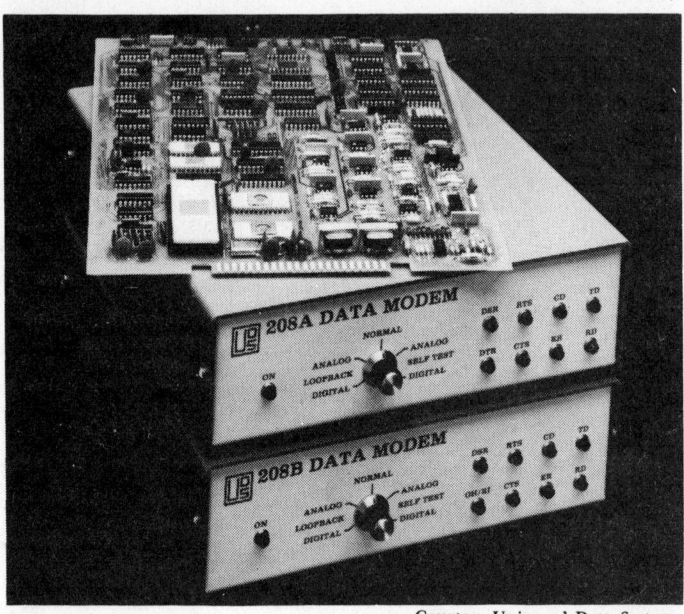

Courtesy Universal Data Systems

Data modem.

data modem — If users want to communicate over telephone lines, they will require modems. These are used to convert data from digital form into an analog form for transmission over the phone lines, and then to convert from transmission form at the other end back into digital data. Modems are available from low data rates of 110 baud (Teletype-compatible) up to 9600 baud and even higher. Rates above 2400 baud require special phone lines.

data movement instructions — Refers to the movement of bytes (or words) of data, such as: load from memory, store to memory, move register to register, push up stack, push down stack, exchange registers, etc.

data movement, microprocessor — In microprocessor-based systems, data movement is commonly an important aspect of system operation. As new applications evolve, users will be evaluating microprocessors with a critical eye toward i/o transfer. The number of instructions is less important than the nature of the instruction and usable addressing modes. How quick can the MPU respond to a peripheral interrupt and how is the interrupt managed? What is available from the vendor in the way of interface devices? The list of questions extends in proportion to the needs of the user.

data name — A single word or a group of words signifying an item of data; it may be a tag or a label.

data organization — Also known as dataset organization. Pertains to any one of the data management conventions for the spatial or physical arrangements of the records of a data set. The five data management organizing methods are sometimes defined as: 1. sequential, 2. partitioned, 3. indexed sequential, 4. direct, 5. telecommunications.

data origination — The act of creating a record in a machine-sensible form, directly or as a by-product of a human-readable document.

data output — Data obtained or obtainable from a device, such as a logic element, or the output channel of a logic element.

data path (microprocessor) — The data path is a transfer bus for input/output and data handling operations. Data path width is suggested by application where random logic suggests individual bit manipulation. Numeric operations such as calculators suggest a 4-bit width for BCD representation. Alphanumeric data handling suggests an 8-bit representation, and scientific processing suggests larger byte sizes.

dataphone — 1. A word used by A.T.&T. to designate any of a family of devices used to permit data communications over telephone channels. 2. A generic term to describe a family of devices to facilitate data communication.

dataphone digital service, DDS — A communications service of the Bell System in which data is transmitted in digital rather than analog form, thus eliminating the need for modems.

dataplotter — A dataplotter provides fast, accurate, automatic plotting of digital information in the form of points, lines, or symbols. Inputs may come from magnetic tape, punched card or tape, manual keyboard, or direct analog voltages.

data pointer — Refers to a specific register holding the memory address of the data (operand) to be used by the instruction. Thus, the register "points" to the memory location of the data.

data preparation — The process of converting data into a medium suitable for input to and processing by the computer.

data processing — 1. Any procedure for receiving information and producing a specific result. 2. Rearrangement and refinement of raw data into a form suitable for further use. 3. The preparation of source media which contain data or basic elements of information, and the handling of such data according to precise rules of procedure to accomplish such operations as classifying, sorting, calculating, summarizing, and recording. 4. The production of records and reports. (Synonymous with data handling.)

data-processing center — A grouping of automatic data-processing equipment and operating personnel in a separate area under the control of a single management group for the purpose of centralizing and controlling data-processing service for others, sometimes called customers, on a reimbursable or non-reimbursable basis.

data processing, centralized — The processing of all data involved with a given activity at a given location and usually in one building housing the equipment configuration.

data processing, decentralized — The housing of data by individual subdivisions of an organization or at each geographical location of the parts of an organization.

data processing graphic — A letter or other drawn, diagrammed (or an omission of such) character or figure which can be reproduced or transmitted in some way through an electronic data system, usually by an ordered set of pulses.

data processing, in-line — Data processing in which all changes to relevant records and accounts are made at the time that each transaction or event occurs.

data processing, integrated — The processing of data on an organized, systematic, and correlated basis throughout some area of interest as opposed to a series of disjointed operations.

data processing, low activity — The processing of a limited number of input transactions against very large master files.

data-processing machine — A general name for a machine that can store and process numeric and alphabetic information. (Related to analog computer, digital computer, and automatic data-processing equipment.)

data processing, non-numerical — Specific languages developed by symbol manipulation and used primarily as research tools rather than for production programming. Most have proved valuable in construction of compilers and in simulation of human problem solving. Other uses have been generalized and verification of mathematical proofs, pattern recognition, information retrieval, algebraic manipulation, heuristic programming, and exploration of new programming languages.

data processing, on-line — *See* on-line processing.

data processing, scientific — The processing of data involved with solving mathematical functions or equations.

data processing, specialized — Various types of automatic data processing have become distinct enough to be designated by proper names. Among these are: business data processing, automated production management, administrative data processing, and others.

data-processing system — A network of machine components capable of accepting information, processing it according to a plan, and producing the desired results.

data processor — 1. A device capable of performing operations on data, such as a digital computer, analog computer, or a desk calculator. 2. A person processing data. 3. A standardized term representing any and all devices which have the capability of performing the reduction, summarizing, processing, or input and output of data or information, and including calculators, punched card equipment, computers, and subsidiary systems.

data protection, printing — Operation of the printers is checked automatically to ensure that they respond correctly to control-unit printing signals. If this check fails, an indicator, which can be tested by a programmed instruction, is automatically set.

data purification — The reduction of the number of errors as much as possible prior to using data in an automatic data processing system.

data, raw — Data that have not been processed. Such data may or may not be in machine-sensible form.

data record — A record containing data to be processed by a program.

data reduction — The art or process of transforming masses of raw test or experimentally obtained data, usually gathered by instrumentation, into useful, ordered, or simplified intelligence.

data reduction, on-line — The processing of information as rapidly as the information is received by the computing system, or as rapidly as it is generated by the source.

data reduction, real-time — The reduction of data as speedily as it is received at the processor or computer, or as rapidly as it is generated by the source, if the transmission time is not overbearing. The computer must process (reduce) immediately since by storing and then reducing, operations would be on-line but not real-time.

data register, input/output — On some low-cost systems, during an input cycle, this register receives information from the data bus; during an output cycle, contents of the register are transferred onto the data bus.

data registers — Special registers provided in many microprocessor CPUs for the temporary storage of data. These CPU registers may also often be used when performing simple data manipulating operations, such as incrementing or decrementing the value of a number.

data reliability — A ratio that relates the extent to which data meets a specific or given standard, usually concerning the accuracy of data, or the degree to which data is error free. Other examples relate to the probabilities of the correctness of data, i.e., the degree to which data is unchanged after transmission or recording operations.

data retrieval — The retrieval or return of data by selecting, searching, or retransmission of information from a file, data bank, or storage device.

data rules — The unique group of conditions surrounding data elements, sets, and files, and the action to be taken when the conditions are satisfied. The rules are usually expressed in tabular form, rather than narrative, to ensure complete, consistent, and accurate documentation of the processing methodology, and at the same time to provide flexibility for change.

data select — A special selection operation in which one set of items is taken for printing or punching from several sets presented on tape.

data selection and modification — By using the light pen in conjunction with incremental display, data of interest stored in the computer memory may be easily selected and modified. Pointing the light pen at a selected displayed point causes the pen to signal the computer. The computer program may then operate on the data selected in a manner previously determined, or under the immediate control of the user, via switch inputs on the console.

data set — A collection of similar and related data records that is recorded for use by a computer. A recordable medium such as a data file.

data set clocking — A time base oscillator supplied by the data set for regulating the bit rate of transmission. This is referred to by IBM as external clocking.

data set (communications) — Usually, a device that is capable of performing modulation/demodulation and control functions designed to provide compatability between various business machines and communication lines for information transmission.

data set, concatenated — A data set temporarily formed by uniting the data contained in several sets in a specific sequence.

data-set control block (DSCB) — A standard-format control block specifying the parameter, for one data set, needed to describe and manipulate the data set in a direct-access device.

data set, indexed sequential — A particular data set organization which combines the efficiency of sequential organization with the ability to rapidly access records out of sequence but used only on direct-access devices.

data set (modem) — A modem is a device that converts digital data from a computer or terminal to a modulated carrier waveform required by the communication channel. There is one modem at each end of the channel. Modems are also known as data sets and are designed for specific kinds of service and for specific bandwidths or data rates.

data set, partitioned — When a single data set is divided internally into a directory and when one or more sequentially organized subsections (members) reside on a direct access basis for each device, a partitioned data set is developed and is most commonly used for storage or for program libraries. Each member of any individual partitioned data set has the same record format and organization, but the internal structure may differ from one partitioned data set to another.

data sets — Unique combinations or aggregations of data elements. Examples are the sales order, accounts-receivable ledger card, sales summary report, payroll register, etc. It should be noted that a data set is a potential combination of data elements. Not all data elements need be present at one time. For example, a payroll-register entry for a given employee may contain only one or two of several possible deductions.

data set, telephone line — A standard telephone data set. For example, Model 202D dataphone is often used at each end of the telephone line. In each office the data set connects the remote terminal unit to the telephone line and converts that unit's signal into "tones" for transmission over the line. Conversely, the data set converts "tones" received over the line from the processing center into signals for the remote terminal unit. At the processing center, other data sets perform the same conversions for the central terminal unit.

data signaling rate — Used in communications to define the rate at which signal elements (containing one or more bits) are transmitted or received over a transmission path by a data terminal equipment. The data signaling rate is expressed in bits per second and baud; however, bps is the most common usage.

data sink — Relating to a data transmission system, data sink often refers to equipment which accepts data.

data, source — 1. Data created by the individual or organization generating or originating the data. 2. The data transmission equipment supplying the data.

data stations, remote — *See* remote data stations.

data stream — Generally all data transmitted through a channel in a single read or write operation.

data structures, data base — Full consideration of appropriate data structures is inherent to the design of any system which must function under the severe constraints of the microcomputing environment. Data structures appropriate for the microprocessor must afford the power of some rather exotic data structures while preserving valuable computer resources. The suitable data structure can only be identified after extensive study of the available resources. Obviously, RAM must be considered at a premium. The lack of this resource limits filesize, record length, program capabilities, and proper documentation. The asset readily accessible to the analyst is the processor itself. Although the processor is one of the least expensive features of the machine, the analyst can completely dedicate the processor to this function alone, facts that time sharing and multiprogramming systems cannot boast.

data switching — A location where an incoming message is automatically or manually directed to one or more outgoing circuits, according to the intelligence contained in the message.

data switching center — *See* switching center.

data switching center, automatic — *See* switching center.

data systems, communications — *See* communication data systems.

phone circuit permitting the transmission of digital data.

data terminal — 1. A device which modulates and/or demodulates data between one input/output device and a data-transmission link. 2. Various typewriter, audio, or visual devices for inputting or receiving output of computers.

data terminal equipment (DTE) — Equipment comprising the data source, the data sink, or both that provides for the communication control function (protocol). Data terminal equipment is actually any piece of equipment at which a communications path begins or ends.

data terminal, multiplex — A unique data transmission device which modulates and demodulates, encodes and decodes, between two or more input/output devices and data transmission stations.

Courtesy Talos Systems, Inc.

Data tablet.

data tablet — The data tablet is a graphical input device that enables the entry of visual images into a computer. Just as a keyboard enters alphanumeric characters (the elements of text), so a data tablet enters lines and points (the elements of images). Data tablets are now commercially available for personal computer systems (among others). In using a data tablet, a pen-shaped stylus is moved over a flat electromagnetically sensitive board. The position of the pen over the board is monitored by a controller which relays information to a computer. In this way it is possible to "draw" images directly into memory.

data telephone circuit — A specific tele-

data terminal ready — Refers to an EIA RS-232-C designation applied to a control circuit used by a terminal or computer to tell its modem that the terminal or computer is ready for operation. In some applications this circuit is used to enable the modem to answer or terminate calls.

data, test — A set of data developed specifically to test the adequacy of a computer run or system. The data may be actual data that have been taken from previous operations, or artificial data created for this purpose.

data time — The unit of time necessary to fulfill a single instruction.

data, transaction — A set of data in a data-processing area, a record of occurrence of a new event or transaction, in which the incidence of the data is essentially random and unpredictable. Hours worked, quantities shipped, and amounts invoiced are examples from, respectively, the areas of payroll, accounts receivable, and accounts payable.

data transfer — There are generally three types of data transfer: programmed data transfers; program interrupt transfers; and direct memory access transfers. Programmed data transfer is the easiest and most direct method of handling data i/o. Program interrupt transfers provide an extension of programmed i/o capabilities by allowing the peripheral device to initiate a data transfer. The data break system uses direct memory access for applications involving the fastest data transfer rates.

data transfer control — Generally, data transfers are controlled by three elements: control information; formatting; and handshaking procedures. Formatting concerns reserving positions, or fields, in the transmission block for specific information. Control data and transfer error checking data must be included in the transmission block. These are usually called the header, body, and trailer of a block.

data transfer, programmed — Normally, data are transferred between the computer accumulator and an external device under program control. An input bus allows each device to clear the computer accumulator before transferring data into it.

data transfer rate — A particular rate at which data is transmitted through a channel, but measured during the time data is actually being transmitted, i.e., tape transfer rates are measured in terms of characters per second, discounting gaps between blocks, words, etc.

data transfer rate, average — A particular rate of data transmission through a channel over a relatively long period of time to include gaps between blocks, words, or records. Also included in this time are regeneration time and other items not subject to program control. Starting, stopping, rewinding, searching, or other programmed control items are not included.

data transfer rate, effective — *Same as* data transfer rate, average.

data transfer register — The temporary storage device which eases the communication or movement of data within the computer.

data transfer sequence, single chip system — On some systems, data transfers to and from the microprocessor need not be synchronous, or slaved to a particular timing sequence; devices with widely different data rates and all using common system buses can be serviced by the processor. A data transfer between the microprocessor and memory peripherals is a simple and straightforward process.

data transmission — The sending of data from one part of a system to another part.

data transmission bauds — The measure of the speed of a transmission. A baud is equal to one signal element per second.

data-transmission equipment — The communications equipment that is used in direct support of data-processing equipment.

data transmission, synchronous — In this type of data transmission, each character consists of 5, 6, 7, or 8 information bits depending on the code structure. There are no start and stop bits. Timing is derived through synchronizing characters at the beginning of each message or block of data.

data transmission system — A series of circuits, modems, or other devices which transfer or translate information from one site or location to another.

data-transmission trap — Usually a conditional (unprogrammed) jump to a specific location activated automatically to provide communication or signals between specific input/output routines and the related programs.

data-transmission utilization measure — The ratio of useful data output of a data transmission system, to the total data input.

data transmission video display units — Any type of input/output equipment with a special feature of displaying information on a screen, usually a cathode-ray tube.

data under voice (DUV) — A transmission system which carries digital data on a portion of the microwave radio spectrum below the frequency used for voice transmission.

data unit — A set of one or more related characters which is treated as a whole. Often used in place of field to specify a particular unit of information.

data use identifier — A title or name for the use of the data items for a data element; for instance, an occurrence date such as the employment date of an employee that is used for data base information.

data validation — Some data entry systems have extensive arrays of data validation and error checking features. An attempt to enter incorrect data is caught on a field-by-field basis before it gets into the computer system. When an incorrect character is detected, the entry is disallowed, the cursor remains in the field, and an audible "beep" indicates the identified error. The operator merely keys in the correct character to continue.

data validity — A relation or measure of verifiability of data, i.e., the results of specific tests performed on the data such as the forbidden code check. Such tests and checks verify the reliability of the data and thus its validity or degree of acceptability.

data word — A word which may be primarily regarded as part of the information manipulated by a given program. A data word may be used to modify a program instruction, or to be arithmetically combined with other data words. A data word often consists of 36 bits (or six 6-bit characters). Data is transferred on a word basis, 36 bits in parallel (some computers).

data word size — The specific length of data word a particular microprocessor is designed to handle. Thus, the term 2-, 4-, 8-, or 16-bit microprocessor refers to data word length. The length of a data word affects the performance capabilities of the micprocessor. Generally, the longer the word length, the higher the data throughput, the greater the precision for arithmetic operation and the greater memory addressing capability.

date, delivery — The date of physical delivery, on-site, of the components of the computer configuration without regard to whether or not they have been unpacked, placed in final position, or interconnected. Delivery of equipment carries no connotation of operational status.

date, installation — The date new equipment is ready for use. The commencement of rental normally begins on the day following the date on which the contractor officially notifies the using organization that the equipment is installed and ready for use, subject to the acceptance and standard of performance provisions of the applicable contract.

dating routine — A routine which computes and/or stores, where needed, a date such as current day's date, expiration date of a tape, etc.

dating subroutine — *See* subroutine, dating.

datum — Signifies a single computer word or unit of information.

daughter card — Card or board interfaced with a motherboard or backplane of a computer system.

DBDC — Abbreviation for Data Base/Data Communications.

DBMS — Abbreviation for Data Base Management System. A DBMS is often primary control software used in manipulating information files. DBMS data dictionaries are now becoming widely available as primary tools for better data management. They can be used with or without DBMS, as the two package types are complementary, not mutually exclusive.

DBMS, CODASYL standard — Some DBMS conform to the CODASYL standard. CODASYL's specifications, formulated over a 10-year period, represent the result of a comprehensive research program by a prominent group of computer users and manufacturers. Based on real-life data processing experiences, the CODASYL standards have become the accepted language tools for the efficient management of complex data bases. DBMS is the first minicomputer data-base management system that conforms to CODASYL standards.

DBOS — Abbreviation for disk-based operating system.

D-bus — Internal designation bus in a microprocessor CPU, from the ALU to its registers.

dc coupled — The connection by a device which passes the steady state characteristics of a signal and which largely eliminates the transient or oscillating characteristics of the signal.

dc dump — 1. The intentional, accidental, or conditional removal of all direct-current power from a system or component. 2. The condition that results when direct-current power is withdrawn from a computer using volatile storage.

dc erasing head — A device which causes the removal of magnetic bits from magnetic tape by the use of a magnetic field developed from a direct current.

d-character — A specific character which is used to modify the operations code in some equipment.

dc signaling — A transmission method which utilizes direct current.

DD — Abbreviation for delay driver, digital data, digital display, decimal display, data demand.

DDA — Abbreviation for digital differential analyzer and digital display alarm.

DDC — Abbreviation for direct digital control.

DDCE — Abbreviation for digital data conversion equipment.

DDCMP — Abbreviation for digital data communication message protocol. A uniform discipline for the transmission of data between stations in a point-to-point or multipoint data communication system. This protocol governs parallel, serial-synchronous, or serial-asynchronous data transmission and receipt.

DDG — Abbreviation for digital display generator.

DDGE — Abbreviation for digital display makeup (U.S. Air Force).

DDL — Abbreviation for Data Description Language.

DDP — An abbreviation for digital data processor.

DDS — 1. Abbreviation for Digital Display Scope. 2. Abbreviation for Dataphone Digital Service.

DDT — *See* debugging package.

dead band — A specific range of values in which the incoming signal can be altered, without also changing the outgoing response. (Synonymous with dead space, dead zone, switching blank, and similar to neutral zone.)

dead file — A file that is not in current use but is retained.

dead halt — *See* halt, dead.

dead space — *Same as* dead band.

dead time — 1. Any definite delay deliberately placed between two related actions in order to avoid overlap that might cause confusion or to permit a particular different event, such as a control decision, switching event, or similar action, to take place. 2. The delay between two related actions, measured in units of time for efficiency study.

dead zone — The specific area in various types of storage media which is not reserved for data store. An example is the space between the bit sites on magnetic tapes.

debatable time — When there is no proof as to what difficulty has caused a delay, such time is labeled debatable time, and a search for evidence ensues to determine if a program mistake, operating mistake, or perhaps a transient fault has occurred.

deblocking — A procedure for reducing a data block into its component records for further processing.

debug — 1. To locate and correct any errors in a computer program. 2. To detect and correct malfunctions in the computer itself. (Related to diagnostic routine.) 3. To test a program on a computer to find whether it works properly. If mistakes are revealed, they must be traced to their source and corrected.

debugger, interpretive (IDB) — A typical IDB is a very sophisticated set of routines which are ideal for debugging assembly language programs. IDB allows the programmer to load and dump programs from cassette or disk, to display large blocks of memory, to examine memory locations in several display formats, to modify memory locations, to single step programs, to set breakpoints which execute on the nth pass, and many more.

debuggers — Debuggers let users examine and change memory content, and start or stop execution at a predetermined location or condition (breakpoint). Other debugging aids include trace and flow checks, which tell when certain address contents (variables) change and how control is transferred within the program.

debugger, simulation — A debugger that uses simulation to run on one machine and facilitate the debugging of a program written to run on another machine.

debugging — The process of isolating and correcting all malfunctions and/or mistakes in a piece of equipment or a program of operations.

debugging-aid routine — A routine to aid programmers in the debugging of their routines. Some typical routines are: storage, print-out, tape print-out, and drum print-out.

debugging aids — A set of routines to aid the programmer in checking out a particular program by furnishing him with the contents of selected areas of memory.

debugging aids, reference — A set of routines which provides a means of utilizing the computer to assist the programmer in debugging his programs. Among the routines included are the following: (a) changed-word post mortem, a routine to compare the contents of program or data areas with a selected image area; (b) address reference search, a routine to detect all words in the computer memory which reference a particular address; (c) dump selected memory area, a routine to provide the contents of all locations within a specified memory area.

debugging, console — The programmer may debug at the machine console or at a remote console by slowly stepping the machine through each instruction and observing the contents of appropriate registers and memory locations.

debugging examples — Various debugging statements are often extensions to many programming languages, options to compilers or interpreters that facilitate detection of program errors at run time. Some types are: identifier cross-reference printouts, trace printings of variable value changes, traces of flow of execution logic from routine to routine, alter or no op statements, and others.

debugging, program — This process is mainly one of making corrections to the program. It is followed by documentation, (which is really a continuing process). The programmer must keep precise records of the entire programming procedure; documentation includes a brief description of the problem, the program, its results, and the process which was used to obtain them.

debugging, remote — The use of remote terminals in a mode suitable for testing of programs, most frequently found in systems devoted to scientific or engineering computation.

debugging, snapshot — A type of diagnostics and debugging technique in which the programmer specifies the start and end of program segments where he wishes to examine the contents of various registers and accumulators. The snapshot tracing may indicate the contents not only of the various accumulators and registers but also of specified memory locations.

debugging, source-language — Debugging information is requested by the user and displayed by the system in a form consistent with the source programming language.

debugging statements — The operating statements provide a wide and flexible variety of methods for manipulating the program itself. The user may: (a) insert or delete statements; (b) execute selectivity; (c) print changes of values as the change occurs and transfer control as the transfer occurs; (d) obtain a static printout of all cross-reference relationships among names and labels, and dynamic exposure of impartial or imperfect execution.

debugging, symbolic — Symbolic commands or macroinstruments are utilized to assist in the debugging procedure.

debug, line monitoring — Refers to use of a line monitor for system debugging, startup and troubleshooting, and so on. It allows for the terminal to be placed into a full-duplex mode in which the traffic of all terminals in the chain may be monitored.

debug macroinstruction — A macroinstruction which generates a debugging or program testing capability within a particular program.

debug macros — Aids built into a program by the applications programmer, in addition to those supplied by the supervisory program. Debugging macros are a type of unit testing.

debug module, development system — A major feature of some development systems is the debug module that allows selected user mode system transactions to be stored in real-time into a special memory. The user can also specify that various types of system transactions can suspend user operation or cause a system to re-enter the monitor mode. A complete record of hundreds of transactions that were recorded in the independent memory just prior to suspension can be conveniently displayed on the system terminal or printed on a line printer.

debug monitor — Refers to a resident debug routine that provides real time breakpoint capabilities specifically for examining and altering memory locations and system status variables. Generally it contains the necessary linking points used to allow the user programs to call the monitor (operating system) routines.

debug on-line — Same as debug, except the computer is performing on-line functions, utilizing another routine which has previously been checked out.

debug program — A debug program provides the programmer with an on-line conversational utility for use in a program debugging operation and offers a wide variety of inspection and control. The commands include memory search/inspect/modify and memory print; memory and/or register initialization; memory to memory copy of specific regions.

debug program patches — Refers to the various debug programs that assist the programmer to find errors in his or her programs while they are running on the system, and allow him or her to replace or patch instructions into (or out of) his or her program.

debug program, single chip systems — On some systems debug programs supervise the operation of a user program during checkout. These types of programs provide the following facilities for testing computer programs: printing selected areas of memory in hexadecimal format, modifying the contents of selected areas in memory, displaying and modifying CPU registers, inserting instruction breakpoint halts, and initiating execution at any point in a program.

debug software packages, development system — The debug software package on some systems allows the user to specify the type of transactions that are to be stored in the memory. The last bit is used as a marker to identify the first transaction that is stored when the user's program begins execution. Any combinations of the following transactions on some systems can be stored: memory reads, memory writes, i/o port reads, i/o port writes.

decade — A group or assembly of ten units, e.g., a counter which counts to ten in one column, or a resistor box which inserts resistance quantities in multiples of powers of 10.

decade counter — *See* counter, decade.

deceleration time — The time which elapses between completion of reading or writing of a tape record, and the time when the tape stops moving. (Synonymous with stop time.)

decentralized data processing — *See* data processing, decentralized.

deciding — An operation whose function is to accept or reject certain items of information. One input is the information, while the other is a fixed reference. The two inputs are combined by the appropriate logical rule to give the output.

decimal — 1. Pertaining to a characteristic or property involving a selection, choice, or condition in which there are ten possibilities. 2. Pertaining to the number-representation system with a radix of ten.

decimal, binary-coded — *See* binary coded decimal.

decimal, binary-coded representation — *See* binary-coded decimal representation.

decimal, coded — Describing a form of notation by which each decimal digit is separately expressed in some other number system; e.g., in the 8–4–2–1 coded-decimal notation, the number twelve is represented as 0001 0010, for 1 and 2; whereas in pure or straight binary notation it is represented as 1100. Other coded decimal notations used are the 5–4–2–1, the excess three, and the 2–3–2–1 codes.

decimal-coded digit — A digit or character defined by a set of decimal digits, such as a pair of decimal digits specifying a letter or special character in a system of notation.

decimal digit — *See* digit, decimal.

decimal notation — *See* number, decimal.

decimal number — *See* number, decimal.

decimal numbering system — A system of reckoning by 10 or the powers of 10 using the digits 0 through 9 to express numerical quantities.

decimal, packed — The storage of two digits in an area which usually stores an alphabetic letter or special character.

decimal point — That base point (radix 10) in decimal numbers which separates integers from fractional values; i.e., values to the left of the point are positive powers of 10, while values to the right of the point are negative powers of 10.

decimal point, actual — A decimal point for "display" purposes; e.g., when a numeric value is listed on a printed report, the decimal point will often appear as an actual printed character. When specified for data to be used within a computer, it requires an actual space in storage.

decimal point, assumed — The point within a numeric item at which the decimal point is assumed to be located. When a numeric item is to be used within a computer, the location of the assumed decimal point is considered to be at the right unless otherwise specified in the appropriate record-description entry. It will not occupy an actual space in storage, but it will be used by the computer to align the value properly for calculation.

decimal-to-binary conversion — The process of converting a number written to the base of ten, or decimal, into the equivalent number written to the base of two, or binary.

decision — The computer operation of determining if a certain relationship exists between words in storage or registers, and taking alternative courses of action. This is effected by conditional jumps or equivalent techniques. Use of this term has given rise to the misnomer "magic brain"; actually, the process consists of making comparisons, by use of arithmetic, to determine the relationship of two terms (numeric, alphabetic or a combination of both), e.g., equal, greater than, or less than.

decision box — The symbol used in flowcharting to indicate a choice or branching in the information-processing path.

decision element — A circuit that performs a logical operation on one or more binary digits of input information (represent "yes" or "no") and expresses the result in its output.

decision gates — A circuit having two or more inputs and one output. The output depends upon the combination of logic signals at the input.

decision instruction — *See* branch.

decision, logic — *See* logic decision.

decision, logical — The choice or ability to choose between alternatives. Basically, this amounts to an ability to answer yes or no with respect to certain fundamental questions involving equality and relative magnitude; e.g., in an inventory application, it is necessary to determine whether or not there has been an issue of a given stock item.

decision-making (game theory) — Game theory is a mathematical theory dealing with decision-making in a competitive situation in which both parties are active and have an effect on the final outcome. The object is to arrive at an optimal course of action by consideration of all possible moves and chance happenings.

decision-making system — One of the basic uses of an on-line, real-time system is to find an optimum answer to every demand according to decision rules which have been previously established, or according to a simulation model.

decision mechanism — The component part of a character reader, in character recognition, that receives the finalized version of the input character and makes a determination as to its probable identity.

decision plan — A system or procedure used for making managerial decisions, i.e., rules either prepared in advance of specific events or developed at the time or on the scene and applied by men, machines, or combinations of these. Such plans include the exception principle, internal decision-making procedures, manual interrupt and intervention, variable or stochastic processing, and various adaptive and heuristic plans.

decision rules — The programmed criteria which an on-line, real-time system uses to make operating decisions. It is important to periodically review the decision rules which are being used by a system, because the nature of the problems to be solved changes over time and because new situations may have arisen which were not at first anticipated.

decision table — *See* table, decision.

deck — A collection of cards, commonly a complete set of cards which have been punched for a definite service or purpose.

deck, tape — The device or mechanism which is designed to control the movement of tape.

declaration — A declaration is represented by one or more instructions which specify the type, characteristics, or amount of data associated with identifiers.

declarative operation — 1. Coding sequence consisting of a symbolic label, a declarative operation code, and an operand. It involves writing symbolic labels and operation codes for data and constants. 2. The process or procedures which provide the object program with various input, output, work ideas, and other constants which may be designed or required.

declaratives — Statements made to a symbolic processor to control the specifics of an assembly.

declarative statement — Instructions in symbolic coding, or systems used to define and designate areas, constants, and symbols.

decode — 1. To apply a code so as to reverse some previous encoding. 2. To determine the meaning of individual characters or groups of characters in a message. 3. To determine the meaning of an instruction from the set of pulses which describes the instruction, command, or operation to be performed. 4. To translate coded characters to a more understandable form.

decoded operations — *See* decoding.

decoder — 1. A device that determines the meaning of a set of signals and initiates a computer operation based thereon. 2. A matrix of switching elements that selects one or more output channels according to the combination of input signals present. (Contrasted with encoder, and clarified by matrix.)

decoder, command — The command decoder preprocesses commands from the user-console. This program is used to convert parameters, etc., before the command is sent to the program for which the command is intended.

decoder, operation — A decoder used to examine and interpret the part of the instruction word specifying the operation to be performed and which sends signals to the circuitry executing the specified operation.

decoding — 1. Performing the internal operations by which a computer determines the meaning of the operation code of an instruction; also sometimes applied to addresses. 2. In interpretive routines and some subroutines, an operation by which a computer determines the meaning of parameters in the routine. 3. Translating a secretive language into the clear.

decollate — The act of separating the parts of a multipart form and the removal of the carbons to then disperse cards or other information or data.

decollator — A device which combines the removal of carbon paper and separation of various copies of a standard multipart continuous form.

decrement — 1. The quantity by which a variable is decreased. 2. A specific part of an instruction word in some binary computers; thus, a set of digits.

decrement field — A portion of an instruction word set aside specifically for modifying the contents of a register or storage location.

decryption — A procedure for the interpretation or deciphering of coded data.

dedicated — 1. Generally refers to machines, programs, or procedures that are designed or set apart for special or continued use. For example, a dedicated microprocessor can be one that has been designed or specifically programmed for a single or special group of applications, such as computerized games, appliances, traffic lights, calculators, etc. ROMs, as control devices, are usually the means of developing dedicated microprocessors. 2. Synonymous with leased or private lines or machines usually referring to communications equipment.

dedicated channel — A specific channel that has been reserved or committed or set aside for a very specific use or application.

dedicated storage — *See* storage, dedicated.

dedicated trap cells — *See* trap, dedicated cells.

deferred addressing — *See* addressing, deferred.

deferred entry/deferred exit — An asynchronous event causes the deferred entry by passing the central processing unit control to a subroutine or to an entry point. This transfer causes a deferred exit from the program having control previously.

deferred processing — Processing which can be delayed or is considered low priority, and is completed when computer time is at nonpeak periods.

define — To establish a value for a variable or symbol or to establish what the variable represents.

definition — 1. The resolution and sharpness of an image, or the extent to which an image is brought into sharp relief. 2. The degree with which a communication system reproduces sound images or messages.

definition, index — The number of times a loop operation is to be repeated. This FORTRAN specification can appear in either do, read, or write statements. It is specified by the starting value, the limit value, and the incremental value.

definition, problem — The art of compiling logic in the form of general flowcharts and logic diagrams which clearly explain and present the problem to the programmer in such a way that all requirements involved in the run are presented.

definition, recursive — A definition which defines something partly in terms of itself.

degradation — A special condition when the system continues to operate but at reduced levels of service. Such circumstances are usually caused by unavailability of various equipment units or subsystems.

degradation, graceful — *See* fail softly.

degradation testing — Measurement of performance of a system at the extreme operating limits. Tests are performed to determine the gradual changes in performance characteristics.

degree of multiprogramming — Refers to the number of transactions handled in parallel by the systems involved in a multiprogram.

delay — 1. The length of time after the close of a reporting period before information pertaining to that period becomes available. Delay may also cover the time to process data, and to prepare and distribute reports. 2. The retardation of the flow of information in a channel for a definite period of time.

delay coding, minimum — *Same as* programming, minimum access.

delay counter — In the control unit of some computers, a counter that can temporarily delay a program long enough for the completion of an operation.

delay, data — *See* data delay.

delay differential — The difference between the maximum and the minimum frequency delays occurring across a band.

delay digit — A logic element which delays its input signal by one digit period.

delay distortion — Also termed envelope delay or phase delay. Distortion resulting from nonuniform speed of transmission of the various frequency components of a signal through a transmission medium.

delayed-output equipment — Equipment which removes the data from the system after processing has been completed or while in process, but which holds it for further instructions or later use.

delay element — The circuitry or electronic mechanism which accepts data temporarily, and emits the same data after a specific interval.

delay, envelope — Characteristics of a circuit which result in some frequencies arriving ahead of the others even though they were transmitted together.

delay, external — Computer down time attributable to circumstances not the fault of the computer system, and beyond the reasonable control of the system operator or maintenance engineer. An example of an external delay would be a failure of the electrical power to the building.

delay line — A device capable of retarding a pulse of energy between input and output, based on the properties of materials, circuit parameters, or mechanical devices. Examples of delay lines are material media such as mercury, in which sonic patterns may be propagated in time; lumped-constant electrical lines; coaxial cables; transmission lines; and recirculating magnetic-drum loops.

delay line register — *See* register, delay line.

delay-line storage — A storage technique in which data is stored by allowing it to travel through some medium such as mercury.

delay loop stores — A method of storing information by transmitting bits or no bits serially through a loop.

delay, operating — During repair time to discover suspected faults, if the investigation shows the equipment to be free of faults, the time lost should count as an operating delay.

delay register line — *See* register delay line.

delay time — The amount of elapsed time between the end of one event and the beginning of the next sequential event.

deleave — 1. The reversing of the collation operation by separating the members of a collated sequence and obtaining a dispersal. 2. Separating the files of a multipart form.

delete — To remove or eliminate, e.g., to remove a record from a master file.

deleted representation — Similar to an erase character, i.e., a particular representation to which any other representation can be converted by further operation or recording. In paper tape, which does not lend itself to erasure or deletions, deleted representation consists of a code hole in all of the code positions. Often called null representation. In graphics, the absence of information can be deleted representation.

deletion record — A record, which, when matched with a master file, results in one or more corresponding records being deleted from the master file.

delimit — To fix the limits of; to bound.

delimiter — A character that limits a string of characters, and therefore cannot be a member of the string.

delta — The difference between a partial-select output of a magnetic core in a 1 state, and a partial-select output of the same core in a 0 state.

delta noise — The difference between the 1-state and the 0-state half-selected noise.

demand — An input/output coding technique in which a read or write order is initiated as the need to read a new block or write a new block of data occurs. Operations do not take place in parallel.

demand fetching — A memory multiplexing design in which segments are kept on a backing storage and only placed in an internal storage when computations refer to them.

demand paging — Generally, demand paging allows a program's required memory area to be noncontiguous and partially nonresident—which permits the maximum utilization of the system's total available memory. Additionally, demand paging permits the computer system to execute programs that are larger than the allocated physical main memory within the processor.

demand paging scheme — An operating system memory management scheme that allows memory to be broken into pages which can be swapped to a high speed disk when more memory is needed. When the nonresident data or code is referenced, a page fault occurs.

demand processing — *See* processing, demand.

demand processing time sharing — *See* time sharing, demand processing.

demand staging — The act of moving data from disk to main memory when requested by an applications program and not before, as opposed to anticipatory staging.

demodulation — A procedure for retrieving original signals from modulated carrier waves. Such a technique is utilized to make communication signals compatible with business-machine signals.

demodulator — 1. A device which receives tones from a transmission circuit and converts them to electrical pulses, or bits, which may be accepted by a business machine. 2. A device which detects the modulating signals, then removes the carrier signal and reconstitutes the intelligence. (Clarified by modulation code, and contrasted with modulator.)

demonstration testing — An exhibition to show the basic system capabilities and limitations.

demultiplexer — The logical circuit that can route a single line of digital information to other lines. The device acts to switch information to many different points.

demultiplexing — Dividing one or more information streams into a larger number of streams. Contrasted with multiplexing.

denial gate, alternative — *Same as* gate, NAND.

denial gate, joint — *Same as* gate, NOR.

dense binary code — A code in which all possible states of the binary code are used.

density — The closeness of space distribution on a storage medium such as a magnetic drum, magnetic tape, or cathode-ray tube.

density, bit — The number of binary digits that are stored in a given linear area or volume.

density, recording — The number of bits per a given unit length of a linear track in a recording medium.

density, storage — *See* storage density.

density, track — The number of adjacent tracks per unit distance measured in a direction perpendicular to the direction of individual tracks. The inverse of track pitch.

departure time — The time at which control is returned to the supervisory program when a segment of an application program is completed.

dependent variable — *See* variable, dependent.

derail — An instruction to go to a subroutine.

derating, component — To ensure reliable system operation under extremely adverse conditions and with limit-value components, components used in circuit modules are derated far below manufacturers' specification.

descending sort — A sort in which the successive keys compare less-than or equal-to.

description, data — *See* data description.

description, problem — A statement of a problem, possibly a description of the method of its solution, or the solution itself. The transformations of data and the relationship of procedures, data, constraints, environments, etc., may also be included.

description, record — *See* record description.

descriptor — 1. A significant word that helps to classify the components of a document. 2. An elementary term, word, or simple phrase used to identify a subject, concept, or idea.

design — The specification of the working relations between the parts of a system in terms of their characteristic actions.

designating device — A device on certain tabulators which allows the first item of a series of similar data to be printed, and inhibits some or all printing of the rest of the series.

designation register — A register into which data is being placed.

designator — A property of part of an entity serving to classify the entity, such as the speed of a computer determining whether it is a high-, medium-, or low-speed system.

design, functional — Logic is a discipline which deals with the principles relating to switching theory and other techniques as regards design of data processing equipment. The application of this logic between the working relations and basic principles is without primary regard for the equipment used. A type of block diagram is formed using logic symbols, and the practical or working relations between all parts of the system are called the functional design.

design, item — The specification of what fields make up an item, the order in which the fields are to be recorded, and the number of characters to be allocated to each field.

design, logic — The analytical detail of the working relations between the parts of a system in terms of symbolic logic and without primary regard for its hardware implementation.

design, logical — 1. The planning of a data-processing system prior to its detailed engineering design. 2. The synthesizing of a network of logical elements to perform a specified function. 3. The results of definitions 1 and 2, frequently called the logic of a computer or of a data-processing system.

design objective — The planned or projected performance goal or expectation based on or chosen prior to the developed operations. The technical estimates of performance requirements awaiting confirmation.

design, operational — The description in logical, mathematical, or operating terms of how system tasks are to be performed. This also refers to the development of methods to accomplish system tasks.

design, problem system — *See* system, design problem.

design programmer — *See* programmer, design.

design, systems — One which formulates and graphically describes the nature and content of input, files, procedures, and output in order to display the necessary connection processes and procedures.

design verification — The experimental tests and original experiments to determine that the design meets the required specifications.

desk check — A procedure of analyzing or inspecting a written program or specific instructions for errors in logic or syntax without the requirement or use of computing equipment.

desktop computer — A basic desktop computer system includes at least 8k of read/write memory and some "off-line" magnetic storage, responds to English-like language commands, and is relatively easy to use. The minimum configuration, however, is usually not sufficient for "real-world" user applications. As a result, most desktop computers include such extra-cost options as additional memory and an external line printer.

destination source instruction — *See* instruction, source destination.

destination warning marker (DWM) — A reflective spot on the back of a magnetic tape, 18 feet from the physical end of the tape, which is sensed photoelectrically to indicate that the physical end of the tape is approaching.

destructive addition — *See* addition, destructive.

destructive read — To take information from a storage device and, by doing so, destroying the information in that device.

destructive reading — A reading process that destroys the data in the source.

destructive readout — *See* read, destructive.

destructive storage — *See* storage, destructive.

destructive test — *See* test, destructive.

detab-X — Decision Tables, Experimental; a programming language that combines decision tables with COBOL.

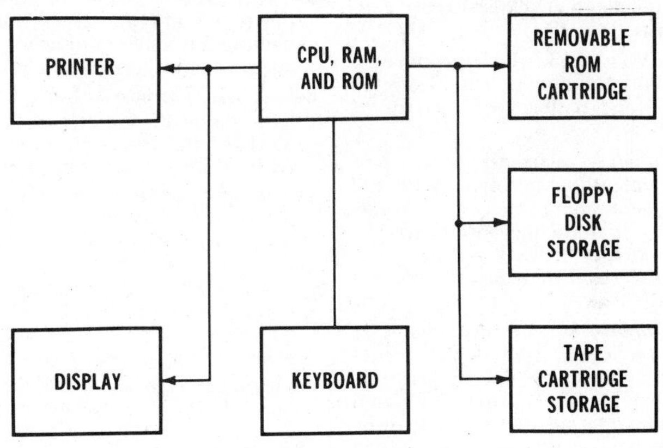

Desktop computer.

despiking — The placing of a capacitor from the supply voltage to ground near the logic circuit, e.g., the process of removing voltage spikes on power lines caused by fast switching logic circuits.

destination address — In computer systems having a source-destination architecture, the destination address is the address of the device register or memory location to which data is being transferred.

detachable plugboard — *See* patchboard.

detail — Most often a file of present or current transactions in the processing plan, such as a record from a file.

detail chart — A flowchart in minute detail of a sequence of operations. The symbols of the detail chart usually denote an individual step or computer operation. A detail chart is more detailed than a logic chart, usually reflects the particular computer characteristics and instructions, and facilitates the actual coding of the program in the manner intended by the programmer preparing the chart.

detail record — The specific listing of data which is a unit part of a major classification of larger segments or a total classification of data.

detecting code, error — *See* code, error detecting.

detection, error (transmission) — Transmission errors are detected by parity and long (channel) checks.

detection, execution errors — Those errors detected during the execution of the user's program.

detection, mark — A type of character recognition system which detects certain intelligence or information from marks placed in areas on paper or cards, called site areas, boxes, or windows. Mark reading results from optical character recognition or mark sensing systems which seek out the presence or absence of pencil marks or graphite particles, such as in college or school exams, census returns, etc.

detector — A circuitry which produces a designed output upon receipt of specific corresponding patterns or patterns of input.

detector (primary element) — The first system element that performs the initial measurement operation and responds quantitatively to the measured variable, i.e., the primary element performs the initial conversion of measurement energy.

detector, property — An optical character recognition (OCR) term which represents the component of a character reader that has the normalized signal for use in extracting a set of characteristic properties on the basis of which a character can be identified.

development system software — Typical programs that would be used during a program-development cycle include an assembler, editor, and a compiler. There are also large programs written in BASIC, variations of PL/1 and FORTRAN that are used first to develop programs in these higher-level languages, then to translate the instructions down to the actual operation code needed to control the processor. These languages, though, generate more code than is necessary.

device — 1. That which is devised, invented, or formed by design. 2. A mechanical contrivance or appliance.

device control character — *See* character, device control.

device controllers, input-output — Input-output controllers consist of the necessary logic circuitry required to interconnect one or more peripheral devices with the input-output interface. An input-output controller is normally identified with a single device; however, certain types of controllers may accommodate multiple devices of the same physical type.

device controllers, microcomputer — On some systems device controllers on the bus may participate in the priority chain, those closest to the CPU having highest priority. Devices interrupt at random for service, or the program may test devices periodically to determine if they are ready for service.

device, conversion — *See* conversion device.

device handlers, i/o — The input/output device handlers are responsible for controlling the activities of all input/output channels and peripheral equipment.

device independence — Refers to the ability to request i/o operations without regard for the characteristics of specific types of input/output devices.

device independence, storage — Logical data storage which isolates the user from the need to know and the ability to know the actual device and location of the data. For example, an operating system may present the user with one disk directory, even though the files are stored on many disk drives.

device-independent i/o programs — On some systems, programs written in any of the languages of the system may make requests to i/o devices and files through a set of modular calling sequences that are device independent.

device, input — The mechanical unit designed to bring data to be processed into a computer, e.g., a card reader, a tape reader, or a keyboard.

device, input/output — *See* input/output device.

device media control language — A language for specifying the physical implementation of the data base logical data structure.

device priority — Basically, each device

has an i/o priority, in some systems, based on its distance from the processor. When two or more devices request interrupt service, the device electrically closer to the microcomputer will receive the interrupt grant (acknowledge). The microcomputer can be inhibited from issuing more grants by setting the processor's priority to a specific number in program status (PS) word.

device, read-out — *See* read-out device.

device ready/not ready — The ability to inform the central computer that an i/o device is prepared to accept data.

device, storage — A device into which data can be inserted, retained, and retrieved.

Dewey decimal system — A classification system, developed by Melvil Dewey, to indicate the arrangement of books.

diagnosis — The process of locating and explaining detectable errors in a computer routine or hardware component.

diagnostic — Pertaining to the detection, discovery, and further isolation of a malfunction or a mistake.

diagnostic check — A specific routine designed to locate a malfunction in a computer.

diagnostic, executive — A part of the executive system is an integrated system of diagnostic routines designed to provide the programmer with information of maximum utility and convenience in checking out programs. The programmer can be highly selective about what is to be printed, and may receive diagnostic listings with source-code symbolics collated with the contents of both registers and central store. Both dynamic (snapshot) and postmortem (PMD) dumps of registers and central store are provided.

diagnostic program results — Basic results from running various diagnostic programs range from "end of pass" indications to numbers of error conditions. Error conditions may result in the program displaying an error message or simply entering Halt mode in some systems. This generally causes the routine to display the contents of the PC (program counter) which will define the address of the Halt and thereby permit ascertaining what the program was testing when it issued the Halt.

diagnostic program utilization — The use of error information obtained is usually described in the documentation of the routines. As the operator becomes familiar with the use of the diagnostic program in use, he or she may wish to invoke certain program options, such as loop on error, etc. This allows an operator to run (or single instruction execute) the program in an area where the hardware error is detected or anticipated.

diagnostic routine — A routine used to locate a malfunction in a computer, or to aid in locating mistakes in a computer program. Thus, in general, any routine specifically designed to aid in debugging or troubleshooting.

diagnostics — Another part of the executive system is an integrated system of diagnostic routines designed to provide the programmer with information of maximum utility and convenience in checking out programs. The programmer can be highly selective about what is to be printed, and may receive diagnostic listings with source-code symbolics collated with the contents of both registers and central store. Both dynamic (snapshot) and post-mortem (PMD) dumps of registers and central store are provided.

diagnostics, compiler — The compiler diagnostics are of four categories: *precautionary*—Print warning message and continue compilation. *correctable*—Try to correct the error, print explanatory message, and continue compilation. *uncorrectable*—If intent of programmer cannot be determined, print a diagnostic message, reject the clause or statement, and continue compilation. *catastrophic*—When so many errors have occurred that no more useful diagnostic information can be produced, terminate the compilation.

Other outputs from the compiler include extensive diagnostic messages, source-language listings, machine-language listings, and special cross-reference listings of name definitions and their references.

diagnostics, error — *See* error diagnostics.

diagnostics, error, time sharing — *See* time-sharing, error diagnostics.

diagnostics, microprogrammed — Diagnostics and service aids may be easily implemented in the control portion of the system with ROMs. Some very small systems store their diagnostics in ROM control. Many models of large systems also do this and this trend will spread.

Microprogrammed implementations are oriented toward servicing and diagnostics. For example, large portions of the control network can be checked by putting parity on the output of the control store. Furthermore, the microprocessor can both set and test internal control states not available to the machine language programmer.

diagnostics, on-line — The running of diagnostics on a system while it is on-line but off-peak to save time and to take corrective action without closing down the system.

diagnostics program — A program used by the supervisory program or the computer operator to check malfunctions and to locate faulty components.

diagnostics, system — A program resembling the operational program rather than a systematic logical-pattern program which will detect overall system malfunctions rather than isolate or locate faulty components.

diagnostic structure — Errors committed by the user may be classified in two broad categories; syntactic and semantic. *See* errors.

diagnostics, unit — A unit diagnostic program used to detect malfunctions in units as the input/output and the arithmetic circuitry.

diagnostic system, executive — A comprehensive diagnostic system is available within the executive system to aid the checkout of user programs. Both allocation time and compilation or assembly time commands are available to trigger snapshot dumps. Postmortem dumps are also available through the executive control statement.

diagnostic test — The running of a machine program or routine for the purpose of discovering a failure or a potential failure of a machine element, and to determine its location or its potential location.

diagnostic trace program — Refers to a particular type of diagnostic program for the performance of checks on other programs or for demonstrating such operations. The output of a trace program may include instructions of the program that is being checked, and intermediate results of those instructions arranged in the order in which the instructions are executed.

diagnotor — A combination diagnostic and edit routine which questions unusual situations and notes the implied results.

diagram — 1. A schematic representation of a sequence of subroutines designed to solve a problem. 2. A coarser and less symbolic representation than a flowchart, frequently including descriptions in English words. 3. A schematic or logical drawing showing the electrical circuit or logical arrangements within a component.

diagram, block — 1. A graphical representation of the hardware in a computer system. The primary purpose of a block diagram is to indicate the paths along which information and/or control flows between the various parts of a computer system. It should not be confused with the term flowchart. 2. A coarser and less symbolic representation than a flowchart.

diagram, dynamic flow — A diagram that shows the operational aspects of a computer program as a function of time. All references to pertinent items, such as tables, index registers, subroutines, etc.

diagram, flow — A graphic representation of the major steps of work in process. The illustrative symbols may represent documents, machines, or actions taken during the process. The area of concentration is on where or who does what, rather than how it is to be done. (Synonymous with process chart.)

diagram, functional — A specific type of block diagram which represents the functional design and special symbols called functional symbols. Functional design relates to the specification between all parts of a system, including the logic design and equipment used. A graphic representation showing the operational aspects of a system.

diagram, logical — A diagram that represents the logical elements of a system and their interconnections, without necessarily expressing construction, engineering, or electrical-schematic circuit details.

diagram, run — *See* run diagram.

diagram, setup — A graphic representation showing how a computing system has been prepared and the arrangements that have been made for operation.

diagram, Veitch — *See* chart, Veitch.

diagram, Venn — A diagram in which each

point represents an individual. Sets are represented by closed regions including all members of the set and excluding all nonmembers. The diagram is used to facilitate determination whether several sets include or exclude the same individuals.

dialectic sensors — A method used in reading data from paper tape by a special sensor.

dial, print-timing — The control knob on the printer which is an adjustment for the printing quality.

dial-up — The service whereby a dial telephone can be used to initiate and effect station-to-station telephone calls.

dial-up lines — Dial-up lines are the 2-wire pairs supplied by the common carriers on the public switched telephone network. Most often these lines are used for half duplex operation, although frequency band splitting modems can facilitate full duplex at 1200 bits per second. An auto-call or auto-answer unit is necessary for unattended operation.

diamond switch — *Same as* storage, core-rope.

dichotomizing search — A search in which the series of items is divided into two parts, one of which is rejected, and the process repeated on the unrejected part until the item with the desired property is found. This process usually depends upon the presence of a known sequence in the series.

dichotomy — A division into subordinate classes, e.g., all white and all nonwhite, or all zero and all nonzero.

dictionary — A book or list of code names or keys used in a program, routine, or system with the description or identification of their designed or intended meaning in that program, routine, or system.

dictionary applications — Containing all of the definitions of the data, the dictionary becomes the information repository for data's attributes, their characteristics, their sources, dispositions of usage, and interrelationships with other data.

dictionary, automatic — The component of a language-translating machine which will provide a word for word substitution from one language to another. In automatic-searching systems, the automatic dictionary is the component which substitutes codes for words or phrases during the encoding operation. (Related to machine translation.)

dictionary code — An alphabetical arrangement of English words and terms associated with their code representations. (Related to reverse-code dictionary.)

dictionary, data base — The purpose of dictionaries is to permit better documentation, control, and management of the corporate data resource, goals which may or may not be achieved through the use of a DBMS. Advanced users of data dictionaries have found them also to be valuable tools in the exercise of project management and systems design.

dictionary, electronic — *Same as* dictionary, automatic.

dictionary, external symbol — *See* external symbol dictionary.

dictionary, relocation — Part of a load module containing directions which enable a fetch program to initialize properly all relocatable address constants within the text section by accounting for the actual starting address of the load module in storage and the incremental difference between the required address and the initial address of the module.

dictionary, reverse-code — An alphabetic or numeric-alphabetic arrangement of codes, associated with their corresponding English words or terms. (Related to dictionary code.)

difference — The number or quantity resulting when one number or quantity (minuend) has another (subtrahend) subtracted from it.

difference engine — A machine capable of computing mathematical tables automatically. It was built in 1812 by Charles Babbage.

difference gate — *Same as* gate, exclusive OR.

difference report — A report noting resulting changes from an original computer program and a program change.

differential delay — The difference between the maximum and the minimum frequency delays occurring across a band.

differential modulation — A type of modulation in which the choice of the significant condition for any signal element is dependent on the choice of the previous signal element.

differentiator — A device whose output function is proportional to a derivative, i.e., the rate of change, of its input function with respect to one or more variables.

digit — 1. One of the n symbols of integral value, ranging from 0 to n-1 inclusive, in a system of numbering with radix n; for example, the ten digts 0, 1, 2, 3, 4, 5, 6, 7, 8, 9 in the decimal system; 0, 1 in the binary system. 2. One of the ideographic characters 0, 1 . . . 9 . . . used to designate a quantity smaller than n for the base n number system. 3. A sign or symbol used to convey a specific quantity of information either by itself or with other numbers of its set; e.g., 2, 3, 4, and 5 are digits. The base or radix must be specified and the value assigned to each digit.

digital — Pertaining to the utilization of discrete integral numbers in a given base to represent all the quantities that occur in a problem or a calculation. It is possible to express in digital form all information stored, transferred, or processed by a dual-state condition, e.g., on-off, open-closed, and true-false.

digital adder — A unit capable of developing the representation of the sum of two or more numbers represented by signals applied to its inputs. Note definitions of half-adders, full-adders, etc.

digital-analog decoder — An analog computer device which translates digital data into variable electrical flow.

digital back-up — A specially designed alternate method of digital process control initiated through the activation of special-purpose digital logic in the event of a failure in the computer system.

digital clock — Clocks which have output signals in digital representation.

digital communications processor — Consists of multimicroprocessors designed for a variety of software programmable functions. The system can act as a data concentrator, speed and code converter, message switch, front-end processor, and multiplexer. Also, various modems, echo suppressors and T-Carrier multiplex equipment can be easily interfaced.

digital computer — 1. A computer that operates by using numbers to express all the quantities and variables of a problem. In most digital computers, the numbers, in turn, are expressed by electrical impulses. 2. A computer that processes information represented by combinations of discrete or discontinuous data as compared with an analog computer for continuous data. More specifically, it is a device for performing sequences of arithmetic and logical operations, not only on data but also on its own program. Still more specifically it is a stored program digital computer capable of performing sequences of internally stored instructions, as opposed to calculators, such as card-programmed calculators, on which the sequence is impressed manually. (Related to machine, data-processing.)

digital data — Information which is expressed in discrete or noncontinuous form. Opposite of analog data.

digital display (DD) — 1. A display of digitally oriented numerals. 2. A visual display, generally on a cathode-ray tube, of alphabetic, numeric, or graphic material.

digital divider — A unit capable of generating a quotient and a remainder from the representation of two numbers.

digital filter — A filtering process performed on a digitized signal by a general or special purpose computer. Although digital filtering is far more flexible than analog filtering, it is also generally slower and more expensive and hence largely limited to experimental applications when relatively few frequencies are being filtered. When a power spectrum is desired across a larger frequency range, however, the fast Fourier transform (FFT) method offers advantages.

digital IC (SSI, MSI, LSI) — A monolithic group of logic elements. May be small-scale integration (e.g., gates, flip-flops, latches); medium-scale integration (e.g., decoders, adders, counters); large-scale integration (e.g., memories, microprocessors).

digital incremental plotter — *See* plotter, digital incremental.

digital logic types — The most "regular" types of digital logic families of elements are the transistor-transistor-logic (TTL), emitter-coupled logic (ECL), and the complementary metal-oxide semiconductor logic (CMOS). Each of these families has its own set of parameters and applications, and each is encountered in many modern microprocessor applications. The TTL family has been the most widely used of the three families.

digital modem — Digital modems provide the necessary modulation, demodulation, and supervisory control functions to implement a serial data communications link over a voice grade channel utilizing frequency shift keying (fsk) techniques. Most microprocessors interface directly to the ACIA.

digital modulator — A typical 2400 bits per second (bps) device provides the necessary modulation and control functions to implement a serial data communications link over voice-grade lines at bit rates of 1200 and 2400 bps.

digital multiplex switching system (DMS) — A family of switching systems utilizing new technology that will provide digital circuit switched service for voice and data transmission. DMS is characterized by the use of pulse code modulation (PCM) and time division multiplexing (TDM) throughout the switched network. The system allows the direct switching of PCM signals used in transmission systems without their conversion to analog format.

digital multiplier — A specific device which generates a digital product from the representation of two digital numbers, by additions of the multiplicand in accordance with the value of the digits in the multiplier. It is necessary only to shift the multiplicand and add it to the product if the multiplier digit is a one, and just shift the multiplicand without adding, if the multiplier digit is a zero, for each successive digit of the multiplier.

digital multiplier unit — A unit which is capable of generating a product from the representations of two numbers, often formed by repeated additions of the multiplicand or multiples of it. See adders, subtracters, etc.

digital output module — On some systems, this module opens and closes contacts to operate valves, energize alarm lights, and control other on/off electrical devices. Its multiplexed termination panels can be remotely mounted to significantly reduce field wiring costs.

digital recorder — A peripheral device that records data as discrete numerically defined points.

digital representation — A representation of variables as data, by means of digits or discrete quantities, as determined by their appearance or nonappearance.

digital signature — A numerical representation of a set of logic states, typically used to describe the logic-state history at one output pin of the device under test during the complete test program.

digital sort — An ordering or sorting according to the least significant digit, followed by a resort on each next higher order digit until the items are completely sorted, most often used in punched card sorting.

digital subtracter — A unit with the capability of developing the representation of the difference between two numbers represented by signals applied to its inputs.

digital-to-analog conversion — Production of an analog signal, whose instantaneous magnitude is proportional to the value of a digital input. Abbreviated D-A conversion.

digital-to-analog converter (DAC) — A typical unit provides two analog output channels ranging from 0 to +10 volts with eight bits per channel resolution. Also provides two logic level outputs for external device control.

digit, binary — A whole number in the binary scale of notation; this digit may only be 0 (zero) or 1 (one). It may be equivalent to an "on" or "off" condition, a "yes" or a "no," etc. The word "bit" is a contraction of binary digit.

digit, binary-coded — *See* binary-coded digit.

digit, check — 1. One or more redundant digits in a character or word, which depend upon the remaining digits in such a fashion that if a digit changes, the malfunction can be detected; e.g., a given digit may be zero if the sum of other digits in the word is odd, and this (check) digit may be one if the sum of other digits in the word is even. 2. One or more redundant digits carried along with a machine word and used in relation to the other digits in the word as a self-checking or error-detecting code to detect malfunctions of equipment in data-transfer operations. (Related to forbidden-combination check, and parity check.)

digit, check-sum — A check digit produced by a sum check.

digit compression — 1. A specific packing process in which an assigned area contains additional digits. Example: storing three digits in two character positions containing six bits. In some computers, a 4-bit pattern represents a single decimal digit. Then two 6-bit character positions can accommodate 12 bits or three 4-bit digits. 2. Any of a number of techniques used to pack digits.

digit, decimal — A single character which represents an integer, i.e., in decimal notation, one of the characters, 0 through 9.

digit, decimal-coded — A digit or character defined by a set of decimal digits, such as a pair of decimal digits specifying a letter or special character in a system of notation.

digit delay — A logic element which delays its input signal by one digit period.

digit delay element — A specific delay element that introduces a delay in a line of signals or pulses of one digit period duration.

digit, forbidden — *Same as* character, illegal.

digit, function — A unique computer code digit that describes the arithmetic or logical operation which is to be carried out.

digit, gap — Digits that are not used to represent data, but are included in a computer word for engineering or convenience purposes, such as spaces.

digit, guard — A low-order hexadecimal zero appended to each operand fraction in a single-word floating-point arithmetic addition or subtraction operation.

digit, high-order — A digit that occupies a more significant or highly weighted position in a numeral or positional notation system.

digitize — 1. To assign digital numbers to characters and words according to fixed rules of ordering. 2. To convert an analog measurement of a physical variable into a numerical value, thereby expressing the quantity in digital form. (Synonymous with quantize.)

digitizer — A device that converts an analog measurement into digital form.

digitizer stability — Assuming the digitizer input device—pen, stylus, or cursor—does not move, stability is the environmental range, including temperature, humidity, and atmospheric pressure, within which the digitizer output remains constant.

digitizing, automatic — In automatic digitizing, the tracking of a line is accomplished as a result of computer and/or optical/electronic sensor hardware. The recording head will automatically follow a line or scan an entire drawing in a raster or grid pattern.

digit, least significant (LSD) — The digit contributing the smallest quantity to the value of a numeral.

digit, low-order — A digit that occupies a low weighted position in a numeral in a positional notation system.

digit, most significant (MSD) — The significant digit contributing the largest quantity to the value of a numeral.

digit, noisy — A specific digit that is chosen to be inserted into the units position of a mantissa during left-shifting manipulation.

digit operation, serial — The capability of handling digits one following another regardless of whether the bits can be handled in serial or parallel fashion.

digit period — The time interval between the occurrence of successive digit signals.

digit place — The site of a digit in a numeral in various positional notation systems.

digit plane — A specific array of cells which are arranged in order to effect three dimensions. The plane therefore contains corresponding bits of every word.

digit position, punching — The area on a punched card onto which a decimal digit may be punched.

digit pulse — A particular drive pulse common to magnetic cells corresponding to a one digit position in some or all of the words in a storage unit. In some techniques it may always be an inhibit pulse or always an enable pulse, which are more acceptable names for the general term.

digit, sexadecimal — A digit that is a member of the set of sixteen digits: 0 thru 9 and then K, S, N, J, F, and L used in a numerical notation system using a radix of 16.

digit, sign — A character, frequently a single bit, used to designate the algebraic sign of the quantity. (Synonymous with sign bit.)

digit(s), significant — A set of digits, usually from consecutive columns beginning with the most significant digit different from zero and ending with the least significant digit whose value is known and assumed relevant; e.g., 2300.0 has five significant digits, whereas 2300 probably has two significant digits; however, 2301 has four significant digits and 0.0023 has two significant digits.

digits, octal — The symbol 0, 1, 2, 3, 4, 5, 6, or 7 used as a digit in the system of notation which uses 8 as the base or radix. (Clarified by number systems.)

digit sorting method, reverse — Sorting which begins with the units position of a given field and proceeds one column at a time (from right to left) until the field is completely sorted.

digit-transfer bus — The main wire or wires used to transfer numerical and other information (but not control signals) among the various registers in a digital computer.

digit transfer trunk — *See* trunk, digit transfer.

digit, unallowable instruction — *Same as* character, illegal.

diminished complement — *Same as* complement, radix-minus-one.

diminished radix complement — *Same as* complement, radix-minus-one.

direct access — The ability to read or write information at any location within a storage device in a constant amount of time. Every site available for data storage on a direct-access device is identified by its own unique, numeric address.

direct access hash — As regards indexing, a hash algorithm which precludes collision. That is, no two elements have the same hash indices. A hash index is the initial estimate of the location of an entry within the table.

direct access inquiry — A storage method which allows direct information inquiry from temporary or permanent storage devices.

direct-access storage — A type of storage device wherein access to the next position from which information is to be obtained is in no way dependent on the position from which information was previously obtained.

direct-access storage inquiry — A process through which information can be directly requested from temporary or permanent storage devices.

direct access unit — A memory device which allows the particular address to be accessed in a manner independent of the location of that address; thus, the items stored in the memory can be addressed or accessed in the same amount of time for each location. Access by a program is not dependent upon the previously accessed position.

direct address — 1. A machine-instruction address of the data to be processed. 2. An address that indicates the location where the referenced operand is to be found or stored, with no reference to an index register or B-box. (Synonymous with first-level address.)

direct addressing — *See* addressing, direct.

direct-address processing — Reading or writing of data from a sector whose address is given.

direct code — A code that specifies the use of actual computer command and address configurations.

direct coding — *Same as* absolute coding.

direct condition testing — On some low-cost systems, on-chip generation of asynchronous control signals for direct interfacing and a capability to use memories of any speed are available.

direct control — *See* control, direct.

direct control connection — A device that permits two systems to be coupled together for control purposes bypassing the channels. Control information can be sent across the connector by a single instruction in each computer.

direct data capture — A technique employed in cash registers or on sales slips whereby customer account numbers, the amount of the purchase, and other information are automatically recorded, read by an optical reading device, and sent to the computer to be processed. The desirability of using direct data capture depends on two factors—the urgency of processing the transactions, and the increased costs of data capture devices compared to manual data preparation.

direct digital control (DDC) — Control action in which control is obtained by a digital device which establishes the signal to the final control element.

directing character code — One or several routing indicators at the start of a message that determine message destination.

direct insert subroutine — A subroutine inserted directly into the linear operational sequence, not entered by a jump. Such a subroutine must be recopied at each point that it is needed in a routine.

direct instruction — An instruction which contains an operand for the operation specified by the instruction.

direction — In flowcharting, the antecedent-to-successor relation, indicated by arrows, lines, or other conventions, between operations on a flowchart.

direction, flow — The antecedent-to-successor relation, indicated by arrows or other conventions, between operations on flowcharts.

direction, grain — The arrangement (direction) of the fibers in the paper in relation to the route or manner in which a document travels through the character reader.

direction, normal flow — *See* flow, normal direction.

directive — An instruction (pseudo-instruction) in a program which has the same general form as a computer instruction but is actually used to control translation.

directives, assembler — The symbolic assembler directives control or direct the assembly processor just as operation codes control or direct the central computer. These directives are represented by mnemonics.

direct memory access — Direct Memory Access (DMA) is a technique that allows a computer user to have direct access to individual memory locations without first having to go through the central processing unit (CPU) of the computer. Also called data break and cycle stealing.

direct memory access controller — On some systems, the DMA circuit is provided for those applications which require data to be transferred directly into memory at a very high rate rather than going through the CPU. In larger systems applications with many high speed peripherals, such as floppy disks, communications channels, etc., the DMA circuit can improve system performance by totally controlling block transfers between i/o circuits and the system memory.

direct memory access (DMA), cycle stealing — For highest speed transfer rates, DMA transfers data on a cycle-stealing basis directly between the memory and the external device, bypassing the central processor.

direct operand addressing — The operand is the content of the selected register.

direct or on-line system — *See* on-line.

directory — A file with the layout for each field of the record which it describes; thus a directory describes the layout of a record within a file.

directory devices — A directory device is one that contains a table of contents with critical information about the files on that device. Besides the file name and date of creation or modification, the directory contains the size and address of the file on the device, although the directory listing on the terminal may not show all of this information. File access times are orders of magnitude faster on directory devices because the hardware can first examine the directory and then go right to the sector where the wanted information resides.

direct output — *See* output, direct.

direct program control (DPC) — The i/o operation is performed in-line to the instruction stream, allowing intimate control of the device by software.

direct reference address — A virtual address that is not modified by indirect addressing, but may be modified by indexing.

disable — A suppression of an interrupt feature.

disabled — Pertaining to a state of the central processing unit that prevents the occurrence of certain types of interruptions. Synonymous with masked.

disabled interrupt — *See* interrupt, armed.

disarmed interrupt — *See* interrupt, armed.

disassembler — Usually refers to a program to translate from machine language to assembly language; e.g. it is generally used to decipher existing machine language programs by generating symbolic code listings of the program.

discrete — Pertains to separate and distinct parts of data such as holes in a card, or graphic characters.

discrete data — A representation for a variable which may assume any of several distinct states, i.e., sex, race. Usually coded. Conventional usage in computing excludes measures of a quantal nature (i.e., number of children in a family). (Contrast with continuous data.)

discrete programming — A class of optimization problems in which the values of all the variables are restricted to integers. Normally, the optimization problem without this integer restriction is linear programming; additional adjectives indicate variations.

Courtesy Micropolis Corp.

Disk drives (multiple floppies).

discrete wired circuits — In discrete wiring, an automatic tool lays down a conductor pattern of insulated wires from point to point. The wired board is then sealed in an epoxy layer to freeze the wires in position.

discrimination — The skipping of various instructions as developed in a predetermined set of conditions as programmed. If a conditional jump is not used, the next instructions would follow in the normal proper sequence. *See* branch, conditional.

discrimination instruction — A more acceptable term for jump or branch instruction. Also called decision instruction. *See* branch.

disjunction — The logical operation which makes use of the OR operator or the logical sum. The disjunction of two variables, or expressions, may be written as A+B, AVB, or AUB. These may also be described as a union when using Venn diagrams. (Clarified by OR operator, OR gate, and contrasted with conjunction.)

disjunction gate — *Same as* gate, OR.

disjunctive search — A search defined in terms of a logical sum, i.e., disjunctive form, in contrast to a conjunctive form or logical product.

disk — A circular metal plate with magnetic material on both sides, continuously rotated for reading or writing by means of one or more read/write heads mounted on movable or fixed arms; disks may be permanently mounted on a shaft, or as a package, they may be removable and others placed on the shaft.

disk access — Disks are usually stacked with each disk rotating in a horizontal plane, as they may be permanent or exchangeable. Access to each disk is by one or more arms which move to definite radial locations on a rotating disk. They are random accessed only in the sense that the read/write heads on the arms move to definite tracks or portions of the disk, and, within a given track, data are transferred sequentially.

disk accessing — Refers to the process of or methods used in transferring data to and from a disk file. Disk units and access routines vary widely in their sophistication. Access can be accomplished either by using physical addresses (actual disk locations) or various levels of symbolic or keyed-record addressing procedures. Some disk drives can locate a desired record using addressing logic contained within the unit itself to find a keyed record, thus leaving more productive time available to the central processing unit while the record is being sought.

disk drives — Typical disk drives are highly reliable, random access, moving-head memory devices, compactly designed for use as peripheral units in large, small and now, microcomputer systems. Typically a photoelectric positioning system, working in conjunction with a velocity transducer and voice coil driven actuator, provides fast and accurate head positioning over a wide temperature range. Cartridge interchangeability is becoming standard.

A typical dual platter disk drive utilizes one permanent disk and one removable cartridge to provide 4.9 million bytes of storage. Some reliable drives have an average access time of less than 30 milliseconds, and a data transfer rate of 2.5 million bits per second.

See illustration, page 159.

diskette — A thin, flexible platter (floppy disk) coated with magnetic material used as the storage medium in a floppy disk unit.

diskette hardholes — Hardholes are small mylar doughnuts which may be affixed to the center hole of a diskette for additional protection. It is possible to damage the center hole of a diskette if it is not properly centered at the time the disk drive door is closed. The mylar doughnut serves to reinforce the center hole of the diskette and give it additional protection against damage. The hardhole also provides for additional friction between the diskette and the clamping hub in order to provent slippage of the diskette during rotation.

diskette sectoring — There are two methods of sectoring: hard-sectoring and soft-sectoring. Hard-sectoring identifies each sector by holes punched in the diskette (one hole per sector). Soft-sectoring identifies the sectors by magnetic codes written on the diskette. Both methods, however, have a hole, called the index hole, in the diskette to identify the beginning of the tracks, which start on the same radius. When the diskette spins, a beam of light is detected by a photoelectric cell that signals the controller that the track has begun.

disk file — 1. Refers to various disk units consisting of a drive, channel, and the fixed or removable disks. 2. An associated set of records of the same format, identified by a unique label.

disk file addressing — The operation which locates information on a random-access file.

disk files — A type of storage medium consisting of numbers of disks that rotate; each disk has a special coating for retaining stored information.

disk, fixed-head — There are some disks which have a head per track. These are called fixed-head disks, in that the heads do not move to get to a particular track. These fixed-head disks have a higher access rate; that is, it takes less time to get to a particular sector since there is no head movement. This arrangement is, typically, more expensive since there are more heads and more electronics required.

disk, hard sector — Generally refers to magnetic disks that are divided into sectors around the disk. These sectors may be marked either by the hardware, called the hard sector, or the software, the soft sector. Hard sectoring is older, consisting of actual holes in the diskette.

disk, hard vs soft sectors — A long-standing difference in the manner by which a disk sector is defined is the hard vs soft sectoring techniques. In the hard-sectored disk system, the physical disk has holes that are used to determine the start of sector 0 and the start of every sector on the disk. This permits simpler hardware since there is no timing requirement to determine the start of each sector. In a soft-sectored disk, there is only a single hole which identifies the start of sector 0. The controller must provide timing circuitry to determine when other sectors are under the head. This generally adds to the expense and complexity of the controller. The advantage is that the controller can define any sector size it requires, whereas the hard-sectored disk must be used with the sector size defined by the physical holes (of perhaps a multiple of sector size, e.g., 2 sectors + 1 sector).

disk, magnetic — A storage device on which information is recorded on the magnetized surface of a rotating disk. A magnetic-disk storage system is an array of such devices, with associated reading and writing heads that are mounted on movable arms. (Related to disk storage.)

disk, moving arm — A type of disk which has a movable arm which contains several heads, each of which covers an area of several tracks of digited information. This is in contrast to a fixed head disk for which the heads are fixed in position, one per track, and the arms are immovable.

disk pack — A set of magnetic disks which have been designed so they can be placed in a processing device for reading and writing. Their design permits them to be interchanged with other disk packs.

disk read-write head — The read-write head of a recording device consists of a coil on a ferromagnetic core. This core has a gap of nonmagnetic material which is brought into contact with the media. (Or very near the media in flying head hard disks.) Current in the coil magnetizes the media as it passes under the gap. The coil responds to a *change* in the magnetic flux of the media. This is accomplished by moving the media. In addition to motion, a change in the magnetic field from the disk is required to produce an output. In other words, the read head can only detect where transitions in polarity occur. Therefore, the information must be encoded in the location of these transitions, and the read system must operate by locating these transitions. This is done by detecting the peaks of the read signal.

disk sectors — A majority of disks are divided into sectors of approximately 128 words. A sector corresponds to a block of data between two successive radials on the disk. The cutting of a disk into sectors is analogous to the way a pie would be sliced.

disk sorting — A sort program that utilizes disk-type memory for auxiliary storage during sorting.

disk sort/merging — *See* sort/merging, disk.

disk storage — 1. A storage device that uses magnetic recording on flat rotating disks. 2. The storage of data on the surface of magnetic disks. (Related to magnetic disk, and magnetic-disk storage.)

disk working storage — *See* storage, working.

disorderly close-down — *See* close-down, disorderly.

dispatching priority — The priority assigned to an active task in a multiprogramming or multitask environment. An active task is nonreal-time and nonforeground. The dispatch priority establishes precedence for the use of the central processing unit (CPU) when the operating system prepares to return control to the problem program.

dispatching systems — Dispatching systems respond to a demand by assigning resources to meet it, then reporting accordingly. A system that assigns inventory to fill orders is an example. In this case a dispatching system must reduce the recorded balances, prepare the appropriate documents for the warehouses where the items are stocked, and issue reorder documents when inventory levels become too low. The dispatching system also performs such functions as financial accounting, payroll, and management reports on daily operations. The equipment for such a system generally consists of a medium or large computer, magnetic tape transports, magnetic disk files, a card reader-punch, a printer, and perhaps several teletypewriter terminals and a buffer.

disperse — 1. The distribution of items among more sets than originally presented. An output item may be distributed to several output sets. 2. A data-processing operation in which input items or fields are distributed or duplicated in more than one output item or field.

dispersing — A designed procedure which results in input data distribution in several output areas rather than one.

dispersion gate — *Same as* gate, NAND.

display — Visible representation of data on a console screen in a printed report, graph, or drawing, subject to alteration by a light pen or "stylus."

display adapter unit — The display adapter unit controls the transmission of data, unit control information, unit status information, and the sequencing and synchronizing of the various units in the system. In addition, digital data received from computer storage is formatted for deflection commands for the crt devices.

display buffer size — The minimum and maximum number of words reserved for display units and used, with automatic refreshing, to present a flicker-free picture.

display capacity — Many displays designed for business uses provide 24 lines of characters with 80 characters per line. To display the full text of an 8½ × 11 letter, or full display of large forms or reports, larger display capacity is needed.

display category — A group, type, class, or array of data or information presented for visual display on cathode-ray tubes.

display character generation — In addition to automatic line generation, the display hardware can display characters specified by 6-bit codes. Each character is displayed in an average of 15 μs (some systems).

display, character-mode — This mode provides a rapid means of displaying alphanumeric characters. Three characters or symbols are contained in each variable bit word with provision for a 128-character or larger alphabet. Characters or symbols may be displayed in one or several sizes. The character generator is capable of performing carriage-return functions upon specific characterlike commands. Escape from the character mode is accomplished with another similar code.

display character sets — Characters include alphabetic letters, symbols, and numerals. Letters may be all capitals (upper case) or may include lower case as well. Alternate character sets such as Cyrillic (Slavic), Farsi (Arabic), or Katakana (Japanese) may be available, as may double-width and double-height characters.

display characters per frame — The maximum number of whole characters which can be drawn flicker-free at the manufacturer's recommended refresher rate.

display console keyboard — An operator control panel for those processors where the display is used in place of the typewriter control console.

display controllers — Display controllers provide an integrated solution to the problem of display-support circuitry. Combined on a single chip are data latching, seven-segment decode, segment drive, and digit multiplex control.

display, control-message — *See* control-message display.

display, crt inquiry — Information is placed into the computer through the alphanumeric keyboard and is simultaneously displayed on its four-inch square (or larger screen) crt. This type of unit then displays a reply to the inquiry on its screen.

display cursors — A cursor is a movable mark that locates a character on the screen. By pressing cursor control keys, the operator can move the cursor from line to line and from character to character. A cursor is used to direct display editing functions such as "delete-character." Thus, if the cursor is moved to underline a certain displayed character, and the delete-character key is then pressed, that character will be removed. Some terminals use a blinking cursor to call the operator's attention to its position.

display, digital (DD) — A display of digitally oriented numerals.

display, direct — Cathode-ray tubes that display various alphameric, graphic, or sketch results from a processor for viewing or photographing for records or animation.

display, direct-access channel — This provides automatic collection of data and control information from core memory with a single instruction. This indexible address register contains the memory address of the next display control or data word in memory. Termination of the transfer is controlled by the stop bit which signals the computer upon completion of plotting. The location of the stop bit may be determined by examining the contents of the channel register (some systems).

display drum — A magnetic, digital, data buffer storage drum which stores data that is to be used for display on a visual device.

display, forced — A display made by the system without the operator requesting it.

display, incremental — The precision incremental display is a powerful new general-purpose incremental cathode-ray tube display which permits rapid conversion of digital computer data into graphic and tabular form. Its combined capabilities offer the user an unusual degree of versatility and accuracy.

display, inquiry and subscriber — *See* inquiry and subscriber display.

display, inquiry-terminal — Information is

placed into the computer through the alphanumeric keyboard and is simultaneously displayed on the screen. The unit then displays a reply to the inquiry on the screen. Information is displayed many times faster than that produced by an operator by means of a typeout. To reuse the display after the inquiry has been answered requires only a press of the erase button.

display modes — Each display mode, such as vector, increment, character, point, vector continue, or short vector specifies the manner in which points are to be displayed on the screen.

display numeric pads — These are numeral key groupings like those used on adding-machines. The pads speed up the entry of numeric data by limiting the hand movement required of the operator.

display, parameter-mode — This mode is used to control the display. It establishes parameter information for each of the other modes. The parameters are changed only when another parameter word is encountered (some computers).

display, point-mode — In this mode, individual points may be established and/or plotted at random locations on the tube face. A point is established by two independent 18-bit words. The first word determines the vertical position; the second word sets up the horizontal position. Once an initial point has been established, subsequent plots may be made by single word changes (some computers).

display printer ports — Some terminals are equipped with connection "ports" to which computer printers can be attached. The printers may simply reproduce material displayed on the terminal screen, or they may be able to print material received from a computer via the terminal.

display, remote (slave) — A slave unit containing only the analog portion of the display. Turn-on may be accomplished independently, or by the master-display control.

display, reverse video — This function shows dark characters on a background of light screen area.

display, subroutining-multilevel — The control state permits the display to jump from accessing one location memory to any other. When it is desired to jump to a display subroutine, the return address is automatically stored in a push-down list.

display, translate — To move, as an image on a screen, from side to side or up and down without rotation of the image.

display tube — A cathode-ray tube used to display information.

display types — Cathode-ray tube, plasma, and liquid crystal displays, light emitting diodes (LEDs), incandescent and fluorescent displays, and "Nixie" tubes are becoming solidly established in circuit design as the trend to digital readout continues. The design engineer faces an unusually formidable task in determining the type of display most suitable and practical for his product.

display unit — A device that provides a visual representation of data.

display unit, graphic — A communications terminal which can display data on a screen.

display unit, remote (visual) — Remote users who can use a typewriter can now talk to a computer and get answers on the spot. The operator of a display unit simply types in the query and presses the transmit key; the answer appears immediately on the screen. Options cover many diverse applications and there are input interfaces for digital computers, telephone subsets, and other digital sources.

display, vector-continue mode — The vector-continue mode is an extension of the vector mode; its word format is the same. This mode is used when it is desirable to draw a vector from any point to the edge of the screen. The vector specified is automatically extended until the edge of the screen is encountered. Upon violation of the screen edge, automatic return is made to the parameter mode. This mode is particularly useful for drawing long, straight lines (for example, grid lines and graph axes) rapidly and efficiently.

dissector — In optical character recognition (OCR), a mechanical or electronic transducer that sequentially detects the level of light in different areas of a completely illuminated sample space.

dissipation, module — The dissipation of the module calculated from the voltage-current product, plus an allowance for transistor dissipation for load current being supplied to other modules.

distance — The number of digit positions

which the corresponding digits of two binary words of the same length are different. (Synonymous with Hamming distance.)

distance gate — *Same as* gate, exclusive OR.

distance, Hamming — *See* Hamming distance.

distance signal — *Same as* Hamming distance.

quirement is not met, distortion is present.

distortion, bias — 1. Bias distortion or bias of start-stop teletypewriter signals is the uniform shifting of the beginning of all marking pulses from their proper positions in relation to the beginning of the start pulse. 2. Distortion affecting a two-condition (or binary) modulation (or restitution) in which all the significant intervals corresponding to one of the two significant conditions have longer or shorter durations than the corresponding theoretical durations.

Courtesy Sperry Univac

Distributed-computer-system processor.

distortion — An undesired change in waveform between the received signal and the original signal.

distortion, asymmetrical — A distortion affecting a two-condition (or binary) modulation (or restitution) in which all the significant intervals corresponding to one of the two significant conditions have longer or shorter durations than the corresponding theoretical durations of the excitation. If this particular re-

distortion, characteristic — 1. A fixed distortion which results in either shortened or lengthened impulses. It generally does not change in degree from day to day. 2. Distortions caused by transients which, as a result of the modulation, are present in the transmission channel and depend on its transmission qualities.

distortion, delay/frequency — That form of distortion which occurs when the envelope delay of a circuit or system is not constant over the frequency range required for transmissions.

distortion, end — *See* end distortion.

distortion, fortuitous — An intermittent distortion which results in either shortened or lengthened impulses. It is caused by battery fluctuations, hits on the line, power induction, etc.

distortion, marking-end — End distortion which lengthens the marking impulse by delaying the mark-to-space transition

distributed computer systems — The arrangement of computers within an organization, in which the organization's computer complex has many separate computing facilities all working in a cooperative manner, rather than the conventional single computer at a single location. Versatility of a computer system is often increased if small computers in geographically dispersed branches are used for simple tasks and a central computer is available for larger tasks. Frequently an organization's central files are stored at the central computing facility, with the geographically dispersed smaller computers calling on the central files when they need them. Such an arrangement lessens the load on the central computer and reduces both the volume and cost of data transmission.

distributed computing — Usually refers to a computation performed in parallel and generally asychronously, but cooperatively, by many processors. It is also a general term for a computing system in which processing and storage facilities are geographically dispersed, but loosely coupled by transmission media.

distributed-intelligence system — Each processor in a distributed-intelligence microcomputer system (DIMS) performs some combination of these four basic activity functions: (1) Local input/output or hardware controller activity. (2) Information concentration and temporary storage. (3) Information processing. (4) Remote input/output and communication.

distributed intelligence system programs — Various sets of programs that use multiple processors, some with their own set of responsibilities but still capable of cooperating as a unit alone or part of a unified system by exchanging information over communication lines.

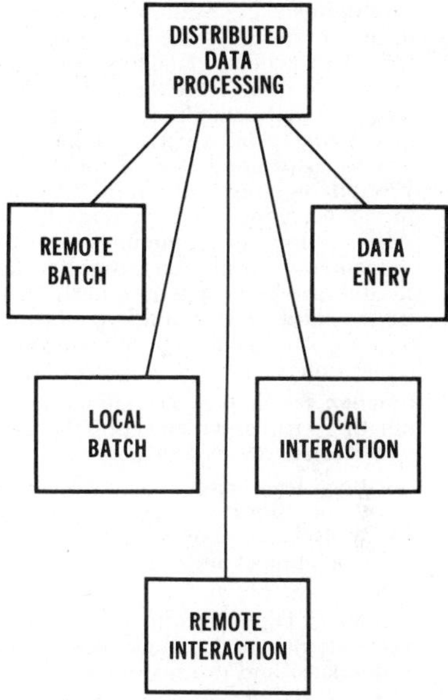

Distributed system.

distributed systems — Refers to various arrangements of computers within an organization in which the organization's computer complex has many separate computing facilities all working in a cooperative manner, rather than the conventional single computer at a single location. Versatility of a computer system is often increased if small computers in geographically dispersed branches are used for simple tasks and a powerful central computer is available for larger tasks.

distributed systems, satellites — Various distributed systems include satellite computer systems for measurement and control, disk-based real-time multiprogramming central systems, and the hardware-software interfacing that establishes, controls, and monitors distributed system communications. Many distributed systems offer capability that is comprehensive. They provide: (1) Quick response to local events, because satellite systems operate independently. (2) Maximum availability; failure at central or a satellite leaves other satellites up and working. (3) Fast, disk-based program processing at central so productive operations of satellites can continue without interruption for program development. (4) A multiprocessor environment in which satellites can call on central to process data for them, and data can be transferred directly between programs in the satellites and in central, maximizing productivity. (5) Easy access to distributed system capabilities through high-level program calls and operator commands speeds and simplifies system programming and implementation, and users can develop the ability to build systems quickly, or to use the software as a building block for tailoring systems for specific customer applications.

distribution frame — A structure for terminating wires and connecting them together in any desired order.

distribution, time-impulse — A device or circuit for allocating timing pulses or clock pulses to one or more conducting paths or control lines in specified sequence.

distributor — The electronic circuit which acts as an intermediate link between the accumulator and drum storage.

diversity gate — *Same as* gate, exclusive OR.

divide check — An indicator which denotes that an invalid division has been attempted or has occurred.

divided slit scan — A device, in optical character recognition (OCR), which scans an input character at given intervals to obtain its horizontal and vertical components. This scanning device consists of a narrow column of photoelectric cells.

dividend — The quantity that is divided by another quantity; also, the numerator of a fraction.

divider, analog — *See* analog divider.

divider, digital — *See* digital divider.

divide time — The period of time required to perform a single division operation with quantities of average length.

division — The parts into which a COBOL program is organized. Identification division provides information to identify the source and object programs. Environment division specifies the equipment to use for translating and running a program. Data division contains entries to define the nature of the data to be processed. Procedure division consists of the processor programs to be run with data.

division, data — *See* data division.

division, identification — The part of COBOL programming in which the programmer gives information to identify the source program and the object program.

division, procedure — The COBOL term for the description of the steps we take in the processing of data into meaningful English.

division subroutine — 1. A set of instructions which simulate division by repetitive subtraction or by series expansion. 2. The approximation of reciprocals. 3. A division simulator.

division, time — Interleaving several message channels, which are separated from each other in time, on a single transmission medium.

divisor — A quantity by which the dividend is divided; also, the denominator of a fraction.

divisor, trial — An initial approximation in the dividing arithmetic process.

DMA (direct memory access) — A procedure or method designed to gain direct access to main storage to thereby achieve data transfer without involving the CPU. This means that the CPU must be periodically disabled while DMA is in progress. The manner and modes of achieving this differ considerably in the many microprocessor models that have DMA capability.

DMA functions — Four typical functions are: data transfer, add to memory, increment memory, or with memory. Other signals specify whether the data transfer is to or from memory; another specifies whether or not to clear memory after reading the word content.

Computers differ greatly in the types of DMA transfer functions allowed, but a well designed CPU will only expect the device controller to strobe data onto the in-bus lines or read data off the out-bus lines; CPU logic will execute any specified memory operations (e.g., add to memory). If data are being output to the device, the CPU places the data on the out-bus lines and pulses other lines on the i/o bus, signaling the device controller to read data.

DMA i/o control — Refers to direct memory access which is a mechanism designed to allow the input/output devices to take control of the CPU for one or more memory cycles, in order to write to or read from memory. The order of executing the program steps (instructions) remains unchanged.

DMA i/o operations — DMA i/o operations involve a peripheral device and, generally, a system memory. A device can transfer data to or from the memory on the processor module or any read/-write memory module along the bus. The actural sequence of operations for executing the data transfer once a device has been granted DMA bus control is quite similar for the majority of microsystems when the DMA device, not the processor, becomes the bus master (controls the operation).

DMA lines, single chip systems — On some low cost systems users can use the microcomputer DMA lines to wire together several CPU chips. This forms a multiprocessor system, in which the CPUs interface to the same address data buses.

DMA, video — In some systems with direct memory access capabilities, the processor memory is shared with video memory but without timing conflicts. Dedicated memory video terminals, on the other hand, give the processor priority in memory operations. If the terminal is writing characters when the processor takes over its memory, the screen becomes undefined, and a "scratch" mark results.

DMCL — Abbreviation for Device Media Control Language.

DML — Abbreviation for Data Manipulation Language.

DMS — Abbreviation for Data Management System.

DNC, direct numerical control — A system connecting a set of numerically controlled machines to a common memory for part program or machine program storage, with provision for on-demand distribution of data to the machines. Direct numerical control systems typically have additional provisions for collection, display, or editing of part programs, operator instructions, or data related to the numerical control process.

document — 1. A form, voucher, or written evidence of a transaction. 2. To instruct, as by citation of references. 3. To substantiate, as by listing of authorities. 4. A medium containing a representation of stored information, such as a sheet of paper, a punched card, etc.

document alignment — The phase of the reading process, in character recognition, in which a transverse or gravitational force is applied to the document to align its reference edge with that of the machine.

documentation — 1. The process of collecting, organizing, storing, citing and dispensing of documents or the information recorded in the documents. 2. The group of techniques necessary for the orderly presentation, organization, and communication of recorded specialized knowledge in order to maintain a complete record of reasons for changes in variables. Documentation is necessary not so much to give maximum utility as it is to give an unquestionable historical-reference record.

documentation book — All the material needed to document a computer application, including problem statement, flowcharts, coding, and operating instructions.

documentation, empirical — The essence of scientific method, i.e., verifiable documentation from observations, experiments, evidence, past recorded experience—without the use of theory or deduction.

documentation, graphic — A process developed for recording data on graphs and films.

document handling — The process of loading, feeding, transporting, and unloading a cutform document submitted for character recognition.

document leading edge — The edge which is first encountered during the reading process in character recognition, and whose relative position indicates the direction of travel for the document.

document misregistration — The improper state of appearance of a document, in character recognition, on site in the character reader, with reference to a real or imaginary horizontal base line.

documentor — A program designed to use data-processing methods in the production and maintenance of program flowcharts, text material, and other types of tabular or graphic information.

document reader — *See* reader, document.

document reference edge — That edge of a source document, in character recognition, which provides the basis of all subsequent reading processes.

document retrieval — The system of searching, indexing, and identifying of specific documents which contain the desired data being sought.

document, source — A document originally used by a data processing system and which supplies the basic data to be input to the data processing system.

documents, software — Relating to all the documents and notations associated with the computer; e.g., manuals, circuit diagrams, etc., or programs and routines associated with the computer; e.g., compilers, special languages, library routines.

document, turnaround — A punched card or the like which has been prepared by a computer, so that when it is returned to the computer it serves as evidence of a completed transaction.

document types — The generic designation of varied printing methods in character recognition, the category of which is of paramount consideration to data preparation.

docuterm — A word or phrase descriptive of the subject matter or concept of an item of information that is considered important for later retrieval of information. (Related to aspect card.)

domain — In terms of relational models of data-base management systems, the domain is the collection of field occurrences in a file. For example, if a file contained ten records, the domain of each field would have ten elements in it.

do-nothing instruction — *See* instruction, dummy.

don't care gate — *See* gate, don't care.

DO statement range — All FORTRAN statements included in the repetitive execution of a DO loop operation.

dot printer — *See* printer, wire.

double fallback — *See* fallback, double.

double length — Pertaining to twice the normal length of a unit of data or a storage device in a given computing system; e.g., a double-length register would have the capacity to store twice as much data as a single-length or normal register; a double-length word would have twice the number of characters or digits as a normal or single-length word.

double-length number — A number having twice as many figures as are normally handled in a particular device. (Synonymous with double-precision number.)

double-length working — For greater precision, oftentimes two or more machine words are used to represent a single number, and this is termed double-length working. *Same as* double precision.

double operand — Some systems use an instruction type containing two address fields, source operand address field and destination operand address field.

double precision — Pertaining to a quantity having twice as many digits as are normally carried; e.g., a double-precision number requires two machine words in a fixed-word machine.

double-precision arithmetic — Arithmetic used when more accuracy is necessary than a single word of computer storage will provide. This is accomplished by using two computer words to represent one number.

double-precision number — A number having twice as many figures as are normally handled in a particular device. The purpose is to carry more significant digits in a computation to thereby avoid the loss of high or low order positions.

double-precision operation — An operation in which two registers are treated as a 64-bit double-word register containing a single quantity.

double-precision quantity — *Same as* double precision number.

double-pulse recording — A specific method for magnetic recording of bits in which each storage cell comprises two regions magnetized in opposite senses with unmagnetized regions on each side.

doubler — An internal component which doubles a given digit and is used in the multiplication routine.

double-rail logic — *See* logic, double-rail.

double-word command — A double word that contains detailed information concerning a portion of an input/output operation.

double word, effective — The double word actually accessed in a double-word operation.

double-word location, effective — The actual storage location pointed to by the effective virtual address of a double-word addressing instruction.

double word, program status — A double

word that indicates all programmable control conditions of a CPU. The program status double word is a set of hardware control registers whose contents are collected and stored as a double word in memory, and whose states can be established by loading a double word from memory.

double-word register — Two registers used to hold a 64-bit double word (some computers).

down-line load — The process by which one node in a computer network transfers an entire system image or a program (task) image to another node and causes it to be executed.

down time — The period during which a computer is malfunctioning or not operating correctly due to machine failures. (Contrasted with available time, idle time, or standby time.)

down time, nonscheduled — This is the idle machine time during which the hardware is being repaired because of failures or unforeseen circumstances other than normal servicing or maintenance time. It is usually expressed as a percent of total available time.

down time, scheduled — The determined or required idle time necessary for normal servicing of computer equipment during which such equipment is unavailable for operations. This is usually expressed as a percent of total available time. It is also known as preventive maintenance time.

DP — Abbreviation for Data Processing.

DPM — The abbreviation for documents per minute, and data-processing machine.

DPMA — Data Processing Management Association.

DPMA certificate — A certificate given by the Data Processing Management Association which indicates that a person has a certain level of competence in the field of data processing. The certificate is obtained by passing an examination that is offered yearly throughout the United States and Canada.

drift error — That part of the error in analog computers due to drift or change in component values caused by changes in temperature or changes in power supply voltages.

drills, network — A final level of testing in a real-time system in which data from all the sites is transmitted and the entire complex of equipment, personnel, interfaces, and programs is tested.

drive — A device that moves tape past a head. (Synonymous with tape transport.)

driven, key — *See* key-driven.

drive pulse — 1. A pulsed magnetomotive force applied to a magnetic core. 2. A particular pulse of current in a winding inductively coupled to one or more magnetic cells which produces a pulse of magnetomotive force.

drive pulse, partial — *See* pulse, partial-write.

driver (buffer) — A driver or a buffer is a circuit designed to isolate a load from the driving source; it is often used between a microprocessor chip and the memory address lines, and to boost a small drive current from the microprocessor IC to a higher value suitable for driving a large number of devices simultaneously.

driver, device — Usually refers to an operating system (OS) module that controls a specific input-output peripheral; e.g., the driver is called by the executive of the operating system in response to a user program i/o call. In most systems, each type of peripheral has a unique driver in the operating system.

drive, tape — The mechanism that moves magnetic or paper tape past sensing and recording heads; usually associated with data-processing equipment. (Synonymous with tape unit, and clarified by magnetic-tape unit, and paper-tape unit.)

DRO (Destructive Read-Out) — The interrogation of a destructive type of storage system.

drop-dead halt — *See* halt, dead.

drop-in — An accidental or unwanted appearance of bits.

drop-out — The accidental failure to read or write a necessary character on a magnetic recording surface.

drops, false — The documents spuriously identified as pertinent by an information-retrieval system, but which do not satisfy the search requirements, due to causes such as improper coding, punching spurious or wrong combinations of holes, or improper use of terminology. (Related to noise.)

drum, display — *See* display drum.

dry running — Relates to the examination

of the logic and coding of a program from a flowchart and written instructions, and record of the results of each step of the operation before running the program on the computer.

DSW — Abbreviation for device status word.

DTE — Abbreviation for Data Terminal Equipment.

dual-channel controller — This controller increases the sorting and merging powers of the systems by permitting simultaneous tape reading and/or writing. All tapes may be accessed from either channel.

dual-gap rewrite head — A character written on tape is immediately read by a read head so that the accuracy of recorded data might be ensured.

dual operation — Most frequent reference is to the Boolean operation whose result is the negation of the result of another Boolean operation.

dual purpose card — Punched cards which contain printed as well as punched information.

dual recordings — The dual recording of critical data makes it possible to machine-compare the two for verification. It is more commonly used in mark-sense recording operations and those card-punch operations in which it is necessary to verify only one or two fields.

dual storage — *See* storage, dual.

dual systems — Special configurations that use two computers to receive identical inputs and execute the same routines, with the results of such parallel processing subject to comparison. Exceptional high-reliability requirements are usually involved.

dummy — An artificial address, instruction, or record of information inserted solely to fulfill prescribed conditions, such as to achieve a fixed word length or block length, but without itself affecting machine operations except to permit the machine to perform desired operations.

dummy address — An artificial address used for illustration or instruction purposes.

dummy instruction — *See* instruction, dummy.

dump — 1. To accidentally or intentionally withdraw all power from a computer. 2. To record the contents of internal storage at a given instant of time, usually as an aid in detecting program mistakes or errors. 3. To print out or punch out a portion or all of the contents of the computer memory. 4. To transfer all or part of the contents of one section of computer memory into another section, or to some output device.

dump, ac — The intentional, accidental or conditional removal of all alternating-current power from a system or component. An ac dump usually results in the removal of all power, since direct current is usually supplied through a rectifier or converter.

dump, change — A printout or output recording of the contents of all storage locations in which a change has been made since the previous change dump.

dump check — A check which usually consists of adding all the digits during dumping, and verifying the sum when retransferring.

dump, dc — The intentional, accidental, or conditional removal of all direct-current power from a system or component.

dump, dynamic — A dump that is performed periodically during the execution of a program.

dumping, dynamic — A specific feature which prints diagnostic data avoiding interruption in the program which is being tested.

dumping, executive — The facility to obtain printable dumps of the contents of areas of film or main memory in case unexpected errors cause premature termination of supposedly debugged programs. The dumps are recorded on tape for later printing on the high-speed printer.

dumping, periodic (time sharing) — *See* time sharing, periodic dumping.

dumping, storage — A procedure or process for transferring data from one particular storage device to another or from one particular area to another.

dump, memory — 1. A listing of the contents of a storage device, or selected parts of it. (Synonymous with main dump and memory printout.) 2. Routine generated automatically according to a programmer's specification and included in an object program to perform, respectively, program-loading operations and a printout of memory contents upon request.

dump point — Refers to a designed point

in a program at which it is desirable to write the program and its data to a backing storage, as a protection against machine failure. Dump points may be selected to effect dumping at specific time intervals or at predetermined events in the running of the program.

dump, post-mortem — A listing of the contents of a storage device taken after a routine has been run in order that the final condition of sections of storage may be recorded for debugging purposes.

dump, power — The accidental or intentional removal of all power.

dump printout — Refers to various program printouts, often in hexadecimal format, of the contents of all memory areas currently assigned to the program (also in many cases, data areas). The output can serve as a valuable diagnostic tool to facilitate troubleshooting and error correction.

dump, priority error — The dumping into tape, etc., of information and main storage so that the cause of an equipment or program error may be assessed by the analysts.

dump, selective — A dump of one or more specified storage locations.

dump, snapshot — A dynamic, partial printout during computing occurring at breakpoints and checkpoints, or at selected items in storage.

dump, static — A dump that is performed at a particular point in time with respect to a machine run, frequently at the end of a run.

dump, storage — A listing of the contents of a storage device, or selected parts of it. (Synonymous with memory dump, main dump, and memory printout.)

dup — Abbreviation for duplication; also, a punched card which is an exact copy of a previous punched card. Improper use of word duplex, but often meant to signify a second set of equipment or computing devices which would substitute for original equipment in case of failure.

duplex — Pertaining to a twin, a pair, or a two-in-one situation, e.g., a channel providing simultaneous transmission in both directions, or a second set of equipment to be used in event of the failure of the primary.

duplex channel — A channel providing simultaneous transmission in both directions.

duplex console — A switchover console connecting two or more computers and used to govern which computer is to be on-line.

duplex equipment — An invalid term but one which usually is given to mean a stand-by, reserve, or fail-safe set of equipment or devices to be used in the event of failure of the primary equipment.

duplex, full — A method of operating a communications circuit so that each end can simultaneously transmit and receive.

duplex, full, service — A service in which the data communication channel is capable of simultaneous and independent transmission and reception.

duplex, half — Permits one-direction electrical communications between stations. Technical arrangements may permit operation in either direction, but not simultaneously. Therefore, this term is qualified by one of the following suffixes: S/O for send only; R/O for receive only; S/R for send or receive.

duplexing, synchro — The scheme of producing a document on a printing device through the synchronous running of a program tape and a master tape or a pure data tape. The operation is completely controlled by function codes in the program tape. A data-processing function.

duplex system — Two computers used in special configuration, one is on-line and the other is standing by ready to be used if a malfunction of the on-line computer occurs. The stand-by computer is often used to complete off-line functions.

duplicate — To reproduce data leaving the original data unchanged.

duplicated record — Images or copies of file records that are located in file modules or frames that are separate from the primary copy. Such duplicate records ensure against loss of urgent or critical files or data.

dwell — The usually adjustable time length of an output pulse that is independent of input signal duration. Pertains to pulsed logic amplifier output, either immediate or delayed.

dyadic Boolean operation — *See* Boolean operation, dyadic.

dyadic operation — An operation on two operands.

dynamic — Pertaining to a quantity that is

affected by time, energy or power, and therefore indicates a relatively transient or unstable condition.

dynamic access, data base — Dynamic access is the capability of combining several of the access to data base methods supported by a system. For example, an indexed file could be accessed randomly by key in order to establish a starting position within the file, and then accessed sequentially to process all records whose keys follow the retrieved record in the collated index.

dynamic control — *See* control, dynamic.

dynamic debug — Pertaining to those debug programs designed for interactive debugging of user-written programs.

dynamic dump — A dump that is performed periodically during the execution of a program.

dynamic dumping — A specific feature which prints diagnostic data, avoiding interruption in the program which is being tested.

dynamic flow diagram — A diagram that shows the operational aspects of a computer program as a function of time. All references to pertinent items, such as tables, index registers, subroutines, etc.

dynamic focus — If the size of the scanning spot is minimized in the center of the screen of a crt, it may grow larger as the beam moves away from the center. Careful yoke design can minimize this location defocusing, or astigmatism, and electron-lens design can minimize the spot size. The only practical way to obtain uniform focus is to apply a correction voltage (dependent on deflection angle) to the focus grid. This procedure, termed "dynamic focus," is available in most high-quality crt display modules.

dynamic handling — This corresponds to interpretation in various respects, but generally means a given feature is not handled fully until the generated machine language program is executed.

dynamic instructions — The sequence of machine steps performed by the computer in a real-time or simulated environment.

dynamiciser — A specific logic element which has the capability of converting a space distribution of simultaneous states representing digits into a corresponding time sequence.

dynamic loading — The loading of a program module or routine into main memory by reference to it by a loaded executing program.

dynamic loop — *See* loop, dynamic.

dynamic memory — The storage of data on a device or in a manner that permits the data to move or vary with time, and thus the data is not always instantly available for recovery, e.g., acoustic delay line, magnetic drum, or circulating or recirculating of information in a medium.

dynamic memory relocation — Frees computer user from keeping track of exactly where information is located in the system's memory. Another important attribute is its ability to keep programs flowing in and out of memory in a highly efficient manner.

dynamic printout — A printout of data which occurs as one of the sequential operations during the machine run.

dynamic program loading — *See* dynamic loading.

dynamic programming (DP) — The essence of dynamic programming is that an optimum decision must be made at every stage of a multistage problem. When considering only a single stage, there may appear to be a number of different decisions of equal merit. Only when the effect of each decision at every stage on the overall goal is determined can the final choice be made. This integrating of the cumulative effect of a path of decisions through each stage of the network is the real essence of DP.

dynamic program relocation — *See* program relocation, dynamic.

dynamic RAM module — A typical 8K dynamic RAM is a 8192 × 8-bit NMOS memory in two 4096-byte arrays. Each array is switch-selectable and can be used as ROM, with cycle stealing refresh, and the refresh capability during power failure.

dynamic relocation — *See* program relocation, dynamic.

dynamic response — The specific behavior of the output of a device as a function of the input, both with respect to time.

dynamic routine — *See* subroutine, dynamic.

dynamic scheduling — Scheduling that changes with the different demands that are made on the system rather than being fixed as in conventional applications.

dynamic stop — A specific stop in a loop which consists of a single jump instruction which effects a jump to itself.

dynamic storage — *See* storage, dynamic.

dynamic storage allocation — Dynamic storage allocation is provided in a separate version of the compiler. Each time a subroutine is called using this feature, the unique storage area for the subroutine is assigned to the first storage available. Thus, all subroutines called on the same level will share the same storage area. This results in a significant storage saving in most cases. In addition, a recursive subroutine call is possible because a new storage area is assigned each time a subroutine is entered. This feature, together with in-line symbolic coding, provides powerful real-time programming capability.

dynamic subroutine — 1. A program or routine which the computer changes, adjusts, or completes to carry out the requirements of the data to be developed or processed. 2. A subroutine which involves parameters, such as decimal point position or item size, from which a relatively coded subroutine is derived. The computer itself is expected to adjust or generate the subroutine according to the parametric values chosen.

dynamic tape and memory dump routines — These routines, particularly valuable when debugging programs, provide automatic "on-the-fly" recording of the contents of memory and of magnetic tape files. Calls to these routines may be programmed in advance by use of macroinstructions, or they may be initiated at object time by the operator.

E

early start dates — Used in an optimistic time estimate in which each job is started as early as possible to estimate the duration of the entire task.

EAROM device (electrically alterable read only memory) — A specialized random access read/write memory with a special slow write cycle and a much faster read cycle; programmed by writing into the array and generally used as a ROM. Contents can be erased en masse. EAROMs have several inherent disadvantages. First the price, when compared to masked MOS ROMs is very high. Reprogrammability does help to reduce true cost of EAROMs but isn't sufficient in large volume applications to warrant EAROM use. The second problem with EAROMs is testing. As it takes a very long time to write a single data pattern into an EAROM, testing multiple data patterns can take up to 20 or 30 minutes while similar tests on R/W RAMs would take a matter of 30 seconds to 1 minute to complete the same test patterns. Another problem with some EAROMs is their comparatively slow speeds. A 340-ns access time prevents some EAROMs from addressing the high speed applications currently served by bipolar PROMs.

EBCDIC — Abbreviation for expanded binary coded decimal interchange code. An 8-bit code used to represent 256 unique letters, numbers, and special characters.

EBCDIC code — An eight-level code similar to ASCII. EBCDIC uses the eighth level for an information bit, which extends the range of characters to 256. ASCII uses its eighth level for a parity bit (odd for synchronous transmission; even for asychronous transmission).

EC — An abbreviation or a notation for error correcting.

echo — Echo is the effect of a wave, which having derived (for example by reflection) from a primary wave, arrives at either end of the same circuit with sufficient magnitude and delay to be distinctly recognized.

echo attenuation — In a four-wire (or two-wire) circuit equipped with repeaters or multiplex equipment in which the two directions of transmission can be separated from each other, the attenuation of the echo currents (which return to the input of the circuit under consideration) is determined by the ratio of the transmitted power (P_1) to the echo power received (P_2).

echo check — A check of accuracy of transmission in which the information which was transmitted to an output device is returned to the information source and compared with the original information to ensure accuracy of output.

ECL (emitter-coupled logic) advantages — Some designers favor computer logic that is essentially designed around ECL (emitter-coupled logic). The ECL approach often is preferred since the devices are inherently very uniform and very stable, and are excellent for driving lines. ECL is very fast, so users must design with the higher speed in mind and follow certain layout rules. The approach also can necessitate use of multilayer printed circuit boards. That is advantageous in terms of packaging density. ECL is also advantageous because it requires only a 1-volt swing in 3 to 4 nanoseconds, while a typical Schottky TTL requires a 5-volt swing in the same time frame. ECL also inherently generates less noise.

ECL microprocessor — A typical ECL microprocessor set contains five chips: a 4-bit slice, a control register function, a timing function, a slice memory interface and a slice look-ahead. The various chips can be used as building blocks to construct a microprocessor with capabilities larger than four bits.

ECMA — European Computer Manufacturing Association.

econometrics — The application of mathematical estimation and inference techniques to economic data in order to set the levels of economic parameters and to verify or disprove economic theorems.

ED — Abbreviation for error detecting, expanded display or external device.

ED (external device) address — The ED address specifies which external device a particular instruction is referring to. Scores of different external devices can be specified.

edge, character — In optical character recognition, there is an imaginary edge which runs along the optical discontinuity between the printed area and the unprinted area of a printed symbol or character. The optical discontinuity is observed by a change in the reflectivity along this imaginary line which is transverse to the character edge.

edge, guide — The edge of a paper tape, magnetic tape, punched card, printed sheet, or other such data containing medium that is used for a determination of its transverse position during movement. The edge of a specific data carrier which is used as a reference, i.e., for dimensioning, and which usually controls its position in actual use.

edge, stroke — An optical character recognition term relating to an imaginary line that is equidistant at all points from the stroke center line and that divides the edge irregularities of the printed stroke in such a way that the unprinted areas on the inside of the center line are approximately equal to the printed areas on the outside of the line.

edge, stroke, irregularity — A term used in optical character recognition referring to the deviation of any point on the edge of a character from the stroke edge.

edit — 1. To prepare for publication. 2. To rearrange data or information. Editing may involve the deletion of unwanted data, the selection of pertinent data, the application of format techniques, the insertion of symbols such as page numbers and typewriter characters, the application of standard processes such as zero suppression, and the testing of data for reasonableness and proper range. Editing may sometimes be distinguished between input edit (arrangement of source data) and output edit (preparation of table formats).

edit capabilities — Edit capabilities permit checking of many characters at a time doing zero suppress, floating dollar sign, asterisk protect, comma and decimal insertions, sign control, and other routines. Editing time in the central processors is reduced.

edit commands — In some systems edit commands are implemented as single, double, or triple letter mnemonics followed by optional command parameters. All commands are terminated by typing a carriage return, ®. Commands may be typed at any time during the edit process in place of entering a source statement. If an error is detected, Edit outputs a question mark (?) and the command is ignored. Typeouts, resulting from a command, may be aborted by depressing the keyboard BREAK key.

edit functions, crt — The edit functions of a crt terminal include the ability to insert or delete characters or entire lines, the ability to position the cursor of the unit and the ability to define certain protected data fields on the screen of the terminal. Generally, the more numerous its editing capabilities, the more "intelligent" users can consider a crt terminal.

editing and modification, text (time sharing) — *See* time sharing text editing and modification.

editing functions, terminal — These allow removal of characters, words or larger pieces of text, insertion of new text, and movement of text from one position to another. Such functions are essential to word processing operations, but they are also very useful features for any display work station. Operators always make mistakes, and editing allows these to be easily corrected.

editing, post — A procedure or process of editing the output of a prior operation, especially those related to accounting, or programs which might have syntax or construction errors.

editing subroutine — *See* subroutine, editing.

editor — An editor is a general-purpose text editing program used to prepare source program tapes. Original text entered via the teletypewriter and held in memory may be changed and corrected. The user can insert, delete or change lines of text, insert, delete and change characters within a line without retyping the line, locate lines containing key words and list or punch any portion of the text.

editor, linkage — A standard service routine to convert outputs of assemblers or compilers to forms which can be loaded and executed, by combining separately developed object modules or incorporating all or parts of previously processed load modules into a new load module. The linkage editor also replaces, deletes, or inserts control sections, creates overlay facilities, or restores symbolic cross references between various input modules. Usually, linkage editors are run before programs are ready for load in OS, DOS, or TOS operations, i.e., disk and tape operating systems.

editor program — *See* program, editor.

editor-programmer — Electronic device through which two or more video tape machines can be controlled to edit programming accurately and, to some extent, automatically.

editor routine — *Same as* program, editor.

editor, symbolic — Permits the editing of source-language programs by adding or deleting lines of text. All modification, reading, punching, etc., is controlled by symbols typed at the keyboard. The editor reads parts or all of a symbolic tape into memory, where it is available for immediate examination, correction, and relisting.

editor, tape — *See* tape editor.

editor types — Editors are aids in preparing source programs, and certain programs have been developed that manipulate text material in various ways. These programs are called editors, text editors, paper tape editors, disk editors, etc., and make it possible to compose assembly language programs on line, or on a stand-along system. They also assist in output formatting, etc.

edit, post — To edit the results of a previous computation.

edit statements — In some systems all statements entered from the keyboard are placed into an internal edit buffer. Each statement entered is preceded by a statement number that specifies the relative order of the statement in relation to all other statements. Statement numbers need not be consecutive, and the sequence in which statements are entered is immaterial; however, statements are buffered in order of increasing statement number and are always listed and dumped in that order. Statement numbers which precede each statement entered into Edit may take many specific forms.

EDP — Electronic data processing. Data processing performed largely by electronic equipment. (Related to automatic data processing.)

EDP center — A complete complex including one or more computers, its peripheral equipment, personnel related to the operation of the center and its functions, and the office space housing the necessary hardware and personnel.

EDP center manager — *See* manager, computer center.

EDPE — Abbreviation for electronic data processing equipment.

EDPM — Electronic data-processing machine.

EDP management science — The field of management science is extending the computer far beyond the automation of routine accounting operations and into the complex decision-making process of management. Through revolutionary computer-programming techniques such as simulation, the objective, scientific approach of management science is providing increased management capability and control.

In addition to the physical or operational processes like inventory management, product planning and control, resource allocation or market forecasting, this also includes the fiscal processes such as bond management, capital investment, risk analysis, profit planning and product pricing.

Manufacturer's broad resources are prepared to meet management's growing demand for this expanded capability and to extend the tradition of "total systems" capability into revolutionary data-processing techniques and applications.

EDPS — Electronic data processing system.

EDUCOM Planning Council — The Planning Council is a cooperative activity of 22 universities that have decided to investigate jointly how the computing needs of their institutions can best be met, assess the means of achieving efficient and effective resource sharing, and develop a national "facilitating network" linking computers at colleges and universities throughout the United States.

edulcorate — 1. To improve by eliminating worthless information. 2. To weed out.

EEROM programmer — A unit that provides a means of programming a single EEROM or an EEROM module from paper tape or from an integral hex keyboard and display.

effective address — 1. A modified address. 2. An address obtained by the combination of the contents of a specific index register with the address of an instruction. 3. The address used for the execution of an instruction. This may differ from that of the instruction in storage.

effective byte — The byte actually accessed in an operation on a single byte or byte string.

effective byte location — The actual storage location pointed to by the effective virtual address of a byte addressing instruction.

effective data transfer rate — *See* data transfer rate, average.

effective double word — The double word actually accessed in a double-word operation.

effective double-word location — The actual storage location pointed to by the effective virtual address of a double-word addressing instruction.

effective half-word — The half-word actually accessed in a half-word operation.

effective half-word location — The storage location pointed to by the effective virtual address of a half-word addressing instruction.

effective instruction — *See* instruction, effective.

effective operand address — An address obtained at the time of execution by the computer to give the actual operand address.

effective speed — Speed (less than rated) which can be sustained over a significant period of time and which reflects the slowing effects of control codes, timing codes, error detection, retransmission, tabbing, hand keying, etc.

effective time — *See* time, effective.

effective transmission rate — *Same as* data-transfer rate, effective.

effective-transmission speed — The rate at which information is processed by a transmission facility, expressed as the average rate over some significant time interval. This quantity is usually expressed as average characters per unit of time, or average bits per unit of time.

effective virtual address — The virtual address value after only indirect addressing and/or indexing modifications have been accomplished, but before memory mapping is performed.

effective word — The word actually accessed in an operation on a single word.

effective word location — The storage location pointed to by the effective virtual address of a word-addressing instruction.

EIA interface — A set of signal characteristics (time duration, voltage, and current) for connection of terminals to modem units, and specific physical coupler dimensions specified by the Electronic Industries Association.

EIA Standard RS-232 B or C — This is a standardized method adopted by the Electronic Industries Association to ensure uniformity of interface between data communication equipment and data processing terminal equipment. It has been generally accepted by a majority of manufacturers of data transmission and business equipment.

eight level — Any teletypewriter code that utilizes eight impulses, in addition to the start and stop impulses, for describing a character.

EITHER-OR operation — *Same as* gate, OR.

electrical impulses — The signals coming from card or magnetic tape readers, and other similar devices, which are converted into the code used by the computer and sent to the computer memory for processing or storage.

electrically alterable memory — A memory device whose contents can be revised with electrical signals.

electrically erasable ROM (EEROM) — An EEROM is a device that can be erased electrically in one second. It can be erased and reprogrammed up to a million times. One type is organized as 512 words of two bits per word.

electromagnetic communications — The electromagnetic-wave conductor is space itself. The electromagnetic frequencies available today for communications fall into two categories: Lightbeam (laser) communication above the ehf frequency band, and nonlightbeam frequency communications in or below the ehf band. The latter devices include radio, television, and radar devices covering the frequency spectrum between the vlf and ehf bands. More elaborate translators are required than for electrical communications.

electromagnetic delay line — A delay line whose operation is based on the time of propagation of electromagnetic waves through distributed or lumped capacitance and inductance.

electromagnetic relay — An electromagnetic switching device having multiple electrical contacts that are operated by an electrical current through a coil. It is used to complete electrical circuits with an applied control current, and also as a mechanical binary counter.

electromechanical device — A piece of equipment which is partially electronic and partially mechanical in nature. While the central processing unit is a pure electronic device, most random access equipment involves moving parts, and are therefore electromechanical devices.

electromechanical printer — A machine capable of printing characters on paper by converting electrical signals into mechanical motion (through motors, cams, levers, linkages, and so forth).

electronic — Pertaining to that branch of science which deals with the motion, emission, and behavior of currents of free electrons, especially in vacuum, gas, or phototubes and special conductors or semiconductors. This is contrasted with electric which pertains to the flow of electrons in metal conductors.

electronically alterable ROM (EAROM) — Electronically Alterable Read Only Memory. This is a type of memory that is similar to EROM (erasable ROM) and RAM, Random Access Memory. EAROMs are nonvolatile (like ROMs) but are electrically erasable while EROMs are erasable only with short wavelength untraviolet light. EAROMs can be written into with standard logic levels, while most EROMs require special equipment and cannot be programmed in circuit. The primary difference is in the write cycle of about 500 nanoseconds for an EROM and the much slower 2 microseconds for EAROM.

electronic data-processing system — 1. A machine system capable of receiving, storing, operating on, and recording data without the intermediate use of tabulating cards, and which also possesses the ability to store internally at least some instructions for data-processing operations, and the means for locating and controlling access to data stored internally. 2. The general term used to define a system for data processing by means of machines utilizing electronic circuitry at electronic speed, as opposed to electromechanical equipment.

electronic data-switching center, automatic — *Same as* automatic data-switching center.

electronic differential analyzer — A form of analog computer using interconnected electronic integrators to solve differential equations.

electronic library — A general-purpose library system where the user sits at a computer terminal and calls for viewing on his crt any author, title, or subject in the card catalogue, or any page of any book in the library. At the press of a button any lines or pages can be printed for him to take home. The tremendous potential of the electronic library can be appreciated if one realizes the materials of several libraries may become available to millions of users through the use of computer utilities.

electronic neuron network simulation — The study and duplication of neuron cells and networks in order to build multiple-purpose systems using analogous electronic components. Computers have been programmed to act as neuron system simulators, and this type of research holds much potential for the future.

electronics — A branch of science dealing with the motion, emission, and behaviour of currents of free electrons and certain ions, especially those in vacuum tubes, gas tubes, semiconductors, and superconductors.

electronic scales — Various microcomputer-based units with electronic weighing indicators that handle most operations involved in static weighing and simple batching. Large LED displays signify overcapacity, motion, minus weights, and zero zone. Some instruments can measure in either pounds or kilograms. Some models accommodate various types of weights, identifications, preset weight control, time and date and related information.

electronic statistical machine — A sorter which can print and add data while sorting.

electronic stylus — A penlike device which is commonly used in conjunction with a crt (cathode-ray tube) for inputting or changing information under program control. The electronic stylus is often called a light pen, and works by signaling the computer with an electronic pulse. The computer acts on these signals and can change the configuration plotted across the tube face or perform other operations using the inputted data according to previously programmed instructions.

electronic switch — A circuit element causing a start and stop action or a switching action electronically, usually at high speeds.

electronic switching system (ESS) — A type of telephone switching system which uses a special-purpose stored program digital computer to direct and control the switching operation. ESS permits the provision of custom calling services such as speed dialing, call transfer, three-way calling, etc.

electronic tutor — A teaching machine which makes use of instructions in the computer to help each student achieve his educational goals. Each student communicates with the computer via his own terminal. The computer will be programmed to adjust its teaching style automatically to the needs of each student, and each student will progress at his own pace, independently of others. Bright students will move from topic to topic rapidly, while slower students will be carefully tutored and given extra practice to raise them to the desired achievement levels.

electrostatic printer — A device for printing an optical image on paper, in which dark and light areas of the original are represented by electrostatically charged and uncharged areas on the paper. The paper is dusted with particles of finely powdered dry ink, and the particles adhere only to the electrically charged areas. The paper with ink particles is then heated, causing the ink to melt and become permanently fixed to the paper.

electrostatic storage — 1. The storage of data on a dielectric surface, such as the screen of a cathode ray tube, in the form of the presence or absence of spots bearing electrostatic charges that can persist for a short time after the electrostatic charging force is removed. 2. A storage device which uses electric charges to represent data.

electrostatic storage tube — A storage device in which information is stored in the form of a pattern of electric charges. This device is generally a crt.

element — A component part.

element, AND — *Same as* gate, AND.

element, anticoincidence — *Same as* gate, exclusive OR.

elementary item — In the COBOL system, a data item containing no subordinate items.

element, code — A discrete condition or event in a code, such as a stroke in a printed character.

element, combinational logic — 1. A device having at least one output channel and two or more input channels, all characterized by discrete states, such that the state of each output channel is completely determined by the contemporaneous states of the input channels. 2. A logic element used in combinational logic.

element, data — A specific item of information appearing in a set of data; e.g., in the following set of data, each item is a data element: the quantity of a supply item issued, a unit rate, an amount, and the balance of stock items on hand.

element, decision — *See* decision element.

element, delay — That circuitry or electronic mechanism that accepts data temporarily and emits the same data after a specific interval.

element, digit delay — A specific delay element that introduces a delay in a line of signals or pulses of one digit period duration.

element, equivalent-to — *Same as* gate, exclusive NOR.

element, function — *Same as* element, logical.

element, logic — A device that performs a logic function.

element, logical — The smallest building block in a computer or data-processing system that can be represented by logical operators in an appropriate system of symbolic logic. Typical logical elements that can be represented as operators in a suitable symbolic logic are the AND gate and the OR gate.

element, majority decision — *Same as* gate, majority decision.

element, NAND — *Same as* gate, NAND.

element, negation — *Same as* gate, NOT.

element, nonequivalent — *Same as* gate, exclusive OR.

element, NOR — *Same as* gate, NOR.

element NOT — *Same as* gate, NOT.

element, NOT-AND — *Same as* gate, NAND.

element, OR — *Same as* gate, OR.

element, sequential — A device having at least one output channel and one or more input channels, all characterized by discrete states, such that the state of each output channel is determined by the previous states of the input channels.

element, sequential logic — A unit or device which has at least one output channel and one or more input channels, designed so that the state of each output channel is determined by the previous states of the input channels, or by the previous states and the concurrent states of the input channels.

element, start — The first element of a character in certain serial transmissions, used to permit synchronization. In Baudot teletypewriter operation, it is one space bit.

element, stop — The last element of a character in certain serial transmissions, used to ensure recognition of next start element.

element, threshold — A device capable of performing the threshhold logic operation. This operation involves the general case of a special majority decision.

element, unit — Alphabetical signal element having a duration equal to the unit interval of time.

elimination factor — The ratio in information retrieval obtained by dividing the number of documents that have not been retrieved by the total number of documents contained in the file.

elimination, zero — The elimination of insignificant zeros (those to the left of a quantity in a field or word) during a printing operation.

else, OR — *Same as* gate, OR.

else rule — A catch-all rule in decision tables designed to handle the conditions not covered by exact and explicit rules; it is written by leaving all conditions blank. Action then to be taken may be to halt processing, note the condition, or to correct the situation and continue processing.

embedded pointers — A technique for implementing associations between records in a data base that uses space in the record to store a pointer, as opposed to storing pointers in some other data structure or using some other means to relate the information.

embossed plate printer — The data preparation device, in character recognition, which prints through the paper medium by allowing only the raised character to make contact with the printing ribbon.

emergency switch — Switch on most control panels which will disconnect all power from the computer system.

emitter — A device, usually used on punch-card machines, to give timed pulses at regular intervals during the machine cycle.

emitter, character — An electromechanical device used to generate and emit, in some code, pulse groups corresponding to characters.

emitter pulse — Relating to a punched card machine, one of the group of pulses that is used to define a particular row within the columns of a card.

empirical — Pertaining to a statement or formula based on experience or experimental evidence rather than on mathematical or theoretical conclusions.

empirical documentation — *See* documentation, empirical.

emulate — The ability of one system to imitate another, with the imitating system accepting the same data and programming and achieving the same results as the imitated system, but possibly with a different time of performance.

emulation — Techniques using software or microprogramming in which one computer is made to behave exactly like another computer; i.e., the emulating system executes programs in the native machine language code of the emulated system. Emulation is generally used to minimize the impact of conversion from one computer system to another, and is used to continue the use of production programs—as opposed to "simulation" which is used to study the operational characteristics of another (possibly theoretical) system.

emulation, remote terminal — Remote terminal emulation is a computer measurement and evaluation technique whereby the teleprocessing workload imposed on a computer system is emulated by another computer. This is a relatively recent development applicable to benchmarking and tuning.

emulation testing — The use of hardware or software to generate in real-time the expected correct output responses for comparison to the DUT (device under test).

emulator — Hardware built into a computer causing the system to accept certain software programs and routines and appear as if it were another system, such as 7094 software running on an IBM 360 computer without translation.

emulator, stand-alone — An emulator whose execution is not controlled by a control program; it does not share system resources with other programs and excludes all other jobs from the computing system while it is being executed.

enable — Restoration of a suppressed interrupt feature.

enabled — The condition of an interrupt level wherein the level is not inhibited from advancing from the waiting state to the active state, except for priority considerations.

enable pulse — A digit pulse which aids the write pulse, which together are strong enough to switch the magnetic cell.

enabling signal — A means of allowing an operation to take place.

encipher — *Same as* encode.

encode — 1. To apply a code, frequently one consisting of binary numbers, to represent individual characters or groups of characters in a message. (Synonymous with encipher.) 2. To substitute letters, numbers, or characters, usually to intentionally hide the meaning of the message except to certain individuals who know the enciphering scheme. (Synonymous with encipher.)

encoded question — A question set up and encoded in a form appropriate for operating, programming, or conditioning a searching device.

encoder — A device capable of translating from one method of expression to another method of expression, for instance in translating a message, "add the contents of A to the contents of B," into a series of binary digits. (Contrasted with decoder and clarified by matrix.)

encoder, exception-item — The exception-item encoder offers the final link in banking's total automation chain. Providing "point of entry" encoding before documents enter a bank's paper flow, the unit eliminates costly disruption caused by nonencoded items in a bank's automated system.

encoding strip — On bank checks, the area in which magnetic ink will be deposited to represent characters.

END — A statement used to indicate the physical end of the source program. This statement is used in both FORTRAN and Assembler language.

end-around carry — The bit carried over from the high-order to the low-order position.

end-around shift — *See* shift, circular.

end data symbol — The representation indicating that no more data will follow this symbol.

end distortion — End distortion of start-stop teletypewriter signals is the shifting of the end of all marking pulses from their proper positions in relation to the beginning of the start pulse.

ending file label — The gummed paper containing a description of the file content, which usually appears at the end of each file and then only once.

ending tape label — The gummed label describing the tape contents which follow all other data on the tape.

end instrument — A device that is connected to one terminal of a loop and is capable of converting usable intelligence into electrical signals, or vice versa. It includes all generating, signal-converting and loop-terminating devices employed at the transmitting and-/or receiving location.

end, leading — That particular end of a wire, tape, ribbon, line, or document that is processed first.

end, logical leading — If the magnetic tape has been recorded in reverse order from that required for decoding, the first end of the tape for the decoding process is termed the logical leading end as contrasted to the regular leading end.

end mark — A code or signal that indicates termination of a unit of information.

end of data — The signal that is read or generated when the final record of a file has been read or written.

end-of-file — 1. Automatic procedures to handle tapes when the end of an input or output tape is reached. A reflective spot, called a record mark, is placed on the physical end of the tape to signal the end. 2. Termination or point of completion of a quantity of data. End of file marks are used to indicate this point. (Synonymous with EOF.)

end-of-file indicator — A device associated with each input and output unit that makes an end of file condition known to the routine and operator controlling the computer.

end-of-file mark — A code that signals the last record of a file has been read.

end-of-file spot — An area used on the tape to signal the end of the file.

end of line — A machine code character which indicates the end or termination of a group of records.

end-of-loop code — *See* code, end-of-loop.

end-of-message — The specific set of characters that indicates the termination of a message.

end-of-message character — *See* character, end-of-message.

end-of-record word — The last word of a record on tape. It has a unique bit configuration and may be used to define the end of a record in memory.

end-of-tape marker — *See* marker, end-of-tape.

end-of-tape or end-of-file routines — Such a routine is part of a tape system's program and is executed when the last record on a reel has been read and processed. It should update the control totals found in the tape label or trailer record, balance and record the record count and any other control totals, rewind the tape, and perform any necessary instruction modification.

end-of-tape warning — A visible magnetic strip on magnetic tape which indicates that a few feet, oftentimes five, of the tape remain available.

endorser — A particular feature now almost standard on most magnetic-ink character readers (MICRs) which is an endorsement record of each bank after the document has been read.

end printing — The conversion of punched information into bold printing across the end of the card simultaneously with gang punching, summary punching, reproducing, or mark-sensed punching. This is similar to interpreting, and makes possible a quick reference to the card.

end, trailing — The last end of a wire, tape, ribbon, or other item that is processed.

energizer — A test system or program designed for a device such as memory, disk, tape, and so on to detect malfunctions prior to use.

engineering improvement time — *See* engineering time.

engineering time — The total machine down time necessary for routine testing, good or bad, for machine servicing due to breakdowns, or for preventive servicing measures; e.g., block tube changes. This includes all test time, good or bad, following breakdown and subsequent repair or preventive servicing. (Synonymous with servicing time.)

English, ruly — A form of English in which every word has one and only one conceptual meaning and each concept has one and only one word to describe it. This is a hypothetical language based on English that complies uniformly to a definite set of rules, without exceptions.

ENIAC — The electronic numerical integrator and calculator which was developed in World War II at the University of Pennsylvania. This computer is represented by many historians to be the first all electronic computer. It contained over 18,000 vacuum tubes and continued to operate until 1955.

entity — An item about which information is stored. An entity may be tangible or intangible, such as an employee, a part, a place, or an event. An entity is further defined by attributes, the characteristics of the entities, such as the first-name, last-name, and age of an employee.

entity identifier — In data base files usually at least one attribute will be defined to disallow redundant values in its corresponding data file. An example would be an employee number in a personnel file. Thus, even though two employees (entities) may have the same name, the records that track their personnel information will be uniquely identifiable. This attribute is the entity identifier.

entrance — The position where the control sequence begins or transfers into a program or subroutine.

entropy — 1. The measure of unavailable energy in a system. 2. The unavailable information in a set of documents. 3. An inactive or static condition (total entropy).

entry — 1. An input received from a terminal device. On receipt, an entry is placed by a control program in an entry block whose address is inserted in a list of entries awaiting processing. 2. A notation written in a stub of a row or in a cell of a decision table. Any row must be in the form of either a limited entry or an extended entry. 3. A statement in a programming system. In general each entry is written on one line of a coding form and punched on one card, although some systems permit a single entry to overflow several cards. 4. A member of a list.

entry and inquiry, keyboard — A technique whereby the entry into and the interrogation of the contents of a computer's storage may be initiated at a keyboard.

entry block — A block of main-memory storage assigned on receipt of each entry into a system and associated with that entry throughout its life in the system.

entry conditions — Various languages or specific conventions of computer centers designate unique entry conditions. They are so specified (often attached with tape to the computer or entry device) and are in effect a special subroutine or addresses of locations of operands, and links or clock signals.

entry, data — The writing, reading, or posting to a coding form or to a terminal or processing medium, of information or instructions, i.e., a datum or item which is usually entered on one line, a single entity of processing.

entry instruction — Usually the first instruction to be executed in a subroutine, i.e., it may have several different entry points each of which corresponds to a different function of the subroutine.

entry, page — The point, in flowchart symbols, where the flowline continues from a previous page, due to space limitations on the original or previous page.

entry point — 1. Most subroutines have specific points or places where control can be transferred and re-entered. The entry point usually corresponds to a new or different function to be performed. 2. Usually the first instruction to be executed in a subroutine or as part of the entry conditions for specific computers or installations. Various subroutines may have a number of different entry points corresponding to different programs, subroutines, or their functions. When an instruction of a subroutine designates a place or point for reentering, it becomes the re-entry point of the major program.

entry, remote job — The inputting of the job information to the main computing system from a remote device. Frequently abbreviated RJE.

entry time — The time when control is transferred from the supervisory to the application program.

entry unit, remote — An input device, frequently a remote terminal, located at a distance from the central computer. Commonly abbreviated REU.

envelope — A byte augmented by a number of additional bits which are required for the operation of the data network. These additional bits can be control address information or error checking control.

environment division, COBOL — *See* COBOL environment division.

EOF (end-of-file) — Termination or point of completion of a quantity of data. End-of-file marks are used to indicate this point.

EOT (end of transmission) — This indicates the end of a transmission, which may include one or more messages, and resets all stations on the line to control mode (unless it erroneously occurs within a transmission block).

epitome — A concise summary of a document.

EPROM — An electrically programmable ROM suited for high performance microcomputer systems where fast turnaround is important for system program development and for small volumes of identical programs in production systems.

equality circuit — *Same as* gate, AND.

equality gate — *Same as* gate, exclusive NOR.

equality unit — *Same as* gate, exclusive NOR.

equalization — The process of reducing frequency and/or phase distortion of a circuit by the introduction of networks to compensate for the difference in attenuation and/or time delay at the various frequencies in the transmission band.

equalizer — A modem or peripheral device designed to compensate for undesired levels of signal strength.

equalizer, delay — A corrective network that is designed to make the phase delay or envelope delay of a circuit or system substantially constant over a desired frequency range.

equal-zero indicator — An internal computer-indicator component which signals "on" if the result of an arithmetic computation is zero.

equation, linear — An equation whose left-hand side and right-hand side are both linear functions of the variables. Such an equation can always be put in the form f(x, y, z, . . .) = C, where f is a linear function and C is a constant.

equations, independent — A set of equations none of which can be expressed as a linear combination of the others. With linear equations, the condition for independence is that the matrix (coefficient columns) shall be nonsingular or, equivalently, have rank equal to the number of equations.

equation solver — A calculating device, usually analog, that solves systems of linear simultaneous nondifferential equations or determines the roots of polynomials, or both.

equipment, auxiliary — The peripheral equipment or devices not in direct communication with the central processing unit of a computer.

equipment compatibility — The characteristic of computers by which one computer may accept and process data prepared by another computer without conversion or code modification.

equipment, conventional — That equipment which is generally considered to be part of the computer system but which is not specifically part of the computer itself. Various card handling devices, tape handlers, disk units, if not built in to the main frame or wired in would be conventional equipment.

equipment, conversion — The equipment that is capable of transposing or transcribing the information from one type of data-processing medium to render it acceptable as input to another type of processing medium.

equipment, data terminal — The modem, device, or unit at either end of a data communication channel, line, station, or link.

equipment, data-transmission — The communications equipment used in direct support of data-processing equipment.

equipment, delayed-output — The equipment that removes the data from the system after processing has been completed or while in process.

equipment, duplex — *See* duplex equipment.

equipment failure — A fault in the equipment, excluding all external factors, that prevents the accomplishment of a scheduled job.

equipment, high-performance — Equipment having sufficiently exacting characteristics to permit its use in trunk or link circuits.

equipment, input — 1. The equipment used for transferring data and instructions into an automatic data-processing system. 2. The equipment by which an operator transcribes original data and instructions to a medium that may be used in an automatic data-processing system.

equipment, low-performance — Equipment having insufficient characteristics to permit its use in trunk or link circuits. Such equipment may be employed in subscriber line circuits whenever it meets the line circuit requirements.

equipment, off-line — The peripheral equipment or devices not in direct communication with the central processing unit of a computer. (Synonymous with auxiliary equipment.)

equipment, on-line — Descriptive of a system and of the peripheral equipment or devices in a system in which the operation of such equipment is under control of the central processing unit. Its information reflecting current activity is introduced into the data-processing system as soon as it occurs. Thus, directly in-line with the main flow of transaction processing. (Synonymous with in-line processing and on-line processing.)

equipment, on-premises-standby — A duplicate set of computer system devices located nearby, available for performance of operations in the event of equipment failures and as regards time sensitive functions or requirements.

equipment, output — The equipment used for transferring information out of a computer.

equipment, peripheral — The auxiliary machines that may be placed under the control of the central computer. Examples of this are card readers, card punches, magnetic-tape feeds, and high-speed printers. Peripheral equipment may be used on-line or off-line depending upon computer design, job requirements and economics. (Clarified by automatic data-processing equipment and off-line equipment.)

equipment, remote — Those units or modules of apparatus which perform prescribed functions remote or distant from the main computer.

equipment, remote-control — The formulating and reformulating apparatus used for performing a prescribed function or functions at a distance by electrical means.

equipment, standby — Automatic data-processing equipment that is not in use and that is available in emergencies, such as machine breakdowns or cases of overload.

equipment, terminal — Data source or data sink equipment such as teletypewriters for input terminals and cathode-ray tube screens for output.

equipment, transmission — That large class of equipment, considered peripheral to the computing equipment, which communicates data rather than computing or processing.

equivalence — A logical operator having the property that if P is a statement, Q is a statement, R is a statement, . . ., then the equivalence of P, Q, R, . . ., is true if and only if all statements are true or all statements are false, false otherwise.

equivalence element — *Same as* gate, exclusive NOR.

equivalence gate — *Same as* gate, exclusive NOR.

equivalent binary digits — The number of binary digits required to express a number in another base with the same precision; e.g., approximately 3⅓ binary digits are required to express in binary form each digit of a decimal number. For the case of coded decimal notation, the number of binary digits required is usually 4 times the number of decimal digits.

equivalent, symbolic — A determination of a combination or pattern of meaningful coding, i.e., using punched holes, magnetic spots, etc.

equivalent-to element — *Same as* gate, exclusive NOR.

equivocation — The measure of the difference between the received and transmitted messages over a channel.

erasability — The ease of removing a printed image, in character recognition, without impairing the surface of the medium.

erasable storage — 1. A storage medium

that can be erased and reused repeatedly, e.g., magnetic-drum storage. 2. A storage device whose data can be altered during the course of a computation, e.g., magnetic tape, drum, and cores. 3. An area of storage used for temporary storage.

erase — To replace all the binary digits in a storage device by binary zeros. In a binary computer, erasing is equivalent to clearing. In a coded-decimal computer where the pulse code for decimal zero may contain binary ones, *clearing* leaves decimal zero while *erasing* leaves all-zero pulse codes.

erase character — *See* character, erase.

erase head — A device on a magnetic tape drive whose sole function is to erase previous information prior to writing new information.

eraser, bulk — A device which erases or destroys the magnetic information on a reel of tape without removing the tape from the reel.

erasure, tape — A process by which a signal recorded on a tape is removed and the tape made ready for re-recording.

EROM (electrically erasable read only memory) — A specific type of ROM that can be programmed electrically. The unique feature is that it retains data even with the power disconnected but can be erased by exposure to short wavelength ultraviolet light, and may be reprogrammed many times.

error — 1. The general term referring to any deviation of a computed or a measured quantity from the theoretically correct or true value. 2. The part of the error due to a particular identifiable cause, e.g., a truncation error, or a rounding error. In a restricted sense, that deviation due to unavoidable random disturbances, or to the use of finite approximations to what is defined by an infinite series. (Contrasted with mistake.) 3. The amount of loss of precision in a quantity; the difference between an accurate quantity and its calculated approximation; *errors* occur in numerical methods; *mistakes* occur in programming, coding, data transcription, and operating; *malfunctions* occur in computers and are due to physical limitations on the properties of materials; the differential margin by which a controlled unit deviates from its target value.

error, absolute — The magnitude of the error disregarding the algebraic sign, or, if a vectorial error, disregarding its direction.

error, balancing — *See* balancing error.

error burst — A group of bits that has two successive erroneous bits always separated by less than a given number (X) of correct bits. Note: the last erroneous bit in a burst and the first erroneous bit in the following burst are accordingly separated by X correct bits or more. The number X should be specified when describing an error burst.

error, call — Too many subroutines have been called by the program. A maximum of fifty subroutines may be called by an object program (some computers).

error character — *See* character, error.

error checking and recovery — Parity is computed or checked on all references to central store. If a parity error occurs, the computer will interrupt to the proper location, an alarm will sound, and the appropriate fault lights will be flashed on the operator's console. For all real-time applications, the system will attempt to recover. Once the computer has satisfactorily recovered, the system will continue normal operation (some systems).

error-checking code — *See* code, error-checking.

error code — 1. A specific character that may be punched into a card or tape to indicate that a conscious error was made in the associated block of data. Machines reading the error code may be programmed to throw out the entire block automatically. 2. Illegal control code on a binary card.

error, composition — Errors of composition and consistency are detected as soon as the user enters the offending statement. He may immediately substitute a correct statement.

error-correcting code — *See* code, error-correcting.

error correction, automatic — A technique, usually requiring the use of special codes and/or automatic retransmission, which detects and corrects errors occurring in transmission. The degree of correction depends upon coding and equipment configuration.

error correction, programmer — When an error is detected from the results of a program, the programmer may cause a print-out which traces step-by-step, the operation of the program on actual data, or he may cause a program dump for analysis and correction.

error-correction routine — A series of computer instructions programmed to correct a detected error condition.

error correction (transmission) — Blocks of data containing transmission errors can be retransmitted correctly. Such retransmission is immediate and fully automatic.

error, data — A deviation from correctness in data, usually an error, that occurred prior to processing the data.

error-detecting and feedback system — A system employing an error-detecting code and so arranged that a signal detected as being in error automatically initiates a request for retransmission of the correct signal.

error-detecting code — *See* code, error-detecting.

error-detecting system — A system employing an error detecting code and so arranged that any signal detected as being in error is (a) either deleted from the data delivered to the data sink, in some cases with an indication that such deletion has taken place, or (b) delivered to the data sink, together with an indication that it has been detected as being in error.

error detection, automatic — *See* error correction, automatic.

error-detection routine — A routine used to detect if an error has occurred, usually without special provision to find or indicate its location.

error detection (transmission) — Transmission errors are detected by parity and long (channel) checks.

error diagnostics — An erroneous statement is printed with the erroneous part of the statement clearly marked. The entire statement is processed, even when an error has been detected, whenever possible. Some compilers will continue to the end of the program. Thus, complete error diagnostics may be obtained in one compilation. The errors are listed on the same device as the source-language listing.

error diagnostics, time sharing — *See* time sharing, error diagnostics.

error dump, priority — The dumping onto tape, etc., by a priority program of information in storage, so that the cause of an equipment or program error interrupt may be assessed by the analysts.

error, dynamic — The error, or part of an error, related to frequency, such as the inadequate dynamic response of some computing device or unit. Similar to drift error.

error, external — A file mark has been read or end-of-tape has been sensed during a loading operation.

error, illegal control-message — A control message has been read that is not defined. If the message is typed in, it may be retyped. Otherwise, only the compile or assemble phase of the job is processed and a job error is given.

error, inherent — The error in the initial values, especially the error inherited from the previous steps in the step-by-step integration. This error could also be the error introduced by the inability to make exact measurements of physical quantities.

error, inherited — An error in quantities, carried over from a previous operation, that serves as an initial step in a step-by-step set of operations.

error interrupts — Special interrupts are provided in response to certain error conditions within the central computer. These may come as a result of a programming fault (e.g., illegal instruction, arithmetic overflow), a store fault (parity error) or an executive system violation (attempt to leave the locked-in area or violation of guard mode). These faults have special interrupt locations in central store and are used by the executive system to take remedial or terminating action when they are encountered.

error interrupt (time sharing) — *See* time sharing, interrupt capability.

error, loading — The error found in the output of the computer which came about as a result of a change in value of the load which was supplied.

error, loading-location misuse — A loading-location specification was made but no load or execute was specified. The loading location specified was not within the available range of memory. The loading location is assigned as the first available location.

error, machine — A deviation from correct data due to an equipment failure.

error, marginal — Such errors irregularly occur in tapes, and most often disappear simply because the writing is done over a slightly different section of tapes.

error, mark-track — A mark-track error indicates that during the course of the previous block transfer a data-parity error was detected, or one or more bits have been picked up or dropped out from either the timing track or the mark track.

error, matching — An error due to inaccuracy in pairing passive components.

error messages — Messages developed by the program to designate a variety of error types.

error, missing — Subroutines called by the program were not found in the library. The names of the missing subroutines are also outputs.

error, no-job definition — The job did not contain a job-definition control card and could not be processed.

error, overflow — A floating-point arithmetic operation resulted in an overflow condition.

error, parity — Indicates that during the course of the previous block transfer of data a parity error was detected, or one or more bits have never been picked up or dropped out from either the timing track or the mark track.

error, program — A mistake made in the program code by the programmer, keypuncher, or a machine-language compiler or assembler.

error, propagated — An error occurring in a previous operation that spreads through and influences later operations and results.

error, quiet — These are errors that occur in manual-mechanical systems and are corrected by competent people close to the system before they spread throughout the process or system.

error range — 1. The range of all possible values of the error of a particular quantity. 2. The difference between the highest and the lowest of these values.

error, range-of-balance — 1. A range of error in which the maximum and minimum possible errors are opposite in sign and equal in magnitude. 2. A range of error in which the average value is zero.

error rate — The total amount of information in error, due to the transmission media, divided by the total amount of information received.

error rate, residual — The ratio of the number of bits, unit elements, characters, and blocks incorrectly received but undetected or uncorrected by the error-control equipment, to the total number that are sent.

error, relative — A ratio of the error to the value of the quantity which contains the error, as contrasted to absolute error.

error, resolution — An error due to or caused by the inability of a computing unit to demonstrate changes of a variable smaller than a given increment.

error, rounding — The error resulting from rounding off a quantity by deleting the less significant digits and applying some rule of correction to the part retained. For instance, 0.2751 can be rounded to 0.275 with a rounding error of 0.0001. (Synonymous with round-off error, and contrasted with truncation error.)

error, round-off — The error resulting from deleting the less significant digit or digits of a quantity and applying some rule of correction to the part retained.

error routine — An error routine provides a means of automatically initiating corrective action when errors occur, such as tape read and write, or disk seek, read, and write. It is executed after the programmed check establishes an error. The error routine should cause the operation to be performed at least one more time (in some cases several). If the error persists, processing is interrupted and the condition is signaled on the console. The operator's instruction manual should include procedures for correction and resumption of processing.

errors, altering — Internal machine generated errors resulting from incorrect data transfer within the machine.

errors, catastrophic — When so many errors have occurred that no more useful diagnostic information can be produced, terminate the compilation.

errors, completeness — Errors of completeness are discovered when the user signifies that his program is complete by entering the END statement. Some errors (e.g., invalid subscript value, reference to an undefined variable, arithmetic spills, etc.) can be detected only during execution. In this case, after a display of the error condition and its location, execution is interrupted and the terminal reverts to READY status.

The user then either immediately corrects his error or proceeds with the rest of his program.

errors, completeness (remote-computing system) — Errors of completeness are detected after the user has indicated that his program is complete. All such errors are then extracted and immediately displayed at the terminal in a sequential list. When all the errors have been listed, the user can then individually correct or disregard them before initiating the execution of his completed program. Any disregarded errors, when redetected during execution, are considered as execution errors.

errors, composition (remote computing system) — Typographical errors, violations of specified forms of statements and misuse of variable names (e.g., incorrect punctuation, mixed-mode expressions, undeclared arrays, etc.). Errors of composition are detected as soon as the user enters the offending statement. The system rejects the offending statement, and the user can immediately substitute a correct statement.

errors, consistency (remote-computing system) — Most errors of consistency are detected as soon as the user enters the offending statement. (They may be of inconsistent statements or format.) The system rejects the offending statement and the user can immediately substitute a correct statement. However, some errors of consistency are not immediately detected. The errors are handled in the same manner as errors of completeness and should be considered as such.

errors, correctable — CPU will try to correct the error, print an explanatory message and continue the compilation.

error, select — Signifies that a tape transport unit select error has occurred, such as more than one transport in the system has been assigned the same select code or that no transport has been assigned the programmed select code.

error, sequence — A card is out of sequence with an object program.

errors, execution (remote-computing system) — An execution error of a program statement causes an immediate execution interrupt at the point at which the error is encountered. The error is extracted and displayed at the terminal. The user may then correct the error and resume the execution of his program. If the user chooses to ignore the error and continue the execution, he may do so.

For all syntactic errors, the diagnostic message is specific (in that the variable in error is named or the column where the error occurred is specified) and often tutorial in suggesting the procedure for obtaining correct results.

error signal — 1. A signal whose magnitude and sign are used to correct the alignment between the controlling and the controlled elements of an automatic control device. 2. Relating to closed loops, that specific signal resulting from subtracting a particular return signal from its corresponding input signal.

error, single — An erroneous bit, preceded and followed by at least one correct bit.

errors, instrumentation — Where input into a system is directly from instruments such as pressure gauges, limit checks are imposed to prevent instrumentation errors. If these limits are violated, control may be assumed by a violation subroutine for immediate corrective action.

errors, intermittent — The sporadic or intermittent equipment error which is difficult to detect as the fault may not occur when the diagnostics are run.

error, size — Occurs when the number of positions to the left of the assumed decimal point exceeds the corresponding positions in the COBOL data-name field.

errors, operator — Errors made by the terminal operator.

errors, precautionary — CPU prints warning message and continues compilation.

errors, scanning — Scanning errors are said to be precluded by an error-scanning format that uses five rows of bar codes and several columns of correction codes. This makes defacement or incorrect reading virtually impossible, and the control codes also help regenerate partially obliterated data.

errors, semantic (remote computing system) — Semantic errors are concerned with the meaning or intent of the programmer and are his responsibility. However, he is provided with an extensive set of debugging aids that allow him to manipulate portions of a program when in search of errors in logic and analysis.

errors, solid — An error that always occurs

when a particular piece of equipment is used.

errors, static — An error that is independent of the time variable, as contrasted with dynamic error, which depends on frequency.

errors, syntactic — Syntactic errors are considered the responsibility of the system and are further categorized as follows:

Composition—Typographical errors, violations of specified form of statements, and misuse of variable names (e.g., incorrect punctuation, mixed-mode expressions, undeclared arrays, etc.).

Consistency—Statements that are correctly composed but conflict with other statements (e.g., conflicting declaratives, illegal statement ending a DO range, failure to follow each transfer statement with a numbered statement, etc.).

Completeness—Programs that are incomplete (e.g., transfers to nonexistent statement numbers, improper DO nesting, illegal transfer into the range of a DO loop, etc.).

errors, tape (read or write) — In reading or writing a tape, quite commonly the machine will detect an error, and one which will quite possibly not appear again if reading or writing is repeated on the same spot. Various recovery routines are used to correct tape errors in most operations.

errors, transient — A one-time nonrepeatable error.

errors, transmission — Such errors are safeguarded by a dual pulse code that effectively transmits the signals and their complements for a double check on accuracy of message.

errors, uncorrectable — If intent of programmer cannot be determined, the CPU prints a diagnostic message, rejects the clause or statement and continues compilation.

error tape — A special tape developed and used for writing out errors in order to correct them by study and analysis after printing.

error, timing — The program was not able to keep pace with the tape transfer rate, or a new motion or select command was issued before the previous command was completely executed.

error, truncation — The error resulting from the use of only a finite number of terms of an infinite series, or from the approximation of operations in the infinitesimal calculus by operations in the calculus of finite differences. It is frequently convenient to define truncation error, by exclusion, as any error generated in a computation not due to rounding, initial conditions, or mistakes. A truncation error would thus be that deviation of a computed quantity from the theoretically correct value that would be present even in the hypothetical situation in which no mistakes were made, all given data were exact, there was no inherited error, and infinitely many digits were retained in all calculations. (Contrasted with rounding error.)

error, unbalanced — Those errors or sets of error values in which the maximum and minimum are not opposite in sign and equal in magnitude, as contrasted to balanced errors; i.e., the average of all the error values is not zero.

error, usage — If prior to a job definition of compile or assemble an equipment usage is declared with a usage control, this error is printed. The job will proceed normally.

error, visual representation — *See* visual error representation.

escape — The departure from one code or language to another code or language, i.e., the withdrawal from existing pattern.

escape code — A code combination that causes the terminal equipment to recognize all subsequent code combinations as having a different or alternate meaning to their normal representation. The FIGS-LTRS shift codes in five-level systems are forms of escape codes. Also known as alternate mode codes.

escape, general — The withdrawal from one of two or more possible alphabets or data sets. Usually the character immediately following the escape character identifies which alphabet is in force.

escape, locking — That escape from one alphabet in which all characters following the escape character will be from the alternative alphabet, much like shifting while typing.

escape, nonlocking — A particular escape in which a specified number of characters, following the escape character, are to be from the alternative alphabet, similar to pressing the shift key for one letter on a typewriter.

ESC, escape character — 1. A control character to signal a change in the meaning of one or more of the characters that follow it. 2. A data communications term representing the use of a control character which, when combined with one or more succeeding characters, forms an escape sequence and the development of additional data communications control operations.

ESS — An abbreviation for Electronic Switching System. A stored program communications system developed by Bell Laboratories. It is a common carrier communications switching system that uses solid-state devices and other computer-type equipment and principles in its operation.

evaluation and review technique, program — *See* program evaluation and review technique (Pert).

evaluation, data — The examination and analysis of data to make an assessment of its inherent meaning, probable accuracy, relevancy, and relation to given situations or context.

evaluation, performance — The analysis in terms of initial objectives and estimates, and usually made on-site, of accomplishments using an automatic data-processing system, to provide information on operating experience and to identify required corrective actions.

even-odd check — *See* check digit, parity.

even parity — *See* check digit, parity.

even parity check — *See* check, even parity.

event — An occasion or action that causes data to affect the contents of the files of a business, e.g., purchases, shipments, sales, returns, etc.

event chain — The series of actions that result from an initial event. An example is order processing, inventory adjustment, shipping document preparation, etc., resulting from a sale.

event, file — A single-file access, either reading or writing. The processing of an action usually requires one or more file events.

event-sensing card — Typical card compares digital input with reference data stored on card. A service request is generated when data sets do not match. Another type generates a service request on positive and/or negative transitions of any of 12 input lines and stores the event.

exceed capacity — The generating of a word or number, the magnitude or length of which is too great or too small to be represented by the computer, such as in an attempt to divide by zero.

except gate — A gate developed due to the presence of a pulse in one or more input lines and the absence of a pulse in one or more input lines.

exception-item encoder — *See* encoder, exception-item.

exception-principle system — An information system or data-processing system that reports on situations only when actual results differ from planned results. When results occur within a normal range they are not reported.

exception reporting — A record of departures from the expected or norm. Often times, maximum or minimum limits are the set parameters and the normal range lies within these end numbers or expectations. Reports that have results which exceed these parameters become the basis for an exception reporting output.

exception scheduling routine — When messages or situations occur that require exceptional action, the exception scheduling routine separates them from the normal scheduling loops or routine. The exception action is performed and the system returns to its normal routine.

excess-three code — *See* code, excess-three.

exchange — To interchange the contents of two storage devices or locations.

exchange, automatic — An exchange in which communication between subscribers is effected, without the intervention of an operator, by means of devices set in operation by the originating subscriber's instrument.

exchange buffering — A technique for input/output buffering which prevents or avoids the internal movement of data. Buffers are either filled, empty, or actively in use, by an input/output device. Exchange buffering relates to distinct areas set aside for work and for buffering.

exchange, central-office — The place where a communication common carrier locates the equipment which interconnects incoming subscribers and circuits.

exchange device, remote computing system — The exchange device controls the flow of information between the computer and the terminals. Characters typed at the terminals are sent to the computer one line at a time via the exchange device. The computer returns an answer to the exchange device, which, in turn, sends it to the proper terminal. The exchange device allows each terminal to send or receive data independent of all other terminals.

exchange, dial — An exchange where all subscribers originate their calls by dialing.

exchange instruction — An instruction to replace the contents of one register (or set of registers) with the contents of another and vice versa.

exchange, manual — An exchange where calls are routed by an operator.

exchange, message — A device placed between a communication line and a computer in order to take care of certain communication functions and thereby free the computer for other work.

exchange, storage — *Same as* memory exchange.

exclusive NOR gate — *See* gate, exclusive NOR.

exclusive OR — A Boolean logic operation performed between specified registers on a bit-by-bit basis. A logic one is left in the results register if either bit in any bit position of either register is a one. A logic zero is left if both are a logic one or both are a logic zero.

exclusive OR function — A logic operation in which the result is logically true when only one input function is true, and false when both inputs are true or false.

exclusive OR, logical — *Same as* gate, exclusive OR.

exclusive segments — *See* segments, exclusive.

execute — To carry out an instruction or perform a routine. To interpret a machine instruction and perform the indicated operation(s) on the operand(s) specified.

execute cycle — The portion of the operational sequence of a computer when the actions required to perform an instruction are actually accomplished. Occurs after a "fetch" cycle has obtained an instruction from memory.

execute phase — 1. The part of the computer operating cycle wherein a command in the program register is carried out upon the address indicated. 2. The act of performing a command.

execution — The processes which are performed by computer devices and circuitry which accomplish a particular instruction or design.

execution cycle — That portion of a machine cycle during which the actual execution of the instruction takes place. Some operations (e.g., divide, multiply) may need a large number of these operation cycles to complete the operation, and the normal instruction/operation alternation will be held up during this time. Also called operation cycle.

execution-error detection — Detection concerned with those errors detected during the execution of the user's program. They include errors that are detectable only during program execution (e.g., invalid subscript value, reference to an undefined variable, arithmetic spills, etc.) along with those errors of completeness detected because either (1) they were disregarded by the user when previously detected or (2) they were not detected in the first place because the user did not indicate that his program was completed.

execution errors, remote-computing — *See* errors, execution (remote-computing system).

execution, interpretive — Permits retention of all of the information contained in the user's original source statements, thereby making source-language debugging possible. Interpretive execution, plus multiprogramming, make the conversational mode of operation a practical reality.

execution, looping — *See* looping execution.

execution of an instruction — The set of elementary steps carried out by the computer to produce the result specified by the operation code of the instruction.

execution path — The principal course or line of direction taken by a computer in the execution of a routine, directed by the logic of the program and the nature of the data.

execution time — 1. The sum total of the amount of time required to complete a given command. 2. The portion of an instruction cycle during which the actual work is performed or operation executed, i.e., the time required to decode and perform an instruction. (Synonymous with instruction time.)

executive capability, mass-storage — *See* storage, mass (executive).

executive command — A command to the executive program to run a subsystem or symbiont.

executive communications — Provides for all communication between the operating programs and the computer operator, and between the executive system and the computer operator. These communications take place via the computer keyboard and the on-line typewriter. This function includes the interpretation of all keyboard inputs addressed to the executive system and the transfer of control to the section of the executive to which the input pertains.

executive control logic, multiprogramming — The specific system is a multiprogram processor and, to initiate or preserve a true multiprogramming environment, the executive system must be in complete control of the total system. Therefore, it is necessary that the system contain sufficient control circuitry to effectively and economically maintain this control.

The multiprogramming capabilities of the system are based upon guard mode operation, the setting aside of certain instructions, registers, and storage locations for the exclusive use of the executive system, assuring maximum protection against the interaction of unrelated programs.

executive control, multiprogramming — Multiprogramming permits many jobs into the computer at the same time—routine jobs, high-priority real-time jobs, or special jobs—without any increased load on the programmer. The system keeps all programs isolated from one another, preventing the unintentional mixing of "apples and oranges." The executive routine keeps the processor constantly computing on work, constantly turning out answers to problems. There is no central processor in the traditional sense of the word. Instead, the separate and combined functions of three modules—processor, memory, and controller—perform the work of the conventional central processor. The system is memory-oriented, not processor-oriented. This means that data bypasses the processor if it isn't needed there, keeping the processor free for productive work.

executive control system — *See* executive system control.

executive control, utility routines — Utility routines are contained as an integral part of the system. These are programs that are useful for data conversion, editing, etc. A description of the individual utility routines provided with the system is given in the individual write-ups of the utility routines. Utility routines are loaded and executed from the master file by an executive control statement. Frequently used object programs may be added to the system as utility routines. These programs may then be called through from the executive master file.

executive deck — A deck of punched cards containing executive programs, routines, and subroutines.

executive diagnostic system — A comprehensive diagnostic system is available within the executive system to aid the check out of user programs. Both allocation time and compilation or assembly time commands are available to trigger snapshot dumps. Postmortem dumps are also available through the executive control statement.

executive dumping — *See* dumping, executive.

executive facilities assignment — Available facilities and their disposition are indicated to the system as system generation time; therefore, the executive system assigns these facilities, as needed and as available, to fulfill the facilities requirements of all runs. The executive system maintains and continually updates inventory tables that reflect what facilities are available for assignment, and which runs are using the currently unavailable facilities.

executive guard mode — Guard mode prevents programs from executing any of a set of instructions reserved for the executive. It also protects certain locations reserved for executive operations.

executive instruction — Similar to supervisory instruction, this instruction is designed and used to control the operation or execution of other routines or programs.

executive program — *Same as* executive routine.

executive, real-time — The executive system is also designed to interface with programs which have real-time requirements. The standard communication subsystem, together with efficient scheduling and interrupt processing features of the executive system, provides an environment satisfactory for any real-time program.

executive, resident — The section of the supervisory program that is always located in main memory. The resident executive is a permanent resident of main memory.

executive routine — 1. The coordinating, directing, or modifying routine that controls the operations of other routines or programs. 2. A routine that controls loading and relocation of routines and in some cases makes use of instructions which are unknown to the general programmer. Effectively, an executive routine is part of the machine itself. (Synonymous with monitor routine, supervisory routine, and supervisory program.)

executive schedule maintenance — The acceptance of job requests from an external medium and the inclusion of these requests in a job request schedule. Executive will reference the job-request schedule to determine the next job to be initiated. Previously submitted requests may be deleted.

executive supervisor — The supervisor is the executive-system component that controls the sequencing, setup, and execution of all runs entering the computer. It is designed to control the execution of an unlimited number of programs in a multiprogramming environment, while allowing each program to be unaffected by the coexistence of other programs. The supervisor contains three levels of scheduling—coarse scheduling, dynamic allocation, and CPU dispatching. Runs entering are sorted into information files, and these files are used by the supervisor for run scheduling and processing. Control statements for each run are retrieved and scanned by the control command interpreter to facilitate the selection of runs for setup by the coarse scheduler.

executive system — 1. An integrated collection of service routines for supervising the sequencing of programs by a computer. Operating systems may perform debugging, input/output, accounting, compilation, and storage-assignment tasks. (Synonymous with monitor system.) 2. A fully integrated system that provides for concurrent operation of multiple programs, plus input/output, plus real-time control of a complete, on-demand computer network. The executive system also provides for automatic logging, simultaneously establishing an automatic and economical computer-accounting system and simplifying its maintenance.

executive system control — Primary control of the executive system is by control information fed to the system by one or more input devices which may be either on-line or at various remote sites. This control information is similar in nature to present control card operations, but allows additional flexibility and standardization.

executive system routine — A routine that automatically accomplishes the execution of program runs in compliance with a predetermined computer schedule. In this capacity, the executive routine extracts the programs that are to be executed, positions them in their operating locations, assigns input/output peripheral equipment, provides for the time sharing of several programs running concurrently, and provides special checking features for the job programs.

executive system utilities — Included within the utilities section of the executive system are diagnostic routines, program file manipulation routines, file utility routines, and cooperative routines for aiding the user in performing such functions as reading cards, printing line images on a printer, transferring files from device to device, and carrying out housekeeping junctions required for file-residence on mass-storage devices.

executive termination — The normal or abnormal termination of an operating program and the return of its assigned facilities to an available status. Termination may be initiated by executive program, by the job program, or by the operator.

executive, time-sharing — *See* time sharing executive.

exerciser, macro — The repeated operation of supervisory programs and other macroinstructions under a variety of conditions to find any program errors.

exercisers — With reference to software

development systems, exercisers are the simplest type. They usually consist of a hexadecimal keyboard and display. The device is designed to handle a specific microprocessor, enabling a user to create and debug programs, interfaces, and so on by manual means. An exerciser is sometimes an analyzer and an evaluation module of the development system.

exit — 1. The time or place at which the control sequence ends or transfers out of a particular program or subroutine. 2. A way of momentarily interrupting or leaving a repeated cycle of operations in a program.

exit macroinstruction — A supervisory program macroinstruction that is the final instruction in an application program, signifying that processing is complete. The supervisory program takes the needed action such as releasing working storage blocks to return control to other processing.

exit, page — The point in flowchart symbols where the flowline continues to a following page due to space limitation of one page.

exit point — The instruction which transfers control from the main routine to the subroutine.

exjunction gate — *Same as* gate, exclusive OR.

explicit address — An address reference that is specified as two absolute expressions. One expression supplies the value of a displacement. Both values are assembled into the object code of a machine instruction.

exponent — A number placed at the right and above a symbol in typography to indicate the number of times that symbol is a factor; e.g., 10 to the 4th (10^4) equals $10 \times 10 \times 10 \times 10$, or 10,000.

exponent, biased — In floating point number systems, some systems bias the exponent by a constant so that all exponents become positive, e.g., 10^{-50} becomes 10^0 and 10^{50} becomes 10^{100}.

exponential smoothing — This is a statistical technique for predicting future demands based on current and past demands activity without storing and saving masses of past history data.

exponentiation — A specific mathematical operation denoting increases in the base number by a factor as previously selected.

expression — A valid series of constants, variables, and functions that may be connected by operation symbols and punctuated, if required, to cause a desired computation.

extended area service — An exchange service at a somewhat higher service rate but without toll charges for an area with a community of interest.

extended precision — A real number requiring three words of core storage. The maximum precision of the mantissa is 2,147,483,647.

extended time scale — *See* time scale.

extension character — *See* code extension character.

extension character, code — *See* code extension character.

extension register — A 16-bit register treated as an extension of the accumulator register. This register is used to hold the remainder after a division operation and couple to the accumulator to hold the product in a fixed point multiply operation. (Some systems.)

extension register, single chip system — The contents of the extension register that can be loaded into the accumulator or can be exchanged with the contents of the accumulator. When the accumulator is loaded from the extension register, the original contents of the accumulator are lost (some systems).

extent — A contiguous area of a physical storage medium. Usually refers to some group of disk sectors or disk blocks.

external clocking — *See* data set clocking.

external delay — *See* delay, external.

external device (ED) address — The ED address specifies which external device a particular instruction is referring to. Scores of different external devices can be specified.

external error — A file mark has been read or end-of-tape has been sensed during a loading operation.

external-interrupt inhibit — The bit, in the program status double-word, that indicates whether (if 1) or not (if 0) all external interrupts are inhibited.

external interrupts — External interrupts are caused by either an external device requiring attention (such as a signal from a communications device), console switching, or the timer going to zero.

external interrupt status word — A status word accompanied by an external interrupt signal. This signal informs the computer that the word on the data lines is a status word; the computer, interpreting this signal, automatically loads this word in a reserved address in main memory. If the programmer or operator desires a visual indication of the status word, it must be programmed.

external labels — Labels are normally defined in the same program in which they are used as operands. However, it is possible to define a symbol in one program, use it in a program assembled independently of the first program, and then execute both programs together.

externally stored program — Programs with instruction routines that are set up in wiring boards or plugboards for manual insertion in older models or small-scale processors.

external memory — A facility or device, not an integral part of a computer, on which data usable by a computer is stored, such as off-line magnetic-tape units or punch-card devices. (Contrasted with internal storage.)

external reference — A distinct reference to a single variable from a range, or an item which is not defined in the particular program, segment, or subroutine. A linkage editor, or a linking load usually integrates various independently written routines which are united before execution. The assembler must be informed that an external symbol is being used to avoid an error condition.

external registers — These registers, which can be referenced by the program, are located in control store as specific addresses. These are the locations (registers) which the programmer references when he desires that some sort of computational function be carried out.

external sense and control lines — *See* sense and control lines, external.

external-signal interrupt — *See* interrupt, external-signal.

external sort — The second phase of a multiphase sort program, wherein strings of data are continually merged until one string of sequenced data is formed.

external storage — *See* storage, external.

external symbol dictionary (ESD) — Part of a load module which contains the names and address locations within a module of all entry points and specific locations that are accessible by name from outside the module; external symbols also include control section names. The ESD also contains external references, or the names of symbols not defined within this load module.

extract — 1. To copy from a set of items all those items which meet a specified criterion. 2. To remove only a given set of digits or characters occupying certain specified locations in a computer word, such as extract the 8, 9, and 10 binary digits of a 44-bit word, as specified by the filter. (Clarified by filter.) 3. To derive a new computer word from part of another word, usually by masking. (Related to unpack.)

extract instruction — An instruction that requests the formation of a new expression from selected parts of given expressions.

extraction — The reading of only selected portions of a record into storage.

extractor — A machine word that specifies which parts of another machine word are to be operated on, thus the criterion for an external command. (Synonymous with mask, and clarified by extract.)

extraneous ink — Ink deposited on a computer printout that is not confined to the printed characters themselves.

extremity routine — This routine is used when initiating a new tape or when reaching the end-of-reel of a multireel file. This routine need not be included in memory if all tapes are set up or initiated automatically by the system supervisor and the open or close macros are not used. The importance of this routine is that it performs necessary tape housekeeping, checks on the operator, and provides necessary information concerning the program being run.

F

F — A subscript symbol which designates "final."

face — In optical character recognition (OCR), a character style with given relative dimensions and line thicknesses.

facility assignment (executive) — The assignment of memory and external facilities to meet the requirements which are defined symbolically in a job program selected for initiation. Executive maintains a list of all allocatable facilities which is updated to reflect assignment of facilities to newly initiated programs, and to reflect release of facilities by programs during, or at termination of, a run.

facility, compare — The ability of a machine to execute set instructions depending upon the outcome of various possible combinations.

facility, hold — The ability of a computer, when its calculations are interrupted, to keep the current value of all the variables.

facsimile — A system for the transmission of images. The image is scanned at the transmitter, reconstructed at the receiving station, and duplicated on some form of paper. Abbreviated fax.

facsimile document system — A system that can send and receive documents over ordinary telephone lines automatically. Most systems can send a complete page in less than two minutes (some under one minute). Many systems also edit documents automatically, have multiple speeds and resolutions, and are compatible with other facsimile systems.

fact correlation — A process which is an integral part of linguistic analysis and adaptive learning which uses methods of manipulating and recognizing data elements, items, or codes to examine and determine explicit and implicit relations of data in files, i.e., for fact retrieval rather than document retrieval.

factor — A number used as a multiplier, so chosen that it will cause a set of quantities to fall within a given range of values.

factor, blocking — The limit of the data records which can be contained in a given block on tape.

factor, elimination — The ratio in information retrieval obtained by dividing the number of documents that have not been retrieved by the total number of documents contained in the file.

factory data collection — *See* data collection stations.

fact retrieval — The automatic recognition, selection, interpretation, and manipulation of words, phrases, sentences,

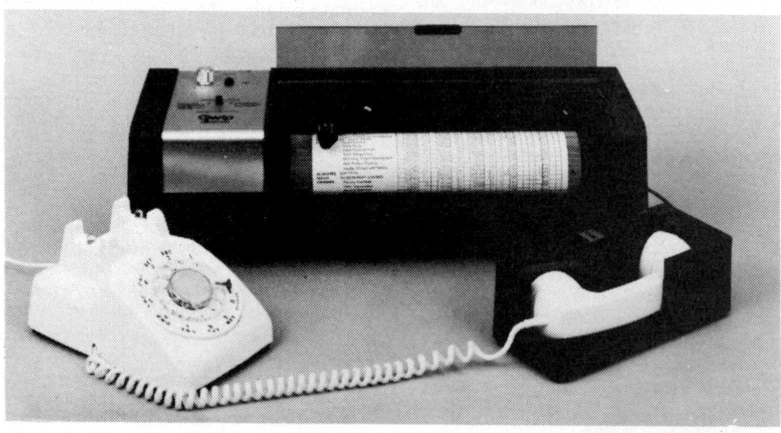

Courtesy Qwip Systems, Div. of Exxon Enterprises, Inc.

Facsimile receiver.

or any data in any form, but particularly in a textual structure, and the relating of these data for conclusions and useful results.

fading — The variation of radio field intensity caused by changes in the transmission medium.

fading, flat — That type of fading in which all components of the received radio signal simultaneously fluctuate in the same proportion.

fading, selective — Fading which affects the different frequencies within a specified band unequally.

fail-safe disconnect — A feature of some systems that causes the terminal to disconnect from the transmission line when certain abnormal conditions occur.

fail-safe system — A system which continues to process data despite the failure of parts in the system. Usually accompanied by some deterioration in performance.

fail soft (softly) — Pertaining to a type or method of system design and implementation that prevents irrecoverable loss of system usage due to failure of any one part or resource of that system. The design of the system is such that provision is made for slow degradation of service, often with a proper warning.

fail soft, time sharing — *See* time sharing, fail soft.

failure analysis — Detailed on-the-spot or laboratory analysis and examination of a failure to determine the exact cause of the failure.

failure, catastrophic — A failure which is total or nearly so, such as breakdown of the power supply, making all circuits inoperative. Any type of failure which renders the useful performance of the computer to zero.

failure, equipment — A fault in the equipment causing improper behavior or preventing a scheduled task from being accomplished.

failure, incipient — An equipment failure that is about to occur.

failure, induced — An equipment failure caused by the environment around the failed item.

failure logging — An automatic procedure whereby the maintenance section of the monitor, acting on machine-check interrupts (immediately following error detection), records the system state. This log is an aid to the customer engineer in diagnosing intermittent errors.

failure, mean-time-to — The average time the system or a component of the system works without faulting. Abbreviated MTTF.

failure prediction — Techniques which attempt to determine the failure schedule of specific parts or equipments so that they may be discarded and replaced before failure occurs.

failures, mean-time-between — The special limit of the ratio of the operating time of equipment to the number of observed failures as the number of failures approaches infinity.

fallback — A condition in processing when special computer or manual functions must be employed as either complete or partial substitutes for malfunctioning systems. Such procedures could be used anywhere between complete system availability and total system failure.

fallback, double — A procedure to circumvent error that has two procedures, or can contend with two separate equipment failures.

fallback, double failure, mean-time-to — The average time the system or a component of the system works without faulting.

fallback procedure — A procedure to circumvent all equipment faults. The fallback may give degraded service and may include switching to an alternate computer or to different output devices and so on.

fallback, recovery — The restoration of a system to full operation from a fallback mode of operation after the cause of the fallback has been removed.

false add — This is addition without carries; the performance of a logic add.

false code — *See* character, illegal.

false code check — *See* check, forbidden-combination.

false drop — An unwanted reference which does not pertain to the subject.

false retrievals — Library references that are not pertinent to, but are vaguely related to, the subject of the library search, and are sometimes obtained by automatic search methods.

fan-in — The maximum number of ON gate terms that can be used to drive an input. Generally the terms cannot all be simultaneously true.

fan-out — The number of circuits which can be supplied with input signals from an output terminal of a circuit or unit. The changes of digital circuits depend basically on the number of devices that can drive or be driven by one circuit of a specific type, and the number of elements that one output can drive is related to the power available from the output and the amount of power required for each input.

FAP — Abbreviation for Fortran Assembly Program. A procedure-oriented software system.

FAST — Acronym for Flexible Algebraic Scientific Translator. Translates complex statements into basic language, saving the tedious task of absolute programming. FAST offers the ability to write a source program in an algebraic format. The source program is entered by means of tape or disk, the translation is made, and the program is executed, all in one computer run. The output is composed of a listing of the program, any error comments, and the result of the program's execution. (NCR)

fast-access storage — The section of the entire storage from which data may be obtained most rapidly.

faster access memory — Various storage media which obtain or release data faster through the use of two or more differing storage devices or media. For example, semiconductor storage is the faster access memory in equipment where both semiconductor storage and magnetic disk storage are built in.

fast-time scale — The ratio of computer time (interval between two events in a simulation) to the problem time (physical system time), when greater than one, is said to be an extended time scale, or slow-time scale. When the ratio is less than one, it is said to be on a fast-time scale. When the ratio is not constant during a run, it is said to be on a variable-time scale. If the ratio is equal to one, it is a real-time system.

fault — A physical condition that causes a device, component, or element to fail to perform in a required manner, e.g., a short circuit, a broken wire, an intermittent connection.

fault defect — An anomaly that prevents the correct operation of the device. "Defect" and "fault" are often used interchangeably, although a fault is the theoretical or practical result of a physical defect.

fault dictionary — A set of fault signatures, each of which indicates the probable faults that could cause the error message matching the signature.

fault isolation — Determination of the cause of a test failure, typically by identifying a defective component or process failure on a board.

fault-location problem — A problem for identification or information regarding faulty equipment. It is designed and used to identify the location or type of fault and is often part of a diagnostic routine.

fault model — A set of data that logically describes the operation of a device or circuit containing one or more faults.

fault, pattern-sensitive — A fault that appears in response to some particular pattern of data.

fault, permanent — Faults are failures in performance in the manner required or specified. Sporadic faults are intermittent while permanent faults are repetitious, but these may either escape attention when they do not result in failure to perform some particular tasks, or be known and easily correctable.

fault processing, time sharing — *See* time sharing, fault processing.

fault, program-sensitive — A fault that appears in response to some particular sequence of program steps.

fault signature — A particular output response or set of responses generated when a test program is executed on a device containing a fault.

faults, intermittent — *Same as* faults, sporadic.

faults, sporadic — Faults are failures in performance in the manner required over specified conditions, and sporadic faults are intermittent faults.

fault time — *See* time, down.

fault-tolerant — Pertaining to those programs or systems which will still execute properly even though parts may fail.

fax — Transmission of pictures, maps, diagrams, etc., by radio waves. The image is scanned at the transmitter and reconstructed at the receiving station. (Synonymous with facsimile.)

Faxcom — A facsimile communications service offered by the TransCanada Telephone System which allows for the transmission of graphics (written, drawn, typed) over the DDD network.

F-conversion — One of the three types of FORMAT specification in FORTRAN. F-conversion is used to convert floating-point data for i/o operations.

FDM — Abbreviation for Frequency-Division-Multiplexing. A technique by which a limited-bandwidth communication channel is partitioned into a group of independent lower-speed channels, each of which utilizes its permanently assigned portion of the total frequency spectrum. Each channel in the sharing group thus uses a frequency slot which contains the unique pair of frequencies needed for transmitting its binary data signals. When FDM is used on a voice grade line, each subchannel may typically transmit data asynchronously at speeds up to 150 bits/s (at faster speeds in special cases).

FDOS — Abbreviation for Floppy Disk Operating System.

feasibility study — Usually the initial procedures and criteria for determination of suitability, capability, and compatability of computer systems to various firms or organizations. A preliminary systems analysis of potential costs savings and new higher level of operations, decision making, and problem-solving capacity as a result of computer procurement.

feasible solution — A solution to the constraint equations in which all variables satisfy their sign restrictions.

feature, checking — Some computers have various built-in capabilities to check their own performance automatically. This is a feature of the particular machine.

feature, multireading — With the utilization of storage, cards are read once only and data is read out of storage on the following cycles, thus avoiding separate cycle reading for each line of print.

Fed Wire system — The Federal Reserve Communications System, a computerized message switch that connects Federal Reserve banks, their branches, and member banks.

feed — 1. To supply to a machine the material to be operated upon. 2. A device capable of feeding, as in definition 1.

feedback — The use of parts or all of the output of a machine, process, or system, as input for another phase, as when used for self-correcting purposes. Such feedback systems or programs use the process of continual comparisons of output with input to make necessary corrections. The feedback system is considered self-correcting if it is a closed loop.

feedback, analog — Normally, feedback in circuits is obtained by means of a resistor from output to input. An important property of this type of amplifier is that if a suitable capacitor is used in the feedback path instead of a resistor, the output will be the integral of the input. Conversely, the input will be the derivative of the output. Hence, the operations of the calculus can be performed, giving the machine great computational power.

feedback and reports (factory) — Feedback is an all-important aspect of the system. Feedback of factory data is collected and analyzed weekly to control and predict stock requirements. Purchase-order receipts, assembly-labor vouchers, and fabrication-labor vouchers are collected and returned to where they are used to update master open-order records. After the feedback data is checked for validity by the computer, it is compared against master records to adjust inventory balances. The receipt of "first operation vouchers" reduces raw-material balances by the amount applied to parts. Last-operation vouchers add to stock on hand for parts and also reduce open-order quantities. A raw-material status report is printed weekly to show usage and balance on hand. Reports are prepared weekly based on feedback data to show labor by individual, labor by area, and labor by shop order. This data also becomes input to the accounting system. A report on rework, extra work, and scrap losses is prepared by reason code. This data also becomes input to the accounting system.

feedback control — A type of system control obtained when a portion of the output signal is fed back to the input in order to obtain a desired effect.

feedback control signal — That portion of the output signal which is returned to the input in order to achieve a desired effect, such as fast response.

feedback control systems — A particular type of control system made up of one or more feedback control loops; it combines the functions of the controlled signals and commands, tending to maintain a prescribed relationship between the two.

feedback, interrupt signal — A steady signal indicating that an interrupt signal has advanced its associated interrupt level to the waiting or active state; the signal is dropped when the interrupt level is reset to the disarmed or the armed state.

feed, card — A mechanism that moves cards serially into a machine.

feeding — A system used by character readers in character recognition, in which each individual input document is issued to the document transport at a predetermined and constant rate.

feeding, cyclic — A system used by character readers, in which each individual input document is issued to the document transport at a predetermined and constant rate.

feeding, form — The rapid, accurate positioning of document forms on a teleprinter or business machine.

feeding, single-sheet — The feeding of individual sheets of paper rather than roll or fan-folded form.

feed pitch — *See* pitch, feed.

feed reel — A specific reel from which tape is unwound during the processing.

feed, tape — A mechanism that will feed tape to be read or sensed.

feed track — The track of a paper tape which contains the small feed holes for the sprockets.

fetch — 1. That portion of a computer cycle during which the location of the next instruction is determined, the instruction is taken from memory, and modified, if necessary, then entered into the control register. 2. To obtain a quantity of data from a place of storage.

fetch and execute cycle, bit-slice machine — Each time the bit-slice microprocessor requires an instruction from the memory, the machine goes through a fetch and execute cycle. The first step is for the machine to fetch an instruction from memory commanding the memory address register (MAR) to access the location to which it is pointing and to pull the information from it and load the information into the instruction decoder in the machine. (Some systems.)

fetch cycle — The portion of an operational sequence in which an instruction or directive is obtained from the location in memory identified by the contents of the program counter.

fetch data — A command that specifies the unit and file to which access is desired.

fetch phase — An alternate part of the cycle of the computer operation wherein the instruction is brought from memory into the program register.

fetch process — A process of addressing the memory and reading into the CPU the information word or byte stored at the addressed location. Most often, fetch refers to the reading out of an instruction from the memory.

fetch sequence — The collective actions of acquiring a memory address and then an instruction or data byte from memory.

fiber optics — A fiber is a transparent material system that conducts or "guides" light. This guiding phenomenon is a result of a dissimilar set of material refractive indices. That is, an optically dense core material (high refractive index n_1) is usually surrounded by a less optically dense cladding material (lower refractive index n_2). The magnitude of the resulting optical density difference between the core and cladding determines the maximum angle at which guiding occurs (numerical aperture). Only rays which are at the maximum angle or less are "accepted" and guided along the fiber, while all other rays escape from the side of the fiber and are "radiated." A very simple fiber structure would consist of a simple strand of glass ($n_1 = 1.5$) surrounded by air ($n_2 = 1.0$).

Because optical fibers are nonmetallic, fiber optic systems provide safe, noise-free communications circuits. Fibers are not susceptible to electromagnetic interference, and they provide isolation from ground-potential rise. Fiber optic systems are also not affected by heavy rain and lightning, which can cause outages in conventional cable and radio systems.

fiber optics cladding — A sheathing or covering, usually of glass, fused to the core or higher index material.

fiber optics components — The fiber has a core, a light-transmitting material of higher index of refraction, surrounded by a cladding, or optical insulating material of a lower index of refraction. Light enters the fiber at an infinite number of angles, but only those rays entering the fiber at an angle less than the critical acceptance angle are transmitted. Light is propagated within the core of a multimode fiber at specific angles of internal reflection. When a propagating ray strikes the core-cladding interface, it is reflected and zigzags down the core.

fiber optics system light sources — Light-producing devices used in fiber-optics transmitters. The three primary sources are gallium arsenide LEDs, GaAs injection lasers, and Neodymium:Yttrium-Aluminum-Garnet (Nd:YAG) lasers. Both LEDs and injection lasers use the basic GaAs diode structure, and the wavelength of the radiated light depends on the device material and the dopant.

and so on. Some sort programs distribute strings of data onto work tapes so that the number of strings on successive tapes form a Fibonacci series.

fiche automated retrieval and display system — A peripheral device for use with an interactive terminal to combine microfiche storage and computer retrieval of large amounts of alphanumeric and/or graphic data.

field — A set of one or more characters (not necessarily all lying on the same word) which is treated as a whole; a set of one or more columns on a punched card consistently used to record similar information.

field, bit-slice machine — A portion of a microprogram word that is designed to represent a group of bits dedicated to controlling a specific piece of hardware.

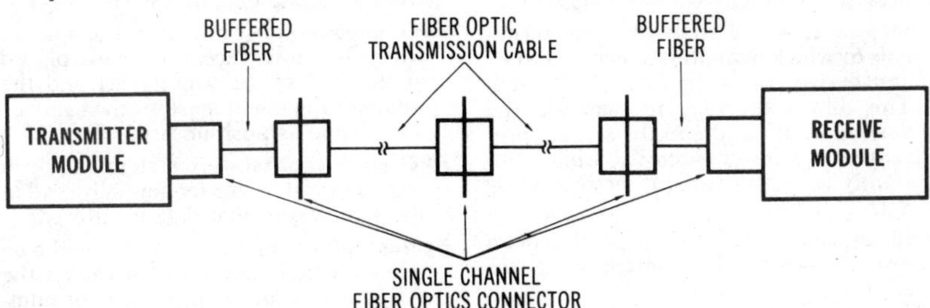

Fiber optics transmission system.

fiber optics transmission system — Abbreviated FOTS. A transmission system utilizing small-diameter glass fibers through which light is transmitted. Information is transferred by modulating the transmitted light. These modulated signals are detected by light-sensitive semiconductor devices.

Fibonacci number — *See* Fibonacci search.

Fibonacci search — A search based on dichotomy and developed in such a way that in each step, the original set or the remaining subset is subdivided in accordance with successive smaller numbers in the specific Fibonacci series. When the number of items in such a set is not equal to a Fibonacci number, the number of items in the set is assumed to equal the next higher Fibonacci number.

Fibonacci series (sorting) — When the number is equal to the sum of the two preceding numbers, i.e., 1, 2, 3, 5, 8,

field checking — On some terminals, the numeric-only and alpha-only field checks can be dynamically performed to find errors when they are made.

field, common — A field accessible to two or more routines.

field, decrement — A portion of an instruction word specifically set aside for modifying the contents of a register or storage location.

field, free — A property of information-processing recording media that permits recording of information without regard to a preassigned or fixed field; e.g., in information-retrieval devices, information may be dispersed in the record in any sequence or location.

field mark — A symbol used to indicate the beginning or the end of some set of data, i.e., group, file, record, block; in this case, a particular field.

field, multiply — A field used to hold the results of the multiplication operation.

field name — A symbolic name a programmer gives to a specific field of data. During assembly, this field is assigned an absolute address.

field, operand — The portion of an immediate-addressing instruction word that contains the immediate operand value, with negative values represented as twos complements.

field, operating code — The portion of an instruction word that contains the operation code.

field, operation — That particular part of the instruction format which specifies the procedure or process which is to be performed.

field programmable logic array — A type of logic array that allows the designer to try out a logic design in an actual system prior to committing to masks. Abbreviated FPLA.

field protect — A feature of some terminals by which delimiters specify the start and end of the field to be protected. This allows the user to maintain the desired information on the screen, presented at a lower intensity, while constantly changing variable or secondary data.

field, register address — The portion of an instruction word that contains a register address.

fields, assembly-language — A language processor that accepts words, statements, and phrases to produce machine instructions. It is more than an assembly program because it has compiler powers. The macroassembler permits segmentation of a large program so that portions may be tested separately. It also provides extensive program analysis to aid in debugging.

field selection — The ability of computers to isolate a particular data field within one computer word (or even in two, three, or four words) without isolating the entire word.

field shifting — The adjustment of the address of a field to realign the item of data.

field, signed — A field that has a plus- or minus-character coding over the units position to designate the algebraic sign of the entire number.

fields, protected — A feature of some systems by which any combination of character positions can be protected against being modified.

field upgrading — Upgrading of equipment by the insertion of functional logic boards such as expanded memory and i/o device controllers, with utilization of the appropriate program.

field utilization — The use of fields (groups of computer characters) as a single data item. Source statements for programming languages are often segmented into several fields for the specification of various syntactical items. Often a 16-bit word is treated as two 8-bit fields or one 8-bit field plus eight 1-bit fields.

field, variable-length — A data field that may have a variable number of characters. This requires item separation to indicate the end of each item.

FIFO — Acronym for First In, First Out. A method of storing and retrieving items from a stack, table, or list.

FIFO queue — First-in-first-out queue in which the most recent arrival is placed at the end of the waiting list and the item waiting the longest receives service first. Same as push-up list.

FIFO stack register — A system in which register outputs are sequentially read in the same order that data is entered.

figures shift — A function performed by a teletypewriter machine that causes the machine to shift to upper case for numbers, symbols, etc., when initiated by the figures-shift character.

figures, significant — 1. Digits of a numeral which have specific meanings for particular purposes. 2. Digits that may not be rounded off without losing accuracy or desired precision.

file — A collection of related records treated as a unit. In a computer system, a file can exist on magnetic tape, disk, punched paper tape, punched cards, or as an accumulation of information in system memory. A file can contain data, programs, or both.

file, active — A file which is being used in which entries or references are made on a current basis.

file activity ratio — A ratio pertaining to the number of file elements in which changes or transactions are made during a specific updating run or in a given period, to the total number of records or elements in the file. If out of a total of 100 records, 20 are updated in a specific month, the activity ratio is thus 20% for this file.

file address checking program — A program to check addresses when macros instruct to write on the file, to see that the program is not writing on the wrong area.

file addressing — Some data records have a particular key or code which identifies the data. When the program is given this key it can locate and use the data at the particular file address.

file addressing, randomizing — The location of a record in a random-access file is located by means of a key set of characters that identify the file. The key is converted to a random number and the random number is converted to the address where the item may be stored. If the item is not in this pocket, an overflow pocket, chained to the first pocket, will be searched.

file analysis — The examination, study, and resolution of file characteristics to determine similarities, number and type of redundancies, and to check labeling and listing of documents which affect file and data elements contained in files.

file, archival quality — A file to be used for historical records; therefore, it has high resistance to deterioration during a specified period of use and storage.

file, chained — To conserve searching time and space, some computer files are in chains. Each data item or key in a record in the chain has the address of another record with the same data or key. To retrieve all data which contain the given key, only the first address need be found, since the next address is adjacent to it, and that one is adjacent to the next, etc.

file, change — A list of transactions processed against the master file.

file checks, magnetic tape — Hardware checks for faulty tapes without loss of computer time or manual intervention.

file components — The parts of a file. A typical file is composed of header or label, data items, and an end of file mark. These components are contained in subdivisions of the file called records or blocks.

file composition — The filing of records within a storage unit.

file conversion — The transformation of parts of records, customer account records, employee records, and the like from their original documents into magnetic files by the computer.

file, data — Aggregations of data sets for definite usage. The file may contain one or more different data sets. A permanent data file is one in which the data is perpetually subject to being updated; e.g., a name and address file. A working data file is a temporary accumulation of data sets which is destroyed after the data has been transferred to another form.

file, dead — A file that is not in current use but is retained.

file density, trailer record — A process used in cases involving identification numbers which match the disk-file addresses.

file, detail — A file of information that is relatively transient. This is contrasted with a master file which contains relatively more permanent information; e.g., in the case of weekly payroll for hourly employees, the detail file will contain employee number, regular time, and overtime, the hours such employee has worked in a given week, and other information changing weekly. The master file will contain the employee's name, number, department, rate of pay, deduction specifications, and other information which regularly stays the same from week to week.

file devices — A computer system is a collection of devices, many of them addressable: disks, magnetic tape drives, cassettes, card or paper tape readers, paper tape punch, printers, terminals, etc. Files can be transferred to and from all of these devices, but of the devices mentioned, only disks are random access devices—devices that allow data to be processed in random order independent of its physical location on the device or its location relative to other information. These devices are sometimes called block replaceable devices. The other devices process information in the same order as the physical order of the data on the device. These are called sequential access devices.

file directory, diskette — Generally, each diskette contains a file directory that identifies what files are stored, where they are located, and other related information such as file size and attributes. Listing the file directory is accomplished with a single command on most systems.

file event — A single file access, either reading or writing. The processing of an action usually requires one or more file events.

file feed — An extension device which increases the punch card capacity of the feed hopper peripheral devices.

file gap — An interval of space or time to indicate or signal the end of a file.

file identification — The coding required to identify each physical unit of the outputs of electronic data-processing machine runs.

file, inactive — A previously active file that, although not currently in use, is expected to be restored to an active status.

file, index — *See* index file.

file index, disk — A table of keyfields identifying the actual disk records in another permanent disk file.

file, inverted — A file containing item labels placed in a single record identified by a label describing the contents of the documents.

file label — A set of alphanumeric characters that uniquely identify the contents of a particular roll of magnetic tape or a portion of a roll of magnetic tape. This file label is written on magnetic tape as a block which contains the file name, reel number, date written, and date expired.

file, magnetic strip — A file storage device which uses strips of material with surfaces that can be magnetized for the purpose of storing data.

file maintenance — Modification of a file to incorporate changes that do not involve arithmetical operations; for example, insertions, deletions, transfers, and corrections.

file maintenance, graphic — The process designed to update physical representations such as microfilm, film prints, crt output copies, etc.

file management — A system design to provide a device-independent interface from a program to data stored on disk.

file manager — A file manager often is an on-line executive program that provides the ability to create, delete, and retrieve programs by name from a bulk storage device. The file manager can be designed to provide program storage for systems as small as 4K words where a full operating system cannot be used. File manager supports disks, magnetic tapes, cassettes, etc.

file mark — An identification mark for the last record in a file. One of the several labels to indicate end-of-file; i.e., file marks may be followed by trailer label, file mark, and reel mark.

file mark, end of — A code that signals the last record of a file has been read.

file, mass storage — A type of secondary, and usually slower, storage, designed to supply the computer with the required information and data for immediate up-to-date reports on a given program segment.

file, master — The overall file or grouping of records having similar characteristics, but which contain the data which is considered permanent by nature of its contents, such as employee pay data, exemptions claimed, department wage rates, etc.

file, master-program — A tape on which all the programs for a system of runs are recorded.

file model — The model is an analog of the processing files. It can be originated, added to (posting), compared with others, held aside, filed for later use, sent somewhere, and so on. Sets of symbols are the simple analogs for these happenings.

file name — Alphanumeric characters assigned to identify a related set of records which constitute a particular file.

file, on-line (central) — The on-line central file may be thought of as a single electronic reservoir, or "data deposit," containing a central-information file index and all major-applications files. The index and the application files are cross-referenced by disk-file memory addresses maintained as integral parts of all records. Under computer control, inquiries may be made directly to any record in the on-line central file. File updating may occur continuously throughout the day. There is no need to accumulate, batch, and sort incoming transactions and other input data for separate application runs.

file organization — The procedure of organizing various information files; these files are often random-access files to develop maximized use of storage and swift retrieval for processing.

file-organization routine — A specifically designed routine for reading input-data files, and sorting them in random-access locations.

file-oriented programming— I/o coding is simplified with the general file and record control program. Programming is file-oriented rather than device-oriented. Information is requested in device-independent fashion.

file-oriented system — If reference to file storage is the principle or key basis of a system, it is considered to be file-oriented. Auxiliary storage used as fundamental or essential in many commercial systems might be file-oriented, while generally considered incidental in scientific systems.

file overflow areas — *See* overflow areas, file.

file packing density — The ratio of available file or data storing space to the total amount of data stored in the file.

file preparation — The ordering, sorting, and handling of parts records, customer account records, employee records, and the like from their original or copied documents into a form suitable for transformation via the computer onto magnetic files for storage.

file, problem — All the material needed to document a program to be run on a computer.

file processing — Modification of a file to incorporate changes that do involve arithmetic operations; for example, receipts, issues, returns, and losses of stock items.

file, program — A flexible, easily updated reference system for the maintenance of the entire software library.

file protection — A device or method that prevents accidental erasure of operative data on magnetic-tape reels.

file reconstruction procedures — The safeguard procedure of protecting against the loss of data should the file be accidentally destroyed by a programmer or operator error, or by an equipment failure.

file record compaction — *See* compaction of file records.

file reel — A magnetic tape reel which feeds toward the rewrite head and is also known as the supply reel.

files, batch transaction — Transactions accumulated as a batch ready for processing against the master file.

files, disk — *See* disk files.

file security — The relative privacy or inaccessibility of files from unauthorized users.

file, sequential — A data file whose key-fields are arranged in a definite sequence. This is contrasted to a random file.

files, permanent data — *See* data files.

file spot, end of — An area on the used tape to signal the end of the file.

files, protected — Files in a computer system that are accessible only to a specific user. Since most files in a system are protected in this way, one user usually cannot obtain access to the information in another user's files.

files, shared — A direct-access device that permits two systems to be linked together. Either system has access to the file.

file storage — A special-purpose storage of relatively large capacity, designed to hold a master file.

file structured devices — Devices that allow the storage of data under assigned file names. Disks, tapes, and cassettes are all file structured devices. Devices that are not file structured, such as a line printer or terminal, contain a single logical collection of data.

file swapping — Some systems attempt to keep as many jobs in memory as possible. When more memory is required to run a job than is available, the system temporarily swaps some jobs out of memory and stores them in one of the swap files defined by the system manager. When it is again their turn to run, the jobs in one of the swap files are swapped back into memory.

files, working data — *See* data files.

file system, backup utility — The backup utility allows the user to ensure against the total loss of data due to hardware failure or software error. When invoked, this utility permits the creation of back-up copies of a single file or a collection of files on some storage medium. Thereafter, if the original files are lost or damaged, these copies can be used to return the files to their original condition.

file system, restore utility — The reverse of the backup utility. Whereas the backup utility creates back-up copies of files, the restore utility takes backup files as input and produces standard files as output. The structure, content, and attributes of these restored files will be those of the original files at the time they were backed up.

file, tape — 1. A record file consisting of a magnetic or punched-paper tape. 2. A set of magnetic tapes in a tape library.

file, transaction — Transactions accumulated as a batch ready for processing against the master file.

file transfer, communications — The process or ability for transfer of sequential ASCII data files between nodes of a computer network. Other types of files may be transferred when formats of participating nodes are compatible.

file transfer, node — The process or ability for transfer of sequential ASCII data files between nodes of a computer network. Other types of files may be transferred when formats of participating nodes are compatible.

file, tub — An open account file which provides ready accessibility to punched cards or other computer storage documents.

file update, master program — *See* master program file update.

file, user (time sharing) — *See* time-sharing user file.

file, variable-length record — A file containing a set of records that vary in length.

file, volatile — A temporary or rapidly changing program or file.

filing system — An organization or set of plans developed to identify records for efficient retrieval. Filing systems may be sequential, alphabetical, numeric, or coded in various ways.

fill, character — *See* character fill.

filler — In order to make some data processing items standard, such as a record, a filler is used as some portion of that item. Thus, the standard size is achieved, and the filler is not an essential part of the data involved.

filler function — A function of some graphics systems that allows the operator to generate arcs of specified radius tangent to two lines and truncates the lines at the point of tangency.

fill, memory — *See* memory fill.

fill, storage — The storing of characters in storage areas not used for data storage or the program for a particular machine run.

film — A base which usually contains a layer of magnetic material often less than one micron thick and used for logic or storage elements.

film, magnetic thin — A layer of magnetic material frequently used for logic or storage elements. Magnetic thin films are commonly less than a micron in thickness.

film reader — *See* reader, film.

film recorder — A mechanism that receives information from a computer and records it in the form of opaque and transparent areas on photographic film.

filter — 1. A device that separates signals or material in accordance with specified criteria. 2. A machine word that specifies which parts of another machine word are to be operated on. Also called extractor or mask.

financial point-of-sale (POS) system — Some terminals provide plastic-card transaction services at small retail stores. With the terminals, financial institutions can enable retail outlets to authorize consumer bank card or personal check transactions. Additionally, banks, savings-and-loan associations, and credit unions can use the terminals to transfer transaction funds directly from a shopper's to a merchant's account.

financial utility — A general-purpose computer utility for handling massive volumes of financial transactions.

finding — The operation which consists of identifying and then selecting. The operation begins when one object in a group is requested to be found. The selection terminates when the object is found.

fine index — A subsidiary or supplemental index of a pair of indexes used to locate a particular file record. The higher or master index would be often considered the "gross" index.

fine sort — *See* sort, fine.

FIPS — Abbreviation for Federal Information Processing Standards. *See* ANSI standards.

firmware — Computer programs that are embodied in a physical device that can form part of a machine. Contrasted with software, which refers to the entire set of programs, procedures, and related documentation associated with a system and especially a computer system, specifically computer programs.

firmware circuitry — Computer circuitry which performs the functions of program instructions. In the firmware concept, many routine operations would be "hard wired" into the machine to relieve the programmer of many repetitive tasks and improve machine efficiency.

firmware instructions — Software instructions committed to a ROM (read-only memory), often as a control block. Firmware can increase the instruction set and control capability of a computer by having the ROM code convert extended instructions into sets of actual machine instructions.

firmware ROM — A ROM containing a control program. The term generally refers to software that has been made operationally permanent by storing it in a type of hardware, e.g., a chip, board, etc.

first generation computer — *See* computer, first generation.

first item list — *Same as* indication, group.

first-level address — An address that indicates the location where the referenced operand is to be found or stored, with no reference to an index register or B-box.

first-order subroutine — *See* subroutine, first-order.

first-pass sorting (own coding) — Computer instructions created by the programmer, in assembly or absolute form, which are executed by a sort during the first pass of the file after input program has been loaded, but prior to execution of first-pass sequencing instructions.

first remove subroutine — *See* subroutine, first-order.

five level — Any teletypewriter code which utilizes five impulses, in addition to the start and stop impulses, for describing a character.

fixed area (FX) — The area on a disk where data files or core image programs may be stored and protected.

fixed block — The number of characters in the block is determined by the logic of the computer.

fixed connector — Used in flowcharting to indicate that only the result indicator can exist after a process completion.

fixed-cycle operation — 1. A type of computer performance whereby a fixed amount of time is allocated to an operation. 2. An operation that is completed in a specified number of regularly timed execution cycles.

fixed data name — The specific reserve term representing a predetermined value.

fixed formats — A state of unchanging description, or a specification of the information content in a particular design or a programmed area.

fixed-form coding — Specific coding instructions with a fixed field assigned to particular labels, operations codes, and operand parts of the instructions.

fixed-head disk — Refers to various disk units that have read/write heads that are specifically fixed in position. In such systems, usually one head is required for each track of information recorded on a disk.

fixed length — Relates to the number of

Courtesy BASF Systems

Fixed-head disk.

characters which can be contained in a specific storage location or data element, and which number of characters to be handled as units cannot be changed by programmers. Opposite of variable length, which if placed in fixed-length storage locations could result in undesired unused spaces in packing density.

fixed-length file records — Enumerable elements each of which has the same number of words, characters, bits, fields, etc.

fixed-length record system — When a system contains all records with the same number of characters, it is called a fixed-length record system. This is contrasted to systems which have a variable number of characters in a record.

fixed-length word — A computer word which always has a fixed number of characters, i.e., one with 16 alphanumeric characters or 32 binary digits without any variation whatever. Registers, storage locations, gating, etc., are designed to handle a fixed number of digits.

fixed-plus-variable structure — A type of computer design in which the logical organization and physical structure of the central processor are arranged to meet the instantaneous needs of different users. This design is a requirement of communication networks, with their thousands of applications.

fixed point — 1. A notation or system of arithmetic in which all numerical quantities are expressed by a predetermined number of digits, with the point implicitly located at some predetermined position. (Contrasted with floating point.) 2. A type of calculation with integers only and without any decimal point or decimal portions.

fixed-point operation — A calculation of numbers in which the arithmetic point, binary or decimal, is assumed to be or is held at a specific relative position for each number.

fixed-point part — That one of the two elements of the floating-point representation of a number which is not the exponent or power of the base.

fixed-position addressing — This permits selective updating of tape information as in magnetic disk or drum storage devices. Units as small as a single computer word may be stored or recorded on tape without disturbing adjacent information. Data blocks are numbered and completely addressable. Inter-record gaps are eliminated, thereby increasing tape storage capacity.

fixed radix scale — *Same as* notation, fixed radix.

fixed routine — A routine which cannot be modified during its execution.

fixed-size records — Denumerable file elements each of which has the same number of words, characters, bits, fields, etc.

fixed word — The limitation of equipment as to the constant number of characters which the equipment will handle.

fixed word length — 1. A term which refers to computers in which data are treated in units of a fixed number of characters or bits (as contrasted with variable word length). 2. All storage fields must have a predetermined length or capacity (in contrast to a variable word length).

flag — 1. A bit of information attached to a character or word to indicate the boundary of a field. 2. An indicator used frequently to tell some later part of a program that some condition occurred earlier. 3. An indicator used to identify the members of several intermixed sets. (Synonymous with sentinel.) 4. Any of various types of indicators used for identification, e.g., a wordmark.

flag bit — A specific information bit that indicates a type or form of demarcation that has been reached. This may be carry, overflow, etc. Generally the flag bit refers to special conditions, such as various types of interrupts.

flag indicator — A signal set up to indicate that a specific condition has occurred in a computer. The flag may be programmed or generated in the machine. For example, when a buffer is full, a flag may be set up to indicate this condition.

flag lines — Inputs to a microprocessor controlled by i/o devices and tested by branch instructions.

flag operand — The third operand of a symbolic instruction, designating which digits of the object-level instruction will be flagged.

flag status register — A type of register used to store the states of the various flag cells. Each flag type is assigned a particular bit position within the register.

flag tests — Single bits used to indicate the result of a simple test. Typical microprocessor systems have flags for such functions as a zero test, positive test, and carry. Flags are generally used as a basis for conditional decisions, such as jump if zero.

flatbed plotter — A device that provides continuous line or point plotting of curves and data.

flat file — A file structure that does not support involvement of hierarchical relationships, such as a CODASYL data set. The term is sometimes used to exclude files with searching mechanisms or direct access capabilities. Typical flat files are simple sequences of records on tape or cards.

flexibility, software — *See* modularity, software.

flip-flop — A bistable device (a device capable of assuming two stable states) which may assume a given stable state depending upon the pulse history of one or more input points and having one or more output points. The device is capable of storing a bit of information, controlling gates, etc. A toggle.

flip-flop register — *See* register, flip-flop.

float — To move or shift one or several characters into positions to the right or left as determined by data structure or programming desires, e.g., to float asterisks to the right or left of numerical fields; dollar signs to the rightmost nonspace positions.

floating address — *See* address, floating.

floating-decimal arithmetic — A method of calculating that automatically accounts for the location of the radix point. This is usually accomplished by handling the number as a signed mantissa times the radix raised to an integral exponent; e.g., the decimal number +88.3 might be written as $+.883 \times 10^2$; the binary number $-.0011$ as $-.11 \times 2^{-2}$.

floating gate — A technique used for ultraviolet-erasable EPROMs in which a silicon gate is isolated inside the silicon dioxide.

floating point — A notation in which a number x is represented by a pair of numbers y and z (and two integers n and m which are understood parameters in any given representation) with y and z chosen so that $x = y \cdot n^z$ where z is an integer. The quantity z is called the exponent or characteristic; e.g., a decimal number 241,000,000 might be shown as 2.41, 8, since it is equal to 2.41×10^8.

floating-point arithmetic — A method of calculation which automatically accounts for the location of the radix point. This is usually accomplished by handling the number as a signed mantissa times the radix raised to an integral exponent.

floating-point arithmetic (operation) — In order to add two floating-point numbers, it is first necessary to equalize the exponents of the numbers. This is accomplished by shifting the mantissa of the smaller expression to the right the number of places that equals the difference of the two exponents. For example, in adding the floating-point decimal numbers 0.3×10^4 and 0.27×10^6, 0.3×10^4 is written as 0.003×10^6 and then the two numbers are added, which gives the result 0.273×10^6.

$$\begin{array}{r} .3 \times 10^4 \\ +\ .27 \times 10^6 \\ \hline \end{array} = \begin{array}{r} .003 \times 10^6 \\ +\ .27\ \ \times 10^6 \\ \hline .273 \times 10^6 \end{array}$$

The same procedure is required for subtraction except that the subtrahend is subtracted from the minuend in the final step of the operation.

$$\begin{array}{r} .27 \times 10^6 \\ -\ .3\ \ \times 10^4 \\ \hline \end{array} = \begin{array}{r} .27\ \ \times 10^6 \\ -\ .003 \times 10^6 \\ \hline .267 \times 10^6 \end{array}$$

To perform this operation with binary numbers, the exponents are first differenced. Then the mantissa of the number with the smallest exponent is shifted right the specified number of places, that is, the difference between the two exponents. When this is accomplished, the two resulting floating-point expressions are added with a double-precision add instruction, and the exponent of the larger number is affixed to the result. The operation is the same for subtraction except that the sign of the subtrahend is changed before the double-precision add is performed. The procedure just outlined is a much simplified analysis of floating point addition and subtraction, but serves to explain the basic principle.

Multiplication and division of the mantissa of the floating-point expression are performed in the same manner as for normal fixed-point numbers. The exponents, however, are added in multiplication, and subtracted in division.

floating-point coefficient — *See* coefficient, floating-point.

floating-point operation — A calculation of numbers in which the arithmetic point, binary or decimal, is movable, not necessarily the same for each number.

floating-point package — A subroutine or hardware device that achieves floating-point hardware function without additional CPU slowed activity. In software, it consists of routines for fixed to floating-point conversion and vice versa, conversion from decimal to floating point and vice versa, plus floating-point move and such floating-point arithmetic functions as addition, subtraction, multiplication, and division.

floating-point precision — The maximum number of binary digits used as the mantissa of a single-precision floating-point fraction.

floating-point subroutines — Special routines that handle floating-point numbers as arguments.

floppy disk — *See* diskette.

floppy disk controller — The devices that provide control of data transfer to and from a floppy disk.

floppy disk controller, intelligent — The intelligent floppy disk controller (FDC) provides software functions which normally have to be implemented in the microcomputer system itself. These functions are accomplished by using separate microprocessors on the controller boards. Typically, an intelligent FDC will provide a file management system with symbolic filing and automatic space allocation on a diskette. It will also provide full editing capabilities and full input-output buffering as well as a variety of optional interfaces. In addition the usual access methods will be provided, such as sequential, random, or direct accessing. Sophisticated error corrections and order retry for soft errors may also be available on some controllers, as well as explicit diagnostics.

floppy disk drives — A disk unit consists of a disk drive—the mechanism within which the disk rotates—and a controller containing electronic circuitry that feeds signals into and from the disk, and that allows the disk unit to work together with the computer central processing unit.

floppy disk, intelligent — Refers to various

Courtesy Pertec Computer Corp.

Floppy disk drive (and two diskettes).

types that have an addition of a microcomputer as a tester that allows for new tests such as amplitude, resolution determination, dropout, extra pulse, and modulation. The microcomputer also allows users to select exactly what tests they desire to have performed, or to develop their own custom tests.

floppy-disk types — There are two sizes of floppy disk, the standard 8-inch diskette unit and the 5¼-inch diskette unit. They are essentially identical in design because they are contact recording devices closely resembling tape drives. These drives record data at basic rates of 125 to 250 bps with recording densities of 6600 bits per radian. By using different data encoding/decoding techniques, the bit densities may be easily doubled without affecting the density of flux reversals on the medium. Since data is recorded on concentric, circular tracks at a constant rate regardless of track radius, data bit cell lengths vary directly with track radius. Radius ratios on the order of 1.8 to 1 in these products tax the ability to read data reliably with cost-effective drive/read channel circuitry.

flow — A general term to indicate a sequence of events.

flow, bidirectional — Flow that can extend over the same flow lines in either direction.

flowchart — A chart to represent, for a problem, the flow of data, procedures, growth, equipment, methods, documents, machine instructions, etc.

flowchart connector — *See* connector, flowchart.

flowchart, data — *See* data flowchart.

flowchart, operations — A graphic representation of the intercommunicated, interconnected logical steps necessary to solve a particular problem.

flowchart, program — A visual representation of a computer problem in which machine instructions or groups of instructions are designated by symbols.

flowchart, structure — Generalized flowcharts showing input, processing, files, and output without indicating the precise methods of processing.

flowchart symbols — The symbols, such as squares, circles, etc., convey no information and must be labeled. They localize a point of interest but convey only the most general notion of intent. The finished model must include adequate description to explain what the operation does. Liberal use of footnotes is recommended to explain the "why" of operations that are not straightforward.

flowchart, systems — Visual representation of the system through which data provided by the source document are converted into final documents.

flowchart technique — Detailed flowcharts showing data and information requirements and the specific methods and calculations for processing the information.

flow control — The time sequence of instruction executions which relate to the maintenance of control of a computer system. Examples are: executive routines, jump instructions, various specific decision programs or instructions.

flow diagram — A chart that graphically describes the functional relationships of the hardware units that make up a system. Such a diagram tends to serve to indicate the various data and control signal paths between the functional units of the system.

flow diagram, dynamic — *See* diagram, dynamic flow.

flow direction — The antecedent-to-successor relation, indicated by arrows or other conventions, between operations on flowcharts.

flowline — A line representing a connecting path between symbols on a flowchart.

flow, normal-direction — A flow in a direction from left to right or top to bottom.

flow, parallel — The system of operations designed so that several of them may be conducted simultaneously, such as in house building, the air-conditioning ducting can be completed, while the plumbing is being worked on, while the landscaping is being developed, etc.

flow-process diagram — A graphic representation of the major steps of work in process. The illustrative symbols may represent documents, machines, or actions taken during the process. The area of concentration is on where or who does what, rather than how it is to be done. (Synonymous with process chart.)

flow, reverse-direction — A flow in a direction other than left to right or top to bottom.

flow tracing — A type of diagnostics

and debugging in which the programmer specifies the start and end of those program segments where he wishes to examine the contents of various registers and accumulators. The program will run at machine speed until it encounters the desired segments, and the printing commences and is terminated when the end of the program segment is encountered.

fluorescent display — A display having segments composed of fluorescent material that glows when bombarded by electrons.

flying-spot scanner — In optical character recognition (OCR), a device employing a moving spot of light to scan a sample space, the intensity of the transmitted or reflected light being sensed by a photoelectric transducer.

follower, curve — *See* curve follower.

font — A complete family or assortment of characters of a given size and style.

font, optical — One of the media that can be used as computer input. An optical font is a variety of type which can be sensed by a computer input device and translated into electronic form within the computer.

font reticle — A system of lines forming various character outlines or dimensions in optical character recognition which is placed over the image of an input character and which determines whether that character conforms to the prescribed shape and range of dimensions. Other outlines on the font reticle check for minimum space between lines and characters, and for the maximum size of punctuation marks.

footing, control — A summary or total at the end of a control group or for various control groups, i.e., a minor total.

footing, page — The summing of the entries on a particular page, usually appearing at the bottom of each page.

footing, report — The summary of the entire report, which most often appears at the termination and which is also known as final footing.

forbidden character code — *Same as* code, illegal.

forbidden code — *See* code, illegal.

forbidden combination — *Same as* character, illegal.

forbidden-combination check — *See* check, forbidden-combination.

forbidden digit — *See* character, illegal.

forbidden-digit check — *Same as* check, forbidden-combination.

force — To manually interrupt and intervene in the operation of a routine and to effect an execution of a computer jump instruction.

forced coding — *Same as* programming, minimum-access.

forced coding program — *Same as* programming, minimum-access.

forced display — *See* display, forced.

foreground — A high priority program, process, or system part which utilizes the computer CPU immediately, or when and where and as needed, but which still allows less critical or subsidiary programs to be worked on as background tasks during the time when the high-priority programs are not being worked. This is the basis of multiprogramming or foreground/background processing.

foreground/background processing — Automatic execution of lower priority (background) programs when higher priority (foreground) programs are not using the system and vice versa. Background program processing is temporarily suspended to service interrupt requests from i/o devices that require foreground processing.

foregrounding — Refers to specific processing procedures in which top-priority processing most often results from real-time entries which usually have precedence, through the use of interrupts into lower priority or background processing.

foreground processing — Top-priority processing most often resulting from real-time entries which usually have precedence, through the use of interrupts, into lower priority or background processing.

foreground program — A program that is initiated via an outside request delaying a background program.

foreground routine — *Same as* foreground program.

foreign attachments — Since the 1969 Carterphone decision, "foreign" (i.e., non-Bell) attachments have been permitted on the direct dial network. Until recently, a Data Access Arrangement (DAA) was required between the customer-owned modem and the line. A low speed asynchronous modem may now be coupled acoustically or inductively through a conventional handset.

foreign exchange line — A line offered by a common carrier in which a termination in one central office is assigned a number belonging to a remote central office.

foreign-exchange service — That service which connects a customer's telephone to a central-office exchange normally not serving the customer's location.

forest coding — Same as minimum latency programming.

form — A printed or typed document which usually has blank spaces for the insertion of information.

formal logic — *See* logic, formal.

format — A predetermined arrangement of characters, fields, lines, punctuation, page numbers, etc.

format, address — *See* address format.

format character — *See* character, format.

format control — *See* control, format.

format, instruction — *See* instruction format.

format, N address instruction — *See* instruction format, N-address.

format order — *See* instruction format.

format, packed — A binary-coded decimal format in which two decimal digits are represented within a single byte of storage, accomplished by eliminating the zone bits.

format storage, local — A system in which frequently used formats are stored at a terminal controller instead of being repeatedly sent down the communications line.

format, symbolic-coding — In writing instructions using the assembly language, the programmer is primarily concerned with three fields: a label field, an operation field, and an operand field. It is possible to relate the symbolic coding to its associated flowchart, if desired, by appending comments to each instruction line or program segment.

formatting — 1. Planning the order of information to or output from a computer or peripheral, such as a printer or crt, usually to assist or ease the human receiver's interpretation of the information. 2. Preparation of various types of magnetic media to accept data structures. Floppy disks, for example, require before use that formatting regarding track and sector information be set for the controller. After it is formatted, the disk can be used for normal i/o and retrieval operations.

format, variable — A changing description of classification for the information content in a particular area.

form, Backus-Naur — *Same as* Backus normal form.

form-feed character — *See* character, form-feed.

form feed out — A form positioning feature provided as an option on sprocket feed teleprinters. The automatic positioning of the typing unit to the first line of typing on the next form, at the same time feeding out the form in use so it may be torn off.

forms creation, terminals — Forms can be created with display features to make data entry easier and reduce the chance of errors. The forms used are similar to paper forms except that they are displayed on the terminal screen. Forms are made by defining "fields" of one or more characters. Each character can be given one or more of the display features. With some units, once a form is created, it can be stored and displayed as needed.

forms display, fill-in-blanks — A type of forms display that provides "fill in the blank" operation with protected fixed fields. Variable areas are established for operator entry of the required information corresponding to each of the protected (forms) fields. Only variable fields are transmitted when operating in the forms mode.

form stop — On a printer, the automatic device that stops the machine when paper has run out.

Forth language — Forth is a programming language system which can be implemented readily on microcomputers, and which offers high-level means of expressing solutions to a wide range of problems. A major feature of Forth is that user-defined operators (procedures, functions or commands) can be used just as though they were primitives. This makes the language truly extensible. Extensions may be added at the user-program level or at the Forth-interpreter level.

FORTRAN — 1. FORmula TRANslator. A compiler language developed by the IBM Corporation, originally conceived for use on scientific problems but now widely adapted for most commercial problems as well. 2. Pertaining to a computer program which translates a FORTRAN-language program into a machine-language program.

FORTRAN, commercial — Some systems combine FORTRAN IV with elements of BASIC and COBOL for business and computational applications.

FORTRAN compiler system — The FORTRAN compiler system consists of two basic elements: a source language (FORTRAN IV), whose structure closely resembles the language of mathematics, and a compiler that translates the statements and formulas written in the source language into a machine-language program.

FORTRAN continue — A statement which does not generate machine code. It is useful as the last statement in a DO loop.

FORTRAN-80, microcomputer — One type initial compiler is a fully implemented ANSI standard FORTRAN with the exception of the double precision and complex data types. It allows three data types: logical (one byte), integer (two byte) and real (four byte floating point). Logical variables under FORTRAN-80 can represent, and store, both logical values (ones and zeros) and integer quantities from −128 to +127. This allows programmers to minimize data storage, and take advantage of fast logical arithmetic operations—with integers within that range. It is a one-pass compiler that reads source code, concurrently translates it into relocatable object code, that may be placed in ROM, and prints an optional code listing. (12 Kbytes memory required.)

FORTRAN IV — FORTRAN IV is a language that is problem oriented. The programmer may think in terms of the problem, rather than thinking in terms of the computer which is used to solve the problem. Initially designed for scientific applications, it has proved quite convenient for many commercial and industrial applications.

FORTRAN IV cross assembler — A typical program or group of programs designed to convert microcomputer assembly language to microprocessor machine code. Assembly language is fully symbolic, and symbolic cross-referencing is provided together with diagnostics of programming errors. Special assembler features are typically provided to enable efficient use of unique architectural features of specific microprocessors.

FORTRAN IV logical capabilities — FORTRAN IV logical capabilities include: type-declaration statements, logical operators, logical expressions, relational operators, logical assignment statements, and the logical IF statement.

FORTRAN IV simulator — Programs designed to functionally simulate execution of various host computer programs. Simulators are interpretive and provide bit-for-bit duplication of microprocessor instruction execution timing, register contents, etc. The system usually provides direct user control over execution conditions, RAM/register contents, interrupts, i/o data, etc.

FORTRAN language — Programs are written directly as algebraic expressions and arithmetic statements. Various symbols are used to signify equality, addition, subtraction, exponentiation, etc. Additional statements are provided to permit control over how the algebraic expressions and arithmetic statements are to be processed. These include transfer, decision, indexing, and input/output statements.

FORTRAN real constants — *See* constants, real (FORTRAN).

FORTRAN real variables — *See* variables, real (FORTRAN).

FORTRAN subscripts — *See* subscripts (FORTRAN).

forward — Operations involved in interconnecting circuits in order to establish a temporary communication between two or more stations.

forward-backward counter — A device which is capable of adding or subtracting input so that it can count in either an increasing or decreasing direction.

forward scan — An editing operation which makes an output word conform to the control word by comparing positions from right to left and adding punctuation, such as decimals and dollar signs.

four address — 1. A method of specifying the location of operands and instructions in which the storage location of the two operands and the storage location of the results of the operation are cited, and the storage location of the next instruction to be executed is cited.

2. Having the property that each complete instruction specifies the operation and addresses of four registers.

Fourier analysis — The decomposition of a signal into its simplest harmonic curves (sines and cosines).

Fourier series — A mathematical analysis that permits any complex waveform to be resolved into a fundamental plus a finite number of terms involving its harmonics.

four tape sort — *See* sorting, four tape.

fox message — A standard message that is used for testing teletypewriter circuits and machines because it includes all the alphanumerics on a teletypewriter as well as most of the function characters, such as space, figures shift, letters shift, etc. The message is: The quick brown fox jumped over a lazy dog's back 1234567890 ——— sending. The sending station's identification is inserted in the three blank spaces which precede the word "sending."

FPLA device — Abbreviation for Field Programmable Logic Array device. A programmable logic array in which the internal connections of the AND and OR gates can be programmed by passing high current through fusible links.

fragment — One of the parts of the contents of a document, program, or routine, or the act of rearrangement of contents of documents into smaller series or parts.

fragmentation — 1. The process of loading a program into noncontiguous areas of main memory to achieve maximum utilization of storage space. The memory map feature automatically provides this capability. 2. A situation in which a mass memory has many separate holes (available spaces) and needs compacting.

fragmenting — The breaking down of a document into a series of terms or descriptors.

frame — 1. The array of bits across the width of magnetic or paper tape. In paper tape systems, one frame is equivalent to one character. 2. A structure which allows a receiver to uniquely identify an information channel.

frame, main — The central processor of the computer system. It contains the main storage, arithmetic unit, and special register groups. (Synonymous with CPU and central processing unit.)

free field — A property of information-processing recording media which permits recording of information without regard to a preassigned or fixed field; e.g., in information-retrieval devices, information may be dispersed in the record in any sequence or location.

free float, PERT — Certain stops used to halt particular tasks when action will result in an overall delay in the project.

freeze mode — *Same as* hold mode.

freeze point in specifications — A point reached in programming any complex system when the functional specifications of the operational program are frozen.

frequency — In ac signaling, the number of complete cycles transmitted per second. Usually expressed in hertz (cycles per second) kilohertz (kilocycles per second), megahertz (megacycles per second), etc.

frequency-analysis compaction — *See* compaction, frequency-analysis.

frequency, clock — The master frequency of periodic pulses that schedules the operation of the computer.

frequency division multiplexing — A multiplex system in which the available transmission frequency range is divided into narrower bands, each used for a separate channel. Channels are derived by allocating or "splitting up" a wider bandwidth into several narrower bandwidths. Abbreviated fdm.

frequency doubling, recording — *See* recording-frequency doubling.

frequency, maximum operating — The maximum repetition or clock rate at which the modules will perform reliably in continuous operation, under worst-case conditions, without special trigger pulse (clock) requirements.

frequency, pulse repetition — *See* pulse repetition rate.

frequency-shift keying — Abbreviated fsk. A form of frequency modulation in which the carrier frequency is raised or lowered to represent binary 1 or binary 0. For example, if a frequency of 1700 Hz is shifted plus or minus 500 Hz, a frequency of 1200 Hz represents a 0, and a frequency of 2200 Hz represents a binary 1. Generally, fsk techniques are suitable for low-speed devices such as teleprinters and allow operation at speeds as high as 1800 bps.

front-end preprocessor systems — Systems

that serve as an interface between a host computer and its peripherals, local terminals, and remote communication lines. Messages are assembled, stored, and formatted so that i/o interruptions of the host computer are held to a minimum.

front-end processing — Refers to minor microprocessors that are used to interface communication terminals to a "host" data processing system (an information processor).

front-end processor — A small computer that serves as a line controller for a large processor. The small computer not only can serve as a line scanner and controller, but can handle a number of "supervisory" tasks that would normally be done by the large processor, such as error detection, character echoing (on a full duplex line), user validity checking, etc. There are two basic design approaches to the communication front end of a small processor: single bit buffers and line scanning.

front end, programmable — Since front-end processors can be configured with their own peripherals, they are capable of storing a portion of the system load. This can be a distinct advantage during peak-load situations and can help smooth system throughput. The programmable front end can also be configured as a standard data processor. When not functioning in a communications mode, it can be used to perform data processing.

fsk — Abbreviation for Frequency Shift Keying.

fsk mark/space states — In frequency-shift keying, the higher frequency is the mark state, and the lower frequency is the space state.

FSL — Abbreviation for Formal Semantics Language, a program acting as a compiler-compiler.

full adder — A half-adder circuit arrangement which has an additional input of a carry bit or a no bit from a previous position.

full ASCII keyboard — A full ASCII keyboard enables the user to generate lower-case data from the keyboard for direct transmission and print lower-case data. Some systems have an upper-case only key which prevents the full ASCII keyboard from generating lower-case data for those applications where the user does not desire lower case.

full subtracter, parallel — *See* subtracter, full (parallel).

full subtracter, serial — *See* subtracter, full (serial).

fully inverted data base — A data base which is inverted on every field. Such data bases are rare due to the large overhead of additions and deletions.

function — 1. A special purpose or characteristic action. 2. The relation or association of one item from a set with each item from another set. 3. A means of referring to a type or sequence of calculations within an arithmetic statement.

function address instruction format — *See* address instruction, functional.

functional address instruction — *See* address instruction, functional.

functional board tester — A tester that verifies the correct logical operation of a logic board by applying test patterns at the board-edge connector. The output responses usually are monitored at the connector, although some test points may be used.

functional design — *See* design, functional.

functional diagram — *See* diagram, functional.

functional element — A combination of logical and delay elements which performs an elementary computer function.

functional generator — A device that produces a given function of an independent variable.

functional interleaving — *See* interleaving, functional.

functional modularity — The addition of modules to a basic data-processing system which broadens the scope or concept of the system as well as adds capacity.

functional multiplier — A device which will take in the changing values of two functions and put out the changing value of their product.

functional symbols — *See* symbols, functional.

functional unit — A combination of logical and nonlogical elements grouped to perform an elementary computer function such as adding, complementing, or pulse generation.

function buttons — *See* buttons, function.

function codes — *See* codes, function.

function, control — *See* control function.

function digit — A unique computer code digit that describes the arithmetic or logical operation which is to be carried out.

function element — A device that performs a logic function.

function key — 1. A specific key on a keyboard (for example, CR, LF, LTRS, FIGS, etc.) which, when operated, causes a receiving device to perform a certain mechanical function so that a message will be received in proper form. 2. A special key or set of keys which allows functions to be specified characteristic of given applications environment. 3. Keys on keyboards of input/output or specialized terminals which are used to query the system or have it perform certain operations. For example, on a remote-inquiry terminal used in a stock quotation system, a three letter combination identifies any stock, and earnings, sales, dividends, volume, etc., can be displayed, by punching the right function key.

function keys, cathode-ray tube (crt) — Fixed and variable function keys have been added to various crt consoles. A function key when depressed transmits a signal to the computer which can be equated to a prestored typewriter message of many strokes. Function keys by thus saving user actions provide convenience and ease of operation and increased response rate of the user. Special consoles of various types have been developed for a particular user. Examples are: airline agent's sets, badge readers, and stock broker's inquiry consoles.

function keys, user programmable — Various keys that enable the operator to issue a string of display and device commands with a single keystroke. Such a feature can be supported by main memory alone; it does not require secondary storage. These keys may be compared to the various user-definable function keys that are found on programmable calculators.

function objective — That function of the independent variables whose maximum or minimum is sought in an optimization problem.

function part — *Same as* operation part.

function, recursive — *See* recursive function.

function, search-read — *See* search-read function.

functions, software (time-sharing) — *See* time-sharing software functions.

functions, utility — Auxiliary operations such as tape searching, tape-file copying, media conversion, and dynamic memory and tape dumps.

function switch — A circuit having a fixed number of inputs and outputs designed such that the output information is a function of the input information, each expressed in a certain code, signal configuration, or pattern.

function table — 1. A device or routine that can decode multiple inputs into a single output, or encode a single input into multiple outputs. 2. Two or more sets of data so arranged that an entry in one set selects one or more entries in the other sets.

function table tabulation — A tabulation relating all output digital levels to all necessary or possible input digital levels for sufficient successive time intervals (tn, tn+1) to completely characterize the static and dynamic functions of the logic microcircuit. Digital levels may be expressed in electrical values directly or by predefined symbolic equivalents.

fusible link — Refers to a specific type of programmable ROM (Read Only Memory) integrated circuit in which circuits form bit patterns by being "blasted" open (by a heavy destructive current) or left closed or intact. This process is sometimes called "burning" a PROM.

G

gain — The ratio between the output signal and the input signal of a device.

game chip — A typical game chip controls six game tunctions: tennis, squash, soccer, practice, and two rifle shooting games. The chip, when implemented, features four 2-person games and two

1-person games plus automatic scoring and realistic sounds.

game theory — A mathematical process of selecting an optimum strategy in the face of an opponent who has a strategy of his own.

gap — 1. An interval of space or time used as an automatic sentinel to indicate the end of a word, record, or file of data on a tape, e.g., a word gap at the end of a word, a record or item gap at the end of a group of words, and a file gap at the end of a group of records or items. 2. The absence of information for a specified length of time or space on a recording medium as contrasted with marks and sentinels which are the presence of specific information to achieve a similar purpose. (Related to file gap and terminating symbol.) 3. The space between the reading or recording head and the recording medium such as tape, drum, or disk. (Related to gap, head.)

gap, block — The space on magnetic tape separating two blocks of data or information.

gap, controlled head — A microscopic gap is maintained between read/write heads and the disk surface—with absolute reliability. A fail-safe head retraction mechanism prevents any contact with the disk. Heads are completely self-adjusting.

gap digits — Digits sometimes included in a machine word for various technical reasons. Such digits are not used to represent data or instructions.

gap, file — An interval of space or time associated with a file to indicate or signal the end of the file.

gap, head — 1. The space between the reading or recording head and the recording medium such as tape, drum, or disk. 2. The space or gap intentionally inserted into the magnetic circuit of the head in order to force or direct the recording flux into the recording medium.

gap, interblock — The space on magnetic tape separating two blocks of data or information.

gap, interrecord — An interval of space or time deliberately left between recording portions of data or records. Such spacing is used to prevent errors through loss of data or over-writing and permits tape stop-start operations.

gap, interword — The time period and space permitted between words on a tape, disk, drum, etc. Usually, such space allows for controlling specific or individual words, for switching.

gap, record — An interval of space or time associated with a record to indicate or signal the end of the record.

gap scatter — The deviation from true vertical alignment of the magnetic read-head gaps for the several parallel tracks.

gap, word — *Same as* gap, interword.

garbage — Unwanted and meaningless information carried along in storage.

gate — 1. A device having one output channel and one or more input channels such that the output channel state is completely determined by the input channel states, except during switching transients. 2. A signal to trigger the passage of other signals through a circuit. 3. An electrode in a field-effect transistor.

gate, A AND-NOT B — A binary logic coincidence (two-input) circuit for completing the logic operation of A AND-NOT B, i.e., result is true only if statement A is true and statement B is false.

gate, A AND-NOT B or gate, B AND-NOT A — A logic operator possessing the property that if A is a statement and B is a statement, the NOT (if A then B) is true if A is true and B is false, and false if A is false and B is true, and false if both statements are true.

gate, add without carry — *Same as* gate, exclusive OR.

gate, A except B — *Same as* gate, A AND-NOT B.

gate, A ignore B — A binary logic (two input) coincidence circuit which permits the gate to function as a pass for the A input signal while disregarding the B input signal; i.e., the output is the same as the A input signal regardless of the B input signal.

gate, A ignore B negative — A binary logic (two input) coincidence circuit which permits the logic operation of negative A ignore B, i.e., the result is true when A is false and false when A is true, the output being independent of B, same as A ignore B whose output is negated.

gate, A implies B — *Same as* gate, B OR-NOT A.

gate, A implies B negative — *Same as* gate, A AND-NOT B.

gate, alteration — *Same as* gate, OR.

gate, alternative denial — *Same as* gate, NAND.

gate, amplitude — A transducer which transmits only portions of an input wave lying between two amplitude boundaries. Note: The term is used especially when the two amplitude boundaries are close to each other as compared with the amplitude range of the input.

A
B
OUTPUT

Gate, AND (symbol).

gate, AND — A circuit element whose output is a logical one when, and only when, all of the inputs are in a logical one state.

gate, AND negative — *Same as* gate, NAND.

gate, AND-NOT — *Same as* gate, A AND-NOT B or gate, B AND-NOT A.

gate, AND positive — *Same as* gate, AND.

gate, anticoincidence — *Same as* gate, exclusive OR.

gate, A OR-NOT B — A binary (two-input) logic coincidence circuit for completing the logic operation of A OR-NOT B; i.e., the result is false only if A is false and B is true.

gate, B AND-NOT A — A binary (two-input) logic coincidence circuit for completing the logic operation of B AND-NOT A; i.e., the result is true only if B is true and A is false.

gate, B EXCEPT A — *Same as* gate, B AND-NOT A.

gate, biconditional — *Same as* gate, exclusive NOR.

gate, B ignore A — A binary (two-input) logic coincidence circuit for completing a function which permits the B input signal to pass and disregard A input signal; i.e., the output signal is the same as B input signal and is independent of the A input signal.

gate, B ignore A negative — A binary (two-input) logic coincidence circuit for completing a function which is identical to the negative A ignore B gate, but with the labels on the input leads reversed; i.e., the result is true if B is false and false if B is true. The result is the negated or reversed value of B and is independent of A.

gate, B implies A negative — *Same as* gate B AND-NOT A.

gate, B OR-NOT A — A binary (two-input) logic coincidence circuit for completing the logic operation of B OR-NOT A, i.e., the reverse of A OR-NOT B; the result is false only when A is true and B is false.

gate, buffer — *Same as* gate, OR.

gate, conjunction — *Same as* gate, AND.

gate, difference — *Same as* gate, exclusive OR.

gate, disjunction — *Same as* gate, OR.

gate, dispersion — *Same as* gate, NAND.

gate, distance — *Same as* gate, exclusive OR.

gate, diversity — *Same as* gate, exclusive OR.

gate, don't care — A gate whose normal operation can be changed or interrupted upon receipt of a control signal. The output is independent of the inputs.

gate, equality — *Same as* gate, exclusive NOR.

gate, equivalence — *Same as* gate, exclusive NOR.

gate, except — A gate which yields an output corresponding to a one, when one or more input lines are true and one or more other input lines are zero or false.

gate, exclusive NOR — A two input (binary) logic circuit designed to perform the logic operation of exclusive-NOR; i.e., if A and B are input statements, the result is true or 1 when both A and B are true or when both A and B are false. The result is false when A and B are different.

gate, exclusive OR — A binary logic coincidence circuit for completing the logic operation of exclusive OR; i.e., the result is true when A is true and B is false, or when A is false and B is true, and the result is false when A and B are both true or when A and B are both false.

gate, exjunction — *Same as* gate, exclusive OR.

gate generator — A circuit or device that produces one or more gate pulses.

gate, identity — A specific n-input gate which yields an output signal of a particular kind when all of the n-input signals are alike.

gate, if A then B — *Same as* gate, B OR-NOT A.

gate, if A then NOT-B — *Same as* gate, NAND.

gate, if B then NOT-A — *Same as* gate, NAND.

gate, inclusive NOR — *Same as* gate, NOR.

gate, inclusive OR — *Same as* gate, OR.

gate, intersection — *Same as* gate, AND.

gate, join — *Same as* gate, OR.

gate, joint denial — *Same as* gate, NOR.

gate, logic product — *Same as* gate, AND.

gate, logic sum — *Same as* gate, OR.

gate, majority decision — A binary input unit which has the capability of implementing the majority logic operation. The result is true if more than half of the statements are true, and false if half or more of the input statements are false.

gate, match — *Same as* gate, exclusive NOR.

gate, mix — *Same as* gate, OR.

gate, modulo-two sum — *Same as* gate, exclusive OR.

gate, NAND — A logical operator having the property that if P is a statement and Q is a statement, then the NAND of P.Q.R. is true if at least one statement is false and false if all statements are true.

gate, negative (B implies A) — *Same as* gate, B AND NOT A.

gate, negative OR — *Same as* gate, NOR.

gate, neither-NOR — *Same as* gate, NOR.

gate, nonconjunction — *Same as* gate, NOR.

gate, nondisjunction — *Same as* gate, NOR.

gate, nonequality — *Same as* gate, exclusive OR.

gate, nonequivalence — *Same as* gate, exclusive OR.

gate, NOR — A gate whose output is energized when all inputs are absent.

gate, NOT — A logic element which has only one binary input signal; the variable represented by the output signal is the negation of the variable represented by the input signal, i.e., an element whose output signal is 1 when its input signal is 0 and vice versa.

gate, NOT-AND — *Same as* gate, NAND.

gate, NOT-both — *Same as* gate, NAND.

gate, null — A gate which produces signals representing strings of zeros in a particular system as long as power is applied.

gate, one — *Same as* gate, OR.

gate, OR — An electrical gate or mechanical device which implements the logical OR operator. An output signal occurs whenever there are one or more inputs on a multichannel input. An OR gate performs the function of the logical "inclusive OR operator." (Synonymous with OR circuit and clarified by disjunction.)

gate, partial sum — *Same as* gate, exclusive OR.

gate, positive AND — *Same as* gate, AND.

gate, positive OR — *Same as* gate, OR.

gate pulse — Extended duration signals designed to increase the possibility of coincidence with other pulses. Gate pulses present with other pulses cause circuits or devices to perform intended operations.

gate, rejection — *Same as* gate, NOR.

gate, Sheffer stroke — *Same as* gate, NAND.

gate, sine-junction — *Same as* gate, A AND-NOT B or gate, B AND-NOT A.

gate, subjunction — *Same as* gate, A AND-NOT B or gate, B AND-NOT A.

gate, symmetric difference — *Same as* gate, exclusive OR.

gate, synchronous — A synchronous gate is a time gate wherein the output intervals are synchronized with an incoming signal.

gate, time — A time gate is a transducer that gives output only during chosen time intervals.

gate, union — *Same as* gate, OR.

gate zero-match — *Same as* gate, NOR.

gathering, data — *See* data collection.

general assembly program (GAP) — Allows the programmer to write his own program in symbolic code rather than in the absolute code of the computer. One symbolic code instruction is translated into one computer word—a simple one-for-one arrangement.

general escape — *See* escape, general.

generalized data manipulation — The performance of those data-processing chores common to most users, such as sorting, input/output operations, and report generation.

generalized routine — A routine designed to process a large range of specific jobs within a given type of application.

generalized subroutine — Subroutines

that are written for easy and ready use in several various programs with only minor adjustments or adaptations by the programmer or systems analyst.

general program — A program, expressed in computer code, designed to solve a class of problems or specializing on a specific problem when appropriate parametric values are supplied. (Synonymous with general routine.)

general-purpose computer — 1. A computer designed to operate on a program of instructions for the purpose of solving many types of data-processing problems rather than being designed to fulfill a single function or type of function. *See* special-purpose computer. 2. A computer designed to solve a wide variety of problems, the exact nature of which may be unknown before the computer was designed. Also called a stored-program computer.

general purpose operations programs — *See* programs, general-purpose operating.

general purpose simulation program (GPSS) — An IBM discrete system simulation language.

general register — One of a specified number of internal addressable registers in a CPU that can be used for temporary storage, as an accumulator, an index register, a stack pointer, or for any other general-purpose function.

general routine — A program, expressed in computer code, designed to solve a class of problems or specializing on a specific problem when appropriate parametric values are supplied. (Synonymous with generator routine.)

general utility functions — Auxiliary operations such as tape searching, tape-file copying, media conversion, dynamic memory, and tape dumps.

generate — 1. To construct a computer program by use of a generator. 2. To develop or produce various required subroutines from parameters of outline skeleton coding.

generated address — *See* address, calculated.

generated error — The total error accrued by combining the effect of using an exact or imprecise argument with the inexact formula. These errors are compounded by rounding off.

generating program — *See* program, generating.

generating routine — *See* routine, generating.

generation — Under control of parameters supplied to a generator routine, a technique for producing a complete routine from one which is in skeleton form.

generation, automatic character — *See* automatic character generation.

generation, macro — *See* macrogeneration.

generation, report — *See* report generation.

generation, synthetic display — Logical and numerical processing to display collected data or calculated data in symbolic form.

generation, systems — *See* systems generation.

generator — 1. A routine designed to create specific routines from specific input parameters or conditions and skeletal coding. 2. In programming, a program that constructs another program from specifically designed sets of instructions by selecting, adjusting, and arranging them in accordance with given specifications.

generator, function — A specific unit with one or more input and output variables, each output variable being equal to some particular function of the input variable or variables.

generator, number — A set of manual controls on which a computer operator can set a word.

generator, random-number — A special machine routine or hardware designed to produce a random number or series of random numbers according to specified limitations.

generator, report — A technique for producing complete data-processing reports given only a description of the desired content and format of the output reports, and certain information concerning the input file.

generator, report-program — *See* report program generator.

generator routine — A designed set of instructions for production of required subroutines.

generic PROMS — Some PROM manufacturers have developed what they call "generic families" of PROMs. Since units within a family require the same programming voltages, currents, and timing relationships, they can usually be programmed by one programmer with a change of socket.

geodetic system — A computer application system used to reduce the costs of mining and drilling by performing seismographic studies by a computer. Geodesy is the branch of applied mathematics which determines the curvature, shape, and dimensions of the earth. Computers are used for advanced geodetic survey work by mining companies to locate oil and ore deposits.

geometric solution — A graphic method of solving a linear programming problem, by plotting the half-planes determined by the constraints and the lines of constant value for the functional. Its use is restricted to problems with, at most, two structural variables.

geometry — The study of space and of spatial relationships; the investigation of the nature and properties of curves, surfaces and other configurations of points in space.

get — 1. An activity to develop or make a record from an input file available for use by a routine in control of the machine. 2. To obtain or extract a coded or transformed value from a field (as to GET a numerical value from a series of decimal digit characters). 3. To locate and transfer a record or item from storage. (Opposite of put.)

gibberish — *See* hash.

GIGO (garbage in, garbage out) — Unwanted and meaningless information carried along in storage; a result of undesirable input data or information.

glitch — A pulse or burst of noise or other nuisance item that becomes an annoyance and causes error dropouts, types of crashes, or failures.

global — That part of an assembler program that includes the body of any macrodefinition called from a source module and the open code portion of the source module. Contrast with local.

global variable — A variable whose value is accessible throughout the program. This is opposed to a local variable, which is accessible only within the block where it is defined.

glossary — A vocabulary with annotations for a particular subject.

go ahead — A polling signal sent from the computer to a terminal, or from one terminal down-line to another, to direct the terminal to begin transmission to the computer.

GP — Abbreviation for generalized programming, general processor, and general purpose.

GPC — Abbreviation for general-purpose computer.

GPIB interface adapter — One type adapter allows users to interconnect the IEEE parallel GPIB (general-purpose interface bus) with RS 232C systems. It provides two-way transmission of data and can be used to adapt older instruments and terminals to control and processing systems that use the newer GPIB parallel format.

GPS — Abbreviation for general problem solver. A general programming procedure developed in the 1950s on the IBM 704 computer by Rand Corporation.

GPSS — A general purpose simulation system developed by IBM.

graceful degradation — *See* fail soft (softly).

graceful degradation, time sharing — *See* time sharing, fail soft.

grade, teleptypewriter — Represents the lowest type circuit in terms of speed, cost, and accuracy.

grain direction — Important in optical character recognition, it is the arrangement (direction) of the fibers in the paper in relation to the route or manner in which a document travels through the character reader.

grandfather cycle — The period during which magnetic-tape records are retained before reusing so that records can be reconstructed in the event of loss of information stored on a magnetic tape.

grandfather tape — *See* tape, grandfather.

graph — A sheet of paper onto which have been placed curves, lines, points, and explanatory alphabetic and numerical information representing numerical data.

grapheme — A written or machine code that represents a single semanteme.

graphetic level — An example is a character, either handwritten or printed, usually then capable of being copied, reproduced, transmitted, or manipulated by an ordered set of pulses. This is said to be a representation at a graphetic level.

graph follower — A device that reads data in the form of a graph, usually an optical sensing device.

graphic data processing — *See* data processing, graphic.

graphic display unit — A communications terminal which can display data on a screen.

graphic documentation — A process developed for recording data on graphs and films.

graphic file maintenance — The process designed to update physical representation such as microfilm, film prints, crt output copies, etc.

graphic form — A physical or pictorial representation of data, such as printing plotting output, or crt engineering drawings.

graphic panel — A master-control panel which pictorially and usually colorfully traces the relationship of control equipment and the process operation. It permits an operator to check at a glance on the operation of a far-flung control system by noting dials, valves, scales, and lights.

graphics — The use of diagrams or other graphical means to obtain operating data and answers. The use of written symbols and visual displays.

graphics digitizer — A device that converts line drawings and other graphic representations into digital values that are processed through its control console and sent to the computer (graphic processor) for analysis, storage or computation.

graphics display, raster systems — Some basic definitions refer to this class of displays. The screen is invariably divided into discrete addressable elements, usually called X and Y, and are referred to by coordinates with numerical values. The intensity of the image at a given X-Y point is usually represented by a third coordinate, usually called Z. Almost all raster systems have programmable intensity, called Z modulation. The display of continuous-tone pictures is very easy with that capability. Typical graphics systems have 256–2048 (8–11 bits) resolution elements in X and Y, and 16–256 (4–8 bits) gray levels for resolution in Z.

graphics input devices — A character may be entered, erased, or modified by use of a joystick or a track ball. The location of the character on the screen is dictated by positioning a mark called a cursor with one of these devices. On the other hand, a light pen or a data tablet can perform these functions without the aid of a cursor. In repetitive applications, certain characters may be positioned automatically in the desired locations by software.

graphics interface — A typical high-quality graphics interface converts an asynchronous serial data stream into fully buffered and internally refreshed X, Y, and intensity analog signals. When applied directly to the user's X-Y crt display unit or laboratory oscilloscope, the signals generate lines that are exceptionally clean and straight. Under computer control the lines are drawn at arbitrary length/orientation providing full vector graphics capability.

graphics manipulation — Software and hardware for manipulating pictures or to highlight certain portions are offered by most graphics-display makers. These capabilities include zooming-in, magnifying, reducing, rotating a diagram drawn in 3-dimensional perspective about a point, labeling axes, making characters blink, and silhouetting.

graphic solution — A solution obtained with graphs or other pictorial devices, as contrasted with solutions obtained by the manipulation of numbers.

graphics routines — Routines that convert output data into analog form (vectors). They range from a small program that plots a simple graph on a TTY to complex systems that provide multicolored three-dimensional displays, complete with legends—even in different character sizes and fonts.

graphic type machine — A machine used to record and reproduce various operations.

Gray code — *See* code, cyclic.

grid — In optical character recognition (OCR), two mutually orthogonal sets of parallel lines used for specifying or measuring character images.

grid chart — A representation of the relation between inputs, files, and outputs in matrix form.

grid, control — The electrode of a vacuum tube other than a diode upon which a signal voltage is impressed in order to regulate the plate current, usually electrode or grid number 1.

gross index — The first of a pair of indexes consulted to locate particular records, etc.; the secondary or supplemental index is the fine index.

ground, signal — This conductor establishes the electrical ground reference potential for all interchange circuits except the frame-grounding circuit.

group code — *See* code, group.

grouped records — *See* record group.

group indicate — The printing of indicative information from only the first record of a group.

group indication — *See* indication, group.

grouping — When a mass of data having common characteristics are arranged into related groups.

grouping of records — The combining of two or more records into one block of information on tape to decrease the wasted time due to tape acceleration and deceleration and to conserve tape space. This is also called blocking of records.

group, link — Consists of those links which employ the same multiplex-terminal equipment.

group mark — A special character used in a write instruction to designate the end of a record in storage.

group printing — The function of a machine which does not print data from every card. Instead, it summarizes the data contained in a group of cards and prints only the summarized total.

group, record — *See* record group.

group theory — A study, in the mathematical sense of the rules, for combining groups, sets, and elements, i.e., the theory of combining groups.

guard, memory — *See* memory guard.

guard mode, executive — *See* executive guard mode.

guard mode, real-time — The guard mode is activated only by the instruction load internal function which establishes certain operation parameters. When operative, any attempt to perform a restricted operation will result in an interrupt to an address in central store. Guard mode is terminated by the occurrence of any interrupt.

It is possible for any program to use the prevent-all-interrupts and jump instruction, thereby allowing real-time programs to operate effectively when guard mode is established.

guard signal — 1. A signal which allows values to be read or converted only when the values are not in a changing state. 2. An extra output, which is generated when all values are complete, to be used as a guard signal. Used in digital-to-analog or analog-to-digital converters or other converters or digitizers.

guide edge — The edge on which paper and magnetic tape is guided while being fed, if such a method is used.

guide margin — When measuring across a paper tape, it is the distance between the guide edge and the center of the closest track of the tape.

gulp — A small group of bytes, similar to a word or instruction.

H

half-digit — In digital meters, an additional most-significant digit provided at the left of the readout, capable of displaying the numeral 1 when the measurement exceeds the full-scale range.

half duplex — A system permitting electrical communications in only one direction between stations. Technical arrangements may permit operation in either direction, but not simultaneously. This term is therefore qualified by one of the following suffixes: S/O for send only; R/O for receive only; S/R for send or receive.

half-duplex channel — A channel capable of transmitting and receiving signals, but in only one direction at a time.

half-duplex circuit — A duplex intercity facility with single loops to the terminals capable of two-way nonsimultaneous operation.

half-duplex operation — Half-duplex or single-telegraph operation refers to communication on a circuit in only one direction at a time, with or without a break feature. The break feature enables the receiving station to interrupt the sending station.

half-duplex service — A type of communication channel that is capable of transmitting and receiving signals, but is not capable of simultaneous and independent transmission and reception.

half subtracter — *See* subtracter, half.

half-subtracter, parallel — *See* subtracter, half (parallel).

half subtracter, serial — *See* subtracter, half (serial).

halftime emitter — A device that emits synchronous pulses midway between the row pulses of a punched card.

halftone plotting — Production of gray-scale halftones through controlled variation in dot clusters (halftone cells) produced on electrostatic plotters.

half-word — A group of characters that represent half of a computer word for addressing purposes as a unit in storage.

half-word location, effective — The storage location pointed to by the effective virtual address of a half-word addressing instruction.

Hall-effect keyswitch — A type of switch in which a magnet on a plunger assembly is moved near a sensitive Hall-effect transducer.

halt — A condition which occurs when the sequence of operations in a program stops. This can be due to a halt instruction or to some unexpected halt or interrupt.

halt, dead — A machine halt from which there is no recovery. Such a halt may be deliberately programmed. A drop dead halt may occur through a logical error in programming. Examples in which a drop dead halt occur are division by zero and transfer to a nonexistent instruction word.

halt, drop-dead — *Same as* halt, dead.

halt instruction — A machine instruction that stops the execution of the program.

halt instruction, optional — An instruction that can stop the computer either before or after the halt instruction is obeyed, depending on the governing criterion.

halt, nonprogrammed — An inadvertant machine stoppage, not due to the results of a programmed instruction, such as an automatic interrupt, manual intervention, machine malfunction, power failure, or other cause.

halt, optional — *See* halt instruction, optional.

halt, program — *Same as* program stop.

halt, programmed — A machine stoppage or interruption of machine operations caused deliberately by a program instruction. The halt is automatic with this instruction in the program.

Hamming code — One of the error-correction code systems in use today.

Hamming distance — The number of digit positions by which the corresponding digits of two binary words of the same length are different.

handler — A section of the program used to control or communicate with an external device.

handshaking — The required sequence of signals for communication between system functions. The i/o bus protocol for a system defines its handshaking requirements. (This is especially true for asynchronous i/o systems in which each signal requires a response (reply) to complete an i/o operation).

hands-on background — Prior work experience developed by actually operating the hardware and often used as a criterion of programmer capability and knowledge.

hang-up — A nonprogrammed stop in a routine. It is usually an unforeseen or unwanted halt in a machine pass. It is most often caused by improper coding of a machine instruction or by the attempted use of a nonexistent or improper operation code.

hang-up prevention — The computer logic must be designed or modified so that no sequence of valid or invalid instructions can cause the computer to come to a halt or to go into a nonterminating uninterruptible state. Examples of this latter case are infinitely nested executions or nonterminating indirect addressing.

hard copy — 1. Typewritten or printed characters on paper, produced at the same time information is copied or converted into machine language that is not easily read by a human. 2. A printed copy of machine output in a visually readable form, e.g., printed reports, listings, documents, summaries, etc.

hard-copy output, plotters — Images developed on a graphics terminal that are documented on plotters or printers.

Plotters consist of one or more pens that are automatically moved according to the input data, whereas printers develop pictures by forming images with electrostatic printing methods.

hard copy video interface — A device that allows production of hard-copy output on an electrostatic printer/plotter from a video source.

hard error rate — The error rate attributable to equipment, transmission techniques, recording media, and the like. A typical rate might refer to the act of storing or recovering data to or from various bulk storage units.

hard-sectored — Pertaining to a disk on which the sectors are marked by holes in the disk itself.

hardware — 1. The electric, electronic, and mechanical equipment used for processing data, consisting of cabinets, racks, tubes, transistors, wires, motors, and such. 2. Any piece of automatic data-processing equipment. (Slang)

hardware check — A provision constructed in hardware for verifying the accuracy of information transmitted, manipulated, or stored by any unit or device in a computer.

hardware, compatible — Components, peripheral equipment, or other devices which can be used on more than one system with little or no adjustment.

hardware monitors — A simple hardware monitor consists of sensors (probes) that monitor the state of the measured system, a logic plugboard that enables it to perform a variety of Boolean functions on monitored state bits, a set of counters that either count event occurrences or time duration of system activities, and a display or recording unit. More advanced monitors include features such as data comparators, sequencers, random access memory, and associative memory.

hardware priority interrupts — A programmed or designed hardware implementation of priority interrupt functions.

hard-wire logic — Logic designs for control or problem solutions that require interconnection of numerous integrated circuits formed or wired for specific purposes and relatively unalterable. A hand-wired diode matrix is hard-wired logic whereas a RAM, ROM, or CPU can be reprogrammed with little difficulty to change the purpose of operation. Hard-wired interconnections are usually completed by soldering or by printed circuits and are thus hard-wired in contrast to software solutions achieved by programmed microcomputer components.

hash — 1. Considered to be computer or program garbage specifically recorded on tapes to fill or comply with restrictions on conventions of starting procedures, block sizes, and others. 2. Same as garbage.

hash index — The initial estimate of the location of an entry within the table.

hashing — As regards indexing, a nonlinear algorithm for storing data in and retrieving it from a table.

hashing function — The algorithm or procedure for calculating a hash index. A hash index is the initial estimate of the location of an entry within a table.

hash total — A sum formed for error-checking purposes by adding fields that are not normally related by unit of measure, i.e., a total of invoice serial numbers.

HASP — Acronymn for Houston Automatic Spooling Processor. An IBM computer configuration for its 360 and 370 computer series. Several companies have provided their own remote job-entry system to fit the IBM equipment.

HDLC — Abbreviation for High-level Data Link Control.

head — A device that reads, records, or erases information in a storage medium, usually a small electromagnet used to read, write, or erase information on a magnetic drum or tape, or the set of perforating or reading fingers and block assembly for punching or reading holes in paper tape.

head, combined — A small electromagnetic unit used for reading, recording, or erasing information on a magnetic tape, disk, or drum.

header — A file record that contains common, constant, or identifying information for a group of records which are to follow. Also the first part of a message containing all necessary information for directing the message to its destination.

head, erase — A magnetic head used to erase or obliterate the old information prior to writing new information.

header card — A punched card which serves to identify types and characteristics of records maintained on the following cards.

header, record — *See* record header.

headers and trailers — Repetitive words, phrases, or sentences placed at predetermined locations on each page of a document.

header table — *Same as* record header.

head, fixed — Pertaining to the use of stationary, rigidly mounted reading and writing heads on a bulk memory device in contrast to movable heads.

head gap — 1. The space between the reading or recording head and the recording medium such as tape, drum, or disk. 2. The space or gap intentionally inserted into the magnetic circuit of the head in order to force or direct the recording flux into the recording medium.

heading — A string of characters, usually placed at the beginning of a message, that represents message routing and destination information and that is machine readable.

heading, page — The description of a page context of a report; usually appears at the top of each page.

heading record — A record which contains an identification or description of the output report for which following records are related to and concerned with the body of the report.

heading, report — Description of the report content which is often produced at the beginning of the report.

head, magnetic — *Same as* head, read/-write.

head-per-track — An arrangement in which a separate read/write head is fixed over each track of information on the disk surface. Electronic switching replaces mechanical arm accessing.

head, playback — A head that is used for reading data on a medium such as tape, disks, drums, cards, or an optical sensor.

head, preread — A read head that may be used to read data on the track of a moving medium such as tape, disk, or drum before the data reaches the read head.

head, read — A head that is used for reading data from a medium such as tape, disks, drums, or cards.

head, read/write — A small electromagnet used for reading, recording, or erasing polarized spots that represent information on magnetic tape, disk, or drum.

head, record — *See* read/write head.

head, recording — A head used to transfer data to a storage device such as a drum, disk, tape, or magnetic card.

head stack — A group of recording heads all recording a set of tracks simultaneously, i.e., a recording channel or band. Such heads are usually mounted and used together for other purposes.

head-to-tape contact — The degree to which the surface of the magnetic coating approaches the surface of the record or play heads during normal operation of a recorder. Good head-to-tape contact minimizes separation loss and is essential in obtaining high resolution.

head, write — A head used to transfer data to a storage device such as a drum, disk, tape, or magnetic card.

HELP — An aid available to inexperienced user personnel. HELP gives users convenient access to a direct self-teaching facility, which accepts questions on the usage of several software subsystems framed in the natural language of the user and provides appropriate answers in English text (some computers).

hertz — A unit of frequency equal to one cycle per second. Abbreviated Hz.

hesitation — A temporary halt or temporary suspension of operations in a sequence of operations of a computer in order to perform all or part of the operations from another sequence.

heterogeneous multiplex — A multiplex structure in which all the information-bearer channels are not at the same data signaling rate.

heuristic — 1. Procedures or methodology designed to develop a plan or program that will obtain desired results or output as an improvement over current procedures and is satisfactory in relation to the constraints of time, cost, personnel, and the limited use of the result. 2. Pertaining to exploratory methods of problem solving in which solutions are discovered by evaluation of the progress made toward the final result. (Contrast with algorithmic.)

heuristic approach — An approach that encourages further experimentation and investigation. An intuitive trial-and-error method of attacking a problem (as opposed to the algorithmic method).

heuristic problem solving — A series of rules that systematically varies models through formal mutation and regenerative reading.

heuristic program — *See* program, heuristic.

heuristic programming — *See* programming, heuristic.

heuristic routine — *See* program, heuristic.

hexadecimal digit — A digit that is a member of the set of sixteen digits: 0 through 9 and then A, B, C, D, E, or F used in a numerical notation system using a radix of 16. Some systems use letters other than A-F for the last six digits.

hexadecimal notation — Notation of numbers in the base 16.

hexadecimal number — A number, usually of more than one figure, representing a sum in which the quantity represented by each figure is based on a radix of sixteen.

hexadecimal number system — A number system using the equivalent of the decimal number sixteen as a base.

hierarchical data base — 1. A data-base structure that allows files to be related to other files in a one-to-n mapping. For example, a record in employee files may be related to zero to n records in a dependents file. One of these records may be related to zero to n records in a med-history file, recording all of the dependent's trips to the doctor. 2. An access method to a data base involving hierarchical menus. From an evening-out menu users may select the movie category and be presented with another menu. Comedy might then be selected from the choices, and a list of movies in this category showing locally would be printed.

hierarchical network nodes — The processing nodes at the top of the hierarchy are generally large host computers, while the nodes at the bottom generally have only limited intelligence or none at all. But intermediate nodes, such as a remote job entry work station, can have significant processing and data-base capabilities.

hierarchy — A specified rank or order of items. A series of items classified by rank or order.

hierarchy, data — *See* data hierarchy.

hierarchy, memory — A set of memories with differing sizes and speeds and usually having different cost-performance ratios (i.e., expensive/fast to less expensive/slower). Faster access sections contain a main computer memory hierarchy and might consist of a very high-speed, small semiconductor memory, a medium-speed disk memory, and a large, slow-speed tape.

high-activity data processing — A condition in which only a comparatively small number of records are updated or referred to frequently.

higher order language — *See* language, higher order.

high-level compiler — A program that translates statements in high-level language into their machine-language equivalents. The compiler for a given high-level language varies with the computer it serves.

high-level data link control — Abbreviated HDLC. A bit-oriented data link control procedure. All data transfer takes place via frames, which are ended with a frame check sequence for error detection. The control field at the beginning of each frame allows error detection and data link set-up and shut-down.

high-level language — Computer language which uses symbols and command statements an operator can read. Each statement typically represents a series of computer instructions. Examples of high-level languages are BASIC, FORTRAN, FOCAL, and COBOL.

high-level source code — Statements or statement lines as original directives that a programmer prepares to direct the operation of a computer when using a high-level language such as BASIC, FORTRAN, COBOL, etc.

highlighting — Distinguishing or emphasizing data on a crt display by reversing the field, blinking, underlining, changing color, changing light intensity, or some combination of these methods.

high-low bias test — A preventive-maintenance procedure in which certain operating conditions are varied about their normal values in order to detect and locate defective units; e.g., supply voltage or frequency may be varied. (Synonymous with marginal test, and related to check.)

high-low limits — The maximum and minimum values of data expected. These values are used to check the program and results.

high order — Pertaining to the weight or significance assigned to the digits of a number; e.g., in the number 123456, the highest order digit is 1; the lowest order digit is 6. One may refer to the three high-order bits of a binary word as another example.

high-order digit — *See* digit, high-order.

high-performance equipment — Equipment having sufficiently exacting characteristics to permit its use in trunk or line circuits.

high-positive indicator — An internal computer-indicator component that indicates "on" if the result of an arithmetic operation is positive and not zero (some systems).

high-speed carry — A type of carry in which: (1) a carry into a column results in a carry out of that column because the sum without a carry in that column is 9; (2) instead of a normal adding process, a special process is used that takes the carry at high speed to the actual column where it is added. Also called standing-on-nines carry.

high-speed memory — *See* memory, high-speed.

high-speed printer — A printer that operates at a speed more compatible with the speed of computation and data processing so that it may operate on-line.

high-speed reader — *See* reader, high speed.

high-speed storage — *See* storage, high-speed.

hi-low — Used in exception reporting to relate the maximum and minimum limits beyond which an exception is reported and acted upon.

history command, development system — On some systems, history is normally issued after a break from a user program. This instruction lists on the terminal the state of the address, data, and control buses of the CPU during execution of up to several hundred bus transactions that occurred in the user's program just prior to a break.

history run — The printing out of all transactions of a process for reading or recording purposes.

hit — 1. A term used in mechanical retrieval systems to represent an answer found by the machine. 2. In file maintenance, the finding of a match between a detail record and a master record.

hit-on-the-fly system — A printer where either the paper, the print head, or both are in continual motion.

hit on the line — 1. A momentary open circuit on a teletypewriter loop. 2. General term used to describe errors caused by external interferences such as impulse noise caused by lightning or man-made interference.

hit/pick, graphics — A feature that provides the operator with the ability to step through a noncontiguous display list using input devices such as data tablet, joystick, etc., and highlight (brighten) elements on the crt screen for identification and editing.

hold — The function of retaining information in one storage device after transferring it to another device, in contrast to clear.

hold, automatic — In an analog computer, attainment of the hold condition automatically through amplitude comparison of a problem variable, or through an overload condition.

hold button, analog — The hold button causes the solution to be temporarily suspended, permitting the user to study the various quantities.

hold facility — The ability of a computer, when its calculations are interrupted, to keep the current value of all the variables.

holding beam — A diffuse beam of electrons for regenerating the charges stored on the dielectric surface of an electrostatic memory tube or cathode-ray storage tube.

holding time — The total time during which a given channel is occupied for each transmission or call. Consists of both operating time and text or conversation time.

hold instruction — *See* instruction, hold.

hold mode — In the hold mode, also called the freeze or interrupt mode, the computing action is stopped and all variables are held at the value they had when the computation was interrupted.

holistic masks — The set of characters which reside within a character reader and which theoretically represent the exact replicas of all possible input characters in the machine's repertory. Only perfect specimens will be accepted.

Hollerith — A widely used system of encoding alphanumeric information onto cards; hence, Hollerith cards is synonymous with punch cards. Such cards were first used in 1890 for the US Census and were named after Herman Hollerith, their originator.

holographic-based system — A system that utilizes laser and holographic technology in a microform setting.

holographic recorder — A system designed to acquire and record electronic digital data in high-density holographic form on photographic film. A reader retrieves the holographic data and reconverts it to the original electronic form according to the presentation that accompanies the programmed instructions.

home loop — An operation involving only those input and output units associated with the local terminal.

home record — *See* record, home.

homogeneous multiplex — A multiplex structure in which all the information-bearer channels are at the same data signaling rate.

homostasis — The dynamic condition of a system wherein the input and output are balanced precisely, thus presenting an appearance of no change; hence, a steady state.

horizontal processor — A microprogrammed computer that uses a wide microinstruction with many fields. It is usually fast, executing many microorders at the same time, but also quite difficult to microprogram.

horizontal table — In indexing, a table whose entries are stored sequentially; that is, entry one, byte one; entry one, byte two; etc.

host computer — A computer that is connected to a stored-program multiplexor and which is the base or independent computer upon which the multiplexor is dependent for certain vital functions, such as program read-in, etc. In an arrangement of this sort, the multiplexor could have stand-alone capacity in the event the host computer is not always available.

host computer processing — A host computer performs applications processing, accessing of bulk memory (disk packs, for example) and storing data bases. Centralized processing means that all data processing functions are carried out in a single host computer, large or small, attached to the network. Distributed processing, however, means that two or more host computers, probably with associated bulk storage for necessary data bases, are connected to the network. The host computers connected to the network can be close together or far apart.

housekeeping — 1. Pertaining to administrative or overhead operations or functions which are necessary in order to maintain control of a situation; e.g., for a computer program, housekeeping involves the setting up of constants and variables to be used in the program. (Synonymous with red tape.) 2. A general term used to describe coding which reserves, restores, and clears memory areas. 3. Those parts of a program that pertain to the setting up or cleaning up of programs in contrast to those parts of the program which are distinctly input and output operations.

housekeeping operation — A general term for the operation that must be performed for a machine run usually before actual processing begins. Examples of housekeeping operations are: establishing controlling marks, setting up auxiliary storage units, reading in the first record for processing, initializing, set-up verification operations, and file identification.

housekeeping routine — The initial instructions in a program that are executed only one time, e.g., clear storage.

housekeeping runs — Operations required for file maintenance such as sorting, merging, and editing.

Houston Automatic Spooling Processor — *See* HASP.

HP-IB — Abbreviation for Hewlett-Packard Interface Bus. Hewlett-Packard's implementation of IEEE Standard 488-1975 for digital interfacing of programmable instrumentation.

HSM — Abbreviation for high-speed memory.

HSP — Abbreviation for high-speed printer.

HSR — Abbreviation for high-speed reader.

hub — A socket on a control panel or plugboard into which an electrical lead or plug wire may be connected in order to carry signals, particularly to distribute the signals over many other wires.

hub, bus — A location on the control panel which permits several entries or exits of pulse signals.

hub, combination — An electrical jack connection which will omit or receive electrical impulses on a control panel.

human factors, terminal — Key elements of human factors include the size of the screen; the number, shape, and size of the characters on the screen; the color and appearance of the screen; the arrangement of the keyboard; and the sound of the keyboard. The designs should provide comfort to humans.

hunting — 1. A continuous attempt on the part of an automatically controlled system to seek a desired equilibrium condition. The system usually contains a standard, a method of determining deviation from this standard, and a method of influencing the system such that the difference between the standard and the state of the system is brought to zero. 2. Searching operations performed in switching systems to locate the called line or the next available line in an equivalent group.

hybrid computer — A computer that combines the functions of analog and digital computers.

hybrid computer interface — Sometimes called the "linkage." An interface that generally includes DACs, DAMs, ADCs with multiplexers, plus control and sense lines between the analog and digital processors, along with priority interrupt lines.

hybrid input/output — The input/output group of programs consists of a system monitor and programs to control operation of analog/digital conversion equipment and special devices such as an oscilloscope display or a digital plotter.

hybrid office systems — Computerized systems for full office automation, encompassing both word processing (WP) and data processing (DP). They may appear as extensions to existing WP or DP services, or be introduced outright as "hybrid" systems, capable of handling both text editing and numerical, file-oriented data.

hybrid problem analysis — Programs in the problem analysis group help the hybrid programmer decide which parts of the problem to solve on a digital computer and the mathematical techniques that should be used. For example, multivariable function generation that may be difficult to perform on the analog computer is well suited to digital solution.

hypertape units — High-speed tape units that use cartridges which house the supply and takeup reels to permit automatic loading.

hyphenation, automatic — A feature of some word-processing systems in which a dictionary of hyphenated words is held in memory so that the system provides hyphenation automatically without the need for an operator decision.

hysteresis — The lagging in the response of a unit of a system behind an increase or a decrease in the strength of a signal.

I

i address — The location of the next instruction to be executed in some brands of equipment based on whether or not a branch operation occurs.

IAL, International Algebraic Language — The forerunner of ALGOL.

IAR — Instruction address register which contains the address of the next instruction to be executed.

IBM card — A type of paper card that may have information recorded on it by means of punched holes, and which may be read by a computer.

IC — The abbreviation for both integrated circuit and instruction counter.

ICA — Abbreviation for integrated communications adapter. An integrated adapter that allows connection of multiple communication lines to a processing unit.

icand — Abbreviation for multiplicand.

icand register — That register which is used in multiplication to hold the multiplicand.

ICC — Abbreviation for International Computation Center. Sponsored by UNESCO in Rome. This computer center makes computer services available to member nations.

ICIP — Abbreviation for International Conference on Information Processing.

IC memory systems — Although a primary advantage of an IC system is its potential for decreased cost, it has other advantages as well. For example, an IC memory has all of its sensing, driving and decoding circuits built in, so it requires very little additional support electronics on its memory card other than circuits to handle a few control signals, byte controls, data and address buffers, sense amplifiers and chip enable drivers. A typical 16K × 18 IC memory system contains 72 4K memory chips, 10 timing and control devices, 6 data buffers, 6 address buffers, and 2 chip enable drivers. Miscellaneous capacitors and resistors raise the total component count in the system to approximately 130. (A core memory with the same capacity would contain over 600 components.)

iconographic model — A pictorial representation of a system and the functional relations within the system.

identification — A code number or code name that uniquely identifies a record, block, file or other unit of information.

identification, coded — 1. The process of providing personal, equipment, or organizational characteristics or codes to gain access to computer programs, processes, files, or data. 2. The process of determining personal, equipment, or organizational characteristics or codes to permit access to computer programs, processes, files, or data.

identification division — The part of COBOL programming in which the programmer gives information to identify the source program and the object program.

identification, file — The coding required to identify each physical unit of the outputs of electronic data-processing machine runs.

identifier — 1. A symbol whose purpose is to identify, as to indicate or name a body of data. 2. A key.

identifier, data use — A title or name for the use of the data items for a data element; for instance, an occurrence date such as the employment date of an employee that is used for data base information.

identifier, location — An identification, by label of some kind, assigned to a specific location, for instance, a city, neighborhood, or address, or a specific location in computer storage.

identifier word — A full-length computer word which is associated with a search or a search-read function. In a search or search-read function, the identifier word is stored in a special register in the channel synchronizer and compared with each word read by the peripheral unit (some systems).

identify — To attach a unique code or code name to a unit of information.

identifying — The procedure that identifies the source of a given information mark and, therefore, of an object or a location. The operation involves selection and translation.

identifying code — A code placed in perforated tape or punched cards to identify the contents, or their origin.

idle character — A control character that is sent when there is no information to be sent. Sometimes called a null character.

idle time — The time that a computer is available for use, but is not in operation.

IDP, Integrated Data Processing — 1. A system that treats as a whole all data-processing requirements to accomplish a sequence of data-processing steps or a number of related data-processing sequences, and that strives to reduce or eliminate duplicating data entry or processing steps. 2. The processing of data by such a system in which all procedures are tied to the computer.

IEEE 583/CAMAC — A hardware/software standard developed originally for the nuclear industry but currently widely adopted by other industrial users.

ier — Short for multiplier.

if-A then B gate — *Same as* gate, B OR-NOT A.

if-A then NOT-B gate — *Same as* gate, NAND.

if-B then NOT-A gate — *Same as* gate, NAND.

IFCS — Abbreviation for International Federation of Computer Sciences.

IFIPS — Abbreviation for International Federation of Information Processing Societies.

IF-THEN-ELSE — A program statement often used in high level languages. When the IF statement is true, THEN means the next expression is to be executed. If the expression is not true, the ELSE expression is to be executed.

ignore — 1. A typewriter character indicating that no action whatsoever be taken; e.g., in teletypewriter or flexowriter code, a character code consisting of holes punched in every hole position is an ignore character. This convention makes possible erasing any previously punched character. 2. An instruction requiring nonperformance of what normally might be executed, i.e., not to be executed. This instruction should not be confused with a NO OP or Do-Nothing instruction, since these generally refer to an instruction outside themselves.

ignore character — *See* ignore.

ignore character block — *See* character, ignore block.

ignore instruction — *See* ignore.

illegal character — *See,* character, illegal.

illegal code — *See* code, illegal.

illegal command — *See* character, illegal.

illegal control-message error — *See* error, illegal control-message.

illegal operation — The process which results when a computer either cannot perform the instruction part or will perform with invalid and undesired results. The limitation is often due to built-in computer constraints.

image — An exact logical duplicate stored in a different medium.

image dissector — In optical character recognition (OCR), a mechanical or electronic transducer that sequentially detects the level of light in different areas of, a completely illuminated sample space.

image processor — *See* processor, image.

immediate access — Pertaining to the ability to obtain data from or place data in a storage device or register directly, without serial delay due to other units of data, and usually in a relatively short period of time.

immediate access storage — *See* storage, immediate access.

immediate address — The designation of an instruction address that is used as data by the instruction of which it is a part.

immediate addressing — *See* addressing, immediate.

immediate address instruction — *See* address instruction, immediate.

immediate data — Data that immediately follows an instruction in memory. This is used as an operand by that instruction.

immediate processing — *Same as* processing, demand.

imperative operations — An instruction which requires the manipulating of data by the computer.

imperative statements — Action statements of a symbolic program that are converted into actual machine-language instructions.

implementation — The several steps concerned in installing and starting successful operation of computer systems or related machines. The steps begin with feasibility studies, applications studies, equipment selection, systems analysis (present) and design of proposed new system, physical location of equipment, operations analysis, and critical review.

implicit address instruction format — *See* instruction format, implicit address.

implicit prices — Same as marginal values, shadow prices, dual variable levels, etc. —that is, numbers giving the incremental worth of a relaxation of one unit in the right-hand side of a constraint.

implied addressing — *Same as* addressing, repetitive.

imprinter — A device which causes the name and account number of a credit card holder to be transferred to the sales slip. Most credit cards show this information in raised, special type that can be automatically read from the sales slip by the computer.

improper character — *Same as* character, illegal.

improper code — *See* code, illegal.

improper command — *See* character, illegal.

improper command check — *Same as* check, forbidden-combination.

improvement time, system — *See* system-improvement time.

impulse noise — A pulse, appearing at the output of a circuit, which was not transmitted from the originating input to the circuit. These pulses usually are induced from circuit functioning or from sources outside the circuit and its associated input/output equipment.

IMS — Abbreviation for Information Management System. A program product that uses OS (operating system) BTAM to allow IMS applications to operate on the remote terminal system. Remote display stations require nonswitched lines.

inactive file — *See* file, inactive.

inadmissible character, automatic checking — *See* character checking, inadmissible.

incidentals time — Time which is usually allotted to training, demonstrating, or other useful but nonproductive purposes, but not including program development.

incipient failure — An equipment failure that is about to occur.

Courtesy Futuredata Computer Corp.

In-circuit emulator.

in-circuit emulation — Concerns the hardware/software facilities for real-time i/o debugging of chips. The actual microprocessor is replaced by a connector whose signals are generated by an emulation program. The emulated microprocessor can be stopped, its registers examined or modified, and so on. The i/o devices can be controlled from the development system's console or from a time-sharing terminal. Programs can reside in (simulated) RAM memory, or they can actually be ROMs or PROMs.

in-circuit emulation bus — The use of RAM memory for some development system programs eliminates costly and time-consuming PROM programming in the early phases of software development. The in-circuit emulation bus allows the user to connect his own peripheral devices or memory to the system and use them with the system elements.

inclusive NOR gate — *Same as* gate, NOR.

inclusive OR — The Boolean operator that gives a truth table value of true if either or both of the two variables it connects are true. If neither is true, the value is false.

inclusive OR gate — *Same as* gate, OR.

inclusive segment — In a program overlay structure two or more different segments can be in the main memory simultaneously, whereas normally all inclusive segments lie on a single path from the root segment to the lowest segment.

incomplete program — *See* program, incomplete.

incomplete routine — A routine in a library of a programming system that requires parameters to be supplied by a macrostatement or main routine.

increment — 1. The quantity by which another is modified. An increment is usually positive; however, a negative quantity, when added, is also called an increment. 2. To modify a quantity by adding a smaller quantity.

incremental compaction — *See* compaction, incremental.

incremental display — *See* display, incremental.

incremental integrator — *See* integrator, incremental.

incremental plotter control — Provides for high-speed plotting of points, continuous curves, points connected by curves, curve-identification symbols, letters, numerals under program control.

incremental representation — Representation of changes in variables rather than the changes of the variables themselves —changes such as increases and decreases as results of equalities or relations expressed in the equations or model.

incremental tape units — Various types of magnetic tape modules which require a tapeflow for the process of reading or writing.

independent equations — A set of equations none of which can be expressed as a linear combination of the others. With linear equations, the condition for independence is that the matrix (coefficient columns) shall be nonsingular or, equivalently, have rank equal to the number of equations.

independent interrupt processor — *See* interrupt, processor independent.

independent, machine — *See* machine-independent.

independent modularity, program — *See* program-independent modularity.

independent sector — A device on certain tabulators which allows the first item of a series of similar data to be printed and inhibits some of the rest of the series.

in-depth audit — Detailed examination of all manipulations performed on a single transaction or piece of information.

indeterminate (X) state — The unknown logic state of a memory element caused by critical races or oscillations, or existing after power is applied and before initialization. Some simulators can model indeterminate states and typically assign an X to indicate an indeterminate state.

index — 1. A table of computer words or fields containing addresses of records located in file storage. 2. An ordered reference list of the contents of a document, such as names, subjects, etc. 3. A symbol or number used to identify a particular quantity in an array of similar quantities; e.g., the terms of an array represented by X(1), X(2) . . . X(100) have the indexes 1, 2, . . . 100, respectively. 4. Pertaining to an index register.

index addressing, multiple (time-sharing) — *See* time sharing, multiple index addressing.

index, citation — An index or reference list of documents that are mentioned in a specific document or document set. The references are mentioned or quoted in the text. The citation index lists these references.

index, cooperation — An index number constructed by using the product of the drum diameter, expressed in inches, and the line scan advance, expressed in scanning lines per inch. Used in facsimile image transmission.

index, cycle — The number of cycle iterations in digital computer programming. A cycle index register may be used to set the number of cycles desired. Then with each cycle iteration, the register count is reduced by one until the register reaches zero and the series of cycles is complete.

indexed — An addressing mode in which the actual address is obtained by adding a displacement to a base address. In most microprocessor systems, the displacement is contained in the index register, the base address in the instruction field.

indexed addressing — Indexed addressing in some systems means that the address in the second byte of the instruction is added to the low order bits of the index register with any carry propagating into the index register high order bits. The result then becomes the address to be accessed during instruction execution. This facility is very useful in handling elements in arrays and tables. In relative addressing, an offset, contained in the second byte of the instruction, is added to the program counter's low order bits. While this method is used for program jumps, it finds its greatest appeal in facilitating relocatable program code, code that can be loaded into any memory locations and relocated without altering or changing the code.

indexed file — A file that provides a directory-supported random access method based on a record identifier whose size is user-specified. File operations include record addition, insertion, modification, deletion, and retrieval using either a random or sequential access method. A multiway balanced tree directory provides random access with extremely low disc access for search.

indexed sequential access method — The indexed sequential access method (ISAM) provides advanced keyed accessing for fast, on-line retrieval of large data bases. Programmers use ISAM's variable-length record keys to save index space. ISAM permits keyed and keyed-relative processing.

indexed sequential data set — *See* data set, indexed sequential.

index entry — An individual line or item of data contained in an index, such as an entry in a dictionary.

index file — 1. A table of key fields identifying the actual disk records in another permanent disk file. 2. A file of terms in an automatic information retrieval system which is searched by the computer until it finds the index entry which will answer the relevant question. The index entry or the original document can then be printed.

index, fine — A subsidiary or supplemental index of a pair of indexes used to locate a particular file record. The higher or mass index would often be considered the gross index.

index, gross — The first of a pair of indexes consulted to locate particular records, etc. The secondary or supplemental index is the fine index.

index hole — A hole punched in a floppy disk to indicate the beginning of the first sector.

indexing — 1. The indexing method of random-access file organization in which a part of the file is set aside as an index in order to locate information in other parts of the file. 2. The modification of an instruction by the contents of an index register in order to obtain a new effective address. 3. The storing of copy in electronic form permits rapid and automatic indexing for information-retrieval purposes.

indexing, aspect — A method of indexing single units of information by the joint use of two or more terms, usually of equal rank, with retrieval performed by logical associations among the terms and logical connections to couple the terms, so that all units of information relating to a specific item may be searched out.

indexing, association — A study following two approaches—the automatic generation of word-association maps based on lists of words from the text, and representations based on the number of times words appear in the text.

indexing, coordinate — *See* coordinate indexing.

indexing, correlative — *Same as* coordinate indexing.

indexing, cumulative — In a digital computer, the practice of assigning two or more indices to a single address in the instruction word.

indexing, datacode — *Same as* indexing, coordinate.

indexing, manipulative — 1. A system of indexing individual documents by descriptors of equal rank, so that a library can be searched for a combination of one or more descriptors. 2. An indexing technique where the interrelations of terms are shown by coupling individual words. 3. An indexing scheme by which descriptors may be correlated or combined to show any interrelations desired for purposes of more precise information retrieval.

indexing, multiple-aspect — *See* indexing, manipulative.

indexing, zatacode — *Same as* coordinate indexing.

index mode — On some systems, the contents of the selected general register, and an index word following the instruction word, are summed to form the address of the operand. The contents of the selected register may be used as a base for calculating a series of addresses, thus allowing random access to elements of data structures. The selected register can then be modified by program to access data in the table. Index addressing instructions are of a specific form and generally unique to each system.

index, permutation — An index alphabetically listing all of the major, plus minor if desired, words of a title or document so that each word appears once as the first word, followed by the other words rotated in a circular fashion. This is done so that the documents can be retrieved by numerous permutations.

index, permuted-title — *Same as* index, permutation.

index point — One of the equally spaced rotational reference positions of the main shaft of card punch machines, labeled according to the row or column to which it corresponds.

index register — 1. A register that contains a quantity to be used under direction of the control section of the computer hardware, e.g., for address modification and counting. 2. A device that permits automatic modification or an instruction address without permanently altering the instruction in memory. 3. A register to which an arbitrary integer, usually one, is added (or subtracted) upon the execution of each machine instruction. The register may be reset to zero or to an arbitrary number. Also called cycle counter and B-box.

index sort — Provides an indexing capability for sequential and direct accessing from a random-data file via the Index Access Method (IAM). SORT produces a separate index file containing the key field of each data record and a pointer to its location in the data file.

index, word — 1. A storage position or register the contents of which may be used to modify automatically the effective address of any given instruction. 2. An index based on the selection of words as used in a document, without giving thought to synonyms and more generic concepts related to the term selected.

indicate, group — To select and print indicative information from the initial record of a record group.

indication, group — A device on some tabulators which permits the first item of a series of same or similar data or information to be printed and also inhibits some of the printing of the rest of the set or series.

indicator — A device often used as a control unit when it is designed to determine the selection from alternative processes. It can be set into a prescribed state according to the results of a previous process. An example is an overflow indicator. The state of such indicators may be displayed on a control panel for the benefit of programmers and operators.

indicator, branch-on — Branching takes place when appropriate indicators (switches, keys, buttons, etc.), or conditions, have been set to point to a particular group of registers; i.e., a branch may occur dependent upon whether the magnetic tape units are ready to receive a new block of data.

indicator, check — A device that displays or announces an error has been made, or a checking operation has determined that a failure has occurred.

indicator, check divide — An indicator which denotes that an invalid division has been attempted or has occurred.

indicator, end-of-file — A device associated with each input and output unit that makes an end-of-file condition known to the routine and operator controlling the computer.

indicator, equal-zero — An internal computer indicator component which signals ON if the result of an arithmetic computation is zero.

indicator, high-positive — An internal computer-indicator component that indicates ON if the result of an arithmetic operation is positive and not zero.

indicator, instruction-check — A signaling device that is turned on automatically to alert a machine operator's attention to a machine malfunction, program error, or other malfunction in instructions currently being executed.

indicator, machine check — A protective device that will be turned on when certain conditions arise within the machine. The machine can be programmed to stop or to run a separate correction routine or to ignore the condition.

indicator, overflow — A signaling device that indicates the occurrence of an overflow; for instance, a number too large to be contained in a given register.

indicator, overflow check — A device that is turned on by incorrect or unplanned for operations in the execution of an arithmetic instruction, particularly when an arithmetic operation produces a number too large for the system to handle.

indicator, role — A code assigned to a keyword to indicate the role of the keyword; e.g., a keyword may be a noun, verb, adjective, or adverb; therefore, an indicator is used to identify the specific role of the keyword.

indicator, routing — An identifier, such as a label, that defines the route and destination or addressee of a piece of information such as a message.

indicators — 1. The devices that register conditions, such as high or equal conditions resulting from a computation. A sequence of operations within a procedure may be varied according to the position of an indicator. 2. The display device that usually indicates various conditions.

indicators, comparison — Three comparison indicators are: high, low, and equal. They are set on the basis of comparisons of operands in the arithmetic or index registers with operands in memory. The equal indicator is also set and reset by add and subtract instructions. If the result of an addition or subtraction is zero, the equal indicator is set. If the result is not zero, the equal indicator is reset.

indicator, sign check — An error-checking device, indicating no sign or improper signing of a field used for arithmetic processes. The machine can, upon interrogation, be made to stop or enter into a correction routine.

indicators, priority — *See* priority indicators.

indirect address — *See* address, indirect.

indirect addressing — *See* addressing, indirect.

indirect addressing mode — Generally, when indirect addressing is specified, the address calculations determine the address of a memory location which in turn contains the address of the operand. Indexing and relative addressing are also applicable to indirect address mode.

indirect control — *See* control, indirect.

indirect or off-line system — *See* off-line or indirect system.

indirect reference address — *See* address, indirect reference.

indirect relative — On some systems the 8-bit displacement field specifies an address relative to the address of the instruction being executed. This relative address contains the address of the operand. Relative address calculation is the same as in the direct relative mode.

indirect self-relative — Generally applicable only to the preindexed indirect mode. In this mode, the preindexed indirect address is determined; then the contents of the indirect address are added to the indirect address itself, forming the effective operand address.

individual line — A subscriber line arranged to serve only one main station, although additional stations may be connected to the line as extensions. An individual line is not arranged for discriminatory ringing with respect to the stations on that line.

induced failure — *See* failure, induced.

industrial data processing — Data processing designed for industrial purposes, often numerical control (n/c).

industrial process control — Industrial processing applications are as wide and varied as the degrees of control that individual processes may require. Some general process-control application areas are: precious metals production, cement production, environmental control, pilot plants, chemical processes, petroleum refining and many others. The data acquisition and control system provides maximum flexibility in the types of process data that it can accept, and the variety of output signals and data format that a computer may exercise.

inequalities, linear programming — The mathematical problem of minimizing or maximizing a linear function of n variables, subject to n independent restrictions, such as requirements that each variable be nonnegative, and also subject to a finite number of other linear constraints. The latter are either equalities or weak inequalities ($\leq$ or $\geq$); strict inequalities of the form $<$ or $>$ are not admissible. An exact solution or other termination to this problem is furnished by the simplex method or one of its variants.

inequality — A proposition (or relation) which relates the magnitudes of two mathematical expressions or functions A and B. Inequalities are four types; A is greater than B ($A > B$); A is less than B ($A < B$); A is greater than or equal to B ($A \geq B$); A is less than or equal to B ($A \leq B$). The first two types are called strict, and the last two are relaxed or weak. The process of identifying a functional argument or range of arguments which makes the proposition true is called solving the inequality, or obtaining a feasible solution to the inequality.

infinite-pad method — A procedure or method of measuring reflectiveness of paper stock used in optical character recognition. A doubling of the number of backing sheets of the same paper, however, does not appreciably change the measured reflectiveness.

infinity — Any number larger than the maximum number that a given computer is able to store in any register.

infix notation — A method of forming one-dimensional expressions (e.g., arithmetic, logical, etc.) by alternating single operands and operators. Any operator performs its indicated function upon its adjacent terms which are defined, subject to the rules of operator precedence and grouping brackets which eliminates ambiguity.

information — 1. Knowledge that was not previously known to its receiver. Information can be derived from data only to the extent that the data are accurate, timely, unexpected, and relevant to the subject under consideration. 2. Aggregation of data that are presented in various forms. Sets of symbols that specifically indicate one out of a number of alternatives. 3. The meaning assigned to data by the known conventions used in its representation.

information, administrative — Information of a textual nature, originated and prepared by one person for scrutiny by another.

information bearer channel — A channel provided for data transmission which is capable of carrying all the necessary information to permit communication including users' data synchronizing sequences, control signals, etc. It may, therefore, operate at a greater signaling rate than that required solely for the users' data.

information bits — Those bits which are generated by the data source and that are not used for error-control by the data transmission system.

information channel — The transmission and intervening equipment involved in the transfer of information in a given direction between two terminals. An information channel includes the modulator and demodulator, and any error-control equipment irrespective of its location, as well as the backward channel when provided.

information, communication — The physical means of connecting one location to another for the purpose of transmitting information.

information efficiency — A ratio of the actual negative entropy to the maximum possible entropy, using the same set of signs.

information-feedback system — An error-control system using message feedback with reception of the erroneous group from the sending station.

information flow analysis — The development of organizing and analyzing techniques to obtain facts and information about the organization, initialization, and flow to the final users of reports throughout the enterprise or organization.

information, machine-sensible — Information in a form that can be read by a specific machine.

information marker, beginning of — A reflective spot on the back of a magnetic tape, 10 feet from the physical beginning of the tape, which is sensed photoelectrically to indicate the point on the tape at which recording may begin.

information processing — The processing of data representing information and the determination of the meaning of the processed data.

information processing system — A system that receives and delivers information, changing the information in the process.

information rate — The product of the average information content per symbol and the average number of symbols per second.

information requirements — The actual or anticipated questions that may be posed to an information system.

information retrieval — 1. A method for cataloging vast amounts of data, all related to one field of interest, so that one can call out any or all of this data at any time it is needed with accuracy and speed. 2. A branch of computer science relating to the techniques for storing and searching large or specific quantities of information that may or may not be a real-time system.

information-retrieval system — A system for locating and selecting, on demand, certain documents or other graphic records relevant to a given information requirement from a file of such material. Examples of information-retrieval systems are classification, indexing, and machine searching systems.

information source — An information generator. This output is assumed to be free from error.

information system — The network of all communication methods within an organization. Information may be derived from many sources other than a data-processing unit, such as by telephone, by contact with other people, or by looking at an operation.

information system, management — *See* management information system.

information system, real-time — *See* real-time information system.

information theory — The mathematical theory concerned with the information rate, channels, channel width, noise and other factors affecting information transmission. Initially developed for electrical communications, it is now applied to business systems, and other phenomena that deal with information units and flow of information in networks.

information utilities — Data-processing centers are strategically located throughout the United States. These centers offer to management the opportunity of obtaining detailed reports interrelating department activities, with direct phone contact to a computer.

The reports are created from punched paper tape, magnetic tape, disks, and optical reading of journal tapes. All the necessary data required by the center are prepared as an automatic by-product of a machine operation within a department on the customer's premises. Reports and problem solutions are automatically fed back to the teletypewriter unit or crt device of the customer.

information word — An ordered set of characters bearing at least one meaning and handled by a computer as a unit, including separating and spacing, that may be contrasted with instruction words. (Related to machine word.)

inherent storage — *See* storage, inherent.

inherited error — The error in the initial values. Especially the error inherited from the previous steps in the step by step integration. This error could also be the error introduced by the inability to make exact measurements of physical quantities. (Synonymous with inherent error).

inhibit — 1. To prevent an event from taking place. 2. To prevent a device or logic element from producing a specified output.

inhibit, counter — The bit, in the program status double-word, that indicates whether (if 1) or not (if 0) all (clock) count zero interrupts are inhibited.

inhibit, external interrupt — The bit, in the program status double-word, that indicates whether (if 1) or not (if 0) all external interrupts are inhibited.

inhibiting input — A gate input which, if in its prescribed state, prevents any output which might otherwise occur.

inhibiting signal — A signal that prevents an operation from occurring.

inhibit, input/output interrupt — *See* interrupt, input/output, inhibit.

inhibition rule — Priority and inhibition rules are usually implemented in the time-sharing hardware to resolve possible conflicts when two interrupts occur simultaneously, or when a second interrupt occurs before a previous one is completely processed.

inhibit pulse — A pulse that tends to prevent a reversal of the magnetic state in a magnetic core by other drive pulses.

initial condition — The value of a variable at the start of computation.

initial error — *See* error, inherent.

initialize — To originate or establish the basic conditions or startup state. Such procedures might be used to set an initial value for the address of an operand, establish the initial control value for a loop, set all registers to a preset value prior to running, begin a bootstrap operation with a control digit or word, etc.

initialized — The preliminary steps required before execution of iterative cycles to determine efficient start procedures. Usually a single, nonrepetitive operation after a cycle has begun and/or until a full cycle is again begun.

initializer routine — The functions such as error checking performed on a message after it is entered into a system, but before the application program begins its processing.

initial program loading (IPL) — *See* program loading, initial.

initiate — The initiate operation is performed by means of a manually controlled jump to the entry point in older type computers, but bootstrap operations cause entry automatically; i.e., the program is then said to be self-triggered.

initiate button — *See* button, initiate.

initiate key — *See* button, initiate.

ink bleed — In optical character recognition (OCR), the capillary flow of ink beyond the original edges of a printed character.

ink, extraneous — Ink deposited on a computer printout that is not confined to the printed characters themselves.

ink, magnetic — A special ink that contains particles of a magnetic substance whose presence can be detected by magnetic sensors.

ink reflectance — The reflectance of the special ink which is used in optical character recognition as compared to some particular reference standard.

ink smudge — *See* ink bleed.

ink squeezout — *See* ink bleed.

ink uniformity — The degree of light intensity variation over the area of printed characters, specifically within the character edges.

in-line checks — The reliability of a system of software can be improved by including code in the system to check the validity of data structures each time they are processed by system routines. This is called "in-line checking." If data structures are checked before they are used, errors previously introduced by any system component will be identified and should not be propagated. If data structures are checked just after they are modified, the routine causing an error will usually be identified.

in-line coding — A portion of coding which is stored in the main path of a routine.

in-line data processing — *See* data processing, in-line.

in-line processing — 1. The processing of data in a random order not subject to preliminary editing or sorting. 2. A method of processing in which each individual input activity is completely processed, and all pertinent records are updated without previously having been batched or grouped.

in-line subroutine — *See* subroutine, in-line.

in-plant system — A procedure for data handling that might be confined to one building or group of buildings in one locality.

input — 1. Information or data transferred or to be transferred from an external storage medium into the internal storage of the computer. 2. Describing the routines with direct input as defined in (1), or the devices from which such information is available to the computer. 3. The device or collective set of devices necessary for input as defined in (1).

input area — *See* input block.

input block — 1. A section of internal storage of a computer reserved for the receiving and processing of input information. (Synonymous with input area.) 2. An input buffer. 3. A block of computer words considered as a unit and intended or destined to be transferred from an external source or storage medium to the internal storage of the computer.

input buffer register — That device which accepts data from input units or media such as magnetic tape or disks and which then transfers this data to internal storage.

input channel — *See* channel, input.

input (communications) — 1. The current, voltage, power, or driving force applied to a circuit or device. 2. The terminals or other places where current, voltage, power, or driving force may be applied to a circuit or device.

input data — *See* data, input.

input device, optical reader — This device reads printed and typewritten material, and inputs data directly without converting it into punch tape, punch cards, or other intermediate formats. Optical readers recognize all letters of the alphabet, standard punctuation, 0 to 9, and special symbols used in programmed functions. It handles documents and continuous fanfold sheets. This high-speed reader can be used simply as an input device, or it can be used as a complete small system for data processing and storage.

input devices — Devices that convert facts into electronic impulses.

input devices simulation — This type of simulation is the testing of one set of input equipment by using another set of equipment, specially programmed so that the behavior is similar. Tape input is programmed to appear as terminal input.

input editing — Refers to various types of input that may be edited to convert to a more convenient format for processing and storage than that used for entry into the system; and to check the data for proper format, completeness, or accuracy. Often, input must be formatted as most convenient for preparation by humans, and then must be reformatted for computer use.

input equipment — 1. The equipment used for transferring data and instructions into an automatic data-processing system. 2. The equipment by which an operator transcribes original data and instructions to a medium that may be used in an automatic data-processing system.

input expander, analog — This unit allows a complete analog input system to be configured around the data-adapter unit.

input, inhibiting — A gate input which in its prescribed state prevents any output that might otherwise occur.

input limited — The time necesary for the central processing unit to wait for further delivery of input items restricts the speed of the operation.

input loading — The amount of load imposed upon the sources supplying signals to the input.

input, manual — The entry of data by hand into a device at the time of processing.

input, on-line — When the input device transmits data directly to, and under the control of, the control processing unit.

input/output — 1. Commonly called i/o. A general term for equipment used to communicate with a computer. 2. The data involved in such communication. 3. The media carrying the data for input/output. 4. The process of transmitting information from an external source to the computer or from the computer to an external source.

input/output area — *Same as* storage, working.

input/output board — On some systems, this type of board allows the computer to be expanded via the backplane bus to allow additional input-output interface channels. One typical system allows 64K programmable i/o lines per board.

input-output, buffered — All peripheral equipment contains an input/output buffer register for storage of data to be transferred to the computer so that various devices can be operated simultaneously at their maximum speed. The processor does not wait for a device to complete its cycle before continuing the program.

input-output bus — An input-output bus often provides a number of parallel lines for data, command, device address, status, and control information. This eliminates the timing problems created when data and address lines are time-shared. It makes interfacing easier, faster, and less expensive. Memory and input-output interfaces connect directly to the main bus. Each operates at its own pace. Under direct memory access (DMA), this means that transfers can be made directly between external devices and memory without affecting the central processor, if desired.

input/output cable — Specific cables which have groups of wires which connect various input and output equipment to the mainframe units of the computer.

input/output, central computer — Communication between the central computer and the peripheral units of the same computer system may be performed over all input/output channels. Each of the several channels allows bidirectional transfers of data and control signals between the central computer and the peripheral devices. The input/output section acts as an autonomous processor that runs independently of the instruction-execution cycle, scanning the input channels for the presence of input or output word-transfer requests, and transferring data between the channels and central storage.

input/output centralized coordination, time sharing — *See* time sharing, centralized input/output coordination.

input/output channel — *See* channel, input/output.

input/output channel, programmed — Program control of information transfer between the central processor and an external device provides the fastest method of operating on data received from peripheral equipment. The programmed input/output channel allows input directly to the accumulator where the data can be acted on immediately, thus eliminating the need for a memory reference by either the channel or the program. Likewise, output data may be sent directly from the accumulator to an external device.

input/output channels, buffered — *See* input/output section, buffered.

input/output channel selection — Permits the computer to designate a particular channel in the terminal.

input/output channels, multiple (time sharing) — *See* time sharing, multiple i/o channels.

input/output, concurrent — The acceptance, listing, and processing of all requests for i/o functions from the operating programs. This function of the executive system makes possible the concurrent operation of several programs using the same i/o channels without the danger of one program interferring with another program's i/o functions. Requests for i/o operations are submitted to the executive in the form of a parameter specifying the location of an execution packet which defines the function to be performed. An attempt is made to recover from i/o errors whenever feasible.

input/output control — 1. There are several portions of control which direct interactions between the processing unit and input and output equipment. One is written to control actions with tape, card, and printer equipment. A second control is specifically designed for random processing of records stored on direct access devices. It is a separate control in order to minimize seek times. 2. This program assigns equipment, controls the i/o devices, controls data transfers between memory and the i/o device, and controls the buffering of data for the device.

input/output control program — The control of the execution of all input and output operations by the supervisory program.

input/output control section — The input/output section functions as a small processor. Programmed input/output instructions load the access-control word locations and establish desired peripheral activity. From this point, i/o control automatically scans the input/output channels, accepting data from the peripheral subsystem at the natural rate of the equipment. When a peripheral subsystem presents or asks for a word of data, its associated access-control register is referenced and i/o control transfers the data word to or from central store, updates the access-control word, and tests for a terminal condition. All of the access-control word indexing and testing is performed in the index section in effectively zero-time, in parallel with normal construction execution and indexing.

input/output control systems (IOCS) — 1. Various library routines which a programmer or systems analyst can select to custom-fit an application by means of macro programs or instructions and various facts supplied in the source program for handling input and output for tapes, cards, etc., and printer. A description of machine logic configuration, definition of files, sequencing and interrupts. 2. A group of computer routines designed to automatically control the performance of input/output operations and direct other functions such as error correction, checkpoint, label processing, restart, and others.

input/output control unit — There are several portions of control that direct interactions between the processing unit and input and output equipment. One is written to control actions with tape, card, and printer equipment. A second control is specifically designed for random processing of records stored on direct-access devices. It is a separate control in order to minimize seek times.

input/output cycle — On some systems, once the microcomputer has control of the address and data buses, the input-output cycle begins. Basically, the i/o cycle consists of inputting (reading data) from or outputting (writing data) into a specified memory location. Timing is for memory-access, read-data, and write-data operations.

input/output device — A unit that accepts new data, sends it into the computer for processing, receives the results, and converts them into a usable form, like payroll checks or bills.

input/output device (communications) — Any subscriber (user) equipment which introduces data into or extracts data from a datacommunications system.

input/output device handlers — The input/output device handlers are responsible for controlling the activities of all input/output channels and peripheral equipment.

input/output drivers — The list includes: Teletypewriter Driver, to assist the programmer in writing efficient teletypewriter i/o routines; Paper Tape Driver documentation to assist the programmer in writing efficient reader/punch subroutines; Card Reader Driver, provides for input from an 80 column punched card reader and code conversion from Hollerith to ASCII; Line Printer Driver, documentation to assist the programmer in writing efficient line printer output subroutines; Cassette I/O Driver, for convenient operation of digital cassettes. Supports high speed search as well as normal input/output functions; Magnetic Tape Driver, provides for all read, write, rewind and skipping functions for 9-track magnetic tapes; Moving Head Disk Driver, sets up and controls all disk positioning functions and data transfers via Direct Memory Access (DMA) . . . supports overlapped seeks on up to four drives; CRT Driver, documentation to assist the programmer in writing efficient crt i/o subroutines, and others.

input/output, hybrid computer — The input/output group of programs consists of a system monitor and programs to control operation of analog-digital conversion equipment and special devices such as an oscilloscope display or a digital plotter.

input/output instructions — Computer instructions which operate input-output devices like card readers, printers, and terminals.

input-output interface — A typical input-output interface might incorporate two input-output channels, a processor input-output (PIO) channel, and a direct memory access (DMA) channel. The PIO channel interfaces with the processor via the data input bus and provides simplex character-oriented data transfer capability. The DMA channel interfaces directly with the memory, via the data input bus, and provides high-speed, record-oriented data transfer capability at rates of up to 500,000 or more words per second. (Some systems.)

The typical input-output interface incorporates two or more input-output channels, a processor input-output channel, and a direct memory access input-output channel.

input/output interrupt identification — I/o interruptions are caused by an i/o unit ending an operation or otherwise needing attention. Identifications of the device and channel causing the interruption are stored in the old PSW (program status word); in addition, the status of the device and channel is stored in a fixed location (some computers).

input/output interrupt indicators — Input-/output interrupt instructions are used to determine the input/output unit originating an interrupt and the cause of the interrupt by testing the indicators associated with each input/output channel. When the cause of the interrupt has been determined and corrective action, if required, has been taken, the indicators may be reset and the interrupted program resumed. These instructions also provide the facility for setting, resetting, and testing the inhibit input-/output interrupt indicator.

input/output interrupt inhibit — *See* interrupt, input/output, inhibit.

input/output (i/o) devices — Computer hardware by which data is entered into a computer, or by which the finished computations are recorded for immediate or future use.

input/output library — Relieves the programmer of having to be familiar with the functional and instructional differences among the peripherals.

input/output limited — Pertaining to a system or condition in which the time for input and output operation exceeds other operations.

input/output operations, nondata — Processes which relate to input/output operations as differentiated or exclusive of data manipulations, such as tape rewinding.

input/output port control — In some systems, the data and address ports of the microprocessor are connected to i/o devices via two system buses—an 8-bit bidirectional data bus and a 12-bit address bus. High-speed data transfers are made in parallel; however, for slow rate peripherals, a serial input/output capability is often provided.

input/output priority and interrupt — It can be used to divert program attention to new input data, the completion of output buffer transfers, or emergency conditions (inquiries, errors) existing on peripherals. Interrupt feature relieves need for much program checking of status of units.

input/output processor (IOP) — A unit that handles normal data input/output control and sequencing.

input/output, programmed — Program control of information transfer between the central processor and an external device provides the fastest method of operating on data received from peripheral equipment. The programmed input/output channel allows input directly to the accumulator where the data can be acted on immediately, thus eliminating the need for a memory reference by either the channel or the program. Likewise, output data may be sent directly from the accumulator to an external device.

input/output, random access — This is an i/o control capability that permits efficient random processing of records stored on a direct-access device. Random access i/o efficiency is achieved by the system in two ways: (1) Seeks are issued in an order which minimizes the average seek time, rather than in the order in which they were requested. (2) Seeks are overlapped with other processing. Because records must sometimes be processed sequentially (for example, when a report is being written), the ability to call for records sequentially is also available.

input/output, real-time control — All input/output data transfers are automatically controlled by signals emanating from the central processor or from the peripheral subsystems themselves. Any general-purpose input/output channel can accommodate a real-time system peripheral device. All i/o channels are buffered. Each input/output device has associated with it a control unit which, once activated by the central processor, carries out the entire operation of the instruction given it while the central processor proceeds with other tasks.

input/output referencing — References to data on tape or disk are made symbolically. Instead of describing the address of a certain disk or tape, the programmer need not keep in mind where data will be coming from.

input/output register — *See* index register.

input/output, remote message — This is an i/o control for obtaining messages from and sending messages to remote terminals. For remote-message control, the i/o control handles the following functions: receipt of messages from remote terminals; sending of messages to remote terminals; automatic dial-up; and code conversion. The user supplies the system with line-control specifications and installation-oriented routines to analyze message headers. Messages received can be stored in processing queues or output-terminal queues. Macrostatements enable the installation program to obtain messages for processing and to send messages. A log of all message traffic may be stored on a secondary storage device.

input/output request — *See* input/output request words.

input/output request words — Control words for input/output requests that are stored in the message reference block until the i/o is completed.

input/output routines — A set of routines that simplify the programming of input and output functions for standard peripheral equipment.

input/output section, buffered — The buffered input/output permits the processor to continue with computation while input and output communications are proceeding. The transfer of data to or from the central processor is conducted via input/output channels which communicate directly with the magnetic-core memory. Access to the memory is time shared between the operating program and input/output data transfer. Access also is automatically controlled by the i/o rate of the external device; it is not a programming consideration. Any cycle of the memory time is available for input/output data transfer in preference to its use by the program.

The input/output system is provided with program interrupt features so that testing of the condition of the external devices by the running program is not necessary, although possible, if desired.

input/output, simultaneous — Relates to the types of computers which can handle other operations concurrently with input and output operations, most often using buffers which hold input/output data and information as it arrives and on a temporary basis, while other operations are executed by the CPU. Thus, the computer need not wait for data from the very slow i/o units and may instead take it from the faster part of the buffer in massive quantities instead of as it arrives from slower units or terminals.

input/output storage — A specific storage area in a computer reserved for data or instructions, received by or ready to be transferred from or to, an external (peripheral) input or output device or to another specific section of storage.

input/output switching — By linking certain input or output units to more than one channel, a variety of ways are open to reach the device, even if other units are occupying one or more of the available channels. A single unit can be linked through channel switching to one channel at the start of processing on a job, and then to another channel at the end of processing of the same job.

input/output system subroutines — *See* system subroutines.

input/output terminal coordination, (time sharing) — *See* time sharing, terminal input/output coordination.

input/output, time shared, section — *Same as* input/output section, buffered.

input/output traffic control — 1. Input-/output traffic control directs the time sharing of the main memory by the various peripheral devices and the central processor. This control element makes possible the concurrent performance of central processor computing and up to eight simultaneous input/output operations. For example, the computer can simultaneously read or write tape, read cards, punch cards, store information in a random-access disc storage unit, read information from a random-access drum device, print two separate reports, and compute. 2. The coordination of peripheral simultaneity with internal computation is performed by the central processor element called the input/output traffic control.

input pulse, partial select — *See* pulse, partial write.

input queue, new — A group or a queue of new messages that are in the system and waiting for processing. The main scheduling routine will scan them along with other queues and order them into processing order.

input reference — The reference used to compare the measured variable resulting in a deviation or error signal. Also referred to as set point, or desired value.

input register — *See* register, input.

input routine — A routine which directs or controls the reading of programs and data into a computer system. Such a routine may be internally stored, wired, or part of a bootstrap operation, and may perform housekeeping or system control operations according to rules.

input section — *See* input block.

inputs, real-time — Real-time systems are those which have instantaneous input or entry and acceptance, most often determined by the requirements of another independent system; i.e., they are on-line inputs flowing directly to the computer as the activity occurs.

input stacker — The card-feed magazine in a reader, or read-punch unit.

input state — The determination of the condition of that specified set of input channels, i.e., positive, negative, etc.

input storage — 1. Holds each bundle of facts while it awaits its turn to be processed. This allows successive bundles to be compared to make sure they are in the right order or for other control purposes. 2. Any information that enters a computer for the purpose of being processed or to aid in processing. It is then held until signaled for use by the control program.

input stream — Concerns the sequence of job control statements and data submitted to an operating system on an input unit especially activated for this purpose by the operator. Synonymous with input job stream, job input stream.

input, substantive — The transferral of data from an external storage device to an internal storage device, usually from a mass storage unit and off-line, but not always so.

input, tape — *See* tape input.

input tape, problem — An input tape, either punched paper tape or magnetic tape, that contains problem data for checking out a given computer system.

input translator — Refers to a section of some computer programs that converts the incoming programmer's instructions into operators and operands understood by the computer. This scan or search also checks the input items for desired properties and, in many cases, outputs appropriate error messages if the desired properties of the input do not conform to the proper syntax.

input unit, manual — A set of manual controls or devices from which operators can set a specific word for input.

input units — Electronic machines that feed or introduce data into the system. Such machines can be paper tape readers, card readers, magnetic document sorter-readers, optical readers, and others.

input work queue — *See* work queue, input.

inquiries, banking — By indexing the account number and the status entry key, the teller may inquire into the status of an account for information relative to the savings balance, available balance, or any unposted items. If mortgages are on-line, inquiry may also be made as to principal balance, escrow balance, delinquency status, or any other information pertinent to the account.

inquiry — A request for information from storage, e.g., a request for the number of available airline seats or a machine statement to initiate a search of library documents.

inquiry and communications systems — Computer systems are now provided with facilities for diversified on-site and long distance inquiry and data-communications networks. Centralized records and data-processing operations can be tied in with information sources at remote locations and will provide instant on-line response to interrogations and input data from a large number of inquiry stations. Communication networks may include standard teletypewriter stations, and electric typewriter stations.

inquiry and subscriber display — The inquiry and subscriber display is a low-cost unit designed to service multiple subscribers requiring real-time access to stored information, or subscriber to subscriber message communication. Under operator control, the display can compose, correct, transmit, and receive formatted alphanumeric text. Operator composed text is automatically assembled and organized for common carrier or direct computer communication links. Operation of the display is independent of the location or type of data source. The display unit makes available the full capabilities of a remote data processor from a subscriber's own location, in his own operational language, when required. For handling restricted data, secure codes and formatting devices are provided to maintain information integrity.

inquiry answer (remote) — In an operating teleprocessing network, several inquiries simultaneously might come into the system from distant cities concerning information that is contained in a disk file. The appropriate records would then be taken from the disk file and the appropriate responses would be prepared and returned to the original cities. Although this appears to be a simple function, it requires design balance to achieve the required variety of terminal speeds and functions. It requires simultaneous operation of many devices operating through a single economical channel. It requires the time-sharing and space-sharing programs that control these devices. It requires the range of disk file capacity and speed. Furthermore, it has to do all these things concurrently with batch job processing.

inquiry application — Transportation reservation and inventory control systems are examples of inquiries which can be handled on an on-line or interrupt basis. Regular running programs are interrupted or halted until an inquiry is completed. Inquiries can also be queued and held up for batches. Inquiries can be introduced by card, tape, direct console, or remote station inquiry. Bank teller processing also is an example of simultaneous inquiry and batch.

inquiry, data base — Data base inquiry is simply the retrieval of a fairly small amount of information from a centrally situated data base for display at the local site. The classic example is an airlines reservation system. Here, the terminal has a keyboard for requesting specific flight data and a cathode ray tube (crt) screen for displaying the answers. Often data base inquiry requires a hard copy—for example, a completely filled-in airline ticket, which is produced by a teleprinter. The inquiry function has much in common with the transaction function.

inquiry, direct-access — A storage method which allows direct information inquiry from temporary or permanent storage devices.

inquiry display terminal — *See* display, inquiry-terminal.

inquiry, keyboard — Interrogation of program progress, storage contents, or other information by keyboard maneuvering.

inquiry, remote — Inquiry stations when operated on-line permit humans to interrogate the computer files and receive immediate answers to inquiries. In industry they can be located at dozens of remote locations such as office, factory, warehouse, branch locations hundreds of miles away. Such an on-line real-time system permits all levels of industrial management to obtain immediate answers to questions about inventories, work in process, sales, and other facts for effective management.

inquiry station — Device or unit from which an information request is made.

inquiry unit — A device used to "talk" to the computer, usually to get quick answers to random questions like "How many hammers do we have in stock?" or "When did we last order soap powder and in what quantity?"

in-read, out-read — An optical feature that may be added to certain off-line office machinery permitting on-line operation.

inscribe — The action of reading the data recorded on documents and writing the same data on the same document. The document thus becomes available and suitable for the application of automatic reading by optical character readers or other reading devices.

inscribing — In optical character recognition, the preparation of source documents for automatic reading and which includes both handwritten and printed characters.

inserted subroutine — *See* subroutine, direct-insert.

insertion, switch — The insertion of information into a computer system by an operator who operates the switches manually.

insert with automatic justify — Text is automatically justified on completion of all insertions or, optionally, at any insertion.

inside plant — In communication practice, inside plant is that part of the plant within a central office, intermediate station or subscriber's premises that is on the office or station side of the point of connection with the outside plant. Note: The plant in a central office is commonly referred to as central office plant, and the plant on the station premises is referred to as station plant.

installation, computer — *See* computer installation.

installation date — The date new equipment is ready for use. The commencement of rental normally begins on the day following the date on which the contractor officially notifies the using organization that the equipment is installed and ready for use, subject to the acceptance and standard of performance provisions of the applicable contract.

installation processing control — In an effort to reduce job turn-around time and to minimize time wasted in setup, the scheduling of applications and jobs is automated.

installation tape number — A number permanently assigned to a plastic or metal spool to identify a particular roll of magnetic tape.

installation, terminal — A grouping, at one site, of operable data terminals and related equipment.

installation, terminal, for data transmission — Installation comprising the data-terminal equipment, the signal-conversion equipment, and any intermediate equipment. Note: In some instances, the data-terminal equipment may be connected directly to a data processing machine or may be a part of it.

installation time — Time spent in testing, installing, error-checking, and diagnosing of such basic electronic but nonprogramming checks, as dry runs, etc. This time does not include reliability tests which are defined as supplementary maintenance time.

instantaneous data-transfer rate — *See* data transfer rate.

instantaneous storage — Storage, usually

in several locations, with an access time which is slight in comparison with operation time.

instantaneous transfer rate — *See* data transfer rate.

instants, significant (of a modulation or a restitution) — Instants limiting significant intervals of modulation or restitution.

instruction — 1. A coded program step that tells the computer what to do for a single operation in a program. 2. A set of characters, together with one or more addresses (or no address), that defines an operation and which, as a unit, causes the computer to operate accordingly on the indicated quantities. 3. A set of identifying characters designed to cause a computer to perform certain operations. A machine instruction to specific functions.

instruction, absolute — A particular computer instruction which specifies completely a specific computer operation and is capable of causing the execution of that operation.

instruction, actual — *Same as* instruction, effective.

instruction address — *See* address, instruction.

instruction, address, functional — *See* address instruction, functional.

instruction address register — Contains address of next instruction to be executed.

instructional constant — A constant written in the form of an instruction but not intended to be executed as an instruction. One form of dummy instruction.

instructional cycle — The steps involved in the processing of an instruction.

instruction, alphanumeric — The name given to instructions that can be used equally well with alphabetic or numeric kinds of fields of data.

instruction area — 1. A part of storage allocated to receive and store the group of instructions to be executed. 2. The storage locations used to store the program.

instruction, arithmetic — *See* arithmetic instruction.

instruction, blank — *See* instruction, dummy.

instruction, branch — *See* branch instruction.

instruction, branch-on-zero — If the arithmetic accumulator is zero, the computer operation will then proceed to an alternate location.

instruction, breakpoint — 1. An instruction which will cause a computer to stop or to transfer control in some standard fashion to a supervisory routine which can monitor the progress of the interrupted program. 2. An instruction which, if some specified switch is set, will cause the computer to stop or take other special action.

instruction, breakpoint (conditional) — A conditional jump instruction which, if some specified switch is set, will cause the computer to stop, after which either the routine may be continued as coded or a jump may be forced.

instruction byte — Some systems offer byte instructions that load or store any byte in memory or swap bytes in a register and are valuable in data communications or data processing.

instruction character — *See* character, command.

instruction, character ignore — *Same as* ignore.

instruction check — *See* check, forbidden-combination.

instruction, check-indicator — *See* check-indicator instruction.

instruction code — The list of symbols, names and definitions of the instructions that are intelligible to a given computer or computing system.

instruction codes, mnemonic — *See* codes, mnemonic operation.

instruction complement — A built-in feature designed to provide a number of instructions for each programmer instruction.

instruction, computer — *Same as* machine instruction.

instruction, conditional breakpoint — A conditional-jump instruction which, if some specified switch is set or situation exists, will cause the computer to stop, after which either the routine may be continued as coded, or a jump may be forced.

instruction, conditional jump — *Same as* branch, conditional.

instruction, constant — *Same as* constant instruction.

instruction counter — Refers to a multiple-bit register that keeps track of the address of the current instruction and is used as the input to the memory-address register (MAR).

instruction, decision — *See* branch.

instruction decode and control — On low-cost systems, this operation decodes the instruction and provides all control and gating functions required for execution of the specified operation.

instruction decoder — The part of the CPU that interprets the program instructions in binary into the necessary control signals for the ALU, registers, and control bus.

instruction decoder, bit-slice microprocessor — Once the information is fetched from the memory, it goes into the instruction decoder where it is interpreted. The command is then to the control store to start the sequence to be executed. The sequence, in turn, fulfills the instruction. Instruction after instruction is executed in this manner until the desired result is obtained. Each time an instruction is completed, the control store modifies the MAR so that it points to the next location.

instruction digit, unallowable — A character or combination of bits which is not accepted as a valid representation by the machine design or by a specific routine. Instruction digits unallowable are commonly detected and used as an indication of machine malfunction.

instruction, discrimination — A more acceptable term for conditional jump instruction or branch instruction. Also called decision instruction. *See* branch.

instruction, do-nothing — *See* instruction, dummy.

instruction, dummy — 1. An artificial instruction or address inserted in a list to serve a purpose other than execution as an instruction. (Related to constant instruction.) 2. A specifically designed artificial instruction to serve a purpose other than its meaningful or purposeful execution; i.e., it is not data. Such an instruction is usually inserted in the sequence for a purpose, but if it is executed no disturbance to the run will occur. It is frequently a no-operation, a do-nothing, or a waste instruction.

instruction, effective — To alter a presumptive or unmodified instruction when using a stored program computer. Such alteration produces a complete instruction, and when it is actually executed it is called an effective instruction or an actual instruction. The modification process uses words or parts of words specifically called modifiers or index words. These are added to or combined with the presumptive or unmodified instruction by means of arithmetical or logical operations.

instruction, entry — Usually the first instruction to be executed in a subroutine. It may have several different entry points each of which corresponds to a different function of the subroutine.

instruction, execution — The set of elementary steps carried out by the computer to produce the result specified by the operation code.

instruction execution time — Generally, execution time for an instruction depends on the instruction itself, the modes of addressing used, and the type of memory referenced. Again, generally, the instruction execution time is the sum of Basic Time, a Source Address (SRC) Time, and a Destination Address (DST) Time. Thus, the Instruction Time equals the Basic Time + SRC Time + DST Time. (Basic Time = Fetch Time + Decode Time + Execute Time.) Timing is in microseconds, unless otherwise noted, and process time can vary plus or minus 20 percent.

instruction, executive — Similar to a supervisory instruction, this instruction is designed and used to control the operation or execution of other routines or programs.

instruction, extract — An instruction that requests formation of a new expression from selected pairs of given expressions.

instruction format — 1. The allocation of bits or characters of a machine instruction to specific functions. 2. Instructions are coded in a two-address, variable-length format. However, one or perhaps both addresses may often be omitted, thereby saving memory space and speeding up instruction execution. 3. The allocation of instructions according to some particular machine or installation conventions or rules. 4. An allocation of characters of various instructions differentiating between the component parts of the instructions, such as address part, operation part, etc.

instruction format, addressless — *See* addressless instruction format.

instruction format, functional address — This format contains no operation part because the operation is implicitly specified by address parts.

instruction format, implicit address — This particular format contains no address part because it is used either when no address is required or when it is implicitly shown in some way.

instruction format, N-address — A specific arrangement of component parts of a computer instruction word that references N storage locations, specifically, a three-address instruction format, etc.

instruction format, N plus one address — An instruction format which contains one, two, three, ..., (N+1) address parts, respectively. The plus-one address is that of the instruction to be executed next.

instruction format, one plus one address — *Same as* address, two.

instruction format, three address — *Same as* address, three.

instruction format, two address — *Same as* address, two.

instruction format, two plus one address — *Same as* address, three.

instruction format, zero-address — *Same as* addressless instruction format.

instruction, four-address — *See* address, four.

instruction, functional address — *See* address instruction, functional.

instruction, halt — *See* halt instruction.

instruction, hold — A computer instruction which causes data called from storage to be also retained in storage after it is called out and transferred to its new location.

instruction, ignore — *See* ignore.

instruction, immediate address — *See* address instruction, immediate.

instruction, internal manipulation — A computer instruction that changes the format or location of data within the computer system.

instruction, jump — A computer instruction causing a jump in the sequence of instructions. *See* branch.

instruction, logic — An instruction causing the execution of an operation defined in symbolic logic statements or operators, such as AND, OR, etc., and to be distinguished from arithmetic instructions, such as add, multiply, and divide.

instruction, logical — An instruction that carries out a logical operation, such as an AND, OR, NOR.

instruction, look up — An instruction designed to allow reference to systematically arranged and stored data.

instruction loop, closed — Indefinite repetition of a group of instructions.

instruction, machine — An instruction that the particular machine can recognize and execute.

instruction, macro — 1. An instruction consisting of a sequence of microinstructions that are inserted into the object routine for performing a specific operation. 2. The more powerful instructions that combine several operations in one instruction.

instruction, macro (linkage) — A macroinstruction that provides logical linkage between programs and subroutines and that will save data needed by another program.

instruction, micro — A small, single, short, add-shift or delete type of command.

instruction mix — Specific computer instructions selected to complete particular problems. The optimum mix of instructions determines the speed and accuracy in most cases, and programmers try to achieve this optimum.

instruction, mnemonic — *See* codes, mnemonic operation.

instruction modification — A change in the operation-code portion of an instruction or command such that if the routine containing the instruction or command is repeated, the computer will perform a different operation.

instruction multiaddress — *See* multiaddress.

instruction, multiple — *See* multiaddress.

instruction, multiple-address — An instruction consisting of an operation code and two or more addresses. Usually specified as a two-address, three-address, or four-address instruction. *See* multiple-address code.

instruction, no-address — An instruction specifying an operation that the computer can perform without having to refer to its storage unit.

instruction, nonprint — An instruction that is usually transmitted in a form which prevents the printing of a line or character.

instruction, no-op — 1. An instruction that specifically instructs the computer to do nothing but process the next instruction in sequence. 2. A blank instruction. 3. A skip instruction.

instruction, one-address — An instruction consisting of an operation and exactly one address. The instruction code of a single-address computer may include both zero and multiaddress instructions as special cases.

instruction, one-plus-one address — *Same as* address, two.

instruction, operational address — *See* instruction, source-destination.

instruction operation codes — *See* codes, instruction operation.

instruction path, microprocessor — The instruction path is a transfer bus for retrieving instructions from the program memory. Instruction word width is determined by the size of the instruction set which affects processing power.

instruction, presumptive — An instruction that will most likely be modified before it is used for the final program.

instruction, pseudo — *See* pseudoinstruction.

instruction, reference — An instruction designed to allow reference to systematically arranged and stored data.

instruction register — *See* register, instruction.

instruction register, control — A particular register in which the content is the address of the next instruction.

instruction repertory — *See* repertory, instruction.

instruction, repetition — An instruction whose execution is repeated an indicated number of times before the next instruction is processed.

instructions, control — The instructions in this category are used to manipulate data within the main memory and the control memory, to prepare main-memory storage areas for the processing of data fields, and to control the sequential selection and interpretation of instructions in the stored program.

instructions, dynamic — The sequence of machine steps performed by the computer in a real-time or simulated environment.

instruction set — Instruction sets consist of an operator part, one or more address parts, and some special indicators, usually, and serve to define the operations and operands for the computer. It is the total-structured group of characters to be transferred individually to the computer as operations are executed.

instruction, short — The use of an index specification in a FORTRAN read or write statement.

instruction, single-address — *Same as* instruction, one-address.

instruction, single-operand — *See* single-operand instruction.

instructions, input/output — Computer instructions which operate input/output devices like card readers, printers, and terminals.

instructions, interpretive — *See* interpretive instructions.

instruction, skip — An instruction having no effect other than directing the processor to proceed to another instruction designated in the storage portion. (Synonymous with skip, and no-op instruction.)

instructions, microprogrammable — All instructions which do not reference core memory (do not contain a memory address) can be microprogrammed, allowing the programmer to specify several shift, skip, or input/output transfer commands to be performed within one instruction.

instructions, monitored — As shown in the input/output instruction repertoire, instructions calling for input, output, or function transfers may be executed either with or without monitor. When executed with monitor, an internal interrupt will be generated upon completion of the transfer. When an instruction is executed without a monitor the interrupt is inhibited.

instruction, source designation — *Same as* address instruction, functional.

instruction, source-destination — A computer instruction that has no operation part, but rather has the operation implicitly specified by the address parts.

instructions, privileged — Protection against one problem subprogram misusing another problem subprogram's i/o devices is provided by restricting all i/o commands to the supervisor state. A subprogram requests i/o action by issuing a supervisor call instruction. The supervisory subprogram can then analyze this request and take the appropriate action.

instructions, programmed — Special subroutines called programmed instructions may be used as if they were single commands by employing one of the programmed instructions of the repertoire. This capability allows the programmer to define his own special command, through the use of subroutines, which may be changed by the operating routine if desired.

instructions, return — The specific group of instructions which are subroutined at the end of a program to provide for the transfer of control from the return subroutine to the main routine.

instructions, shift — Specific instructions which will shift the number either to the left or to the right within an arithmetic register. A shift operation is principally equivalent to multiplying or dividing by the number base in use, depending upon the direction of the shift. In a decimal computer, a shift of one place to the right is equivalent to dividing by 10, a shift one place to the left is equivalent to multiplying by 10.

instruction statement, machine — *See* machine instruction statements.

instruction, stop — *See* halt instruction.

instruction storage — *Same as* instruction area.

instructions, variable-length — *See* variable-length instructions.

instruction, symbolic — *See* symbolic instruction.

instruction, table-look-up — An instruction designed to allow reference to systematically arranged and stored data.

instruction tape — *Same as* tape, program.

instruction tape, master — A particular magnetic tape which contains most or all of the routines or programs for the basic run or run series. Also a main part of an operating system.

instruction, three-address — *Same as* address, three.

instruction, three-plus-one address — *Same as* address four.

instruction time — 1. The portion of an instruction cycle when the control unit is analyzing the instruction and setting up to perform the indicated operation. 2. The portion of an instruction cycle when the actual work is performed or operation executed, i.e., the time required to decode and perform an instruction.

instruction, transfer — An instruction to a computer that enables the programmer to instruct the computer to choose between alternative subprograms depending upon the conditions determined by the computer during the execution of the program.

instruction, two address — *Same as* address, two.

instruction, two-plus-one address — *Same as* address, three.

instruction, two- three- or four-address — An instruction consisting of an operation and 2, 3, or 4 addresses, respectively. The addresses may specify the location of operands, results, or other instructions.

instruction, unconditional-jump — *See* branch, unconditional.

instruction, unconditional transfer — *Same as* branch, unconditional.

instruction, unmodified — An instruction which is to be modified in some prescribed way by means of a stored program computer available for a particular purpose, to produce the completed executable instruction.

instruction, waste — *Same as* instruction, dummy.

instruction word — 1. A grouping of letters or digits handled by the computer as a distinct unit to signify the provision of definitions of operations to be performed or the description of further data. 2. A part of a word or all of a word which is executed by the computer as an instruction.

instruction, zero-address — An instruction specifying an operation in which the locations of the operands are defined by the computer code, so that no address need be given explicitly.

instrumentation errors — Where input into a system is directly from instrumentation such as pressure gauges, etc. Limit checks are imposed to prevent instrumentation errors. If these limits are violated, control may be assumed by a violation subroutine for immediate corrective action.

instrument, end — A device that is connected to one terminal of a loop and is capable of converting usable intelligence into electrical signals or vice versa. It includes all generating, signal-converting, and loop-terminating devices employed at the transmitting and/or receiving location.

integer — A complete entity; a whole (not fractional or mixed) number.

integer programming — A class of optimization problems in which the values of all of the variables are restricted to be integers. Normally, the optimization problem without this integer restriction is a linear program; additional adjectives indicate variations—for example, integer quadratic programming.

integers — The natural or whole numbers; concepts intimately connected with the process of counting or enumeration. Because integers can be written down in endless series, they are used to indicate order or sequence, i.e., the ordinal aspect of integers. The cardinal aspect of integers concerns how many things are observed or noted and provides a basis of measurement.

integer, single-precision — A fixed-point number that occupies one word of core storage. The value varies depending on the word length of the computer.

integer variables (FORTRAN) — An integer variable consists of a series of not more than six alphameric characters (except special characters), of which the first is I, J, K, L, M, or N (some systems).

integral — In numeric notation, the integral or integer is contained in the places to the left of the assumed point. The decimal 2345.67 has four integral places.

integrand — 1. When a unit has two input variables (x and y) and one output variable (z) which is proportional to the integral of (y)—the y is the integrand. 2. A calculus expression, i.e., the math expression or function which is operated upon in the process of integration.

integrated data processing — *See* data processing, integrated.

integrated system — The combination of processes which results in the introduction of data which need not be repeated as further allied or related data is also entered. For example, shipment data may also be the basis for inventory inquiries, invoicing marketing reports, etc.

integrator — A device whose output function is proportional to the integral of the input function with respect to a specified variable.

integrator, incremental — A digital integrating device with an output signal which is a maximum negative, zero, or a maximum positive value depending on a negative, zero, or positive instantaneous input signal.

integrator, storage — In an analog computer, an integrator used to store a voltage in the hold condition for future use, while the rest of the computer assumes another computer control state.

integrator, summing — An analog computer amplifier which forms the time integral of the weighted sum of the input voltages or currents as an output.

intelligence — The developed capability of a device to perform functions that are normally associated with human intelligence, such as reasoning, learning, and self-improvement. (Related to machine learning.)

intelligence, artificial — The study of computer and related techniques to supplement the intellectual capabilities of man. As man has invented and used tools to increase his physical powers, he now is beginning to use artificial intelligence to increase his mental powers. In a more restricted sense, the study of techniques for more effective use of digital computers by improved programming techniques.

intelligent controller — Generally a device designed to originate control that is equipped with local interpreting functions such as editing, input validity checks, and complex command decoding.

intelligent terminal applications — Intelligent terminals are capable of data processing with storage and a stored program available to the user. Advances in LSI technology greatly increased the capabilities of such terminals, with the trends being simultaneously more local processing and more on-line interaction with a central data base. The first significant use of LSI was the replacement of magnetostrictive delay line with MOS shift register and later with low-cost MOS random-access memory. Terminals are also using other LSI products. Becoming standard are the universal asynchronous receiver/transmitter (UART), "smart" Point of Sale (POS) terminals, automatic bank "teller" terminals, and scores more.

intelligent terminals, special purpose — These terminals contain some logic and are usually polled by the computer, or, conversely, the computer polls some intermediate device, such as magnetic tape or disk. If the computer goes down, the terminal can continue to operate in a limited mode for a certain period of time. Applications include department stores, supermarkets, hotel systems—front desk, coffee shop, bar, etc.—and banks.

intelligent voice terminal — An intelligent terminal operated by human voice in which the software resident in the terminal is often user-programmable. It is best for applications suiting an intelligent terminal but where hands-free data entry is cost advantageous.

intelligent work station — An intelligent terminal work station can embody all of the basic functions performed by a business computer; it can be a complete small business computer in itself—a system that is capable of operating completely on its own, and also of communicating and cooperating with other computers. The built-in large-scale integrated electronics that plays such an important role in intelligent terminals and "dumb" terminals alike, is now making it possible to add further features economically.

intensity — The density of a black or colored image produced on paper for optical character recognition.

interactive debugging — The interactive debugging program often generates full screen hexadecimal memory dump displays instantaneously. Commands include display, store, execute, change memory, dump memory, find data in memory, set, reset and display breakpoints, on many systems.

interactive system — Pertaining to an application in which each entry elicits a response as in an inquiry system. An interactive system may also be conversational, implying a continuous dialogue between the user and the system.

interactive terminal processing — A procedure that provides for interactive communications between the system and local or remote terminals. Features include an interface to support multiuser interactive applications programs, interactive file editing, remote job entry, and job status retrieval.

interactive time sharing — Time sharing apportions computer resources among many simultaneous users, giving each a seemingly dedicated system to apply to the task at hand. Interactive time sharing maximizes the use of the computer as a working tool by integrating user input and machine output in a dynamic give-and-take process.

interblock — 1. To prevent a machine or device from initiating further operations until the operation in process is completed. 2. To avoid or prevent the operations of one part of a computing system while other parts are operating.

interblock gap — The space on magnetic tape separating two blocks of data or information.

interblock space — That part of a magnetic tape between blocks of information on which nothing is written. Also called inter-record gap.

intercepting trunk — A trunk to which a call for a vacant number, changed number, or a line out of order is connected for action by an operator.

interchangeable card feed — A device which usually converts an 80 column card feed to a 51 column card feed.

interchangeable type bar — A printer type bar which can be removed by the operator to change from one alphabet to another.

intercomputer communication — Data is transmitted from one computer to another so that the data can be reprocessed in order to facilitate handling and increase transmission speed.

intercycle — A step in the sequence of steps made by the main shaft of a punched-card machine. At this time the card feed is stopped, usually due to a control change. In some machines the number of intercycles that are to arise for a control change can be predetermined; in others this determination is made solely by the machine.

interface — 1. A common boundary between automatic data-processing systems or parts of a single system. In communications and data systems, it may involve code, format, speed, or other changes as required. 2. A common boundary, e.g., the boundary between two systems or two devices.

interface adaptor (device adaptor) — A unit that provides a mechanical and electrical interconnection between the tester and the device under test may include special stimulus, measurement, load, and switching circuitry unique to a device or family of devices, but is not provided in the tester.

interface, analog — Analog interfaces

allow the personal computer to monitor and control the nondigital world. These circuits are the key elements in environmental sensors, dc motor controls, and other interfaces to linear peripheral devices.

interface cards, data communications — Data communication interface cards permit computer users to transmit data using a wide variety of privately owned and common-carrier communication facilities. Most communications interfaces conform to EIA specification RS-232C and CCITT specification V.24.

they will fabricate these units for particular systems under close supervision by the same engineers that designed them. These engineers, who are naturally quite familiar with the logic and requirements, are best qualified to do this important work.

interface design, system — *See* system interface design.

interface, EIA Standard RS-232 B or C — A standardized method adopted by the Electronic Industries Association to ensure uniformity of interface between data communication equipment and

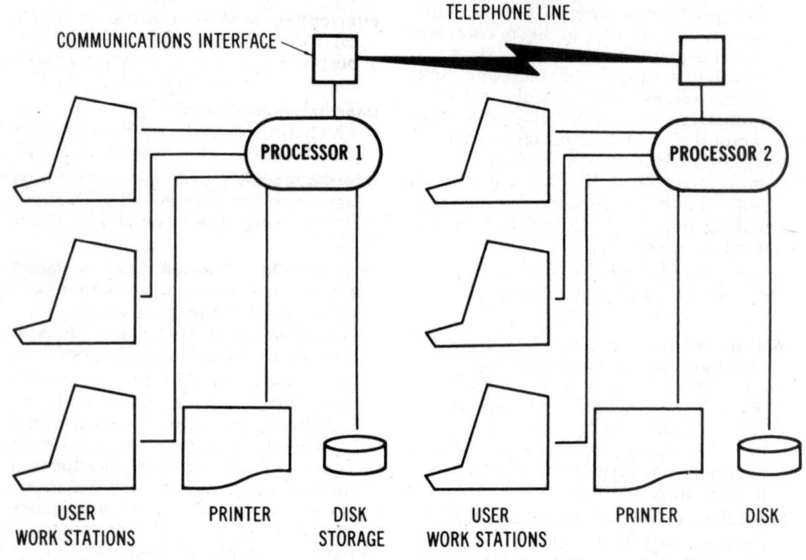

Interface, communications.

interface, communications — The transfer of data between the processor and the standard communication subsystem takes place through input data leads, connected to the processor input channel, and output data leads, connected to the processor output channel. In addition to the data leads, there are several control leads which are used to control the flow of data.

interface design — For unique user applications such as on-line installations which require specialized input/output equipment, engineering staffs will design the necessary interface units as part of services to their customers. Then,

data processing terminal equipment. It has been generally accepted by most manufacturers of data transmission and business equipment.

interface i/o module — A typical device has four 8-bit input/output ports for parallel oriented peripheral interfacing with eight controlled interrupt lines. Each i/o port is individually selectable as a memory device with three-state TTL compatible i/o lines.

interface, Kansas City standard — Named for the meeting place of the symposium at which it found acceptance, the Kansas City standard describes a modern technique for reading and writing digital data on audio cassette recorders and could influence developments in the hobby computer market. Low-speed, fsk modems use different pairs of frequencies for originating and answering calls and thus do not talk to themselves. Recording and replaying data from tape requires a modem that uses only a single pair of mark/space frequencies, because the recorded data consists of these keyed frequencies. Using harmonically related frequencies permits deriving the clock frequency from the data and accommodates the wide speed variations of inexpensive cassette recorders. The standard provides both speed and software independence.

interface latch chip — On some systems that use latches for interfacing, the interface latch chip can be used as a bidirectional input/output port, a dedicated input port, or as a dedicated output port. A control signal (dynamic for bidirectional mode and static for dedicated modes) is supplied by the user, in many cases. Separate control lines enable the i/o ports, in some systems; thus, the latch may be a high-impedance device; i.e., it does not load the system bus unless an enable signal is present.

interface (MIL STD 188B) — The standard method of interface established by the Department of Defense. It is presently mandatory for use by the departments and agencies of the Department of Defense for the installation of all new equipment. This standard provides the interface requirements for connection between data communication security devices, data processing equipment, or other special military terminal devices.

interface types — Various interfaces can be categorized into three distinct types for some systems. 1. Slave—This interface usually has no provision in its control logic to become master. It will only transfer data onto and off the bus by command of a master device. 2. Interrupt—This interface generally has the ability to gain mastership of the bus in order to give the central processor the address of a subroutine which the processor will use to service the peripheral. 3. DMA—This interface has the ability to gain mastership of the bus in order to transfer data between itself and some other peripheral.

interfacing, single chip system — On some low cost systems, interfacing has the following characteristics: static operation, bidirectional, tri-state 8-bit data bus with TTL or CMOS compatible options, relatively simple and powerful interrupt functions.

interference — The presence of undesirable energy in a circuit, caused by electrostatically or electromagnetically coupled external circuits.

interference, adjacent-channel — Adjacent-channel interference occurs when two modulated carrier channels are placed close together in frequency so that one or both sidebands extend from one channel into the other.

interfix — A technique that allows the relationships of keywords in an item or document to be described so that very specific inquiries can be answered without false retrievals due to crosstalk.

interior label — *See* label, interior.

interlanguage — A modification of common language, suitable for automatic translation by the equipment into machine or computer usable language.

interleave — To insert segments of one program into another program so that the two programs can, in effect, be executed simultaneously, e.g., a technique used in multiprogramming.

interleaving, functional — The process of having i/o and computing operations proceed independently of one another but interleaved in their sharing of the memory.

interleaving, memory — Two or more memory banks operating at a fraction of a cycle apart and significantly reducing cycle time and improving memory speed.

interleaving, multiprocessing — *See* multiprocessor interleaving.

interlock — To arrange the control of machines or devices so that their operation is interdependent in order to assure their proper coordination.

interlock (communications) — Any protective feature which helps to prevent interference to normal transmission or processing of data by other operations, such as sending from the keyboard while an automatic transmission is in progress, or to prevent sending more than one character at a time from the keyboard.

interlock time, print — The required time for the printer to accept data from the print storage area and to complete the printing.

interlude — A minor subprogram designed for preliminary computations or data organization, such as calculating the value of some parameter or clearing parts of the storage. It is usually overwritten after it has served its purpose, as it is usually no longer needed in the program.

intermediate control — The group of various minor controls into a category other than beginning or ending.

intermediate cycle — *See* cycle, intermediate.

intermediate memory storage — An electronic scratchpad for holding working figures temporarily until they are needed, and for releasing final figures to the output.

intermediate product — *See* product, intermediate.

intermediate storage — *See* storage, intermediate.

intermediate total — A total which lies somewhere between a major and a minor total, i.e., a summation developed for some other purpose or in some hierarchy of sums, or due to a termination in a program.

intermittent errors — *See* errors, intermittent.

intermittent faults — *Same as* faults, sporadic.

intermix tape — A specific feature of some computer equipment which allows for combinations of different models of tape units to be interconnected to a single computer.

internal and external interrupts — *See* interrupts, internal and external.

internal arithmetic — The computations performed by the arithmetic unit of a computer.

internal buffer — Buffering can be performed by input/output media such as punched or magnetic tape, and often is (e.g., in teletypewriter ASR terminals). However, some manufacturers provide an internal buffer (usually composed of a semiconductor shift register), which is used to gather keyed or received data prior to transmitting or printing, respectively. The internal buffer capacity in characters is presented where applicable.

internal checking — The equipment characteristics which are designed for the improvement of accuracy, such as hole counts, parity checks, validity checks, and others.

internal control systems — Programmed controls built into the system to govern the flow of computer operations.

internal instruction, manipulation — A computer instruction that changes the format or location of data within the computer system.

internal interrupt — A feature of peripheral equipment using an external device which causes equipment to stop in the normal course of the program and perform some designated subroutine.

internally stored program — *See* program, internally stored.

internal magnetic recording — Storage of information within the material such as used in magnetic cores.

internal memory — Any one of the internal parts of an automatic data-processing machine capable of retaining data.

internal sort — The sequencing of two or more records within the central computer memory; the first phase of a multipass sort program.

internal storage — *See* storage, internal.

internal storage locations — *Same as* storage, working.

International Algebraic Language — The forerunner of ALGOL.

interoffice trunk — A direct trunk between local central offices in the same exchange.

interpret — 1. To print on a punched card the graphic symbols of the information punched in that card. 2. To translate nonmachine language into machine language. 3. To decode. 4. The translation of coded characters into standard letters, numbers, and symbols.

interpreter — 1. A punch-card machine that will take a punch card with no printing on it, read the information in the punched holes, and print a translation in characters in specified rows and columns on the card. 2. An executive routine that, as the computation progresses, translates a stored program expressed in some machinelike pseudocode into machine code and performs the indicated operations, by means of subroutines, as they are translated. An interpreter is essentially a closed subroutine that operates successively on an indefinitely long sequence of program parameters, the pseudoinstructions, and operands. It may usually be entered as a closed subroutine and left by a pseudocode exit instruction.

interpreter code — An interim, arbitrarily designed code which must be translated to computer coding in order to function as designed, usually for diagnostic or checking purposes.

interpreter (program) — An essentially closed subroutine (executive) which translates a stored pseudocode program into machine and performs the desired and specified operations. Such an interpreter program usually consists of sequences of pseudoinstructions and operands (program parameters) which are introduced as a closed subroutine and exit by a specific pseudocode instruction.

interpreter routine — An executive routine that, as the computation progresses, translates a stored program expressed in some machinelike pseudocode into machine code and performs the indicated operations, by means of subroutines, as they are translated.

interpreting — Interpreting consists of sensing alphabetical or numerical data punched in a card and printing it on the same card.

interpretive code — A routine that decodes and immediately executes instructions written as pseudocodes. This is contrasted with a compiler which decodes the pseudocodes into a machine-language routine to be executed at a later time. The essential characteristic of an interpretive routine is that a particular pseudocode operation must be decoded each time it is executed.

interpretive execution — Permits retention of all of the information contained in the user's original source statements, thereby making source-language debugging possible. Interpretive execution plus multiprogramming make the conversational mode of operation a practical reality.

interpretive instructions — Various segments of interpreters which automatically reproduce or translate an old program code into a new program code or the interpretation of the old program code on a new machine.

interpretive language — *See* language, interpretive.

interpretive mode — In tracing (debugging) routines when a program is simulated in its execution by using pseudo accumulators and pseudo index registers, branch instructions are inserted at various points to place the machine and program in an interpretive mode for error tracing, and when an error is found, control is transferred back to the main program.

interpretive program — *See* program, interpretive.

interpretive programming — *See* programming, interpretive.

interpretive program translation — *Same as* program, interpretive.

interpretive routine — A routine that decodes instructions written as pseudocodes and immediately executes those instructions, as contrasted with a compiler that decodes the pseudocodes and produces a machine-language routine to be executed at a later time.

interpretive tracing — *See* tracing, interpretive.

interrecord gap — 1. The unrecorded portion between records on magnetic tape. 2. An interval of space or time, deliberately left between recording portions of data or records. Such spacing is used to prevent errors through loss of data or overwriting, and permits stop-start tape operations.

interrecord gap length — The length of the unused recording area between records written by the unit.

interrogation — A simple inquiry to the system for which a quick reply is expected.

interrupt — 1. A break in the normal flow of a system or routine such that the flow can be resumed from that point at a later time. An interrupt is usually caused by a signal from an external source. 2. An interrupt is a special control signal that diverts the attention of the computer from the main program, because of a particular event or set of circumstances, to a specific address which is directly related to the type of interrupt that has occurred. 3. To stop current control sequence, i.e., to jump when affected by signals from on-line peripheral equipment or to skip as triggered by results of programming test techniques.

interrupt, armed — Interrupts may be armed or disarmed. An armed interrupt accepts and holds the interruption signal. A disarmed interrupt ignores the signal. An armed interrupt may be enabled or disabled. An interrupt signal for an enabled condition causes certain hardware processing to occur. A disabled interrupt is held waiting for enablement.

interrupt, automatic — Interruption caused by program instruction as contained in some executive routine; interruption not caused by programmer but due to engineering of devices. Error interrupt.

interrupt, batch-processing — An outstanding feature of any real-time system is its capacity to process real-time and batch-processing applications concurrently. This real-time data-processing innovation is made possible through a unique feature that permits remote external units with information of high precedance to interrupt computer processing. Whenever transaction data for a real-time problem are entered into a remote external unit, the computer's batch-processing program may be interrupted to permit handling the high priority real-time transaction and the sending of processed results back to the external unit.

interrupt capability, time sharing — *See* time sharing, interrupt capability.

interrupt code — The programmed or arbitrarily selected code which requires translation to computer code in order to result in machine language.

interrupt, contingency — The program is interrupted if any of the following events occur at the operator's console: the operator requests use of the keyboard to type in information; a character has been typed in or out; a type-in has been completed; or the operator requests a program stop. Contingency interrupt also occurs if an arithmetic operation resulted in an overflow, an invalid operation code was specified, or the clock was addressed after clock power was removed.

interrupt control and reset logic — Interrupt and reset logic functions include bus error and power-fail on some systems. On a specific system, the interrupt functions include power-fail (impending), Halt mode (console microcode control), refresh interrupt, event (or line time clock) interrupt, and external interrupts.

interrupt control routine — A routine entered when an interrupt occurs that provides for such details as the storage of the working details of the interrupted program, an analysis of the interrupt to decide on the necessary action, and the return of control to the interrupted program.

interrupt, count-zero — An interrupt level that is triggered when an associated (clock) counter pulse interrupt has produced a zero result in a clock counter.

interrupt, cycled — The change (by sequence or specific operation cycle) of control to the next or a specific function in a predetermined manner or order.

interrupt, disabled — *See* interrupt, armed.

interrupt, disarmed — *See* interrupt, armed.

interrupt-driven transfers — Interrupts allow various processors to continue a programmed operation (sometimes called a background program) without waiting for a device to become ready to transfer data. When the device does become ready, it interrupts the processor background program execution and causes execution of a device interrupt service routine. After the service routine of the device has been executed, the background program is restored and program execution resumes at the point where it was interrupted.

interrupt, external, inhibit — The bit, in the program status double-word, that indicates whether (if 1) or not (if 0) all external interrupts are inhibited.

interrupt, external-signal — This facility allows signals from external equipment to interrupt the program and initiate a subroutine that services the equipment issuing the signal. Operations using this facility speed the transfer of the data and control information between the computer and peripheral equipment by allowing conditions in the equipment to initiate a transfer of program control to a subroutine that enacts a transfer, rather than waiting for the main routine to sample the condition and initiate the subroutine.

interrupt feedback signal — A steady signal, indicating that an interrupt signal has advanced its associated interrupt level to the waiting or active state; the signal is dropped when the interrupt level is reset to the disarmed or the armed state.

interrupt handling — When an interrupt occurs, the control program saves the interrupted program's registers and status, and routes control to routines that handle the interrupt cause. When the interrupt is handled, the original program's registers and status are restored, and control is restored so that the original program continues as if no interrupt had taken place.

interrupt identification — Various i/o interruptions are caused by an i/o unit ending an operation or otherwise needing attention. Identifications of the device and channel causing the interruption are often stored in the old Program Status Word (PSW). In addition, the status of the device and channel is stored in a fixed location.

interrupt indicators, input/output — *See* input/output interrupt indicators.

interrupt, input/output, inhibit — The bit, in the program status double-word, that indicates whether (if 1) or not (if 0) all internal interrupts of the i/o group are inhibited.

interruption — A brief curtailing or suspension of operations or its sequence of instructions, usually followed by the start of another sequence or a revision to the one stopped. Examples are the stops in priority processing.

interrupt, i/o parity — Each time control is given to the monitor the i/o parity trap is armed and the interrupt location is patched with an instruction. When an i/o parity occurs the computer halts to the instruction at which the parity occurred with the console i/o parity indicator light on.

interrupt latency — Refers to the delay between an interrupt request and acknowledgement of the request.

interrupt linkage — Refers to the technique which causes the computer to switch to (and then return from) the "interrupt handling" portions of the program as various interrupts occur.

interrupt logging — The logging or listing of interrupts during program testing, or when a system is being monitored, so that possible program errors caused by interrupts may be classified and corrected.

interrupt log word — The setting of bits into an interrupt log record which indicates the number and type of interrupts that occur during the running of each segment of a program. The output is on a medium such as tape for analysis.

interrupt mask — Some of the program interruptions, all external interruptions, and all i/o interruptions can be masked (ignored); when this is done, the external and i/o interruptions are held pending and taken at a later time (governed by the control program).

interrupt, master-control — A signal generated by an input/output device, or by an operator's error, or by request of the processor for more data or program segments, or the like, which permits the master control program to control the computer system.

interrupt, microcomputer — Interrupts are asynchronous events typically triggered by peripherals needing attention from the CPU. On some 16-bit microcomputers, there are three interrupts: nonmaskable interrupt (NMI), nonvectored interrupt (NVI), vectored interrupts (VI), and five traps (system call, illegal instruction, privileged i/o instruction, other privileged instructions, and the segmentation trap).

interrupt module — In some systems, a specific device acts as the monitor for a number of priority-designated field contacts and immediately notifies the computer when any of these external priority requests have been generated. This assures servicing of urgent interrupt requests on the basis of programmer-assigned priorities when requests occur simultaneously.

interrupt, not-busy — When an external device recognizes its address and is not busy, it sends a response on the not-busy line to the computer. If no such response is received, the processor will assume that the addressed device is busy. The processor will send a start signal only if a not-busy response is received. If a device is disconnected, it will appear as busy to the computer (some computers).

interrupt, operator — The operator interrupt trap is armed and the fixed interrupt location is patched each time the monitor receives control. When an operator interrupt occurs, control is given to a routine in the monitor. This routine signifies to the operator the type-in is desired by ringing the bell, returning the carriage, and typing.

interrupt oriented — Some programs are not encumbered with instructions that check system components for status or service. Interrupt signals are generated by processors as well as all i/o devices.

interrupt, override — An optional group of power on/off interrupts which have the highest priority and which cannot be disabled or disarmed.

interrupt (peripheral) — The stop resulting from the signal of readiness for or completion of a task by a peripheral device.

interrupt, power-fail — Only a priority interrupt can interrupt a nonpriority interrupt routine. Power fail is the highest priority interrupt and may interrupt any other program or interrupt routine as long as the power-fail interrupt trap is armed.

interrupt priority system — Using various priority interrupt systems, each class of interrupts is assigned a priority, where interrupts of a given class inhibit all interrupts of lower priorities until the higher priority interrupt is completely processed. However, an interrupt of higher priority can interrupt an interrupt of lower priority before it is completely processed.

interrupt priority table — When a computer does not have a fully automatic interrupt handling capability a table is set up that lists the priority sequence of handling and testing interrupts.

interrupt processing, time sharing — *See* time sharing, interrupt processing.

interrupt, processor-dependent — An example of a processor-dependent interrupt condition is the "presence bit condition" caused by a program being executed on a processor that is executing an operand call which addresses a descriptor with a presence bit of zero.

interrupt, processor-error — If a word accessed in any part of the system is found to contain incorrect check bits, or if an error occurs in the addressing of a memory location, processor-error interrupt occurs.

interrupt, processor-independent — An example of a processor-independent interrupt condition is an i/o finished condition caused by the i/o hardware when an i/o operation has been completed.

interrupt, program-error — Program interrupts occur because of programmer errors such as an invalid operation.

interrupt program, i/o — The interrupt-program control approach requires a smaller i/o overhead than that of programmed transfer. The i/o devices can signal the microprocessor by an interrupt whenever they are ready to transmit or receive information. When information is received and identified, the microprocessor interrupts its normal program, stores its state and jumps to a subroutine that allows it to perform the transfer operation. Once the interrupt has been serviced, the microprocessor returns to the state at which it was interrupted or some other predetermined state, and it resumes its normal operation.

interrupt program time-out — Some systems permit the user to set a limit on the length of time the interrupt system may be inhibited (selectable by jumpers from 20 to 640 microseconds). If a program or a system fault inhibits interrupts beyond the limit, a noninhibitable interrupt is generated for corrective procedures. All features on a Memory Parity and Protect (MPP) option can be independently enabled.

interrupt request signal — Refers to signals to the computer that temporarily suspend the normal sequence of a routine and transfer control to a special routine. Operation can be resumed from this point later. Ability to handle interrupts is very useful in communication and debugging where it allows the microprocessor to use breakpoints and to service many channels.

interrupt response time — The elapsed time between interrupt and the start of the interrupt-handling subroutine is called the "response time." The difference between the total time elapsed and the actual execution time is referred to as the "overhead." Both times should be kept as low as possible.

interrupt routine — A program that performs interrupt action to coordinate the timing i/o with processing.

interrupt routine, tape-driver — *See* tape-driver interrupt routine.

interrupts and control logic — The synchronization of input/output activities and responses to real-time situations is accomplished through interrupts. The interrupt is a control signal that may be received from a peripheral subsystem (external interrupt) or from the control section of the central processor. Each interrupt has a unique fixed address in central store. These interrupt locations are programmed to enter interrupt response subroutines in the executive system.

interrupts, automatic check — Input/output interrupts occur upon successful completion of an input/output operation, if a programmer has specified an input/output operation incorrectly, or if a machine malfunction (such as a parity error) occurrs in the path to or from the input/output device. These interrupts permit an automatic check of the status of the operation and of any errors that may have occurred, and initiation of an error-recovery procedure when practical. In the event of intermittent errors, statistics can be kept and logged out between jobs. This automatic checking as provided by the "interrupt" technique makes for highly efficient and accurate programming.

interrupt, scanner — External devices are continuously scanned for interrupt requests. A scanner counts through the nonpriority external-device addresses sequentially, asking if the addressed device is requesting an interrupt. When an interrupt request is found, the scanner will stop at that address and attempt to interrupt the computer program. This feature (ED interrupt) is the important invention which is the basis for real-time computing time sharing.

interrupt schemes, time sharing — *See* time sharing, interrupt schemes.

interrupts, error — Special interrupts are provided in response to certain error conditions within the central computer. These may come as a result of a programming fault (e.g., illegal instruction, arithmetic overflow), a store fault (parity error) or an executive system violation (attempt to leave the locked-in area, or violation of guard mode). These faults have special interrupt locations in central store and are used by the executive system to take remedial or terminating action when they are encountered.

interrupt service routine — Refers to a special routine or program designed to properly store away to the stack the present status of the machine in order to respond to an interrupt request, perform the real work required by the interrupt, restore the saved status of the machine, and then resume the operation of the interrupted program.

interrupts, external — External interrupts are caused by either an external device requiring attention (such as a signal from a communications device), console switching, or by the timer going to zero.

interrupt signal — One of the more powerful control signals governing the input-/output operations of the central computer and the peripheral subsystems is the interrupt signal. This signal is used to demand the immediate attention of the central computer. It causes program control to be switched to a special address connected with the event or circumstances that initiated the interrupt. Interrupts from external sources serve primarily to synchronize the computer program with the status of the subsystem units, and to indicate error conditions occurring within the peripheral subsystems. Internal interrupts synchronize the computer program with the termination of input/output transfers.

interrupts, internal and external — An interrupt is a special control signal which diverts the "attention" of the computer to "consider" an extraordinary event or set of circumstances; that is, it causes program control to be transferred to a special subordinate which corresponds to the "stimulus." Many levels of control can be exercised by the numerous forms of interrupts provided. The interrupts from external sources serve primarily to synchronize the computer program with the readiness of peripheral devices, including other computers, to transmit or receive data. Internal interrupts serve primarily to synchronize the computer program with the termination of input/output transfers and to signal the occurrence of an error. An interrupt causes the next instruction to be procured from a fixed address corresponding to the interrupt source. This fixed address serves as a subroutine entrance by containing a return jump instruction.

interrupts, machine — Machine interrupts occur because of a malfunction in the processor. For these interrupts, the control program may call in machine diagnostic routines from the system library. The current program may either be ended with an abnormal end-of-program or restarted after the diagnostic routines have been executed, and the results stored for later analysis.

interrupts, machine-check — Machine-check interrupts are caused by the machine-checking circuits detecting a machine error. The system is automatically switched to a diagnostic procedure.

interrupts, multiprogramming — Some computers are equipped with a set of control signals which are referred to as interrupts. Whenever certain conditions exist, a control signal will direct the central computer to execute the word (instruction) at a specified address in central store. Each interrupt is activated by unique conditions and directs the computer to a correspondingly unique address in central store. The occurrence of an interrupt terminates guard mode, program lock-in, and central-store address assignments.

interrupts, optional — *See* optional priority interrupts.

interrupts, optional priority — *See* optional priority interrupts.

interrupts, processor — *See* processor interrupt.

interrupts, standard — Various events can lead to a program interrupt. Each interrupt is to a unique fixed memory address which is associated with the event that caused it. Each external device has an interrupt address which is equal to its external-device address. An external device may have more than one interrupt event, and each event may have its own interrupt address. Interrupts may occur only at the end of program instructions. It is important to the programmer that each type of interrupt results in transfer of control to a different memory address. This makes it unnecessary for the program to scan interrupt events to see what has happened. A subroutine for each interrupt event may be in memory.

interrupts, supervisor — *See* supervisor interrupts.

interrupts, supervisor-call — Supervisor-call interrupts are caused by the program issuing an instruction to turn over control to the supervisor (the operating system). The exact cause for the call is shown in the old PSW (program status word) (some computers).

interrupts, system-call — System-call interrupts are programmed requests from a processing program to the control program for some action, such as initiation of an i/o operation.

interrupt system — Some processors feature an interrupt system in which an interrupt source, whether internal or external, meets automatic and immediate response. The interrupt source is properly identified, and a change in program sequence to service the interruption is automatically executed.

interrupt, trapped program — Events can cause the program of the computer to be interrupted: (1) memory parity error, (2) add overflow, (3) programmed i/o channel, (4) operator, (5) external device, (6) multilevel priority interrupts, and (7) power failure. An interrupt trap associated with each event may be set under program control to either respond when the event occurs or to ignore it.

interrupt trigger signal — A signal that is generated, either internal or external to the CPU, to interrupt the normal sequence of events in the central processor.

interrupt vector — Refers to a two memory location identification assigned to an interrupting device. It contains the starting address and the processor status word for its service routine.

interrupt vectoring — Handling interrupts in some systems is a problem of software polling. A polling sequence usually has a corresponding program. Such a polling approach is usually the lowest cost alternative for identifying interrupts, but may in some instances be too slow. For many applications, hardware may be added to the system to achieve priority encoding of the various interrupt requests. The encoded value of the interrupt request can then be used as a system address to transfer control to the appropriate response routine. This is referred to as "interrupt vectoring."

intersection — 1. The Boolean operator that gives a truth table value of true only when both of the variables connected by the logical operator are true. 2. A logical operator that has the property that if P is a statement and Q is a statement, when P AND Q are true, both statements are true, and false if either is false or both are false. Truth is normally expressed by the value 1; falsity by 0. 3. The logical operation which makes use of the AND operator or logical product.

intersection gate — *Same as* gate, AND.

interval, significant — A time interval during which a given significant condition according to the code and the signal to be transmitted is, or should be, transmitted.

interval timer — With the interval timer, the control program provides the facility to keep track of time of day and to interrupt periodically as required. More than one interval can be controlled at once. For example, a five-second interval between successive polling of a teleprocessing line can be specified, and at the same time a two-minute limit on the duration of a new program undergoing test can be in effect.

interval, time-write — The determination of the interval during machine operation when output data is available for an output operation, i.e., the net time exclusive of transmission which it takes to perform an output operation such as printing or writing on tape.

interval, unit — In a system using an equal-length code, or in a system using an isochronous modulation, the intervals of time, such as the theoretical duration of the significant intervals of a telegraph modulation (or restitution), are whole multiples of this interval.

intervention button — *See* button, emergency.

intervention switch — *See* button, emergency.

interword gap — *See* gap, interword.

interword space — *Same as* gap, interword.

introspective program — A self-monitoring program.

inversion — 1. The operation of taking the reciprocal of a value, that is, unity divided by the value. 2. In Boolean operations, it is the same as NOT.

invert — To change any logical, mathematical, or two-state value to its direct opposite state.

inverted file — *See* file, inverted.

inverter — *Same as* gate, NOT.

invigilator — This type of equipment is used to discern whether some prescribed condition is present, usually within a predetermined time period. It is often connected to a control unit, as in process control equipment, to give an alarm if the response time of some machinery or process has been exceeded or interrupted.

i/o — The abbreviation for input/output.

i/o buffer — Permits data-word transfers to and from memory to proceed without main program attention. May be programmed so that when i/o transfer is complete, the computer generates an internal interrupt.

i/o bus lines — Parallel lines and control logic are referred to collectively as the i/o bus. They transfer information between microprocessor and i/o devices. The bus contains three types of lines: data, device address, and command. Data lines consist either of one bidirectional set or two unidirectional sets. In the latter case, one set is used exclusively for inputting of data to the CPU and the other for outputting of data. In most cases the width of the bus—number of lines—equals the word length of the microprocessor.

i/o bus structures — The i/o bus structures employ several schemes. A radial system is one of the simplest, but it limits the number of i/o units. A party-line system reduces the number of lines needed for a distributed system. The latter system also comes in a daisy-chain version, which connects devices serially.

ioc — Abbreviation for input/output controller.

i/o cable — A wire bus or trunk connecting the various input or output devices to the computer.

i/o cabling — Some systems have card frames (stand-alone or in the packaged mini or microcomputer) that can be chained together via a variable 16-line (or more) flat ribbon i/o bus cable, often up to 100 feet. Fifty-line ribbon cables are available to connect controller cards to free-standing devices. Generally no wire wrapping is required, since card frame chaining and device cabling is often done with simple plug-in connectors. The result is convenient, reliable and economical cabling for i/o.

i/o channel — A central computer and its connected terminals use the data communications network to interchange information. The general facility of a computer for transferring information between itself and the outside world is its input/output (i/o) channel. Particular devices are connected with a hardware interface. In the case of a communications line, the modem terminating the line must be interfaced with the CPU.

i/o communications modes — Some devices have been designed to satisfy a wide variety of input/output requirements by providing three modes of i/o operation: synchronous i/o—processing is suspended until the completion of the i/o event; asynchronous i/o—an i/o event is started, processing continues until a user-defined point is reached, and processing is then suspended until the i/o event is completed; event-driven i/o—an i/o event is started, processing continues until the i/o event completes, and processing is then interrupted to service the completed i/o event.

i/o concurrent — Pertaining to terminals that are capable of performing i/o tasks such as communications to the host computer, printing, and file management without halting ongoing data entry operation.

i/o control sequence, single chip systems — On some systems the input-output control sequence can be summed as follows: bus request from the microprocessor; request granted or denied—if denied, bus request remains active until bus request is granted; address and address-valid strobe from the microprocessor; data valid and inputted or outputted, as required.

iocs — An abbreviation for input/output control system.

i/o equipment — Equipment of the peripheral nature which has a primary purpose of feeding input to the computer and taking output from the computer.

i/o hardware, single chip system — On some low-cost systems i/o hardware has the following characteristics: separate serial-data input and output ports, two sense inputs, direct interfacing to standard memory parts, direct interfacing to CMOS logic and memory, as examples.

i/o instruction — Generally an instruction that results in information being inputted or outputted to or from a CPU.

i/o interface — Types of circuit modules that adapt the signal requirements of external equipment to those of a computer and vice versa.

i/o interface control module — These microcircuit modules handle all computer inputs and outputs, with the number and type determined by system applications and the peripheral equipment used. There is also provision to directly connect an i/o interface with a memory module, under program control, to allow an efficient method of resolving conflicts in memory access.

i/o interrupt (programmed i/o bus) — Some systems provide such interrupts for real time clock, TTY ready, operator interrupt, and external i/o (unlimited number).

i/o line, dedicated — Processors with dedicated i/o lines usually have special instructions for manipulating bits, setting mask codes and even performing operations directly on the bits in the port. General-purpose processors usually don't have any i/o port lines, but there are many specially designed support circuits available to provide both serial and parallel i/o ports.

i/o modules, serial and parallel — Serial and parallel i/o modules are generally available for interfacing various processor buses with external devices. These modules simplify connection to peripherals when and if required, and also facilitate assembly of prototype systems without penalizing later development of customized interfaces.

iop (input/output processor) — A unit that handles normal data input/output control and sequencing.

i/o port — Refers to a connection to a CPU that is designed and configured for provision of data paths between the CPU and the external devices, such as keyboards, displays, readers, etc. An i/o port of a microprocessor may be an input port or an output port, or it may be bidirectional.

ior — Abbreviation for input/output register.

i/o routines, random-access — Direct, serial, and random processing of drum and disk files are provided by these routines. Macroinstructions are available to direct the input/output functions.

IPC — Abbreviation for industrial process control.

IPL — 1. Abbreviation for Information Processing Language. 2. Abbreviation for Initial Program Loader or Initialize Program Load. This is the initialization routine used in various intelligent controllers and some computers.

IPL (Initial Program Load) PROM — On some systems several optional autoload PROMs are offered. Some are a combined 256-word PROM for TTY/PTR/CR/floppy disk/moving head disk/head per track disk. This IPL PROM mounts on the system console interface module which contains a small switch to select the desired autoload routine.

IPL PROM routines — Initial Program Load PROM routines are bootstrap loaders so the first block of data which the user puts on his or her autoload media is the standard loader, which the IPL PROM loads into RAM on one manufacturer's system console interface module. The loader then proceeds to load the full program.

IR — Refers to the instruction register that holds the current instruction being decoded and executed by the central processor control section.

IRL — Abbreviation for information retrieval language.

irregularity stroke-edge — A term used in optical character recognitión referring to the deviation of any point on the edge of a character from its stroke edge.

ISAM — Abbreviation for Indexed Sequential Access Method. In sequentially retrieving indexed records, the order of record processing depends on the collating sequence of key values within the index (primary or alternate) being used for access. One system simply reads one record via the first key in the index, turns the corresponding data over to the application program, then reads the next record via the next key in the index, and so on. Thus, sequential access is provided, even though the system is accessing the data in a physically random order. This method of retrieval is commonly called the indexed sequential access method (ISAM).

isochronous — Having a regular periodicity.

isochronous modulation (or restitution) — Modulation (or restitution) in which the time interval separating any two significant instants is theoretically equal to the unit interval or to a multiple of the unit interval.

ISO (International Standards Organization) code — Codes authorized by the ISO to represent alphabetic, numeric, and special characters.

item — 1. A field or set of fields holding related data or information that concerns an individual object, event, transaction, or operation. 2. The word is used in a similar sense to the word file and means each of the unit organizations of information of which the file is comprised. 3. Consecutive fields can be combined to form a larger unit of information called an item. Grouping fields to form an item simplifies the manipulation of related data fields, and minimizes the number of instruction executions required to move consecutive fields within the main memory.

item, addition — An item that is to be added at a specific place to an already established file. Addition master item would be the proper term if the file is a master file.

item advance — A technique in the grouping of records for operating successively on different records in storage.

item, data — Sometimes called a datum. A specific member of a data set denoted by a data element, for instance, Monday, the name of a specific member of the set of the days of a week. The week is the data element, Monday the data item, and 05 could be the data code.

item design — The set or collection of records or fields to compose an item as delineated, or the sequence in which fields are to be recorded; the type or group of characters to be allocated to each field.

item, elementary — In the COBOL system, a data item containing no subordinate terms.

item, line — An item of data, in data processing, that is on the same level as a given set of items for a given application and which could logically be printed on the same line on a printer page, for instance, stock number, item, quantity, and cost.

item list, first — *Same as* indication, group.

item separation symbol — A control symbol which indicates beginning of an item.

item size — 1. The magnitude of an item, usually expressed in numbers of words, characters, or blocks. 2. The number of characters in an item.

iterate — To execute successively a series of instructions, for instance, to execute repeatedly a loop in a routine until some condition is satisfied. An example would be to square each value of N from one to ten and accumulate the squared values before exiting the loop and continuing with the program. This is usually done with a series of arithmetic or logical operations on a digital computer.

iteration — 1. A single cycle of operations in a solution algorithm made up of a number of such cycles. 2. The technique of repeating a group of computer instructions. 3. One repetition of such a group.

iterative — Describing a procedure or process which repeatedly executes a series of operations until some condition is satisfied. An iterative procedure can be implemented by a loop in a routine.

iterative operation — The standard, usual, or automatic repetition of the solution, for example, of a set of equations with successive or changed combinations of initial conditions, or simply the use of different parameters and the use of the same computing program.

iterative process — A process for calculating a desired result by means of a repeating cycle of operations that comes closer and closer to the desired result; e.g., the arithmetical square root of N may be approximated by an iterative process using additions, subtractions, and divisions only.

Iverson notation — A special set of symbols developed by Dr. Kenneth Iverson to describe the formal structure of computer languages. Used in APL.

J

jack panel — *See* control panel.

jargon — A vocabulary used by a specific group of people but not generally nor universally accepted in fields other than the one in which it originated. The jargon of the computer industry is colloquially known as computerese.

JCL — Abbreviation for Job Control Language (IBM). A system which interprets instructions that are given to it by the user and then processes them in order to tell the central processor what to do with the user's program. Used on batch and time sharing systems.

jitter — 1. Short-time instability of a signal. The instability may be in either amplitude or phase, or both. The term is applied especially to signals reproduced on the screen of a cathode-ray tube. The term "tracking jitters" is used to describe minor variations in the pointing of an automatic-tracking radar. 2. The maximum peak-to-peak value of the timing variations in synchronous data expressed as a percentage of the ideal bit period.

job control language — Specifies an environment in which a job is to be run, and optional output desired.

job control program — A program that is called into storage to prepare each job or step to be run. Some of its functions are to assign i/o devices to certain symbolic names and set switches for program use.

job control, stacked — Under sequential-stacked job control, the jobs are performed in the sequence in which they are received by the system.

job control statements — Individual statements used to direct an operating system in its functions, as contrasted to information needed to process a job but not intended directly for the operating system itself.

job flow control — Job flow control includes: i/o transition between jobs and job segments, unit assignments, initial loading and initialization when the computer is first turned on; control between jobs; and control over the type of operation mode, ranging from simple stacked jobs through teleprocessing systems performing concurrent operations.

job library — A concatenation of user-identified partitioned data sets used as the primary source of load modules for a given job.

job management — Relates to specific functions that are performed by special programs such as job schedulers or master schedulers in tandem or combination.

job management procedure — A procedure to provide the facilities for job submission, resource allocation, job initiation, execution management, and job termination. The number of jobs active is limited only by available resources

job-oriented language — *See* language, job-oriented.

job-oriented terminal — 1. A terminal designed for a particular application. 2. A terminal specially designed to receive source data in an environment associated with the job to be performed, and capable of transmission to and from the system of which it is a part.

job output device — A device assigned by the operator for common use in recording output data for a series of jobs.

job processing — The reading of job control statements and data from an input stream, the initiating of job steps defined in the statements, and the writing of system output messages.

job-processing control — The job-processing control is the portion of the control program which starts job operations, assigns input/output units, and performs functions needed to proceed from one job to another.

job processing, master file — The master file contains the programs necessary for job processing. The programs in the master file are sectioned into four categories: (1) input/output drivers, (2) system programs, (3) utility routines, (4) library subroutines.

job-processing system — One monitor system is composed of a series of individual programs that work together to form a complete operating system. Manuals describe the total monitor system. They also contain a complete description of the primary operating system routines—the monitor program, executive program, system loader, system-preparation routine, and input-/output routines. The compiler, assemblers, utility routines, and library subroutines are described in the sense in which they are used as part of the monitor system. The complete description of these routines is provided in separate manuals. The words "monitor system," "operating system," and "system" are used interchangeably in manuals and refer to the monitor system (some systems).

job-program mode — In the job-program mode, both read/write and jump-storage protection is in effect. Therefore, job programs are limited entirely to those areas assigned by the executive. If the job program reads, writes, or jumps to an out-of-limits address, an interrupt will return control to the executive for remedial action. Read/jump protection allows the executive to stop the program at the point of error, terminate it, and provide diagnostic information to the programmer, thereby minimizing wasted time and smoothing the checkout process. A particular advantage of read/jump protection is that programs of a classified nature can be confidently run together; they are fully protected from audit (inadvertant or otherwise) by other programs.

job-request selection — The use of information contained in the job-request schedule to select the next job to be initiated. Selection is based on the priority and precedence assigned to the job, the sequence relationship of this job to other jobs with the same priority and precedence, and the availability of facilities required by the job.

job schedule — A control program that is used to examine the input work queue and to select the next job to be processed.

job scheduling, executive — Various executive programs will sequence the loading and execution of programs as directed by the user via system commands to the executive. Users can enter instructions at the teletypewriter, or commands may be supplied with the user program (as on cards placed at the beginning of a job deck). The control program function controls input job streams and system output, obtains input/output resources for jobs and job steps, attaches tasks corresponding to job steps, and otherwise regulates the use of the computing system by jobs.

job statement control — Individual statements used to direct an operating system in its functions, as contrasted to information needed to process a job, but not intended directly for the operating system itself.

job step — A job step consists of the external specifications for work that is to be done as a task or set of tasks. It is also used to denote the set of all tasks which have their origin in a job step specification. A job stream consists of a set of computer jobs or job steps in an input queue awaiting initiation and processing.

join gate — *Same as* gate, OR.

joint denial gate — *Same as* gate, NOR.

JOSS (johnniac open-shop system) — A time-sharing language developed by the Rand Corporation to make quick calculations that were too complicated for a calculator.

joystick — The stick or lever that can be

tilted in various directions to control or indicate direction of movement of cursors, game activities, and other movement or measurement.

jump — The jump is a departure from the normal one-step incrementing of the program counter. By forcing a new value or address into the program counter, the next instruction can be fetched from an arbitrary location, either farther ahead or behind. A program jump can be used to go from the main program to a subroutine, from a subroutine back to the main program, or from the end of a short routine back to the beginning of the same routine to form a loop. *Also see* branch.

jump, conditional — *See* branch, conditional.

jump instruction — A computer instruction causing a jump in the sequence of instructions. *See* branch.

jump instruction, conditional — *Same as* branch, conditional.

jump instruction, conditional transfer — *See* branch, conditional.

jump instruction, unconditional — *See* branch, unconditional.

jump operation — The computer departs from the regular sequence of instruction executions and jumps to another routine or program, or even some preceding or forward instructions to alter control, repeat a process or loop, etc.

jump to subroutine instructions — Some systems offer special jump instructions that jump to subroutines and return via addresses stored in the E register. This method of return via a hardware register decreases subroutine and interrupt overhead. Using a register also permits subroutines to be executed in ROM.

jump, unconditional — *See* branch, unconditional.

junction hole — *Same as* control punch.

junk — A slang expression that refers to garbled or otherwise unintelligible sequence of signals or other data, especially as received from a communications channel, i.e., hash or garbage.

justification — The act of adjusting, arranging, or shifting digits to the left or right to fit a prescribed pattern.

justified margin — Arrangement of data or type printed on pages in a manner such that the left or right end characters of each horizontal line lie in the same column.

justified, right hand — When a quantity in storage or in a register has no zeros in the low order (right hand) positions it is considered right hand justified.

justify — 1. To adjust exactly, as by spacing; to align a set of characters horizontally (or vertically) to right or left margins. To develop exact format or spacing in words, fields, items, or data as designed by context of exact specifications. 2. To move a data item so that a particular part of the item assumes a particular position relative to some reference point in a storage medium; for instance, to adjust the print on a printed page so that the left, right, or both margins are aligned; also to shift the item in a register to position specifically the most or least significant digit.

justify, right — To format a right margin for the type on a printed page. More difficult and expensive than left justification.

juxtaposition — The positioning or placing of items adjacent to each other or side by side.

K

K — A symbol which is equivalent to the numeral 1024. For example, 8 K would be equivalent to 8192.

Kansas City Standard, audio cassette — Early standardization has been of great benefit to personal computing. A meeting of manufacturers and technical editors in Kansas City produced the so-called "Kansas City Standard" for computer data encoding on standard audio cassettes using standard cassette recorders. The computer interface required is simple and inexpensive. By using audio cassettes, a hobbyist can easily store long programs, such as a BASIC interpreter, and load them into his computer in less than 30 seconds.

If the data transfer rate of a cassette is too slow, the computer hobbyist has his choice of several floppy disk systems that have been mated to the S-100 bus.

Karnaugh map — A tabular arrangement which facilitates combination and elimination of duplicate logical functions by listing similar logical expressions.

KCS — An abbreviation for 1000 characters per second. The generally accepted measurement of data transmission speed.

key — 1. A group of characters usually forming a field, utilized in the identification or location of an item. 2. A marked lever manually operated for copying a character, e.g. typewriter paper-tape perforater, card punch manual keyboard, digitizer or manual word generator. 3. That part of a word, record, file, etc., by which it is identified or controlled. 4. The field by which a file of records is sorted into order, e.g. the key for a file of employee records by a number, department, or letter.

key, activate — *Same as* button, initiate.

key, actual — A data item, in the COBOL language, which can be used for a machine address and which will express the location of a record in a storage medium.

keyboard — A device for the encoding of data by key depression, which causes the generation of the selected code element.

keyboard and display control — Refers to various systems that provide up to 64-key (and more) strobing, key debounce, 2-key rollover protection, multiple key buffering, and character display buffers with automatic segment/digit strobing.

keyboard, ANSI — The American National Standards Institute keyboard is a typewriter-standard unit that offers a choice of upper-case characters only or upper-case and lower-case combined. By contrast, the Data Communications (ASR-33) keyboard offers only upper-case and some punched-tape control functions.

keyboard, ASR type (automatic send-receive) — This is modeled after the standardized teletypewriter unit, a 33-compatible alphanumeric device. The control characters are used for special functions such as moving the cursor or shifting the keyboard into a mode for defining or calling symbols.

keyboard classes — Keyboards fall into two basic types—alphanumeric and numeric. Alphanumeric keyboards are used for word processing, text processing, data processing, and teleprocessing. Numeric-only keyboards are used on Touch-Tone telephones, accounting machines and calculators. The Touch-Tone telephone has come into significant use as a calculator and data input and voice output device.

keyboard, companion — An auxiliary keyboard device which is usually located remotely from the main unit.

keyboard components layout — Most available keyboards incorporate single-contact switches followed by an encoder to eliminate the effect of noise and switch bounce and convert the key closures into ASCII. There are two types of key arrangements, typewriter and data entry. The latter, a calculator-style alphabetic arrangement and numeric keypad, provides greater speed and lower error rates for nontypists. For users who touch-type long text messages, the typing layout proves superior. In either system, be sure keytops are dished inward to home the typist's fingers.

keyboard computer — A computer, the input of which employs a keyboard, possibly an electric typewriter.

keyboard contact bounce — The momentary (and decreasing) rebounds occurring between two contact surfaces suddenly thrust together before they attain firm closure. As a switch rating, bounce is stated as a time interval required for reaching firm closure after the initial closure.

keyboard control keys — On most crt terminals, control keys move and control the cursor, switch the terminal from one application to another, switch the communication disciplines, and cause the performance of other functions.

keyboard features — Keyboards are the part of the terminal that interfaces with the operator; they should be designed in a manner that makes the operator as comfortable and efficient as possible. The most important design features are layout, N-key rollover, edit keys, function keys, numeric pad, and control keys.

keyboard function keys — Many suppliers offer terminal function keys that make it possible to strike one or two keys to call out strings of characters and formats,

Courtesy DatagraphiX, Inc.

Keyboard labels.

send a unique distinct code to the computer which may represent any amount of data, and to conveniently activate the terminal peripherals.

keyboard inquiry — Interrogation of program progress, storage contents, or other information by keyboard maneuvering.

keyboard labels — Generally, labels can be placed on special keys to identify user-defined escape and other sequences called up by individual keys.

keyboard lockout — An interlock feature that prevents sending from the keyboard while the tape transmitter or another station is sending on the circuit.

keyboard send/receive set (KSR) — A combination transmitter and receiver with transmission capability from keyboard only.

key, carriage restore — A button which returns the printer carriage to the start position.

key-driven — Any device for translating information into machine-sensible form, which requires an operator to depress a key for each character, is said to be key-driven.

keyed sequential access method (KSAM) — A file structure and a group of library routines which together allow users to directly read records from a file base on content of key fields, or in sequential order, based on the ordering of key field contents.

key, index — As regards indexing, a field within an entry that is used to locate the entry. For example, surnames are the key field for the entries of a telephone directory.

keying error, rate of — Ratio of number of alphabetic signals incorrectly transmitted to the number of alphabetic signals of the message.

key, initiate — *See* button, initiate.

key, load — A control key, or similar manual device, which is used to input data or instructions into a computer or control system.

key, major — The most significant key in a record.

keypad — A small keyboard or section of a keyboard containing a smaller number of keys, generally those used on simple calculators. These 10, 12, or 16-key units are often the simplest input devices to microcomputers or function as an extension of ASCII keyboards to permit more extensive computational capability.

keypad, numeric — On some systems this is used in alternate-keypad mode. Numeral, decimal point, and enter keys transmit unique escape sequences, distinguishing them from alphanumeric keys.

keypunch — 1. A special device to record information in cards or tape by punching holes in the cards or tape to represent letters, digits, and special characters. 2. To operate a device for punching holes in cards or tape.

keypunch and verifier operator — Employees who operate numerical and alphabetical keypunch and verifying machines to transcribe routine or easily identified data from various documents onto punched cards.

key, single cycle — A push button on printers, which causes an additional line to be printed despite an end-of-form indication.

key, symbolic — In COBOL, contrast with actual key.

keytape — A device used to record data directly onto magnetic tape. Consists of a tape drive, keyboard, control and logic circuitry, and occasionally other input devices such as adding machines or paper tape readers.

key, tape load — A specific control push button which causes the first tape unit to read and transfer data into internal storage until the interrecord gap is sensed, at which time the internal storage is read for the first instruction.

key-verify — To use the punch-card machine known as a verifier, which has a keyboard to make sure that the information supposed to be punched in a punch card has actually been properly punched. The machine signals when the punched hole and the depressed key disagree.

keyword — Refers to the word in a high-level language statement line that defines the primary type of operation to be performed.

keyword-in-context index (KWIC) — The keyword-in-context index lists available programs arranged alphabetically by the keywords in the program titles. There is an index entry for each significant keyword in the title. Certain words are not accepted as indexing words but will be printed as part of the title.

A KWIC index is prepared by highlighting each keyword of the title in the context of words on either side of it and aligning the keywords of all titles alphabetically in a vertical column.

keywords — The most informative words in a title or document which describe the content of that document; the significant words.

kilo — A prefix meaning one thousand. Its abbreviation is K; e.g., 8K means 8000. In computer use it may also refer to the power of two closest to a number; e.g., 4K word memory is actually 4096 words.

kilobauds — New and higher capacity data channels. For special applications, some data channels capable of 20 kilobauds have been placed in service.

kilobit — One thousand binary digits.

kilomega — A prefix meaning one billion; e.g., a kilomegacycle means one billion cycles (same as billicycle and gigacycle), and a kilomegabit means one billion bits (same as billibit).

kilomegabit — One thousand million binary digits or one billion binary digits, such as a one-billion-bit storage device.

kit, breadboard — In general, a collection of parts and sockets, and full instructions, designed for insertion into a breadboard. These usually come with an assortment of sockets for custom circuitry. A number of circuit kits are available which allow the user to add special functions to the modular microcomputer system. Such kits are available for interfacing to ASCII keyboards, to 8-bit parallel TTL input/output sources, to the ASR33, and to other makes of printers.

kit, major system — A major system kit is a complete stand-alone system for writing, debugging, and executing programs on one of the major microprocessors. Unlike other microcomputer systems, these kits include not only the processor and memory but have complete sets of low cost peripherals. These standard systems come with an alphanumeric crt display, an ASCII keyboard, and two cassette tape units. Many also incorporate a number of other features, the most significant being universal system buses which allow memory and peripherals to be used as the basis of microcomputer systems using many types of processors with both 8- and 16-bit processors accommodated by simply plugging in a new CPU module. Such kits become a development tool for the new microprocessor.

kludge — A computer mimic or humorous term indicating the black box or computer. A kludge is slang for, or representation of, an endearment of the pet computer, i.e., "our kludge."

KSAM — Abbreviation for Keyed Sequential Access Method.

KSR — Abbreviation for Keyboard Send-/Receive. A combination teletypewriter transmitter and receiver with transmission capability from keyboard only.

KWIC — Abbreviation for Key Word In Context.

L

label — 1. A set of symbols used to identify or describe an item, record, message, or file. Occasionally it may be the same as the address in storage. 2. To assign a symbol, acronym, or word, as a means of identification, to a body of data, tape, card deck, block, etc.; to create a specialized associated record or filing "handle."

label, file — A set of alphanumeric characters that uniquely identifies the contents of a particular roll of magnetic tape or a portion of magnetic tape. The file label is written on magnetic tape as a block which contains the file name, reel number, date written, and date expired.

label, interior — A label accompanying the data it identifies. As in the case of magnetic tape, the interior labels are usually read by the computer under the control of a program.

label, operational — Tape files are identified, as far as the operator is concerned, by means of an operational label.

label record — A record used to identify the contents of a file or reel of magnetic tape.

labels, future — Future labels are labels which are referenced by the programmer in the operand field of a statement and have not been defined previously. Since an address cannot be assigned to this reference, the label is put into a symbol table as an unassigned label, accompanied by the address of the command which referenced it.

labels, tab — Those particular labels which are part of a continuous form and thus can feed through a tabulator or printer. After printing, the labels can be detached and affixed to a product, envelope, etc.

label, tape — A tape label consists of two blocks. The first block is an installation tape number which should be assigned on introducing a new reel of tape into the system. This number never changes. The second block identifies the information which will follow on the tape and contains dating information that will be used by special programs to further identify the tape, and to protect information from being destroyed prematurely.

label, trailer — The end-of-tape file record that lists summary information concerning that file.

language — A defined set of characters that is used to form symbols, words, etc., and the rules for combining these into meaningful communications, e.g., English, French, ALGOL, FORTRAN, COBOL, etc.

language, absolute — *Same as* machine language.

language, algebraic — A language which uses symbols and letters, both Greek and English, to express relations, variables, constants, parameters, operators, operands, and mathematical or logical relations. Each algebra has its own set of rules and is designed to delineate situations, relations, operations, and equalities and inequalities.

language, algorithmic — An arithmetic language by which numerical procedures may be precisely presented to a computer in a standard form. The language is intended not only as a means of directly presenting any numerical procedure to any suitable computer for which a compiler exists, but also as a means of communicating numerical procedures among individuals.

The language itself is the result of international cooperation to obtain a standardized algorithmic language. The

International Algebraic Language is the forerunner of ALGOL.

language, artificial — A language specifically designed for ease of communication in a particular area of endeavor, but one that is not yet natural to that area. This is contrasted with a natural language which has evolved through long usage.

language, command — A source language which is usually structured with procedural instructions. Such a language has capabilities of causing the execution of many functions, most of which are basic or used repetitively.

language, common — A language or macrocode which can be read or written by many different machines or by various groups of users.

language, common business-oriented — A specific language by which business data-processing procedures may be precisely described in a standard form. The language is intended not only as a means for directly presenting any business program to any suitable computer for which a compiler exists, but also as a means of communicating such procedures among individuals. (Synonymous with COBOL.)

language, common machine — A machine-sensible information representation which is common to a related group of data-processing machines.

language, common (OCR) — Universally acceptable language for optical character readers (OCR) approved by most manufacturers and which usually includes commonly accepted character shapes.

language, computer-dependent — *Same as* language, machine-oriented.

language, computer-oriented — A related term for a programming language requiring a low degree of translation. Such programs usually run very efficiently on a related computer but require very extensive translation or compiling on another variety of computer.

language, computer-sensitive — A computer programming language which is dependent totally or in some part upon the type of machine that is to execute programs written in the language.

language, conversational — A language utilizing a near-English character set which facilitates communication between the computer and the user. For example, BASIC is one of the more common conversational languages.

language converter — A data-processing device designed to change one form of data, i.e., microfilm, strip chart, etc., into another (punch card, paper tape, etc.).

language, FORTRAN — *See* FORTRAN.

language, higher order — A computer programming language that is less dependent on the limitations of a specific computer, for instance, pseudolanguages; problem oriented languages; languages common to most computer systems, such as ALGOL, FORTRAN, and COBOL; and the assembly languages.

Language, International Algebraic — The forerunner of ALGOL. Abbreviated IAL.

language interpreter — A general term for any processor, assembler, or other routine that accepts statements in one language and produces equivalent statements in another language. (Illustration page 276.)

language, interpretive — A special program writing language which translates and executes each source language expression serially, i.e., before translating and executing the following one, much as an interpreter of languages or speeches might do.

language, job-oriented — Specific types of programming languages which are means of communicating instructions to equipment by using terms distinctly pertinent to the area or type of job which is being processed.

language list, assembly — A listing that contains the symbolic instructions equivalent to the binary-code output of the compiler. This assembly-output listing is useful as a debugging aid. By including certain pseudo-operation codes in in-line assembly language, the assembly-language output can be assembled by the assembler (if output is obtained on either cards, paper tape, or magnetic tape). This will allow modification of programs at the assembly-language level.

language listing, symbolic-assembly — This binary output program of the compiler is optional at compile time. The listing contains the symbolic instructions equivalent to the binary-code output of the compiler. This assembly language output listing is useful as a debugging aid. By including certain pseudo-operation codes in "in-line" assembly language, the assembly language output can be assembled by the assembler (if output is obtained on either cards, paper tape, or magnetic tape). This will allow modification of programs at the assembly language level.

language, list-processing — A language developed by symbol manipulation used in construction of compilers, in simulations, etc.

language, low-level — A language close to the machine code of a computer, whose instructions usually bear a one-to-one relationship with machine code.

language, machine — Information recorded in a form that may be made available to a computer; e.g. punched paper tape may contain information available to a machine, whereas the same information in the form of printed characters on a page is not available to a machine.

language, machine-independent — A programming language which is not written for application or use with any specific computer system or class of computers. Such languages are usually problem-oriented and widely accepted, such as FORTRAN, COBOL, ALGOL, etc.

language, machine-oriented — A system for expressing information that is intelligible to a specific machine; e.g., a computer or class of computers. Such a language may include instructions that define and direct machine operations, and information to be recorded or acted upon by these machine operations.

language, meta — A formal language which uses special symbols to describe the syntax of computer languages, for example, Backus normal form.

language, native — A communication language or coding between machine units or modules which is peculiar to or usable for a particular class or brand of equipment.

language, natural — A language whose rules reflect and describe current usage rather than prescribed usage.

language, object — A language which is the output of an automatic coding routine. Usually object language and machine language are the same; however, a series of steps in an automatic coding system may involve the object language of one step serving as a source language for the next step, and so forth.

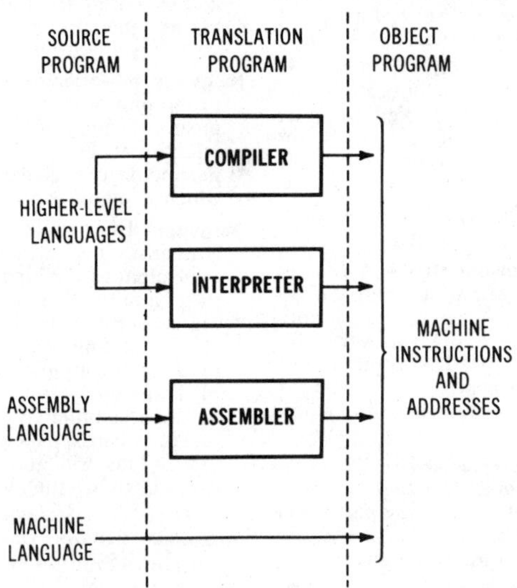

Language interpreter.

language, original — *See* language, source.

language, problem — *Same as* language, problem-oriented.

language, problem-oriented — A machine-independent language where one needs only to state the problem, not the how of solution. (Contrasted with procedure-oriented language.)

language, procedure-oriented — A machine-independent language which describes how the process of solving the problem is to be carried out, e.g., FORTRAN. (Contrasted with problem-oriented language.)

language, program — A language, not a machine language, which is used to express computer programs such as assembly, symbolic machine, macroassembly, procedure-oriented, problem-oriented, algebraic, string-manipulation, multipurpose, list processing, etc.

language, programming — A specific language used to prepare computer programs.

language, pseudo — *See* language, artificial.

language rules — Rules basically designed to: prevent the programmer from making nonsensical or disallowed statements of computer operations and to allow a "shorthand" for commonly made code sequences.

languages, list processing — Specific languages developed by symbol manipulation and used primarily as research tools rather than for production programming. Most have proved valuable in construction of compilers and in simulation of human problem solving.

language, source — The original form in which a program is prepared prior to processing by the machine.

languages, time sharing — *See* time sharing languages.

languages, user-oriented (time sharing) — *See* time sharing user oriented languages.

language, symbolic — The discipline that treats formal logic by means of a formalized artificial language or symbolic calculus, whose purpose is to avoid the ambiguities and logical inadequacies of natural languages. Advantages of the symbolic method are greater exactness of formulation, and power to deal with complex material.

language, synthetic — A pseudocode or symbolic language. A fabricated language.

language, target — The language into which some other language is to be properly translated.

language translation — The translation of information from one language to another.

language translator — 1. A program used to convert a language to equivalent statements in another computer language, usually for a different computer. 2. A routine which aids in the performance of natural language translations such as French to English. 3. Any assembler or compiling program which brings forth same or equivalent output from human-readable statements.

large-scale integration — The accumulation of a large number of circuits (say 1000 to 10,000) on a single chip of semiconductor. Characteristic of many CPU circuits and memories introduced since 1970.

laser — Acronym for Light Amplification by Stimulation of Emission of Radiation. An amplifier and generator of coherent energy in the optical, or light, region of the spectrum. Sometimes called an optical maser.

laser COM — Laser Computer Output Microfilm. Pertaining to products that combine laser and dry-film technologies to cause the laser to write directly on microfilm to produce instantaneous micrographic storage without intermediate steps.

latch — A device or circuit that maintains an assumed position or condition until it is reset to its former state by external means.

latch, bistable — A type of flip-flop that can be enabled to store a logical one or a logical zero. One bistable latch device is commonly used in memory and register circuits for the storage of each bit.

latching — Arrangement whereby a circuit is held in position, e.g., in read-out equipment, until previous operating circuits are ready to change this circuit. Also called locking.

latency — In a serial storage device, the time required to locate the first bit (or character) in a particular storage location. Access time for such a device includes latency plus the time to read out or write in a complete word.

latency code, minimum — *Same as* minimum-access code.

latency time — 1. The time lag between the completion of instruction staticizing and the initiation of the movement of data from its storage location. 2. The rotational delay time from a disk file or a drum file.

latest start dates, PERT — Used in estimating the completion date of a particular task. Each job is arranged to start as late as possible so that the entire task is completed on the required date.

layout — The overall plan or design, such as schematics, flowcharts, diagrams, format for card columns or fields, outline of the procedure, makeup of a book or document, etc.

layout character — *See* character, layout.

layout, data — *See* data layout.

layout, record — *See* record layout.

LCD — Abbreviation for Liquid-Crystal Display. A liquid-crystal display consists of a thin sandwich, or cell, of two glass plates with sealed edges, containing nematic liquid-crystal material. Transparent electrodes are deposited on the inner surfaces of the glass plate in the shape or shapes of the segments and areas that form the display. When voltage is applied to the front and back electrodes, the molecular orientation of the liquid-crystal material between them is altered, modifying the amount of light that can pass through it.

LDM — Abbreviation for Line-Driver Modem.

LDRI — Abbreviation for Low Data-Rate Input.

LDT — Abbreviation for Logic Design Translator.

leader — 1. A record that precedes a group of detail records, giving information about the group not present in the detail records, e.g., beginning of batch 17. 2. An unused or blank length of tape at the beginning of a reel of tape preceding the start of the recorded data.

leader record — A specific record containing the description of information contained in a classification or group of records, which follow this initial document.

leading control — A title or short definition of a control group of records which appears in front of each such group.

leapfrog test — A program designed to discover computer malfunctions. It is characterized by performing a series of arithmetical or logical operations on one group of storage locations, transferring itself to another group of storage locations, checking the correctness of the transfer, and beginning the series of operations all over again.

learning, computer — That process by which computers modify programs according to their own memory or experience, i.e., changes of logic paths, parameter values. An example is the now famous chess-playing computer. In process-control, an analog computer can alter its parameters by a continuous process according to temperatures or other gauge reports it receives. Examples are adaptive autopilots for aircraft, which explore different alternatives.

learning, machine — The capability of a device to improve its performance based on its past performance.

learning program — *See* program, learning.

leased circuit data transmission service — A service whereby a circuit (or circuits) of the public data network is made available to a user or group of users for their exclusive use. Where only two data circuit-terminating equipments are involved, it is known as a point-to-point facility; where more than two are involved, it is known as a multipoint facility.

least frequently used memory — Abbreviated LFU memory. When information must be read into main memory, other already resident information must be overwritten. Several algorithms may be used to decide which page or segment of memory is to be overwritten. The LFU algorithm replaces the area which is being or has been accessed the least.

least recently used memory — An algorithm for determining which page or segment of main memory is to be overwritten based on the length of time since the last access to that memory. Abbreviated LRU memory.

least significant character — The character in the rightmost position in a number or a word.

least significant digit — The significant digit contributing the smallest quantity to the value of a numeral.

left justified — Data is left justified when the left-hand digit or character (or its sign) occupies the left-hand position of the space allotted for that data.

left justify — To format a left margin for the type on a printed page. Typewriters produce left justified copy.

leg — A course or path taken in a routine from one branch point to the next.

legal retrieval — *See* retrieval, legal.

length — The number of bits or other characters in a word.

length, block — The total number of records, words, or characters contained in one block.

length, double — Pertaining to twice the normal length of a unit of data or a storage device in a given computing system; e.g., a double-length register would have the capacity to store twice as much data as a single-length or normal register; a double-length word would have twice the number of characters or digits as a normal or single-length word.

length, field — The physical extent of a field. On a punch card it refers to the number of columns. On a tape it refers to bit positions.

length, fixed — *See* fixed length.

length, gap — The dimension of the gap of a head measured from one pole face to the other. In longitudinal recording, the gap length can be defined as the dimension of the gap in the direction of tape travel.

length, interrecord gap — The length of the unused recording area between records written by the unit.

length, record — The number of characters necessary to contain all the information in a record.

length, register — The number of digits, characters, or bits that a register can store.

length, string — The number of records in a string.

length, variable — The number of characters which may be available in a particular storage location or data element. Since it is variable, it is possible that each successive block may have a different, varying number of words, but the word packing density usually remains constant.

length, word — *See* word length.

letter — One of a set of symbols combined to represent written words.

letter code — In the Baudot code, the function that causes machines to shift to lower case. This code is used to "rub-out" errors in tape, as it is made up of intelligence pulses in each of the five channels, and causes receiving machines to print nothing.

letter shift — A function performed by a teleprinter, when initiated by the letters-shift character, that causes the machine to shift from upper case to lower case.

level — 1. A COBOL term indicating the status of one data item relative to another; indicates whether one item includes subsequent ones or whether, as reflected in the numbering scheme which must follow certain rules, data items are independent of each other. 2. The number of bits in each character of an information coding system. 3. The number of discrete signal elements which can be transmitted in a given modulation scheme.

level, activity — The value taken by a structural variable in an intermediate or final solution to a programming problem.

level, addressing — *See* addressing level.

level, circuit noise — The circuit noise level at any point in a transmission system is the ratio of the circuit noise at that point to some arbitrary amount of circuit noise chosen as a reference. This ratio is usually expressed in decibels above reference noise, abbreviated dBm, signifying the reading of a circuit noise meter, or in adjusted decibels, abbreviated dBa, signifying circuit noise-meter reading adjusted to represent interfering effect under specified conditions.

level, data — *See* data level.

level, graphetic — An example is a character, either handwritten or printed, usually then capable of being copied, reproduced, transmitted, or manipulated by an ordered set of pulses. It is said to be a representation at a graphetic level.

level indicator — In the COBOL system, a symbol or level-number used in a data division entry to indicate level. For example, FD is a level indicator.

level-number — A numeric level indicator.

level of addressing — *See* address, indirect.

level, overload — The operating limit of a system, component, etc.; that point at which operation ceases to be satisfactory as a result of signal distortion, overheating, damage, etc.

levels, source language — Especially in ALGOL several levels of source languages are noted. Provisions are made for the use of reference level, several publication levels, and many hardware levels.

level status blocks — *See* level status register.

level status register — In some systems, level registers are replicated on each priority level and are also called level status blocks (LSB). The LSB contains the execution time essence of a task and is available to the program in execution.

lexeme — The written word, particle, or stem that denotes the meaning.

lexicon — A vocabulary, not necessarily in alphabetical order, with definitions or explanations for all terms.

LFU — *See* least frequently used memory.

librarian — A program that creates, maintains, and makes available the collection of programs, routines, and data that make up an operating system. Librarian functions may include system generation and system editing.

librarian, magnetic-tape — Arranges the installation program in acceptable formats on the library tape. While the librarian provides the information needed by the system supervisor to automatically manipulate the running of one program after the other, features within the librarian allow the programmer to control the sequence in which the program will be run.

librarian program — The librarian-program portion of the control function provides maintenance of library programs used as part of the operating system. The library may be stored on a single secondary storage unit, or it may be distributed over several different storage units. In either case, the librarian program keeps this library up to date by adding, deleting, and modifying as required. User-written application programs can be incorporated into the library along with subroutines, the control program itself, compilers, sort/merge, and utility programs.

library — 1. A collection of documents for study or reference. 2. Groups of proven or standard routines, or parts of routines, used to solve problems with or without further modification to adapt to particular individual provisions; most often stored in symbolic coding or compiler programs and subdivided into various volumes according to type of arithmetic or computational technique used.

library, COBOL — A COBOL library processor is available to store and retrieve data and procedure division descriptions, and it provides dynamic dumps of specified data areas to facilitate program checkout.

library, electronic — A general-purpose library system in which the user sits at a computer terminal and calls for viewing on a crt of any author, title, or subject in the card catalog, or any page of any book in the library.

library facilities — A basic library of general-purpose software is furnished by manufacturers to perform common jobs; to this the user can add his own often-used programs and routines. Programs in the library can be conveniently assembled into an object program by the use of macroinstructions.

library file editor — Some systems use a library file editor that lets users combine compiler or assembler output to form binary libraries. The result is a set of central, updatable program libraries that eliminate program duplication.

library, input/output — Relieves the programmer of having to be familiar with the functional and instructional differences among the peripherals.

library, job — One or several partitioned data sets used as the primary source of object programs for a definite job and a source of runable programs from which all or most of the necessary programs for a given job will be selected.

library, macro — An assemblage of prepared and specialized but unparticularized programs, which are located in mass storage and which may be selectively found by an assembler which reads them, particularizes them by replacing general parameters with specific parameters, and incorporates them into programs.

library, object program — *See* library, program.

library, program — An assemblage or organized set of computer programs, routines, or common or specifically designed software, i.e., catalog of program titles, abstracts, etc., reels of magnetic tapes or cabinets of punched cards, tapes containing various programs or routines, source or object programs classified for intelligence or retrieval, etc.

library programming — A distinct program to form an assemblage or to retrieve from or input to a library, instead of one written for a particular job. It is a program which may be called simply by reference to an index of library program names.

library, routine — 1. An ordered set or collection of standard and proven routines and subroutines, usually stored in relative or symbolic coding, by which problems and parts of problems may be solved. (A library may be subdivided into various volumes, such as floating-decimal, double-precision, or complex, according to the type of arithmetic employed by the subroutines.) 2. A checked-out routine which may be incorporated into a larger routine and is maintained in a library as an aid to programmers. 3. A routine for building and maintaining a library of special programs and subroutines. It is capable of inserting, deleting, changing, or replacing routines in the library. With this routine, the library may be altered at will to conform to individual customer requirements.

library, subroutine — A set of standard and proven subroutines which is kept on file for use at any time.

library tapes — Library tapes will have tape labels, skip records, and CM's (control marks) exactly as outlined for data tapes. However, the programs themselves must be stored on magnetic tape according to a particular format. Library tapes may contain two types of intermixed formats—standard format (running programs as set up by the librarian), and debugging format (this includes check data as well as the programs to be checked). Various CM's are used in this intermixing of formats.

library tracks — Tracks used to store reference data, such as titles, key words, document numbers, etc., on tapes, drums, disks, or mass storage devices.

library, user — A basic library of general-purpose software is furnished by manufacturers to perform common jobs; to this the user can add his own often-used programs and routines. Programs in the library can be conveniently assembled into an object program by the use of macroinstructions.

LIFO — Acronym for Last In First Out. 1. Refers to push-down-stack procedures; a buffer procedure. 2. A queue discipline wherein the newest entry in a queue or file is the first to be removed.

light-A — A control-panel light which monitors the A-register and signals parity check errors.

light-B — A control-panel light which monitors the B-register and signals parity check errors.

light, check — A control-panel indicator light which indicates parity errors or arithmetic overflow conditions.

light gun — *See* light pen.

light, logic — *See* logic light.

light pen — 1. A hand-held light-sensing device that detects the crt beam when pointed toward a portion of the screen. Routines are provided to allow the user to point the light pen at objects or instructions on the screen for identification or control purposes. In addition, a facility may be provided for light-pen tracking, which allows the user to point at a tracking object displayed on the screen and move it rapidly anywhere across the screen. 2. A hand-held reader for bar-code labels and tags.

light pen attention — An interruption generated by a light pen when it senses light on the screen of a crt display device.

light, ready — An indicator light on the display panel which, when on, indicates that a piece of equipment is ready for operation.

light stability — In optical character recognition (OCR), the resistance to change of color of the image when exposed to radiant energy.

light, storage — The light on a control console panel which indicates that a parity check error has occurred on a character as it was read into storage.

light, tape — A light usually found on the control console which indicates an error during the read or write cycle.

light, thermal — A display signal which is visible to machine operators when internal equipment temperature is higher than a designed level.

limit check — *See* check, limit.

limited — A word often attached to another word or term to indicate the particular machine activity that needs the most time, e.g., tape-limited, input-limited, computer-limited, etc.

limited, computer — *See* computer limited.

limited, computer (sorting) — A sort program in which the execution time of the internal instructions determines the elapsed time required to sort.

limited, input — The time that the central processing unit waits for delivery of input items. This restricts the speed of the operation.

limited, input/output — On buffered computers, a section of a routine in which the time required for computation is exceeded by the time required for input-/output operations.

limited, output — The speed restriction on a process or on equipment which causes other operations to await the completion of an output operation. This causes other equipment to have idle time.

limited, printer — The restrictions on a process due to the slowness or inadequacy of the printing equipment. Other operations must await the completion of the printing unit.

limited, tape — Just as some computers are limited to the slower speeds of cards for adequate performance, others are bound or limited in performance speeds by the time required for reading, writing, or punching tapes. When computers execute various types of business or large batch data processing, and much of the time is used in moving tapes, the computer or processor must wait and is said to be tape limited.

limiter — A device that reduces the power of an electrical signal when it exceeds a specified value. The amount of reduction or compression increases with an increase of the input power.

limit, priority — The upper bound to the priority list for dispatching or designing a priority rating to various tasks or subtasks, i.e., active, inactive, top priority, lowest priority, or batch processing.

limits, high-low — The maximum and minimum values of data expected. These values are used to check the program and results.

limits, scanning — The action of comparing input variables against either prestored or calculated high and/or low limits to determine if an alarm condition is present.

linear equation — An equation whose left-hand side and right-hand side are both linear functions of the variables. Such an equation can always be put in the form f(x, y, z, . . .)=c, where f is a linear function and c is a constant.

linear programming — 1. A technique used in mathematics and operations research to find a best solution for a certain type of problem; e.g., to determine the ratio of quantities to mix, blend, select, etc., for an optimum mixture. Sometimes called optimum programming and mathematical programming. 2. The analysis of problems in which the linear function of a number of variables is to be maximized (or minimized) when those variables are subject to a number of constraints in the form of linear inequalities, or the solution of these problems. 3. A technique of mathematics and operations research for solving certain kinds of problems involving many variables, where a best value or set of best values is to be found. This technique is not to be confused with computer programming, although problems using the technique may be programmed on a computer. Linear programming is most likely to be feasible when the quantity to be optimized, sometimes called the objective function, can be stated as a mathematical expression in terms of the various activities within the system, and when this expression is simply proportional to the measure of the activities, i.e., is linear, and when all the restrictions are also linear.

linear programming (product mix) — Given a set of raw materials with given characteristics and a given set of market prices for finished products, linear programming will indicate how these raw materials should be combined to produce the highest possible profits for the company. Blending of gasoline is an example of this type of application.

linear programming, resource allocation — Linear programming (LP) is a mathematical technique in which the best allocation of limited resources may be determined by manipulation of a series of linear equations. Each factor in the problem is evaluated against all other factors in relation to the long-range goals, yielding optimum paths of action for management consideration.

linear programming (transportation) — Given a large number of warehouses with limited capacities and a large number of distributers with known demands, linear programming enables the design of a shipping schedule that will minimize total costs.

linear search — A symbol table search that examines each item starting with the first item and proceeding sequentially.

linear selection — One of the methods of selecting memory or input-output devices that dedicates one address line per chip selection. This results in overlapping memory, noncontiguous memory.

linear unit — A device which follows the rules of mathematical linearity, i.e., in which the change in output due to a change in input is proportional to the magnitude of that change and does not depend on the values of the other inputs, i.e., adders, scalers, and integrating amplifiers, whereas multipliers and function generators are often designed as nonlinear.

line-B — *Same as* index register.

line, character spacing reference — *See* character-spacing reference line.

line, code — A single instruction, usually written on one line in a code for a specific computer, to solve a problem. This instruction is usually stored as a whole in the program register of the computer while it is executed, and it may contain one or more addresses of registers or storage locations in the computer where numbers or machine words are to be obtained or sent, and one or more operations to be executed. (Synonymous with program line.)

line conditioning — The process by which the telephone company maintains the quality of a specific, privately leased line to a certain standard of permissible delay distortion and signal attenuation. AT&T has two types of conditioning referred to as C and D. There are five categories of C conditioning (C1 through C5) and two categories of D conditioning (D1 and D2). C conditioning attempts to equalize the drop in signal voltage and envelope delay for all frequencies transmitted; D conditioning controls the signal-to-noise ratio and harmonic distortion. Both may be used on the same communication channel.

line, control — *See* control line.

line-control block — Abbreviated LCB. An area of main storage containing control data for operations on a line. The LCB can be divided into several groups of fields; most of these groups can be identified as generalized control blocks.

line-control procedures — Information transmitted over a communication line contains both data and control characters. Line-control procedures, which increase transmission efficiency by establishing rules of protocol between transmitter and receiver, include ASCII, SDLC, and BSC disciplines. BSC (Binary Synchronous Control) and SDLC (Synchronous Data Link Control) are the industry standards for synchronous transmission. For asynchronous transmission, ASCII procedures are the industry standard. Line-control procedures are generally implemented in software, but the choice of a particular line-control procedure depends on the hardware and transmission technique required.

line control unit — A multiplier or line control computer—a special-purpose computer for controlling input and output from communication lines when these lines are not directly accessed to the computer.

line, delay — A device capable of retarding a pulse of energy between input and output, based on the properties of materials, circuit parameters, or mechanical devices. Examples of delay lines are material media such as mercury, in which sonic patterns may be propagated in time; lumped-constant electrical lines; coaxial cables; transmission lines; and recirculating magnetic-drum loops.

line, delay, register — *See* register, delay line.

line discipline — Procedures that act to adjust the operating parameters of transmission systems to achieve correct or desired line control; includes considerations of contention, polling, queuing priority, etc.

line distortion — As data in the form of analog signals is sent down a line between modems, it suffers from the effects of envelope delay and amplitude distortion. Signals of different frequencies are delayed or attenuated by differing amounts as they are transmitted. To compensate for these effects, two techniques are employed: line conditioning and modem equalization.

line drivers — *Same as* bus drivers, output.

line editor program — A program that allows additions, deletions, and corrections to be made to the text on a line by line basis.

line, end of — A machine code character which indicates the end or termination of a group of records.

line interface — In order for a computer to communicate over a particular line and with a particular terminal or another computer, the computer manufacturer must provide a communications interface to handle that specific line-terminal or line-computer combination. The line interface provides a way for the remote device (terminal or computer) to talk to the host computer site. It usually conforms to ASCII code and discipline, meets the electrical and logical requirements of the Electronic Industries Association (EIA) RS-232 standard, and connects to a modem or acoustic coupler at speeds between 110 and 9600 bits per second.

line item — An item of data, in data processing, that is on the same level as a given set of items for a given application and which could logically be printed on the same line on a printed page; for instance, stock number, item, quantity, and cost.

line keys, crt system — Keys for such functions as double space, print (to activate the printer), stop (to deactivate the printer), read (to display stored text), recall (to retrieve text from the "save" area of the diskette), save (to save a portion of text for later retrieval), store (to store text to diskette), line end (to eliminate text to the right of the cursor up to a full line), line enter (to spread text open or move text down for better framing), and page end (to clear the screen from the cursor position to the end of the displayed text).

line misregistration — The improper or unacceptable appearance of a line of characters or numerals in optical character recognition, usually so gauged on or with respect to the real or imaginary horizontal base line.

line noise — Noise originating in a transmission line.

line printer — A printing device which prints an entire line of data at a time and then advances to the next line. Such printers normally use rotating drums or chains on which the desired characters are engraved. Line printers operate much faster than character-at-a-time printers. They are normally associated with computers or medium to high-speed terminal services.

line printing — Printing one line of characters across a page, i.e. 100 or more characters simultaneously, as continuous paper advances line by line in one direction past type bars or a type cylinder that contains all characters in all positions.

line protocol — Line protocol is a set of rules for controlling the sequence of transmissions on a synchronous line. These rules explain bidding for a line, methods for positive and negative acknowledgements, requests for retransmissions, receiver and transmitter timeout constraints, and other controls necessary for the orderly flow of message blocks from one terminal to another.

line skew — A type of line misregistration, in which a string of characters to be read by an optical character reader appears in a uniformly slanted or skewed condition with respect to a real or imaginary base line.

lines, select — The core memory circuits on various equipment which carry selecting coincident pulses. These pulses

Courtesy Radio Shack

Line printer.

select the core position which is to be used in the ensuing operation.

line status — The status of a communication line, such as receive, transmit, or control.

line, voice-grade — The common communications line used in normal telephone communications. It is an essential part of most communications systems involving computers and data transmission. A typical voice-grade line has a bandwidth of up to 3000 hertz.

link — 1. That part of a subprogram that connects it with the main program. 2. A process to gather or unite two or more separately written, assembled, or compiled programs or routines into various single operational entities, i.e., to complete linkage. Some computer systems have special programs called linkage editors to correct address components into symbols or to perform relocation to avoid overlapping.

linkable program — A program with extra information in the object module which defines internal and external symbols. The loader uses this information to connect, or link, external references to internal symbols.

linkage — 1. Specific instructions that are related to the entry and re-entry of closed subroutines. 2. The instructions which connect one program to another, providing continuity of execution between the programs.

linkage, communications — Common-carrier equipment provided by such companies as American Telephone and Telegraph, Western Union, and American Cable and Radio provide high-speed communication facilities for two-way transmission of data between the central computer site and remotely located input/output units. Transactions originating at these remote points are conveyed along linkage wires directly to the computer where they are immediately evaluated and processed. Then the result is returned to the originator and other appropriate distant points. The whole transaction is handled in a matter of seconds.

linkage editor — A standard service routine to convert outputs of assemblers or compilers to forms which can be loaded and executed by combining separately developed object modules, or incorporating all or parts of previously processed load modules into a new load module. The linkage editor also replaces or inserts control sections, creates overlay facilities, or resolves symbolic cross references between various input modules. Usually linkage editors are run before programs are ready for load in OS, DOS, or TOS operations, i.e., disk and tape operating systems.

linkage macroinstruction — *See* macroinstruction, linkage.

link bit — A specific one-bit diagnostic register which contains an indicator for overflow from the accumulator, and usually other registers, and which can be tested under program control.

link, communication — The physical means of connecting one location to another for the purpose of transmitting information.

link control — An agreed procedure on how message data passes between the terminal and the processor and which ensures message integrity by including an error-control discipline.

link control procedure — A procedure by which data is transferred in an orderly and accurate manner over a communications link. Abbreviated LCP.

link, data — Equipment that permits the transmission of information in data format.

linked sequential file — A file that has an access interface identical to that used for the various sequential devices (magnetic tape, line printer, card reader, etc.). Consistency between sequential device and disk is achieved with the linked sequential file.

linked subroutine — *Same as* subroutine, closed.

link group — Consists of those links which employ the same multiplex equipments.

linking loader — A loader used to link compiled/assembled programs, routines, and subroutines and transform the results into tasks.

linking loader executive — An executive program that connects different program segments so they may be run in the computer as one unit.

linking, program — *See* program linking.

link overflow — *See* overflow, link.

LISP — Acronym for LISt Processing. An interpretive language, developed for manipulation of symbolic strings of recursive data, i.e., used to develop higher-level languages.

list — 1. A string of items written in a meaningful format that designates quantities to be transmitted for input-/output. 2. An individual series of similar items, as the names of cities and the current population of each, i.e., a one-dimensional array of numbers. 3. To print every relevant item of input data.

list, assembly — A printed list that is the byproduct of an assembly procedure. It lists in logical instruction sequence all details of a routine, showing the coded and symbolic location next to the actual notations established by the assembly procedure. This listing is highly useful in the debugging of a routine.

list, chained — A set of items each of which contains an identifier for the next item in a particular order, but such order does not have any particular relation to the order in which they are stored.

list, command — A sequence of steps, generated by the CPU, pertaining to the performance of an i/o operation.

list, first item — *Same as* indication, group.

list, indexed — A FORTRAN instruction in read and write statements to form special indexed arrays.

listing, assembly-language — This binary-output program of the compiler is optional at compile time. The listing contains the symbolic instructions equivalent to the binary-code output of the compiler. This assembly-output listing is useful as a debugging aid. By including certain pseudo-operation codes in in-line assembly language, the assembly-language output can be assembled by the assembler (if output is obtained on either cards, paper tape, or magnetic tape). This will allow modification of programs at the assembly-language level.

listing, proof — *See* proof listing.

listing, selective — The output printing of data which needs various sets of predetermined criteria.

list, memory-map — The memory map is a listing of all variable names, array names, and constants used by the program with their relative address assignments. The listing will include all subroutines called and the last location when called (some systems).

list, polling — *See* polling list.

list processing — A specific technique for programming, using list structures to organize storage. Computer storage is organized into many lists or structures of data items, each with a symbolic name, a leader, starting record, and number of entries.

list processing languages — Specific languages developed by symbol manipulation and used primarily as research tools rather than for production programming. Most have proved valuable in construction of compilers and in simulation of problem solving. Other uses have been generalized and verification of mathematical proofs, pattern recognition, information retrieval, algebraic manipulation, heuristic programming, and exploration of new programming languages.

list processing program — A particular type of program called EULER is an extension of ALGOL 60 and has specific list processing capabilities.

list, punch-down — A list of items where the last item entered is the first item of the list, and the relative position of the other items is pushed back one.

list, push-down — *Same as* list, punch-down.

list, push-up — A list of items where each item is entered at the end of the list, and the other items maintain their same relative position in the list.

list structure — A specific set of data items combined because each element contains the address of the successor item or element, i.e., a predecessor item or element. Such lists grow in size according to the limits of fixed storage capacity, and it is relatively simple to insert or delete data items anywhere in a list structure.

literal — A word, number, or symbol which names, describes, or defines itself and not something else that it might represent.

literature search — A systematic and exhaustive search for published material on a specific subject, and usually the preparation of abstracts on that material.

live keyboard — A keyboard that lets users interact with the system while a program is running to examine or change program variables or perform keyboard calculations.

load — To enter or add to the internal storage of a computer various information from auxiliary, intermediate, or external storage.

load-and-go — A computer operation and compiling technique in which the pseudo-language is directly converted to machine language and the program run without an output machine-language program being created.

load cards — The punched cards which contain the program instructions and the constant values.

loader — A program required on practically all systems that loads the user's program along with required system routines into the central processor for execution; used on time-sharing, real-time, and batch systems. Loaders transfer the object code from some external medium (tape or disk) into RAM. Linking loaders can, in addition, string different program modules together, and a relocation feature permits loading into different address blocks, as they are assigned by the translator. Obviously, in this case, loader and translator must be able to communicate.

loader, automatic — A loader program often implemented in a special ROM (read-only memory) that allows loading of binary paper tapes or the first record or sector of a mass-storage device. The program is equivalent to a bootstrap loader plus a binary loader. When an automatic loader is installed, it is seldom necessary to key in a bootstrap program to load the binary loader.

loader, binary — A program used to load a binary format, such as those produced by the binary-dump program, the link editor, or an assembler, into memory.

loader, bootstrap — *See* bootstrap loader.

loader, bootstrap (microprocessor) — Enables users to enter data or a program into the RAMs from a teletypewriter, paper tape, or keyboard, and execute the program from the RAMs. Often consists of a PROM that plugs into the phototyping board.

loader (FORTRAN) — The FORTRAN loader is a two-pass relocating loader that can load separately compiled programs into storage and complete the linkages between them.

loader, initial program — The procedure that causes the initial part of an operating system or other program to be loaded such that the program can then proceed under its own control. Contrast with bootstrap. Abbreviated IPL.

loader programs — Programs that take information being entered into the computer or coming from external memory and transfer it into the internal memory of the computer. They also help keep track of where the information is in memory.

loaders and linkage editors (microprocessors) — Loaders and linkage editors perform a number of services for the programmer. Generally they take machine code or object code as input, along with possible programmer commands, and produce the desired "memory image." Their characteristics are influenced by the available translators and the machine architecture. Relocating loaders are needed with assemblers that can generate relocatable object code. Linkage editors are needed when the assembly language allows for reference across object modules. If separately assembled (or compiled) subroutines are allowed, subroutine linkages must be accomplished. Loaders can be considered a form of translator.

loader, system — The system loader loads binary object programs output from compilations and assemblies into computer memory. The system loader is capable of loading binary main programs, binary subprograms, library subroutines, and input/output drivers. The linkage between these programs is performed automatically during loading. The system loader loads input/output drivers from the specified logical equipment for a program and performs all linkages within the monitor. Programs may be loaded from cards, paper tape, or from the master file. Intermixed programs may be loaded in part of each of these devices in one load operation. The loader is resident in upper computer memory and is capable of overlaying itself in part with library subroutines. Common data-storage areas are placed in the loader area to allow complete overlay of the loader. Thus, a program may use all of computer memory. No memory storage is lost because of the size of the loader (some systems).

loader types — A number of microcomputer loaders are available to complete various coding processes. Many types can be stored in ROMs. Assembled programs are often loaded into read-only memory. They can also be loaded into RAMs, in which case a bootstrap type is often used. A relocating loader automatically adjusts program addresses and loads the resulting instructions. Some loaders have linking capability that lets users employ routines with undefined labels. These types supply the missing cross-references between separate routines.

load facility — The hardware facility designed to allow program loading.

loading, block — A technique for program loading in which the control or other sections of the program or program segment are loaded into adjacent positions in the main memory.

loading, bootstrap — 1. A particular routine placed in storage for the purpose of reading into storage another program, routine, or various data. 2. A single subprogram that loads a complete object program.

loading, dynamic program — The loading of a program module or routine into main memory through reference to it by a loaded executing program.

loading error — The error found in the output of the computer which came about as a result of a change in value of the load which was supplied.

loading, input — Amount of load imposed upon the sources supplying signals to the input.

loading, initial program — *See* program loading, initial.

loading-location misuse errors — A loading-location specification was made but no load or execute was specified; the loading location specified was not within the available range of memory; the loading location is assigned as the first available location.

loading procedure — System, object, and library routines are loaded in a similar manner. A program may have a fixed origin or may be relocatable. Fixed origin programs are loaded into the specified memory address. Programs are relocated by a base address initially set by the executive routine. After the main program has been loaded, any library subroutines or equipment drivers called will then be loaded. When all the necessary routines are in memory, the loader returns to the job processor.

loading, program — *See* program loading.

loading routine (bootstrap) — 1. A developed routine placed in storage for the purpose of reading into storage another program, routine, or various data. 2. A single subprogram that loads a complete object program.

loading routine, program — The procedure for inserting instructions and the constant values of the program into the computer.

load key — *See* key, load.

load key, tape — *See* key, tape load.

load mode — In load mode, data transmission is such that data delimiters are carried along with the data transmitted, as in contrast with move mode.

load on call — When a program is too large to fit into core memory of the central processing unit, sometimes it can be segmented so that some subprograms reside on the disk, to be loaded into core on call.

load point — The preset point at which magnetic tape is initially positioned under the read/write head to start reading or writing

load sharing — Computers placed in tandem (duplexing or triplexing) to share the peak-period load of a system.

local — In some systems, a mode in which data entered from the keyboard is displayed on the screen but is not transmitted on the communications line.

LOCAL — Acronym for Load On CALl.

local format storage — A method by which frequently used formats can be stored at a terminal controller instead of being repeatedly sent down the communications line.

local forms control — Abbreviated LFC. A system for off-line data-entry operations by diskette storage of fixed formats and data at the local site.

local loop — The service provided by the common carrier to connect a customer's location to a central office. This always includes the circuit and some circuit termination equipment, but may also include input/output equipment. Sometimes referred to as subscriber station.

local mode — The state of a data terminal equipment that cannot accept incoming calls or data because it is engaged in some internal activity.

local side — Data-terminal connections to input/output devices.

local validation and arithmetic — A data-reliability function which acts to ensure that entered data is error-free by the time it reaches the host computer. A variety of edit checks and arithmetic operations identify bad entries and verify totals, freeing the application program of error processing and the communications line of error messages. Control records indicating the appropriate checks for each field in a format may be stored in buffer memory or on diskette or disk at the terminal controller.

local variable — A variable whose name is known only to the subprogram to which it belongs.

locate — A tape is searched for the first occurrence of specific information.

location — A place in main memory or auxiliary storage where a unit of data may be stored or retrieved.

location, bit — A storage position on a record capable of storing one bit.

location counter — *Same as* register, control.

location, effective byte — The actual storage location pointed to by the effective virtual address of a byte addressing instruction.

location, effective double-word — The actual storage location pointed to by the effective virtual address of a double-word addressing instruction.

location, effective half-word — The storage location pointed to by the effective virtual address of a half-word addressing instruction.

location, effective word — The storage location pointed to by the effective virtual address of a word-addressing instruction.

location identifier — *See* identifier, location.

location, memory — A position in a computer storage device.

location, run — A routine which locates the correct run on a program tape, whether initiated by another routine or manually.

locations, protected — Locations reserved for special purposes, and in which data cannot be stored without undergoing a screening procedure to establish suitability for storage therein.

location, storage — A storage position holding one computer word, usually designated by a specific address or a specific register.

locking escape — *See* escape, locking.

locking shift character — *See* character, locking shift.

lock, memory write — A p-bit write-protect field optionally provided for each 512-word page of core memory addresses (some computers).

lockout — A portion of the buffer cycle in which the logic or arithmetic unit must cease operation or neither will be able to communicate with the memory unit.

lockout, keyboard — An interlock feature that prevents sending from the keyboard while the tape transmitter or another station is sending on the same circuit.

lockout module — An electronic circuit that prevents keying of more than one keyboard output signal at a time. When two or more keys are depressed simultaneously, it either accepts only the first signal registered or prevents entry of all signals and transmits an error signal to warn the operator.

lockout, write — In various time-sharing computers, a lockout prevents all programs (usually) from writing to any particular portion of a store, but still allows unimpeded reading of that part of storage by all concurrent programs.

lock-up table — A method of controlling the location to which a jump or transfer is made. It is used especially when there are a large number of alternatives, as in function evaluation in scientific computations.

log — 1. A record of everything pertinent to a machine run, including identification of the machine run, record of alteration, switch settings, identification of input and output tapes, copy of manual key-ins, identification of all stops, and a record of action taken on all stops. 2. To print or record one or more values. The values might be the instantaneous values of input variables, or averaged or calculated values.

logarithm — The logarithm of a number is the exponent indicating the power to which it is necessary to raise a given number, called the base, to produce the original number.

logger — A device that automatically records physical processes with respect to time.

loggers, system utilization — A program or a device that collects statistical information about how the system is operating.

logging, failure — An automatic procedure whereby the maintenance section of the monitor, acting on machine-check interrupts (immediately following error detection), records the system state. This log is an aid in diagnosing intermittent errors.

logging, interrupt — *See* interrupt logging.

logic — 1. The science that deals with the canons and criteria of validity in thought and demonstration; the science of the formal principles of reasoning. 2. The basic principles and applications of truth tables, the relationships of propositions, the interconnection of on-off circuit elements, etc., for mathematical computation in a computer.

logical AND — *Same as* gate, AND.

logical capabilities, FORTRAN IV — *See* FORTRAN IV logical capabilities.

logical comparison — The act of comparing A and B. The result of the execution of such an operation is 1, or yes, if A is the same as B, and 0, or no, if A is not the same as B (or vice versa).

logical connectives — The operators or words, such as AND, OR, OR ELSE, IF THEN, NEITHER NOR, and EXCEPT, that make new statements from given statements and also have the property that the truth or falsity of the new statements can be calculated from the truth or falsity of the given statements and the logical meaning of the operator.

logical data independence — The quality of a data-base environment that allows the conceptual or logical (as opposed to physical) structure of the data to be changed without affecting the programs that manipulate data that is not changed.

logical decision — 1. The choice or ability to choose between alternatives. Basically this amounts to an ability to answer yes or no with respect to certain fundamental questions involving equality and relative magnitude; e.g., in an inventory application, it is necessary to determine whether or not there has been an issue of a given stock item. 2. The operation of selecting alternative paths of flow depending on intermediate program data.

logical design — 1. The logic of the system, machine, or network. 2. Computer design from the viewpoint of data flow within the computer without consideration of the hardware.

logical diagram — A diagram representing logical elements and their interconnections without construction or engineering details. The graphic representation of the logic elements and their relations in a computer. The graphic presentation of logic processes which are to be performed in a distinct order to achieve a solution.

logical element — The smallest building block in a computer or data processing system that can be represented by logical operators in an appropriate system of symbolic logic. Typical logical elements are the AND gate and the OR gate; they can be represented as operators in a suitable symbolic logic.

logical expressions — *Same as* logic expressions.

logical file — 1. A data set that is composed of one or more logical open records. 2. A data file that has been described to the disk or tape operating systems through the use of a file-definition (DTF) macroinstruction. Note that a data file is described to the operating system through a different defining method. Operating system publications refer to a data file described in this different manner as a data set.

logical flowchart — A detailed solution of the work order in terms of the logic, or built-in operations and characteristics, of a specific machine. Concise symbolic notation is used to represent the information and describe the input, output, arithmetic, and logical operations involved. The chart indicates types of operations by use of a standard set of block symbols. A coding process normally follows the logical flowchart.

logical group instructions — A group of instructions that usually includes AND, OR, exclusive-OR, compare, and rotate or complement data in registers or in memory.

logical IF — A FORTRAN IV statement will execute when the logical expression is true, or will bypass the statement if it is false.

logical instruction — An instruction that carries out a logical operation, such as AND, OR, NOR.

logical multiply — *See* AND.

logical number — The number assigned to a peripheral unit during autoload or system generation time. This number can be altered whenever convenient, in contrast to a physical unit number.

logical operation — An operation in which a decision affecting the future sequence of instructions is automatically made by the computer. The decision is based upon comparisons between all or some of the characters in an arithmetic register, and their counterparts in any other register on a less than, equal to, or greater than basis; or, between certain characters on arithmetic registers and built-in standards. Also, a shifting operation in which the digits dropped off one end of a word are returned to the other in circular fashion. Operations on a word on a character-by-character basis without regard for other characters as in logical OR operations.

logical operations — The comparing, selecting, making references, matching, sorting, merging, etc., where in essence 1s and 0s (corresponding to yes's and no's) constitute the elements being operated on.

logical operator — A mathematical symbol that represents a mathematical process to be performed on an associated operand. In FORTRAN IV, an operation which acts on one or two logical variables or logical expressions. Such operators are AND, the logical product, OR, the logical sum, and NOT, the logical complement.

logical OR instructions — Specific Boolean logic operations performed between specified registers on a bit-by-bit basis. A logic 1 is left in the results register if any bit in any bit position of either register is a logic 1.

logical product — *Same as* gate, AND.

logical record — A record whose scope, direction, or length is governed by the specific nature of the information or data which it contains instead of by some feature or limitation of the storage device that holds it. Such records differ in size from the physical records in which they are contained. Physical records might be limited to a 400-character physical record size (example, an airline standard), but many logical records might require fewer or more than the limit.

logical relation — In assembler programming, a logical term in which two expressions are separated by a relational operator. The relational operators are EQ, GE, GT, LE, LT, and NE.

logical shift — *See* shift, circular.

logical sum — *See* sum, logical.

logical switch — An electronic device used for directing input cards to one of a number of outputs.

logical symbol — 1. A sign used as an operator to denote the particular operation to be performed on the associated variables. 2. A symbol used to graphically represent a logical element.

logical tracing — Tracing as performed only on jump or transfer instructions.

logical variable — In FORTRAN IV, a variable which may have only true or false value.

logic analysis — The delineation or determination of the specific steps required to produce the desired output or intelligence information from the given or ascertained input data.

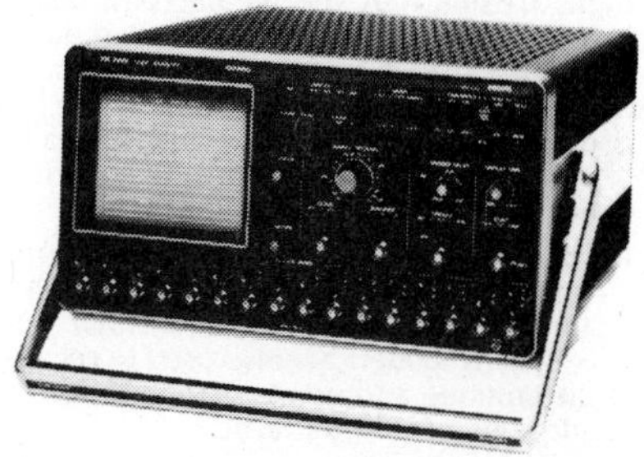

Courtesy Philips Test and Measuring Instruments, Inc.

Logic analyzer.

logic analyzers — Logic analyzers generally fall into three categories: state analyzers, timing analyzers, and trigger generators. State analyzers display digital data, in the form of 1s and 0s on a cathode-ray tube or via light-emitting diodes, in a word-versus-event format. This concentration on word sequences makes state analyzers useful in examining the functional behavior of binary systems. They are especially useful in the design of microprocessor-controlled digital products for examining the flow of command and data words on multiline buses.

logic, Boolean — A mathematical analysis of logic.

logic card — A group of electrical components and wiring circuitry mounted on a board which allows easy withdrawal from and replacement in a socket in the equipment. Each such card is related to a basic machine function, and, on discovery of a bug in that function, the card can be replaced.

logic chart — A flowchart of a program or portions of a program showing the major logical steps intended to solve a problem.

logic circuit — An electronic circuit that is used to complete a logical function. Some examples are: OR, NOR, AND, NAND and exclusive OR. The output of the circuit is dependent on the state (1 or 0) of the inputs.

logic comparison — *See* comparator.

logic convention, positive — Logic defined such that a logic 1, or high signal, corresponds to a more positive voltage level and a logic 0, or low signal, corresponds to a more negative voltage level.

logic decision — A specific decision made in a computing system or environment as a direct result of the internal organization of the system, but one of the binary or yes or no type, and basically relating to questions of equality, inequality, or relative magnitude.

logic decoder — A logic device that converts data from one number system to another (e.g., an octal-to-decimal decoder). Decoders are also used to recognize unique addresses, such as a device address, and bit patterns.

logic design — The specification of the working relations between the parts of a system in terms of symbolic logic and without primary regard for its hardware implementation.

logic diagram — A diagram that represents a logic design or its hardware implementation.

logic, double-rail — Each logic variable in these circuits is represented by a pair of electric lines. Three states can actually be assumed, such as zero, one, and undecided.

logic element — A device that performs a logic function.

logic element, sequential — *See* element, sequential logic.

logic expressions — A logic expression consists of logical constants, variable array elements, function references, and combinations of those operands, separated by logical operators and parentheses. A logical expression may contain arithmetic expressions, separated by relational operators, and separated by other elements specified by logical operators and parentheses. Logic expressions are most often used in logical IF statements but can also be used in logical assignment statements and as arguments of functions. The logical expression may take on only two values, true or false. When a logical expression appears in a FORTRAN statement, it is evaluated according to specified rules. It will always yield one of the two values, true or false.

logic, formal — An objective study of the structure, form, and design of valid arguments, and disregarding for this purpose the meaning and importance of the terms of the argument itself.

logic, hard-wired — A logic design that requires interconnection of numerous integrated circuits formed or wired for specific purposes and which are relatively unalterable. A hard-wired diode matrix is hard-wired logic, whereas a RAM, ROM, or CPU can be reprogrammed with little difficulty to change the purpose of operation. Hard-wired interconnections are usually completed by soldering or by printed circuits and are thus "hard-wired" in contrast to software solutions.

logic instruction — An instruction that executes an operation that is defined in symbolic logic, such as the operations AND, OR, NOR.

logic light — The control-console light which indicates that an error has occurred in an operation.

logic, machine — *See* machine logic.

logic, mathematical — Exact reasoning concerning nonnumerical relations by using symbols that are efficient in calculation.

logic multiply — A Boolean operation performed on two binary digits so that the result is one, if and only if both digits are one, and zero if either digit, or both, is a zero.

logic, negative — Logic in which the more negative voltage represents the 1 state and the less negative voltage represents the 0 state.

logic, N-level — A particular arrangement or design of gates connected in such a way that no more than N gates are in series in a specific component or frame.

logic operation — 1. Nonarithmetic operations that are expressible in terms of the propositional calculus or a two-valued

Boolean algebra operating on individual pairs of bits. 2. Sometimes, nonarithmetic operations, such as compare, shift, and jump.

logic probe — A logic-testing tool designed to give a direct readout of logic levels without the set-up and calibration time needed for logic analyzers and scopes. Logic probes use one or more lamps to indicate whether a point in a digital signal path is at a logic 1, a logic 0, or is toggling between these levels. Some units, for example, use three lamps—red for 1, white for 0, and blue for toggling. The relative brightness of the red and white lamps gives some indication of the duty cycle, and all lamps off indicates the absence of logic signals. Other units have a single lamp—on for 1, off for 0, and blinking for toggling. A constant half-brightness indication means no signal is present.

logic product — The result developed from the AND operation as contrasted with product arithmetic.

logic product gate — *Same as* gate, AND.

logic, programmed — The internal logic design which is alterable in accordance with a precompleted program which controls the various electronic interconnections of the gating elements; i.e., the instruction repertory can be electronically changed, or the machine capability can be matched to the problem requirement.

logic shift — A shift which is similar to a cyclic shift and which can affect all positions, i.e., a nonarithmetic shift.

logic spectrum, programmable — The programmable logic spectrum breaks down into two distinct categories—programmable logic devices and programmable logic systems. Each of these categories can be further broken down and ordered by the flexibility and capability of their individual elements. Programmable logic devices can be defined as relatively simple entities which, of themselves, do not comprise an entire computing system. Included in this category are random logic, FPLAs, PLAs, ROMs, EAROMs, RAMs, CAMs, and microprocessors.

logic states — The binary (1 or 0) values at the nodes of logic elements and ICs at a particular time. Also called logic signals.

logic sum — *See* sum, logical.

logic sum gate — *Same as* gate, OR.

logic symbol — 1. A symbol used to graphically represent a logic element. 2. A symbol used to represent a logic connective.

logic, symbolic — 1. The study of formal logic and mathematics by means of a special written language which seeks to avoid the ambiguity and inadequacy of ordinary language. 2. The mathematical concepts, techniques, and languages as used in definition (1), whatever their particular application or context.

logic system analyzer — A test instrument capable of monitoring the operation of a microprocessor-based system. The primary instrument for verification and troubleshooting in the design, manufacture, and field service of various microprocessor-based products.

logic, transistor-transistor — Abbreviated TTL. An integrated circuit in which two transistors are combined in one monolithic structure. These circuits are generally faster, easier to construct, and hence cheaper than DTL circuits.

logic types — The most common types of digital-logic families of elements are the transistor-transistor-logic (TTL), emitter-coupled logic (ECL), and metal-oxide-semiconductor (MOS) or complementary metal-oxide-semiconductor (CMOS) logic. Each of these families has its own set of parameters and applications, and each is encountered in many modern microprocessor applications. The TTL family has been the most widely used of the three families.

logic, variable — The internal logic design which is alterable in accordance with a completed program which controls the various electronic interconnections of the gating elements.

login — A procedure for user access to a system involving identification, access control, and exchange of network information between user and system. Also called logon.

logout — A procedure for user exit from a system which frequently provides usage statistics to the user. Also called logoff.

log, real-time clock — This built-in clock is used for a wide variety of programming-time purposes. It can be used to log the receipt times of periodic real-time input data. Each input message and its receipt time may be recorded together. This clock is also used in connection with the preparation of statistical and analytical reports dealing with the frequency of certain transactions.

log, remote computing-system — The remote computing system maintains a log of operations that take place between the computer and each terminal. The log contains such information as the number of statements handled, the number and types of errors detected, and the volume of output produced. The information in the log can be used for various purposes. For example, the number of errors may indicate that additional training might be helpful. Similarly, if an individual terminal is busy, it might indicate the need for an additional terminal. If the cost of the system is shared among terminals according to usage, the information in the log can be used for billing purposes.

log, system — A data set in which job-related information, operational data, descriptions of unusual occurrences, commands, and messages to or from the operator may be stored. Abbreviated SYSLOG.

log word, interrupt — *See* interrupt log word.

longitudinal check — A system of error control based on the check that some preset rules for the formation of the group of bits in the same numerical order in all the character signals in a block are observed.

longitudinal circuit — A circuit formed by one telephone wire (or by two or more telephone wires in parallel) with the return through the earth or through any other conductors except those which are taken with the original wire or wires to form a metallic telephone circuit.

longitudinal parity check — The data line terminal at the transmitting end generates a longitudinal parity character during the transmission of the data characters. This is essentially a count for even parity of all of the bits in each one of the bit levels for all data characters in the message including the start-of-message code but not the end-of-message code. This same count is also being generated for the bits of the data characters entering the data-line terminal of the receiving end.

longitudinal redundance — A condition in which the bits in each track or row of a record do not total an even (or odd) number. The term is usually used to refer to records on magnetic tape, and a system can have either odd or even longitudinal parity.

longitudinal redundancy check — Abbreviated LRC. A system of parity checking for transmission errors. Data organized into blocks has a block-check or LRC character following the block. The LRC character is developed by forming a parity check on all bits in the same bit position in the block. This is equivalent to forming a parity bit for all bits located on each "channel" or "level" of paper or magnetic tape.

longitudinal transmission check — An even or odd parity check at fixed intervals during data transmission.

long word — *See* word, long.

look ahead — A feature of the CPU that permits the machine to mask an interrupt request until the following instruction has been completed. This is also a feature of adder circuits and ALUs that permits these devices to look ahead to anticipate that all carries generated are available for addition.

look-at table — Finding elements of a table by direct calculation rather than by a comparison search.

look-up — A procedure for obtaining the function value corresponding to an argument from a table of function values.

look-up instruction — An instruction designed to allow reference to systematically arranged, stored data.

look-up table — A collection of data in a form suitable for ready reference, frequently as stored in sequenced machine locations or written in the form of an array of rows and columns for easy entry, and in which an intersection of labeled rows and columns serves to locate a specific piece of data or information.

look-up, table, instruction — *See* instruction, table-look-up.

look-up, table, techniques — *See* table-look-up techniques.

loop — 1. The repeated execution of a series of instructions for a fixed number of times. 2. A coding technique in which a group of instructions is repeated, usually with modified instructions or modified data values. 3. A sequence of instructions that is repeated until a terminal condition prevails.

loopback test — A type of test in which signals are looped from a test center through a data set or loopback switch and back to the test center for measurement.

loop box — A register for modifying instructions in a loop.

loop, central processing unit (CPU) — The main routine or a control program and that which is associated with the control of the internal status of the processing unit, in contrast to those control programs of routines developed with terminals and file storage input-output.

loop, central scanning — A loop of instructions which determines which task is to be performed next. After each item of work is completed, control is transferred to the central scanning loop which searches for processing requests in order to determine which is the next item to be processed. The computer may cycle idly in the central scanning loop if no item requires attention, or it may go into a wait state which is interrupted if the need arises.

loop checking — A method of checking the accuracy of transmission of data in which the received data are returned to the sending end for comparison with the original data, which are stored there for this purpose.

loop, closed — A programming technique, system, or device to develop feedback of data for various control, modification, or checking purposes.

loop counter — A specific register used to implement high-speed loop branching, including simple instruction loops.

loop, dynamic — A specific loop stop consisting of a single jump instruction which causes a jump to itself. A loop stop is usually designed for operating convenience, such as to indicate an error.

loop, feedback — A closed signal path in which outputs are compared with desired values to obtain corrective commands.

loop, feedback control — A closed transmission path which includes an active transducer and consists of a forward path, a feedback path, and one or more mixing points arranged to maintain a prescribed relationship between the loop input and output signals.

loop feedback signal — That part of the loop output signal that is fed back to the input to produce the loop actuating signal.

loop, home — A specific operation involving only those input and output units associated with the local terminal, i.e., as when a teletypewriter is being used to punch a data tape while not connected to the computer.

looping — A computer operation in which a sequence of steps is repeated.

looping execution — The execution of the same set of instructions where for each execution some parameter or sets of parameters have undergone a change. Such change may be a new value for a variable, or addresses of various data may be modified, often through the use of an index register.

loop initialization — The instructions immediately prior to a loop proper which set addresses and/or data to their desired initial values.

loop input signal — An external signal applied to a feedback control loop in control systems.

loop, nesting — Nesting loops usually contain a loop of instructions which then also contains inner loops, nesting subroutines, outer loops, and rules and procedures relating to in and out procedures for each type.

loop, open — Pertaining to a control system in which there is no self-correcting action for misses of the desired operational condition as there is in a closed loop system.

loop, operation — A loop which has an associated set of instructions which restore modified instructions or data to their original or initial values at each entry to the loop, or a sequence of instructions which may be obeyed repetitively.

loop, rapid-access — A section of storage, particularly in drum, tape, or disk-storage units, which has much faster access than the remainder of the storage. Synonymous with revolver.

loop, recirculating — In drum computers, a small section of memory which has much faster access than the remainder of memory.

loop, self-checking — A self-checking loop assures the integrity of the i/o circuits of the control computer. A subroutine in the control computer compares the value received with the value transmitted. If the values are not identical, corrective action is taken.

loop, self-resetting — A loop that contains instructions restoring all locations affecting the operation of the loop to their initial condition as at entry of the loop.

loops, outside — Outside loops are most often considered for nested loops when loops within it are entirely contained. The outside loop executes the control parameters that are being held constant while the current loop is being carried through possible values.

loop, stop — A small closed loop usually designed and used for operator convenience, i.e., to indicate an error, improper use, or special result.

loop storage — *See* storage, loop.

loop stores, delay — A method of storing information by transmitting bits or no-bits serially through a loop.

loop system, closed — A system in which the computer controls an external program or process without human intervention. An example of a closed-loop process-control system would be a computer connected directly to instrumentation through a digital-to-analog converter to complete the feedback loop. The computer could then take control directly of the process by setting controllers, activating switches, valves, etc.

loop termination — Many ways exist to terminate loops. For example, when reading data from cards, the cards can simply be let to run out, causing a hang-up or stop. More commonly, however, in reading data, the last card contains some particular code number which may be tested and used to terminate the loop. Most often, the first card contains the number of data sets to be read, and this number is put into a counter location, and tested for zero to end the loop.

loop testing — Those instructions of a loop which determine when the loop function has been completed.

loop transfer function — The mathematical function expressing the relationship between the output of a properly terminated feedback loop system and the input.

loop update — The process of supplying current parameters associated with a particular loop for use by the control algorithm of that loop in calculating a new control output.

loss, gap — The loss in output attributable to the finite gap length of the reproduce head. The loss increases as the wavelength decreases, amounting to approximately 4 dB when the wavelength is equal to twice the gap length, and subsequently increases rapidly toward a complete extinction of output when the wavelength is approximately equal to 1.15 times the gap length.

loss, transmission — A general term used to denote a decrease in signal power in transmission from one point to another. Transmission loss is usually expressed in transmission units.

low-activity data processing — The processing of a limited number of input transactions against very large master files.

low order — Pertaining to the weight or significance assigned to the digits of a number; e.g., in the number 123456, the low order digit is 6. One may refer to the three low-order bits of a binary word as another example.

low-order digit — A digit that occupies a less significant position in a number.

low-order position — The rightmost position in a number or word.

low-performance equipments — Those equipments having insufficiently exacting characteristics to permit their use in trunk or link circuits. Such equipment may be employed in subscriber line circuits whenever it meets the line-circuit requirements.

low speed — Pertaining to data communications systems operating at speeds of less than 2400 bits per second.

LP — Abbreviation for Linear Programming. A mathematical technique whereby the best allocation of limited resources may be determined by manipulation of a series of linear equations. Each factor in the problem is evaluated against all other factors in relation to the long-range goals, thus yielding optimum parts of action for management consideration.

LPM — Abbreviation for Lines Per Minute.

LRC — Abbreviation for longitudinal redundancy check. An error-checking technique based on an accumulated Exclusive OR of transmitted characters. An LRC character is accumulated at both the sending and receiving stations during the transmission of a block. This accumulation is called the block-check character (BCC) and is transmitted as the last character in the block. The transmitted BCC is compared with the accumulated BCC character at the receiving station for an equal condition. An equal comparison indicates a good transmission of the previous block.

LRU — Abbreviation for Least Recently Used.

LSC — Abbreviation for Least Significant Character (right-most).

LSD — Abbreviation for Least Significant Digit (right-most).

LSI — Abbreviation for Large-Scale Integration. High-density integrated circuits for complex logic functions. LSI circuits can range up to several thousand transistors on a silicon chip with an area of one-tenth square inch or so.

LSI microprocessor — An LSI microprocessor is essentially a complete system on one chip, or at most a few chips. Sometimes called a microcomputer, the system normally consists of a CPU, a RAM, an i/o, and a ROM. The ROM is predesigned and can be customized by programming. In examining the semantics of microprocessing, it should be pointed out that the CPU was introduced first. Most people call the combination of CPU with a ROM and a RAM a microprocessor. Some LSI microprocessor systems are complete sets with no interfacing circuitry needed, and they contain a variety of LSI i/o circuits. Therefore, some industry people now call a completed system a microcomputer—a set of system-designed LSI circuits which have been programmed in the ROM to perform unique functions. All microcomputers contain a small memory which is satisfactory for any manual input, such as a keyboard.

M

MAC — Abbreviation for (a)—multiple access computer, (b) machine aided cognition, (c) memory assisted cognition. Most usually related to the government supported, large computing research and technique implemention being carried out at the Massachusetts Institute of Technology, and initially meaning, multiple access computer.

machinable — *See* data, machine readable.

machine address — An absolute, direct, unindexed address expressed as such, or resulting after indexing and other processing has been completed.

machine-available time — Power-on time less maintenance time.

machine check — 1. An automatic check. 2. A programmed check of machine functions.

machine-check indicator — A protective device that will be turned on when certain conditions arise within the machine. The machine can be programmed to stop, to run a separate correction routine, or to ignore the condition.

machine-check interruption — An interruption that occurs when the machine-checking circuits detect a machine error. Often, a system is then automatically switched to a diagnostic procedure.

machine code — 1. The absolute numbers, names, or symbols assigned by the machine designer to any part of the machine. 2. Same as operation code.

machine coding — *See* coding, machine.

machine cognition — Artificial perception in optical machine reading and pattern recognition. Certain machines have the capability of optically sensing a displayed character and selecting from a given repertoire of characters the specific character which is nearest in shape to the character which is displayed. The various shapes of characters are based on statistical norms, and if different shapes arise, new characters join the repertoire. This suggests a type of artificial learning, i.e., perception and interpretation are based on experience. Optical character recognition must be part of the scheme.

machine cycle — 1. The specific time interval in which a computer can perform a given number of operations. 2. The shortest complete process of action that is repeated in order. 3. The minimum length of time in which the foregoing can be performed.

machine error — A deviation from correctness in data resulting from an equipment failure.

machine fault time, no charge — The unproductive time due to computer fault such as nonduplication, transcribing error, input/output malfunction, and machine malfunction resulting in an incomplete run.

machine-independent — An adjective used to indicate that a procedure or a program is conceived, organized, or oriented without specific reference to the operating characteristics of any one data-processing system. Use of this adjective usually implies that the procedure or program is oriented or organized in terms of the logical nature of the problem, rather than in terms of the characteristics of the machine used in solving it.

machine-independent language — *See* language, machine-independent.

machine-independent solution — Procedures or programs that are organized in terms of the logical nature of the problem rather than in relation to or concerning the various computer equipment used to solve them or process them.

machine instruction — A code element, which upon machine recognition, causes a predefined sequence of operations.

machine instruction statements — The direct counterparts of machine instructions. A typical statement consists of tag, mnemonic operation code, one or more operand addresses (or literal operands), and one or more variant characters.

machine interruption, check — Machine-check interruptions are caused by the machine-checking circuits detecting a machine error. The system is automatically switched to a diagnostic procedure.

machine language — 1. A set of symbols, characters, or signs, and the rules for combining them, that conveys instructions or information to a computer. 2. A language for writing instructions in a form to be executed by the compiler; the language can be directly interpreted by the control section of the machine. 3. Information or data expressed in code that can be read directly, used, or written by the computer or peripheral machines without further processing.

machine-language code — A system of combinations of binary digits used by a given computer. (Synonymous with machine code, and contrasted with symbolic code.)

machine-language coding — Coding in the form in which instructions are executed by the computer. (Contrasted to relative, symbolic, and other nonmachine-language coding.)

machine language programming, ROM — Machine language programming involves programming in assembly language and then assembling by hand into the machine code, which is then entered into the control ROM (read only memory). This process is slow and cumbersome and requires the cooperation of the process engineer(s) and programmers experienced in assembly language programming. Programmers with these qualifications are expensive, and completion dates of this type of programming are difficult to predict. The only advantage of machine language programming is that the machine resources can be efficiently utilized.

machine learning — Concerns the ability of a device to improve its performance based on its past performance. (Related to artificial intelligence.)

machine-length word — *See* word, machine.

machine logic — 1. Built-in methods of problem approach and function execution; the way a system is designed to do its operations, what those operations are, and the type and form of data it can use internally. 2. The capability of an automatic data-processing machine to make decisions based upon the results of tests performed.

machine, object — The computer on which the object program is to be executed.

machine, (optical) character recognition — The technology of using a machine to sense and encode into a machine language characters that are written or printed to be read by human beings.

machine-oriented language — *See* language, machine-oriented.

machine-oriented programming system

—A system that uses a language that is oriented to the internal language of a specific computer. Systems that are considered to be machine oriented are assembly systems and macrosystems.

machine, pinboard — A machine in which pins are inserted in holes in a panel to call for a function or storage.

machine programming, cross-assembler — An improvement over machine language programming is the use of a cross-assembler running on a larger computer (possibly on a time-sharing system). This is mainly a programming aid, since it relieves the programmer of the tedious task of assembling the machine code. It also provides accurate hard copy of the programs and associated documentation. However, the computer running the cross-assembler is generally not local to the process controller, and so the programmer must make field patches between trips to his assembly computer.

machine readable — *See* data, machine readable.

machine-readable, data — *See* data, machine-readable.

machine-readable medium — The device or material which is used to convey data to a sensing device or unit such as punched cards or tapes.

machine recognizable — *See* data, machine readable.

machine run — The execution of one or several machine routines which are linked to form one operating unit.

machinery, computing — *See* computing machinery.

machine, scanning — A machine which facilitates the input of data. Two types of scanning machines are the magnetic-ink scanners and the optical scanners.

machine script — *See* data, machine readable.

machine, self-organizing — A class of machine that may be characterized loosely as containing a variable network in which the elements are organized by the machine itself, without external intervention, to meet criteria of successful operation. (Synonymous with self-organizing machine.)

machine sensible — *See* data, machine readable.

machine-sensible information — Information in a form that can be read by a specific machine.

machine, source — The computer on which the source program is translated into the object program.

machine-spoiled time — The wasted computer time due to a computer malfunction during production runs, i.e., part of down time.

machine time, available — The elapsed time when a computer is in operating condition, whether or not it is in use.

machine tool control — A powerful and versatile program for production of tapes for numerically controlled point-to-point and contouring machines.

machine tools, numerically controlled — Computer-controlled machinery used in manufacturing operations. Some numerically controlled machines use paper tape which has been prepared by a specially programmed computer to control the movements of complex machine tools. Computers can control drafting machines, conveyer belts, and many other complicated physical processes.

machine translation — The automatic transmission from one representation to another representation. The translation may involve codes, languages, or other systems of representation. (Related to automatic dictionary.)

machine, Turing — A mathematical abstraction of a device that operates to read from, write on, and move an infinite tape, thereby providing a model for computerlike procedures. The behavior of a Turing machine is specified by listing an alphabet, i.e., collection of symbols read and written, a set of internal states, and a mapping of an alphabet and internal states which determines what the symbol written and tape motion will be, and also what internal state will follow when the machine is in a given internal state and reads a given symbol.

machine, universal-Turing — A Turing machine that can simulate any other Turing machine.

machine word — A unit of information of a standard number of characters which a machine regularly handles in each transfer; e.g., a machine may regularly handle numbers or instructions in units of 36 binary digits; this is then the machine word. Related to word, information.

macro — Pertaining to a specific type of instruction in assembly language that is implemented in machine language by more than one machine-language instruction, e.g., a group of instructions often designed to serve as an additive command or group of commands.

macroassembler facilities — An assembler is available for use in the operating system in assembling object programs from source programs written in a flexible but easy-to-use symbolic language. The assembler language is a versatile, machine-oriented language that can be used for a variety of applications, both commercial and scientific. A number of facilities for assisting the programmer are provided by the assembler. These include macrofacilities as well as facilities for defining constants, for defining data-storage areas, for referring to files and storage locations symbolically, and for using literals.

macroassembly program — A language processor that accepts words, statements, and phrases to produce machine instructions. It is more than an assembly program because it has compiler powers. The macroassembler permits segmentation of a large program so that portions may be tested separately. It also provides extensive program analysis to aid in debugging.

macrocode — A coding system that assembles groups of computer instructions into single code words; the system therefore requires interpretation or translation so that an automatic computer can follow it.

macrocoding — Procedures for providing segments of coding which are used frequently throughout a program and can be defined at the beginning and used and referenced by a mnemonic code with parameters. This increases coding efficiency and readability of the program.

macrocommand — Programs that are formed by strings of standard, but related, commands. Such strings are usually brought into operation by means of a single macrocommand or instruction. Any group of frequently used commands or routines can be combined into a single macrocommand—and the many individual instructions thus become one.

macrodefinition — The specification of a macrooperation. This includes specifying the name of the macrooperation and the prototype cards, which indicate the fields which are to be fixed and the fields which are to be variable (substitutable arguments).

macrodefinition library — A macrodefinition stored in a program library; for example, the various manufacturer supplied supervisor and data management macrodefinitions.

macroexerciser — The repeated operation of supervising programs and other macroinstructions under a variety of conditions to find any program errors.

macroexpansion, conditional — A certain number of lines of coding within a macroinstruction will be included or excluded during expansion, depending upon certain conditions.

macroexpansion instruction — A statement in symbolic source language that is expanded by the assembler into one or more machine-language instructions, relieving the programmer of having to write out frequently occurring instruction sequences.

macroflowchart — Tables and charts utilized in designing the logic of a specific routine in which the various segments and subroutines of a program are represented by blocks.

macrogeneration — The many-for-one concept or process of generating several machine-language instructions from one macrostatement in source programs.

macroinstruction — An instruction consisting of a sequence of microinstructions which is inserted into the object routine for performing a specific operation.

macroinstruction, debug — A macroinstruction which generates a debugging or program testing capability within a particular program.

macroinstruction, exit — A supervising program macroinstruction that is the final instruction in an application program signifying that processing is complete. The supervising program takes the needed action such as releasing working storage blocks to return control to other processing.

macroinstruction, linkage — A macroinstruction that provides logical linkage between programs and subroutines and that will save data needed by another program.

macrolibrary — An assemblage of prepared and specialized but unparticularized programs which are located in mass storage and which may be selectively found by an assembler which reads them, particularizes them by replacing general parameters with specific parameters, and incorporates them into programs.

macro (macrocode or macroprogram) — A source-language statement, routine, or program that is understandable to a processor or compiler with or without aid of an interpretive routine. Production of many-for-one instructions in machine language; an open-ended sequence of machine instructions, may be linked to consecutive or closed subroutines.

macroparameter — The symbolic or literal that is in the operand part of a macrostatement and which will be substituted into specific instructions in the incomplete routine to develop a complete open subroutine.

macroprogramming — The process of writing machine-procedure statements in terms of macroinstructions.

macros, debug — Aids built into a program by the applications programmer, in addition to those supplied by the supervisory program. Debugging macros are a type of unit testing.

macros, programmer-defined — Segments of coding, which are used frequently throughout a program, can be defined at the beginning and used and referenced by a mnemonic code with parameters. This increases coding efficiency and readability of the program.

macrostatement number — A number that is associated with a single macrostatement so that the reference may be made to that statement.

macrosystem — A programming system with symbolic capabilities of an assembly system and the added capability of many-for-one or macroinstruction development.

macrotrace — An error detection aid such as main memory and file dumps, loggings, and simulators. A macrotrace records pertinent information when macroinstructions are being executed. The macrotrace can print out the record of macros or it can record them and also dump working storage and the needed registers.

magnetic-bubble storage — The storage medium of a bubble memory is a very thin layer of magnetic garnet material. This material has ribbon-shaped stripes (magnetic domains) in its natural state. When an external magnetic field is applied to the material, the domains contract into stubby cylinders, which look and behave like bubbles when viewed from the top through a microscope. Under the influence of external fields, the bubbles are manipulated to represent information bits.

magnetic card — *See* card, magnetic.

magnetic card storage — *See* card, magnetic.

magnetic cell — *See* cell, magnetic.

magnetic core — A magnetic material, usually toroidal in shape, which is pulsed or polarized by electric currents carried in a wire or wires wound around it. This device is capable of assuming and remaining at one of two conditions of magnetization, thus providing storage, gating, or switching functions.

magnetic document sorter-reader — Magnetic ink character recognition (MICR) was developed through the efforts of the banking profession and the machine manufacturers. Special properties of the ink used to print the data on the documents can be given small charges of electricity. As a by-product of reading these electrical impulses, the sorter transmits the data to the memory of the computer for processing.

magnetic head — A small electromagnet used for reading, recording, or erasing polarized spots on a magnetic surface. Also called R/W head, read head, write head.

magnetic ink — Ink containing particles of magnetic substance which can be detected or read by automatic devices; e.g., the ink used for printing on some bank checks for magnetic ink character recognition (MICR).

magnetic ink character recognition — *See* MICR (Magnetic Ink Character Recognition).

magnetic ink scanners — Machines which read numbers designed in a special type font and printed in a magnetic (iron oxide) ink.

magnetic memory — Any portion of the

memory that uses the magnetic properties of a material to store information.

magnetic recording — A method by which data is recorded by impressing a pattern of magnetization on a thin layer of magnetic material. In general, data is written by passing current through an inductive recording head as the tape (or disk) moves past the head, causing a flux transition to be recorded. The polarity of the flux reversal is determined by the direction of the current through the write head. As the tape is read, each flux reversal is sensed by the read head, and this causes peaks to occur in the read signal.

magnetic storage — A device (or devices) that utilizes the magnetic properties of materials to store information.

magnetic strip file — A file storage device which uses strips of material with surfaces that can be magnetized for the purpose of storing data.

magnetic tape — *See* tape, magnetic.

magnetic tape, file checks — Hardware checks for faulty tapes without loss of computer time or manual intervention.

magnetic-tape file operation — Magnetic tape is provided for the storage of information to accomplish sequential file updating. It is also used as an interim means of storage in off-line conversion of input to magnetic tape, and when working tapes are utilized in operations such as sorting.

magnetic-tape librarian — Arranges the installation program on the library tape in acceptable formats. While the librarian provides the information needed by the system supervisor to automatically manipulate the running of one program after the other, features within the librarian allow the programmer to control the actual sequence in which the program will be run.

magnetic-tape master file — *See* tape, master file.

magnetic-tape parity — During writing operations, the processor generates and transmits a parity bit with each character sent to a tape unit. As each character is written, it is automatically read back to verify the write operation. Each character within a record is checked for parity. At the end of each record, the handler writes a check character which is checked by the processor both for a vertical and an accumulated transverse parity.

magnetic-tape reader — A device capable of sensing information recorded on a magnetic tape in the form of a series of magnetized spots.

magnetic-tape sorting — A sort program that utilizes magnetic tapes for auxiliary storage during a sort.

magnetic tape station — A specific tape device which contains a magnetic-tape drive, including reading and writing heads, various controls, etc., for storage or transfer of data.

magnetic-tape storage — A storage device consisting of metal or plastic tape coated with magnetic material. Binary data are stored as small, magnetized spots arranged in column form across the width of the tape. A read/write head is usually associated with each row of magnetized spots so that one column can be read or written at a time as the tape is moved relative to the head.

magnetic-tape terminal — The magnetic-tape terminal converts the character pulses from serial-bit form to parallel-bit form while checking for odd parity and translating the code to the desired magnetic-tape code for entry into a buffer storage. The longitudinal parity count at the end of the message is verified. The integral part of the magnetic-tape terminal performing this function is called a coupler. The coupler of the magnetic-tape terminal performs a function similar to that of the data line terminal.

magnetic tape unit — The mechanism, normally used with a computer, that handles magnetic tape. It usually consists of a tape transport, reading or sensing and writing or recording heads, and associated electrical and electronic equipments. Most units may provide for tape to be wound and stored on reels; however, some units provide for the tape to be stored loosely in closed bins.

magnetostriction — A phenomenon in which certain materials increase in length in the direction of the magnetic field when subjected to such a field, and restore to their original length when demagnetized.

magnetostrictive delay line — A delay line that utilizes the physical principle of magnetostriction.

magnitude — The size of a quantity as distinct from its sign. Thus +10 and −10 have the same magnitude.

mag tape — The informal or slang expression for magnetic tape.

mail box — A set of locations in a common RAM storage area, an area reserved for data addressed to specific peripheral devices as well as other microprocessors in the immediate environment. Such an arrangement enables the coordinator CPU and the supplementary microprocessors to transfer data among themselves in an orderly fashion with minimal hardware.

main frame — The fundamental portion of a computer, i.e., the portion that contains the CPU and control elements of a computer system, as contrasted with peripheral or remote devices usually of an input-output or memory nature.

main memory — Usually the fastest storage device of a computer and the one from which instructions are executed. (Contrasted to auxiliary storage.)

main-memory mapping — On some units, the main memory is mapped for protection and relocation in four separate maps: system data, system code, user data, and user code. Memory mapping automatically reallocates the user code or the noncritical operating system code to alternate physical memory pages upon detection of a parity or uncorrectable memory error.

main operation — The primary application or designed procedure which the equipment performs. (Contrasts with by-product.)

main path — The principal course or line of direction taken by a computer in the execution of a routine, directed by the logic of the program and the nature of the data.

main program — *Same as* program, master control.

main routine — *Same* as program, master control.

main storage — Usually the fastest storage device of a computer and the one from which instructions are executed. (Contrasted with auxiliary storage.)

maintenance — 1. Tests, measurements, replacements, adjustments, and repairs intended to keep equipment or programs in satisfactory working order. 2. Updating of object program master files, selection of programs to be run, and control of checkout and production operation.

maintenance and operation of programs — Updating of object-program master files; selection of programs to be run, and control of checkout and production operation.

maintenance contracts, preventive — Preventive-maintenance contracts provide either resident field engineers or periodic visit arrangements that are tailored to the user's specific needs. Competent and experienced personnel ensure peak performance of all equipment.

maintenance, corrective — When a known fault or malfunction is repaired or corrected using adjustments or replacements after measurements and tests to locate, diagnose, and remove the fault, the service is called corrective maintenance.

maintenance, file — The periodic modification of a file to incorporate changes that occurred during a given period.

maintenance, preventive — Maintenance performed on a computer system to keep equipment in top operating condition and to preclude failures during production runs.

maintenance, program — *See* program maintenance.

maintenance program chain — An instruction set that will permit the deletion of records from a file.

maintenance, remedial — The maintenance performed by the contractor following equipment failure; therefore, remedial maintenance is performed, as required, on an unscheduled basis.

maintenance, routine — That machine time which is specifically devoted to repairs, and usually on some regular pattern or schedule, during which time preventive maintenance activities are also performed.

maintenance, scheduled — Maintenance activities that are performed in accordance with a planned or established schedule or timetable.

maintenance schedule, executive — *See* schedule, maintenance (executive).

maintenance standby time — Time during which the maintenance staff is on duty (and presumably being paid) but during which they are not engaged in scheduled maintenance, installation, repair, or supplementary maintenance, i.e., they may perform other tasks.

maintenance time — The elapsed time during scheduled working hours between the determination of a machine failure and placement of the equipment back into operation.

maintenance time, routine — *Same as* maintenance, routine.

maintenance time, supplementary — This time is designed to modify or change equipment in some major way to improve reliability, but usually without additions of equipment. This time is usually considered part of scheduled engineering time and/or scheduled maintenance time.

major cycle — 1. The maximum access time of a recirculating serial-storage element 2. A number of minor cycles.

majority — A logic operator which has the property that if P, Q, and R are statements, the function P, Q, R . . . is true if more than one-half of the statements are true and false if half or less are true, as applied in majority voting logic, which is a form of hardware organization used where reliability is required and involves duplicating all functional elements an odd number of times and supplying each duplicate element with identical parts and comparing the outputs. Majority is concerned with the fact that an output must be generated in identical form by an absolute majority of the redundant units in order to be considered valid.

majority decision element — *Same as* gate, majority decision.

majority decision gate — *See* gate, majority decision.

majority element — Related to a threshhold element or a decision element, if the weights are equal to 1 and the threshhold is equal to (n+1) /2, the element is called a majority element.

major key — The most significant key in a record.

major state — The control state of a computer. Major control states in some systems include fetch, defer, execute, etc.

major total — The summation or tally of the group of intermediate totals and, therefore, often called the most significant total.

make-break operation — A type of telegraph-circuit operation where the flow of current is interrupted as pulses are transmitted.

malfunction — A failure in the operation of the hardware of a computer.

malfunction, program-sensitive — A malfunction that occurs only when some unusual combination of program steps occurs.

malfunction routine — A routine used to locate a malfunction in a computer, or to aid in locating mistakes in a computer program. Thus, in general any routine specifically designed to aid in debugging or troubleshooting. (Related to debugging, definition 2.)

management, data base — A systematic approach to storing, updating, and retrieval of information stored as data items, usually in the form of records in a file, where many users, or even many remote installations, will use common data banks.

management information — The required data or program results considered the primary prerequisites for decision making with regard to business operations and control.

management information system — 1. Specific data-processing system that is designed to furnish management and supervisory personnel with information consisting of data that are desired, and which are fresh or with real-time speed. 2. A communications process in which data are recorded and processed for operational purposes. The problems are isolated for higher-level decision making, and information is fed back to top management to reflect the progress or lack of progress made in achieving major objectives.

management programming system data — A system of progress designed to provide an operator with the capability for querying, augmenting, and manipulating large computer-stored data bases in a natural language.

management science, EDP — The field of management science is extending the computer far beyond the automation of routine accounting operations and into the complex decision-making process of management. Through revolutionary computer programming techniques such as simulation, the objective, scientific approach of management science is providing increased management capability and control. In addition to the physical or operational processes like inventory management, product planning and control, resource allocation or market forecasting, this also includes the fiscal processes such as bond management, capital investment, risk analysis, profit planning, and product pricing. Manufacturer's broad resources are prepared to meet management's growing demand for this expanded capability and to extend the tradition of total systems capability into revolutionary data-processing techniques and applications.

management science operation research — *See* operations research (management science).

management, storage (time sharing) — *See* time sharing, storage management.

management system, total — *See* system, total management.

management workstation, financial — A station used in account and operations managers' duties. These stations tie into transaction-processing systems for monitoring of customer-account status, lines of credit, investigations, quality and timeliness of service delivery, etc.

management workstation, manufacturing — A station to give production planners and managers access to inventory and plant-capacity data, providing up-to-date reports on sales, distribution, special promotions, competitive activity, etc.

manager, computer center — A major function of data processing management, which requires constant attention, is to establish standards and maintain high quality. This means recruiting qualified personnel, training new employees, and updating existing ones. In addition, the manager must develop quantity and quality evaluation systems, develop job descriptions, and constantly review individual and group performance.

manager, operations — This individual is responsible for the operations and scheduled use of data processing equipment.

manager, programming — This individual is responsible for planning, scheduling, and supervising program development and maintenance work.

manager, systems analysis — This individual is responsible for planning, scheduling, and supervising systems analysis and design activities.

manifolding — Relates to the use of many sheets of paper and carbon sheets to produce multiple copies at single printings; i.e., four-part paper suggests an original and three copies.

manipulated variable — In a process that is desired to regulate some condition, a quantity or a condition that is altered by the computer in order to initiate a change in the value of the regulated condition.

manipulation, byte — The ability to manipulate, as individual instructions, groups of bits such as characters. A byte is considered to be eight bits in most cases, and forms either one character or two numerals.

manipulation data — *See* data, manipulation.

manipulative — *See* indexing, manipulative.

man-machine dialogue — A specialized form of interactive processing between people and machines in which the human operator carries on a dialogue with the computer through a console or some other device.

man-machine digital system — An organization of people, digital computers, and equipment to regulate and control events and achieve system objectives.

man-machine system — An organization of people, digital and/or analog computers, and equipment to regulate and control events and achieve system objectives.

mantissa — The fractional part of a logarithm; e.g., in the logarithm 2.5, 2 is the characteristic and 5 is the mantissa.

manual address switches — The external control switches used by the operator to select an address manually for read-off in the storage address display lights or to transfer the contents to a register without disturbing the address contents or area.

manual analysis — The generation of input and output test patterns by a test engineer or technician who studies the function or structure of a logic circuit.

manual control — The direction of a computer by means of manually operated switches.

manual entry — The manual insertion of data, usually from remote typewriter units or keyboard modules or terminals.

manual exchange — An exchange where calls are completed by an operator.

manual input — Entry of data into a computer or system by direct manual manipulation of a device.

manual-input unit — *See* input unit, manual.

manual load key — *See* key, load.

manual mode — *See* mode, manual.

manual operation — Processing of data in a system by direct manual techniques.

manual read — An operation in which the computer does the sensing of the contents or settings of manually set switches or registers.

many-for-one languages — The higher-level languages (COBOL, FORTRAN, APL, others) are many-for-one languages because they take a single functional statement and translate it into a series of instructions or subroutines in machine language, in contrast to a low-level (assembly) language in which statements translate on a one-for-one basis.

many-to-one — Relates to ratios or measured relations between members of one set and members of another set, in which correspondences are stated that two or more members of one set correspond to one (only) member of another set. When several expressions in a source language are equivalent to one statement in a target language, a many-to-one relation exists.

map — 1. To transform information from one form to another. 2. To establish a correspondence between the elements of one set and the elements of another set.

map, Karnaugh — A tabular arrangement which facilitates combination and elimination of duplicate logical functions by listing similar logical expressions.

map, memory — *See* memory map.

map, memory list — *See* memory map list.

mapped memory, multiprogramming — In a multiprogramming mapped-memory system, several blocks may be assigned to users. Each user has access only to his own block while he is connected. Blocks are correlated with multiple-mapping registers that translate addresses for various blocks. Before a user can go to work, a mapping register must be loaded to define his block.

mapping — 1. A transformation from one set to another set. 2. A correspondence.

mapping, data-base — A description of the way in which different record types (files) of a data base are associated with one another.

mapping, memory — An optional mode of computer operation wherein the eight high-order bits of any virtual address greater than 15 are replaced by an alternative value, thus providing for dynamic relocatability of programs (some computers).

mapping mode — The mode of computer operation in which virtual addresses above 15 are transformed through the memory map so that they become references to actual main memory locations (some computers).

maps, status — A status report of programs and i/o operations—usually in tabular form.

map, storage — *See* storage map.

margin — 1. The difference between the actual operating point and the point where improper operation will occur. 2. Also called range or printing range. In telegraphy, the interval between limits on a scale, usually arbitrary, in which printing is error-free.

marginal check — A preventive-maintenance procedure in which certain operating conditions (e.g. supply voltage or frequency) are varied about their nominal values in order to detect and locate incipient defective parts.

marginal checking — A means of testing circuits for incipient or intermittent failures by varying the voltages applied to the circuit.

marginal cost — The rate of change of cost as a function of quantity.

marginal error — Such errors irregularly occur in tapes, and most often disappear simply because the writing is done over a slightly different section of tapes.

marginal revenue — The rates of change of income as a function of quantity.

marginal test — A preventive-maintenance procedure in which certain operating conditions are varied about their normal values in order to detect and locate incipient defective units, e.g., supply voltage or frequency may be varied. (Synonymous with high-low bias test, and related to check.)

marginal testing — A form of test, usually

as part of preventive maintenance or as a fault-finding or correcting operation, to test against safety margins for faults.

marginal tests (voltage and registers) — Built into some computers is a network for marginal test of computer subsections. Two features of the marginal test system make routine checks fast and accurate. The marginal check voltage is continuously variable, and all working registers are displayed simultaneously on the console lights.

margin guide — *See* guide, margin.

margin, justified — *See* justified margin.

margin, justify — *See* justify.

mark — 1. In communications, an impulse which, in a neutral circuit, causes the loop to be closed, or in a polar circuit, causes the loop current to flow in a direction opposite to that for a space impulse. 2. A sign or symbol used to signify or indicate an event in time or space, e.g., end of word or message mark, a file mark, a drum mark, an end-of-tape mark.

mark, admissible — Specific rules or conventions determine which marks, symbols, and numerals or characters are permitted in various areas of computing for all installations and for various languages.

mark detection — A type of character recognition system which detects from marks placed in areas on paper or cards, called site areas, boxes, or windows, certain intelligence or information. Mark reading results from optical character recognition or mark-sensing systems which seek out the presence or absence of pencil marks or graphite particles, such as on college or school exams, census returns, etc.

mark, end — An indicator to signal the end of a word or the end of a unit of data.

marker — A symbol used to indicate the beginning or the end of some set of data, e.g., the end of a record, block, field, file, etc.

marker, beginning-of-information — abbreviated BIM. A reflective spot on the back of a magnetic tape, 10 feet from the physical beginning of the tape, which is sensed photoelectrically to indicate the point on the tape at which recording may begin.

marker, destination-warning — A reflective spot on the back of a magnetic tape, 18 feet from the physical end of the tape, which is sensed photoelectrically to indicate that the physical end of the tape is approaching.

marker, end-of-tape — A special mark, character, long blank, or other coding used to indicate the end of a tape or recording. Often, this is an easy-to-see reflective strip, a transparent section, or a special bit pattern on paper tape.

mark, file — An identification mark for the last record in a file, or one of the several labels to indicate end-of-file. File marks may be followed by trailer label, file mark, and reel mark.

mark, group — A special character used to designate the end of a record in storage for a write instruction.

mark, hold — The normal no-traffic line condition whereby a steady mark is transmitted.

marking bias — Bias distortion that lengthens the marking impulses by advancing the space-to-mark transition.

marking-end distortion — End distortion that lengthens the marking impulse by delaying the mark-to-space transition.

mark matching — A method employed in optical character recognition to correlate or match a specimen character with each of a set of masks representing the characters to be recognized; i.e., the characters are deliberately registered on the reference masks and no allowance is made for character misregistration. Mask types are: holistic masks (exact), peep-hole masks (more lenient but still exacting), and weighted area masks.

Mark I — An early electromechanical computer, utilizing both mechanical and electrical components to perform computational processes.

mark reading — *See* reading, mark.

mark, record — A special character used in some computers either to limit the number of characters in a data transfer, or to separate blocked or grouped records in tape.

mark, record-storage — A special character that appears only in the record-storage unit of the card reader to limit the length of the record read into storage.

mark scan — To mark scan is to read a document for a specific mark in a particular location. The mark may be made by a pen or pencil, since the operation is usually based on optical scanning and light reflectance. Mark scanning differs from mark sensing because mark sensing requires an electrographic pencil with conductive ink.

marks, control — Abbreviated CM. A control mark is a one-slab block written on magnetic tape to indicate the type of data that follows, or to indicate the end of useful information. The control mark (any one-slab block) supplies special control features which can be utilized by the programmer. However, several specified CM configurations have been reserved for particular features on data tapes, as FF for end of file.

mark, segment — A special character written on tape to separate one section of a tape file from another.

mark sense — A technique used to recognize pencil marks on cards or documents for conversion to electrical signals or punchings in a medium.

mark sensing — A technique for detecting special pencil marks entered in special places on a card, and automatically translating the marks into punched holes.

mark, single-quote — A special FORTRAN character used to enclose literal messages.

mark-space multiplier — A specific analog multiplier, in which one input variable is represented as a current or a voltage, and is used to control the mark-to-space ratio of a repetitive rectangular wave and whose amplitude is made proportional to the other variable, which is also represented by a voltage or a current.

mark, storage — The name given to a point location which defines the character space immediately to the left of the most significant character in accumulator storage. An example would be:

---

a 7 4 6 7 4 8 9

---

in which the letter "a" would be the storage mark.

mark, tape — The special character that is written on tape to signify the physical end of the recording on tape.

mark, track-error — Indicates that during the course of the previous block transfer a data parity error was detected, or one or more bits have been picked up or dropped out from either the timing track or the mark track.

mark, word — An indicator to signal the beginning or end of a word.

mask — 1. A machine word that specifies which parts of another machine word are to be operated on. Also called extractor or filter. 2. Act of replacing characters in the accumulator with characters from a specified storage location that corresponds to the "ones" position in the mask, which is in a specific storage location or register. 3. To extract a selected group of characters from a string of characters.

masking — 1. An operation that replaces characters in the accumulator with characters from a specified storage location or register. 2. The process of extracting a nonword group or field of characters from a word or a string of words. 3. The process of setting internal program controls to prevent transfers which otherwise would occur upon setting of internal machine latches.

mask, interrupt — *See* interrupt mask.

mask, logical — The pattern used to force 0s or to inhibit (normally 1s) signals. A logical AND is used with a mask to force 0s selectively.

mask, preset — A technique for detecting the presence or absence of specific binary conditions. The process of masking performs some logical operation (AND, OR, etc.) between a program variable and a preset mask, hence the name. Masking is often used for setting or resetting binary conditions in other variables.

mask processing, programmable read-only memories — Integrated circuit devices are fabricated from a wafer of silicon through a number of processing steps, including photomasking, etching, and diffusing in order to create a pattern of junctions and interconnections across the surface of the wafer. One of the final steps in the manufacturing process is to coat the entire surface of the silicon wafer with a layer of aluminum, and then to selectively etch away portions of the aluminum, leaving the desired interconnecting pattern. In the manufacture of mask programmed read-only memories, the row-to-column contacts are selectively made by the inclusion of aluminum connections in the final aluminum etch process.

masks, holistic — *See* holistic masks.

masks, peephole — A set of characters in a character-recognition unit, which resides as a set of strategically placed points and which would theoretically show all input characters as being unique regardless of their style, i.e., for any one character there is only one set of points.

mask vs bipolar ROM — The primary difference in read-only memories is in the forming of the open or closed contact, that is, in the design of the cell. In mask-programmable read-only memories, the contact is made by selectively including or excluding a small conducting jumper during the final phase of semiconductor manufacture. In bipolar programmable read-only memories (PROMs), the contact is made with a fusible material such that the contact can later be opened, allowing the data pattern to be configured by the user after the device has been manufactured.

mask words — The mask word modifies both the identifier word and the input word which is called up for a search comparison in a logical AND operation.

mass data — *See* data, mass.

mass data, multiprocessing — *See* multiprocessing mass data.

mass storage — Peripheral devices into which large amounts of data can be deposited and recovered. Sometimes referred to as "secondary" storage to differentiate from memory.

mass storage device — A type of memory with a very large capacity in comparison to internal or main memory. Typically, these devices are tape, disk, cartridge, or other exterior memories but still directly addressable by the CPU.

mass storage dump/verify program — A program that allows the user to dump a specified area of memory to a mass storage device such as a disk, magnetic tape, or cassette. In an autoloadable format, the accuracy of the dumped program is automatically verified.

mass-storage executive capability — *See* storage, mass (executive).

mass storage file — *See* file, mass storage.

master — 1. A file of data considered permanent or semipermanent, i.e., an arrangement or ordering of a series of records. 2. A single record from such a file.

master card — A card containing fixed or indicative information for a group of cards. It is usually the first card of that group.

master clock — The electronic or electric source of standard timing signals, often called "clock pulses," required for sequencing computer operation. This source usually consists of a timing-pulse generator, a cycling unit, and sets of special pulses that occur at given intervals of time. In synchronous computers the basic time frequency employed is usually the frequency of the clock pulses.

master clock frequency — The number of pulses per second produced by the master clock.

master clock, microprocessor — Clocks are generally required for most microprocessors. A trend is for newer processors to require only a frequency-controlling two-terminal device (crystal or RC net). Some of the vendors offer clock or clock-driver chips. In many designs, the DIP-socket sized crystal oscillators are used. In others, crystal-controlled stability is not important. Clock frequency has little to do with relative data manipulation speed, and should not be used as a selection criterion. The number of phases, however, is important; four phases are harder to generate than one or two. In clock schemes with multiple phases particularly common in MOS processors, the requirements for overlapped or closely controlled relative rise for periods should be investigated. Sometimes four phases are easier to make than overlapped, synchronized two-phase clock signals.

master-control interrupt — Signal generated by an input/output device, or by an operator's error, or by request of the processor, for more data program segments, or the like, which permits the master control program to control the computer system.

master control program — *Same as* program, master control.

master control routine — 1. In a program consisting of a series of subroutines, a routine that controls the linking of the other subroutines and may call the various segments of the program into memory as required. 2. A program which controls the operation of a hardware system.

master data — A set of data which is altered infrequently and supplies basic data for processing operations. The data content of a master file. Examples include: names, badge numbers, or pay rates in personnel data; or stock number, stock descriptions, or units of measure in stock-control data.

master file — 1. A file of relatively more permanent information, which is usually updated periodically. 2. A main reference file of information.

master file inventory — Permanently stored inventory information retained for future use.

master file, magnetic tape — *See* tape, master file.

master file tape — *See* tape, master file.

master-file–update program — A process in which programs from the old master file are deleted, corrected, or left unchanged and new programs are added from the transaction tape. Updating can include changing of program job assignments. A new program master file is then produced.

master instruction tape — Abbreviated MIT. A tape on which all the programs for a system of runs are recorded.

master mode — The mode of computer operation in which all legal basic operations are permissible.

master payroll data file — The information bank where data on each employee is kept.

master program — *Same as* program, master control.

master program file — A tape on which all the programs for a system of runs are recorded.

master program file update — Programs from the old master file are deleted, corrected, or left unchanged, and new programs are added from the transaction tape. A new program master file is produced.

master program tape — *See* tape, master.

master record — The basic updated record used in the next file-processing run. A master record is most often a magnetic tape item. Visual copies for possible analysis and alteration are usually developed.

master routine — *Same as* executive routine.

master scheduler — The control scheduler that permits the function of a control program that allows an operator to initiate special actions or to cause requested information to be delivered which can override the normal control functions of the system.

master/slave computer — *See* master/-slave system.

master/slave mode — This feature guarantees that one program cannot damage or access another program sharing memory.

master/slave multiprogramming — A system designed to guarantee that one program cannot damage or access another program sharing the same memory.

master/slave system — A special system or computer configuration for business or scientific use (as production automation) in which one computer, usually of substantial size or capability, rules with complete control over all input/output and schedules and transmits tasks to a slave computer. The latter computer often has a great capacity, and it performs the computations as directed and controlled by the master unit.

master slice — An unmetalized wafer containing arrays of circuit elements as determined by subsystem requirements. These circuit elements can then be interconnected in a variety of ways to achieve different functions.

master station — A type of station that has control of a channel at a given instant for the purpose of sending numbered messages to a slave station (whether or not it actually does). Also referred to as a transmitting station or data source.

master synchronizer — A primary source of timing signals. Often a ring counter synchronized by a crystal-controlled oscillator.

master system tape — This is a monitor program that allows for the centralized control of program operation. It provides a load-and-go operation with one magnetic-tape unit without operator intervention. The operator can specify loading and execution of any program on the master system tape by a simple on-line typewriter directive.

master tape — *See* tape, master.

master terminal — In some networks, any terminal in the network can be the master, but only one terminal is master at any one time. As master, the terminal can communicate with all other terminals in the network.

master timer — *See* master clock.

match — 1. A data processing operation similar to a merge, except that instead of producing a sequence of items made up from the input, sequences are matched against each other on the basis of some key. The following is a schematic of a two-item match:

SEQUENCE A	SEQUENCE B
1	1
2	3
3	3
4	4
5	5
6	6
7	7
8	11
9	11
10	13
11	
12	
13	

2. Comparison of keys (records) that are identical. (Synonymous with a hit or strike.)

match gate — *Same as* gate, exclusive NOR.

matching — The matching technique is generally used to verify coding. Individual codes are machine-compared against a group of master codes to select any that are invalid.

matching error — An error due to inaccuracy in pairing passive components.

matching, mark — *See* mark matching.

match-merge — The comparison of two files, usually based on key words designed to place them in the prearranged sequential order of those records which match the arbitrarily selected key words.

material dispersion, fiberoptics — Light-impulse broadening due to differential delay of various wavelengths of light in a waveguide material.

mathematical analysis — Includes arithmetic and algebra; deals with numbers, the relationships between numbers, and the operations performed on these relationships.

mathematical check — A check that uses mathematical identities or other properties, occasionally with some degree of discrepancy being acceptable; e.g., checking multiplication by verifying that A × B = B × A. (Synonymous with arithmetic check.)

mathematical model — A series or organization of equations that are a mathematical representation of a "real world" problem or process in a skeletonized form, but with precise measurements of the relationships of the variables, parameters, and constants. Each model has some objective function (goal or target) and decision rules (values to be determined) which will solve the problem to develop the answer or range of alternatives.

mathematical operator — A symbol that indicates briefly a mathematical process, which describes the relations and restrictions which exist between the input variables and the output variables of a system.

mathematical parameter — A secondary variable in an application. For example, the analytic geometry description of a line, y = ax plus b can be replaced by the parametric expression $y = a^t x + b$ where t is regarded as a parameter. The constants, a and b, and the variables, x and y, are not considered as parameters.

mathematical power — *See* power, mathematical.

mathematical program — *See* program, mathematical.

mathematical programming — *Same as* linear programming.

mathematical simulation — The use of a model of mathematical equations in which computing elements are used to represent all of the subsystems.

mathematical subroutines — Subroutines including sine, cosine, square root, exponent, log, etc.

mathematics — Involves the definition of symbols of various kinds and describes the operations to be performed, in definite and consistent ways, upon the symbols; a symbolized and extended form of logic to form the patterns of scientific phenomena, the laws obeyed, and the uniformities displayed. Although mathematics does not provide these, it expresses and interprets them and helps to deduce their consequences, or to forecast what will happen if they hold. Mathematics points and advises where to look for verification or contradiction of hypotheses.

matrix — 1. A rectangular array of numbers subject to mathematical operations, such as addition, multiplication, and inversion, according to specified rules. Any table is a matrix. 2. An array of circuit elements such as diodes, wires, magnetic cores, and relays, arranged and designed to perform a specified function; for example, conversion from one number system to another.

matrix algebra tableau — The current matrix, with auxiliary rows and/or columns, as it appears at an iterative stage in the standard simplex method computing form of solution.

matrix, coefficient — The matrix of left-side coefficients in a system of linear operations. It is to be distinguished from the matrix obtained by appending the right side, which is called the augmented matrix of the system. It may be thought of as including a full set of logical vectors to convert inequality constraints to equations, and in the case of the modified simplex array it also contains the objective function coefficients.

matrix, constraint — In linear programming, the augmented matrix of the constraint equations; it is the matrix formed by the coefficient columns, or left sides, and the column of constants.

matrix, dot — A dot-matrix display uses individual character displays arrayed in any length. Each unit contains dots arranged in rows and columns, which can be selected in the proper pattern to display a letter, number, or other symbol when energized. Display assemblies can be obtained with power supply, programming and decoding electronics, and scanning circuitry that causes the message to traverse the display from left to right for displaying continuous messages.

matrix, interconnect — A network or array of conductors arranged to facilitate rapid and convenient interconnection between them by way of switches, pins, jumpers, or other means.

matrix, photocell — *See* photocell matrix.

matrix printer — *See* printer, wire.

matrix printing — The printing of alphanumerical characters by means of the appropriate selection of pins contained in a rectangular array on the printing head.

matrix, program timing — A unique array of connections which supply timing pulses at regular intervals and in proper sequence to permanently selected groups of lines in the normal execution of operations, i.e., the clock pulses for a clock pulse generator in sychronous digital computers.

matrix, semantic — A graphical device for plotting in a standard conventional form whatever precise elements of meaning have been ascertained from the semantic analysis of a concept.

matrix, storage — *See* storage matrix.

matrix table — A specific set of quantities in a rectangular array according to exacting mathematical rules and designs.

maximal — Highest or greatest.

mean time between failures — The special limit of the ratio of operating time of equipment to the number of observed failures as the number of failures approaches infinity.

mean time to failure — The average time the system or component of the system works without faulting.

mean time to repair — The average time to repair a fault or a component of the system.

measure, data-transmission utilization — The ratio of useful data output of a data-transmission system to the total data input.

measurement and control systems — Measurement and control systems are designed for scientific and industrial applications requiring acquisition, storage, computation, reduction, presentation, and output of high- and low-level analog signals from sensors such as thermocouples, strain gauges and RTDs in medical and biomedical research, quality assurance laboratories, product development and testing programs, process simulation, and pilot plants for process control.

measurement, work — *See* work measurement.

mechanical differential analyzer — A form of analog computer using interconnected mechanical surfaces to solve differential equations; e.g., the Bush differential analyzer, developed by Vannevar Bush at M.I.T., used differential gear boxes to perform addition, and a combination of wheel disk spherical mechanisms to perform integration.

mechanical translation — A generic term for language translation by computers or similar equipment.

mechanism, decision — *See* decision mechanism.

mechanism, tape transport — *See* tape transport.

mechanized data — *See* data, mechanized.

media — The plural form of medium. Magnetic cards, disks, and cartridges and paper tapes are examples of the various media types devised to carry data or information.

medium — The material or basis on which data and instructions are recorded. Examples are punched cards, punched or magnetic tape, disk or diskette, cartridges, etc. (Plural, media.)

medium, input/output — 1. The vehicle or material designed and used to carry recorded data, i.e., a magnetic card, magnetic tape, microfilm, etc. The medium is the carrier of data and instructions to and from a computer. 2. A specific register that contains modifiers of instructions before execution, or a register that controls actions under the direction of the computer or program.

medium, machine readable — *See* data, machine readable.

medium, nonerasable — Paper tapes and most ROMs are examples of nonerasable media used to drive various production machines. It is quite uncommon to use paper tape or ROM as an intermediate memory because it is nonerasable.

medium-scale integration — Abbreviated MSI. Integrated circuits containing logic functions more complex than small-scale integration but less complex than large-scale integration (LSI). Examples of MSI relate to 40-bit counters, latches, data multiplexers, etc.

medium, storage — The material on which data is recorded and which may be paper tape, cards, magnetic tape, strips, or devices such as magnetic cartridges, disks, etc.

medium, transfer — The material, such as sheets, ribbons, or plastic film, which enables the transfer of ink during printing.

mega — A prefix meaning million.

megabit — One million binary bits.

megacycle — A million cycles per second; 10^6 cycles per second. (The preferred term is megahertz.)

member, print — *See* print member.

memories, associative — With associative-memory capability, high-speed memory searches within computers are based on content or subject matter rather than being limited to locating data through specified addresses.

memorize — Typically, meaning to transfer data or information to internal storage.

memory — A device into which information can be copied, which will hold this information, and from which the information can be obtained at a later time. (The terms memory and storage are interchangeable.)

memory access, quick — *Same as* storage, high speed.

memory, acoustic — A computer memory that uses a sonic delay line.

memory, add-on and add-in — Minicomputer storage devices range from add-on solid-state MOS or bubble memories to various types of disk and tape drives. Add-on memory is generally supplied with an enclosure, a power supply, and a cable connecting the memory to the mini. Add-in memories are normally circuit boards that slip into the chassis or expansion cabinets of a mini or micro.

memory, addressed — Memory sections containing each individual register.

memory addressing modes — Methods of specifying the memory location of an operand. Common addressing modes are, in general: direct, immediate, relative, indexed, and indirect. These modes are important factors in program efficiency.

memory address register — A register containing the address of the selected word in memory. *See* register.

memory address, virtual — Often interpreted as addressing (1) a particular character relative to the beginning of a page, (2) a particular page relative to the initial point of that segment, and (3) a particular large memory segment or book. Thus programs can be addressed into noncontiguous areas of memory in relatively small blocks.

memory annex — A small memory unit as a go-between for the input and output units and the main memory.

memory applications, virtual — Virtual memory has been used primarily on large, multiprogrammed computers in order to have a larger number of active programs in main memory. In some cases, however, the minicomputer being used will be dedicated to a single program rather than being multiprogrammed. With this consideration, the virtual memory system allows a user to run large programs without having to go to the expense of buying more than a minimal amount of main memory for the machine.

memory array — Memory cells arranged in a rectangular geometric pattern on a chip, usually organized into rows and columns as in a matrix.

memory, associative — Data storage based on the data actually stored in the memory, not the location of the data. This leads to its alternate name, content-addressable memory (CAM). Associative memory is a method of organization and memory design that permits the access of all information that matches certain "tag" bits of the address.

memory, backing — Considered to be the same as auxiliary storage, i.e., those units whose capacity is relatively larger than working (scratchpad or internal) storage but of longer access time, and in which transfer capability is usually in blocks between storage units.

memory bank select — The memory that can be directly addressed by most microprocessors is not sufficient for many applications. This has led to the incorporation of memory-bank select in RAM memory cards. An eight-position DIP switch on such cards is used to select one (or more) of eight banks of memory in which the card is to reside. Each bank consists of a maximum of 64K bytes of memory. One output port address of the microprocessor is reserved for selecting the active bank (or banks) of memory. With eight banks of 64K, microprocessor memory space can be expanded to a half-megabyte. In addition to memory expansion, bank select is also convenient in implementing small time-shared systems. In such a system, each user is restricted to just one bank of memory, thus protecting against accidental accessing of another user's memory space. (Some systems.)

memory, bootstrap — The bootstrap memory is a time-saving device built into the main computer. It is programmed to fit the specialized needs of various computer users. The program and words in the bootstrap memory cannot be altered by the computer but can be manually changed when necessary. The purpose of the bootstrap memory is to provide for the automatic reading of new programs into the computer with protection against erasing its vital instructions (some systems).

memory, bubble — Magnetic-domain, or "bubble," memories may be thought of as patterns of vertically oriented bar magnets moving on tracks within a thin horizontal film or platelet. The polarity of the bar magnets (actually tiny cylindrical magnetic fields) is always perpendicular to the film plane and opposite to their surrounding region. In the most simplified model of bubble memory, the presence of a bubble is detected when its reverse magnetic field is sensed during its passage under a permanently magnetized material that changes resistance with a change in polarity. The bubbles are unaffected by their passage under the sensor.

memory bus — The CPU communicates with memory and i/o devices over a memory bus. In different computers this bus has various names, including i/o bus, data bus, or one of a host of proprietary names.

memory, cache — Units with limited capacity but very fast semiconductor memory which can be used in combination with lower-cost, but slower, large-capacity memory, giving effect to a larger and faster memory. Look-ahead procedures are required in the progress of the programs to effect locating and depositing the right information into the fast memory when it is required.

memory capacity — The number of elementary pieces of data that can be contained in a storage device. Frequently defined in terms of characters in a particular code or words of a fixed size that can be so contained.

memory character format — Memory storing techniques of storing one character in each addressable location.

memory chip, bubble — Contained in a small module, bubble memory is an electronic chip that stores digital information by changing the magnetic polarity of tiny areas in the chip called bubbles. The bubbles are actually cylindrical magnetic islands polarized in a direction opposite from that of a film in which the bubbles function. The memory has no moving parts. Because it works magnetically, it retains information even when the power is turned off. Bubble memory has advantages over electromechanical mass memory devices, such as paper tape, cassettes, or floppy disks; it offers solid-state reliability, higher access speeds, smaller size, and less weight and power consumption.

memory, content-addressed — A memory

in which the storage locations are identified by their contents rather than their addresses. Enables faster interrogation to retrieve a particular data element.

memory, core — A storage device composed of ferromagnetic cores, or an apertured ferrite plate, through which select lines and sense windings are threaded.

memory cycle — The operations required for addressing, reading, writing, and/or reading and writing data in memory.

memory, cycle stealing — Many applications require the fastest possible transfer of large amounts of data between the microcomputer memory and peripheral devices. System efficiency can be increased by avoidance of time-consuming programmed word transfers in which the microprocessor supervises each operation. Increased efficiency can be achieved by addition of a direct-memory access (DMA) facility. It allows an i/o device interface to "steal" a memory cycle from the program and transfer a word of data directly from or to a memory address specified in a special address register. With an automatic increment of the address register after each word transfer, successive words of data can be transferred into successive memory locations.

memory data register — Abbreviated MDR. A memory data register is a 4-, 8-, 12-, or 16-bit register that holds the last data word read from or written into the memory location addressed by the contents of the memory address register.

memory dump — 1. A listing of the contents of a storage device, area, or selected parts of it. 2. A process of writing the contents of memory consecutively in such a form that it can be examined for computer or program errors. 3. Routine generated automatically according to a programmer's specification and included in an object program to perform, respectively, program-loading operations and a printout of memory contents upon request.

memory dump (monitor control) — A memory dump may be specified in the control information for a job. Upon termination of the job, the dump routine is loaded from the system unit and executed. The dump routine overlays the monitor and produces a complete dump of the object program. Upon completion of the dump, the monitor is reloaded to process the next job. Programs terminate normally by returning control to the monitor. A job may be terminated by the operator or the monitor. Once a job has terminated, the monitor automatically initiates processing of the next job. If for any reason the resident monitor becomes destroyed and processing is not continuous, the system may be reloaded and initialized by the bootstrap loader.

memory, external — A facility or device, not an integral part of a computer, in which data usable by a computer is stored. Examples are off-line magnetic-tape units and other magnetic devices. (Contrasted with storage, internal.)

memory fill — Placing a pattern of characters in memory registers not in use in a particular problem to stop the computer if the program, through error, seeks instructions taken from forbidden registers.

memory guard — Electronic or program guard inhibiting or preventing access to specific sections of storage devices or areas especially concerning the main or internal memory of the central processor.

memory hierarchy — A set of memories with differing sizes and speeds, and usually having different cost-performance ratios. A hierarchy might consist of a very high speed, small semiconductor memory, a medium-speed disk memory, and a large, slow-speed tape memory.

memory, high-speed — A unit which is capable of producing information at relatively higher speeds than other peripheral or memory units connected or related to a computer system; also an indication of the lower average access time.

memory interleaving — Interleaving, like cache, takes advantage of the fact that most computer programs tend to reference sequential addresses. In interleaving, sequential addresses are placed on sequential memory boards (some systems can interleave two, four, or eight memory modules at a time) so that the CPU can fetch a word, manipulate it, then fetch the next word without having to wait for completion of the memory cycle of one board.

memory, internal — 1. The storage of data in a device that is an integral part of a computer. 2. The storage facilities forming an integral physical part of the computer and directly controlled by the computer. In such facilities all data are automatically accessible to the computer, e.g., main memory and magnetic disk or tape on-line. (Contrasted with storage, external.) 3. All memory or storage which is automatically accessible to the computer without human intervention.

memory load and record operation — A type of operation that allows users to suspend processing and store the complete contents of memory on tape for continuation later.

memory location — A specific position in a computer storage device.

memory locations, standard — These are various areas of storage which are reserved for mathematical tables, or for the automatic storage of final contents of registers.

memory, magnetic — Any portion of the memory that uses the magnetic properties of a material to store information.

memory management — Addressing extension hardware options available for some computers. The memory management option controls the operation of user programs in a multiprogram environment.

memory, main — Usually the fastest storage device of a computer and the one from which instructions are executed. (Contrasted with auxiliary storage.)

memory map — A special type of listing of addresses or symbolic representations of addresses which define the boundaries of the memory address space occupied by a program or a series of programs. Often memory maps can be produced by a high-level language such as APL, FORTRAN, etc. In addition, under operation of some computer memory management options, a dynamic memory map is maintained to guide automatic allocation of memory space to overlay programs.

memory map list — A memory map is provided at compile time on an optional basis. The memory map is a listing of all variable names, array names, and constants used by the program, with their relative address assignments. The listing will include all subroutines called and last location when called.

memory mapping — An optional mode of computer operation wherein the eight high-order bits of any virtual address greater than 15 are replaced by an alternative value, thus providing for dynamic relocatability of programs (some computers).

memory map, virtual addresses — An automatic device for transforming virtual addresses into physical addresses in some time-sharing systems.

memory module — A magnetic or semiconductor module providing storage locations for 4K, 8K, 12K, 16K, or more words (where K = 1024).

memory, nonvolatile — A storage medium which retains information when power is removed from the system.

memory page — A section of memory, typically 256 words. This arises from the fact an 8-bit computer handles memory addresses in 8-bit bytes. One byte can address 256 locations, so most 8-bit microprocessors use a total of 2 bytes to give one 16-bit word capable of addressing 65,536 (2^{16}) locations. The upper 8 bits are referred to as the page number. Thus the address in octal page form 012 125 is location 125 (octal) on page 012 (octal).

memory parity — A procedure that generates and checks parity on each memory transfer and provides an interrupt if an error is detected.

memory parity and protect option — Abbreviated MPP. On some systems with 18-bit memories, the memory system generates and checks byte parity. The MPP option provides a means for dealing with parity errors by "capturing" the following information and generating a noninhibitable interrupt for corrective action by the user's program: CPU or DMA generated parity error, address and content of memory location causing parity error, upper or lower byte caused parity error. On these systems, intentional parity errors can be produced by a special instruction for maintenance purposes.

memory, permanent — Storage of information that remains intact when the power is turned off. Also called nonvolatile storage.

memory pointer registers — Special registers that direct (point) the CPU to the location of a word in memory that contains data.

memory print — *See* memory dump.

memory print-out — A listing of the contents of a storage device, or selected parts of it. (Synonymous with memory dump and core dump.)

memory protect — Memory protect is available for use in many processors. It protects the integrity of operating systems against accidental modifications. Memory protect divides memory space into two segments, separating the operating system from user programs. If any part of a user program seeks to modify system space, the system interrupts and takes control. This is a necessity for many real-time environments and other highly interactive systems.

memory protect, multiprogramming — *See* multiprogramming memory protect.

memory protect no-operation — *See* no-operation, memory protect.

memory protect privileged instruction — A feature that provides a "hardware protected" environment so that an executing program cannot destroy the operating system or another job.

memory, pseudostatic (microcomputer) — A type of memory in which all refresh and overhead operations are taken care of on the card.

memory, quick-access — *Same as* storage, high speed.

memory, random-access — A storage technique in which the time required to obtain information is independent of the location of the information most recently obtained. This strict definition must be qualified by the observation that we usually mean relatively nonrandom access when compared to semiconductor types for main stores, but relatively random access when compared to magnetic tapes for file storage. (Contrasted with sequential-access storage.)

memory, rapid — That section of the whole memory from which information may be obtained in the shortest possible time.

memory, rapid-access — *Same as* storage, high-speed.

memory, read-only — A memory that cannot be altered in normal use of the computer. Usually, a small memory that contains often-used instructions such as microprograms or system software.

memory, regenerative — A memory device where contents gradually vanish if not periodically refreshed.

memory register — A register in the storage of the computer, in contrast with a register in one of the other units of the computer.

memory, scratchpad — A high-speed memory device used to store the location of an interrupted program and to retrieve the latter after the interrupting program has been completed.

memory, secondary — A particular storage which is usually of large capacity, but also with longer access time, and which most often permits the transferring of blocks of data between it and the main storage.

memory, semiconductor — A memory whose storage medium is a semiconductor circuit. Often used for high-speed buffer memories and for read-only memories, ROM, or random access memories, RAM.

memory, standard units — Storage from which the data to be operated on is normally obtained. This storage may be under the control of the computer, but data to be operated on must be transferred to secondary or internal storage before operations commence; it is returned to external storage only after operations are completed. External storage devices usually have larger capacities and lower access speeds than internal and secondary storage.

memory, static — 1. A memory device that contains no mechanical moving parts. 2. A memory device that contains fixed information.

memory, virtual — A technique that permits the user to treat secondary (disk) storage as an extension of main memory, thus giving the virtual appearance of a larger main memory. A type of memory with the capability of using a type of algorithm of the paging or segmenting type. In this manner, a larger memory is simulated than actually exists.

memory, virtual (pointer) — Virtual memory systems are designed for storage efficiency. Some computers are structured so that parts of programs and data may be scattered through main memory and auxiliary storage. Various pointers or sets of pointers automatically keep track of the location of these program portions. The user of computers so designed may be unaware of this scattering procedure and most often operates computing procedures as though he were using normal memory.

memory, volatile — A storage medium in

which information is destroyed when power is removed from the system.

memory, working — The internal memory which stores information for processing.

memory workspace — The amount of memory required by a program over and above the amount of memory required to store the program itself. Workspace is generally used for input/output device buffer areas and for various other locations required by a program during its execution.

merge — To produce a single sequence of items, ordered according to some rule (that is, arranged in some orderly sequence), from two or more sequences previously ordered according to the same rule, without changing the items in size, structure, or total number. Merging is a special kind of collating.

merge, order of — The number of input files to a merge program. Also power of the merge.

merge-sort — The production of a single sequence of items in a specific order as programmed or according to some rules developed without changing the items in structure, size, or total number.

merging sort — *See* sort, merge.

mesh — To combine in an arrangement according to some rule, two or more sequences previously arranged according to the same rule, to obtain a single sequence of items without any change in the number or type of items.

message — A transmitted series of words or symbols that are designed and intended to convey information. In message switching, a message consists of a header, text, and an end-of-message symbol.

message, automatic — A location in which incoming data from one circuit is transferred to the proper outgoing circuit.

message block — In order to reduce the transmission overhead, messages exchanged between various devices and the application programs may be blocked and unblocked at various points in the system. The blocking operation consists of the concatenation of several messages into a single transmission or physical record. This is done to reduce the frequency of the delays due to changing the transmission direction of the communication link.

message concentrator — Generally, concentrators keep host computer overhead low by preformatting and editing messages to fit the host system before transmission. The concentrator saves time by intercepting messages with errors, eliminating spurious transactions to the host computer. Most message concentrators are built around a mini or microcomputer that runs under a real-time operating system. It receives messages of various speeds and formats through a data control unit. The micro or minicomputer reformats the messages to suit the host system, checks for errors, and, when necessary, stores messages on the moving-head disk until line bandwidth is available. The messages are then sent in a high-speed (sometimes 50-kilobaud) burst to the host system, directly or through a packet switching network.

message, end of — The specific set of characters that indicates the termination of a message.

message, enquiry — Abbreviated ENQ. A signal that is used as a request for a response to obtain identification and/or an indication of station status, transmitted as part of an initialization sequence (line bid) in point-to-point operation, and as the final character of a selection or polling sequence in multipoint operation.

message error, illegal control — A control message has been read that it is not defined. If the message is typed it may be retyped. Otherwise, only the compile or assembled phase of the job is processed, and a job error is given.

message exchange — A device placed between a communication line and a computer to take care of certain communication functions and thereby free the computer for other work.

message format — The specific identification and placement of portions of a message, such as its heading, address, text, end of message, etc.

message, fox — A standard message which is used for testing teletypewriter circuits and machines because it includes all the alphanumerics on a teletypwriter as well as most of the function characters such as space, figures shift, letters shift, etc. The message is: "The quick brown fox jumped over a lazy dog's back 1234567890---sending." The sending station's identification is inserted in the three blank spaces which precede the word "sending."

message header — That part of a message that contains the transmission-control information preceding the text.

message, multiple-address — A message that is to be delivered to more than one destination.

message polling — A technique for calling or signaling by the designated master station to other stations in a multipoint or multichannel network.

message queuing — Controls the order in which messages are stored, processed, and transmitted.

message reference block — *See* block, message reference.

message-response time — For terminal-oriented systems, two types of response time are most meaningful. The terminal-response time is the time required from the instant the "transmit" or equivalent key on a keyboard is depressed to the moment the reply message begins to appear at the terminal. The overall-response time is the elapsed time from the instant the user generates a message to the moment a complete reply is received. This criterion includes the print or display time of the terminal and the time it takes to transfer the message from the user's location to the terminal location.

message retrieval — The capacity to retrieve a message some time after it has entered an information system.

message routing — The function of selecting the route, or alternate route, for a message.

messages, error — Messages developed by a program to designate a variety of error types.

message, single-address — A message which is to be delivered to only one destination.

message switch — A term for one of the routing points in a store and forward switching system.

message switching — 1. The technique of receiving a message, storing it until the proper outgoing circuit is available, and then retransmitting it. 2. A system in which data transmissions between stations on different circuits within a network are accomplished by routing the data through a central point.

message switching, packet — A form of message switching in which the message size is restricted to a relatively small length, normally several thousand bits at most, and in which no long-term storage is provided in the switching centers. The switching center to which the sender is connected frequently has the ability to break longer messages into shorter segments called packets; if not, the user terminal (computer) must perform this function. Each packet can be routed individually toward the destination switching center, where the message is reassembled in proper order for transmission to the destination. Packet systems are customarily encoded for extremely rapid delivery rates, on the order of tenths of seconds, and packets which cannot be delivered within some fixed maximum are discarded.

meta language — A formal language which uses special symbols to describe the syntax of computer languages.

methods analyst — Designs systems and supervises their implementation. Also plans, controls, and coordinates conversion to new systems.

MICR — Abbreviation for Magnetic Ink Character Recognition. A check-encoding system employed by banks for the purpose of automating check handling. Checks are imprinted (using magnetic ink) with characters of a type face and dimensions specified by the American Banking Association. There are fourteen characters—ten numbers (0–9) and four special symbols.

MICR code — *See* code, MICR.

microcircuit — A specialized electronic circuit composed of elements which are fabricated and interconnected to make them inseparable and miniaturized. Microcircuits frequently reduce cost, increase reliability, and operate faster than tubes and many transistors. They are common to the so-called third generation of computer equipment. (Illustration, page 320.)

microcircuit, analog — A type of linear microcircuit intended to be used so that the output is a mathematical continuous function of the input. An operational amplifier is an example of an analog microcircuit.

microcircuit, digital — A type of microcircuit which is intended to accept particular logic states, changes between logic states, or sequences of logic states at its

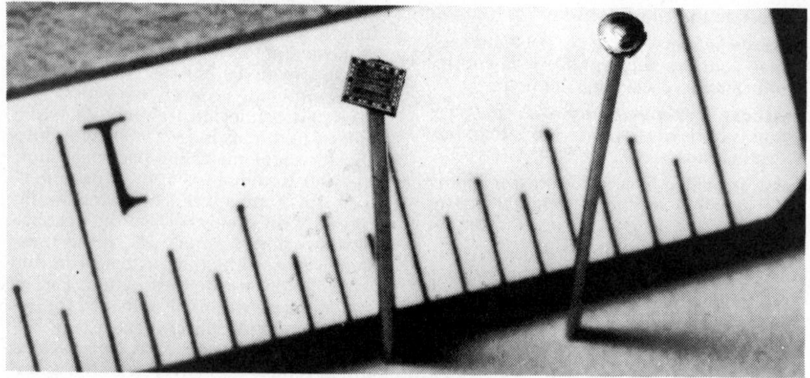

Courtesy NCR Corp.

Microcircuit.

input terminals, and convert these to logic states at the output terminals according to a set of logic equations or function tables.

microcode — 1. A list of small program steps. Combinations of these steps, performed automatically in a prescribed sequence, form a macrooperation like multiply, divide, and square root. 2. A set of control functions performed by the instruction decoding and execution logic of a computer system. The microcode defines the instruction set (repertoire) of a specific computer. It is often not accessible to programmers if the system is a large one and designed for nonuse by the owners and users, e.g., proprietary to the manufacturer. Most microcomputers are ready for microcode use by hobbyists and designers.

microcoding — A system of coding that uses suboperations not ordinarily accessible in programming.

microcomputer — A general term referring to a complete tiny computing system, consisting of hardware and software, whose main processing blocks are made of semiconductor integrated circuits. In function and structure, it is somewhat similar to a minicomputer, with the main difference being price, size, speed of execution, and computing power. The hardware of a microcomputer consists of the microprocessing unit (MPU), which is usually assembled on a printed circuit board with memory and auxiliary circuits. Power supplies, control console, and cabinet are separate.

microcomputer architecture — The basic interrelationships between the principal parts of the microsystem and the methods (or paths) by which data can be made to flow within a system. Architecture includes number of registers available, how registers are used, instruction sets, input-output operations, number of stacks available, how stacks are used, hardware interrupt structure, data paths into memory (number and types), data paths into CPU (number and types), and others. Most architectures are classified into either CPU oriented, memory oriented, or bit-slice.

microcomputer bus, S-100 — The S-100 microcomputer bus consists of a bank of 100-contact connectors wired in parallel on a common mother board. The 100 lines of the bus carry address, data, and control signal information. Several of the lines are left undefined for use in customized systems. A ground trace between the signal lines is used for shielding to reduce cross talk and assure reliable operation.

microcomputer, communications — A communications-oriented system for facilitating the firmware implementation of custom communications controllers. Generally, the system is designed to perform such functions as data concentration, channel contention, message routing, polling control, speed and code conversion, protocol conversion, and voice response.

microcomputer components — Microcom-

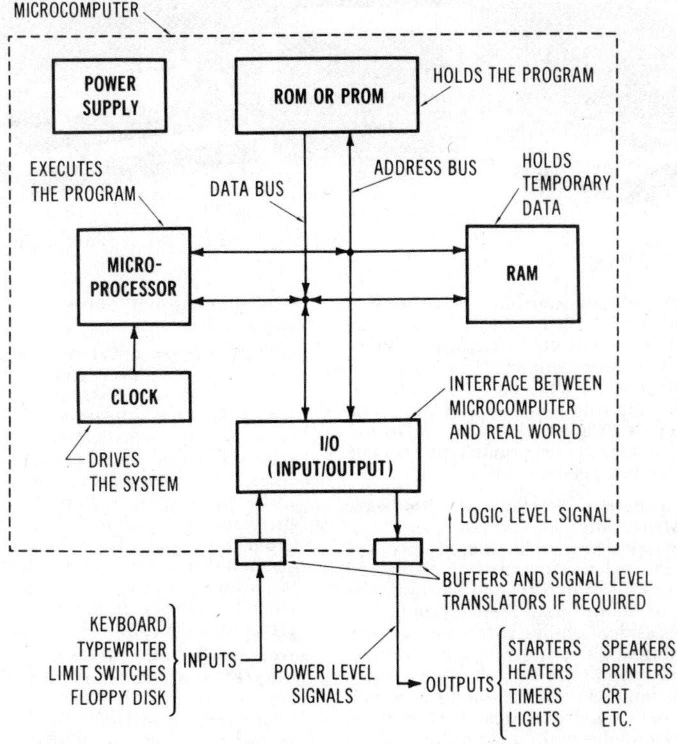

Microcomputer components.

puters are tiny digital computers developed from a few large-scale integrated circuit (LSI) chips. A central processor (CPU) may be on a single LSI chip (microprocessor chip) or several such chips. A microcomputer system also requires ROM storage for programs and data, clock circuits, input/output interfaces, selector registers, and control circuits.

microcomputer components, high-level system — The major components of a high-level MPS are a second generation, high performance CPU; a programmable input/output controller (PIO); a programmable serial input/output controller (SIO); a versatile counter timer circuit (CTC); and a high-speed direct memory access controller (DMA).

microcomputer control, ACIA — An asynchronous communications interface adapter (ACIA) interfaces an MPU to devices requiring an asynchronous serial data format.

microcomputer CPU — In general aspects, the CPU consists of the following: program counter (PC), instruction register (IR), instruction execution logic, a memory-address register (MAR), a general-purpose register (GPR) file, and an arithmetic and logic unit (ALU).

microcomputer data base system — With the data-base management system, the user's computer and intelligent terminals can communicate with the disk file through high-level commands, while the intelligent disk system carries out the detailed commands for indexing, searching, and deblocking operations required to access or store the needed data. Thus, the communications lines almost exclusively carry requested data, while a minimum of control information flows back and forth between the terminal and the disk system. Since most sys-

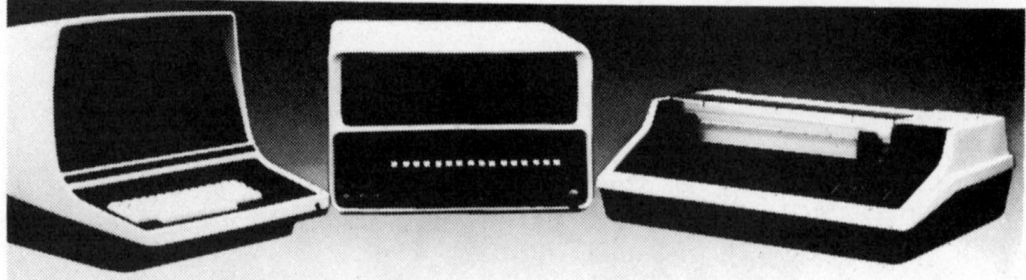

Courtesy Fairchild Camera and Instrument Corp.

Microcomputer development hardware.

tems communicate through the EIA standard interface RS-232-C, they can be easily connected to many different types of host computers or terminals. And the use of a high-level language for communications means that any computer or terminal that can talk to another computer or terminal can also talk to the disk system.

microcomputer development hardware — Microcomputer development systems are designed to simplify product design cycles. They provide a test bed for interfaces and related hardware, as well as full program preparation facility with resident on-line hardware and software debugging aids. Peripheral interfaces include TTY, high speed paper tape equipment, serial line printer with magnetic tape cassettes. Various card level modules of the systems range from microcomputers, memory and i/o modules, to general-purpose arrays.

microcomputer development system — These systems, often purchased by large users of microprocessors for program development and debugging, are specially designed tools to employ software devices such as exercisers, emulators, etc., to eliminate manual i/o and the need for the user to be fluent in hexadecimal. They often include terminals, tapes, cassettes, floppy disks, etc.

microcomputer, front-end — Special performance features can be provided by a front-end mini- or microcomputer. For example, in many applications it is desirable to identify specific terminals as they generate messages. A front-end microcomputer can be programmed to identify the caller and to provide the proper interface between the terminal and the host processor. Another communications feature allows direct access to the network for monitoring and evaluating common-carrier performance, providing instant notification of network faults.

microcomputer i/o architecture — The i/o architecture of a microcomputer generally breaks down into these areas: transfer techniques, instruction formats, buses, bus structures, interrupt schemes, and memory-access techniques. Most microprocessors allow for three types of i/o transfer techniques: programmed transfer, interrupt-program control, and hardware control. In the first two cases, found in most simple applications, the microprocessor controls the transfer. In the third case, system hardware controls the transfer.

microcomputer POS systems — Point-of-sale (POS) systems, in which the cash register is actually a special-purpose computer terminal that can monitor and record transactions directly in the store's data files, perform checks on credit card validity, and handle other marketing data functions. The microcomputer constitutes a natural device for use in the control of automated checkout counters and can also be used for product label printing control. Microcomputers also appear in standalone electronic cash registers.

microcomputer, single-board — A typical single-board microcomputer is designed to operate as a complete computer with its own self-contained memory plus serial and parallel i/o ports. It might feature the use of CPU (central processing unit), CTC (counter timer circuit), and PIO (parallel input-output) devices.

microcomputer system basic components — Additive to the basic CPU components of various microcomputer systems are additional parts, generally including single-chip modems; clock generators; and assorted controllers, adapters, and expanders.

microcomputer system monitor — Most system monitors give complete control over the operation of the microcomputers. All necessary functions for program loading and execution are provided, while additional commands implement extensive debugging facilities. These facilities include the capability to examine and modify memory or CPU register contents, set program breakpoints, and initiate program execution at any given address. Users can dynamically reassign system peripherals via monitor commands through calls to the system-monitor i/o subroutines.

microcomputer, training — A typical training unit is designed to teach microcomputer principles and programming. It allows analysis and display of the CPU with registers, flags, program counter, and stack pointer; and it permits visualization of elements such as memory, inputs, and outputs. This enables debugging of various structure addressing modes and interrupts.

microcomputer types — Some of the various microcomputer types (in popular jargon) are: an inexpensive computer, a personal computer, a very small computer, a dedicated computer, a few-chip computer, an 8-bit processor, a single-chip processor, and an MOS-LSI processor.

microcomputer word processing — Microcomputer applications include an office equipment application, word processing, i.e., controlling one or more typewriters that edit text stored on cassettes or floppy disks.

microcontroller — 1. A microprogrammed machine, a microprocessor, or a microcomputer used in a control operation, that is, to direct or make changes in a process or operation. 2. Any device or instrument that controls a process with high resolution, usually over a narrow region.

microcontroller applications — There are generally three classes of control applications: device control, in which a single machine tool or computer peripheral is sequenced through its different operations; data control, in which data from one or more sources must be moved to one or more destinations or multiple low-speed data paths are concentrated into a higher-speed data path; and process control, in which discrete inputs from measured process variables are used in a closed loop environment.

microcontroller functional components — A typical microcontroller is a complete microcomputer system consisting of a central processing unit and an interpreter; read-only program storage; optional read/write data storage, called working storage, with variable field access to 1 to 8 bits; and a complete bit addressable input/output system called the interface vector. (Some types.)

microcontroller i/o system — A typical microcontroller i/o system is treated as a set of internal registers. Therefore data from external devices may be processed (tested, shifted, added to, etc.) without first being moved to internal storage. In fact, the entire concept is to treat data at the i/o interface no differently than internal data. This concept extends to the software which allows variables at the input/output system to be named and treated in the same way as data in storage.

microcontroller registers — There are three types of registers in some systems. These are input registers, working registers, and output registers. The input registers are capable of accepting data from the outside world and placing it on a data bus to the arithmetic unit. By devoting these registers exclusively to inputting data, the logic to implement these registers becomes extremely simple. In a controller, these registers could be used to accept input data from a computer data bus, a magnetic tape, push buttons, etc.

microcycle — Often, manufacturers use a basic cycle time or period, sometimes called a microcycle, to specify the instruction execution speed. This may be the inverse of the clock frequency or of a multiple (possibly two or three times) of the clock frequency. Each instruction is then defined as requiring several microcycles for execution. As a result, a three-microcycle instruction may actually require three, six, or nine clock cycles. Longer instructions such as multiply and divide can require tens or even hundreds of microcycles.

microelectronic devices — Devices made up of transistors, resistors, capacitors, and similar components, fabricated along with their interconnections on a single substrate in a single series of op-

Courtesy Pertec Computer Corp.

Microfloppy-diskette drive.

erations. The primary material of microelectronic circuits is usually silicon.

microfiche — One type of COM format. A typical microfiche measures approximately 4 × 6 inches (105 × 148 millimeters). It can include an eye-readable title row, up to 269 data frames at a 48 × reduction ratio, and an index frame.

microfilm — A fine-grain, high-resolution film containing an image that is greatly reduced in size as compared to its original paper form. The recording of microimages onto microfilm utilizes numerous techniques and film types. Film widths of 16 mm, 35 mm, 82.5 mm, and 105 mm are used in COM.

microfilm computer output — A microfilm printer that will take output directly from the computer, thus substituting for a line printer or tape output. *See also* COM.

microfloppy-diskette drive — One type of diskette drive accepts a 5.25-inch diskette used for applications in word-processing systems, microcomputers, smart terminals, portable computers, and program/load/storage devices.

microform media — Types of photographic data storage, including microfiche (a sheet of microfilm containing multiple microimages in a grid pattern), 16-mm roll film (available on open spools or various self-feeding cartridges), aperture cards (containing a 35-mm image or multiple images on punch cards), 105-mm film, microcircuitry (tight-tolerance, high-resolution precision photography), and other standard photographic reproduction methods.

micrographics/computer information-display system — A combination of multiple crt computer terminals with graphic buffers, central automatic microfilm selector, video-generator modules, and a computer programmed to search, index, and update.

microinstruction — 1. A small, single, short add, shift, or delete type of command. 2. A bit pattern that is stored in a microprogram memory word and specifies the operation of the individual LSI computing elements and related subunits, such as main memory and input/output interfaces.

microinstruction sequence — The series of microinstructions that the microprogram control unit (MCU) selects from the microprogram to execute a single macroinstruction or control command. Microinstruction sequences can be shared by several macroinstructions. These are normally selected by the operation codes (op codes) supplied by the microinstructions, such as control commands or user instructions in main memory. The MCU decodes these commands by using their bit patterns to determine which is to be the next microprogram address. Each decoding results in an n-way program branch to the desired microinstruction sequence.

microinstruction storage — In most applications, the microprocessor-based system will be built with microprograms residing in ROMs or PROMs. Therefore, it is important that a form of ROM simulation which offers facilities to easily load, examine, and modify storage be available during microprogram development. Easily alterable microcode is essential during development so that trial-and-error techniques may be used for debugging. A large number of short sequences of one or more instructions will be executed in order to become familiar with the microprocessor chip set and to exercise all of the combinations that the microinstruction set offers. Most of the familiarization programming must be done before the final version of the microprogram can be started. During microprogram development, hundreds of changes will be made to the program to locate errors quickly and to experiment with different routines to develop a more efficient program. Without the ability to alter program content quickly, debugging becomes tedious and time consuming.

microkit microcomputer system — The basic microkit system consists of a mainframe, keyboard, crt display and two cassette tape units. The computer itself can contain four microcomputer modules (CPU; RAM; crt and keyboard i/o; tape, RTC, and EIA i/o), power supplies, and i/o connectors. Often, all are packaged in a compact, desk-top enclosure. Some microkit systems are built around a universal system bus through which all the system modules communicate. A specific CPU module interfaces to the bus and controls the operation of the system. One typical microkit has 8K bytes of RAM memory, which is expandable to 56K bytes. Each 1K page of memory is separably write protectable under software control.

microprocessing unit — Abbreviated MPU. The main constituent of the hardware of a microcomputer. One MPU consists of the microprocessor, the main memory (composed of read/write and read-only memory), the input/output interface devices, and the clock circuit, in addition to a buffer, driver circuits, and passive circuit elements. The MPU does not contain power supplies, cabinet, or control console, and it is normally understood to be an assembled printed circuit board. The level of sophistication of the MPU is that of the named microcomputer.

microprocessor — The semiconductor central processing unit (CPU), and one of the principal components of the microcomputer. The elements of the microprocessor are frequently contained on a single chip or within the same package, but sometimes they are distributed over several separate chips. In a microcomputer with a fixed instruction set, the microprocessor consists of the arithmetic logic unit and the control logic unit. In a microcomputer with a microprogrammed instruction set, it contains an additional control memory unit.

microprocessor analyzer — A digital diagnostic instrument for testing and debugging of MPU hardware and software.

microprocessor architecture — Architectural features include general-purpose registers, stacks, interrupts, interface structure, choice of memories, etc. General-purpose registers are used for addressing, indexing, and status and as multiple accumulators. They simplify programming and conserve main memory by eliminating memory buffering of data. Multiple accumulators are especially important for ROM programs that have no writable memory.

microprocessor cache memory — A typical cache memory consists of a cluster of bipolar units arranged in four blocks of four words each. Each memory board contains one cache. When addressing memory, the CPU checks cache and main memory. If the work is in cache, the data are transferred. An error check does not require extra CPU time. Error-detection/correction memories use five bits more than noncorrecting units. The extra bits are for a computation made by both memory and CPU when they exchange data. (Some systems.)

microprocessor chip — An integrated circuit that contains all the essential elements of a central processor, including the control logic, instruction decoding, and arithmetic-processing circuitry. To be useful, the microprocessor chip or chips are combined with memory and i/o integrated circuit chips to form a microcomputer.

microprocessor chip sets — Microprocessor chip sets can be combined with ROMs or PROMs, R/W RAMs, and i/o logic to form the hardware of a microprogrammable minicomputer. RALU (Register-Arithmetic Logic Unit) chips are available with 2- and 4-bit word widths. In addition, most suppliers offer a control chip (MCU) as an aid in designing a processor. The most widely accepted uses for these microprocessor chips are as controllers for high-speed peripheral devices, high-speed data acquisition preprocessors, and military-airborne or industrial control systems, and in wide ranges of instrumentation.

microprocessor classifications — There are at least four major classifications of microcomputer systems: calculators, controllers, data processors, and general-purpose computers. Controllers and calculators are the most likely candidates for single-chip CPUs. Data processors and general-purpose computers require more flexibility and are better served by a multichip system. Most microprocessors claim to be microprogrammable, since they make use of ROM to store an intermediate-level program or a higher-level program.

microprocessor compiler — A program that translates the source program into machine language. These compilers, which can be run on medium- or large-scale computers, are available from several time-sharing services.

microprocessor cross-assembler — If the software that converts the programmer's listing into object code resides in a computer other than the selected microprocessor, it is called a cross-assembler. On the other hand, if conversion software resides in a computer using the selected microprocessor, it is called an assembler. Both forms produce identical outputs.

microprocessor "intelligence" — In an MPU-based design, "intelligence" refers to the control program, a sequence of instructions that guides the MPU through the various operations it must perform. During system development, users have a predefined instruction set to prepare a satisfactory control program. The program, usually called "software" at this point, is then stored in memory that can be accessed by the MPU during operation, thus becoming the system's intelligence. Once in ROM memory, the program is usually called "firmware."

microprocessor memory interface — For applications requiring more than the RAM located on the CPU, several memory interface circuits can be included in the microprocessor. Each device can generate more address lines and the signals necessary to interface with up to 65K or more bytes of RAM, PROM, or ROM memory. Other devices may be used in conjunction with standard static semiconductor memory devices.

microprocessors, support — System components for expanded multiprocessor applications, such as i/o processors, special instruction set extension processors, memory management, and distributed intelligence configurations.

microprogram — 1. Computer instructions which do not reference the main memory. Microprogramming is a technique to design subroutines by programming very minute computer operations. As regards microprocessors, microprograms can implement a higher-language program by storing microinstructions in ROM. 2. A program of analytic instructions which the programmer intends to construct from the basic subcommands of a digital computer. 3. A sequence of pseudocommands which are translated by hardware into machine subcommands. 4. A plan for obtaining maximum utilization of the abilities of a digital computer by efficient use of the subcommands of the machine. 5. A type of program that directly controls the operation of each functional element in a microprocessor.

microprogram assembly language — Computer-dependent machine language using mnemonics for the basic instruction set. In a microprogrammed computer, each assembly language instruction is implemented by a microprogram.

microprogram, bipolar — The microprogrammed approach is useful for bipolar microcomputers because complex macroinstruction sets can be realized as sequences of relatively primitive microinstructions. The logic of the final macromachine remains relatively simple, with most of the complexity being represented by the contents of the control memory. When used with the central processing element (CPE) slice, the basic microinstruction functions are established, although additional logical elements drawn from standard TTL families may be added which will alter or enhance the microinstruction set.

microprogram, bit-slice machines — The microprogram on bit slice machines is the sequence of instructions held in the control store. It determines what operations the processor performs for each command given to it by the main memory.

microprogram control — A ROM and counter form the basis for execution control logic. To select and generate a timing sequence, users set the counter to the start value and increment it for each step. The ROM decodes each counter value to activate appropriate ROM-output lines. This technique is called microprogram control, since the contents of the ROM control the sequence of operations.

microprogram control logic — The hardware needed to implement machine instructions. A hardwired computer uses much more control logic than a microprogrammed computer.

microprogram control store — The memory, used by the control processor, in which microprograms are stored. It may be implemented with ROM, PROM, or WCS.

microprogram fields — Parts of a microinstruction that specify one micro-operation. Each of several fields may be independent of any other.

microprogram instruction set — The repertoire of machine-dependent instructions available to the assembly-language programmer.

microprogrammable computer, user — A computer in which part of the control store is set aside for the user, and the user is able to put microprograms in and access them.

microprogrammable instructions — *See* instructions, microprogrammable.

microprogrammable ROM computer — A computer in which the internal CPU control signal sequence for performing instructions is generated from a ROM. By changing the ROM contents, the instruction set can be changed. This contrasts with a fixed instruction computer, in which the instruction set cannot be changed readily.

microprogram machine instructions — The binary-coded bit patterns that actually control the operations of the computer through the control processor. Programs written in symbolic languages like FORTRAN are translated into machine instructions by compilers, assemblers, or interpreters.

microprogram map (system user) — A group of addresses stored in computer hardware that is used to access specific program and data storage space in main memory.

microprogrammed diagnostics — Diagnostics and service aids may be easily implemented in the control portion of the system with ROMs. Some very small systems and many models of large systems store their diagnostics in ROM control. Microprogrammed implementations are oriented toward servicing and diagnostics. For example, large portions of the control network can be checked by putting parity on the output of the control store. Furthermore, the microprocessor can both set and test internal control states not available to the machine-language programmer.

microprogrammed microprocessor — In a microprogrammed processor, operations on the fundamental register-transfer level can be programmed. These basic operations are the elements of conventional machine instructions. With minicomputers or large-scale computers, microprogramming employs a single high-speed memory whose outputs control the data paths in the systems either directly or through decoding logic. This memory is then programmed—in a manner analogous to conventional machine or assembly-language coding—to provide the functions needed for the processor's instruction set.

microprogram microassembler — A program that translates microprograms in symbolic form (similar to assembly language) into bit patterns that are then loaded into the control store.

microprogram microcode — Another name for the microinstructions that make up a microprogram, either in source language or in object-code form.

microprogramming — The technique of using a certain special set of computer instructions that consists only of basic elemental operations which the programmer can combine into higher-level instructions as he chooses, and can then program using only the higher-level instructions.

microprogramming, bit-slice microprocessor — The changing of the way the ALU (arithmetic-logic unit) reacts to instructions by altering the microprogram held in the control store. When several bit slices and a controller are connected together with a control store, a complete processor is built.

microprogramming, diagonal — A control-processor implementation technique that combines horizontal and vertical microprogramming by encoding the contents of control store. It yields high performance with simple machine-language format instructions.

microprogramming, horizontal — A control processor implementation technique in which many micro-operators are used in each microinstruction to provide intimate high speed control almost at the gate level of the computer's operation. The technique is usually associated with very wide word widths.

microprogramming techniques — There are very few techniques that have been widely publicized for writing efficient microprograms or developing efficient microcode. A few of the more frequently used techniques discussed often which are finding application in microprogramming are: indexing, subroutines, and paramaterization. Many arithmetic operations are made up of a sequence of repetitive operations. For example, a multiply is made up of a sequence of adds and shifts. This sequence will be executed over and over again until the operation is completed. Index registers have been used in computers to count the number of times one goes through a sequence of instructions. The same technique is applicable to microprogramming.

microprogramming, vertical — A control processor implementation technique in which fewer micro-operators are employed in each microinstruction to simplify user microprogramming at the expense of performance.

microprogram, single-chip system — In some systems, the operation of the microprocessor consists of repeatedly accessing or fetching instructions from the program stored in external memory and executing the operations specified by the instructions. These two steps are carried out under the control of an internal microprogram. (Some systems are not user-microprogrammable.) The microprogram is similar to a state table specifying the series of states of system control signals necessary to carry out each instruction.

micropublishing system — Hardware and software that make up a complete publishing system, which begins by accepting typed, error-free author copy and ends in the production of quantity microfiche documents for distribution to users.

microsecond — A millionth part of a second. One second = 1,000,000 microseconds.

MICR scan — The sensing of characters, marks, or codes printed in magnetic ink. The technique was developed by American Bankers' Association and is used on bank checks. The character size, shape, and ink are standardized by the USA Standards Institute.

middle punch — *Same as* eleven punch.

migration, data — The moving of data from an on-line device to an off-line or low-priority device, as determined by the system or as requested by the user. Contrast with staging.

milestone — A task or event that cannot be considered completed until all tasks that feed into it are completed.

millimicrosecond — One thousandth of a millionth of a second. Written symbolically as 10^{-9} second. The preferred term is nanosecond.

millisecond — One thousandth of a second (10^{-3} second); abbreviated msec or ms.

miniassembler program — A typical mini-assembler program is designed to simplify machine-level programming on various microprocessor systems. The program allows the operator to type mnemonic program symbols on the terminal directly in assembler language, while the program generates the correct object code, placing it in the proper memory location, and printing it out simultaneously on the terminal. Relative branches are calculated from the absolute address which is entered following branch instructions.

Minicard — An Eastman Kodak trademark designating its photographic system for information storage and retrieval.

minicomputer — Usually, a minicomputer is a parallel binary system with 8-, 12-,

Courtesy Interdata, Inc.

Minicomputers.

16-, 18-, 24-, or 32-bit word length incorporating semiconductor or magnetic core memory offering from 4K words to 64K words of storage and a cycle time of 0.2 to 8 microseconds or less. These units are characterized by higher performance than microcomputers or programmable calculators, richer instruction sets, higher price and a proliferation of high-level languages, operating systems, and networking methodologies.

minicomputer i/o — Minicomputers employ two types of i/o transfers. (A) In a program i/o, the program issues instructions to execute data transfers between the minicomputer and the peripheral devices. These low-rate data transfers are directed through the minicomputer accumulators. (B) In a direct memory access (DMA) transfer, the peripheral interface controls the transfers of information directly between the minicomputer memory and the peripheral data register. This type of transfer usually moves data in blocks, not single units.

minidiskette — A storage medium similar to, but smaller than the standard flexible disk. Available in hard- or soft-sectored formats, it shares the same oxide formulation, technology, and technique of manufacture. The protective jacket is 5.25 inches square.

minimum-access code — A system of coding that minimizes the effect of delays for transfer of data or instructions between storage and other machine components. (Related to optimum code.)

minimum-access coding — *See* coding, minimum access.

minimum-access programming — *See* programming, minimum-access.

minimum-access routine — *Same as* programming, minimum-access.

minimum delay coding — *Same as* coding, minimum-access.

minimum-latency code — *Same as* minimum access code.

minimum-latency programming — *Same as* programming, minimum-access.

minor control — The least significant or lowest category of report grouping of basic detail.

minor control change — When control changes of different levels of significance are used, they can be given distinguishing titles—minor control change, then intermediate, or next major—to establish a hierarchy related to the importance of the data.

minor cycle — The time interval between the appearance of corresponding parts of successive words in a storage device that provides serial access to storage positions.

minuend — The quantity from which another quantity is subtracted or is to be subtracted.

minus zone — The bit positions in a computer code that represent the algebraic minus sign.

MIS — *See* management information system.

misfeed — When cards, tapes, or other data or storage media fail to pass into or through a device properly. Causes may be damaged, misprogrammed, or missensed input.

misregistration, character — The improper state of appearance of a character, in character recognition, with respect to a real or imaginary horizontal base line in a character reader.

misregistration, document — The improper state of appearance of a document, in character recognition, on site in the character reader with reference to a real or imaginary horizontal base line.

misregistration, line — The improper or unacceptable appearance of a line of characters or numerals in optical character recognition, usually gauged with respect to the real or imaginary horizontal baseline.

missing error — Subroutines called by the program were not found in the library. The names of the missing subroutines are also output.

mistake — A human failing, e.g., faulty arithmetic, use of incorrect formula, or incorrect instructions. Mistakes are sometimes called gross errors to distinguish from rounding and truncation errors. Thus, computers malfunction and humans make mistakes. Computers do not make mistakes and humans do not malfunction, in the strict sense of the word. (Contrasted with error.)

mistake, systems — A human error developed in the creation of instructions, programs, etc.

mixed-base notation — A method of expressing a quantity by using two or more characters, where each character is of a different radix.

mixed-base number — A number consisting of two or more characters representing a sum, in which the quantity represented by each character is based on a different radix.

mixed radix — Relates to a numeration system that uses more than one radix, such as the biquinary system.

mixed radix notation — *See* mixed-radix number.

mixed-radix number — A number consisting of two or more characters representing a sum, in which the quantity represented by each character is based on a different radix. (Synonymous with mixed-base number.)

mixer, OR — *See* OR gate.

mix gate — *Same as* gate, OR.

mnemonic — Pertaining to or intending to assist the human memory. A mnemonic term is an abbreviation or acronym that is easy to remember.

mnemonic code — A technique to assist the human memory. A mnemonic code resembles the original word and is usually easy to remember, e.g., mpy for multiply and acc for accumulator.

mnemonic instruction — *Same as* codes, mnemonic operation.

mnemonic operation codes — *See* codes, mnemonic operation.

mnemonic symbol — Frequently used symbols for representation of information, selected to assist the memory in recalling meaning, as mpy for multiply.

mod/demod — Abbreviated form for modulating and demodulating units.

mode — 1. A method of operation, e.g., the binary mode, the interpretive mode, the alphameric mode, etc. 2. The most frequent value in the statistical sense. 3. The characteristic of a quantity being suitable for integer or for floating-point computation.

mode, alter — A program condition which permits changing or updating data in storage.

mode, analysis — A mode of operation in which special programs monitor the performance of the system for subsequent analysis. Program testing data or statistical data may be automatically recording when the system is running in the analysis mode.

mode, binary — *See* binary mode.

mode, burst — A mode of communications between the processor and i/o devices. When a signal from an i/o device operating through the multiplexor channel indicates burst mode, the receiving unit continues to fetch bits until the unit is finished.

mode, byte — An alternate mode of communications between the processor and i/o devices. Byte mode allows the multiplexor channel to accept data from multiple low-speed devices simultaneously.

mode, card — The status of the computer while cards are being read or punched.

mode, conversational — This mode of operation means that real-time man-machine communications are maintained. In this mode the system is often used for servicing remote terminals, word processing, and other "people-oriented" systems.

mode, conversational operation — In this mode, the system is used for servicing remote terminals. Real-time man-machine communications are maintained for transaction processing operations.

mode, freeze — *Same as* hold mode.

mode, hold — *See* hold mode.

mode, interpretive — In tracing (debugging) routines, when a program is simulated in its execution by using psuedo accumulators and pseudo index registers, branch instructions are inserted at various points to place the machine and program in an interpretative mode for error tracing, and when found, control is transferred back to the main program.

mode, job-program — *See* job-program mode.

model — 1. Mathematical representation of a process, device, or concept. 2. A general, often pictorial representation of a system being studied.

model, file — The model is an analog of the processing of files. It can be originated, added to (posting), compared with others, held aside, filed for later use, sent somewhere, and so on. Sets of symbols are the simple analogs for these happenings.

modeling, conceptual — A method of making a model to fit the results of a biological experiment, then conducting another experiment to find out whether the model is right or wrong. The models are created continuously, and are tested and changed in a cyclic manner. The physical sciences have developed through the years in this way, but there has been little use of the approach in biology, mainly because the kind of mathematics that developed is not well suited to biology. But now computers can get around this problem, and the important technique of conceptual modeling is beginning to be used in biology, business, psychology, etc.

model, mathematical — The general characterization of a process, object, or concept, in terms of mathematics, thus enabling the relatively simple manipulation of variables to be accomplished in order to determine how the process, object, or concept would behave in different situations.

mode, load — In load mode, data transmission is such that data delimiters are carried along with the data transmitted, in contrast with move mode.

model, pilot — A model of a system that is not so complex as a complete model and is used for program testing.

model symbols — The symbols such as squares, circles, etc., convey no information and must be labeled. They localize a point of interest, but convey only the most general notion of intent. The finished model must include adequate description with each symbol to explain what the operation does. Liberal use of footnotes is recommended to explain the "why" of operations which are not straightforward.

modem — Acronym for MOdulator DEModulator unit. A modem is a device that converts data from a form which is compatible with data-processing equipment to a form that is compatible with transmission facilities, and vice-versa. (Illustration, page 332.)

modem, acoustic — A device that combines the functions of a modulator-

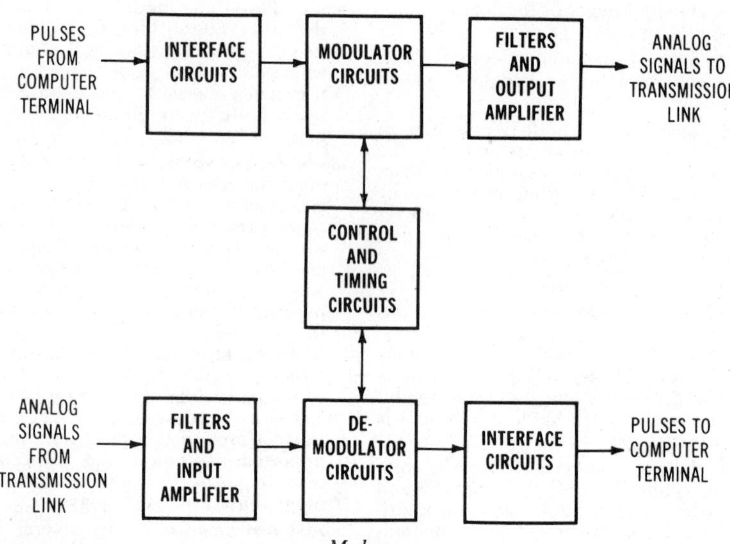

Modem.

demodulator with an acoustic coupler, into which a telephone handset may be placed to connect to dialup lines.

mode, manual — The condition existing when all automatic features are off and the computer is prepared to accept operator instructions directly from the control console.

mode, master — The mode of computer operation in which all legal SIGMA operations are permissible.

modem diagnostics — One of the more valuable outgrowths of modem development is the inclusion of diagnostic capabilities within the modem. One of the more common means for this is through loopback, where a piece of transmitting equipment can have its digital signal routed directly back to it through the modem interface (local digital loopback), through the modem and back (local analog loopback), to the opposite end of the communication line (remote analog loopback), or actually through the far end modem and back (remote digital loopback). Related to this is the self-test facility, which incorporates a random pattern generator in the modem.

modem-encryption devices — Some systems, by placing encryption devices at the modem interfaces, have all data on the link encrypted and decrypted in a manner that is essentially transparent to the sending and receiving stations. The clear bit stream entering the encryptor is reproduced at the exit from the decryptor. Thus, all synchronizing, delimiting, and control characters can be recognized by the receiving station as usual. If a transmission error occurs that modifies the ciphertext, the resulting cleartext will contain an error. The error detection mechanism thus operates as it would without the encryption devices.

modem equalization — Modem compensation for amplitude and envelope-delay distortion of the line. Equalization is often not required in lower-speed modems attached to a leased line, since minimum line conditioning is sufficient. However, conditioning and equalization are required when higher-speed modems (4.8K and 9.6K bits per second) are attached. Modems used for high-speed transmission over the dial-up network must have equalization, since it is never certain exactly which unconditioned telephone line will be used.

modem functions — Functionally, a modem is divided into two logical segments, the modulator and the demodulator. The modulator accepts digital inputs from devices such as computers and remote terminals and converts the squared dc pulse voltages to analog audio signals which are sent over the transmission link. At the other end of the link, the demodulator of a second modem reconverts the analog signals to digital outputs.

modem operation — Because most data-communication applications require the use of telephone lines as channels, modems operating at low transmission rates, up to 9600 bps, must take full advantage of limited bandwidths. At low speeds, frequency-shift modulation (using alternating tones to represent ones and zeros) suffices, but high-rate modems employ 4-, 8-, or 16-phase shift keying.

modem sharing unit — Abbreviated MSU. A device that enables multiple terminals to share one modem. MSUs are particularly valuable in networks that require clusters of terminals at remote sites, because the number of modems and transmission lines is reduced. Operation is polled half-duplex.

modem standards — To perform correctly, a modem must match the data-communications equipment at the digital interface as well as the telephone line at the analog interface. Numerous standards that govern both mechanical interfaces and language protocols currently exist; computer and terminal manufacturers as well as suppliers of data communications equipment and networks usually offer products and services compatible with these standards. Because of standards development by the EIA, most modems accept data in RS-232C format, which specifies signal levels and pin connections. The European data-input standard is termed CCITT V.24.

modem synchronization — There are basically two ways for a modem to handle the transmission of data, in spurts or in a continuous stream. The former is called asynchronous, the latter synchronous. Asynchronous transmission is appropriate for data from sources like keyboards, but is not as efficient. Modems which transmit asynchronously generally can operate at any rate up to their maximum. Modems designed for synchronous operation run only at fixed speeds, although they may be able to operate at many rates within their overall range.

modem types — TWX and Telex machines contain integral nonacoustic modems hardwired to the telephone lines. Packaged modems, usually separate from the data terminal equipment, are self-contained. Standalone modems are offered in rack-mount packages as well as other forms. Modem cards fit into a terminal manufacturer's card file to form an integral part of the terminal. Semiconductor houses offer chip modems, although these devices usually lack receiving filters. Voice-grade units are used with telephone lines, and wideband devices are used with coaxial cables or twisted pairs.

modem, wideband — Wideband modems, as supplied by telephone companies and subject to specific tariffs, provide synchronous data transmission at data rates from 19,200 to 230,400 bits per second. They operate with special wideband lines (actually groups of voice-grade lines) provided by the telephone companies. They are primarily used in computer-to-computer applications.

mode, off-line — Means that the devices are not hooked up together. Perhaps the printer is printing the payroll checks, while the computer is solving a completely unrelated mathematical problem. Both are independent operations.

mode, on-line — Means that all devices are hooked up directly, say with the computer. Although the devices work on different phases of the procedure, all are connected in some way and usually depend on each other for desired results.

mode, operational — The combination of machine operating modes currently in effect.

mode, program (remote-control system) — *See* program mode (remote control system).

mode, ready (time sharing) — *See* time sharing, ready mode.

mode, real-time — Real-time is a mode of operation in which data that are necessary to the control and/or execution of a transaction can be processed in time for the transaction to be affected by the results of the processing.

mode, real-time guard — *See* guard mode, real-time.

mode, recording — In the COBOL system, the representation in external media of data associated with a data-processing system.

mode, reset — In analog computing, the integrators are inoperative, and the required initial conditions are applied or reapplied, as contrasted to the operate mode.

mode, service — An operational mode for the handling of malfunctions or errors in words, etc.

mode, slave — The mode of computer operation in which most of the basic controls affecting the state of the computer are protected from the program.

modes of priority — The organization of the flow of work through a computer. The mode depends upon the sophistication of the system and the machine, and will vary from a normal noninterrupt mode to a system in which there are several depths of interrupt. There also may be different modes in different functions such as the i/o mode.

mode, supervisor — A mode of operation under which certain operations, such as memory-protection modification instructions, and input/output operations, are permitted.

modes, user (time sharing) — *See* time sharing, user modes.

mode, training — The training of terminal operators and the testing of a system in which normal operations are defined and carried on by the operator, in which he is encouraged to enter all types of transactions from normal to exceptional. The randomness and inventiveness of the input operator are used to check the formal test input and any inconsistencies.

modification — The changing of one or more words or parts of words, called modifiers or index words, which are added to the presumptive instruction by means of an arithmetical or a logical operation.

modification, address — *See* address modification.

modification, instruction — *See* instruction modification.

modification, program — The ability of a program to modify itself or to set a switch so that a set of events occurring at one time can affect the action of the program at a later time.

modifier — A quantity used to alter the address of an operand; e.g., the cycle index.

modifier register — *Same as* index register.

modify — 1. To alter a portion of an instruction so its interpretation and execution will be other than normal. The modification may permanently change the instruction or leave it unchanged and affect only the current execution. The most frequent modification is that of the effective address through use of index registers. 2. To alter a subroutine according to a defined parameter.

modify instruction — An instruction that will most likely be modified before it is used for the final program.

modular — A degree of standardization of computer-system components to allow for combinations and large variety of compatible units.

modularity — 1. A condition in the determination of the design of the equipment and programming systems such that the hardware and software components can be readily identified, altered, or augmented without replacements of particular units or sections. 2. Operating system programs conform to specific standards, so that control programs will have an identical interface with all processing programs. These standards are well documented so that user-written programs can follow the same conventions. The user is free to supplement supplied programs to meet special situations. By following the rules indicated in the standards, portions of control or processing programs can be changed or replaced in modular fashion.

modularity design — The processor, memory, device interfaces, backplane, and interconnecting hardware can be modular in design. Module selection, such as memory type and size and device interfaces, enables custom tailoring to meet specific application requirements.

modularity, functional — Addition of modules to a basic data-processing system, thus broadening the scope or concept of the system as well as adding capacity.

modularity, program-independent — The property of a system which allows it to accept changes and adjust processing accordingly to yield maximum utilization of all modules without reprogramming. This system is used in multiprocessing.

modulation — The process of varying

some characteristic of a carrier wave in accordance with the instantaneous value of samples of the intelligence to be transmitted. Types of modulation include differential, frequency, phase, phase-amplitude, pulse code, and others.

modulation, bi-phase — An encoding method for recording data on magnetic tape. In this method, zero is a positive change (low- to-high transition) during the bit time, and one is a negative change (high-to-low transition).

modulation, differential — A type of modulation in which the choice of the significant condition for any signal element is dependent upon the choice for the previous signal element. Differential phase-shift keying (dpsk) modulation is an example.

modulation, digital — The actual digital signal is not suitable for transmission over public phone systems. Three properties of an analog signal can be exploited for carrying digital data: frequency, phase, and amplitude. Thus the techniques used for carrying data involve frequency modulation (fm), phase modulation (pm), and amplitude modulation (am). In practice, the techniques also involve encoding levels (two levels can be used to represent 0 and 1; four levels can represent the combinations 00, 01, 10, and 11; etc.) The most frequently used kinds of modulation are frequency-shift keying (fsk), am, and pm.

modulation, phase — Abbreviated pm. A form of modulation in which the angle relative to the unmodulated carrier angle is varied in accordance with the instantaneous value of the amplitude of the modulating signal.

modulation, pulse amplitude — Abbreviated pam. A form of modulation in which the amplitude of the pulse carrier is varied in accordance with successive samples of the modulating signal.

modulation, pulse code — Abbreviated pcm. A form of modulation in which the modulating signal is sampled and the sample quantized and coded so that each element of the information consists of different kinds and/ or numbers of pulses and spaces.

modulation types — Frequency-shift keying (fsk) is a two-level frequency modulation technique used almost universally for low-speed operation. Amplitude modulation (am) is frequently used in specialized forms like QAM (Quadrature Amplitude Modulation, a four-level form). Pulse code modulation (pcm) is a form in which the periodic nature of the signals is ignored, and the presence or duration of the signal is used for encoding. Other, less common, forms of modulation include Duobinary (used only in GTE Lenkurt equipment) and baseband (where digital pulse trains are reshaped for transmission over analog lines, usually for sending over short distances only).

modulator/demodulator — A device that converts data from a form which is compatible with data-processing equipment to a form that is compatible with transmission facilities, and vice versa. Acronym: modem.

module — 1. A segment of core storage. 2. A piece of peripheral equipment with specific capacity for storage (memory). 3. An interchangeable plug-in item containing components. 4. An incremental block of storage or other building block for expanding the computer capacity.

module checking — *Same as* module testing.

module dissipation — The dissipation of the module calculated from the voltage-current product, plus an allowance for transistor dissipation for load currents being supplied to other modules.

module, memory — *See* memory module.

module, programming — *See* programming module.

module testing — The destructive read-off or use caused by overloading or underloading the computer components, causing failure of substandard units and thereby minimizing nonscheduled downtime.

modulo — A mathematical operation that yields the remainder function of division. Thus 39 modulo 6 = 3.

modulo-N check — 1. A check that makes use of a check number that is equal to the remainder of the desired number when divided by N; e.g., in a modulo 4 check, the check number will be 0, 1, 2, or 3 and the remainder of A when divided by 4 must equal the reported check number B; otherwise an equipment malfunction has occurred. 2. A method of verification by congruences, e.g., casting out nines. (Related to self-checking number.)

modulo-N count — *See* count, modulo-N.

modulo-N counter — *See* counter, modulo-N.

modulo-N residue — The remainder from a division of a number by another number, i.e., the residue for 58 modulo-8 is 2 since 58 divided by 8 is 7 with a remainder of 2.

modulo-two sum gate — *Same as* gate, exclusive OR.

MOL — An abbreviation for Machine Oriented Language.

monadic Boolean operation — A specific Boolean operation on only a single operand.

monadic operation — An operation on one operand, e.g., negation. (Synonymous with unitary operation.)

monitor — 1. To control the operation of several unrelated routines and machine runs so that the computer and computer time are used advantageously. 2. To test, check, or sequence, i.e., supervise the operation of a computer; a master schedule. 3. A black-and-white or color crt (cathode ray tube) display consisting of rows and columns of elements. Alphanumeric characters are formed in dot-matrix elements. Multiple elements can often be combined to form larger symbols.

monitoring — A monitor checks for error conditions that can occur when a program is being executed (e.g., numerical overflow, infinite loops, or an attempt to access a protected area of core memory). The monitor attempts to provide error recovery and diagnostics.

monitoring and automatic alarms — Features contained in various types of technical control equipment to give the operator a warning as certain line parameters deviate from their specified settings. This warning allows preventive action to be taken prior to actual circuit failure.

monitor operating system — The monitor exercises primary control of the routines that compose the operating system. It is this operating system which turns the computer into a flexible tool allowing the user to achieve maximum use of the hardware's advanced design features.

monitor program — 1. A specific program developed to indicate the progress and other characteristics of work in various computer systems. 2. A program that enables an operator to direct a computer to perform frequently required tasks, such as loading or storing programs, examining or altering the contents of locations in memory, executing programs under controlled conditions, etc.

monitor routine — *See* executive routine.

monitor, sequence — *See* sequence monitor.

monitor system — *Same as* executive system.

monitor system, time-sharing — *See* time-sharing monitor system.

monitor, time-sharing — The monitor system is a collection of programs remaining permanently in memory to provide overall coordination and control of the total operating system. It performs several functions. First, it permits several users' programs to be loaded into main memory simultaneously. The monitor makes use of the time-sharing hardware to prevent one user's program from interfering with another user's program. Each program is run for a certain length of time; then the monitor switches control to another program in a rotating sequence.

monitor unit — A device which is supervisory and which is capable of verifying the operation of another device or group in data processing systems, production automation systems, message routing systems, etc. When significant departure from the normal procedures, measurements or guides (criteria) occur, the state of the system is observed, measured, and operators alerted or various departures corrected.

monolithic — Pertaining to the single silicon substrate in which an integrated circuit is constructed.

monostable — Pertaining to a device that has one stable state.

Monte-Carlo method — A trial-and-error method of repeated calculations to discover the best solution of a problem. Often used when a great number of variables are present, with interrelationships so extremely complex as to forestall straightforward analytical handling.

morpheme — An element of language which relates and connects images or ideas in sentences, i.e., the relation between a noun and a verb.

morphology — The branch of linguistic

study that deals with the history and functions of derivational forms and inflections.

mortem, post — *See* post mortem.

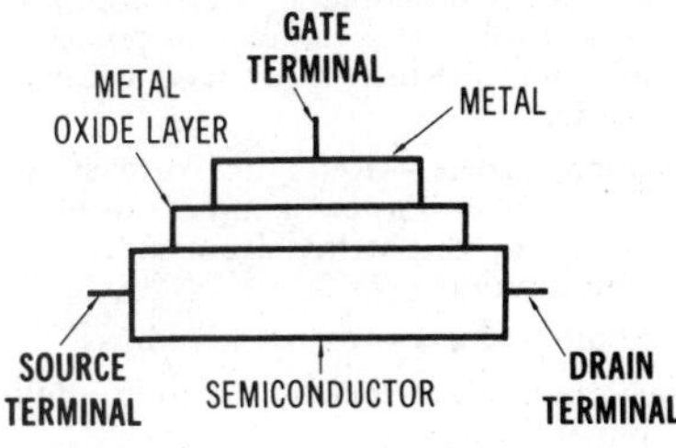

MOS gate structure.

MOS — Abbreviation for Metal Oxide Semiconductor. This refers to the three layers used in forming the gate structure of a field-effect transistor (FET).

MOS circuits — Circuits based on metal-oxide-semiconductor technology, which offers very low power dissipation and hence makes possible circuits that jam transistors close together before a critical heat problem arises. Most monolithic memories, calculators, and electronic watches use this technology.

most significant character — The character in the left-most position in a number or word.

most significant digit — Abbreviated MSD. The significant digit contributing the largest quantity to the value of a numeral, i.e., the left-most digit.

mother board — A circuit board onto which various processor boards are plugged.

motion register — This two-bit register contains a go/stop flip-flop and a forward/reverse flip-flop which control the motion of the selected tape drive. The register is set under program control.

m out of n code — A form of fixed-weight binary code in which m of the n digits are always in the same state.

movable random access — *See* random access, movable.

moving arm disk — *See* disk, moving arm.

moving-head disk system — A disk unit in which a read/write head is capable of moving across the surface of the disk to access any one of a number of circular tracks of data.

MPS — Abbreviation for MicroProcessor System or MicroProcessor Series.

MPU — The microprocessing unit (MPU) performs the central control function of a microcomputer, and its architecture determines the eventual applications for which the system is best suited. Some MPUs are especially oriented toward the process control and data communications fields; others are designed for alarm functions, games, calculators, or other purposes. Guiding characteristics for superior systems are maximum power, versatility, system throughput (operating speed), and design ease.

MPU hardware — Microprocessor unit (MPU) hardware consists of microprocessor chips that differ in the number needed to complete, with support chips, a microcomputer system. To implement a functioning computer, the CPU chip generally requires timing, i/o control, buffering, and interrupt control —most as external components to the CPU.

MPU, single-chip system architecture — Typically, the one-chip microcomputer system has all the basic features of a general-purpose microcomputer, including an input/output capability, a memory-access capability, a data-processing capability, and a powerful instruction set, all implemented on a single chip.

MSC — Abbreviation for Most Significant Character (left-most).

MSD — Abbreviation for Most Significant Digit (left-most).

MT — Abbreviation for Mechanical Translation or Machine Translation.

multiaccess — Pertaining to large systems that permit several people or groups to transact with the computer through the operator's console or many on-line terminals. Access points are generally connected to the central processor by data transmission lines from remote terminals, which can be typewriters, visual display units, crt's, or satellite processors. Multiaccess multiprogramming systems have been installed by many universities, laboratories, businesses, and research groups. Most operate in a conversational mode with fast response times and are controlled by operating systems.

multiaccess computing — This implies that more than one identical input/output terminal may be directly used with the system. Usually, they are remote, such as teletypewriter or similar units, or cathode-ray-tube types in the more modern systems.

multiaddress — A type of instruction that specifies the addresses of two or more items which may be the addresses of locations of inputs or outputs of the calculating unit, or the addresses of locations of instructions for the control unit. The term multiaddress is also used in characterizing computers, e.g., two-, three-, or four-address machines.

multiaddress instruction — *See* multiaddress.

multiaspect — Pertaining to searches or systems that permit more than one aspect or facet of information to be used in combination, one with the other, to effect identifying and selecting operations.

multifile sorting — The automatic sequencing of more than one file, based upon separate parameters for each file, without operator intervention.

multifont optical arena — Basic character reading equipment, having the ability to discern many fonts or formats of characters, usually from hard copy.

multifunction instruction set — In some systems, single-word instructions move data between random memory locations and any register. Other single-word instructions can execute arithmetic or logical operations from any pair of registers, and also shift, test, and store the resulting quantity. Hardware multiply and divide instructions are a standard part of the advanced microcomputer's instruction repertoire.

multilayer — Pertaining to a type of printed circuit board that has several layers of circuit etch or pattern, one over the other and interconnected by electroplated holes. Such holes can also receive component leads, and a given component lead can connect to several circuit points, reducing the required dimensions of a printed circuit board.

multilevel address — *Same as* address, indirect.

multilevel subroutining (display) — The control state permits the display to jump from accessing one location in the memory to any other. When it is desired to jump to a display subroutine, the return address is automatically stored in a push-down list.

multipass sort — A sort program designed to sort more data than can be contained within the internal memory of a central computer. Intermediate storage, such as disk, tape, or drum, is required.

multiple — A system of wiring so arranged that a circuit, a line, or a group of lines is accessible at a number of points, to any one of which a connection can be made.

multiple access — Reference to a system from which output or input can be received or dispatched from more than one location.

multiple address — *See* multiaddress.

multiple-address code — *See* code, multiple-address.

multiple addressing modes — Some microcomputer CPUs use a variety of addressing modes, including absolute, relative, indexed, deferred and auto-increment/decrement. These single-word, bit-efficient instruction formats minimize memory use.

multiple-address instruction — *Same as* multiaddress.

multiple-address message — A group of words to be delivered to more than one address, as coded for more rapid, less repetitious communication.

multiple arithmetic — *See* arithmetic, multiple.

multiple-aspect indexing — *See* indexing, manipulative.

multiple connector — A connector to indicate the merging of several lines of flow into one line, or the dispersal of one line to flow into several lines.

multiple graphs — More than one graph plotted, utilizing a set or sets of data. Thus, a set of data may furnish data required for plotting more than one graph.

multiple i/o channels, time sharing — *See* time sharing, multiple i/o channels.

multiple-length number — A number having two, three, or more times as many figures as are normally handled in a particular device.

multiple-length numeral — *See* numeral, multiple-length.

multiple-length working — Refers to the use of two or more machine words to represent a number, and to thus increase precision, i.e., the use of double-length procedures, double precision, etc.

multiple operations — The characteristic of being able to perform two or more computer processes concurrently.

multiple precision — The use of two or more computer words to represent a single numeric quantity or numeral, i.e., with twice as many or more digits as are normally carried in a fixed-length word.

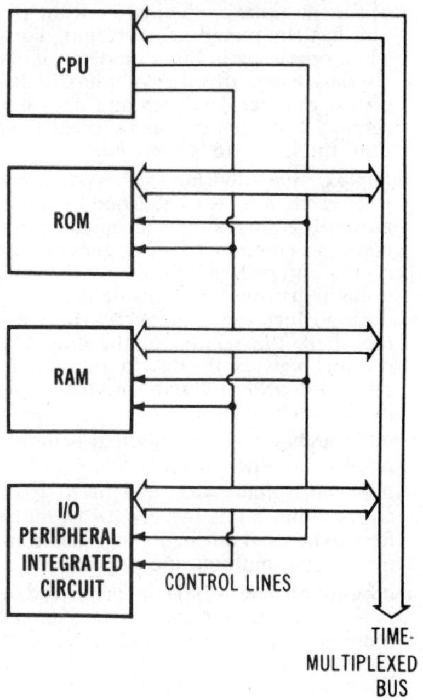

Multiplexed bus.

multiple programming — The programming of a computer by allowing two or more arithmetical or logical operations to be executed simultaneously. (Contrasted with serial programming.)

multiple punch — *See* punch, multiple.

multiplex — 1. The process of transferring data from several storage devices operating at relatively low transfer rates to one storage device operating at a high transfer rate in such a manner that the high-speed device is not obliged to "wait" for the low-speed units. 2. The concurrent transmission of more than one information stream on a single channel.

multiplex data terminal — A device that modulates and/or demodulates data between two or more input/output devices and a data transmission link.

multiplexed bus — A type of bus structure that time-multiplexes control, address, and data information. Several independent control lines support the multiplexed bus and signal external circuits (with respect to the microprocessor CPU) with the particular type of information and its stability on the bus. This bus structure provides a suitable means of circuit interconnection with inherent minimal requirements for support circuits, primarily because each peripheral circuit (memory or i/o) requires the connection of the data transfer path. All peripheral ICs essentially receive the

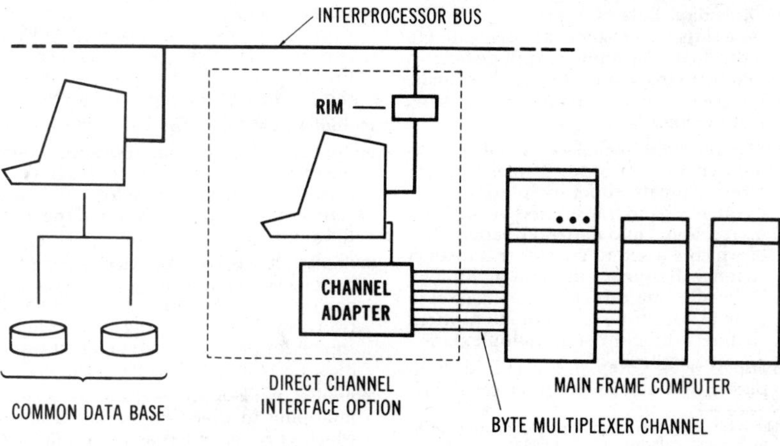

Multiplexed operation.

full address and control information for free. Device selection (enabling a specific memory location or i/o register) can thus take place within the memory or i/o peripheral or integrated circuit.

multiplexed operation — A process in which simultaneous operations share the use of a common unit of a system in such a way that they can be considered to be independent operations. (Illustration, page 339.)

multiplexer[1] — A device that takes low-speed inputs from a number of terminals and combines them into one high-speed data stream for simultaneous transmission on a single channel. At the other end of the link, a demultiplexer reconverts the high-speed data stream into a series of low-speed inputs to the host computer. The channel is split into time slots (time division multiplexing, tdm) or frequency bands (frequency division multiplexing, fdm).

multiplexer IOP — An input/output processing unit that is capable of performing bidirectional data transfer between main memory and standard-speed peripheral devices, with up to 32 such devices operating concurrently (some computers).

multiplexer simulation — A testing program which simulates the function of the multiplexer.

multiplexing — A process of transmitting more than one signal at a time over a single link, route, or channel in a communications system.

multiplexing, byte — A process in which time slots on a channel are delegated to individual slow input/output devices so that bytes from one after another can be interlaced on the channel to or from main memory.

multiplex, multichannel — Use of a common channel in order to make two or more channels, either by splitting of the frequency band transmitted by the common channel into narrower bands, each of which is used to constitute a distinct channel (frequency-division multiplex), or by allotting this common channel in turn, to constitute different intermittent channels (time-division multiplex).

multiplexor[1] — Often a specialized computer, with stored program capability, for handling input/output functions of a real-time system.

multiplexor, burst mode — The multiplexor channel can service high-speed devices by operating in burst mode. In burst mode, the i/o unit keeps control of the multiplexor channel until the i/o unit has completed its operation. Thus when operating in burst mode, a single i/o device captures the complete multiplexor channel data path and does not relinquish it from the time it is selected until the last byte is serviced.

multiplex, time-division — A system in which a channel is established by intermittently connecting its terminal equipment to a common channel, generally at regular intervals and by means of an automatic distribution. Outside the times during which these connections are established, the section of the common channel between the distributors can be utilized in order to establish other similar channels in turn.

multiplicand — The quantity that is multiplied by another quantity.

multiplication table — A specific area of storage that holds the groups of numbers to be used during the tabular scanning of the multiplication operation.

multiplication time — The time required to perform a multiplication. For a binary number it will be equal to the total of all the addition times and all the shift time involved in the multiplication.

multiplier — The quantity that is used to multiply another quantity.

multiplier, analog — The analog device which develops the analog product from two or more analog input signals; i.e., the output variable is proportional to the product of the input variables.

multiplier, digital — *See* digital multiplier.

multiplier factor — In multiplication, when the method of performance makes a distinction between two factors, they are called the multiplier factor and the multiplicand.

multiplier, function — A device causing the generation of a continuously varying analog representation of a product of two continuously varying analog input signals, as particular independent variables, i.e., time or distance change.

multiplier, mark-space — A specific analog multiplier in which one input variable, which is represented as a current or a voltage, is used to control the mark-to-

[1]The terms multiplexer and multiplexor are used by different manufacturers to denote the same or similar meaning.

space ratio of a repetitive rectangular wave and whose amplitude is made proportional to the other variable, which is also represented by a voltage or a current.

multiplier-quotient register — A register in which the multiplier for multiplication is placed, and in which the quotient for division is developed.

multiplier unit, digital — *See* digital multiplier unit.

multiply/divide instructions — Some systems provide special multiply/divide instructions that perform these functions up to five times faster than software routines.

multiply field — A designated field in a character unit used to hold the results of the multiplication operation. The field capacity must exceed by one character the number of characters required in the multiplier and multiplicand fields.

multiply, logic — *See* logic multiply.

multiply, logical — A logical operator which has the property that if P is a statement and Q is a statement, then P AND Q is true if both statements are true, false if either is false or both are false. Truth is normally expressed by the value 1, falsity by 0. The AND operator is often represented by a centered dot (P·Q), by no sign (PQ), by an inverted "u" or logical product symbol (P∩Q), or by the letter "x" or multiplication symbol (P×Q). Note that the letters AND are capitalized to differentiate between the logical operator AND, and the word *and* in common usage.

multiply operation — An arithmetic operation in which the operands are factors and the result is the product, as obtained by adding the multiplicand the number of times specified by the multiplier.

multipoint circuit — A circuit interconnecting several stations that must communicate on a time-shared basis.

multiprecision arithmetic — A form of arithmetic similar to double-precision arithmetic except that two or more words may be used to represent each number.

multipriority — A queue of items waiting for processing. The queue is made up of items of different priorities and in effect is a queue of queues.

multiprocessing — 1. The utilization of several computers to logically or functionally divide jobs or processes, and to execute various programs or segments asynchronously and simultaneously. 2. Two or more processors in a system configuration; one processor to control the system, with the others subordinate to it. All processors have direct access to all memory; each can perform computations and request input/output on individual programs stored in system core memory. Devices request memory access and wait until memory is available. They start immediately upon receipt of a memory access, and need not wait for the next clock cycle. 3. Processing several programs or program segments concurrently on a time-shared basis. Each processor is only active on one program at any one time, while operations such as input/output may be performed in parallel on several programs. The processor is directed to switch back and forth among programs under the control of the master-control program.

multiprocessing, executive system — *See* executive system multiprogramming.

multiprocessing, mass-data — Multiprocessor systems handle vast masses of general-purpose data. Handling scientific, engineering, and business data with equal ease, such a system tied into coast-to-coast communications network gives a consolidated data-processing operation. Two or more processors, each with direct access to banks of common memory, continuously process a conventional work load, and provide answers to special projects, such as product analysis, market research, site analysis, and operations research. The total system is under executive control of one processor. This results in the most efficient use of the expensive central processor and is the basis for time sharing of single processors among multiple users, each processor having access to the mass data memories of each other's system.

multiprocessing, microcomputer — A form of distributed processing is the multiprocessor type of organization. In the architecture, multiple independent microcomputers are interconnected to provide increased computing power. While this structure provides a more powerful overall processing system than the single CPU/intelligent controller organization, the multiprocessor system

Courtesy Sperry Univac

Multiprocessing operation.

is several times more expensive because each CPU requires its own support chips, large amounts of software must be written, and the interaction of processors in the system can make the control software very complex.

multiprocessing operation — A type of operation in which two (or more) central processors perform as one system. This configuration enables the system to perform overlapped simultaneous processing to a greater extent than does a single computing system. Multiprocessing configurations may consist of a host computer and a front-end processor, or both may be host computers. In either case, both are processing (either on segments of the same job or on entirely different jobs) simultaneously.

multiprocessing system — A system that is organized to contain two or more interconnected computers, which perform functionally or geographically specialized processing tasks.

multiprocessor — A computer with multiple arithmetic and logic units for simultaneous use and capability.

multiprocessor interleaving — Interleaving is a special process of addressing adjacent storage modules in an even/odd fashion. It significantly reduces storage-access conflicts in a multiprocessor system, and thereby increases overall system performance. With interleaving, the modules are divided into even and odd locations (although the addressing structure within the modules themselves remains unchanged). Thus, in a fully expanded eight module system, modules 0, 2, 4, 6 are referenced for even addresses while modules 1, 3, 5, 7 are referenced for odd addresses.

multiprocessor, overlapping — The processor is capable of determining whether its current operand and next instruction lie in different storage modules. It is also capable, if this situation is present, of retrieving these two words in parallel, at an effective 100% performance increase. Since the i/o controller is not required to reference instructions in main storage except on command transfers, it does not have, nor does it need, the overlapping feature. The overlapping feature permits the separation of the instruction and data of a program into separate physical banks. Furthermore, the basing register of the processor allows either the instruction or data area of a program to be relocated independently—a significant advantage in memory compacting to overcome fragmentation. (Some systems.)

multiprocessor system, modular — Some distributed processing systems use modules containing individual microprocessors and firmware. A typical system is designed for long-term use, is modular in design, and is processor independent, including RAM memory.

multiprocessor-system types — Categories of multiprocessor systems include: common-bus, crossbar-switch, multimemory/multibus, pipeline, and array processors. The primary advantage of multiprocessor systems is improved reliability. This is because these systems are modular in nature and hence readily reconfigurable under software control, or they are fully duplexed through parallel processing but permit either portion of the system to carry the full load.

multiprogramming — A technique for handling numerous routines or programs simultaneously by overlapping or interleaving their execution; i.e., permitting more than one program to time share machine components.

multiprogramming, degree of — Refers to the number of transactions handled in parallel by the systems involved in a multiprogram.

multiprogramming, executive control — *See* executive control multiprogramming.

multiprogramming (executive control logic) — *See* executive control logic, multiprogramming.

multiprogramming, executive-system — *See* executive system multiprogramming.

multiprogramming, foreground/background — Programs that require immediate response to high-priority (foreground) tasks and which utilize system resources on demand. Background tasks (typically batch processing jobs), wait for execution until foreground interrupts, calls, etc., are executed before resuming. That is, background programs are executed only during idle times of the foreground program; they must always yield to the demands from foreground programs.

multiprogramming interrupts — Some computers are equipped with a set of control signals which are referred to as interrupts. Whenever certain conditions exist, a control signal will direct the central computer to execute the word (instruction) at a specified address in central store. Each interrupt is activated by unique conditions and directs the computer to a correspondingly unique address in central store. The occurrence of an interrupt terminates guard mode, program lockin, and central-store address assignments. (Some systems.)

multiprogramming, master/slave — A system designed to guarantee that one program cannot damage or access another program sharing memory.

multiprogramming memory protect — This hardware function provides positive protection to the system executive routine and all other programs. It not only protects against processor execution, but also against i/o data area destruction. Because it is a hardware function rather than software, it reduces multiprogramming complexities.

multiprogramming, priority — Priority multiprogramming is oriented toward concurrent operation of several types of applications. Assignment of priority levels is at the discretion of the user. For example, one priority level can be reserved for a program that must provide rapid responses to real-time devices, such as communications control. Another can be reserved for the peripheral control package to accomplish several media conversions—card to tape, tape to printer, etc. The third priority level could then be used to run either a production or a monitor job.

multiprogramming, program competition — Multiprogramming is a process by which several related or unrelated programs or portions of programs are performed concurrently, provided that enough processing, storage, and input/output facilities are available. While one program is awaiting an occurrence, such as the completion of an input/output operation or the end of a time interval, control of the processing unit is directed to another program in accordance with a pre-established order of priority. The competition among several programs for the processing, storage, input/output, and programming facilities of the system helps to ensure that as much of the system as possible is kept busy performing useful work as much of the time as possible. As a result, the total throughput of the system, that is, the total volume of work performed by the system during a given interval of time, is significantly increased.

multiprogramming requirements — Multiprogramming requirements are: a supervisory program, referred to as executive, monitor, or supervisor; an interrupt processing system; memory protection facilities to prevent one program from destroying others; dynamic program and data relocatability so that the same routine can be reentrant (that is, the routine can be used, unmodified, in different memory locations at different times); direct access facilities, or at least the facility for the convenient addressing of peripheral equipment. (For personal computers the floppy disk is the typical example of a direct access device.)

Typically, user programs to be run are stored in auxiliary memory, usually disk, readily accessible so that the supervisory program can switch them into main memory when their times to operate arrive. Each program is allocated the required area in main memory, and that area is protected, by either hardware or software, from interference by other programs. Any instruction attempting to address an area outside the allocated memory block is trapped and prompts an error message.

multiprotocol communication chips — Several data-link control chips support more than one data-link control procedure. These chips ease the problem posed by the increasing number of data-communications systems that must support both character-controlled and bit-oriented protocols within the same equipment. In a multiline controller, each line protocol may be different. A multiplexer or data concentrator, for instance, might service character-controlled protocols on its low-speed terminal side and bit-oriented ones on its high-speed backbone link.

multireel sorting — The automatic sequencing of a file having more than one input tape, without operator intervention.

multisequencing — The simultaneous execution of several parts of a program by separate central processing units.

multistation — Any network of stations capable of communicating with each other, whether on one circuit or through a switching center.

multitasking — Procedures in which several separate but interrelated tasks operate under a single program identity. Differs from multiprogramming in that common routines and dataspace as well as disk files may be used. May or may not involve multiprocessing.

multitasking/multiprogramming — Special methods and systems designed to achieve concurrency by separating programs into two or more interrelated tasks that share the same code, buffers, files, and equipment.

multithread processing — *See* processing, multithread.

Mylar — A DuPont trademark for polyester film often used as a base for magnetically coated or perforated information media.

N

N-address instruction format — *See* instruction format, N-address.

name — A term of one or more words to identify one of a general class of items, e.g., to identify a person, machine component, operation code, function, etc.

name, data — *See* data name.

name, file — Alphanumeric characters assigned to identify a related set of records which constitute a particular file.

name, program — The brief reference in a program to another program or portion of another program.

name, record — In COBOL, the name given to a record within a file and assigned the level number 01. Data names for elements within a record have lower-level numbers, 02, 03, etc.

names — In COBOL, a combination of one to thirty alphanumeric characters containing at least one alpha and no blanks, not starting or ending with a hyphen. Names are used for conditions, data, and special procedures or purposes.

name, section — The distinct qualifying term available for a paragraph name.

name, set — An identifier.

name, variable — An alphanumeric name selected by a programmer to represent a specific program variable. Rules for naming variables vary between compilers (FORTRAN, BASIC) and computing equipment.

NAND — A logical operator having the property that if P is a statement, Q is a statement . . . then the NAND of P.Q.R. . . . is true if at least one statement is false, false if all statements are true.

NAND element — *Same as* gate, NAND.

NAND gate — *See* gate, NAND.

NAND operation — *Same as* gate, NAND.

NAND operator — *Same as* gate, NAND.

nanosecond — A billionth of a second. Nanosecond speeds were first introduced to the data-processing industry with a thin-film memory computer.

NASORD — A programming reference to a file not in sequential order.

native language — A communication language or coding between machine units or modules which is peculiar to or usable for a particular class or brand of equipment.

natural language — A language whose rules reflect and describe current usage rather than prescribed usage.

N/C language processor — In numerical control, a computer program developed to serve as a translating system for a parts programmer to develop a mathematical representation of a geometric form with the use of symbolic notation.

N/C (numerical-control) machines — A punched paper or plastic tape with magnetic spots is used to feed digital instructions to a numerical-control machine, i.e., an automated cutting or forming machine thus guided. Tolerances as fine as 1/10,000 of an inch are achieved on unattended units. Tapes are developed from digital computer programs.

N-cube — A term used in switching theory to indicate two N-1 cubes with corresponding points connected.

N-dimensional cube — *See* N-cube.

NDRO — An abbreviation for nondestructive read out.

negate — 1. To perform the NOT logic operation. 2. The conversion of an initially true value to false or vice versa or change signs.

negation — *Same as* NOT operation.

negative A-implies-B gate — *Same as* gate, A AND-NOT B.

negative AND gate — *Same as* gate, NAND.

negative B-implies-A — *Same as* gate, B AND-NOT A.

negative OR gate — *Same as* gate, NOR.

negative-true logic — A logic system in which the voltage representing a logical 1 has a lower or more negative value than that representing a logical 0. Most parallel i/o buses use negative-true logic due to the nature of commonly available logic circuits.

negator — *Same as* gate, NOT.

neither-NOR gate — *Same as* gate, NOR.

neither-OR operation — *Same as* gate, NOR.

nest — 1. To embed a subroutine or block of data into a larger routine or block of data. 2. To evaluate an nth degree polynomial by a particular algorithm which uses N−1 multiply operations and N−1 add operations in succession.

nested macros — The power of a macro instruction may be increased by calling another macro from within the macro instruction. Such a macro within a macro is called a nested macro. When a nested macro call is encountered during macro expansion, the state of the macro currently being expanded is saved, and expansion then begins on the nested macro. Upon completing expansion of the nested macro, expansion of the original macro continues. Nested macros may themselves contain macros. However, the depth of nesting is limited by parameter list sizes.

nesting — 1. Including a routine or block of data within a larger routine or block of data. 2. The relationship between the statements contained in two perform statements. The statements included in the second or inner perform statement must be wholly included in or excluded from the first, or outer, perform statement. Note special FORTRAN nesting rules for inner loops.

nesting level — In assembler programming, the level at which a term or subexpression appears in an expression, or the level at which a macrodefinition containing an inner macroinstruction is processed by an assembler.

nesting loop — *See* loop, nesting.

nesting storage — *Same as* storage, pushdown.

nest of subroutines — *See* subroutines, nest of.

network — 1. A series of interconnected points. 2. The interconnection of a number of points by communications facilities.

network access control — Various tasks related to network administrative controls, including monitoring of system operation, ensuring of data integrity, user identification, recording system access and changes, and methods for granting user access.

network, analog — A circuit or circuits that represent(s) physical variables in such a manner as to permit the expression and solution of mathematical relationships between the variables, or to permit the solution directly by electric or electronic means.

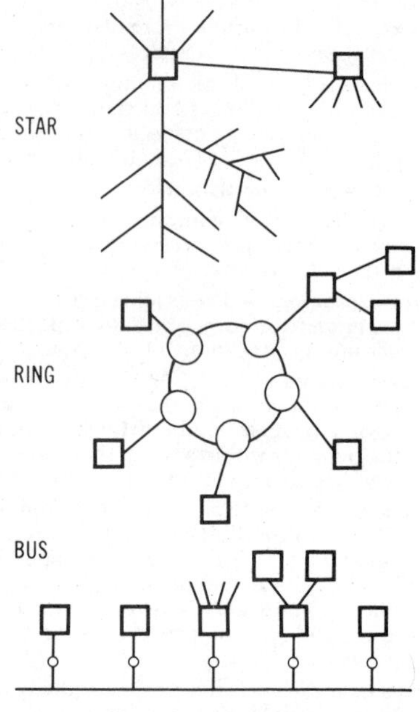

Network configurations.

network analyzer — 1. A simulator for the study of a network, e.g., electrical supply network. 2. An analog computer using electrical circuit elements to represent electrical phenomena to solve problems concerning the behavior of these electrical phenomena.

network awareness — A condition in which the central processor is cognizant of the status of the network.

network components — In large systems, the host processors, remote computer systems, remote terminals, and transmission paths or channels that link all the components to each other.

network, computer — Basically, two or more interconnected computers with advantages for permitting geographical distribution, and thus economy of computer operations. Such a network also permits parallel processing (usually time sharing), combinations of send-receive communications, multipoint remote entry and output, locally controlled data banks and switching centers, and less requirement for centralized facilities.

network configurations — The three most common known methods of configuring systems with many mini or microcomputers are the star, ring, and shared-bus arrangements—and the specific hardware and software to implement each type.

network drills — A final level of testing in a real-time system in which data from all the sites is transmitted and the entire complex of equipment, personnel, interfaces, and programs is tested.

network load analysis — A listing of the flow of messages between stations to organize and create station characteristics by volumes of documents, frequency of processing, and special time requirements.

network standalone systems — Generally, dedicated networks that can include both local and remote data sources. Typical is a system that interconnects branch offices with a headquarters computer or provides communications between various departments within an office complex, e.g. inquiry/response processing of a dynamic data base.

network, star — A system of remote computers configured so that all report to a central computer and tap its data file. It is often a two-level hierarchy but differs in that it entails a heavy flow of back-and-forth communications between the small processors and the central unit, as in an airline reservation and ticketing system.

network timing — Timing signals transferred from the data circuit-terminating equipment to the data terminal equipment on an interchange circuit which controls the transfer of digits across the transmitted and received data circuits.

new input queue — A group or a queue of new messages in the system that are waiting for processing. The main scheduling routine will scan them along with other queues and order them into processing in order.

new-line character — *See* character, new-line.

new sync — Allows for a rapid transition from one transmitter to another on multipoint private-line data networks.

next-available-block register — *See* register, next available block.

nexus — A connection or interconnection. A tie or link.

nibble — Generally considered to be a 4-bit word, in contrast to a byte, which is generally considered to be an 8-bit word.

NI (noninhibit) interrupts — Some systems provide various noninhibit interrupts such as: powerfail, auto restart, TTY break, Memory Parity and Protect, Interrupt Program Time Out, nonimplemented Op code and others.

node — A point of convergence on a diagram, chart, or graph. Nodes can be used to designate a state, event, time convergence, or a coincidence of paths or flows.

node computer — The most extensive distributed processing system is the ARPA net which links many different computers in the continental US, Hawaii, and Europe via satellite. The ARPA net consists of a set of node computers which store and forward data, messages, and programs. Each node computer can connect several host computers. The host computers must go through the node to get into the communications network. Some host computers are connected to the node computers via high speed communication links; others can be connected via modems and dial-up telephone lines.

The ARPA net is distributed geographically as well as functionally, with many different kinds of computers interacting. The node processors are transparent to the user.

noise — 1. Meaningless extra bits or words that must be ignored or removed from the data at the time the data is used. 2. Errors introduced into data in a system, especially in communication channels. 3. Random variations of one or more characteristics of any entity such as voltage, current, and data. 4. Loosely, any disturbance tending to interfere with the normal operation of a device or system.

noise, broadband (white) — The thermal noise that is uniformly distributed across the frequency spectrum at a wide range of energy levels.

noise characteristics — The most critical consideration in the use of digital circuit modules is noise. In large module assemblies, the spurious signals introduced by noise can cause false operations that, due to their random and transient nature, are extremely difficult to correct. Noise is probably the most frequent source of malfunction in large logic arrays, particularly in a field environment. One error of this type can degrade or destroy the data from a critical test or operation and consequently delay important programs and schedules.

noise factor — The ratio consisting of the difference between the number of documents retrieved and the number of relevant documents retrieved, divided by the number of documents retrieved. A measure of the efficiency of the information retrieval system in which a zero would be optimum.

noise, impulse — A pulse appearing at the output of a circuit that was not transmitted from the originating input to the circuit. These pulses usually are induced from circuit functioning or from sources outside the circuit and its associated input/output equipment.

noise, line — Noise originating in a transmission line.

noise margin, voltage — The voltage amplitude of extraneous signal that can be algebraically added to the noise-free worst-case "input" level before the output voltage deviates from the allowable logic voltage level. The term "input" is used here to refer to logic-input terminals, power-supply terminals, or ground-reference terminals.

noise, random — Noise due to the aggregate of a large number of elementary disturbances with random occurrence in time.

noise, reference — The magnitude of circuit noise that will produce a circuit noise-meter reading equal to that produced by 10 watts of electronic power at 1000 hertz.

noisy digit — A specific digit that is chosen to be inserted into the units position of a mantissa during left-shifting manipulation associated with the normalizing of various floating-point numbers.

nonconjunction — *Same as* gate, NAND.

nonconjunction gate — *Same as* gate, NOR.

nondisjunction gate — *Same as* gate, NOR.

nonequality gate — *Same as* gate, exclusive OR.

nonequivalence — *See* exclusive OR.

nonequivalence element — *Same as* gate, exclusive OR.

nonequivalence gate — *Same as* gate, exclusive OR.

nonequivalent element — *Same as* gate, exclusive OR.

nonexistent code — *See* character, illegal.

nonexistent code check — *See* check, forbidden-combination.

nonlocking escape — *Same as* character, nonlocking shift.

nonlocking shift character — *See* character, nonlocking shift.

nonnumeric — Any character or symbol other than a digit.

nonnumerical data processing — Specific languages have been developed by symbol manipulation and used primarily as research tools rather than for production programming. Most have proved valuable in construction of compilers and in simulation of human problem solving. Other uses have been generalized and verification of mathematical proofs, pattern recognition, information retrieval, algebraic manipulation, heuristic programming, and exploration of new programming languages.

nonnumeric character — Any allowable character except a numeric digit.

nonnumeric coding — *See* coding, nonnumeric.

nonprint instruction — *See* instruction, nonprint.

nonprogrammed halt — *See* halt, nonprogrammed.

nonrealtime processing — Processing historical data such as batch processing. Also used to describe as unsuccessful real time information processing systems.

nonreflective coatings — Materials that can be applied to the outer surface of the video screen to reduce glare that may be present in some office environments. The coating tends to make the images on the screen slightly fuzzy, but it is useful in situations where glare causes operator problems.

nonresident simulator computer system — A system that involves the utilization of an in-house larger computer to simulate the MPU hardware in the development of microcomputer programs. This use features a lower cost than conventional time sharing and usually offers access to faster peripherals as well.

nonreturn-to-zero — A method of writing information on a magnetic surface in which the current through the write head winding does not return to zero after the write pulse.

nonvolatile memory — A storage medium which retains information when power is removed from the system.

nonvolatile storage — A storage medium which retains information in the absence of power and which may be made available upon restoration of power, e.g., magnetic tapes, cores, drums, and disks. (Contrasted with volatile storage.)

no operation — An absent or omitted instruction left blank deliberately, often to permit later insertion of data or information without any rewriting, or for the program itself to develop one or more instructions. Often, a specific instruction which merely advances the instruction content and performs no other function.

no-operation instruction — *See* no-op instruction.

no operation, memory protect — A special procedure developed to protect the contents of specific sections of storage from alteration, by inhibiting the execution of any type of memory modification instruction upon detection of the presence of a guard bit associated with the accessed memory location. Such instructions which access protected memory are most often executed as a no operation, or a special violation program interrupt is generated.

no-op instruction — 1. An instruction that specifically instructs the computer to do nothing but process the next instruction in sequence. 2. A blank instruction. 3. A skip instruction. 4. A waste instruction. (Synonymous with waste instruction and skip.)

NOR — The Boolean operator that gives a truth table value of true only when both of the variables connected by the logical operator are false, i.e., the negation of inclusive OR.

NOR circuit — A circuit that has an output only when all inputs are down.

NOR element — *Same as* gate, NOR.

no return point — A first instance in a program in which a rerun is no longer possible, since data may no longer be available.

NOR gate — *See* gate, NOR.

normal-direction flow — In flowcharts, the normal flow is from left to right and from top to bottom.

normal form, Backus — *See* Backus normal form.

normalize — 1. In programming, to adjust the exponent and fraction of a floating-point quantity so that the fraction lies in the prescribed normal, standard range. 2. In mathematical operations, to reduce a set of symbols or numbers to a normal or standard form. (Synonymous with standardize.) 3. To alter or position into a regular or standard format as to right- or left-justify.

normalized — A mantissa is normalized if its first digit is not zero.

normalizer — An electronic component of an OCR (optical character reader) which changes or modifies the signal from the scanner to receive a processed rendition of the input character which is more suitable for a detailed or more sophisticated analysis, i.e., essentially a quality improving usage which does not alter the basic character shape. Magnetic ink character normalizers perform a similar function, filling in any voids and cancelling extraneous additions due to erasures, etc.

normally closed contacts — A pair of contacts on a relay that open when the relay is energized.

normally open contacts — A pair of contacts on a relay that close when the relay is energized.

normal orientation — Although most OCRs (optical character readers) can be programmed, and do thus accept a wide variety of character styles and even oddities, they must be normally oriented to direct the reader to perform the scan across the width of the source document. The line elements of the source document appear in parallel with this edge.

normative testing — Standards of performance that are established for the testing of both quantitative and qualitative system performance.

NOR operation — *Same as* gate, NOR.

NOR operator — *Same as* gate, NOR.

NOT — A logical operator having the property that if P is a statement, then the NOT of P is true if P is false, and false if P is true.

NOT-AND element — *Same as* gate, NAND.

NOT-AND gate — *Same as* gate, NAND.

NOT-AND operation — *Same as* gate, NAND.

notation — 1. The act, process, or method of representing facts or quantities by a system or set of marks, signs, figures, or characters. 2. A system of such symbols or abbreviations used to express technical facts or quantities, e.g., as mathematical notation. 3. An annotation or note.

notation, base — An annotation consisting of a decimal number, in parentheses, written as a subscript suffix to a number, its decimal value indicating the radix of the number; e.g., $11_{(2)}$ indicates the number 11 is in the radix of two, $11_{(8)}$ indicates the number 11 is in the radix of eight. A number written without its radix notation is assumed to be in the radix of ten.

notation, binary — *See* number, binary.

NOT-both gate — *Same as* gate, NAND.

NOT-BOTH operation — *Same as* gate, NAND.

NOT circuit — *Same as* gate, NOT.

NOT element — *Same as* gate, NOT.

NOT gate — *See* gate, NOT.

NOT-IF-THEN operation — *Same as* gate, NAND.

NOT operation — A Boolean operation on one operand in which the result has the alternative value of the operand, i.e., if the two possible states of the operand are represented by a zero or a one, the corresponding results are one or a zero. Same as negation, Boolean complementation, or inversion.

NOT operator — *Same as* gate, NOT.

N-plus-one-address instruction — *See* instruction format, N plus one address.

N-tuple — A collection of N elements, usually ordered, e.g., x1, x2. . . .

nucleus — A part of an operating system which resides in main memory or storage. Control routines are grouped in the resident nucleus, and the balance of the operating system (OS) is relegated to auxiliary storage devices as disks, drums, and sometimes tapes. The nucleus loads parts of the nonresident routines into storage as programmed and as required.

null — 1. An absence of information, as contrasted with zero or blank for the presence of no information. 2. Zero. 3. Pertaining to no deflection from a center or end position.

null cycle — The time necessary to cycle through a program without introducing data. This establishes the lower bound for program processing time.

null gate — *See* gate, null.

null string — An empty string.

number — 1. A figure or word, or group of figures or words, representing graphically an arithmetical sum; a numeral, as the number 45. (Clarified by number systems.) 2. A numeral by which a thing is designated in a series, as a pulse number. 3. A single member of a series designated by consecutive numerals, as a part number. 4. A character, or a group of characters, uniquely identifying or describing an article, process, condition, document, or class, as a 6SN7 tube. 5. To count; enumerate. 6. To distinguish by a number.

number, ABA — A coding number assigned to banks by the American Bankers Association to assist in check clearing.

number, base — The quantity of characters for use in each of the digital positions of a numbering system. In the more common numbering systems the characters are some or all of the Arabic numerals as follows:

System Name	*Characters*	*Radix*
BINARY	(0,1)	2
OCTAL	(0,1,2,3,4,5,6,7)	8
DECIMAL	(0,1,2,3,4,5,6,7,8,9)	10

Unless otherwise indicated, the radix of any number is assumed to be 10. For positive identification of a radix 10 number, the radix is written in parentheses as a subscript to the expressed number, i.e., $126_{(10)}$. The radix of any nondecimal number is expressed in similar fashion, e.g., $11_{(2)}$ and $5_{(8)}$.

number, binary — A number, usually consisting of more than one figure, representing a sum, in which the individual quantity represented by each figure is based on a radix of two. The figures used are 0 and 1.

number, binary-coded decimal — A number usually consisting of successive groups of figures, in which each group of four figures is a binary number that represents but does not necessarily equal arithmetically a particular digit in an associated decimal number; e.g., if the three rightmost figures of a decimal number are 362, the three rightmost figure groups of the binary coded decimal number are 0011 0110 0010.

number, biquinary — A number consisting of a pair of digits representing a sum, in which the left digit is based on the radix two, and the right digit is based on the radix five. The figures 0 or 1 (a 1 represents 5) are used for the left digit, and 0, 1, 2, 3 or 4 are used for the right digit. Example, 13 (5 + 3) is the decimal digit 8. The left digit of each pair of digits has a weight of 0 or 5.

number, biquinary-coded decimal — A number usually consisting of successive pairs of digits, in which each pair is a biquinary number; e.g., if the digits of a decimal number are 3671, the biquinary-coded decimal number would be 03 11 12 01. The left digit of each pair of digits has a weight of 0 or 5.

number, call — 1. A group of characters identifying a subroutine and containing: (a) information concerning parameters to be inserted in the subroutine, (b) information to be used in generating the subroutine, or (c) information related to the operands. 2. A call word if the quantity of characters in the call number is equal to the length of a computer word.

number, check — A number composed of one or more digits and used to detect equipment malfunctions in data-transfer operations. If a check number consists of only one digit, it is synonymous with check digit. (Related to digit, check.)

number, coded decimal — A number consisting of successive characters or a group of characters in which each character or group of characters usually represents a specific figure in an associated decimal number; e.g., if the figures of a decimal number are 45, the coded decimal number might be represented as GQ, or LIZZ, or 0100 0101.

number complements, octal — *See* octal number complements.

number control — This is the quantity of a number (value) which must be the result of a process or problem in order to prove the accuracy.

number control, serial — The control of messages by assigning a number at the time of origination and adding additional numbers as the message passes through specific points.

number, decimal — A number, usually of more than one figure, representing a sum, in which the quantity represented by each figure is based on the radix of ten. The figures used are 0, 1, 2, 3, 4, 5, 6, 7, 8, and 9.

number, designation — Used in truth tables, which are representations of all possible combinations of binary states of a set of variables. A designation numeral thus is the set of digits which represents a particular Boolean expression as a line or a column in such a table.

number, double-length — A specific numeral which contains twice as many digits as ordinary numerals in particular computers and ones which usually require two registers or storage locations. Such numerals are most often used for double-precision computing.

number, double-precision — *See* double-precision number.

number, duodecimal — A number, consisting of successive characters, representing a sum in which the individual quantity represented by each character is based on a radix of twelve. The characters used are 0, 1, 2, 3, 4, 5, 6, 7, 8, 9, T(for ten), and E(for eleven). (Related to number systems.)

number, Fibonacci — A numeral which is part of a unique set for a highly specific search method.

number, floating-point — In many cases, the solution of a problem requires values of numbers that are either too large or too small to be expressed by the computer. The physical size of the number can be reduced by "scaling" or shifting the number to the right or left a predetermined number of places so that the most significant bits of the number may be used. For instance, the decimal number 6510 may be expressed as 0.651×10^7, 0.0651×10^8, 0.00651×10^9, etc. The exponent of the number-system base is the scale factor or the number of places the number is shifted. Some systems are fixed-point arithmetic, and there is no automatic hardware feature for handling the scaling factor or exponent. The programmer is responsible for remembering the scale factors. Also, the possibility of an overflow during intermediate operations must be considered.

number generator — A set of manual controls on which a computer operator can set a word for input.

number generator, random — *See* generator, random-number.

number, hexadecimal — A specific numeration system which uses the radix 16; i.e., 16 symbols are used, 0 through 9 plus the characters A, B, C, D, E, and F for digits beyond 9. Each hexadecimal digit thus can be represented by a group of four binary digits, which is called a tetrad.

number, identification — The number from 0000000 to 9999999, assigned to input data.

number, installation-tape — A number permanently assigned to a plastic or metal spool to identify a particular roll of magnetic tape.

number, logical — The number assigned to a peripheral unit during autoload or system generation time. This number can be altered whenever convenient, in contrast to a physical unit number.

number, mixed-base — A number consisting of two or more characters representing a sum, in which the quantity represented by each character is based on a different radix.

number, mixed-radix — *Same as* number, mixed base.

number, multiple-length — A number having two, three, or more times as many figures as are normally handled in a particular device.

number, octal — A number of one or more figures representing a sum, in which the quantity represented by each figure is based on a radix of eight. The figures used are 0, 1, 2, 3, 4, 5, 6, and 7. (Clarified by octal.)

number, operation — 1. A number designating the position of an operation or its equivalent subroutine in the sequence of operations comprising a routine. 2. A number, stated in symbolic code, identifying each step in a program.

number, polyvalent — A number, consisting of several figures, used for description, wherein each figure represents one of the characteristics being described.

number, positional — A method for expressing a quantity using two or more figures, wherein the successive right to left figures are to be interpreted as coefficients of ascending integer powers of the radix.

number, radix — *Same as* number, base.

number, random — *See* random number.

number range — The span or dimension or range of values which a number (variable) can assume, and usually expressed within beginning and ending limits or using N, if such limits are unknown.

number, read-around — The number of times a specific spot, digit, or location in electrostatic storage may be consulted before spillover will cause a loss of information stored in surrounding spots. The surrounding information must be restored before the loss occurs.

number, real — An element of a set of all positive and negative numbers, including all types, integers, zeros, mixed, rational, irrational, etc., but not imaginary or complex.

number, reel — A sequence number that identifies a particular reel in a series of reels that make up a file.

number representation system — *See* numeration system.

number, section — A sequence number that identifies a particular section in a series of sections that make up a file.

number, self-checking — A number, with a suffix figure related to the figure(s) of the number, used to check the number after it has been transferred from one medium or device to another. (Related to check bit, modulo-N check, and error-detecting code.)

number, septinary — A number, usually of more than one figure, representing a sum in which the quantity represented by each figure is based on a radix of seven. The figures used are 0, 1, 2, 3, 4, 5, and 6.

number, serial — Numerals usually attached to a device, machine, item, or a sequence or position of an item relative to other items, i.e., numbers representing a label or identifier.

number, sexadecimal — A number, usually of more than one figure, representing a sum, in which the quantity represented by each figure is based on a radix of sixteen. (Synonymous with hexadecimal number.)

number, statement — *See* statement number.

number, symbolic — A numeral used in writing routines for referring to a specific storage location; such numerals are converted to actual storage addresses in the final assembling of the program.

number system — A systematic method for representing numerical quantities in which any quantity is represented as the sequence of coefficients of the successive powers of a particular base with an appropriate point. Each succeeding coefficient from right to left is associated with and usually multiplies the next higher power of the base. The first coefficient to the left of the point is associated with the zero power of the base. For example, in decimal notation, 371.426 represents $(3 \times 10^2) + (7 \times 10^1) + (1 \times 10^0) + (4 \times 10^{-1}) + (2 \times 10^{-2}) + (6 \times 10^{-3})$. The following are names of the number systems with bases 2 through 20: 2, binary; 3, ternary; 4, quaternary; 5, quinary; 6, senary; 7 septenary; 8, octal, or octonary; 9, novenary; 10, decimal; 11, undecimal; 12, duodecimal; 13, terdenary; 14, quaterdenary; 15, quindenary; 16, sexadecimal, or hexadecimal; 17, septendecimal; 18, octodenary; 19, novemdenary; 20, vicenary. Also 32, duosexadecimal, or duotricinary; and 60, sexagenary. The binary, octal, decimal, and sexadecimal systems are widely used in computers. (Synonymous with duodecimal number and binary-number system; related to positional representation; and clarified by octal and binary digit.)

number system, binary — *See* number, binary.

number, user — The unique number assigned to each user of a time-shared system enabling him to identify himself to the system when he communicates with it through a remote terminal. (Synonymous with identification number.)

numeral — A digit or digits normally used to represent a number.

numeral, binary — *Same as* number, binary.

numeral, decimal — *Same as* number, decimal.

numeral, designation — Used in truth tables which are representations of all possible combinations of binary states of a set of variables. A designation numeral thus is the set of digits which represents a particular Boolean expression as a line or a column in such a table.

numeral, double-length — *See* number, double-length.

numeral, duodecimal — *Same as* number, duodecimal.

numeral, hexadecimal — *Same as* number, hexadecimal.

numeralization — The use of digits to represent alphabetic data.

numeral, multiple-length — Numeral representation of quantities of items which have two, three, . . . times as many digits as the numeric words usually encountered. Such numerals require two or more registers or storage locations to achieve higher precision calculations.

numeral, octal — *Same as* number, octal.

numeral, self-checking — A unique and very specific numeral containing check digits for even- or odd-parity checking, i.e., a six-bit numeral may have a seventh bit serving as an odd-parity, in which the total number of ones in the numeral must always be odd.

numeral, sexadecimal — *Same as* number, hexadecimal.

numeration system — A system for the representation of numbers, e.g., the decimal system, the roman numeral system, the binary system.

numeric — Composed of numerals; the value of a number as opposed or contrasted to character representation.

numerical analysis — The study of methods of obtaining useful quantitative solutions to problems that have been expressed mathematically, including the study of the errors and bounds on errors in obtaining such solutions.

numerical code — A restrictive type of code which has a character set consisting of digits only.

numerical control — *See* APT (Automatically Programmed Tools).

numerical control, direct (DNC) — A system connecting a set of numerically controlled machines to a common memory for part program or machine program storage, with provision for on-demand distribution of data for the machines. Direct numerical control systems typically have additional provisions for collection, display or editing of part programs, operator instructions, or data related to the numerical control process.

numerically controlled machine tools — *See* APT.

numeric-alphabetic — *Same as* alphabetic-numeric.

numerical tape — A punched paper or plastic tape used to feed digital instructions to a numerical control (N/C) machine.

numerical word — *See* word, numerical.

numeric character — An allowable digit in a computer system of representing numbers.

numeric code — A system of numerical abbreviations used in the preparation of information for input into a machine, i.e., all information is reduced to numerical quantities.

numeric coding — Coding that uses only digits to represent data and instructions.

numeric control — That field of computer activity which centers around the control of machine tools by mechanical devices; e.g., a computer can control assembly-line tools for machining.

numeric data code — *See* code, numeric.

numeric key punch — A key punch that processes only numeric data.

N-way switch — *See* switch, programmed.

O

object code — The code produced by a compiler or special assembler which can be executed on the target computer.

objective function — The function of the independent variables whose maximum or minimum is sought in an optimization problem.

object language — 1. The machine language developed by the compiler from the source language; the machine language is directly comprehensible to the computer without further refinement or definition by interpreters, assemblers, or compilers. 2. A result of transforming or translating a source language by any of the many devices or procedures.

object-language program — *See* object routine.

object machine — The computer on which the object program is to be executed.

object phase — An occasion on which the target program is run is often called run phase, target phase, or object phase. Most often this terminology is used when compiling has taken place.

object program — The binary form of a source program produced by an assembler or a compiler. The object program (the final translation) is composed of machine-word or machine-coded instructions that the specific computer can execute.

object program library — *See* library, program.

object-program preparation — Conversion of programs from one of several easy-to-use source languages, or from certain competitive system languages, to a specific machine code.

object routine — The machine-language routine that is the output after translation from the source language.

object time — The time at which an object program is executed, as opposed to the time at which a source program is translated into machine language to create an object program.

occurs — In COBOL, describes a sequence of data items of the same format. Subscripting is used to refer or designate a particular item in a procedure statement.

OCR — Abbreviation for Optical Character Recognition. Recognition by machines of printed or written characters based on inputs from photoelectric transducers. Contrast with MICR.

OCR-A code — A major type of magnetic character "language." This is a special type font that is both human and machine readable. It has been adopted by the National Retail Merchants Association as the standard for marking merchandise sold in department stores and other general retail outlets.

OCR applications, business — Uses such as scanning for credit authorization, banking, postal uses, government health care, retailing transactions, word processing, and others.

OCR, common language — *See* language, common (OCR).

OCR wand — A typical device provides automatic reading that can be employed on irregular-sized documents or pages. The wand scans any sized document at the rate of 100 characters per second which is comparable to the production of 20 key operators. When operating at a crt or other display station, any data read with the wand can be displayed facilitating key correction.

OCR wand readers — Various types of OCR wand readers are connected directly to terminals, computers, and other data processing equipment. They are designed to optically lift human-readable source data from a document and transmit the information directly to the host device. Typical applications are reading financial transaction documents including utility bills, purchase orders, charge slips, claim reports, remittance forms, and order entry documents. Several types read OCR-A type font established by the National Retail Merchants Association, and OCR-B, a type font used widely in Europe.

octal — Pertaining to eight; usually describing a number system of base or radix eight; e.g., in octal notation, octal 214 is 2 times 64, plus 1 times 8, plus 4 times 1, and equals decimal 140. Octal 214 in binary-coded octal is represented as 010,001, 100; octal 214, as a straight binary number is written 10001100. Note that binary-coded octal and straight binary differ only in the use of commas; in the example shown, the left hand zero in the straight binary is dropped. (Clarified by octal number.)

octal, binary-coded — A coding system in which binary numbers are used to represent the octal digits of an octal number.

octal digit — The symbol 0, 1, 2, 3, 4, 5, 6, or 7 used as a digit in the system of notation that uses 8 as the base or radix. (Clarified by number systems.)

octal notation — *See* octal number.

octal number — A number of one or more figures, representing a sum in which the quantity represented by each figure is based on a radix of eight. The figures used are 0, 1, 2, 3, 4, 5, 6, and 7. (Clarified by octal.)

octal number complements — Octal notation is used in source language and program testing diagnostic printouts. The octal or base 8 number system expresses values as multiples of powers of 8. Octal notation is a fixed-length system of binary notation. The binary number is interpreted octally by grouping the bits into bytes of three, starting from the right, and interpreting each byte into its octal equivalent. Within each byte the bit positions are weighted with the value of 4, 2, and 1, or 2^2, 2^1, and 2^0. If, after grouping the bits in the fashion described, the most significant byte contains less than three bits, as many binary zeros are implied to the left as are required to bring the numbers of bits in that group to three. For example, the binary number 10011101101 is interpreted octally as follows:

(0)10	011	101	101
2	3	5	5

octal number system — A number system which expresses values as multiples of powers of eight. (Clarified by octal number complements and octal number.)

octal numeral — *Same as* octal number.

octet — A sequence of eight binary digits operated on or considered as a unit and usually concerned with an 8-bit byte, i.e., representing one character or two numerals.

octonary — Pertaining to the number representation system with a base of eight.

odd-even check — *See* check digit, parity.

oersted (video-tape) — A measure of video-tape performance such that the higher the oersted rating, the higher the signal level from the tape. Most ferric tapes today are in the range of 300 oersteds, and most chromium tapes operate at about 500 oersteds.

office, central — A common facility that performs the necessary circuit-switching functions required in the operation of communication networks.

off-line — Descriptive of a system and of the peripheral equipment or devices in a system in which the operation of peripheral equipment is not under the control of the central processing unit. (Clarified by off-line equipment.)

off-line equipment — The peripheral equipment or devices not in direct communication with the central processing unit of a computer. (Synonymous with auxiliary equipment.)

off-line mode — A way of computer operation; it means that the devices are not hooked up together. Perhaps the printer is printing the payroll checks, while the computer is solving a completely unrelated mathematical problem. Both are independent operations.

off-line operation — *Same as* off-line processing.

off-line or indirect system — A remote system in which a mechanical, electronic, or thermal sensing device is used for input and a mechanical, electronic, or thermal controlling device is used for output, but none of these is directly connected to the computer. If there is no human action required in the communications linkage, the system is a direct or on-line system when units are connected to a computer.

off-line output — *See* output, off-line.

off-line processing — Processing not directly associated with or required for main program or real-time communication and control. In an off-line mode, human intervention and control is required between data entry and ultimate processing.

off-line storage — Storage not under control of the central processing unit.

off-line unit — Input/output device or auxiliary equipment not under direct control of the central processing unit.

off-line working — *Same as* off-line operation.

off premise — Standby equipment, usually a back-up or duplicated set of computer equipment at another location. Available for performance of operations under circumstances where the failure of the prime equipment is acute as regards the time sensitivity of the operation being completed.

offset — An unintentional transfer of ink to spoil readability of a document, such as from two freshly printed sheets with the back of one document smearing the face of the other.

off-the-shelf — 1. Pertaining to production items that are available from current stock and need not be either newly purchased or immediately manufactured. 2. Pertaining to computer software or equipment that can be used by customers with little or no adaptation, thereby saving them from the time and expense of developing their own software or equipment.

on-board regulation — The practice of placing small voltage regulators on each circuit board in a system rather than having one large power supply for the entire system. Advantages include the ability to expand the system gradually, the isolation of electrically noisy circuits, and no noise pickup on the power supply wiring. The disadvantages include the necessity for a large number of voltage regulators and the placing of heat sources on the cards.

on call, load — *See* load on call.

on-chip control logic — Logic contained on the microprocessor chip that decodes instructions and coordinates instruction execution with memory and i/o operations which are managed by the system controller.

one-address — Single address; a system of machine instruction such that each complete instruction explicitly describes one operation and one storage location.

one-address instruction — An instruction consisting of an operation and exactly one address. The instruction code of a single address computer may include both zero and multiaddress instructions as special cases.

one-ahead addressing — *Same as* addressing, repetitive.

one-for-one — A phrase often associated with an assembly routine where one source-language instruction is converted to one machine-language instruction.

one-for-one translation — The specific process in which each programming instruction is equal to one machine language instruction.

one gate — *Same as* gate, OR.

one-level address — *Same as* direct address.

one-level code — A code using absolute addresses and absolute operation codes; i.e., a code that indicates the exact location where the referenced operand is to be found or stored. (Synonymous with specific code and related to address, absolute.)

one-level subroutine — A program or subroutine which cannot use either subroutines or itself during its execution, i.e., a closed subroutine.

one output — The voltage response obtained from magnetic core in a "1" stage by reading or resetting process.

one output signal — The output of a magnetic cell in the one condition when a read pulse is supplied.

one-plus-one address — An instruction system having the property that each complete instruction includes an operation and two addresses; one address for the location of a register in the storage

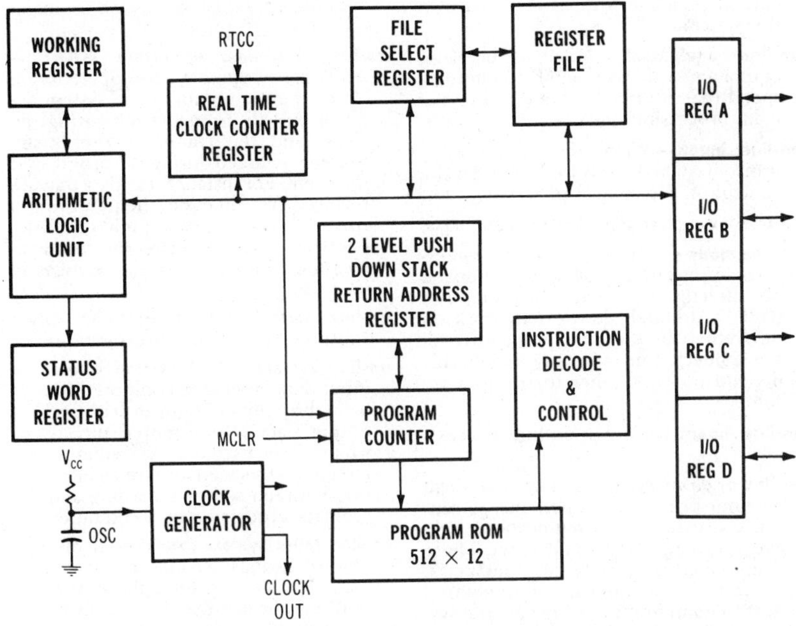

On-chip control logic (8-bit microcomputer).

containing the item to be operated upon, and one for the location containing the next instruction.

one-plus-one address instruction — An instruction containing two or four addresses one of which specifies explicitly the location of the next instruction to be executed. It is usually used on computers whose storage has a latency factor, e.g., a drum computer.

ones complement — *See* complement, ones.

one-shot operation — *See* operation, single-step.

one-step operation — *See* operation, single-step.

one-to-one — A relation between individual members of one set and individual members of another set, i.e., each member of one set has a specific relation to one member of the other set.

one-to-one assembler — *See* assembler, one-to-one.

one-to-one translator — *Same as* assembler, one-to-one.

one-to-partial select ratio — The ratio of a 1 output to a partial select output.

on-line — Descriptive of a system and peripheral equipment or devices in a system in which the operation of such equipment is under control of the central processing unit. Information reflecting current activity is introduced into the data processing system as soon as it occurs. It is directly in line with the main flow of the transaction processing. (Clarified by on-line equipment, and synonymous with in-line processing and on-line processing.)

on-line, central file — *See* file, on-line (central).

on-line data processing — *See* on-line processing.

on-line data reduction — The processing of information as rapidly as the information is received by the computing system or as rapidly as it is generated by the source.

on-line, debug — *Same as* debug, except the computer is performing on-line functions, utilizing another routine which has previously been checked out.

on-line diagnostics — The running of diagnostics on a system while it is online but off-peak to save time and to take corrective action without closing down the system.

on-line equipment — Major processing equipment of compatible computer speed that is directly connected to the main processing unit.

on-line input — When the input device transmits data directly to, and under the control of, the control processing unit.

on-line mass storage — *See* storage, mass.

on-line mode — A way of computer operation—means that all devices are hooked up directly, i.e., with the computer (CPU). Although the devices work on different phases of the procedure, all are connected in some way and usually depend on each other for desired results.

on-line operation — *See* on-line processing.

on-line or direct system — A system which has four principal components—a central processor, a communications linkage, a terminal device, and a user. These components interact to carry out a task, but if there is no human action required in the communications linkage, the system is direct or on-line.

on-line plotter — A local or remote digital incremental plotter—in either on-line or off-line operation with a digital computer—provides a high speed plotting system of versatility and reliability. For on-line operation with medium-size computers, a small adapter unit converts the computer output signals to a form suitable for driving a plotter. No modification to the basic computer circuitry is required. Adapters are available for all standard medium-scale digital computers. The plotter can be used for off-line operation with virtually any medium or large-scale computer.

on-line processing — The operation of terminals, files, and other auxiliary equipment under direct and absolute control of the central processor to eliminate the need for human intervention at any stage between initial input and computer output.

on-line process optimization — An important part of process control is the job of ensuring operating conditions or combinations of conditions for optimum profit. On-line analog computers can be used to adjust one or more process conditions to compensate for uncontrolled variations so that operation is maintained at the optimum level.

on-line, real-time operation (OLRT) — A special system plan and operation in which the input data to the system are given directly from the measuring devices, and the computer results are thereby obtained during the progress of the event. For instance, the data that are received from measurements during a run, with real-time computation of dependent variables during the run, enables the computer to make changes in its output.

on-line storage — Storage under direct control of the central processing unit.

on-line system — 1. A system where the input data enters the computer directly from the point of origin and/or in which output data is transmitted directly to where it is used. 2. A system which eliminates the need for human intervention between source recording and the ultimate processing by a computer.

on-line teller system (bank) — If the volume of savings account and mortgage loan activity warrants, these transactions may be handled in real time by the on-line teller system. Teller consoles at each window at each office may be linked to the computer and the on-line central file.

"on-line" teller systems — On-line teller systems have four major elements: (1) a large random access memory tied directly to the computer, used to store account records and auxiliary information; (2) teller consoles, for keyboard entry of transaction information and computer-controlled printing of replies to passbooks, tickets, and journals; (3) data-communication equipment and telephone lines, linking the teller consoles to the computer; (4) an electronic computer system for control and computation.

on-line unit — Input/output device or auxiliary equipment under direct control of the computer.

on-line working — *See* on-line processing.

onomasticon — A vocabulary of proper or special names, e.g., a list of titles, chemical compounds, companies, executives, etc.

on-premise stand by equipment — A duplicate set of computer system modules located nearby, available for performance of operations in the event of equipment failures and as regards time sensitivity functions of requirements.

on, sign — The instruction which commences communication with the computer system. On a remote terminal, the user can generally gain access to the system by typing in his identification number and an appropriate password.

OP code — A command, usually given in machine language.

open collector — A type of output structure found in certain bipolar logic families. The output is characterized by an active transistor pulldown for taking the output to a low voltage level, and no pullup device. Resistive pullups are generally added to provide the high level output voltage. Open collector devices are useful when several devices are to be bused together on one i/o bus such as IEEE-488-1975 (HP-IB).

open-ended — 1. The quality by which the addition of new terms, subject headings, or classifications does not disturb the pre-existing system. 2. Having the capability of being extended or expanded.

open-ended system — *See* system, open-ended.

open loop — An arrangement in which a computer monitors a process or device and presents the results in real time so that an operator can make adjustments to the process or operation, if required.

open-loop system — A system in which the computer does not directly control a process or procedure but instead displays or prints information for the operator to assist in determination of required action. Most real-time systems are basically open-loop systems.

open-routine — A routine that can be inserted directly into a larger routine without a linkage or calling sequence.

open running — A condition in which a teletypewriter is connected to an open line or a line without battery. A teletypewriter receiver under such a condition appears to be running, as the type hammer continually strikes the type box but does not move across the page.

open shop — A computing installation at which computer programming, coding, and operating can be performed by any qualified company employee.

open subroutine — 1. A separately coded sequence of instructions that is inserted in another instruction sequence directly in low order of the line. A subroutine that must be relocated and inserted into the main routine at each place it is used.

operand — 1. Any one of the quantities entering into or arising from an operation. An operand may be an argument, a result, a parameter, or an indication of the location of the next instruction. 2. A piece of data upon which an operation is performed. 3. The address or name portion of an operation, e.g., x is the operand of the operation (and x).

operand address — *See* address, operand.

operand address, effective — *See* address, operand effective.

operand field — The portion of an immediate-addressing instruction word that contains the immediate operand value, with negative values represented as twos complements.

operand, flag — The third operand of a symbolic instruction, designating which digits of the object-level instruction will be flagged (some computers).

operand/operator — Computer statements consist of an operand that is the data to be operated on and an operator, the instruction itself. The statement consists of a register instruction together with an operand address.

operands, source vs destination — Operations which imply two operands such as add, subtract, move, compare, etc., are handled in many systems, by instructions that specify two addresses. The first operand is called the source operand, the second the destination operand. Bit assignments in the source and destination address fields may specify different modes and different registers.

operating console, microcomputer — The operating console is generally mounted on the front of the processor enclosure, contains all controls and indicators necessary for the operation of the processor. The controls and indicators can include the following: run indicator, run switch, halt indicator, halt switch, reset switch, link indicator, interrupt on indicator, display switch, accumulator position, program counter position, memory data position, alter switch, etc.

operating control, concurrent — *See* concurrent operating control.

operating programs — *See* programs, operating.

operating ratio — The ratio of the number of hours of correct machine operation to the total hours of scheduled operation. For example if a 168-hour week is scheduled, if 12 hours of preventive maintenance are required and 4.8 hours of unscheduled down time occurs, then the operating ratio is (168-16.8/168). This is equivalent to a 90% operating ratio. (Synonymous with computer efficiency.)

operating system — 1. An organized collection of techniques and procedures for operating a computer. 2. A part of a software package (program or routine) defined to simplify housekeeping as input/output procedures, sort-merge generators, data-conversion routines, or tests.

operating system, floppy disk — Several firms have developed floppy disk operating systems for microprocessor development systems that obviate any need for paper tape or cards. Source programs written and edited at the system keyboard and stored on the floppy may then be assembled immediately with macroassembler units under operating system control. Assembled programs may be stored on disk in binary form, then loaded into the processor through a DOS Linking Loader, along with other object modules and the DEBUG programs. DOS packages include dual-drive floppy disk, interface, cable, software, and documentation.

operating system functions — The system software controlling the overall operation of a multipurpose computer system, including such tasks as input and output distribution, interrupt processing, memory allocation, job scheduling, message switching, and other allocation and communication functions.

operating system monitor — *See* monitor, operating system.

operating system supervisor — Operating system consists of a supervisory control program, system programs, and system subroutines. Included are a symbolic assembler and macroprocessor, a FORTRAN or other compiler, and debugging aids. A library of general utility programs is also provided.

operating system, time sharing — The operating system is a collection of programs remaining permanently in memory to provide overall coordination and control of the total operating system. It performs several functions. First, it permits several users' programs from interfering with other users' programs. Each program is run for a certain length of time, then the monitor switches control to another program in a rotating sequence. Switching is frequent enough so that all programs appear to run simultaneously. Another function of the time-sharing monitor is to process input/output commands.

operation — 1. A defined action; the action specified by a single computer instruction or pseudoinstruction; an arithmetical, logical, or transferral unit of a problem, usually executed under the direction of a subroutine. 2. A combination of at least one operator and one operand, e.g., add x. 3. The process of executing a defined action.

operation address instruction — *See* instruction, source-destination.

operational address instruction — A computer instruction having no operation part but rather has the operation implicitly specified by the address parts.

operational character — A specific character that, when used as a code element, can initiate, modify, or stop a control operation. Characters may be used, for example, to control the carriage return, etc.

operational, design — *See* design, operational.

operational mode — The combination of machine operating modes currently in effect.

operational unit — A combination of devices or circuitry which performs a computer process.

operational use time — *See* time, effective.

operational word — A COBOL term used to denote a word which improves readability of the language but need not be on the reserved list.

operation, arithmetical — An operation in which numerical quantities form the elements of the calculation, e.g., addition, subtraction, multiplication, division.

operation, asynchronous — The method of processing in which one operation is completed before the next operation is initiated, i.e., initiation and execution are independent on a portion of the equipment while the remainder of the equipment is free.

operation, attended — In data set applications, individuals are required at both stations to establish the connection and transfer the data sets from talk (voice) mode to data mode.

operation, auxiliary — An operation performed by equipment not under continuous control of the central processor unit.

operation, average calculating — A representative operation which might serve as a base or indication of calculating speeds of various machines, i.e., a number representing, for example, two additions and one multiplication and the time to calculate this, or more commonly accepted, nine additions and one multiplication.

operation, bidirectional — Reading, writing, and searching may be conducted in either direction.

operation, binary — *See* binary operation.

operation, binary arithmetic — *See* arithmetic operation, binary.

operation, binary Boolean — *See* Boolean operation, binary.

operation, bookkeeping — *Same as* housekeeping.

operation, Boolean — *See* Boolean operation.

operation character — *Same as* character command.

operation code — 1. The symbols that designate a basic computer operation to be performed. 2. A combination of bits specifying an absolute machine-language operator, or the symbolic representation of the machine-language operator. 3. That part of an instruction that designates the operation of arithmetic, logic, or transfer to be performed.

operation code, augmented — A particular code which is further defined or limited by information found in another position of an instruction, i.e., an instruction word but one which has addresses considered as the operation code.

operation code field — The portion of an instruction word that contains the operation code.

operation codes — The number of internal machine instructions available.

operation codes, mnemonic — The writing of operation codes in a symbolic notation which is easier to remember than the actual operation codes of the machine.

operation, combination — Relates to the performance of two or more operations simultaneously and as a unit.

operation, complementary — *See* complementary operations.

operation, complete — An operation that includes obtaining the instruction, obtaining all the operands from storage, performing the operation, and returning the results to storage.

operation, computer — *See* computer operation.

operation, concurrent — *See* concurrent operation.

operation control — The control device that directs the arithmetic operation involved in the execution of an instruction in a computing system.

operation-control switch — *See* switch, operation-control.

operation, conversational — *See* conversational mode.

operation cycle — That portion of a machine cycle during which the actual execution of the instruction takes place. Some operations (e.g., divide, multiply) may need a large number of these operation cycles to complete the operation, and the normal instruction/operation alternation will be held up during this time. Also called execution cycle.

operation, dagger — *Same as* gate, NAND.

operation, declarative — *See* declarative operation.

operation, decoded — *See* decoding.

operation decoder — A switching circuit that interprets the operator portion of the machine instruction to be executed, and sets other circuitry for its execution.

operation, double precision — An operation in which two registers are treated as a 64-bit double-word register containing a single quantity (some computers).

operation, dual — Most frequent reference is to the Boolean operation whose result is the negation of the result of another Boolean operation or negation of operand.

operation, dyadic — An operation of two operands.

operation dyadic, Boolean — *See* Boolean operation, dyadic.

operation, EXCEPT — *Same as* gate, NAND.

operation field — That particular part of the instruction format which specifies the procedure or process which is to be performed.

operation, fixed-cycle — A type of computer performance whereby a fixed amount of time is allocated to an operation; synchronous or clocked-type arrangement within a computer in which events occur as a function of measured time.

operation, fixed-point — *See* fixed-point operation.

operation, floating-point — *See* floating-point operation.

operation, housekeeping — A general term for the operation that must be performed for a machine run usually before actual processing begins. Examples of housekeeping operations are: establishing controlling marks, setting up auxiliary storage units, reading the first record for processing, initializing, set-up verification operations, and file identification.

operation, illegal — *See* illegal operation.

operation, iterative — The standard, usual, or automatic repetition of the solution. For example, a set of equations with successive or changed combinations of initial conditions, or simply the use of different parameters and the use of the same computing program.

operation, jump — The computer departs from the regular sequence of instruction executions and jumps to another routine or program, or even some preceding or forward instructions to thus alter control, repeat a process or loop, etc.

operation, logical — 1. A logical or Boolean operation on n-state variables which yields a single n-state variable. Operations such as AND, OR, and NOT on two-state variables which occur in the algebra of logic, i.e., Boolean algebra. 2. The operations of logical shifting, masking, and other nonarithmetic operations of a computer. (Contrasted with arithmetic operation.)

operation, loop — A loop which has an associated set of instructions which restore modified instructions or data to their original or initial values at each entry to the loop, or sequence of instructions which may be obeyed repetitively.

operation, main — The primary application or designed procedure which the equipment performs.

operation, make-break — A type of telegraph-circuit operation where the flow of current is interrupted as pulses are transmitted.

operation mode, conversational — *See* conversational mode.

operation mode, real-time — Real-time is a mode of operation in which data necessary to the control and/or execution of a transaction can be processed in time for the transaction to be affected by the results of the processing. Real-time processing is most usually identified with great speed but speed is relative. The essence of real time is concurrency—simultaneity. Real-time is refinement in the integration of data-processing with communications. Real-time eliminates slow information-gathering procedures, dated reporting techniques and lax communications; ensures that facts within the system are as timely as a prevailing situation, as current as the decisions which they must support. Real-time provides answers when answers are needed, delivers data instantly whenever the need for that data arises. Incoming information is edited, updated, and made available on demand at every level of responsibility. Imminent departures from established standards are automatically detected, and management is notified in time for action.

operation, monadic — An operation on one operand, e.g., negation.

operation, monadic Boolean — *See* Boolean operation, monadic.

operation, multijob — The simultaneous, concurrent, or interleaved execution of job parts, steps, or segments from more than one job. A type of multiprogramming, when each job or part waits for some external event to occur before it can continue processing: or each job, job part, or step has its own instruction and data areas and may be shared.

operation, multiplexed — A simultaneous operation which shares the use of a common unit of a system in such a way that it can be considered as an independent operation.

operation, multiply — *See* multiply operation.

operation, NAND — *Same as* gate, NAND.

operation, neither-OR — *Same as* gate, NOR.

operation, NOR — *Same as* gate, NOR.

operation, NOT — A Boolean operation on one operand in which the result has the alternative value of the operand, i.e., if the two possible states of the operand are represented by a zero and a one, the corresponding results are one and zero. *Same as* negation, Boolean complementation, or inversion.

operation, NOT-AND — *Same as* gate NAND.

operation, NOT-BOTH — *Same as* gate, NAND.

operation NOT-IF-THEN — *Same as* gate, NAND.

operation number — 1. A number designating the position of an operation, or its equivalent subroutine in the sequence of operations comprising a routine. 2. A number identifying each step in a program stated in symbolic code.

operation, off-line — *See* off-line processing.

operation, one-shot — *See* operation, single-step.

operation, one-step — *See* operation, single-step.

operation, on-line — *Same as* on-line processing.

operation, OR — *Same as* gate, OR.

operation overhead — *Same as* housekeeping.

operation, parallel — The simultaneous performance of several actions, usually of a similar nature, through provision of individual similar or identical devices for each such action. Parallel operation is performed to save time over serial operation. Parallel operation usually requires more equipment.

operation part — In an instruction, the part that usually specifies the kind of operation to be performed, but not the location of the operands.

operation, peripheral — *See* peripheral operation.

operation protection, nonstop — Ensures against program hang-ups due to infinite indirect address loops or execute instruction loops.

operation, push-to-type — A teletype operation in one direction at a time by using a switch depressed during transmission.

operation ratio — That proportion of the total number of hours during which the equipment is actually operating, including time for operator or programmer errors, to the total number of hours of scheduled equipment operation.

operation, real-time — *See* real-time operation.

operation, real-time (concurrency) — *See* real-time concurrency operations.

operation, real-time on-line (OLRT) — *See* on-line real-time operation.

operation, red-tape — *Same as* housekeeping.

operation register — *See* register, operation.

operation, repetitive — Operations frequently used in computing such that repeated solutions of the same set of equations, with the same set of initial conditions and parameters, are developed. In crt (cathode-ray tube) usage, a steady-state solution becomes apparent when displayed on the screen.

operation, representative calculating — *See* time, representative-computing.

operations analysis — *See* analysis, operations.

operation, scale — The process of changing a quantity by a specific factor for the purpose of bringing its range within prescribed limits.

operation, scatter-write — The process of obtaining various data elements from one location and simultaneously transferring them to several output areas, for contrast.

operations, complementary — *See* complementary operations.

operations control — Operations control of installation administration and work flow includes instructions from and to the computer operator, administrative records, logs of system operation, and the control over library programs.

operations control, non-data — Processes which relate to input/output operations as differentiated or exclusive of data manipulation, such as, tape rewinding.

operations, decoded — *See* decoding.

operation, sequential — The performance of actions one after the other in time. The actions referred to are of a large scale as opposed to the smaller scale operations referred to by the term serial operation. For an example of sequential operation, consider Z × (B×C). The two multiplications indicated follow each other sequentially. However, the processing of the individual digits in each multiplication may be either parallel or serial.

operation, serial — The flow of information through a computer in time sequence using only one digit, word, line, or channel at a time. (Contrasted with parallel operation.)

operation, serial digit — Capability of handling digits, one following another, regardless as to whether the bits can be handled in serial or parallel fashion.

operation, serial-parallel — The combined type of serial and parallel operations used, for example, in handling bits in parallel fashion but characters in serial fashion.

operation, serial word — The specific feature of certain handling equipment in which words are read immediately after another in groups.

operations, evolutionary — A statistical technique useful for improving plant operations by slight perturbation of operating conditions repeatedly over a long period of time.

operations flowchart — *See* flowchart, operations.

operation, Sheffer-stroke — *Same as* gate, NAND.

operation, single-shot — *Same as* operation single-step.

operation, single-step — A method of operating an automatic computer manually, in which a single instruction or part of an instruction is performed in response to a single operation of a manual control. This method is generally used for detecting mistakes.

operations manager — *See* manager, operations.

operations, multiple — The characteristic of being able to perform two or more computer processes concurrently.

operations multitask — Concurrent processing of two or more job steps.

operations research — The use of analytic methods adopted from mathematics for solving operational problems. The objective is to provide management with a more logical basis for making sound predictions and decisions. Among the common scientific techniques used in operations research are the following: linear programming, probability theory, information theory, game theory, monte-carlo method, and queuing theory.

operations research, computerized — Operations research (O.R.) takes on a new dimension with the computer because it can now be applied to an extent previously prohibitive in time and costs. Most data needed for problem solving may be quickly accessible and computer-ready as a by-product of such routine computer operations as billing, inventory, or accounts receivable. Capability is another factor. The worth of any OR solution is directly related to the percentage of factors taken into consideration. As a problem becomes more complex, the problem-solving procedure becomes more lengthy and costly using human efforts, or people often economize by oversimplifying the problem and excluding all but the important factors. In so doing, they may arrive at the solutions that are far less than optimal. Using a computer, however, a great number of factors can be handled and manipulated at electronic speeds.

operations research (management science) — The field of management science is extending the computer far beyond the automation of routine accounting operations and into the complex decision-making process of management. Through revolutionary computer-programming techniques such as simulation, the objective, scientific approach of management science is providing increased management capability and control. In addition to the physical or operational processes like inventory management, product planning and control, resource allocation or market forecasting, this also includes the fiscal processes such as bond management, capital investment, risk analysis, profit planning, and product pricing. Manufacturers' broad resources are preparing to meet management's growing demand for this expanded capability and to extend the tradition of "total systems" capability into new revolutionary data-processing techniques and applications.

operations, split-word — *See* split-word operations.

operation, step-by-step — *Same as* operation, single-step.

operation stroke — *Same as* gate, NAND.

operation table, Boolean — *See* Boolean operation table.

operation time — The elapsed time required by the equipment in order to execute a specific operation.

operation time, average — That time which is required for a computer to perform specific sets of operations divided by the exact number of operations, such as the average time to perform a single add, multiply, divide, with that sum divided by the total of these operations, or three.

operation time, average calculating — *See* operation time, average.

operation, transfer — 1. An operation that moves information from one storage location or one storage medium to another (e.g., read, record, copy, transmit, exchange). Transfer is sometimes taken to refer specifically to movement between different media. 2. Storage to movement within the same medium.

operation truetime — *See* on-line real-time operation.

operation, unary — An operation on one operand, e.g., negative. (Synonymous with monadic operation.)

operation use time — In Federal Government ADP contracts, the time during which the equipment is in operation, exclusive of idle time, standby time, maintenance time, or rerun time due to machine failure, is called the use time. Components not programmed for use in a specific computer run are not considered to be in use even though connected into the computer system.

operation, variable-cycle — A specific operation in which any operation is initiated immediately after the previous cycle is completed, although each cycle time period need not necessarily be of the same length.

operator — 1. The what-to-do portion of an operation, e.g., add is the operator of the operation (add x). 2. The person who actually manipulates the computer controls, places information media into the input devices, removes the output, presses the start button, etc.

operator, AND — *See* AND.

operator, complementary — An operator whose result is not of a given operator, for example, NOR and NAND.

operator control — A central control console provides supervision of computer systems. Through the console, the operator can control the processor and peripheral units . . . observe . . . and monitor processing functions. A console typewriter provides direct communication with the processor memory.

operator errors — Errors made by the terminal operator.

operator, exclusive OR — A logical operator that has the property that if P and Q are two statements, then the statement P*Q, where the * is the exclusive OR operator, is true if either P or Q, but not both, are true, and false if P and Q are both false or both true, according to the following table, wherein the figure 1 signifies a binary digit or truth.

P	*Q*	*P*Q*
0	0	0 (even)
0	1	1 (odd)
1	0	1 (odd)
1	1	0 (even)

Note that the exclusive OR is the same as the inclusive OR, except that the case with both inputs true yields no output; i.e., P*Q is true if P or Q are true, but not both. Primarily used in compare operations.

operator, inclusive OR — A logical operator which has the property that P or Q is true, if P or Q, or both, are true; when the term OR is used alone, as in OR-gate, the inclusive OR is usually implied.

operator intervention section — That portion of the control equipment in which operators can intervene in normal programming operations on control.

operator, logical — In FORTRAN IV, an operation which acts on one or two logical variables or logical expressions. Such operators are AND (the logical product), OR (the logical sum), and NOT (the logical complement).

operator, mathematical — A symbol that indicates briefly a mathematical process which describes the relations and restrictions that exist between the input variables and the output variables of a system.

operator, NAND — *Same as* gate, NAND.

operator, NOR — *Same as* gate, NOR.

operator, NOT — *Same as* gate, NOT.

operator, OR — A logical operator that has the property such that if P or Q are two statements, then the statement that P or Q is true or false varies according to the following table of possible combinations:

P	*Q*	*P or Q*
False	True	True
True	False	True
True	True	True
False	False	False

operator part — *Same as* operation part.

operators — The characters that designate mathematical operations, such as +, −, etc.

operator's console — Equipment that provides for manual intervention and for monitoring computer operation.

operator's control panel — The operator's control panel contains all the switches and indicators for the operation of the central processor. Bit-by-bit register display and manual entry into the registers are provided by convenient indicator push buttons. The control panel is used primarily for initial set-up prior to a program run or for debugging purposes, rather than to exercise control over a running program. Control of an operating routine is maintained by the use of the on-line typewriter or by sense switches.

operators, postfix — A notation system where the operator appears after the operand, for example, AB+ =A+B. It is used in Polish notation.

operator's request control panel — *See* control panel, operator's request.

operators, suffix — *Same as* operators, postfix.

op register — That specific register in which the operation code of the instruction set is stored.

optical arena, multifont — Basic character reading equipment having the ability to discern many fonts or formats of characters, usually from hard copy.

optical bar-code reader — This device is available with the data station to read coded information from documents such as premium changes, bills, invoices, and coupons at the rate of hundreds of characters per second. The data station features a high-speed printer, and thus can be used for on-line operations. Card and paper-tape equipment also can be connected to the data station.

optical-character readers, magnetic — *See* readers, optical-character (magnetic).

optical-character reader, videoscan — A unit that combines OCR (optical character reader) with mark sense and card read. It can read printing and marks in the same pass. It can also read holes in cards.

optical character recognition (OCR) — The identification of graphic characters by use of photosensitive devices.

optical document reader — *See* reader, document.

optical font — *See* font, optical.

optical font sensing — *See* font, optical.

optical isolation — It is often necessary in control circuits to electrically isolate the control (logic) section of the control system from the input and output sections. This isolation has been commonly provided by relays, isolation transformers, and line drivers and receivers. Solid-state control systems often make use of another device called an optically coupled isolator (OCI) to effectively provide isolation. The OCI couples the two systems together by transmission of light energy from a sender (LED) to a receiver (phototransistor).

optical marked-page reader — *See* reader, marked-page.

optical memories — Memory systems in which light waves (e.g., laser beams) are used to read or write information from photosensitive films, semiconductors or ferroelectric materials.

optical reader — 1. This system is based on the principle that the special shape of each character printed on the input media is capable of being identified by a reading device. For example, the audit-journal from a cash register, if printed in a distinctive optical font, could be used as the input media to a computer. As the optical reader reads each character from the input media, it translates the data into electrical impulses that in turn are transmitted to the computer for processing. 2. Reads printed and typewritten material directly, without converting it into punchtape, punchcards, or other intermediate formats. It recognizes all letters of the alphabet, standard punctuation, 0 through 9, and special symbols used in programmed functions. It handles documents, and continuous fanfold sheets.

optical reader input device — *See* optical reader.

optical scanner — A special optical device which scans patterns of incident light and generates analog/digital signals which are functions of the incident light synchronized with the scan, the primary purpose being to generate or "read" digital representations of printed or written data.

optical scanner, bar-code — An optical-scanning unit that can read documents encoded in a special bar code, at a hundreds character-per-second speed, is an element in the data station. The scanner opens up various systems concepts for such tasks as billing, couponing, retail-item control, and other forms of returnable media. The scanner can read either lithographed or computer-printed bar codes. As it scans, it transfers the encoded data to a buffer for direct transmission or to punched paper tape and printer for pretransmission editing (some systems).

optical scanning — A technique for machine recognition of characters by their images.

optima, alternate — Distinct solutions to the same optimization problem.

optimization — A method by which a process is continually adjusted to the best obtainable set of operating conditions.

optimization, linear — Procedures for locating maximum or minimum values of a linear function of variables which are subject to specific linear constraints which may or may not be inequalities.

optimization, nonlinear — A mathematical technique or procedure for the determination of a maximum, minimum, or an attempted optimum value of variables which are subject in the model to predetermined nonlinear constraints, as expressed by sets of inequalities or equations. This is contrasted to linear optimization in which constraints are linear, i.e., in a certain sense, proportional.

optimization, on-line process — *See* on-line process optimization.

optimize — To arrange the instructions or data in storage so that a minimum amount of machine time is spent for access when instructions or data are called out.

optimum code — A computer code that is particularly efficient with regard to a particular aspect, e.g., minimum time of execution, minimum or efficient use of storage space, and minimum coding time. (Related to minimum-access code.)

optimum programming — *See* programming, optimum.

optional halt — *See* halt instruction, optional.

optional halt instruction — *See* halt instruction, optional.

optional interrupts — *See* optional priority interrupts.

optional priority interrupts — Many levels of optional priority interrupts are available on the computer. Any priority interrupt takes precedence over a lower priority interrupt and may interrupt any lower priority program. Each level of priority interrupt may be separately allowed or disallowed by the program, and each leads to a unique interrupt routine. As an option, the several computers may be provided with a programmed input/output channel that sends information to or from the accumulator by programmed instructions. The instructions specify which device is to communicate; thus, the time sharing of the programmed input/output lines is controlled directly by the program.

optional word — Words introduced in a COBOL program to improve readability.

options — During the execution of any program, including a processor program, options are available to the programmer in the construction, extension, or printing of the results. Updated source code can replace or augment the original code, with listings completely or partially inhibited. Other options control the execution, punching, and timing of the programs.

options, prewired — Optional equipment that is closely related to the processor device, such as the extended arithmetic element, memory extension control, and one of the analog-to-digital converter options, is prewired so that the time, effort, and cost involved in adding this option at the factory or in the field are a minimum.

O. R. (operations research) — The use of analytic methods adopted from mathematics for solving operational problems. The object is to provide management with a more logical basis for making sound predictions and decisions. Among the common scientific techniques used in operations research are the following: linear programming, probability theory, information theory, game theory, monte-carlo method, and queuing theory.

OR — 1. A logical operator having the property that if P is a statement and Q is a statement, then the OR of P.Q. is true if and only if at least one is true; false if all are false. P or Q is often represented by P+Q, PUQ. 2. *See* inclusive OR and exclusive OR.

OR circuit — A circuit in which the phase or polarity of the output signal results from the inclusive OR function applied to the phase or polarity of the input signals.

order — 1. A defined successive arrangement of elements or events. This term is losing favor as a synonym for instructions, due to ambiguity. 2. To sequence or arrange in a series. 3. The weight or significance assigned to a digit position in a number.

order, code — *See* code, operation.

order expanded — *See* pseudoinstruction.

order format — *See* instruction format.

ordering — Sorting or sequencing.

ordering bias — *See* bias, ordering.

ordering by merge — A technique of repeated merging, splitting, and remerging can be and is often used to place items into an order.

orderly close-down — *See* close-down, orderly.

order of the merge — The number of input files to a merge program.

order structure — *See* instruction format.

ordinary binary — *See* binary.

OR element — *Same as* gate, OR.

OR else — *Same as* gate, OR.

organization, computer service — *See* computer service organization.

organization, data — *See* data organization.

organization, file — *See* file organization.

organization, processor — *See* processor organization.

organizing — Relates to the ability of a system to arrange its internal structure.

OR gate — *See* gate, OR.

OR gate, exclusive — *Same as* gate, exclusive OR.

OR gate, negative — *Same as* gate, NOR.

OR gate, positive — *Same as* gate, OR.

orientation, normal — *See* normal orientation.

oriented, procedure — A programming language that is similar to the language used in the job, and is relatively independent of the data-processing system.

oriented, word — *See* word-oriented.

origin — 1. The absolute storage address of the beginning of a program or block. 2. In relative coding, the absolute storage address to which addresses in a region are referenced.

original language — *See* language, source.

origination — A process to determine the type, nature, and origin of a document.

origination, data — The act of creating a record in a machine-sensible form directly, or as a by-product of a human readable document.

origin counter — *See* counter, origin.

OR mixer — The circuitry which emits an output upon receiving at least one input from any of several alternate sources.

OR operation — *Same as* gate, OR.

OR operator — A logical operator that has the property such that if P or Q are two statements, then the statement that P or Q is true or false varies according to the following table of possible combinations:

P	*Q*	*P or Q*
False	True	True
True	False	True
True	True	True
False	False	False

ORSA — Abbreviation for Operations Research Society of America.

OS — Abbreviation for operating system.

oscillator and timing generator — A circuit or device used on low-cost systems to generate the basic timing for microprocessor control functions.

oscilloscope — An instrument for showing visually the changes in a varying voltage.

OS (operating system) functions — Generally there are five functional areas in operating systems: the executive, the task scheduler, the i/o handler, the data management section, and the system management section.

outconnector — A flowchart symbol which signifies a place at which a flowline is broken or interrupted for continuation at another location, as contrasted with inconnector.

out device — The unit that translates computer results into usable or final form. *See* input/output device.

outline, character — *See* character outline.

out-of-line coding — A portion of coding which is stored away from the main path of a routine.

out of range — A value which does not lie within a specific range of a linear program problem is out of range, or simply a term used to refer to over capacity.

out of service time — *See* time, out of service.

out plant system — A data-transmission system consisting of one or more centrally located terminals and one or more remote terminals.

output — 1. Computer results, such as answers to mathematical problems, statistical, analytical or accounting figures, production schedules, etc. 2. Information transferred from the internal storage of a computer to secondary or external storage; information transferred to any device exterior to the computer. 3. The state of a sequence of states occurring on a specified output channel. 4. The device or collective set of devices used for taking data out of a device. 5. A channel for expressing a state on a device or logic element.

output area — 1. The area of internal storage from which data is transferred to external storage. 2. A specific storage area designated to control and hold information that will be written by an output unit or used in visual scanning. 3. A block of computer words considered as a unit, and intended or desired to be transferred from an internal storage medium to an external designation.

output block — A portion of the internal storage reserved primarily for receiving, processing, and transmitting data that is to be transferred out.

output, buffer — *See* buffer output.

output buffer register — *See* register, output buffer.

output bus drivers — *See* bus drivers, output.

output capability — The number of unit loads that can be driven by the output of a circuit.

output data — Data obtained or obtainable from a device, such as a logic element, or the output channel of a logic element.

output delay — The typical delay of the circuit measured at the 50 percent signal levels, with half of rated dc load and half of the specified wiring capacity.

output device — The part of a machine that translates the electrical impulses representing data processed by the machine into permanent results such as printed forms, punched cards, and magnetic writing on tape.

output, direct — Printed, visual, or communicated data which results from online output or output equipment, i.e., the final output is produced by equipment directly connected to the computer and directly under computer control as contrasted to printouts from generated tapes, etc., which are processed from stored equipment or offline.

output equipment — The equipment used for transferring information out of a computer.

output module — The part of a machine that translates the electrical impulses representing data processed by the machine into permanent results such as printed forms, displays, tapes, and so on.

output, off-line — Output which may have

come from a computer system originally but which is obtained from off-line equipment, or data from off-line origination. Indirect output is usually considered so because it was produced by equipment not directly connected to the computer system.

output program — *See* program, output.

output queue — Messages that are in line or queued which have been produced by the system and are waiting to be scheduled for transmission.

output register buffer — The buffering or transfer device which receives data from internal storage and transfers it to an output media such as magnetic tape.

output routine — That set of instructions which organizes, directs, or controls the handling of output data by starting the output equipment, specifying the output format, speed, monitoring, etc.

output routine, typewriter (TYPOUT) — *See* typewriter output routine (TYPOUT).

output state — The determination of the condition of that specified set of output channels, i.e., positive, negative, or one or zero, etc.

output storage — *See* output area.

output stream — Diagnostic messages and other output data issued by an operating system or a processing program on output devices especially activated for this purpose by the operator. Also called job-output stream, output-job stream, and so on.

output table — *See* board, plotting.

output tape(s) sorting — Tapes containing a file in specified sequence as a result of a specified sort/merge process.

output test, processor — An automated processing of the output so that errors may be more easily tracked down.

output unit — The unit which delivers information in acceptable language to a point outside the computer.

output work queue — *See* work queue, output.

output writer — A service program which moves data from the output work queue to a particular output device, a printer, card punch, or terminal. The output writer thus transfers the actual output, often from an output work queue to an output device, after it has determined the normal rate of speed of the device to be used.

outside loops — *See* loops, outside.

over capacity — Values which are not in the range of a quantity are said to be out of range or over capacity.

overflow — In an arithmetic operation, the generation of a quantity beyond the capacity of the register or location which is to receive the result; over capacity; the information contained in an item of information which is in excess of a given amount. Overflow develops when attempts are made to write longer fields into a field location of a specific length; a 12-digit product will overflow a 10-digit accumulator.

overflow areas, file — In random addressing, the overflow area is an available storage location that is chained to a particular pocket so that when that pocket is full, the generated addresses use the overflow area.

overflow check — Overflow check, a feature associated with arithmetic operations, is a means of immediately recognizing results that exceed the capacity of the counter or accumulator in which they are developed. In order to recognize an overflow and associate it with the proper calculation, the check should be performed immediately after the arithmetic operation. A machine or system which employs this feature can be programmed to detect and signal the condition.

overflow check indicator — A device that is turned on by incorrect, or unplanned for, operations in the execution of an arithmetic instruction, particularly when an arithmetic operation produces a number too large for the system to handle.

overflow error — An overflow condition resulting from a floating-point arithmetic operation.

overflow (FORTRAN) — In FORTRAN, overflow occurs when the characteristic of a floating-point number exceeds the machine capacity (generally 10^{+38}). In assembler language, overflow occurs when a fixed point number is divided by zero or when an algebraic sum is larger than the accumulator register can hold.

overflow indicator — 1. A bistable trigger that changes state when overflow occurs in the register with which it is associated. It may be interrogated and/or restored to the original state. 2. An internal computer-indicator component that is indicated to be "on" if an overflow condition exists due to an arithmetic miscalculation in programming designs.

overflow, link (L) — This one-bit register serves as an extension of the accumulator. The content of this register can be program sampled and program modified. Overflow into the link from the accumulator can be checked by the program to greatly simplify and speed up single- and multiple-precision arithmetic routines.

overflow position — An extra position in the register in which the overflow digit is developed.

overflow, product — *Same as* overflow.

overflow, types — Two types of overflow may occur in computers—add and divide. Overflow may also occur in certain algebraic subtraction operations, such as a negative quantity subtracted from a positive quantity. In reality, of course, this is the same as an additive operation.

overflow (underflow), test conditions — *See* test conditions, overflow (underflow).

overhead bit — A bit other than an information bit, e.g., a check bit, a framing bit, or some other procedure or format bit.

overhead operation — *Same as* housekeeping.

overlap — *See* processing, overlap.

overlapping — A type, process, or procedure for concurrent operation in which various phases of two consecutive instructions are executed simultaneously, i.e., multiplication can take place while reading from storage is also being completed.

overlapping, multiprocessor — The processor is capable of determining whether its current operand and next instruction lie in different storage modules. It is also capable, if this situation is present, of retrieving these two words in parallel, at an effective 100% performance increase. Since the i/o controller is not required to reference instructions in main storage, except on command transfers, it does not have, nor does it need, the overlapping feature.

overlay — A technique for bringing routines into high-speed storage from some other form of storage during processing, so that several routines will occupy the same storage locations at different times. Overlay is used when the total storage requirements for instructions exceed the available main storage.

overlays — Programs or runs too large for memory can be divided into logical segments or overlays. One overlay overlays another, or several segments may be in memory at one time. Overlays are also used when various operations occur infrequently, such as deductions for community chest, union dues, etc. The overlays are called in only when the functions they perform are required. An overlay subroutine is provided to call in these overlays. This subroutine functions in a manner similar to the system supervisor.

overlays program — *Same as* overlays.

overlays, segments — A segment of a program is defined as that portion of memory which is committed by a single reference to the loader. Usually a segment overlays some other segment and may have within itself other portions which in turn overlay one another, i.e., subsegments. That part of a segment which is actually brought into memory when the loader is referenced is called the fixed part of a segment. Segments are built up from separate relocatable elements, common blocks, or other segments.

overlay supervisor — A specific subroutine which controls the location and execution sequence of parts of computer programs during conditions of restricted storage space availability.

overload level — The operating limit of a system, component, etc.; that point at which operation ceases to be satisfactory as a result of signal distortion, overheating, damage, etc.

overloads — When the rate of input into a system is so concentrated that the computer cannot process the flow of messages on a real-time basis.

overload simulator — In order to test a system under overload conditions, an artificial condition is created that makes the program act as it would during an actual overload or overflow.

overprinting — An optical character reading term designating marks placed in clear bands or areas which are set aside for machine reading after the document has been prepared for machine sensing.

override interrupt — An optional group of power on/off interrupts which have the highest priority and which cannot be disabled or disarmed.

override, operator's — On some systems, operators may be allowed to force the system to accept "illegal" data. Records containing override fields are usually flagged and may be retrieved for subsequent update or correction prior to transmission.

overrun error — An occurrence that can happen when previous characters in a register were not read by the microprocessor at the time a new character was loaded again in the register.

own code — *See* code, own.

own coding, intermediate-pass — Computer instructions created by the programmer, in assembly or absolute form, which are executed by a sort during the intermediate passes of the file after the execution of instructions for comparisons of keys, but prior to output of the selected records. May also be executed during the internal sort, but after the selection of records.

own coding, last pass — Computer instructions created by the programmer, in assembly or absolute form, which are executed by a sort during the last pass of the file after the final merging instructions have been executed but prior to unloading the output record.

own coding (sorting) — Special coding provided by the programmer, which is integrated with sort/merge coding.

oxide spots, ferrous — The medium by which information is represented on magnetic tape. These ferrous oxide spots represent information in binary form which is interpreted by the magnetic tape drive and then stored in computer memory for processing.

P

PA — Abbreviation for paper advance.

PABX (Private Automatic Branch Exchange) — A private automatic exchange that provides for the transmission of calls to and from the public telephone network.

pack — 1. The combination or consolidation of several short fields into one larger field. 2. To combine two or more units of information into a single physical unit to conserve storage. For example, the fields of an employee's pay number, weekly pay rate, and tax exemptions may be stored in one word, each of these fields being assigned a different location within the word. 3. The procedure which reduces the amount of storage required to hold information by changing the method of coding data or blanks. For example, storing two or more data items into a single word by using a contiguous subfield, or by dividing words into convenient parts, etc.

package, application — Sets of programs and/or subroutines used to solve problems of a specific type or in a typical manner, i.e., business, scientific, financial, and so on.

packaged programs — Those common programs written for various major applications in a manner such that a user's specific problems of data or organization will not make the package less useful.

package, floating-point — A subroutine or hardware device that achieves floating-point hardware function without additional CPU slowed activity. In software, it consists of routines for fixed to floating-point conversion and vice versa, conversion from decimal to floating point and vice versa, plus floating-point move and such floating-point arithmetic functions as addition, subtraction, multiplication, and division.

package, program — A group or collection of logically related operational program segments, i.e., all those having to do with the processing of a certain type of inquiry.

pack, disk — *See* disk pack.

packed decimal — A system means of data representation. Two digits per character can be used to increase speed and capacity in fields where alphabetics and special characters are not being used.

packet — 1. Stacker. 2. A short block (1000 to 2000 bits) of data prefixed with addressing and other control information that is used to carry information through a packet-switching network.

packet assembly — A user facility which permits nonpacket-mode terminals to exchange data in the packet mode.

packet disassembly — A user facility which enables a packet destined for delivery to a nonpacket-mode terminal to be delivered in the appropriate form; e.g., in character form at the applicable rate.

packet-mode terminal — A data terminal which can control and format packets and transmit and receive packets.

packet switched data transmission service — A service involving the transmission and, if necessary, the assembly and disassembly of data in the form of packets.

packet switching — The transfer of data by means of addressed packets whereby a channel is occupied only for the duration of transmission of the packet. The channel is then available for the transfer of other packets. In contrast with circuit switching, the data network determines the routing during, rather than prior to, the transfer of a packet.

packing density, file — The ratio of available file or data storage space to the total amount of data stored in the file.

packing factor — *See* packing density, file.

packing sequence — A procedure for loading the upper half of an accumulator with the first data word, shifting this into the lower half, loading the second datum, shift, etc., so that the three data words are thus packed in sequence.

pad — A process of filling or completing a unit of data such as a word, block, or file, most often with zeros or smaller units of dummy or meaningless characters.

pad character — Character introduced to use up time while a function (usually mechanical) is being accomplished, e.g., carriage return, form eject, etc.

pad character, transmission — If the data line control (DLC) is implemented in a half-duplex channel, bit transitions will not occur during line turnaround and synchronization will be lost. To assist the initial establishment of bit synchronization following each line turnaround, a pattern of alternating zeros and ones is often sent to precede each transmission. This pattern is called an opening pad character.

padding — 1. A technique used to fill out a block of information with dummy records, words, or characters. 2. Adding characters to a record to enlarge it to a predetermined block length, to make it easier to handle in a specified record-length routine.

P address — Location to which the program branches or to which data is transparent (certain equipment).

pad, scratch — A useful and informal term referring to or designating a unique internal storage area, supposedly reserved for intermediate results, various notations, or working area, quickly erasable storage.

page — A quantity of determination of main-memory capacity and used when allocating memory and for partitioning programs into units or control sections. A page is quite standardized, usually 512 to 4096 bytes or words and/or 8 to 64 lines of source program coding, as used for displaying the coding on crt's (cathode ray tubes) i.e., in crt's used in conversational time sharing a single page of program can be displayed at one time for the programmer or user inspection, the size varying with the size and capacity of the crt, and not related to the memory page stated above.

page check — *See* check, page.

paged machine — A computer that divides memory addresses into "blocks" of words referred to as "pages." Special directives are necessary in order to reach locations outside the current page pointed to by the program counter because the program counter is not provided with the capability to increment itself across a page boundary. It must be specifically set to a new page value.

page, entry — The point, in flowchart symbols, where the flowline continues from a previous page due to space limitations on the original or previous page.

page, exit — The point, in flowchart symbols, where the flowline continues to a following page due to space limitation on the page on which the flowchart is drawn.

page fault — A program interrupt that occurs when an accessed piece of data or program is not currently in main memory and must be read in from disk. Only applicable to operating systems featuring demand paging.

page footing — The summing of the entries on a particular page, usually appearing at the bottom of each page.

page heading — The description of a page context of a report, usually appears at the top of each page.

page, invalid (time sharing) — *See* time sharing, page type.

page printer — *See* printer, page.

page reader — An optical character reader which can process cut-form documents of differing sizes and which might be able to read information in reel form.

page swap, virtual memory — Page swapping is often based on parameters such as program priority, page usage, and whether the page has been modified. If a nonresident page is referenced, in many systems an executive interrupt is generated.

page-turning — 1. A technique of providing large single level memory, usually with dynamic memory relocation. 2. A procedure for moving complete pages of information between main memory and auxiliary storage units, to permit several simultaneous programs in execution to share main memory, or to permit cyclic scheduling for time allotments.

page type, time sharing — *See* time sharing, page type.

paging — A procedure for transmitting pages of information between main storage and auxiliary storage, especially when done for the purpose of assisting the allocation of a limited amount of main storage among a number of concurrently executing programs.

paging, crt — When stated in relation to crt's, paging involves switching from one "page" of information to the next. As regards memory, a page is a logical block of storage used for memory management, the address specified by a page address number, with a displacement number as the address within the page, on some systems.

paging terminal — A crt terminal that permits the user to recover buffered information that has been rolled off the screen—top and bottom—by the push of a button. Buffer memory provides storing of more lines of data than can be displayed at one time, reducing the need for computer use and memory and lowering the number of times the computer must be accessed, thus reducing overall transmission time and cost.

pairs, sorting comparison — The comparison of the keys in two records and placement of the higher value ahead of the smaller value for descending sequences.

panel — *See* control panel.

panel, central control — *See* control panel.

panel, control — *See* control panel.

panel, control console — *See* control panel or console.

panel, graphic — A master control panel that pictorially and usually colorfully traces the relationship of control equipment and the process operation. It permits an operator, at a glance, to check on the operation of a far-flung control system by noting dials, valves, scales, and lights.

panel, jack — A specific control panel which uses electrical connectors, i.e., short wires, plugs, etc., to control the operation of particular devices such as older type punched card machines.

panel, maintenance control — *See* control panel, maintenance.

panel, operator's control — *See* operator's control panel.

panel path — *See* control panel.

panel, programming control — *See* control panel, programming.

panic button — *See* button, emergency.

paper, coordinate — Marginally punched, continuous-form paper, normally used for printout of an XY plotter.

paper, slew — *Same as* paper throw.

paper tape — A strip of paper on which data is recorded in the form of groups of holes arranged in binary format along the length of the tape. The tape is divided into columns that run the length of the tape, and channels that extend across the width of the tape.

paper tape channels — *See* tape channels, paper.

paper-tape output device — Output data comes to this device from the computer.

Blank paper tape is placed in the device, and the data is punched into the tape. Some computer paper-tape units combine the input and output functions.

paper tape, perforated — *See* punched tape.

paper tape, punched — *See* tape, punched paper.

paper tape punches — A device which punches paper tape.

Courtesy Heath Co.

Paper-tape reader and punch.

paper-tape reader — A device that senses and translates the holes or information on tape into machine code.

paper tape speed — The rate, in characters per second, at which the unit reads or punches paper tape.

paper-tape systems — Systems having paper tape equipment with no mass storage device have an operating system contained on binary paper-tape reels. The binary reels are of two types—format binary and absolute binary. Format binary programs are loaded by the system loader. Absolute binary programs may be loaded by the monitor or by a "PRESET" operation.

paper tape type — Indicates the function of the unit: reader only (RD), punch only (PN), or reader-punch (RP).

paper throw — When paper in a printer moves through a distance greater than the normal line spacing without printing, it is called a paper throw or a paper slew, i.e., the speed for throw is usually greater than for single-line feed.

paragraph — A pertinent or allied group of sentences, or those which are related logically and which are smaller or subgroups of pages as described in some computer systems.

parallel — 1. The internal handling of data in groups, all elements of a group being handled simultaneously. 2. Objects (programs) considered simultaneously (or nearly so) rather than in sequence or some specific order. 3. Pertaining to simultaneous processing of the individual parts of a whole, such as the bits of a character and the characters of a word, using separate facilities for the various parts. 4. Handled simultaneously in separate facilities. 5. Operation on two or more parts of a word or item simultaneously.

parallel access — 1. Simultaneous access to all bits in a storage location comprising a character or word. Equal access time for any bit, character, or word in a storage device. 2. The process of obtaining information from or placing information into storage where the time required for such access is dependent on the simultaneous transfer of all elements of a word from a given storage location. (Synonymous with simultaneous access.)

parallel arithmetic — *See* arithmetic, parallel.

parallel ASCII keyboard — A parallel keyboard input that is provided to permit the use of a standard ASCII keyboard and a video display module in many personal computer systems.

parallel by bit — Handling all the binary digits (or bits) of a character simultaneously in separate equipment.

parallel by character — The handling of all the characters of a machine word simultaneously in separate lines, channels, or storage cells.

parallel computer — A computer in which the digits or data lines are handled concurrently by separate units of the computer. The units may be interconnected in different ways as determined by the computation to operate in parallel or serially. Mixed serial and parallel machines are frequently called serial or parallel according to the way arithmetic processes are performed. An example of a parallel computer is one which handles decimal digits in parallel, although it might handle the bits which comprise a digit either serially or in parallel. (Contrasted with serial computer.)

parallel data controller — Such devices provide a flexible programmable interface to external devices or for interfacing multiple family computer devices. Some units provide two independent bidirectional input/output channels, each of which operates in a variety of parallel data transfer modes.

parallel data medium — A medium for recording or entering data and as an input/output media for computers such as cards, tapes, paper, and disks. Usually the data carrier is easily transportable.

parallel data transfers, single chip system — Parallel data transfers occur during each instruction fetch and during the ensuing read/write cycle associated with execution of the memory-reference instructions. The class of instruction could perhaps more properly be called "Input/Output Reference Class" in the case of some microprocessors, since all data transfers, whether with memory, peripheral devices, or a central processor data bus, occur through the execution of these instructions. This is a unified bus structure.

parallel digital computer — Specific equipment which processes digits in concurrent procedures as contrasted to serial computing.

parallel flow — The system of operations designed so that several of them may be conducted simultaneously, such as in house-building the air-conditioning ducting can be completed, while the plumbing is being worked on, while the landscaping is being developed, etc. This is opposite from serial development where each task must wait until the completion of one before another can begin.

parallel full subtracter — *See* subtracter, full (parallel).

parallel half-subtracter — *See* subtracter, half (parallel).

parallel input-output — A typical unit is bus compatible with various family microcomputers and provides 24 bidirectional, TTL compatible i/o lines. Most are programmable to operate in static, clocked, or discrete modes.

parallel input/output controller (PIO) — A programmable circuit that permits a direct interface to a wide range of peripherals without other external logic.

parallel input/output (PIO), high-level system — On some systems, the PIO circuit uses an advanced interrupt driven, program controlled i/o transfer technique for easy handling of a great many peripherals with a parallel interface. Without other logic, the PIO can interface most line printers, paper tape readers or punches, card readers, keyboards, electronic typewriters, and other devices.

parallel input/output (PIO) interrupt logic — On some high-level systems, the PIO contains all the interrupt control logic necessary for nested priority interrupt handling with very fast response time. Generally the additional interrupt control circuits are not needed and servicing time is minimized. The PIO can handle high speed i/o ports, and it interrupts the CPU after each i/o transfer is complete.

parallel input/output (PIO) peripheral interrupt — A major feature of the PIO on some systems is its ability to generate an interrupt on any bit pattern at the i/o pins, thus eliminating the need for the processor to constantly test i/o lines for a particular peripheral status condition. This feature greatly enhances the ability of the processor to easily handle peripherals, while also reducing software overhead.

parallel input port — A port is some arrangement for getting data signals into or out of a computer. An input port gets them in. A parallel port is one that has the signals running in parallel—meaning that a number of signals travel through the port at once. (The alternative is a serial port, through which the signals travel one after the other.)

parallel interface — A type of interface in which all bits of data in a given byte (or word) are transferred simultaneously, using a separate data line for each bit.

parallel i/o universal — Universal parallel i/o can be programmed on some systems to define any direction and data-transfer characteristics for several ports. Full flexibility in buffering and terminating the parallel ports is provided by uncommitted driver/termination device locations. Data transfer can be accomplished under full interrupt control.

parallelism — Concurrent operation of several parts of a computer system. This could be simultaneous processing of multiple programs or simultaneous operation of multiple computers.

parallel operation — The flow of information through the computer or any part of it using two or more lines or channels simultaneously.

parallel processing — The operation of a computer so that programs for more than one run are stored simultaneously in its storage, and executed concurrently. *See* multiprocessing, concurrent processing, and multiprograming.

parallel programming — *See* programming, parallel.

parallel reading — When a data card is read row-by-row.

parallel running — 1. The checking or testing of newly developed systems by running comparatively in conjunction with previously existing systems. 2. The running of a newly developed system in a data processing area in conjunction with the continued operation of the current system. 3. The final step in the debugging of a system; this step follows a system test.

parallel-serial — *See* serial-parallel.

parallel, serial operation — The combined type of serial and parallel operation used, for example, in handling bits in parallel fashion but characters in serial fashion.

parallel storage — 1. A storage device wherein characters, words, or digits are dealt with simultaneously. 2. Storage in which all bits, characters, or (especially) words are essentially equally available in space, without time being one of the coordinates.

parallel transfer — 1. A method of data transfer in which the characters of an element of information are transferred simultaneously over a set of paths. 2. Simultaneous transfer of all bits (in a storage location) comprising a character or word.

parallel transmission — A system for sending all bits of a particular character simultaneously.

parameter — 1. In a subroutine, a quantity which may be given different values when the subroutine is used in different main routines or in different parts of one main routine, but which usually remains unchanged throughout any one such use. 2. A quantity, in a mathematical calculation, that may be assigned any arbitrary value. 3. In generators, the quantity used to designate input/output devices to specify subroutines to be included, or to define the routine to be generated. 5. A constant or a variable in mathematics that remains constant during some calculation. 6. A definable characteristic of an item, device, or system.

parameter block — A table of user-created information that is consequent to each operating system call. The information, for example, allows the operating system to provide the requested service correctly.

parameter, mathematical — *See* mathematical parameter.

parameter mode (display) — This mode is used to control the display. It establishes parameter information for each of the other modes. The parameters are changed only when another parameter word is encountered. Special features of this mode include: an automatic stop bit —signals the computer when plotting is completed and brings the display to a halt; individual parameter inhibit bits— permit each parameter to be independently established.

parameter, preset — A parameter incorporated into a subroutine during input.

parameter, program — A parameter incorporated into a subroutine during computation. A program parameter very frequently comprises a word stored relative to either the subroutine or the entry point and dealt with by the subroutine during each reference. It may be altered by the routine and/or may vary from one point of entry to another.

parameters, report generation — Manufacturers furnish a program for automatic creation of reports according to user specifications. To use the report generator, the programmer merely prepares a set of parameters defining control fields and report lines. These parameters are used as input to the report generator that produces a symbolic program. The assembled version of this program accepts raw data as input, edits it, and generates the desired reports.

parameters, sorting — The response to the requirement for specifications for a sort/merge generator. Parameters are used to fix input and output formats, computing configuration, location of keys, and so on.

parameter, statement — A parameter

statement assigns specified integer values to specified variables at compile time; e.g., parameter I = 2 causes the integer 2 to replace I whenever it occurs in the source program. This facilitates the assignment of different values to frequently referenced parameters in different compilations of the same program.

parameter testing — Tests of individual sections or subroutines of a program to assure that specified inputs produce the desired outputs.

parameter word — A word in a subroutine which contains one or more parameters which specify the action of the subroutine, or words which contain the address of such parameters.

parametric programming — A method for investigating the effect on an optimal linear-programming solution of a sequence of proportionate changes in the elements of a single row or column of the matrix. Most commonly, the method is applied to either the objective-function row or the right-side column.

parity — As regards computer operations, parity relates to the maintenance of a sameness of level or count, i.e., keeping the same number of binary ones in a computer word to thus be able to perform a check based on an even or odd number for all words under examination.

parity bit — 1. A redundant bit added to a group of bits so that an inaccurate retrieval of that group of bits is detected. 2. A parity bit is most often used to develop a total of bits, either odd or even, for each character. It is usually associated with the frame for each 6-bit character on tape, and parity bits can be placed at intervals to associate them with the seven rows of bits, i.e., six for data and one for parity. 3. The total or summation check in which the binary digits in a single character or word in storage are added to check against a single, previously specified digit; e.g., a check of the test to determine whether the number of ones or zeros is odd or even. 4. A technique in parallel addition wherein some or all of the carries are temporarily stored instead of being allowed to propagate immediately. 5. A binary digit appended to an array of bits to make the sum of all the bits always odd or always even.

parity, block system — A system of using an additional bit to a block of information to detect single bit errors in the block.

parity check — 1. A summation check in which the binary digits, in a character or word, are added, and the sum checked against a single, previously computed parity digit; i.e., a check tests whether the number of ones in a word is odd or even. (Synonymous with odd-even check, and related to redundant check and forbidden-combination check.) 2. Use of a redundant and the least significant digit (called the parity digit) carried along as a check of a binary (machine) word. It is 1 if the total number of 1's in the machine word is odd, and 0 if the total number of 1's in the machine word is even, for the even parity check. The digit value is 0 for an odd number of 1's, and 1 for an even number of 1's when the odd parity check is used. *See* check digit, parity.

parity check, character (communications) — During transmission, as the core storage readout is being converted from parallel to serial bit form, the data line terminal at the transmitting end functions to add a parity bit, where necessary, to make each data character odd or even parity. As the data characters are being received, the data line terminal makes a parity check as the conversion from serial to parallel bit form takes place for the storage entry. The parity and synchronizing bits are dropped off at this time. If the wrong parity is detected, an error is signaled by the receiving computer.

parity check digit — *See* check digit, parity.

parity check, even — *See* check, even parity.

parity check, horizontal — A parity check applied to the group of certain bits from every character in a block.

parity check, longitudinal (communications) — The data line terminal generates a longitudinal parity count character as the data characters are being transmitted. This is essentially a count for even parity of all bits in each one of the bit levels for all data characters in the message. This same count is also generated for the bits of the data characters entering the data line terminal when it is receiving. The longitudinal parity-count character generated by the magnetic tape terminal at the sending end follows immediately after the end of the block character, to be compared with the longitudinal parity count character generated at the computer.

parity check procedure — A method of checking the correctness of binary data after that data has been transferred from or to storage. An additional bit, called the parity bit, is appended to the binary word or character to be transferred. The parity bit is the single-digit sum of all the binary digits in the word or character and its logical state can be assigned to represent either an even or an odd number of 1s making up the binary word. Parity is checked in the same manner in which it is generated.

parity-check, vertical — *See* check, even parity.

parity-count character (longitudinal) — *Same as* parity check, longitudinal (communications).

parity error — *See* error, parity.

parity, even — *See* check digit, parity.

parity flag — A specific indicator that signals whether or not the number of digits in the logic one condition is an odd or even value. The indicator is often used for error checking purposes during i/o operations.

parity, i/o interrupt — *See* interrupt, i/o parity.

parity-line circuit — A multistation net in which all stations are on a single circuit. The stations must share the circuit since only one station may transmit at a time.

parity, magnetic-tape — *See* magnetic-tape parity.

parity, odd — *See* check digit, parity.

parity or mark-track error — Indicates that during the course of the previous block transfer, a data parity error was detected or one or more bits have been picked up or dropped out from either the timing track or the mark track.

parity, storage — A particular application of parity checking codes or devices when transferring data to or from storage devices such as disk, drum, auxiliary core, etc.

parity, tape — That particular application of parity checking codes or devices when transferring data to or from magnetic or paper tape.

parser — A routine that controls decoding of an external program statement by establishing its syntactic tree, according to the specified syntax of the programming language.

parsing, language theory — The breaking down of the components of a sentence into structural forms.

part — A part of an instruction word that specifies the address of an operand. Loosely, the operator part of an instruction.

part, address — 1. A part of an instruction word that specifies the address of the operand. 2. The part of an instruction word that defines the address of a register or location.

part, function — *Same as* operation part.

partial arithmetic, multiple — *See* arithmetic, multiple.

partial carry — *See* carry, partial.

partial drive pulse — *See* pulse, partial write.

partial product — *See* product, partial.

partial-read pulse — Any one of the applied currents that will cause selection of a core for reading.

partial-select input pulse — *Same as* pulse partial write.

partial-select output pulse — *Same as* partial-read pulse.

partial sum — *See* sum, partial.

partial sum gate — *Same as* gate, exclusive OR.

partial word — A programming device which permits the selection of a portion of a machine word for processing.

partial write pulse — *See* pulse, partial write.

partitioned data set — *See* data set, partitioned.

partitioning — Subdividing one large block into smaller subunits that can be handled more conveniently, e.g., partitioning a matrix.

part, operation — *See* operation part.

part, operator — *Same as* operation part.

PASCAL — A language designed to enable teaching of programming as a systematic discipline and to do systems programming. Based on the language, ALGOL, it emphasizes aspects of structured programming.

PASCAL P-code — Some manufacturers have designed a microcomputer around a language instead of the other way around. The language is PASCAL. One way to compile this high-level programming language is to do it in two steps. First, PASCAL source code is compiled into its intermediate code, P-code. Then the P-code is executed interpretively on the host machine. This interpreter is actually an idealized stack machine and can be implemented in software. That is, with the proper routines, a processor can be turned into a pseudomachine whose native language is the P-code.

PASCAL structure — PASCAL is a block-structured programming language in the style of ALGOL. Programs consist of two parts: a heading names the program and specifies the variables it will use, and the body of the program, called a block, follows. A block is further subdivided into six sections. The first four declare the labels, constants, data types, and variables. The fifth names and precedes an actual procedure or function. The last section, called the statement section, contains the executable code for the named function or procedure.

Labels identify statements so they can be referenced. Constants equate numbers with names for use throughout a program, like pi = 3.14. Data types are numerous; furthermore, structured types can be defined to include arrays, records, sets, and files. Each named variable must be followed by its type. Procedures can be put within procedures, and the statements for each must be preceded with the keyword "begin" and terminated with the word "end." Operators are defined for multiply, divide, add, subtract, logical, and relational, and numerous control statements are allowed.

pass, sorting — The processing of each file record once, for the purpose of reducing the number of strings of sequenced records and increasing the number of sequenced records per string.

pass (sorting), intermediate — Any phase of a merging operation which, because of the number of strings or otherwise, does not reduce the file to a single sequenced string.

password — The unique set of digits or characters assigned to a user as part of his identification number in communicating with the computer.

patch — 1. A section of coding inserted into a routine (usually by explicitly transferring control from the routine to the patch and back again) to correct a mistake or alter the routine. 2. A special routine linked to the program by unconditional transfers of control; used for checking or correcting programs. 3. To correct or change the coding at a particular location by inserting transfer instructions at that location and by adding the new instructions and the replaced instructions elsewhere.

patchboard — A removable board containing hundreds of terminals into which patch cords (short wires) are connected, which determine the different programs for the machine. To change the program, the wiring pattern on the patchboard or the patchboard itself must be changed.

patch cord — A handy flexible connector conductor with receptacles or connectors at each end and which is used to interconnect sockets of plugboards.

patching plug program — A relatively small auxiliary plugboard patched with a specific variation of a portion of a program and designed to be plugged into a relatively larger plugboard patched with the main program.

patch panel — *See* control panel.

patchplug — A specialized plug of metal or plastic which functions as a patchcord. The patchplug is cordless in contrast to a standard plug which has a wire for jumping or connecting two terminals. A patchplug usually has an insulating handle.

patch-program plugboard — *See* plug, program patching.

patch routine — 1. Enables octal changes (or corrections) to be made to specified programs at object program execution time. Changes occur in main memory only and do not affect the object program stored on the run tape. 2. A specific correcting routine written of a sequence on the program chart and referring to a correct sequence.

path — The logical course or line of direction taken by a computer in the execution of a routine.

path, critical — The longest time path in a project which has to be done as quickly as possible. Because the overall time required to complete the project cannot be less than that required along the critical path, it requires the most careful monitoring. Any delay along this path causes the project to be delayed, while minor delays along noncritical paths does not. *See* PERT.

path, main — The principal course or line of direction taken by a computer in the execution of a routine, directed by the logic of the program and the nature of the data.

pattern, bit — *See* bit pattern.

pattern compaction, curve — *See* compaction, curve fitting.

pattern recognition — 1. The identification, by automatic means, of shapes, forms, or configurations. 2. The recognition of shapes or other patterns by a machine system. The patterns may be either a physical shape or a speech pattern.

pattern-sensitive fault — A fault which is brought forth only as a result to one or certain patterns or sequences of data, i.e., a program for testing for positive, negative, or zero in that order and which could respond incorrectly to minus zero, but would respond properly to all other numbers, or a fault brought on by excessive heat dissipation.

paycheck run — Refers to the processing and actual printing of payroll checks.

PCI (Process Control Interface), home system — A process control interface board permits an interface with home computers to a variety of electromechanical devices such as relays, switches, motors, contacters, thermostats, and so on. One type of PCI uses eight relay outputs and eight optically isolated inputs that transmit sensory and control information to and from the computer. Applications, practically unlimited, include monitor environmental conditions (heat, light, humidity) in the home or laboratory; control warning devices; control automatic sorting and grading of products on an assembly line; and read and respond to scientific test results, such as changes in pressure, pH, or viscosity.

PCM — 1. Punched card machine—The set of conventional punch card equipment including sorters, collators, and tabulators. (Synonymous with EAM and clarified by tabulating equipment.) 2. Pulse code modulation—Modulation of a pulse train in accordance with a code.

PC-relative addressing — In some systems, a PC (program counter) relative address is formed by adding the displacement value specified in the operand field of the instruction to the current contents of the program counter.

peak data transfer — *See* data transfer rate.

pen, light — An optional device, used in conjunction with the incremental display, that can greatly extend its usefulness. It is a high speed, photosensitive device that can cause the computer to change or modify the display on the cathode-ray tube. As the pertinent display information is selected by the operator, the pen signals the computer by generating a pulse. Acting upon this signal, the computer can then instruct other points to be plotted across the tube face in accordance with the pen movements, or exercise specific options previously programmed without the need for separate input devices.

pen (light) control — A light pen for communication between operator and processor. When this penlike device is pointed at information displayed on the screen, it detects light from the cathode-ray tube when a beam passes within its field of view. The pen's response is transmitted to the computer, which relates the computer's action to the section of the image being displayed. In this way, the operator can delete or add text, maintain tighter control over the program, and choose alternative courses of action.

perception, artificial — *See* artificial cognition.

performance evaluation — The analysis (in terms of initial objectives and estimates and usually made on site) of accomplishments, using an automatic data-processing system to provide information on operating experience and to identify any required corrective actions.

performance period — A particular time interval in which a device is to operate, i.e., the scheduled hours of operation, but not including various test or preparatory schedules or hours rescheduled due to equipment malperformance.

period, action — The time during which the stored data is read or new data is written in a storage location, specifically in electrostatic storage tubes.

period, digit — The time interval between the occurrence of successive digit signals.

periodic dumping, time sharing — *See* time sharing, periodic dumping.

period, performance — *See* performance period.

period, scan — *See* scan period.

peripheral — Operation of input/output and other devices not under direct computer control; most commonly used to designate the transfer of information between magnetic tapes and other media.

peripheral addressing, single chip systems — On some low-cost systems users address peripherals the same way as memory. Thus, powerful memory-reference instructions (and addressing mode) may be used for peripheral data i/o as well. Some systems offer straightforward handshaking i/o that allows simple interfacing in DMA (Direct Memory Access) and multiprocessor applications.

peripheral bus — On many systems, i/o interfaces and peripherals often plug right into the bus slots. The result is a simple and powerful method of i/o interfacing.

peripheral circuit, programmable — Many new peripheral circuits for microprocessors offer a new dimension for LSI support chips in that they are all programmable. This allows the system designer maximum flexibility which results in lowered system cost. Many circuits provide functions for serial i/o timing, byte-oriented i/o, direct memory access, and interrupt control.

peripheral control, Direct Memory Access (DMA) — For high-speed transfer rates, DMA transfers data on a cycle-stealing basis, on some computers, directly between the memory and the external device, bypassing the central processor.

peripheral controls — Peripheral controls regulate the transfer of data between the central processor and peripheral devices. Specifically, they reconcile the mechanical speeds of the peripheral devices with the electronic speed of the computer.

peripheral control transfers — Peripheral controls often regulate the transfer of data between the central processor and peripheral devices. Specifically, they reconcile the mechanical speeds of the central processor, and minimize the interruption of central processor activity due to peripheral data transfers.

peripheral control unit — An intermediary control device that links a peripheral unit to the central processor, or in the case of off-line operation, to another peripheral unit.

peripheral conversion program — Handles all those jobs normally done by a separate peripheral processor. The priority interrupt system and multiple memory accumulators in the computer eliminate virtually all loss in running time. Such processing is done through the arithmetic processor.

peripheral devices — Various kinds of machines that operate in combination or conjunction with a computer but are not physically part of the computer. Peripheral devices typically display computer data, store data from the computer and return the data to the computer on demand, prepare data for human use, or acquire data from a source and convert it to a form usable by a computer.

peripheral devices, programmable — The programmable devices represent a distribution of computing power. The UPI (or universal peripheral interface) is, in fact, an entire ROM- or EPROM-based microcomputer that serves as a custom programmble interface for more complex peripherals. Preprogrammed versions of the device are available as data encryption units, printer controllers and other functions.

peripheral equipment — 1. Various units or machines that are used in combination or conjunction with the computer but are not part of the computer itself, such as typewriters, sorters, tape readers, and others. 2. Operations considered not a part of processing, computing or logic, but instead mainly input and output operations, such as magnetic tape conversion, card punching, printing, reading. *See* auxiliary equipment.

peripheral, input-output — Typical input-output peripherals include diskettes, cartridge disks, hardcopy terminals, video display terminals, magnetic tape units, disc pack drives, line printers, paper tape punches and readers, cassettes, plotters, and card readers. Also generally included are A/D and D/A (analog and digital) converters, digital i/o and general-purpose interfaces.

peripheral interface adapter (PIA) — Some microprocessors have incorporated LSI devices exclusively dedicated to enhance their i/o capabilities and thus simplify the interfacing task of the design engineer. For example, several firms provided microprocessors with special peripheral interface adapters (PIA) that act like a universal i/o interface. The typical PIA offers two 8-bit, 3-state buses to interface with peripherals, along with the ability to service four independent interrupt lines. The unit also provides handshake control logic signals for synchronizing i/o devices to the microprocessor.

peripheral interface channel — That interface form (matching) previously designed or agreed on so that two or more units, systems, programs, etc., may be easily joined, transconnected, or associated to function properly together in communication of information.

peripheral interfaces — A number of optional interface cards are available for practically all systems, for a selected set of standard peripherals. The interfaces are implemented as printed circuit cards that plug into the chassis assembly.

peripheral interrupt — The stop resulting from the signal of readiness for or completion of a task by a peripheral device.

peripheral operation — Operation of input/output and other devices not under direct computer control; most commonly used to designate the transfer of information between magnetic tapes and other media.

peripheral plotters — *See* plotters, peripheral.

peripheral processing, concurrent — Service functions can be performed on a peripheral computing system that serves as an auxiliary to a larger system, or they can be performed on one system concurrently with other types of processing, such as stacked job processing, in a way that ensures that the data-processing facilities of the system are efficiently employed. When peripheral and stacked job processing are performed concurrently, it is possible to incorporate in the operating system optional features that are designed to enable the operator to mount files for one job while other jobs are being processed.

peripheral processor — For some environments, input and output are best processed by two interconnected computers wherein one computer handles the input/output for the other. The control programs of operating system provide the capability to handle this mode of operation for a configuration of equipment in which a very high-speed, high-storage capacity central processing unit performs calculations upon data supplied by a smaller computer that schedules, buffers, and controls the flow of input data, intermediate results, and output data to and from the larger unit. Usually in this configuration the larger unit is termed the "host" and the smaller one is called "peripheral," but either one may actually be in control of the other's operations and schedule.

peripheral subsystems — A subsystem consists of one or more peripheral units of the same type connected to an available input/output channel. Each subsystem is controlled by a channel synchronizer/control unit that interprets the control signals and instructions issued by the central processor, effects the transfer of data to or from the selected unit and the central processor, indicates to the central processor the status of the available peripheral units, and informs the central processor when errors or faults that affect the operation of the subsystem occur.

peripheral transfer — A procedure or process for transferring data between two units of peripheral or auxiliary equipment.

peripheral trunks — The basic systems are equipped with many input/output trunks, each of which can be connected to a peripheral control. A control which handles both reading and writing (e.g., a magnetic tape control) connects to a pair of trunks. Data are transferred between main memory and a trunk (and thus a peripheral device) via the read/-write channel specified in the instruction which initiates the transfer. Additional peripheral devices can be connected to the system simply by adding eight more input/output trunks to the basic configuration. The number of peripheral devices in a system depends only on the number of input/output trunks available.

permanent data files — *See* data files.

permanent fault — *See* fault, permanent.

permanent memory — Storage information that remains intact when the power is turned off. Also called nonvolatile storage.

permanent storage — *Same as* storage, nonvolatile.

permanent virtual circuit — A permanent association existing between two DTEs.

It is effectively a point-to-point, nonswitched circuit over which only data, reset, interrupt, and flow-control packets can flow.

permutated-title index — *Same as* index, permutation.

permutation — Any of the total number of changes in position or form that are possible in a group.

permutation index — *See* index, permutation.

permuted-title index — *Same as* index, permutation.

personal computers, video- and cassette-based — Some users have a tv set as an output display, a full alphanumeric keyboard for input, and an audio cassette for program storage and exchange. Video-based systems provide full user to system interaction at minimal cost. The speed of system response is practically instantaneous. Operations may be performed in almost complete silence. Reliability is enhanced as electromechanical mechanisms are limited to the keyboard and cassette recorder. Data media storage density is increased with audio cassettes over paper tape.

personal computing — Personal computers are often defined as those that are low cost (relative to mini and standard systems), based on tiny microcomputer chips and thus portable, personally controllable, and easily used. There are several classifications—home, hobbyist, professional, business, very small business, appliance, and more.

personality cards — Inside some PROM programers, a microcomputer tailors the program to the PROM the development team has decided to use. A programer often directs the data to be stored through "personality" cards that provide the appropriate timing patterns, voltage levels, and other requirements. The programer is partitioned so that new personality cards can be inserted as new PROMs are developed.

personality module — A typical personality module contains the specialized interfacing, power supplies and programming instructions unique to the particular PROM or family of PROMs being programmed (pulse width, number of pulses, duty cycles and threshold level). In many cases, a single module enables the user to program several types of PROMs.

PERT/COST — A PERT program for providing management with cost control for all phases of a project.

PERT/COST system — A generalized program designed to facilitate planning, scheduling, control, and monitoring of

Courtesy Ohio Scientific, Inc.

Personal computer, video- and cassette-based.

both large- and small-scale research and development projects.

PERT, early start dates — Used in an optimistic time estimate in which each job is started as early as pòssible to estimate the duration of the entire task.

PERT, free float — Certain stops used to halt particular tasks where no action would have resulted in an overall delay in the project.

PERT, latest start dates — Used in estimating the completion date of a particular task. Each job is arranged to start as late as possible so that the entire task is completed on the required date.

PERT (Program Evaluation and Review Technique) network — Use of PERT requires an extensive analysis of an overall project in order to list all the individual activities, or jobs which must be performed in order to meet the total objective. These activities are then arranged in a network that displays the sequential relationship among them. This analysis must be extremely thorough and detailed if it is to be realistic. PERT provides a means of reporting and analysis for project administrators. Information required can be developed and areas which impose the greatest time restrictions on the completion of a product can be high-lighted. Areas with an excess of time for completion, called stack areas, are also highlighted.

PERT, start dates — Used in estimating the completion date of a particular task. Each job is arranged to start as late as possible so that the entire task is completed on the required date.

PERT/TIME — A PERT program which allows management to plan, schedule, and direct programs and projects, as well as evaluate progress during project execution.

phase, compiling — *See* compiling phase.

phase encoding, redundant — An encoded system in which zeros and ones are represented by different width pulses. Each pulse can be given once or repeated for a certain amount of time. It is called redundant (repeated) phase encoding; e.g., the hobbyist cassette Kansas City Standard is redundant because all of the information is contained in the first portion of the pattern. Redundant phase encoding is actually frequency-shift keying (fsk).

phase, execute — 1. The part of the computer operating cycle wherein a command in the program register is carried out upon the address indicated. 2. The act of performing a command.

phase hits — Abrupt shifts in the phase of a transmitted carrier. Excessive phase hits can cause errors in high-speed, phase-modulated or QAM modems. Phase hits generally originate in radio carrier systems.

phase jitter — Peak-to-peak phase deviation of a transmitted carrier signal. An excessive phase jitter causes errors in high-speed, phase-modulated or QAM modems. Phase jitter generally originates in frequency-division multiplexers in carrier systems.

phase, object — *Same as* phase, run.

phase, run — An occasion on which the target program (after compiling) is run and often called the run phase, the target phase, or the object phase.

phase, shift — The time difference between the input and output signal or between any two synchronized signals of a control unit, system, or circuit.

phase, sorting — An arbitrary segmentation of a sort program. Many sorts are segmented into three phases: initialization phase, internal phase, merge phase.

phase, target — *Same as* phase, run.

phoneme — A primitive unit of auditory speech in a given language.

phonetic system — The specific equipment which has features for starting and acting upon data from the voice source or having a voice-form output.

photocell light checks — Checks performed on data read from cards passing through a card reader.

photocell matrix — An optical character recognition term which is a device capable of projecting an input onto a fixed two-dimensional array of photocells to develop a simultaneous display of the horizontal and vertical components of the character. The time necessary to scan the character is related to the response time of the photocells.

photoelectric reader — *See* reader, photoelectric.

photographic storage — 1. Photographic copies of data shown on direct-display cathode-ray tubes. 2. High-density storage of data in binary form on photographic disks for quick reference purposes. 3. Facsimile copies of readable documents or of direct output of the processor.

photogravure — A method of printing in which the small cells of the characters contain the ink on a recessed surface. This method is often used in preparing documents for character recognition.

photomultiplier light pen — A fiber optic light pipe and photomultiplier in the light pen allow high-speed detection of information displayed on the various optical displays. Detection of information by the pen can be sampled by the computer to alter the program.

photo-optic memory — A memory that uses an optical medium for storage. For example, a laser might be used to record on photographic film.

phototypesetting — A reproduction process for typed matter from computer outputs to photographic film or paper, and basically using optical character recognition after phototypesetting has been used to perfect or normalize character irregularities off-line. Computer-controlled phototypesetting is also used for computer-generated output for clean appearance, rapid processing, and for the use of unusual type characters which ordinary line printers cannot provide, for example, to produce phone directories.

physical simulation — The use of a model of a physical system in which computing elements are used to represent some but not all of the subsystems.

PIA bus interface — The PIA in many systems is used to provide 8 or 16 bits of external interface and 4 control lines at addressable locations in standard system memory. Often, i/o bits can be accessed in 2 words of 8 bits each, but each i/o bit is individually programmable to act as either an input or an output.

PIAs, single-multiple — Peripheral Interface Adapters (PIAs) permit parallel oriented peripherals to be connected to various microprocessors usually without any additional circuit requirements. A typical PIA contains two i/o circuit blocks, each capable of controlling an independent 8-bit peripheral i/o bus. Often, multiple PIAs can be used with a single system and selectively addressed by means of Chip Select Inputs.

pica — A unit of measure in printing approximating one-sixth of an inch.

pickup — Refers to a memory location from which the processor will obtain specific information.

picosecond — One thousandth of a nanosecond, or 10^{-12} seconds; abbreviated psec.

pictorial — A series of specifications and total layout of columns, blank spaces, margins, headings, stubs, etc., to develop the plan or format for the contemplated reports.

picture — In COBOL, a symbolic description of each data element according to specified rules concerning numerals, alphanumerics, location of decimal points, and length.

pilot — An original or test program, project, or device.

pilot model — A model of a system that is not so complex as a complete model and is used for program testing.

pilot system — The collection of file records and supplementary data obtained from the actual operations of a business over an extended period and used to effect a realistic system for testing by closely simulating the real world environment.

pilot tape — A tape that contains all the data used on a pilot model, and is used for loading the files.

PIO interface — Abbreviation for Parallel Input-Output interface. PIO interfaces allow the computer to input and output parallel data to and from an external parallel device such as a keyboard and tv terminal. Parallel means that all of the data bits are output at the same time.

pipelining — The beginning of one instruction sequence before another has been completed. Once a technique used on supercomputers, pipelining is now used to speed execution on machines of all sizes.

pipelining, bit-slice machines — The hardware arrangement that permits different sections of a bit-slice processor to work simultaneously instead of sequentially, and, thus, speeds up processing.

pitch array — *See* pitch, row.

pitch, character — That specific difference from the vertical reference axis of a character to the vertical reference axis of the adjacent character in a line of text or in a printed word.

pitch, feed — The distance between the centers of adjacent feed holes in perforated tape. Feed pitch and row pitch are often the same because there is one row of holes at each feed hole.

pitch, row — The distance measured along punched paper tape between the centers of adjacent holes.

pitch, track — The distance between centers of adjacent tracks on magnetic tapes, disks, drums, cards, or on paper tape, i.e., the distance between centers of holes is measured across the longitudinal axis or traverse to the motion of the recording device or medium.

PIU programming — The PIU can be programmed into one of three basic modes of operation. The interface, normally a single byte wide, can be optionally extended to be two bytes wide. Data transfer rates of one megabyte in the former implementation and two megabytes in the latter are projected at thirty meter separations.

Additional programming capability involves the ability to configure and control the signals which generate interrupts. One type PIU is packaged in a 68-pin package with all i/o signals being TTL compatible.

pixel scan — The basic element derived through various types of scanning processes is the picture element called a pixel. In these systems, the computer receives input data from the scanner and digitizer. The scanner views photographs or film transparencies that are illuminated by the light table. The brightness of the image is sampled at many points and digitized into data that are compatible with the computer. The display allows the analyst to observe the image being viewed and processed. Joystick or other type cursors allow the analyst to point to any pixel—picture element as a single bit.

PLA (programmed logic arrays) — A PLA is an orderly arrangement of logical AND and logical OR functions. A programmable logic array is an alternative to ROM which uses a standard logic network programmed to perform a specific function. PLAs are implemented in either MOS or bipolar circuits.

PL/M-86 — A high-level language, developed by Intel Corporation, that has been designed for both 8-bit and 16-bit systems and applications programming, particularly the Intel 8086 and 8088 microcomputers. It is completely compatible with PL/M-80, facilitating upgrading from 8080 and 8085 Intel machines to the 16-bit design.

PL/1 (programming language) — Compilers are provided for use in compiling object programs from source programs written in this programming language. This language has some features that are characteristic of FORTRAN and incorporates some of the best features of other languages, such as string manipulation, data structures, and extensive editing capabilities. Further, it has features not currently available in any language. The language is designed to take advantage of recent developments in computer technology and to provide the programmer with a flexible problem-oriented language for programming problems that can best be solved using a combination of scientific and commercial computing techniques. It is designed to be particularly useful for the increasing number of semicommercial, semiscientific applications such as information retrieval and command and control applications.

place — In positional notation, a position corresponding to a given power of the base, a given cumulated product, or a digit cycle of a given length. It can usually be specified as the nth character from the right end of the numerical expression.

place, digit — The site of a digit in a numeral in various positional notation systems.

place value — The representation of quantities by a positional value system.

plant — The usage in programming is to put or place an instruction which has been formed during the execution of a routine in a storage location, in such a way that it will be obeyed at some later stage in the execution. Thus, plants give the computer the ability to control and execute its own programs by using the ability of the computer to prepare or select instructions or subroutines on the basis of results obtained.

platen — A backing, commonly cylindrical, against which printing mechanisms strike to produce an impression.

playback head — *See* head, playback.

plot — To map or diagram. To connect the point-by-point coordinate values.

plotter — 1. A visual display or board in which a dependent variable is graphed by an automatically controlled pen or pencil as a function of one or more variables. 2. A device that inscribes a visual display of a dependent variable.

plotter control, incremental — Provides for high-speed plotting of points, continuous curves, points connected by curves, curve identification symbols, letters, and numerals under program control.

plotter, digital incremental — Digital incremental plotters in either on-line or off-line operation with a digital computer provide a high-speed plotting system of high versatility and reliability. For on-line operation with medium size computers, a small adapter unit converts the computer output signals to a form suitable for driving the plotter. No modification to the basic computer circuitry is required. With adapters available for all of the units, the plotter can be used off-line with virtually any medium- or large-scale computer.

plotter, on-line — *See* on-line plotter.

plotters, peripheral — Digital incremental plotters offer varied paper size, speeds, and plotting increments. Since the control unit does not require the use of a computer i/o channel, simultaneous plotting and other i/o channel operations on the same channel are possible.

plotter, XY — A device used in conjunction with a computer to plot coordinate points in the form of a graph.

plotting — The process of placing any type of information on the graph.

plotting, automatic — In many diverse areas of industry and science, a clear graphical representation of results is essential for rapid interpretation and evaluation of data. From weather mapping to business and stock market reports, from engineering design investigations to insurance actuarial graphs, in research laboratories and in computer laboratories, graphs of X vs Y plots are required for summarizing and presenting information in concise form. This need has been further accentuated by modern high-speed computers. The rapid production of vast quantities of data by these machines requires especially fast and accurate plotting equipment.

plotting board — *See* board, plotting.

plotting system, magnetic-tape — This system is very versatile, reliable, and almost completely automatic. Zero position, scale-factor adjustment, curve identification, symbol selection, axis generation, etc., are handled entirely by subroutines within the computer. For this reason the plotting system may be operated by unskilled personnel. The operator is required only to select the desired plot by means of the automatic-search feature, then initiate the plotting action by pressing either the single or multiple plot button. These systems produce completed graphs from data recorded on magnetic tape. Information read from the tape is used to drive a digital incremental plotter which reproduces the data in either a continuous curve or discrete points. Versatility of the system permits the use of subroutines for generation of any desired symbols, letters, numerals, or scale markings.

plotting table — *See* board, plotting.

plugboard chart — *See* chart, plugboard.

plugboard computer — A computer that has a punchboard input and output, and to which program instructions are delivered by means of interconnecting patch cords on a removable plugboard.

plugboard, detachable — *Same as* patchboard.

plugboard, patch-program — *See* plug, program-patching.

plugboard, removable — *Same as* patchboard.

plug-compatible — Pertaining to the capability of various devices to be interchangeable without modifications to them or the connecting or replacement devices.

plugging chart — *Same as* chart, plugboard.

plug-in unit — 1. An assembly of electronic components of a standard type, wired together, which can be plugged in or pulled out easily. 2. A self-contained circuit assembly.

plug, patch — *See* patchplug.

plug, program-patching — A relatively small auxiliary plugboard patched with a specific variation of a portion of a program and designed to be plugged into a relatively larger plugboard patched with the main program.

plugs, cordless — On patchcords, if connectors do not include a flexible portion, they are termed cordless plugs.

plus-90 orientation — An optical character recognition term which represents that specific position which indicates line elements on a document.

pocket — In sorters and other like equipment, the stacker assigned for each key position, i.e., a card storage temporary location or pocket for a given key for which totals are developed.

pockets, file addressing — In a random file, a small area or pocket in which one or more records are kept—an economical method of holding a small number of records.

pocket-size reels — Handy to carry, easy to load. Each 3½ inch reel holds up to 3 million bits, the equivalent of 4000 feet of paper tape, assuming 6-bit words are used.

point — In positional notation, the character or implied character that separates the integral part of a numerical expression from the fractional part, e.g., a decimal point or binary point.

point, arithmetic — *See* point, radix.

point, base — *See* point, radix.

point, binary — The radix point in a binary number system; i.e., the dot that marks the position between the integral and fractional, or units and halves, in a binary number.

point, branch — A given condition or instruction at which the computer may either continue on the present logical path, or jump (transfer control of the program) to another or one of several possible paths.

point, check — *See* checkpoint.

point, decimal — *See* decimal point.

point, entry — *See* entry point.

pointer — A table look-up technique that permits each datum (X_1) to be stored with a pointer pointing to a list of associated functions of X_1, as a variant technique to ordered or sequential or even indirect addressing techniques.

pointer operation — An address that is used to identify the location in memory where something can be stored or found. The item pointed to could be a numeral or a character, a variable, an interrupt handling routine, a table, or about any type of program or data structure.

pointer register, four address — On some low-cost systems, the microprocessor provides flexible addressing to 65K bytes of memory or peripheral addresses by means of its four address-pointer registers. Also users can use the flag outputs of the status registers in several ways other than simply to supply internal software flags.

pointer/registers, single-chip system — On some systems, the pointer registers are 16-bit general-purpose registers that are loaded normally under program control with reference addresses that serve as page pointers, stack pointers, and subroutine pointers. In applications having minimal memory addressing requirements, these registers may be used alternately as data storage registers.

point, exit — The instruction that transfers controls from the main routine to the subroutine.

point, fixed — Pertaining to a number system in which the location of a point is fixed with respect to one end of the numerals, according to some convention.

point, floating — Pertaining to a number system in which the location of the point does not remain fixed with respect to one end of the numerals.

point, index — One of the equally spaced rotational reference positions of the main shaft of card punch machines, labeled according to the row or column to which it corresponds.

point, load — A preset point at which magnetic tape is initially positioned under the read/write head to start reading or writing.

point-mode display — *See* display, point-mode.

point of no return — A first instance in a program in which a rerun is no longer possible, since data may no longer be available.

point-of-sale — Abbreviated POS. Pertaining to systems for automating various aspects of retail operations. The general types of functions performed by POS systems are: (1) Inventory control and other functions internal to the retail establishment. Data entered on an electronic cash register becomes input to a store-wide or chain-wide file of such data. (2) Credit authorization. A purchaser's credit card is read by a terminal, and a central computer verifies that the card is valid and that the purchaser's credit is sufficient to cover a sale. Such systems provide the means for establishing a zero floor

Courtesy NCR Corp.

Point-of-sale system.

limit for all credit transactions. (3) Credit verification. A merchant obtains verification from a bank's central computer that a purchaser's demand account balance is sufficient to cover a sale. (4) Electronic funds transfer. Some FET projects include POS terminals which are card-activated and which debit a customer's account and credit a merchant's account in order to effect payment for a sale.

point, radix — The dot that delineates the integer digits from the fractional digits of a number; specifically, the dot that delineates the digital position involving the zero exponent of the radix from the digital position involving the minus-one exponent of the radix. The radix point is often identified by the name of the system, e.g., binary point, octal point, or decimal point. In the writing of any number in any system, if no dot is included the radix point is assumed to follow the right most digit. (Synonymous with point.)

point, reentry — The point at which an instruction or a program is reentered from a subroutine or main program.

point, rerun — *See* rerun point.

point, restart — *Same as* restart.

point, restart (sorting) — The point at which a restart (or rerun) can be initiated. Memory registers, and the position of tapes are recorded at this point.

point, set — The specific desired value for the quantity being controlled; usually in a feed back control loop.

point shift, floating — A shift in 4-bit increments, performed on a short-format or long-format floating-point number.

points, rescue — *See* rescue points.

point, summing — Relates to any distinct point at which signals are added algebraically.

point-to-point transmission — Transmission of data between two points.

point, variable — Pertaining to a number system in which the location of the point is indicated by a special character at that location.

POKE statement — A command in BASIC which will cause the computer to change part of its own program in the manner commanded by the programmer. This "self-modifying" feature is one of the most potentially powerful capabilities of a computer. It is also one of the most risky, since it can lead to "crashes."

polar — When a logical "true" input is represented by an electrical voltage with a polarity opposite to the voltage representing a logical "false" input, the signal is defined as bipolar. If both "true" and "false" inputs are represented by the same voltage polarity, the signal is defined as unipolar.

polar operation — A type of circuit operation where the flow of current is reversed as pulses are transmitted. Polar differs from make-break operation in that with polar operation, current always flows when the circuit is closed. Only the direction of current flow is reversed by transmission.

Polish, Cambridge — Used in the LISP language, the Polish operators = and × are allowed to have more than two operands.

Polish notation — 1. A distinct technique or device credited to the Polish logician J. Lukasieqicz for treating algebraic statements as manipulatory strings of symbols followed by manipulatory strings of operations. 2. A specific form of prefix notation.

poll — A flexible, systematic method centrally controlled for permitting stations on a multipoint circuit to transmit without contending for the line.

polling — 1. An alternative to contention networks wherein terminals are polled in sequence to see if they have anything to send. Polling prevents any one terminal from an overly long wait. 2. A procedure which relates to the integration in succession of all terminals of a system on a shared communications line to determine which of the terminals requires the services of the mainframe or CPU. The sending device must be ready and the receiving device must be prepared and set to receive, much like a party-line telephone service, and each terminal can demand the attention from the CPU by a signal. Sophisticated computers have automatic polling circuitry, while others require special programming to poll.

polling characters — A set of characters designed to be peculiar to a terminal and the polling operation. Response to these characters indicates to the computer whether or not the terminal has a message to send.

polling, display station — Polling offers the cost-saving benefits of shared communications resources—modems, data lines, and computer i/o channels—as well as improved transmission error checking and communications compatibility with a wide range of computer systems. One type of terminal operates as a single unit or can be daisy-chained to other units on a single communication line. Synchronous multipoint (binary synchronous multipoint communications, bisync) and asynchronous multipoint (patterned after bisync) can optionally be used for polled communications networks.

polling list — Polling is a means of controlling communication lines by polling or asking the terminals if they have anything to send. The polling list is the device which controls the sequence of polling for every channel.

polling technique, remote — The importance of instantaneous responses to control messages can be best appreciated by this brief description of one on-line system's "polling" technique. The system is controlled through constant polling of teller consoles on each line by the central terminal unit. Polling is a request to each console for a message or for readiness to receive a reply. Because the full-duplex line permits the remote terminal unit to respond instantly to polls (less than 1/10th of a second), as many as 16 teller consoles can be efficiently serviced on one line. The turn-around delay inherent in a half-duplex line greatly reduces the number of consoles which can be polled and serviced efficiently, thereby requiring more lines.

polling, time sharing — Polling is a technique for controlling the use of lines by an agreed protocol between devices trying to share a common transmission path. The devices are rigidly controlled (so that only one of them sends information along a line at any instant) by an exchange of control signals or messages between them. Sometimes polling is governed by the central computer which sends a control message to each terminal in turn, inviting it to transmit an information message. The terminal replies either with such a message or with a control message.

polymorphic — Relates to the mode of a computer organization or configuration of the major parts or units in such a way that all components at a particular installation are held in a common pool. As each program is selected for execution, a specific set of components is selected from the pool and connected for execution of the program, after which they are returned to the pool; i.e., each configuration of equipment is matched to a program. Thus, many programs can be run concurrently if enough matched sets can be made available from the pool.

polyphase — A unique sorting technique that permits sorting with either an odd

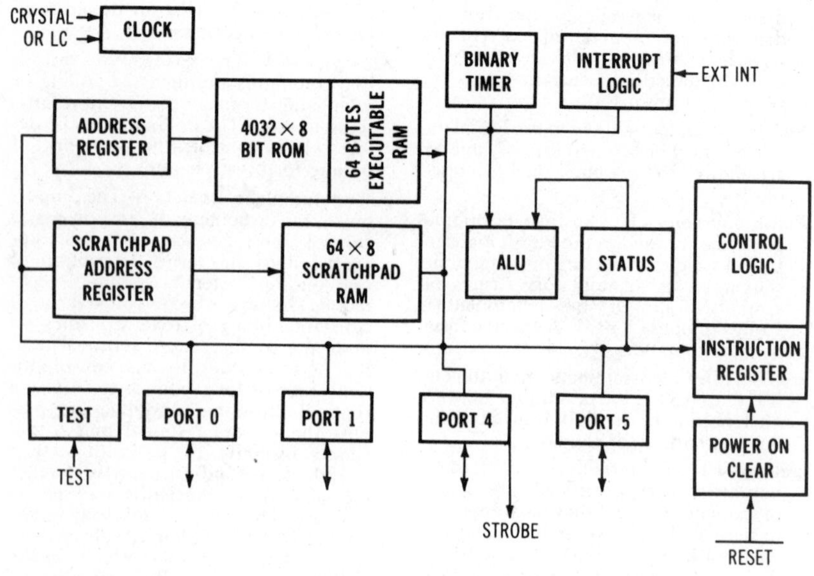

Ports, input-output.

or even number of tapes, thus permitting greater system flexibility than conventional methods.

polyphase merging — A technique used in a sort program to merge strings of sequenced data. Given T work tapes, merging is performed at the power of T − 1. The effective power of the merge varies between T − 1 and T/2, depending on the amount of input data and the number of strings.

polyvalence — The property of being interrelated in several ways.

polyvalent notation — A method for describing salient characteristics, in condensed form, using two or more characters, where each character or group of characters represents one of the characteristics.

polyvalent number — A number, consisting of several figures, used for description, wherein each figure represents one of the characteristics being described. (Similar to polyvalent notation.)

pop — Basically the process of removing information from the top of a stack, and then preparing to be able to access the next piece of information stored on the stack. This process generally involves changing the value of a stack pointer register so that it points to the next piece of data on the pile of data stored in memory.

port — The entry channel to which a data set is attached. The port is in the central computer, and each user is assigned one port. (Some systems.)

port, input-output — Each processor can have a number of i/o ports. Some are associated with external system activity; others, for information exchange with other system processors. In practice, ports are part of the i/o section of a processor. Low-cost microcomputers are particularly adaptable to communications via their i/o ports.

port sharing unit (PSU) — One type connects to a communication controller or CPU port and transmits or receives data from two to six terminals or modems. Less costly than a multiplexer, the PSU reduces the number of controller ports in a polled-terminal data communications configuration and makes more efficient use of connected ports.

position — 1. A site on a punched tape or card where holes are to be punched. The position at which the sign of a number is located. 2. An identifiable place in a program, set of instructions, or within a context.

positional notation — 1. The procedure

used in conventional number systems wherein the value assigned to a particular digit is determined by the symbol used (for example, 3) and by the position of the symbol relative to the radix point (for example, 300.0). 2. A number representation by means of an ordered set of digits, such that the value contributed by each digit depends on its position as well as on the digit value. 3. A method of representing numbers in which the digits are arranged sequentially, each succeeding digit is interpreted as the coefficient of successive powers of an integer referred to as the base of the number system. For example, in the decimal number system each succeeding digit is interpreted as successive coefficient powers of the integer or base 10.

position independent code — A type of machine-coded program that uses only relative addressing that thereby permits the program to reside in any portion of the system memory.

position, low-order — The extreme right digit or character position in a number or word.

position, overflow — An extra position in the register in which the overflow digit is developed.

position, pulse — *See* pulse.

positive AND gate — *Same as* gate, AND.

positive OR gate — *Same as* gate, OR.

post — To enter a unit or information on a record.

post edit — To edit the results of a previous computation.

post-edit programs — A test of the application or operational program that is edited, formatted, and sorted into a test result tape.

post-indexed — Generally, applicable only to the preindexed indirect mode. In this mode, the preindexed indirect address is determined, the operand address is fetched from the indirect address, then the contents of the specified index register is added to that operand address to determine the effective operand address.

postfix operators — A notation system where the operator appears after the operand, for example, AB + = A + B as it is used in Polish notation.

post mortem — A check routine that prints out information, either automatically or when called for, concerning the contents of all or a specified part of storage after a problem has "died" on the computer. Its purpose is to assist in the location of a program error or a machine malfunction.

post mortem dump — A static dump, used for debugging purposes, that is performed at the end of a machine run.

post-mortem routine — 1. A routine that either automatically or on demand prints data concerning registers and storage locations when the routine is stopped in order to assist in locating a mistake in coding. 2. Pertaining to the analysis of an operation after its completion. 3. Specific routine used in diagnostics and debugging operations after an error has been committed and must be located. 4. A service routine useful in analyzing the cause of a failure, such as a routine that dumps out the content of a store after a failure.

postmultiply — To multiply a matrix "A" by some conforming matrix "B," that is, by a matrix "B" that has as many rows as the given matrix "A" has columns (A ×B).

postnormalize — To normalize the result of an arithmetic operation.

postprocessor — A set of computer instructions which transform tool centerline data into machine motion commands using the proper tape code and format required by a specific machine control system. Instructions such as feed rate calculations, spindle speed calculations, and auxiliary function commands may be included.

post-write disturb pulse — *See* pulse, post-write disturb.

powder, anti-setoff — Finely powdered limestone or starch applied to paper immediately after printing that allows for a more optically acceptable document in optical character recognition. The powder reduces the unintentional transfer of ink between stacked printed sheets.

power dump — The accidental or intentional removal of all power.

power fail/auto restart — Some systems monitor ac primary voltage and send a signal to the CPU when voltage drops below a pre-set level. This initiates a noninhibitable interrupt through the power fail vector, to execute the user's power-down routine. It also starts a timer that allows 250 microseconds for an orderly shutdown; then the CPU automatically goes to the WAIT condition.

power-fail circuit — A logic circuit that protects an operating program if primary power fails. Typically, power-fail circuits inform the computer when power failure is imminent. This initiates a routine that saves all volatile data. After restoration of the power, the circuit is designed to initiate a routine that restores the data and restarts the computer operation.

power-fail interrupt — *See* interrupt, power-fail.

power-fail, restart — Often logic can be incorporated as a standard feature to prevent power dips or outages from damaging the ability of the computer to accomplish its tasks. On return of power, the system software can immediately restart the system.

power-line monitor — Some models plug into the same ac line as the computer and when a high-speed transient occurs, an audible alarm signals the occurrence while simultaneously recording the amplitude and duration of the pulse. Also, a built-in digital clock can stop at the exact time of transient entry to aid in determining where errors occurred in the computer data.

power management system — A typical power management system is sensitive to external factors such as temperature change. It monitors and regulates energy consumption. It is also capable of forecasting and making corresponding adjustments in power use. Since commercial electricity customers are billed on the basis of both total-power usage and peak-power requirements at any one time during the billing period, the system can be programmed to put a ceiling on maximum use.

power, mathematical — Relates to the number of times a number or quantity is to be multiplied by itself, i.e., 8^3 is eight cubed, or eight multiplied by itself as, $8 \times 8 \times 8$ or 512.

power, memory — A hierarchy of memories within a system makes information in main storage available at varying speeds. Small local store memories operate in as little as 200 billionths of a second. Control memories operate in as little as 250 billionths of a second. Powerful main memories—containing up to 524,000 characters of information—range from 2.5 millionths of a second down to one millionth of a second.

power of a number — The exponent.

power supply, uninterruptible — On some systems, optional batteries in chassis provide an uninterruptible power supply to the program and data RAM memories to ride through a 10-minute power outage. Newer flat and breadboard plug-in batteries offer even more efficient power storage.

PPS — Abbreviation for pulses per second.

p-pulse — *See* pulse.

preanalysis — An initial review of the task to be accomplished by the computer in order to increase the efficiency of that task.

precision — The degree of exactness with which a quantity is stated; a relative term often based on the number of significant digits in a measurement. Contrast with accuracy, which refers to the absence of error regardless of precision. For example, a two-digit number is accurate if correctly stated; whereas a five-digit number may be inaccurate, despite having greater precision.

precision, double — *See* double precision.

precision, floating-point — The maximum number of binary digits used as the mantissa of a single-precision floating-point fraction.

precision, multiple — *See* multiple precision.

precision, single — The number of words or storage positions used to denote a number in a computer. Single-precision arithmetic is the use of one word per number; double precision, two words per number, and so on. For variable word-length computers, precision is the number of digits used to denote a number. The higher the precision, the greater the number of decimal places that can be carried.

precision, triple — The retention of three times as many digits of a quantity as the computer normally handles; e.g., a computer whose basic word consists of ten decimal digits is called upon to handle thirty decimal digit quantities.

precomplier program — A unique program which is designed to detect errors and provide source program correction before the computation of the object, deck, or program.

predefined process — *See* process, predefined.

predicate — To affirm or deny, in mathematical logic, one or more subjects.

pre-edit — To edit input data prior to computation.

pre-edit checking programs — *See* pre-edit programs.

pre-edit programs — A checking of the application or operational program before the test run. A pre-edit run can remove such things as disobedience to established supervisory, core, program segmentation rules, etc.

prefix notation — A method of forming one-dimensional expressions without need for brackets by preceding, with a string or vector of operators, an operand string or vector that may itself contain operators upon operands.

preliminary proposal review — An on-site review to provide guidance to proponent agencies in the preparation of ADP (automatic data-processing) system proposals.

preliminary review — *See* review, preliminary-proposal.

premultiply — To multiply a matrix "B" by some conforming matrix "A"—that is, by a matrix "A" that has as many columns as the given matrix "B" has rows (A×B).

prenormalize — To normalize the operands of an arithmetic operation before the operation is performed.

preparation aids, program — Program preparation aids convert programs from easy-to-use source languages into computer machine language.

preparation, data — The process of converting data into a medium suitable for input to and processing by the computer.

preparation, file — *See* file preparation.

preparation, object-program — Conversion of programs from one of several easy-to-use source languages, or from certain competitive system languages, to a specific machine code.

preread disturb pulse — *See* pulse, preread disturb.

preread head — *See* head, preread.

prerecorded tracks — A preliminary tape, disk, or drum recorded routine that simplifies programming, relieves the programmer of the responsibility of furnishing timing, or counting instructions and permits block and word addressability.

preselection — 1. A technique for storing data from the next input tape in the computer memory before the data being processed by computer is absorbed. The selection of the next input tape is determined by instruction to the computer. 2. A programming technique in buffered computers in which a block of information is read into the input buffer register from the next input tape to be called upon.

presence, bit — *See* bit, presence.

preset — A preset relates to a variable whose value is established initially for some routine or operation, while to preset is the act of initializing a value of a variable.

preset mode — Some systems may be operated in the preset mode of operation. In this mode of operation the monitor is not resident in memory. Each absolute program is loaded into memory with the present button on the computer console. The processing of individual jobs is the same as in the batch processing mode, except that the EOJ (end of job) stop places the computer in a halt state. To begin processing a new job, the absolute compiler, assembler, loader, or utility program for the job must be preset into memory.

preset parameter — A parameter incorporated into a subroutine during computation. A program parameter frequently comprises a word stored relative to either the subroutine or the entry point, and dealt with by the subroutine during each reference. It may be altered by the routine, or it may vary from one point of entry to another.

presort — The first part of a sort, in which records are arranged into strings that equal or exceed some minimum length.

prestore — 1. To store a quantity in an available or convenient location before it is required in a routine. 2. To set an initial value for the address of an operand or a cycle index. 3. To restore.

presumptive address — A number that appears as an address in a computer instruction, but which serves as the base, index, initial or starting point for subsequent addresses to be modified. (Synonymous with reference address.)

presumptive instruction — An instruction

that will most likely be modified before it is used for the final program.

prevention, hang-up — *See* hang-up prevention.

preventive maintenance — 1. A maintenance plan that is designed to prevent failures rather than correct malfunctions. 2. The maintenance of a computer system that attempts to keep equipment in top operating condition and to preclude failures during production runs.

preventive maintenance contracts — Preventive maintenance contracts provide either resident field engineers or periodic-visit arrangements that are tailored to the user's specific needs. Competent and experienced personnel ensure peak performance of all equipment.

previewing — An optical character recognition (OCR) term defining a process of trying to gain initial or prior information about characters which appear on an incoming source document. Such intelligence could be the range of ink density, relative position, etc., to be used as an aid to normalization or attempted perfecting of the oncoming reading operations.

prewired options — Optional equipments that are closely related to the processor, such as the extended arithmetic element, memory extension control, and one of the analog-to-digital converted options, are prewired in the basic computer so that the time, effort, and cost involved in adding these options at the factory or in the field is a minimum.

PRF — Abbreviation for pulse repetition frequency.

prices, implicit — Same as marginal values, shadow prices, dual-variable levels, etc. —that is, numbers giving the incremental worth of a relaxation of one unit in the right-hand side of a constraint.

primary equipment — *Same as* working equipment.

primary key — Files permitting keyed access usually required that one of the key fields be given highest priority. Retrieval speed and efficiency are usually optimized for this key. The values in the fields of the primary key usually must be unique.

primitive — 1. The most basic or fundamental unit of data, i.e., a single letter, digit, element, or machine code is primitive when related to the ultrasophisticated codes or languages now available. 2. First or second generation computer equipment.

principle, unit record — Refers to a punched card used to record information about one transaction only in its 80 columns.

print and punch, combined — The simultaneous printing and punching of data onto a punched card.

print control character — *See* character, print control.

printer — 1. A device that expresses coded characters as hard copy. 2. An output device for spelling-out computer results as numbers, words, or symbols. Printers range from electric typewriters to high-speed printers which prepare invoices, checks, statements or documents at 10 lines per second and faster.

printer, bar — 1. A specific printer which has its type at each print position in a box or magazine. The desired character is selected by moving the box vertically until that character is opposite the printing position. 2. A printing device which utilizes several side-by-side type bars. Printing data involves activating specific bars which move vertically until the characters they contain are properly aligned. Then, the data are printed simultaneously.

printer, chain — A typical high-speed printer with type carried on a moving closed loop chain or belt which is hit on the fly by a component hammer as the type moves across the paper.

printer, character — A device capable of producing hard copy, the printing being accomplished one character at a time.

printer, character-at-a-time — This type of printer is similar to an electric typewriter or teleprinter, or a printing keypunch.

printer, console — An auxiliary output printer used to relay messages to the computer operator.

printer controller — A typical high-speed line printer controller contains the circuitry necessary to interface a high volume printing device to the microcomputer. The controller includes a character serial PIO interface that permits data to be transmitted to the line printer's data buffer at rates up to 66,-000 characters per second. The controller also includes circuitry to support printers equipped with variable forms unit options.

printer controller, microcomputer — A unit that provides character print buffers and automatic control and timing for commercially available printers.

printer dot — *Same as* printer, wire.

printer,electrostatic — A device for printing an optical image on paper in which dark and light areas of the original are represented by electrostatically charged and uncharged areas on the paper. The paper is dusted with particles of finely powdered dry ink and the particles adhere only to the electrically charged areas. The paper with ink particles is then heated, causing the ink to melt and become permanently fixed to the paper.

printer, high-speed (HSP) — A printer which operates at a speed more compatible with the speed of computation and data processing so that it may operate on-line. At the present time a printer operating at a speed of 1000 lines per minute and 100 characters per line, is considered high-speed.

printer, ink-jet — A printing device in which dot-matrix characters are formed by drops of ink ejected from electrically controlled nozzles.

printer interrupts — One common way to utilize a computer more effectively during relatively slow output is to use the interrupt system. The microcomputer sends a byte to a peripheral, then returns to another task. When the byte has been printed, the device signals the computer through an interrupt line. The computer stops what it is doing (is interrupted), saves the contents of its registers, and determines the source of the call. In this case, it sends another byte to the printer, then returns to its previous work. With an interrupt system, the computer is not spending large amounts of time waiting for the printer.

printer limited — Often, the timing restrictions on a process due to the slowness or inadequacy of the printing equipment, whereby other operations must await the completion of the printing unit.

printer, matrix — *Same as* printer, wire.

printer, page — A unique printer which composes a full page of characters before printing this full page during a cycle of operations. Such types are xerographic printers, crt (cathode-ray tube) printers, photographic devices.

printer, serial — A device capable of printing characters, one at a time across a page. Many variations in serial printers exist, e.g., typewriter; stylus or matrix serial printer; and high-speed, multiple-line stylus or matrix serial printer.

printer, skip — A skip function may be signaled on any step. When skip is signaled on a step that also impulses print, the skip function is effective after the line has been printed. If skip is signaled on any other step, the skipping action is initiated immediately.

printer skipping — The rate at which the unit advances a form through the carriage without printing.

printer spacing chart — A form for developing a layout and spacing, or general design of printed output, as well as the preparation of the carriage control tape.

printer speed — The rate at which the unit operates when it is actually printing data.

printer, stick — An antiquated printer consisting of a stick which prints one character at a time as the stick moves from left to right.

printer, stylus — *See* printer, wire.

Courtesy Digital Equipment Corp.
Printer terminal.

printer terminal components — Basically a printer terminal consists of a keyboard, power supply, control unit, data-communications interface, optional memory, and printer mechanism. Generally, a message entered through the keyboard communicates with the printer mechanism and another terminal or host-computer system via an interface circuit. Conversely, the computer may also transmit digital signals via the terminal interface back to the terminal.

printer-terminal interface — Most terminals use a current loop (20 or 62.5 mA) or EIA RS232 interface to exchange data between the terminal and computer. Some employ a modem for communications with a remote computer or terminal via a phone line. Future units will probably incorporate IBM's SDLC communications discipline or microprocessors to accept various disciplines or protocols.

printer type bar — A narrow box or magazine contains the type bars and when a particular character is selected a vertical movement of the box proceeds until the selected character is opposite the printing position. Each bar contains the entire alphabet and may be interchangeable or fixed.

printer type bar, interchangeable — A printer type bar which can be removed by the operator to change from one alphabet to another.

printer, wheel — A printer which has the type face mounted or engraved on the outside of a rim of a disk or a wheel, i.e., a wheel exists for each line of print and is keyed to a shaft which is rotated at high speed. Printing is accomplished by a hammer pressing the paper against the ribbon.

printer, wire — A high-speed printer that prints characterlike configurations of dots through the proper selection of wire-ends from a matrix of wire-ends, rather than conventional characters through the selection of type faces. (Synonymous with matrix printer.)

printer, xerographic — A device for printing an optical image on paper in which dark and light areas of the original are represented by electrostatically charged and uncharged areas on the paper. The paper is dusted with particles of finely powdered dry ink and the particles adhere only to the electrically charged areas. The paper with ink particles is then heated, causing the ink to melt and become permanently fixed to the paper.

printing control — A specific list of control group identifications or particulars through a procedure which omits listing of detail records.

printing counter — This counter on the magnetic-tape terminal advances by one for each tape block transmitted or received. At the end of transmission, the total number of tape blocks for the run is printed automatically. During a run upon the detection of an error block when receiving, the number of that tape block is printed.

printing, data-protection — Operation of the printers is checked automatically to ensure that they respond correctly to control-unit printing signals. If this check fails, an indicator, which can be tested by a programmed instruction, is automatically set.

printing, line — The printing of an entire line of characters at once.

printing matrix — *Same as* printer, wire.

print interlock time — The required time for the printer to accept data from the print storage area and to complete the printing of its output.

print local function — Some terminals can pass data to the auxiliary interface at a speed that is independent from the main communication interface, by use of the Print Local function. Data can be received by the terminal from the host at one speed and then transferred from the display buffer at a completely different speed to the peripheral attached to the serial, EIA interface. This enables the use of slower and less costly peripherals.

print manager, data base — The Print Definition Language (PDL) defines the printer characteristics (lines and columns) and standard header, page, and overflow print conditions. Information may be queued for spooling, printed, or converted to an ASCII or other format for transmission. Special headings may be inserted, and printers may be dynamically assigned. The programmer is only concerned about the logical information to be printed.

print member — The particular part or component of a printer which is the element developing the form of the printed character, such as the print bar, type bar, or wheel.

print-on-alarm RAM — A data-system condition in which continuous scanning of data channels takes place, but output of data is initiated only when an alarm condition is interpreted by the CPU. RAMs are programmed to designate and signal such conditions.

printout — Sometimes an instruction to cause the printing of data in storage or from other external storage media into hard copy.

printout, dynamic — A sequential operation of printing as part of a computer run and during the run instead of at the end of the run.

printout, memory — A listing of the contents of a storage device, or selected parts of it. (Synonymous with memory dump and core dump.)

printout, static — The printing of data after the run instead of as part of the run, which is called a dynamic printout.

print positions — The maximum number of characters which can be printed on a single line.

print timing dial — The control knob on the printer which is an adjustment of the printing quality.

print transparent — A mode in which a terminal will pass all received data to an auxiliary port and neither display nor act upon it.

print wheel — A single element providing the character set at one printing position of a wheel printer.

print-wheel assembly — An assembly of print wheels keyed and fastened to a shaft which is rotated at a high speed with a print wheel at each print position. A hammer forces the ribbon against the paper at the instant the desired character to be printed at a position is aligned with the line of the print.

prioritize — To arrange a group of similar things in some order based on their relative importance to one another. The ordering can be in terms of either location or time.

priority — 1. The sequence in which various entries and tasks will be processed by the analysis of action codes and other priority-real-time systems, as controlled by program level indicators. 2. The positioning of various routines as input/output ahead or taking precedence over the normal control sequence of the basic routine. (Clarified by priority circuits.)

priority circuits — *See* circuits, priority.

priority, dispatching — *See* dispatching priority.

priority error dump — *See* dump, priority error.

priority execution, I/O operations — Hardware and software associated with i/o operations have unique priorities. Hardware priority is determined by the position of the device-controller card on the i/o bus. Therefore, the controller card closest to the computer has the highest priority and is serviced first. Software, or device handler, priority is assigned at system generation time. The handlers run on task levels and usually have higher priorities than normal tasks. "More important" handlers are normally assigned the higher priorities so they may have control whenever necessary. Whenever tasks waiting for a handler are unsuspended, the highest priority task awaiting the handler is given control. The task scheduler on some systems maintains this priority scheme and ensures its integrity at all times.

priority indicators — 1. Groups of characters used in the header of a message to define the order of transmitting messages over a communication channel. 2. Information that is used to order a queue.

priority-interrupt controller — Usually, a bipolar LSI circuit that adds high-speed "priority interrupt" capability to low-price microcomputer systems often encompassing up to eight peripherals. It eliminates the necessity for the MPU to poll all its peripherals to determine their service requirements and priority ratings. The circuit is of particular importance in systems utilizing many peripherals with interrupt requirements.

priority interrupt controller chip — A special chip that manages several external interrupts and provides automatic vectoring, i.e., responds to the interrupt acknowledge from the microprocessor by supplying one of n branching addresses corresponding to the start address of the interrupt handler, on some systems.

priority interrupt input/output — *See* input/output priority and interrupt.

priority interrupts, multilevel — Interrupt provisions have been made to facilitate the priority requirements of various subroutines. The interrupt requests of these subroutines are handled by the central processor in the sequence of the highest priority. If a priority subroutine requests an interrupt, it will have priority over all subroutines of lower priority, even though they have previously requested an interrupt.

priority interrupts, optional — Many levels of optional priority interrupts are available on the computer. Any priority interrupt takes precedence over a lower priority program. Each level of priority interrupt may be separately allowed or disallowed by the program and each leads to a unique interrupt routine. As an option, the several computers may be provided with a programmed input-/output channel that sends information to or from the accumulator by programmed instructions. The instructions specify which device is to communicate; thus, the time sharing of the programmed input/output lines is controlled directly by the program.

priority interrupt system — A priority interrupt system allows high-speed interrupt processing without the customary wasted time for saving registers and status. This is facilitated by providing a separate register set for each interrupt level, so an interrupt routine can use a full register set without affecting the registers of the interrupted routine. Each interrupt level can be individually enabled or disabled. The priority interrupt system provides for internal processor interrupts, i/o peripheral device interrupts, and groups of individual external interrupts, each with its own unique interrupt memory address and priority assignment.

priority interrupt table — When a computer does not have a fully automatic interrupt handling capability, a table is set up that lists the priority sequence of handling and testing interrupts.

priority limit — The upper bound to the priority list for dispatching or designing a priority rating to various tasks or subtasks, i.e., active, inactive, top priority, lowest priority, or batch processing.

priority, modes of — *See* modes of priority.

priority (multiplexing) — Some specific standard communications subsystems have been designed to handle a multiplicity of different speed communications facilities in the most efficient manner possible. The communication multiplexer contains priority logic which permits high-speed facilities to be serviced more frequently than low-speed facilities on a completely random basis.

priority, multiprogramming — This priority is oriented toward the concurrent operation of several types of applications. Assignment of priority levels is at the discretion of the user. For example, one priority level can be reserved for a program that must provide rapid responses to real-time devices, such as communications control. Another can be reserved for the peripheral control package to accomplish several media conversions—card to tape, tape to printer, etc. The third priority level could then be used to run either a production or monitor job.

priority ordered interrupts — Some time-sharing computers can have over 200 priority ordered interrupts for external lines. This extensive interrupt capability allows a terminal to be attached to more than one interrupt line. If the attached interrupts cover a range of priorities, by selectively arming and disarming the external interrupt lines, the executive program can change the relative priority of a terminal's attention requests, allowing different classes of service or response to be given to the terminal.

priority processing — *See* processing, priority.

priority routine — In an interrupt, the leaving of one program by the processor to work on the program connected with the interrupt or the priority routine.

priority rules — Priority and inhibition rules are usually implemented in the time-sharing hardware to resolve possible conflicts when two interrupts occur simultaneously or when a second interrupt occurs before a previous one is completely processed.

priority selection — The use of information contained in the job request schedule to select the next job to be initiated. Selection is based on the priority and precedence assigned to the job, the sequence relationship of this job to other jobs with the same priority and precedence, and the availability of facilities required by the job.

priority structure — The organization of a system for processing. The priority structure of the system depends not upon the number of instructions but upon the complexity of the programs. The structure can range from systems with no priority to multicomplex organizations with multilayers of interrupts and multilevels of priority.

priority-structured i/o interrupt system — Devices electrically closest to the microcomputer module receive highest priority, for either DMA or programmed i/o transfers. (DMA devices have a higher priority than programmed i/o devices.) This structure allows nesting of interrupts to as many levels as there are devices connected to the bus. Upon receipt of an interrupt grant, the device directs the processor to an interrupt vector location which contains the starting address of the device interrupt service routine and the new processor status word.

privileged instruction operation — Often various measures for protection against one problem subprogram misusing another problem subprogram i/o devices are provided by restricting all i/o commands to the supervisor state. A subprogram requests i/o action by issuing a supervisor call instruction. The supervisory subprogram can then analyze this request and take the appropriate action.

privileged instructions — Protection against one problem subprogram misusing the i/o devices of another problem subprogram is provided by restricting all i/o commands to the supervisor state. A subprogram requests i/o action by issuing a supervisor call instruction. The supervisory subprogram can then analyze this request and take the appropriate action.

problem — A set of circumstances, situations, or states which develop when some unknown information is to be discovered, i.e., a solution is sought from some known information and a procedure is understood to acquire the unknown.

problem, check — A problem chosen to determine whether the computer or a program is operating correctly.

problem definition — The art of compiling logic in the form of general flowcharts and logic diagrams that clearly explain and present the problem to the programmer in such a way that all requirements involved in the run are presented.

problem description — A statement of a problem and possibly a description of the method of its solution, or the solution itself. The transformations of data and the relationship of procedures, data, constraints, environments, etc., may also be included.

problem, fault-location — *See* fault-location problem.

problem file — All the material needed or for use to document a program to be run on a computer.

problem folder — *Same as* problem file.

problem input tape — An input tape, either punched paper tape or magnetic tape, that contains problem data for checking out a given computer system.

problem language — *Same as* language, problem-oriented.

problem-oriented language — 1. A source language oriented to the description of a particular class of problems. 2. A specific language designed for solutions to problems of a particular class of problems. COBOL AND FORTRAN programs are designed for various classes of problems whether scientific or commercial types, and although they require elaborate and extensive translation and compilation, they are relatively simply developed and quite easily understood even by the novice computer personnel.

problem, test — A problem chosen to determine whether the computer or a program is operating correctly.

problem time — Often called physical system time, it is the time interval between corresponding events in the physical system being simulated.

problem, trouble-location — A test problem whose incorrect solution supplies information on the location of faulty equipment. It is used after a check problem has shown that a fault exists.

problem, troubleshooter — The unique program for or designed as a series of test computations whose incorrect answers will isolate a fault. This type of procedure is used most often after a check problem shows that a fault exists.

procedural and exception tests — Procedural and exception tests are designed to check machine control and operation before processing. They consist of test data (generally punched into cards) covering all or most conditions which can arise during the run, as well as a control panel and/or program which will process the test data and check out machine components. The control panel is inserted, or the program loaded, or both; the test data is then read into the machine and processed. The results are compared against predetermined ones. If they are satisfactory, actual processing can begin. In some installations these tests are made only at the beginning of each working day; in others they are made before specific runs.

procedural testing — Tests of alternative human responses in system operations. This is distinguished from hardware or software tests.

procedure — A precise step-by-step method for effecting a solution to a problem.

procedure analysis — The analysis of a business activity to determine precisely what must be accomplished and how.

procedure, bypass — *See* bypass procedure.

procedure division — A routine in COBOL that describes the procedures to be used in processing the data described in the data division; it contains all the necessary steps to solve a given problem. Procedures are written as sentences which are combined to form named paragraphs. Likewise, paragraphs may be combined to form sections. Paragraph and section names are assigned by the programmer so that control may be transferred from one section or paragraph to another.

procedure, fallback — *See* fallback procedure.

procedure, loading — System, object, and library routines are loaded in a similar manner. A program may have a fixed origin or may be relocatable. Fixed origin programs are loaded into the specified memory address. Programs are relocated by a base address initially set by the executive routine. After the main program has been loaded, any library subroutines or equipment drivers called will then be loaded. With all the necessary routines in memory, the loader returns to the job processor. (Some systems.)

procedure name — The brief reference in a program to another program or portion of another program.

procedure-oriented — A programming language that is similar to the language used in the job, and is relatively independent of the data-processing system.

procedure-oriented language — A source language oriented to the description of procedural steps in machine computing.

procedures, in-line — A COBOL term for procedural instructions which are part of the main sequential and controlling instructions of the program.

proceed-to-select signal — *See* signal, proceed-to-select.

process — A generic term that may include compute, assemble, compile, interpret, generate, etc.

process, batch — *See* batch process.

process chart — *Same as* flowchart.

process control — 1. Pertaining to systems whose purpose is to provide automation of continuous operations. This is contrasted with numerical control that provides automation of discrete operations (e.g., machines). 2. Automatic control of continuous-manufacturing industrial processes by using, for example, hybrid computers.

process control, industrial — *See* industrial process control.

process controller, microcomputer-based — A typical unit provides logic storage and control for a variety of instruments, inputs, etc., in desired profiles, e.g., stored and retrieved using digital and microcomputer techniques. Capacity for one typical unit is up to 40-line segments with process resolution to one part in 1000. Programming entry into the micro memory is via keyboard on the front panel; 16 push buttons allow the operator to select 28 functions.

process-control system — A system whose primary purpose is to provide automation of continuous operations.

process control system organization — One industrial microcomputer system consists of a central processor unit (CPU) module which provides system control and performs the various arithmetic and logical functions; one or more programmable read-only memories (PROMs) which store the system instructions or program; one or more random access memories (RAM) which are used for data storage; possibly an interrupt control module which is used to handle interrupt signals from devices being controlled; one or more input/output modules which accept inputs from the system being controlled and transmit control signals to that system; a power supply and regulators; a communications bus flat cable which provides the signal path to tie the various modules together; and the necessary mounting hardware.

processing, automatic data — Data processing performed by a system of electronic or electrical machines so interconnected and interacting as to reduce to a minimum the need for human assistance or intervention. (Related to automatic data-processing system.)

processing, background — Work which has a low priority and is handled by the computer when higher priority or real-time entries are not occurring. Batch processing such as inventory control, payroll, housekeeping, etc., are often treated as background processing but can be interrupted on orders from terminals or inquiries from other units.

processing, batch — A technique by which items to be processed must be coded and collected into groups prior to processing.

processing, batch data — *See* batch processing.

processing, business-data — Data processing for business purposes, e.g., recording and summarizing the financial transactions of a business.

processing capacity — Often the maximum limitation of places of a number which can be processed at any one time. An example is a 12-place number.

processing, centralized data — Data processing performed at a single, central location on data obtained from several geographical locations or managerial levels. Decentralized data processing involves processing at various managerial levels or geographical points throughout the organization.

processing, concurrent — *See* concurrent processing.

processing, continuous — The technique of constantly processing input items. This is sometimes referred to as on-line or real-time processing and is contrasted to batch processing.

processing control sequence — The control program initializes job operations, assigns input/output units, and performs the functions needed for automatic transition from one job to another, whether concurrent operations are under way or not. When the computing system is restarted after being turned off for some period of time, the control program is initially loaded, establishes initial control over all i/o units, and starts processing-program operation according to the schedule established by the user.

processing, conversational — The user is said to be communicating with the system in a conversational manner when each statement he enters through the terminal is processed (translated, verified, and, if desired, executed) immediately. The system then sends a reply to the terminal. The information contained in the reply varies. For example, it might be a message indicating that the previous statement contained an error. Operations in the conversational manner must be in either of two possible modes—the program mode, or the command mode (some computers).

processing, data — *See* data processing.

processing, deferred — Processing which can be delayed or is considered low priority, and is completed when computer time is at nonpeak periods.

processing, demand — The processing of data as quickly as it becomes available or ready. This is real-time and thus avoids the need for storage of any appreciable amount of unprocessed data.

processing, demand (time sharing) — *See* time sharing, demand processing.

processing, direct-address — Reading or writing of data from a sector whose address is given.

processing, electronic data — Data processing performed largely by electronic equipment. (Related to automatic data processing.)

processing, fault (time sharing) — *See* time sharing, fault processing.

processing, file — *See* file processing.

processing, foreground — High-priority processing, usually resulting from real-time entries, given precedence by means of interrupts, over lower priority "background" processing.

processing, image — Processing by those computer systems that simulate the human brain, which "sees" images like a scanner. They can manipulate images in various ways that are contributory to the extraction of specifically desired information. The two primary end products of these systems are (1) an enhanced reconstruction of the original image, and (2) a numeric or graphic report that relates specific information contained in the image.

processing, industrial data — Data processing designed for industrial purposes, often numerical control.

processing, information — A less restrictive term than data processing, encompassing the totality of scientific and business operations performed by a computer.

processing, in-line — *Same as* on-line processing.

processing, integrated data (IDP) — 1. A system that treats as a whole, all data-processing requirements to accomplish a sequence of data-processing steps, or a number of related data-processing sequences, and that strives to reduce or eliminate duplicating data entry or processing steps. 2. The processing of data by such a system in which all operations are in some way connected or associated with a computer.

processing, interactive — Processing that involves the constant interplay of creative and routine activities with the routine jobs being relegated to the computer so that man is left free to exercise his imagination and judgment.

processing (LISP) — *See* LISP.

processing list — *See* list processing.

processing machine, data — A general name for a machine that can store and process numeric and alphabetic information. (Related to analog digital computer and automatic data-processing equipment.)

processing multithread — A sequence of events in programs required for the computer processing of a message known as a thread. In single-thread processing all work is completed before work is begun on a new message. In multithread processing, message threads are handled in parallel.

processing, off-line — *See* off-line processing.

processing, on-line — *See* on-line processing.

processing, overlap — Processor operations performed at the same time by using different parts of the circuitry, for example, read-process-write, or any two of these.

processing, parallel — The operation of a computer so that programs for more than one run are stored simultaneously in its storage, and executed concurrently.

processing, priority — A type of time sharing or facility sharing in which the programs to be run are selected by priority rules or criteria.

processing programs — Processing programs actually accomplish work such as updating inventory records, preparing reports and compiling new programs. They include both support programs and application programs. The application programs will be written making use of FORTRAN, COBOL, and other macrostatements of the assembly program wherever possible.

processing, random — Transfer of an item between core memory and a drum or disk location. The address of the item is determined by mathematical transformation of its key.

processing, random-access (central file) — *See* random-access processing (central file).

processing ratio — The end result in the calculation of the time the equipment is being properly used, including lost time because of human error and the total available time.

processing, real-time — *See* real-time processing.

processing, real-time (bank) — *See* real-time processing (bank).

processing, remote — *See* remote message processing.

processing, scientific — The processing of data involved with solving mathematical functions or equations.

processing, single thread — The complete processing of all programs and events of one message before starting in another message. *See* processing, multithread.

processing system, job — *See* job-processing system.

processing unit — A part of a computing system which is the primary arithmetic and logical performing modules.

process, input/output (IOP) — A unit that handles normal data input/output control and sequencing.

process interrupt card — The process interrupt card provides a means by which the user, or processes that he specifies, can generate interrupts and request service on a priority basis. The typical card has eight channels, which may be optionally isolated. Each input can be programmed to trigger an interrupt on a low-to-high transition, a high-to-low transition, a change in input state; or it can be ignored. When mechanical contacts are used, the input can be programmed to be ignored (disabled) after interrupt for approximately 10ms, to inhibit switch-bounce from causing further interrupts. The card will stack and hold up to eight interrupts for as long as power is applied and the interrupts are serviced on a user-determined priority basis. The user process requesting an interrupt is identified via a software routine. (Some systems.)

process, iterative — A process for calculating a desired result by means of a repeating cycle of operations that comes closer and closer to the desired result; e.g., the arithmetical square root of N may be approximated by an iterative process using only additions, subtractions, and divisions.

process, limited — The speed of the central processing unit controls the processing time and not the input/output speeds or capability.

process, limited (sorting) — A sort program in which the execution time of the internal instructions determines the elapsed time required to sort.

process optimization — An extensive process-controller program, based on the model of the process, directs the DAC (data aquisition and control) system. Process data is continuously collected and analyzed for computation of optimum operating instructions. These instructions are given to the process operator via an on-line typewriter.

processor — 1. A device capable of receiving data, manipulating it, supplying results usually of an internally stored program. 2. A program used in compiling a source program that will produce, when completed, an execution of the objective function of the program or process. 3. A generic term that includes assembly, compiling, and generation. 4. A shorter term for automatic data processor or arithmetic unit.

processor, attached support ASP — The utilization of multiple computers, usually two, connected via channel-to-channel adapters, to increase the efficiency in processing many short duration jobs.

processor basic instructions — Processor modules execute basic instructions which can be functionally grouped into five categories: register operations, accumulator operations, program counter and stack control operations, input/output operations, machine operations.

processor, bit-slice — A processor based on the approach that allows microcomputer organizations of variable word sizes, with processor units separated into 2-, 4- or 8-bit slices on a single chip. These devices can be parallelled to yield an 8-, 12-, 16-, 24-, or 32-bit microcomputer when assembled with the other necessary "overhead" components of the system. The 16-bit microprocessors constructed from these components can be assembled into microcomputers that perform in the minicomputer class.

processor, bit-slice word — Normally, a programmed bit-slice processor may require anywhere from 100 to 1024 words of microprogram memory to control all the operations. Each word, in turn, can consist of many bits since it can be used to control more than just the processor slice. It can also control peripherals, memories, and other processor subfunctions. Depending on the application, a microprogram-control word can be from about 10 to 60 bits long. The advantages of microprogramming your own processor versus buying a programmed chip include the ability to write your own macroinstructions and thus customize for your application.

processor, central — *See* processor unit, central (CPU).

processor-controller applications — Processor-controller (P-C) can be used for editing, supervisory control, direct control, or data analysis. A control and data path provides for the attachment of the system where more powerful supervision is required. For example, the aspects of an application with the controlling operations exercised by an analog computer. This multiprocessor system capability enables the handling of real-time applications of any size or complexity.

processor, cycle time — *See* cycle time, processor.

processor, data — *See* data processor.

processor-dependent interrupt — *See* interrupt, processor-dependent.

processor-error interrupt — Processor-error interrupt occurs if a word accessed in any part of the system is found to contain incorrect check bits, or if an error occurs in the addressing of a memory location.

processor front-end — A small computer that serves as a line controller for a large processor. The small computer not only can serve as a line scanner and controller, but can handle a number of "supervisory" tasks that would normally be done by the large processor, such as error detection, character echoing (on a full duplex line), user validity checking, etc. Two basic design approaches to the communication front end of a small processor are single bit buffers and line scanning.

processor, graphics — Those computer hardware and software systems that follow and interpret operator commands, provide stored symbol information and integrate all instructions and commands to develop displays of charts, graphics, line drawings, and so on.

processor, image — The image processor provides the input and output of data in graphic form. Some units contain two photographic-film transport units which are similar in operation but which differ in the function that they perform. For convenience, they are designated as transport A and transport B. Transport A exposes film from the high-resolution recording cathode-ray tube, exposes processes, and scans processed film for computer input at the read station using a high-resolution scanning crt and it projects the processed film from the read station to a 20 × 22-inch read-projection screen located at the front of the unit. Transport B exposes film from the record crt, processes, and projects exposed film. The large screen projector permits the operator to study the output image off line from the computer. The image is larger and of higher quality than can be obtained on the graphic console and the image can be studied and compared with drawings or other graphic console images.

processor input-output (PIO) channel — The processor input-output channel is used to communicate with low-speed, character-oriented devices which are asynchronous in nature. Each item of data is transferred to or from an addressed device, via the accumulator, by executing an input-output instruction for each transfer. Input-output instructions, in addition to transferring data, are also used to test the status of a device and to initiate input or output operations. The processor input-output channel enables data transfer between the accumulator and a selected input-output controller and device, as directed by the execution of a series of input-output transfer (IOT) instructions.

processor interface — The transfer of data between the processor and the standard communication subsystem takes place through input data leads, connected to the processor input channel, and output data leads, connected to the processor output channel. In addition to the data leads, there are several control leads that are used to control the flow of data.

processor interface routines — The processor interface routines, provide a simple, standard interface for all processors within the system. Complete facilities are provided for the input of source-language statements and the output of the resulting relocatable binary code.

processor interrupt — As the computer is sequencing through a set of instructions, there are definite times when it is desirable to interrupt the program for such things as handling a machine error, an i/o device, a supervisor call, or a program exception such as an arithmetic overflow. Electronic circuitry instead of complex programming recognizes and handles these interrupts. This results in the most efficient utilization of the processor. Interrupts are automatic procedures that alert the system to conditions arising that may affect the sequence of instructions being executed. To make possible the operation of a system in a nonstop environment, and to increase the efficiency of i/o equipment, the system must have the ability to switch to the appropriate routine when a supervisory call or exceptional condition arises, and then resume the processing that has been interrupted. Records of the complete status of the system are automatically stored as soon as an interrupt occurs, together with an identification of the cause of the interrupt.

processor interrupt chips — Processor chips can be equipped with an interrupt line which allows the enabling or disabling of interrupts. Input to the interrupt recognition logic can be generated by an external event detection module which implements the detection of, and response to, application-defined events or power failure conditions. Enabling and disabling interrupts can be performed under program control. Serial communication between the processor and external equipment is often furnished by an integral universal asynchronous receiver/transmitter. Through this interface, programs can be loaded from an external peripheral device such as a paper-tape loader and MPS systems communicating directly with external data bases.

processor, interrupt dependent — An example of a processor-dependent interrupt condition is the presence bit condition caused by a program being executed on a processor that is executing an operand call. This addresses a descriptor with a presence bit of zero (some computers).

processor interrupt facility — The interrupt facility provides a processor interrupt when an input-output device is ready to send or receive data, or a power failure is detected. If the interrupt facility is enabled when an interrupt occurs, the processor disables the interrupt facility, stores the contents of the program counter in location 0, and executes location 1.

processor, interrupt independent — An example of a processor-independent interrupt condition is an i/o finished condition caused by the i/o hardware when an i/o operation has been completed (some computers).

processor, microprogrammed — A microprogrammed processor is really a computer within a computer. The microprocessor can often emulate the instruction set of earlier computers, control the front panel in the halt mode, operate the automatic bootstrap, and implement the enhanced instruction set. Compatibility at the base instruction set level is far more important than at the microprogram level. Microprograms are typically small compared to applications programs, and experience has shown that it is relatively easy to convert these small programs from one type microcode to another microcode.

processor module — A typical processor module (PM) contains a single chip MOS/LSI microprocessor along with the integrated logic and control circuitry necessary to operate as a parallel 8-bit central processing unit. The microprocessor support logic consists of a clock; an input multiplexer; data, memory, and address bus gating; i/o control logic; interrupt recognition logic; and a universal asynchronous receiver/transmitter. Single-chip microprocessors often contain various general-purpose registers, condition flip-flops, instruction control and decoding logic, and a memory stack.

processor module, development system — The processor module in some systems is a single card containing all elements necessary to function as a standalone computer. A serial asynchronous i/o port is provided for operation of a teletypewriter or crt terminal. The card might also contain 3K or up to 8K bytes of ROM and 1K or more of RAM in which resides the operating system, peripheral drivers, bootstrap loader, and debug software. The peripheral driver routines can usually be accessed by the users.

processor organization — The computer can be divided into three main sections: arithmetic and control, input/output, and memory. The arithmetic and control section carries out the directives of the program. The calculations, routing of information, and control of the other sections occur in this part of the central processor. All information going into and coming out of the central processor is handled by the input/ output section. It also controls the operation of all peripheral equipment. The memory section is the heart of the central processor; it provides temporary storage for data and instructions. Because of its importance, the total cycle time of the memory is the main determining factor in the overall speed of the processor.

processor organization, central — *See* central processor organization.

processor, output test — In a complex system an automated processing of the output so that errors may be more easily tracked down.

processor, peripheral — For some environments, input and output are best processed by two interconnected computers wherein one computer handles the input/output for the other. The control programs of the operating system provide the capability to handle this mode of operation for a configuration of equipment in which a very high-speed, high-storage-capacity central processing unit performs calculations upon data supplied by a smaller computer that schedules, buffers, and controls the flow of input data, intermediate results, and output data to and from the larger unit. Usually in this configuration the larger unit is termed the host and the smaller one is called peripheral, but either one may actually be in control of the other's operations and schedule.

processor, program — *See* program processor.

processor, satellite — A smaller processor used to support a large processor to increase its productivity. The smaller processor is used for card to tape conversion, off-line printing, and communication interface.

processors, auxiliary — Contained within the executive system is a set of auxiliary processors for performing functions complementing those of the source language processors such as FORTRAN. This set of processors includes the collector for linking relocatable subprograms, the procedure-definition processor for inserting and modifying procedure definitions in a library, the COBOL library processor for manipulation of COBOL library elements, and the data-definition processor for introducing data descriptions.

processor status word — The processor status word (PSW) typically contains the current processor status. This information includes the current processor priority, the condition codes describing the arithmetic or logical results of the last instruction, and an indicator for detecting the execution of an instruction to be trapped during program debugging, on some systems. The PS word format permits certain instructions to allow programmed manipulation of code bits and loading or storing (moving).

processor status word (PSW), 16-bit — A 16-bit register that records errors and exception conditions in the processor that must be handled by the operating system. Extensive error checking is evidenced within the processors by noting the bit conditions reported in the PSW. The program check interrupt lists errors detected in software. The soft exception trap interrupt lists exceptions where no error has occurred but where software intervention is required; for example, a stack overflow requires that more storage be allocated to the stack.

processor unit, central (CPU) — The principal unit of the computer that controls the processing routines, performs the arithmetic functions, and maintains a quickly accessible memory. It also often contains the console.

processor verbs — Verbs which specify to the processor the procedures by which a source program is to be translated into an object program. Such verbs do not cause action at object time.

process, predefined — A type of identified process which is defined and delineated in another location in greater detail than the subject one.

process, read/write — To read in one block of data while simultaneously processing the previous block and writing out the results of the preceding processed block.

process, recursive — In data processing, a method of computing values of functions in which each stage of processing contains all subsequent stages, i.e., the first stage is not completed until all other stages have been completed.

process study — The processor-controller rapidly collects the process data that is necessary for the development of a model of the process. The model is developed by using a combination of empirical techniques and observing past methods of running the process. When a more complete and more precise description of the process is required, a model is constructed by using such mathematical techniques as correlation analysis and regression analysis. The process-control program is then tested on the mathematical model prior to its use on the process. Extensive operator guide information is obtained. In addition, the model represents considerable progress toward complete supervisory control.

process time — The time for translating a source program into an object program through the action of a processor program and the computer.

product — The quantity that results from multiplying two quantities.

product area — Some computers have an area in main storage to store results of multiplication operations specifically.

product, intermediate — When multiplying the multiplicand by just one of the digits of the multiplier, the result is a partial product, i.e., a series of first partial product, etc. The partial sums then are simply shifted and added to obtain the final or total product, which is then called *product.*

production control — As applied by computers, a data acquisition system from the floor of a product in line or process for the speed up and simplification of the flow of production information for management.

production, language theory — In formal language theory (BNF), the translation of an input string to an output string.

production routine — That routine which produces the results of the problem or program as it was designed, as contrasted with the routines which are designed for support, housekeeping, or to compile, assemble, translate, etc.

production run — A run that fulfills the program objective. It occurs after the projected program has been successfully checked out.

production time — That time which is used to accomplish designed, desired, or useful work and during which the computer is running properly, satisfactorily—without faults, malfunctions, or important errors, i.e., not idle or using development or incidentals.

productive time — That time which is spent in processing work without the occurrence of faults or errors.

product, logical — *Same as* gate, AND.

product of sums — A boolean expression which has been transformed into pairs of ORed variables which are sequentially ANDed. Such as f (A,B,C) = (A·B) + (A·C).

product overflow — *Same as* overflow.

product, partial — A particular result developed by multiplying the multiplicand by one of the digits of the multiplier; i.e., there are as many partial products in a multiplication operation as there are significant digits in a multiplier, as partial sums are shifted and added to obtain the final product.

program — 1. A plan for the automatic solution of a problem. A complete program includes plans for the transcription of data, coding for the computer, and plans for the absorption of the result into the system. The list of coded instructions is called a routine. 2. A set of instructions or steps that tells the computer exactly how to handle a complete problem—payroll, production scheduling, or other applications. Most programs include alternate steps or routines to take care of variations. Generally, program steps form a complete cycle. Each incoming bundle of facts (unit of information) sets off the whole cycle from start to finish, the succeeding unit sets it off again, and so forth. 3. To plan a computation or process from the asking of a question to the delivery of the results, including the integration of an operation into an existing system. Thus, programming consists of planning and coding, including numerical analysis, specification of printing formats, and any other functions necessary to the integration of a computer into a system. 4. To plan the method of attack for a defined problem. 5. To plan the whole operation from input to output and set the control section to handle it.

program-address counter — A register in which the address of the current instruction is recorded. (Synonymous with instruction counter.)

program allocation and loading — Relocatable binary elements produced by compilation are linked together for execution or for future use by an allocation program that is resident in the system at all times. An extensive selection of subroutines is directly available from the system library, enabling the allocator to incorporate them dynamically as the compiled elements are being constructed into a program. The relocatable element is the common denominator output of processors, allowing applications to be programmed in several different languages, compiled, and properly linked at execution time (some computers).

program, assembler — *See* assembly routine.

program, assembly — *Same as* assembly routine.

program, automatic recovery — A program enabling a system to remain functioning when a piece of equipment has failed. The automatic recovery program often activates duplex circuitry, a standby computer, or switches to a mode of degraded operation.

program, background — This program is of lower priority than the foreground or main program and is at halt or standby while the main program runs.

program, bootleg — A conventional routine or stop-gap program used to begin, capture, and process data in a specifically prescribed manner. Usually to start or initiate the reading of a program by means of its own action.

program bootstrap, input — *See* bootstrap input program.

program breakpoint — A location at which execution of a program can be halted to permit visual check, printing out, or other performance analysis.

program card — A prepunched card that serves to instruct the machine in the steps or operations it is to perform.

program, chain additions — A specific set of instructions which adds new records to individual files.

program check — 1. A system of determining the correct program and machine functioning either by running a sample problem with similar programming and a known answer, or by using mathematical or logic checks such as comparing A times B with B times A. 2. A check system built into the program or computers that do not have automatic checking. This check system is normally concerned with programs run on computers that are not internally self-checking. (Synonymous with routine check, and related to automatic check.)

program checking — *See* checking program.

program check interruption — An interruption caused by unusual conditions encountered in a program, such as incorrect operands. Abbreviated PCI.

program checkout — A standard run-through of a program on a computer to determine if all designs and results of a program are as anticipated.

program, coded — A program that has been expressed in the code or language of a specific machine or programming system.

program compatibility — A distinctive feature of most programming aids and the objective programs that they produce is operational compatibility. This property enables the operating system to integrate all elements.

program compilation — Programs written in the languages of ALGOL, COBOL, FORTRAN IV, or the other assembly languages are compiled at several thousand statements per minute without sacrificing object code efficiency.

program, compiler — *Same as* compiler.

program, computer — *See* computer program.

program, control — 1. A sequence of instructions that prescribes the series of steps to be taken by a system, a computer, or any other device. 2. Descriptive of a system in which a computer is used to direct an operation or process and automatically to hold or to make changes in the operation or process on the basis of a prescribed sequence of events.

program, control command — A program that handles all commands addressed to the system from the user-consoles. These commands would include requests to log in or out, a request to use the edit program, requests to have a program placed on the run queue, requests to load a program, etc.

program counter — A specific CPU register that holds the address value of the memory location where the next CPU directive is to be obtained.

program counter (as a general register) — The program counter (PC) is unique from other general-purpose registers in one important respect on most systems. Whenever the processor retrieves an instruction, it automatically advances the PC (often by 2). By combining this automatic advancement of the PC with, for example, four of the basic addressing modes, one can produce four special PC modes—immediate, absolute, relative, and relative deferred.

program counter/pointer register — A combination that performs program bookkeeping; i.e., the program counter is continually modified to point to the next sequential instruction of the program.

program counter, single chip system — On some systems, the program counter is a 16-bit register that contains the address of the instruction being executed. The contents of this register are automatically incremented by one just before each instruction is fetched from memory to enable sequencial execution of the stored instruction. Under program control, the contents of this register also may be modified or exchanged with the contents of a pointer register to effect subroutine calls and program branches.

program, cross-assembler — Microcomputers generally do not have enough memory or are not equipped with the

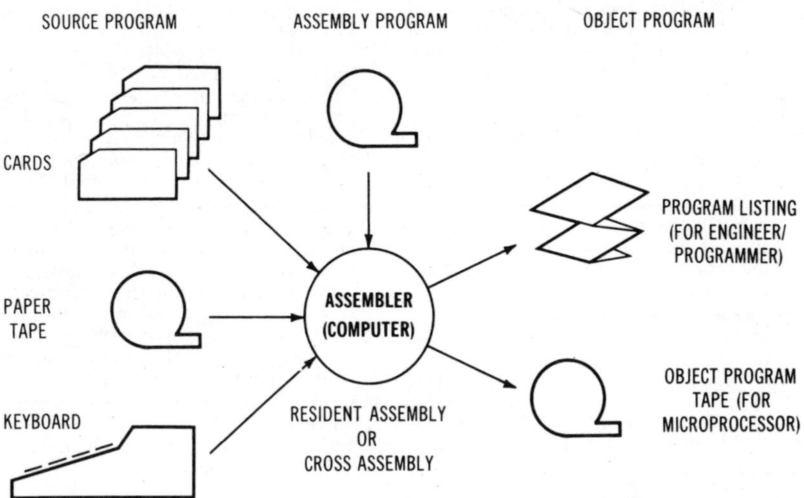

Program development tools.

necessary peripheral devices to support many utility programs. In such a situation, another computer is used to perform the assembly or compilation, and the programs used are called cross-assemblers or cross-compilers. For example, a microcomputer program might be cross-assembled on a time-sharing system. Punched tape output from the time-sharing terminal would then be loaded into the microcomputer for testing.

program debugging — *See* debugging, program.

program design, microprocessor — The program design, the single most important part of the software development, bridges the gap between hardware and software—or firmware when the program is put into ROMs. Involved here are the overall system operation, the hardware design and the kind of programs to be written. The program design should define every step of the system operation from the point of view of the microprocessor. It should establish the necessary "handshaking" between the peripherals and the microprocessor and between the peripherals and external circuitry.

program development system — For program development, some suppliers provide a microprogramming development package, whereby users can make, simulate, and debug programs on a system that has a crt display, keyboard, dual or single floppy disk drives and optional hard copy printer.

program development time — That time used by computers to test or debug programs, or to perform trials of new procedures, processes, or techniques, i.e., part of uptime (effective) but not part of production or incidentals time, which both have specific definitions.

program development tools — Usually included are compilers and cross-assemblers that translate source code into machine language, edit programs that permit changes to be made easily in source code as the design evolves, linking loaders that merge independently assembled object modules for execution, library systems that enable a designer to maintain and retrieve current versions of multiple application programs simultaneously, and simulators that are used to test and debug application programs.

program development worksheet — A paper form used to assist in the organized development of a complex computer program. Columns for recording various types of pertinent information are provided. They are filled in as a programmer works through successive stages in the program development and assembly process.

program, diagnostics — A program used by the supervisory program or the computer operator to check malfunctions and to locate faulty components.

program, diagnostic trace — A particular type of diagnostic program for the performance of checks on other programs or for demonstrating such operations. The output of a trace program may include instructions of the program which is being checked and intermediate results of those instructions arranged in the order in which the instructions are executed.

program documentation — This is a vital part of programming. Documentation is required so that programs can be modified, so that people can be trained, and so that machine operators know how to run programs and diagnose the problems if they occur.

program drum — A revolving cylinder on which the program card is mounted.

program, editor — A program that provides a means for manipulating the text of a named file on a microtape or in the user area of the drum. This program may be used for the creation of the text, or for later use as data or as a program to be translated by the FORTRAN compiler, etc. The commands provided by the editor allow text to be created, deleted, or moved about.

program error — A mistake made in the program code by the programmer, keypuncher, or a machine-language compiler or assembler.

program-error interrupt — Program interrupts occur because of programmer errors such as an invalid operation code, an attempt to violate storage protection, and exceptional results of a calculation. When a program interrupt occurs, control may be passed to an error routine in the current program segment, or the program may be ended with an abnormal end-of-program indication.

program evaluation and review technique (PERT) — Use of PERT requires an extensive analysis of an overall project, in order to list all the individual activities or jobs which must be performed in order to meet the total objective. These activities are then arranged in a network that displays the sequential relationships among them. This analysis must be extremely thorough and detailed if it is to be realistic, and it will require application of all the talents and experience available to the organization. PERT provides a means of reporting an analysis for project administrators. Information required can be developed and areas that impose the greatest time restrictions on the completion of a product can be highlighted. Areas with an excess of time for completion, called slack areas, are also highlighted.

program, executive — One of various programs that control loading and relocation of routines and in some cases make use of instructions which are unknown to the general programmer. Effectively, an executive routine is part of the machine itself (synonymous with monitor routine, supervisory routine, and supervisory program).

program, externally stored — A program which is stored in one of many input devices or media and which must be read from the medium or device by connection and interrogation or interpretation, i.e., programs on tapes, cards, disks, etc., rather than wired or internally stored types.

program, fault-location — A program for identification of information regarding faulty equipment. It is designed and used to identify the location or type of fault and is often part of a diagnostic routine or system.

program fetch — A routine to obtain a requested phase, load it into main storage at the locations assigned by the linkage editor, and transfer control to the phase-entry point.

program file — A flexible, easily updated reference system for the maintenance of the entire software library.

program flowchart — *See* flowchart, program.

program, general — A program expressed in computer code designed to solve a class of problems, or specializing on a specific problem when appropriate parametric values are supplied. (Synonymous with general routine.)

program, generating — A designed program for construction of other programs, i.e., for performing particular types of operations such as sorting programs, output programs, etc. The generating program can select among various broad methods for performing a task and adjust those details of the selected method to provide a program with specific characteristics, which then are matched to the characteristics of the data to be handled by the generated program. It may include an assembly program.

program generator — Generally a large detailed program which permits a computer to write other programs automatically. Generators are usually of two types—(1) the character controlled generator, which operates like a compiler in that it takes entries from a library tape, but unlike a simple compiler in that it examines control characters associated with each entry, and alters instructions found in the library according to the directions contained in the control characters; (2) the pure generator is a program that writes another program. When associated with an assembler a pure generator is usually a section of program which is called into storage by the assembler from a library and then writes one or more entries in another program. Most assemblers are also compilers and generators. In this case, the entire system is usually referred to an an assembly system. (Related to problem-oriented language.)

program generator, report — *See* report program generator.

program halt — *Same as* program stop.

program, heuristic — 1. A routine by which the computer attacks a problem not by a direct algorithmic procedure, but by a trial and error approach frequently involving the act of learning. 2. A set of computer instructions that simulates the behavior of human operators in approaching a similar problem.

program, incomplete — A specific program not complete in itself and usually a specification of a process to be performed on data. It may be used at more than one point in any particular program, or it might be made available for inclusion in other programs, i.e., a subroutine. Often called subprogram, incomplete program, etc.

program-independent modularity — Defined as the property of a system which allows it to accept changes and adjust processing accordingly to yield maximum utilization on all modules without reprogramming. This system is used in multiprocessing. To achieve this objective, the computer system incorporates master control programs to exercise an unprecendented degree of automatic control.

program instruction — Designed sets of characters, together with one or more addresses (or no address), that define an operation and which, as a unit, cause the computer to operate accordingly on the indicated quantities; a machine instruction to specific functions. Types include actual, arithmetic, blank, branch, control, direct, effective, execution, executive, extract, halt, hold, jump, machine, macro, programmed, and pseudo.

program, internally stored — A program which is stored or contained within the computer, such as in the same area in which the data is stored or in some high-speed on-line auxiliary core storage, i.e., immediately accessible to the control and arithmetic or CPU units.

program, interpreter — An essentially closed subroutine (executive) which translates a stored pseudocode program into a machine and performs the desired and specified operation. Such an interpreter program usually consists of sequences of pseudo instructions and operands (program parameters) which are introduced as a closed subroutine and exist by a specific pseudocode instruction.

program, interpretive — A specialized program which relates and handles the execution of a program by translating each instruction of the source language into a sequence of computer instructions and allows these to be executed before translating the next instruction, i.e., the translation of an instruction is performed each time the instruction is to be obeyed. If the interpretative program allows for programs written for one type of a computer to be run on a different type, it is often called a simulator program.

program, interpretive trace — A trace or diagnostic program used for performing a desired check on another program may include instructions as its output, and intermediate results of those instructions can be arranged in the order in which the instructions are executed. When such a trace program is an interpretive type, it is called an interpretive trace program.

program-interrupt signal — *Same as* interrupt, external-signal.

program interrupt (trapped) — Six events can cause the program of the computer to be interrupted: (1) busy, (2) add overflow, (3) divide overflow, (4) operator, (5) external device, and (6) index overflow. An interrupt trap associated with each event may be set under program control to either respond when the event occurs or to ignore it. Many addresses in memory are reserved for external device interrupt. Each interrupt occurs at its own address so it can lead to its own unique subroutine. Upon completion of the subroutine, control can be returned to the original program at the point of interruption (some computers).

program, introspective — A self-monitoring program.

program language — *See* language, program.

program language types — Basically, the major kinds of programming languages are as follows: 1. Assembly, or symbolic machine languages—one-to-one equivalence with computer instructions, but with symbols and mnemonics as an aid to programming. 2. Macroassembly languages, which are the same as assembly or symbolic machine languages, but permit macroinstructions for coding convenience. 3. Procedure-oriented languages for expressing methods in the same way as expressed by algorithmic languages. Procedure-oriented languages may be further divided into: (a) algebraic languages (numerical computation), (b) string-manipulating languages (text manipulation), (c) simulation languages (such as GPSS, DYNAMO), and (d) multipurpose languages (such as PL/I). 4. Problem-oriented languages for expressing problems.

program, learning — The unique program designed to alter itself by making changes based on the experience of the program and results unknown until portions of the program have been run. For example, a program designed to increase efficiency and provide instructions for program modification or a predestined basis, concerning various analysis techniques built into the program itself resulting in corrective action or alternations of program instruction based on various criterion established within the program.

program, librarian — The librarian program portion of the control function provides for maintenance of library programs used as part of the operating system. The library may be stored on a single secondary storage unit or it may be distributed over several different storage units. In either case the librarian program keeps this library up to date by adding, deleting and modifying as required. User-written application programs can be incorporated into the library along with subroutines, the control program itself, compilers, sort/merge, and utility programs.

program library — *Same as* library, program.

program line — A single instruction usually written on a standard coding format stored as a single entity.

program linking — If a program is too large to be stored in memory, the programmer can divide it into "links" by means of a FORTRAN link statement. At run time, routines in the monitor system automatically handle the execution of the segments of the linked program (some computers).

program listing — An operational and maintenance tool that shows both the source and object language and a symbol table cross reference. Changes in programs involve making object-level language changes to compensate for deficiencies in logic or in compilation, or to handle situations not adequately provided for by the source language. The listing should be cross-referenced to the diagrams and the comments in the coding.

program, list processing — A particular type of program called EULER is an extension of ALGOL 60 and has specific list processing capabilities. Several others also exist.

program loading — During the execution of a processing program, and as a result of many different actions of the control programs, additional programs or program segments may be brought into main storage. The loader alters all necessary addresses in the object program to allow loading at an address of main storage assigned by the control program. The loader has the capability to load separately assembled program segments as if they were a single program, to call in segments from the system program library and combine them with other programs, to link one program segment with another through the use of symbolic references, and to enable different program segments to refer to common data areas. The loader can also

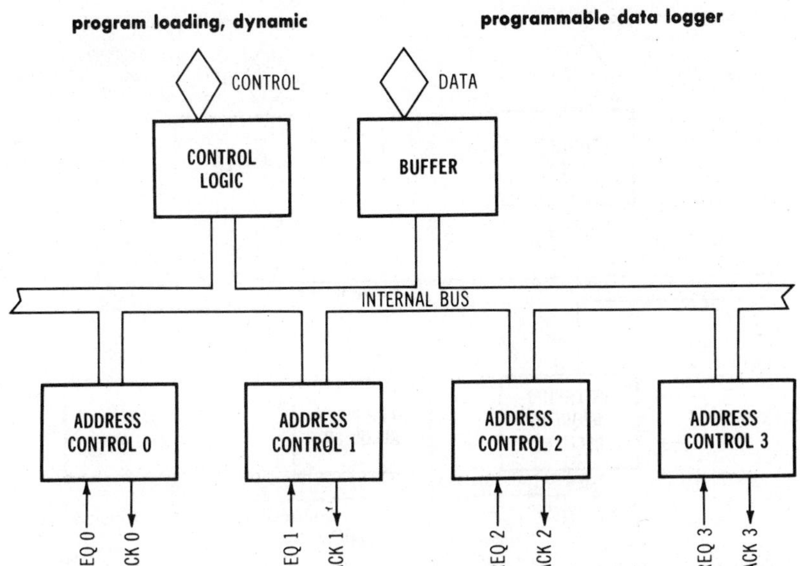

Courtesy National Semiconductor Corp.

Programmable DMA controller.

perform program overlays, and enable patching of object programs.

program loading, dynamic — The loading of a program module or routine into main memory by reference to it by a loaded executing program.

program loading, initial — An initiation process which brings a program or operating system into a computer with the data records which participate in the process. A routine such as the above is established in memory, making it possible to load and execute any other desired program—a first record loading, the second, etc.

program loading routine — The procedure for inserting instructions and the constant values of the program into the computer.

programmable communication interface (USART) — The typical universal synchronous/asynchronous receiver/transmitter (USART) chip is designed for data communications. It is used as a peripheral device and is programmed by the central processing unit to operate with virtually any serial data transmission technique (including the IBM Bi-Sync). One type USART accepts data characters from the CPU in a parallel format and converts them into a continuous serial data stream for transmission. It can simultaneously receive serial data streams and convert them into parallel data characters for the CPU. A signal is transmitted to the CPU when the unit can accept a new character for transmission or when it has received a character for the CPU. Also, the CPU can read the complete status of the unit at any time, including data transmission errors and control signals. Most USARTs have TTL compatible inputs and outputs, operate from a single 5-volt power supply, and have a single TTL clock.

programmable data control unit — Usually referred to as front-end systems, some programmable data control units are FORTRAN-written application software-control communication systems. These systems can preformat messages to the format of the host processor and maintain disk files for message queuing and system backup. They can handle multiple protocols and support up to 256 synchronous, asynchronous or SDLC lines for some systems.

programmable data logger — A typical microcomputer-based field programmable data logger and monitor features: acquisition rates up to 100 points per second, capacity to 1000 points with four multi-

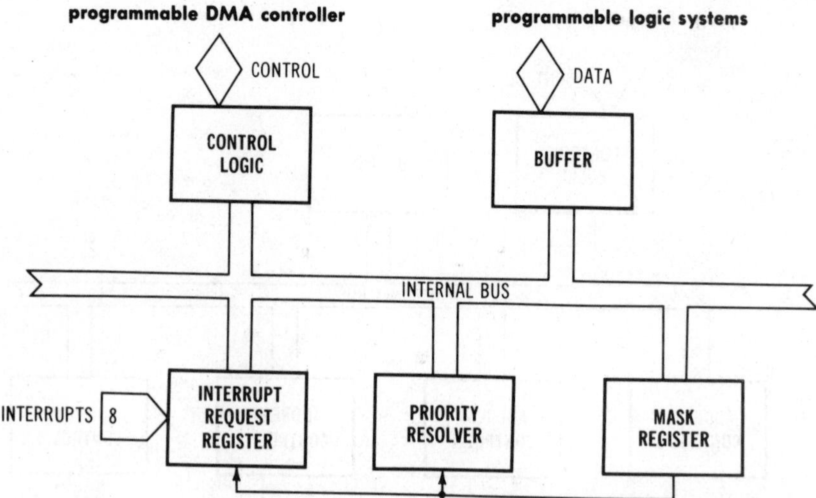

Courtesy National Semiconductor Corp.

Programmable interrupt controller.

plexing assemblers, programmable alarms, and battery-protected programming.

programmable DMA controller — A four-channel, direct-memory-access (DMA) controller facilitates high-speed data transfers between memory and peripheral devices. It generates, on peripheral request, a string of sequential memory addresses for block data movement; and it can handle blocks up to 16K or more bytes in length for one to four peripherals.

programmable function key — A feature that allows the user to key in a program and assign it to a function key and also display the program and edit it using normal terminal functions.

programmable input-output chip (PIO) — An input-output chip, often an 8-bit interface chip that multiplexes one connection to the data bus into two or more 8-bit ports.

programmable interface unit (PIU) LSI device — The PIU is a general-purpose programmable LSI device designed for readily adapting microprocessor or hardwired controllers to the system. Its primary function is to eliminate the extensive hardwired logic that is usually needed for handshaking interfaces between various system components, such as processors and peripherals, processors and channels, channels and peripherals, or processors and processors. An additional feature is the provision for high current bus drivers and compatible line receivers within the LSI device, allowing for direct connection to the bus cables. The functional configuration of the PIU is programmable by the system so that normally a minimal amount of external logic is required.

programmable interrupt controller — Usually an eight-level, vectored, priority interrupt controller, the device receives peripheral interrupts, resolves priority conflicts, and passes an interrupt request to the processor along with a pointer to the interrupt handling routine.

programmable interval timer — A chip equipped with a separate clock and several registers used to count time independently of the microprocessor, for real-time applications. At the end of the time period, it sets a flag or generates an interrupt, or merely stores the time elapsed.

programmable logic array — Abbreviated PLA. A general-purpose logic circuit (an integrated circuit) that contains an array of logic gates that can be connected (programmed) to perform various functions.

programmable logic systems — Programmable logic systems are self-contained and include all of the elements of computer-control, arithmetic and logic functions, memory, i/o and the required software to make them implement the desired functions. Included in this category are microcomputers, programmable calculators, minicomputers, and large scale computers. This spectrum is wide, overlapping and replete with jargon that blurs distinctions between devices, systems, and categories.

programmable peripheral interface — Typically, a circuit that provides three 8-bit ports, which are used independently or together to provide bidirectional communications with peripheral devices.

programmable read only memory — Acronym PROM. A user-programmable ROM.

programmable remote display terminal — A typical programmable display terminal with a microprocessor operates as an intelligent remote terminal station or as a cluster of stations. It can be used for data entry, data processing, control and monitoring, conversational interaction and off-line operation. Featured on some systems are peripheral sharing, buffered peripheral transfers, keyboard control of peripherals, data editing, and extensive screen control. Often, the terminal can be supplied in various screen format changes.

program, macroassembly — A language processor that accepts words, statements and phrases to produce machine instructions. It is more than an assembly program because it has compiler powers. The macroassembler permits segmentation of a large program so that portions may be tested separately. It also provides extensive programming analysis to aid debugging.

program main — *Same as* program, master control.

program maintenance — A specific computer program most often consisting of various diagnostic routines, checking or test routines, and other types designed to complete the removal or reduction of malfunctions, mistakes, and errors and to thus repair or maintain programs and routines.

program, master control — The master control program: (1) Controls all phases of a job set-up; directs program compiling and debugging, allocates memory, assigns input-output activity, schedules and interweaves multiple programs for simultaneous processing. (2) Directs all equipment functions and the flow of all data; provides for comprehensive automatic error detection and correction. (3) Directs the operator with printed instructions. (4) Adjusts system operation to changes in system environment.

Thus, the program-independent modularity of the computer, combined with the automatic schedule and control features of the master control system, provides true multiprocessing ability of the system. A good example of this is shown by the ability of a system to perform four read/write operations simultaneously with the program executions on two processors (some systems).

program master file update — Programs from the old master file are deleted, corrected, or left unchanged and new programs are added from the transaction tape. Updating can include changing of program job assignments. A new program master file is produced.

program, mathematical — Considered by many to be the same as linear programming but not committed to be so defined because of sophisticated uses of research-type operations used as decision tools by modern management science enthusiasts.

programmed check — A check procedure designed by the programmer and implemented specifically as a part of his program. (Contrasted with automatic check.)

programmed data transfer — *See* data transfer, programmed.

programmed halt — *See* halt, programmed.

programmed input/output channel — Program control of information transfer between the central processor and an external device provides the fastest method of operating on data received from peripheral equipment. The programmed input/output channel allows input directly to the accumulator where the data can be acted on immediately, eliminating the need for a memory reference by either the channel or the program. Likewise, output data may be sent directly from the accumulator to an external device.

programmed instructions — Special subroutines may be used as if they were single commands by employing one of the programmed instructions of the system repertoire. This capability allows the programmer to define his own special commands through the use of subroutines which may be changed by the operating routine if desired. The number of instructions required in a typical program is reduced because each subroutine may be called by a single instruction instead of 2 or 3. Programmed instructions also provide, with standard recommended subroutines, complete instruction compatibility.

programmed i/o bus, microcomputer — The programmed i/o bus on some systems is generally regarded as the "workhorse" bus of the system and, because of its simplicity, most interfaces designed by users are placed on this bus.

programmed i/o transfers — Programmed i/o transfers are executed by single- or double-operand instructions. The instruction can be used to input or output 8- or 16-bit data words. By including the device address as the effective source or destination address, the user selects the input or output operation. In many instances, the programmer inputs a byte from the device control/status register (CSR) to determine that the device has input data ready or that it is ready to accept the output of the processor.

programmed logic — *See* logic, programmed.

programmed operators system (SYSPOP) — A function which makes monitor mode service routines available to USER mode programs without loss of system control or use of user memory space.

programmed switch — *See* switch, programmed.

programmer — 1. One who prepares programs for a computer. 2. A person who prepares instruction sequences without necessarily converting them into the detailed codes. 3. A person who prepares problem solving procedures and flowcharts and who may also write and debug routines.

programmer defined macros — *See* macros, programmer-defined.

programmer, design — This individual designs and tests the program logic, and selects the subroutines and other software aids for use in the program.

programmer/duplicator — A typical unit consists of a master control unit and a plug-in PROM personality module. When the unit is connected to a tty or similar terminal, it can be commanded to program, list, duplicate, and verify PROMs.

programmer, EEROM — A unit that provides a means of programming a single electrically erasable ROM (EEROM) or an EEROM module from paper tape or from an integral hex keyboard and display. EEROMs are electrically erasable and, therefore, need not be removed from the module or socket to be erased and reprogrammed. Often included is a RAM buffer which permits editing of any EEROM. The equipment may also be used as a ROM emulator. Optional expansion capability sufficient to interface with modem and cassette devices has become available.

program, micro — 1. A program of analytic instructions which the programmer intends to construct from the basic subcommands of a digital computer. 2. A sequence of pseudocommands which will be translated by hardware into machine subcommands. 3. A means of building various analytic instructions as needed from the subcommand structure of a computer. 4. A plan for obtaining maximum utilization of the abilities of a digital computer by efficient use of the subcommands of the machine.

programming — 1. The process of creating a program. 2. The art of reducing the plan for the solution of a problem to machine-sensible instructions.

programming accessories — Some microcomputer single-board systems offer a wide variety of accessories that facilitate programming, troubleshooting, and fabrication. A PROM burner, for example, lets users burn debugged programs into PROM assemblies. An extender board gives convenient access to printed-circuit assemblies for design and maintenance. A typical 9-slot backplane/card frame and a power-supply assembly simplify board packaging—and other devices and aids are also generally available.

programming, applications — Applications programs range from sorting, payroll processing, and billing, to linear programming, matrix manipulation, and simulation. Whenever applications programs can be sufficiently generalized, the computing system provides and maintains them. Among the standard applications programs available are (1) linear programming, (2) APT III, (3) PERT/COST, and (4) mathematical subroutines.

programming, audit — A program designed to enable use of the computer as an auditing tool.

programming, automatic — A computer process which helps to prepare various programs. Such capability includes various translators as compilers, generators, assemblers, and coders. Other types of automatic programming capabilities might be integration of subroutines into master programs or interpretation of instructions, e.g., much research is in process to make computers fully automatic program generators or developers by assembling or locating programs by simple statements of problems.

programming by prompting — Because users often lack familiarity with any kind of programming, current instruments simplify this task through prompting techniques. Typically, users can turn these units on and have them guide them through the proper sequence of setup steps via questions or directions appearing on a display. An instrument of this type prompts its operator in English-language sentences displayed on its alphanumeric readout. Some units also provide step-by-step guidance but use a built-in crt display. Other manufacturers invest a considerable effort in creating an easy-to-read front panel that permits unambiguous programming.

programming capabilities, single chip systems — On some low-cost systems, programming capabilities include multiple addressing modes—program counter relative, pointer relative, immediate data, and auto-index.

programming compatibility — Many systems are modular by a "building block" principle or technique. They can be augmented and increased in power as needed. Programs are generally upward compatible; that is, programs written for a less powerful system of the same class or series can be run, in many cases, without modification on a more powerful system.

programming competition, multiprogramming — *See* multiprogramming, program competition.

programming, conversational — A technique used in instructing the computer to perform its operations, whereby common vocabulary can be utilized by the user to describe his procedures most accurately. If a statement cannot be understood by the computer, it asks the user for a clarified instruction. This conversational procedure continues until the user has selected the series of statements in the proper sequence which will solve his problem. Conversational programming saves the user the inconvenience of having to study other programming languages extensively before he can solve his problem.

programming, convex — An operations research term for the development of nonlinear programming procedures in which the function to be optimized and the constraints are convex or concave functions of the independent variables, i.e., not related to programming in a computer sense.

programming, dynamic — The essence of dynamic programming is that an optimum decision must be made at every stage of a multistage problem. When considering only a single stage, there may appear to be a number of different decisions of equal merit. Only when the effect of each decision at every stage on the overall goal is determined can the final choice be made. This integrating of the cumulative effect of a path of decisions through each stage of the network is the real essence of DP (dynamic programming).

programming, dynamic (cost problem) — A method for optimizing a set of decisions that must be made sequentially. Characteristically, each decision must be made in the light of the information embodied in a small number of observables called state variables. The incurred cost for each period is a mathematical function of the current state and decision variables, while future states are functions of these variables. The aim of the decision policy is to minimize the total incurred cost or, equivalently, the average cost per period. The mathematical treatment of such problems involves the theory of functional equations, and usually requires a digital computer for implementation.

programming, file-oriented — The i/o coding is simplified with the general file and record control program. Programming is file-oriented rather than device-oriented. Information is requested in a device-independent fashion.

programming, heuristic — Most programming is algorithmic, that is, one sets out the various conditions in advance and the computer follows a preset path through the program depending on the input data received. Under a heuristic programming procedure, the computer searches through a number of possible solutions at each stage of the program, it evaluates a good solution for this stage, and then proceeds to the next stage. Essentially, heuristic programming is similar to the problem solving techniques by trial and error methods that we use in everyday life.

programming, hybrid — Routines in the hybrid programming library are designed to help the engineer decide which parts of the problem should be solved in a digital domain. They also deal with timing, function generations, integration, and the general simulation problems provide a diagnosis of the hardware operation, and check whether the analogue device is scaled or wired correctly.

programming, integer — A class of optimization problems in which the values of all the variables are restricted to be integers. Normally, the optimization problem without this integer restriction is a linear program; additional adjectives indicate variations—for example, integer quadratic programming.

programming, interpretive — The writing of programs in a pseudomachine language that is precisely converted by the computer into actual machine-language instructions before being performed by the computer.

programming language — A specific language used to prepare computer programs.

programming language, automatic (APL) — A device, technique, or language which permits the computer to aid in doing part of the coding and programming.

programming, linear — A technique of mathematics and operations research for solving certain kinds of problems involving many variables where a best value or set of best values is to be found. This technique is not to be confused with computer programming, although problems using the technique may be programmed on a computer. Linear programming is most likely to be feasible when the quantity to be optimized, sometimes called the objective function, can be stated as a mathematical expression in terms of the various activities within the system. When this expression is simply proportional to the measure of the activities, and all the restrictions are also linear, it is a linear program.

programming manager — This individual is responsible for planning, scheduling, and supervising program development and maintenance work.

programming, mathematical — Techniques of finding an optimum value of a function of many variables when these variables are subject to restrictions in the form of equations or inequalities. The term is usually restricted to problems so complex that they require a digital computer for their solution. Special types of programming are linear programming, quadratic programming, and nonlinear programming.

programming, micro — The programmer technique of using a certain special set of instructions for an automatic computer that consists only of basic elemental operations, and combining them into higher-level instructions. He may then program using only the higher level instructions; e.g., if a computer has only basic instructions for adding, subtracting, and multiplying, the instruction for dividing would be defined by microprogramming.

programming, minimum-access — Programming in such a way that minimum waiting time is required to obtain information out of storage. (Synonymous with minimum-latency programming, and contrasted with random-access programming.)

programming, minimum latency — *Same as* programming, minimum-access.

programming module — Specific name for a set of programming instructions which is treated as a unit by an assembler, compiler, loader, or translator.

programming, multiple — The programming of a computer by allowing two or more arithmetical or logical operations to be executed simultaneously. (Contrasted with serial programming.)

programming, nonlinear — An inclusive term covering all types of constrained optimization problems except those where the objective function and the constraints are all linear. Special types of nonlinear programming for which some theory has been developed are convex programming, concave programming, and quadratic programming.

programming, optimum — Programming in order to maximize efficiency with respect to some criteria, e.g., least-storage usage, least time share of peripheral equipment, or least use of time between operations.

programming, parallel — The feature of programming which provides for two or more results when concurrent operations are to be performed simultaneously. Contrast with serial programming.

programming, parametric — A method for investigating the effect on an optimal linear-programming solution of a sequence of proportionate changes in the elements of a single row or column of the matrix. Most commonly, the method is applied to either the objective function row or the right hand column.

programming, piece work — The programming technique of using an outside service organization to prepare programs for which payment is arranged by accomplishment, other than on a time-cost basis. Software companies are usually consulted for the above.

programming, quadratic — A program of an objective quadratic function stated in maxims that are subject to linear constraints. This is one of the few convex programming problems, aside from linear programming, which have solution algorithms that terminate in a finite number of steps.

programming, random-access — Programming without regard to the time required for access to the storage positions called for in the program.

programming, sequential — Programming of a special type in which only one logic or arithmetic operation is performed at a time, i.e., all programming is sequential, one step after another, unless a specific modifier labels it otherwise, such as time sharing, interleaving, etc.

programming, serial — The programming of a computer by which only one arithmetical or logical operation can be executed at one time, e.g., a sequential operation. (Contrasted with multiple programming.)

programming, stochastic — A generalization of linear programming in which any of the unit costs, the coefficients in the constraint equations, and the right hand sides are random variables subject to known distributions. The aim of such programming is to choose levels for the variables which will minimize the expected (rather than the actual) cost.

programming, symbolic — The use of arbitrary symbols to represent addresses in order to facilitate programming.

programming system — An assemblage of programs, programming languages, routines and subroutines for use in specific computing systems, i.e., such are the bases for operating systems of data processing and computing.

programming system, machine-oriented — A system that uses a language that is oriented to the internal language of a specific computer. Systems that are considered to be machine-oriented are assembly systems and macrosystems.

program mode (remote control system) — 1. When a program is active at a given terminal, that terminal is in the program mode. In this mode, the user enters program statements that make up the substance of his program, and he operates on the program (i.e., modifies, tests, executes, and debugs it) by using operating statements. While the terminal is in the program mode, the user can also enter single statements that are executed immediately, but are not retained in storage. 2. When a program is active at a given terminal, that terminal is in the program mode.

program, modification — The ability of a program to modify itself or to set a switch so that a set of events occurring at one time can affect the action of program at a later time. *See also* executive routine and system, monitor-operating.

program, monitor — A specific program developed to indicate the progress and other characteristics of work in various computer systems.

program, object — The program that is the output of an automatic-coding system. Often the object program is a machine-language program ready for execution, but it may well be in an intermediate language. (Synonymous with target program, and contrasted with source program.)

program, object-language — *See* object routine.

program, output — A program which organizes the output procedures of computers, i.e., which starts the output equipment, presents data to them at suitable intervals of time, specifies formats, etc.

program, overlays — Programs or runs too large for memory can be divided into logical segments or overlays. (One program overlays another or several segments may be in memory at the same time.) Overlays are also used when various operations occur infrequently, such as deduction for union dues, etc. The overlays are called in only when the functions they perform are required. An overlay subroutine is provided to call in these overlays. This subroutine functions in a manner similar to the system supervisor.

program package — A group or collection of logically related operational program segments, i.e., all those having to do with the processing of a certain type of inquiry.

program parameter — 1. A parameter incorporated into a subroutine during computation. A program parameter frequently comprises a word stored relative to either the subroutine or the entry point and dealt with by the subroutine during each reference. It may be altered by the routine and/or may vary from one point of entry to another. 2. The arbitrarily selected or given outer limits of the data being processed; often constraining the results of programming itself.

program, partial — A specific program not complete in itself and usually a specification of a process to be performed on data. It may be used at more than one point in any particular program, or it might be made available for inclusion in other programs, i.e., a subroutine, and that which is often called subprogram, incomplete program, etc.

program patching plug — A relatively small auxiliary plugboard patched with a specific variation of a portion of a program and designed to be plugged into a relatively larger plugboard patched with the main program.

program post-edit — A test of the application or operational program that is edited, formatted, and sorted into a test result tape.

program, precompiler — A unique program which is designed to detect errors and provide source program correction before the computation of the object, deck, or program.

program preparation aids — These convert programs from easy-to-use source languages into machine language.

program preparation (object) — Conversion of programs from one of several easy-to-use source languages, or from certain competitive system languages, to a machine code.

program processor — A programming aid which reads symbolic instructions and then compares and converts them into a suitable computer language.

program read-in — The procedure and means of developing, by either hardware or software techniques, the programs that do not normally reside in main memory and that must be read in from auxiliary storage when required for processing. These techniques are required in any system that cannot retain all computer instructions in main memory at one time.

program, recycling — An organized arrangement for recycling programs through a computer when alterations have been made in one program that may change or have an effect on other programs.

program register — *See* register, program.

program, relocatable — A special routine whose instructions are written in a special manner so that it can be located and executed in many areas of the memory. Some modification to the instructions originally coded relative to a fixed starting place in the memory may be involved before execution. Relocatable programs allow for the highly flexible real-time use of the main memory.

program relocation — The execution of a program in a location that is different from the location for which the program was originally assembled.

program relocation, dynamic — The moving of a partially executed program to a different location in main memory without detrimentally affecting the ability to complete normal processing.

program runs — A run is the same as a program except that a program refers to the writing or coding of the job, whereas the run refers to the actual running of the program. Consequently, programs and runs are synonymous except to denote the time and action being performed.

programs, applications — Problem-solving programs are given maximum operating efficiency when functioning under an operating system. Standard functions, such as i/o control, are furnished the user so that he need only program the data-handling portion of his job. In addition, operating systems provide a standardized operating procedure for all application programs.

program scheduler — Called at regular intervals to decide which program in memory is to be run. A running program is temporarily terminated each time its allotted time has run out, or when it requires input/output operations with a device that is busy. A program may be terminated temporarily by user intervention to the scheduler, or it may suspend its own operation. Temporary termination does not remove the program from memory. A program may be dumped on backing storage and permanently discontinued by calling the scheduler and allocator.

programs, compaction — A series of techniques used for the reduction of space, bandwidth, cost, transmission, generating time, and storage of data. These techniques are designed to perform elimination of repetition and removal of irrelevancies.

programs, conversion — Conversion programs enable users of several competitive systems to take advantage of the improved throughput and cost-performance characteristics of these computers without incurring the prohibitive reprogramming costs.

program segment — Various computer instructions set in groups of an artificially fixed size to fit into standard-sized areas of main storage in order to facilitate memory allocation and program read-in.

program, segmented — A program written in separate segments or parts. Only one, or some, of the segments may fit into memory at any one time, and the main portion of the program, remaining in memory, will call for other segments from backing storage when needed, each new segment being utilized to overlay the preceding segments.

program segmenting — Programs that do not fit into memory may be segmented by use of the source-language linking statements. This allows sections of the program to be loaded and executed independently. Common storage is used by each link for passing data.

program segment size — Programs are usually divided into segments, and in most systems the infrequently used segments which may well be the greater part of the program are kept in file rather than core. The question of variable or fixed segment size is determined by the complexity of the program, the response or read-in time and the frequency of use.

program selection — To change from one job to another, the operator simply changes the program selector switch. There are no control bars, wired panels or control tapes to change. Switching from one job to another is a matter of seconds not minutes.

program, self-modification — The ability of a program to justify itself or to set a switch so that a set of events occurring at one time can affect the action of the program at a later time.

program, self-triggered — The initial operation is performed by means of a manually controlled jump to the entry point in older computers, but bootstrap operations cause entry automatically, i.e., the program is said to be self-triggered.

program-sensitive error — An error arising from the unforeseen behavior of some circuits when a comparatively unusual combination of program steps occurs during a run.

program-sensitive fault — A fault that appears in response to some particular sequence of program steps.

program-sensitive malfunction — A malfunction that occurs only during some unusual combination of program steps.

program, service — A particular program which is designed to indicate a progress of work, i.e., one which provides a service to another program, an input program, a monitor program, an output program.

programs, generalized data-manipulation — Generalized data-manipulation programs perform common data-processing chores such as sorting, input/output operations, and report generation.

programs, general-purpose operating — Plans or instructions for controlling input/output operations, remote data transmission, and multiple users which can be used and reused to control these operations. Since these control programs are generally applicable to all users, they are usually prepared by computer manufacturers and offered as part of the free service. They are called by various names such as input/output control system, operating system, or executive system.

program simulation, supervisory — When the supervisory program is not available, this refers to the use of a replacement program that initiates the supervisory program.

program, simulator — A program that causes one computer to emulate (imitate) the logical operation of another computer. The purpose is to measure and evaluate and to exercise program logic independent of hardware environment. It is most often used for debugging logic prior to committing it to ROM.

programs, manual — Programmable calculators, many of which are computers in their own right, make use of manual keystroke programming (a series of keystrokes which, when executed in sequence, will perform a calculation), which with memory, allows execution of sequences resulting in complex program entry and execution.

programs, manufacturer — Utility routines, assemblers, application package programs, and a large array of other programs, subroutines and programming aids developed and proved in use for customers, are available for direct use.

program, snapshot — *See* snapshot program.

programs, operating — Operating programs direct the loading, segmentation, library search, space and time sharing of memory for a group of programs running both sequentially and concurrently.

program, sort/merge — *See* sort/merge program.

program, source — A computer program written in a language designed for ease of expression of a class of problems or procedures by humans, e.g., symbolic or algebraic. A generator, assembler, translator or compiler routine is used to perform the mechanics of translating the source program into an object program in machine language. (Contrasted with object program.)

programs, packaged — These are various programs or routines which have been written by various individuals or organizations that are available from computer manufacturers or software companies.

program, specific — A program which can only be used to solve a particular problem, i.e., one which is thoroughly unique to that problem and not reusable with any other.

program specification — The precise and ordered definitions of logic and scope of processing functions that are performed by particular programs or program segments.

programs, post-edit — A test of the application or operational program that is edited, formulated, and sorted into a test result tape.

programs pre-edit — A checking of the application or operational program before the test run. A pre-edit run can remove such things as disobedience to established supervisory, core, or program segmentation rules, etc.

programs, processing — Complementing the control programs and functioning under them are those programs necessary to handle users' specific data processing needs. These programs, known collectively as processing programs, include application programs both manufacturer- and user-written, compilers, report program generator, sort/merge, and utility programs. Although they rely upon the control programs for such functions as job scheduling, loading, and i/o control, processing programs function independently of one another, each performing a specific job or segment.

programs, pseudo applications — An operational program that is written to test the supervisory program.

programs, standard procedures — Suggested programming methods set by the manufacturer.

programs, support — Those programs which support or aid the supervisory programs and the application programs and include diagnostics, testing, data generators, etc.

programs, systems — These are the programs designed to implement system functions that may be requested from the user console. This is in contrast to system subroutines that may be called by system programs or other programs. System programs are normally provided by manufacturers, but they may be developed by the programmer. The programs contain a termination mode to return the communication link to the system program.

programs, system support — Those processing programs that contribute directly to the use and control of the system and the production of results: the job control program, the linkage editor, and the utility programs.

program, standard — Such a program meets certain specific criteria such as one written in a standard FORTRAN, COBOL, or ALGOL language and which brings forth an approved solution to a problem, such as a square root problem, or a standardized payroll problem which is very commonly used on thousands of machines.

program, star — A handwritten program independently designed by a programmer and checked so that no mistakes or bugs are contained, i.e., the star program should run correctly the first time, excepting machine malfunctions.

program statements — The user's program is made up of program statements. When entered from a terminal, these statements are always retained in storage as part of the active program. If the user has a statement in his program that refers to an executable program statement within the program, he should assign a statement number to the statement referred to.

program status double-word — *See* double word, program status.

program status information, microcomputer — The program status is a group of words containing the flags, control bits, and program counter. Upon the occurence of an interrupt or trap, CPU program status information is saved and a new program status is loaded. In the nonsegmented type of microcomputer, program status consists of two words: the flag and control word (FCW), and the value of the program counter (PC).

program step — 1. A phase of one instruction or command in a sequence of instructions; thus, a single operation. 2. An increment, usually one instruction, of a program.

program stop — A stop instruction built into the program that will automatically stop the machine under certain conditions, or upon reaching the end of the processing, or completing the solution of a problem.

program storage — A portion of the internal storage reserved for the storage of programs, routines, and subroutines. In many systems protection devices are used to prevent inadvertent alternation of the contents of the program storage. (Contrasted with working storage.)

program, storage print — A program that produces a printout of storage and registers to aid the user in locating the reason(s) for a program malfunction.

program, stored — A series of instructions in storage to direct the step-by-step operation of the machine.

program, subject — *Same as* program, source.

program, supervisory — *Same as* executive routine.

program switching — On a single transaction the control program initiates several switches among the various programs; therefore, the processor must be designed to accomplish very rapid program switching.

program system testing — Test and checkout of complete programs as opposed to parameter or assembly testing.

program tape — *See* tape, program.

program tape or drum — A tape or drum used to store a complete routine for future input. In the event that the length of the routine exceeds the available internal storage capacity, it will be read in and operated on by the computer, one segment at a time.

program, tape-to-card — Transfers binary or EBCDIC data from cards to magnetic tape.

program, tape-to-printer — Transfers data from magnetic tape to printer.

program, target — The program that is the output of an automatic coding system. Often the target program is a machine-language program ready for execution, but it may well be in an intermediate language. (Synonymous with object routine, and contrasted with source program.)

program test — A system of checking before running any problem, in which a sample problem of the same type with a known answer is run.

program tester — A program tester is available that enables a program or part of a program to be loaded and dynamically and selectively tested in accordance with simple and concise specifications expressed in terms of symbols and definitions used in the original source program. A variety of testing and monitoring facilities are provided by the program tester including file and storage display facilities designed to simplify the analysis of programming errors.

program testing — This is completed to discover whether the program is successful in meeting the defined systems requirements.

program testing time — The machine time expended for program testing, debugging, and volume and compatibility testing.

program, test supervisor — A supervisory program that is used only for testing.

program test tape — That specific tape which contains both program instructions and preapproved test data or coding to be used for analysis diagnostics, or checkout runs.

program timing matrix — *See* matrix, program timing.

program, trace — A particular type of diagnostic program for the performance of checks on other programs for demonstrating such operations. The output of a trace program may include instructions of the program which is being checked and intermediate results of those instructions arranged in the order in which the instructions are executed.

program, trace-interpretive — A trace or diagnostic program used for performing a desired check on another program may include instructions as its output, and intermediate results of those instructions can be arranged in the order in which the instructions are executed. When such a trace program is an interpretive type, it is called an interpretive trace program.

program translating — A particular program (often called a translater) which translates from one language into another, i.e., from one programming language into another programming language.

program translation, interpretive — *See* program, interpretive.

program, translator — This program uses the source language program as input and produces from it a programming machine language. Like any other machine program, this may either be run immediately or stored for later use.

program, utility — A standard routine used to assist in the operation of the computer, e.g., a conversion routine, a sorting routine, a printout routine, or a tracing routine.

program verbs — Verbs which cause the processor to generate machine instructions that will be executed by the object program.

PROM — Acronym for Programmable Read-Only Memory. Generally, any type of memory which is not recorded during its fabrication but which requires a physical operation to program it. Some PROMs can be erased and reprogrammed through special physical processes.

PROM blank check — A PROM programmer operation used to determine that a PROM about to be programmed contains no preprogrammed data; i.e., it is clear of data, or blank.

PROM continuity test — A PROM programmer operation that checks each PROM pin for adequate contact at the socket. Also detects faulty PROM internal diode clamps.

PROM, electrically erasable — One PROM form is the electrically alterable, metal-nitride MOS array. It can be electrically programmed in much the same way as uv (ultraviolet) PROMs, but users can erase either the entire array or just one word without using light sources.

PROM illegal bit check — A PROM programmer operation in which the PROM about to be programmed is checked for illegal bits, or preprogrammed bits in the PROM that do not exist in the input truth table.

PROM intelligent programming — A MOS PROM programming technique in which the number of program pulses (n) applied to a word is a function of the number of pulses (x) required to program the word, and a multiplier (A) according to the equation:

$$n = x + A(x+1) - 1$$

PROM Nichrome links — Programmable read-only memory (PROM) programming is accomplished by burning out fusible links at each memory cell in the mask structure. This is done by causing a large current to pass through the Nichrome link. The programming is permanent and is a useful way to store programs.

PROM programmer — A PROM programmer peripheral is a device used to program programmable read-only memories.

PROM uv eraser — A high-intensity ultraviolet-light source emitting short-wave radiation which is used to erase programmed data in MOS PROM devices.

PROM verify — A PROM programmer operation in which two data fields are checked, one against the other, for identical data content. Typically, data fields may be contained on paper tape, in RAM buffers, in PROMs, or in other storage devices.

proof listing — A specific report, prepared by a processor, that indicates the coding as it was originally devised and written plus the comments that have been written, and the machine language that has been produced. In accounting, it is an itemized list of the transactions and their detail together with the control totals, sequence checks, or other data for proofing and audit trial.

proof total — One of a number of check totals which can be correlated in some manner for consistency or reconciliation in a range, set, or distinct calculation.

proof, zero — *See* zero proof.

propagate — One of the two signals supplied by an adder for carry prediction by a carry look-ahead circuit.

propagated error — An error occurring in one operation that spreads through and influences later operations and results.

propagation delay — The time required for a pulse or a level transition to propagate through a device.

propagation time — This is the time required for an electrical impulse to travel from one point to the other.

property — A characteristic quality.

property detector — *See* detector, property.

property sort — *See* sort, property.

proportional band — The range of values of a condition being regulated that will cause the controller to operate over its full range. Usually expressed by engineers in terms of percentage of instrument full scale range.

proportional control — A method of control in which the intensity of action varies linearly as the condition being regulated deviates from the condition prescribed.

proportional spacing — Some letters, such as M and W, are wide; others, such as i, l, and j, are narrow. Proportional spacing allows for these differences when advancing the print head, which gives a document the appearance of having been typeset and makes it more legible and compact.

proprietary program — When the development of a program is controlled by an owner through the legal right of possession and title, it is a proprietary program. Commonly, the title remains with the owner, and its use is allowed with the stipulation that no disclosure of the program can be made to any other party without prior agreement between the owner and user.

protected field — A display field in which the user cannot enter, modify, or erase data from the keyboard.

protected-fields terminal — When fill-in forms are displayed on a video screen, some of the material—like "Name," "Address," and other instructive items —should not normally be altered by the operator. Some terminals provide for these items (locations on the screen are referred to as "fields") to be protected from inadvertent changes by operators.

protected files — *See* files, protected.

protected formatting — A method that permits the computer to write protected data on the screen. The operator can fill in the blank (unprotected) areas but cannot change the protected data, format, or programming.

protected location — A storage location reserved for special purposes in which data cannot be stored without undergoing a screening procedure to establish suitability for storage therein.

protection character — *See* character, protection.

protection, file — A device or method that prevents accidental erasure of operative data on magnetic-tape reels.

protection, memory — *Same as* storage protection.

protection, nonstop operation — Ensures against program hang-ups due to infinite indirect address loops or execute instruction loops.

protection, read/jump — Read/jump protection allows the executive to stop the program at the point of error, terminate it, and provide diagnostic information to the programmer, thereby minimizing wasted time and smoothing the checkout process. A particular advantage of read/jump protection is that programs of a classified nature can be confidently run together; they are fully protected from audit (inadvertent or otherwise) by other programs.

protection, storage — *See* storage protection.

protocol — A set of conventions between communicating processes on the format and contents of messages to be exchanged. The simplest protocols define only the hardware configuration. More complex protocols define timings, data formats, error detection and correction techniques, and software structures. The most powerful protocols describe each level of the transfer process as a layer, separate from the rest, so that certain layers, such as the interconnecting hardware, can be changed without affecting the whole.

protocol, data base — Under the data base access protocol imposed by most information storage and retrieval applications, only host commands and specified data fields will pass between the host and the controller according to standard procedures.

protocol, data communications — A protocol is a set of rules that must be obeyed to ensure an orderly information exchange between two or more parties. In data communications, a protocol defines the rules for the electrical, physical, and functional characteristics of the communications link. Such a protocol contains the control procedures required to facilitate data transfer across the link interfaces and to and from the user's applications programs.

protocol emulator — A software package that allows a digital node to communicate with a variety of foreign (nondigital) vendor equipment by emulating the communication protocols of the foreign host.

protocol functions — In most communications systems, protocols are required for bit synchronization, so that the receiver knows when a bit starts and ends so that it can be sampled; for character synchronization, so that the receiver can determine which bits belong to a character; and for message synchronization, so that the receiver can recognize the special character sequences which delineate messages. Typical protocols include the blocking of transmission into messages employing start of text and end of text (STX/ETX) or other similar markers, and a positive/negative acknowledgment procedure (ACK/NAK). Additional error detection and correction is provided by longitudinal redundance checks (LRC).

protocol, network — A basic procedure or set of rules that governs and controls the flow of messages between computers. Also, a set of conventions between communicating processes on the format and content of messages to be exchanged.

proving time — The time which is used for the testing of the machine or system to ensure that no faults exist or malfunctions are present, by using special diagnostic routines of circuit testing or to discern status or conditions of components. Such time could be included in fault time after the repair of the fault and in scheduled maintenance time.

PRT (production run tape) — A tape containing checked-out and scheduled production running on various computers.

pseudo application programs — An operational program that is written to test supervisory programs.

pseudocode — 1. An arbitrary code, independent of the hardware of a computer, that must be translated into computer code. 2. Computer instructions written in mnemonic or symbolic language by the programmer. These instructions do not necessarily represent operations built into the computer. They must be translated into machine language and have absolute addresses assigned them before they can become a finished and assembled program that the computer can use to process data.

pseudo file address — The use of a false address by the application program to obtain a record from file. The pseudo address is converted by the supervisory program into an actual machine address. The actual machine address may change as different file units are used in duplexing and fall-backs.

pseudoinstruction — 1. A symbolic representation in a compiler or interpreter. 2. A group of characters having the same general form as a computer instruction, but never executed by the computer as an actual instruction. 3. An instruction written in an assembly language designating a predetermined and limited group of computer instructions for performing a particular task. 4. A user-defined instruction, such as a macroinstruction, that does not belong to the basic instruction set of the microprocessor.

pseudolanguage — An artificial language which is uniquely constructed to perform a distinct task; i.e., a special set of rules is devised with particular meanings assigned to chosen expressions. Some types of programs are quite easily written in pseudolanguage, especially various problem or procedure-oriented types, and most of these have some English-type statements in either semantics, syntax, logic, or mnemonics.

pseudo–offline working — *Same as* working, pseudo–offline.

psuedo-op — *Same as* pseudoinstruction.

pseudo-operation — An operation that is not part of the computer's operation repertoire as realized by hardware; hence, an extension of the set of machine operations.

pseudopaging — A procedure or way of viewing memory locations whereby programmers refer to memory addresses as being organized into blocks of words referred to as "pages" for reference purposes only. The machine being used may not be a true paged machine in that the program counter is able to advance routinely from the end of one block of addresses to the start of the next group —an operation that cannot be performed by a true paged machine.

pseudorandom — This relates to the desire for satisfaction of one or more criteria for statistical randomness, which is briefly defined as equal probability of occurrence of given digits or events occurring in an equal number of times in large numbers of digits or events. The randomness is produced by definite calculation processes. Pseudorandomness is not full random status, but often partial or close, and designed and known to be such.

pseudorandom number sequence — A sequence of numbers, determined by some defined arithmetic process, that is satisfactorily random for a given purpose, such as by satisfying one or more of the standard statistical testing for randomness. Such a sequence may approximate any one of several distributions, e.g., uniform distribution or a normal (Gaussian) distribution.

PSW — Abbreviation for Processor Status Word. A special-purpose CPU register that contains the status of the most recent instruction execution result, trap bit, and interrupt priority (some systems).

PTS (Program Test System) — A specific system that automatically checks out programs, producing diagnostic information where necessary to aid in production run organization.

pull (from stack) — The process of fetching the element or data item which is currently on the top of the stack.

pulse — 1. A pulse developed at a particular instant in time relative to a specific reference pulse, which may be a major or minor cycle pulse, and one which is often used to mark, clock, or control a particular binary digit position in a computer word. 2. One of a group of pulses which are used to define particular digit periods within a word period.

pulse amplitude — Maximum instantaneous value of a pulse.

pulse, clock — A pulse positioned next to recorded characters on tapes, drums, disks, etc., to control the timing of read circuits, count characters, or develop and perform related type functions which a clock pulse would perform.

pulse code — 1. A code in which sets of pulses have been assigned particular meanings. 2. The binary representations of characters.

pulse, commutator — A pulse developed at a particular instant in time relative to a specific reference pulse, which may be a major or minor cycle pulse, and one which is often used to mark, clock, or control a particular binary digit position in a computer word.

pulse decay time — That specific time which is required for the trailing edge of a pulse to decline and which is measured as the time required to drop from 90% of full amplitude to 10%. (Illustration, page 430.)

pulse, digit — A particular drive pulse corresponding to one digit position in some or all the words in a storage unit. In some techniques it may always be an inhibit pulse or always an enable pulse which are more acceptable names for the general term.

pulse-double recording — A specific method for magnetic recording of bits in which each storage cell comprises two regions magnetized in opposite senses with unmagnetized regions on each side.

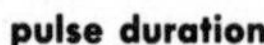

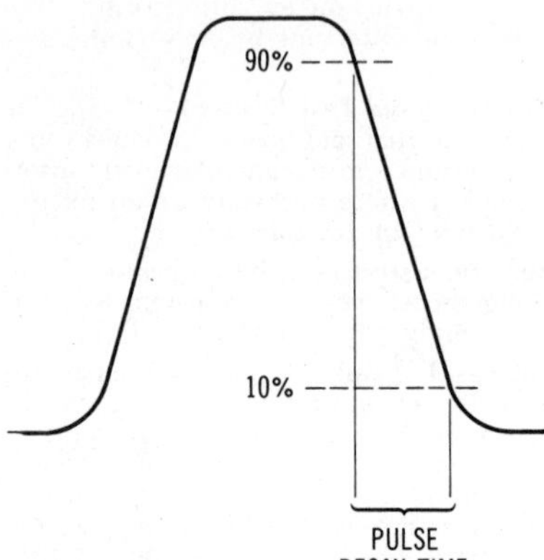

Pulse decay time.

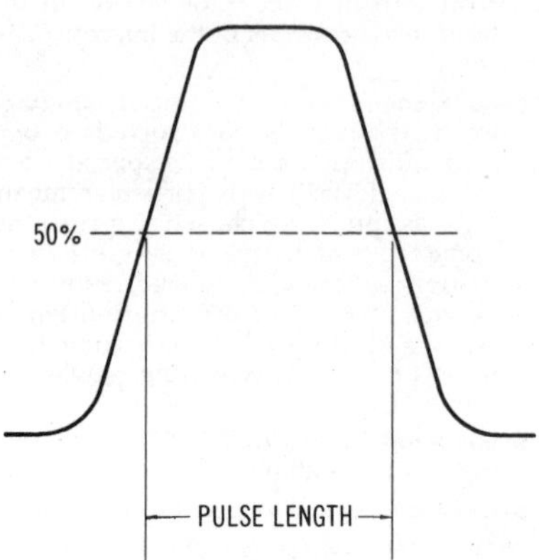

Pulse length.

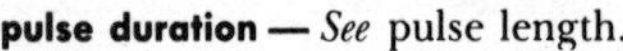

pulse duration — *See* pulse length.

pulse (electric) — A momentary and significant rise or fall in voltage level. A pulse provides the primary means for the transmission of data into a computer. The presence or absence of a pulse during a particular time period is interpreted as binary information.

pulse, emitter — Relating to a punched card machine, one of the group of pulses that is used to define a particular row within the columns of a card.

pulse, enable — A digit pulse which aids the write pulse, so when they are together they are strong enough to switch the magnetic cell.

pulse, full drive — *See* pulse, full read.

pulse, full read — In coincident-current selection, the resultant of the partial drive pulses which, when applied together, cause the selection of, for example, full read pulse, or full write pulse.

pulse, gate — A pulse that enables a gate circuit to pass a signal; usually, the gate pulse is of longer duration than the signal, to make sure that a coincidence in time occurs.

pulse, inhibit — A specific pulse which prevents an action which might otherwise occur if such a pulse were not present, i.e., close a gate, prevent reading, etc.

pulse length — Nominal duration of a standard pulse which is the time interval between the half amplitude points of the rise and decay points of the curve. For pulses of other shapes, the points on the curve must be stated. Time interval between the points on the leading and trailing edges at which the instantaneous value bears a specified relation to the pulse amplitude. Note: Frequently the specified relation is taken as 50%.

pulse, marking (teletypewriter) — A marking pulse or "mark" is the signal pulse which, in dc neutral operation, corresponds to a "circuit closed" or "current on" condition.

pulse, P — *See* pulse.

pulse, partial drive — *Same as* pulse, partial write.

pulse, partial select input — *Same as* pulse, partial write.

pulse, partial write — In coincident-current magnetic-core storage devices, one of two or more pulses that are required to effect the selection or the switching of a core, when entering or storing data.

pulse, position — *See* pulse.

pulse, post-write disturb — In a coincident-current magnetic-core storage device, a pulse applied after a write pulse to put all cores in the disturbed state, as contrasted with pulse, preread disturb.

pulse, preread disturb — In a coincident-current magnetic core storage device, a pulse applied before a read pulse to ensure that the core about to be read is in the disturbed state, as contrasted with pulse, post-write disturb.

pulse rate — The time interval of periodic pulses which are integrated with the control of the computer or the entire system.

pulse, read — In coincident-current core storage devices, a specific pulse or the sum of several pulses (simultaneous) which are capable of switching a core, or producing a change in its residual flux density so as to produce an output signal on the read winding provided for this purpose.

pulse regeneration — A pulse regeneration is the process of restoring a series of pulses to the original timing, form, and relative magnitude.

pulse repetition rate — The number of electric pulses per unit of time experienced by a point in a computer; usually the maximum, normal or standard pulse rate.

pulse, reset — A pulse designed and used to position a binary storage cell, i.e., a flip-flop, or a magnetic core, back to its original reset state.

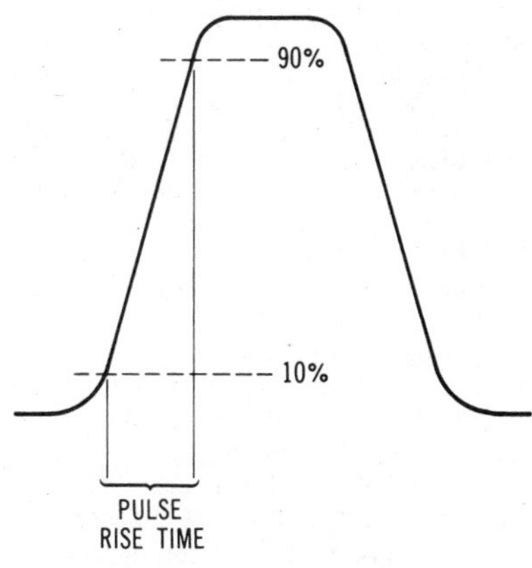

Pulse rise time.

pulse rise time — That specific time which is required for the leading edge of a pulse to rise, i.e., for the amplitude to reach a specified value, such time being measured as the time required to rise from 10% to 90% of full amplitude.

pulse, set — A pulse designed and used to position a binary storage address, i.e., a flip-flop or magnetic core, into a specified state or original condition or state.

pulse shaping — *Same as* pulse regeneration.

pulse, shift — A pulse which causes the characters in a register to shift.

pulse, spacing (teletypewriter) — A spacing pulse or "space" is the signal pulse which, in dc neutral operation, corresponds to a "circuit open" or "no current" condition.

pulse, sprocket — 1. A pulse generated by a magnetized spot which accompanies every character recorded on magnetic tape. This pulse is used during read operations to regulate the timing of the read circuits and also to provide a count on the number of characters read from tape. 2. A pulse generated by the sprocket or driving hole in paper tape which serves as the timing pulse for reading or punching the paper tape.

pulse standardization — *Same as* pulse regeneration.

pulses, transmission — Electrical impulses which can be transmitted and received through communication lines. Transmission pulses may be either voice or data communications in nature. In the latter case, computer interface equipment converts incoming pulses into the proper binary code and delivers the data to storage.

pulse string — A particular group of pulses which happen in time sequence at a point in a circuit, i.e., an amplitude vs time plot of the pulses appears as though the pulse group occurs in space sequence or along a line, thus the terms pulse string or pulse train.

pulse, teletypewrite marking — A unique signal pulse which corresponds to a circuit-closed or a current-on state, in dc or neutral operation.

pulse, timing — *See* pulse, clock.

pulse width — *See* pulse length.

pulse, write — That drive pulse (or the sum of several simultaneous drive pulses) which under suitable conditions can write into a magnetic cell or set a cell, i.e., usually to a one condition.

punch card — A heavy stiff paper of constant size and shape, suitable for punching in a pattern that has meaning, and for being handled mechanically. The punched holes are sensed electrically by wire brushes, mechanically by metal fingers, or photoelectrically by photocells. (Related to 80 column card and 90-column card.)

punched tape — Tape, usually paper, upon which data may be stored in the form of punched holes. Hole locations are arranged in columns across the width of the tape. There are usually 5 to 8 positions (channels) per column, with data represented by a binary-coded alphanumerical decimal system. All holes in a column are sensed simultaneously in a manner similar to that for punched cards. Mylar and other plastic tapes are used instead of paper tapes for more permanent purposes and when such tapes are frequently used and reused.

punched tape machine — Any tape punch that automatically converts coded electrical signals into perforations in tape.

punch-tape code — A code used to represent data on punch tape.

punctuation bits — The use of a variable-length data format requires that there be a method of indicating the actual length of a unit of information. This requirement is fulfilled by two punctuation bits associated with each memory location. These bits can constitute a word mark, used to define the length of a field; an item mark, used to define the length of an item; or a record mark, used to define the length of a record. In addition to defining the lengths of data fields, word marks are also used to define the lengths of instructions in memory.

purification, data — The reduction of the number of errors as much as possible prior to using data in an automatic data-processing system.

push — The process of placing information on the top of a stack and then preparing to be able to place the next piece of information on the stack. This process generally involves changing the value of a stack pointer register so that it points to the next address where data may be stored.

push-button switching — A switching system in a reperforator that permits the selection of the outgoing channel by an operator.

push-down — A last-in, first-out method of queuing in which the last item attached to the queue is the first to be withdrawn.

push-down list — A list of items where the last item entered is the first item of the list, and the relative position of the other items is pushed back one.

push-down nesting — As data is transferred into storage, each word in turn enters the top register and is then "pushed down" the column from register to register to make room for the subsequent words as they are assigned. When a word is transferred out of the storage, again only from the top register, other data in the storage moves back up the column from register to register to fill the space left empty. This is accomplished either through programs or the equipment itself.

push-down queue — A last-in, first-out (LIFO) method of queuing in which the last item attached to the queue is the first to be withdrawn.

push-down stack — A type of dedicated consecutive temporary storage using the registers of the computer. It is sometimes part of the system memory and is structured so that the data items retrieved are the most recent items stored in the stack, e.g., a LIFO (last-in, first-out) arrangement.

push-down storage — *See* storage, push-down.

push (from stack) — The process of adding onto a stack an element or data item which forms the new top of the stack.

push-to-type — A teletypewriter operation in one direction at a time by using a switch depressed during transmission.

push-up list — A list of items where the first item is entered at the end of the list, and the other items maintain their same relative positions in the list.

push-up storage — *See* storage, push-up.

putaway — Refers to a memory location in which the processor will store specific information.

Q

Q — A register used as an accumulator extension, necessary for efficient multiply-divide programming.

Q address — A source location in internal storage in some types of equipment from which data is transferred.

QAM — Abbreviation for Quadrature Amplitude Modulation. A high-speed modem modulation technique employing both differential phase modulation and amplitude modulation.

QTAM — Abbreviation for Queued Telecommunications Access Method. An access method that provides the capabilities of BTAM plus the capability of queued messages on direct-access storage devices. It may be employed for data collection, message switching, and many other teleprocessing uses.

Q test — A comparison test of two or more units of quantitative data for their equality or nonequality.

quad — An assembly of four separately insulated conductors, twisted together in such a manner as to provide two pairs.

quad bus transceiver — A component that consists of four separate receiver-transmitter combinations, designed for use with a bidirectional bus system such as a data bus.

quadratic programming — Maximization, subject to linear constraints, of an objective function that is a quadratic function. This is one of the few convex programming problems, aside from linear programming, that have solution algorithms that terminate in a finite number of steps.

quadrature — Quadrature expresses the phase relationship between two periodic quantities of the same period when the phase difference between them is one fourth of a period.

quadripuntal — Pertaining to four punches, specifically having four random punches on a punch card. This term is used in determinative documentation.

quadruplex system — A system of Morse telegraphy arranged for the simultaneous independent transmission of two messages in each direction over a single circuit.

qualification — In COBOL, the technique of making a name unique by adding IN or OF and another name, according to defined rules and procedures.

qualifier — A name used to qualify another name with an action similar to an adjective in English grammar, i.e., to give additional information about a name or to distinguish the named thing from other things having the same name.

quality control — That process whereby systematic and regular review of the timeliness, accuracy, completeness, etc., of data entry is accomplished.

quantification — An act of quantifying or giving numerical value to the measurement of an item, i.e., to attempt to give discrete values to human characteristics using statistical terms, numerical indicators, or weights.

quantity — 1. A constant, variable, function name, or expression. 2. A positive or negative real number in the mathematical sense. The term quantity is preferred to the term number in referring to numerical data; the term number is used in the sense of natural number and reserved for "the number of digits," the "number of operations," etc.

quantity, double-precision — A quantity having twice as many digits as are normally in a specific computer.

quantity, scalar — *See* scalar, quantity.

quantity, variable — A quantity that may assume a succession of values.

quantity, vector — A quantity which has both magnitude and direction, such as field intensity, velocity, etc., as contrasted with scalar quantities.

quantization — The subdivision of the range of values of a variable into a finite number of nonoverlapping subranges.

quantization distortion — In communication, quantization is a process in which the range of values of a wave is divided into a finite number of smaller subranges, each of which is represented by an assigned (or quantized) value within modifying various forms of modulation; for example, quantized pulse-amplitude modulation.

quantize — To subdivide the range of values of a variable into a finite number of nonoverlapping subranges or intervals, each of which is represented by an assigned value within the subrange; e.g., to represent a person's age as a number of whole years.

quantizer — A device that converts an analog measurement into digital form.

quantum — One of the ranges or discrete values resulting from quantization.

quantum, timesharing — A unit of processing time in a time-sharing system that may be allocated for operating a program during its turn in the computer. More quanta may be allocated to higher-priority programs than to lower-priority programs.

quasi-instruction — *See* pseudoinstruction.

queries, time sharing — Many organizations have problems requiring retrieval from data or document libraries. Remote terminals are being used to browse through the data file searching for material fulfilling the requirements.

query — A specific request for data, instructions, characteristics of states of switches, position in a queue, etc., while the equipment is computing or processing.

query languages — A class of English-like languages that allows nonprogrammers to inquire about the contents of a data base and receive fast responses. Although the ability to specify the contents of the output is usually powerful and flexible, formatting and arithmetic abilities are usually limited. More sophisticated reports are better developed with a report writer.

query station — A specific unit of equipment which introduces requests or queries for data, states of processing, information, etc., while the equipment is computing or processing or communicating.

question, encoded — A question set up and encoded in a form appropriate for operating, programming, or conditioning a searching device.

queue — A line or group of items waiting for the attention of the processor—usually in core and chained together by address words.

queue, automatic — An arrangement in which a specific series of interconnected registers are designed to implement either a LIFO (last in, first out) queue or a FIFO (first in, first out) queue without program manipulation. For a FIFO queue, new entries to the queue are placed in the last position and automatically jump forward to the last unoccupied position, while removal of the front entry results in all entries automatically moving forward one position. Also called push-down storage and push-up storage.

queued access method — Any access method that automatically synchronizes the transfer of data between the program using the access method and input/output devices, thereby eliminating delays for input/output operations. (The primary macroinstructions used are GET and PUT.)

queue discipline — The methods selected to determine order of service in a queue, i.e., LIFO (last in, first out), FIFO (first in, first out), etc.

queued sequential access method — A version of the basic sequential access method (BSAM). When this method is used, a queue is formed of input data blocks that are awaiting processing or output data blocks that have been processed and are awaiting transfer to auxiliary storage or to an output device. Abbreviated QSAM.

queued telecommunications access method — A method used to transfer data between main storage and remote terminals. Application programs use GET and PUT macroinstructions to request the transfer of data, which is performed by a message control program. The message control program synchronizes the transfer, thus eliminating delays for input/output operations. Abbreviated QTAM.

queue, input work — *See* work queue, input.

queue, multipriority — *See* multipriority.

queue, new input — A group or a queue of new messages waiting for processing. The main scheduling routine will scan them along with other queues and order them into processing in order.

queue, output — Messages that are in line or queued which have been produced by the system and are waiting to be scheduled for transmission.

queue, output work — *See* work queue, output.

queue, push-down — A first-out method of queuing in which the last item attached to the queue is the first to be withdrawn.

queues, direct-access — A group of queues, or, more specifically, message-segment chains of queues, residing on a direct-access storage device. The group can include destination and process queues.

queue, sequential — The first-in first-out method of queuing items waiting for the processor.

queue, task — Queues (lines in waiting) that contain control information for all tasks in a system at a given time.

queue, work-in-process — Items that have had some processing and are queued by and for the computer to complete the needed processing.

queuing — A study of the patterns involved and the time required for discrete units to move through channels, e.g., the elapsed time for auto traffic at a toll booth or employees in a cafeteria line.

queuing analysis — The study of the nature and time concerning the discrete units necessary to move through channels, e.g., the time and length of queue at service centers of grocery check-out stands, harbors, airports, etc. Queuing analysis is employed to determine lengths of lines and order, time, and discipline of service.

queuing list — A list frequently used for scheduling actions in real time on a time-priority basis. Appends are made following the ending item. The beginning item is always the removed item.

queuing, message — Controls the order in which messages are stored, processed, and transmitted.

queuing theory — A form of probability theory useful in studying delays or line-ups at servicing points.

queuing-theory problems — When a flow of goods (or customers) is bottlenecked at a particular servicing point, losses accumulate in the form of lost business, idle equipment, and unused labor. Minimizing such costs involved in waiting lines, or queues, is the object of queuing theory, an OR (operations research) technique for the most efficient handling of a line at a particular point of service.

queuing time — Time spent waiting to send or receive a message because of contention on the line.

quibinary code — A binary-coded decimal code for representing decimal numbers in which each decimal digit is represented by seven binary digits that are coefficients of 8, 6, 4, 2, 0, 1, 0, respectively.

quick-access storage — *Same as* storage, high-speed.

quiescent — At rest. Specifically, the condition of a circuit when no input signal is being applied or of a system waiting to be operated.

quiescent carrier telephony — That form of carrier telephony in which the carrier is suppressed whenever there are no modulating signals to be transmitted.

quiescing — The stopping of a multiprogrammed system by means of the rejection of new jobs.

QUIP — A 64-lead integrated-circuit package developed jointly by Intel and the 3M Co. It has two rows of pins instead of one along each longitudinal edge, so that the 64 pins are contained in 1⅝ inches of length. This size enhances strength and rigidity, and the consequent shortening of the internal metalized conductors results in low pin-to-pin capacitance, lead resistance, and inductance. A QUIP can be dismantled with a small screwdriver, and a special set of probe contacts along the top of the unit allows access for measurements while the QUIP is operating in its socket.

quoted string — In assembler programming, a character string enclosed by apostrophes that is used in a macroinstruction operand to represent a value that can include blanks. The enclosed apostrophies are part of the value represented.

qwerty — Refers to the typical typewriter keyboard which starts with these six letters, left-to-right, in the top row below the numerals.

R

radial transfer — A procedure or process for transferring data between peripheral equipment and the internal memory of the machine.

radix — *See* number base.

radix complement — *Same as* complement.

radix complement, diminished — *Same as* complement, radix-minus-one.

radix-minus-1 complement — A complement on N-1 is obtained by subtracting each digit of the given quantity from N-1 (where N = radix); e.g., the ones complement of binary 11010 is 00101; the nines complement of decimal 456 is 543.

radix mixed — Relates to a numeration system that uses more than one radix, such as the bioprimary system.

radix notation — *See* notation base.

radix number — *See* number base.

radix point — The dot that marks the separation between the integral and fractional parts of a number. In the decimal number system, the decimal point; in the binary number system, the binary point.

radix scale — *Same as* notation base.

rail logic, double — *See* logic, double rail.

Rajchman selection switch — *Same as* storage, core rope.

RAM — Acronym for Random Access Memory. This type of memory is random because it provides access to any storage location point in the memory immediately by means of vertical and horizontal coordinates. Information may be "written" in or "read" out in the same very fast procedure.

RAM dump — To copy the contents of all or a part of a storage, usually from an internal storage, such as a RAM, into an external storage, such as a printout. The process of copying, and also the data resulting. The dump does not eliminate the data stored. A snapshot dump is the copying of the contents stored in memory at one address into a display.

RAM loader — A program to read a program from an input device, and usually into some type of random access memory (RAM).

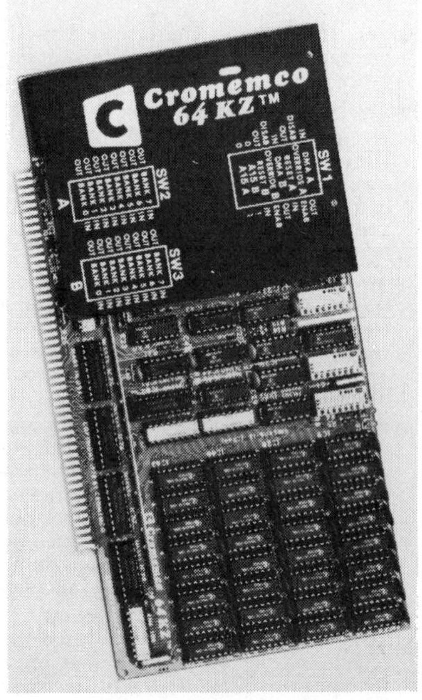

Courtesy Cromemco, Inc.

RAM.

RAM mail box — A mail box is often referred to as a set of locations in a common RAM storage area, an area reserved for data addressed to specific peripheral devices as well as other microprocessors in the immediate environment. Such an arrangement enables the coordinator CPU and the supplementary microprocessors to transfer data among themselves in an orderly fashion with minimal hardware.

RAM memory expansion — Expansion of RAM in 8K byte increments up to totals of 64K bytes and more to permit tailoring memory sizes to exact application requirements.

RAM print-on-alarm — A data system condition in which continuous scanning of data channels takes place, but output of data is initiated only when an alarm condition as interpreted by the CPU in a RAM is encountered.

RAM refresh cycle (dynamic) — Memory is extended without a decrease in performance by taking advantage of a characteristic of dynamic MOS RAMs. These memories require a small amount of inactive time between operations (or clocks). This time is sufficient to allow address translation and its associated delay to take place without system performance loss when the memory is equipped with a dynamic mapping system. Refreshing of the entire physical address space is accomplished by the refresh timer, control circuitry, and memory modules.

RAM refresh operation — All dynamic MOS random access memories require a periodic refresh operation to ensure that stored data is retained. A refresh operation consists of a specified number of write cycles (some memories require a read cycle) on the least significant address bits of the memory within a given period of time. The number of write or read cycles will vary depending on the memory circuit.

RAM text editor — The RAM resident character-oriented text editor contains search, substitute, insert and delete commands which facilitate rapid program alteration.

random access — 1. Pertaining to the process of obtaining data from, or placing data into, storage when there is no sequential relation governing the access time to successive storage locations. 2. A quality of memory device that allows data to be written in, or read from, the memory through direct locating rather than locating through reference to other data in the memory. No search is required; the machine can proceed directly to the desired memory location.

random-access input/output — This is an i/o control capability that permits efficient random processing of records stored on a direct-access device. Random-access i/o efficiency is achieved by the system in two ways: (1) Seeks are issued in an order that minimizes the average seek time, rather than in the order in which they were requested. (2) Seeks are overlapped with other processing. Because records must sometimes be processed sequentially (for example, when a report is being written), the ability to call for records sequentially is also available.

random-access i/o routines — Direct, serial, and random processing of drum and disk files are provided by these routines. Macroinstructions are available to direct the performance of the input-/output functions.

random-access memory — *See* memory, random-access.

random-access memory (RAM) (Bank) — Provides storage of on-line account records containing all information—account balance, available balance, unposted dividends and previous no-book transactions, account holds, etc.—required for complete processing of transactions and inquiries, as well as for updating of passbooks.

random access memory system, bipolar — A unit designed to meet the needs of control memory, disk controllers, scratch pad and signal processing applications. The unit provides fast access and cycle times in a TTL compatible memory system. Utilizing bipolar technology and solid-state integrated circuitry, the memory provides high reliability and performance at low costs. Some memory systems feature a basic size of 1024 words by 10 bits per memory card. They can be expanded to any word or bit length by the use of additional memory cards. Each system includes all address and data registers.

random access, movable — Describes a feature of a storage device like disk packs, tape strips, or card strips which can be physically removed and replaced by another, thereby allowing for a theoretically unlimited storage capacity.

random-access processing (central file) — Application records stored in the on-line central file may be updated quickly because transactions may be processed as soon as they arrive at the bank's processing center, in any sequence or mix of transaction types.

random-access programming — Programming without regard to the time required for access to the storage positions called for in the program. (Contrasted with minimum-access programming.)

random-access software — A comprehensive array of programming and operating aids that includes a loader/monitor, a program for updating program files, a special sort, input/output routines, and utility routines.

random-access sorts — Separate programs are furnished by manufacturers to sort data stored on random-access disks and drums. These programs strip off the item keys of data stored on a random-access device, sort the keys, and then store on the disk or drum a table containing the keys and the addresses of the corresponding file items. Items may be brought in from the disk or drum in the order of the sorted keys by using macroinstructions.

random-access storage — 1. A storage medium in which the time required to obtain information is statistically independent of the location of the information most recently obtained. 2. A type of storage in which access can be made directly to any storage regardless of its position, either absolute or relative to the previously referenced information.

random-access system — A particular method of filing data in a manner which approximates equal time to the processing of the data, i.e., usually that type of core storage or auxiliary storage which is ultrafast.

random distribution — A distribution of events where the probability of any event occurring at any given time is the same for it occurring at any other time.

randomize — The procedure for making numbers, data, or events random, i.e., without bias as to the selection of each number or event by assigning pseudo-random codes or characters to particular locations in storage.

randomizing, file addressing — *See* file addressing, randomizing.

randomizing scheme — Plans for the distribution of file records among several file storage modules designed so that the accesses to these records will be distributed equally and the waiting times for file information will be set evenly.

random noise — Noise due to the aggregate of a large number of elementary disturbances with random occurrence in time.

random number — 1. A set of digits constructed of such a sequence that each successive digit is equally likely to be any of N digits to the base n of the number. 2. A number formed by a set of digits selected from a random table or sequence of digits.

random-number generator — A special machine routine or hardware unit designed to produce a random number or a series of random numbers according to specified limitations.

random-number sequence — An unpredictable array of numbers produced by chance, and satisfying one or more of the tests for randomness.

random number, uniform — A set of digits constructed in such a sequence that each successive digit is equally likely to be any of n digits to the base of the number.

random processing — 1. Information and data records are processed in the particular order specified by the control system and not in the order in which they are stored. 2. Transfer of an item between core memory and a drum or disk location whose address is determined by mathematical transformation of the item's key.

random sequence — A sequence that is not arranged by ascending or descending keys, as in alphanumeric or numeric sequences, but is instead arranged in an organized fashion in bulk storage, by locations determined by calculations performed on keys to develop addresses. The calculations are repeated in order to acquire the address and locate the item desired.

random sequential access — *See* access, random sequential.

random topology — The arrangement of computers in a distributed computing network without regard for a predefined network configuration or hierarchy.

random variable — 1. Also called variate. The result of a random experiment. 2. A discrete or continuous variable which may assume any one of a number of values, each having the same probability of occurrence.

range — 1. All the values that a function or word may have. 2. The difference between the highest and lowest of these values.

range, balanced error — An error range in which the highest and lowest error values are opposite in sign and equal in magnitude.

range check — On some systems, this seeks the presence of one or more pairs of table entries that data must fall within. Each pair of table entries consists of a low- and a high-data value, in table lookup procedures.

range, dynamic — The dynamic range of a transmission system is the difference in decibels between the noise level of the system and its overload level.

range, error — 1. The range of all possible values of the error of a particular quantity. 2. The difference between the highest and the lowest of these values. 3. The binary program with its associated subroutines will not fit into the available main memory. The names of any missing subroutines are listed following this message.

range limit or limit priority — The upper boundary to the priority list for dispatching or designing a priority rating to various tasks or subtasks, i.e., active, inactive, top priority, lowest priority, or batch processing.

range, out of — A value which does not lie within a specific range of a linear program is out of range, or simply a term used to refer to overcapacity.

range, proportional — The band, range, or set of values of a specific condition which is being controlled and which will cause the controller to operate over its full linear range. A proportional range is most often expressed by engineers or design teams in terms of percentage of full scale of the associated instrument.

rank — To arrange in an ascending or descending series according to importance.

rapid access — Rapid access is often synonymous with random access and is contrasted with sequential access, i.e., dependency upon access of preceding data.

rapid-access memory — In computers having memories with different access times, the section that has much faster access than the remainder of the memory.

rapid-access storage — *Same as* storage, high speed.

RAS — Abbreviation for Row Address Strobe. A signal that is used in dynamic RAMs to reduce the pin count by multiplexing the address.

raster scan — Raster scan means that the beam of a cathode ray tube is swept completely across the phosphor surface of the tube 50 or 60 times (depending on the power line frequency) in a second. Information, generated via the memory, turns the beam on and off, intensifying dots on the phosphor at the proper time to produce characters and graphics on the video screen. This is basically the same method used by consumer television sets.

rate, action — A type of control action in which the rate of correction is made proportional to how fast the condition is going awry. This is also called derivative action.

rate, bit — The rate at which binary digits, or pulses representing them, pass a given point on a communications line or channel. (Clarified by baud and channel capacity.)

rate, clock — The time rate at which pulses are emitted from the clock. The clock rate determines the rate at which logical or arithmetic gating is performed with a synchronous computer.

rate, data signaling — *See* data signaling rate.

rate, effective data transfer — *See* data-transfer rate, average.

rate, error — The total amount of information in error, due to the transmission media, divided by the total amount of information received.

rate, instantaneous data-transfer — *See* data-transfer rate.

rate, modulation — Reciprocal of the unit interval measured in seconds. (This rate is expressed in bauds.)

rate of error, keying — Ratio of numbers of alphabetic signals incorrectly transmitted to the number of alphabetic signals in the message.

rate pulse — The time interval of periodic pulses which are integrated with the control of the computer or the entire system.

rate, pulse-repetition — The number of electric pulses per unit of time experienced by a point in a computer; usually the maximum, normal, or standard pulse rate.

rate, read — *See* read, rate.

rate, reset — The number of corrections per unit of time made by the control system.

rate, residual-error — The ratio of the number of bits, unit elements, characters and blocks incorrectly received but undetected or uncorrected by the error-control equipment, to the total number of bits, unit elements, characters, blocks that are sent.

rate, sampling — The time developed during the sampling of physical quantities for measurement, i.e., to obtain data to feed into a computing system so that the results of the computations can be made available to complete a specific task or purpose. Some examples are on-line processing for controlling weather data, time sharing of equipment, future positions for missile guidance, etc.

rate, scan — A frequency at which data is compared or read to various predetermined sense of criteria, for the purpose of seeking certain data.

rate, signaling — The rate at which signals are transmitted.

rate, storage data transfer — *See* data transfer rate, average.

rate, transmission — *Same as* data transfer rate.

rate, undetected-error — *Same as* rate, residual-error.

ratio, availability — The ratio of total service time to the total of fault time, regular maintenance time, supplementary time, and serviceable time.

ratio, break-make — The ratio of the break period to the make period.

ratio control — That specific limitation in the relation between two quantities as expressed in direct or percentage comparison.

ratio, file activity — *See* file activity ratio.

ratio, operating — The ratio of the number of hours of correct machine operation to the total hours of scheduled operation; e.g., on a 168-hour week scheduled operation, if 12 hours of preventive maintenance are required and 4.8 hours of unscheduled down time occurs, then the operating ratio is (168-16.8)/168, which is equivalent to a 90% operating ratio. (Synonymous with computer efficiency.)

ratio, processing — The end result in calculating the time equipment is being used properly, including lost time because of human error and the total available time.

ratio, read-around — The number of times a specific spot, digit, or location in electrostatic storage may be consulted before the spillover of electrons will cause a loss of data stored in the surrounding spots.

ratio, read time-working — *See* time scale.

ratio, recall — *See* recall ratio.

ratio, reflectance — *See* reflectance ratio.

ratio, relevance — *See* relevance ratio.

ratio, signal-to-noise — The ratio of the amount of signals conveying information to the amount of signals not conveying information.

ratio, variable time — *Same as* time scale, extended.

raw data — Data that has not been processed; it may or may not be in machine-sensible form.

RDY — The control signal for slow memory to indicate if data are valid (some systems).

reactive mode — A condition of communication between one or more remote terminals and a computer, in which each entry (usually batch) causes certain actions to be performed by the computer, but not necessarily including an immediate reply. Contrasts with conversation mode.

read — 1. The process of introducing data into a component or part of an automatic data-processing machine. 2. To copy, usually from one form of storage to another, particularly from external or secondary storage to internal storage. 3. To sense the meaning by arrangements of hardware. 4. To accept or copy information or data from input devices or a memory register, i.e., to read out; to position or deposit information into a storage or output medium, or a register, i.e., to read in. 5. To transcribe information from an input device to internal or auxiliary storage.

readable, machine — *See* data, machine readable.

read after write verify — A function for determining that information currently being written is correct as compared to the information source.

read amplifier — A set of circuitry which increases the level of current received from the read head or various other sensing devices.

read-around number — The number of times a specific spot, digit, or location in electrostatic storage may be consulted before spillover of electrons will cause a loss of information stored in surrounding spots.

read-back check — A specific check for accuracy of transmission in which the information that was transmitted to an output device is returned to the information source and compared with the original information, to ensure accuracy of output.

read, backward — A feature available on some magnetic-tape systems whereby the magnetic-tape units can transfer data to a computer storage while moving in a reverse direction. Normally used, if available, during the external sort phase to reduce rewind time.

read, destructive — The sensing of data using a process which inherently destroys (erases) the record of the data which has been read. In some storage, reading is destructive, but such data is usually regenerated after each readout. In tapes, drums, disks, etc., reading is usually accomplished without destruction.

reader — Any device, which has the capability of sensing, detecting, or converting data, i.e., transferring to another form or medium.

reader, character — A specialized device that can convert data (represented in one of the type fonts or scripts readable by human beings) directly into machine language. Such a reader may operate optically; or, if the characters are printed in magnetic ink, the device may operate magnetically or optically.

reader, document — An input device which can read documents as a human would, so that data can be directly and easily put into the computer for processing. Although document readers cannot read human script as yet, they can read a large variety of hand-printed and typed documents; for example, bank checks with the account numbers in magnetic ink and specially formed numbers made by the raised letters on credit cards.

reader, film — A unit of peripheral equipment which projects film to permit reading by clients or customers of the data stored on the film, such as microfilm or microfiche, or a device which converts patterns of opaque and transparent spots on a photofilm to electrical pulses which correspond to the patterns.

reader/interpreter — A specific service routine that reads an input stream, stores programs and data on random-access storage for later processing, identifies the control information contained in the input stream, and stores this control information separately in the appropriate control list. A reader-/interpreter may be considered very nearly as the opposite of an output writer.

reader, magnetic-tape — A device capable of restoring information recorded on a magnetic tape to a train or sequence of electrical pulses, usually for the purpose of transferring the information to some other storage medium.

reader, mark — A device capable of reading pencil marks on documents up to a size of 13 × 8 inches. The marks can be positioned anywhere on the document. The sensing cells of the reader are switched on by special clock track marks.

reader, marked-page — Optical marked-page readers can be attached to a system for direct reading of marks made by an ordinary lead pencil in specified positions (like the marks made for an electronic test scoring) on 8½ x 11-inch sheets of paper. The sheets can be read at a maximum rate of 2000 per hour, or one each 1.8 seconds. The reader is normally attached to the multiplexor channel and operation is in the multiplex mode. Applications for the reader are in payroll, order entry, accounts payable, inventory control, sales analysis, general ledger work, and many other phases of business, government, and institution (some units).

reader, optical — 1. This system is based on the principle that the special shape of each character printed on the input media is capable of being identified by a reading device. For example, the audit-journal from a cash register, if printed in a distinctive optical font, could be used as the input media to a computer. As the optical reader reads each character from the input media, it translates the data into electrical impulses that in turn are transmitted to the computer for processing. 2. Reads printed and typewritten material directly, without converting it into punch-paper, punch cards, or other intermediate formats. It recognizes all letters of the alphabet, standard punctuation, zero through nine, and special symbols used in programmed functions. It handles documents, and continuous fan fold sheets.

reader, optical bar-code — This device is

available with the data station to read code information from documents such as premium changes, bills, invoices, and coupons at the rate of hundreds of characters per second. The data station features a high-speed printer, and thus can be used for on-line operations. Card and paper-tape equipment also can be connected to the data station.

reader, optical document — *See* reader, document.

reader, page — An optical character reader which can process cut-form documents of differing sizes and which might be able to read information in hand-written form.

reader, paper-tape — A device capable of restoring the information punched on a paper tape to a train or sequence of electrical pulses, usually for the purpose of transferring the information to some other storage medium.

reader, photoelectric — A unit of peripheral equipment which has the capability of converting data in the form of patterns of holes in storage media as tapes or cards, into electric pulse patterns by means of photosensitive diodes and transistors, i.e., a reader used for rapid input to a computer and one which usually can also drive a printer, plotter, etc.

readers, optical-character (magnetic) — Magnetic character readers can be attached directly to channels for the fast and direct reading into the system of the magnetically inscribed information on checks and other banking transactions. Readers differ mainly in document-reading rates; some read up to 950 documents per minute, others as many as 1600 documents per minute. As the documents are read, they may be sorted into many classifications. All magnetic inscriptions can be checked for validity. The documents read may be of intermixed size and thickness, as typically encountered in check-handling operations. The standard minimum length is 6 inches; shorter documents may be read at appreciably higher rates, but these are not sorted unless a special feature for that purpose is installed. Many other special features are available.

reader-sorter — A unit of punch card equipment which senses and transmits input while sorting documents.

read-gather, write-scatter — *See* gather-write/scatter-read.

read head — A head that is used for reading data or a medium, such as tape, disks, drums, cards, or an optical sensor.

read-in — To sense information contained in some source and transmit this information to an internal storage.

readiness review — An on-site examination of the adequacy of preparations for the effective utilization of a new computer installation, and to indicate any necessary corrective actions.

reading access time — The elapsed time before data may be read or used in the computer during the equipment read cycle.

reading, destructive — A reading process that destroys the source data.

reading, mark — A form of mark detection using a photoelectric device to locate and verify information as coded or marked in special boxes or windows on preprepared forms. The unit, a scanner, reads by detecting the reflected light from the document.

reading, nondestructive — A reading process that does not destroy the data in the source.

reading, parallel — When a data card is read row-by-row.

reading, rate of — Number of characters, words, fields, blocks or cards sensed by an input sensing device per unit of time.

reading station — 1. The keypunch area where a data card is aligned to be read by a sensing mechanism. 2. A specific location in the reading device in which data is obtained from media, such as punched cards or magnetic tape.

read-in program — *See* program, read-in.

read-in, read-out — An optical feature that may be added to certain off-line office machinery permitting on-line operation.

read/jump protection — *See* protection, read/jump.

read, manual — An operation in which the computer does the sensing of the contents or settings of manually set switches or registers.

read, nondestructive — A reading of the information in a register without changing that information.

read-only memory — Abbreviated ROM. The ROM is used to store the microprogram or a fixed program depending upon the microprogrammability of the

CPU. The microprogram provides the translation from the higher-level user commands, such as ADD, SUBTR, etc., down to a series of detailed control codes recognizable by the microprocessor for execution. The size of the ROM varies according to user requirements within the maximum allowed capacity dictated by the addressing capability of the microprocessor.

readout — 1. The act of removing and recording information from a computer or an auxiliary storage. 2. The information that is removed from computer storage and recorded in a form that the operator can interpret directly.

read out — To sense information contained in the internal storage of a computer and transmit this information to an external storage unit.

readout, destructive — The act of retrieving information from memory by using a process which erases the contents of the cells. With a nondestructive readout, the contents are not erased.

read-out device — A device that records the computer output either as a curve or as a group of printed numbers or letters.

readout, nondestructive — 1. The copying of information from a computer storage device without altering the physical representation of the information in the device.

read-process-write — The process of reading in one block of data, while simultaneously processing the preceding block and writing out the results of the previously processed block. Some special processors can perform concurrently on any two or three of these operations, others are limited to read/write.

read pulse — *See* pulse, read.

read rate — The particular rate which measures the number of units of data that are sensed by a device in a unit of time, usually expressed as bits, words, or pages per second or minute.

read release — A feature of some equipment which permits more computer processing time by releasing the read mechanism.

read reverse — The unit can read tape under program control in either direction.

read-scatter — The ability of a computer to distribute or scatter data into several memory areas as it is being entered into the system on magnetic tape.

read time — 1. The time it takes a computer to locate data or an instruction word in its storage section and transfer it to its arithmetic unit where the required computations are performed. 2. The time it takes to transfer information that has been operated on by the arithmetic unit to a location in storage. (Synonymous with read time, and related to write time and word time.)

read while writing — The reading of a record or group of records into storage from a tape at the same time another record or group of records is written from storage onto tape.

read/write channels — The data path between the main memory and a peripheral device that is completed by a programmer-assigned read/write channel. This channel is not a fixed connection to any one unit but is rather a floating link that can be used by any device. As opposed to the conventional method of complex and costly high-speed and low-speed transmission lines, the read/write channel can be assigned to any device regardless of speed or mode of data transfer.

read/write check — *See* check, read/write.

read/write check indicator — A device incorporated in certain computers to indicate upon interrogation whether or not an error was made in reading or writing. The machine can be made to stop, retry the operation, or follow a special subroutine depending upon the result of the interrogation.

read/write counters — Data is transferred between the main memory and peripheral devices via read/write channels. Associated with each channel are two read/write counters. These counters store the starting and current addresses of the data being transferred by the read/write channel.

read-write cycle — The sequence of operations required to read and write, e.g., restore memory data.

read/write head — A small electromagnetic unit used for reading, recording, or erasing polarized spots that represent information on a magnetic tape, disk, or drum.

read-write memory — Abbreviated RWM. Some systems are implemented with ROM (read only memory) program memory only. In addition, often the main PROM has all the control lines available for implementing RWM (read/write memory) program memory. In small systems ROM program memory is used for systems in fixed applications. RWM memory is used where it is desired to change the system application by the operator. RWM is a considerable step in small system complexity in hardware and programs.

read/write scatter — An operation performed under program control that reads a block of data from tape and breaks it up into processable elements. After processing, data is recombined and written on the tape as a block.

ready — The status or condition of being ready to run. A program, task, or hardware device that is in a ready condition needs only a start signal in order to begin operation.

ready condition — A specification or circumstance of a job or task signified when all of its requirements for execution other than control of the central processor have been satisfied.

ready light — An indicator light on the display panel which, when on, indicates the equipment is ready for operation.

ready mode, time sharing — *See* time sharing, ready mode.

ready-record — A specific signal from a file-access mechanism to the computer that a record whose address was previously provided by a seek command has now been located and may be read into memory.

ready status word — A particular status word indicating that the remote computing system is waiting for entry from the terminal.

real constants — A real constant is written with a decimal point, using the decimal digits 0, 1, . . . , 9. A preceding + or − sign is optional. An unsigned real constant is assumed to be positive. An integer exponent preceded by an E may follow a real constant. The exponent may have a preceding + or − sign. An unsigned exponent is assumed to be positive.

real number — An element of a set of all positive and negative numbers, including all types: integers, zeros, mixed, rational, irrational, etc., but not imaginary or complex.

real ratio (time) — One computer time ratio is the time interval between two events in a simulation by a computer to the problem time, or the physical system time, i.e., the time interval between corresponding events in the physical system being simulated. When this ratio is greater than 1, the operation is considered to be on an extended time scale, which is a slow-time scale. When it is less than 1 it is said to be on a fast-time scale, and when it is not constant during the run it is said to be on a variable time scale. Real-time working is involved when it is equal to 1.

real time — 1. In solving a problem, a speed sufficient to give an answer within the actual time the problem must be solved. 2. Pertaining to the performance of a computation during the actual time that the related physical process transpires in order that results of the computation can be used in guiding the physical process.

real-time address — *Same as* address, immediate.

real-time addressing — *Same as* addressing, immediate.

real-time application — Real-time processing is accomplished on a time-current basis. It handles the flow of data from widespread manufacturing inventories and production lines such as the shifting pattern of transportation schedules, or the scattered operations of the utility industry. For example, in airlines reservation control, the real-time system provides an instantaneous picture of seat availability, cancellations, sales, and flight data for the whole airline. The airline agent simply presses buttons.

real-time, batch processing — The requirements for real-time action are known frequently to occur in peaks and valleys. In many businesses these requirements tend to increase from early morning through the middle of the day and to taper off from then on. In other businesses the occurrence of these demands may be sporadic. The real-time system is so designed that it will automatically, as its facilities are freed from the dynamic demands of real-time processing, load them up with the ordinary day to day backlog of less urgent work of the familiar batch-processing type—typically, the sequential processing of sequentially ordered files such as accounts receivable, payable, or payrolls.

real-time channel — The various units of equipment that provide interface between the end of communication and the computer memory. Such a channel performs the identical basic function as a multiplexer but has more limited storage capability and does not have stored-program capacity.

real-time clock — A real-time clock develops readable digits or periodic signals for the computer to allow computation of elapsed time between events, and to initiate the performance of time-initiated processing.

real-time clock interrupt — On some systems the real-time clock (RTC) interrupt is disabled when the interrupt system is inhibited; thus, its priority is lower than the noninhibitable class of interrupts. It has the highest priority among all other interrupts.

real-time clock logs — This built-in clock is used for a wide variety of programming-time purposes. It can be used to log the receipt times of a periodic real-time input data. Each input message and its receipt time may be recorded together. This clock is also used in connection with the preparation of statistical and analytical reports dealing with the frequency of certain transactions.

real time clock module — Some units can provide 13 or more programmable time bases from one microsecond to one hour. A 1-MHz crystal controlled oscillator typically generates the frequency standard of the module. When enabled, the module informs the computer at the completion of each time interval.

real-time clock pins (RTC) — On some systems the microcomputer provides two or more real-time clock input pins, one for the RTC enable and one for an external frequency which triggers the RTC interrupt. The input signal may come from the ac line frequency, a precision counter, the OEM system clock or other sources, on these systems.

real-time clock routine — On some systems the real-time clock (RTC) routine is written by the customer (Original Equipment Manufacturer, in many cases) programmer for the particular requirements of his or her system. Some generalized software operating systems use the 1-ms RTC interrupt for time of day, elapsed time, and a variety of task scheduling operations.

real-time clock, time sharing — *See* time sharing, real-time clock.

real-time concurrency operations — The great point is that the real-time system is at no moment necessarily committed to real-time operations or to batch processing operations exclusively. Both may proceed concurrently and several kinds of each may proceed concurrently under the control of an internally stored executive program. But the real time operations always have priority and the system will assign its facilities as these priorities require, relinquishing them to other activities, such as engineering calculations or normal business processing tasks, as soon as they no longer need to keep pace with real time events. In this way maximum use may be made of the components of any desired configuration of the real-time system; and the advantages of its enormous storage capacity, speed, flexibility, and communications capabilities may be obtained at a low cost per unit of work accomplished. To sum up, it should be said that experience indicates that the real-time system will quite probably outperform, by a wide margin, any other system of its kind in a wide range of applications.

real-time control, input/output — All input/output data transfers are automatically controlled by signals emanating from the central processor or from the peripheral subsystems themselves. Any general-purpose input/output channel can accommodate a real-time system peripheral device. All i/o channels are buffered. Each input/output device has associated with it a control unit that, once activated by the central processor, carries out the entire operation of the instruction given it while the central processor proceeds with other tasks.

real-time control, single-chip system — On some systems, real-time control is accomplished via a sense input, an interrupt, and flags. Other hard-wired control signals provide bus access, access priority, data-flow supervision, and general control of the processor. The bus-access and access-priority control lines can be used to cascade several processors—all with direct interface to the address and data buses.

real-time control system — A computer system that processes the data and makes the necessary decisions in real time. For example, the automatic control of manufacturing processes by a computer in an oil refinery.

real-time data reduction — *See* data reduction, real-time.

real-time, executive — The executive system is designed to interface with programs that have real-time requirements. The standard communication subsystem, together with the efficient scheduling and the interrupt processing features of the executive system, provides an environment satisfactory for any real-time program.

real-time information system — A real-time information system is a system that can provide information about the process it is describing fast enough for the process to be continuously controlled by an operator using this information (for example, a scientist controlling the path of a space rocket).

real time input/output — Information in a system in which a machine accepts the data as it is generated by a sensor, processes or operates on the data, and furnishes the results so as to affect the operations of the data generator or some other device; e.g., the data received from an industrial process under the control of a computer or the data received from a missile under the guidance control of a computer.

real-time inputs — *See* inputs, real-time.

real-time mode — *Same as* real-time concurrency.

real-time monitor — The executive system is an operating and programming system designed to monitor the construction and execution of programs, to optimize the utilization of available hardware, and to minimize programmer effort and operator intervention. The executive system, as a monitor, provides for concurrent processing and real-time operation in a classical monitor environment. The executive system is of modular construction, tailored to each user's equipment configuration and applications requirements. Extensions to the system for peripheral devices and application programs may be added, altered, or deleted as required.

real-time multicomputing — Real-time command and control situations requiring maximum reliability utilize two or more computers in multicomputer systems. Two or more essentially independent computing systems communicate directly, with access to each other's memory. Capable of tremendous computing power, such systems have the added advantage of reserve equipment. Typical real-time applications demanding this degree of reliability include manned space-vehicle launching and airport traffic control. The concept of individual modules for processor, memory, and controller provides multiprocessor and multicomputer systems with multiple functions without duplication of hardware.

real-time on-line operation (OLRT) — The processing of data in synchronism with a physical process, in such a fashion that the results of the data-processing are useful to the physical operation.

real time operating system — Abbreviated RTOS. Some systems provide for disk-based real-time multiprogrammed operations in the foreground with batch processing in the background and automatic overlay and roll-out of programs to disk, with dynamic memory allocation.

real-time operation — Concurrent operations for data processing (computing) and physical processing in such a way that the results of the computing operations are available immediately whenever needed by the physical processing operations, and vice versa.

real time option boards — Various option boards contain the major interfaces and options that most users need. Some of these include: real time clock, programmers console control, input/output interface, 12-bit parallel i/o and an asynchronous serial line unit. Extended option boards include: memory extension and time-share control, power fail with auto restart and bootstrap loaders.

real-time processing — A procedure that provides for multitasking on a priority scheduling basis. The processor may be switched from task to task by an i/o request, a supervisor call, a device interrupt or at the end of a task. It provides a roll-out/roll-in feature to ensure real-time response to high priority requests.

real-time processing (bank) — If the volume of savings account and mortgage-loan activity warrants, these transactions may be handled in real-time by the on-line teller system. Teller consoles at each window at each office may be linked to the computer and the on-line central file.

real-time processing communication —

A real-time system is a combined data processor and communicator of transaction data between remote locations and a certain computer, via communication lines, and allows the data to be processed while the business transaction is actually taking place. A real-time system may be thought of as a communications-oriented data-processing system which is capable of performing batch-processing functions while concurrently processing inquiries or messages, and generating responses in a time interval directly related to the operational requirements of the system.

real-time processing, inventory — The remotely located sales offices are supplied with an inquiry/answer device capable of communicating directly with the computer itself. To place an order, the required information is entered into the system by the input device. Since the device is connected directly to the computer, complete information, including the availability and status of the item ordered, is confirmed in seconds. If the items are available, the invoice is printed automatically, along with associated shipping information, at the sales office, indicating to the salesman that the order has been filled as requested. If any particular item on the order depleted the inventory to the recorder point, the computer automatically sends a message to the recorder source, connected directly to the computer, requesting an updating in inventory. All these operations are accomplished in a matter of seconds.

real-time, remote inquiry — On-line inquiry stations permit users to interrogate the computer files and receive immediate answers to their inquiries. In industry, the stations can be located at dozens of remote locations such as office, factory, warehouse, and remote branch locations. Such a system permits all levels of industrial management to obtain immediate answers to questions about inventories, work-in-process, sales, etc.

real-time satellite computer — A satellite computer in the real-time system relieves the larger computer system of time consuming input and output functions as well as performing preprocessing and postprocessing functions such as validity editing and formatting for print.

real-time simulation — A particular operation of a simulator or simulation program, such that the instants of occurrence of many basic events in the simulator occur at the same times as they would in the system being simulated.

real-time software, microprocessor — The software distinguishes various real-time microprocessor systems. Software ties together the processor and peripheral capabilities of the systems. Software is organized around two major operating systems, one for program development and one for on-line real-time operation. These two systems must be totally compatible, with the programs developed capable of being directly loaded for execution. In larger configurations, they operate on-line as a background task system.

real-time system — The processing of information or data in a sufficiently rapid manner so that the results of the processing are available in time to influence the process being monitored or controlled.

real-time system, executive — The real-time executive system controls, sequences, and provides for the efficient allocation of facilities for operating the real-time system. Normally, the real-time executive system controls a real-time program operating concurrently with one or more batch programs. The real-time executive system eliminates the need for the programmer to plan concurrently. It maintains and restores the operational environment of each program so that as far as the programmer is concerned, his program operates as if it were the only one being run in the system. The real-time executive system also provides a number of basic subroutines that assist in matters of console control, rerun, the loading of segments or overlays, and input/output control for the various subsystems (some systems).

real-time working — The use of the computer as an element of a processing system in which the times of occurrence of data transmission are controlled by other portions of the system, or by physical events outside the system, and cannot be modified for convenience in computer programming. Such an operation either proceeds at the same speed as the events being simulated or at a sufficient speed to analyze or control external events happening concurrently.

real-time working ratio — *See* time scale.

real variables (FORTRAN) — A real variable consists of a series of not more than six alphanumeric characters (except special characters) of which the first is alphabetic but cannot be one of the integer indicators, i.e., I, J, K, L, M, or N.

reasonableness check — Tests made on data received by a computer to ensure that the data in question lie within a given range. A means of protecting a system from errors.

reasonableness tests — These tests provide a means of detecting a gross error in calculation or, while posting to an account, a balance that exceeds a predetermined limit. Typical examples include payroll calculations and credit-limit checks in accounts receivable. In some cases both an upper and a lower limit are established; each result is then machine-compared against both limits to make certain that it falls between the two.

recall ratio — In information-retrieval systems, the ratio of the number of pertinent documents retrieved by a single query to the total number of pertinent documents in the total collection, as determined by the query criteria.

recall signal — A signal originated by the user, after the call set-up has been completed, used to control the data network in some way other than disconnect.

receive only — The description of a teletype device which has only printer capabilities. Such a machine can receive information from the computer but cannot send it.

receive-only service — Service in which the data-communication channel is capable of receiving signals, but is not equipped to transmit signals.

receiver — Also called the card stacker, it is that part of the machine in which punched cards are deposited after passing through the machine.

receiver signal — Equipment controlled by signaling currents transmitted over the line and used generally to send out new signals.

receive/send keyboard set (KSR) — A combination transmitter and receiver with transmission capability from keyboard only.

receiving margin — Sometimes referred to as range or operating range. The usable range over which the rangefinder may be adjusted. The normal range for a properly adjusted machine is approximately 75 points on a 120-point scale.

reciprocal — The mathematical expression establishing the relation of a number which exists when that number is divided into a single unit or one, i.e., the process of multiplying by the reciprocal of the number is equivalent to dividing by that number.

recirculating loop — In drum computers, a small section of memory that has much faster access than the remainder of memory.

reckoner, Lincoln — An on-line, time-sharing executive program developed by Lincoln Laboratories.

recognition accuracy, voice system — The degree to which voice recognition equipment will correctly encode the input utterance without repeated inputs or corrections; higher recognition accuracy provides faster data input.

recognition, character — The technology of using a machine to sense and encode into a machine language characters that are written or printed to be read by human beings.

recognition, magnetic ink — *See* MICR.

recognition, pattern — The recognition of shapes or other patterns by a machine system. Patterns may be such as physical shapes or speech patterns.

recognizable machine — *See* data, machine readable.

recognizer, syntax — A subroutine which recognizes the phase class in an artificial language, normally expressed in backus normal form (BNF), formal language theory.

recomplementation — An internal procedure that performs nines or tens complementation, as required, on the result of an arithmetic operation.

record — 1. A set of one or more consecutive fields on a related subject, as an employee's payroll record. Although a record need not be a block in length, such an arrangement is often useful. 2. A listing of information, usually in printed or printable form; one output of a compile consisting of a list of the operations and their positions in the final specific routine and containing information describing the segmentation and storage allocation of the routine. 3. To make a transcription of data by a systematic alteration of the condition, property, or configuration of a physical medium, e.g., placing information on magnetic tapes or a drum by means of magnetized spots. 4. A group of related facts or fields of information treated as a unit, thus a listing of information usually in printed or printable form. 5. To put data into a storage device. 6. To group related facts or fields of information treated as a unit.

record, addition — A record that results in the creation of a new record in the updated master file.

record block — A specific storage area of fixed size which is usually in a main memory or file storage; it is organized into such standard blocks to allow more flexibility in storage allocation and control. (Synonymous with physical record.)

record, chained — Physical records, located randomly in main or auxiliary memory modules, that are linked or chained by means of a control field in each record which contains the address of the next record in the series or chains. Long waiting lists or files can be connected or chained in this way.

record check time — The elapsed time which is required to verify a record transfer on tape. The volume of time or duration that is based on tape speed or distance between the rewrite heads.

record control schedule — A type of master record or schedule designating all activities involved regarding disposition of business records, i.e., transfers, retention, etc.

record, data — A record containing data to be processed by a program.

record, deletion — A new record added to a file, or removing and replacing an existing record in a file as contrasted with record, addition.

record description — In COBOL, a record is described in terms of the data elements it contains. For each element in a record, a character picture is used to specify its level, name, and format.

record, detail — The specific listing of data which is a unit part of a major classification of larger segments or a total classification of data.

record, duplicated — Images or copies of file records that are located in the file modules, or frames that are separate from the primary copy. Such duplicate records ensure against loss of urgent or critical files or data.

recorder, digital — A peripheral device that records data as discrete, numerically defined points.

recorder, film — A unit of equipment which has the capability of making records or placing data on film by using light, dark, opaque, or transparent spots on photographic roll film or some of the latest digital type of photography of shadow or depths of gray. Such data may be digital output from a computer or from a sensor. Some types use a light beam passing through the film to a photocell to read data.

record file, fixed-length — *See* record, fixed-length.

record file, variable-length — A file containing a set of records that vary in length.

record, fixed-length — A record in which the number of characters is fixed. The restriction may be deliberate to simplify and speed processing, or it may be caused by the limitations of the equipment used.

record gap — 1. The space between records on a tape, usually produced by tape acceleration or deceleration during the writing stage of processing. 2. A gap used to indicate the end of a record.

record group — Several records which, when placed together, associate or identify with a single key which is located in one of the records. Grouping is efficient in time and space-saving on magnetic tapes.

record head — A head used to transfer data to a storage device, such as a drum, disk, tape, or magnetic card.

record header — A specific record containing the description of information contained in a classification or group of records which follows this initial document. Also known as header table.

record heading — A record which contains an identification or description of the output report to which following records are related and which is concerned with the body of the report.

record, home — Usually the first record in a chain of records, i.e., the home record is used with the chaining method of file development or organization.

recording — The operation by which an input device facilitates the presentation of source data to be processed.

recording density — The number of bits per a given unit length of a linear track in a recording medium.

recording density, tape — *See* tape recording density.

recording double-pulse — A specific method for magnetic recording of bits, in which each storage cell comprises two regions, magnetized in opposite senses with unmagnetized regions on each side.

recording-frequency doubling — Magnetic recording of bits by a specific method in which each storage cell comprises two magnetized regions with unmagnetized regions on each side. The magnetized regions are magnetized in opposite senses to represent zero and in the same sense to represent one. The sense of the magnetization is changed in passing from one cell to the next.

recording head — A head used to transfer data to a storage device, such as a drum, disk, tape, or magnetic card.

recording, magnetic — That special method of recording data by impressing a pattern of magnetization on a thin layer of magnetic material, usually on a nonmagnetic base, such as a disk, drum, tape, etc.

recording mode — In the COBOL system, the representation in external media of data associated with a data-processing system.

recording phase, redundant — *See* redundant phase recording.

recordings, dual — The dual recording of critical data makes it possible to machine-compare the two for verification. It is more commonly used in mark-sense recording operations and those card-punch operations in which it is necessary to verify only one or two fields.

recording, source — The recording of data in machine-readable documents, such as punched cards, punched paper tape, magnetic tapes, etc. Once in this form, the data may be transmitted, processed, or reused without manual processing.

record, label — A record used to identify the contents of a file or reel of magnetic tape.

record layout — A record must be organized or arranged in sequence as to occurrence of items and the size, distribution, etc., i.e., as the two-dimensional format of a printed page.

record length — 1. In a computer, the number of characters necessary to contain all the information in a record. 2. An arbitrarily chosen number of characters that comprise the records in a given program. To secure this record length, it is sometimes necessary to pad the records. (Clarified by padding.)

record length or word — The number of characters, digits or words which comprise a data set of fixed or variable size.

record, logical — A record that contains pertinent information about a common subject. The most basic subdivision of a record is called a field.

record mark — A special character used in some computers either to limit the number of characters in a data transfer, or to separate blocked or grouped records in tape.

record, master — The basic updated record used in the next file-processing run. A master record is most often a magnetic tape item. Visual copies for possible analysis and alteration are usually developed.

record name — In COBOL, the name given to a record within a file and assigned the level number 01. Data names for elements within a record have lower-level numbers, 02, 03, etc.

record, physical — Punched cards are each a physical record, and magnetic tapes and disks have physical records as bounded by interrecord gaps.

record ready — A signal from a file-access mechanism to the computer that a record whose address was previously provided by a seek command has now been located and may be read into memory.

record, reference — An output of a compiler that lists the operations and their positions in the final specific routine, and contains information describing the segmentation and storage allocation of the routine.

records — Any unit of information that is to be transferred between the main memory and a peripheral device is defined as a record. Records can be of any length.

records/blocks — Many mass-storage systems organize data into blocks called records. Often when a data transfer between the storage system and the computer is performed, an entire record must be transferred. Some systems utilize a fixed record size, which means that all records are of the same length. Most tape systems, however, allow a variable record size, which means that a record may be as short as one byte or as long as desired. Note that the use of short records may reduce the storage capacity substantially due to gaps between records.

record, semifixed length — A particular fixed-length record which has a length subject to change at the choice of the system analyst or programmer, although such lengths usually remain fixed for a given problem, run, specific operation, or routine.

records, grouped — A set of records sharing the same label, tag, or key.

records, grouping of — The combining of two or more records into one block of information on tape, to decrease the wasted time due to tape acceleration and deceleration and to conserve tape space. This is also called blocking of records.

records management — A specific program designed to provide economy and efficiency in the creation, organization, maintenance, use, and disposition of records. Thus, needless records will not be created or kept and only the valuable records will be preserved.

record sorting — The basic element of a file such that the sorting of file constitutes the reordering of file records; also referred to as item.

records, overflow — Records which cannot be accommodated in assigned areas of a direct access file and which must be stored in another area where they can be retrieved by means of a reference stored in place of the records in their original assigned area.

record-storage mark — A special character that appears only in the record-storage unit of the card reader to limit the length of the record read into processor storage.

record, strip — A recording method in which information is stored vertically with strips visible for information location.

records, variable-length (sorting) — Denumerable file elements for which the number of words, characters, bits, fields, etc., is not constant.

record system, fixed-length — *See* fixed-length record system.

record, trailer — A record that follows a group of records and contains pertinent data related to the group of records.

record, transaction — Specific information which modifies information in a file.

record type — A data structure defined to contain the information describing the entities being racked by a data base, and their associated attributes. Data bases generally contain files with records of a homogeneous data type. Some less sophisticated file systems may contain files that possess mixed record types.

record, unit — 1. A separate record that is similar in form and content to other records, e.g., a summary of a particular employee's earnings to date. 2. Sometimes refers to a piece of nontape auxiliary equipment, e.g., card reader, printer, or console typewriter.

record, variable length — A record which has a loose or unfixed number of constituent parts, i.e., blocks, words, etc., are subject to particular installation or chief programmer rules, constraints, conventions, or by the equipment design.

recovery fallback — The restoration of a system to full operation from a fallback mode of operation after the cause of the fallback has been removed.

recovery procedures, error — Procedures designed to help isolate and, where possible, to recover from errors in equipment. The procedures are often used in conjunction with programs that record the statistics of machine malfunctions.

recovery program, automatic — The process in a system built on providing a high degree of reliability, where a diagnostic routine locates the trouble and the automatic recovery program shifts to duplexed or standby equipment, or to a fallback mode of operation.

recovery routine — Most commonly in tape operations a reading or writing error will occur. Usually the record is reread or rewritten several times before any appropriate action is taken. If the error does not disappear, the program is halted, but preferably a record should be made of the error and the program continued, as devised by scores of special recovery routines.

recursion — The continued repetition of the same operation or group of operations.

recursive — Pertaining to a process that is inherently repetitive. The result of each repetition is usually dependent upon the result of the previous repetition.

recursive function — A mathematical function which is defined in terms of itself; for example, an operation which takes advantage of the recursive definition of the function, resulting in either repetition of the calculations using the same function, or using the same function with a slight modification.

recursive process — In data processing, a method of computing values of functions in which each stage of processing contains all subsequent stages, i.e., the first stage is not completed until all other stages have been completed.

recycling of programs — An organized arrangement for recycling programs through a computer when alternates have been made in one program that may change or have an effect on other programs.

redact — To edit or revise input data.

redaction — A new or revised edition of input data.

redefine — In COBOL, to reuse the same storage area for different data items during program execution by means of appropriate instructions in the data program.

red tape — 1. Pertaining to administrative or overhead operations or functions that are necessary in order to maintain control of a situation; e.g., for a computer program, housekeeping involves the setting up of constants and variables to be used in a program. 2. A general term that reserves, restores, and clears the memory areas.

red-tape operation — A computer operation that does not directly contribute to the solution; i.e., arithmetical, logical, and transfer operations used in modifying the address section of other instructions, in the counting cycles, and in the rearrangement data.

reduction, data — The transformation of raw data into a more useful form, e.g., smoothing to reduce extraneous noise.

reduction, data, real time — *See* data reduction, real time.

redundance, longitudinal — A condition in which the bits in each track or row of a record do not total an even (or odd) number. The term is usually used to refer to records on magnetic tape, and a system can have either odd or even longitudinal parity.

redundance, vertical — An error condition that exists when a character fails a parity check, i.e., has an even number of bits in an odd-parity system, or vice versa.

redundancy — 1. In the transmission of information, redundancy is the fraction of the gross-information content of a message that can be eliminated without the loss of the essential information. Numerically, it is one minus the ratio of the net information content to the gross information content, expressed in percent. 2. An extra piece of information used to assist in determining the accuracy of moved digits or words in a computer. (Clarified by redundant check.)

redundancy check — A checking technique based on the presence of extra (redundant) information which is used only for checking purposes. Parity checking, check digits, control totals, and hash totals are all examples of redundancy checks.

redundancy check character, longitudinal — On a tape where each character is represented in a lateral row of bits, a character used for checking the parity of each track in the longitudinal direction. Such a character is usually the last character recorded in each block and is used in some magnetic recording systems to reestablish the initial recording status. Abbreviated RCL.

redundancy check, cyclic — A cyclic parity check character for longitudinal error control calculated from a devisor polynomial. A typical one is: $X^{16} + X^{15} + X^2 + 1$.

redundancy check, longitudinal — An error control device or system based on the arrangement of data in blocks according to some preset rule, the correctness of each character within the block being determined on the basis of the specific rule or set.

redundancy check, vertical — An odd parity check performed on each character of a transmitted block of ASCII-coded data as the block is received. Abbreviated RCV. *See also* redundancy check, cyclic; redundancy check, longitudinal.

redundancy, communication — Duplication or partial duplication of circuitry or information designed to decrease the probability of a system or communication failure. Redundancy is also used to refer to inadvertent communication of more information or detail than is required with a consequent waste of available communication capacity.

redundant character — A character specifically added to a group of characters to ensure conformity with certain rules that can be used to detect a computer malfunction.

redundant check — The use of extra bits in machine words for the purpose of detecting malfunctions and mistakes.

redundant checking — *See* checking, redundant.

redundant code — A code using more signal elements than necessary to represent the intrinsic-processing information.

redundant phase recording — Ensures transfer reliability, reduces problem of skew in bidirectional operation. Each tape track is redundantly paired with a second, nonadjacent track. Use of phase (rather than amplitude) recording reduces the dropouts due to variations in amplitude.

reel — A spool of tape; generally refers to magnetic tape.

reel, feed — A specific reel from which tape is unwound during the processing.

reel number — A sequence number that identifies a particular reel in a file of reels.

reels, pocket-size — Handy to carry, easy to load. Each 3½-inch reel holds up to 3 million bits, the equivalent of 4000 feet of paper tape, assuming 6-bit words are used.

reel, take-up — A specific reel on which tape is wound or may be wound during processing.

reenterable — A special attribute of a program that describes a routine which can be shared by several tasks concurrently ("reusable reentrant"), or which can "call" itself or a program which calls it. Special provisions are required: (1) to externalize all intermediate variables used (the "prototype control section" of the calling program), and (2) to avoid destruction of the return address by circular calling sequences.

reenterable load module — A type of load module which can be used repeatedly or concurrently by two or more jobs or tasks.

reentrant — That property of a program that enables it to be interrupted at any point by another user, and then resumed from the point of interruption. Reentrant programs are often found in multiprogramming and time-sharing systems, where there is a requirement for a common store of so-called public routines that can be called by any user at any time. The process is controlled by a monitor that preserves the routine's environment (registers, working storage, control indicators, etc.) when it is interrupted and restores that environment when the routine is resumed for its initial use.

reentrant code — A specific set of instructions that form a single copy of a program or routine that is shared by two or more programs, as contrasted to the conventional method of embedding a copy of a subroutine within each program. Typically, reentrant routines are composed completely of instructions and constants that are not subject to modification during execution.

reentrant code generation — In some systems, the FORTRAN IV and BASIC compilers automatically produce a reentrant code that is compatible with ASSEMBLY language object code. This feature provides the user with the convenience of an efficient, high-level language in conjunction with the more basic assembly language and standard library routines for applications software.

reentrant program — A program (or portion) that can be used simultaneously by different routines. Programs can call themselves repeatedly or may call a routine that in turn calls a reentrant coded program again.

reentry point — The point at which an instruction or a program is reentered from a subroutine or main program is called the reentry point.

reference — An indication of where to find specific information, e.g., by reference to a document, an author, an instruction, etc.

reference address — 1. Addresses that are used in converting related addresses to machine-language addresses. 2. An address used as a reference for a group of related addresses.

reference address, indirect — *See* address, indirect reference.

reference axis — A line drawn across the plotting grid at the location of a selected value such as at the zero of an axis.

reference block, message — *See* block, message reference.

reference debugging aids — *See* debugging aids, reference.

reference, direct address — *See* address, direct reference.

reference, external — *See* external reference.

reference-input signal — A signal that is specifically external to a control loop which serves as the standard of comparison for the directly controlled variable.

reference instruction — An instruction designed to allow reference to systematically arranged or stored data.

reference line, character-spacing — *See* character-spacing reference line.

reference listing — A list printed by a compiler to indicate instructions as they appear in the final routine including details of storage locations.

reference programming, library — A distinct program to form an assemblage, or to retrieve from or input to a library, instead of one written for a particular job. It is a program which may be called simply by reference to an index of library program names.

reference record — An output of a computer that lists the operations and their positions in the final specific routine. The output also contains information describing the segmentation and storage allocation of the final routine.

reference table, program — That section of storage used as an index for operations, subroutines, and variables.

reference time — An instant near the beginning of a switching routine, chosen as an origin for time measurements. It is the instant when the drive pulse reaches a specific fraction of its instantaneous value. The drive pulse is also called magnetic cell response pulse, and integrated voltage pulse.

referencing, input/output — References to data on tape or disk are made symbolically. Instead of describing the address of a certain disk or tape, the programmer refers to such data with a functional name. This means the programmer need not keep in mind where data will be coming from.

reflectance — In OCR (optical character recognition) the diffuse reflectivity of ink-free areas of the substrate on which the printing exists.

reflectance, background — An optical character recognition term related to the reflectance of the background of a document surface within the area reserved for printing (clear band), as compared to a reference standard.

reflectance ink — *See* ink, reflectance.

reflectance ratio — The reciprocal of the ratio of the intensity of the light reflected from the image area of a picture to the intensity of light reflected from the background or light area.

reflectance, spectral — The determined reflectance related or caused by a specific wavelength of incident light from a specified surface.

reflected binary — *See* binary, reflected.

reflected code — Any binary code that changes by only one bit when going from one number to the number immediately following. (Synonymous with reflected-binary code and cyclic code.)

reflection, coefficient — The ratio of incident to reflected light intensity at a point on a surface.

reflective scan — A scan technique in which the light source is aimed at a reflecting surface to illuminate the photosensor.

reflective spot — An evident mark which indicates the beginning or end of a tape.

refresher rate, display — The manufacturer's recommended number of frames per second for regenerating the display.

refreshing — A process of constantly reactivating or restoring information that decays or fades away when left idle. For instance, the phosphor on a crt screen needs to be constantly reactivated by an electron beam in order to remain illuminated. Cells in dynamic memory elements must be repeatedly accessed in order to avoid a fading away of their contents.

refresh-RAM — A dynamic RAM that loses its contents within a few milliseconds. Refresh logic must then rewrite the contents of the complete RAM within a two-millisecond period.

regenerate — The restoring of information that is electrostatically stored in a cell, on the screen of a cathode-ray tube in order to counteract fading and other disturbances that are prevalent with this type of information.

regeneration — 1. The process of returning a part of the output signal of an amplifier to its input circuit in such a manner that it reinforces the excitation and thereby increases the total amplification. 2. Periodic restoration of stored information. 3. The inclusion of logic in a system design to permit the generation of data (when required) from basic formulae as opposed to storage of large volumes of static data.

regeneration pulse — *See* pulse, regeneration.

regenerative feedback — A technique which returns part of the output of a machine, system, or process to the input in a way that causes a larger feedback.

regenerative memory — A memory device whose contents gradually vanish if not periodically refreshed.

regenerative reading — A specific read operation which involves the automatic writing of data back into the positions from which it is extracted.

regenerative repeater — A repeater in which retransmitted signals are practically free from distortion.

regenerative storage — *See* storage, circulating.

regenerative track — *Same as* loop, high speed.

region — 1. In relative coding, a group of location addresses that are all relative to the same specific reference address. 2. A group of machine addresses that refer to a base address.

regional address — An address of a machine instruction within a series of consecutive addresses; e.g., R18 and R19 are specific addresses in an "R" region of "N" consecutive addresses, where all addresses must be named.

register — 1. A device for the temporary storage of one or more words to facilitate arithmetical, logical, or transferral operations. Examples are the accumulator, address, index, instruction, and M-Q registers. 2. The hardware for storing one or more computer words. Registers are usually zero-access storage devices. 3. A term to designate a specific computer unit for storing a group of bits or characters.

register-A — *Same as* register, arithmetic.

register, accumulator — That part of the arithmetic unit in which the results of an operation remain; into which numbers are brought from storage, and from which numbers may be taken for storage.

register, address — A register that stores an address.

register, addressable — That specific temporary storage unit or device as represented by particular storage location numbers.

register address field — The portion of an instruction word that contains a register address.

register, arithmetic — That particular register in the logic unit which holds the operands required for a specific operation. i.e., it can hold the addend for addition, the multiplier for multiplication, or particular words to be compared or shifted, etc.

register, B — *Same as* index register.

register, base — *Same as* index register.

register, block — An address register of available blocks of storage that are chained together for use by the line control computer, for the allocation of incoming information.

register, boundary — A special register used in a multiprogrammed system to designate the upper and lower addresses of each user's program block in the core memory.

register, buffer output — The buffering or transfer device which receives data from internal storage and transfers it to an output media such as magnetic tape.

register capacity — The upper and lower limits of the numbers that may be processed in a register.

register, check — A register used to store information temporarily where it may be checked with the result of a succeeding transfer of this information.

register, circulating — 1. A shift register in which the stored information is moved right or left, and the information from one end is reinserted at the other end. In the case of one-character right shift, the right-most character reappears as the new left-most character and every other character is shifted one position to the right. 2. A register in which the process, as in the preceding statement, is continuously occurring. This can be used as a delaying mechanism.

register, control — 1. A register which holds the identification of the instruction word to be executed next in time sequence, following the current operation. The register is often a counter that is incremented to the address of the next sequential-storage location, unless a transfer or other special instruction is specified by the program. (Synonymous with program counter, and contrasted with program register.) 2. The accumulator, register, or storage unit that stores the current instruction governing a computer operation; an instruction register.

register, current-instruction — The control-section register that contains the instruction currently being executed after it is brought to the control section from memory. Also called instruction register.

register, data (microcomputers) — The data registers, when addressed, store the data present on the MPU data bus during an MPU write operation. This data will also appear on those peripheral lines that have been programmed as PIA outputs. If a peripheral line is serving as an input, the corresponding bit position of the data register can still be written into by the MPU; however, the information on the data bus will not appear on that peripheral data line. During an MPU read operation, the data present on peripheral lines programmed as inputs is transferred directly to the MPU data bus. The PIA control registers allow the MPU to establish and control the operating modes of the peripheral control lines. By means of these four lines, control information is passed back and forth between the MPU and peripheral devices.

register, delay line — A unique register incorporating a delay line plus a means for a signal regeneration, and a feedback channel. Thus, the storage of data in serial representation is achieved through continual circulation.

register, designation — A register into which data is being placed.

register, double-word — Two registers used to hold a 64-bit double-word (some computers).

register, E — A register treated as an extension of the accumulator register and/or the quotient register. This register is used to perform arithmetic requiring double-words.

register, extension — On some small systems this 8-bit register supports the accumulator in performing arithmetic operations, logic operations, and data-transfer operations. The serial i/o capability is also implemented via the extension register.

register, external — These registers, which can be referenced by the program, are located in control storage as specific addresses. These are the locations (registers) which the programmer references when he desires that some sort of computational function be carried out.

register file — A bank of multiple-bit registers that can be used as temporary storage locations for data or instructions and is often referred to as a stack.

register, flip-flop — Chainlike connections of flip-flops used to store binary digits which are stored in parallel or, if desired, serially, wherein data may be fed from one end and shifted bit by bit. If chained in parallel, all flip-flops can be set to the desired state simultaneously.

register, icand — That register which is used in multiplication to hold the multiplicand.

register, ier — That register which holds the multiplier during a multiplication operation.

register, index — A specific register that contains a quantity which may be used to modify memory addresses.

register, indirect addressing — A procedure or addressing mode that utilizes the contents of memory pointer registers to indicate a memory address

register, input — A specific register which receives data from input devices to hold only long enough to complete transfer to internal storage, i.e., to an arithmetic register, etc., as directed by the program.

register input-buffer — That device which accepts data from input units or media such as magnetic tape or disks and which transfers this data to internal storage.

register input/output — *Same as* index register.

register, instruction — A temporary storage device which retains the instruction code of the instruction currently being executed. Also, known as instruction counter. The arrangement of information; an item of data which is discernible as the equivalent to a command to perform a certain operation; the sequence of operations for equivalent or programming sequences.

register length — The number of digits,

characters, or bits that a register can store.

register, magnetic-shift — A register that makes use of magnetic cores as binary storage elements, and in which the pattern of binary digital information can be shifted from one position to the next left or right position.

register, mask — The mask register functions as a filter in determining which portions of words in masked operations or logical comparisons are to be tested. In repeated masked-search operations, both the mask register and the repeat counter must be loaded prior to executing the actual search command (some systems).

register, memory — A register in the storage of the computer, in contrast with a register in one of the other units of the computer.

register mode — On some systems, register mode means any of the general registers may be used as simple accumulators and the operand is contained in the selected register. Since they are hardware registers, in these systems, and within the processor, the general registers operate at high speeds and provide speed advantages when used for operating on frequently addressed variables. The assembler interprets and assembles instructions in a specific form as register mode operations. Also, assembler syntax requires that a general instruction be specifically defined.

register, modifier — *Same as* index register.

register, MQ — Multiple-quotient register.

register, multiplier-quotient — A specific register in the arithmetic or logic portion of a computer in which the multiplier for multiplication is placed and in which the quotient for division is formed.

register, next available block — An address register of available blocks of core storage that are chained together for use by the line control computer for the allocation of incoming information.

register, op — That specific register in which the operation code of the instruction set is stored.

register, operation — 1. A register in which an operation is stored and analyzed in order to set conditions for the execution cycle. 2. A temporary storage device which retains the operation number while that number is being analyzed. 3. A register which stores the operation code of the instruction or program in process.

register, output buffer — The buffering or transfer device which receives data from internal storage and transfers it to an output media such as magnetic tape.

register, payroll — A payroll system which records the employees and the amount due each of them.

register pointer — The portion of the program status double-word that points to a set of 16 general registers to be used as the current register block.

register, program — 1. Register in the control unit that stores the current instruction of the program and controls computer operation during the execution of the program. 2. A temporary storage device or area which retains the instruction code of the instruction being executed.

register, R — The register that holds the ten low-order digits.

register, return code — A particular register which is used to store data which controls the execution of follow-on or subsequent programs.

register select — Register pins are usually connected to the address bus. This refers to one or more lines used to select one register out of n units within a device.

register, sequence — Controls the sequence of the instructions.

register, sequence control — A hardware register which is used by the computer to remember the location of the next instruction to be processed in the normal sequence, but subject to branching, execute instructions, and interrupts.

registers, general — Very fast registers which can be used for any purpose (usually as scratchpad). More recently they are used in place of special registers such as the accumulator.

register, shift — A register in which the characters may be shifted one or more positions to the right or left. In a right shift, the rightmost character is lost. In a left shift, the leftmost character is lost.

register, standby — A register in which accepted or verified information can be stored so as to be available for a rerun in case the processing of the information is spoiled by a mistake in the program, or a malfunction in the computer.

register, stepping — *Same as* register, shift.

register, storage — A register in the storage of the computer, in contrast with a register in one of the other units of the computer. (Synonymous with memory register.)

register, time delay — *Same as* delay line storage.

registration — The accuracy of the positioning of punched holes in a card.

regression, multiple — An efficient analysis program for determining the mathematical relations and relative significances of manufacturing parameters associated with a given problem.

regular binary — *See* binary.

rejection — A logical operation applied to two operands which will provide a result depending on the bit pattern of the operands; e.g., operating on the following 6-bit operands; p=110110, q=011010, then r=000001.

rejection (discrimination accuracy), voice systems — The degree to which equipment will not accept unwanted or invalid inputs, including extraneous noise, thereby allowing operation in a high-noise environment.

rejection gate — *Same as* gate, NOR.

relation — 1. A phase in a programming language comparing two elements with a relational operator. 2. In a relational data-base vocabulary, a relation is a file in normalized form. Pragmatically, a flat file that is inverted.

relational expression — In the COBOL language, an expression that describes a relationship between two terms; for example, A is less than B.

relational operator — In assembler programming, an operator that can be used in an arithmetic or character relation to indicate the comparison to be performed between the terms in the relation.

relational symbols

Symbol	Sample Relation	Explanation
=	A = B	A is equal to B
<	A < B	A is less than B
<=	A<= B	A is less than or equal to B
>	A > B	A is greater than B
>=	A >= B	A is greater than or equal to B
<>	A <> B	A is not equal to B

relative address — 1. An address of a machine instruction that is referenced to an origin; e.g., R + 15 is a specific address relative to R, where R is the origin; the other R + machine addresses do not need to be named. 2. A label used to identify a word in a routine or subroutine with respect to its relative position in that routine or subroutine. A relative address is translated into an absolute address by addition of some specific address for the subroutine within the main routine.

relative addressing — *See* addressing, relative.

relative addressing, real-time — *Same as* relative addressing, timesharing.

relative code — A code in which all addresses are specified or written with respect to an arbitrarily selected position, or in which all addresses are represented symbolically in machine language.

relative coding — 1. Coding in which all addresses refer to an arbitrarily selected position. 2. Coding using relative addresses.

relative error — A ratio of the error to the value of the quantity which contains the error, as contrasted to absolute error.

relative frequency — A measure or calculation of the ratio of numbers of observations in a class (subset) to the total number of observations or elements constituting a population, i.e., universal subset.

relative magnitude — The magnitude relationship or comparison of one quantity to another, most often related to base magnitude and expressed as a difference from or a percentage of the base or reference.

relative record file — A file that provides a low overhead direct disk access to a contiguous section where i/o transfers may be either blocked or unblocked.

relative time clock (RTC) — Using a relative time clock, the executive keeps track of time. At every relative time clock (RTC) interrupt, the interrupt service routine returns control to the executive, which checks if a higher priority device is seeking execution or if a program wants to be turned "on".

relay — An electromagnetic switching device having multiple electrical contacts and energized by electrical current through its coil. It is used to complete electrical circuits.

relay center — A location where an incoming message is automatically directed to one or more outgoing circuits according to intelligence contained in the message. (Clarified by switching center.)

relay, tape — A method used, (using perforated tape as the intermediate storage), for relaying messages between the transmitting and receiving stations.

release-guard signal — *See* signal, release guard.

release read — A feature of some equipment which permits more computer processing time by releasing the read mechanism.

relevance ratio — An information retrieval term expressing the ratio of the number of pertinent documents retrieved by a particular query to the total number of documents retrieved by the query criteria, as contrasted with recall ratio.

reliability — 1. A measure of the ability to function without failure. 2. The amount of credence placed in the result. 3. A word to indicate a measurement trustworthiness and dependability, and frequently used to imply a reliability factor or coefficient.

reliability, channel — The percentage of time the channels meet the established abitrary standards.

reliability, circuit — The percentage of time the circuit meets arbitrary standards set by the user.

reliability data — *See* reliability.

reliability (of a transducer) — A measure of the probability that a transducer will continue to perform within specified limits of error for a specified length of time under specified conditions.

relocatability — A capability whereby programs or data may be located in a place in memory at different times without requiring modification to the program. In some units, segments of the program and all data are independently relocatable with no loss in efficiency.

relocatable — Pertaining to object programs that can reside in any part of system memory. The actual starting address is established at load time by adding a relocation offset to the starting address. Relocatable code is typically composed of position-independent code.

relocatable linking loader — The relocatable linking loader on some systems lets users combine multiple independent binary modules into an executable program. Capabilities include automatic library search, conditional load, comprehensive load map listings, and origin definition flexibility.

relocatable program — A special routine whose instructions are written in a special manner so that it can be located and executed in many areas of the memory. Some modification before execution may be involved to the instructions originally coded relative to a fixed starting place in the memory. Relocatable programs allow for the highly flexible real-time use of the main memory.

relocatable program loader — A program that assigns absolute origins to relocatable subroutines, object programs, and data, assigns absolute locations to each of the instructions or data, and modifies the reference to these instructions or data.

relocatable subroutine — A subroutine that can be located physically and independently in the memory—its object-time location is determined by the processor.

relocate — 1. To modify the instructions of a routine in such a way that the routine can be moved to another location and then executed at that location. 2. To modify the addresses relative to a fixed point or origin.

relocating object loader — A device that is used to load and link object programs produced by assemblers. Binary programs produced by the binary dump and link editor programs can also be loaded. This program satisfies external references between separate program segments, generates linkages to externals as required and maintains a common literal pool for usage by the completed program complex. When loading library subroutine packages, this program selectively loads only those segments required to satisfy external references.

relocation dictionary — Abbreviated RLD. A part of a program that contains information necessary to change addresses when it is relocated.

relocation, dynamic-memory — Frees programmer from keeping track of exactly where certain information is located in the system's memory. Another important attribute is its ability to keep programs flowing in and out of the memory in a highly efficient manner.

relocation, dynamic page — The segmentation of internal storage into blocks whose addressing is automatically controlled by a memory-protected set of addressable registers.

relocation, program — The execution of a program or location which is different than the location from which the program was originally assembled.

REM — Acronym for REcognition Memory. A simplified associative memory, designed to be easily interfaced with ordinary computers.

remark — Part of a statement providing an explanation of the use or function. This is contrasted to a comment which is a separate statement.

remedial maintenance — *See* maintenance, remedial.

remember — That instruction referring to nondestructive readout.

remote batch — *See* batch, remote.

remote batch access — *See* access, remote batch.

remote batch, off-line — An off-line remote batch or procedure that can involve the preparation of punched cards or magnetic tapes from source documents, then the transmission of data to produce duplicate punched cards or magnetic tapes at the computer site. In an on-line system, data is fed directly into the host computer through some form of communications adapter. There are several limitations to the hard-wired communication adapters associated with most large processors, and the trend is to replace them with communications preprocessors, sometimes called "smart front ends."

remote batch processing (remote job entry) — Abbreviated RJE. A process in which computer programs or data are entered into a remote terminal for transmission to the central processor. Jobs can be "batched" before transmission. Results of the processing may be transmitted back to the originating point.

remote command submission — The process or ability of a program or utility to transfer a batch command file to a remote system and cause it to be executed.

remote communications, microprocessor — Remote communications systems disseminate information to destinations outside the system. These destinations can be interfaced to a larger host computer. The communications link and message frequency determine the resources that should be dedicated. The communications function can be carried out either with a dedicated processor in the system or combined with the concentration or processing activities. Remote i/o considerations are (1) parallel or serial interface, (2) single or multiple ports, (3) synchronous or asynchronous, (4) baud rate, (5) communication link, (6) information block size, (7) simplex, half-duplex or duplex, (8) dedicated or common bus. The remote i/o interface can be treated like any other i/o interface, in terms of activity-rate calculations.

remote-computing system completeness errors — *See* errors, completeness (remote-computing system).

remote-computing system error detection — Those errors detected during the execution of the user's program. They include errors that are detectable only during program execution (e.g., invalid subscript value, reference to an undefined variable, arithmetic spills, etc.) along with those errors of completeness detected because either (1) they were disregarded by the user when previously detected or (2) they were not detected in the first place because the user did not indicate that his program was complete.

remote-computing system execution errors — *See* errors, execution (remote-computing system).

remote console — One of various terminal units in a remote computing system. Some of the distant consoles are available with each equipped with facilities to transmit and receive data to and from the central processor. Connection to the processor is normally made through a remote computing system exchange.

remote control — Any system of control performed from a distance. The control signal may be conveyed by intervening wires, sound (ultrasonics), light, or radio.

remote-control equipment — *See* equipment, remote-control.

remote control signals — Some microcomputers have signal lines for the RUN, HALT, and RESET functions as well as LOAD and POWER-ON. These signals permit the processor to be operated from a remote control panel located up to 50 feet or more from the processor. The function of each remote control signal is indicated. Examples are: Remote halt indicator, remote run indicator, remote power on, etc.

remote-control system, program mode — *See* program mode (remote-control system).

remote data stations — Remote data stations can be installed by any normal office environment without special cooling or electrical requirements. They can be linked as single remote units, or as multiple stations, to one or more computers, using conventional voice-grade telephone lines.

remote debugging — The use of remote terminals in a mode suitable for testing of programs, most frequently found in systems devoted to scientific or engineering computation.

remote device — An input/output unit, or other piece of equipment, which is removed from the computer center but connected by a communication line. In a typical on-line, real-time communications system, the remote device is usually a teletypwriter, an audio answer back device, or a crt visual display unit.

remote display, slave — A slave unit containing only the analog portion of the display. Turn-on may be accomplished independently, or by the master-display control.

remote display unit, visual — *See* display unit, remote (visual).

remote entry unit — *See* entry unit, remote.

remote file access (remote resource access) — The ability to read from, and write to, files located on a remote system. Some programs can also cause program commands to be executed at the remote system.

remote inquiry — *See* inquiry, remote.

remote inquiry (real time) — On-line inquiry stations permit users to interrogate the computer files and receive immediate answers to their inquiries. In industry, the stations can be located at dozens of remote locations such as office, factory, warehouse, and remote branch locations. Such a system permits all levels of industrial management to obtain immediate answers to questions about inventories, work-in-process, sales and other facts.

remote job entry — *See* entry, remote job.

remote job entry (RJE) processing — Processing of stacked jobs over communication lines via terminals typically equipped with line printers. Small computers also can operate as RJE stations if equipped with communications adapters.

remote job entry terminals — Remote job entry terminals are no longer one-function machines. Most terminal systems now are supported by microcomputer-based multitasking real-time disk operating systems. They not only support RJE functions but also bring on-line processing capability with high-level language support to the place where transactions and data originate. If mass data is added, users can store data and easily write application programs to access it.

remote message processing — The operating system can be used to process messages received from remote locations by way of communication lines and telecommunication equipment. Remote message processing is, in effect, an extension of the full power of the data processing and programming facilities of the computer to remote locations. A message received from a remote location may be in the nature of a request to the system for a particular service, and may or may not be accompanied by data. The requested service may be simply the routing of a message to another remote location or it may be the processing of a job or transaction similar to jobs and transactions that are received locally. By extending the services of the system, via communication lines, directly to the user, the turnaround or response time of the system is reduced from hours to seconds. Consequently, the system can directly participate in and control various commercial and scientific activities as they are being carried on. For example, the system may be used to centrally control a geographically dispersed banking activity. In such a system, master files containing account records for thousands of depositers are stored in direct-access storage. By entering pertinent data into the system, tellers at widely separated locations can check balances, update passbook records, and handle other similar transactions, all within a few seconds.

remote polling technique — *See* polling technique, remote.

remote processing — *Same as* remote message processing.

remote station — *See* station, remote.

remote subsets — Input and output devices located at points other than the central computer site. Information is indexed on the subset and transmitted by wire to the computer. When the information has been processed by the central-site computer, it is returned over the common-carrier lines to the subset that reproduces the final results at the remote location—all in seconds or minutes.

removable plugboard — *Same as* patchboard.

remove subroutine, first — *See* subroutine, first order.

repair time — That time which is devoted or used to diagnose, clear, or repair machines or systems, including fault location, detection, correction, and consequent tests. This is part of down time, including proving time after a repair is made; also if the case exists, repair delay time, machine spoiled work time, and scheduled engineering time.

repeatability — The closeness of agreement among a number of consecutive measurements of a constant signal, approached from the same direction. Repeatability is expressed as maximum nonrepeatability in percent of span or counts of error.

repeat counter — The repeat counter is used to control repeated operations such as block transfer and repeated search commands. To execute a repeated instruction "k" times, the repeat counter must be loaded with "k" prior to the execution of the instruction. A repeated sequence may be suspended to process an interrupt, with circuitry providing for the completion of the repeated sequence after the interrupt has been processed.

repeater — A device used to amplify and/or reshape signals.

repeater, regenerative — A repeater in which signals retransmitted are practically free from distortion.

repertory — The many sets of operations that can be represented in a given operation code.

repertory code — *Same as* code, instruction.

repertory, instruction — 1. The set of instructions that a computing or data-processing system is capable of performing. 2. The set of instructions that an automatic coding system assembles.

repetition instruction — An instruction that causes one or more instructions to be executed an indicated number of times.

repetitive addressing — *Same as* addressing, one ahead.

repetitive operation — Operations frequently used in computing, such that repeated solutions of the same set of equations with the same set of initial conditions and parameters are developed. In crt (cathode-ray tube) usage, a steady-state solution becomes apparent when displayed on the screen.

replacement — The substitution of various types of equipment for other units which perform the same or similar operations.

replacement, mechanical — The computer contracter substitutes another unit for customer's original machine. Such action usually is warranted by the poor mechanical condition of the original equipment.

replica reproduction — Facsimile copies of documents produced by copiers or photocopiers.

report delay — *See* delay.

report footing — The summary of the entire report, which most often appears at the termination and which is also known as final footing.

report generation — A technique for producing complete machine reports from information that describes the input file and the format and content of the output report.

report generator — A software program that can direct the production of output reports if the computer is provided with format and specifications, input file detail, sorted input data, inout/output procedure rules and other information.

report heading — Description of the report content which is produced, usually at the beginning of the report.

reporting, exception — A record of departures from the expected or norm. Often times, maximum or minimum limits are the set parameters and the normal range lies within these end numbers or expectations. Reports that have results which exceed these parameters become the basis for an exception reporting output.

reporting period — The length of time covered by a report.

report interval — The measure of the length of the time between the preparation of two issues of a corresponding report. The interval may be variable in length when events, rather than the passage of time, trigger the preparation of reports, as in inventory-control routines when "order points" are reached.

report program generator — The report program generator provides a convenient programming method for producing a wide variety of reports. The generator may range from a listing of a card deck or magnetic-tape reel to precisely arranged, calculated, and edited tabulation of data from several input sources.

report program generator language — Abbreviated RPG. A popular problem-oriented language for commercial programming, especially in smaller installations. Like COBOL, RPG has powerful and relatively simple input/output file manipulation (including table look-up), but is relatively limited in algorithmic capabilities.

report, progress — A current status report of a specific activity or group of activities in the form of a summary of results, i.e., of a run at a point, etc.

reports and feedback, factory — *See* feedback and reports (factory).

reports, difference — A report noting resulting changes from an original computer program and a program change.

representation — A combination of one or more characters to represent a unit.

representation, analog — A representation that does not have discrete values but is continuously variable.

representation, binary incremental — *See* binary incremental representation.

representation, calculating operation — *See* time, representative computing.

representation, deleted — *See* deleted representation.

representation, digital — *See* digital representation.

representation, number — Any system designed to represent the numbers with an agreed upon set of rules.

representation, positional — A number representation or number system in which the significance or value of each digit depends upon its place or position with respect to a radix point. (Related to number system).

representation system, numeration — *See* numeration system.

representation, variable point — *See* variable point representation.

reproducer, tape — A particular machine which is used to either copy or edit paper tape or to do both.

reproduction codes — Function codes in a master tape that are carried through the data operations and also appear in the produced tape. (Clarified by nonreproducing codes.)

reproduction replica — Facsimile copies of documents produced by copiers or photocopiers.

request control panel, operator — *See* control panel, operator's request.

request-repeat system — A system employing an error-detecting code and so arranged that a signal detected as being in error automatically initiates a request for retransmission of the signal that was detected as being in error.

request-send — *See* circuit send-request.

request words for input/output — Control words for input/output requests that are stored in the message reference block until the i/o is completed.

requirements, information — The actual or anticipated questions that may be requested of an information system.

rerun — 1. To repeat all or part of a program on a computer. 2. A repeat of a machine run, usually because of a connection, an interrupt, or a false start.

rerun point — 1. That stage of a computer run at which all information pertinent to the running of the routine is available either to the routine itself or to a rerun in order that a new run may be reconstituted. 2. One of a set of planned-for points in a program used so that if an error is detected between two such points, to rerun the problem it is only necessary to go back to the last rerun point. Rerun points are often three to five minutes apart, so that little time is required for a rerun. All information pertinent to a rerun is available in standby storage during the whole time from one rerun point to the next. 3. The initialization of a restart after the discovery of an error or computer stoppage.

rerun routine — A routine designed to be used after a computer malfunction or a coding or operating mistake to reconstitute a new routine from the last previous rerun point. (Synonymous with rollback routine.)

rescue dump — A rescue dump (R dump) is the recording on magnetic tape of the entire contents of the memory, which includes the status of the computer system at the time the dump is made. R dumps are made so that in the event of power failure, etc., a run can be resumed from the last rescue point (R point) rather than rerunning the entire program.

rescue points — For many applications it is very desirable, indeed essential, to create rescue points (R points) from which it is known that the program can be resumed in a proper manner. If a processing mishap does occur after creating a rescue point, the operator can restart his run at any rescue point by use of the restart routine. For long runs, the liberal use of rescue points will mean that the run is, in essence, segmented. A mishap will affect only one segment and all the valid processing that preceded the establishing of the latest point is saved and need not be reprocessed.

reserve — *Same as* allocate.

reserved words — The words which are set aside in COBOL language which cannot be used as data names, file names, or procedure names, and are of three types: connected, optional words, and key words.

reset — 1. To return a device to zero or to an initial or arbitrarily selected condition. 2. To restore a storage device to a prescribed initial state, not necessarily that denoting zeros. 3. To place a binary cell into the zero state.

reset cycle — The return of a cycle index to its initial or some preselected condition.

reset key, error — A push button that when pushed acknowledges an error and resets the error detection mechanism indicated by the check light. This is required to restart a program after an error has been discovered in batch mode.

reset mode — In analog computing, the integrators are inoperative and the required initial conditions are applied or reapplied, as contrasted to the operate mode when the input signals are connected to the computing units including integrators, for the generation of the solution.

reset procedure — An input is used to reset and start the MPU from a power down condition, resulting from a power failure or an initial start-up of the processor. If a positive edge is detected on the input, this will signal the MPU to begin the restart sequence. This will start execution of a routine to initialize the processor from its reset condition. All the higher order address lines will be forced high. For the restart, the last two locations in memory will be used to load the program that is addressed by the program counter. During the restart routine, the interrupt mask bit is set and must be reset before the MPU can be interrupted.

reset pulse — *See* pulse, reset.

reset rate — The number of corrections, per unit of time, made by the control system.

reset switch — The reset switch, when toggled, generates a master reset condition. The processor is halted, all internal registers are set to zero, the interrupt facility is disabled, the input-/output interface is initialized, and the program counter is set to a specific range. The reset switch also functions as an indicator test in that all indicators are illuminated when the reset switch is toggled.

reset-to-n — The procedure to set a device as a register, counter, etc., for storing or displaying a particular value, say n, by returning a counting device to its initial state, thus representing n, i.e., some number as it was predetermined or desired.

resident — Pertaining to programs that reside in the main memory of the system. Often it is convenient to have the editor, assembler, and various debuggers simultaneously resident.

resident assemblers — The development of programs that convert an uneducated microcomputer into a dedicated machine can be accomplished directly on the machine to be programmed or on other types of computers. A typical assembler "on board" the system is thus resident and translates the MPU mnemonic instructions into the specific language of the MPU in operation. Assemblers usually work along with editors which are software routines that permit programmers to use a computer to make whatever changes are required to create, correct, or revise a program.

resident compiler — Although many microprocessors require a cross-compiler —one that runs only on a larger machine—resident compilers that use the microcomputer itself to produce their programs are technically feasible with the advanced state of microcomputer development and inexpensive peripherals. Such a compiler requires several passes to reduce a source program to machine language, using the developmental system itself, and eliminating the need for large-system support.

resident, executive — The section of the supervisory program that is always located in core. The resident executive is a permanent resident of core.

resident macroassembler — A resident macroassembler translates symbolic assembly-language instructions into the appropriate machine-operation codes. In addition to eliminating the errors of hand-translation, the ability to refer to program addresses with symbolic names makes it easy for the user to modify programs by adding or deleting instructions. Full macro capability eliminates the need to rewrite similar sections of code repeatedly and greatly simplifies the problem of program documentation.

resident modules — The resident module keeps track of program execution status and which overlay modules are required. Nonmemory resident programs are often stored on disk. Thus, while monitoring system programs, memory could hold various other programs. When the system monitoring service is complete, if the overlays contain data tables or have alterations which must be preserved, the operator can store the overlays back on disk; this is called rollout. If the operator is going to compile some FORTRAN programs next, he rolls the FORTRAN compiler. If data transfers between disk and memory are fast enough, a user can look upon the disk as an extension of usable memory.

resident program — A program that is permanently located in storage. For example, the nucleus in main storage or a system library on direct access storage.

residual error — The difference between an optimum result derived from experience or experiment and a supposedly exact result derived from theory.

residue check — *Same as* check, modulo-N.

residue, modulo-N — *See* modulo-N check.

resistor, pull-down — A resistor connected across the output of a device or circuit to hold the output equal to or less than the zero input level of the following digital device. It also serves or is used to lower the output impedance of a device. It also refers to a resistor connected to a negative or to ground.

resistor, pull-up — A resistor connected to the positive supply voltage of a transistor circuit, as from the collector supply to the output collector.

resolution error — *See* error, resolution.

resolver — A small section of storage, particularly in drum, tape or disk storage units, that has much faster access than the remainder of the storage.

resource-sharing — The sharing of one central processor by several users and several peripheral devices. Principally used in connection with the sharing of time and memory.

resource-sharing control — The tying together of multiple computers in distributed processing systems whereby several computers work together sharing the work load.

response — The response of a device or system is an explicit quantitative expression of the output as a function of the input. The response characteristic, often presented graphically, gives the response as a function of some independent variable, such as frequency.

response time — The amount of time which elapses between generation of an inquiry at a terminal and the receipt of a response at the terminal. Response time would be: transmission time to the computer, processing time at the computer, access time to obtain any file records needed to answer the inquiry, and transmission time back to the terminal.

response unit, audio — *See* audio-response unit.

restart — 1. One of a set of preselected points located in a program such that if an error is detected between two points, the problem may be rerun by returning to the last such point instead of returning to the start of the problem. 2. To return to a previous point in a program and resume operation from that point.

restart checkpoint and procedures — *See* checkpoint and restart procedures.

restart point — *Same as* rerun point.

restart point (sorting) — *Same as* restart sorting.

restart routine — *Same as* rerun routine.

restart, sorting — The return to a previous point in the program where processing may begin. The previous point may be the beginning of the program or it may be a checkpoint.

restitution — A series of significant conditions resulting from decisions based on demodulated telegraph signals.

restore — 1. To return a variable address or other computer word to its initial or preselected value. 2. To return a register, trigger, error-condition signal, etc., to zero or to a specific initial condition.

restore pulse generator — *Same as* generator, clock pulse.

restorer, direct-current — A method of restoring the dc or low-frequency components to a transmitted signal.

restore, tape-skip — A function that permits certain portions of tape to be idled through a tape reader without being acted upon. This function is initiated by depressing the tape-skip key. Skipping continues until the reader finds a tape-skip restore character in the tape. This character must have been included in the original programming.

result, address — That address into which the results of an arithmetic process are transferred.

reticle, font — *See* font, reticle.

retrieval — 1. The recovery of research material. 2. The act of finding stored material.

retrieval, coordinate — *Same as* concept coordination.

retrieval data — *See* data retrieval.

retrieval, document — *See* document retrieval.

retrieval, fact — *See* fact retrieval.

retrieval, information — The recovering of desired information or data from a collection of documents or other graphic records.

retrieval, legal — A language developed at the University of Pittsburgh to retrieve legal information such as citations, references, specific literature, court decisions, and which has a rather elaborate indexing system. The service is offered to lawyers and provides assistance concerning Pennsylvania state laws. An expansion of this program into other areas appears imminent with more elaborate use of KWIC indexing programs.

retrievals, false — The library references that are not pertinent to, but are vaguely related to, the subject of the library search and are sometimes obtained by automatic search methods.

retrieval system, information — *See* information-retrieval system.

retrieve — To find and select specific information in the record of a file storage.

retrieving — Searching of storage to locate the data required, and selecting or removing the required data from storage.

retrofit — The adjusting of existing systems or programs for the purpose of fitting in or accommodating a new part and performing all other changes necessary in related systems or programs.

retrofit testing — Testing to assure system operation after replacing some equipment or programs.

return — 1. The mechanism providing for a return to a previous point in the usual sense. In particular, a set of instructions at the end of a subroutine that permits the system control to be returned to the proper point in the main routine. 2. To go back to a specific, planned point in a program, usually when an error is detected, for the purpose of rerunning the program. Rerun points are usually three to five minutes apart to avoid long periods of lost computer time. Information pertinent to a rerun is available in standby registers from point to point.

return, carriage — The operation that causes the next character to be printed at the left margin of printout.

return instructions — The specific group of instructions which are subroutined at the end of a program to provide for the transfer of control from the return subroutine to the main routine.

return point (sorting) — *Same as* restart, sorting.

return-to-zero (RZ) — A method of writing information on a magnetic surface in which the current through the write-head winding is returned to zero after the write pulse.

reverse capstan — A rotating shaft with minimal tolerances which controls the reverse or rewind movement of magnetic tape at uniform speed.

reverse channel — Specifically, a channel used for transmission of supervisory or error-control signals. The direction of flow of these signals is in the direction opposite to that in which information is being transferred. The bandwidth of this channel is usually less than that of the forward channel, i.e., the information channel.

reverse-code dictionary — An alphabetic or numeric-alphabet arrangement of codes associated with their corresponding English words or terms. (Related to dictionary code.)

reverse-direction flow — A flow in a direction other than left to right or top to bottom.

reverse Polish notation — Abbreviated RPN. A type of logic in calculators that allows the user to enter every problem from left to right exactly as it is written. There is no need to worry about operational hierarchy, as the logic system handles it all automatically. This type of logic is distinguishable because the electronic calculator has no equals key. It has an enter key instead.

reverse, read — The unit can read tape in either direction under program control.

reverser sign — *See* sign changer.

reverse solenoid — That electrical-mechanical device which provides pressure via a roller to force magnetic tape against the reverse capstan and move the tape in a reverse direction.

reverse video — This function shows dark characters on a background of light screen area. The effect is useful for situations where information is being entered on a fill-in-the-blanks basis. Reverse video can also be used when material is being edited, to show which characters are being inserted or deleted, and for special comments and warnings to the operator.

reversible, counter — *See* counter reversible.

review, preliminary-proposal — An on-site review to provide guidance to proponent agencies in the preparation of ADP system proposals.

review, readiness — An on-site examination of the adequacy of preparations for the effective utilization of a new computer installation, and to indicate any necessary corrective actions.

revolver — *Same as* loop, high speed.

revolver track — *Same as* loop, high speed.

rewind — The process of returning a film or magnetic tape to its initial data point.

rewind time — The measurement of elapsed time required to transfer tape to the supply reel.

rewind time (sorting) — Elapsed time consumed by a sort/merge program for restoring intermediate and final tape files to original position.

rewrite — The process of restoring the information in the storage device to its prior-to-reading state.

rewrite dual gap head — A character written on tape is immediately read by a read head so that the accuracy of recorded data might be ensured.

RF — Abbreviation for Report Footing.

RH — Abbreviation for Report Heading.

right hand justified — *See* justified, right hand.

right justified — Data are right justified when the right-hand digit or character occupies its allotted right-hand position.

right justify — *See* justify, right.

right shift instruction — Specifically, an operation that shifts the contents of all bit positions in a register to the right. The least significant bit value is shifted out of the register. The MSB portion is typically set to a value of zero.

rigid disk — Disk storage wherein the medium is a magnetic alloy mounted on a thick metallic substrate. Rigid disks may take the form of "nonremovable" disks, which have the medium in a sealed container, and "disk packs" or "disk cartridges" wherein the medium may be removed from the drive mechanism. Rigid disks have a capacity range from 5 to greater than 200 Mb.

ring counter — A loop of interconnected bistable elements such that one and only one is in a specified state at any given time and such that, as input signals are counted, the position of the element in the specified state moves in an ordered sequence around the loop.

ring network — A network topology in which computers are connected in a circular configuration.

ring network node — In a "ring" network, each computer node controls its own function and all are equal—there is no dependence on a single machine. Each has similar hardware and software. Usually, each computer can communicate with every other one, and may have access to their files. Each node can back up any of the others.

ring network structure — Many organizations design their computer networks in the form of loop or ring structures. With this arrangement, many of the remote stations (terminals or computers) connected to the ring do not communicate with the main-site or host processor individually. Instead, the data to be transmitted is looped around the stations. The loop or ring structure is economical when several remote stations and host processors are located near each other. When remote stations are geographically dispersed over long distances, line costs would be very expensive if a loop structure were used. In such cases, it would be more economical to use a distributed-type structure.

ring shift — *See* shift, circular.

ripple-through carry — *Same as* carry, high speed.

rise time — The time required for the leading edge of a pulse to rise from one-tenth of its final value to nine-tenths of its final value. Rise time is proportional to the time constant of the circuit.

RJE — Abbreviation for Remote Job Entry.

RLD — Abbreviation for Relocation Dictionary. *See* dictionary, relocation.

RMW — Abbreviation for the Read-Modify-Write cycle in a RAM.

robot — A device equipped with sensing instruments for detecting input signals or environmental conditions but with a reacting or guidance mechanism, which can perform sensing, calculations, etc., and with stored programs for resultant actions, i.e., a machine running itself.

robot capability — Properly programmed, the robot can solve problems in the two general areas of visual inspection and identity and attitude analysis. Available routines have the capability to extract the 2-dimensional outline of the image of an object, locate corners, find holes and separate multiple objects, identify an object on the basis of its distinguishing features, specify the grip points, acquisition and orientation of a workpiece. In one set of laboratory experiments the developmental system has identified each of four different foundry castings and determined their position and orientation so that its manipulator can pick them up off a conveyor belt.

role indicator — A code assigned to an individual word, indicating the nature or particular function that this specific word is to play in any textual occurrence.

rollback — A system that will restart the running program after a system failure. Snapshots of data and programs are stored at periodic intervals and the system rolls back to restart at the last recorded snapshot.

rollback routine — *Same as* rerun routine.

rollover — The action of depressing two or more keys simultaneously. A quality keyboard controller will include debouncing and multiple-key rollover protection.

ROM — Acronym for read-only memory. A blank ROM can be considered to be a mosaic of undifferentiated cells. Many types of ROMs exist. A basic type of ROM is one programmed by a mask pattern as part of the final manufacturing stage. PROMs are "programmable" ROMs. ROMs are relatively permanent although they can be erased with the aid of an ultraviolet irradiation instrument. Others can be electrically erased and are called EPROMs. Information is stored permanently or semipermanently and is read out, but not altered in operation.

ROM bipolar technologies — Bipolar devices offer higher speeds than MOS devices. For very high volume usage with those devices whose data patterns never change, mask programmable read-only memories, commonly called ROMs, provide the lowest cost. Electrically programmable read-only memories or PROMs allow the data pattern to be defined when the device is used rather than when the device is manufactured.

ROM bootstrap — Nearly every computer uses at least one ROM program, the most common one being a ROM bootstrap loader. The bootstrap loader is a minimum program which, if everything in memory has been wiped out, will allow the programmer to recreate his main memory load.

ROM bus interface (TTL) — A ROM bus interface can demonstrate a simplicity of interface with many systems. In many cases, all microbus components operate at the same TTL levels and with the same drive capability, data, address, and control lines can be connected without buffers. Timing of the memories can be set to permit simple operation at full speed with the processor. The chip selects of the same buses have been used to partially decode the system address lines. In small- and medium-sized systems, this partial address decoding will be sufficient to distinguish all packages in the system without using any additional address decoding packages.

ROM controlled terminals — Some terminal MPUs control internal peripherals by means of instructions stored in the read-only memory (ROM). Such operations as accessing of a peripheral device for data, keeping track of sales for inventory control, and performing tax computation are possible. In essence, the MPU can provide the usual cash register functions plus additional retail system management capability. For example, the data communications channel permits remote interrogation to obtain the terminal's current sales.

ROM custom changes — Special-purpose adaptations can be made of the device by changing a few program words. Just about every system designer is faced with the selection of devices which would be perfect if only this or that feature were present in the basic structure. Microprogrammed devices are inherently open-ended and features can be easily added to adapt the device to the environment. For example, some manufacturers of microprogrammed systems offer the customer special options to make the system operate in a communications environment. In this way, the system can be tailored to specific environment.

ROM functions — ROM is used to store the microprogram or a fixed program depending upon the microprogrammability of the CPU. The microprogram provides the translation from higher-level user commands, such as ADD, MPY, etc. down to a series of detailed codes recognizable by the microprocessor for execution. The size of the ROM varies according to user requirements within the maximum allowed capacity dictated by the addressing capability of the microprocessor.

ROM, instruction words — ROM portions of memory are often used to store instructions, although in some situations the RAM is also used. Instructions residing in ROM are hardwired and once entered cannot be changed without cost and difficulty. The instructions are in the form of a string of binary (1 and 0) bits called words. The length of the words is 4, 8, or 16 bits as required by the design of the microprocessor. When decoded, the words spell out the procedure for the processor to use in carrying out the instruction.

ROM microprogramming — By microprogramming a ROM on the microprocessor chip, a logic designer can implement in one package, together with some ancillary memory, a function that often took 50 or more TTL packages. Designs can be changed by a simple software program—and reprogrammable ROMs can be used to change systems in the field. In effect, design engineers must soon become programmers to discard many tedious but formerly essential logic optimization techniques.

ROM module board — A provision for ROM replacement of up to 48K or more bytes of main memory for applications requiring program security or other special purposes.

root segment — The master or controlling segment of an overlay structure which always resides in main memory. Usually this is the first segment within the program, and it is always the first to be loaded at program initiation time.

rope storage — *Same as* storage, core rope.

ROPP — Abbreviation for Receive Only Page Printer. A teleprinter unit with printer only for stations which do not generate messages.

RO (Receive Only) — A receive-only printer.

rotate — A specific instruction that results in pushing the contents of a register or word by one position to the left or the right. The bit coming in is often the one "falling off" the other end. Sometimes it is the old value of the carry bit.

round — To adjust the least significant digits retained in truncation to partially reflect the dropped portion; e.g., when rounded to the digits, the decimal number 2.7561 becomes 2.76.

rounding error — The error resulting when dropping certain less significant digits and some adjustment is applied to the more significant retained. Also called round-off error. A common round-off rule is to take the quantity to the nearest digit.

round-off error — The error resulting from rounding off a quantity by deleting the less significant digits and applying some rule of correction to the part retained; e.g., 0.2751 can be rounded to 0.275 with a rounding error of .0001. (Contrasted with error truncation.)

route — 1. The route followed, or to be followed, for the transmission of a telegram or the establishment of a connection. 2. The means of transmission (wire, cable radio) used, or to be used, for the transmission of a telegram or the establishment of a connection.

routine — 1. A sequence of machine instructions that carry out a well-defined function. 2. A set of coded instructions arranged in proper sequence to direct the computer to perform a desired operation or series of operations.

routine, algorithmic — *See* algorithmic routine.

routine, alternate — Assignment of a secondary communications path to a destination if the primary path is unavailable.

routine, assembly — *See* assembly routine.

routine, automatic — A routine that is executed independently of manual operations, but only if certain conditions occur within a program or record, or during some other process.

routine, auxiliary — A routine designed to assist in the operation of the computer and in debugging other routines.

routine, check — A check system built into the program or computers that do not have automatic checking. This check system is normally concerned with programs run on computers that are not internally self-checking. (Related to automatic check.)

routine, checkpoint — *See* checkpoint routine.

routine, closed — A routine that is not inserted as a block of instructions within a main routine, but is entered by basic linkage from the main routine.

routine, compile — A computer instruction that is also called a compile, compiler, compiling routine, and a compilation. An executive routine that, before the desired computation is started, translates a program expressed in pseudocode into machine code (or into another pseudocode for further translation by an interpreter). In accomplishing the translation, the compiler may be required to adapt or to specialize the instructions.

routine, complete — A routine that does not require modification before it is used. Such routines are usually in company or manufacturer libraries.

routine, condensing — A routine used to convert the machine language, i.e., the one-instruction per card output format, from an assembly program or system into several instructions per card.

routine, control — *Same as* executive routine.

routine, conversion — A flexible and generalized program which can be used by a programmer to change the presentation of data from one form to another, such as changing from card to disk.

routine, correction — A routine which is designed to be used in or after a computer failure or malfunction or a program or operator error and which thereby reconstitutes the routine being executed before the error or malfunction and from the most recent or closest rerun point.

routine, dating — A routine that computes and/or stores, where needed, a date such as current date, expiration date of a tape, etc.

routine, debugging-aid — A routine to aid programmers in the debugging of their routines. Some typical routines are: storage, printout, tape printout, and drum printout.

routine, diagnostic — 1. A routine used to locate a malfunction in a computer, or to aid in locating the mistakes in a computer program. Thus, in general any routine specifically designed to aid in debugging or troubleshooting. (Synonymous with malfunction routine, and related to debugging.) 2. A specific routine designed to locate either a malfunction in the computer or a mistake in coding.

routine, direct-insert — *Same as* subroutine, direct insert.

routine, dynamic — *Same as* subroutine, dynamic.

routine, editor — *Same as* program, editor.

routine, error — *See* error routine.

routine, error-correction — A series of computer instructions programmed to correct a detected error.

routine, error-detection — A routine used

to detect whether or not an error has occurred, usually without a special provision to find or indicate its location.

routine, executive — *See* executive routine.

routine, executive system — *See* executive system routine.

routine, file-organization — A specifically designed routine for reading input-data files, and sorting them in random-access locations.

routine, fixed — A routine which cannot be modified during its computer execution.

routine, floating-point — A set of coded instructions arranged in proper sequence to direct the computer to perform a specific set of operations that will permit floating-point operation; e.g., enable the use of a fixed-point machine to handle information on a floating-point basis from an external point of view. Floating-point routines are usually used in computers that do not have built-in floating-point circuitry, in which case floating-point operation must be programmed.

routine, general — A routine expressed in computer coding designed to solve a class of problems specializing to a specific problem when appropriate parametric values are supplied.

routine, generating — A compiling routine that is capable of handling less fully defined situations.

routine, generator — *See* generator routine.

routine, heuristic — A routine by which the computer attacks a problem not by a direct algorithmic procedure, but by a trial and error approach frequently involving the act of learning. (Synonymous with heuristic program.)

routine, housekeeping — The initial instructions in a program that are executed only one time, e.g., clear storage.

routine, incomplete — A routine in a library programming system that requires parameters to be supplied by a macrostatement or main routine.

routine, initializer — The functions such as error checking performed on a message after it is entered into a system, but before the application program begins processing.

routine, input — *See* input routine.

routine, intepreter — An executive routine which translates a stored machinelike pseudocode into a machine code and performs the operations indicated by subroutines during computation.

routine, interpretive — 1. An interpretive routine is essentially a closed subroutine that operates successively on an indefinitely long sequence of program parameters. It may usually be entered as a closed subroutine and executed by a pseudocoded exit instruction. 2. A routine that decodes and immediately executes instructions written as pseudocodes. This is contrasted with a compiler that decodes the pseudocodes into a machine-language routine to be executed at a later time. The essential characteristic of an interpretive routine is that a particular pseudocode operation must be decoded each time it is executed. (Synonymous with interpretive code.)

routine, interrupt — A program that performs interrupt action to coordinate the timing i/o with processing.

routine, interrupt control — A computer routine entered when an interrupt occurs (for analysis of the interrupt cause).

routine interrupt (tape driver) — *See* tape driver interrupt routine.

routine, library — *See* library, routine.

routine, loading — That set of instructions which brings other data and instructions into storage and which is frequently built into various computer models.

routine maintenance time — *Same as* maintenance routine.

routine, malfunction — A routine used to locate a malfunction in a computer, or to aid in locating mistakes in a computer program. In general, any routine specifically designed to aid in debugging or troubleshooting. (Related to debugging.)

routine, minimum-access — A routine so coded that by judicious arrangement of data and instructions in storage, the actual access time is less than the expected random-access time. Such a routine is used with serial storage systems. (Synonymous with minimum-latency routine.)

routine, minimum-latency — *See* routine, minimum-access.

routine, monitor — *Same as* executive routine.

routine, object — The program that is the output of an automatic coding system.

Often the object program is a machine-language program ready for execution, but it may well be in an intermediate language. (Synonymous with target program, and contrasted with source program.)

routine, open — A routine that can be inserted directly into a larger routine without a linkage or calling sequence.

routine, output — *See* output routine.

routine, patch — A specific correcting routine written of a sequence on the program chart and referring to a correct sequence.

routine, post mortem — 1. A routine that either automatically or on demand prints data concerning contents of registers and storage locations, after the routine stops, in order to assist in locating errors or mistakes in coding. 2. A service routine useful in analyzing the cause of a failure, such as a routine that dumps out the content of a store after a failure. (Related to post mortem.)

routine, priority — *See* priority routine.

routine, production — *See* production routines.

routine program — The procedure for inserting instructions and the constant values of the program into the computer.

routine, program loading — The procedure for inserting instructions and the constant values of the program into the computer.

routine, recovery — *See* recovery routine.

routine, relocatable — A specific routine designed and stored such that it may be moved quickly and conveniently to other locations.

routine, rerun — A routine designed to be used in the wake of a computer malfunction or a coding or operating mistake to reconstitute a routine from the last previous rerun point. (Synonymous with rollback routine.)

routine, restart — *Same as* routine rerun.

routine, rollback — *Same as* routine rerun.

routine, selective tracing — A tracing routine designed to permit only specific instructions to be selected and evaluated, i.e., as i/o instructions.

routine, service — A broad class of routines that are standardized at a particular installation for the purpose of assisting in maintenance and operation of the computer as well as the preparation of programs, as opposed to routines for the actual solution of production problems. This class includes monitoring or supervisory routines, assemblers, compilers, diagnostics for computer malfunctions, simulation of peripheral equipment, general diagnostics and input data. The distinguishing quality of service routines is that they are generally standardized so as to meet the servicing needs at a particular installation, independent of any specific production-type routine requiring such services.

routines, input/output random-access — *See* random access i/o routines.

routine source — *Same as* program source.

routine, specific — A routine expressed in computer coding designed to solve a particular mathematical, logical, or data-handling problem in which each address refers to explicitly stated registers and locations.

routine, static — A subroutine that involves no parameters other than the addresses of the operands.

routine, storage — 1. A part of storage allocated to receive and store the group of instructions to be executed. 2. The storage locations used to store the program.

routine, stored — *Same as* program, stored.

routine, supervisory — *See* executive routine.

routine, target — *Same as* object program.

routine, test — A routine designed to show whether a computer is functioning properly or not.

routine, trace — A routine used to observe how the object program operates while it is being executed.

routine, tracing — A diagnostic routine used to provide a time history of one or more machine registers and controls during the execution of the object routine. A complete tracing routine would reveal the status of all registers and locations affected by each instruction each time the instruction is executed. Since such a trace is prohibitive in machine time, traces which provide information only following the execution of certain types of instructions are more frequently used. Furthermore, a tracing routine may be under control of the processor, or may be called in by means of a trapping feature. (Related to trap.)

routine, translating — *Same as* translator.

routine, utility — Subroutines for handling

machine operations necessary to data processing but not contributing directly to the required output; such routines might be copying, loading and organizing disks, printing, etc. (Synonymous with utility program.)

routine, working — That routine which produces the results of the problem or program as it was designed, as contrasted with the routines which are designed for support, housekeeping, or to compile, assemble, translate, etc.

routing — The assignment of a communications path for the delivery of a message.

routing, alternate — Assignment of a secondary communications path to a destination if the primary path is unavailable.

routing indicator — An address, or group of characters, in the message header that defines the final circuit or terminal.

routing, message — The function performed at a central message processor of selecting the route, or alternate route if required, for delivery of a message.

row scanning — A technique that is used in decoding which key of a keyboard was pressed. Each row is scanned in turn by outputting a "1." The output on the columns is examined, resulting in identification of the key.

RPG, disk — On some systems, this is a simplified, problem-oriented programming language that provides the user with the facilities for assimilating data, producing printed reports, and creating, updating and maintaining files. It often consists of a programming language and a compiler program.

R register — *See* register, R.

RS-232 interface — The interface between a modem and the associated data terminal equipment, and standardized by EIA Standard RS232. For voice-band modems the interface leads are single leads with a common ground return.

RS-422 standard — There is a standard for interfacing serial data transmission between peripherals, systems, and modems. The Electronic Industries Association (EIA) of America has, by consent of various manufacturers and users, standardized a 25-pin connection with appropriate signal levels called the RS-232 interface. There is also a new EIA standard that has been introduced, called the RS-422 standard, that is more suitable to TTL.

RTE — Abbreviation for Real-Time Executive. A software system that provides a multiprogramming, foreground-background system, with priority scheduling, interrupt handling, and program load-and-go capabilities.

rubber banding — In interactive graphics, rubber banding refers to attaching constraints to the beginning and end points of a line.

rules, decision — The programmed criteria which an on-line, real-time system uses to make operating decisions. It is important to periodically review the decision rules which are being used by a system because the nature of the problems to be solved changes over time and because new situations may have arisen which were not at first anticipated.

rules, inhibition — *See* inhibition rules.

rules, priority — *See* priority rules.

rules, syntax — The rules governing sentence structure in a language or statement structure in a language, such as that of a compiler program.

run — 1. The act of processing a batch of transactions while under the control of one or more programs, and against all the files that are affected to produce the required output. 2. One performance of a program on a computer. 3. Performance of one routine, or several routines automatically linked so that they form an operating unit, during which manual manipulations are not required of the computer operator.

run book — All materials needed to document a computer application, including problem statement, flowcharts, coding, and operating instructions.

run chart — A flowchart of one or more computer runs in terms of input and output.

run diagram — A graphic representation of the files, transactions, information, and data that are to be handled together under the program control to produce the newly updated files, list of changes, or specific reports.

run duration — On the occasion on which, after compiling, the target program is run during the run phase or target phase, the duration or the run is called the run duration, and the compiling is called the compiling duration.

run, history — The printing out of all transactions of a process for reading or recording purposes.

run, location — A routine which locates the correct run on a program tape, whether initiated by another routine or manually.

run, machine — The execution of one or several machine routines that are linked to form one operating unit.

run mode — A mode in which the computer is considered to be operating when it is automatically executing instructions contained in its memory cards and cells.

running accumulator — *Same as* storage, push-down.

running dry — The examination of the logic and coding of a program from a flowchart and written instructions, and recording of the results of each step of the operation before running the program on the computer.

running mode, time sharing — *See* time sharing, running mode.

running, parallel — 1. A test run in which a newly developed program is processed along with the current program in the computer. 2. The final step in the debugging of a system; this step follows a system test.

run phase — An occasion on which the target program (after compiling) is run is often called the run phase or the target phase or the object phase.

run schedule — A specific listing of work to be performed under time required to perform such work.

runs, housekeeping — The activities of sorting, editing, or merging runs needed for the file maintenance—the nonproduction runs. In a special sense, the set-up and clean-up parts of programs in contrast to actual production processing.

runs, program — A run is the same as a program except that a program refers to the writing or coding of the job, whereas the run refers to the actual running of the program. Consequently, programs and runs are synonymous except to denote the time and action being performed.

run, test — A diagnostic run of the program, using manufactured data. The results of this run are checked against the correct answers for this problem.

run time — The time required to complete a single, continuous execution of an object program.

run, trial — The procedure for using equipment with a sample card deck or part of data which is used on the actual run designed to promote the check for accuracy of methods.

RWD — A shortened program term of designated added instruction to rewind a reel of tape.

R/W (read/write) head — A small electromagnet used for reading, recording, or erasing polarized spots on a magnetic surface. Also called magnetic head, read head, and write head.

S

salesman's portable computer terminal — A portable computer terminal that can be taken into homes or offices and used to communicate directly with host computers. Usually, it couples acoustically through a standard telephone receiver.

sample-and-hold amplifier — Sample-and-hold amplifiers are used to capture and store analog signals. They are particularly useful in conjunction with successive approximation analog-to-digital converters in digitizing time-varying input signals. If the input to a successive approximation A/D varies more than 2 or 3 LSBs during the conversion period, large errors in the digital output may result. A sample-and-hold amplifier in front of the A/D, commanded to the hold mode just prior to the beginning of the A/D conversion, will store the analog value present when the hold command was received during the conversion period of the A/D. This will ensure that the digital value generated by the A/D is an accurate representation of the analog input.

sampling — 1. Obtaining a value of a variable at regular or intermittent intervals. 2. A procedure of systems analysis in which traffic volumes, file activity, and other transfers are estimated on the basis of representative samples taken. 3. A method of communication line control in which messages on a circuit are sampled by a computer that selects only those for which computer processing is required. 4. A random method of checking and control in which a transaction or item is selected and the processing that it undergoes is checked in detail. This provides an indication of accurate and complete processing.

sampling, analog — The process by which the computer selects individual hybrid input signals from the process, converts them to an equivalent binary form, and stores the data in memory.

sampling rate — The rate at which measurements of physical quantities are made, e.g., if it is desired to calculate the velocity of a missile and its position is measured each millisecond, then the sampling rate is 1000 measurements per second.

Satellite ACS — Abbreviation for Satellite Advanced Communications Service. An AT&T service that provides the necessary code conversion, protocol translation, and speed matching to allow otherwise incompatible terminals and computers to communicate freely with each other. ACS supports a variety of stand-alone and clustered, synchronous and asynchronous terminals using code sets such as ASCII and EBEDIC, and operating at speeds from 110 to 9600 bps in character or block mode with polled or contention line control.

satellite computer — A processor connected locally or remotely to a larger central processor, and performing certain processing tasks—sometimes independent of the central processor, sometimes subordinate to the central processor.

satellite computer compatibility — Some satellite computers connected to the host may utilize a special compatibility module that allows programs to execute in satellite computers under a simulated node environment. This type of module converts all necessary monitor calls issued by a satellite program into compatible communication calls and sends them to the host computer which actually performs the indicated operations.

satellite computer network — A configuration in which a group of satellite computers are tied to a larger central computer through asynchronous or synchronous communications links. This configuration can be used to support large systems, because each remote computer has some data processing capability of its own.

satellite processor — The usually small processor designed especially and primarily for card-to-tape conversion, printing of tape contents, and other selected high-volume operations; frequently used to support and add to the capacity of a large processor to further increase its productivity.

satellite XTEN network — A service by Xerox in which leased satellite capacity, radio links, and communications processing are used to provide switched 256-kbps digital transmission service between user premises. Typically, a user's message moves from his terminal through Xerox-supplied equipment interfaces on his premises and to transceivers linked to a rooftop antenna. From there, the message is beamed to a substation or city station and then to an earth station for transmission to a satellite. At the user's option, documents, messages, and data can be transmitted to a network control center, where they may be recorded for subsequent retrieval.

saturating integrator — *Same as* integrator, incremental.

saturation testing — The testing of a program by pushing through a great many messages in an attempt to find errors.

SBC — Abbreviation for Single Board Computer.

scalar product — The product of two vector quantities when the result is a scalar quantity, e.g., work = force × displacement. Known as the inner product and denoted algebraically by a dot between the vectors (or by a round bracket enclosing them). Its magnitude is given by the product of the amplitudes and the cosine of the angle between them, i.e., $A \cdot B = AB \cos \theta$.

scalar quantity — A specific quantity which has magnitude but not direction, i.e., the magnitude of a vector quantity, as contrasted to vector cells of multiple values. Scalars are single, such as volume, size, temperature, etc., while vector quantities, such as wind velocity, have both magnitude and direction.

scale — 1. A rulerlike drawing placed on the graph to aid in the determination of values within the plotting grid. 2. A range of values frequently dictated by the computer word length or routine at hand. 3. To alter the units in which the variables are expressed, in order to bring all quantities within a given range.

scale, binary — *See* binary scale (or numbering system).

scale coefficient — *Same as* scale factor.

scale factor — 1. A number used as a multiplier or divisor that is chosen because it will cause a set of quantities occurring in a problem to fall within an acceptable range of values. 2. The coefficient necessary to convert a scale or instrument reading to the value of a quantity being measured.

scale factor, time — *Same as* time scale.

scale, label — Numerical labels placed next to the scale to indicate the value of the scale at that point.

scale operation — *See* operation, scale.

scaler — A specific unit with an output variable which equals the input variable multiplied by some constant.

scale radix — *Same as* radix notation.

scale, time — *See* time scale.

scale, variable time — *See* time scale.

scaling — 1. The conversion of a standard signal into the corresponding engineering units. 2. Use of a factor to multiply the results obtained in a problem so that the results will be within a range that can be expressed by the machine.

scan — 1. To examine stored information for a specific purpose as for content or for arrangement. 2. To examine the status of communication lines or other input/output channels to determine whether data is being received or transmitted.

scan, divided slit — A device, in optical character recognition (OCR), which scans an input character at given intervals to obtain its horizontal and vertical components. This scanning device consists of a narrow column of photoelectric cells.

scan, forward — An editing operation which makes an output word conform to the control word by comparing positions from right to left and adding punctuation, such as decimals and dollar signs.

scan, mark — To mark scan is to read a document for a specific mark in a particular location. The mark may be made by a pen or pencil, since the operation is usually based on optical scanning and light reflectance. Mark scanning differs from mark sensing because mark sensing requires an electrographic pencil with conductive ink.

scan, MICR — *See* MICR scan.

scanner — 1. An instrument which automatically samples or interrogates the state of various processes, files, conditions, or physical states and initiates action in accordance with the information obtained. 2. A photoelectric control light source and/or photoreceiver.

scanner, analog input — A device which will, upon command, connect a specified sensor to measuring equipment and cause the generation of a digit count value which can be read by the computer.

scanner, bar-code — An optical scanning unit that can read documents encoded in a special bar code.

scanner, flying-spot — An optical character reading device which uses a moving spot of light to scan a sample space or area by applying a photoelectric transducer to sense the intensity of the transmitted or reflected light, which varies in accordance with the data being sent, i.e., differing reflectances and intensities.

scanner, interrupt — External devices are continuously scanned for interrupt requests. A scanner in the computer counts through the nonpriority external device addresses sequentially, each time asking if the addressed device is requesting an interrupt. When an interrupt request is found, the scanner will stop at that address and attempt to interrupt the computer program.

scanner, magnetic ink — A machine which reads numbers designed in a special type font and printed in a magnetic (iron oxide) ink.

scanner, optical — A special optics device that scans patterns of incident light and generates digital signals that are functions of the incident light synchronized with the scan, the primary purpose being to generate or "read" digital representations of printed or written data.

scanner types — Typically, the function of a scanner is conversion of a printed character into electrical signals for analysis by the recognition unit. The most common scanner types are mechanical disk, flying spot scanner, laser scanner, parallel photocells, and the vidicon scanner.

scanner, visual — A device that scans optically and usually generates an analog or digital signal.

scanner, voice-output — A device in which an electronic camera scans printed text, feeding signals into a minicomputer which produces speech sounds. Thousands of components go into one machine, making it an extremely complicated consumer device.

scanning — The action of comparing input variables to determine a particular action.

scanning limits — The action of comparing input variables against either prestored or calculated high and/or low limits to determine if an alarm condition is present.

scanning loop, central — *See* loop, central scanning.

scanning machine — A machine which automatically reads printed data and converts it into machine language. There are two basic types—optical scanners and magnetic-ink scanners.

scanning, optical — A technique for machine recognition of characters.

scanning rate (or speed) — The speed at which a computer can select, convert, and compare an analog input variable to its high and/or low limits.

scan period — The time during which the screen is swept by the electron beam in electrostatic storage tubes for the sole purpose of regenerating or restoring the charge distribution which represents the stored data.

scan rate — The rate at which a control computer periodically checks a controlled quantity.

scan, reverse — The specific editing operation which supresses zeros, i.e., replaces zeros with blanks, and thus eliminates the zeros, and the zero suppression word mark.

scan, slit-divided — A device, in optical character recognition (OCR), which scans an input character at given intervals to obtain its horizontal and vertical components. This scanning device consists of a narrow column of photoelectric cells.

scatter gap — The alignment deviation (of magnetic recording head gaps) for groups of heads for several racks of a magnetic tape handler.

scatter loading — A procedure or process of loading a program into main memory such that each section or segment of the program occupies a single, connected memory area (in some systems a "page") but the several sections of the program need not be adjacent to each other. Usually implemented by a virtual memory structure.

scheduled down time — The determined or required idle time necessary for normal servicing of computer equipment during which such equipment is unavailable for operations. This is usually expressed as a percent of total available time. It is also known as preventive maintenance time.

scheduled engineering time — *See* time, scheduled engineering.

scheduled maintenance time — *See* time, scheduled maintenance.

scheduled operation — The periods of time during which the user plans to use specified equipment. Hours rescheduled as a result of equipment failure usually are not considered as scheduled hours of operation in computing equipment effectiveness.

schedule job — A control program that is used to examine the input work queue and to select the next job to be processed.

schedule maintenance (executive) — The acceptance of job requests from an external medium and the inclusion of these requests in a job request schedule. The executive will reference the job request schedule to determine the next job to be initiated. Previously submitted requests may be deleted.

scheduler — A special system of the executive software section. The scheduler controls the time when the execution of the program will be performed.

scheduler, job — The control program function that controls input job streams and system output, obtains input/output resources for jobs and job steps, attaches tasks corresponding to job steps, and otherwise regulates the use of the computing system by jobs.

scheduler, master — The control scheduler that permits the function of a control program that allows an operator to initiate special actions or to cause requested information to be delivered that can override the normal control functions of the system.

scheduler, program — The scheduler is called at regular intervals to decide which program in memory is to be run. A running program is temporarily terminated each time its alloted time has run out, or when it requires input/utput operations with a device that is busy. A program may be terminated temporarily by user intervention to the scheduler, or it may suspend its own operation. Temporary termination does not remove the program from memory. A program may be dumped and permanently discontinued by calling the scheduler and allocator.

schedule, rung — A specific listing of work to be performed under time required to perform such work.

scheduler, work process — Schedules the operating time of the overall electronic data processing activity in order to ensure that the data-processing equipment is effectively and efficiently utilized.

scheduling algorithm — A set of rules that is included in the scheduling routine of the executive program. The scheduling algorithm determines the length of a user's quantum and the frequency with which this quantum is repeated.

scheduling, dynamic — Scheduling that changes with the different demands that are made on the system rather than being fixed as in conventional applications.

scheduling rules, time sharing — *See* time sharing, scheduling rules.

schema — The description of the logical structure and content of a data base.

scheme, randomizing — *See* randomizing scheme.

schemes, interrupt (time sharing) — *See* time sharing, interrupt schemes.

Schottky bipolar microcomputer set — Various families of Schottky bipolar LSI circuits are microprogrammed in the sense that their control logic is organized around a separate read-only memory called the microprogram memory. Control signals for the various processing elements are generated by the microinstructions contained in the microprogram memory. In the implementation of a typical central processor, the microprogram interprets a higher level of instructions called macroinstructions, similar to those found in a small computer. For device controllers, the microprograms directly implement the required control functions.

Schottky diode — A special diode characterized by nanosecond switching speed, but relatively low voltage (45 volts maximum) and limited temperature range (125–150°C).

scientific application — Various uses of the computer which are classified as nonbusiness and related to various scientific or research problem-solving questions or programs. Such programs are relatively characterized by a low volume of input and distinctly lack volumes of processing and, again, a low volume of output.

scientific computer — Scientific problems are characterized by a minimum of input, a maximum of compute, and a maximum of iteration. Management science applications have these attributes, plus the massive data loads of the normal commercial applications. The requirements for a computer to handle these special applications are a very large memory, extremely high-speed arithmetics, and a very large variety of floating-point arithmetic commands.

scientific data processing — The processing of data involved with solving mathematical functions or equations.

scientific notation — A notion in which quantities are expressed as a fractional part (mantissa) and a power of ten (characteristic).

scientific system — A particular system devoted principally to computation, in contrast to a commercial or data-processing system in which the main emphasis is on file updating rather than performance of calculations.

scrambled — Pertaining to the encoded or private form of a signal which is unintelligible except when decoded or descrambled.

scramblers, data security — Devices that protect access to large data base management systems through synchronous data encryption. Typically this security system is used to protect remote-terminal-to-computer and computer-to-computer transmissions.

scramble time — *See* time, scramble.

scratchpad memory — Any memory space used for the temporary storage of data. More specifically, scratchpad memories are high-speed integrated circuits that are addressed as internal registers.

scratchpad memory, RAM — Generally, the registers that are used to store temporary intermediate results (data) in some type of random-access memory (RAM); this could relate to the memory addressed (with pointers).

scratchpad storage — *Same as* scratchpad memory.

scratch tape (sorting) — Tape(s) used to store intermediate-pass data during a sort program.

screen — 1. The surface in an electrostatic cathode-ray storage tube where electrostatic charges are stored, and by means of which information is displayed or stored temporarily. 2. To make a preliminary selection from a set of entities, the selection criteria being based on a given set of rules or conditions.

script, machine — *See* data, machine readable.

scrolling — A feature that allows text to be moved up or down, so as to show material that does not fit on the display screen. When the scrolling key is pressed, the entire displayed text moves up or down. The first line in the direction of motion disappears and a new line appears at the opposite edge of the screen. An alternate approach is to display the text in "pages." Then, when the page advance key is pressed, the currently displayed text is succeeded by a new screenful of text.

SDLC — Abbreviation for Synchronous Data Link Control. A uniform discipline for the transfer of data between stations in a point-to-point, multipoint, or loop arrangement, using synchronous data transmission techniques.

SDLC frame — An SDLC frame can perform message-transmission, supervisory, or management functions. The message field is absent in a supervisory frame and may provide link-oriented instructions in a management frame.

SE — 1. Abbreviation for Sign Extend. An operation used during a multiply or divide during a shift, to ensure that the bit shifted in is identical to the sign bit. 2. Abbreviation for Stop Element. In start-stop transmission, the last element in each character, to which is assigned a minimum duration, during which the receiving equipment is returned to its rest condition in preparation for the reception of the next character.

search — A systematic examination of the available information in a specific field of interest.

search, area — An area search relates to information retrieval by examining a collection of data or documents, but specifically those within a particular subset according to some criteria determination, i.e., belonging to some class, category, geographical area, location, etc.

search, binary — A technique for finding a particular item in an ordered set of items by repeatedly dividing in half the portion of the ordered set containing the sought-for item until only the sought-for item remains.

search, chain — *See* chain search.

search, chaining — *See* chain search.

search, conjunctive — A search defined in terms of a logical product, i.e., conjunctive form, in contrast to a disjunctive form, or logical sum.

search cycle — The sequence of events or the time interval needed for the occurrence of a fixed number of events required to complete a single search operation, such as carrying out a comparison.

search, dichotomizing — A search in which the series of items is divided into two parts, one of which is rejected, and the process is repeated on the unrejected part until the item with the desired property is found. This process usually depends upon the presence of a known sequence in the series of items.

search, disjunctive — A search defined in terms of a logical sum, i.e., disjunctive form, in contrast to a conjunctive form or logical product.

search, Fibonacci — *See* Fibonacci search.

OPEN FLAG	ADDRESS	CONTROL	MESSAGE	FRAME CHECK	CLOSE FLAG

SDLC frame.

searching storage — *Same as* storage, content addressed.

search, literature — A particularized search of published items of information which is usually made in order to become aware of unique characteristics of certain subjects prior to developing full research on the subject.

search-read function — In a search or search-read function, the identifier word (a full length computer word) is stored in a special register in the channel synchronizer and compared with each word read by the peripheral unit.

search time — Time required to locate a particular field of data in storage. Searching requires a comparison of each field with a predetermined standard until an identity is obtained. A contrast with access time, which is based upon locating data by means of the address of its storage location.

secondary key — All keys of a keyed access file other than the primary key are secondary keys. The retrieval speed for searches based on these fields is usually half the speed of searches based on the primary key. Secondary key values are not usually required to be unique.

secondary storage — *Same as* storage, external.

second generation computer — *See* computer, second generation.

second-level address — *Same as* address, indirect.

second, millimicro — *Same as* nanosecond. One billionth of a second.

second order subroutine — *See* subroutine, second order.

second remove subroutine — *See* subroutine, second order.

section — In the COBOL system, a sequence of one or more paragraphs designed in accordance with COBOL rules. Also defined as one of the portions of the program.

section, input — *Same as* input block.

section name — The distinct qualifying term available for a paragraph name.

section number — A number that identifies a particular section in a series of sections that make up a file.

section text — Part of a load module which has computer instructions in final form and data defined with specified initial values.

sector — Similar to a binary word except it may include characters or bits not allotted to the programmer. Example: A word can be 27 bits, plus sign. However, the sector can contain 32 bits—the remaining 4 bits may be used by the logic in the computer for spacing, etc.

sector, disk — A triangular section of a disk surface. A block of data is addressed by its track and sector numbers.

sector, independent — A device on certain tabulators which allows the first item of a series of similar data to be printed, and inhibits some or all printing of the rest of the series.

sectors — The smallest addressable portion of an auxiliary storage track or band.

secure terminal, auto mode — A mode used for telephone communication. Data entered through the keyboard or cassette playback is assumed to be "in the clear" and is enciphered into the telephone transmitter. However, it also appears as clear text on the display, printer, or recording channel. Data received at the telephone receiver is assumed to be encoded, and is deciphered before appearing "in the clear" at the display, cassette recording channel, or printer. In this mode, private telephone communication is carried out, while the outputs at both ends are clear.

secure terminal, decipher mode — A mode in which all inputs (keyboard, telephone reception, or cassette playback) are assumed to be enciphered. The system will decipher the information and present it in the deciphered (decoded) form to all outputs (display, telephone transmitter, printer, or cassette record channel). This mode is used for deciphering data that has arrived in the enciphered form, such as a recorded cassette.

security — The protection of information against unauthorized disclosure, transfer, modifications, or destruction, whether accidental or intentional.

security features, terminal — Features intended to preserve data and systems integrity. Such features include passwords, sign-ons, physical terminal locks, software lockouts, and so on. Regardless of the form or feature, good protection demands that the system prevent entry into individual record fields, individual records, single or multiple files, and individual terminals. There should be no access to specific commands.

security, file — *See* file security.

security, network — The measures taken to protect a network from unauthorized access, accidental or willful interference with normal operations, or destruction. This includes protection of physical facilities and software, and personnel security.

seek — The process of obtaining specific records from a random-access file. The number of seeks is the number of file items inspected before the desired item is found. To look for data according to information given regarding that data; occasionally used interchangeably and erroneously for search, scan, and screen.

seek time — The time required to make the auxiliary storage unit ready to access a specified location by selection or positioning. The range is from the minimum time for the best possible case to the maximum time for the worst possible case.

segment — 1. In a routine too long to fit into internal storage, a part short enough to be stored in the internal storage. These parts contain the addresses of succeeding parts of the routine. Routines that exceed internal storage capacity may be automatically divided into segments by a compiler. 2. The process of dividing a routine into an integral number of subroutines with each part capable of being completely stored in the internal storage and containing the instructions to jump to other segments. 3. To store part of a program or routine separately, usually in external or intermediate storage areas and devices to be brought in as needed to high-speed storage.

segmentation — A programmer-defined and monitor-implemented technique of dividing a program into essentially self-contained segments so that only certain parts need be in memory at any instant. Segmentation may be performed to allow several programs to be in memory at the same time or to allow a program to be operated that is too large for the available memory space.

segmentation, COBOL — COBOL programs can be segmented by use of priority numbers on each section.

segment, inclusive — In a program overlay structure, two or more different segments can be in the main memory simultaneously, whereas normally all inclusive segments lie on a single path from the root segment to the lowest segment.

segmenting — The act of dividing information into unique sections which can be handled as a unit.

segmenting, program — *See* program segmenting.

segment mark — A special character written on tape to separate each section of a tape file.

segment, program — *See* program segment.

segments, exclusive — Relating to an overlay program structure that is not resident in main memory simultaneously with other parts. Very large programs are often segmented into overlays, and such segments are called into memory from auxilliary storage and thus main memory capacity is not overstrained. Overlay segments are ordered as first-level, second-level, etc.

segment size, program — *See* program segment size.

segments overlays — *See* overlays, segments.

segregating unit — A segregating unit pulls or separates individual cards from a group. This machine is equipped with two feeding magazines and four receivers that interfile or segregate the cards in various sequences—at the rate of hundreds of cards per minute from each feeding magazine.

seizing signal — A specific signal that is often translated at the start of a message to initiate a circuit operation at the receiving end of a circuit.

select — 1. To choose one of several alternate subroutines from a file of subroutines. 2. To activate the control and data channels to and from an i/o (input/output) unit, preparatory to "reading from" or "writing on" the selected device. 3. To take alternative A if the report on a condition is of one state, and alternative B if the report on the condition is of another state.

selectable-length word — *See* word, selectable-length.

select, data — A special selection operation in which one set of items is taken for printing or punching from several sets presented on tape.

select-error — Signifies that a tape-transport unit "select-error" has occurred;

e.g., that more than one transport in the system has been assigned to the same select code or that no transport has been assigned the programmed select code.

selecting — A data-processing function of pulling from a mass of data certain items that require special attention. Typical selections are: items containing specific digits, items for a specific date, items higher than a specific number, items below a specific number, items below two specific numbers, etc.

selecting data — The process of extracting pertinent or specific information from a large body of data or the removal of certain records from the file.

select input pulse, partial — *See* pulse, partial write.

selection check — A check (usually an automatic check) to verify that the correct register, or other device, is selected in the interpretation of an instruction.

selection control — *See* control, selection.

selection, job-request — *See* job-request selection.

selection, priority — *Same as* job-request selection.

selection ratio — The ratio of the least magnetomotive force used to select a cell or core, to the maximum magnetomotive force used which is not intended to select a cell or core.

selection-replacement technique — A technique used in the internal portion of a sort program. The results of the comparisons between groups of records are stored for later use.

selection time — The time from the delivery of the proceed-to-select signal until all the selection signals have been transmitted.

selective assembly — Run tapes that contain specific programs selected by the programmer from both an input deck of new programs and a tape file of previously processed symbolic programs.

selective calling — 1. The ability of a transmitting station to specify which of several stations is to receive a message. 2. A form of teletypewriter communications system. One loop may include several machines, but with selective calling, only the machine selected will respond. The device that controls the individual machines in response to a selective call (call-directing characters) is called a stunt box.

selective dump — A dump of a selected area of internal storage.

selective erase — A feature that permits an operator to revise any part of an image on a display by removing only the offending portion instead of having to redraw the entire picture less the part to be changed.

selective listing — The output printing of data which meets various sets of predetermined criteria.

selective trace — A tracing routine that uses only specified criteria. Typical criteria are: instruction type (arithmetic jump), instruction location (specific region), and data location (specific region).

selector — A switch used in step-by-step switching systems. The selector responds to each dialed digit by moving up a band of contacts the prescribed number of steps according to the digit dialed and then searching across that level for a free selector or connector which will accept the next dialed digit(s).

selector channel — Selector channels are used where high-speed devices are to be attached to a system. A single channel can operate only one i/o (input/output) device at a time. Two or more channels connected to any computer system provide the ability to read, write, and compute from multiple input/output devices.

selectors — Automatic switches that provide flexibility in system processing. They allow a computer to consider a variety of values and operations at any time during a program and to pick out the appropriate one, based on input coding or processed results up to that point. They permit the computer to reuse earlier steps in a program with new factors and functions.

select switch, tape — *See* switch, tape select.

self-adapting — Pertaining to the ability of a computer system to change its performance characteristics in response to its environment.

self-checking code — A code in which errors produce forbidden combinations. A single-error detecting code produces a forbidden combination if a digit gains or loses a single bit. A double-error detecting code produces a forbidden combination if a digit gains or loses either one or two bits and so forth. (Related to self-checking number and code, error-detecting.)

self-checking number — A number with a suffix figure related to the figure(s) of the number, used to check the number after it has been transferred from one medium or device to another. (Related to check bit, modulo-N check, and error-detecting code.)

self-checking numeral — *See* numeral, self-checking.

self-complementing code — A machine language in which the code of the complement of a digit is the complement of the code of the digit.

self-demarcating — *See* code, self-demarcating.

self-demarking code — 1. A code in which the symbols are so arranged and selected that the generation of false combinations by interaction of segments from two successive codes is prevented. 2. *Same as* self-checking code.

self-learning — A special capability of a device or machine such that it can improve its capability in decision-making as programmed with instructions and based on information received, new instructions received, results of calculations, or environmental change; i.e., error histories and historical performance can and do relate to improving techniques.

self-modification program — *See* program, self-modification.

self-organization — The capability of a machine to organize a program automatically into a logical sequence or efficient steps of execution.

self-organizing — Having the capability of classification or internal rearrangement, depending on the environment, in accordance with given instructions or a set of rules.

self-organizing machine — A class of machine that may be characterized loosely as containing a variable network in which the elements are organized by the machine itself, without external intervention, to meet the criteria of successful operation.

self-organizing system — A system that is capable of internal reconfiguration in response to externally occurring events.

self-relative addressing — In relative addressing, if the number added corresponds to the address of the instruction under consideration, the term is usually self-relative addressing.

self-repairing — An unusual characteristic or capability of some machines to detect, locate, repair, remove, or change (sidetrack) various types of malfunctions (or parts) during its operations and without human intervention other than supplementing such repairs as making components or parts available for automatic insertion, connections, etc.

self-test capability, printer — Some printers are equipped with a built-in self-test feature for checking all the electronic and electromechanical assemblies of the printer. If the printer is working normally during test, a rotating test pattern covering the full character set will continuously print until the test mode is terminated.

self-test, network — A test of the master console of the network control system. Internal test loops verify proper execution of tests, address decoding, control functions and so on.

semanteme — An element of language that expresses a definite image or idea, e.g., the word "tree." (Contrasted with morpheme, an element of language that conveys relations between nouns, verbs, etc.)

semantic errors — Semantic errors are concerned with the meaning or intent of the programmer and are definitely his responsibility. Consequently, he is provided with an extensive set of debugging aids for manipulating and referencing a program when in search of errors in the logic and analysis.

semantic matrix — A graphical device for plotting the precise elements of meaning that have been ascertained from the semantic analysis of a concept in a standard conventional form.

semantics — The study of meanings; the significance and connotation of words.

semantics, formal — A language for computer-oriented languages which acts as a compiler-compiler and contains formal semantics.

semantics, language theory — The meaning of a sentence as contrasted to syntax, which is the structure of a sentence.

semiautomatic message-switching center — A center at which an operator routes messages according to information contained in them.

semiautomatic-switching center — A point at which messages are routed by an operator according to the message content.

semicompiled — Pertaining to a specific program which has been converted from source language into object code by a compiler, but which has not yet had included those subroutines explicitly or implicity called by the source program.

semiconductor memories — Semiconductor memories use active transistor circuits as memory cells. They are classed into two major groups: unipolar metal oxide semiconductor (MOS) and bipolar MOS. MOS random access read-write memories can be either static flip-flops or dynamic charge storage circuits. The static flip-flops typically use six transistors per bit and store information as one of two stable states. Dynamic circuits generally consist of three field-effect transistor (FET) cells which use the presence or absence of charge on a capacitor to store information. MOS devices are classified according to different fabrication techniques, i.e., p-channel (PMOS), n-channel (NMOS), and complementary (CMOS). Two variations of MOS fabrication technology, metal-nitride-oxide-silicon (MNOS) and silicon-on-sapphire (SOS), are also used in semiconductor memories. The main difference between unipolar and bipolar technologies is the number and sequence of diffusion operations during manufacture. Bipolar processes are identified by the type of logic circuit used, either TTL (Transistor Transistor Logic) or ECL (Emitter Coupled Logic). Charge coupled devices (CCD) comprise a subsection of semiconductor memories.

semifixed length record — *See* record, semifixed length.

sender/receiver buffers — Using buffers, the controller in a sender fills memory with bits from the input device and then empties it bit by bit in proper sequence onto a communications line. The reverse occurs when the terminal is a receiver. Buffer control may be quite complex, as when the controller simultaneously manages separate buffers for send and receive functions in the same terminal, or when the terminal employs double buffering to improve terminal speed. (In double buffering, one buffer is being filled while the other is being emptied; then the buffers reverse roles, and so on.) Control of simultaneous and double buffers, while complex, is a relatively fixed function and well within the capability of hard-wired logic.

sender/receiver terminals — Remote data terminals can be categorized as senders, receivers, and sender/receivers. Each has a controller and a buffer memory. The sender has a data input mechanism, most commonly a keyboard, while the receiver has a data output mechanism, most commonly either a character or line printer or a crt display. The printer supplies hard, or permanent, copy, while the crt displays the message temporarily. The sender/receiver consolidates the send/receive functions into one physical device as, for example, in a keyboard/printer terminal.

send-only service — Service in which the data-communication channel is capable of transmitting signals, but is not equipped to receive signals.

send-receive, automatic — A combination teletypewriter transmitter and receiver with transmission capability from either keyboard or paper tape. Most often used in a half-duplex circuit.

send-request circuit — *See* circuit, send-request.

sense — 1. To examine data particularly relative to a set of criteria. 2. To determine the present arrangement of some element of hardware, especially a manually set switch. 3. To detect special signals. 4. To read holes in paper or cards and magnetic spots on tape, drums, etc.

sense amplifiers — Sense amplifiers respond to induced voltage impulses during the read cycle. In some systems, they are strobed during a critical time of the cycle, producing an active (high) output when a logical 1 is read, regardless of the induced polarity on the two ends of the sense/inhibit wires for each bit.

sense and control lines, external — These lines can be used to inform the central processor of the condition of any two-level possibility, such as: switch on or off, temperature normal or abnormal, voltage in regulation or out, etc. The same lines may be used for control purposes, each capable of providing a two-level control signal to any external device. Typical applications include: turn indicating lights on or off at remote areas, control of relays in special equipment, initiation of analog sequences, etc.

sense light — A light that may be turned on or off and may be interrogated by the computer to cause a program branch.

sense, mark — To mark a position on a punched card by an electrically conductive pencil, for later conversion to machine punching.

sense switch — A switch on the console of a computer that may be set up or down. Statements may be included in a program to test the condition of these switches and to vary program execution based on these settings. Also called alteration switch.

sensible, machine — *See* data, machine readable.

sensing, automatic display flags — Control state or mode permits the visual display to jump, conditioned on the states of its own flags (light pen flag, edge flag, stop flag, etc.). This reduces the number of program interrupts.

sensing element — The specific portion of a device which is directly responsive to the value of the measured quantity.

sensing, mark — A technique for detecting special pencil marks entered in special places on a punch card, and automatically translating the marks into punched holes.

sensing signal — A specific signal which is often translated at the start of a message for the purpose of initiating circuit operation at the receiving end of a circuit.

sensitive-language, computer — *See* language, computer-sensitive.

sensitivity — The degree of response of an instrument or control unit to change in the incoming signal.

sensitivity analysis — A test or trial of a range or number of input values to determine the response, interdependence, or friction of the output values. Sensitivity analysis is often called parametric programming because, in such investigations, one or more parameters are permitted to vary in order to determine whether or not a solution should be modified.

sensor — A device that permits a computer to obtain analog information concerning temperatures, flows, pressure, and so forth.

sensor-based computer — A type of computer designed and programmed to receive real-time data (analog or digital) from transducers, sensors, and other data sources that monitor a physical process. The computer may also generate signals to elements that control the process. For example, the computer might receive data from a gauge or flowmeter, compare the data with a predetermined standard, and then produce a signal that operates a relay, valve, or other control mechanism.

sensor-based system — A type of organization of components including a computer whose primary source of input is data from sensors and whose output can be used to control the related physical process.

sensor, dielectric — A special sensor used in reading data from paper tape.

sensor/entry device, data collection — The sensor/entry device in the closed-loop system is matched to the input documents. It can be an optical reader, a tag reader, a magnetic-ink reader, or a mark reader. The sensor/entry device can also be a key-to-tape or key-to-disk station, or even a crt tied directly to the computer on line.

sentence — In COBOL, a sequence of one or more statements specifying one or more operations, according to certain rules, and terminated by a period.

sentinel — A symbol to mark a unit of information, e.g., the end of an item, field, block, tape, file, etc.

separating character — *See* character, separating.

separation symbol, item — A control symbol which indicates beginning of an item.

separator — A flag that separates and organizes items of data.

separator, word — A character in machine coding that segregates fields.

SEPOL — Acronym for Soil-Engineering Problem-Oriented Language.

septenary number — A number, usually of more than one figure, representing a sum, in which the quantity represented by each figure is based on a radix of seven. The figures used are: 0, 1, 2, 3, 4, 5, and 6.

sequence — 1. To put a set of symbols into an arbitrarily defined order. 2. An arbitrarily defined order of a set of symbols; i.e., an orderly progression of items of information or of operations in accordance with some rule.

sequence break (sorting) — That point in a file between the end of one string and start of another.

sequence, calling — A specified arrangement of instructions and data necessary to set up and call a given subroutine.

sequence check — A data-processing operation designed to check the sequence of the items in a file.

sequence checking — A sequence check is used to prove that a set of data is arranged in either ascending or descending order before it is processed. It is generally a mechanized operation performed in a separate machine run or simultaneously with another operation run.

sequence-checking routine — A routine that checks every instruction executed and prints out certain data; e.g., to print out the coded instructions with addresses, and the contents of each of several registers, or it may be designed to print out only selected data, such as transfer instructions and the quantity actually transferred.

sequence, collating — A sequence of characters as arranged in the order of their relative precedence. The collating sequence of a particular computer is determined as part of its design; each character acceptable to the computer has a preassigned place in this sequence. A collating sequence is used primarily in comparing operations.

sequence, control — The normal order of selection of instructions for execution. In some computers one of the addresses in each instruction specifies the control sequence. In most computers, the sequence is consecutive except where a transfer occurs.

sequence control register — *See* register, sequence control.

sequence control tape — A tape that contains the sequence of instructions required for solving a problem.

sequence counter — *Same as* register, sequence control.

sequence error — A condition in which a card is out of sequence within an object program.

sequence error checking — Protocols often include alternating acknowledgments and block sequencing. The technique used depends on the protocol. The receiving station sends back an indication of a sequence error with a negative acknowledgment or some other control message.

sequence monitor — Computer monitoring of the step-by-step actions that should be taken by the operator during a startup and/or shutdown of a power unit. As a minimum, the computer would check that certain milestones had been reached in the operation of the unit. The maximum coverage would have the computer check that each required step is performed, that the correct sequence is followed, and that every checked point falls within its prescribed limits. Should an incorrect action or result occur, the computer would record the fault and notify the operator.

sequence packing — A procedure for loading the upper half of an accumulator with the first data word, shifting this into the lower half, loading the second datum, shifting, etc., so that the three data words are thus packed in sequence.

sequence, pseudorandom number — A sequence of numbers, determined by some defined arithmetic process that is satisfactorily random for a given purpose, such as satisfying one or more of the standard statistical tests for randomness. Such a sequence may approximate any one of several statistical distributions, e.g., uniform distribution or a normal (Gaussian) distribution.

sequence, queue (any) — A collection of items in the system which are waiting for the attention of the processors. The any-sequence queue is organized so that items may be removed from the collection without regard to the sequence in which they entered it.

sequencer — 1. A machine which puts items of information into a particular order; e.g., it will determine whether A is greater than, equal to, or less than B and sort or order accordingly. 2. A circuit that pulls information from the control store memory (microprogram store), based upon external events or conditions.

sequence, random — A sequence that is not arranged by ascending or descending keys, as in alphameric or numeric sequences, but is instead arranged in an organized fashion in bulk storage by locations determined by calculations performed on keys to develop addresses.

The calculations are repeated in order to acquire the address and locate the item desired.

sequence, random-number — An unpredictable array of numbers produced by change, and satisfying one or more of the tests for randomness.

sequence register — A special register that, when activated, designates the address of the next instruction to be performed by the computer.

sequence timer — A succession of time-delay circuits arranged so that completion of the delay in one circuit initiates a delay in the following circuit.

sequencing — The act which puts into order various data as to rank, time, or other predetermined order classification.

sequencing, automatic — The ability of equipment to put information in order or in a connected series without human intervention.

sequencing by merging — A technique of repeated merging, splitting, and remerging can be and is often used to place items into an organized arrangement.

sequencing criteria (sorting) — The fields in a record which determine, or are used as a basis for determining, the sequence of records in a file.

sequencing key (sorting) — The field in a record which determines, or is used as a basis for determining, the sequence of records in a file.

sequencing, time — Switching signals generated by a program purely as a function of accurately measured elapsed time.

sequential access, data base — In some systems, files can be accessed sequentially. In sequential access mode, records are processed in consecutive order. Sequential access is best used for those files in which all or most of the records in the file are processed each time the file is opened. In various systems, relative files are accessed sequentially through the relative record number that represents the beginning of a given file. Some systems begin with a given relative record and successively return the next existing record until processing is completed. Indexed files permit the sequential access of records as well. In indexed processing, records are retrieved from files based on the values of data items, known as key fields, in the records. The collection of all existing values in a given key field is an index. Each record has at least one primary and zero or more alternate keys all of which point to the same record and each of which comprises an entry in an individual index.

sequential-access storage — A storage technique in which the stored items of information become available only in a one after the other sequence, whether or not all the information or only some of it is desired, e.g., magnetic-tape storage. (Related to serial storage, and contrasted with random-access storage.)

sequential alarm module — In some systems, the specific device which continuously monitors a group of alarm contacts; i.e., whenever one or more of these contacts close, the module immediately signals a priority interrupt to the computer. The computer then reads the module contact input states to thereby establish a trip sequence from current and previous readings.

sequential collating — Sequencing a group of records by comparing the key of one record with another record until equality, greater than, or less than, is determined.

sequential computer, logic-controlled — A specific sequential computer with the capability of executing instructions in a sequence designed by particular built-in logic, i.e., a fixed sequence, but one which can be overridden or changed by an instruction; a highly unique and almost single-purpose computer with little or no concurrent action.

sequential control — A mode of computer operation in which instructions are executed in consecutive order, unless otherwise specified by a jump.

sequential data set, indexed — *See* data set, indexed sequential.

sequential file — To get to an item in a sequential file, the user must first read all the preceding items (records, sectors, blocks, or bytes). In a random-access file, individual bytes can be directly addressed because information within the file is usually segmented or delimited by a number of bytes. A sequential file might use record separators or end-of-file marks as delimiters, with a correspondingly larger lower limit on the size of the smallest amount of information transferred. The same applies when a file is updated.

sequential logic — A circuit arrangement in which the output state is determined by the previous state of the input.

sequential logic element — *See* element, sequential logic.

sequential operation — The performance of actions one after the other in time. The actions referred to are of a large scale as opposed to the smaller scale operations referred to by the term serial operation. For an example of sequential operation consider A*(B*C). The two multiplications indicated follow each other sequentially. However, the processing of the individual digits in each multiplication may be either parallel or serial.

sequential operation, automatic — To develop a series or family of solutions from a set of equations, various initial conditions are recalculated with other parameters.

sequential processing — The procedure of processing information or data records in the same order in which they happen.

sequential programming — *See* programming, sequential.

sequential queue — The first-in-first-out method of queuing items waiting for the processor.

sequential sampling — Sampling inspection in which the decision to accept, reject, or inspect another unit is made following the inspection of each unit.

sequential table search, data base — A sequential search table is an unordered pairing of arguments and results. The entire table is searched sequentially from the beginning until a match is found.

sequential testing — A series of tests performed in a predetermined order and requiring repeated observations.

serial — Pertaining to the time-sequential processing of the individual parts of a whole, such as the bits of a character, the characters of a word, etc., using the same facilities for successive parts.

serial access — Sequential access to elements of data (bits, characters, or words) within all or part of a storage device. For example, storage in which words, within a group of words (as on a track of a magnetic drum), appear one after the other in time sequence is said to be serial by word. Access may still be parallel by character or by bit, despite being serial by word.

serial addition — *See* addition, serial.

serial arithmetic — *See* arithmetic, serial.

serial-by-bit — Pertaining to the handling of bits of a character in a fashion of one immediately following another. Characters may be handled either serially or in parallel.

serial-by-character — *See* serial-by-bit.

serial data controller — A digital receiver-transmitter that interfaces specific microcomputers to a serial communications channel. Many are capable of half and full-duplex operation at synchronous rates up to 250K bps for some systems and asychronous rates up to 18K bps or more. Most are capable of programmable transmission modes; character lengths of 5, 6, 7, and 8 bits; even, odd, or no parity; one or two stop bits; etc.

serial digit operation — *See* digit operation, serial.

serial flow — The system of operations such that each operation is performed singly and not at the same time other tasks are being completed; i.e., the work moves along a single line or channel where one type of operation is performed in succession or at each station and none are performed at the same time or simultaneously with other tasks. Opposite from parallel flow.

serial input-output — A method of data transfer between a computer and a peripheral device in which data are transmitted for input to the computer or output to the device bit by bit over a single circuit.

serial input/output, high level systems — The serial input/output (SIO) circuit is a programmable i/o device similar to the PIO, except that it is designed to handle peripherals with a serial data interface, such as floppy disks, crt's, and communications terminals.

serial i/o — *See* serial input-output.

serialize — To change from parallel-by-bit to serial-by-bit.

serial number control — *See* control, serial number.

serial numbering — The serial numbering of orders, invoices, checks, etc., provides control while the data is in transit. Each item or document in the series or group is assigned a successive number; an indication of the beginning and ending of numbers accompanies the group.

serial operation — Sequential performance of arithmetic or data transmission on one character at a time.

serial-parallel — 1. A combination of serial and parallel; e.g., serial by character, parallel by bits comprising the character. 2. Pertaining to a device that converts a serial input into a parallel output.

serial printer — The specific output device which prints one character at a time, such as typewriters and some types of printers.

serial printer interface — A device that employs a switch that determines whether data are to be routed from the display to the printer or from the computer to the printer. A line printer, as opposed to a character printer, requires a large output buffer, but the basic system architecture should not be affected.

serial processing — Reading or writing of the item following the one currently being processed.

serial programming — The programming of a computer by which only one arithmetical or logical operation can be executed at one time, e.g., a sequential operation. (Contrasted with multiple programming.)

serial storage — *See* storage, serial.

serial transfer — In a serial transfer, the bits stored in a string of flip-flops are caused to move along the string from one flip-flop to the next, toward one end of the string, so that all of the bits eventually pass through the end flip-flop. This process is generally called shifting, and a string of flip-flops connected in this manner make up a shift register. The bits shifted out of one register can be shifted into another similar register, thereby shifting the contents from one register to another.

serial transmission — The method of information transmission in which the bits that compose a character are transmitted sequentially as contrasted with parallel or simultaneous transfer. There are two types of serial transmission. Asynchronous data words can arrive at irregular intervals and must be preceded by start bits and followed by stop bits to aid identification. Conversely, in synchronous transmission, system timing determines the flow of data words, which are locked into the timing scheme. This transmission mode, both fast and complex, requires an elaborate timing-recovery circuit.

serial word operation — The specific feature of certain handling equipment in which words are read one after another, in groups.

series — 1. Pertaining to the connecting of components end to end in a circuit, to provide a single path for the current. 2. An indicated sum of a set of terms in a mathematical expression (e.g., in an alternating or arithmetic series). 3. Lines in a spectrum described by a formula related to the possible energy levels of the electrons in outer shells of atoms.

series, time — The discrete or continuous sequence of quantitative data assigned to specific moments in time, and usually studied with respect to their distribution in time.

service bits — Those overhead bits that are not check bits, e.g., request for repetition, numbering sequence, etc.

service bureau — A computer service that packages its services so that all users have to do is to supply the input data and pay for the results. It happens to provide the service on a computer, but users are not directly concerned with the computer at all. Many financial services, such as payroll, billing, and bookkeeping, are offered this way.

service engineering — Service engineering provides support capability for systems engineering and planning; installation and checkout; maintenance and operator training; contractual preventive maintenance; regional service and parts; factory equipment repair; and equipment modernization, rehabilitation, and expansion.

service, full-duplex — A service in which the data-communication channel is capable of simultaneous and independent transmission and reception.

service, half-duplex — A type of communication channel which is capable of transmitting and receiving signals, but is not capable of simultaneous and independent transmission and reception.

service, mode — An operational mode for the handling of malfunctions or errors in words, etc.

service organization, computer — *See* computer service organization.

service program — *See* program, service.

service, receive-only — Service in which the data-communication channel is capable of receiving signals, but is not equipped to transmit signals.

service request interrupts — Interrupts used for servicing buffer channel requests. They are an internal machine function and are not directly under the control of the programmer.

service routine — A set of instructions to perform a programmed operation, typically in response to an interrupt.

service, send-only — Service in which the data-communication channel is capable of transmitting signals, but is not equipped to receive signals.

services, setup — The action or services performed on a message before it meets the application program. Services include error checking, analyzing the action code, etc.

servicing time — *Same as* engineering time.

servomechanism — A device to monitor an operation as it proceeds, and to make necessary adjustments to keep the operation under control. A furnace thermostat is an example of a servomechanism.

servomultiplier — An analog computer device or unit which has a position control and a capability of multiplying each of several different variables by a single variable, represented by analog voltages. The multiplier is used as an input signal to a mechanism that turns shafts.

set — 1. To place a storage device in a prescribed state. 2. To place a binary cell in the one state. 3. A collection of elements having some feature in common or which bear a certain relation to one another; e.g., all even numbers, geometrical figures, terms in a series, a group of irrational numbers, all positive even integers less than 100, may be a set or a subset.

set breakpoint — A user debug command that is designed to cause the setting of a breakpoint in a specific memory location. At program execution, this breakpoint, when encountered, causes a temporary program suspension and a transfer of control to the system debug routine.

set name — An identifier.

set of data — The x values and y values representing points which will be drawn as a set of curves on a graph. Thus, a set of data consists of the multiple x values and associated y values required to define the curve.

set point — The specific desired value for the quantity being controlled, usually in a feedback control loop.

set-point control — A process may be intelligently controlled at the site, thus eliminating hard-wired logic and extensive master-remote communications. In set-point control, an analog signal is checked against specified limits, and commands are sent to a relay driver or electronic circuit to actuate control points. Gas or water flow is a typical example. If the meter signal exceeds its upper (lower) limits, a close (open) command is sent to the valve that controls the flow rate.

set pulse — *See* pulse, set.

sets, data — *See* data sets.

set symbol — A variable symbol used to communicate values during conditional assembly processing.

set theory — The study of the use and application of groups or sets.

settings, trap — *See* trap settings.

settling time — The time required for a dot to move to a new point on the screen and stay put without vacillating. It is an important specification for displays made from dots. Dot writing time and settling time, taken together, determine the maximum rate at which one can produce a clean, stored display using binary data.

set up — The preparation of pieces of equipment for operation, i.e., placing paper in printers, adjusting paper feeds for tape units, etc.

set up, single — *Same as* single step.

set-up time — The portion of the elapsed time between machine operations that is devoted to such tasks as changing reels of tape and moving cards, tapes, and supplies to and from the equipment.

several-for-one — A transaction which often is considered to mean the creation of a number of machine instructions from one program instruction. This is an indication of the various types of software.

sexadecimal — Pertaining to a characteristic or property involving a selection, choice, or condition in which there are 16 possibilities. Also called hexadecimal.

sexadecimal number — *See* number, sexadecimal.

sexadecimal numeral — *See* number, sexadecimal.

shaping, pulse — *Same as* pulse regeneration.

shaping, signal — *Same as* pulse regeneration.

share — To use a device for two or more interleaved purposes.

shared files — A direct-access device that permits two systems to be linked together. Either system has access to the file.

shared-files system — A special file system configuration in which two computers have access to the same file-storage device, though not necessarily at the same time.

shared logic systems — If the "logic" (computational power) of a central computer is parceled out to numerous word-processing terminals, the result is a shared logic word-processing system.

shared storage — The ability to share core storage between two computers. This means that either machine can insert information into storage, and either machine can access the data and use it.

share operation system — The particular process or translation of symbolic instructions into a machine instruction. Often abbreviated as SOS.

sharing — Interleaved time use of a device —hence, a method of operation in which a computer facility is shared by several users concurrently.

sharing, load — An arrangement in which computers are placed in tandem (duplexing or triplexing) to share the peak-period load of a system.

sheet, coding — A form upon which computer instructions are written prior to being punched into cards.

Sheffer stroke function — The Boolean operator that gives a truth table value of true only when both of the variables connected by the logical operator are not true.

Sheffer stroke gate — *Same as* gate, NAND.

shift — A movement of bits, digits, or characters to the left or right. For a number, this is equivalent to multiplying or dividing by a power of the base number.

shift, arithmetic — To multiply or divide a quantity by a power of the number base; e.g., if binary 1101, which represents decimal 13, is arithmetically shifted twice to the left, the result is 110100, which represents 52, which is also obtained by multiplying (13 by 2) twice; on the other hand, if decimal 13 were to be shifted to the left twice, the result would be the same as multiplying by 10 twice, or 1300. (Related to shift and cyclic shift.)

shift, carrier — Difference between the steady-state, mark, and space frequencies in a data-carrier system using frequency-shift modulation.

shift, case — The changeover of the translating mechanism of a telegraph receiving machine from letters case to figures case or vice versa. This shift is normally performed in telegraph apparatus by preceding the transmission of letters-case characters or functions by a figures-shift signal.

shift character, nonlocking — *See* character, nonlocking shift.

shift, circular — A shift in which the digits dropped off at one end of a word are returned at the other in a circular fashion; e.g., if a register holds eight digits, 23456789, the result of a circular shift two columns to the left would be to change the contents of the register to 45678923. (Synonymous with end-around shift, logical shift, nonarithmetic shift, ring shift, and cyclic shift.)

shift, computer — To move the characters of a unit of information columnwise left or right.

shift, cyclic — *Same as* shift, circular.

shift, end-around — *Same as* shift, circular.

shift, figures — A function performed by a teletypewriter machine, when initiated by the figures-shift character, that causes the machine to shift to upper case for numbers, symbols, etc.

shift, floating point — A shift in 4-bit increments, performed on a short-format or long-format floating-point number.

shift, frequency — A system of telegraph-teletypewriter operation in which the mark signal is one frequency and the space signal is a different frequency.

shift-in character — A code extension character that can be used by itself to cause a return to the character set in effect prior to the departure caused by a shift-out character. Abbreviated SI character.

shifting — The arithmetic process during which each movement of value to the left multiplies a number by the radix in use, and each movement to the right divides the number by the radix. Shifting may also feed a process for other radix points.

shift instructions — Numerous variations of the shift instruction are implemented on different computers; typically you can shift right or you can shift left. A right shift is more useful, because it is equivalent to dividing by 2, while the left shift is equivalent to multiplying by 2 and can be reproduced by adding the contents of a register to itself. A shift may be continuous through a status bit or branched or it may bypass the status bit. The shift may also be arithmetic and propagate the high order bit (sign bit) to the right. A shift may be circular, in which case, with every right shift, the low order bit moves to the high order bit, or the shift may be logical, in which case the low order bits are lost and zeros replace the high order bits (for a right shift). A computer could provide shift instructions with any permutation of right or left shift; circular or logical shift; bypassing a status bit, or through it (continuous or branched); arithmetic (bypassing the sign bit), or through the sign bit.

shift, letters — A function performed by a teleprinter, when initiated by the letters-shift character, which causes the machine to shift from upper case to lower case.

shift locking character — *See* character, locking shift.

shift, logic — *Same as* shift, circular.

shift, logical — *Same as* shift circular.

shift, nonarithmetic — Same as shift circular.

shift out — To move information within a register toward one end so that as the information leaves this same end, zeros enter at the opposite end.

shift-out character — *See* character, locking shift.

shift, phase — The time difference between the input and output signal or between any two synchronized signals of a control unit, system, or circuit.

shift pulse — A pulse which causes the characters in a register to shift.

shift register — A register in which binary data bits are moved as a contiguous group a prescribed number of positions to the right or to the left.

shift register, flip-flop — A type of digital storage circuit which uses a chain of flip-flops to shift data from one flip-flop to its adjacent flip-flop on each clock pulse. Data may be shifted several places to the right or to the left depending on additional gating and the number of clock pulses received. Depending on the number of positions shifted, in a right shift the right-most characters are lost; in a left shift the left-most characters are lost.

shift register, magnetic — *See* register, magnetic-shift.

shift, ring — *Same as* shift, circular.

shortest word — A word of the shortest length a computer can use, and which is most often half of the full length word.

short instruction — The use of an index specification in a FORTRAN READ or WRITE statement.

short instruction format — A "standard" length (i.e., one-word) instruction as opposed to a "long" instruction. Most instructions are of this type.

short-term storage — Data stored in core memory for a short period of time.

short word — A fixed word of lesser length in a system that is capable of handling words of two different lengths. In many computers, this is referred to as a half-word because the length is exactly the half-length of a full word.

SI — Abbreviation for SuperImpose. The process that moves data from one location to another, superimposing bits or characters on the contents of specified locations.

side circuit — One of two physical circuits in a phantom group.

sideways sum — *See* sum, sideways.

sign — An indication of whether a quantity is greater than zero or less than zero. The signs often are the marks + and −, respectively; other arbitrarily selected symbols may be used, such as a 0 and 1, or 0 and 9. These symbols must be interpreted by a person or the machine.

signal — An event, phenomenon, or electrical quantity that conveys information from one point to another.

signal, analog — An electrical signal that varies continuously in amplitude or frequency with the information being transmitted.

signal, carry-complete — A signal generated by a digital parallel adder, indicating that all carries from an adding operation have been generated and propagated and the addition operation is completed.

signal, clock — *Same as* pulse, clock.

signal conditioning — 1. Any manipulation of transducer or transmitter outputs to make them suitable for input to the computer peripheral equipment. 2. Operations such as linearizing and square-root extraction performed within the computer.

signal, correcting — In synchronous systems, a special signal that may be sent recurrently for correction of data.

signal detection, modem — Besides modulating digital data into an analog form, a modem must demodulate the carrier signals to reproduce the data. In general, this is accomplished by comparing the signal pulses with a known reference, detecting the difference, and generating the proper sequence of digital pulses. A high-speed modem using 8-phase dpsk, for example, receives a signal, compares its phase with that of the preceding pulse (information which is stored in a modem memory facility), and produces a 3-bit binary number corresponding to the difference.

signal, digital — A discrete or discontinuous electrical signal; one whose various states are discrete intervals apart.

signal distance — The number of digit positions in which the corresponding digits of two binary words of the same length are different. (Synonymous with Hamming distance.)

signal element — The basic unit by which data is transmitted on communication channels. Each signal element is a state or condition on a channel which represents one or more bits of digital information. A signal element might be a dc pulse or an ac signal of some amplitude, frequency, or phase which the receiving equipment can recognize and translate into the original format. Signaling speed is the number of such signal elements occurring in one second and is measured in bauds.

signal element, start-stop — A part of a digital signal, distinguished from others by its duration, position, and sense, or by some of these features only. In start-stop operation, a signal element has a minimum duration of one unit interval. If several unit intervals of the same sense run together, a signal element of duration of more than one unit element may be formed. Signal elements may be start elements, information elements, or stop elements.

signal-enabling — A means of allowing an operation to take place.

signal, feedback-control — The portion of the output signal that is returned to the input in order to achieve a desired effect, such as fast response.

signal, ground — A conductor establishing electrical ground reference potential for all transmitting circuits in a communications network.

signal, guard — A signal which allows values to be read or converted only when the values are not in a state of change, i.e., to avoid errors or ambiguity. Used in digital-analog or analog-digital converters or other converters or digitizers.

signaling, binary — A communications mode in which information is developed by the presence and absence, or the plus and minus variations, of only one parameter of the signal.

signaling, closed-circuit — That type of signaling in which there is current in the idle condition, and a signal is initiated by increasing or decreasing the current.

signaling, data rate — Relating to data transmission, an expression in bits per second relating to data transmission capacity of a particular channel.

signaling, dc — A transmission method which utilizes direct current.

signaling in band — Signaling which utilizes frequencies within the intelligence band of a channel.

signaling out of band — Signaling which utilizes frequencies outside the intelligence band. Also used to indicate the use of a portion of a channel bandwidth provided by the medium such as a carrier channel, but denied to the speech or intelligence path by filters. It results in a reduction of the effective available bandwidth.

signal inhibiting — A means of preventing an operation from happening.

signal, interrupt — A signal that interrupts a running program so that some other task can be performed. Sometimes interrupts are given priorities so that the central processor will suspend its current task only if the priority is great enough for immediate execution.

signal, interrupt feedback — *See* interrupt feedback signal.

signal, interrupt trigger — *See* interrupt trigger signal.

signal level — An optical character recognition term which relates to the amplitude of the electronic response which occurs from the contrast ratio between the area of a printed character and the area of a document background.

signal normalization — *Same as* pulse regeneration.

signal notation — In some cases, a circuit may be enabled when a signal label such as ENABLE is high and in other cases when it is low. To distinguish one case from another, use is made of signal notation furnished in various equipment charts.

signal, one output — The output of a magnetic cell in the one condition when a read pulse is supplied.

signal, proceed-to-select — The signal returned from distant automatic equipment over the backward signaling path, in response to a calling signal, to indicate that selecting information can be transmitted. Note: In certain signaling systems, this signal can be one and the same as the "call-confirmation signal."

signal, program-interrupt — *See* interrupt, external-signal.

signal, pulsing — Signals which are transmitted in the forward direction and carry the selective information to route the call in the desired direction.

signal ratio — 1. Broadly, the comparison of light seen by a photosensor when the object to be detected is blocking the beam, to the light seen when the beam is not blocked. 2. More specifically, the comparison of photocell resistance when the sensor is dark to when it is illuminated.

signal, read output — *Same as* read out.

signal regeneration — *Same as* pulse regeneration.

signal, release-guard — A signal sent back in response to the clear-forward signal to indicate that the circuit has become free at its incoming end. This signal is provided to protect the circuit at its outgoing end against subsequent seizing before the release operation, controlled by the clear-forward signal, has been completed at the incoming end.

signal reshaping — *Same as* pulse regeneration.

signals, control — Various signals are provided to control and to ensure an orderly flow of information words between the central computer and the peripheral subsystems. These signals do not transmit data, but are used to command and identify the transfer of information words at the proper times and in the proper sequence. These control signals travel over the control lines of the input/output channel.

signals, correction from — A system of correction in which the maintenance of synchronous equipment is controlled, not by a special correcting signal, but by the position of the characteristic instants of restitution of telegraph signals comprising the text.

signal, seizing — In semiautomatic or automatic working, a signal transmitted at the commencement of a call to initiate circuit operation at the incoming end of the circuit.

signal shaping — *Same as* pulse regeneration.

signal standardization — *See* pulse regeneration.

signal, start-dialing — In semiautomatic or automatic working, a signal transmitted from the incoming end of a circuit, following the receipt of a seizing signal, to indicate that the necessary circuit conditions have been established for receiving the numerical routine information.

signal, start (in a start-stop system) — Signal servicing to prepare the receiving mechanism for the reception and registration of a character, or for the control of a function.

signals, timing — Electrical pulses sent throughout the machine at regular intervals to ensure absolute synchronization.

signal, stop (in a start-stop system) — Signal serving to bring the receiving mechanism to rest in preparation for the reception of the next telegraph signal.

signal strength — A measure of the amplitude of the signal obtained from reading devices such as photocells, magnetic tape read heads, etc.

signature analysis — A means of isolating digital logic faults at the component level. Although considered most useful in servicing microprocessor-based products, the technique is applicable to all digital systems. Basically, the technique involves the tracing of signals and the conversion of lengthy bit streams into four-digit hexadecimal "signatures." Using logic diagrams and schematics specially annotated with correct signatures at each data node, and guided by troubleshooting trees, the serviceman traces back until he finds a point in the circuit which has a correct input signature and incorrect output signature. Signatures are traced under the direction of a test PROM (programmable read-only memory). The manufacturer produces the PROM which replaces the product's application program for test purposes.

signature testing — Comparison of the actual output digital signatures, such as transition counts, with the expected correct signatures recorded from a known-good device.

sign bit — A binary digit used to designate the algebric sign of a quantity, plus or minus.

sign changer — As regards scalers, when the constant which is used as a multiplier has the value of –1, the scaler may be called a sign changer, an inverter, or a sign reverser.

sign check — It is possible to detect a change in sign during arithmetic operations and either stop the machine or signal for subsequent review. In payroll applications, the sign check is used to indicate the condition in which deductions exceed gross pay. This sign is also used in accounts receivable, accounts payable, inventory, and general ledger applications. The sign check can be used to recognize any balance that becomes negative.

sign-check indicator — A device that detects and signals the occurrence of an error in the sign of a number or of a field.

sign digit — *Same as* sign bit.

signed field — A field that has a plus or minus character coding over the units position to designate the algebraic sign of the entire number.

sign flag — An indicator that is set to a logic 1 if the MSB of a register being tested is a binary 1. When using the "twos complement" arithmetic convention, this condition indicates that the register contains a negative number.

sign, flip-flop — The specific flip-flop used to store the algebraic sign of numbers.

significance — 1. Circumstances or solutions discerned to be unlikely to arise out of chance factors alone. 2. The arbitrary rank, priority, or order of relative magnitude assigned to a given position or column in a number.

significant character, least — The character in the rightmost position in a number or a word.

significant character, most — The character in the leftmost position in a number or word.

significant conditions of a modulation — Distinct conditions, assumed by the appropriate device of the sending apparatus, which serve to characterize the variety of the elements of the alphabetic telegraph signals to be transmitted.

significant conditions of a restitution — Distinct conditions, assumed by the appropriate device of the receiving apparatus, which serve to characterize the variety of the elements of the alphabetic telegraph signals received.

significant digit — *See* digit(s), significant.

significant digit, least — *See* digit, least significant (LSD).

significant figures — *See* figures, significant.

significant interval — A time interval during which a given significant condition according to the code and the signal to be transmitted is, or should be, transmitted.

sign off — The closing instruction to the computer system which terminates communication with the system. On a remote terminal, the user generally signs off by typing the command OFF or SIGN OFF.

sign on — The instruction which commences communication with the computer system. On a remote terminal, the user can generally receive access to the system by typing in his identification number and an appropriate password.

sign position — The position at which the sign of a number is located.

sign reverser — *See* sign changer.

sign, special — *Same as* character, special.

silicon gate — Pertaining to an MOS process in which silicon instead od metal is used as one of the transistor elements to make possible lower operating voltages and increased dynamic response.

silicon on sapphire technology — The technology whereby monocrystalline films of silicon are epitaxially deposited onto a single-crystal sapphire substrate to provide the basic structure for the fabrication of dielectrically isolated active and/or passive elements. Abbreviated SOS.

simplex — Pertaining to a circuit capable of one-way operations only. The term is seldom used today because no such circuit is offered by the common carriers. Terminal equipment may limit transmission to one direction only, but the circuit used will be half-duplex.

simplex channel — A channel that permits transmission in one direction only.

simplex/duplex modems — Modems may be designed to operate in three modes: (1) simplex, where data is transmitted in only one direction; (2) half-duplex, where data can be transmitted in only one direction at a time, but that direction can be reversed; and (3) full-duplex, where data may be transmitted in both directions simultaneously.

simplex system — A system configuration that does not include standby equipment.

simulate — To represent the functioning of one system by another; e.g., to represent one computer by another, to represent a physical system by the execution of a computer program, or to represent a biological system by a mathematical model.

simulated real-time on-line operation — The processing of data in synchronism with a physical process in such a manner that the results of the data processing are useful to the physical operation.

simulate/emulate, microprocessor — A simulator is a device used to imitate one system with another, using a software program written in assembly or high level language. The simulator accepts the same data, executes the programs and accomplishes the same results as the system imitated. The simulator is generally much slower than the machine being simulated and bears no physical resemblance to it. Simulators may be used to get a finer insight or control of workings of the imitated machine. Generally, larger minicomputers, such as software development systems, will be used to simulate smaller microprocessors for the purpose of developing and debugging software.

An emulator differs from a simulator, inasmuch as the latter uses software to imitate. The emulator uses a microprogram and specific hardware to imitate the desired system at the same speed as or faster than the imitated system's cycle time. The slice microprocessors are used to emulate large minicomputers with fewer components and faster cycle times. The emulator can be made to resemble physically the imitated machine.

simulating the multiplexer — A testing program which simulates the multiplexer.

simulation — 1. The representation of physical systems and phenomena by computers, models, or other equipment, e.g., an imitative type of data processing in which an automatic computer is used as a model of some entity such as a chemical process. When information enters the computer to represent the factors of the process, the computer produces information that represents the results of the process, and the processing done by the computer represents the process itself. 2. In computer programming, the technique of setting up a routine for one computer to make it operative as nearly as possible like some other computer.

simulation, design and monitoring — The building of a model of a system in the form of a computer program by the use of special languages. The models of a system can be adjusted easily, and the system that is being designed can be tested to show the effect of any change.

simulation, deterministic — A simulation in which a fixed relationship exists between input parameters and output results for each action, value, event, etc., such that given input parameters will always result in the same output.

simulation input devices — *See* input devices. simulation.

simulation, man-machine — The scope of simulation includes models of systems in which human beings participate (operational or behavioral models). However, the possibility also exists of incorporating people within the model. In other words, the model is no longer completely computer-based but requires the active participation of a man.

simulation, mathematical — The use of a model of mathematical equations in which computing elements are used to represent all of the subsystems.

simulation, physical — The use of a model of a physical system in which computing elements are used to represent some, but not all, of the subsystems.

simulation, real-time — *See* real-time simulation.

simulation, representative — A model of a system in which the components, processes, and interactions of the model bear a clear relation to the system under study. This tends to rule out highly abstract, mathematical models.

simulation, static vs dynamic — In a dynamic system the activity is time-dependent. This activity may be further classified as stable or unstable (under given conditions). One may choose to study steady-state or transient behavior of a dynamic system.

simulation, supervisory programs — The use of a replacement program that imitates the supervisory program.

simulator — 1. A routine that runs on one computer and imitates the operations of another computer. 2. A computer or model that represents a system or phenomenon and mirrors or maps the effects of various changes in the original, enabling the original to be studied, analyzed, and understood by means of the behavior of the model.

simulator, overload — In order to test a system under overload conditions, an artificial condition is created that makes the program act as it would during an actual overload or overflow.

simulator program — *See* program, simulator.

simulator software program — Various simulators are computer programs written in the FORTRAN IV language and are often called interpreters. These aid program development interpreters accept machine code produced by assemblers, along with execution commands from a time-sharing terminal, card reader, or disk file. The execution commands allow the manipulation of the simulated memory and the CPU registers. In addition, operator and instruction breakpoints may be set to stop execution at the crucial points in the program. Tracing features are also available which allow the CPU operation to be monitored. Interpreters accept symbol tables from either compilers or cross-assemblers to allow debugging, tracing and braking, and display of programming using symbolic names. Compilers, assemblers, and simulators as software packages may be procured from suppliers on tapes or from time share services.

simulator, table — *See* table simulator.

simultaneity — The simultaneous operation of peripheral devices.

simultaneity, tape-processing — *See* tape-processing simultaneity.

simultaneous access — The process of obtaining information from or placing information into storage where the time required for such access is dependent on the simultaneous transfer of all elements of a word from a given storage location.

simultaneous input/output — *See* input-/output, simultaneous.

simultaneous-operation computer — *Same as* computer, simultaneous.

sine-junction gate — *Same as* gate, A AND-NOT B or gate, B AND-NOT A.

single address — A system of machine instruction such that each complete instruction explicitly describes one operation and involves one storage location. (Related to one-address instruction.)

single address code — *See* code, single-address.

single-address instruction — An instruction having one operand address. (Contrast with multiple-address instruction.)

single-address message — A message to be delivered to only one destination.

single-chip systems, configurations — Such chips used in a minimal configuration might include a few switches for control, a ROM for implementing instructions, and a few indicators for monitoring purposes. A maximum system might include several input/output peripherals, read/write as well as read-only memory (RAM and ROM), a full-featured control panel, and so on.

single circuit — A telegraph circuit capable of nonsimultaneous two-way communications. *See* half-duplex circuit.

single cycle key — A push button on printers, which, when depressed, causes an additional line to be printed despite an end-of-form indication.

single error — An erroneous bit, preceded and followed by at least one correct bit.

single-level address — *Same as* address, direct.

single-operand addressing — A method in which one part of the instruction word specifies a register; the second part provides information for locating the operand. Examples: clear, increment, test, etc.

single-operand instruction — An instruction that contains a reference to a single register, memory location, or device.

single precision — The number of words, or storage positions, used to denote a number in a computer. Single-precision arithmetic is the use of one word per number; double-precision arithmetic, two words per number, and so on. For variable word-length computers, precision is the number of digits used to denote a number. The higher the precision, the greater the number of decimal places that can be carried.

single precision integer — *See* integer, single-precision.

single quote mark — A special FORTRAN character used to enclose literal messages.

single setup — Pertaining to a method of operating a computer in which each step is performed in response to a single manual operation.

single-sheet feeding — The feeding of individual sheets of paper rather than roll or fanfolded form.

single-shot operation — *Same as* operation, single-step.

single step — Pertaining to a method of operating a computer in which each step is performed in response to a single manual operation.

single-step debugging — An important first step in system debug is to check out in a single-step mode the simplest instructions which enable information to be entered into registers and which permit system states to be set up. Once this has been done, short routines which set up system states can be written. Then the response of the microprocessor to these states can be checked.

single-step mode — A mode that allows an operator to have the computer execute just one instruction at a time; thus the operator can closely examine the results of each operation to determine if an algorithm performs as planned.

single-step operation — A method of operating an automatic computer manually in which a single instruction or part of an instruction is performed in response to a single operation of a manual control. This method is generally used for detecting mistakes.

single thread processing — *See* processing, single thread.

single vertical key — A push button on a printer which produces an additional printed line for indication.

sink — A device capable of accepting data signals from a transmission device. It may also check these signals and originate error control signals. Opposite of source.

sink, network — The point of usage of data in a network. A data terminal installation that receives and processes data from a connected channel.

SIO interface — Abbreviation for Serial Input-Output interface. An interface that accepts data from an output device (typically a tty keyboard or a cassette recorder) in consecutive (serial) form and converts this data stream into, generally, 8-bit parallel words. The interface is also designed to convert 8-bit parallel words from computers into serial data streams to output to a serial device. Each serial word, both input and output, consists of a start bit, eight data bits, in many cases a parity bit, and one or two stop bits, for a total of ten to twelve serialized bits per word.

site, bit — A location on magnetic recording media where a "bit" of information is stored.

size, address — The maximum number of binary digits in an instruction used in directly addressing memory.

size, character — The number of binary digits in a single character in the storage device.

size, error — A condition that occurs when the number of positions to the left of the assumed decimal point exceeds the corresponding positions in the COBOL data-name field.

size, item — The magnitude of an item, usually expressed in numbers of fields, words, characters or blocks.

skeletal code — The framework of a routine that is formed by a generalized routine using input parameters.

sketchpad — A tool for engineers developed by Massachusetts Institute of Technology. The user draws with a light pen on a computer display scope. If he sketches a rough circle, it becomes perfect. He may erase, or he may magnify and reduce at a ratio of 2000 to 1. He may also sketch a part in perspective, then rotate the sketch to see the top, side, or bottom views of the sketched part.

skew — The percentage of bit errors which were caused by "ones" which were read as "zeros." Skew is an indication of possible threshold misalignment in modem receivers.

skew, character — *See* character skew.

skew, line — A type of line misregistration in which a string of characters to be read by an optical character reader appears in a uniformily slanted or skewed condition with respect to a real or imaginary baseline.

skip — An instruction to proceed to the next instruction; a "blank" instruction.

skip code — A functional code which instructs the machine to skip certain predetermined fields in memory.

skip flag — A one bit, in a specific position, that causes bytes to be skipped until the count equals zero. This skip instruction permits the computer to ignore portions of the input record to the memory.

skip instruction — An instruction having no effect other than directing the processor to proceed to another instruction designated in the storage portion.

skip (printer) — A skip function may be signaled on any step. When a skip is signaled on a step that also impulses a printout, the skip function is effective after the line has been printed. If skip is signaled on any other step, the skipping action is initiated immediately.

skip, tape — A machine instruction to forward space and erase a portion of a tape when a defect on the tape surface causes a write error to persist.

skip test — A specific type of microinstruction designed and utilized for conditional operations based on the state of readiness of various devices or the conditions of a register.

slave application — *See* computer, slave.

slave computer — *See* computer, slave.

slave, group select — In some systems, a particular group of terminals, when addressed by the master, can receive data sent by the master. Terminals not having this particular group address do not receive data even though they are within the same communications network.

slave mode — The mode of computer operation in which most of the basic controls affecting the state of the computer are protected from the program.

slave system — A particular system which is connected to another system and in which the commanding or master system discharges commands and orders which are thus imitated by the slave system.

slave system/terminal — A remote system or terminal whose functions are controlled by a central "master" system. It is similar in concept to a host system in that it responds to remotely generated requests, but unlike a host system, it is usually capable of performing a limited range of operations.

slave, unique select — In some systems, each terminal can have a unique address which is different from its group address. When a terminal is addressed with this unique code by a master, it is possible to establish two-way communication between those two terminals and no others in the network. Also, the master can inhibit this uniquely selected terminal from transmitting.

slew, paper — *Same as* paper throw.

slew rate — Fast signal response, measured in volts per second. Used in operational-amplifier specifications.

slice — 1. A special type of chip architecture that permits the cascading or stacking of devices to increase word bit size. 2. Those parts of a waveform lying inside two given amplitude limits on the same side of the zero axis.

slice architecture — In a "slice" architecture, a section of the register file and ALU in a computer is placed in one package. In some systems the registers are all four bits wide; others accommodate two bits. Each end of each register is accessible through the ALU at the chip edge; two or more of these "slices" can be cascaded together to form larger word sizes. Whether instruction lengths are identical to data word size or not depends upon how the control portion of the processor is organized. In some systems, another chip in the set provides eight microprogrammed control sections.

slice architecture microcomputers — Modular component building blocks, called bit slices, are used to fabricate microprocessors of varying word width such as 8 bit, 12 bit, 16 bit, 24 bit, etc. The completed products are generally customized and offer higher performance than conventional machines. Unlike conventional machines that have a fixed predefined instruction set, the slice architectures require an instruction set to be defined and implemented via a microprogram. This provides a system that is efficiently tailored to a particular application. Often, the high-performance slice component products are used to emulate existing older technology computer architectures. In this case, a microprogram is used to make the slice machine execute the instruction of the emulated computer. For one application, there are two levels of programming: first, the microprogram firmware, and second, the software of the emulated machine. This two-level complexity has discouraged universal acceptance of these devices compared to fixed instruction microprocessors. Applications that require high performance and efficient architectures are the domain of the slice approach.

slice, time — An allotment of computer time for a particular task to be accomplished (a concept in multiprogramming or time sharing).

slit scan, divided — *See* scan, divided slit.

slot — On a magnetic drum, all the cells under a set of read/write heads at one instant of time.

slow memory — Those portions of the memory with a relatively slow access rate from which information may be obtained automatically.

SLSI — Abbreviation for Super Large Scale Integration. Often related to 100,000 or more transistors per chip.

small-scale integration — Abbreviated SSI. The earliest form of integrated-circuit technology. Typically an SSI circuit contains from one to four logic circuits.

"smart" interactive terminal — An interactive terminal in which part of the processing is accomplished by a microcomputer or microprocessor contained in the terminal itself. This type of terminal is sometimes referred to in the literature as an "intelligent terminal." To be considered a smart terminal the computing capability of the minicomputer in the terminal must be available to the user in a way that permits him to program it to perform part of his unique application.

"smart" terminal components — In its most rudimentary form, a smart terminal contains a crt, a keyboard, a serial communication i/o device, and a microcomputer. The microcomputer controls text editing, formatting, and the protocol of communication with the host computer system. Such terminals can incorporate peripheral memory devices like tape cassettes, can be programmed independently of their roles in the larger computer system, and can therefore serve several useful functions, both on- or off-line. For example, the microcomputer can serve as a communications controller and handle tasks like line switching.

"smart" terminal, editing — Editing can mean anything from character delete and insert, to line delete and insert, to field delete and insert, to page delete and insert, to clear line (clear to end of line from cursor location), to clear page (clear to end of page from cursor location except for protected fields), to clear memory (clear all refresh memory including protected fields), to automatic justification of text, or any combination of these.

"smart" vs "intelligent" terminal — By one definition, a truly intelligent terminal is user programmable, while a smart terminal provides built-in capability not alterable by the user. For example, a terminal that can implement special functions if one plugs in a new ROM is smart, but not intelligent. At the low end of the spectrum, dumb terminals can talk only with computers and find use as low-cost teleprinter replacements.

smudge — In OCR (optical character recognition), the displacement of ink under shear beyond the original edges of a printed character.

smudge resistance — The property of ink that tends to prevent the inadvertent smudging of a printed image in normal use.

SNA — Abbreviation for Systems Network Architecture. The IBM standardized relationship between its virtual telecommunication access method (VTAM) and the network control program (NCP/VS).

snapshot copy — In some systems, with the snapshot command, the entire contents of one disk drive are copied to another similar drive while user activity is suspended. However, this type of copy may be initiated off-site, at a time of little or no system activity.

snapshot debugging — *See* debugging, snapshot.

snapshot dump — A selective dynamic dump performed at various points in a machine run.

snapshot program — When a trace program is an interpretive program, it is called an interpretive trace program, and when a trace program gives output only on selected instructions or for a selected set or single condition it is called a snapshot program.

snapshots — The capture of the entire state of a machine (real or simulated)—the memory contents, registers, flags, etc.

SNOBOL 4 — Abbreviation for StriNg-Oriented symBOlic Language. A programming language used mainly for advanced string manipulation. Some examples of this are in artificial intelligence, compiler construction, and text preparation. Used on batch, real-time, and time-sharing systems. (Bell Labs.)

soft error rate — A specific type of bit-error-rate attributable to transient conditions in a bulk storage system. Such errors may theoretically be eliminated by repeating the transfer operation.

soft-fail — Often called fail-soft. Pertaining to techniques that preserve a degree of system operation despite failures.

soft key terminal — A type of terminal which the user can personalize for specific job functions. For instance, the user could assign one key to generate a computer log-on sequence and another to call up an order entry form. These "soft keys" are simple to program, with each of them capable of storing up to 80 characters on some terminals.

soft sector — A sector (section) on a disk marked by information written on the disk. Sector marks are used by the disk controller to locate specific areas of the disk. For example, the controller may be looking for sector 3, track 4. New floppy disks typically come preformatted, meaning the sector codes are already written on the disk between the data portions.

soft-sectored disk system — A disk format in which the beginning of every sector is decided by the user and is so recorded on the disk, in contrast to hard-sectored.

soft-sector formatting — The standard diskette is designed for use with a format in which the sector information is prerecorded on the diskette during an initialize operation. In this case, a single hole on the diskette serves as a reference point. The format in which the sector information is prerecorded on the diskette is referred to as the soft-sectored format.

software — Various programming aids that are frequently supplied by the manufacturers to facilitate the purchaser's efficient operation of the equipment. Such software items include various assemblers, generators, subroutine libraries, compilers, operating systems, and industry-application programs.

software, common — Programs or routines which usually have common and multiple applications for many systems, i.e., report generators, sort routines, conversion programs which can be used for several routines in language common to many computers.

software, communication — *See* communication software.

software, compatible — Languages which can be used on more than one computer system.

software control, microprocessor — The changing control of computers as a result of software or programs. The memory portion of the computer stores the program and data; the microprocessor portion of the system executes the stored programs. In most cases where the data rates dictated by the external environment are faster than the execution cycle time of the program, provisions for this condition must be made, usually in the form of hard-wired logic in the external hardware; the microprocessor communicates with the resulting hardware.

software cross-products (microprocessor) — These include assemblers, simulators, and various compilers. They develop versions of programs which are used for assembly, simulation, or compilation of programs. A cross-assembler, for example, is functionally identical to other resident assemblers. Compilers are machine-oriented systems programming languages designed specifically to generate various internal codes. Assemblers often have full macro capability and allow for conditional assembly (meaning that at the time of assembly, one of several sections of code may be chosen).

software documentation — Program listings and/or documentation consisting of technical manuals describing the operation and use of programs.

software documents — *See* documents, software.

software driver — A series of instructions the computer follows to reformat data for transfer to and from a particular peripheral device. The electrical and mechanical requirements are different from one kind of device to another, and the software drivers are used to standardize the format of data between them and the central processor. Software drivers are often provided to interface the system to floppy disks, crt or printing terminals, electronic typewriters, line printers, and paper-tape peripherals.

software emulation — That group of techniques (software programs) often in microprograms that permit one computer to execute the machine-language code of another computer, generally for the purpose of minimizing reprogramming during conversion of one system to another or for use in a development system.

software error interrupts — Nearly all software errors eventually result in an interrupt indicating an invalid operation, addressing error, or a protection violation. The major problem with using only this approach is that there may be a significant time lapse between the occurrence of an error and the use of damaged data in a way which causes a hardware-detectable violation. During this time period, damage may be propagated, obscuring the original error and making successful repair and recovery less likely.

software, floppy-disk — Software is required for a floppy-disk system to function. This software is called an operating system, and is often called a DOS. The operating system handles such functions as controlling the drive motor, positioning the read/write head, locating specific data on the surface of the floppy disk, creating files, transferring data, etc. It also provides communication with the user via command instructions.

software functions, time-sharing — *See* time-sharing software functions.

software house — A company that offers software support service to users.

software interrupts — Some systems allow interrupts to be enabled or disabled, through software, during program operation. Such masking allows priorities to change dynamically in response to system conditions. For example, a real-time program can disable data entry terminals whenever critical analog data is being collected. As soon as the scan is complete, the terminals can be automatically enabled and ready to input data.

software, key-to-disk — Key-to-disk software permits, in most cases, validation of original source data as well as operator entry checks, data reformatting, separate data files for storage of constant data, validation tables, and information retrieval and execution of application programs.

software, microcomputer (typical system) — Standard software for many micros includes an assembler, loader, debugging utility, source edit utility, and diagnostic programs. The assembler translates symbolic assembly language programs into executable machine programs. The loader loads object tapes produced by the assembler or debugging utility. The debugging utility aids program checkout and features multiple breakpoints, instruction trace, and several other standard functions. The source edit utility is used to generate assembly language source tapes or modify existing source tapes. The diagnostics are used to verify processor operation.

software, microprocessor — Software, by directing the hardware, enables the microprocessor to perform a functional system related task. In a fixed-instruction microprocessor, a set number of instructions or operations are defined with fixed word lengths, and these exercise the CPU independent of the data. Software is alterable and accessible by the user.

software monitor — The package of software usually stored on PROMs that gives the computer a fundamental interactive intelligence. The monitor is a type of executive secretary for the user. It tells the computer how and where to acquire the programs and data, where to store them, and how to run them. The monitor usually contains software routines and i/o drivers needed by the user to perform system operations.

software package — Various computer programs or sets of programs used in a particular application such as a payroll/personnel package, scientific subroutines package, etc.

software package, terminal — Most terminal makers offer data-processing and communications software packages that interface to specific communications software and operating systems in host computers. The data-processing portions of these packages consist of graphics application programs and compilers in high-level languages such as FORTRAN.

software prototyping — One software development approach uses a combination of hardware and software called a prototyping system. Prototyping systems provide program assembly, online execution, and debugging. A general-purpose prototyping system allows the designer-programmer to be more creative and productive in the design of a particular microcomputer application. As a result, companies in this business either design a prototyping system as their first product or buy it. Using an on-line teleprinter, the designer-programmer assembles, edits, and stores the program in RAM associated with a computer in the prototype system. Switching to the "operate" mode, the microprocessor in the application system accesses the program in the prototyping system as if it were in its own ROM, and check-out begins.

software, random access — *See* random-access software.

software, remote — Program downloading, remote operation of peripherals and file manipulation programs, remote editing, debugging, and program preparation functions. All this requires communications routines with redundancy checks and retry capability.

software requirements, time-sharing — *See* time-sharing software requirements.

software "sealed-in" — A method by which it is feasible to preserve the secrecy of a program in ROM, even though the ROM is in the customer's possession. This is accomplished by packaging in one sealed unit on a circuit board both the ROM memory necessary to hold the proprietary program and a separate, dedicated micro CPU. The sealed-in dedicated CPU stands between the proprietary code and the outside world. The sealed package of the circuit board is designed to be piggybacked into the host computer. There it gets its power and works in cooperation with the host CPU, host memory, and host peripherals. The addressing buses within the sealed package are arranged so that the host computer cannot address any of the ROM in the sealed package.

software stack — An area in read-write memory set aside under program control. An on-chip hardware stack provides increased performance. For hardware stacks to be generally useful, there should also be on-chip indicators for stack full and stack empty, which increases chip area. However, the on-chip hardware required for a software stack consists primarily of a stack-pointer register and appropriate increment/decrement control. An indication of overflow and underflow is not so critical as for an on-chip hardware stack, since the software stack can be easily expanded in system memory.

software support systems — Software support systems execute the object program in the same manner as the microprocessor would. Thus, the programmer can check to determine if the original source program performs its functions correctly.

software system, microprogram assembler — One system is designed to microprogram all control signals and memory to reduce prototype time for various systems. The microprogram assembler provides software assistance and documentation for writing and modifying microprograms and generating tapes for PROM programmers. Such systems can include a framework for a common language, automatic accounting information, and billing control. Many such systems are available on time-sharing services of major service companies.

software trace mode — A mode in which the program halts and the internal status of the microprocessor is made available to the outside world wherever breakpoint conditions are met. In addition to the mnemonic instructions and the memory addresses, the user can view register contents, program counter location, stack pointer, and condition codes or flags. Breakpoints can be set at every instruction if desired. The primary advantage of this mode is the depth of insight it gives into program operation. The capability is fully interactive, enabling the user easily to alter register contents, make source code changes to correct program errors, reassemble programs, and rerun to test corrections.

software, universal development system — Generally, a system that provides users with all software required for evaluation and development of system concepts and final design of applications programs. It includes cross-assembler, editor, loaders, i/o drivers, host/target debug, and other features.

SOH—Abbreviation for Start Of Header — A communication control character used at the beginning of a sequence of characters which constitute a machine-sensible address or routing information. Such a sequence is referred to as the header.

solenoid, forward — An electromechanical device which, when energized, maintains pressure via a roller, forcing magnetic tape against the forward capstan, which moves the tape in a forward direction.

solenoid, reverse — That electromechanical device which performs a maintenance of pressure via a roller, forcing magnetic tape against the reverse capstan which moves the tape in the reverse direction.

solid error — An error that always occurs when a particular piece of equipment is used.

solid-logic technology — Abbreviated SLT. Microelectric circuits, the product of solid-logic technology, are the basic components of some systems. Called logic circuits because they carry and control the electrical impules that represent information within a computer, these tiny devices operate at speeds ranging from 300 down to six billionths of a second. Transistors and diodes mounted on the circuits are as small as 28 thousandths of an inch square and are protected by a film of glass 60 millionths of an inch thick.

solid-state circuitry — The solid-state components in circuits of computers.

solid-state component — A component whose operation depends on the control of electric or magnetic phenomena in solids, e.g., a transistor, crystal diode, or ferrite core.

solid-state computer — A computer built primarily from solid-state electronic circuit elements.

solid-state devices — The electronic components that convey or control electrons within solid materials, e.g., transistors, germanium diodes, and magnetic cores. Thus, vacuum and gas tubes are not included.

solid-state logic — *Same as* solid-logic technology.

solution check — A solution to a problem obtained by independent means to verify a computer solution.

solution, feasible — A solution to the constraint equations in which all variables satisfy their restrictions (linear programming).

solution, geometric — *See* geometric solution.

solution, graphic — A solution obtained with graphs or other pictorial devices. (As contrasted with solutions obtained by the manipulation of numbers.)

solution, machine independent — A solution procedure developed in terms of a logical solution to a problem rather than in terms of a particular mechanized processing system.

solver, equation — A calculating device, usually analog, that solves systems of linear simultaneous nondifferential equations or determines the roots of polynomials, or both.

S-100 bus — A specific assembly of 100 parallel common communication lines, each of which is capable of carrying one bit or signal through the entire computer. Typically, the computer bus itself consists of a bank of printed-circuit card-edge connectors soldered to a common mother board. The connectors are used to accept the CPU card, memory cards, and i/o cards for the computer system. The standard S-100 bus card is 5 × 10 inches with a 100-contact edge connection (50 on each side of the card). In order to accommodate a large number of cards, a large mother board with long bus traces is required. To avoid problems associated with capacitive coupling between traces, shielded mother boards may be necessary. To keep the cost of the main frame low, an unregulated power supply is normally used. Each computer card provides distributed regulation via three-terminal regulators. The S-100 bus requires nominal supply voltages of +8 volts, +18 volts, and −18 volts. The existence of three supply voltages on the bus is important in providing flexibility in mating with a variety of memory and i/o interface cards.

sonic delay line — A delay line using a medium (such as mercury or quartz) providing acoustic delay. (Related to mercury delay line.)

sophisticated vocabulary — An advanced and elaborate set of instructions. Some computers can perform only the more common mathematical calculations such as addition, multiplication, and subtraction. A computer with a sophisticated vocabulary can go beyond this and perform operations such as linearize, extract square root, and select highest number.

sort — 1. To arrange items of information according to rules dependent upon a key or field contained in the items. 2. A systems program which arranges a file of items in a logical sequence according to a designated key word contained within each item (e.g., the arranging of items according to date, code number, etc.).

sort, ascending — A sort in which the final sequence of records is such that successive keys compare greater than or equal to.

sort, block — A sort of one or more of the most significant characters of a key to serve as a means of making workable-size groups from a large volume of records.

sort, bubble — A sorting technique which exchanges a pair of numbers if they are out of order.

sort (COBOL) — Some systems provide for SORT as used with the COBOL language to create sorted records in ascending order or descending order on the basis of multilevel key fields.

sort, descending — A sort in which the final sequence of records is such that the successive keys compare less than or equal to.

sort, digital — *See* digital sort.

sorter, magnetic-character — Equipment designed to read, translate, and sort documents imprinted with the various magnetic-ink type fonts.

sort, external — The second phase of a multipass sort program, wherein strings of data are continually merged until one string of sequenced data is formed.

sort, fine — Usually off-line detail sorting by the sorter especially used in banks; for example, fine sorting could be the function of arranging checks and deposits into customer account number order.

sort, four-tape — *See* sorting, four-tape.

sort, generalized — A sort program which will accept the introduction of parameters at run time and which does not generate a program.

sort, generated — A production program which was produced by a sort generator.

sorting — The process of arranging data into some desired order according to rules dependent upon a key or field contained by each item.

sorting, balanced — A technique used in a sort program to merge strings of sequenced data.

sorting, checkpoint — *Same as* sorting, restart.

sorting, collating — A sort which uses a technique of continuous merging of data until one sequence is developed.

sorting, comparison-of-pairs — Determination of the order of two records by the comparison of the keys in the two records.

sorting, computer limited — A sort program in which the executive time of the internal instructions determines the elapsed time required to sort.

sorting control card — A card which is used to specify the parameters for a sort.

sorting control field — A continuous group of characters within a record which form all or part of the control word.

sorting, digital — To sort first the keys on the least significant digit, and then to resort on the next higher-order digit until the items are sorted on the most significant digit. A punched-card technique.

sorting, disk — A sort program that utilizes disk-type memory for auxiliary storage during sorting.

sorting, Fibonacci series — Some sort programs distribute strings of data onto work tapes so that the number of strings on successive tapes form a Fibonacci series. (The current number is equal to the sum of the two preceding numbers, i.e., 1, 2, 3, 5, 8, and so on.)

sorting, first-pass (own coding) — Computer instructions created by the programmer, in assembly or absolute form, which are executed by a sort during the first pass of the file after the input program has been loaded but prior to execution of first-pass sequencing instructions.

sorting, four-tape — Merge sorting in which input data are supplied on two tapes and are sorted into incomplete sequences alternately on two output tapes. The output tapes are used for input on the succeeding pass, resulting in longer and longer sequences after each pass until the data are all in one sequence on one output tape.

sorting, input tape(s) — Tape(s) containing a file in arbitrary sequence to be introduced into a sort/usage program.

sorting, insertion method — A method of internal sorting where records are moved to permit the insertion of records.

sorting, intermediate pass — Any phase of a merging operation which, because of the number of strings or otherwise, does not reduce the file to a single sequenced string.

sorting item — The basic element of a file such that the sorting of the file constitutes the reordering of file records.

sorting key — The fields in a record which determine, or are used as a basis for determining, the sequence of records in a file.

sorting, magnetic-tape — A sort program that utilizes magnetic tapes for auxiliary storage during a sort.

sorting, merge — To produce a single sequence of items, ordered according to some rule, from two or more previously unordered sequences, without changing the items in size, structure, or total number. Although more than one pass may be required for a complete sorting, items are selected during each pass on the basis of the entire key.

sorting, multifile — The automatic sequencing of more than one file, based upon separate parameters for each file, without operator intervention.

sorting, multireel — The automatic sequencing of a file having more than one input tape, without operator intervention.

sorting, own coding — Special coding provided by the programmer, which is intergrated with sort/merge coding.

sorting, pass — The processing of each file record for the purpose of reducing the number of strings of sequenced records and increasing the number of sequenced records per string.

sorting, phase — An arbitrary segmentation of a sort program. Many sorts are segmented into three phases; initialization phase, internal phase, and merge phase.

sorting, process-limited — A sort program in which the exception time of the internal instructions determines the elapsed time required to sort.

sorting restart — The return to a previous point in the program where processing may begin. The previous point may be the beginning of the program or it may be a checkpoint.

sorting, return point — *Same as* sorting, restart.

sorting rewind time — Elapsed time consumed by a sort/merge program for restoring intermediate and final tape to original position.

sorting scratch tape — Tape(s) used to store intermediate-pass data during a sort program.

sorting sequencing criteria — *Same as* sorting, sequencing key.

sorting sequencing key — The field in a record which determines, or is used as a basis for determining, the sequence of records in a file.

sorting string — A group of sequential records, normally stored in auxiliary computer storage, i.e., disk, tape, or drum.

sorting, tape-limited — Also input/output limited. A sort program in which the effective transfer rate of tape units determines the elapsed time required to sort.

sorting variable-length records — Denumerable file elements for which the number of words, characters, bits, fields, etc., is not constant.

sorting, von Neuman — A technique used in a sort program to merge strings of sequenced data. The power of the merge is equal to T/2.

sorting work tape(s) — Tape(s) used to store intermediate-pass data during a sort program.

sorting, Xmas-tree — A technique used in

the internal portion of a sort program. The results of the comparisons between groups of records are stored for later use.

sort, internal — The sequencing of two or more records within the central computer memory; the first phase of a multipass sort program.

sort/merge — A set of routines to arrange random items in an ordered sequence. These routines can also be used to combine two or more ordered sequences into a single file.

sort/merge generator — Custom programs for sorting files of data.

sort/merge program — The sort/merge program is designed to satisfy the sorting and merging requirements of tape- or random-storage–oriented installations. It is a generalized program that can produce many different sorting or merging programs in accordance with control information specified by the user.

sort/merging, disk — Sort/merging of data on disks may often be programmed to avoid excessive positioning or waiting time until the disk rotates to a desired position. This is accomplished by placing the blocks of data so that after reading data block N, and the processing of data block N, the reading (or writing) of block N + 1 will take place just at that point to which the disk has rotated or the head has moved.

sort, multipass — A sort program which is designed to sort more data than can be contained within the internal memory of a central computer. Intermediate storage, such as disk, tape, or drum, is required.

sort, property — A sort completed by selecting from groups of items which have particular characteristics which meet selected criteria and according to certain keys, such that the priority or ordering of the sort relates to a specific property of the key, e.g., sorting by countries, then by states, then by counties, then by cities, and each according to population sizes within their individual groups.

sorts, random-access — Separate programs are furnished by manufacturers to sort data stored on random-access disks and drums. These programs strip off the memory-item keys of data stored on a random-access storage unit, sort the keys, and then store on the disk or drum a table containing the keys and the addresses of the corresponding file items. Items may be brought into memory from the disk or drum in the order of the sorted keys by using the macroinstructions.

sorts, tape — Generalized programs that adapt themselves, as directed by programmer-specified parameters, to operate in a particular configuration and to sort data in a particular format. Many of these programs take advantage of the polyphase-sorting technique developed by Honeywell. Tailored for use in small card-oriented systems is a sort program that requires only three tape units and receives its specialization parameters by card. This program sorts fixed-length records on up to seven keys, and provides facilities for self-coding.

sort, tag — A tag sort extracts only the keys from each record and sorts them. Thus, the information from fixed or variable length records can be retained in a minimum amount of memory by the key-sort method. Some types of tag sorts have an exclusion capability permitting selection of records that are not to participate in the sort.

sort utility — The activity or function performed by a program, often a utility package, in which items in a data file are arranged or rearranged in a logical or specifically defined sequence as designated by a key word or field in each item in the file. Hundreds of different types of sort techniques are available for highly selective operations and data use applications.

SOS — Abbreviation for Silicon On Sapphire. Refers to the layers of material, and indirectly to the process of fabrication, of devices which achieve bipolar speeds through MOS technology by insulating the circuit components from each other.

sound output, programmable — Most personal computers with sound output have a single bit port which can produce sound only with the constant attention of the microprocessor. This means that an interactive game must stop processing animation while it is outputting sound. Some firms have solved this with a programmable divider which will constantly output a tone as specified by the contents of one memory location. Thus, a BASIC program can easily support a real-time animated game with sound output because the "overhead" for sound generation is minimal. The programmable divider sound output is specified by the contents of the one memory location and can be turned on and off via another register.

source address — In computer systems that have a source-destination architecture, the source address is the address of the device or memory location from which data is being transferred.

source address instruction — *Same as* address instruction, functional.

source code — The original mnemonic or high-level statement versions of a program. The starting information or "source" from which the final "object" (machine language or final code) is derived.

source computer — The computer that is utilized to prepare problems as input for other computer operations.

source data — *See* data, source.

source data collection — Source data collection involves devices such as optical character readers and printers, magnetic strip encoders and readers, embossed badge systems, digitizers, point-of-sale systems, environmental monitors, and tag readers in commercial, scientific, and military applications. It also covers key-to-tape, key-to-disk, key-to-diskette, key-to-cassette, etc., except key-to-cards, since source data automation is usually concerned with replacing keypunch functions in a data-processing system. Source data collection usually includes three distinctive elements: an encoding device, almost always computer-controlled; an automatically sensible element (such as a credit card), which uniquely identifies one entry in the data base; and a sensor, or high-speed conversion device for capturing the data for computer entry.

source data entry, OCR — Source data entry by means of optical character recognition (OCR), in which human-readable documents are optically scanned and read into the computer directly, without keying or rekeying. In mixed media systems, OCR is combined with keyboard-to-storage in the same equipment. An advantage is that misread or unreadable characters rejected by the OCR can be keyed in by a data-entry operator.

source-destination instruction — *See* instruction, source-destination.

source document — *See* document, source.

source editors — Programs that facilitate the entry and modification of the source code into a computer system for later translation, on-line storage, off-line storage, or listing on a printer for later reference. Without a source editor the programmer would have to go through a tedious process of building his program on a unit record physical medium like cards, or through a virtually impossible process using a sequential medium like paper tape. Source editors are best designed when they take into consideration the characteristics of the language being entered and the type of communications terminal used.

source file editor — A line-oriented editor that operates in an OS environment. Editing of programs can be done sequentially by their assembler produced source statement line numbers. The source file editor produces a resultant updated file while preserving the original master file.

source language — The original form in which a program is prepared prior to processing by the machine.

source-language debugging — Debugging information is requested by the user and displayed by the system in a form consistent with the source programming language.

source language translation — The translation of a program to a target program, for example, to FORTRAN, ALGOL, etc., to machine language, the instructions being equivalent in the source program and to the automatic or problem-oriented language as FORTRAN, the translating process being completed by the machine under the control of a translator program or compiler.

source machine — The computer on which the source program is translated into the object program.

source module — A particular organized set of statements in any source language recorded in machine-readable form and suitable for input to an assembler or compiler.

source operand register — In some systems, a register that contains the last source operand of a double operand instruction. The high byte may not be correct if the source is a forbidden mode.

source program — A program coded in other than machine language that must be translated into machine language before use.

source recording — *See* recording, source.

source routine — *Same as* program, source.

source utility — The source utility facilitates the preparation and modification of symbolic assembly language source tapes. Edit is an interactive program which enables the user to perform the following functions, often by way of the teletypewriter: construct a symbolic source tape; insert, delete, replace, and modify statements in an existing source program, and obtain a new source tape which incorporates the modifications; obtain a state-numbered listing of the program being edited.

space — 1. A site intended for the storage of data, e.g., a site on a printed page or a location in a storage medium. 2. A basic unit of area, usually the size of a single character. 3. One or more space characters. 4. To advance the reading or display position according to a prescribed format, e.g., to advance the printing or display position horizontally to the right or vertically down.

space code — Similar to skip code, but restricted to one space at a time.

space, dead — A specific range of values in which the incoming signal can be altered without also changing the outgoing response. (Synonymous with dead zone, and similar to neutral zone.)

space, interblock — *Same as* gap, interrecord.

space, interword — *Same as* gap, interword.

space suppression — The withholding of the movement of platen and/or paper for a line of printing.

space, switching — *Same as* gap, interword.

space-to-mark transition — The transition, or switching, from a spacing impulse to a marking impulse.

space, word — The actual area or space occupied by a word in serial digital devices such as drums, disks, tapes, and serial lines.

space, working — A portion of the internal storage reserved for the data upon which operations are being performed. (Synonymous with temporary storage, and contrasted with program storage.)

spacing bias — Bias distortion which lengthens the spacing impulse by delaying the space-to-mark transition.

spacing chart, printer — *See* printer spacing chart.

spacing-end distortion — End distortion which lengthens the spacing impulse by advancing the mark-to-space transition.

spacing, reference line character — *See* character-spacing reference line.

speaker dependent — Pertaining to a class of voice-operated hardware that uses pattern recognition techniques and requires the operator to give the equipment a sample of speech patterns before words can be recognized.

speaker identification, voice systems — An area of application wherein a previously spoken utterance is processed and analyzed according to its acoustic components for the purpose of isolating one from a group of speakers, not unlike fingerprint matching.

speaker independent — Pertaining to a class of voice-operated equipment requiring no prior speech sampling.

speaker verification, voice system — An area of application wherein the speaker's voice pattern is matched to previously entered patterns in storage to verify and authorize the speaker. Typical usage is for facility access controls.

special character — A character other than a digit or letter, e.g., *+−$=.

special-instruction repertoire — *See* repertory, instruction.

specialized data processing — *See* data processing, specialized.

specialized processing — *See* data processing, specialized.

special-purpose computer — A computer designed to solve a specific class or narrow range of problems.

special sign — *Same as* character, special.

specific address — An address that indicates the exact storage location where the referenced operand is to be found or stored in the actual machine-code address-numbering system. (Related to absolute code.)

specific addressed location — *See* addressed location, specific.

specific addressing — *See* addressing, specific.

specification — 1. For programming, a precise definition of the records and programs needed to carry out a particular processing function. 2. As an equipment concept, a technical or engineering description of the hardware.

specification, program — The precise and ordered definitions of logic, and scope of processing functions, that are performed by a particular program or program segments.

specification statements — *See* statements, specification.

specific code — *See* code, absolute.

specific coding — *Same as* addressing, specific.

specific program — A program for solving a specific problem only.

specific routine — A routine to solve a particular mathematical, logical, or data-handling problem in which each address refers to explicitly stated registers and locations.

specific symbol — *Same as* character, special.

spectroradiometer, computer-controlled — With a computer-controlled spectroradiometer, calibration is a simple operation, and calibration can be accomplished immediately prior to measurement. When the absolute values of the calibrated source are entered into one of the computer memory registers, the spectroradiometer can quickly calibrate itself by dividing its response at various wavelengths into this stored absolute value of the calibrated source at that wavelength. A correction table to be applied to measurements is thereby generated and stored, thus making possible accurate absolute power measurements of unknown sources in terms of the calibrated source.

speech control, variable — Abbreviated VSC. A method of speeding or slowing the playback of recorded speech without altering its pitch or tone.

speech input — A method of data entry in which a particular utterance is recognized within the terminal, then converted to a code such as ASCII, and transmitted to the host computer. The host sees it as data keyed in. The method is usually used in applications where an individual's hands and eyes are busy, such as in quality control, shipping, and receiving.

speech processor, digital — Some types of speech processors convert audio input from telephones to 2400-bit/s digital speech for transmission simultaneously with computer data. Linear predictive coding techniques are enhanced by microprocessor control.

speech synthesizer — A device that produces speech sounds from input in another form. One type of hobbyist speech synthesizer is a hard-wired analog of the human vocal tract; various portions of the circuit simulate the vocal cords, the lungs, and the variable-frequency resonant acoustic cavity of the mouth, tongue, lips, and teeth. Information necessary to produce speech sounds of standard American English is programmed into ROMs that reside on the synthesizer board. The unit accepts a string of ASCII characters (each character representing a particular phonetic sound, or phoneme) in exactly the same fashion as a printed peripheral. Because the synthesizer is primarily an analog circuit which is commanded digitally, new programming information is required only at the end of each completed phoneme. The maximum information transfer rate is about 50 bytes (phonemes) per second (25 bytes per second typical). The output audio signals are variable in pitch and speed, so the voice can be adjusted male or female and can speak slowly or quickly as desired.

speed, effective transmission — The rate at which information is processed by a transmission facility, expressed as the average rate over some significant time interval. This quantity is usually expressed as average characters per unit of time, or average bits per unit of time.

speed, paper tape — The rate, in characters per second, at which the unit reads or punches paper tape.

speed, printer — The rate at which the unit operates when actually printing data, ranging from the slowest to the fastest speed of the unit.

speed, tape — The rate at which the tape moves past the recording head during a data transfer.

speed, transmission — The number of information elements sent per unit time, usually expressed as bits, characters, items, word groups, or records per second or per minute.

spelling — The order of signs as they appear within printed or written words.

SPL — *see* system programming language.

split — The formation of two ordered files from one regular file, as contrasted with merged, i.e., usually unordered.

split catalog — A library catalog in which the different varieties of entry are filed separately, e.g., subject entry, author entry, title entry.

split-screen crt — A display format in which different sections or areas of each crt are dedicated to the display of specific types of information.

split-word operations — Either addition or subtraction can be performed on whole words, half words, or third words simultaneously, but there is never any interaction between the partial words. The right halves of two operands, for example, are added and the sum is stored in the right half of the selected accumulator. At the same time, the left halves of the same two operands are added and the result is stored in the left half of the same accumulator. Again, there is no carry interaction between the halves. (The same holds true for whole and third words.) Thus, split-word arithmetic increases computer speed and saves storage space due to shorter operands.

spool — The mounting for a magnetic, paper, or plastic tape.

spooled print — A process in which print data, which can clog a communication line and reduce response times, can be transmitted during times of low communication activity and spooled onto a disk or diskette. Later, this information may be printed locally without any host intervention.

spooling — A technique by which output to slow devices is placed into queues on mass storage devices to await transmission. This allows more efficient use of the system, since programs using low-speed devices can run to completion quickly and make room for others.

sporadic faults — *See* faults, sporadic.

spot, carbon — Carbon paper carbonized on some areas only so that certain entries will not be reproduced on the copy.

spot, flying — A small, rapidly moving spot of light, usually generated by a cathode-ray tube and used to illuminate successive spots of a surface containing dark and light areas. The varying amount of light reflected is detected by a phototube and used to produce a time succession of electronic s[illegible] effectively describe the surfa[illegible]

spot, reflective — An evident ma[illegible] indicates the initial beginning o[illegible] tape.

spread — The time interval, at either side of an ideal instant of modulation or restitution of a modulated carrier signal, in which occur the actual significant instants of the modulation or restitution.

sprocket holes — Feed holes punched in a tape to control the movement and positioning of the tape.

SPS — Abbreviation for Symbolic Programming Systems. A programming language in which terms may represent quantities and locations.

square chip carrier — A type of chip packaging device that occupies about one-third to one-sixth the area of a DIP. The longest trace on a 64-pin DIP is over six times as long as the corresponding trace on a 64-lead chip carrier. Thus, chip carriers have reduced longest-lead capacitance, resistance, and inductance.

squeal — As related to magnetic tape, subaudible tape vibrations, primarily in the longitudinal mode, caused by frictional excitation at heads and guides.

squeezeout — In optical character recognition (OCR), the displacement of ink from the center to the edges of a character during printing, resulting in a character with "darker" outlines than the center.

stability — In optical character recognition (OCR), the resistance to change of color of the image when exposed to radiant energy.

stability, computational — That particular degree to which a computational process becomes or remains valid and reliable when subjected to various conditions which tend to produce errors or malfunctions.

stability, light — The ability of an image to hold its spectral appearance when exposed to light or radiant energy in optical character reading equipment.

stack — 1. That portion of a computer memory and/or registers used to hold information temporarily. 2. A dynamic, sequential data list, usually contained in system memory, having special provisions for program access from one end or the other. Storage and retrieval of data from the stack is generally automatically performed by the processor.

stack architecture — Many microcomputers have a stack architecture wherein any portion of the external memory can be used as a last-in, first-out stack to store/retrieve the contents of the accumulator, the flags, or any of the data registers. Many units contain a 16-bit stack pointer to control the addressing of this external stack. One of the major advantages of the stack is that multiple level interrupts can easily be handled since complete system status can easily be saved when an interrupt occurs and then be restored after the interrupt. Another major advantage is that almost unlimited subroutine nesting is possible.

stack, dual hardware — Some systems offer dual hardware stacks implemented by the extended instructions. They are equivalent to large systems with overflow and underflow protection on all stack operations, regardless of stack placement in memory.

stacked graph — A graph with two or three x scales and the same number of y scales plotted in such a way that there are discrete plotting grids placed one above the other.

stacked multiprocessor — A multiprocessor system is a collection of two or more independent CPUs tied together via some kind of network and communication link. A tightly coupled (stacked) system has all its CPUs on a common bus sharing common memory and i/o facilities. A loosely coupled system has the CPUs with their own independent memory and i/o facilities communicating with one another on a message basis via a parallel or serial bus link. The tightly coupled systems are on a parallel bus and interleave access to the memory and i/o, on a cycle-by-cycle basis. Subgrouping of multiprocessor systems also includes master/slave and master/master networks. In a master/slave network, one processor (the master) controls the communication and activity assignments of the other processors (slaves). The slaves are generally not self-initiating. In a master/master scheme, each processor is independent and self-initiating. An arbitration algorithm and specific hardware control the communication flow. Each processor has a preassigned function.

stack facility, microcomputer — The stack facility available on many micros is limited, in contrast to the ones on standard minicomputers. The micro stack often requires the explicit handling of both the stacking data and the stack pointer register. A few micros implement a stack in a separate small memory space within an organization that effectively has an open bottom. Once the stack is filled, any attempt to push additional data onto the stack will destroy the first entry on the stack without any warning or hardware protection. In this organization, the size of the stack memory absolutely limits the depth of the stack. This stack limitation may restrict subroutine call nesting or the permitted level of context switching that the computer can handle, since these actions normally require entries on the stack.

stack, last in, first out — A stack as used in some systems is an area or memory set aside by the programmer for temporary storage or subroutine/interrupt service linkage. The instructions which facilitate stack handling are useful features found only on a few low-cost systems. They allow a program to dynamically establish, modify, or delete a stack and items on it. Some systems use the last-in, first-out concept; i.e., various items may be added to a stack in sequential order and retrieved or deleted from it in reverse order. Thus, this type of stack starts at the highest location reserved for it and expands linearly downward to the lowest address as items are added to the stack.

stack manipulation — In some systems, instruction addressing mode combinations facilitate temporary data storage structures. This can be used for convenient handling of data that must be accessed frequently and is known as stack manipulation. The register used to keep track of stack manipulation is generally known as the stack pointer. In these systems, any register can be used as a stack pointer under program control; however, certain instructions associated with subroutine linkage and interrupt service automatically use specific registers as a "hardware stack pointer."

stack pointer — A special register that enables a CPU to process "stacks" ("piles" or "nests") of data using a first-in, last-out (push-pop) or similar method. The stack pointer register "points" to (contains the address of) the current "top" or entry point of a stack of information.

stack pointer operation — Stack pointers are coordinated with the storing and retrieval of information in the stack. The stack pointer is decremented by one immediately following the storage in the stack of each byte of information. Conversely, the stack pointer is incremented by one immediately before retrieving each byte of information from the stack. The stack pointer may be manipulated for transferring its contents to the index register or vice versa. The address of a location is at the top of the stack.

stack, push-down — A push-down stack is essentially a last in, first out (LIFO) buffer. As data are added, the stack moves down, with the last item added taking the top position. Stack height varies with the number of stored items, increasing or decreasing with the entering or retrieving of data. The words "push" (move down) and "pop" (retrieve the most recently stored item) are used to describe its operation. In actual practice, a hardware-implemented push-down stack is a collection of registers with a counter which serves as a "pointer" to indicate the most recently loaded register. Registers are unloaded in the reverse of the sequence in which they were loaded. The principal benefit of the push-down stack is an aid to compiling. By reducing the use of registers necessary for temporary storage, stack architecture can greatly decrease the number of steps required in a program, thereby reducing costs.

stack, storage — *See* storage stack.

staging — The moving of data from an off-line or low-priority device back to an on-line or higher-priority device, usually on demand of the system or on request of the user.

stand-alone — Pertaining to a device that requires no other piece of equipment along with it to complete its own operation. It can operate independently.

stand-alone interactive terminal — Typically, a terminal built around a flexible processor programmed to take over some of the processing handled by the host computer.

stand-alone system — Usually, a microcomputer software development system that runs on a microcomputer without connection to another computer or a time-sharing system. This system then includes an assembler, editor, and debugging aids. It may include some of the features of a prototyping kit. Other stand-alones refer to terminals that contain a microcomputer to make the terminal in effect a full microcomputer with an add-on display capability.

stand-alone terminal components — Generally these include: interactive CPU, display, keyboard, memory, printer, mass storage, and interface ports.

stand-alone terminal, touch-screen — A special type of stand-alone terminal in which the user can initiate data transfer or other functions by touching the crt screen.

standard — The accepted, approved, or established criteria or requirements for controlling the technical performance and practices of programmers and others responsible for system organization and integration. Standards must necessarily be precisely developed and written, thoughtfully reviewed, and widely distributed in order to be of maximum effectiveness and acceptability.

standard graph — A graph plotted with one x scale and one or two associated y scales forming a single plotting grid.

standard interface — That specific form of interface (matching) previously designed or agreed upon so that two or several units, systems, programs, etc., may be easily joined or associated.

standard interrupts — Various events can lead to a program interrupt. Each interrupt is to a unique fixed-memory address that is associated with the event that caused it. Addresses are reserved for these interrupts. Each external device has an interrupt address. An external device may have more than one interrupt event, and each event may have its own interrupt address. Interrupts may occur only at the end of program instructions.

standardization — The establishment of specific procedural methods for the processing of data.

standardization, international data communication — ISO/TC97/SC-6: Internationally, there are a number of organizations involved either directly or indirectly with the development of data communication standards. Foremost among these is the International Organization for Standardization (ISO), Technical Committee (TC) 97, Subcommittee (SC) 6, concerned with digital data transmission. Membership in this subcommittee, as in all ISO activities, is provided by the national standards organizations of the participating countries. The US member is ANSI X3S3. The scope and program of work of this group include the continual surveillance of the telecommunication environment as it affects the development of data communication standards and the ability to build, install, operate, and maintain data-processing systems using telecommunications.

standardization, pulse — *Same as* pulse regeneration.

standardization, signal — *See* pulse regeneration.

standardize — 1. To cause conformity with established standards. 2. To establish standards. 3. To change a floating-point result so that the exponent and mantissa lie in a range that can vary according to the computer's design (mantissas represented by numbers between 1 and 9.99, e.g., 6.28×10^{18}, or numbers between 0 and .999, e.g., $.628 \times 10^{19}$).

standard memory locations — *See* memory locations, standard.

standard procedures, program — Suggested programming methods set by the manufacturer.

standard program — *See* program, standard.

standards, EIA, CCITT — These are two almost identical and widely followed standards defining the electrical and some of the mechanical properties of the interface between modems and data sets and data processing ("data terminal equipment") stations. These standards are the Electronic Industries Association Standard RS-232C (commonly referred to as "the EIA spec" or "RS-232"), and the International Telephone and Telegraph Consultative Committee Recommendation V.24 ("CCITT V.24").

standards, systems — System standards are either of the following: (1) the minimum required electrical performance characteristics of communication circuits that are based on the measured performance of existing developed circuits under the same operating conditions for which the new circuits were designed, (2) the specified characteristics necessary in order to permit interoperation of the system. (For example, the values for center frequencies for telegraph channels, test tone, etc.)

standard subroutine — A subroutine that is applicable to a class of problems.

standard, system — *See* system standard.

standard, working — A specified combination of a transmitting and receiving system, or subscriber's lines and feeding circuits (or equivalent systems), connected by means of a distortionless variable attenuator, and employed under specified conditions to determine by comparison the transmission quality of other telephone systems or parts of systems.

standby — 1. A condition of some equipment that will permit complete resumption of stable operation within a short period of time. 2. A duplicate set of equipment to be used if the primary unit becomes unusable because of malfunction.

standby application — An application in which two or more computers are tied together as part of a single overall system and which, as in the case of an inquiry application, stand ready for immediate activation and appropriate action.

standby block — 1. Locations always set aside in storage for communication with buffers in order to make more efficient use of such buffers. 2. An extra or reserve block of information stored in the internal computer memory so that the central computer need not wait for an input device to feed in, or an output device to take out, information.

standby, cold — A backup system that has to be turned on manually.

standby computer — The computer that is used in a dual or duplex system and is waiting to take over the real-time processing burden whenever the need arises.

standby equipment — Automatic data-processing equipment that is not in use and that is available in emergencies, such as machine breakdowns or cases of overload.

standby, hot — A backup system that is automatically switched into operation when a malfunction of the active system is detected.

standby register — A register in which accepted or verified information can be stored so as to be available for a rerun in case the processing of the information is spoiled by a mistake in the program, or by a malfunction in the computer.

standby time — 1. The elapsed time between inquires when the equipment is operating on an inquiry application. 2. The time during which two or more computers are tied together and available to answer inquiries or process intermittent actions on stored data.

standby time unattached — *Same as* standby unattended time.

standby unattended time — The time in which the machine is in an unknown condition and not in use working on problems. This includes time in which the machine is known to be defective and work is not being done to restore it to operating condition. It also includes breakdowns that render it unavailable due to outside conditions such as power shortages.

standby, warm — A backup system in which there may be a delay of seconds before it can be switched into operation after the active system malfunctions.

standing-on-nines carry — A carry out of a digit position generated by a carry into the digit position; the normal adding circuit is by-passed.

star network — Type of system in which all users communicate with a central point that has supervisory control over the system. Users communicate with each other only by permission of this central processor. Data movement is outward from or inward toward the host. If communication becomes necessary between the remote processors or terminals, the host acts as a central message switcher to pass data between them. This configuration makes the network simple to control.

star program — *See* program, star.

start bit — That specific bit that indicates the beginning of asychronous serial transmission.

start button — *Same as* button, initiate.

start dates, PERT — *See* PERT, start dates.

start element — A specific first element of a character in some serial transmissions. It is used to permit synchronization.

starting-dialing signal — In semiautomatic or automatic working, a signal transmitted from the incoming end of a circuit, following the receipt of a seizing signal, to indicate that the necessary circuit conditions have been established for receiving the numerical routine information.

start key — The push button on the control panel which initiates or resumes the operations of the equipment after an automatic or programmed stop.

start signal — *See* start-stop system.

start-stop — Pertaining to a system in which each code combination is preceded by a start signal which serves to prepare the receiving mechanism for the reception and registration of a character, and is followed by a stop signal which serves to bring the receiving mechanism to rest in preparation for the reception of the next character. The start and stop signals are referred to as "machine information" or synchronizing bits. *Also see* asynchronous.

start-stop system — A system in which each group of code elements corresponding to an alphabetical signal is preceded by a start signal which serves to prepare the receiving mechanism for the reception and registration of a character, and is followed by a stop signal which serves to bring the receiving mechanism to rest in preparation for the reception of the next character.

start-stop system, stepped — A start-stop system in which the start signals occur at regular intervals.

start-stop transmission — Asynchronous transmission in which each group of code elements corresponding to a character signal is preceded by a start signal which serves to prepare the receiving mechanism for the reception and registration of a character, and is followed by a stop signal which serves to bring the receiving mechanism to rest in preparation for the reception of the next character.

start time — The time between the interpretation of the tape instructions to read or write and the transfer of information to or from the tape into storage, or from storage into tape. (Synonymous with acceleration time.)

state — A computing term relating to the condition of all the units or elements of the system, i.e., the storage data, digits in registers, settings on switches, etc., including the question, what is their state?

state code — A coded indication of the state of the CPU, such as responding to an interrupt, servicing a DMA request, executing an i/o instruction, etc.

state, input — *See* input state.

statement — 1. In computer programming, a meaningful expression or a generalized instruction in a source language. 2. An instruction (macro) to the computer to perform some sequence of operations.

statement, arithmetic — A type of FORTRAN statement that specifies a numerical computation.

statement, declarative — Instructions in symbolic coding, or systems used to define and designate areas, constants, and symbols.

statement, job control — *See* job control statement.

statement number — A number that is associated with a single macrostatement so that reference may be made to that statement in terms of its number.

statement, parameter — A parameter statement assigns specified integer values to specified variables at compile time, e.g., parameter I = 2 causes the integer 2 to replace I whenever it occurs in the source program.

statement range, DO — All FORTRAN statements included in the repetitive execution of a DO loop operation.

statements, control — *See* control statements.

statements, data-formatting — Statements that instruct the assembly program to set up certain constants and to designate reserved memory areas and also to punctuate the memory to indicate field boundaries.

statements, imperative — Action statements of a symbolic program that are converted into actual machine-language instructions.

statements, program (communications) — A user's program is made up of program statements. When entered from a terminal, these statements are always retained in storage as part of the active program. If the user has an executable program statement within the program, he should assign a statement number to the statement referred to. Numbers 1 through 999 may be used as statement numbers, with no two statements having the same number. The statements acceptable to the remote-computing system are described in tables which give each statement in general form, its purpose, and one or more examples of its use.

statements, specification — These are nonexecutable FORTRAN compiler information required to define variables, allocate storage, and define subprograms to be used. The statements are type statements: REAL, INTEGER, EXTERNAL, DIMENSION, COMMON, EQUIVALENCE, DATA, and DEFINE FILE statements.

statements, type — Statements in FORTRAN used to overide the normal mode of assigning variable names and to reserving arrays.

state, output — The determination of the condition of a specified set of output channels, i.e., positive or negative, one or zero, etc.

state table — Sometimes called state transition table. A list of the outputs of a logic circuit based on the inputs and previous outputs. This type of circuit has memory and cannot be described by a simple truth table.

static — Nonmovable or unchanging.

static check — *See* check, static.

static dump — A dump that is performed at a particular point in time with respect to a machine run, frequently at the end of a run.

static error — An error that is independent of the time variable, as contrasted with a dynamic error.

static handling — Handling done completely by the compiler program.

staticize — 1. To convert serial or time-dependent parallel data into static time form. 2. Occasionally, to retrieve an instruction and its operands from storage prior to its execution.

staticizer — A storage device for converting time-sequential information into static time parallel information.

static memory — That type of MOS memory that uses flip-flops as storage elements. It does not need to be refreshed and does not require a clock. It does not lose its contents as long as power is applied.

static memory elements — Semiconductor memory devices that retain data stored in them indefinitely without further attention or refreshing as long as power is supplied.

static MOS circuits — MOS memories are produced with either static or dynamic circuits. Static memory cells are cross-coupled bistable circuits wherein information is stored by one of the two stable states. Most static MOS memory cells use six transistors for each cell or bit location.

static printout — *See* printout, static.

static storage — *See* storage, static.

static subroutine — A subroutine that involves no parameters other than the addresses of the operands.

station — 1. A device containing a tape drive, together with reading and writing heads and associated controls. (Synonymous with tape station.) 2. An independently controllable configuration of data terminal equipment from or to which messages are transmitted on a data link. It includes those elements that serve as sources or sinks for the messages, as well as those elements that control the message flow on the link, by means of data communication control procedures. *See also* terminal installation.

station, called — In communications switching, a called station is the one which receives the request from a calling station.

station, calling — In communications switching, the calling station directs the operations of selecting, polling, etc.

station, control — The station on a network which supervises the network control procedures such as polling, selecting, and recovery. It is also responsible for establishing order on the line in the event that contention or any other abnormal situation arises between any stations on the network. Compare tributary station.

station error detection — The process by which a slave station determines whether a message it receives is an accurate copy of what the master station transmitted. The process usually involves some sort of comparison or parity check.

station, inquiry — *See* inquiry station.

station, magnetic tape — *See* magnetic tape unit.

station, master — In a switching network, a station which sends data to a slave station.

station, multipoint — *See* tributary station.

station, net-control — A station on a network which coordinates the use of the network (or circuit) by all of the stations on the net.

station, point-to-point — A station that can be called by the central station, or can call the central station if it has a message to send.

station, remote — Usually input/output devices which are not at the immediate site of the computer and which permit additional input queries for data or information.

station, repeater — An intermediate station arranged to receive a signal from an adjacent station and amplify and retransmit it to another adjacent station.

station, secondary — A station that has been selected to receive a transmission from the primary station. The assignment of secondary status is temporary, under control of the primary station, and continues for the duration of a transmission.

station, slave — A station that receives data from a master communications station which it either monitors or with which it complies, or in some cases, repeats to other stations, but whose output is not part of the original output.

station, subscriber — The service provided by the common carrier to connect a customer's location to a central office. This always includes the circuit and some circuit-termination equipment, but may also include input/output equipment. Sometimes referred to as "local loop."

station, tape unit — *See* magnetic tape unit.

station, tributary — A station, other than the control station, on a centralized multipoint data communications system, which can communicate only with the control station when polled or selected by the control station.

station, way — A telegraph term for one of the stations on a multipoint circuit.

statistical analysis — One of the four main techniques of operations research. Data gathering, arranging, sorting, sequencing, and evaluating are all common statistical analyses. Statistical analysis combines mathematical techniques and computer technology to handle a wide range of business and scientific problems wherever large amounts of information or data must be evaluated and analyzed.

statistical data recorder — Under disc operating system (DOS), a feature that records the cumulative error status of an i/o device on the system recorder file. Abbreviated SDR.

statistical error — Inaccuracy arising in measurements of average count rate for random events, as a result of statistical fluctuations in the rate.

statistical universe — A statistical universe (or statistical population) is a complete group of things or phenomena which are similar in certain stated respects. For example, the heights of white native-born males between the ages of 21 and 65 constitute a universe of heights similar in that they all belong to a stated class of individuals (i.e., white, native-born males).

status — The current condition of a device. This usually indicates the flag flip-flops or special registers.

status bits, microprogram — Parameterization is a technique of recording parameters which characterize a system in storage elements such as status bits. Status bits are frequently used in information processing systems to store information about the conditions of the device. Frequently, program words can be saved if it is possible to set certain bits based on a condition of the network and then test these bits at subsequent instruction times. Microprograms can frequently be shortened by the use of status bits. Branches in the microprogram frequently can be made a number of instruction cycles after the status bits are set. This eliminates premature branching and the unnecessary duplication of microinstructions.

status flag latch — For functional control, in some systems, the status flags are generally latched. The latching arrangement can be anything from a simple flip-flop to an MSI device such as a 4-bit or 8-bit latch.

status, program (double-word) — *See* double word, program status.

status register — A register that is designed to hold status information inside a functional unit such as an MPU, DMA, and so on. A typical MPU has a status register that provides carry, overflow, sign, and zero interrupt. It could also include parity, enable, interrupt, and others.

status-register copy, single-chip systems — In some systems, the contents of the status register can be copied into the accumulator to enable status modification or conditional-branch testing. When the status register is copied into the accumulator, the contents of the status register are not altered, but the original contents of the accumulator are lost.

status scan — A command or key that automatically causes scans of all modems, on a selected line, and displays the status of modem/terminal power, key EIA interface signals, and test or back-up modes.

status table, subroutine — *See* table, subroutine.

status word — Information necessary to resume processing following the handling of an interruption of operations.

status word CANCL — A status word that indicates that the remote computing system has deleted some information.

status word (communications) — The status word is sent to the central processor in the same manner as the input data word, except that an external interrupt signal is generated after the channel synchronizer has placed the word on the input data lines. In this way, the central processor can distinguish status words from input data words.

status word, device — Abbreviated DSW. A computer word containing bits whose condition indicates the status of devices.

status word ERROR — A status word that indicates that the remote computing system has detected an error.

status word, programs — Abbreviated PSW. In most systems, the PSW is stored at a fixed location, the address of which depends on the type of interruption. The system then automatically fetches a new PSW from a different fixed location, the address of which is also dependent on the type of interruption. Each class of interruption has two fixed locations in main storage, one to receive the old PSW when the interruption occurs and the other to supply the new PSW that governs the servicing of that class of interruption. After the interruption has been serviced, a single instruction uses the stored PSW to reset the processing unit to the status it had before the interruption (some computers).

status word READY — A status word that indicates that the remote computing system is waiting for a statement entry from the terminal.

status word register — A group of binary

numbers that inform the user of the present condition of the microprocessor. In some systems, the status register provides information as follows: plus or minus sign, overflow indication, carry bit, all zeros in the accumulator, and interrupt bit status.

status words — 1. Words that either indicate something about the status of the system or indicate that the system is making response to, or diagnosis of, a statement that has been entered. The majority of status words are responses to program-debugging statements. 2. Words that contain control information generated by the peripheral control unit and the channel synchronizer. The status word is transmitted to the central processor over the data lines.

steady-state characteristics — Those particular characteristics relating to a condition, such as a value, rate, periodicity, or amplitude, which exhibit only negligible change over an arbitrarily long period of time. They may describe conditions in which some characteristics are static while others are dynamic.

step — 1. One instruction in a computer routine. 2. To cause a computer to execute one instruction.

step-by-step operation — *See* single step.

step change — The change from one value to another in a single increment and in negligible time.

step counter — A counter used in the arithmetical unit to count the steps in multiplication, division, and shift operation.

step, job — A single unit of work from the user's viewpoint. A job is made up of one or more job steps. A job step is composed of one or more tasks, each task being a single unit of processing.

stepped start-stop system — A start-stop system in which the start signals occur at regular intervals.

stepper motor — A mechanical device that rotates by a fixed amount each time it is pulsed, as in various floppy-disk systems.

stepping register — *Same as* register, shift.

step, program — A phase of one instruction or command in a sequence of instructions. Thus, a single operation.

stochastic — Pertaining to trial-and-error procedures as contrasted with the fixed step-by-step procedures of algorithms; results defined in probability terms.

stochastic programming — A generalization of linear programming in which any of the unit costs, the coefficients in the constraint equations, and the right-hand sides are random variables subject to known distributions. The aim of such programming is to choose levels for the variables which will minimize the expected (rather than the actual) cost.

stochastic simulation — Properties of the representation rather than of the system itself. The introduction of random variables as essential elements of the model provides the basis for the label "stochastic" or "probabilistic." Example: a model of an inventory system in which the timing or quantity of demands for items and/or replenishment lead times are randomly distributed is stochastic. If these and other elements are taken as determined (not necessarily constant), the model is deterministic.

stock report, inventory — A report showing the current amount of inventory on hand for each item carried in inventory.

stop, automatic — An automatic halting of a computer-processing operation as the result of an error detected by built-in checking devices.

stop bit — The last element of a character designed for asynchronous serial that defines the character space immediately to the left of the most significant character in accumulator storage.

stop code — A code read in the reader of tape-operated equipment (other than tape-to-card converters) that stops the reader and suspends machine operations.

stop, coded — A stop instruction built into the routine.

stop control, analog — The stop control terminates the solution, enabling the final values to be observed.

stop, dynamic — A specific stop in a loop which consists of a single jump instruction which effects a jump to itself.

stop element — The last element of a character in certain serial transmissions, used to ensure recognition of the next start element.

stop, form — The automatic device on a printer that stops the machine when the paper has run out.

stop instruction — A machine operation or routine that requires manual action other than the use of the start key to continue processing.

stop key — A push button on the control panel which can halt the processing. This often happens only after the completion of an instruction being executed at a given moment.

stop loop — A small closed loop usually designed and used for operator convenience, i.e., to indicate an error, improper use, or special result.

stopper — The highest memory location in any given system.

stop, program — A stop instruction built into the program that will automatically stop the machine under certain conditions, or upon reaching the end of the processing, or completing the solution of a problem.

stop signal (in a start-stop system) — Signal serving to bring the receiving mechanism to rest in preparation for the reception of the next telegraph signal.

stop time — The time that elapses between completion of reading or writing of a tape record and the time when the tape stops moving.

storage — A device capable of receiving data, retaining them for an indefinite period of time, and supplying them upon command.

storage address display lights — The various indicator lights on the control panel to specify the bit pattern in a selected address.

storage allocation — The assignment of blocks of data to specified blocks of storage.

storage, annex — *Same as* associative storage.

storage area — A specifically designated location in various types of storage units, i.e., for programs, constants, input/output buffer storage, etc.

storage area, disk — *See* storage, working.

storage, automatic — *Same as* storage, computer.

storage, auxiliary — *Same as* storage, external.

storage, backing — *Same as* storage, external.

storage block — A portion or section of storage usually within a storage area. A storage block is considered a single element for holding a specific or fixed number of words.

storage, buffer — *See* buffer storage.

storage, built-in — *Same as* storage, internal.

storage, bulk — *See* storage, external.

storage capacity — Number of units of data that may be stored in a given storage device at one time. It is variously expressed in terms of bits, characters, or words.

storage, cathode-ray tube — Storage accomplished by beams of electrons accessing storage cells and operating on them. This does not include storage tubes used for display purposes which are cathode-ray tubes of special designs for continuously holding images on the screen.

storage cell — 1. An elementary unit of storage, e.g., binary cell, decimal cell. 2. One of the actual areas of a magnetic surface that are separately and distinctly magnetized by the storage information.

storage, changeable — Data is not destroyed (nondestructive) in this peripheral or storage device in the process of changing medium (disks, paper-tape magazines, or tape reels). The parts of this storage device which contain the data can be removed and replaced by other parts containing different data.

storage charge — The expense per unit of storage on a peripheral device like disks, drums, or tape. The storage charge is usually levied by time-sharing service companies on a monthly basis and usually involves the data which the customer desires to be saved on a fairly permanent basis.

storage, circulating — A device or unit that stores information in a train or pattern of pulses, where the pulses issuing at the final end are sensed, amplified, reshaped, and reinserted into the device at the beginning end.

storage, common — Since COBOL programs can be chained (an executive function), intermediate data results can be maintained between programs using the common storage provision of COBOL.

storage, common block — A block of storage locations in a digital computer which is associated with information or data required both in the main program and in a specific subprogram.

storage compacting — Certain hardware features make feasible the dynamic relocation of programs residing in the central storage—a necessity in order to provide an effective multiprogramming environment. At program termination, the storage assigned is returned to the pool of the available central storage. Storage compacting is initiated if, and only if, a requirement exists for contiguous storage, and compacting can meet this requirement. Compacting is never performed unnecessarily, as the storage-contents control routine always attempts to fit the programs into the gaps in the in-use store, if possible.

storage, computer — Often called automatic storage. A designed part of the automatic data processing system or hardware that may be controlled automatically and without the need for human intervention.

storage concept, add to — The process which immediately enters the final sum of the accumulator into the computer memory.

storage, constant — A part of storage designated to store the invariable quantities required for processing.

storage, content-addressed — A memory mechanism which interrogates the computer memory for content rather than memory location. Normally, a computer memory is accessed by address location such as 04267 rather than by content, such as "Print Total Balance of J. J. Jones."

storage control, diskette — A feature of some systems that permits control of diskette storage allocation. Program routines provide for control of diskette resources and for formatting allocated space.

storage, coordinate — A storage unit whose elements are arranged in a matrix so that access to any location requires the use of two or more coordinates, e.g., a cathode-ray tube store and a core store using coincident-current selection.

storage cycle — A periodic sequence of events occurring when information is transferred to or from the storage device of a computer. Storing, sensing, and regeneration form parts of the storage sequence.

storage, cyclic — *Same as* storage, circulating.

storage data, carrier — This type of storage usually requires some action by an operator such as selection and loading before automatic control becomes operable.

storage, dedicated — The allocation of, reservation of, or obligation of, set-aside, earmarked, or assigned areas of storage which are committed to some specific purpose, user, or problem, i.e., exclusively reserved space on a disk storage unit for an accounting procedure, problem, or data set.

storage, delay-line — A storage technique in which data are stored by allowing them to travel through some medium such as mercury (acoustic storage).

storage density — The number of characters stored per unit length or area of storage medium (for example, number of characters per inch of magnetic tape).

storage, destructive — Some storage devices are designed so that contents at a location need to be regenerated after being read, if they are to be retained. Cathode-ray–tube storage and others are of the destructive type, and regeneration is most often automatic when retention is desired.

storage device — A device in which data can be inserted, retained, and then retrieved for later use.

storage device, mass — Mass storage devices are the means of collecting, organizing, and retrieving large volumes of data. Many manufacturers offer small mass storage devices tailored to a customer's needs. One dual cassette magnetic tape drive provides a total of 180,000 characters of on-line storage at low cost. Where higher capacity and speed are required, a dual floppy disk drive might be the appropriate device. It uses diskettes for low-cost random-access mass memory.

storage, di-cap — A device capable of holding data in the form of an array of charged capacitors and using diodes for controlling information flow.

storage, direct-access — A type of storage device wherein access to the next position from which information is to be obtained is in no way dependent on the position from which information was previously obtained.

storage, disk — The storage of data on the surface of magnetic disks. (Related to magnetic disk and magnetic-disk storage.)

storage, dual — Storage in devices that permit storage of logic of a particular programmer's own design as well as specific instructions and data, i.e., the programmer's instruction code is utilized to write a program of instructions.

storage dump — 1. To copy, or the process of copying, the contents of all or part of a storage, usually from an internal storage into an external storage. 2. A printout of the contents of all or part of a particular storage device. 3. The data resulting from the process in definition 1. (Synonymous with memory dump, memory printout, and dump.)

storage dump trap — In some personal systems, a storage dump trap may be inserted in the instructions to catch and display all registers, flags, and storage contents at any specific point in the execution of a program. This has proven to be a powerful debugging tool for software development.

storage, dynamic — Storage that involves mobility of stored data in time and space. Acoustic delay lines, in which stored data is constantly in motion relative to the storage medium and require continuous regeneration, are an example of a dynamic storage device. Magnetic-core storage, in which the stored data is fixed in time and space, is an example of a static storage device.

storage, electrostatic — 1. The storage of data on a dielectric surface, such as the screen of a cathode-ray tube, in the form of the presence or absence of spots bearing electrostatic charges; these spots can persist for a short time after the removal of the electrostatic charging force. 2. A storage device used as in the foregoing description.

storage element — One unit in a memory, capable of retaining one bit of information. Also the smallest area of the surface of a charge storage tube which retains information different from that of neighboring areas.

storage, erasable — 1. An area of storage used for temporary storage. 2. A medium that may hold information that can be changed. The medium can be reused, e.g., magnetic tape, drum, or core.

storage exchange — 1. The interchange of the total contents of two storage devices or locations, such as two registers. 2. A switching device capable of controlling and handling the flow or exchange of data between storage units or other elements of a system.

storage, external — Storage facilities divorced from the computer itself but holding information in the form prescribed for the computer, e.g., magnetic tapes, magnetic wire, punched cards, etc. The storage is the source of operating data. It may be under the control of the computer, but data to be operated upon must be transferred to secondary or internal storage before operations commence, and they are returned to external storage only after operations are completed. External storage devices usually have larger capacities and lower access speeds than internal secondary storage.

storage, fast — High-speed input or access storage, usually in a hierarchy of storage units and related relatively. An imprecise term.

storage, fast-access — The section of the entire storage from which data may be obtained most rapidly.

storage, file — A specific-purpose type of storage designed to contain a master file, usually relatively large and uniformly accessible.

storage fill — The storing of characters in storage areas not used for data storage or the program for a particular machine run.

storage flip-flop — A bistable storage device which stores binary data as states of flip-flop elements.

storage, high-speed — A specific storage device which has relatively short access time, as compared to main memory of the CPU, i.e., at least significantly shorter than other devices in the same computer system, such as disk-tape storage.

storage, immediate access — Storage, usually in several locations, which has access time that is slight in comparison with operation time, i.e., very fast or real-time capabilities.

storage, inherent — Often called computer or automatic storage. A designed part of the automatic data processing system or hardware, and may be controlled automatically and without human intervention.

storage, input — *See* input storage.

storage, input/output — A specific storage area in a computer reserved for data or instructions received by or ready to be transferred from or to an external (peripheral) input or output device or another specific section of storage.

storage inquiry, direct access — A process through which information can be directly requested from temporary or permanent storage devices.

storage, instantaneous — Storage, usually in several locations, having access time which is slight in comparison with operation time, i.e., very fast or real-time capabilities.

storage, instruction — *Same as* instruction area.

storage integrator — In an analog computer, an integrator used to store a voltage in the hold condition for future use while the rest of the computer assumes another computer control state.

storage, intermediate — A kind of an electronic scratchpad. As input is turned into output, it usually goes through a series of changes. An intermediate memory storage holds each of the successive changes just as long as it is needed. It can hold data picked up or developed in one program cycle for use in succeeding program cycles. It can accumulate data from cycle to cycle.

storage, internal — 1. The storage of data on a device that is an integral part of a computer. 2. The storage facilities forming an integral physical part of the computer and directly controlled by the computer. In such facilities all data are automatically accessible to the computer, e.g., magnetic core, and magnetic tape on-line. (Synonymous with internal memory and contrasted with external storage.)

storage key — A special set of bits designed to be associated with every word or character in some block of storage, which allows tasks having a matching set of protection key bits to use that block of storage.

storage light — The light on a control console panel which indicates that a parity-check error has occurred on a character as it was read into storage.

storage list, available — The queuing or chaining of uncommitted core blocks together for allocation by the supervisory program.

storage list, uncommitted — Blocks of storage that are chained together which are not allocated at any specific moment.

storage location — 1. A storage position holding one machine word and usually having a specific address. 2. The character position used to address a data field in a character-addressable machine.

storage locations, buffer — *See* buffer storage locations.

storage locations, internal — *Same as* storage, working.

storage location, temporary — A specific area of memory which has been set aside for data which is in process of intermediate states of computation. In the CPU, such storage is often called "scratch-pad" memory.

storage, loop — A particular storage device which uses continuous closed loops of magnetic tape with read/write heads as a storage medium. Such tapes are read forward or backward to increase speed and efficiency of access, and a significant number of such ready for read/-write loops compose a tape bin.

storage, magnetic — A storage device that utilizes the magnetic properties of materials to store data, e.g., magnetic cores, tapes, and films.

storage, magnetic-disk — A storage device or system consisting of disks, on whose surfaces information is stored in the form of magnetic spots arranged in a manner to represent binary data. This data is arranged in circular tracks around the disks and are accessible to reading and writing heads on an arm that can be moved mechanically to the desired disk and then to the desired track on that disk. Data from a given track are read or written sequentially as the disk rotates.

storage, magnetic-drum — The storage of data on the surface of a magnetic drums.

storage, magnetic-tape — A storage device in which data is stored in the form of magnetic spots on iron oxide or coated plastic tape. Binary data is stored as small magnetized spots arranged in column form across the width of the tape. A read/write head is usually associated with each column of magnetized spots so that all columns can be read or written at a time as the tape traverses the head.

storage, main — Usually the fastest storage device of a computer and the one from which instructions are executed. (Contrasted with auxiliary storage.)

storage management, time sharing — *See* time-sharing storage management.

storage map — A pictorial aid that the

programmer uses to estimate the proportion of storage capacity to be allocated to data.

storage mark — The name given to a point location that defines the character space immediately to the left of the most significant character in accumulator storage. An example would be:

a 7 4 6 7 4 8 9

in which the letter "a" would be the storage mark.

storage, mass — The type of memory device now available in many designs and media forms which is capable of retaining and communicating vast amounts of data, often in the trillion-bit range.

storage, mass (executive) — The executive system is designed to provide installations with an effective and efficient utilization of the mass storage devices available. The result is an ability to relieve operators and programmers of responsibilities in maintaining and physically handling cards, magnetic tapes, etc., thus eliminating many of the errors that heretofore inherently accompanied the use of large-scale software systems. At the same time, the overall efficiency of operating is considerably improved. Provisions are made for the maintenance of permanent data files and program files on the mass storage devices, with full facilities for modification and manipulation of these files. Security measures are invoked by the executive system to ensure that files are not subjected to unauthorized use. Provisions are also made within the executive system for automatic relocation of files of low usage-frequency to magnetic tape, as unused mass storage space approaches exhaustion. When the use of files related in such a manner is requested, they are retrieved and restored, under control of the executive system, with no inconvenience to the user.

storage, matrix — A storage unit whose elements are arranged in a matrix so that access to one location requires the use of two or more coordinates, i.e., a cathode-ray tube store and a core store using coincident-current selection.

storage, microprocessor — Storage and memory are terms that are used interchangeably. The most important types of storage for microprocessors are ROM, RAM, PROM, paper and magnetic tape cassettes, disks, etc.

storage, modifier — Storage where a set of locations is used primarily to hold modifiers.

storage, minidisk — Storage based on smaller, lower-capacity versions of the disk storage units used with larger computers. The simplest has a single disk and fixed magnetic heads. Popular configurations combine one fixed with one removable disk. Storage capacity is several million bits and up. However, larger units may be too expensive for microcomputer applications and may offer more capacity than is needed.

storage, mixed — A type of storage whose elements are arranged in a matrix so that access to any location requires the use of two or more coordinates, i.e., cathode-ray-tube storage, core storage, etc., which use coincident-current selection.

storage monitors, crt — Various crt types permit a display to be retained on the screen even after the input signal has ceased. The image may be held for a few seconds or several hours. Units with storage capability may also be operated in the nonstore mode.

storage, nesting — *See* storage, push-down.

storage, nondestructive — A type of storage whose location is regenerated after it is read, since it is desired and designed into the unit that the contents are to be retained at the location after reading. Drums, some semiconductor types, most magnetic tapes, disks, etc., are examples of nondestructive storage.

storage, nonvolatile — Storage in which information is retained in the absence of power and may be made available upon restoration of power, e.g., magnetic tapes, drums, or cores.

storage, off-line — Storage not under control of the central processing unit.

storage, on-line — A storage device under direct control of the central processing unit.

storage, on-line mass — *See* storage, mass.

storage, output — *See* output area.

storage, parallel — Storage in which all bits, or characters, or (especially) words are essentially equally available in space, without time being one of the coordinates. Parallel storage contrasts with serial storage. When words are in parallel, the storage is said to be parallel by words; when characters within words (or binary digits within words or characters) are dealt with simultaneously, not one after the other, the storage is parallel by characters or parallel by bits, respectively.

storage, parallel-search — A storage device in which storage locations are identified by their contents. (Synonymous with content-addressed storage and associative storage.)

storage parity — *See* parity, storage.

storage, permanent — *Same as* storage, nonvolatile.

storage, photographic — Any storage scheme utilizing photographic processes. This includes various microimage systems, computer-output microfilm, and binary data storage on photographic mediums.

storage, primary — *Same as* storage, main.

storage-print program — A program that produces a printout of storage and registers to aid the user in locating the reason(s) for a program malfunction.

storage, program — A portion of the internal storage reserved for the storage of programs, routines, and subroutines. In many systems, protection devices are used to prevent inadvertent alteration of the contents of the program storage. (Contrasted with working storage.)

storage protect — A hardware function that provides protection to the system executive routine and all other programs. It not only protects against processor execution, but also against i/o (input/output) data area destruction. Because it is a hardware function rather than software, it reduces multiprogramming complexities.

storage protection — Continued existence of a stored program requires protection from all contemporary programs and, in particular, that each stored program have inviolate storage areas. This is accomplished by independently establishing reserved areas in each storage module and inhibiting a program of reading, writing, or transferring to a location that is not within its reserved areas. Every instruction that references the central store has the final address checked to ensure that it falls within a permissible area. Storage protection allows several programs to reside in core storage at the same time while one is being executed. It also allows transfer of data from peripheral equipment to memory while other programs already are in memory. Storage protection eliminates danger that one program would inadvertently be placed over, and thereby destroy, another program.

storage, push-down — A storage which works as though it comprised a number of registers arranged in a column, with only the register at the top of the column connected to the rest of the storage. Each word, in turn, enters the top register and is then "pushed down" the column from register to register to make room for the next words to arrive. As the words are transferred out of the storage units (out of the top register), other data in storage moves back up the column from register to register to fill the top register.

storage, push-up — Special storage which operates so as to maintain a push-down list so that the next item of data to be retrieved is the oldest item on the list, i.e., it is pushed up in a type of queue arrangement wherein the word at the top came from the bottom in steps and has been in the longest and will go out first.

storage, quick-access — *Same as* storage, high-speed.

storage, random-access — A storage technique in which the time required to obtain information is independent of the location of the information most recently obtained. This strict definition must be qualified by the observation that we usually mean relatively random. Thus, magnetic drums are relatively nonrandom access when compared to semiconductors for main storage, but are relatively random access when compared to magnetic tapes for file storage. (Synonymous with random-access memory and contrasted with sequential-access storage.)

storage, rapid access — *Same as* storage, high-speed.

storage, regenerative — *See* storage, circulating.

storage register — A register in the storage of the computer, in contrast with a register in one of the other units of the computer. (Synonymous with memory register.)

storage registers, associative — Those registers which are not identified by their name or position but which are known and addressed by their content.

storage resolver — A small section of storage, particularly in drum, tape, or disk storage units, that has much faster access than the remainder of the storage.

storage retrieval, flying-head — The flying-head (air-floating head) technique combines aerodynamic and pneumatic principles. Read/write heads float on a boundary layer of air, generated by the rotation of the drum, at 0.0005 inch or less from the oxide-coated surface of the drum. The read/write head is suspended in this position by the opposing forces of the boundary layer of air and the head-positioning mechanism.

storage, routine — *Same as* instruction area.

storage, scratchpad — A high-speed memory device used to store the location of an interrupted program and to retrieve it after the interrupting program has been completed.

storage, searching — *Same as* storage, content addressed.

storage, secondary — *Same as* storage, external.

storage, sequential-access — A storage technique in which the items of information stored become available only in a one-after-the-other sequence, whether or not all the information or only some of it is desired, e.g., magnetic-tape storage. (Related to serial storage, and contrasted with random-access storage.)

storage, serial — Storage in which time is one of the coordinates used to locate any given bit, character, or (especially) word. Storage in which words within given groups of several words appear one after the other in time sequence, and in which access time, therefore, includes a variable latency or waiting time of zero to many word-times, is said to be serial by word. Storage in which the individual bits comprising a word appear in time sequence is serial by bit. Storage for coded-decimal or other nonbinary numbers in which the characters appear in time sequence is serial by character; e.g., magnetic drums are usually serial by word but may be serial by bit or parallel by bit, or serial by character and parallel by bit, etc.

storage, shared — The ability to share main storage between two computers. This means that either machine can insert information into the storage, and either machine can have access to the data and use it.

storage, slow — A storage module or device whose access time is longer in relation to the speeds of arithmetic operations of the central processing unit (CPU) of a computer and more lengthy when compared to other faster access peripheral units.

storage stack — A group of storage elements connected together in some fashion, i.e., a stack of data could be operated on a first-in, first-out basis.

storage, static — Storage of information that is fixed in space and available at any time.

storage, tape-loop — *See* storage, loop.

storage tape, magnetic — A tape or ribbon or any material impregnated or coated with magnetic material on which information may be placed in the form of magnetically polarized spots.

storage, temporary — Internal-storage locations reserved for intermediate and partial results.

storage, time accounting — In some systems, the accounting system supplies the control and master accounts with a report of user account storage and connect time. Specifically, one report lists the user account storage limit, current storage, and peak storage used; it also shows the user's time limit and time used, with a separate record of time used as a private (dedicated) port. One utility program writes the report information to a file opened by the control or master account. The information may then be conveniently drawn from this file for the purpose of billing master or user accounts for system utilization.

storage, uniformly accessible — That particular storage which is designed to reduce the effect of variation of access time for an arbitrary sequence of addresses.

storage unit — Any of several registers in the memory or storage of the computer.

storage, variable field — An indefinite limit of length for the storage field.

storage, virtual — A conceptual form of main storage which does not really exist, but is made to appear as if it exists through the use of hardware and programming.

storage, volatile — Storage media such that if applied power is cut off, the stored information is lost e.g., acoustic delay lines, electrostatic tubes.

storage, word-organized — A specific type of storage which is composed of magnetic cells in which each word of the storage has a separate winding common to all the magnetic cells of the word, i.e., carrying the read and possibly the write pulse also. (Some older types.)

storage, working — 1. The portion of the internal storage reserved for the data of a current program and for intermediate and partial results. 2. The area on a disk used to hold dynamic or working data. This is contrasted to a reserved area containing permanent information such as compilers, track and sector information, etc., and user area for semipermanent storage.

storage, zero-access — 1. The storage for which the latency (waiting time) is small. Though once widely used, this term is becoming less acceptable, since it constitutes a misnomer. 2. Storage for which the waiting time is negligible at all times.

store — 1. To transfer an element of information to a device from which the unaltered information can be obtained at a later time. 2. To retain data in a device from which it can be obtained at a later time. 3. The British term for storage.

store and forward — Pertaining to communication systems in which messages are received at intermediate routing points and recorded (stored). They are then retransmitted to a further routing point or to the ultimate recipient.

store-and-forward blocks — Blocks of data that are routed from switching node to switching node, momentarily queuing at each node before being forwarded to the next. Typically, each block is examined for transmission errors on arrival and is discarded if damaged.

store-and-forward switching center — A message-switching center in which the message is accepted from the sender whenever he offers it, held in a physical store, and forwarded to the receiver whenever he is able to accept it.

store, B — *See* index register.

store, computer — *Same as* storage.

stored program — A set of instructions in the computer memory specifying the operations to be performed and the location of the data on which these operations are to be performed.

stored-response testing — Comparison of the actual output responses of the device under test with the expected correct output responses stored within the tester. The expected correct responses can be recorded from a known-good device or determined by manual analysis or software simulation. Stored-response testing often implies storage of the actual logic states, although such digital signatures as transition counts could be the stored responses.

stored routine — A series of instructions in storage to direct the step-by-step operation of the machine. (Synonymous with stored program.)

store form key — In some systems, this key causes the current form on the screen to be added to the forms file, and a corresponding entry is made in the forms directory.

storing, associative — *Same as* storage, content addressed.

straight binary — *See* binary.

straight-line code — The repetition by explicit instructions for each repetition, of a sequence of instructions, with or without address modification. Generally, straight-line coding will require less execution time and more space than equivalent loop coding. If the number of repetitions is large, this type of coding is tedious unless a generator is used. The feasibility of straight-line coding is limited by the space required as well as by the difficulty of coding a variable number of repetitions.

straight-line coding — Coding in which loops are avoided by the repetition of parts of the coding when required.

stream, bit — A term commonly used in conjunction with a transmission method in which character separation is accomplished by the terminal equipment, and the bits are transmitted over the circuit in a consecutive line of bits.

stream bit transmission — The method of transmitting characters at fixed time intervals. No stop-start elements are used, and the bits making up the characters follow each other without pause.

streaming — The condition of a terminal or modem that has locked into a constant carrier signal, preventing normal transmission of data.

stream, input job — An input source of documents, usually punched cards or card images, which is the first part of an operating system. The stream contains the beginning-of-job indicators, directions, optional programs, etc.

STRESS — Acronym for Structural Engineering System Solver.

string — 1. A connected sequence of characters, words, or other elements. 2. A set of records arranged in an ascending or a descending sequence according to the increasing or decreasing magnitude of their keys.

string, alphabetic — A sequence of letters from the same alphabet, i.e., a character string.

string, bit — *See* bit string.

string break — The point at which a sort can find no more records with sufficiently high control keys to fit on the current output string.

string, character — *See* character string.

string, character (BASIC) — Character strings are any sequence of letters, numbers, and symbols enclosed in quotation marks. Character strings are sometimes called string constants, literal strings, literals, or simply strings. Normally, a character string represents a message to be printed on the GS display or a piece of written text. Digits entered as part of a character string cannot be used in math computations; they are treated just like any other symbol. The length of a character string is limited only by the size of the random-access memory.

string file — Tape, wire, or string used to arrange documents for convenient reference and use.

string length — The number of records in a string.

string manipulation — A technique for manipulating strings of characters.

string manipulation, data-base — In some systems, operations are provided for manipulating strings of textual information. The user can scan a line of text from left to right and from right to left, and search for a specific data item which can be automatically counted and/or substituted by specified characters. A combine operator links two character string fields and places the combined character string in a result field.

string of bits — *See* bits, string of.

string sorting — A group of sequenced records, normally stored in auxiliary computer storage, i.e., disk, tape, or drum.

string, symbol — *See* symbol string.

string variable, alphanumeric — Some versions of BASIC provide an additional variable form, the alphanumeric string variable. It is distinguished from numeric variables by the manner in which it is named, a letter or a letter and a digit followed by a $. String variables can be used in a program for the input, loading, storing, transferring, comparing, and printing of alphanumeric data.

string variable ROM — A string variable ROM provides a computer with the ability to accept and manipulate alphabetic as well as numerical information. It expands the language of the computer to include string variables without sacrificing any of the special function keys or read/write memory. The new commands provided by the string ROM are of three main types: input, manipulation, and output.

strip-chart recorder — A recorder that automatically makes a plot of a variable versus time on graph paper. The paper is moved at a constant speed under a pen or other writing device as the variable is recorded.

stripe card reader — A device that decodes information contained in a stripe of magnetic tape imbedded in a plastic card.

strip, encoding — On bank checks, the area in which magnetic ink will be deposited to represent characters.

stripe recording, magnetic — Recording on a magnetic material deposited in stripe form on a document or card.

strip file, magnetic — *See* file, magnetic strip.

strip, magnetic-file — A file storage device which uses strips of material with surfaces that can be magnitized for the purpose of storing data.

strip, magnetic-tape — On each magnetic-tape strip is listed hundreds of individual records. As a specific record is needed, a computer signal similar to the combination to a safe causes the proper strip to drop from the deck. The strip then whips around the fast-moving drum that searches for the current record, reads or writes on it, and transmits its data to the computer for further processing.

strip record — *See* record, strip.

strobe — A selection signal that is active when data are correct on a bus.

strobe pulse — A pulse to gate the output of a core-memory sense amplifier into a trigger in a register. Also called sample pulse.

stroke — A line segment, point, or other mark used in the formation of characters.

stroke, character — *See* character stroke.

stroked characters — Stroked characters are similar in concept to dot-matrix characters because the characters are formed through the use of a series of short strokes. The advantage over dot-matrix characters is the variety of different fonts that can be formed.

stroke edge — *See* edge, stroke.

stroke edge irregularity — *See* edge, stroke, irregularity.

stroke gate, Sheffer — *Same as* gate, NAND.

stroke, Sheffer — *Same as* NAND.

structure, block — A technique allowing program segmentation into blocks of information or subroutines of a total program.

structured analysis — Structured analysis is often a formal, top-down decomposition of a problem (or process) into a model that offers a complete, precise description of what the problem is. What follows is a document that describes what is called the functional specifications of the problem. These functional specifications are used to produce a design, a model of how the system will attack the problem. A typical model thus depicts the relationships of program modules to each other and to such mechanisms as computers, input-/output devices, data files, and so on. The model is used as a basis for the coding effort.

structured programming — The phrase originally applied to coding and is used as a shorthand for a collection of techniques designed to be used to make the programming art more rigorous. The techniques include restricting the size of the code being produced to one coding sheet, restricting the numbers and kinds of program structures, allowing only one entrance and one exit, and avoiding the GO TO. However, the phrase is now used by many to encompass a whole range of techniques that apply to every stage of producing and managing software systems.

structured programming documentation — In the structured programming procedure, documentation is designed in and becomes a byproduct of every stage, rather than being carried out after the system has been built.

structured program testing — In structured programming, testing is done in stages as is documentation. Instead of waiting until all of the program modules have been completed and linked together for the first time, each module is debugged and tested as a unit. As the modules are hooked together (first two, then three, and so on), a series of integration tests, using sample code and dummy data where necessary, is performed. As a result, the final system test, using real data, is made less difficult.

structure flowcharts — *See* flowchart, structure.

structure, list — *See* list structure.

structure, order — *See* instruction format.

structure, priority — The organization of a system for processing. The priority structure of the system depends not upon the number of instructions, but upon the complexity of the programs. The structure can range from systems with no priority to multicomplex organizations with multilayers of interrupts and multilevels of priority.

structure, system — *See* system structure.

study, application — The detailed process of determining a computer system or set of procedures for using a given computer for definite functions or operations, and establishing the specifications to be used as the basis for the selection of computer equipment.

study, process — *See* process study.

study, systems — *See* systems study.

stunt box — A device to control nonprinting functions of a teletypewriter terminal.

STX — Abbreviation for Start of TeXt. A communication control character which precedes a sequence of characters that is to be treated as an entity and entirely transmitted through to the ultimate destination. Such a sequence is referred to as text. STX may be used to terminate a sequence of characters (heading) started by SOH.

style — A construction, without any size restriction, that is used in optical character recognition. Different sizes of the given character style are proportional in all respects.

stylus, electronic — *Same as* light pen.

stylus, light (pen) — When this penlike device is pointed at information displayed on the screen, it detects light from the cathode-ray tube when a beam passes within its field of view. The response of the pen is transmitted to the computer, which relates the computer action to the section of the image being displayed. In this way, the operator can delete or add text, maintain tighter control over the program, and choose alternative courses of action.

stylus printer — *See* printer, wire.

subaddress — A portion of an input/output device that is accessible through an order code. For disk storage units, the module number is the subaddress.

subalphabet — A subset of an alphabet, e.g., any group of less than 26 letters.

subchannels, multiplexer — The multiplexer permits simultaneous operation of attached low-speed devices through a time-sharing (byte-interleaved mode) principle. Each device sends an identifier to the channel each time it requests service. The multiplexer channel, using this identifier, updates the correct control counts, etc., and stores the data in the correct locations.

subcommand — A request for an operation that is within the scope of work requested by a previously issued command.

subcomponents, system, time-sharing — *See* time-sharing system subcomponents.

subject program — *Same as* program, source.

subjob — A routine or machine run. A program may be broken into several subjobs or tasks to utilize more effectively the computer CPU.

subjunction gate — *Same as* gate, A AND-NOT B or gate, B AND-NOT A.

suboptimization — The process of fulfilling or optimizing some chosen objective that is an integral part of a broader objective. Usually the broad-level objective and lower-level objective are different.

suboptimization, pricing — When using a multiple-pricing alogrithm, suboptimization enters the first variable into the basic program which gives by itself the greatest improvement in the objective; the next variable entered gives the greatest additional improvement, and so on. This technique tends to prevent the first entering variable from being removed by the second, etc.

subpictures — In many applications, combinations of points, lines, and text form special symbols that are repeated many times in a complete picture. An example of a repeated graphic symbol might be a resistor which is labeled with a certain value. A programmer can define such a graphic symbol as a subpicture and then call it each time the symbol is to be repeated.

subprogram — 1. A part of a larger program that can be compiled independently. 2. *See* routine.

subprogram types — Various mechanisms exist in different assemblers and compilers for providing subprograms. These include subroutines, functions, procedures, and macroinstructions. These differ primarily in the manner in which they are referenced and in which they are linked to the program which references them. There are basically two methods of linkage: (1) each subprogram reference is replaced by a jump to the appropriate procedure, or (2) each subprogram reference is replaced by the actual statements associated with that procedure.

subroutine — A program that defines desired operations and which may be included in another program to produce the desired operations. A subroutine can be arranged so that control may be transferred to it from a master routine and so that, at the conclusion of the subroutine, control reverts to the master routine. Such a subroutine is usually called a closed subroutine. A single routine may simultaneously be both a subroutine with respect to another routine and a master routine with respect to a third. Usually control is transferred to a single subroutine from more than one place in the master routine, and the reason for using the subroutine is to avoid having to repeat the same sequence of instructions in different places in the master routine.

subroutine call instructions — In some systems, the subroutine call provides for automatic nesting of subroutines, reentrancy, and multiple entry points. Subroutines may call other subroutines (or even themselves) to any level of nesting without making special provision for storage of return addresses at each level of subroutine call. The subroutine calling mechanism in these systems does not modify any fixed location in memory, thus providing for reentrancy. This allows one copy of a subroutine to be shared among several interrupting processes.

subroutine calls — The linkage between a call to a subroutine and the actual entry to the subroutine is made in a manner similar to future patching. All calls to a particular subroutine are linked in the same way. When a call to a subroutine is indicated to the loader, the address where it was last called and the name of the subroutine are entered in a subroutine call table (SCT). A subroutine should not be loaded twice; therefore, a check is made to determine if it has been previously called or loaded. If a subroutine is called which is already in the table, the first call in the new program is linked to the last call specified in the new subroutine call record. When a subroutine is loaded, its name and entry address are entered in the SCT, and any previous calls are patched and directed to the subroutine entry point with use of the ink-back process.

subroutine, closed — A frequently used subroutine which can be stored in one place and then connected to a routine using various linkages or calling sequences or commands, at one or more locations, i.e., when it is stored separately from the main routine, jump instructions from program control will fetch or call the beginning of this subroutine, and, at its end, another transfer instruction will return it.

subroutine, dating — A specific subroutine which computes and stores associated dates and times and is programmed for file updating relating to work with computer runs of various types, but usually time-sensitive.

subroutine, direct-insert — A subroutine inserted directly into the linear operational sequence rather than by a jump. Such a subroutine must be recopied at each point that it is needed in a routine.

subroutine, division — *See* division subroutine.

subroutine, dynamic — A subroutine which involves parameters, such as decimal-point position or item size, from which a relatively coded subroutine is derived. The computer itself is expected to adjust or generate the subroutine according to the parametric values chosen.

subroutine, editing — This subroutine has parameters whose values are selected prior to execution and are used for performing various operations, usually on input and output data and before main program operations.

subroutine, first-order — A subroutine entered directly from the main routine or program and subsequently returned to it.

subroutine, first remove — *Same as* subroutine, first order.

subroutine, generalized — A subroutine written for easy and ready use in various programs with only minor adjustments by the programmer.

subroutine, in-line — A subroutine inserted directly into the linear operational sequence. Such a subroutine must be recopied at each point that it is needed in a routine.

subroutine, inserted — 1. A separately coded sequence of instructions that is inserted in another instruction sequence directly in low order of the line. 2. A directly inserted subroutine to the main line program specifically where it is required. 3. A subroutine that must be relocated and inserted into the main routine at each place it is used.

subroutine instructions — In most systems, subroutines called programmed instructions may be used as if they were single commands by employing one of the programmed instructions of the repertoire. This capability allows the programmer to define his own special command, through the use of subroutines, which may be changed by the operating routine if desired.

subroutine library — A set of standard and proven subroutines which is kept on file for use at any time.

subroutine linkage — In some systems, subroutines provide a facility for maintaining a single copy of a given routine which can be used in a repetitive manner by other programs located elsewhere in memory. In order to provide this facility, generalized linkage methods must be established for the purpose of control transfer and information exchange between subroutines and calling programs. In some systems, the instruction sets contain several instructions that are useful for this purpose.

subroutine, linked — *See* subroutine, closed.

subroutine, microprogram — The use of subroutines in computer programming is well known and well understood. Frequently many microinstructions can be saved by using subroutines and using sections of microcode as subroutines in many different programs. If this is to be done, a provision must be made for storing and restoring the current address for the ROM. Many techniques for accomplishing this are known. In many microprogrammed systems, this will be accomplished by placing the output from the address register onto one of the data buses where it can be stored in a register. This temporary storage register can then become one of the address sources for setting the ROM program counter.

subroutine, one-level — A program which cannot use other subroutines or itself during its execution, i.e., a closed subroutine.

subroutine, open — *Same as* direct insert subroutine.

subroutine, relocatable — A subroutine that can be located physically and independently in the memory. Its object-time location is determined by the processor.

subroutines, arithmetic — Often includes all the arithmetic subroutines required for FORTRAN, such as sine, cosine, $\log_e$, $\log_{10}$, exponent, tangent, arctangent, and square root.

subroutine, second-order — A subroutine is entered from a first-order subroutine and returned to it or to the main routine, whereas, the first-order subroutine is entered directly from the main program.

subroutine, second remove — *Same as* subroutine, second-order.

subroutines, floating-point — Special routines that handle floating-point numbers as arguments.

subroutines, i/o (input/output) system — Input/output format control that provides for the various format statements used in the FORTRAN language. These subroutines are also available to other programs and may be called from the systems library tape.

subroutines, mathematical — Subroutines that provide complete sets of mathematical subroutines including sine, cosine, square root, exponent, logarithm, etc.

subroutines, nest of — The process of sublevels for subroutines, wherein one subroutine will transfer control to another subroutine and so on with ultimate control climbing back through the array of subroutines to the subroutine which first transferred control.

subroutines, scientific — Several subroutines that perform standard mathematical operations are available in computer systems. These operations include fixed-point multiplication and division; floating-point addition, subtraction, multiplication, and division; square-root extraction; matrix and statistical functions; and calculation of logarithmic and trigonometric functions.

subroutine, standard — A subroutine that is applicable to a class of problems.

subroutine, static — A subroutine that involves no parameters other than the addresses of the operands.

subroutine status table — *See* subroutine table.

subroutines, violation — When the input does not conform to preset criteria or limits, a violation subroutine takes over.

subroutine table — The routine for maintaining a listing of the subroutines in core and for bringing from file the subroutines as needed by the application program.

subroutine, test — A routine designed to show whether a computer is functioning properly.

subroutining, multilevel (display) — The control state permits the display to jump from accessing one location in the memory to any other. When it is desired to jump to a display subroutine, the return address is automatically stored in a push-down list.

subschema — A specification of part of the data base. Visually, an applications program is only interested in dealing with a part; thus, only a subschema is declared and opened for access.

subscriber and inquiry display — *See* inquiry and subscriber display.

subscriber's loop — The service provided by the common carrier to connect a customer's location to a central office. This always includes the circuit and some circuit termination equipment, but may also include input/output equipment.

Sometimes referred to as subscriber station.

subscriber station — The service provided by the common carrier to connect a customer's location to a central office. This always includes the circuit and some circuit-termination equipment, but may also include input/output equipment. Sometimes referred to as local loop.

subscript — 1. A letter or symbol in typography written below a set name to identify a particular element or elements of that set. 2. An indexing notation. 3. An integer used to specify a particular item in a list or table according to COBOL rules, and consisting of a numeric data literal-name. 4. A notation used to specify a particular member of an array where each member is referenced only in terms of the array name.

subscripted variable — A variable followed by one or more subscripts enclosed in parentheses.

subscripts (FORTRAN) — An array is a group of quantities. It is often advantageous to be able to refer to this group by one name and to refer to each individual quantity in this group in terms of its place in the group. For example, suppose it is desired to refer to the second quantity in a group, in ordinary mathematical notation this would be (the variable) $NEXT_2$. The quantity 2 is called a subscript. In FORTRAN, it is expressed NEXT(2), and if the array consists of 15, 12, 18, 42, 19, then the second (position) value or subscripted NEXT(2) would have the value 12.

subsegment — A segment of a program is defined as that portion of memory which is committed by a single reference to the loader. Usually a segment overlays some other segment and may have within itself other portions which in turn overlay one another, i.e., subsegments. That part of a segment which is actually brought into memory when the loader is referenced is called the fixed part of a segment. Segments are built up from separate relocatable elements, common blocks, or other segments.

subsegment tables — For each segment which itself has subsegments, a table is automatically associated with its fixed part. One table contains a seven-word entry for each of the subsegments. The entry holds information for the loader that describes the action necessary to load the corresponding subsegment and the limits of memory in each bank that is used by the segment. It also contains some pointer addresses to allow the diagnostic system to analyze the current state of a program. Using the information in this entry, it is possible to maintain up-to-date indications as to which segments are currently intact in memory and which were destroyed by the loading of some other segment.

subsequent counter — *See* counter, subsequence.

subset — 1. A set contained within a set. 2. A contraction of the words "subscriber set" which has been used for many years to refer to the device which is installed on a subscriber's premises. A data subset is a modulation/demodulation device designed to make business-machine signals compatible with the communications facilities and vice versa. It accepts digital information, converts it into a suitable form for transmission over the telephone circuits, and then reconverts the data to its original form at the receiving end.

subset, character — A smaller set of certain characters from a larger or universal set, all with specified common features.

subsets, remote — *See* remote subsets.

substantive input — The transferral of data from an external storage device to an internal storage device, usually from a mass storage unit and off-line, but not always so.

substep — A part of a step.

substitute — To replace an element of information by some other element of information.

subsystem — An organization of computer components (e.g., a tape drive and controller) that comprises a functional unit that is part of a larger system.

subsystems, communications — To allow their central processors to function most effectively as real-time systems, computers are designed with standard communication subsystems. Some members of the family of subsystems enable a central processor to exchange data simultaneously with a number of remote locations over standard common-carrier communications facilities. The subsystem consists of a multiplexer or multiplexers, each of which allows simplex communication circuits to share a computer i/o channel, and communication-line terminal units which properly terminate the communication circuits and translate the data from these circuits to a form compatible with the central processor.

subtracter — A particular unit capable of forming the representation of the difference between two numbers represented by signals applied to its inputs.

subtracter, full (parallel) — As regards digital subtracters (full), when parallel representation is involved, a parallel full subtracter may be formed from as many three-input subtracters as there are digits in the input words, with the borrow output of each connected to the borrow input of the three-input subtracter corresponding to the digit position of next higher significance.

subtracter, full (serial) — As regards digital subtracters, when serial representation is used, a serial full subtracter may be formed from a three-input subtracter with a digit delay element connected between the borrow output and the borrow input.

subtracter, half — A unit or device capable of representing the difference between two numbers, usually restricted to permitting the subtrahend to have only one nonzero digit.

subtracter, half (parallel) — A special half subtracter resulting from as many half subtracters as permitted digits in the input numerals, but with the borrow output of each half subtracter connected to the subtrahend input of the half subtracter matching the next higher significant digit position, i.e., forming a full parallel subtracter.

subtracter, half (serial) — When serial representation is used, a serial half subtracter may be formed from a two-input subtracter with a digit delay element connected between the borrow output and the subtrahend input.

subtracter, one digit — *Same as* subtracter, half.

subtracter, two-input — *Same as* subtracter, half.

subtract time — A determination of the elapsed time required for one subtraction operation, but excluding the time required to obtain and return the quantities from storage.

subtrahend — The number or quantity that is subtracted from another number, called the minuend, giving a result usually called the difference, or sometimes called the remainder.

suffix — A label often used in the description of an item by a programming language in order to select that item from a table in which it occurs.

sum — The quantity that results from adding two quantities.

sum, check digit — A check digit produced by a sum check.

sum, logical — A result, similar to an arithmetic sum, obtained in the process of ordinary addition, except that the rules are such that a result of one is obtained when either one or both input variables is a one, and an output of zero is obtained when the input variables are both zero. The logical sum is the name given the result produced by the inclusive OR operator.

summarizing — For control of operations in which data is summarized and then recorded in summary form, a final total of a key field or fields can be accumulated from the summarized data and balanced to one accumulated from the detail data. In card-to-card and tape-to-tape runs, the stored program should develop the necessary final totals of the summary data when it is recorded on the output tape; it should also balance it at the end of the run to a control total read from a control card or the tape label.

summary — A report that is lacking in details.

summation check — *See* check, summation.

summer — In analog representation, a unit with two or more input variables and one output variable which is equal to the sum, or a weighted sum, of the input variables.

summing amplifier — By introducing multiple input paths to an operational amplifier, a summing amplifier is created. The device adds, inverts, and multiplies each input variable.

summing integrator — By replacing the feedback resistor of a summing amplifier with a capacitor, continuous integration of the sum, with respect to time, is performed over a time base which depends on the value of the capacitor. Conceptually, the integrator constitutes the most important element of the analog computer.

summing point — *See* point, summing.

sum, partial — A particular result obtained

from the addition of two or more numbers without considering carries, i.e., in binary numeration systems, the partial sum is the same result as is obtained from the exclusive OR operation.

sum, sideways — A specific sum which is developed by adding digits without regard to position, i.e., sideways sums are brought forward by attaching various weights to the different digit positions and most often form check digits through odd or even parity techniques.

superimposed circuit — An additional channel obtained from one or more circuits, normally provided for other channels, in such a manner that all the channels can be used simultaneously without mutual interference.

superimpose (SI) — Moves data from one location to another, superimposing bits or characters on the contents of specified locations.

superposed circuit — *See* superimposed circuit.

superscript — In mathematical and model-building notation, a symbol written above and to the right of the base symbol to indicate a specified function or differentiation from some other similar or same base letter or character. Also the power to which a number is to be raised is placed in the superscript location, and most often to indicate a cell of a matrix or a derivation, or a unit of a particular set, if the character indicates the universal set.

supervising system — 1. A program that controls loading and relocation of routines and in some cases makes use of instructions which are unknown to the general programmer. Effectively, an executive routine is part of the machine itself (synonymous with monitor routine, supervisory routine, and supervisory program). 2. A set of coded instructions designed to process and control other sets of coded instructions. 3. A set of coded instructions used in realizing automatic coding. 4. A master set of coded instructions.

supervisor — An executive routine.

supervisor, computer — An individual who is responsible for the operation and scheduled use of computer and peripheral devices.

supervisor, executive — The supervisor routine is the executive-system program component that controls the sequencing, setup, and execution of all runs entering the computers. It is designed to control the execution of an unlimited number of programs in a multiprogramming environment, while preventing each program from being affected by the coexistence of other programs. The supervisor contains three levels of scheduling; coarse scheduling, dynamic allocation, and central processor unit dispatching. Runs entering are sorted into information files, and these files are used by the supervisor for run scheduling and processing. Control statements for each run are retrieved and scanned by the control-command interpreter to facilitate the selection of runs for setup by the coarse scheduler. (Some systems.)

supervisor interrupts — Supervisor call interruptions are caused by the program issuing an instruction to turn over control to the supervisor (a type of master-control program). The exact reason for the call is shown in the PSW (program status word).

supervisor mode — A mode of operation under which only certain operations, such as memory-protection modification instructions and input/output operations, are permitted.

supervisor (monitor) — The section of the operating system that accepts operator commands that relate to system control. The supervisor is often considered to be the man-machine interface for many control functions of the computer system.

supervisor, overlay — *See* overlay supervisor.

supervisor program test — A supervisory program that is used for nothing else except testing.

supervisor, system — *See* system supervisor.

supervisory control — 1. A control system that furnishes intelligence, usually to a centralized location, to be used by an operator to supervise the control of a process or operation.2. Characters or signals that automatically actuate equipment or indicators at a remote terminal.

supervisory control, operating system — The operating-system software consists of a supervisory control program, system programs, and system subroutines. Included are a symbolic assembler and macroprocessor, a language compiler, and debugging aids. A library of general utility programs is also provided as well as other software packages.

supervisory packet, telecommunications — Various access systems offer telecommunications supervisory packages that can automatically direct the output from the host system to a particular device specified by the user, or to a file in the user's library. Automatic supervision frees the user's port for execution of other on-line programs and allows the user to make periodic checks on the status of a job for remote job entry systems.

supervisory programs — Computer programs that have the primary function of scheduling, allocating, and controlling system resources rather than processing data to produce results.

supervisory programs simulation — *See* simulation, supervisory programs.

supervisory routine — *Same as* executive routine.

supervisory system — All of the supervisory programs used by one given system.

supplementary maintenance time — *See* maintenance time, supplementary.

support chips — Chips that are required to assist the CPU chip for complete operation beyond the basic processor operation, such as peripheral control chips.

support processor, attached — The utilization of multiple computers, usually two, connected via channel-to-channel adapters, to increase the efficiency in processing many short-duration jobs.

support programs — Those programs which support or aid the supervisory programs and the application programs, and include diagnostics, testing, data generators, etc.

support software — Most microcomputer manufacturers offer users the opportunity to develop fixed programming routines that convert a microprocessor system into a dedicated control element. This is accomplished by means of software that emulates or simulates the actual system. Software support consists of tape, disk, and card libraries that permit user program development with test and debug system devices.

support systems — 1. Programming systems that are used to develop or support the normal translation functions of any of the machine, procedural, or problem-oriented languages. 2. A collection of computer programs to aid the production and checkout of a system. 3. The combination of the skills, techniques, and equipment to operate and maintain a system.

suppression — An optional function in either on-line or off-line printing devices that permits them to ignore certain input characters or groups of characters.

suppression, space — *See* space suppression.

suppression, zero — The elimination of the zeros to the left of the significant digits, usually before printing.

suppressor, echo — A voice-operated device for connection to a two-way telephone circuit to attenuate echo currents in one direction caused by telephone currents in the other direction.

surface recording — Storage of information on the ferric-oxide coating on magnetic tape, magnetic drums, etc.

swapping — In time sharing, the transfer of a currently operating program from system memory to an external storage device, the replacement of that program by a program of higher priority, and the restoration of the temporarily stored program following execution of the higher priority program.

swapping, pulse — *Same as* pulse regeneration.

swap time — The time required to transfer a program from external memory to high-speed internal memory and vice versa.

SWIFT — Acronym for the Society for Worldwide Interbank Financial Telecommunication, an organization similar to the Bank Wire connecting approximately 400 member banks in Europe and North America.

swing, frequency — Pertaining to a modulated wave, the variation due to modulation, of the instantaneous frequency above and below the carrier frequency.

switch — 1. A point in a program from which a program may proceed to one of several possible courses of action, depending on conditions established by the programmer; conditional statements are often used to establish switches of this kind; a branch point. 2. A mechanical, electromechanical, or electronic device, built into a unit of equipment, that can be interrogated in order to select a course of action. 3. A symbol used to indicate a branchpoint, or a set of instructions to condition a branch. 4. A device that can alter flow. Switches may be activated manually or under program control.

switch and search capability — A means by which a sequence of searching instructions may be recorded on one cassette to drive a second cassette, enabling the operator to merge variable information with standard paragraphs or other unchanging material.

switch, breakpoint — A manually operated switch that controls conditional operation at breakpoints, used primarily in debugging.

switch-control computer — A computer designed to handle data transmission to and from remote computers and terminals.

switched circuit — A circuit or channel that may be connected and disconnected by action of one or more of the associated stations, or by external means.

switched line — A communications link for which the physical path may vary with each usage, e.g., the dial-up telephone network.

switched-message network — A service offered by the common carrier in which a customer may communicate with any other customer receiving the same service. Examples are TELEX and TWX.

switch, electronic — A circuit element causing a start and stop action or a switching action electronically, usually at high speeds.

switch, function — A circuit having a fixed number of inputs and outputs designed so that the output information is a function of the input information. Each circuit expresses a certain code, signal configuration, or pattern.

switching — Provisions of point-to-point transmission between dynamically changing sources and sinks (i.e., different sources and different sinks are connected and disconnected as required).

switching applications — Message-handling applications in which the computer is used to accept messages from terminals, route the messages over trunk lines at perhaps higher speeds to remote message switching computers, and provide certain reliability functions such as an audit trail and error control. Message switching is a somewhat different application of computer communications in that there is no user processing involved. The sole purpose of the system is to communicate messages from one point to another point.

switching, blank — A specific range of values in which the incoming signal can be altered without also changing the outgoing response. (Synonymous with dead space and dead zone, and similar to neutral zone.)

switching center — A location at which incoming data from one circuit is transferred to the proper outgoing circuit.

switching center, automatic message — A location where an incoming message is automatically directed to one or more outgoing circuits according to intelligence contained in the message.

switching center, semiautomatic message — A location where an incoming message is displayed to an operator who directs the message to one or more outgoing circuits according to information read from the message.

switching center, torn-tape — A location where operators tear off the incoming printed and punched paper tape and transfer it manually to the proper outgoing circuit.

switching circuit — A circuit which performs a switching function. In computers, this is performed automatically by the presence of a certain signal (usually a pulse signal). When combined, switching circuits can perform a logical operation.

switching, circuit or line — A switching technique where the connection is made between the calling party and the called party prior to the start of a communication (for example, telephone switching).

switching coefficient — The derivative of the applied magnetizing force with respect to the reciprocal of the resultant switching time.

switching, cross-channel — An optional feature that permits direct-program access to attached input/output devices through two channels.

switching, elastomeric contact — A type of switch construction usually used in low-cost, low-profile keyboards, like those for pocket calculators. A "soft" contact eliminates problems of contact bounce, and the relatively high contact resistance is no problem with the MOS circuits found in many calculator chips and microprocessors.

switching, message — The technique of receiving a message, storing it until the proper outgoing circuit is available, and then retransmitting it.

switching, packet — A data transmission process, utilizing addressed packets, whereby a channel is occupied only for the duration of transmission of the packet. In certain data communication networks the data may be formatted into a packet or divided and then formatted into a number of packets (either by the data terminal equipment or by equipment within the network) for transmission and multiplexing purposes.

switching, push-button — A reperforator switching system which permits the selection of the outgoing channel by an operator.

switching space — *Same as* gap, interword.

switching, store and forward — *Same as* message switching.

switching theory — A particular branch of theory relating to combinational logic, its operation, behavior, and consequences, i.e., concerning such devices as computer Turing machines, logic elements, and switch networks.

switching time — 1. The interval between the reference time and the last instant at which the instantaneous voltage response of a magnetic cell reaches a stated fraction of its peak value. 2. The interval between the reference time and the first instant at which the instantaneous integrated voltage response reaches a stated fraction of its peak value.

switch insertion — The insertion of information into a computer system by an operator who operates the switches manually.

switch, logical — An electronic device used for directing input cards to one of a number of outputs.

switch, manual — The hand operated device designed to cause alternate actions. Contrasted with the electronic switch.

switch matrix — An array of circuit elements interconnected specifically to perform a particular function as interconnected, i.e., the elements are usually transistors, diodes, and relay gates completing logic functions for encoding, transliteration of characters, decoding number system transformation, word translation, etc., and most often input is taken along one dimension while output is taken along another.

switch, N-way — *See* switch, programmed.

switch, operation-control — A particular type of matrix switch that selects the input lines of a matrix. The output of the matrix controls the logic elements which execute specific operations.

switchover — The act of transferring the real-time processing work load from one specific or multiplexer program to another in a duplex system. Switchover must be initiated manually in some systems; in many others, it can be accomplished automatically.

switch, programmed — A particular instruction which may be in the form of a numeral and may be placed in a routine to allow the computer to select one of a number of alternative paths in its program; i.e., switch settings on the console equipment can be inspected by operators or the computer and result in changes or branches in the main program.

switch, reed — A special switching device which consists of magnetic contactors which are sealed into a glass tube. The contactors are actuated by the magnetic field of an external solenoid, electromagnet, or permanent magnet.

switch register — A function performed by a physical switch that can also be implemented by software, with switches being set through a terminal device or a memory location. Generally, it is a physical register made up of a number of manual switches, typically equal to the number of bits in the computer, and often located on the computer control panel. The switch register is used for manual entry of addresses and data into computer memory and for manual intervention in program execution.

switch, sense — The sense switches on the operator's console provide manual control of program branching. Testing of the sense-switch settings occurs when the sense-switch instruction is given.

switch setting, branch-on — *See* branch-on switch setting.

switch, storage — A manually operated switch or group of switches, most often on computer consoles to permit operators to read register contents.

switch, tape-feed — A switch that causes the reperforator to meter a predetermined length of blank tape.

switch, tape select — A particular control rotary switch which has the capability of selecting either a neutral mode during automatic operation or the use of one of the on-line tape units.

switch, toggle — 1. A manual electric switch operated with a small projecting arm. 2. An electronically operated circuit that holds either of two states until changed.

syllable — A term used to describe groups of characters or portions of machine words.

symbiont control — Symbionts, besides being routines from main programs, may be concurrently performing typical off-line operations, such as tape-to-printer, independent of the main program. Symbionts may be initialized by the operator, or by a main program. Symbiont operations may be suspended, terminated, or reinitiated at any time.

symbionts — Small routines, called symbionts, run concurrently with the series of main programs. These symbionts move information back and forth between the peripherals and magnetic drum. Main programs desiring communication with these peripherals reference input/output subroutines that transfer data images between the drum and peripherals.

symbol — 1. A simplified design representing a part in a schematic circuit diagram. 2. A letter representing a particular quantity in formulas. 3. In some systems a symbol consists of up to eight letters and digits beginning with a letter. Symbols are defined by their appearance as statement labels or equality symbols. The value of a symbol, defined as a label, is the value of the location counter at the time the label was encountered. The value of a symbol, defined by equality, is the value of the expression appearing on the right of the equal sign. 4. A conventional representation of a concept or a representation of a concept upon which agreement has been reached.

symbol, abstract — A specific symbol whose shape or pattern is not indicative of its meaning or use, and which almost always requires definition for each particular application.

symbol, breakpoint — A symbol that may be optionally included in an instruction (as an indication, tag, or flag) to designate it as a breakpoint.

symbol, check — *See* check symbol.

symbol cross-reference table, microcomputer — An alphabetic list of all identifiers used in a program module, their attributes and values, and a list of the input source records on which they were referenced.

symbol dictionary, external — *See* external symbol dictionary (ESD).

symbol, external — A symbol for a location name which appears in the external symbol dictionary of a program. The program must permit the named location to be referred to by other programs. Since in most programming, separately written subroutines must be united before execution by a linkage loader or editor, they must not occupy overlapping regions of memory, but instead must occupy adjacent areas. Thus, the programs must refer to a data item or instruction in other programs by external symbols.

symbol, flowchart — A symbol used to represent an operation, data, or equipment in data-processing problems.

symbolic address — A label assigned to a specific word in a routine for the convenience of the programmer. The symbol used is independent of the location of a word within a routine. It identifies the field of data to be operated on or the operation to be used, rather than its storage location.

symbolic addressing — *See* addressing, symbolic.

symbolic assembler — An assembler that lets the programmer code instructions in a symbolic language. The assembler allows mnemonic symbols to be used for instruction codes and addresses. Constant and variable storage registers can be automatically assigned. The assembler produces a binary object tape and lists a symbol table with memory allocations and useful diagnostic messages.

symbolic assembly-language listing — A listing that contains the symbolic instructions equivalent to the binary code output of the compiler. This assembly-language output listing is useful as a debugging aid. By including certain pseudo-operation codes in "in-line" assembly language, the assembly-language output can be assembled by the assembler routine. (If output is obtained on either cards, paper tape, or magnetic tape.) This will allow modification of programs at the assembly-language level.

symbolic assembly system — A program system developed in two parts: a symbolic-language program and a computer program (processor). The processor translates a source program developed in symbolic language to a machine object program.

symbolic code — This code expresses programs in source language, i.e., by referring to storage locations and machine operations by symbolic names and addresses that are independent of their hardware determined names and addresses. (Synonymous with pseudocode and contrasted with machine-language code.)

symbolic coding — 1. Coding in which the instructions are written in nonmachine language; i.e., coding using symbolic notation for operators and operands. 2. Writing programs in any language other than absolute machine language.

symbolic-coding format — In writing instructions using the assembly language, the programmer is primarily concerned with three memory fields: a label field, an operation field, and an operand field. It is possible to relate the symbolic coding to its associated flowchart, if desired, by appending comments to each instruction line or program segment. All of the memory fields are in free form, providing the greatest convenience possible for the programmer. Consequently, the programmer is not hampered by the necessity to consider fixed form boundaries in the design of his symbolic coding.

symbolic conversion program — Abbreviated SCP. A one-to-one compiler for symbolic addresses and operation codes designed for systems of the International Telephone and Telegraph Corp. (ITT).

symbolic debugging — Symbolic commands (or marcoinstructions) are utilized to assist in the debugging procedure.

symbolic deck — A deck of punched cards containing programs written in symbolic language as opposed to programs written in binary language.

symbolic editor — Permits the editing of source-language programs by adding or deleting lines of text. All modification, reading, punching, etc., is controlled by symbols typed at the keyboard. The editor reads parts or all of a symbolic tape into memory where it is available for immediate examination, correction, and relisting.

symbolic input/output referencing — References to data on tape or disk are made symbolically. Instead of describing the address of a certain disk or tape, the programmer refers to such data with a functional name. This means the programmer need not keep in mind where data will be coming from. It also means that there is a good deal of flexibility for the machine operator. He can mount tapes in the most efficient way each day. The control programs set up an input and output assignment table indicating the whereabouts of data files. These tables are used as directories when programs are run.

This flexibility helps the operator schedule work so that jobs can be loaded, tapes mounted, and disk packs attached before a job is called by the control program.

symbolic instruction — An instruction in an assembly language directly translatable into a machine code. An instruction using symbols to represent or express the operator part and the address parts.

symbolic key — In COBOL, contrast with actual key.

symbolic language — The discipline that treats formal logic by means of a formalized artificial language or symbolic calculus whose purpose is to avoid the ambiguities and logical inadequacies of natural languages. Advantages of the symbolic method are greater exactness of formulation, and power to deal with complex material.

symbolic logic — 1. The study of formal logic and mathematics by means of a special written language that seeks to avoid the ambiguity and inadequacy of ordinary language. 2. The mathematical concepts, techniques and languages as used in the foregoing definition, whatever their particular application or context. (Synonymous with mathematical logic, and related to logic.)

symbolic names — 1. Names assigned by programmers to represent addresses or locations in a program. 2. Names given to variable values in high-level language programs.

symbolic notation — A method of representing a storage location by one or more figures.

symbolic number — A numeral, used in writing routines, for referring to a specific storage location; such numerals are converted to actual storage addresses in the final assembling of the program.

symbolic parameter — In assembler programming, a variable symbol declared in the prototype statement of a macrodefinition. A symbolic parameter is usually assigned a value from the corresponding operand in the macroinstruction that calls the macrodefinition.

symbolic programming — The use of arbitrary symbols to represent addresses in order to facilitate programming.

symbol, item separation — A control symbol which indicates beginning of an item.

symbol, logic — 1. A symbol used to represent a logic element graphically. 2. A symbol used to represent a logic connective.

symbol, logical — A sign used as an operator to denote the particular operation to be performed on the associated variables.

symbol, mnemonic — Frequently used symbols for representation of information and so selected to assist the programmer's memory in recalling meaning, as MPY for multiply.

symbols, atomic — In list processing languages, atomic symbols are sometimes referred to as atoms when using list processing languages and may either be numeric or nonnumeric. The external representation of a nonnumeric atomic symbol is a string of letters or digits starting with a letter, such as AB5,W or epsilon.

symbols, functional — A block diagram term representing the functional design, i.e., the practical specification of the working relations between all parts of a system.

symbol, specific — *Same as* character, special.

symbols, standard language — Prescribed graphical shapes used to represent special meanings or functions in any computer program.

symbol string — A concatenation of items or characters, i.e., a one-dimensional array of such items ordered only by reference to the relations between adjacent members.

symbol table — *See* table, symbol.

symbol table control — Symbols that have been defined and used, but are no longer required, may be deleted from the symbol table. This allows room for new symbols. Thus, a very large program can be assembled with a relatively small symbol storage area.

symbol, terminating — A symbol on the tape indicating the end of a block of information. (Related to gap.)

symmetric difference gate — *Same as* gate, exclusive OR.

symmetric linear programming — A fast, efficient mathematical technique for solving distribution and allocation problems in manufacturing operations.

symmetric list processor — A high-level list processing language.

synch — Synchronizing signal that identifies the start of a block.

SYN character — Character synchronization is accomplished by recognizing one or two "phasing" characters, often called SYN or sync characters. The receiver senses these SYN characters and phases its receive logic to recognize, by bit count, the beginning and end of each subsequent character. To ensure character synchronization throughout a message, SYN sequences are sometimes inserted in the transmitted data stream at one- or two-second intervals. This permits receiving stations to verify that they are in sync. If a SYN is not received within the prescribed time interval, the receiver will reject the message and begin searching for the SYN sequence that will precede the next message.

synchro-duplexing — The scheme of producing a document on a printing device through the synchronous running of a program tape and a master tape or a pure data tape. The operation is completely controlled by function codes in the program tape. A data-processing function.

synchronization — In the COBOL system, the alignment of data with respect to the left or right boundaries of machine words. (Compare with justification.)

synchronization, bit — Bit synchronization is achieved through a received clock signal which is coincident with the received serial data stream. Most modems or terminals derive this clock by means of phase-locked loops from the 0 to 1 and 1 to 0 transitions occurring in the received data.

synchronization sequence — In transmitting a continuous stream of data bits (synchronous transmission), some form of synchronization is required between the sender and the receiver. The most efficient method is to precede a group of characters (message or block) to be transmitted with a unique group of bits called a synchronization sequence. The receiver searches for this unique sequence bit pattern so that it can properly frame and get into phase with the control or data characters in the incoming bit stream. Ideally, the synchronization sequence and the transmission code should be so designed that the sequence could never be reproduced within the actual data stream, so that false synchronization might never occur. This is not always possible, especially when, as in ASCII code, all 128 combinations of the seven bits within characters are utilized. Protocols differ in the number of synchronizing characters used and the code of the characters.

synchronizer — A storage device used to compensate for a difference in the rate of flow of information or the time of occurrence of events when transmitting information between two devices.

synchronizer, channel — The channel-synchronizer signals provide for orderly transfer of the digital information. These signals do not transmit data, but are used to command and identify the transfer of data words, function words, etc., at proper times and in proper sequence.

synchronizer, master — *Same as* master clock.

synchronizer, tape — A tape device which controls the exchange of data between the central processor (CPU) and the various tape units, i.e., a buffer for programmed control of the events.

synchronizing pilot — A reference signal for the purpose of maintaining the synchronization of the oscillators of a carrier system. The signal is also used to compare the frequencies and phases of the currents generated by these oscillators.

synchronous — A term applied to a computer in which the performance of a sequence of operations is controlled by equally spaced clock signals or pulses.

synchronous clock — Even in the case of static circuitry, a clock frequency is generally used to keep the various events in the computer in step and running at the proper rate. This action results in synchronous operation, as contrasted with asynchronous operation.

synchronous clock operation — System operation governed by (and synchronized to) a master timing source. Synchronous refers to the constant frequency and phase of the source, e.g., computer data transfers that occur at definite intervals relative to a system clock.

synchronous communication — A method of transferring serial binary data between computer systems or between a computer system and a peripheral device; binary data is transmitted at a fixed rate, with the transmitter and receiver synchronized. Synchronization characters are located at the beginning of each message or block of data to synchronize the flow.

synchronous computer — A computer in which each event or the performance of each operation starts as a result of a signal generated by a clock. (Contrasted with asynchronous computer.)

synchronous data link control — Abbreviated SLDC. An advanced line control discipline for communication between terminals and computer. It is a key element of systems network architecture.

synchronous data message block — The message block is usually composed of one or two synchronization characters, a number of data and control characters (typically 100 to 10,000), a terminating character, and one or two error control characters. Between messages, the communication line may idle in SYN characters or be held to mark. Synchronous modems can be used to transmit asynchronous data, and, conversely, asynchronous modems can be used for synchronous data if the receiving terminal can derive the clock from the data.

synchronous data transmission — In this type of data transmission, each character consists of 5, 6, 7, or 8 information bits depending on the code structure. There are no start and stop bits. Timing is derived through synchronizing characters at the beginning of each message or block of data.

synchronous gate — A synchronous gate is

a time gate wherein the output intervals are synchronized with an incoming signal.

synchronous inputs — 1. Those terminals on a flip-flop, allowing data to be entered but only upon command of the clock. These inputs do not have direct control of the output such as those of a gate but only when the clock permits and commands. Called JK inputs or ac set and reset inputs. 2. Those terminals in a flip-flop which can affect the output state of the flip-flop independent of the clock. Called set, preset, reset or dc set and reset, or clear.

synchronous operation — Operation in which each event or the performance of each operation starts as a result of a signal generated by a clock.

synchronous serial data adapter — A device that provides interface between various types of MPUs and synchronous data terminals such as floppy-disk equipment, cassette or cartridge tape controllers, numerical control systems, and other systems requiring movement of data blocks.

synchronous system (communications) — A system in which the sending and receiving instruments are operating at the same frequency, and the phase is maintained by means of feedback.

synchronous terminals — Machine-input terminals and manual-input batch terminals that accumulate slow input data, generally deliver output data at a fast rate to the line, and use synchronous transmission. In synchronous transmission, long data blocks made up of a string of character codes are transmitted, with each block—rather than each character—framed by a special synchronizing code.

synchronous time-division multiplexers — Devices that share a synchronous communication line by cyclically scanning incoming lines, peeling off bits or characters, and interleaving them into frames on a single high-speed data stream. This effect is similar to that of a high-speed conveyer belt picking up objects arriving at a common point from several lower speed conveyer belts.

synchronous transfer — An i/o transfer which takes place in a certain amount of time without regard to feedback from the receiving device.

synchronous transmission — That type of communication in which the sending and receiving instruments are operating continuously at substantially the same frequency and may be maintained, by means of adjustment or correction, in a desired phase relationship, e.g., a constant time interval between successive bits, characters, or events.

sync, new — A feature of some data sets that allows for a rapid resynchronization during transition from one transmitter to another on a multipoint private-line data network.

syndetic — 1. Having connections or interconnections. 2. Pertaining to a document or catalog with cross references.

synergic — The combination of every organ of a system, e.g., a coordinated system.

SYN register — In some units, an 8-bit register (synchronous character code) that is loaded from the data access line (DAL) lines by a write operation and holds the synchronization code used for receiver character synchronization. It serves as a fill character when no new data is available in the transmitter holding register during transmission. This register cannot be read onto the DAL lines. It must be loaded with logic zeros in all unused high-order bits.

SYN synchronous idle — A character used as a time fill in the absence of any data or control character to maintain synchronization. The sequence of two continuous SYNs is used to establish synchronization (character phase) following each line turnaround.

syntactic errors, remote computing system — Syntactic errors are considered the responsibility of the system and are further categorized as follows:

Composition—Typographical errors, violations of specified forms of statements, and misuse of variable names (e.g., incorrect punctuation, mixed-mode expressions, undeclared arrays, etc.).

Consistency—Statements that are correctly composed but conflict with other statements (e.g., conflicting declaratives, illegal statement ending a DO (FORTRAN) range, failure to follow each transfer statement with a numbered statement, etc.).

Completeness—Programs that are incomplete (e.g., transfers to nonexistent statement numbers, improper DO nesting, illegal transfer into the range of a DO loop, etc.).

syntax — The rules governing sentence structure in a language, or statement structure in a language such as that of a compiler program.

syntax checker — A program that tests source statements in a programming language for violations of the syntax of that language.

syntax-directed compiler — A compiler based on the syntactical relation of the character string.

syntax node, voice system — A recognition structure that permits vocabulary subsets to be associated with the context of a user's format, thus achieving higher recognition accuracies within larger vocabularies.

syntax recognizer — A subroutine which recognizes the phase class in an artificial language, normally expressed in Backus normal form (BNF).

syntax transducer — A subroutine designed to recognize the phase class in an artificial language, normally expressed in Backus normal form (formal language theory BNF).

synthesis — The combining of parts in order to form a whole; e.g., to develop a circuit, computer, or program from performance requirements. This can be contrasted with analysis of a given circuit or program.

synthesis, systems — Procedural planning to solve problems. This involves: analysis of the problem, preparation of a flowchart, detailed preparation, development of subroutines, location of storage locations, specification of input and output formats, and the incorporation of a computer run into a complete data processing system.

synthetic address — *Same as* address, calculated.

synthetic-display generation — Logical and numerical processing to display collected data or calculated data in symbolic form.

synthetic language — A pseudocode or symbolic language. A fabricated language.

system — 1. An assembly of components united by some form of regulated interaction to form an organized whole. 2. A devised and designed regular or special method or plan or methodology or procedure. The organization of hardware, software, and people for cooperative operation to complete a set of tasks for desired purposes.

system, accuracy-control — An error-detection and correction system.

system analyzer — An instrument that can be used as an independent, portable troubleshooting unit for field service of MPU equipment, or in conjunction with various full-line development systems to enhance the capabilities of the latter as a design tool. In field service application, a system analyzer derives operating power and i/o signals directly from the system under test. It stops the system at any point in its program, steps through the program, changes the contents of the system memory, and monitors and records the MPU operation during a selected portion of the program.

system, assembly — An automatic programming software system that includes a programming language and a number of machine-language programs. These programs aid the programmer by performing different programming functions such as checkout, updating, etc.

systematic inaccuracies — Inaccuracies due to limitations in equipment design.

system, automatic data-processing — An interacting assembly of procedures, processes, methods, personnel, and automatic data-processing equipment to perform a complex series of data-processing operations.

system, back-up — Such systems combine error-detection and correction techniques that spot and correct computer and transmission errors.

system, BASIC — *See* BASIC.

system, binary notation — *See* binary number.

system, binary number — *See* binary number.

system, binary-weighted error-detection — A system based on the concept of assigning binary one values to all marking pulses of each code combination.

system, biquinary — *See* number, biquinary.

system call interrupts — *See* interrupts, system-call.

system capacity (throughput) — The maximum traffic a system can carry with a specified response time.

system chart — A flowchart of an overall

procedure or system showing the flow of information and/or documents.

system check — A check on the overall performance of the system, usually not made by built-in computer check circuits, e.g., control totals, hash totals, and record counts.

system check module — A device that monitors system operability if power fails or deviations from desired computer operations develop. It initiates appropriate emergency actions by the computer.

system commands — A typical executive accepts and interprets a collection of system commands by a user allowing him to: log in and out; save and restore program and data files; compile and execute a program; interrupt and terminate a running program; edit, manipulate, and list program and data files; request status of system and user programs; and specify systems subcomponent desired.

system commands, time-sharing — *See* time-sharing system commands.

system, communications — *See* communications system.

system communications processing — The transmission of data to the central computer for processing from a remote terminal as opposed to a terminal connected directly to the central computer.

system constants — Permanent locations contained in the monitor (control unit). These locations contain data used by system programs. Some constants contain data that may be used by certain programs.

system, control — A system of the closed-loop type in which the computer is used to govern external processes.

system controller — The system controller regulates and coordinates all communications between major computer-system components (processor, memory, input/output controller, and real-time devices). The independent operation of these two functions provides a means of expansion, and provides for the maximum utilization of the components.

system, data-acquisition — *See* data-acquisition system.

system data bus — Most communication between modules in microprocessors occurs over a system data bus. This bus is independent of the processor and handles communications between any two devices connected to the bus. In order to transfer information over the bus, a device first requests access through the bus priority network of the bus control. If no higher priority request is present, control of the bus is granted, and the device then becomes bus master for one bus cycle. During this cycle, the master may address any other bus-connected device (which becomes the slave) and may command a transfer of data to or from the slave. In some systems the system data bus is composed of three signal buses. The data bus often consists of 16 bidirectional data lines. The timing bus provides the basic system clocks as well as address and data strobes which indicate when data is valid on the bus. The control bus provides a priority system for bus access, signals to indicate whether the current transaction is a read or write from memory or a peripheral, an extended cycle signal, and a response line to indicate that a peripheral device has accepted an order sent over the system bus.

system, decimal numbering — A system of numerals using digits 0 through 9 and thus having a base, or radix, of 10.

system definition, microprocessor — System definition involves the major tasks to be performed by the microprocessor —which is assumed to be the central control device of the system. Data formats should be established to maximize processor control. The overall system timing is included in this design phase to ensure that all functions can be handled within the timing constraints. Based on the system definition, the basic program structure can now be defined. Each input channel to the microprocessor represents a major program, assuming the use of more than one input device. In addition, an executive program should be written to control the overall operation of the system. Various routines—based on the different functions or command codes supplied—further subdivide the main program.

system design — The specification of the working relations between all the parts of a system in terms of their characteristic actions.

system design problem — The proposition of designing document which describes the optimum (or close to optimum) realization of the specified desired properties of a system. This is almost entirely an information-handling process.

system, diagnostic — A program resembling the operational program rather than a systematic logical pattern program which will detect overall system malfunctions rather than isolate or locate faulty components.

system, direct or on-line — *See* on-line or direct system.

system documentation — Usually, the technical description that provides in-depth coverage such that benchmarks for the equipment can be established, programs can be written and rewritten, and preliminary design of systems can be accomplished. User manuals are the primary item, and data sheets provide a functional description of the CPU chip and parametric specifications, plus other data and information.

system, duplex — Two computers used in special configuration; one is on-line and the other is standing by ready to be used if a malfunction of the on-line computer occurs. The stand-by computer is often used to complete off-line functions.

system engineering — The analysis and implementation of the procedures and plans adopted involving all the elements in an industrial process, business problem, or control situation.

system, error-detecting — *See* error-detecting system.

system, error-detecting and feedback — A system employing an error-detecting code and so arranged that a signal detected as being in error will automatically initiate a request for the retransmission of the incorrectly received signal.

system, error-detection — A system employing an error-detecting code and so arranged that any signal detected as being in error is deleted from the data delivered to the data link (in some cases with an indication that such a deletion has taken place), or delivered to the data link along with an indication that it has been detected as being in error.

system, exception principle — An information system or data-processing system that reports on situations only when the actual results differ from the planned results. When the results occur within a normal range, they are not reported.

system, executive — *See* executive system.

system, executive-control — Primary control of the executive system is by control information fed to the system by one or more input devices that may be either on-line or at various remote sites. This control information is similar in nature to present control-card operations, but allows additional flexibility and standardization.

system, fail-safe — A system which continues to process data despite the failure of parts in the system. Usually accompanied by some deterioration in performance.

system, file-oriented — *See* file-oriented system.

system, fixed-length record — *See* fixed-length record system.

system handbook — A concise distillation of the major characteristics of the instruction set including operation codes, addressing modes and microprocessor status for each instruction. Also includes reference to the primary aspects of system implementation including chip interfaces and timing. This document is aimed at the experienced user who understands the basics of the family and requires a concise reference book.

system hardware, industrial control — A typical industrial microcomputer system can be divided into five basic parts. They are the microprocessor and its associated memory; the interface modules which connect the microcomputer system to external devices such as limit switches, push buttons or motor starters; the equipment to program the microcomputer; a program analyzer which is used to analyze and diagnose the operation of the microcomputer based system; and a system tester which allows the user to check the microprocessor memory and interface modules to see if they are functioning properly.

system, horizontal — A programming system in which instructions are written horizontally, i.e., across the page.

system image preservation utility — An on-line utility task that can save the image of a running system on a load medium such as paper tape, cassette, floppy disk, or magnetic tape. The saved system image can subsequently be restored by bootstrapping it from the load device.

system-improvement time — The machine down time needed for the installation and testing of new components, large or small, and machine down time necessary for modification of existing components. This includes all programming tests to check out the modified machine.

system, indirect or off-line — *See* off-line or indirect system.

system, information — The network of all communication methods within an organization. Information may be derived from many sources other than a data-processing unit, such as by telephone, by contact with other people, or by studying an operation.

system, information-feedback — An error-control system using message feedback when an erroneous group is received from the sending station.

system, information-processing — A system that receives and delivers information, changing the information in the process.

system, information-retrieval — A system for locating and selecting on demand certain documents or other graphic records relevant to a given information requirement, from a file of such material. Examples of information-retrieval systems are classification, indexing, and machine-searching systems.

system, information-transmission — A system which receives and delivers information without changing it.

system, in-plant — A data-handling system confined to one building or a number of buildings in one locality.

system, integrated — *See* integrated system.

system interface design — For unique user applications, such as on-line installations that require specialized input/output equipment, liaison engineering staffs design the necessary interface units as part of the services to the customers. Then, the manufacturer will fabricate these units, at a normal product cost, for the particular system under close supervision by the same engineers that designed them.

system interface (microprocessor) — Devices that interconnect all other support hardware and often a tty (teletypewriter unit) for program assembly, simulation, PROM programming, prototype operations, and debugging.

system interrupts — System call interrupts are programmed requests from a processing program to the control program for some action, such as initiation of an input/output operation.

system language — In a system language, program statements generally correspond directly with machine-level instructions, and. conversely, every machine operation is reflected in a high-level language statement. Because of this correspondence, system-language programs usually translate efficiently to the machine-language level, and the programmer finds all the facilities of the machine directly available.

system librarian — An individual who issues and stores data files and other records of the installation and also maintains a list of all the up-to-date programs.

system loader — *See* loader, system.

system log — A data set in which job-related information, operational data, descriptions of unusual occurrences, commands, and messages to or from the operator may be stored. Abbreviated SYSLOG.

system log file — In some operations, the system maintains a log of many activities helpful to the system manager for billing and general system supervision. The transactions monitored are: all user log on/off, all user changes to baud rate, execution of sleep procedure, system load, exercise of date command, snapshot copy, and power fail/auto restart. A report of the most recent transactions is printed out on request by a control account.

system, macro — A programming system with symbolic capabilities of an assembly system and the added capability of many-for-one or macroinstruction development.

system, macroinstruction — Various macroinstructions control the translation procedure and do not necessarily develop usable machine-language programs or instructions.

system management (accounting) — The system manager authorizes users by assigning them system-recognizable user names and passwords. A user name and password enable the user to log into the system through a user interface. A well-designed operating system enables the system manager to account for the user of the system and to control the kinds of activities each user can perform.

system, management-information — A communications process in which data are recorded and processed for operational purposes. The problems are isolated for higher-level decision making, and information is fed back to top management to reflect the progress or lack of progress made in achieving major objectives.

system modularity — Modularity generally refers to a complete assortment of equipment that can be initially tailored to the unique needs of the application (whether instrumentation and control, communications, computation, or data systems), then expanded later by simply adding to the configuration.

system, monitor — *Same as* executive system.

system, monitor-operating — The monitor (control unit) exercises primary control of the routines that compose the operating system. It is this operating system that turns the computer into a flexible tool—allows the user to achieve maximum use of the design features of the hardware.

system, multicomputer — The use of more than one computer in a system.

system, multiprocessing — A system that is organized to contain two or more interconnected computers, but which performs functionally or geographically specialized processing tasks.

system, network operating — A network system requires extension to a multiprogramming executive which permits the implementation of multicomputer networks consisting of microcomputors and other processors. Connection may be local via i/o bus, interconnection, or remote via communication facilities. It provides inter-CPU communication, control procedures, and operating system commands to support "virtual device" activation. This facility allows user programs executing in a local CPU to communicate with user programs and/or peripheral devices in a remote CPU. High-reliability systems may be configured to provide modular redundance with increased performance by full utilization of back-up elements.

system, notation — *See* numeration system.

system, number — *See* number system.

system, numeration — *See* numeration system.

system numeration, representation — *See* numeration system.

system, numerical — *See* numeration system.

system, octal — *See* octal.

system, octal number — *See* octal number system.

system, on-demand — A system from which timely information or service is available on request.

system, open-ended — In optical character recognition, a system in which the input data is taken from sources other than the computer with which the character reader is associated or data which is part of the system.

system, operating — *Same as* executive system.

system organization, industrial — An industrial microcomputer system consists of a central processor unit (CPU) module which provides system control and performs the various arithmetic and logical functions; one or more programmable read only memories (PROMs) which store the system instructions or program; one or more random access memories (RAM) which are used for data storage; possibly an interrupt control module which is used to handle interrupt signals from devices being controlled; one or more input/output modules which accept inputs from the system being controlled and transmit control signals to that system; a power supply and regulators; a communications bus flat cable which provides the signal path to tie the various modules together; and the necessary mounting hardware.

system or section, operator control — A portion of the controlling equipment which is readily available to operators for controlling the systems equipment; this is usually a major portion of the console.

system, out-plant — A data-transmission system consisting of one or more centrally located terminals and one or more remote terminals.

system, PERT/COST — A generalized program designed to facilitate planning, scheduling, control, and monitoring of both large- and small-scale research and development projects.

system, phonetic — The specific equipment which has features for starting and acting upon data from the voice source.

system, polymorphic — A specific or particular system which can take on various forms ideally suited to the problems at hand, usually by altering, under its own control, its interconnections and the functions of its component parts.

system, process control — A system whose primary purpose is to provide automation of continuous operations.

system, programming — An assemblage of programs, programming languages, routines, and subroutines for use in specific computing systems, i.e., the basis for operating systems or total systems of data processing and computing.

system programming language — A language that has been developed for writing systems oriented software packages. The syntax and semantics of these languages are usually compromised to produce small and fast load modules for a particular machine.

system, quadruplex — A system of Morse telegraphy arranged for the simultaneous independent transmission of two messages in each direction over a single circuit.

system, real-time — *See* real-time processing.

system reliability — The probability that a system will accurately perform its specified task under stated tactical and environmental conditions.

system reliability, time-sharing — *See* time-sharing system reliability.

system, request-repeat — A system employing an error-detecting code and so arranged that a signal detected as being in error automatically initiates a request for retransmission of the signal detected as being in error.

system reset, network — An operation that halts all testing operations and resets the master console to an idle condition. The system awaits the next line/drop address and test command.

system, rollback — *See* rollback.

system safe signal — On some systems and for some applications, external system logic uses the system safe signal to trigger recovery procedures which may transfer operation to a back-up computer, notify a host computer which would attempt to download program or diagnostics, or direct the microcomputer to PROM for program reload or diagnostic procedures.

systems analysis — The examination of an activity, procedure, method, technique, or business to determine what must be accomplished and the best method of accomplishing the necessary operations.

systems analyst — *See* analyst, systems.

systems and procedure — Organization of *all* the manual and machine data processing operations required to produce information about one particular activity.

systems approach — Looking at the overall situation rather than the narrow implications of the task at hand; particularly, looking for interrelationships between the task at hand and other functions which relate to it.

system, scientific — A particular system devoted principally to computation, in contrast to a commercial or data-processing system in which the main emphasis is on file up-dating rather than performance of calculations.

systems consultant — An individual who supplies technical assistance and direction with specific emphasis on problem identification, organization analysis, conversion planning, forms control and analysis, and reports control.

systems design — The formulation and graphic description of the nature and content of input, files, procedures, and output in order to display the necessary connection processes and procedures.

system, self-organizing — A system that is capable of internal reconfiguration in response to externally occurring events.

systems flowchart — *See* flowchart, systems.

systems generation — In some computers, a systems disk must be generated by the user, who specifies the configuration, file protected area, error handling, etc.

system, shared-files — A special file system configuration in which two computers have access to the same file-storage device, though not necessarily at the same time.

system, share operation — The particular process or translation of symbolic instructions into a machine instruction. Often abbreviated SOS.

systems, hybrid — There have been a number of efforts to utilize the best properties of both digital and analog computers by building hybrid systems. In the hybrid system, a digital computer is used for control purposes and provides the program, while analog components are used to obtain the more lengthy solutions.

system, simplex — A system configuration that does not include standby equipment.

system simulation — An assemblage of interacting components and processes. The interactions are largely internal to the system, although links to an external environment will be recognized.

systems, inquiry and communications — Computer systems are now provided with facilities for diversified on-site and long-distance inquiry and data-communications networks. Centralized records and data-processing operations can be tied in with information sources at remote locations, and will provide instant, on-line response to interrogations and input data from a large number of inquiry stations. Communication networks include standard teletypewriter stations and electric typewriter stations.

system, slave — *See* slave system.

systems network architecture — Abbreviated SNA. A development by IBM intended to provide a unified design for interactive and batch applications in a communications system. It combines a single access method, a single network control program, and a single communications line control. SNA and the products that implement it include a single, standardized line discipline, called synchronous data-link control (SDLC); a standardized access method, called virtual telecommunications access method (VTAM); a network control program (NCP); and a family of standardized, mutually compatible terminals.

system software types — Supervisory and support modules as opposed to application programs. Types include such programs as operating systems, assemblers, debug routines, text editors, compilers, library maintenance, utilities, linking loaders, and i/o drivers.

systems, open-loop — Systems in which the computer does not directly control a process or procedure but instead displays or prints information for the operator to assist in determination of required action. Most real-time systems are basically open-loop systems.

systems, paper-tape — Systems having paper-tape equipment with no mass-storage device have a storage system contained on binary paper-tape reels. The binary reels are of two types: formatted binary, and absolute binary. Formatted binary programs are loaded by the system loader. Absolute binary programs are loaded by the monitor.

systems, procedure (and) — Organization of all the manual and machine data processing operations required to produce information about one particular activity.

systems, programs — *See* programs, systems.

systems study — The detailed process by which a set of procedures is determined in order to use a computer for definite functions or operations. Also, specifications are established to be used as a basis for the selection of equipment suitable for the specific needs.

systems synthesis — *See* synthesis, systems.

system standard — A specified characteristic often necessary to permit system operation.

system, start-stop — A system in which each group of code elements corresponding to an alphabetical signal is preceded by a start signal which serves to prepare the receiving mechanism for the reception and registration of a character, and is followed by a stop signal which serves to bring the receiving mechanism to rest in preparation for the reception of the next character.

system statistics — Some systems provide a supervisor program that provides detailed statistics on operator performance including the number of keystrokes; number of records written, verified, or updated; number of constraint errors; number of fields changed; and number of sign-ons.

system, stepped start-stop — A start-stop system in which the start signals occur at regular intervals.

systems test — 1. The running of the whole system against test data. 2. A complete simulation of the actual running system for purposes of testing out the adequacy of the system. 3. A test of an entire interconnected set of components for the purpose of determining proper functioning and interconnection.

system structure — The consideration of the specific nature of a chain of command and its origin, sequence, and type of data collected, the form and destination of the results, and the procedures used to control these operations.

system subcomponents, time-sharing — *See* time-sharing system subcomponents.

system subroutines — Input/output format control that provides for the various format statements used in the FORTRAN language. These subroutines are also available to other programs and may be called from the systems library tape.

system supervisor — The system supervisor is designed to allow an installation to proceed automatically from run to run with little or no computer time loss because of setting up the "next program." It is also designed to accomplish as many of the set-up and control functions as is possible prior to reading in the actual program. It is assumed that the programs are located on tape in the exact order that they are to be run. This order can be superseded by the operator. Each program on completion should transfer control to the "finish" entry point of the control program. This program will read in the next system supervisor from the library tape. Control is then transferred to the supervisor.

system, supervisory — All of the supervisory programs used by one system.

system, support — 1. A collection of computer programs to aid the production and checkout of a system. 2. The combination of the skills, techniques, and equipment to operate and maintain a system.

system, synchronous (communications) — A system in which the sending and receiving instruments are operating continuously at the same frequency and are maintained, by means of correction if necessary, in a desired phase relationship.

system, tandem — A special system configuration in which the data proceeds through one central processor into another processor. This is the system of multiplexers and master/slave arrangements.

system terminal — The center of many system operations is the crt (cathode-ray-tube) terminal. The crt terminal consists of a video display and a keyboard for data entry and system commands. The crt terminal contains a character generator, memory, and control logic such that refreshing of the video display is performed within the crt terminal. The control logic allows characters to be put on the display either from the keyboard or from a remote device, such as a computer, depending on the state of the terminal. The typical crt allows for the display of 1920 characters formed by 80 columns and 24 rows. One industry standard on screen size appears to be 12 inches diagonal; however, screen sizes of 14 and 15 inches and larger are available.

system testing program — Test and checkout of complete programs as opposed to parameter or assembly testing.

system, time-shared — A specific system in which available central-computer time is shared among several jobs, as directed by a scheduling plan or formula.

system, time-sharing (monitor) — *See* time-sharing monitor system.

system timing, microprocessor — Typically, a processor instruction cycle consists of five states: two states in which an address is sent to memory, one for the instruction or data fetch, and two states for the execution of the instruction. If the processor is used with slow memories, a ready line synchronizes the processor with the memories.

system, total — *See* total system.

system, total management — A management-oriented system conceived and designed by management as a singular entity to control the entire organization. Some of the systems which are integrated to form the total management system are accounting, inventory control, quality control, purchasing, receiving, and financial control. The total management system is an integrated management information and control system, and it is the prevailing application type of third generation computers. It blends both the administrative and operational applications into a single information system which provides management with timely and meaningful business information.

system, uniterm — An information-retrieval system that uses uniterm cards. Cards representing words of interest in a search are selected and compared visually. If identical numbers are found to appear on the uniterm cards undergoing comparison, these numbers represent documents to be examined in connection with the search.

system, upset-duplex — A direct-current telegraph system in which a station between any two duplex equipments may transmit signals by opening and closing the line circuit, thereby causing the signals to be received by upsetting the duplex balance.

system, utility — A system or program that is developed to perform miscellaneous or utility functions such as card-to-tape, tape-to-printer, and other peripheral operations or suboperations.

system utilization logger — A program or a device that collects statistical information about how the system is operating.

system, zatacode — *Same as* coordinate indexing.

T

tab — 1. A label, marker, or indicator used at one or both ends of a medium, such as a tape, to permit quick awareness of its message. 2. A slang term or abbreviation for tabulating equipment.

tab command — On some units, a command that moves the cursor to the next tab stop.

tab key, editing — On one type of system, a tab key permits the operator to move the cursor to the last character of the field. This key can be used when it is desired to add information to an existing field.

table — A collection of data in a form suitable for ready reference. It is frequently stored in sequenced machine locations or written in the form of an array of rows and columns for easy entry, in which an intersection of labeled rows and columns serves to locate a specific piece of data or information.

table, addition — The area of core storage that holds a table of numbers to be used during the table-scan concept of addition.

tableau, matrix-algebra — The current matrix, with auxiliary rows and/or columns, as it appears at an interactive stage in the standard-simplex method solution.

table block — A distinct portion or subset of a table of data or instructions, usually specifically identified for convenient access.

table, Boolean operation — *See* Boolean operation table.

table, decision — A tabulation or array of possible courses of action, selections, or alternatives which can be possible and thus considered in the analysis of various problems, i.e., a graphic aid to problem description, flow, and potential results, much as the purpose of a flowchart.

table development — In some systems, table development includes table creation, modification, deletion, printing, and viewing operations, together with printing or viewing of the names of the tables that have been created. There are two types of tables users can develop, verification and extraction. While a form is being created, the user specifies that a particular variable field is to be associated with a verification or extraction operation. In these systems, each time a form containing a verification or extraction operation is being used for data entry, the associated operation occurs whenever the applicable field in the form is filled.

table entry/look-up, data-base — In some systems, each table entry contains an argument (coded value) and a result (decoded value). A table is used for translation by comparing the input field with the argument values in the table until a matching argument is found. The corresponding result is the look-up result field value. Both basic and automatic table look-up can be used in the same request. In these systems, both allow tables to be referenced sequentially, by displacement, or using a binary search.

table, function — 1. Two or more sets of information so arranged that an entry in one set selects one or more entries in the remaining sets. 2. A dictionary. 3. A device constructed of hardware, or a subroutine, which can either decode multiple inputs into a single output or encode a single input into multiple outputs. 4. A tabulation of the values of a function for a set of values of the variable.

table, header — Specific records that contain the description of information designated in a classification or group of records which follows this initial document.

table lock-up — A method of controlling the location to which a jump or transfer is made. It is used especially when there are a large number of alternatives, as in function evaluation in scientific computations.

table look-at — Finding elements of a table by direct calculation rather than by a comparison search.

table look-up — 1. Any of various processes or procedures for searching identifying labels in a table so as to find the location of a desired associated item. The techniques used primarily to (1) obtain a derived value for one variable given another where the relationship cannot be easily stated in a formula or algorithm, (2) convert a discontinuous variable from one form to another (e.g., convert from one code to another), or (3) provide conditional (logical) control functions (e.g., converting disk keys from symbolic to actual addresses or determining which of several discrete processes should be applied for a given state. 2. A digital computer instruction which directs that the above operation be performed.

table look-up, data-base automatic — In some systems, special features provide two methods of performing table look-up operations: basic table look-up and automatic table look-up. With basic table look-up the user specifies the input argument field, the table, and the field where the result is to be stored. Automatic table look-up differs from the basic method in that the user defines the look-up operation in the file definition rather than specifying it in a request. When the look-up result field name is later referenced for processing or report output, the contents of the specified argument field will be used to search the specified table automatically. In these systems, definitions of look-up result fields can be changed easily during dictionary maintenance runs.

table-look-up instruction — An instruction designed to allow reference to systematically arranged, stored data.

table-look-up techniques — (1) If particular variables are associated with a table of functions, e.g., X_i links with F_i, G_i, . . . , and if the values of X_i are equally spaced, locations of associated functions can be conveniently generated by some simple linear relation. (2) If arguments are not equally spaced, the addresses of each X_i and others can be separated with an appropriate constant. Compare-type order codes can be invoked to locate and the addresses of the associated function can be computed. (3) Each datum X_i can be stored with a pointer pointing to a list of associated functions of X_i. (4) Indirect addressing may be used to jump from an ordered sequential storage of arguments to nonsequential, nonordered stores of associated functions (some systems).

table, multiplication — A specific area of storage that holds the groups of numbers to be used during the tabular scanning of the multiplication operation.

table, output — *See* board, plotting.

table, plotting — *Same as* board, plotting.

table, program reference — That section of storage used as an index for operations, subroutines, and variables.

table simulator — A specific computer program which has the capability of computing the values in a table rather than simply looking them up as stored.

table, subroutine — The routine for maintaining a listing of the subroutines in core and for bringing from file the subroutines as needed by the application program.

table, symbol — A mapping for a set of symbols to another set of symbols or numbers. In programming, the assembler builds a table of labels used in an assembler language program and assigns to those labels a set of relative or absolute core locations.

table, symbol control — Symbols that have been defined and used, but are no longer required, may be deleted from the symbol table. This allows room for new symbols. Thus, a very large program can be assembled with a relatively small symbol storage area.

table, terminal — An ordered collection of information consisting of a control field for the table and blocks of information on each terminal from which a message can originate, and each terminal, group of terminals, and processing program to which a message can be sent.

table, transfer — *See* transfer table.

table, translation — In some systems, data may be translated through a table. Tables may translate either individual items or a range of items through table look-up techniques.

table, truth — A representation of a switching function, or truth function, in which every possible configuration of argument values 0 and 1 (or true and false) is listed, and beside each is given the associated function value 0 or 1 (or true or false). The number of configurations is 2^n, where n is the number of arguments, unless the function is incompletely specified, i.e., don't-care conditions. An example of a truth table for the AND function and the (inclusive) OR function is:

Variable		*AND Function*	*OR*
A	B	AB	A + B
0	0	0	0
0	1	0	1
1	0	0	1
1	1	1	1

tactile keyboard — Designed for calculators, digital tv and fm receivers, terminals, and other applications, the typical tactile keyboard has three component layers. Just below the keys (not provided with some units) is a sheet of Mylar, first screened on its bottom side with a conductive pattern and then "bubbled" by heat and pressure deformation. These bubbles invert when depressed by keys into spaces in the second layer, a Mylar sheet with a circular opening at each key position. As a bubble inverts, the conductive area on its underside contacts the third layer, a screened circuit board, to complete switch closure.

tag — A unit of information, whose composition differs from that of other members of the set so that it can be used as a marker or label. A tag bit is an instruction word that is also called a sentinel or a flag.

tag converting unit — A machine that performs automatic reproduction of information from perforated price tags to punched cards. This machine provides cards for the tabulation of detailed and up-to-date merchandise reports, including size, color, priceline, fabric, and style.

takedown — Those actions performed at the end of an equipment-operating cycle to prepare the equipment for the next setup, e.g., removal of tapes from the tape handlers at the end of a computer run according to a takedown procedure.

takedown time — The time required to take down a piece of equipment.

take-up reel — A specific reel on which tape is wound or may be wound during processing.

talk, cross — Cross talk occurs when signals on one telephone circuit appear on another circuit as interference. The circuit which is the source of the signals is known as the disturbing circuit, and that on which the signals are heard is the disturbed circuit.

talker, echo — A portion of the transmitted signal returned from a distant point to the transmitting source with sufficient time delay to be received as interference.

talking computer — One type of talking computer is used to tutor the blind and visually handicapped in vocational class work. The pupil communicates with specially designed instructional programs through a typewriterlike keyboard and hears responses generated by a voice synthesizer.

talking-computer synthesizer — One type of speech synthesizer is a hardwired analog of the human vocal tract. Various portions of the circuit simulate the vocal cords, the lungs, and the variable-frequency resonant cavity of the mouth, tongue, lips, and teeth. The information necessary to produce the speech sounds of American English is programmed into ROMs which reside on the synthesizer board. The unit accepts a string of ASCII characters (each character representing a particular phonetic sound or phoneme) in the same fashion as a printing peripheral. Because the synthesizer is primarily an analog circuit which is commanded digitally, new programming information is required only at the end of each completed phoneme.

tally — To add or subtract a digit "1" from a quantity, usually the contents of a register.

tandem switching — The use of an intermediate switch or switches to interconnect circuits from the switch of one serving central office to the switch of a second serving central office in the same exchange.

tandem system — A special system configuration in which the data proceeds through one central processor into another processor. This is the system of multiplexors and master/slave arrangements.

tape — 1. Magnetic, punched paper, sometimes other types of tape as paper loops, etc., used to control vertical formatting of printers, or plastic tapes used to control automatic typewriters. 2. A strip of material that may be punched, coated, or impregnated with magnetic or optically sensitive substances, and used for data input, storage, or output. The data is stored serially in several channels across the tape, transversely to the reading or writing motion.

tape, advance-feed — Perforated paper tape that has the leading edge of the feed holes directly in line with the leading edges of the intelligence holes. This characteristic makes it possible to readily identify and differentiate between the front end and the tail end of an uninterpreted tape. While some applications still use advance-feed tape, most new ones no longer use it. *See* tape, center-feed.

tape alternation — A selection, usually controlled automatically by a program, of first one tape unit and then another, normally during input or output operations, that permits successive reels of a file to be mounted and removed without interrupting the program.

tape beginning control — A special perforation, reflective spot, or transparent portion of the first part of a magnetic tape to indicate its start.

tape bootstrap routine — One load tape has as its first block a bootstrap routine that serves to bring in the remainder of the resident and various other parts of the system. Some bootstrap routines also provide a simple card-load routine, a panic dump, and a method of patching the resident system prior to writing it to disk or tape.

tape bound — *Same as* tape limited.

tape, carriage control — A tape that contains the control codes related to the movement of the carriage of the printer, and thus controls the vertical and horizontal positioning of the carriage as well as the paper feed unit.

tape, center-feed — Perforated paper tape that has the feed holes centered directly in line with the centers of the intelligence holes. The most common method in use today.

tape certification — To certify magnetic computer tape to zero errors is to assure or make certain the reel of tape has zero errors. This is generally done on a tape certifier and is accomplished by saturating the magnetic tape or writing on it with 100% of a signal and instantaneously reading it back to see whether a parity is achieved. Normal industry standards call for reading back at least 50% of the signal at 800 bits/inch, 35% of the signal at 1600 bits/inch, and 40% of the signal at 6200 bits/inch. All of the specifications give a reasonable margin of safety on any normal computer. Most computers are set so they will read back a signal and receive parity as long as they can read between 12% and 20% of the original signal placed on the computer tape.

tape, chadded paper — A paper tape with the holes fully punched.

tape, chadless paper — A paper tape with the holes partially punched. It is commonly used in teletypewriter operations.

tape, change — A paper or magnetic tape carrying information that is to be used to update filed information on a master tape. (Synonymous with transaction tape.)

tape channels, paper — The presence of a hole in the tape indicates the presence of a code bit. The holes are punched in channels parallel to the edge of the tape, and paper tape of 5, 6, 7, or 8 information channels is in use at present. An 8-channel tape (with an additional sprocket channel for guiding the tape or for code synchronization) will commonly be of 1-inch width with codes spaced at 10 per inch along the tape.

tape channels, punched paper — The parallel tracks along the length of the tape.

tape character — Information consisting of bits stored across the several longitudinal channels of a tape.

tape coil, blank paper — A coil of paper tape that has to be punched with the feed holes and can be punched with a pattern of holes that represent data.

tape coil, paper — The roll of paper tape as coiled and ready for use at the punch station, but one which may be blank or punched in preparation for working.

tape comparator — A machine which automatically compares two tapes which are expected to be identical. The comparison is row by row, and the machine stops when a discrepancy occurs.

tape conditioning — Conditioning a tape means to run the tape forward to the end of the tape, reverse it, and run the tape backward to the beginning of the tape. Conditioning is necessary for smooth, continuous operation of a cartridge. Whenever a cartridge has been subjected to sudden environmental changes (such as being transported by air), users should condition the tape before use. Also, if the read fail message occurs while a particular cartridge is being read, it may be due to uneven tension in the tape. Conditioning restores proper tension.

tape, control — A paper or plastic tape used to control the carriage operation of some printing output devices.

tape-controlled carriage — An automatic paper-feeding carriage controlled by a punched paper tape.

tape-control unit — The unit, including associated buffering, for controlling the operation of the magnetic tape transport.

tape, cycling — An updating procedure which creates a new tape file.

tape drive — The mechanism that moves magnetic or paper tape past sensing and recording heads and is usually associated with data-processing equipment. (Synonymous with tape transport and feed, tape, and related to tape unit and magnetic-tape unit.)

tape drive controller functions — A typical magnetic tape drive controller consists of four functional sections: a motion control section, a read section, a write section, and a direct memory access interface section.

tape-driver interrupt routine — In the interrupt routine, the driver determines whether a fail condition has occurred on the addressed unit. A fail condition is recognized when the unit is at the end of the tape, at a file mark, or if a parity fail

Courtesy Wangco Div., Perkin-Elmer Corp.
Tape drive.

has occurred. If no fail has occurred and the operation requested requires a series of commands, the driver will give the next command and exit to the interrupt point.

tape dump — The transfer of complete contents of information recorded on tape to the computer or another storage medium.

tape editor — The symbolic tape editor program is used to edit, correct, and update symbolic program tapes using the computer and the teletypewriter unit. With the editor in the core memory, the user reads in portions of his symbolic tape, removes, changes, or adds instructions or operands, and gets back a corrected symbolic tape. The user can work through the program instruction by instruction, spot-check it, or concentrate on new sections.

tape erasure — A process by which a signal recorded on a tape is removed and the tape made ready for re-recording. Erasure may be accomplished in two ways: in ac erasure, the tape is demagnetized by an alternating field which is reduced in amplitude from an initially high value; in dc erasure, the tape is saturated by applying a primarily unidirectional field.

tape, error — A special tape developed and used for writing out errors in order to correct them by study and analysis after printing.

tape feed — A mechanism that will feed tape to be read or sensed by the machine.

tape-feed switch — A switch that actuates the reperforator to meter a predetermined length of tape.

tape file — 1. A record file consisting of a magnetic or punched-paper tape. 2. A set of magnetic tapes in a tape library.

tape file checks, magnetic — Hardware checks for faulty tapes without loss of computer time or manual intervention.

tape format, paper — A binary object tape consists of one or more records which are organized in a sequential fashion along the length of the tape. Each record consists of a maximum of 67 and a minimum of 1 consecutive tape columns. Blank tape may appear before, between, or after records. The arrangement of records on a binary object tape is not standardized.

tape, fully perforated (chad tape) — Perforated paper tape in which the perforations are complete—that is, in which the punch makes a complete hole in the tape (as opposed to chadless tape, where the hole is not completely punched out).

tape, grandfather — A magnetic tape which contains basic or initial information, which is used on a second tape, and this second tape is the one which is updated according to the latest transactions or changes. When this second tape is copied, it becomes the new grandfather tape, and a series of grandfather tapes is the historical record or statistical base for further manipulation, analysis, or an audit trial. They are also backup tapes in case of accidental erasure or loss of latest developed tapes.

tape input — A method of introducing data to an input device by the use of plastic or metallic magnetic tape, perforated paper tape, or fabric tape loops; the mechanical method by which data is read from tape and fed into a machine.

tape, instruction — *Same as* tape, program.

tape, intermix — A specific feature of some computer equipment which allows for combinations of different models of tape units to be interconnected to a single computer.

tape labels — A tape label appears on each reel of magnetic tape in the form of a leader and/or a trailer record; its contents will be determined to some extent by the application and the type of data found on the tape. The leader record appears as the first and the trailer record as the last on the tape. Together they provide the means for machine-performed accounting control of tape operations. Types of information which may be included in a tape label are: a name or code for the tape which identifies the application and tape data type, reel number or sequence number if there is more than one, frequency of use, record format, date of preparation or date last used, purge date, operation in which the tape was written (generally a code), name of individual chiefly responsible, output number if there are several tapes, record count, control totals, any instructions to be typed out to the operator as well as an end-of-reel or end-of-file code.

tape leader — Section at the beginning of a reel of magnetic or punched tape which is often left blank to allow for initial threading or to contain some sort of marker or code to indicate the nature of the data stored on the tape. Holes, notches, some special magnetization, etc., are used for such purposes.

tape, library — *See* library tapes.

tape limited — Just as some computers are limited to the slower speeds of input for adequate performance, others are bound or limited in performance speeds by the time required for reading, writing, or interpreting tags. When computers execute various types of business or large batch data processing and much of the time is used in moving tapes, then the computer or processor must wait and is said to be tape limited.

tape limited (sorting) — A sort program in which the effective transfer rate of tape units determines the elapsed time required to sort.

tape loadpoint — The initial position of the magnetic tape under the heads, at which point magtape reading or writing can begin.

tape-loop storage — *See* storage, loop.

tape, mag — The informal or slang expression for magnetic tape.

tape, magnetic — A tape or ribbon of any material impregnated or coated with magnetic material on which information may be placed in the form of magnetically polarized spots.

tape mark — The special character that is written on a tape to signify the physical end of the recording on tape.

tape marker, beginning — A special perforated reflective spot or a transparent portion of the first part of a magnetic tape to indicate its start. Abbreviated BIM.

tape, master — Usually a magnetic tape containing the main program or the data master file, which is updated by data contained in a change tape.

tape, master-file — The word "file" is used in a general sense to mean any collection of informational items similar to one another in purpose, form, and content. Thus a magnetic tape master file is a file; the term may also be applied to a punched paper tape of input items, or, if convenient, to a set of cassettes that is equivalent in nature to either the magnetic or paper tape. File may even be applied to an accumulation of information in the processor memory if the need arises to refer in a general way to this collection of data.

tape, master-instruction — Abbreviated MIT. A tape on which all the programs for a system of runs are recorded.

tape master program — *See* tape master.

tape, master-system — A monitor (control unit) program that allows for centralized control of program operation. It provides a load-and-go operation, without operator intervention, with one tape unit. The operator can specify loading and execution of any program on the master-system tape by a simple on-line typewriter directive.

tape, Mylar — A specific data-processing tape manufactured by E.I. Du Pont de Nemours & Co., Inc. It consists of a polyester film backing with a magnetic oxide coating.

tape, numerical-control — A punched paper or plastic tape with magnetic spots used to feed digital instructions to a numerical control (N/C) machine, i.e., an automated cutting or forming machine thus guided. Tolerances as fine as 1/10,000 of an inch are achieved on unattended units. Tapes are developed for digital-computer programs.

tape operating system — Abbreviated TOS. Some operating systems have component modules (i.e., compilers, linkage-editor, etc.) stored on a system tape and use tape libraries for storage of user program and data files. (Contrasts with disk operating system, DOS.)

tape or disk program — A tape or disk used to store a complete routine for future input. In the event that the length of the routine exceeds the available internal storage capacity, it will be read in and operated on by the computer, one segment at a time.

tape, paper — A strip of paper capable of storing or recording information. Storage may be in the form of punched holes, partially punched holes, carbonization or chemical change of impregnated material, or by imprinting. Some paper tapes, such as punched paper tapes, are capable of being read by the input device of a computer or a transmitting device by sensing the pattern of holes that represent coded information.

tape parity — *See* parity, tape.

tape, perforated — *See* tape, punched paper.

tape perforating — The recording of data in paper tape by means of punched holes. This is generally done by a card-to-tape converter which automatically senses the information from punched cards and perforates a 5-channel or 8-channel tape used in telegraphic transmission and other common-language applications.

tape perforator — An off-line, keyboard-operated device for punching code holes in paper tape.

tape, pilot — A tape that contains all the data used on a pilot model. It is often used for loading the files.

tape, problem input — An input tape, either punched-paper tape or magnetic tape, that contains problem data for checking out a given computer system.

tape-processing simultaneity — A feature of some computers is tape processing simultaneity. All tape units are capable of transferring data simultaneously with other central processor operations. The ability to perform tape operations simultaneously is further enhanced by the fact that the central processor is involved in a tape read or write operation during only two microseconds per character transferred. Thus, the majority of a tape-processing interval is available to the central processor to perform computations or direct other peripheral operations.

tape-processing unit — Tape processing includes the functions of recording, transcribing, transmitting, receiving, and converting data recorded in perforated paper tape. Data recorded in paper tape can be processed to: produce punched cards by automatic conversion, provide input for electric computers, provide automatic wire transmission of all or selected data, type subsequent related records and documents, and provide master tapes or cards for use in repetitive data operations.

tape, program — A tape that contains the sequence of instructions required for solving a problem.

tape, punch — A tape, usually paper, upon which data may be sorted in the form of punched holes. Hole locations are arranged in rows across the width of the tape. There are usually 5 or 8 channels per row, with data represented by a binary-coded decimal system. All holes in a column are sensed simultaneously in a manner similar to that for punch cards. (Synonymous with perforated tape.)

tape, punch, code — A code used to represent data on punch tape.

tape-punch control keys — Keys that control functions such as power on, feeding tape at beginning and end of reel, tape error, and punch on and off.

tape, punched paper — Paper or plastic material from 300 to 1000 feet long into which data is recorded in the form of small round holes punched into prescribed positions. An input and/or output medium, used primarily in systems where information is received over wire communication circuits.

tape reader — 1. A device capable of sensing information punched on a paper tape in the form of a series of holes. 2. A device capable of sensing information recorded on a magnetic tape in the form of a series of magnetized spots.

tape recording density — Common recording densities are 200 characters per inch, 556 per inch, 800 per inch, or even higher in the newest "packed" tapes. Blocks or records are usually separated by blank gaps on tapes, most commonly of ¾ in.

tape reproducer — A machine used either to copy or to edit paper tape or to do both.

tape, scratch (sorting) — Tape(s) used to store intermediate-pass data during a sort program.

tape, sequence control — A tape that contains the sequence of instructions required for solving a problem.

tape skew — The deviation of a tape from a linear path when transported across the heads, causing a time displacement between signals recorded on different tracks and amplitude differences between the outputs from individual tracks owing to variations in azimuth alignment.

tape skip — A machine instruction to space forward and erase a portion of tape when a defect on the tape surface causes a persistent write error.

tape skip, tape-skip restore — A function that permits certain portions of the tape to be idled through a tape read head without being read. This function is initiated by depressing the tape-skip key. Skipping continues until the read head finds a tape-skip restore character in the tape. This character must be included in the original programming.

tapes, library — Library tapes have tape labels, skip records, and control marks. However, the programs must be stored on magnetic tape according to a particular format. Library tapes may contain two types of intermixed formats—standard format (running programs as set up by a librarian), and debugging format (this includes check data as well as the programs to be checked).

tape sort and collate programs — Generalized programs that adapt themselves, as directed by programmer-specified parameters, to operate in a particular configuration—sort and collate data into a particular format.

tape sort, four — *See* sorting, four tape.

tape speed — The speed at which tapes are transported from feed to take-up reels during normal recording or reproduction.

tape station — *Same as* tape unit.

tape storage — Various storage devices in which data are stored in the form of magnetic spots on metal or coated plastic tape. Binary data are stored as small magnetized spots arranged in column form across the width of the tape. A read-write head is usually associated with each row of magnetized spots so that one column can be read or written at a time as the tape traverses the head.

tape storage, magnetic — *See* storage, magnetic-tape.

tape synchronizer — *See* synchronizer, tape.

tape, test input — A method of testing and simulation, wherein a test input tape is prepared from an input message tape, which is then read by the test supervisory program in a manner as if it had actually arrived from regular input devices.

tape-to-head speed — The relative speed of tape and head during normal recording or replay. The tape-to-head speed coincides with the tape speed in conventional longitudinal recording, but is considerably greater than the tape speed in systems where the heads are scanned across or along the tape.

tape-to-printer program — Transfers data from magnetic tape to printer.

tape-to-tape converter — A device for changing from one form of input/output medium or code to another, i.e., magnetic tape to paper tape (or vice versa), or eight-channel code to five-channel code, etc.

tape trailer — A special strip or tape length at the end of tape reels, usually containing a type of end-of-tape marker, i.e., a hole, long blank, special magnetic spots, etc.

tape, transaction — Information on a paper tape or magnetic tape that is to be used to update filed information on a master tape.

tape transmitter, automatic — A peripheral unit which senses data on paper, magnetic, or mylar tape and which holds, feeds, controls, and reels the tape. They are used basically for computer input units, and often used to drive printers, plotters, card punches, or transmission modems.

tape transmitter distributor — *Same as* tape reader.

tape transport — The mechanism that moves magnetic or paper tape past sensing and recording heads. This mechanism is usually associated with data-processing equipment. (Synonymous with drive, tape and tape feed; related to tape unit and magnetic-tape unit.)

tape unit — A device consisting of a tape transport, controls, a set of reels, and a length of tape that is capable of recording and reading information on and from the tape, at the request of the computer.

tape unit perforator — *See* tape processing unit.

tape units, incremental — Various types of magnetic tape modules which require a tape flow "halt" for the process of reading or writing.

tape verifier — A device designed for checking the accuracy of punched tape by comparing previously punched tape with a second manual punching of the same data, with the machine signaling discrepancies.

tape, work (sorting) — Tape(s) used to store intermediate-pass data during a sort program.

target interface, development system — The provision the user has with software/hardware traceability features. This ensures that the final design is acceptable.

target language — The language into which some other language is to be translated.

target phase — An occasion on which the target program is run is often called the run phase or the target phase or the object phase. Most often, target phase terminology is used when compiling has taken place.

target program — *Same as* object program.

target routine — *Same as* object program.

task — A routine or machine run. A program may be broken into several subjobs or tasks to utilize more effectively computer CPU time.

task checkpoint — On some systems, once a task is in memory, the executive normally allows it to run to completion in a multiprogrammed fashion, even if its memory is required for the execution of a higher-priority, nonresident task. However, if it is desirable to free memory for execution of a higher-priority task, a task can be declared checkpointable when created. A checkpointable task currently active in a partition can be interrupted and swapped out of memory to disk when a higher-priority task requests the partition in which it is active. Later, after the higher-priority task has completed its execution, the checkpointed task will be rolled in and restored to active execution at the point where it was interrupted.

task dispatcher — The task dispatcher provides the ability to initiate parallel tasks and to synchronize their execution.

task dispatcher routine — A control routine or function which selects from the task queue or lists the next task to be processed and gives it control of the central processor.

tasking — In order to facilitate implementation of systems involving several independent processes, the processor must be able to maintain the illusion that several routines are running simultaneously. Therefore, to relieve the programmer of the job of creating this illusion, some form of multitasking facility must be supplied. The basic parts of such a facility include a real-time monitor to provide a task scheduling capability and a number of commands to allow activation, deactivation, and synchronization of tasks. Other desirable features include a timing facility and a provision for interrupt handling.

task management — A set of functions of the control program or routine which controls the use of system resources other than the input/output devices by tasks.

task management functions — The procedural functions for task creation, scheduling, synchronization, and termination. Multitasking is supported both across several programs and within a single program.

task processing, terminal — In order to facilitate fast response in various types of processing environments, tasks are created to process transactions from a terminal almost immediately upon their arrival at the system (after the input is edited and formatted). A task is one or more application programs (modules) that have been loaded into the system to process a transaction. Since a rule of thumb in a transaction-oriented environment is that programs must execute in a half second or less, message processing priorities must be established immediately, based on the operator, transaction, terminal, or a combination thereof.

task queue — A queue that contains all the task control blocks which are in the system at any one time.

task scheduler — The task scheduler is used in real-time operating systems to organize and schedule the processing of events not directly connected to user interrupts and to provide multiple execution paths through a program. This concept is called multitasking. The task scheduler activates, terminates, suspends, or readies tasks either individually or in groups. In the activation stage, the scheduler prepares a task to receive identification, priority, and program variables that define the environment in which the task operates. It then places the activated tasks in a ready queue, and they are processed on the basis of priority numbers assigned by the user. The operating system makes sure that control of the central processor is always given to the highest-priority task capable of using it.

task scheduler supervision control — The scheduler suspends tasks under a number of circumstances: when ordered to do so by another task, when a specific time delay or outside event must occur before the task can resume, while waiting for a message from another task or completion of i/o and system calls, or when a task is ordered to resume at a certain time of day. When the time elapses or the awaited event occurs, the scheduler again readies the task for execution.

task scheduling, event-driven — Task scheduling in some systems is primarily event driven, in contrast to systems which use a static scheduling mechanism for determining the eligibility of a task to execute. The basis of event-driven task scheduling is the software priority assigned to each active task. When a significant event (such as i/o completion) occurs, the executive interrupts the executing task and searches for the highest-priority task capable of executing.

task, serial — A task is a logically complete execution path through a program that can be executed independently of any other task in the same program. In serial tasking, each task gains control of the system resources it needs, uses the resources to complete its function, and then relinquishes control of the resources to the next task.

task-to-task communication — The process by which a user program on one node of a computer network exchanges messages or data with a user program on another node.

TCAM — Abbreviation for TeleCommunications Access Method. A specific method for controlling the transfer of messages between the application program and remote terminals that provides a high-level message control language. TCAM can be custom tailored to applications requirements through selection of the appropriate macroinstructions and operands.

teaching machines — Most such units have the following characteristics: (1) A computer monitored or controlled with continuous and active response to each unit of information presented or queried, (2) immediate and recorded feedback from questions of the student's responses and an acknowledgment of correct or incorrect answers to the student with other alternative or remedial information and instructions, and (3) a scheduling which allows students to work at their own pace and a modular presentation allowing teacher-programmers to present materials sufficiently varied to suit individual student capabilities. The teaching machine consists of both programs and hardware. The programs are either linear or branching types, or a mixture of both. Linear programs usually consist of one or two sentences, followed by a sentence containing blanks. Progress through the program is linear in the sense that one follows the other in sequence, although skipping some frames, usually planned. Branching programs have larger units of information, such as two or three paragraphs. The student usually answers multiple-choice questions. The main path is followed if the answers are correct. Branches provide remedial teaching or instructions for incorrect answers. The teaching machines physically have a storage unit, a display mechanism, a response panel, and communication with a central computer. Some machines can be combined with slides, film strips, and microfilm.

technical control center — A modular electronic system that functions to help data-center personnel locate and diagnose problems which can occur anywhere in a network. A technical control center allows any line to be patched to any modem and any modem to be patched to any port. It can be determined whether a problem lies in the data terminal, the transmission equipment (modems), the front end, the CPU, or perhaps an erring operator. The technical control center permits on-line checks to be performed with its test equipment which can pinpoint a malfunction with a minimum of disruption to the network.

technique — The method used to collect, process, convert, transfer, and retrieve data to prepare reports.

technique, advance item — A programming technique which groups records in specific arrangements disregarding location aspects of the data.

technique, flowchart — *See* flowchart technique.

technology, solid-logic — Microelectronic circuits, the product of solid-logic technology, make up the basic components of some systems. Called logic circuits because they carry and control the electrical impulses that represent information within a computer, these tiny devices operate at speeds ranging from 300 down to six billionths of a second.

telecommunication — The transmission or reception of signals, writing, sounds, or intelligence of any nature by wire, radio, light beam, or any other electromagnetic means.

telecommunications access method — Abbreviated TCAM. A communication subsystem designed to exchange messages between the communication network and a set of message queues, according to information contained in control blocks and message headers. The program which controls these operations, called the message control program (MCP), is coded for each particular installation using a set of system macros which invoke various parts of the TCAM software.

telecommuting — The replacement of "physical" commuting from home to workplace with "logical" commuting, in which one works at home through a computer and telecommunications channel.

teleconference — A conference between persons who are remote from one another but linked together by a telecommunications system.

teledata — A device that introduces parity bits to punched paper tape for transmission. The receiving unit checks parity for code accuracy and repunches paper tape with valid data.

telefile — An early on-line banking system

developed for Howard Savings Institution of Newark, New Jersey.

telemanagement — A service which features computerized management of a customer's long-distance system, automatically routing each call over the least costly line available at the time the call is made and logging each call for accounting control.

telemeter — 1. An electric telemeter is the formulating and reformulation apparatus for indicating and/or recording the value of a measured quantity by electrical means at a remote station. 2. To transmit digital and/or analog data by radio waves; e.g., data can be telemetered from a missile and recorded at a ground station.

telemetering — Also called telemetry or remote metering. Measurement which, through intermediate means, can be interpreted at a distance from the primary detector. A receiving instrument converts the transmitted electrical signals into units of data, which can then be translated by data reduction into appropriate units.

telemeter service — Metered telegraph transmission between paired telegraph instruments over an intervening circuit adapted to serve a number of such pairs on a shared-time basis.

telemetry — Transmission to a distance of measured magnitudes by radio or telephony, with suitably coded modulation (e.g., amplitude, frequency, phase, pulse).

Telenet — Telenet Communications Corp., a USA communications carrier offering packet switching transmission.

telephone communication units — The data sets as used with the many data communications systems provide half-duplex capability. They are used for sending and receiving but not for both operations simultaneously. The data set at the transmitting end takes the character pulses from the data-line terminal and converts them to modulated information-bearing signals that can be transmitted over the telephone line. The data set at the receiving end converts the signals from the telephone line back to the same character pulses as those delivered by the transmitting data-line terminal and delivers these pulses to the receiving data-line terminal. A data set conditions itself in the receiving mode unless instructed to be in the transmitting mode. The turnaround of the data set at the transmitting end is performed by the "request to transmit step" in the program of the computer at the sending end. It may be used with either the private line or the exchange telephone facilities.

telephone couplers — Mechanisms for putting a regular telephone handset into service as a modem. Usually, they work acoustically, but they may also work inductively.

telephone dialer — Under program control, this circuit divides the output of an on-chip crystal oscillator, thus providing the tone frequency pairs needed by the telephone system. The tone pairs are selected through a latch by means of a BCD code from the bus.

telephone dialer circuit — An MOS telephone dialer circuit converts push-button closures to rotary dial pulses directly compatible with a standard telephone system.

teleprinter — 1. Descriptive name for telegraphic terminals. 2. Generally an electric typewriter that can be operated manually or electrically by reading a reperforating paper tape. 3. The typewriter usually connected to a leased or dial-switched telegraph-grade circuit for transmitting text or data messages in a readable form. 4. An input/output terminal device, normally used on low-speed circuits, that includes at least a page printer.

teleprinter grade service — This term originally referred to a service provided by the common carriers which included a communication circuit of narrow bandwidth that was capable of speeds no greater than 180 bauds and furnished a compatible dc signal to the terminal input/output device directly. This definition is no longer completely valid because much of the low-speed data transmission is accomplished over circuits utilizing ac signaling, so a dataset must be provided between the circuit and the terminal equipment. The term now is used primarily to distinguish this type of service from voice-grade service in reference to the tariffs of regulatory agencies.

teleprocessing — The most generalized concepts relate to the forms and procedures of information handling in which a data processing system uses communication facilities.

teleprocessing terminal — A teleprocessing terminal is used for on-line data transmission between remote process locations and a central computer system. Connection to the computer system is made by a data adapter unit or a transmission control. Some systems facilitate the control of natural gas and petroleum pipe lines, utility distribution operations, and the collection of process data in petroleum refineries, chemical plants, paper mills, iron and steel works, batch processes in manufacturing, and many other applications.

teletext and viewdata — Teletext is a generic term used to describe the broadcast of text and graphics as part of the television video signal. Viewdata refers to the transmission of such information on an interactive basis, usually via telephone lines. Television sets must be equipped with suitable decoding circuits to enable the sets to receive transmissions and display them on the tv screen. Teletext and viewdata are essentially compatible and use the same decoder with only minor differences.

Best-known among the broadcast teletext systems are probably Ceefax, short for See-Facts, developed by the BBC, and Oracle, a similar (and compatible) teletext service developed by the British Independent Broadcasting Authority. In Ceefax, the viewer presses a button on a special keypad and makes an index appear on the screen. On the index are three-digit combinations corresponding to categories, such as weather, news, sports, travel information, and tv programming, among others. The viewer presses the three-digit combination desired and, after a pause of up to 25 seconds, gets either a lower-level index (showing, for example, the kinds of sports news categories that are available) or the short message sought.

The process is feasible because the electron-beam scanning of the normal tv set is temporarily inhibited each time it is shifted from the bottom of the picture to the top. It is during this brief vertical-blanking interval that a digitized data signal can be received at the set, decoded, and generated into meaningful characters on the screen without interfering with the regular tv signal. The British television standard, for example, specifies 625 scanning lines for a picture, split into two consecutive fields of 312½ lines each. In actuality, only 287½ lines of each field appear on the screen, with the remaining 25 lines being produced during the vertical-blanking interval. Teletext data are carried on four of these empty scanning lines.

When the teletext data are extracted by a decoder inside the receiver, the page of text and graphics can be displayed in color on the screen instead of the transmitted program. A main feature of television teletext systems allows the viewer to choose any one of the transmitted pages by selecting the appropriate page number on the keyboard. The desired page is decoded by the decoding system and stored in memory for display on the screen.

Teletype — A trademark of the Teletype Corporation. It usually refers to a series of different types of teleprinter equipment, such as transmitters, tape punches, reperforators, and page printers, utilized for communications systems.

teletypewrite marking pulse — *See* pulse, teletypewrite marking.

teletypewriter — An electromechanical machine consisting of a typewriterlike keyboard and printer. Such machines were originally used to transmit information in communications systems. They are now frequently used to communicate with a computer. Many of the machines are designed to utilize ASCII or other codes.

teletypewriter controller — A teletypewriter controller is often incorporated on the same circuit board as the control panel logic module; thus, it is usually available at no additional expense. This "minimum cost" interface then operates under program control by the CPU to allow full duplex communication with a single teletypewriter.

teletypewriter/crt utility package — A library of programs that performs the most common i/o functions for a teletypewriter or crt (cathode-ray tube) terminal.

teletypewriter entry systems — Many personal computer systems are teletypewriter-based systems. They usually have some form of monitor in ROM that allows the operator to type in code and helps isolate him or her from errors. The total program is printed out in hard copy, and paper tape is usually available.

teletypewriter exchange services (Telex & TWX) — Services that provide direct-dial point-to-point connections using teleprinter equipment, such as keyboard printers, paper tape readers, and tape punches. Facilities are also available to permit computers to interface to these services. These are Western Union services.

teletypewriter grade — Represents the lowest-type communication circuit in terms of speed, cost, and accuracy.

teletypewriter KSR — Abbreviation for Keyboard Send-Receive unit. A unit that receives the line signal and prints the same as an RO, but, in addition, has a keyboard that is used for manually sending line signals. It has no paper-tape capability but is often used for conversational time sharing and inquiry-response applications.

teletypewriter network — A system of points, interconnected by private telegraph channels, which provide hard copy and/or telegraphic coded (5-channel) punched paper tape, as required, at both sending and receiving points. Typically, up to 20 way stations share send-receive time on a single circuit and can exchange information without requiring action at a switching center. If two or more circuits are provided, a switching center is required to permit cross-circuit transmission.

teletypewriter pulse, spacing — A spacing pulse or "space" is the signal pulse which, in dc neutral operation, corresponds to a "circuit open" or "no current" condition.

teletypewriter service, private-line — A form of teletypewriter service differing from exchange service in that it is limited to service between certain specified stations. The service may be contracted for on a full-time or part-time basis.

teletypewriter 20-mA current loop — An interface that accommodates terminals with a current-loop 7-bit ASCII interface.

teletypewriter utility package — A library of commonly required programming functions involving i/o through a teletypewriter. Various teletypewriter utility package routines provide i/o operating on a single character or a line of characters. Other routines perform conversion of data for i/o purposes where that data is octal, decimal, or hexadecimal. The package may be selectively loaded to conserve memory since only the required routines will be included in the load.

Telex — An automatic dial-up teletypewriter switching service provided on a worldwide basis by various common carriers; e.g., within Canada, CNCP Telecommunications provides Telex service, while in the United States, Western Union is the carrier.

teller consoles (bank) — Consoles that accept teller-indexed transaction messages for transmission to the computer and print the processed replies (received from the computer) onto customer passbooks, transaction tickets, and the transaction journal.

teller/dispenser units — Automated teller-machines/cash-dispensers interface directly with the customer. Each machine generally includes a cash-dispensing mechanism, a keyboard for activation by the customer, a display panel on which a series of instructions is flashed to the customer, and a data-processing module. While technologies vary from one manufacturer to another, all of these machines are used essentially to perform and process cash withdrawals from checking and savings accounts, cash advances from credit cards, deposits to checking and savings accounts, third-party payments, and balance inquiry.

teller systems, on-line — No matter what the application, all "on-line" computer systems have one common trait; they permit direct access to a computer, including the pertinent records stored in its electronic memory. This direct access may come from one or many inquiry stations of various types, which may be located either close by the computer or miles away, connected to the computer over various communication devices such as telephone or telegraph lines. In on-line teller systems, all tellers are in direct communication with, and are under complete control of, a computer that is connected, via communications lines, to each teller console. On-line teller systems have four major elements: a large random-access memory tied directly to the computer, used to store account records and auxiliary information; teller consoles for keyboard entry of transaction information and computer-controlled printing of replies to passbooks, tickets, and journals;

data-communication equipment and telephone lines, linking the teller consoles to the computer; and an electronic computer system for control and computation.

Telpak — A service offered by telephone companies for leasing of wideband channels between two or more points. Telpak channels can be leased in groups of 60 or 240 voice-grade channels.

temporary storage — Internal-storage locations reserved for intermediate or partial results.

tens complement — The radix complement of a numeral whose radix is ten. It is obtained by subtracting each digit of a number from 9, and adding 1 to the least significant digit of the resultant number. For example, the tens complement of 2456 is 7544.

terminal — 1. A point at which information can enter or leave a communication network. 2. An input/output device designed to receive data in an environment associated with the job to be performed, and capable of transmitting entries to, and obtaining output from, the system of which it is a part.

terminal, addressable-pollable — A terminal is addressable when it has its own unique identifier. All data sent to the terminal must be preceded by their addresses. Pollable means that the terminal responds to status inquiries from the computer. Each terminal in the system is queried by the computer in succession. The ability of the terminal to respond to the poll and to identify itself makes it pollable.

terminal, ASCII — American Standard Code for Information Interchange is a standard code used by many computers, video-display terminals, teleprinters and computer peripherals. A full 8-bit ASCII word may be transmitted in parallel or serial form, with the eighth bit often providing parity information. In an ASCII terminal, keyboard encoders convert a single switch closure into an ASCII word; character generators convert stored ASCII data words (and some timing commands) into groups of dots suitable for raster-scan display.

terminal, basic — An input-output device that allows a human operator to encode characters in computer-readable form and allows a computer to produce printed or displayed characters in a human-readable form via a communications link. Sometimes called a dumb terminal.

terminal brightness — Variable brightness takes several forms in video displays. One type, a standard feature in most displays, is an overall brightness control that operates like the one on a television receiver. This control can adapt the screen to the operator's working environment, helping to counteract possible eye-straining effects by allowing the operator to select a comfortable screen brightness. Another type of variable brightness, called dual intensity, allows specific characters, words, or screen areas to be highlighted. This can be a useful device for finding errors. It is particularly useful when data are being entered into the keyboard. Then the entered characters can be shown more brightly, while the other material remains less bright in the background.

terminal code, ASCII — The American Standard Code for Information Interchange (ASCII), which assigns a 7-bit binary number for each letter of the alphabet, number, and punctuation mark. Certain machine functions, such as carriage return, end of transmission, line feed, tab, etc., are also assigned codes. ASCII is the standard code used in tv typewriters, many video driver systems, and the newer teletypewriters (the older models used the Baudot code).

terminal components — Components needed to perform most functions: keyboard, display, microprocessor, memory, storage, printers, modems, and adapters.

terminal, control — A unit that supervises communication between the consoles and the processing center. It receives incoming messages at random intervals, stores them until the central processor is ready to process them, and returns the processed replies to the remote consoles which originated the transactions.

terminal controller, minicomputer — Front-end computers, in addition to acting as larger host-computer interfaces, can also function as terminal controllers and often as peripheral controllers.

terminal control, remote — A facility that allows the central-site technician to perform diagnostic checks without the need to send anyone to a remote point that is giving trouble. Each remote terminal and connecting link shares the services of the controller, thus reducing manpower as well as the skill and training needed to maintain network continuity. Shared standby equipment at the central site reduces the amount of standby equipment needed.

terminal control system — A control program which handles multiterminal operations on some computer systems. It schedules the input/output processing and the use of hardware resources in a multitasking, multiterminal environment.

terminal control system, disk — Typically, a control program which efficiently handles multiterminal operations in conjunction with the disc operating system. It provides task scheduling, i/o management, file access, priority dispatching, and fast task handling.

terminal cursor — A cursor is a movable mark that locates a character on a crt screen. Most terminals have a cursor of some sort. On the smarter terminals, the cursor can be moved around freely, but usually the movements are more restricted. Typical cursors include a line under the character at hand, a nondestructive blinking white block, and a white block on which an existing character on the screen is reversed. Typical cursor keyboard commands are up, down, left, right, home, and return left to next line on new line command. With the up, down, left, and right keys, there is usually a repeating feature for rapid long-distance cursor movement. When cursor control keys are not enough, other interactive control devices are sometimes available as options. These include a joystick, a light pen, a track ball, and a set of thumbwheel controls. These techniques are most useful on graphic terminals.

terminal daisy-chaining — Daisy-chaining is generally the same as multidropping, except that no modems are used; however, the terminals share the same data link. The data link comes from the computer, goes to the first terminal, comes out of the first terminal and on to the second terminal, etc. All terminals share the same data link and the same computer port.

terminal, data — A device that modulates and/or demodulates data between one input/output device and a data-transmission link.

terminal, data-communication — A data station is an all-purpose remote-communication terminal that can be used for a broad range of applications. These applications involve direct on-line data transmission to and from company branch offices or warehouses, and remote locations throughout a plant. When not being used for actual on-line transmission (remote mode), the data station can be used for off-line (local mode) data preparation and editing.

terminal, dedicated memory — Dedicated memory terminals are prevalent in microprocessor systems. A typical terminal contains 1k or 2k bytes of memory for screen data. The memory is used almost continuously for screen refresh, and hence is dedicated to the terminal. The processor may have both read and write access to the video memory. Dedicated memory terminals include bit mapped terminals. Every dot location on a bit mapped display is addressable. Many bit mapped terminals allow read access as well as write access.

terminal-digit posting — The arranging and recording of serial numbers of documents on the basis of the final configuration of the digits of the serial number.

terminal, direct memory access — This kind of terminal is connected to a processor bus. The video memory actually resides in processor memory. It is not dedicated memory, so the information must be transferred from the processor to the screen for each screen refresh. Usually, processor operation is suspended for refresh, resulting in lower processor throughput.

terminal-distributed systems — Various arrangements of computers within an organization in which the computer complex has many separate computing facilities all working in a cooperative manner, rather than the conventional single computer at a single location. Versatility of a computer system is often increased if small computers in geographically dispersed branches are used for simple tasks and a powerful central computer is available for larger tasks. Frequently, the central files of an organization are stored at the central computing facility, with the geographically dispersed smaller computers calling on the central files when they need them.

terminal, duplex — For computer operations, when referring to interactive terminals, half- and full-duplex must be understood in the broader context of computer network conventions. Half-duplex refers to the case in which the user's keyboard is connected to the printer at the terminal, and to the convention that when the computer is producing output it does not respond to input from the user (except perhaps for a special "break" signal). When the computer is not typing, it is in a mode to accept input from the user. Full-duplex refers to the case in which the user's keyboard is locally disconnected from the printer mechanism. When characters are received at the computer, they are returned to the user.

terminal, editing — A system for providing capabilities such as replacement of characters; insertion, deletion, and movement of characters, words, sentences, paragraphs, and blocks; field checks which include the number of, sequences of, and types of digits; zero fill, left or right; batch balancer; and check digit verification.

terminal edit operations — Operations such as clear entire screen, clear unprotected positions, character type-over, character insert/delete, line insert/delete, erase to end of page, and erase line/field.

terminal electric buzzers — Buzzers that have the striker and sounder connected into the circuit in the form of a normally closed switch. Current through the switch contacts generates a magnetic field around a coil. This field attracts the striker arm, which moves toward it, opening the switch contacts and interrupting the field. With the field gone, the striker is pulled back into its resting position by spring tension, closing the switch contacts and re-energizing the field, which causes the operation to repeat itself.

terminal electromechanical buzzers — Buzzers in which the striker arm and sounder are removed from the electrical circuit. The magnetic field is instead modulated by an on-board oscillator circuit consisting of discrete components or an IC. The striker arm is alternately attracted to and repelled by the electromagnetic field, causing the arm to oscillate around its resting position. The back-and-forth movement of the striker against a plastic drumhead generates the audible buzz.

terminal emulation — The ideal of emulation is that if a "regular" terminal is unplugged from a system, a "foreign" unit can be plugged in and will immediately perform all the functions of the regular terminal. To accomplish this, a microcomputer built into the terminal stores the procedures needed to make proper use of a variety of different control codes. By properly matching procedures to codes, one terminal can emulate another. The matching is done by a special program stored in the internal memory of the terminal.

terminal end-to-end control — A means whereby, during the data phase of a call, interconnected DTEs may exchange control and data signals without loss of information.

terminal equipment — Data source or data sink equipment such as teletypewriters for input terminals and crt (cathode-ray–tube) screens for output.

terminal equipment, data — *See* data terminal equipment.

terminal, graphics — A display system with keyboard and/or graphics input devices (light pen or stylus) for the display and manipulation of graphic as well as alphanumeric images.

terminal human factors — Key elements of human factors include the size of the screen; the number, shape, and size of the characters on the screen; the color and appearance of the screen; the arrangement of the keyboard; and the sound of the keyboard. The designs should provide comfort to humans.

terminal independence — Monitors support a wide variety of terminal devices. Terminal independence, which allows application programs to be coded without regard to special terminal-dependent control characters, is generally provided for on most or all terminals supported by a monitor. Line-control functions such as polling, addressing, queuing, and rerouting, are often handled automatically. Some monitors also provide extensive editing capabilities.

terminal, inquiry, display — *See* display, inquiry terminal.

terminal installation — A grouping, at one site, of operable data terminals and related equipment.

terminal installation for data transmission — Installation comprising the data-terminal equipment, the signal-conversion equipment, and any intermediate equipment. Note: In some instances, the data-terminal equipment may be connected directly to a data-processing machine or may be a part of it.

terminal intelligence, ROM/RAM — One form of intelligence for terminals is developed with a compromise approach. Read-only memory (ROM) is used to implement cursor control, communication protocols, and other well understood functions. Random access memory (RAM) and PROM (programmable ROM) are added so that users can use special programs, giving the terminal the important characteristic of user programmability.

terminal, interactive — A type of terminal that is generally equipped with a display, a keyboard, and an incremental printer. Optionally, it may also include a tape subsystem. Such terminals support interactive, conversational, demand, inquiry, and transaction-oriented applications.

terminal interchange — A buffering device at a location remote from the processing center. Such a device provides temporary storage for messages originating at the terminals that it serves and at the processing center.

terminal interface — The Electronic Industries Association has standardized connections, fixing the voltage levels, impedances, connector type, and pin assignments. The standard is called: "EIA Standard RS-232-C, Interface Between Data Processing Terminal Equipment and Data Communication Equipment." A similar standard has been prepared by the Consultive Committee on International Telegraphy and Telephony.

terminal interface functions — Terminal interfaces connect the display unit to the communications-computer system. In effect, the interface has three functions: to reorganize the computer data word into the word structure required by the display; to convert the computer logic voltages into display-logic levels; and to match the data structure and communication characteristics of the display with those of the communication facilities. Communication between the display device and the computer can be initiated by either the computer or the display operator.

terminal, job-oriented — A terminal specially designed to receive the job-source data in the environment of the job. The terminal also is capable of transmission to and from its computer system.

terminal-keyboard types — Generally, there are two basic types of keyboards, alphanumeric and numeric. Alphanumeric keyboards are used for word processing, text processing, data processing, and teleprocessing. Numeric-only keyboards are used on Touch-Tone telephones, accounting machines, and calculators.

terminal/light-pen system — A system consisting of a specially configured terminal and light pen. Pointing the pen to the desired character position and pressing its tip to the screen selects the data for action by the system.

terminal, magnetic-tape — The magnetic-tape terminal converts the character pulses from serial-bit form to parallel-bit form, while checking for odd parity and translating the code to the desired magnetic-tape code for entry into a buffer storage. The longitudinal parity count at the end of the message is verified. The integral part of the magnetic-tape terminal performing this function is called a coupler. The coupler of the magnetic-tape terminal performs a function similar to that of the data-line terminal.

terminal memory — Like any other computer system, the microcomputer module is useful only if it has a program to execute and memory in which to store data. This is the function of the terminal memory modules, which are of two types, RAM (random-access memory) and ROM (read-only memory) for storing terminal programs. Terminal programs are called firmware because the ROM makes them more permanent than software but less permanent than hardware. In some units, one half of the available memory is dedicated to ROM or program memory, and the balance of the available memory locations are used for RAM.

terminal, microcomputer-upgrade — Microcomputers allow simple terminals, such as low-speed crts and keyboard devices, to be upgraded into programmable or intelligent terminals. This is because the micro allows logic and memory for data editing and some limited processing to be added. As a result, the intelligent terminal has flexible design for simplified user interface including custom keyboards, modularity to meet a variety of user requirements including control of other terminals, and buffering capability to simplify the communications interface and the impact on host computer software. More and more of the communications function can be done inside the terminal rather than at the host computer site. Microprocessors are also being used in all functional areas of terminal design, including print mechanisms, carriage control, interface control, and maintenance testing.

terminal, microprocessor-controlled — The operating characteristics of "smart" terminals are controlled through firmware. The terminal microprocessor manages memory allocation, data communications, keyboard scanning, and display control.

terminal modem eliminator — A device that permits direct terminal-to-terminal or terminal-to-computer connection and eliminates the need for two modems operating back to back.

terminal-modem interfaces — The interfaces between the terminal and modem. They contain not only digital data signals, but signals for controlling the modem and the data link. For example, when the line is turned around in half-duplex communication, the sending modem must be switched to the receiving condition, and the receiving modem must be switched to the sending condition. A modem is switched from receive to send through the EIA interface by raising to a predetermined voltage level the control lead designated as "Request to Send." When the "Clear to Send" status lead of the modem turns on, it is a signal to the computer or terminal that the modem is ready to transmit data over the data link.

terminal, multiplex-data — A device that modulates and/or demodulates data between two or more input/output devices and a data-transmission link.

terminal network — Some terminal systems are optimized to perform message switching best, others to do input/output functions, and still others to carry out arithmetic calculations; and in a complex computer application, the designer configures a system to utilize the unique strengths of each minicomputer type. A network results whenever two or more of these processors are linked together by communications lines as opposed to connections by an internal bus. Thus, a terminal network, in essence, distributes computer functions among its elements according to the most cost-effective arrangement in a specific application.

terminal operating modes — Types of terminal operation, such as conversational (character at a time) transmission, message (line at a time) transmission, and page (full or partial screen at a time) transmission.

terminal peripherals — Various devices can be interfaced to a system for communication, mass storage, hard-copy printing, or other data-processing applications. These may augment standard terminal functions or serve to expand the terminal itself into a complete small-business or laboratory system.

terminal polling — A technique for asking each terminal if it has any messages to send or for watching for an interrupt signal, which forces the computer to read the message from the interrupting terminal.

terminal processor functions — Generally, terminals must assemble each sequence of incoming bits into a full character, strip off the start and stop bits, translate the data from transmission code into computer-processable code, test the parity bit to see if an error has occurred, and place the character in the correct location in its memory for assembly into words and messages. Furthermore, the processor must determine whether the received character is a message character or a control character. A control character sets up a different level of activity within the computer. For example, it could indicate the end of a message that allows the computer to disconnect the terminal and go on to other communications or data-processing tasks.

terminal protocols — The heart of terminal-to-computer or computer-to-computer communications lies within the "protocols" used to control the flow of information through the network. A protocol is a set of agreements on the format, relative timing, and interpretation of control messages. There are many types and levels of protocols. For example, a link protocol is a procedure that regulates the transfer of data between two or more devices over a single circuit. An end-to-end protocol is a procedure that regulates the transfer of data between devices connected via a data network.

terminal self-diagnostics — Many designers add troubleshooting aids, or self-diagnostic routines. Such diagnostic aids can be special test lights that indicate a circuit malfunction, test points with which to attach scope and meter clips, or extension racks that hold additional printed-circuit boards.

terminal self-testing — A process in which a terminal automatically tests the major portion of a system, either when the power is turned on or upon the depression of a switch by the operator.

terminal, smart, interactive — An interactive terminal in which part of the processing is accomplished by a microcomputer or microprocessor contained in the terminal itself. This type of terminal is sometimes referred to in the literature as an intelligent terminal. For a terminal to be considered a smart terminal, the computing capability of the microcomputer in the terminal must be available to the user in a way that permits programming it to perform part of a unique application.

terminal storage capability — Some terminals containing microprocessors, PROM, and RAM, and working with disks can store programs like a batch terminal and also serve the inquiry/response activities of an on-line system. They can store noncritical data during the day and transmit it to the CPU during the evening. Data can be processed at night and sent back, unattended, to the diskette for printing the following morning, avoiding peak loads on communications lines or at the central computer.

terminal system control units — Some system control units (SCUs) incorporate microcomputers which enable them to function as a method for controlling a network of terminals. They serve by polling each terminal to extract data being entered, analyzing received data to verify operation of the terminal, and transmitting prompting information to lead terminal operators through the data entry sequence.

terminal tailoring — Various devices and schemes are available to tailor terminals. Among the most common are: numeric keyboard and LED display, special function keys (user defined), prompting lights (for signals or messages), custom key labeling, audible warning indicators, and others.

terminal, teleprocessing — *See* teleprocessing terminal.

terminal, touch-sensitive digitizing screen — A system in which a high-frequency pulse-echo ranging technique is used to locate electronically the point of finger contact on a crt screen. This location data is converted into computer-compatible binary or BCD format.

terminal transaction systems — Transaction-oriented systems process transactions by running the appropriate programs against each transaction and returning the results to the terminal operator, usually within a few seconds. Some of the better-known examples of such systems are found in the airline, banking, insurance, utility, distribution, and retail industries and in law enforcement and medicine.

terminal transmission interface — Some peripheral devices handle parallel data; others require a serial format. One peripheral interface adapter (PIA) interfaces parallel structured devices to the 8-bit i/o bus of the MPU. The asynchronous communications interface adapter (ACIA) is used for formatted serial data (referred to as "asynchronous" data). To be transmitted over a communications link, this serial data must often be converted to analog form by a modem.

terminal unit — A part of the equipment in a communication channel that may be used for either input or output to the channel.

terminal, user-designed — A terminal that has user-defined prompting lights to indicate which functions are to be performed and in which order. A user-defined alphanumeric keyboard can be set for specific operations or alphanumeric entry.

terminal, visual display — Abbreviated VDT. A device which permits input to a computer (by a user, not a computer operator) through a keyboard and/or some other manual input method (light pen, cursor controls, function buttons), and whose primary output method is a visual (i.e., volatile or soft copy) display of alphanumeric and/or graphical information. Excluded are devices with only a few characters of display capacity—say, under 100—since that normally implies that they have a special purpose.

Many terminal devices, e.g., POS, banking, credit verification, industrial data collection terminals, etc., now employ visual-display devices using various technologies.

terminating symbol — A symbol on the tape indicating the end of a block of information.

termination, executive — The normal or abnormal termination of an operating program and the return of its assigned facilities to an available status. Termination may be initiated by executive program, by the job program, or by the operator.

termination, loop — *See* loop termination.

terminator/initiator — A specific program which makes a job step ready to run in some computers and which also performs regular housekeeping tasks after a job has ended. Used in conjunction with job schedulers which select a job or jobs part waiting to be executed after allocating and clearing memory space of extraneous data.

ternary — 1. Pertaining to a characteristic or property involving a selection, choice, or condition in which there are three possibilities. 2. Pertaining to the number-representation system with a radix of three.

ternary code — A code in which only three states are considered.

test — To examine, particularly relative to a criterion; to determine the present arrangement of some element of computer hardware, e.g., a manually set switch.

test and verify programs — Test and verify (T & V) programs enable the user to determine whether the hardware is functioning properly or to isolate a malfunction. Such programs are provided for processor, memory, and many standard peripherals and controllers.

test, bias — A form of test, usually as part of preventive maintenance or as a fault-finding or correcting operation, to test against safety margins for faults.

test, branch instruction — *See* branch instruction test.

test card, diagnostic — A special input/output card used to test all i/o functions and strappable operation configurations.

test case — Verification for accuracy or completeness by using a sample of the input data as a testing or checking exercise.

test, compatability — Specific tests run to check acceptability of both software and hardware as a system, i.e., to test component workability.

test conditions, overflow (underflow) — Often tests are made for conditions called underflow and overflow which occur when a result too large or too small for the arithmetic register has been generated; i.e., once an underflow or an overflow occurs, the appropriate indicator can remain "set" until it is tested. After the test, it is conventional for the overflow or underflow condition to be restored to normal.

test control points or pins — Input pins provided for testing or fault-isolation purposes that can control the state of internal memory elements.

test, crippled-leapfrog — A variation of the leapfrog test, modified so that it repeats its tests from a single set of storage locations rather than a changing set of locations. (Related to test, leapfrog.)

test data — A set of data developed specifically to test the adequacy of a computer run or system. The data may be actual data that has been taken from previous operations, or artificial data created for this purpose.

test, destructive — A test of equipment capability in which results prove to be a cause of permanent degradation due to the type of performance exacted from the equipment tested; for example, the application of excess power, voltages, heat, etc., which eventually causes the circuits or elements to burn, shatter, burst, or otherwise be destroyed.

test, diagnostic — The running of a machine program or a routine for the purpose of discovering a failure or a potential failure of a machine element, and to determine its location or its potential location.

test equipment, digital — Compact, lightweight probes, pulsers, test clips, comparators, oscilloscopes, and other devices that have features suited to the digital service technician or designer.

test generation, automatic — Abbreviated ATG. Calculation of a specific set of input test patterns with a computer program providing algorithmic and heuristic routines. Also called automatic test-pattern generation (ATPG).

test, high-low-bias — A preventive-maintenance procedure in which certain operating conditions are varied about their normal values in order to detect and locate incipient defective units; e.g., supply voltage or frequency may be varied. (Synonymous with marginal test, and related to check.)

testing — The method for examining to determine the real character or specific aspects of an item, program, or system. Acceptance testing for equipment determines capacity, capability, and reliability. Program testing determines whether programs do what they are supposed to do when used with the test, simulated, or live data.

testing, bias — *See* testing, marginal.

testing, comparison approach — A test method in which the CPU is compared with a known good device. With both devices mounted close to each other, input data are sent simultaneously to both, but with separate drivers. Also, output data are monitored from both devices and are considered valid when data coincidence occurs. Real-time-cycle response testing is possible. Implementation is not difficult, chiefly because output data need not be stored in a memory for comparison.

testing, cross-sectional — A series of tests to get a representative sampling of system performance. These tests are usually one-pass tests such as an acceptance test.

testing, degradation — Measurement of the performance of a system at the extreme operating limits. Tests are performed to determine the gradual change in performance characteristics.

testing, functional — The functional approach to testing makes use of the fact that most operations are made up of a limited number of equipment functions. Since there are a great many combinations of 10 or 15 functions, only a few functions comprise many operations. By testing these functions independently, the entire product can be evaluated in a timely, concise manner, and greater diagnostic capabilities emerge.

testing, longitudinal — Iterative tests which compare earlier performance with later performance.

testing, loop — That particular procedure developed to determine whether or not further loop operations are required.

testing, marginal — A form of test usually as part of preventive maintainance or as a fault-finder or correcting operation, to test against safety margins for faults.

testing, microcomputer development systems — Many programs can be tested to virtual completion on the microcomputer development system. Debugging programs are used during this stage of the operation, and the program being tested is kept in semiconductor random access memory (RAM), where it can be easily modified using the debugging program. Debugging programs allow the programmer to modify and examine the contents of memory locations and set up data and register conditions for the program being tested. Preparation of source tapes, assembly, and debugging is greatly facilitated if the microcomputer development system can be equipped with a high-speed tape reader and punch—the high-speed reader is an especially valuable tool.

testing, normative — Standards of performance that are established for the testing of both quantitative and qualitative system performance.

testing, parameter — *See* parameter testing.

testing, procedural — Tests of alternative human responses in system operations. This is distinguished from hardware or software tests.

testing, program — A procedure completed to discover whether the program is successful in meeting the defined systems requirements.

testing, program system — Test and checkout of complete programs as opposed to parameter or assembly testing.

testing, retrofit — Testing to assure system operation after replacing some equipment or programs.

testing, saturation — The testing of a program by pushing through a great many messages in an attempt to find errors that happen infrequently.

testing, self-diagnostic method — In the self-diagnostic method, some engineers use a ROM to load into CPU memory (RAM) a worst-case sequence of instructions. The CPU chip is placed within its intended operating environment, including interrupts from peripherals. The instruction set terminates at some identifiable error location. Error indication, usually identified by an instruction routine, shows if the unit fails or passes. Most small users of CPU chips test with self-diagnosis, because it can be implemented easily with laboratory equipment or with hardware and assistance from the chip manufacturer. Some shortcomings are: multiple errors may negate each other and be undetected, or the actual cause of a failure may not be diagnosed. Also, without special hardware, external environment conditions, such as interrupts, cannot be tested under worst-case conditions.

testing, sequential — A series of tests performed in a predetermined order and requiring repeated observations.

testing, stored-response — Stored-response testing encompasses various test development methods and various pattern-generation techniques. Each method stores and executes user-written diagnostics quite differently. With stored-response, users keep an emulation, or a simulation program in bulk memory (usually a disk) and then apply the program to the CPU under test to generate output data response. Users can simulate the sequence of operation of a CPU in conjunction with all peripheral devices, such as RAMs and ROMs. To do this requires a large RAM or PROM to store a predefined sequence of instructions associated with the appropriate data set. Simulated outputs can be sampled and their logic states identified at a defined sampling period.

testing time — The time which is used for the testing of the machine or system to ensure that no faults exist or malfunctions are present by using special diagnostic routines for circuit testing or to discern status or conditions of components. Usually such time could be included in fault time after the repair of the fault and included in scheduled maintenance time.

testing time, program — *See* program testing time.

testing, word generator — Some word generators are designed to meet the requirements for testing the new types of digital circuits. They provide multichannel bit patterns and supply them with the flexible clocking, delay, and control of output parameters needed for general-purpose testing. Some have eight data channels plus clock, strobe, and two sync outputs. There are few restrictions other than length on the bit patterns that can be generated by these instruments.

test initialization — Applying input patterns to a logic circuit so that all internal memory elements achieve a known logic state.

test input tape — *See* tape, test input.

test instructions (debugging) — Most good compiler systems are designed to automatically remove various temporary tracing (debugging) instructions after tests are automatically made to ensure accuracy and precision.

test, leapfrog — A program designed to discover computer malfunction, characterized by the property that it performs a series of arithmetical or logical operations on one group of storage locations, transfers itself to another group of storage locations, checks the correctness of the transfer, then begins the next series of operations again. Eventually, all storage positions will have been occupied and the test will be repeated. (Related to test, crippled-leapfrog.)

test, marginal — *Same as* high-low bias test.

test, output processor — In a complex system, an automated processing of the output so that errors may be more easily tracked down.

test-pattern generator — A device used to generate special messages for testing data-transmission equipment.

test points or pins — Output pins provided for testing or fault-isolation purposes that can monitor the nodal responses.

test problem — A problem chosen to determine whether a computer or a program is operating correctly.

test program system — A checking system used before running any problem, in which a sample problem of the same type with a known answer is run.

test routine — A routine designed to show whether a computer is functioning properly.

test run — A diagnostic run of the program, using manufactured data. The results of this run are checked against the correct answers for this problem.

test set, tape — A peripheral device or unit designed to locate defects in magnetic tape before use, such as oxide emissions, uneveness, bubbles, etc.

test simulation, digital — Modeling of the operation of a logic circuit by a computer program containing device models and topology information about their interconnections.

tests, reasonableness — Tests that provide a means of detecting a gross error in calculation or, while posting to an account, a balance that exceeds a predetermined limit. Typical examples include payroll calculations and credit limit checks in accounts receivable. In some cases, both an upper and lower limit are established; each result is then machine-compared against both limits to make certain that it falls between the two.

tests, reliability — Tests and analyses carried out in addition to other types of tests and designed to evaluate the level of reliability in a product, etc., as well as the dependability or stability of this level relative to time and use under various environmental conditions.

test, supervisor program — A supervisory program that is used only for testing.

test, system — 1. The running of the whole system against test data with a verified solution. 2. A complete simulation of the actual running system for purposes of testing out the adequacy of the system. 3. A test of an entire interconnected set of components for the purpose of determining proper functioning and interconnection.

test tape program — That specific tape which contains both program instructions and preapproved test data or coding to be used for analysis diagnostics or checkout runs.

test, volume — The processing of a volume of actual data to check for program malfunctions.

tetrad — A group of four, especially a group of four pulses used to express a digit in the scale of 10 or 16.

text — That part of a message that contains the information to be conveyed.

text editing — Facilities designed into a computer program to permit the original keyboarding of textual copy without regard for the eventual format or medium for publication. Once the copy has been placed in computer storage, it can be edited and justified into any required column width and for any specified type font.

text editing and modification, time sharing — *See* time sharing, text editing and modification.

text editor — A text editor provides the system user with a flexible source text generation system. Source statements are entered via any source input device/file, and the entered text may be output or statements added, deleted, or modified. The text editor permits the order of statements or groups of statements to be altered at any time. The final text is output to a source device/-file for use as input to an assembler.

text editor facilities — A typical text editor provides facilities for editing a source program (usually assembly language) read in from an external device. The program is stored in an area of memory during the editing process and is written back out to an external device when editing is complete. The user can insert, delete or replace lines in the text buffer.

text editor, RAM — Various text editors are used to enter and revise programs directly on the system. Some character-string-oriented text editors reside in RAM in basic systems, and the workspace may often be expanded up to a very large package.

text function — In a graphics system, a function that allows text to be entered into a drawing.

text processing networks — The term "network" does not necessarily imply a geographic separation involving clerical/editorial workers in other buildings or other towns. It is also possible to have a network within a single building, linking workers and their supervisors to a shared data base. The data base can be on-line to all, and changes to that data base may be immediately reflected on the crt screens of all network participants.

text section — Part of a load module which has computer instructions in final form and data defined and with specified initial values.

theory, communication — A branch of mathematics that is concerned with the properties of transmitted messages. The messages are subject to certain probabilities of transmission failure, distortion, and noise.

theory, game — A mathematical process of selecting an optimum strategy in the face of an opponent's strategy.

theory, group — *See* group theory.

theory, information — *See* information theory.

theory, probability — A measure of the likelihood of the occurrence of a chance event that is used to predict behavior of a group,

theory, queuing — A form of probability theory useful in studying delays or lineups at servicing points.

theory, switching — A particular branch of theory relating to combinational logic, its operation, behavior, and consequences, i.e., concerning such devices as computers, Turing machines, logic elements, and switch networks.

thermal light — A display signal which is visible to a computer operator when the temperature in a piece of equipment is higher than it is supposed to be.

thesaurus — 1. An assemblage of alphabetized items (or items grouped in some other concept or meaningful collection) providing the user with very close or direct synonyms or meanings, close to the term so alphabetized and used as an aid to writers, poets, or programmers. 2. In computing, a collection of words or terms used to index, classify, or sort, and then store and retrieve information in a data store or bank; i.e., main terms serve as labels, keywords, or descriptors, and when such references are cited along with the thesaurus, a very useful index is developed.

thin film — 1. Having to do with the branch of microelectronics in which thin layers of material are deposited on an insulating base in a vacuum. 2. A layer which is of (or approximates) monomolecular thickness and is laid down by vacuum deposition. Many types of electronic components and complete microcircuits can be produced in this way.

third generation computer — Generally, a computer based on the use of microcircuits and miniaturization of components to replace vacuum tubes, reduce costs, speed operation, and increase reliability. The third generation of computers began in about 1964 and helped to foster the growth of time sharing.

third-level address — *See* address, third-level.

three address — A method of specifying the location of operands and instructions in which the storage location of the two operands and the storage location of the results of the operations are cited, e.g., addend, augend, and sum addresses all specified in one instruction word.

three, excess (code) — *See* code, excess three.

three input adder — *Same as* adder.

three plus one address — A method of specifying the location of operands and instructions in which the storage location of the two operands, results of the operations, and the next instruction to be executed are specified.

three plus one address instruction — A machine instruction usually consisting of the addresses of two operands, the address for storing the result, the address of the next instruction, the command to be executed, and miscellaneous indices.

three plus one instruction — A specific instruction which contains four addresses, one of which specifies the location of the next instruction which is to be performed.

threshold — 1. A logical operator having the property that if P is a statement, Q is a statement, R is a statement. . . . , then the threshold of P, Q, R, ... , is true if and only if at least N statements are true, false if less than N statements are true, where N is a specified nonnegative integer called the threshold condition. 2. The signal level at which a change in logical state is encountered in a circuit, such as 1 to 0 or 0 to undefined transitions.

threshold element — A device that performs the logic-threshold operation, in which the truth of each input statement (or weight) completes the output determination of the threshold state.

through connection — In computer kits, electrical continuity between patterns on double-sided or multilayer boards established by means of plated through holes or jumper wires.

throughput — The productivity based on all facets of an operation; e.g., a computer with a capability of simultaneous operations of read/write/compute would have a high throughput rating.

throughput, simultaneous — Computer functioning at the same time input and output data is being transferred.

throughput turnaround time — For half-duplex circuits (one way at a time), turnaround measures the time to reverse direction. For full-duplex operation, the analogy is train time or initialization time, the delay in establishing synchronization. For short-haul modems, it is the clear to send delay.

throw, paper — *See* paper throw.

ticket, batch — A control document used to identify groups of source documents, often with group totals.

tie line — A private-line communications channel of the type provided by common carriers for linking two or more points.

time, acceleration — The time between the interpretation of instructions to read or write on tape and the transfer of information from the tape into storage or from storage into tape. (Synonymous with start time.)

time, access — 1. The time it takes a computer to locate data or an instruction word in its storage section and transfer it to its arithmetic unit where the required computations are performed. 2. The time it takes to transfer information that has been operated on from the arithmetic unit to the location in storage where the information is to be stored.

time, actual — *Same as* time, real.

time, add — The time necessary to perform the actual addition of two quantities, but not including the time necessary to either obtain the quantities from storage or to store the sum or result, i.e., usually the time to add two words of fixed word length.

time, add-subtract — The time required to perform an addition or subtraction, exclusive of the time required to obtain the quantities from storage and put the sum or difference back into storage.

time, available — The time during which a computer has the power turned on, is not under maintenance, and is known or believed to be operating correctly.

time, available-machine — *See* time, available.

time, average operation — *See* operation time, average.

time, carry — 1. The time required for transferring a carry digit to the next higher column and adding it there. 2. The time required for transferring all the carry digits to their respective next higher columns and adding them.

time, code-checking — The time spent checking out a problem on the machine making sure that the problem is set up correctly and that the code is correct.

time comparator, word — That circuitry which compares the word time counter with the specified word time at the moment of a coincident pulse. This is done in order to verify that the correct word is being read.

time, conversion — The length of time required to read out all the digits in a given coded word.

time, current — *See* time, real.

time, cycle — The interval between the call for and the delivery of information from a storage unit or device.

time, data — The unit of measurement relating to the time necessary to fulfill a single instruction.

time, dead — Any definite delay deliberately placed between two related actions in order to avoid overlap that might cause an entirely different event such as a control decision, switching event, or similar action to take place.

time, debatable — When there is no proof as to what difficulty has caused a delay, such time is labeled debatable time, and a search for evidence ensues to determine if a program mistake, operating mistake, or perhaps a transient fault has occurred.

time, decay — The time in which a voltage or current pulse will decrease from nine-tenths to one-tenth of its maximum value.

time, deceleration — The time that elapses between completion of reading or writing of a tape record and the time when the tape stops moving. (Synonymous with stop time.)

time, delay — The amount of elapsed time between the end of one event and the beginning of the next sequential event.

time-delay register — *See* delay-line storage.

time, departure — The time at which control is returned to the supervisory program when a segment of an application program is completed.

time-derived channel — Any channel obtained by the time-division multiplexing of a channel.

time division — A communication process in which several messages time share a single transmission channel.

time division multiple access — Abbreviated TDMA. Satellite TDMA is a technique whereby several earthstation terminals time-share a common transponder by transmitting bursts of signals which arrive at, and are repeated by, the satellite in a sequential, nonoverlapping mode.

time-division multiplex — A sequential switching system that connects the terminal equipment to a common channel. Outside the times during which these connections are established, the section of the common channel between the multiplex distributors can be utilized to establish other terminal connections.

time-division multiplexer — A device which permits the simultaneous transmission of many independent channels of varying speeds into a single high-speed data stream.

time-division multiplexing — Time sharing of a channel by preallocating short time slots to each transmitter on a regular basis. There are variations, such as statistical and asynchronous time-division multiplexing, which allocate the slots more flexibly.

time, down — The period during which a computer is malfunctioning or not operating correctly due to mechanical or electronic failure, as opposed to available time, idle time, or stand-by time, during which the computer is functional.

timed recall, automatic — An arrangement in which the attendant is signaled when calls that have been extended to a station are not answered within a certain preset time.

time, effective — That specific time in which equipment is in actual use, such as production time, incidental time, development time (program), etc.

time, engineering — The total machine down time necessary for routine testing, for machine servicing, due to breakdowns, or for preventive servicing measures, e.g., block tube changes. This includes all test time following a breakdown and the subsequent repair or preventive servicing.

time, entry — The time when control is transferred from the supervisory to the application program.

time, execution — The portion of an instructive cycle during which the actual work is performed or operation executed, i.e., the time required to decode and perform an instruction.

time, fault — *Same as* time, down.

time frame — The limits of time needed for a particular situation or event.

time, from movement — An elapsed period of time during which a printing cycle produces the printing and movement of hard copy.

time, idle — The period between the end of one programmed computer run and the commencement of a subsequent programmed run.

time, incidental — Time used for training, demonstrations, or other useful purposes, but not production or program time.

time, ineffective — Time in which the equipment is not working due to operating delays or idle time.

time, installation — Time spent in testing, installing, error-checking, diagnosing of basic electronic but nonprogramming checks, such as dry runs, etc. This time does not include reliability tests which are defined as supplementary maintenance time.

time, instruction — The portion of an instruction cycle during which the control unit is analyzing the instruction and setting up to perform the indicated operation.

time, latency — The delay while waiting for the information called for from the memory to be delivered to the arithmetical unit. More specifically, in a serial-storage system, the access time minus the word time.

time, machine spoiled — The wasted computer time due to a computer malfunction during production runs, i.e., part of down time.

time, maintenance routine — *See* time, scheduled maintenance.

time, maintenance standby — Time in which the maintenance staff is on duty but during which they are not engaged in scheduled maintenance, installation, repair, or supplementary maintenance; i.e., they may perform other tasks.

time, multiplication — The time required to perform a multiplication. For a binary number, it will be equal to the total of all the addition time and all the shift time involved in the multiplication.

time, no-charge — That period of time for which there is no rental charge or cost for the equipment, generally as a result of a machine malfunction and the manufacturer's warranty.

time, no-charge machine fault — The unproductive time due to computer fault such as the following: nonduplication, transcribing error, input/output malfunction, and machine malfunction resulting in an incomplete run.

time, nonscheduled maintenance — The elapsed time during scheduled working hours between the determination of a machine failure and placement of the equipment back into operation.

time, object — The time at which an object program is executed, as opposed to the time at which a source program is translated into machine language to create an object program.

time-of-day clock — A clock that records time in hours, minutes, and seconds, over a 24-hour range. It sends time to the central processor upon command.

time, off — Time when the machine is not in use or intended to be, i.e., work is not being performed by it or on it.

time, operational — The elapsed time required by the equipment in order to execute a specific operation.

time, operation-use — In federal government ADP contracts, the time during which the equipment is in operation, exclusive of idle time, standby time, maintenance time, or rerun time due to a machine failure. Components not programmed for use in a specific computer run are not considered to be in use even though connected into the computer system.

time, out of service — Time periods such as fault time, awaiting repair time, repair delay time, repair time, machine spoiled work time, but not generally debatable time, external delays, or unused time.

time, preventive maintenance — Usually, scheduled maintenance time or supplementary maintenance time.

time, problem — Often called physical system time, the time interval between corresponding events in the physical system being simulated.

time, process — *See* process time.

time, production — *See* production time.

time, productive — That time which is spent in processing work without the occurrence of faults or errors.

time, program development — *See* program development time.

time, program-testing — The machine time expended for program testing, debugging, and volume and compatibility testing.

time, proving — *See* proving time.

time, pulse decay — *See* pulse decay time.

time-pulse distribution — A device or circuit for allocating timing pulses or clock pulses to one or more conducting paths or control lines in specified sequence.

time, pulse rise — *See* pulse rise time.

time-quantum method, time sharing — *See* time sharing, time-quantum method.

timer — A timer provides the system with the ability to read elapsed time and to inform the system when a specified period of time has passed.

time, read — 1. The time it takes a computer to locate data or an instruction word in its storage section and transfer it to its arithmetic unit where the required computations are performed. 2. The time it takes to transfer information which has been operated on from the arithmetic unit to the location in storage where the information is to be stored.

time, real — Relating to the performance of computing during the specific time in which the related process, event, problem, or communication is taking place; i.e., the computing must be fast enough during the process of the happening of the event for the results of this computing to influence the related process or result.

time, record-check — *See* record-check time.

time, reference — An instant near the beginning of a switching routine, chosen as an origin for time measurements. It is the instant when the drive pulse reaches a specific fraction of its instantaneous value.

time, reimbursed — The machine time that is loaned or rented to another office agency or organization either on a reimbursable or reciprocal basis.

time, repair — *See* repair time.

time, representative-computing — A method of evaluating the speed performance of a computer. One method is to use one-tenth of the time required to perform nine complete additions and one complete multiplication. A complete addition or a complete multiplication time includes the time required to procure two operands from high-speed storage, perform the operation, and store the result, and the time required to select and execute the required number of instructions to do this.

time, response — The amount of time which elapses between generation of an inquiry at a terminal and the receipt of a response at the terminal. Response time would be: transmission time to the computer, processing time at the computer, access time to obtain any file records needed to answer the inquiry, and transmission time back to the terminal.

time, rewind — The measurement of elapsed time required to transfer tape to the supply reel.

time, rewind (sorting) — Elapsed time consumed by a sort/merge program for restoring intermediate and final tape files to original position.

timer, internal — An electronic timer which facilitates monitoring or logging events at predetermined intervals.

time, rise — *See* pulse rise time.

timer, master — *Same as* master clock.

timer, programmable — A timer designed to monitor and control i/o servicing delay, instead of using software timing loops. In addition, some units can be used to count external operations, generate operating rates, and perform other functions under program control.

timer, sequence — A succession of time-delay circuits arranged so that completion of the delay in one circuit initiates a delay in the following circuit.

timer, watchdog — A timer set by the program to prevent the system from looping endessly or becoming idle because of program errors or equipment faults.

time scale — A time scale relates to a correspondence between the time required for a process or event set to occur or be completed and the solution time required to, for example, control or analyze the process. In computing, when the machine solution time is greater than the actual physical time of processing, the time scale is considered to be greater than one, and the computation is said to be on extended-time scale or slow-time scale. Time scale is less than one if the opposite occurs, or at unity if computations proceed in the same time period with the actual process; the unity case is referred to as real-time.

time scale, extended — *See* time scale.

time-scale factor — *See* time scale.

time scale, variable — *See* time scale.

time schedule controller — A specific controller in which the reference input signal (or the set point) adheres automatically to a predetermined time schedule.

time, scheduled engineering — That particular time in which a system is scheduled to be out of service due to servicing schedules for engineering improvements and maintenance; i.e., it can be scheduled on a regular basis relative to the running schedules and work loads and is considered out-of-service time but not down time, because the machine is not necessarily malfunctioning.

time, scheduled maintenance — That machine time which is specifically devoted to repairs, and usually on some regular pattern or schedule, during which time preventive maintenance activities are also performed.

time, scramble — Specific computer time set aside for use by programmers who have programs ready to run which are short, urgent, and one-shot types. For example, particular system rules or conventions schedule scramble time, as at some universities, Saturday night after midnight.

time, search — The time required to locate a particular field of data in storage. Searching requires a comparison of each field with a predetermined standard until an identity is obtained. This is contrasted with access time that is based upon locating data by means of the address of its storage location.

time, seek — The time required to make the auxiliary storage unit ready to access a specified location by selection or positioning. The range is from the minimum time for the best possible case to the maximum time for the worst possible case.

time sequencing — Switching signals generated by a program purely as a function of accurately measured elapsed time.

time series — The discrete or continuous sequence of quantitative data assigned to specific moments in time, usually studied with respect to their distribution in time.

time, serviceable — That time which is available for use of any type and which is known to be time when the system is functioning properly, which thus includes production, program development, incidentals, delay idle, or even unused time.

time, servicing — *Same as* engineering time.

time, set-up — The portion of the elapsed time between machine operations that is devoted to such tasks as changing reels of tape and moving cards, tapes, and supplies to and from the equipment.

time share — The use of a device for two or more purposes during the same overall time interval, accomplished by interspersing the computer component actions in time.

time-shared BASIC — Time-shared BASIC is a conversational language designed to provide easy access to computers for the maximum number of people. It is an enhancement of the original BASIC.

time-shared computer utility — The special computational ability of time-shared computer systems. Programs as well as data may be made available to the user. The user also may have his or her own programs immediately available to the central processor, may have them on call at the computer utility, or may load them by transmitting them to the computer prior to using them. Certain data and programs are shared by all users of the service; other data and programs, because of proprietary nature, have restricted access. Computer utilities are generally accessed by means of data communication subsystems.

time-shared input/output — *See* input/output section, buffered.

time-shared system — A system in which available central-computer time is shared among several jobs as directed by a scheduling plan or formula.

time sharing — The use of a device for two or more purposes during the same overall time interval, accomplished by interspersing the computer component actions in time.

time-sharing accounting — The executive must provide for the recognition and login of users. It must keep detailed records as required by the administrators of the system on the amount of central processor time, the amount of storage, and the usage of peripherals to be charged to each other. Other statistics as required may be maintained on idle time, error conditions, and the like.

time sharing, adaptive — An arrangement in which a time-sharing scheduler scans each queue level (from high to low) to find the first ready-to-run task. When this task uses up its time slice or becomes i/o bound, the scanning process is repeated. The time-sharing scheduler also responds to the changing demands of each task for processor time. As a task becomes either more i/o or CPU bound, it is moved to higher or lower queue levels.

time-sharing allocation of hardware resources — User and system programs and data reside on auxiliary random access storage devices with possible backup copies on a slower serial access medium such as magnetic tape. The system executive decides where information is to be stored and maintains necessary directories to permit retrieval. Programs and data must be brought into core memory for execution or modification. The executive assigns and transfers information between auxiliary and core memory as needed. The executive must also manage the assignment of serial access devices and peripheral devices to prevent conflict between concurrent user programs seeking use of peripheral devices. For example, a line printer cannot be used concurrently by several users.

time-sharing allocator (dynamic) — *See* allocator, dynamic.

time sharing, centralized input/output coordination — If the executive is to maintain control of the system, input/output operations must be forbidden to all users and to all system components except the executive. The executive must provide substitutes for these forbidden operations by means of a centralized input/output package. This package accepts requests for input or output, queues these requests, and schedules the input/output capabilities of the hardware in filling the requests.

time-sharing clock — In some systems, several user programs may reside in main memory simultaneously. The operational switching between them is controlled by a clock which is used to generate an interrupt to signal the processor that a certain time period has elapsed. The scheduling algorithm is then entered every time a clock interrupt occurs. If it is found that the program in main memory has exhausted its time slice or has changed its status, that program is swapped for the next program in the queue.

time sharing, command mode — A user is in "command" mode when there is no current task to be performed. Any console actions by a user in the command mode are interpreted by the executive as task requests (system commands). Receipt of a valid task request changes a user status to "ready" or to "waiting to be loaded." If an excessive time interval elapses without a task request, the system logs out the user, returning him to an inactive status.

time sharing, conversational — The simultaneous utilization of a computer system by multiple users at remote locations, each being equipped with a remote terminal. The user and the computer usually communicate by way of a higher-level, easy-to-learn computer language.

time sharing, conversational compilers — General purpose systems usually provide languages and procedures by means of which a user may construct a program, modify it, test it, and, in some cases, add it to the file of system subcomponents. Most of the program preparation languages developed for time-sharing systems are dialects of existing languages. Processors for the languages vary from those borrowed with only slight modification from batch mode processing to conversational mode compilers designed especially for on-line use.

time sharing, conversational guidance — Most time-shared systems operate part of the time in a conversational or dialog mode. Here the user takes some action and the system responds. Then the system requests input or takes other action and the user responds. In this alternating stimulus-response mode, the system can and should provide guidance to the user on the form and content of the user response.

time sharing, data base management and reporting — Most of the business data processing falls into this category. The range is from rather routine processing provided for small businesses who cannot afford their own computer to large dedicated systems operating in real-time, such as stock exchange systems.

time-sharing deferred-batch mode — Deferred-batch processing enables a user at an interactive terminal to submit a job to the time-sharing batch queue. After a job has been initiated by sending keyboard input to the central computer, normal processing can be continued in the interactive mode. To avoid tying up the low-speed terminal when the batch job results are ready for printing, output may be diverted to a high-speed remote batch terminal at the user's own site or elsewhere, or to peripherals at the central computer site.

time sharing, demand processing — Complementing the batch-processing capabilities of the executive system are its time-sharing capabilities, i.e., the simultaneous accommodations by the executive systems of requests and demands from users at numerous remote inquiry terminals, operating in a demand (or conversational) mode. All facilities available to the batch-processing user are also available in the demand mode; the primary difference is that the executive system utilizes its knowledge of the existence of such demand devices to permit the user additional flexibility in the statement of and control of individual runs. The demand user may communicate directly with the executive, or a worker program, or he may communicate with a conversational processor.

time sharing, error diagnostics — It is highly desirable in a remote system that a user's actions be closely monitored by the system, with errors in procedure or entry called to the user's attention as soon after commission as possible. The error message sent to an offending user should be provided whenever possible.

time-sharing executive — A typical executive processes all users' requests (executive commands) and allows users to call for, operate, and modify object programs using all available system services. It provides complete bookkeeping facilities for file storage in, and retrieval from, secondary memory. It includes facilities for collecting accounting data.

time sharing, fail soft — A concept that implies a system which can reorganize itself to isolate and cut off the offending equipment while continuing to operate. The capacity and efficiency of the system decreases, but service to users continues in the best manner with the remaining equipment.

time sharing, fault processing — The executive program of a time-shared system must be in control or able to regain control at all times. User actions or executing user programs may generate unpredictable interrupt and fault conditions. The executive must process all such conditions if it is to maintain control of the system. Clock interrupts must be set up before control is given temporarily to a user program. Interrupts on completion of input/output transmission affect the ready status of deferred tasks. Interrupts from user consoles indicate user actions and requests for attention.

time sharing, graceful degradation — *See* time sharing, fail soft.

time-sharing interchange — Time-sharing interchange allows the interactive user to issue commands which cause batch programs to be executed under various programs. It transfers data and other required input, either entered at the interactive terminal or stored in files, from offices to a batch-processing system operating within the time-sharing network.

time sharing, interrupt capability — A time-shared computer should have a sophisticated interrupt capability with interrupts occurring on internal faults, input/output transmission errors or completion, invalid instructions or operand addresses, and the like. Handling of communications with remote terminals can be accomplished on a polling basis. However, interrupts from a terminal when a message has been transmitted eliminate the necessity for the computer to continuously cycle through all communication lines seeking messages.

time sharing, interrupt processing — Interrupt processing varies in detail from computer to computer. The following functions are usually performed. (1) Normal program sequencing is stopped, usually at some convenient and appropriate point in the instruction cycle. (2) The interrupt conditions are recorded in dedicated memory cells (location may depend on interrupt class). Recorded conditions include: program counter setting at time of interrupt, class of interrupt, type within class, channel or device number, and the like. (3) The next instruction to be executed is taken from a dedicated memory cell (the location may depend on interrupt class).

time sharing, interrupt schemes — One of the features of computers of the third or late second generations is a sophisticated interrupt scheme. An interruption is the cessation of normal sequencing and branching under program control when an internal fault (such as arithmetic overflow) or an event external to the running program occurs. Interrupts may be categorized in five classes: (1) input/output or channel, (2) external, (3) machine malfunction, (4) program fault, (5) supervisory call (on master/slave mode computers).

time sharing, invalid pages — *See* time sharing, page type.

time sharing, languages — There are two types of languages which seem to be suitable for standardization—conversational calculation and text editing. Most of the conversational languages available on present time-shared systems have been modeled after FORTRAN or BASIC. However, added gimmicks, committed capabilities, and differing formats make each version incompatible with any other.

time-sharing monitor system — The monitor system is a collection of programs remaining permanently in memory to provide overall coordination and control of the total operating system. It performs several functions. First, it permits several users' programs to be loaded into core memory simultaneously. The monitor makes use of the time-sharing hardware to prevent one user's program from interferring with other users' programs. Each program is run for a certain length of time; then the monitor switches control to another program in a rotating sequence. Switching is frequent enough so that all programs appear to run simultaneously. Another function of the time-sharing monitor is to process input/output commands. The input/output service routines preprocess data so that all devices appear identical to the user's program, thus simplifying coding. The monitor makes use of the program interrupt system to overlap input/output operations with computation. If a user's program must wait for completion of an input or output operation, the monitor automatically switches to another user's program. A program may be terminated temporarily by user intervention, or it may suspend its own operation. Temporary termination does not remove the program from memory. A program may be dumped on backing storage and discontinued under user control.

time sharing, multiple i/o channels — A time-sharing computer must be able to service numerous communication lines connecting it to the user terminals. This requires multiple input/output channels operating asynchronously with the data processing. An alternate solution is to have a separate computer or processor serving as an input/output coordinator or concentrator. This processor services the individual terminals and accumulates character by character until an entire message is transmitted. Then the main processor is interrupted and the entire message transmitted. The input/output coordinating computer is especially designed for servicing communications networks and has multiple channels attached to it.

time sharing, MUMPS-11 — MUMPS-11 is an interactive multiuser data-base management operating system. The high-level MUMPS language supports string manipulation and a hierarchical file structure. The system is optimized for data-base management functions, including the random retrieval of string-oriented data from large data files. Time sharing is accomplished by a memory partition system.

time-sharing operating system — *See* operating system, time-sharing.

time sharing, page type — Memory protection is accomplished by adding a specific element to the page type. The value of the page type can be used to signal "read-only," "read/write," or "invalid." The system executive can set the value for each physical page of main memory and allow or deny access to it by a user program. Reference to "invalid" pages or attempts to write a "read-only" page cause fault interrupts.

time sharing, periodic dumping — Provisions should be included in a time-shared system for periodic dumping of system and user files onto a back-up medium, such as a magnetic tape. This function, which can be carried out during off-peak hours, guards against catastrophic system failures which destroy current working files.

time sharing, processing interrupt — Interrupt processing varies in detail from computer to computer. The following functions are usually performed: (1) normal program sequencing is stopped, usually at some convenient and appropriate point in the instruction cycle; (2) the interrupt conditions are recorded in dedicated memory cells (location may depend on interrupt class); recorded conditions include program counter setting at time of interrupt, class of interrupt, type within class, channel or device number, and the like; (3) the next instruction to be executed is taken from a dedicated memory cell (the location may depend on interrupt class).

time-sharing queues — Most sophisticated installations of any size find the need to operate a system of queues. The appropriate queue to be serviced by the processor at any particular time is selected according to priority and program type by the scheduling algorithm. Programs are initiated or released for processing by being selected from the tops of the various queues which are formed in accordance with the design philosophy of the particular installation. In addition to systems of queues, the supervisory program normally has to deal with systems of priorities. Again, what determines these priorities is a matter of design philosophy. Various criteria are used in practice. Usually it is possible for the system itself to cause priorities to be modified while programs are being queued. Such modifications are especially desirable in real-time systems because one program might be continually bypassed, or because a deadline is approaching and the program concerned is not being serviced.

time-sharing ready mode — A user task in ready status can be executed or resumed. Usually a separate queue of ready tasks is maintained by the executive. Whenever a processor is available, the executive activates the task at the head of the ready queue, changing its status to "running."

time sharing, real time — A situation in which a process is providing data on a critical real-time basis and requires that immediate processing and response be made if the process is to continue.

time sharing, real-time clock — A real-time clock is capable of being set to interrupt a running program at the end of a specified time. The minimum clock interval must be less than the basic quantum of time during which a user program is to be allowed to run. This clock, under the control of the executive, provides the best, and in some cases the only, means for the executive to regain control of the computer after a user program has exhausted its time allotment.

time-sharing resources, allocation — *See* time-sharing allocation of hardware resources.

time-sharing roll-in, roll-out — From time to time it may be that a program being queued will have to take precedence over a program being serviced. Downgrading of priorities happens often in scheduling systems. To facilitate this, some operating systems provide a roll-in, roll-out facility which enables the supervisory program to make a request for processing time on behalf of a higher-priority program in the queue. This will result in a lower-priority program being rolled out to enable the new program to be processed. Programs rolled out in this way are written into temporary storage along with their current status.

time sharing running mode — A user task is in the running mode when it is in control of a processor and is executing. A task leaves the running mode either voluntarily or involuntarily in accordance with the scheduling rules of the executive. Reasons for leaving the running mode may include: (1) request for input/output, (2) request for console response, (3) suspension on expiration of time quantum, (4) termination.

time sharing scheduling rules — Scheduling rules specify for a time-shared system: (1) the types of status or mode queue to be maintained, (2) the actions which cause a task (or user) to change modes and/or queues, (3) the time intervals which may elapse before one of the actions is taken, (4) the manner in which a task is placed on or taken from a queue.

time sharing, scientific and engineering calculation — Most time-shared systems provide conversational calculation facilities allowing research scientists, engineers, and technicians to use the computer as a large slide-rule.

time-sharing service, packet network — A time-sharing or data-base retrieval service organization can connect its host computer to the packet network in one of three ways. For minimal cost, it can obtain single low-speed terminal lines from the network into its terminal ports. This provides an excellent way to obtain nationwide dial-in terminal service at a minimal starting cost. Alternatively, it can access the network using the host-interface protocol over a leased medium-speed synchronous line between the network and its front-end processor. In this environment, a 9.6-kilobit-per-second synchronous line will support approximately 100 low-speed terminals simultaneously. Customers of the service firm can dial in to any local office of the packet network and then connect to the host computer. A third host-interfacing alternative is the possible use of an on-site controller at the host location to provide immediate compatibility without the requirement of host-interface software.

time-sharing sign on — Access to any time-sharing system is restricted, usually by the requirement that the user sign on with a valid account identification number and password (which can be composed of up to ten printing and nonprinting characters). (Some systems.)

time sharing (slice) — A method of operation in which a computer is shared by several users for different purposes, apparently at the same time. Although the computer actually services each user in sequence for a short period or "time slice," the high speed of the computer makes it appear that all users are being handled simultaneously.

time-sharing software — Necessary software features include: a means of reserving memory and peripherals for exclusive use by individual programs for predetermined periods of time, a means of switching from one program to another to optimize computer performance, and facilities to relocate programs dynamically during execution as the overall pattern of programs in the computer changes. The effect of these routines is to provide multiprogramming facilities which enable many users to initiate programs and to schedule them through the system according to their relative predetermined priorities. The simplest system is based on a circular queue for "round-robin" scheduling. Each program accepted into the system is assigned a fixed time slice, and processor operation is switched from one program to another in round-robin fashion until each program is completed. In this arrangement, only one active user program is in main memory at one time. Other active programs are held on disk.

time-sharing software functions — Software functions required in a time-shared system include: (1) allocation of hardware resources, (2) scheduling of user tasks, (3) interrupt and fault processing, (4) terminal input/output coordination, (5) centralized input/output supervision, (6) accounting, (7) interpretation and execution of system commands, (8) management of subcomponents of system, (9) management of user files, (10) miscellaneous utility functions. These functions are referred to as executive, supervisory, or monitor functions. In some time-shared systems, certain of these functions may be omitted or may be present only in a very limited way.

time-sharing software requirements — Software in a time-shared system may be divided into three categories: (1) The system proper. This is a collection of programs which controls the time-shared system, provides general services to the user, and fulfills user requests. The programs include the executive package, which is not directly callable by a user, and a utility package which is directly usable. (2) The system subcomponents. These are application packages not necessarily vital to the system operations. These programs provide specific services to the user. An example of a system subcomponent is a FORTRAN compiler. (3) The user programs. These are programs prepared by the user for his private purposes or in some cases for availability to some or all other users.

time-sharing storage compacting — Certain hardware features make feasible the dynamic relocation of programs residing in central storage—a necessity in order to provide an effective multiprogramming environment. At program termination, the assigned storage is returned to the pool of available central storage. Storage compacting is initiated if, and only if, a requirement exists for contiguous storage and compacting can meet this requirement. Compacting is never performed unnecessarily, as the storage-contents control routine continuously attempts to fit programs into gaps in the in-use store.

time-sharing storage management — Two of the problems in the time-shared management of storage—the protection of user files and the reduction of constraints on the size of user programs due to limited core space—are common to all time-shared systems and have received considerable attention in software development.

time-sharing supervisory program — A system of priorities is usually implemented. The supervisory program permits the execution of the program with the highest priority until such time as it is suspended for some reason. Priorities are usually determined by a scheduling algorithm which is used by the supervisory program to keep a record of the status of each user program. If, by bringing a program into its area in main memory, there is a storage conflict, the program with the lower priority status must be restored to its place in auxiliary memory. This process is variously called swapping; switching; push-pull; or roll-out, roll-in.

time-sharing system commands — The design of most time-shared systems centers around an executive monitor. This executive accepts, interprets, and schedules task requests from the user. A collection of commands are usually provided by which the user instructs the system as to what task he desires to have performed. The specific commands available and the form in which they are phrased vary widely from system to system, but usually include the following categories: (1) commands governing entry into and exit from the system, (2) commands requesting the establishment of certain system modes, (3) commands controlling allocation of memory, (4) commands modifying scheduling rules or establishing priorities, etc.

time-sharing system reliability — Although reliability of the hardware and software of a computer installation is always an important issue, in a time-shared system it is critical. Malfunction of a computer component in a batch-mode system disrupts only a few users. In a time-shared system, many users may be disturbed. Provisions must be included in a time-shared system to minimize the inconvenience and possible loss of information caused by system failure.

time-sharing system software — *See* time-sharing software requirements.

time-sharing system subcomponents — Time-shared system subcomponents are different from user files only in their availability. System subcomponents may be used by all users, but may not be modified by anybody except those specifically designated as system users. The executive merely maintains records on the location and attributes of the files of data and programs, stores and retrieves them as requested, and if the file is executable binary code, it loads, relocates as required, and executes the file as requested.

time-sharing terminal input/output coordination — If input from a user console is one character at a time, the console coordination program must accumulate these in a message buffer until a "break" or "end-of-message" character is received. Then the executive is interrupted so that it may process the message.

time-sharing text editing and modification — Many time-shared systems provide a text handling component. This facility is used by authors composing reports, by production groups preparing manuals, by secretaries handling correspondence, and in one large system in the preparation of land title reports.

time sharing, time-quantum method — Scheduling rules are highly dependent upon the objectives, constraints, and usage of the system. Usually, a time quantum or interval is allotted to a running task. If the task does not terminate or otherwise relinquish control prior to the expiration of this time quantum, the executive regains control, suspends the task, and places it on the ready queue, usually at the bottom. If the only functions which can be requested by a user are system functions (that is, no user prepared programs are permitted), the time quantum method may not be necessary, since the system functions can be constructed to relinquish control at or before specified time intervals.

time-sharing time slices — Time quanta of a few hundred milliseconds are usually chosen. It has been shown that the smaller the time quantum the better the average response time, if all user tasks are highly interactive. However, very small time slices badly penalize programs requiring a large amount of computation between console interactions. To work out of this dilemma, some systems have two ready queues, one with a small time interval for highly interactive programs, another with a large time interval for long computation problems. This compromise technique reduces the amount of swapping and overhead on the longer running programs caused by frequent interruptions, but provides rapid response for highly interactive programs.

time-sharing user file — Time-shared system subcomponents are different from user files only in their availability. System subcomponents may be used by all users but may not be modified by any except those specifically designated as system users. The executive merely maintains records on the location and attributes of the files of data and programs, stores and retrieves these as requested, and if the file is executable binary code, it loads, relocates as required, and executes the file as requested.

time-sharing user modes — At any given time, a user is in one of the following execution modes: (1) inactive; (2) command; (3) ready; (4) running; (5) waiting (a) for i/o completion, (b) for console action, (c) for task completion, (d) to be loaded.

time-sharing user-oriented languages — The design of languages to be used at remote terminals is more critical than in batch-mode systems. One of the aims of time sharing is to increase the accessibility of computers to nonprogramming problem solvers. One would therefore expect to have a higher percentage of lay users in a time-shared system. Language forms, syntax, and special words should be tailored to these users lacking in computer expertise.

time-sharing waiting mode — Tasks in the "waiting" mode are voluntarily suspended until some operation is complete. Upon completion of the awaited operation, the waiting task is returned to the ready mode (or in some systems to the running mode).

time slice — A designated interval of time during which a job can use a resource without being preempted.

time slice, multiplexing — Minicomputers can support complex kinds of multiplexing and concentration. The simplest kind is fixed-time-division multiplexing where every user is assigned a time slice, and all users are examined in turn. If a user has no traffic to send, the time slice remains empty and is wasted.

time slice, statistical multiplexing — Statistical multiplexing is a scheme in which each user is examined in turn until one is found with traffic to send. No time slices are left empty if any user has any traffic; however, some identification must be sent with the data in each time slice to identify the user.

time slicing — *Same as* time sharing.

time, standby — 1. The elapsed time between inquiries when the equipment is operating on an inquiry application. 2. The time during which two or more computers are tied together and are available to answer inquiries or to process intermittent actions on stored data.

time, standby maintenance — *See* time, maintenance standby.

time, standby unattached — Time in which the machine is in an unknown condition and is not processing a problem. Includes time in which the machine is known to be defective and work is not being done to restore it to operating condition. Includes breakdowns that render the machine unavailable due to outside conditions (power outages, etc).

time, start — The time between the interpretation of instructions to read or write on tape and the transfer of information from the tape into storage or from storage into the tape.

time, stop — The time that elapses between the completion of a reading or writing of a tape record and the time when the tape stops moving.

time, subtract — A determination of the elapsed time required for one subtraction operation, but excluding the time required to obtain and return the quantities from storage.

time, supplementary maintenance — Time designed to modify or change equipment in some sort of major way to improve reliability, but usually without additions of equipment. This time is usually considered part of scheduled engineering time and/or scheduled maintenance time.

time, swap — The time required to transfer a program from external memory to high-speed internal memory and vice versa.

time, switching — 1. The time interval between the reference time, or time at which the leading edge of a switching or driving pulse occurs, and the last instant at which the instantaneous voltage response of a magnetic cell reaches a stated fraction of its peak value. 2. The time interval between the reference time and the first instant at which the instantaneous integrated voltage response reaches a stated fraction of its peak value.

time, system-improvement — All the machine down time needed for the installation and testing of new components, large or small, and machine down time necessary for modification of existing components. Includes all programmed tests following the above actions to prove the machine is operating properly.

time, takedown — The time required to take down a piece of equipment.

time, testing — *See* testing time.

time-to-digital conversion — The process of converting an interval into a digital number.

time, training — The machine time expended in training employees in the use of the equipment, including such activities as mounting, console operation, converter operation, printing operation and related activities, and time spent in conducting required demonstrations.

time, transfer — That specific time interval between the instant the transfer of data to or from a storage commences and the instant it is completed.

time, true — *Same as* time, real.

time, turnaround — The time required to reverse the direction of a transmission in a communication channel.

time, unattended — Time during which the equipment is in an unknown condition and during which it is not in use. This also includes most often time during breakdown.

time, unused — That time which is available for machine operations, but which is left unused and most often unattended by any computer system personnel.

time, up — The time during which equipment is either producing work or is available for productive work. (Contrasted with down time.)

time utilization — The arrangement of a program which allows processing to continue while records necessary for processing are being located in file and read into core and working storage.

time, waiting — Same as latency, the time interval between the instant the control unit signals the details, addresses, etc., of a transfer of data to or from the storage unit and the instant the transfer commences.

time, word — 1. The amount of time required to move one word past a given point. The term is used especially in reference to words stored serially. 2. The time required to transport one word from one storage device to another. (Related to access time.)

time, write — The amount of time it takes to record information. (Related to access time.)

timing and control circuits — Circuits that receive bus and internal control signals and generate appropriate read/write timing and control signals.

timing circuits — For many purposes, it is desirable to produce a signal of a certain duration, starting with a triggering impulse. Signals of this type are frequently needed in connection with input/output devices, where signals occur much more slowly than they do inside the computer. In the case of static circuitry, there are various forms of monostable circuits that can produce pulses of any desired duration. In dynamic circuits, delay lines can be used to produce time delays and pulse trains of a desired length.

timing, clock — A pulse positioned next to recorded characters on tapes, drums, discs, etc., to control the timing of read circuits, count characters, or develop and perform related functions which a clock pulse would perform.

timing control — On many systems, all necessary timing signals are provided by an on-chip oscillator and a timing generator. The frequency of the oscillator, in turn, is selected by connecting an external capacitor or crystal between specific pins. When a crystal is used, the resulting frequency of the oscillator is equal to the resonant frequency of the crystal. When a capacitor is used, the frequency of the oscillator varies according to the capacitance values.

timing error — An error introduced because the program was not able to keep pace with the tape-transfer rate, or a new motion or select command was issued before the previous command was completely executed.

timing matrix, program — *See* matrix, program timing.

timing meter — A device that measures the time duration of an activity by sampling the state of a memory element or elements associated with that activity. One type of timing meter is a binary counter driven by a clock derived either from the basic CPU clock or from a special generator.

timing, microcomputer — There are two ways in which designers can schedule the execution of each instruction step: with asynchronous logic or with synchronous logic. With asynchronous logic, every instruction contains its own logic sequences, with each step triggering the next appropriate step. Only the instruction fetch sequence would be common to all instructions. Asynchronous logic has two severe limitations: (a) it makes the CPU logic far more complex, and (b) it presents formidable timing problems when interfacing the CPU to external logic modules, each of which may impose its own incompatible timing demands. Synchronous logic is far cheaper and simpler to design for. It is based on a clock signal (or signals) which triggers an operation on one edge of each clock pulse. Clock pulses are of fixed length and period.

timing pulse — *See* pulse, clock.

timing signals — Electrical pulses sent throughout the machine at regular intervals to ensure absolute synchronization.

timing track — *See* track, timing.

tiny BASIC — A subset of Dartmouth BASIC. Statements include: let, if . . . then, input, print, go to, go sub, return, end rem, clear, list, and run. Functions include RND (random-number generator) and USR (user subroutine). These functions allow branching, with arguments to assembly-language subroutines.

TLU — Abbreviation for Table Look Up. To obtain a function value corresponding to an argument, stated or implied, from a table of function values stored in the computer.

TNS — Abbreviation for Transaction Network Service. A Bell System metropolitan-area inquiry-response data-exchange service intended to provide a basic communications service for short data messages, such as inquiry-response financial transactions.

toggle — 1. Pertaining to any device having two stable states. 2. A circuit or device containing active elements, capable of assuming either one of two stable states at a given time.

toggle switch — 1. A manually operated electric switch with a small projecting arm. 2. An electronically operated circuit that holds either of two states until changed.

token — A distinguishable unit in a sequence of characters.

tolerance — A permissible deviation from a specified value.

tomographic computerized (CT) body scanning — A system in which a scanner rotates a low-intensity X-ray beam around the body 180° in a transaxial plane. Detectors, placed opposite the beam, monitor and digitally signal the varying degrees to which body tissues absorb radiation. A computer transforms this digital information into a cross-sectional, almost 3-D, image of the body. This process differs from conventional X-ray units which use stationary X-ray sources to produce flat pictures of the body.

tool data management — Tool data management includes tool-length offset storage, cutter diameter-compensation value storage, groups of program-selectable tool-length trims, tool-data tape input, tool-usage monitor, remote tool-management terminal, and electronic tool-gauge interface capabilities.

topological optimization — A designer's task with regard to deciding how to interconnect network locations as economically as possible while meeting all performance goals and constraints. It is the most difficult task for the system planner, especially if the network is large and encompasses many concentrators, multiplexers, and so on.

topology — The physical or logical placement of nodes in a computer network.

topology alternatives — Alternative network topologies include: (1) highly centralized or star; (2) fully distributed, either partially or fully connected; (3) ring, which is a variant of a distributed configuration; and (4) various combinations of these.

topology, centralized — Centralized communications topology is the kind of network in which each terminal has direct access to the single host computer, usually on multipoint, multiplexed, or dial-up lines, and possibly through a front-end processor.

topology, hierarchical — Hierarchical communications topology means a network in which terminals connect to multiplexers, multiplexers to concentrators, and concentrators to front-end processors which, in turn, connect to one or more host computers. In nonhierarchical communications topology, each of the nodes of the network is of roughly the same capability. For example, packet-switching networks, whether private or common carrier, may be used to provide a nonhierarchical structure.

topology, network — Network topologies can be centralized or distributed. Centralized networks are those in which all nodes connect to a single node. The alternative topology is distributed where, in the limit, each node is connected to every other node, although the terminology is commonly applied to topologies approaching this full connectivity.

torn-tape switching center — 1. A location where operators tear off incoming printed and punched paper tape and transfer it manually to the proper outgoing circuit. 2. A center at which messages are produced in a physical form and then retransmitted to the proper destination.

total, batch — The sum of certain quantities, pertaining to batches of unit records, used to verify accuracy of operations on a particular batch of records; e.g., in a payroll calculation, the batches might be departments, and batch totals would be number of employees in the department, total hours worked in the department, total pay for the department. Batches, however, may be arbitrary, such as orders received from 9 am to 11 am on a certain day.

total, check — *See* check total.

total, control — *See* control total.

total, gibberish — *Same as* hash total.

total, hash — *See* hash total.

total, intermediate — A total which lies somewhere between a major and a minor total, i.e., a summation developed for some other purpose, or in some hierarchy of sums, or due to a termination in a program.

totalizing — To register a precise total count from mechanical, photoelectric, electromagnetic, or electronic inputs or detectors.

total, major — The summation or tally of the group of intermediate totals and, therefore, often called the most significant total.

total management system — *See* system, total management.

total, minor — The sum of the least significant type.

total, proof — One of a number of check totals which can be correlated in some manner for consistency or reconciliation in a range, set, or distinct calculation.

total system — Often called the integrated system, it is a plan to place all important and significant operational components of an organization under the complete or partial control of computers. Real-time system configurations, and their immediacy of data collection, processing, and generation are convenient to this total-system concept.

touch-control panel — Some touch-control panels are basic elements for the interfacing of glass keyboards with MOS circuitry. Conductive coatings are fired onto a glass panel and activate controls by touch only; no movement of a switch is involved. The touch-control panel combines electrocapacitive switching, decoration, and transparent windows for digital display devices. The fired-on conductive coatings and ceramic decorations provide an operating surface with the mechanical and chemical durability characteristic of a glass surface.

touch-input system — With some touch-input systems, users may select points of interest by touching them. This is possible by using an array of infrared light beams that are projected directly above the display surface. When interrupted by a user's finger, they signal digital logic to generate the coordinates of the touch point as binary data.

touch interface crt screen — A crt screen equipped with a position sensor such that probe or finger contact at a point on the screen causes the coordinates of the point to be transmitted to a computer or controller.

touch-sensitive digitizer — Abbreviated TSD. A device which, by means of transducers located along two sides of a glass plate, accurately determines the location of a finger or other passive probe and converts the positional information into digital form for computer processing.

touch switching — A solid-state switching system that includes a touch panel and an integrated circuit (IC) that interfaces with the electronic components that control functions. Each touch pad on the panel is a capacitive switch. The pad forms the common plate of two capacitors; two conductive stripes on the back surface opposite each pad form the corresponding plates of each capacitor.

trace — An interpretive diagnostic technique that provides an analysis of each executed instruction and writes it on an output device as each instruction is executed.

trace debug — A debugging program that prints or displays a specific set of registers and/or memory locations as they are encountered throughout the execution of a program, generally without interrupting the program execution. A trace of the contents of key variables and registers is often provided for later problem analysis and debug review.

trace display — A software diagnostic technique used to follow program execution step by step to determine where an error is occurring. A running trace usually displays the contents of all CPU registers as each instruction is executed, thereby enabling the user to determine where values are not changing as predicted.

trace flow — A debugging device which prints out contents of various registers and memory locations in a particular program segment specified by the user.

trace-mode debugging — A method generally used throughout an entire program to determine and indicate any variable changes, where transfers to statements or subroutines occur, and the values of loop counters.

trace program — *See* program, trace.

trace program, interpretive — *See* program, interpretive trace.

trace routine — An executive routine that develops a sequence record of the execution of programs to be checked or traced.

trace, selective — A tracing routine wherein only instructions satisfying certain specified criteria are subject to tracing. The following criteria are typical examples. (a) Instruction type—arithmetic jump. (b) Instruction location—a specific region. (c) Data location—a specific region. For case (a), where tracing is performed on a transfer or a jump instruction, the term logical trace is sometimes used.

tracing — An interpretive diagnostic technique to record on an output device the execution of each instruction and its results. This technique provides a record of each processed instruction by the recording of all instructions, operands, and results for analysis of the computer run.

tracing, flow — A type of diagnostics and debugging in which the programmer specifies the start and end of those program segments where he wishes to examine the contents of various registers and accumulators. The program will run at machine speed until it encounters the desired segments, and the printing commences and is terminated when the end of the program segment is encountered. It is also possible then to include "snapshot" traces which indicate the contents not only of the various accumulators and registers, but also of specified memory locations.

tracing, interpretive — Such routines interpret rather than execute directly each instruction in either source language or machine code. The program is simulated in its execution by using accumulators and pseudo index registers which are not identical to the accumulators and registers used by the tracing program; thus, control does not pass from the tracing program to the program which is being traced when a branch instruction is encountered.

tracing, logical — Tracing which is performed only on specific jump or transfer instructions and for specific purposes.

tracing routine — A routine that supplies automatic tracing.

tracing, selective — Specific tracing on particular data most often related to some highly specific instructions such as transfer instructions only, or for specified locations, registers, storage units, areas, etc.

tracing structure, built-in — Various debugging, diagnostic, or error-tracing routines are built-in parts of programs, i.e., instructions to output partial results during any program execution cycle. Such instructions may be of a temporary nature and can be easily removed using various series of test instructions.

track — 1. A sequence of binary cells arranged so that data may be read or written from one cell at a time in serial fashion; for example, a track on a magnetic drum is a path one bit wide around the circumference of the drum. 2. The portion of a moving-storage medium, such as a drum, tape, disk, that is accessible to a given reading station.

trackball — A ball mounted in a box equipped with position sensors. A trackball does not move the cursor in direct proportion to its position, but instead it transports the cursor in proportion to the speed at which it is rolled and in the direction of its rotation. This method of operation enables a cursor to be precisely positioned because the speed of rotation can easily approach zero. However, by rotating the ball rapidly, the cursor can be moved fast, so as not to cause undue delay.

track density — The number of adjacent tracks per a given unit of distance measured in a direction perpendicular to the direction of individual tracks. The inverse of track pitch.

track, feed — The track of a paper tape which contains the small feed holes for the sprockets.

tracking cross — A crosslike array of bright dots on the display, used for locating points and lines or for drawing curves.

track, library — Tracks used to store reference data, such as titles, key words, document numbers, etc., on tapes, drums, disks, or mass storage devices.

track, magnetic — That part of a moving magnetic medium which is influenced by a magnetic head, i.e., the ring-shaped portion of the surface of a magnetic drum storage as connected with one physical position of one magnetic head.

track pitch — *See* pitch, track.

track, primary — On a direct-access device, the original track on which data are stored.

tracks density — The number of bits which may be written in a single position across the width of the tape, including parity bits.

tracks, prerecorded — A preliminary tape-, disk-, or drum-recorded routine that simplifies programming. Relieves the programmer of the responsibility of furnishing timing or counting instructions and permits block and word addressability.

track, timing — A specific track on magnetic tape, magnetic disks, drums, etc., on which a long string of pulses is recorded developing a clock signal to thus recognize rows of data by counting or by the positioning of the pulses or marks in the track.

traffic control, input/output — *See* input-/output traffic control.

traffic control, microcomputer — A microcomputer at each intersection allows a large central master traffic control system to know the traffic flow at each intersection. The intersection microcomputer can implement light changes operating (1) on its own information, (2) in conjunction with a group of intersections, or (3) under central master control.

traffic information — With respect to a terminal, information concerning the type of message or transaction, the number of transactions per day or hour, message-length distributions for input and output, priority, and others.

traffic statistics — The obtaining of information from a study of communications traffic. Includes statistical study of message headings, receipts, acknowledgments, routing, and so on, plus a tabulation of volumes and types of messages with respect to time.

trail, audit — *See* audit trail.

trailer — 1. A record that follows a group of detail records and gives information about a group not present in the detail records. 2. A record that follows a header.

trailer label — The end-of-tape file record that lists summary information concerning that file.

trailer record — A record that follows a group of records and contains pertinent data related to the group of records.

trailer, tape — *See* tape trailer.

training mode — *See* mode, training.

training time — *See* time, training.

transaction — A collection or grouping of several related actions entered by a terminal operator as in an airline reservation system where the sale of a space on one flight is an action, and the sale of an itinerary or schedule including several alternate flights for the same passenger would be a transaction.

transaction data — Data describing a specific event in a data-processing application area, such as job number, quantity, price, etc.

transaction-driven systems — In batch-oriented systems, data enters the processing cycle on a systematic basis in highly structured groupings or batches, and files are usually updated after the fact. In interactive, transaction-driven systems, data is entered randomly, and files are updated immediately as transactions occur, usually as a byproduct of processing those items. As a result of direct real-time data entry, records dealing with the event or transaction are as current as the latest transaction, wherever the entry is made in the system or network. Often, the system provides direct communication with the operator by asking questions, offering step-by-step entry guidance, and answering operator queries.

transaction file — Transactions accumulated as a batch ready for processing against the master file.

Transaction Network Service — *See* TNS.

transaction-oriented systems — A transaction-oriented system is a specialized type of on-line system designed to handle interactive-type applications that revolve around entering, retrieving, updating and/or manipulating information (normally located in a data base), using one or more user-written programs. A transaction-oriented system typically runs under the operating system as a single, high-priority job in a multiprogramming environment and is generally designed for a set of specific functions, such as airline-reservations handling. A system of this nature tends to be highly user oriented, in that one of its primary goals is to interact effectively with terminal operators in such a way as to provide an efficient flow of information between the operators and the system. This is best accomplished in a transaction environment by providing very fast response time (a few seconds or less, depending upon the situation).

transaction record — Specific information which modifies information in a file.

transaction recorder, automatic — Routines or systems are developed for recording several facts about each transaction with minimum manual input. Worker and job identification are picked up from plates or individual cards, start-stop times are checked by clock notations, completions are developed by recording dials at inquiry stations throughout plants.

transaction tape — A paper or magnetic tape carrying information that is to be used to up-date filed information. This filed information is often on a master tape.

transceiver — A terminal device that can both transmit and receive signals.

transceiver, card — A device that transmits and receives data from a punched card to a punched card. It is essentially a conversion device which at the sending end reads the card and transmits the data over the wire. At the receiving end it punches the data into a card.

transcribe — To copy, with or without translating, from one external storage medium to another.

transcriber — The equipment associated with a computer for the purpose of transferring the input or output data from a record of information in a given language to the computer medium and language, or from a computer to a record of information.

transcription — Conversion of data from one language, medium, or code to another. Includes the reading, translating, and recording (writing) operations.

transcription break — A flowchart symbol or device that shows the relationship between two files. The symbol is directional and suggests the flow of information from one file to the file that is affected by the information. The operation symbol should be on the history lines of the file that is affected.

transducer — A device that converts energy from one form to another; e.g., a quartz crystal imbedded in mercury can change electrical energy to sound energy as is done in sonic delay lines in computer-storage systems.

transducer, incremental — A rotary or linear feedback device with discrete on-off pulses. All pulses are the same, and there is always the same number of signals per unit length or per revolution. Direction is determined by special logic circuits.

transducers, analog/digital — Analog transducers output either voltages or currents. Digital transducers fall into two basic categories. Some incorporate a sensing unit as part of an oscillator circuit and determine the frequency of that circuit as a function of the measured quantity. Others detect the position of a primary sensor and convert that quantity into a coded digital word.

transducer, syntax — A subroutine which recognizes the phase class in an artificial language, normally expressed in Backus normal form.

transducer translating device — A device for converting error of the controlled member of a servomechanism into an electrical signal that can be used in correcting the error.

transfer — 1. To change control by means of an instruction or signal that specifies the location of the next instruction and directs the computer to that instruction; to jump. A transfer is used to alter the normal sequence control of the computer. 2. To copy, exchange, read, record, store, transmit, transport, or write data. 3. To terminate one sequence of instructions and begin another sequence.

transfer, average data, rate — *See* data transfer rate, average.

transfer, block — The conveyance of a group of consecutive words from one place to another.

transfer check — A check on the accuracy of a data transfer.

transfer circuit — A circuit which connects communication centers of two or more separate networks in order to transfer the traffic between the networks.

transfer command — A particular order or instruction which changes control from one part of the program to another part by indicating a remote instruction.

transfer, conditional — *See* branch, conditional.

transfer control, unconditional — *Same as* branch, unconditional.

transfer function — A mathematical expression or expressions that describe(s) the relationship between physical conditions at two different points in time or space in a given system, and also describes the role played by the intervening time or space.

transfer instruction — *Same as* branch instruction.

transfer instruction, conditional — *See* branch, conditional.

transfer instruction, unconditional — *See* branch, unconditional.

transfer medium — The material which enables the transfer of ink during printing, i.e., sheets, ribbons, plastic film.

transfer of control — *Same as* branch.

transfer operation — An operation that moves information from one storage location or one storage medium to another, e.g., read, record, copy, transmit, or exchange. Transfer is sometimes taken to refer specifically to movement between different storage media.

transfer, parallel — In a parallel transfer, all the bits stored in one string of flip-flops are transferred simultaneously to another string, using one wire (or a pair of wires) for each flip-flop.

transfer peak — *See* data transfer rate.

transfer, peripheral — A procedure or process for transferring data between two units of peripheral or auxiliary equipment.

transfer, radial — A procedure or process for transferring data between peripheral equipment and the internal memory of the machine.

transfer rate, character — The speed at which data may be read from or written to the unit, exclusive of seek or latency delays.

transfer rate, data — The speed at which data may be read from or written to the device, from the lowest to the highest speed and density available.

transfer rate, instantaneous — *See* data transfer rate.

transfer rate, maximum — The maximum number of binary digits per second which can be accommodated on the channel. For a duplex channel (input-/output) the transfer rate is usually shown for one direction only.

transfer rate, system — A measure of how fast data can be read from or written into the storage medium. Often this is qualified further by specifying a burst transfer rate and an average transfer rate. The burst rate is the actual speed during reading or writing. The average rate is measured for a long transfer of several thousand bytes. It is usually less than the burst rate because of the gaps between blocks of data or time spent searching for the next block of data.

transfers, automatic-word — An instruction that uses the data-break facility to allow concurrent information processing and data acquisition during block transfers.

transfer, serial — A system of data transfer in which the characters of an element of information are transferred in sequence over a single path in consecutive time positions.

transfer table — A table that contains a list of transfer instructions of all the programs that are in core, which enables transfers of control to be made from one program to another.

transfer time — That specific time interval between the instant the transfer of data to or from a storage commences and the instant it is completed.

transfer, unconditional — *Same as* branch, unconditional.

transfer vector — *See* transfer table.

transfer, word — Transmission of entire words. All word bits are transferred between the computer and the external device at one time. This means that no breakdown of words into characters on output, or assembling of characters into words on input, takes place.

transform — To change the structure or composition of information without altering its meaning or value; to normalize, edit, or substitute.

transient — 1. A disturbance intermediate to two steady-state conditions. 2. Pertaining to rapid change.

transient error — Some errors arise which are not caused by any inherent defect in tapes, machines, or programs, but because of the presence of some dust, which will disappear when the tape is physically moved again. Such errors are termed to be transient.

transistor — A device made by attaching three or more wires to a small wafer of semiconducting material (a single crystal which has been specially treated so that its properties are different at the point where each wire is attached). The three wires are usually called the emitter, base, and collector. They perform functions somewhat similar to those of the cathode, grid, and plate of a vacuum tube, respectively.

transistor, bipolar — A transistor in which electrical conduction depends on the flow of both majority and minority carriers.

transistor, field-effect — A transistor in which the conduction is due entirely to the flow of the majority carriers and in which the conduction can be varied by an electric field produced by an auxiliary source.

transistor, metal-oxide-semiconductor field-effect — Abbreviated MOSFET. An insulated-gate field-effect transistor in which the insulating layer between each gate electrode and the channel is an oxide material or an oxide and nitride material.

transistor, npn — A transistor formed by sandwiching a narrow block of p-type semiconductor material between two larger blocks of n-type material. In the construction of the transistor, measures are taken to ensure that the flow of current from emitter to base is not reduced by much when it continues on to the collector; the base material is only slightly doped and is much narrower than the crystals on either side of it. The emitter-base junction is usually forward biased, and the base-collector junction is usually reverse biased. *See also* transistor, pnp.

transistor, pnp — A transistor formed by sandwiching a narrow block of n-type semiconductor material (the base) between two larger blocks of p-type material (the emitter and collector). In normal operation, the emitter-base junction is forward biased while the base-collector junction is reverse biased. *See also* transistor, npn.

transition — The change from one circuit condition to another, such as the change from mark to space or from space to mark.

transition card — A card, used in the loading of a deck of program cards, that causes the termination of the loading process and initiates the execution of the program.

transition, mark-to-space — The transition, or switching, from a marking impulse to a spacing impulse.

transition, space-to-mark — The transition, or switching, from a spacing impulse to a marking impulse.

translate — To change information from one language to another without significantly affecting the meaning, e.g., problem statements in pseudocode, data, or coding to machine.

translate (display) — To move, as an image on a screen, from side to side or up and down without rotation of the image.

translating program — A particular program (often called a translator) which translates from one language into another.

translating routine — A program whose input is a sequence of statements in some language and whose output is an equivalent sequence of statements in another language.

translation — The operation that reestablishes the text of a message from the restored signals and includes printing of the text.

translation, algorithm — A specific, effective, essentially computational method for obtaining a translation from one language to another.

translation, error rate of (communication) — Ratio of the number of alphabetic characters incorrectly translated to the number of alphabetic characters in the undistorted and restored message at the input of the receiving apparatus.

translation, frequency — The transfer, en block, of the signals occupying a definite frequency band from one position in the frequency spectrum to another so that the arithmetic frequency difference of the signals is unaltered.

translation, language — The translation of information from one language to another.

translation, machine — The automatic translation from one representation to another representation. The translation may involve codes, languages, or other systems of representation. (Related to automatic dictionary.)

translation, mechanical — A generic term for language translation by computers or similar equipment.

translation, one-for-one — The specific process in which each programming instruction is equal to one machine-language instruction.

translation program, interpretive — *Same as* program, interpretive.

translator — 1. A program whose input is a sequence of statements in some language and whose output is an equivalent sequence of statements in another language. (Synonymous with translating routine.) 2. A translating device.

translator, language — *See* language translator.

translator, one-to-one — *Same as* assembler, one-to-one.

translator program — A program that uses

the source language program as input and produces from it a programming machine language.

translator routine — A routine that compiles (translates) a source program expressed in problem-oriented language into an object program in machine code.

transliterate — To represent the characters or words of one language by corresponding characters or words of another language.

transmission — The electrical transfer of a signal, message, or other form of intelligence from one location to another.

transmission, analog — Analog transmission sends a continuous signal range (amplitude, frequency, or phase) over a channel; filters and linear amplifiers maintain signal quality. Analog voice channels are interfaced to the digital output of terminals and computers by a modem, within which digital pulses modulate a phone-channel compatible carrier. This carrier then passes through the telephone network as though it were a voice signal. The receiving end demodulates the signal back to digital form.

transmission, asynchronous — The transmission process such that between any two significant instants in the same group (block or character), there is always an integral number of unit intervals. Between two significant instants located in different groups, there is not always an integral number of unit intervals.

transmission, binary — The information exchanged by computers and other data terminals is generally in binary, or pulse-type, form, consisting of a simple voltage on-off pattern. Transmission media linking data-processing equipment should, ideally, be capable of handling this pulse-type signal format. In an effort to provide such media, networks are in service which are intended solely for transmitting digital signals. The analog voice telephone system offers the most readily accessible, widespread communications facility. These telephone circuits were originally designed to accommodate a limited quantity of low-speed telegraph traffic; they were not meant to carry high-volume, high-speed digital data. To make transmission of such data possible on voice-channel facilities, the binary language of data processing must be translated into the analog language of voice communication.

transmission channels — There are three basic channel configurations: point-to-point, multipoint, and circuit-switched. A point-to-point channel connects just two parties. Even nonswitched, these channels can operate in either the half- or full-duplex mode. In multipoint setups, several secondary stations share a common line. The primary station solicits its transmissions from its tributary secondaries by polling them, and picks which secondaries are to receive a data transmission. Usually, nonswitched multipoint systems are restricted to half-duplex transmission. However, it is possible for the primary to transmit to one secondary while receiving from another. A circuit-switched arrangement establishes a transmitter-to-receiver path for every call. Calls are initiated by pulse or DTMF dialers either manually from rotary or keypad devices, or automatically.

transmission codes, fixed ratio — Error detection codes that use a fixed ratio of one bit to the total number of bits.

transmission codes, recurrent — Codes in which check symbols are used to detect against the burst type of error.

transmission codes, spiral parity checking — A method used to detect single bit errors. Each check character is obtained by shifting the level for each successive checking character.

transmission control unit — Abbreviated TCU. An input/output control unit that addresses messages to and receives messages from a number of remote terminals.

transmission, data — The sending of data from one place to another, or from one part to another part of the system.

transmission, data, trap — *See* data-transmission trap.

transmission, effective speed of — The rate at which information is processed by a transmission facility, expressed as the average characters per unit time or average bits per unit time.

transmission equipment — That large class of equipment considered peripheral to the computing equipment itself which communicates data rather than computing or processing.

transmission frames, SDLC — All SDLC

transmissions occur in well-defined frames. Information frames incorporate the transmitted message intelligence. Supervisory frames carry no data; they convey such signals as ready or busy indications, polls or acknowledgments, and requests for retransmission after detecting errors. Management frames provide the data needed for such functions as activating, initializing, and controlling the response mode of secondary stations as well as reporting errors in transmission procedures. Each message frame has six distinct fields. The standardized format minimizes the amount of signaling needed for data-link control by permitting multiple-frame transmission sequences that do not require an acknowledgment.

transmission interface converter — The transmission interface converter controls information transfer between a transmission channel and a transmission adapter.

transmission level — The expression in transmission units of the ratio P/P_0, where P represents the power at the point in question, and P_0 the power at the point chosen as the origin of the transmission system.

transmission link — A section of a channel (or circuit) between: (1) a transmitter station and the following telegraph repeater, (2) two successive telegraph repeaters, (3) a receiving station and the preceding telegraph repeater.

transmission modes — Basic types of transmission are: simplex (one way only), simplex with back channel (one way with limited backtalk handshaking), half duplex (bidirectional but in one direction at a time), and full duplex (simultaneously bidirectional).

transmission packet — Use of short standardized packets. A packet-switching network is able to store and forward messages very rapidly, typically within a fraction of a second. This is made possible by the use of very high-speed switching computers in which messages (packets) are stored in fast-access memory exclusively, rather than on the slow-access storage devices (electromechanical disk drives) employed in conventional message switching systems. Flow control techniques are designed to ensure that main storage does not become overloaded, while still maintaining line loadings as close to maximum as possible. Thus, packets are stored only momentarily at each node and pass very rapidly from node to node through the network. Delay is but a fraction of a second.

transmission, parallel — A system for sending all bits of a particular character simultaneously.

transmission, point-to-point — Transmission of data between two points.

transmission ratio, utilization — The data transmission ratio of useful or acceptable data output to the total input of data.

transmission reversal, terminal systems — In some systems, transmission reversal, under operator control, permits suspension of transmission from the host CPU to the terminal to allow transmission from the terminal to the host.

transmission, serial — To move data in sequence, one character at a time, as contrasted with parallel transmission.

transmission speed — The number of information elements sent per unit of time, usually expressed as bits, characters, word groups, or records per second (or per minute).

transmission, start-stop — Asynchronous transmission in which a group of code elements corresponding to a character signal is preceded by a start element and is followed by a stop element.

transmission system codes — Method of using a character parity check as well as a block check to detect errors.

transmission system, information — A system which receives and delivers information without changing it.

transmission, transparent mode — Transmission of binary data with the recognition of most control characters suppressed. In binary synchronous communications, entry to and exit from the transparent mode is indicated by a sequence beginning with a special data-link escape (DLE) character.

transmit — To move data from one location to another.

transmit flow control — A transmission procedure which controls the rate at which data may be transmitted from one terminal point so that it is equal to the rate at which it can be received by the remote terminal point.

transmitted-data circuit — Signals in this circuit are originated by the data-terminal equipment for transmission on the data-communication channel. This circuit is not required for receive-only service.

transmitter — In telephony, a device to convert sound to electrical energy. In radio and television, a device to generate and radiate electrical energy.

transmitter distributor — The device in a teletypewriter that makes and breaks the line in timed sequence. Modern usage of the term refers to a paper-tape transmitter.

transmitter-distributor, tape — *Same as* tape reader.

transmitter ready — An interrupt triggered by a universal synchronous-asynchronous receiver transmitter. It indicates that the processor is ready to send out another character to a remote terminal.

transmitter register — A register the purpose of which is to serialize data and present it to the transmitted data output.

transmitter-start code — Usually a two-letter call that is sent to an outlying machine and automatically turns on its tape transmitter.

transparent — Pertaining to a function not noticed or seen or directly implemented by the operator or user. Many code conversions are completed without the operator seeing them or being aware of them.

transparent data communication code — A mode of data communication that uses a code-independent protocol and does not depend for its correct functioning on the character set or code used.

transparent text — Text which may contain any sequence of bits and which does not perturb and is not perturbed by the channel or the protocol.

transparent transmission — A method of transmission in which the transmission medium will not recognize control characters or initiate any control function.

transport — 1. To convey as a whole from one storage device to another. 2. A device that moves tape past a head. (Synonymous with tape transport.)

transportation, document — The phase in the reading process in character recognition which makes the effective delivery of the source document to the read station.

transport mechanism, tape — *See* transport, tape.

transport, tape — The mechanism that moves magnetic or paper tape past sensing and recording heads, and is usually associated with data-processing equipment. (Synonymous with tape transport mechanism, tape drive, and tape feed; related to tape unit and magnetic-tape unit.)

transport unit — A specific piece of peripheral equipment or media handling device, such as a card feed.

transverse check — A system of error control based on some preset rules for the formation of characters.

trap — 1. A special form of a conditional breakpoint that is activated by the hardware itself, by conditions imposed by the operating system, or by a combination of the two. Traps are an outgrowth of the old idea of switch-controlled halts or jumps. Frequently, a number of internal triggers or traps exist in a computer. Since these traps are usually set only by unexpected or unpredictable occurrences, and since the execution time and number of instructions for testing them can be burdensome, it is usual for these triggers to cause an automatic transfer of control, or jump to a known location. The location from which the transfer occurred, and the cause of the transfer are recorded in other standard locations. Some trapping features can also be enabled or inhibited under program control, e.g., an overflow trap. (Related to tracing routine.) 2. A routine to determine indirectly the setting of internal triggers in the computer.

trap, arithmetic mask — The bit, in the program status doubleword, that indicates whether (if 1) or not (if 0) the fixed-point arithmetic trap is in effect.

trap/breakpoint — Various halts that are designed and inserted in object code with the purpose of causing a branch to a debug program at appropriate times and places.

trap control settings — Trap control settings which interrupt signals will be allowed to interrupt a program in process. If a trap is armed, then the associated interrupt conditions will be permitted to interrupt the main program when they occur. A trap that has not been armed, or has been disarmed, inhibits the occurrence of interrupt signals.

trap, data transmission — *See* data transmission trap.

trap, dedicated, cells — The executive of a time-sharing system regains control when an interrupt occurs by prestoring in the dedicated trap cells. The program then jumps to the appropriate interrupt processing subroutines. The dedicated cells are in a protected area of core memory and cannot be modified by a user program. Arming and enabling operations are usually privileged instructions forbidden to user programs. Exceptions to this may be certain program faults, such as arithmetic overflow.

trapped instruction — 1. A special instruction which is executed by a software routine in cases where the necessary hardware is absent and in cases where the CPU is not in the state required. 2. An instruction whose execution was stopped or cancelled.

trapping — A feature of some computers whereby an unscheduled (nonprogrammed) jump is made to a predetermined location in response to a machine condition (e.g., a tagged instruction, or an abnormal arithmetic situation). Such a feature is commonly used by monitor routines to provide automatic checking, or for communication between input-/output routines and their programs.

trapping mode — A scheme used mainly in program-diagnostic procedures for certain computers. If the trapping mode flip-flop is set and the program includes any one of certain instructions, the instruction is not performed but the next instruction is taken from location 0. Program-counter contents are saved in order to resume the program after executing the diagnostic procedure.

trap settings — Trap settings that control interrupt signals will be allowed to interrupt a program in process. If a trap is armed, then the associated interrupt conditions will be permitted to interrupt the main program when they occur. A trap that has not been armed, or has been disarmed, prevents the occurrence of interrupt signals.

traverse — The area through which a punched card is transported through the machine.

tray — The flat file drawer used to store punched cards.

tree — This term is often used for some types of decoders because their diagrammatic representation can resemble the branches and trunk of a tree.

tree-form language — A language in which the files are structured in a hierarchical, or tree, form.

tree-structure network — In industrial environments, a hierarchical, or tree, structure is often used to supervise and control a variety of real-time process-control applications. In such systems, a hierarchy of computers is used to control processes, synchronize them, and report their status. Small sensor-based systems provide real-time process-control handling while recording the occurrences of events at each process and reporting them to a supervisory level. The computers at the supervisory level coordinate the sensor systems and report status, parts count, etc., to a host computer for corporate planning, inventory control, etc.

tree structures, file addressing — Specific switching or data file addressing structures designed to select an element by reduction cascading or all members of a set by expansion cascades. If used in chained data structures, the addresses associated with each item have multiple pointers to other items, i.e., to the next row member and the next column member.

trend — To print or record variable values.

triad — A group of three bits or three pulses usually in sequence on one wire or simultaneously on three wires.

trial divisor — An initial approximation in the dividing arithmetic process.

trial run — The procedure which is used to check for accuracy of methods. A sample card deck or part of the actual-run data may be used for the check.

tributary circuit — A circuit that connects as an individual drop, or drops, to a switching center.

tributary station — A station (on a channel) which is not a control station.

trigger — A bistable electronic device used to store information, to generate gates, and to condition AND and OR circuits, etc.

trigger bistable — A circuit which has two stable states requiring excitation triggers to cause a change from one state to the other. The excitation may be caused by first one and then the other of two inputs or by alternating two signals or excitations of a single input. Same as binary pair and flip-flop.

triggering — The starting of circuit action, which then continues for a predetermined time under its own control.

trip computer — A small computer used in a vehicle to obtain current information on fuel consumption, driving range on remaining fuel, number of miles to destination, and other information.

triple address — *Same as* address, three.

triple-length working — The use of three machine words to represent a number to enhance precision.

triple precision — The retention of three times as many digits of a quantity as the computer normally handles; e.g., a computer whose basic word consists of 10 decimal digits is called upon to handle quantities with 30 decimal digits.

tristate — Pertaining to an output configuration found in several logic families which is capable of assuming three output states: high, low, and high impedance. This feature is useful for interconnecting large numbers of devices on the same wires while allowing only one to control the levels of the lines at a given time.

trouble-location problem — A test problem that, when incorrectly solved, supplies information on the location of the faulty component. It is used after a check problem has shown that a fault exists.

troubleshoot — To isolate and remove the mistakes in a program caused by the malfunction of a computer. (Related to diagnostic routine.)

troubleshooter problem — *See* problem, troubleshooter.

true complement — *Same as* complement.

true time — *Same as* time, real.

true-time operation — *See* on-line, real-time operation (OLRT).

truncate — 1. To drop digits of a number of terms of a series, thus lessening precision; e.g., the number 3.14159265 is truncated to five figures in 3.1415, whereas one may round off to 3.1416. 2. To terminate a computational process in accordance with some rule.

truncation error — Error resulting from the use of only a finite number of terms of an infinite series.

trunk — 1. One or more conductors used for distributing signals or power from one or more sources to one or more destinations. (Synonymous with bus.) 2. A path for the transfer of data or signals.

trunk circuit — A circuit that connects two data-switching centers.

trunk (communications) — A trunk is a telephone line between two central offices that is used to provide communications between subscribers.

trunk, digit transfer — A set of wires used to transfer numbers (electrical pulses) which represent data and instructions to various registers and counters. However, on-off and similar transfer lines or control signals are not considered digit transfer trunks.

trunks, peripheral — *See* peripheral trunks.

truth table — A listing which presents all possible input and output states of a logical function.

truth table tabulation — A tabulation relating all output logic states to all necessary or possible combinations of input logic states for sufficient successive time intervals (t_n, t_{n+1}) to completely characterize the static and dynamic functions of the logic microcircuit, expressed in logic states or appropriate symbols.

TTL — Abbreviation for Transistor Transistor Logic (Sometimes abbreviated T^2L.) A family of integrated circuit logic elements with a specific output structure. The output stage consists of a pair of transistors. In a zero state (output low), the upper transistor is off and the lower transistor is on. In the one state (output high), the lower transistor is off and the upper transistor is on. In this way, the output stage has the ability to source or sink a large amount of current if necessary, but does not have to dissipate this power if not needed since only one transistor is on at a time. In addition, the active current source of TTL allows higher speeds.

TTL, Schottky — A type of TTL with a speed twice to three times that of conventional TTL.

tty — Abbreviation for teletypewriter.

tty asynchronous operation — Generally, the input of a tty (teletypewriter) to a computer is an asynchronous operation because the inputs occur at a rate not constant in frequency and phase with respect to a master clock; that is, they occur at random times determined by the system operator, not the computer clock.

tty replacement crt's — In a tty replacement crt terminal, incoming information appears character by character on the screen and forms into lines that scroll on the screen as new information arrives. When the screen is filled, the appearance of a new character causes the oldest line to disappear. Used as an input device, a tty replacement crt terminal exhibits each character of input information as the operator types that character. Again, when the screen fills, the next character extinguishes the oldest line.

tube — A tube in EDP (electronic data-processing) systems refers usually to a cathode-ray tube that is used to display data.

tube, cathode-ray — Abbreviated crt. A vacuum tube in which an electron beam can be focused to a small diameter on a luminescent screen. The concentrated beam can be varied in position and intensity to produce a visible pattern.

tube, display — A cathode-ray tube used to display information.

Turing machine — *See* machine, Turing.

turnaround document — *See* document, turnaround.

turnaround system — In character recognition, a system in which the input data to be read are printed by the computer with which the reader is associated.

turnaround time — 1. The particular amount of time that is required for a computation task to get from the programmer to the computer, onto the machine for a test or production run, and back to the programmer in the form of the desired results. 2. The elapsed time between submission of a job to a computing center and the return of results. 3. In communications, the actual time required to reverse the direction of transmission from sender to receiver or vice versa when using a two-way alternate circuit.

turning, page — *See* page turning.

turnkey console — In personal computers, a low-cost switch control panel for operator control of power, initialize, and execution.

turnkey system — A system for which the supplier has total responsibility for construction, installation, and testing, including hardware and software.

TUTOR, electronic teaching — A teaching machine which makes use of programmed instructions in a computer to help each student achieve the desired educational goals. Each student communicates with the computer via an individual terminal. The computer is programmed to adjust its teaching style automatically to the needs of each student, and each student progresses independently of others.

tutorial lights — On some "intelligent" terminals, programmable indicator lights can be interlaced with the transaction sequence providing tutorial lead-through to an operator and/or providing a pictorial history of keyboard action while entering a transaction.

tv magazine — In the Ceefax system, data is arranged into 100-page magazines. The average access time to any page in the magazine is 12.5 seconds.

tv monitor terminals — Many microcomputer hobbyists and small-business users adapt standard tv sets for many applications as terminals. Although outboard radio-frequency modulators allow input connection directly on the antenna terminals on the set, such interface circuits must first meet stringent FCC regulations for legal operation.

tv terminal — Abbreviated TVT. A computer terminal that generally consists of a keyboard and a crt display. Typically, this unit utilizes an ordinary or modified tv set as a display.

twin check — A continuous duplication check achieved by the duplication of hardware and/or an automatic comparison of data.

two-address — An instruction that includes an operation and specifies the location of an operand and the result of the operation. *See* code, multiple-address.

two-address code — A specific instruction code containing two operand addresses.

two-address instruction — *See* multiaddress.

two-address instruction system — A machine-language instruction that has two addresses, but both may reference data.

two-input subtracter — *Same as* subtracter, half.

two-key rollover — To prevent the wrong code from being entered when more than one key is struck, most encoders furnish two-key rollover. When two keys are pressed, the first switch closure delays the second key command until the first key returns home.

two-level address — *See* address, indirect.

two-out-of-five code — A code in which each decimal digit is represented by five binary digits of which two are ones and three are zeros, or vice versa.

two-pass assembler — An assembler which requires scanning of the source program twice. The first pass constructs a symbol table. The second does the translation.

two-phase modulation — A method of phase modulation in which the two significant conditions differ.

two plus one address — *See* address format.

two-plus-one address instruction — *See* address, three.

twos complement — *See* complement.

two-state variable — A variable which assumes values in a set containing exactly two elements, often symbolized as 0 and 1. This is often confused with double-value variable, i.e., $y = \pm\sqrt{x}$. (Synonymous with binary variable.)

two-, three- or four-address instruction — An instruction consisting of an operation and 2, 3, or 4 addresses, respectively. The addresses may specify the location of operands, results or other instructions.

two-valued — *Same as* binary variable.

two-wire channel — A channel for transmission in only one direction at a time.

TWX — Teleprinter exchange service with real-time direct connection between subscribers.

type bar — *See* printer type bar.

type bar, fixed — A type bar on a printer which cannot be removed by an operator and thus giving to that printer unit a fixed alphabet.

type bar, interchangeable — A printer type bar which can be removed by the operator to change from one alphabet to another.

type face — In optical character recognition (OCR), a character style with given relative dimensions and line thicknesses. (Contrasted with type font.)

type font — A type face of a given size, such as 12-point Gothic.

type font, optical — A font developed as a medium that can be read by both people and machines.

typeout key respond — A particular push button on a console inquiry keyboard which locks the typewriter keyboard and permits the automatic processing to continue.

U

UA — Abbreviation for User Area.

UART — Abbreviation for Universal Asynchronous Receiver Transmitter. A specific device that will interface a word parallel controller or data terminal to a bit serial communication network.

UART transmitter/receiver — An abbreviation for Universal Asynchronous Receiver/Transmitter that accepts parallel input data and transmits it serially. The receiver converts serial input data to parallel output data by inserting the desired number of start bits at the beginning of the transmitted word and stop bits at the end of the word. Parity bits can be inserted. Data is transmitted out at a data rate (baud rate) determined by the transmitter data clock. The receiver section checks for a valid start bit at the beginning of a serial data word, converting the incoming data to a parallel output word. The receiver checks for parity and overrun errors.

UCS — Abbreviation for User Control Store. A part of the control store set aside for the user's microprogram.

UDC — Abbreviation for Universal Decimal Classification.

ultraviolet erasable PROMs — ROMs are usually thought of as having permanent binary information programmed into their memories. Once information is programmed into an ordinary ROM, it cannot be altered. However, various types of PROMs are erasable. These types of PROMs permit information stored semipermanently to be erased and new information to be reprogrammed in. One type of erasable PROM can be erased by concentrated shortwave ultraviolet light. It is housed in a 16-pin dual in-line package (DIP) with a quartz top that is transparent to shortwave ultraviolet light. When it is desired to change the contents of the device, the unwanted information is simply erased by directing ultraviolet light through the quartz "window" of the IC and reprogramming as desired.

ultraviolet light erasing — EPROM, erasable programmable read-only-memory, chips may be erased by exposure to high intensity shortwave ultraviolet light at wavelength 2537 A. The recommended integrated dose (i.e., UV intensity × intensity time) is 6 Ws/cm². The devices are made with a transparent quartz lid covering the silicon die. Conventional room light, fluorescent light, or sunlight has no measurable effect on stored data, even after years of exposure. However, after 10 to 20 minutes under a suitable ultraviolet concentrated light source, the device is erased to a state of all zeros or all ones. It is recommended that no more ultraviolet light exposure than necessary to erase the EPROM should be used to prevent damage to the device. CAUTION: WHEN USING AN ULTRAVIOLET SOURCE OF THIS TYPE, ONE SHOULD BE CAREFUL NOT TO EXPOSE ONE'S EYES OR SKIN TO THE ULTRAVIOLET RAYS BECAUSE OF THE DAMAGE TO VISION, OR BURNS WHICH MIGHT OCCUR. IN ADDITION, THESE SHORTWAVE RAYS MAY GENERATE CONSIDERABLE AMOUNTS OF OZONE WHICH IS ALSO POTENTIALLY HAZARDOUS.

unallowable code — *See* check, forbidden-combination.

unallowable code check — *Same as* check, forbidden-combination.

unallowable digit — A character or combination of bits which is not accepted as a valid representation by the computer or the machine design or by a specific routine and suggests malfunction.

unallowable instruction digit — *See* instruction digit, unallowable.

unary operator — An arithmetic operator having only one term. The unary operators that can be used in absolute, relocatable, and arithmetic expressions are positive (+) and negative (−).

unattended concentrator program — Programs for concentrators aid the host computer by guarding against system failure. If an unattended concentrator's program is randomly lost, on some systems, down-line load features are available to let the host processor reload the program automatically, getting the remote system back on-line almost immediately.

unattended data acquisition system — Generally these compare performance with preset criteria and record the out of tolerance specification for later transmission. Often they also provide multiple-diagnostic tests that can automatically sequence from "gross" tests to more definitive tests, thus providing the operator with more specific data.

unattended operation — Operation of a terminal without the intervention or assistance of an operator. Implies that automatic answering and remote device control features are incorporated in the system.

unattended standby time — *See* time, standby unattached.

unbalanced error — *See* error, unbalanced.

unblind (blind) — The selective controlling of a transmission printer or reperforator. Used, for example, to prevent prices from typing on a receiving teletypewriter.

unblocking — The process of separating and obtaining one or more records from a block in the memory.

uncommitted storage list — Blocks of storage that are chained together and not allocated at any specific moment.

unconditional — 1. Subject to a specific instruction only. 2. Without any conditions; e.g., an unconditional statement is executed whenever it is encountered during a routine or program.

unconditional branch — An instruction of basic importance that develops a deviation from the program-execution sequence despite existing conditions.

unconditional control transfer instruction — An instruction which always causes a jump, i.e., an unconditional jump.

unconditional jump — *Same as* unconditional branch.

unconditional transfer — *Same as* unconditional branch.

unconditional transfer of control — *Same as* unconditional branch.

underflow — 1. In an arithmetical operation, the generation of a quantity too small to be stored by the register or location that is to receive the result. 2. The generation of a quantity smaller than the accepted minimum, e.g., floating-point underflow.

underflow characteristic — A situation developed in floating-point arithmetic if an attempt is made to develop a characteristic less than −99.

undetected-error rate — The ratio of the number of bits (unit elements, characters, blocks) incorrectly received but undetected or uncorrected by the error-control equipment, to the total number of bits, unit elements, characters, and blocks that are sent.

unidirectional — A connection between telegraph sets, one of which is a transmitter and the other a receiver.

uniformity, ink — *See* ink uniformity.

uniform system — *See* system, uniterm.

union catalog — Often means a compiled list of the contents of two or more tape libraries.

union gate — *Same as* gate, OR.

unipolar (in contrast with bipolar) — 1. When both true and false inputs are represented by the same electrical voltage polarity, the signal is defined as unipolar. 2. When a logical true input is represented by an electrical-voltage polarity opposite to that representing a logical false input, the signal is defined as unipolar.

unit, AND — *Same as* gate, AND.

unit, anticoincidence — *Same as* gate, exclusive OR.

unit, arithmetic — The portion of the hardware of a computer in which arithmetic and logic operations are performed. The arithmetic unit generally consists of an accumulator, some special registers for the storage of operands and results, supplemented by the shifting and sequencing circuitry for implementing multiplication, division, and other pertinent operations. Synonymous with ALU (arithmetic and logic unit).

unitary code — A code having only one digit; the number of times it is repeated determines the quantity it represents.

unit, audio-response — *See* audio-response unit.

unit, control — The portion of a computer that directs the sequence of operations, interprets the coded instructions, and initiates the proper instructions to the computer circuits.

unit, data — A set of one or more related characters that is treated as a whole group. Often used in place of a field (memory) to specify a particular unit of information.

unit, data-adapter (communications) — *See* data-adapter unit (communications).

unit diagnostics — A unit diagnostic program is used to detect malfunctions in such units as the input/output and the arithmetic circuitry.

unit, digital multiplier — *See* digital multiplier unit.

unit, display — Generic term used to describe any of the scores of output devices which provide visual representation of data.

unit element — Alphabetic-signal element having a duration equal to the unit interval of time.

unit, equality — A device with output signals that represent 1 when signals representing identical n-bit numbers are applied to both inputs.

uniterm — A word, symbol, or number used as a descriptor for retrieval of information from a collection, especially such a descriptor used in a coordinate indexing system. Related to card, aspect, descriptor, indexing, coordinate docuterm.

uniterming — The selection of words, considered to be important and descriptive of the contents of a paper for later retrieval of the articles, reports, or other documents. The selected words are then included in a uniterm index.

uniterm system — A data-recording system used by libraries, based on classifying keywords in a coordinate indexing system.

unit, functional — *See* functional unit.

unit, hypertape — Magnetic tape units which use cartridges, house the supply and take-up reels, and perform automatic loading.

unit interval — The length of time of the signal element in an equal length code signaling system. Usually, the duration of the shortest signal element in a coding system using isochronous modulation.

unit, linear — *See* linear unit.

unit, logic — *Same as* unit, arithmetic.

unit, magnetic tape — *See* magnetic tape unit.

unit, manual input — *See* input unit, manual.

unit, monitor — *See* monitor unit.

unit, on-line — Input/output device or auxiliary equipment under direct control of the computer.

unit, operational — A combination of devices or a circuitry which performs a computer process.

unit, OR — *Same as* gate, OR.

unit, processing — A part of a computing system which is the primary arithmetic and logical performing module.

unit record — 1. A separate record of information which is similar to other records. 2. The medium, usually punched cards, used to record the "unit record." 3. The equipment and methods used to repetitively process unit records in order to sort, calculate, and produce various summary reports of the data contained in unit record form.

unit, segregating — *See* segregating unit.

units position — The furthermost right position or the low order location. In the number 1054, the 4 is in the units position.

unit string — A string of characters but one which has only one member, much like a null string which has no members.

unit, tape — *See* tape unit.

unit, tape-processing — *See* tape-processing unit.

unit, transport — A specific piece of peripheral equipment or media handling device such as a card feed.

universal button box — A coined term for a set of push buttons whose functions are determined by the computer program.

universal decimal classification — An expansion of the Dewey decimal classification started by P. Otlet in Brussels; sometimes referred to as the Brussels system.

universal synchronous receiver/transmitter — Abbreviated USRT. A typical USRT is a single chip MOS/LSI device that can totally replace the serial-to-parallel and parallel-to-serial conversion logic required to interface a word-parallel controller or data terminal to a bit-serial, synchronous communication network. The USRT consists of separate receiver and transmitter sections with independent clocks, data lines, and status. Common with the transmitter and receiver are word length and parity mode. Data is transmitted and received in an NRZ format at a rate equal to the respective input clock frequency. Data messages are transmitted as a contiguous character stream, bit synchronous with respect to a clock and character synchronous with respect to framing or "sync" characters initializing each message. The USRT receiver compares the contents of the internal Receiver Sync Register with the incoming data stream in a bit transparent mode. When a compare is made, the receiver becomes character synchronous, formatting a 5-, 6-, 7-, or 8- bit character for output each character time.

universal Turing machine — A Turing machine that can simulate any other Turing machine.

UNIX — A multiprogramming operating system developed at Bell Laboratories that features sophisticated software and text-developing utilities.

unload — To remove information in massive quantities as in unloading the storage contents onto a magnetic tape.

unmodified instruction — *See* instruction, unmodified.

unpack — 1. To decompose packed information into a sequence of separate words or elements. 2. To recover the original data from packed data. 3. To separate combined items of information each into a separate machine word.

unscheduled maintenance — *See* maintenance, corrective.

unscheduled maintenance time — *Same as* maintenance time.

unused combination — *Same as* check, forbidden-combination.

unused command — *Same as* character, illegal.

unused time — That time which is available for machine operations but which is left unused and most often unattended by any computer system personnel; i.e., since seven 24-hour periods per week total 168 hours, total time is the addition of attended time and unused time, i.e., just rest time.

unwind — To code, explicitly, at length and in full all the operations of a cycle, thus eliminating all red-tape operations in the final problem coding. Unwinding may be performed automatically by the computer during assembly, generation, or compilation of a program.

update — 1. To modify a master file with current information according to a specified procedure. 2. To apply all current changes, additions, and deletions (substitutions) to a new file. 3. To modify an instruction so that the address numbers it contains are increased by a stated amount each time the instruction is performed. 4. During the checkout period, the updating run deletes and adds programs, corrections, test data, etc., to the master program file.

update cursor — Circuitry that allows a user to add new material into a video terminal memory and display. The cursor, which locates the current entry location, is generally a blinking underline (although some are overlines or boxes).

update, program master-file — Programs from the old master file are deleted, corrected, or left unchanged and new programs are added from the transaction tape. Updating can include changing of program job assignments. A new program master file is produced.

up time — The time during which equipment is either producing work or is available for productive work. (Contrasted with down time.)

usage error — *See* error, usage.

USASCII — Abbreviation for USA Standard Code for Information Interchange. The standard code, using a coded character set consisting of 7-bit coded characters (eight bits, including parity check), used for information interchange among data processing systems, communications systems and associated equipment. The USASCII set consists of control characters and graphic characters. (Usually seen as ASCII.)

user — The person or company using a remote terminal in a time-shared computer system for the purpose of entering a program for execution by the computer.

user area (UA) — The area on a disk where semipermanent data may be stored. This area is also used to store programs, subprograms, and subroutines. This area is contrasted with reserved areas that contain compilers, track and sector information, etc., which may not be written into.

user class of service — A category of data transmission provided in a network in which the data signaling rate and terminal operating mode is standardized.

user file, time-sharing — *See* time-sharing user file.

user modes, time-sharing — *See* time-sharing user modes.

user number — *See* number, user.

user-oriented languages, time-sharing — *See* time-sharing user-oriented languages.

user's group — Organizations made up of users of various computing systems to give the users an opportunity to share knowledge they have gained in using a digital computing system and exchange programs they have developed.

USRT — Abbreviation for Universal Synchronous Receiver/Transmitter. A general-purpose communications interface that allows a high-speed synchronous communications device to transmit data to and receive data from a microcomputer system. It connects to the peripheral device via separate serial transmit and receive lines and to the system address bus through PIA. Often the USRT has separate internal receiver and transmitter sections, which can be blocked by two separate clocks. Many have the capability to handle different word lengths, generate and check parity and other conditions, detect sync during receive, and send a fill character during transmit operation.

utilities — The standard routines that are usually furnished free with the purchase of a computer system that are, in effect, "housekeeping" programs.

utilities, executive-system — Included within the utilities section of the executive system are diagnostic routines, program file-manipulation routines, file-utility routines, and cooperative routines for aiding the user in performing such functions as reading cards, printing line images on a printer, transferring files from device to device, and carrying out housekeeping functions required for file residence on mass-storage devices.

utilities, interactive — Routines (interactive) that load and punch, display and alter memory and registers, trap, step, search memory for value, fill memory with value, hex add and subtract, relocate programs, display block of memory, and so on.

utility control console — A computer console that is primarily used to control utility and maintenance programs.

utility functions — Auxiliary operations such as tape searching, tape-file copying, media conversion, and dynamic memory and tape dumps.

utility program — A standard routine used to assist in the operation of the computer, e.g., a conversion routine, a sorting routine, a printout routine, or a tracing routine.

utility routine — 1. A standard routine, usually a service or housekeeping routine. 2. A subroutine for controlling machine functions or machine-produced conditions that have little relation to the actual processing of data.

utility routines, executive-control — Utility routines are contained as an integral part of the executive system. These are programs that are useful for data conversion, editing, etc. A description of the individual utility routines provided with the executive system is given in the individual write-ups of the utility routines. Utility routines are loaded and executed from the master file by an executive-control statement. Frequently used programs may be added to the system as utility routines. These programs may then be called, through the executive, from the master file.

utility routines (Honeywell) — Update and select program. A program under control of input director cards, this program performs master-file update, program selection and directory listing.

utility system — A system or program that is developed to perform miscellaneous or utility functions such as card-to-tape, tape-to-printer, and other peripheral operations or suboperations.

utilization loggers system — A program or a device that collects statistical information about how the system is operating.

utilization ratio, data-transmission — The data-transmission ratio of useful or acceptable data output to the total input of data.

utilization, time — The arrangement of a program which allows processing to continue while records necessary for processing are being located in file and read into main and working storage.

V

VAB — Abbreviation for Voice Answer Back. An audio response unit is a device which can link a computer system to a telephone network to provide voice responses to inquiries made from telephone-type terminals. The audio response is composed from a vocabulary prerecorded in a digital-coded voice or a disk-storage device.

vacuum servo — That peripheral device which maintains a magnetic tape reservoir, maintained by the absence of air pressure on one side of the tape. *See also* tape reservoir.

validity — 1. Correctness; especially the degree of the closeness by which the repeated results approach the correct result. 2. A relative measure of the quality of being sound, correct, efficient, etc.

validity check — 1. A check for accuracy of character representation. 2. A checking technique based on known reasonable limits on data or computed results. For instance: a man cannot work 400 hours in one week, a month does not have 32 days, an hourly classified man very seldom has a net pay greater than $350.00 per week, etc. Also called a reasonableness check.

validity, data — *See* data validity.

value — A value designed to serve as a minimum or maximum control value and often compared with the value of some index, count, or signal to determine if the anticipated maximum or minimum has been attained.

value, absolute — A particular quantity, the magnitude of which is known by the computer but the algebraic sign is not relevant.

value, index field — The contents of the 3-bit index (X) field of an instruction word (bit 12–14), designating one of the current general registers 1–7 as an index register.

value, place — The representation of quantities by a positional value system.

valve control amplifier — *See* amplifier, valve control.

variable — 1. A symbol whose numeric value changes from one repetition of a program to the next, or changes within each repetition of a program. 2. In COBOL, a data item in storage that assumes different values during execution of the object program.

variable address — An address that is to be modified or has been modified by an index register or similar device.

variable, binary — *See* binary variable.

variable, binary-state — *See* binary variable.

variable block — The number of characters in a block of memory is determined by the programmer.

variable connector — *See* connector, variable.

variable, controlled — A quantity, condition, or part of a system which is subject to mainipulation, regulation, or control by computer.

variable-cycle operation — *See* operation, variable-cycle.

variable, dependent — A variable whose value is determined by some function of another quantity or representation, i.e., the standard expression is y =f (x), where y is considered the dependent variable because its value is determined by the value of x and the nature of the function to be performed.

variable field — A field in which the scalar (or vector) at any point changes during the time under consideration.

variable field length — A data field that may have a variable number of characters. This requires item separators to indicate the end of each item.

variable field storage — An indefinite limit of length for the storage field.

variable format — *See* format, variable.

variable (FORTRAN) — A variable is a symbolic representation (name) that will assume a value. This value may change either for different executions of the program, or at different stages within the program. For example, in the following statement, both I and K are variables: K = 3 I.

variable function generator — A particular function generator which operates with reference to a set of values of the function which are present within the device with or without interpolation between these values, i.e., a cam for mechanical analog representation.

variable, integer (FORTRAN) — An integer variable usually consists of a series of not more than six alphameric characters (except special characters), of which the first is I, J, K, L, M, or N. The value of I will be assigned by a preceding statement and may change from time to time, and the value of K will vary whenever this computation is performed with a new value of I. As with constants, a variable may be integer or real, depending on whether the value that it will represent is to be integer or real, respectively. In order to distinguish between variables that will derive their value from an integer as opposed to those that will derive their value from a real number, the rules for naming each type of variable are different.

variable length — *See* length, variable.

variable-length fields — Information is stored in variable-length memory areas called fields. A field is defined as a group of consecutive memory locations whose contents are treated as a unit. Each location within a field stores either six binary digits or one alphanumeric character. Since fields can be of any length (from one memory location up to virtually the maximum number of locations), information units of varying lengths can be stored without wasting memory capacity.

variable-length instructions — A feature which increases memory efficiency by using only the amount necessary for the application and increases speed because the machine interprets only the fields relevant to the application. Halfword (2 byte), two-halfword (4 bytes), or three-halfword (6 bytes) instructions may be used.

variable-length record — *See* record, variable length.

variable-length record file — A file containing a set of records that vary in length.

variable-length word — A computer word in which the number of characters is not fixed but is variable and subject to the discretion of the programmer, i.e., storage locations, registers, parallel logic wiring, and gating are arranged in such a way as to handle a character or digit singly, but in storage each character is addressable and thus may be considered a word.

variable, local — A variable whose name is known only to the subprogram to which it belongs.

variable, manipulated — In a process that is desired to regulate some condition, a quantity is altered by the computer in order to initiate a change in the value of the regulated condition.

variable name — *See* name, variable.

variable point — Pertaining to a number system in which the location of the point is indicated by a special character at that location.

variable-point representation — A specific radix notation in which each number is represented by a single set of digits, the position of the radix point explicitly indicated by the inclusion of an appropriate character.

variable-precision coding compaction — A data compaction procedure accomplished using precision which is reduced in relation to the magnitude of the function, the time, the independent variable, or some other parameter.

variable quantity — A quantity that may assume a succession of values.

variables, integer (FORTRAN) — An integer variable consists of a series of not more than six alphanumeric characters (except special characters), of which the first is I, J, K, L, M, or N.

variables, real (FORTRAN) — A real variable consists of a series of not more than six alphanumeric characters (except special characters), of which the first is alphabetic but not one of the integer indicators, i.e., I, J, K, L, M or N.

variable symbol — In assembler programming, a variable symbol that does not have to be declared because the assembler assigns them read-only values.

variable time — *See* time scale.

variable time scale — *See* time scale, extended.

variable time scaler — *See* time scale.

variable, two-state — *See* binary variable.

variable, two-valued — *See* binary variable.

variable word — The specific feature in which the number of characters handled in the unit is not constant. For contrast, *see* fixed word.

variable word length — 1. A phrase referring to a computer in which the number of characters addressed is not a fixed number but is varied by the data or instruction. 2. The number of positions in a storage field is determined by the programmer.

variation indicator — An instruction that changes an operand or command.

VDT — Abbreviation for Visual Display Terminal. VDTs include all devices which permit input to a computer (by a user, not a computer operator) through a keyboard and/or some other manual input method (light pen, cursor controls, function buttons), and whose primary output method is visual (i.e., volatile or soft copy) display of alphanumeric and/or graphical information. Excluded are devices with only a few characters' worth of display capacity—say, under 100—since that normally implies that they have a special purpose. Many terminal devices—POS, banking, credit verification, industrial data-collection terminals, etc.—now employ visual display devices using various technologies.

vector — 1. The term for a symbol which denotes a directed quantity, i.e., one which cannot be completely described except in terms of both magnitude and direction (e.g., wind velocities, voltage and currents of electricity, and forces of all kinds). 2. A 1-dimensional array.

vector algebra — Manipulation of symbols representing vector quantities according to laws of addition, subtraction, multiplication, and division which these quantities obey.

vector diagram — An arrangement of vectors showing the relationships between alternating quantities having the same frequency.

vectored interrupt — An interrupt scheme where each interrupting device causes the operating system to branch to a different interrupt routine. This scheme is useful for very fast interrupt response.

vectored priority interrupts — Various maskable products that can be used with time counters for external inputs or dedicated external inputs. Each vector jumps the program to a specific memory address.

vectored restart — The capability of automatically clearing the system during restart, saving program steps.

vector graphics — The most common class of graphics is called vector graphics. All vector output consists of lines and curves drawn point-to-point by the output device as ordered by the computer. The other class is called raster graphics. The computer orders each picture element (PIXEL) darkened or not, usually in a regular pattern such as a television scan.

vector, interface — In some systems, the interface vector is the input/output path between the microcontrolled system and the user equipment. Each bit in the interface provides a program addressable, buffered, bidirectional path. Both the microcontroller and the user have simultaneous access to each bit for read or write operations. Bits are often grouped into 8-bit interface vector bytes to simplify user control of the interface and access by the program. In one system the processor treats the interface vector as an n-word, variable field, random access storage. Control elements in the interpreter specify the word to be accessed as well as the bit position and length of the data field to be read or written.

vector, transfer — A table that contains a list of transfer instructions of all the programs that are in core, which enables transfers of control to be made from one program to another program.

Veitch chart — *See* chart, Veitch.

Venn diagram — A diagram in which sets are represented by closed regions.

verb — In COBOL, an instruction word that specifies one or more operations to be performed by a data processor.

verbs, processor — Verbs which specify to the processor the procedures by which a source program is to be translated into an object program. Such verbs do not cause action at object time.

verbs, program — Verbs which cause the processor to generate machine instructions that will be executed by the object program.

verification — That act which attempts to make analytical comparisons of data and which indicates or rejects two sets of data which fail to compare accurately.

verification mode — In systems with time sharing, a mode of operation under the EDIT command in which all subcommands are acknowledged and any textual changes are displayed as they are made.

verifier — 1. A manually operated punchcard machine that reports, by means of visual signals, whether a card is punched as intended. 2. A device, similar to a card punch, for checking the inscribing of data by rekeying.

verifier, tape — A device designed for checking the accuracy of punched tape by comparing previously punched tape with a second manual punching of the same data, with the machine signaling discrepancies.

verify — 1. To check, usually with an automatic machine, one typing or recording of data against another in order to minimize the number of human errors or mistakes in the data transcription. 2. In preparing data for a computer, to make certain that the data prepared is correct.

verify, key — *See* key-verify.

vertical feed — Indicates the attitude in which a card is placed in the hopper, enters, and traverses the card track.

vertical format — Pertaining to the vertical arrangement of data, as viewed by an observer of a document.

vertical parity check — *Same as* check, even parity.

vertical processor — A microprogrammed computer that uses a narrow microinstruction word. This restricts the number of micro-orders per microinstruction, but makes microprogramming easier.

vertical redundance — An error condition that exists when a character fails a parity check; i.e., has an even number of bits in an odd-parity system, or vice versa.

vertical table — A table where the bytes of each entry are stored sequentially. That is, entry one, byte one, entry two, byte one, etc. FORTRAN stores arrays in this manner.

V format — A data record format designed so that the logical records are of variable length and each record begins with a record length indication.

video-data interrogator — A terminal unit that is comprised of a keyboard and separable associated display, providing a terminal facility for conventional communications lines.

videodisc computer system — The simplest system consists of a television receiver, a videodisc player, and a remote-control key pad with which to operate the player. The typical disc is thin, flexible, and transparent. In practice, one never sees or touches the disc itself; it is stored in a cardboard cassette. When the cassette is placed in the player, the machine removes the disc and then reinserts it into the cassette when playback is finished.

videodisc microprocessor — A microprocessor that facilitates the interfacing of a videodisc player with computers and other data processors. The microprocessor also lets the viewer control the display in self-instructional audiovisual devices using search, etc.

videodisc, optical — In an optical unit, the pickup system involves a low-power laser beam so that no physical structure touches the tracks on the disc. The laser is located under the disc surface, which is sealed with a plastic coating to prevent contamination of the information by dust or fingerprints. The laser reads the video and two audio tracks through this protective covering.

videodisc parameters — Some of the pertinent parameters that apply to all videodisc systems are playing time, signal-to-noise ratio, track width, and highest spatial frequency. The three classes of systems are mechanical, capacitive, and optical.

video display units, data transmission — Any type of input/output equipment with a special feature of displaying information on a screen.

video generator — A device that accepts commands from the keyboard and drives the tv monitor. On many units, a 2K × 16 RAM is included in the module for storing display area patterns and microcode for graphic symbols.

videograph — High-speed cathode-ray printer.

videoscan optical character reader — A unit that combines OCR (optical character reader) with mark sense and card read. It can read printing and marks in the same pass. It can read holes in cards.

video-screen management — Such activities relate to direct cursor positioning, cursor control functions, programmable character blink features, screen erase and character repeat keys, and others.

violation subroutines — *See* subroutines, violation.

virgin coil — Tape completely devoid of punches.

virgin medium — That storage medium in which no data is recorded, i.e., paper which is completely unmarked, or paper tape which has no holes punched in it.

virtual — Apparent, as contrasted with actual or absolute.

virtual address — The immediate address or real-time address.

virtual address, effective — The virtual address value after only indirect addressing and/or indexing modifications have been accomplished, but before memory mapping is performed.

virtual addressing — *Same as* addressing, immediate.

virtual address space — In virtual storage systems, the virtual storage assigned to a job, terminal user, or system task.

virtual call — A user communications facility in which a call set-up procedure and a call clearing procedure will determine a period of communication between two DTEs, in which user's data will be transferred in the network in the packet mode of operation. All user's data is delivered from the network in the same order in which it is received by the network.

virtual circuit — A synthetic equivalent of a real circuit (point to point) derived from a store-and-forward packet network. Data packets are kept in sequence at the deliver point (though not necessarily in transit).

virtual copy — The production of an essentially exact copy of the contents of locations in the memory of a computer onto an external bulk storage device, including reproducing the information regarding the exact memory addresses in which the data being stored resides. The addressing information is required so that the data can be restored later to the exact same locations in the exact same format in the computer as though the memory contents had never been altered. The process of making a "virtual copy" allows a program to be completely removed and then later restored to a computer leaving no trace of the interruption.

virtual memory — *See* memory, virtual.

virtual memory address — *See* memory address, virtual.

virtual memory concepts — Two important concepts of virtual memory systems are those of address space and memory space. The address space is the set of all locations used by a program, both instruction and data. The memory space is the set of actual hardware locations available on the machine. Programs running under virtual memory will generally have their address space much larger than the memory space. A mapping or function from the address space to the memory space is needed. Normally virtual memory space is needed. In other words, the address used by a program may not correspond to the actual hardware address of the item being referenced. Therefore, something is needed to translate a program or virtual address into a hardware address. Normally virtual memory systems have special hardware which will intercept all program addresses and send them to be translated. In addition, many systems also have hardware address translation routines which generally involve a hardware table with entries for each page in memory.

virtual memory pointer — An aid for storage efficiency. Some computers are designed so that parts of programs and data may be scattered through main memory and auxiliary storage. Various pointers or lists of pointers automatically keep track of the location of these program portions. The user of computers so designed may be unaware of this scattering procedure and most often operates computing procedures as though he were using normal memory.

virtual memory types — Demand-paged virtual memory uses a mapping concept. It breaks up a program into "pages" of small equal size and stores them on a fast disk or drum. It also logically divides physical memory into page-sized frames with hardware and manages the process of filling active physical memory with appropriate program pages on a demand basis. Segmented virtual memory does not use a map. Rather, a program is divided into a root portion and a number of other segments. The root remains memory resident and calls other segments as needed. The compiler generates the root and its segments, but the user must be sure that the real memory, or the part that he is using, usually his partition, is at least as large as the largest segment.

visible file — The grouping or systematic arrangement of forms, cards, or documents, so that data placed on the margin may serve as an index which the user can quickly see without the necessity of withdrawing each item.

visual display interface — A numeric or alphanumeric visual display that conveys the results of computation or measurement to the observer.

visual display terminals — Abbreviated VDTs. VDTs include all devices which permit input to a computer (by a user, not a computer operator) through a keyboard and/or some other manual input method (light pen, cursor controls, function buttons), and whose primary output method is visual (i.e., volatile or soft copy) display of alphanumeric and/or graphical information. Excluded are devices with only a few characters' worth of display capacity—say, under 100—since that normally implies that they have a special purpose. Many terminal devices—POS, banking, credit verification, industrial data collection terminals, etc.—now employ visual display devices using various technologies.

visual error representation — When a transmission has not been properly received after three successive tries, the third transmission will be printed. The line will be transmitted again and may be printed for comparison with the third transmission.

visual inquiry station — Usually an input/output unit which permits the interrogation of an automatic data processing system by the immediate processing of data from a human or terminal (automatic) source, together with the display of the results of the processing . . . in many cases, on a cathode ray tube (crt).

visual scanner — 1. A device that scans optically and usually generates an analog or digital signal. 2. A device that optically scans printed or written data and generates their representation.

visual terminal types — There are several alternative technologies to crt terminals, including plasma panel displays, magneto-optic displays, and injection electroluminescence light-emitting diode (LED) displays. In displays having a very small number of characters, plasma panel and LED techniques are being used. From a longer range standpoint the LED technology is perhaps the most promising because of its compatibility with other semiconductor LSI technologies.

vocabulary — 1. A list of operating codes or instructions available to the programmer for writing the program for a given problem for a specific computer. 2. A group of characters occupying one storage location. This unit of information is treated and transported by the computer circuits as an entity; it is treated by the control unit as an instruction, and by the arithmetic unit as a quantity.

vocabulary size, voice system — The number of utterances (words or short phrases) that can be distinctly recognized and digitally encoded. The larger the vocabulary, the more complex the source data that can be handled without special software.

vocabulary, sophisticated — An advanced and elaborate set of instructions. Some special chips can perform only the more common mathematical calculations such as addition, multiplication, and subtraction. A computer with a sophisticated vocabulary in chip form can go beyond this and perform operations such as linearization, extract square root, and select highest number.

voice answer back — *Same as* VAB.

voice frequency — A frequency lying within a part of the human audio range. Voice frequencies used for commercial transmission of speech usually lie within the range of 200 to 3000 hertz.

voice-grade channel — A channel which is suitable for transmission of speech, digital or analog data, or facsimile.

voice-grade service (voice channel) — This term originally referred to a service provided by the common carriers that included a circuit capable of carrying a voice transmission. Now, when used in reference to the transmission of data, it also refers to a circuit of sufficient bandwidth to permit a data-transfer rate up to 2400 bits per second. Primarily the term distinguishes this service from teleprinter grade service in reference to regulatory agencies' tariffs.

void — In character recognition, the undesired absence of ink within the outline of a character as might occur in magnetic ink characters or optical characters and is most often due to defects in the inks, paper, or printing process.

volatile — A characteristic of becoming lost or erased when power is removed, i.e., the loss of data where it is not returned or recovered when power is restored. Some such units, as tape units, are in a volatile condition if such a power loss occurs.

volatile file — A temporary or rapidly changing program or file.

volatile memory — This is a standard read/write memory whose content is irretrievably lost when operating power is removed by accident or as contrived. Virtually all types of read/write semiconductor memory are volatile, but new technologies are being introduced to avoid this possible calamity.

volatile storage — A storage device in which stored data are lost when the applied power is removed, e.g., an acoustic delay line.

volatility — The aspect of loss or alteration of electrical energy in storage.

volatility of storage — The tendency of a storage device to lose data when the electric power is cut off. Storage media may be classed as volatile (e.g., electrostatic storage tubes) or nonvolatile (e.g., magnetic tape).

volume statistics — The groups of various pertinent facts in relation to the nature and level of operations of an area under consideration expressed in numbers (e.g., number of sellers, number of different items, orders, purchases, etc.), plus, or including, subclassifications of these data to obtain a clear understanding of the pattern of the operations.

volume test — The processing of a volume of actual data to check for program malfunctions.

voluntary interrupt — An interrupt to the processor or operating system caused by an object program's deliberate use of a function known to cause an interrupt, and hence under program control.

von Neumann sort — A technique used in a sort program to merge strings of sequenced data. The power of the merge is equal to T/2.

VS — Abbreviation for Virtual System. A type of operating system under which the user utilizes the system in a method that appears to be accessing more main storage than the system actually has. A virtual system emulates this extra storage. Used on batch and time-sharing systems.

VTAM — Abbreviation for Vortex Telecommunications Method. A special data communications software package that organizes and simplifies data-communications programming to serve remote workstations for a host computer.

VTR — Abbreviation for Video Tape Recorder. VTRs are open-reel machines that do not take video cassettes or cartridges. (VCR is the abbreviation for Video Cassette Recorder.)

W

wait — The condition a real-time program meets when it requires information from a file-storage unit and is forced to "wait" until the required file record is accessed and brought into the main memory. File-oriented systems have this characteristic that leads to multiprogrammed approaches by interleaving and overlapping "wait" times for one program to achieve process time for another program.

waiting lines (queuing theory) — When a flow of goods (or customers) is bottlenecked at a particular servicing point, losses accumulate in the form of lost business, idle equipment, and unused labor. Minimizing such costs involved in waiting lines, or queues, is the object of queuing theory, an O/R (operations research) technique for the most efficient handling of a waiting line at a particular service point.

waiting list — A procedure for organizing and controlling the data of unprocessed operational programs. These lines are ordinarily maintained by the control program.

waiting mode time sharing — *See* time sharing, waiting mode.

waiting state — The state of an interrupt level that is armed and has received an interrupt trigger signal, but is not yet allowed to become active.

waiting time — *Same as* latency, the time interval between the instant the control unit signals the details, addresses, etc., of a transfer of data to or from the storage unit and the instant the transfer commences.

WAIT macroinstruction — In multithread processing, the presentation of a request on one message that causes a delay so that no processing can go on. A WAIT macro is given which shifts control to a supervisory program so that work may continue on other messages. Work on the delayed message will continue only when the cause of the delay is removed.

wait time — The time interval during which a processing unit is waiting for information to be retrieved from a serial access file or to be located by a search.

warning marker, destination (DWM) — A reflective spot on the back of a magnetic tape, 18 feet from the physical end of the tape, which is sensed photoelectrically to indicate that the physical end of the tape is approaching.

waste instruction — *Same as* instruction, dummy.

watchdog — This type of equipment is used to discern whether some prescribed condition is present, usually within a predetermined time period. Also called invigilator.

watchdog timer — A timer set by the program to prevent the system from looping endlessly or becoming idle because of program errors or equipment faults.

WATS (Wide Area Telephone Service) — A service that provides a special line allowing the customer to call a certain zone (or band), on a direct-distance dialing basis, for a flat monthly charge. The continental United States is divided into six bands for the purpose of determining rates.

waveform generator — A circuit driven by pulses from the master clock; it operates in conjunction with the operation decoder to generate timed pulses needed by other machine circuits to perform the various operations.

way-operated circuit — A circuit shared by three or more stations on a party-line basis. One of the stations may be a switching center.

way station — A telegraphic term used to refer to one of the stations on a multipoint network.

wear resistance — Manufacturers of printing ribbons advise that they have built-in resistance to resist severe reduction to produce images after first-runs and normal use.

weighted average — A moving average performed on data in which some of the values are more heavily valued than others.

wheel, printer — *See* printer wheel.

wheels, type — *Same as* print wheel.

Wide Area Telephone Service — *See* WATS.

Williams tube — A cathode-ray tube used as an electrostatic storage device of the type designed by F. C. Williams, Manchester University.

Williams-tube storage — *See* Williams tube.

winding — A conductive path, usually of wire, that is inductively coupled to a magnetic device.

wire board — *See* board.

wired OR — Externally connecting separate circuits or functions so that the combination of their outputs results in an "OR" function. The point at which the separate circuits are wired together will be a "1" if any circuit feeding into this point is "1."

wire, magnetic — A wire made of, or coated with, a magnetic material and used for magnetic recording.

wire printer — *See* printer, wire.

wire wrap — A method of making an electrical connection in an electrical circuit by wrapping wires around specially designed terminals.

wiring board — *See* control panel.

word — 1. A set of characters that occupies one storage location and is treated by the computer circuits as a unit and transported as such. Ordinarily a word is treated by the control unit as an instruction, and by the arithmetic unit as a quantity. Word lengths are fixed or variable, depending on the particular computer. 2. A unit of data. A set of characters that may be of any length and occupies one storage location. A word is usually treated as a unit by a data processing machine. Quantities, dollar amounts and names are examples of words. 3. In telegraphy, 5 characters plus 1 space, or 6 keystrokes.

word, alphabetic — A specific word entirely of characters of an alphabet or special signs and symbols—hyphens, semicolons, etc.

word arrangement, communications — The standard communication subsystem accommodates four types of computer input/output words. They are the function word, input-data word, output-data word, and output-data request word.

word, banner — The first word in a file record.

word/byte/nibble — These terms are often misused in describing microprocessor data. For a specific microprocessor, a word is the number of bits associated with the instruction or data length. This can be 4, 8, 16 bits, etc., depending on the machine. A byte specifically refers to an 8-bit word; a byte can be manipulated by a 4, 8, or 16-bit microprocessor. For example, instructions are often provided to deal with byte data in 4- or 16-bit processors. This is called byte handling, and is independent of the natural word size of the machine.

A nibble is 4 bits, and it takes two nibbles to make a byte. Nibble (or 4 bit) control can be found on many 8-bit word machines as well as on some 16-bit machines. Four-bit operations are usually associated with hexadecimal (HEX) or binary coded decimal (bcd) operations.

word, call — That set of characters designed to identify, label, or place a subroutine or data into the subroutine itself or into a program of which a subroutine is a part. The call word acts as the identifier.

word capacity — The selection of one of the word lengths of the equipment as a datum and thus to classify different operations as partial or multiples of these lengths for working.

word, check — A machine word is often used to represent a check symbol and this is appended and printed to the block, thus signifying the check.

word, communications status — The status word is sent to the central processor in the same manner as the input data word, except that an external interrupt signal is generated after the channel synchronizer has placed the word on the input data lines. In this way, the central processor can distinguish status words from input data words.

word, computer — A group of characters

(bits) which are treated as a unit and which are stored in one computer storage location, each word being addressable, such words being instruction words with address and operation parts or a data word with alphanumeric characters of fixed or real numbers. Parts of computer words are syllables, bytes, etc.

word, connective — A COBOL reserved term to denote the presence of a qualifier. It may also be used to form a compound condition.

word, control — A word in the memory, usually the first or last of a record, or first or last word of a block, that carries indicative information for the following words, records, or blocks.

word, duoprimed — A computer word containing a representation of the 6, 7, 8, and 9 rows of information from an 80-column card.

word, ERROR status — This status word indicates that the remote computing system has detected an error.

word, fixed — The limitation of equipment as to the constant number of characters which the equipment will handle.

word, fixed-length — *See* fixed-length word.

word generator, manual — *Same as* generator, manual number.

word-half — A group of characters that represent half of a computer word for addressing purposes as a unit in storage.

word index — The contents of a storage position or register that may be used to automatically modify the effective address of any given instruction.

word, information — *See* information word.

word, instruction — *See* instruction word.

word key — *See* key.

word length — The number of bits or characters which are handled as a unit by the equipment, as a size of the field.

word length computer, variable — A computer designed to treat information having a variable number of bits.

word length, data — *Same as* word capacity.

word length, double — Many arithmetic instructions produce two word results. With fixed-point multiplication, a double-length product is stored in two A registers of control storage for integer and fractional operations. Integer and fractional division is performed upon a double-length dividend with the remainder and the quotient retained in the A registers.

word location, effective — The storage location pointed to by the effective virtual address of a word-addressing instruction.

word, long — The longest or lengthiest computer word which a particular computer can handle. They may be made up of full words, two full words, or a double-length word.

word, machine — A unit of information of a standard number of characters which a machine regularly handles in each transfer; e.g., a machine may regularly handle numbers or instructions in units of 36 binary digits. This is then the machine word.

word-mark — An indicator to signal the beginning or end of a word.

word, numerical — A word which consists entirely of digits of some numeration system, as a decimal system, and not of characters of an alphabet, which is not normally used to assign number value.

word, operational — A COBOL term used to denote a word that improves readability of the language but need not be on the reserved list.

word, optional — Words introduced in a COBOL program to improve readability.

word-organized storage — A specific type of storage which is composed of magnetic cells in which each word of the storage has a separate winding common to all the magnetic cells of the word, i.e., carrying the read and possibly the write pulse also.

word-oriented — Refers to the type of memory system used in early computers. The memory system is divided into sections called "words," each of which has a location number and contains enough bits of binary digits to hold about 10 numeric positions.

word, parameter — A word in a subroutine which contains one or more parameters which specify the action of the subroutine or words which contain the address of such parameters.

word, partial — A programming device which permits the selection of a portion of a machine word for processing.

word pattern — The smallest meaningful language unit recognized by a machine.

It is usually composed of a group of syllables and/or words.

word period — The size or magnitude of the time interval between the occurrence of signals representing digits occupying corresponding positions in consecutive words.

word processing — Abbreviated WP. Operations including interactive information-retrieval systems, management information systems, text editing, translation, and typesetting.

word-processing communication — When word processors are equipped with communications capability, some of the initial input and much of the editing can be done remotely. Word processors communicating in a dial-up mode can establish a network allowing a draft to be routed for review and comment before being delivered to a central facility for final composition.

word-processing/computer hybrid system — One type of hybrid system allows users to perform applications such as order entry, inventory control, sales analysis, and payroll. Word-processing applications include the preparation of general correspondence, form letters, and standard reports. The unit facilitates the preparation and editing of reports that may require several drafts before the final printing, the creation of documents from a library of stored paragraphs, and the printing of form letters from stored documents with addresses supplied from a mailing list that is also stored.

word processor, microcomputer-based — One of many types of office automation systems. A typical unit has super and subscripts, repagination, document assembly capability, and standard editing functions. Such units typically include diskette drive and daisy wheel printer.

word, ready status — This status word indicates that the remote computing system is waiting for a statement entry from the terminal.

words, constant — Descriptive data that is fixed and does not generally appear as an element of input.

word, selectable-length — The ability of a programmer to assign a number of characters to each item of data. The words must be long enough to handle the longest item, and spaces not used are filled with blanks or zeros.

word separator — A character in machine coding that segregates fields.

word, serial operation — The specific feature of certain handling equipment in which words are read one immediately after another in groups.

words, function — The function word contains the operating instructions for the peripheral units, its format depending upon the particular subsystem.

word, shortest — A word of the shortest length a computer can use, and which is most often half of the word length of the full length word.

word sizes — Since a single bit can represent 0 or 1, programmers must code larger numbers by grouping bits into words in some rational way. Common word sizes include 6, 8, 12, 16, 18, 24, 32, and 64 bits. Thus a computer that groups bits in 16-bit words is referred to as a 16-bit machine; a computer whose logic is based on 8-bit words is referred to as an 8-bit machine.

By common convention, the bits of a word are numbered from right (0 for the low order bit) to left (7 for the high order bit). Some computer manufacturers reverse the convention, numbering from left to right.

words, mask — The mask word modifies both the identifier word and the input word which is called up for a search comparison in a logical AND operation.

word space — The actual area or space occupied by a word in serial digital devices such as drums, disks, tapes, and serial lines.

words, reserved — The words which are set aside in COBOL language which cannot be used as data names, file names, or procedure names, and are of three types: connected, optional, and key words.

word, status — This status word indicates that the remote computing system has deleted some information.

word time — 1. The time required to transfer a machine word from one storage position to another. 2. Especially in reference to words stored serially, the time required to transport one word from one storage device to another. *See* access time.

word time comparator — That circuitry which compares the word time counter with the specified word time at the moment of coincident pulse. This is done in order to verify that the correct word is being read.

word transfer — Transmission is of entire words (24 bits in parallel). The 24 bits are transferred between the computer and the external device at one time. This means that no breakdown of words into characters, on output, or assembling of characters into words, on input, takes place. This provides an increase of four times the input/output speed over character transfer, assuming the external device can accept or send words at that rate (some systems).

word, variable-length — A computer word in which the number of characters is not fixed but is variable and subject to the discretion of the programmer, i.e., storage locations, registers, parallel logic wiring and gating are arranged in such a way as to handle a character or digit singly, but in storage each character is addressable and thus may be considered a word.

work area — A portion of storage in which a data item may be processed or temporarily stored. The term often refers to a place in storage used to retain intermediate results of calculation, especially those results which will not appear directly as output from the program.

work cycle — The series or sequence that is necessary to perform a task, job, or execution and yield a unit of production, and which recurs in similar order for each task or unit of work. As the last element of the task is completed, the first part of the series is started anew for the succeeding job or unit of production.

work-distribution chart — 1. A listing or inventory of the duties, responsibilities, and sequence of the personnel in the job or task force under study. 2. The establishment of each duty relationship performed by the individual in relation to the specific task or function, which includes brief volumes-of-occurrence indicators, and the estimated and projected times to perform each item of work.

work flow — Operations designed so that several tasks may be conducted simultaneously. This is opposite from serial development, in which tasks must wait until the completion of one before another can begin.

working area — *See* storage, working.

working data files — *See* data files.

working, double-length — *Same as* double precision.

working equipment — The basic or primary set of equipment for modules in which more than one set is available and the other sets are standby equipment in the event of a failure of the working equipment.

working memory — The internal memory which stores information for processing.

working, multiple length — Refers to the use of two or more machine words to represent a number and to thus increase precision, i.e., the use of double-length procedures, double precision, etc.

working, on-line — The performance of operations on data in such a way that the circuits of the equipment operating are under the control of central processor or mainframe, i.e., when on-line, data from the connected peripheral equipment or from another system is processed as soon as it is received and without manual intervention.

working, pseudo-off-line — A type of operation on data in such a way that the operations are completed on equipment connected to the mainframe, but under the control of a separate routine which is running in parallel or concurrently with the mainframe, i.e., the transfer of data from cards to tape while under mainframe control, but for later use.

working ratio, real-time — *See* time scale.

working, real-time — *Same as* real-time operation.

working routine — That routine which produces the results of the problem or program as it was designed, as contrasted with the routines which are designed for support, housekeeping, or to compile, assemble, translate, etc.

working, simultaneous — *Same as* simultaneous operations.

working space — A portion of the internal storage reserved for the data upon which operations are being performed. (Synonymous with temporary storage, and contrasted with program storage.)

working standard — A specified combination of a transmitting and receiving system, or subscriber's lines and feeding circuits (or equivalent systems), connected by means of a distortionless variable attenuator, and employed under specific conditions to determine, by comparison, the transmission quality of other telephone systems or parts of systems.

working storage — *See* storage, working.

working, synchronous — *See* synchronous computer.

working, triple-length — The use of three machine words to represent a number to enhance precision.

work-in-process queue — Items that have had some processing and are queued by and for the computer to complete the needed processing.

work load — The assigned amount of work to be performed in a given period.

work measurement — A procedure or set of rules for the establishment of a relationship between the quantity of work performed and the man (and/or machine) power used. Some systems also measure this relationship with a quality base, or a productivity quantum or ratio.

work process schedule — Under general direction, schedules operating time of the overall electronic data processing activity in order to ensure that the data-processing equipment is effectively and efficiently utilized.

work queue, input — A list or line of jobs ready or submitted for processing but not yet begun or in process. Usually, these tasks are input on a first-come, first-served basis, such as an input queue consisting of programs, data, and control cards settled and waiting in the input job stream. Schedulers and special operating systems handle and control such queues differently.

work queue, output — Various data which are output are often not immediately printed or processed into final form, but are stored on some type of auxiliary storage device and become part of a queue which is programmed with control information for disposition of this information. Often the computer system is printer-bound or can operate only as fast as the printer can perform.

work, serial — *Same as* serial flow.

workspace — The amount of memory required by a program, over and above the amount of memory required to store the program itself. Workspace is typically used for input/output device buffer areas and for various other locations required by a program during its execution.

work-time, machine spoiled — Time wasted due to a computer malfunction during a production run.

worst case access time — The maximum amount of time required to go between the two most widely separated points (addresses) on a bulk storage device. For a tape unit, this would be the time required to traverse the entire length of the tape. For a fixed-head disk unit, it would be the time required for the disk to make one revolution.

worst-case design — The worst-case design approach is an extremely conservative one in which the circuit is designed to function normally even though all component values have simultaneously assumed the worst possible condition that can be caused by initial tolerance, aging, and a temperature range of 0°C to 100°C. Worst-case techniques are also applied to obtain conservative derating of transient and speed specifications.

worst-case noise pattern — Sometimes called a checkerboard or double-checkerboard pattern. Maximum noise appearing when half of the half-selected cores are in a 1 state and the other half are in a zero state.

WP — Abbreviation for Word Processing.

writable control store (WCS) — Control store implemented with RAM so that the user can dynamically alter the microprogram.

write — To transfer information to an output medium; to copy, usually from internal storage to external storage; to record information in a register, location, or other storage device or medium.

write addressing — Write addressing is controlled by a binary counter. Following reset, the first word entered is stored in address 000. Since the positive edges of many write clock pulses also toggle the write address counter, each data entry automatically increments the counter to the next memory location. Outputs are available on the binary counter and allow the register file to be enabled without additional decoding logic.

write after read — A technique of writing (restoring) previously read data into a memory device following completion of the read cycle.

write/backspace/read — In some units, when the terminal is in the write/backspace/read mode, all tape-write operations are verified. After each record is written, the tape is backspaced and read to make sure that the data are correct. If there is an error, the terminal attempts to write the data again up to nine times. This process is time consuming and is not normally required.

write data, disk — This operation is used to transfer data from the host to the system to be written onto the disk. The system uses the word count and disk address specified by functions (0) and (1) to write the data onto the disk. The system transfers data until the word count reaches zero or an error occurs. The disk address is updated after each sector transfer. The interface handshake procedure is the same as for functions (0) and (1), except that it is repeated once for each transfer as determined by the word count (some systems).

write head — A head used to transfer data to a storage device, such as a drum, disk, tape, or magnetic card.

write interval — The determination of the interval during machine operation when output data is available for an output operation, i.e., the net time exclusive of transmission which it takes to perform an output operation such as printing or writing on tape.

write key — A code in the program status doubleword that is used in conjunction with a memory lock to determine whether or not a program may write into a specific page of actual addresses.

write key field — The portion of the program status doubleword that contains the write key.

write lockout — *See* lockout, write.

write memory lock — A 2-bit write-protect field optionally provided for each 512-word page of core memory addresses (some computers).

write-only — The operation of transferring information from logic units or files.

write-process-read — The process of reading in one block of data, while simultaneously processing the preceding block and writing out the results of the previously processed block. Some special processors can perform concurrently on any two or three of these operations; others are limited to read/write.

write-read head — A small electromagnet used for reading, recording, or erasing polarized spots that represent information on magnetic tape, disk, or drum.

writer, output — A service program which moves data from the output work queue to a particular output device, i.e., a printer, voice output, or terminal. The output writer thus transfers the actual output, often from an output work queue to an output device, after it has determined the normal rate of speed of the device to be used.

write time — The amount of time it takes to record information.

writing head — A magnetic head that is designed and used to write as contrasted with the read head, with which it is often combined.

writing rate — The maximum speed at which the spot on a cathode-ray tube can move and still produce a satisfactory image.

writing speed — The speed of deflection of the trace on the phosphor, or the rate of registering signals on a charge storage device.

writing-while-read — Reading a record or group of records into storage from a tape at the same time another record or group of records is written from storage onto tape.

WS — Abbreviation for Working Storage. The specific area on a disk used to hold dynamic or working data. This area is contrasted to reserved area containing permanent information such as compilers, track and sector information, etc., and user area for semipermanent storage.

X

XEC — An instruction to execute register contents. This instruction allows the programmer to load the binary machine code representation into a working register and then have the CPU treat the contents of a working register as an instruction. If the programmer wishes to include optional features in a ROM program, he can include an XEC instruction in the ROM, then select and load the appropriate instruction code into the working register before branching to the ROM program. Read/write memory is usually manufactured in 4096-word modules, where each memory module occupies one slot on the memory bus. There are only a limited number of memory slots available on the memory bus.

xerography — A dry copying process involving the photoelectric discharge of an electrostatic charge on the plate. The copy is made by tumbling a resinous powder over the plate; the remaining electrostatic charge is discharged, and the resin is transferred to paper or an offset printing master.

X.25 packet switch protocol — A packet-switching protocol that has been adopted as an international standard for data sharing and file transfer between different vendors' hardware. This message protocol uses higher level data link control mechanisms, but the US protocol and IBM protocol are similar.

X-Y loading — An option that enables some RO terminals to be written from a data source that specifies, in parallel, both a character and the X-Y position on the screen at which the character is to be displayed.

X-Y plotter — A device used in conjunction with a computer to plot coordinate points in the form of a graph.

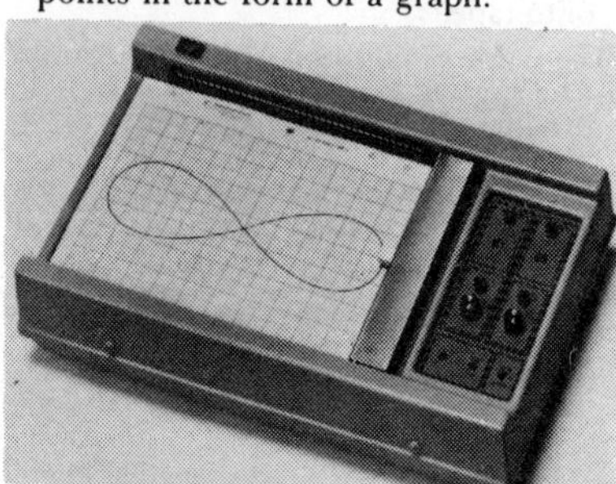

Courtesy Linear Instruments Corp.
X-Y recorder.

X-Y recorder — A recorder that automatically plots on graph paper two variables against each other, one on an X axis and the other on a Y axis. The paper, which can be of any type—linear, log-log, etc.—remains stationary, and the pen is moved across the paper in accordance with signals to the X and Y inputs of the recorder.

X-Y recorder acceleration — The peak pen acceleration of an X-Y recorder when the pen responds to a step input. Acceleration decreases as the pen approaches its maximum speed. Acceleration is the most significant specification in applications requiring fast dynamic response. Typical acceleration values range from about 150 to 3000 in/s² (381 to 7620 cm/s²).

X-Y recorder deadband — The largest input signal within the bandwidth of the recorder to which the pen will not respond, expressed as a percentage of full scale. Typical deadband ratings range from about 0.05 to 0.25 percent.

X-Y recorder dynamic specifications — Those specifications that relate to the motion of the pen (or other writing device); e.g., acceleration, slewing speed, etc.

X-Y recorder linearity — Terminal-based linearity is the maximum difference between the actual pen position and the theoretical position, based on the assumption that the zero point corresponds exactly to zero signal and that the full-scale point corresponds exactly to full-scale signal. Expressed as a percentage of full scale, a typical figure is 0.1 percent. (Some manufacturers use the "best straight line" definition of linearity, which is less precise than terminal-based linearity.)

X-Y recorder resettability — The measurement of the total distance separating the final resting points of the pen when the same point is approached from different directions. It is expressed as a percentage of full scale, and a typical value is 0.1 percent.

X-Y recorder response time — The time it takes for a strip-chart recorder to travel full scale. A typical response time is about 0.5 second.

X-Y recorder retrace — A quick test used to check the general performance of an X-Y recorder. An identical ramp voltage is applied to each axis, causing a straight line to be drawn. The ramp is then reversed, and the pen retraces the line. The smoothness of the lines indicates absence of mechanical binds and slide-wire nonlinearity. The opening between the lines at slow speeds indicates the amount of deadband and resettability. The opening between the lines at faster speeds indicates the phase shift between axes.

X-Y recorder slewing speed — The maximum speed attainable along either the X or Y axis of an X-Y recorder. Slewing speed is expressed in inches per second or centimeters per second; a typical slewing speed ranges from about 20 to 30 in/s (51 to 76 cm/s). Many recorder specifications include slewing speed as the only dynamic specification. A common misconception is that slewing speed is the single major contributor to good dynamic performance. In many applications, however, it is sometimes the least important. Most applications demanding fast pen response are limited not by slewing speed but by acceleration.

X-Y recorder static specifications — Specifications such as sensitivity, accuracy, deadband, etc., that are determined by the electrical characteristics of the recorder. Most static specifications are generally very close to the readability limitations imposed by the human eye.

Y

yoke — A group of heads in magnetic recording which are rigidly fastened and moved together for reading and writing on channels consisting of two or more tracks on magnetic tapes, disks, or similar media.

Z

zatacode indexing — *Same as* coordinate indexing.

zatacoding — A system of superimposing codes by edge-notched cards.

zero — 1. Nothing. 2. The combination of coded bits that the computer recognizes as zero. Positive-binary zero is usually indicated by the absence of digits or pulses in a word; negative-binary zero in a computer operating on ones complements is usually indicated by a pulse in every pulse position in a word; in a coded-decimal machine, decimal zero and binary zero may not have the same representation. In most computers, distinct and valid bit structures are used for positive and negative zero.

zero access — *See* access, zero.

zero-access addition — *See* addition, zero-access.

zero-access storage — The storage for which the latency (waiting time) is small.

zero address code — An instruction code which contains no instruction code for the next address.

zero-address instruction — Any of a number of techniques used to eliminate the storage of nonsignificant leading zeros.

zero-address instruction format — *Same as* addressless instruction format.

zero balancing (accounting) — Zero balancing is an effective method of verification when both detail items (e.g., accounts payable distribution cards or records) and their summary (e.g., an accounts payable disbursement card or record) are processed together. Each detail item is accumulated minus, and the summary plus. The result is a zero balance if both are correct.

zero, binary — *See* binary zero.

zero bit — The two high-order bits of the program counter are labeled the Z (zero) and L (link) bits. Typically the Z bit will be set to 1 whenever an operation results in the accumulator bits all being clean (accumulator contains zero value); the Z bit will be zero otherwise.

zero complement — *Same as* complement.

zero compression — That process which eliminates the storage of insignificant leading zeros to the left of the most significant digits. *See also* zero suppression.

zero condition — Relating to a magnetic cell, the state of representing one.

zero control, floating — The bit, in the program status doubleword, that indicates whether (if 0) or not (if 1) the result of a floating operation is stored if the characteristic is reduced below zero.

zero count interrupt — An interrupt level that is triggered when an associated (clock) counter pulse interrupt has produced a zero result in a clock counter.

zero elimination — *See* zero suppression.

zero-error reference — A constant ratio of incremental cause and effect. Proportionality is a special case of linearity in which the straight line passes through the origin. Zero-error reference of a linear transducer is a selected straight-line function of the input from which output errors are measured. Zero-based linearity is transducer linearity defined in terms of a zero-error reference where zero input coincides with zero output.

zero fill — A procedure which fills in characters with the representation of zeros but which does not change meaning or content.

zero flag — An indicator that is set to a logic 1 condition if a register being tested contains all 0s in its cell positions. It is set to a logic 0 state if any cell in the register is in a 1 condition.

zeroize — The procedure to fill storage space or to replace representations with zeros; i.e., the storage location may be cleared to zero, although doing so may not necessarily be the same as the meaning of zeroize.

zero kill — A specific feature of some sorters which determines that only zeros remain in the high order positions of documents while the documents are being sorted in lower order positions.

zero-level address — An instruction address in which the address part of the instruction is the operand.

zero-level addressing — *Same as* addressing, immediate.

zero-match gate — *Same as* gate, NOR.

zero page addressing — In some systems the zero page instructions allow for shorter code and execution times by only fetching the second byte of the instruction and assuming a zero high address byte.

zero page addressing, indexed (x,y indexing) — This form of addressing is used in some systems in conjunction with the index register and is referred to as "zero page, X" or "zero page, Y." The effective address is calculated by adding the second byte to the contents of the index register. Since this is a form of zero page addressing, the content of the second byte references a location in page zero. Additionally, due to the zero page addressing nature of this mode, no carry is added to the high order eight bits of memory, and crossing of page boundaries does not occur.

zero proof — A procedure or process of checking computations by adding positive and negative values so that if all computations are accurate the total of such proof would be zero.

zero state — The condition of a magnetic core in which the direction of the flux through a specified cross-sectional area has a negative value as determined by an arbitrarily specified direction for the negative normal to that area.

zero suppression — The elimination of insignificant zeros (those to the left of a quantity in a field or word) during a printing operation.

zone — 1. That portion of a character code that is used with the numeric codings to represent nonnumeric information. 2. A portion of internal storage allocated for a particular purpose.

zone bits — The bits other than the four used to represent the digits in a dense binary code.

zoned format — A binary-coded decimal format in which one decimal digit consists of zone bits and numeric bits and occupies an entire byte of storage.

zone, minus — That set of characters in a particular code which is associated with the adjacent bit which represents a minus sign.

zone, neutral — A range of values in the parameters of a control system in which no control action occurs.

zone, plus — A set of characters in a particular code which is associated with the adjacent bit which represents a plus sign.

APPENDIX A

Introduction to Modern Computer Technology

SECTION I

Introduction to the "All Digital" Era and the World of "Throwaway Computers"

A noted scientist[1] has commented, "We will have one digital world in which transmission, processing, computing, storage, and switching of voice, pictures, and data will be inextricably intertwined both in communications facilities and in their use." To accommodate the requirements of digital computers and to simultaneously increase speed and improve accuracy, reliability, and equipment cost effectiveness, many nationwide telephone systems are moving toward becoming all digital. "If it isn't digital, it will be" is a statement heard at practically all conventions and conferences that relate to appliances, automobiles, sound, broadcasting, music, and so forth. Many feel that the distinction between computers and communication has already been lost. Communication is as much a part of computing as computing is of communication. IBM is deeply involved as a partner with Comsat and Aetna Insurance in Satellite Business Systems, which will connect computers everywhere by way of "rooftop" antennas on homes and businesses. And AT&T, General Telephone and Electronics, and other telephone and communications companies are marketing computer equipment through subsidiaries.

The computer-communications confluence is evident among computer buyers, too, since industry figures reveal that 30 to 40 percent of computing budgets are now targeted to communications. Thus, we must be concerned not only with computerese but also with the language of communications, digital audio/video products, and so on; the languages of these technologies form a new language that might best be called "Electrospeak." Millions of electronically unsophisticated consumers now speak of bits, bytes, and bauds, of laser scanners, CCD cameras, and LVR video recorders.

Perhaps no single invention in history has influenced our evolving lifestyle so quickly and so radically as has the microcomputer. We are finding a changed world with sophisticated electronic devices in one form or another in virtually every household and industry. They are inside our refrigerators, tv sets, automobiles, traffic signals, industrial process controllers, and laboratory equipment. They are found in banks, retail stores, and doctors', lawyers', and dentists' offices. Practically every child loves computerized games. And, the new "game computers" quickly become practical major information and control systems for a few hundred dollars.

What is the basis for all this? It is the "chip"—the tiny ¼-inch square that contains an entire computer (Figs. A-1, A-2, and A-3). The microprocessor that manipulates information, the memory with the program to control the processing, the input-output ports that accept and transmit the information and data, and the timing systems that keep everything scheduled as designed and programmed are all on a single chip. And this chip often costs less than $5 in large quantities. (Some game and calculator chips cost as little as 99¢. Others, very complex and superfast, are as expensive as $90, but

[1] Dr. John A. Pierce, of California Institute of Technology, who while at Bell Labs received many awards for work in electron tubes, microwaves, and satellite communications, speaking at the Wescon meeting in San Francisco, Sept. 17, 1979.

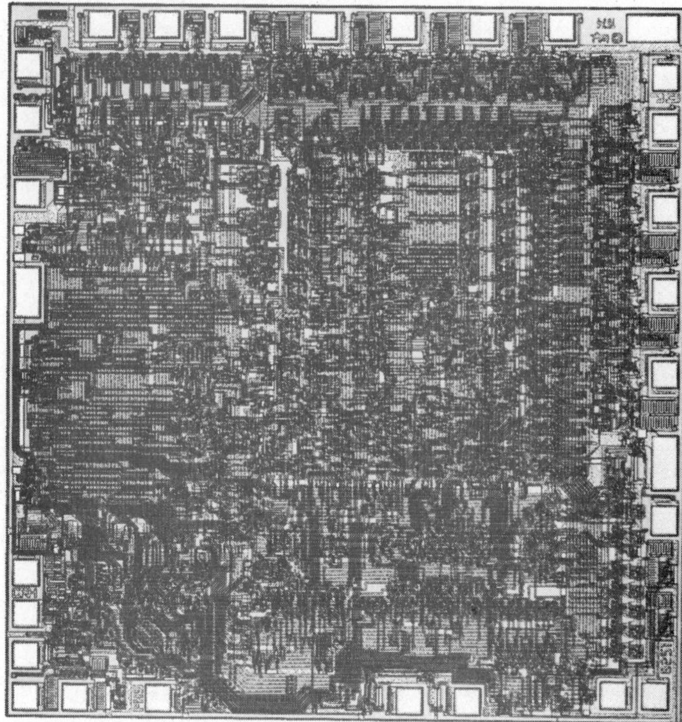

Courtesy Intel Corp.

Fig. A-1. Example of a microprocessor chip.

these have tremendous power and versatility.) The impact is that much of the world is moving into a new competitive nationalism based on an "information economy." The technological advances are changing basic institutions drastically. Information machines control military, energy, production, telecommunication, and business decisions. Offices, transportation, and entertainment systems are being automated. Already, some Third-World countries are not asking for steel mills—they want silicon production facilities.

What will be the major driving force for continually expanding applications of microelectronics? Many feel the strongest push will come from the massive use of these

Courtesy Intel Corp.

Fig. A-2. One type of package in which a chip may be mounted.

Courtesy Apple Computer, Inc.

Fig. A-3. Example of computer constructed with printed circuit board in which chip packages may be installed.

tiny "intelligence" controllers in communications. In 1978, some of the editors of *Scientific American* closely examined "the impact of this revolution in technology on virtually every area of contemporary life." In one of their microcomputer single-topic issues, they reported on "the ultimate ephemeralization of the computer." Perhaps the key sentence was: "Riding on integrated microelectronic circuits, the computer is disappearing into the devices and the machines that it operates, or that operate it."[2]

One of the major "futurist" braintrusters in the US enumerates the three great societal upheavals in the world to date as: (1) mankind's changeover from hunting to farming, (2) the 19th century Industrial Revolution move to factory production, and (3) the era of "cheap" computers which are expected to become as "pervasive as wristwatches." A prediction more easily related to everyday life was reported in the May 1979 issue of *Telecommunications:* " 'If computer technology costs continue to decline, the home terminal could become the ultimate two-way communication device for Americans,' says Security Pacific National Bank's futurist, Hank Koehn. Home computers are expected to penetrate the market significantly in the 1980s. 'By the 1990s, they may be commonplace. Americans may be able to stay home and take educational courses, access reference material from the library, prepare their taxes, do their grocery shopping, keep personal records, and even regulate their household security and environment.' Home terminals, video cassettes, and interactive visual devices will reduce commuting needs and permit increased leisure time. These remarks are based on information prepared for a forthcoming bank publication, *Tomorrow Begins Today,* which assesses societal trends and their potential future impact."

The revolutionary aspects of the microcomputer—low cost, small size, great computing power, automated mass production with annual output in the tens of millions, ease of programming, and so on—have had dramatic impact on the entire computer industry. The microcomputer has practically obsoleted many of the "giant" machines of the 1970s. Because the massive acceptance of microcomputers is so strong and so pervasive and because major manufacturers are rapidly switching many machines to "chip" architecture, all new computers are having positive effects on world inflation. The costs of computing are falling drastically while productivity and the number of workers who use computers increase at least as dramatically. Distributed processing places computers in many business settings where they have never been before—on the desks of accountants, lower-level managers, foremen, clerks, executives—and automated and "paperless" offices are being designed. This is all working successfully toward reduced costs and increased profits for both large and small enterprises. Computer customers are finding so many new thing to do with their computers that the investment payback periods are

[2] Quoted from a *Scientific American* advertisement as it appeared in *Computer*, July, 1978, p. 95.

running from three years down to as little as a single year, and this characteristic alone practically forces managers to see that such systems are available throughout the operations they control.

PERSONAL COMPUTERS—FROM HOBBYIST TOYS TO A SUPERGIANT INDUSTRY IN FIVE YEARS

A few hobbyist-kit computer companies experimented with a 4-bit chip in 1974. In 1975, Intel's first 8-bit microprocessor chip, the 8008, was used as the basis for crude computers that sold for about $400. *Popular Electronics* ran a cover picture and story on the MITS Altair kit and system in the December 1975 issue, and the small company (later absorbed into the Pertec Computer Company) was flooded with orders. Within a year or so, Commodore's PET mass-produced computer was in strong demand, first at $495, then $595, then $795. PET sales increased 192% to reach 25,000 in 1978 with practically no advertising expenditure. Apple Computer, Inc. moved from a small beginning to sales of $100,000,000 in 1979, strongly challenging Tandy Corp.'s Radio Shack, which had sales of 105,000 systems in 1978 after some near-saturation tv advertising. Cromemco, Inc. doubled its 1978 sales to $30 million in 1979, financing its growth entirely from profits.

Courtesy Texas Instruments Inc.

Fig. A-4. Home computer with slide-in software ROM cartridge.

Existing companies like Radio Shack and Commodore Business Systems and startup companies like Apple, Cromemco, Ohio Scientific, etc., rang up combined sales approaching a half billion dollars in 1978. Major toy companies—Atari, Bally, Mattel, APF, and others—demonstrated $500 to $1000 computers. Texas Instruments entered this market with the 99/4 model (Fig. A-4) and followed with several other models. The Hewlett-Packard Co. entered with products including floppy disks, light pens, plotters, and strong software. The Atari Model 800 for less than $1000 has power, utility, and expandable capability beyond those of a "game-type" computer. General Telephone and Electronics obtained a license to market Mattel's Intellivision under GTE's subsidiary names of Sylvania and Philco. The Mattel machine is being sold to cable customers as a "Playcable" machine. GTE is also heavily involved in tv data-base systems such as viewdata and teletext home and business tv information retrieval systems both with and without telephone assistance. Low-cost personal computers can be used for this two-way direct and instant data-base information retrieval tv capability. Zenith purchased the Heath Company in late 1979. Heath had earlier made a very successful entry into personal computers, doubling its sales each year to rise from nothing to 25% of its total $80 million business in 1978.

AT&T through its Canadian subsidiary had a long lead with computer-controlled tv data-base retrieval systems. Continental Telephone purchased a strong position in American Satellite. As early as July 1979, AT&T had conducted experiments with a phone-fed videotext Electronic Information Service. The company reported about 100 subscribers in Albany, N.Y. were loaned video terminals and keyboards for several weeks. Users had direct access to AT&T computers with directory listings and public service data such as sports, weather, and time. Its Canadian subsidiary had two previous years of experience.

SELLING COMPUTERS BY THE MILLIONS TAKES MASS MARKET MEDIA AND MILLION-DOLLAR PROMOTION BUDGET

Radio Shack's successful tv and print media campaign in 1978, which sold 105,000 computers, taught an important lesson: Ordinary people are really not afraid of computers or of complex systems, if they are properly presented, if they prove real value for dollars spent, and if the products are designed for easy use.

In late 1979, Atari ordered 2 million 16K (bit) dynamic RAMs on a split contract from four major suppliers: Hitachi, Motorola, National Semiconductor, and Toshiba. Memory capacity of 8000 bytes is shipped with each system, which makes this order sufficient to equip 500,000 systems. Atari had considerable market strength to back up this order. J. C. Penny used their most important catalog page, page 2, in their 1979-80 catalog to display the Atari machines. Sears pushed this brand hard in its catalogs and stocked the machines, disk drives, printers, and other equipment in 500 of its largest stores. Penny's stocked the Atari 400 initially but then went to the 800 also. Atari's tv campaign for fall 1979 included spots daily for 6 weeks on all three major networks. Atari added some other promotion pluses. One was an invoice discount of 5% to pay for 50% of local print and tv ads used by stores to follow through on the national tv and magazine campaigns. The big discount stores and catalog houses jumped on this program as did several major computer clubs and other marketing organizations, many with discounts to customers of up to 20% and special premiums of free or half-price Atari program cartridges. Because printed programs can be input from the keyboard, thousands of software types of games, home and business control programs, and so on would be advertised as designed specifically for the Atari with prices from $1 to $500—available in print, on cassettes, on disks, etc.

In 1979, IBM had 26 "retail" stores providing highly advertised computer lectures, and Digital Equipment Corp. had 15 stores. Texas Instruments and Heath had stores in many states and were expanding, while Radio Shack, besides its 7000 worldwide outlets, established 100 computer-only stores. Apple Computer, Inc. was at work to use tv, music, and appliance stores as outlets for its computers, and Bell & Howell had a franchise to sell Apple computers to educational institutions.

In 1978 more than 14 million microprocessors were sold. The great majority were 4-bit machines for games, appliances, and controllers. The million or so 8-bit microprocessors were the central processing units (CPUs) for personal computers, many onboard systems for design engineers, for computer students, for hobbyists. The 16-bit microcomputers that became popular in late 1979 are somewhat faster and more efficient.

Some of the other developments that "broke the dam" for the personal computer deluge were the entries into computer markets by paper and forms suppliers, by typewriter companies, by small European countries, and even by some Third World countries such as Nigeria. In 1979, Moore Business Forms, Inc. had sold office and computer supplies for 97 years and was an established leader in this area. Suddenly, in late 1979, it offered a complete office computer system, the MBS 20/50 based on a Texas Instruments microcomputer, the TI DS 990. It was initially priced at about $15,000, and it was competing against a word-processing–oriented computer system offered by the

A. B. Dick Co., a major supplier of duplicating machines and supplies. Both of these companies were competing against some electronic typewriters that were really computer systems—one, for example, from a transcriber company, Lanier, and another from Royal Business Machines, Inc. Its 9500 business computer with hard disk storage and special software for wholesalers and accountants was competing with another typewriter company turned computer company, Olivetti, Inc. These companies, thus, are preparing for the coming of the "paperless office."

Major office machines companies are active in the computer-communications sectors. Xerox products stretch from top-line word-processing systems to computerized, communicating copiers to satellite networks (XTEN) through new distributed processing systems. Exxon, the giant oil company, also has become a major factor in the computer-communications business. Zilog, Inc. is one of the major microprocessor chip makers, and it is owned and strongly backed by Exxon Enterprises, Inc. Exxon also has communication companies, voice input-output machine and laser companies, and several others. One of its newest and most intriguing is Xonex. It began developing an integrated electronic office network system. This is composed of management work stations that integrate filing, data-base access, word processing, electronic mail, the telephone, and other key office functions in a distributed environment. The firm's controller unit connects all these elements so that each work station can vary depending upon specific needs.

Integration of telephones and computers has become a distinctly important advance. For example, a telephone voice-input system that recognizes the speech of most callers and converts each word of a limited vocabulary into a unique digital code for computer entry is a significant accomplishment. Giving remote voice commands to computers and being identified specifically is a most desirable capability in industry, business, hospitals, laboratories, and even the home. Hitachi Ltd. of Japan is one firm that markets a system that uses standard word patterns stored in the system which have derived from the pronunciation of 100 persons, male and female, young and old, and disregards the individual differences among these speakers. The HR-150 speech-recognition system is designed to be connected to a single telephone circuit. For most applications, it is combined with a "confirming" display and an audio programmable speech-response system, both of which are readily available from Hitachi and others. The system is built around a fast 8-bit microcomputer, with one model using patterns for 16 words and another with patterns for 128 words.

In Europe, the British and West Germans began to move quickly into personal computers. The Online 1979 Microcomputer Show in London expanded its attendance from 3000 in 1978 to 9000 eager students, scientists, and business people a year later. One of its several popular small systems was a home/personal computer from Technologics Ltd. that provided viewdata, teletext data-base retrieval, and color computing designed for use with a standard domestic tv set. The system was available for from about $2000 to $2500 depending on peripherals wanted. Despite competition from American brands such as Apple, PET, Radio Shack, and others, a Belgian company, Data Applications International (DAI) successfully introduced its under $1000 personal computer. The Dutch educational tv system ordered 1000 of them to supply to its 13,000 students taking a computer hardware course and another 10,000 students taking a software course.

In Nigeria, Third World Microsystems, Ltd. by mid-1979 had sold shopkeepers, traders, and universities 20 of its systems and had orders for 110 more. It was ready to move into Zaire, Kenya, and Ghana.

A "THROWAWAY" MICROCOMPUTER—BRINGING COMPUTER HARDWARE TO THE LEVEL OF A CONSUMABLE COMMODITY

For under $1000, Computer Automation Inc. offers a full-power microcomputer, the Scout Model 4/04 (Fig. A-5), that is designed in a four-board configuration. Each board incorporates an optional built-in diagnostic capability; a factory-programmed ROM (read-only memory) effects a go/no-go test each time the power is turned on. If the board is functional, an LED lights. Thus, even an inexperienced technician can immediately isolate a system failure to the board level, and a quick repair can be accomplished by means of a board swap. With hardware costs decreasing due to competition

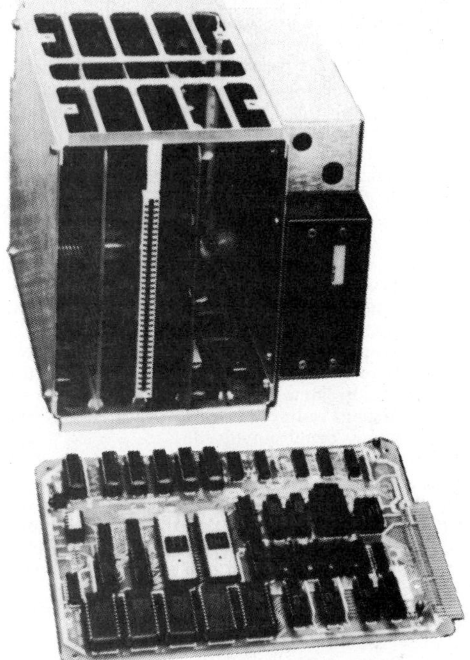

Courtesy Computer Automation, Inc.

Fig. A-5. Microcomputer with replaceable boards.

and mass production, some of the boards list in the $100 to $2000 range. If the system doesn't work, the user can check the status of each board automatically, request the appropriate replacement from the supplier, and throw the defective board away. No serviceman need make a call. With readily available spare boards, system downtime is minimized.

The economic basis for the disposable hardware derives largely from the soaring cost of repair. Even under near-perfect conditions, the supplier suggests it cannot test and fix a board that won't work, pay for the paperwork, and get the board back to the customer for less than $175; it costs something like $100 for administrative paperwork, $50 in parts and labor for even a minimum repair, plus $25 or so for shipping and insurance. And none of that expense reflects probable delay, mishandling, inconvenience, and downtime.

If millions of computers are to be sold, a natural question is, "Who will buy these millions of computers and for what purposes?" To provide some answers to this fundamental question, we offer the next section with some primary categories of users and/or applications for specific types of small computer systems.

SECTION II

The Impact of the Personal Computer

There are school computers, car computers, game computers, very small business computers, translator computers, energy-management computers, data-base computers, and more. Even such "noncomputer" companies as Comsat, General Telephone and

Electronics, AT&T, CBS, Knight-Ridder Newspapers, Associated Press, Dow-Jones, and others are involved in the personal computer business in one way or another.

What is this new and suddenly giant-sized industry all about? In 1977, 43,000 people bought personal computers. By 1978 the number was 240,000, and in 1979 over 825,000 people were projected to become users of personal computers. This does not include the stand-alone and desk-top mini and microcomputers that now appear in thousands of offices. These were generally in the $15,000 to $20,000 price range, and IBM had two in competition. When this manufacturer announced its "supermini" 4300 series, with the bare-bones machine at about $65,000, the rush to purchase was so great that some customers reported receiving delivery positions as far out as three years. IBM had expanded manufacturing capacity as much as practical. In mid-1979, soon after the introduction, it was announced that some $150 million worth of chips would be purchased from semiconductor companies over the next three years because IBM couldn't produce enough. It also went into the capital market for $1 billion in loan funds for expansion. At the same time this company was expanding, its minicomputer competitors as a group were growing at 30% per year, some as high as 50% and higher.

But what about your neighbor's home computer, your daughter's high school pals who take their "portables" to school, and their friends who use their below-$1000 systems to compose music, develop "new art," control model airplanes, and bring in two-way slow-scan tv with their ham radios? How did this all start, where is it going, and who are the companies already deeply involved?

The first mass-produced personal or home computer was the PET from Commodore Business Machines, Inc., which owns its own chip manufacturer, the MOS Technology, Inc. division. It was closely followed by the Apple. Apple was soon joined by ITT, which has the franchise to market the very popular color systems in Europe, and by Bell & Howell with the franchise to market the systems to educational institutions. Each company was moving machines at a rate of about 25,000 per year, but they have now more than doubled that capacity. Other pioneer companies selling more than 5000 each per year are: Ohio Scientific, Southwest Technical, Heath, Vector Graphics, Cromemco, Compucolor, Compal (Xerox part ownership), and a score or more of other companies.

At this point, a distinction must be made between microcomputers, personal computers, minicomputers, and standard computers. The microcomputer is a chip-based system that can become the basic ingredient of a personal computer and even some low-cost minicomputers. Thus, the word "microcomputer" is often used synonymously with "personal computer" but not with "minicomputer." Personal computers have four general characteristics: (1) they are based on tiny chips, (2) they have small and usually portable main frames, i.e., the processor, its main memory, and control circuitry, (3) they are very low cost, seldom over $1000 for the main frame, and (4) they are easy to use. Minicomputers are not usually chip computers, not often portable, not usually priced in the below $10,000 range, and not very easy to use. All microcomputers are not personal computers—they are used in communications, industrial applications, and so no. Standard computers are large, complex, expensive, and very fast.

Texas Instruments announced massive distribution contracts for its five models of personal computers with a price range from $400 to $10,000. Outlets include its own multiplying Texas Instruments Supply Stores (and maintenance centers), plus 500 US outlets of Moore Business Forms, and at least 500 "computer stores" including a half-dozen wholesaling chains. TI software is strongly promoted by using tv, magazines, and promotions by department stores, calculator shops, specialties stores, and so on. Hewlett-Packard announced three systems in the below $10,000 price range, and it already has three minicomputer systems in the below $50,000 range that compete with Data General, Wang, Quantel, Digital Equipment Corp. (200,000 sold to date), Datapoint, and others. Tektronix, one of the biggest names in instruments and crt terminals and display graphics, is strongly pushing its "intelligent" systems. RCA has a new personal computer division, a competitive $400 home system, and several educational models. Rockwell International is moving to compete model for model, and Zenith purchased the Heath Company, which has a "plug-and-go" line.

But, to understand fully the market power immensity of the personal computer market revolution, it is necessary to analyze the types of computer systems and users and the specific appeals to mass market purchasers. Several examples follow:

1. The most widespread use of personal computers may come about as a result of sales of low-cost data-base retrieval computers that will plug into the telephone.
2. Sooner and in equally large numbers will be sales of "game" computers very heavily merchandised on tv, in local ads, and in thousands of stores. These are often full computers with disks, etc.
3. As exciting as the first two are the translator-computers first introduced by Craig and Lexicon as simple translators. TI soon after offered a voice-output foreign language translator, and Quasar announced a competing product to TI. Matsushita, the largest consumer electronics company in Japan, acquired the manufacturing and distribution rights from Craig, and Nixdorf Computer Personal Systems of West Germany acquired the national and international rights of manufacture and sales from Lexicon. Matsushita will use their several brand names (Panasonic, National, Technics, etc.) and mass-produce millions.
4. Staying with the marketing of computers "in the millions," a clear example is the car computer as exemplified by retrofit types, the Avatar, the Autocomp, the CompuCruise, and the Prince On-Board systems for older cars. These cost from $150 to $350. But, the use of computers to control a dozen car functions (saving gas, etc.) may excite millions of users of both domestic and foreign auto models.
5. Energy conservation applications may become the strongest "patriotic" efforts and primary pocketbook issues. The first types for control of appliances, energy systems, etc., in homes were quickly followed by all types of building energy control micro and minicomputers.
6. More than 50 million calculators have been sold in America, many of them programmable types for under $100 or up to $300. Now less than $300, the TI, H-P, Casio, Sharp, and other models are becoming computers in their own right. Casio accepts cassette input; the H-P 41C has much of the full power of computers—alphanumeric output, graphic printing, push-in program cards, snap-in special memory and data. Most have music, some have voice output. Users must know computer language terms.
7. Computerized tv bringing near perfect stereo reception, pure color, scores of accessories and programmability features, near life-sized images, conversion of audio tape to pictures, low-cost printing of screen images, art and music ("light pen") composition, safety and security terminals, 8-12 hour copying of programs, two-way education with graphics, etc., means the use of one or several microcomputers within tv sets. Micros already appear in the best video-cassette recorder-players. Add to all this the microcomputer-controlled videodisc systems and the tv set as an all-around computer output device for data-base retrieval, and microcomputers in music, tv, and most entertainment systems may become near-universal.
8. Very small business systems computers and managers' desk-top computers are often heralded as the "biggest potential market" for micro and minicomputers. IBM, Sperry Univac, NCR, and others have models that sell from $30,000 down to $15,000 (IBM to $4500), and the minicomputer companies like DEC, Datapoint, etc., have models with $5000 to $10,000 price tags. Radio Shack has a $3400 system, TI has a $5000 system, and the new Hewlett-Packard systems range from $800 to $15,000. Cromemco, Inc. sells them by the dozens as time-sharing systems within that price range for the seven-terminal system. Practically every computer store attests to doctors, dentists, lawers, accountants, contractors, real estate agents, and other professionals as being their best customers—and there are 5 million very small businesses in North America.
9. Although managers will use millions of small computers as division and department computers, office automation is the strongest trend in business data processing today. Tens of thousands of firms are integrating their word processing and data processing departments. Telephone computers receive information from distant data banks, and computerized copiers now communicate with distant terminals as they also receive facsimile by satellite from a dozen major equipment suppliers.
10. A strong marketing effort is being conducted by Radio Shack to put their computers in classrooms. Apple computers are being aggressively pushed by Bell & Howell with historically strong ties to education markets. Cluster/One is a system

that permits the interconnection of 30 below $1000 school computers into "self-paced" learning environment classrooms. TI has just begun to enter the educational markets, and Hewlett-Packard is now ready also.

11. Personal computers to control hobbies and as hobbies were the basis for the earliest sales of microcomputers. Several hundred thousand hobby computers have been sold. There are clubs, newsletters, associations, flea markets, etc., and the movement continues to grow. Most of the more than 260,000 ham radio operators may soon have personal computers. A few hundred thousand model train, car, airplane, and boat enthusiasts are a potential market for $200 board-type control computers to make their favorite toys do scores of new tricks, win contests, and so on. The "build-a-robot" craze continues to surprise teachers, scout leaders, etc., as do the home-appliance, safety, and security-control systems being "invented" in garages. The home computer market is expected to be huge, and the "learning systems" at $100 to $400 by RCA, TI, and others are pushing this "computer-chip-and-board" customer hard.

What's Happening in Japan, in Europe, and around the world? One "beginner's guidebook" in Japan sold more than 350,000 in less than 20 months. More PET computers are sold abroad than in the US. Radio Shack computers are selling well in Japan, England, and elsewhere around the globe. But, the American industry is expecting an onslaught of Japanese and Far East computers. Since mid-1979, a dozen Japanese companies have shown and demonstrated their systems to potential American customers, and another dozen have begun selling them in Japan while they are also selling components to Hong Kong and Korean firms. West Germany had three personal computers in the markets in 1979, France two, and England eight, and their governments have contributed (or scheduled) up to $2 billion for educational and industrial development of personal computers. ITT "Apples" are strong in Europe.

The above areas of computer applications or examples of uses of specific types of small computers demonstrate some of the range and scope and particularly the power of "miracle chip" systems. It must be emphasized that many single and properly equipped computer systems can perform any and all of the above applications with the required peripheral equipment and the effective software.

Perhaps the two most significant areas not noted above relate to appliance computers (controllers) and communication-equipment computerized devices. The three forces mandating microcomputers within home and other appliances are: (1) The competitive edge these superfast, pervasive, and convenient controls add to these products forces a "follow-the-leader-or-die" market strategy. (2) The requirement by the Department of Energy for these appliance products to meet strict energy conservation standards and minimum operating efficiencies pushes controllers into practically every major device. (3) The reduction of parts count and thus costs coupled with extra automated diagnostics and redundancy reliability features make the addition of microcomputers wise engineering choices.

As regards communications, the phrase, "If it isn't digital, it will be" says it all. Digital telephone systems are spreading around the world much faster than in the US. Digital tv, music, and every form of communication known are becoming dominant very rapidly. Every movement of every piece of paper suddenly becomes a computer application; every aspect of the processing, transfer, and utilization of information is now designed to be as "paperless" as possible and as free from human intervention as possible. "Managers of information" are now superseding computer people as leading executives. The computer in basic reality is nothing but a "cog"—a manipulator of data and information in the larger aspect of information control. Any information worth anything must be communicated, and the computer is only a part of that processing and distribution machinery. But, it took the low cost of the microcomputer and its wide capability to force this communication revolution.

SECTION III

Who Will Buy the Millions of Computers Being Marketed, and for What Purposes?

The categories of specific types of systems and users are kept quite general, but they do cover wide areas of equipment, capabilities, and applications analysis. They are:

A. Personal-use data-base retrieval computers—instant user-selected information on tv screens
B. Calculator, translator, and game computers. How the kids—from age 8 to 80—moved from fun with computerized games to practical information-control systems
C. Personal computers as energy conservation systems—homes, buildings, and cars
D. Home tv sets are no longer passive devices. New "media rooms" make them centers of personal and family living—with computers
E. The market for very small business systems (VSBS) is fiercely competitive
F. The "computers are for everybody" office automation pressures—and progress

PERSONAL-USE DATA-BASE RETRIEVAL COMPUTERS—INSTANT USER-SELECTED INFORMATION ON TV SCREENS

A conference speaker once stated, "It takes a small computer to make a house a home." The same speaker noted, "If the microcomputer comes, can the home information utility be far behind?"[3] The British, some years ago, developed an experimental tv data-base retrieval system called teletext, which provided "automatic" information selectable by the tv user but without cost or interference with regular programs. Another system, called viewdata, provided much more detailed data-base information that allowed users to use the tv and the telephone to search, with displayed "menus" of information headings, deeply into data bases held by large computers (costs are involved with this). Both systems are now known in the UK as the Prestel systems. The systems went public in 1979 with consumers buying either specially-equipped tv sets or coder-decoder attachments for older sets. The French developed a competing system called Antiope, and the West Germans purchased the rights to the British systems and called their version of it Bildschirmtext. The British used their system to find times and titles of plays and movies, reports of airline schedules, availability of specific products, and a host of other "yellow pages" and directory or scheduling-type services.

It is now obvious that consumers and business people as well as scientists, students, and professionals want access to easy computer power that will allow them to obtain information services quickly, easily, and inexpensively. Because practically everybody owns a tv set and has access to a telephone, only a $250 to $500 computer-decoder device is needed to open whole new worlds. The British estimated that they would have 15 million subscribers (as decoder prices fall to 10 to 20 pounds) to the Prestel systems by the early 1980s. Because the decoders work best with computer chips within them, and because computer chips can do much more than decode, some purchasers were offered a great many computer services as they evaluated various "decoders," and people who already had home computers could use programs to work with the various remote data-base systems.

Home or business tv sets are no longer passive devices for entertainment. Television sets have become teachers for courses offered by "open univerities" around the world. They are playmates for use with video games, are display terminals for home computers, are screens for data-base information retrieval, are blackboards for developing home art (Japanese "touch screen" tv sets), and have become "guards" for home and business security systems. They are "baby sitters" for surveillance of children, pets, etc., when used with computer-controlled closed-circuit tv (cctv) cameras, and they are public and private poll-takers when used with two-way systems such as the American-Express–Warner Cable TV "QUBE" systems. What's important about these systems? The variety, the timing, and the participants, as briefly summarized below.

1. The variety of personal data-base computers extends from viewdata and teletext types to QUBE types (which are slightly more interactive than the first two types) and includes "cable computers" and personal-computer network systems.
2. The timing is most important for the introduction and mass marketing of these computers. Some private data-base computer systems are already in service in the US—particularly the system that provides farmers with selective prices of grains,

[3] Howard Anderson, president, The Yankee Group, a Cambridge, Massachusetts research firm, during a seminar, "Home Information Utility," October 24, 1979.

meat, commodities, etc., and specific types and times of weather reports, without the customer's having to waste time sitting through a mass of unwanted display data. He or she can select precisely the data of interest, as can all users of viewdata- and teletext-type systems. And, Mattel is already distributing its Intellivision computer for cable tests; Oak Industries, Inc. is distributing its head-end computer systems to cable providers. CBS, RCA, Texas Instruments, and a host of others are testing or have already completed satisfactory tests.

3. Perhaps most important about this impending massive use of computers are the participants—their number, corporate size, market power, and geographical locations. A quick scan of the press clippings will yield besides the governments of Great Britain, France, West Germany, Holland, Hong Kong, Canada, and others, such corporations as AT&T (both in the US and Canada), General Telephone and Electronics, RCA, CBS, TI, Philips, Micro TV, General Instruments, Motorola, Thompson CSF, Comsat, GE (UK), the partnership of American Express and Warner Cable, and Zenith and news organizations such as AP, UPI, Reuters, Knight-Ridder Newspapers, Dow-Jones, and others.

What Do the Data-Base Retrieval Systems Offer?

Some of the capabilities claimed for the British system are the following: Insertion of the entire contents of a 60,000-page encyclopedia in the data base; display of movie and theater listings, reviews, curtain times, seat availabilities, and so on; store advertising; capability for viewers to select from displayed merchandise, punch in a credit card number, pay for the selection, and immediately see the delivery data flashed on the screen; and the capability to remove a listing from classified advertising automatically once a job is filled or an item purchased. Living-room supermarket shopping is simple and certainly a saving of time as well as personal and vehicular energy. Because the system is controlled by the viewer's personal computer and is connected to major computers, provisions are available to use it for calculations and for sending messages to other system users. For those who want to record viewdata material, video cassette recorders can be used. In late 1979, Matsushita (Panasonic) announced it would begin marketing in the European teletext and viewdata markets a hard-copy printer capable of printing characters and graphics in seven colors.

Teletext- and Viewdata-Type Projects in the US

In 1979 General Telephone and Electronics announced that it had obtained licenses allowing it to offer the British-developed viewdata home and business information systems. Knight-Ridder Newspapers, Inc. also began conducting tests using 150 to 200 Miami homes. Bell Telephone of Canada tested its Vista system with the Canada-developed Telidon technology. This is second-generation equipment that can reproduce photographs and very accurate graphics, such as detail maps. The Telidon monitors were initially used in the offices of Bell Canada and three publishers who supplied the software for the test—Torstar, the Southam Press, and F. P. Publications, publishers of the Toronto Globe and Mail. The Telidon system uses alphageometric coding, which is different from the alphamosaic scheme used by the British Prestel systems.

KSL-TV in Salt Lake City, in conjunction with Texas Instruments, has conducted tests using its own transmission equipment and software. Their latest system was called Touch-Tone Teletext; a viewer can request a desired page of information by using his telephone, and receive that page over the air on the tv set. There is no connection between the telephone and the tv set, although they must be located fairly close together so that the viewer can watch the tv set for changes in the index pages while the selection for viewing is being made. After making an index page selection, the viewer keys in on the Touch-Tone phone the number of the selected information page; the data is then broadcast to the tv receiver. The Touch-Tone Teletext system combines the regular teletext page sequencing with the expanded data base of the videotex system. The system is designed to combine the advantages of both types of information distribution service in one; the free usage, high data rate, and unlimited audience of teletext is combined with the two-way access and unlimited data base of videotex. KMOX-TV in St. Louis is also an early entrant in the teletext-viewdata sweepstakes. A CBS-owned station, it tried both the British system and the French Antiope system.

Mavis (McDonnell-Douglas Audio Voice Information System) was installed in Detroit under a contract with Michigan Bell after becoming operational in Kansas City, where Southwestern Bell provides its customers with a commodity information service. Such services operate best with small computers and either educate or train users to this computer technology. Texas Instruments, besides gaining experience with KSL-TV, also received an order from the French to provide 100,000 Antiope decoder chips as manufactured by its French subsidiary. United Press International (UPI), signed a 10-year deal with Telecomputing Corp. of America, McLean, Va. for a 200-city viewdata network which was scheduled for operation in June, 1980. At the same time, Associated Press (AP) and Dow Jones began to offer home and office quotation retrieval services for the stock markets. Investors use their tabletop personal computers to punch up issues and prices, check on "historical" tapes, etc. Subscribers can program their home computers with specific stock portfolios and with the service can study the changing values of the portfolios over periods of time and play "what-if" games as well. American Express has provided $175 million to join Warner Communications in joint ventures in cable systems, specifically two-way QUBE types.

Personal Computer Networks, Some Using Satellites, Spread Rapidly Across the US

The financial muscle and the marketing experience and power of many of the participants in the viewdata- and teletext-type systems indicate that hundreds of thousands of systems may be sold for data-base retrieval use both in homes and among businesses, educational institutions, and governmental divisions. Computers become an integral part of these systems as they do also with various personal-computer data-base networks. One example is the SOURCE telecomputing net. SOURCE is available, for a fee, via a local telephone call in more than 250 cities. The SOURCE network provides more than 2000 computer programs and many types of data bases, ranging from United Press International's entire daily file of world, regional, and local news, sports, and financial information to airline schedules. Some of the various business applications packages, for example, include payroll, accounts receivable, and general ledger systems. Real estate can be bought and sold through the system, and numerous educational courses can be taken. Ticketron show reviews and schedules for most major cities add to nationwide restaurant guides. Any personal computer equipped with a 300-word-per-minute telephone interface can gain toll-free access to the system by paying a one-time registration charge. The SOURCE network features both store-and-forward mail capability (Mailcall) and the ability to communicate interactively (Chatting). Electronic mail to the outside world is provided via Datapost, and messages can be left for subscribers from any telephone via Voicegram. Telecomputing Corporation of America (TCA) of McLean, Virginia provides this network. There are many similar services in being or planned. One is offered by the Personal Computer Division of CompuService, Inc. in Columbus, Ohio.

A number of personal-computer users and amateur radio operators who use personal computers extensively have taken to the use of home satellite antennas. K-band frequencies offer an advantage in this application because antennas of a given gain can be smaller and lighter (roof-top size) at 12 to 14 and at 19 to 29 gigahertz. At high K-band operating frequencies, transmission is free from most terrestrial interference, and new antennas take care of the problems of down-link attenuation that could result from rainfall.

Six-Star Cablevision, with a network located near Los Angeles, was one of the first cable companies offering personal-computer services on the cable (on 3 of 42 available channels), including computer programs, menu planning, consumer shopping surveys, and other services. General Instruments Inc., through its Jerrold subsidiary and in cooperation with Mattel, Inc., conducted experiments with cable adapters and players (terminals). "Playcable" provided one-way and two-way capabilities in experimental stages transmitting games, information, programs, and so on to subscribers as they desired. (Japan's HI-OVIS two-way "wired city" systems had been working with such services as requesting entertainment through computer-assisted instruction, cashless shopping, medical assistance, police and fire protection, remote telemetering, and other services. The experimental system began in 1972 and switched to fiber optics communications in 1978.)

Personal Computers As Data-Base Retrieval Controllers in Homes and Business Develop Remote Feed Home Education Centers

As more and more personal computer users discover and use their "information controller" for news, weather, scheduling, etc., either through private microwave or satellite networks or by accepting viewdata-type services, the advantages of two-way video become apparent. Slow-scan tv has been simple and cost-effective for many years over amateur radio. Several companies now offer low-cost, two-way interactive "tv-frame-grabber" systems using ordinary telephone lines, notably Nippon Electric Company (NEC) in the US, Japan, and elsewhere. AT&T Picturephone Meeting Service became available in 12 cities in 1979, but users must go to the AT&T studios in one of the initial 11 cities. Some large corporations began installing their own teleconferencing rooms and private systems. Microphones and cameras are voice-activated to automatically pick up sound and video from individual speakers without assistance from studio operators. Cameras have zoom lenses, some focus on blackboards, and line-scan printers permit participants to receive immediate hard copies. Some systems are in color and offer video-cassette recording for replays or later transmission. Fig. A-6 shows an American Satellite Corp. (ASC) satellite teleconferencing demonstration. Satellite Business Service (SBS) also demonstrates their services using satellites (with small antenna rooftop receptors planned).

Courtesy American Satellite Corp.

Fig. A-6. Satellite teleconferencing demonstration of simultaneous audio, freeze-frame video, and facsimile transmission.

CALCULATOR, TRANSLATOR, AND GAME COMPUTERS—HOW THE KIDS FROM 8 TO 80 MOVED FROM FUN WITH COMPUTERIZED GAMES TO PRACTICAL INFORMATION CONTROL SYSTEMS

As eager youngsters and their skeptical but inquisitive parents entered toy stores and departments, computer electronics stores, and many tv, stereo, and appliance stores, they often became spellbound by the antics of low-cost computers (or as others judged, very expensive toys and games). As many hundreds of thousands followed the pressures of massive and national and local tv and print promotion campaigns, a "let's-find-out-about-this" attitude prevailed. However, once they began to examine the literature, watch the in-store working displays, and personally experiment with the computer keyboards and controls, strange things happened. Many were enthralled, entertained, and educated. They saw computer art, graphics, and animation. They heard computer-synthesized music and voice responses. They watched dazzling electronic and video games and amusements. They quickly became aware of the big names —Radio Shack, PET, Apple, Atari 400 and 800, Mattel Intellivision, APF Imagination Machine, Texas Instruments, Hewlett-Packard, and many more, including strong competitors from Japan: Panasonic, Canon, Sharp, Casio, Hitachi, Nippon Electric Corp. (NEC)—and the list was constantly growing. Words like "peripherals," "ROM" and "RAM," "operating system," "software," "disk," and so on were understood quite quickly, and many more constantly popped up in customer questions to sales personnel. One first impression stayed: "Those computers can do a lot more than just play games. In fact, they provide more value per dollar than anything else."

At the same time, hobbyist magazines, mass-circulation news magazines, and men's "specialty" magazines were crowded with articles about personal-computer capabilities and applications. The editors of all ranges of media were engulfed with personal-computer news. The enthusiastic and intense promoters had done their jobs well. Amateur programmers from everywhere were doing such things as analyzing the cries of babies to determine if they meant real alarm or discomfort or were just frivolous. Computers were producing "in minutes" full-color pictures for portraits or for use directly on T-shirts. Wide publicity was achieved by the personal-computer networks when they offered data from an ever-increasing number of "highest respect" data banks. Home computers for security, safety, and energy management, and voice input and output seemed to make a great deal of sense, especially because the kids could also simultaneously use them for all ranges of educational areas. And, wasn't computer science now really a "premier science" for all to understand?

But, these early customers "hadn't seen anything yet." Who wouldn't buy a "light pen" for his system? They came fully assembled and with a program for only $29.50. What did they do? They allowed direct interaction with information on the crt screen, making programs accessible to persons with no computer background. They also can be used to create any number of unique games and special graphics effects. How many new users would learn computer languages? Most! It was easy to learn BASIC; then some others, specifically PASCAL, were not at all difficult. Those who own video cassette recorders could purchase a half-dozen computer programming visual "instruction classes," and they were just the beginning of many computer "home" course offerings. If the elementary and secondary schools wouldn't teach the kids about computers, their applications and languages, there were hundreds of books, magazines, traveling seminars, shows, conventions, and conferences, and literature by the ton. Anyone could learn fast and practically free. Software of endless variety and even memory was plentiful and inexpensive. New mini and microdisk systems, including one called "Micro-Winnie," 4 to 6 inches in diameter were available for $200. Other full fixed or floppy magnetic disk memory systems became available to make storage low in cost. Matsushita (Panasonic) was making 100 tiny disk drives (70,000 characters and 2 inches high) an hour as they "started" mass production in Japan.

The fun is in computing, but the highest adventures are found using the thousands of new products that match, fit, and extend the capabilities once you have your first computer. Many users found the large-screen video projection systems for computer output were exceptionally valuable. What prestige office, major university, or "edge of technology" high school could not or would not have at least a few of these devices as part of their installation?

Will the Greatest Number of Computer Owners Start With Electronic Toys?

In mid-1979, producers of microprocessors were swamped with orders from toy manufacturers. One manager remarked, "We could probably sell five times our production capacity, and so could everyone else." At Texas Instruments, 60% to 70% of the production of the TMS-1000 microprocessors was being taken by the toy industry. In less than three years, and before the 1979 rush, Texas Instruments had sold 13 million TMS-1000 microprocessors. Mattel, with microprocessor chips supplied mainly by Rockwell International in 1978, sold more than 2 million electronic games that year.

One example of computerized toys is shown in Fig. A-7; it can be programmed by means of a keyboard to follow a desired path. Other examples include computerized chess play systems (Fig. A-8) and voice synthesis toys and learning aids.

Courtesy Milton Bradley Co.

Fig. A-7. Big Trak programmable toy.

The Move-Up From Electronic Games to "Game Computers" and Then "Full Computers"

The Atari Models 400 and 800, which were highly publicized in 1979, offered eight different color graphics modes (using 16 colors), and music with simple control of note, tone, and volume variations, using four audio channels as played through the tv. The ROM cartridge selection was extensive. Educational ROMs covered history, government, counseling, accounting, physics, classics, auto mechanics, economics, etc.

Mattel received significant support for its Intellivision when GT&E purchased the franchise rights to market the machine under its Sylvania and Philco brand names and to offer it for $250 with the keyboard separate but at about the same price. Also, the

Courtesy Fidelity Electronics, Ltd.

Fig. A-8. Computer chess game.

use of this machine on many cable companies plus the heavy promotions and large (toy) customer base made it a major contender. It has color, 3-octave music, 64-key keyboard, microphone, insertable ROMs including educational programs, games, and so on.

Among Japanese products, one machine, Panakit, for about $150 assembled, offers capabilities as follows: "Teaches basic concepts of microprocessor technology; users easily enter and display instructions through convenient keyboard and readouts; it plays music over 3-octave range using instructions for pitch and length of notes; has a built-in audio amplifier with volume and tempo controls and speaker; can perform control tasks over a 24-hour period using a built-in real-time clock; combines user instructions with input signals from any of three input sensors supplied with the unit; and allows users to enjoy simulating various sounds, play games, and so on."

The Radio Shack TRS-80 Model I and Model II are cost-effective machines. The company stresses that these machines are not home computers, though they can both be used in homes. The Model I in 1979 was turning into a "door opener" machine as its price was reduced to below $500, while the TRS-80 Model II (Fig. A-9) is a full service business-oriented system with either 32K or 64K RAM, a 500K-byte floppy disk drive, expandable to 2 million bytes. It includes a 12-inch high-resolution monitor that displays 24 lines of 80 normal characters or 40 expanded characters, uppercase and lowercase.

Early in the development of the Apple II, the Apple Computer Company realized that 90% of necessary repairs could easily be diagnosed by the computer itself, and with the right guidance, all local dealers can perform repairs. Many of the other computer companies began using similar self-checking capabilities. Many firms use toll-free telephone numbers to have technical personnel lead the customer through various tests and procedures interfacing with the self-diagnostic tests built into the machines.

In mid-1979, a directory of over 1000 programs designed for the Apple was available for $4.95. As regards support for both Radio Shack and Apple, business software, real

Courtesy Radio Shack

Fig. A-9. Radio Shack TRS-80 Model II microcomputer with line printer and external disk system.

estate programs, medical programs, stock market reporting programs, several newsletters, and specific journals were available for either and both systems. The personal-computer aftermarket industry invents and distributes several hundred products to support, expand, and interface with every popular computer.

An example of this is a program called SUNSIM-1 that is used on the TRS-80 to simulate solar homes. It calculates energy from the sun in hourly intervals at any specified location on earth, and demonstrates its use for domestic space heating, cooling, and water heating. The home energy distribution system is dynamically shown with graphics. Cumulative energy and temperature values are displayed, including solar energy collected and used, backup energy used, thermal and hot water storage temperature, default values, user's specific inputs and requirements for size of home, volume of thermal storage, and angle of solar collector. The program requires 16K bytes of storage, is available on cassette, and is somewhat typical of how home-computer tinkerers can earn money developing programs from well thought-out and tested programs that many users need.

As an example of the profitability of expertly developed and properly promoted software, one individual developed a text editing program, advertised it, adjusted it for practically any type of computer, and sold more than 1000 sets of programs for $395 per set within two years. A gross profit of almost $400,000 to start with, and license fees from company users started to mount at the rate of about $100,000 a year.

Texas Instruments' first personal computer system was the TI 99/4 (Fig. A-10) using Solid State Software™ cartridges with emphasis on educational programs, color graphics, a solid-state speech synthesizer, and so forth. Milton Bradley, a major toy company, began marketing the cartridges for the TI machines; Moore Business Forms, Inc. began marketing some TI business computers; other outlets include department stores, catalog houses, computer stores, electronics distributers, and direct mail sales.

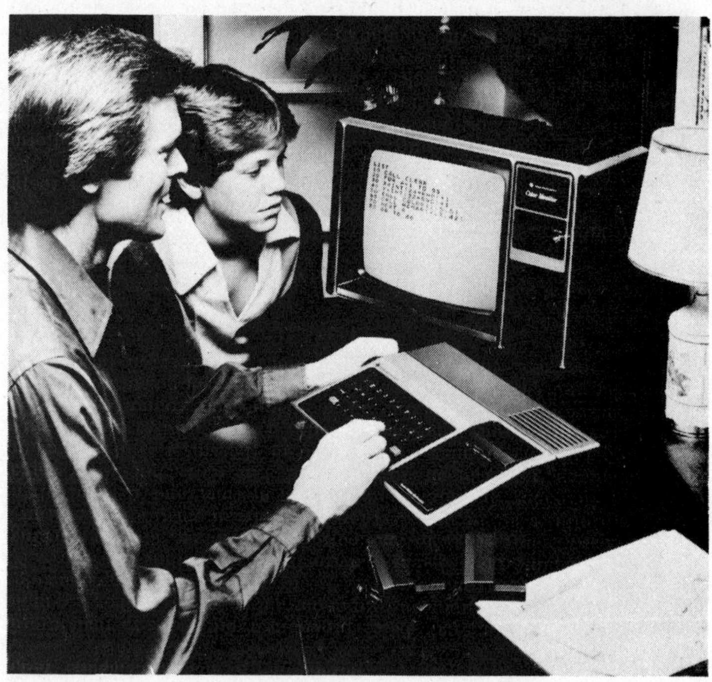

Courtesy Texas Instruments Inc.

Fig. A-10. Model 99/4 home computer system.

The trade-up to computers does not include only millions of computerized games. Tens of millions of calculator users and a few hundred thousand language-translator users are very likely prospects for hand-held computers at first and full systems later. They are convinced of the real dollar value of their "tools" and easily realize that the computer can become a practical "do-everything" machine for them. A quick look at the sudden advances of calculators is followed by an intriguing analysis of how translator systems suddenly became full-system personal computers.

From Simple to Powerful Calculators to Simple and Powerful Small Computers

More than 200 million calculators are in use around the world. Some factories in Japan have capacities to produce more than a million a month while others in Hong Kong can produce from 200,000 to 500,000 a month. While Americans were buying more than 20 million a year, the Japanese felt that their local market had peaked in 1978 at just over 11 million a year. That was before the credit-card-sized calculator appeared to give the industry another shot of expansive mass production. The Casio ML-720 Music Card Calculator (Fig. A-11) is an example; in addition to mathematical operations and a liquid crystal display, it can sound an 11-note musical scale when the individual keys are touched. Another "shot in the arm" for the calculator industry is the "electronic diary" type that sounds alarms and offers voice or display reminder readouts in numbers and words (Fig. A-12).

Courtesy Casio, Inc.

Fig. A-11. Card-size calculator with musical tones.

Examples of two "calculator-computers" follow: The alphanumeric Hewlett-Packard HP-41C provides a full range of mathematical, scientific, and statistical functions. The power of the unit can be scaled up with the addition of a series of options: (1) up to four memory modules increase memory to up to 2k lines or 319 registers; (2) a plug-in card reader lets you enter programs from recorded magnetic cards or record your own programs; (3) a thermal printer furnishes hard copy of calculations, plots, and complete alphanumeric output; and (4) 16 plug-in application modules provide preprogrammed solutions to problems in specific areas. Programs can automatically compare data, constants, or results, test flags, and alter execution based on tests. The Heath OC-1401 navigation computer is a hand-held, on-board computer for private pilots and aviation enthusiasts. It features continuous flight data update, storage for up to nine flight leg entries, clock/timer, diagnostic circuitry, scientific functions, and no requirement for external programs. Computations include magnetic heading, true air speed, ground speed, true course, ETA to next check point, ETA to destination, clock time to next check point, and clock time to destination. The display shows distance and time to check point or destination and shows the amount of fuel remaining. The unit has internal rechargeable batteries (charger included) to keep data in memory, or it may be powered from the aircraft cigarette lighter using the converter and cable supplied with the unit.

People who use these types of calculators or who have "grown up" with other complex programmable calculators such as the HP-67 and 97 and the TI-57, 58, and 59 are likely to become quick personal-computer customers and avid users.

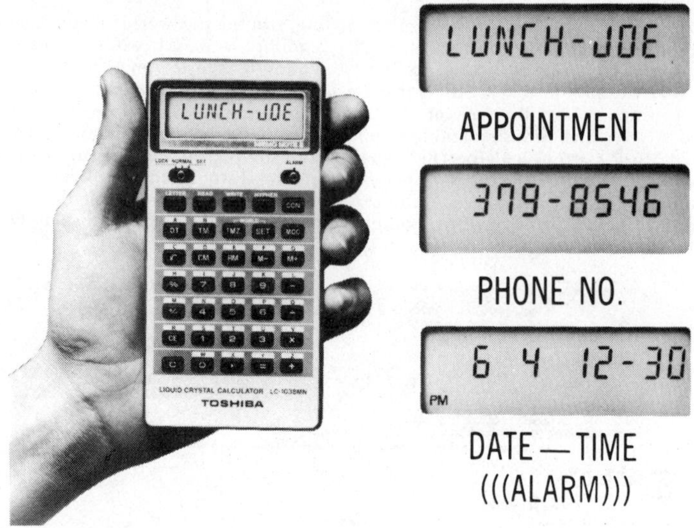

Courtesy Toshiba America, Inc.

Fig. A-12. "Electronic diary" type of calculator.

Language Translator Computer With Voice Answerback, Memory, and Programmability

Whereas the translator systems began as rather elementary display systems much like a calculator for languages, the concept and the products have now become the center of full hand-held computers. These pocket computers deserve a closer look. It all started when Craig and Lexicon within months both introduced relatively simple but highly saleable language translators that allowed users the simplicity of tapping in, for example, English words, questions, and so on with an immediate readout of those inputs in another language, such as French, German, Spanish, Russian, and so on. Specific phrases in foreign languages, such as "where is ——," could be called to the display with single coded key punches. Texas Instruments then introduced their "talking" language translator. It has the ability to form thousands of spoken phrases by linking together its vocabulary words. Each module contains about 1000 words, of which half are spoken and displayed and half are displayed only. Internally, components include a speech synthesizer chip, a controller, and four ROMs (memory chips). An earplug is included for personal use. Twenty-five common phrases, such as "I need a doctor," are preprogrammed. A "memory" mode drills users on pronunciation and translation of user-selected words. In the "learn" mode, a programmed drill assists the user in learning.

To illustrate how simple and low-cost speaking capabilities really became, one company demonstrated a talking clock and a talking watch in practically any language for less than $100. Special messages can be programmed in (for up to 30 years) for anniversaries, graduations, and so on, so that the watch will do more than simply say, "Time to wake up" or "Time's up."

When Nixdorf of West Germany bought the Lexicon line, Lexicon was already offering software modules that made the translator into a portable personal computer. Its 189 module for the LK-3000 translator enabled clerks to file and retrieve documents without precoding sorting and without performing elaborate computations. Users also are able to program into a blank module up to 1000 characters of programmable storage, causing the unit to display phone numbers, addresses, appointments, and so on on demand. Lexicon also offers an RS-232 interface so that the user can transmit and receive messages through a standard modem. The competing Craig translator that was purchased by Matsushita (Panasonic) was to have voice translations much like the TI machine, a wide range of new software, programmability using BASIC and FORTH languages, an optional printer, a coupler for use with telephones to access data banks, and other capabilities.

What About Voice Input at a Cost of a Few Hundred Dollars or Less?

A press release from a conference on "Paperless Computerized Communications for Office Workers" read, "Most office systems involve typing input into terminals for transmission, storage, and retrieval. So pity the poor executive who can't or won't type. After all, that's clerical work. According to the communications experts at this meeting, these machines might employ voice input systems. This concept takes the familiar dictating machine one step further and automatically transposes spoken input into written letters or retrieves information in response to verbal commands." Another item in the press stated, "Two companies—Heuristics Inc. and Votrax Division of Federal Screw Works—feel so strongly about the use of voice response and voice input that they have developed units that connect to personal/home computers such as the TRS-80, Apple II, and S-100 bus computers of other makes. Sales in late 1979 were reported to be brisk, both companies admitted, for units that retail at $169 and up." These systems enhance data entry, especially in "eyes busy" work areas within a company, such as sorting, testing with hands, remote checking, etc.

Voice answerback warnings are far superior to displayed ones or bells and other alarms. In the cockpit of an airliner a voice saying "pull-up!" is far better than a flashing light or constant beep, and this type of system is just as easy to use. Voice answerback systems used by the phone companies to give correct phone numbers by computer, and computerized price reports on commodities are "pure" automation. Recognition accuracy of words spoken into some systems is as high as 98% to 99%. An Exxon affiliate, Periphonics Corp., installs voice response systems in a variety of application areas. Some include "bank from home" systems for banks and thrift institutions, a national order entry system used by more than 600 sales representatives of Lever Brothers, and others.

Will there be many more systems of this type soon? Sanyo Electric Co. has introduced a voice control unit that allows tv set owners to play video games or switch channels through oral commands. It recognizes 30 types of words from at least two different people. When the person orally commands the tv set to turn on the power or switch channels, the memory compares the verbal instructions with the voice pattern and commands registered in the RAM and executes the order. The voice recognition is more than 95% accurate. Nippon Telegraph and Telephone Public Corp. has developed a single-chip speech synthesizer that codes and decodes speech signals using linear predictive coding schemes and analyzes human speech and codes it into sound-source (the vocal chords) and filter (the roof of the mouth) parameters. Sharp Corp. of Japan has a prototype voice synthesizer that enables computer or microwave ovens to give instructions and results orally. With this capability, a "talking calculator" at a reasonable price was also offered. The "voice" informs operators if an error is made or allows the user to verify his or her figures by pressing a key to trigger the unit to recite orally the input data and the results of instructions. This type of voice input and voice output is installed at low cost—the talking calculator was under $200; the voice added only about $20 to the total. Voice provides "magic" to appliances (microwave ovens that orally provide recipes or reminders of instructions, safety hazards, and so on) and certainly increases the marketability of personal computers, toys, other appliances, and many other products and tools.

PERSONAL COMPUTERS AS ENERGY CONSERVATION SYSTEMS FOR HOMES, BUILDINGS, AND CARS

Many financial periodicals have carried various articles with headlines something like, "Home Security: The Next Consumer Boom?" Others are even stronger concerning another area: building energy conservation. A brief list that combines these and other functions that are quite easily serviced by a personal computer follows:

1. Alarm monitoring/police notification
2. Environmental control (heating, air conditioning, humidification, dehumidification, air purity, etc.)
3. Fire and smoke detection
4. Appliance control (microwave oven, gas oven, refrigerator)
5. Perimeter system control (sprinklers, outdoor lights, gates)
6. Solar and/or auxiliary energy source control
7. Watering system control based on soil moisture
8. Fuel economizing systems
9. Maintenance alert system for household devices (key component sensing and periodic preventive maintenance)

There are many products designed to conserve energy. Electronic thermostats and energy monitors cover much of the needed assistance. The Dupont Energy Management Corp. Energy Monitor (Fig. A-13) allows the owner to program an energy budget and watch the device flash warnings when energy use exceeds the budget. The digital display shows eight functions: current dollar cost for energy used, projected amount of next bill, amount of last bill, billing date, chosen energy budget, cost per kilowatt hour, date, and time of day. This is an optional or add-on device; "controllers" are still needed.

Courtesy Dupont Energy Management Corp.

Fig. A-13. Device for monitoring energy usage.

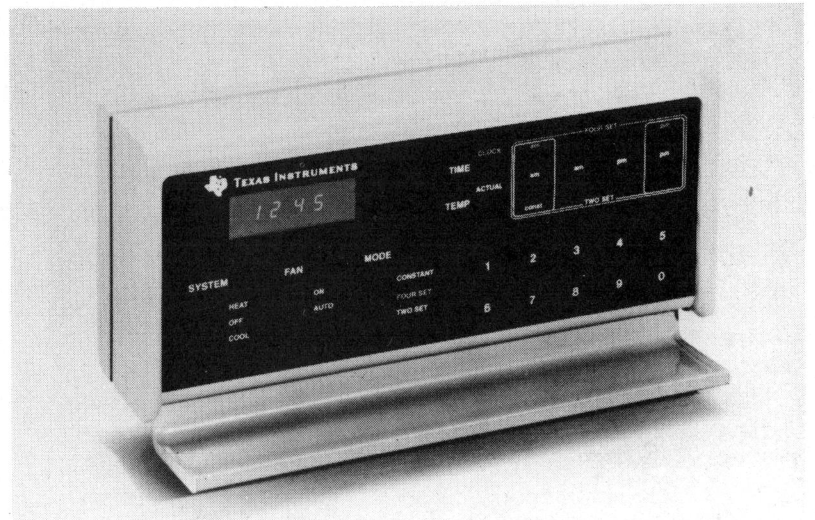

Courtesy Texas Instruments Inc.

Fig. A-14. Digital thermostat.

Also available are digital thermostats such as the one from Texas Instruments pictured in Fig. A-14. (Honeywell and others offer similar devices.) The unit in Fig. A-14 is a programmable thermostat for residential dwellings with central air conditioning and heating. It offers digital display of time and temperature and has a multiple programming feature and a wide range of temperature set-back capabilities. A home owner may install the thermostat himself by using a screwdriver and clipping color-coded wires together. The unit affords three operating modes—constant, two-set, and four-set. The day/night mode (or four-set mode) is useful for families who spend the day away from home, yet desire a comfortably heated or cooled home waiting for them when they return in the evening. For example, in winter, the user can program his unit to come up to a comfort setting of 70° before he arises in the morning, drop to 60° at 8 a.m. before he leaves for work, increase to 70° at 5 p.m., when he comes home from work, and decrease to 65° at 11 p.m. before he retires. In the night mode (or two-set mode), the temperature is automatically decreased at bedtime and raised to a comfort setting before the occupants arise in the morning.

With the Coby I and particularly its successor, the Micro Power Center 168 (Fig. A-15), both from Energy Technology Inc., users can remotely control up to 100 energy-consuming devices to the second. All commands are transmitted directly through existing ac lines by coded pulses that are intercepted and "read" by a specific remote unit that executes the command received. There is no interference with other equipment. The system uses special plug-in remote receptacles, in-line remotes, and thermostat remote devices.

A less ambitious system is the BSR (USA) Ltd. X-10, a home and office environmental control system with a cost under $100. It consists of a small calculator-sized command console, which plugs into any wall socket and can turn off or on up to 16 lights or appliances by remote control, and three different control modules. X-10 sends coded electrical signals through the existing wiring in a building to a small module that plugs between the lamp or appliance and the wall socket or switch.

An example of an energy management system for small buildings without full-time operators is the MCC Powers S170/80 Energy Management System (Fig. A-16). This is a microcomputer-based system which combines energy management and facilities management capabilities. It automatically controls building operations without a full-

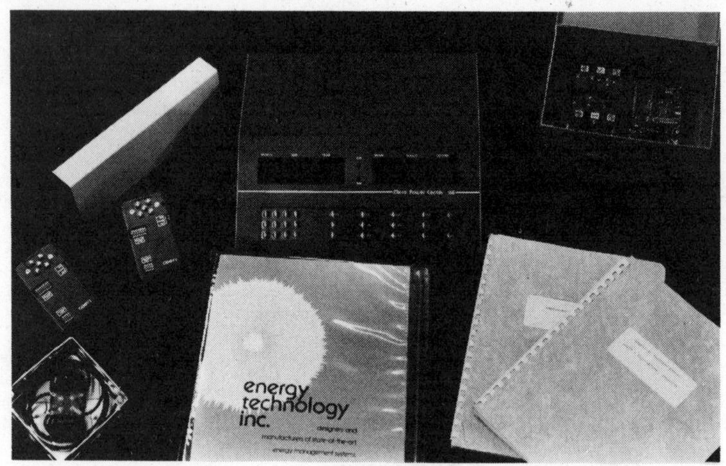

Courtesy Energy Technology, Inc.

Fig. A-15. Left to right: bypass, two control voltage remotes, transmission booster, Micro Power Center 168, in-line remote.

time operator. Features include automatic scan of alarms (analog and binary), including printout and annunciation; remote monitoring of analog values and equipment status; equipment start/stop and mode control; setpoint adjustment of remote controllers; run time totalization; event programming; and English-language printouts and system logs. It is upward-expandable for future growth requirements and management needs. A larger model of the system, the System 600, is available. It is a computer-based building automation system based on Digital PDP-11 computers and quickly retrofit to present structures.

Computer systems continue to become less and less expensive and are being installed in smaller and smaller buildings. It is obvious that we all must become more efficient in the use of electricity in our homes and at work. The potential of microcomputer controls is enormous, and they are rapidly becoming incorporated into many

Courtesy MCC Powers

Fig. A-16. S170/80 Energy Management System.

renovations of existing homes, including those being switched to solar energy installations.

The Market for Car Computers

Car computers not only assist in a dozen or more electronic systems such as optimizing ignition, fuel injection, controlling emissions, etc., but they are also diagnostic alerters for tires, oil, and other consumables. To make it a bit easier on the "I hate computers!" auto mechanics, most of the automakers are incorporating self-test systems with their microcomputer controls. GM had programmed checks on 25 possible failures on a dashboard display in some 1980 cars. Ford offered mechanics a more limited range of computer-controlled checks and required the use of special readout instruments. But, it had a module on its small cars that displays eight failure modes, such as temperature sensor, and so on. Another control system introduced in the 1980 full-sized Fords provided 11 checks, and they were exploring computerized diagnostic service gear with standard English readouts.

A typical use of a microcomputer is a West German system that checks car lights automatically. At its heart is an 8-bit microprocessor with a prime function of giving instructions for activating the lamps, monitoring the signals from the lights and sensors, and informing the driver of any failures via the dashboard indicator. The microprocessor is contained, along with peripheral components, in a small unit behind the dashboard.

Some of the specific uses proposed for microcomputers are: electronic voltage regulator, emission/engine control, electronic transmission control, variable-displacement engine, radar collision avoidance, electronic fuel ejection, electronic ignition, entertainment communications, digital clock, intrusion alarm, dynamic ride control, headlamp dimmer, intoxication tester, on-board diagnostics, climate control, remote garage-door opener, crash protection, automatic speed control and sleep detector, seat-position memory, and others. For dashboard readouts: speed in mph and kph, engine speed, time, voltage, fuel, oil pressure, oil, water, inside/outside temperatures, and so on. Instrument panels on some cars, using three microcomputers, check vehicle functions, flashing specific messages and sounding alerts if something is wrong. The computer determines which messages have highest priority. Simple diagnostics check wiring and sensors, and more advanced tests can be used.

A number of retrofit car computers became available in late 1978. One was the CompuCruise, which sold for between $300 and $400. Features advertised for this unit include the following. Computerized cruise control establishes and maintains a preselected road speed. It also features resume and traffic flow adjust. CompuCruise is programmed to compute the most fuel efficient driving speed; which brand and grade of fuel is most economical in the vehicle; effects of tire brands, types, and pressures; when tune-up and repair is needed; whether tune-ups have been properly performed; and other useful fuel-saving data. When expected trip distance is put into the unit, it will continually display time, distance, or fuel to arrival, updated once per second and based on current vehicle speed and fuel consumption. Automatic data sensors allow it to display time, distance, or fuel to empty, based on current vehicle speed and fuel consumption. Inside temperature and outside temperature (if desired, outside temperature sensor can be located to provide engine coolant temperature) may be displayed in Fahrenheit or Celsius. Battery and charging voltage also are displayed.

Other similar car computers are available, including Avatar ($295), Prince ($350), and Autocomp ($130).

HOME TV SETS ARE NO LONGER PASSIVE DEVICES—NEW "MEDIA ROOMS" MAKE THEM CENTERS OF PERSONAL AND FAMILY LIVING, WITH COMPUTERS

At the time of this writing, the video cassette recorder (VCR) was already an important consumer item, and the videodisc player was expected to become equally important in a short time. However, these devices only barely touch the potential utility of the tv set. Dualvision, art and color manipulation with light pens or touch screens, pictures from audio tape, stereo, facsimile—these are but a few items from a long list of possibilities. With the microcomputer again taking the forefront, the "media room" will indeed become the center of home activity with computer control of these and most other items of entertainment, education, and environment-control automation. This brings with it a need for everybody to know the nomenclature of microcomputer use, components, expansion, and so on.

The various components of the designed media rooms include microcomputers within several of the devices such as tv sets, videodisc players, and video cassette players, but also a central control personal computer which will be programmed to control closed tv surveillance systems (now low in cost—$400-$800 including a small monitor and monochrome camera), various other monitoring systems, inbound and outbound communications, and other services. Projection systems for both tv and computer output also belong in these home information centers, and these have become available with respectable quality for under $2000.

In late 1979, the Japanese television industry offered a number of interactive tv products, and an American tv projection system provided nearly life-sized images. The "Fun and Teach" tv set (Matsushita) had a touch screen allowing even very small children a palette of many colors to demonstrate their feelings for design and art. A color tv facsimile or "home reco.der" (also from Matsushita) produced hard-copy duplicates of images shown on the tv from remote sources, from in-house videodiscs or video cassettes, or as developed through the use of computer programs. Sharp's "DualVision" tv sets permitted two pictures to be shown simultaneously with a switch to make either one the large, or main, picture. A half-dozen competing companies had similar products; one from Taiwan offered three pictures on the same tv set.

Of specific significance was the introduction of low-cost pcm systems. Sharp's "Sono-Pattern" system was a prototype of this sight and sound technology. Utilizing pulse code modulation (pcm) recording technology, the Sono-Pattern is a decoding system which works in conjunction with a computer-type keyboard encoding device, a stereo cassette recorder, a standard television screen, and a high-fidelity system to display graphics or words on the video screen in eight different colors while corresponding background music or narration is simultaneously played through hi-fi speakers. Video patterns are recorded digitally through one channel of a cassette deck on a standard audio cassette tape by programming the patterns with a separate encoder. The audio portion is recorded in a normal manner on the same tape through the other channel, using any sound source. The Sono-Pattern works by rapidly converting the encoded digital (pcm) pulses to video signals, thus permitting continuous display over a standard tv screen.

Without elaborating further on the marvels of tv innovations, the ability to use tv for portrayal of life-size images, develop color newspapers as printed by tv receivers, and combine them with $200-$400 tv cameras that could be used in practically any light, "media rooms" were no longer affordable only by millionaires, but could be incorporated into practically any individual's home, depending upon his or her decision to allocate available funds for these purposes.

Two-way tv in the United States is exemplified by the QUBE system, first offered in Columbus, Ohio, then in Houston, Texas, Cincinnai, Ohio, and other cities. The system is owned by Warner Cable and American Express. The QUBE system allows people to use their home tv sets for interactive education, immediate voting response to talk shows or game shows, instant response to local social and political decisions presented to them, and so on. The QUBE terminal is microprocessor controlled.

A specific example of the variety of services that such two-way systems can offer is the Warner Security System, which is designed to monitor home detection devices such as burglary, fire, and emergency medical monitors on a 24-hour basis. The system is also designed to give police, fire, and medical emergency authorities a computer printout of vital information at the time they respond to a particular situation in the home. The information concerning individual households that is stored by the computer is determined by the person who has the security system installed. The home security and medical alert systems in the home are monitored through the same cable that is used for Warner Cable TV and QUBE. The home security system is monitored by Warner's central station, and signals are processed every few seconds by computers. This system enables the central station not only to know immediately when a detection device reacts, but also where and when a cable has been cut, or when any part of the system has been tampered with.

THE MARKET FOR VERY SMALL BUSINESS SYSTEMS (VSBS)

With up to 5 million small businesses in North America and at least an equal number in Europe, Africa, and Latin America, the press for sales of "under $10,000" computer systems is strong and continuous. The low end of these systems was between $2500 and $3500, with Radio Shack's main entry at $3250. Many others, such as Apple, PET, and Ohio Scientific offered similar systems. Others offered "bare-bones" systems for this price or slightly more and then hoped to sell add-on equipment to build total sales to from $10,000 to $20,000. The economics of these systems is such that the annual wage of only one clerk, with benefits, easily pays for the total computer system and the software. The difference in accuracy, control, on-time record-keeping, and so on, is significant, and the users know they have many more applications for their machines. Besides the always needed data-base storage and retrieval, the primary use of these small systems is in one or more of four general areas as described below.

Technical and Scientific Problem Solving: The problem-solving market may be defined as the market for computers sold to perform the repetitive numerical calculations associated with research, engineering, and statistical analysis within departments of large universities, the federal government, and technically oriented companies. Typical applications include various kinds of statistical and tabulation analysis, operations research, structural analysis, coordinate geometry, financial planning, and modeling. Much of the application software for this market is supplied by small companies. Prices of systems sold in this market range from $4800 to $45,000.

Business Systems: The business-systems market may be defined as the market for computers sold to perform the record keeping and financial data processing requirements of smaller companies, government units, and divisions of larger companies. Typical applications include foreign-exchange currency transactions at major banks, order-entry and inventory management for distribution and manufacturing industries, project management for the construction industry, and accounting within life insurance agencies and other companies. Systems sold to this market segment range in price from $3000 to $8000.

Distributed Data Processing: The distributed–data-processing market may be defined as the market for intelligent terminals or computers coupled with telecommunication capabilities which enable them to perform local on-site jobs and then communicate results to another computer over telephone lines. Users of these multiple systems are large industrial companies and financial institutions as well as federal and state governments. Typical applications include consolidation of remotely gathered data, distributed payroll processing, and order-entry processing. System prices in this market are $8000 to $50,000. Many companies provide a full line of industry-compatible telecommunications options for entire system configurations.

Word Processing: The word-processing market may be defined as the market for computers sold to increase efficiency in text processing and repetitive typing. Typical word-processing applications include client account reporting in public accounting firms, document preparation in law firms, and customer service applications in major retail chains. Many companies have been in the word processing marketplace for several years and currently offer both stand-alone and multiple work-station systems in the $5000 to $30,000 price range.

The types of operations the very small business systems serve are listed in a general fashion below:

- For business offices, stand alone or integrated
- For manufacturing firms, tool control, processing, etc.
- For warehousing, distribution, retail operations
- For CPA and financial organizations, real estate, insurance
- For medical, dental, legal, and engineering time and billing, data base and other services
- Data entry and inquiry operations, remote or on-site
- Distributed and dispersed processing, business, industrial, etc.
- Other applications in education, homes, as related to business

OFFICE AUTOMATION PRESSURES AND PROGRESS

Office automation may start with relatively simple electronic typewriters with limited memory and display characteristics, but microprocessor logic, cassettes, disks, screens, and new communications keyboards are quickly added. Stand-alone multipurpose work stations will follow, and an entirely new environmental appearance results as more and more facets of a true "electronic office" emerge.

The merging of word processing and data processing and the impact of distributed processing (DP) are placing the computers (small systems) in the hands and control of the people who originate the data stream and amend it and use it, instead of placing one behemoth in a distant building. Small computers are under the control of the new "computer scientists," those who know or care about the intrinsic operation of a company. Personal computers have caused this change and have practically revolutionized data processing.

This is the automated office—word processing (WP) ; facsimile; intelligent communicating copiers; "menu" crt screens for input and output to the computer by clerks, secretaries, bosses, top executives; work station computers; data bases accessible in the main by practically everybody in the office for information required by them. Practically all "automated" offices are creating more productivity per worker and more timely, accurate information directly accessible by executives for sounder, quicker decisions.

Managers are indeed becoming their own typists—to more easily access the computer—yet they need not learn to program or to understand the mechanics of the machine itself or the peripherals. However, they quickly discover that they must learn a considerable amount of computerese to get by, and then learn even more to understand, make judgements, and effectively utilize the power and versatility of these systems, or both they and their jobs could move out the door.

The computer has now become a major "tool" for practically every office worker to know, understand, and personally use, whether it is an adjunct to the WP or DP system or part of the integrated whole. The equipment is marvelous, inexpensive for the value, and most convenient for those who learn to use it quickly, properly, and effectively.

An often confusing avalanche of technological development has already descended on many unprepared managers, and more is coming. Even the most alert and change-sensitive managers discover they are being overwhelmed with conflicting information, but to remain competitive, expensive decisions must be made. The new information technology will affect every area of the business and institutional office, from the chief executive officer to the most recently hired clerk. Because of continually falling costs of excellent-capability electronic equipment, and the fierceness of competitive supplier marketing battles, it is poor business judgement to avoid making labor-saving and enhanced-efficiency equipment purchases. It is true that the changes pushed on the personnel are often great and sometimes novel and most often stressful. However, machines are no longer simple adjuncts or tools of these jobs; they are becoming part of the continuous integration of all office work-processing and decision-making procedures. Until recently, people and "things" have been perceived as separate entities, but a type of "people/thing" people seems to be entering the information business scene. When environments become so drastically modified, in order to exist and succeed, people must themselves modify not simply their habits but their method of work functioning also. There seems no really "humane" domination of how or what office automation will occur. The typical hierarchical, pyramidal organization structures that have ruled the bureaucracies in the past can no longer exist with any degree of efficiency. Information processing is already far too costly for humans to perform. And now, "old type" communications are too error-prone and slow between humans to remain unautomated. For example, "direct voice mail" systems, also called computer conferencing, have many advantages over paper mail and phone calls. While the cost of labor in the late 1970s was increasing from 7% to 10%, cost of computers and communications equipment was decreasing at from 11% to 15%. When personal computers began to come on very strong in 1979, costs of computer logic were decreasing at an annual rate of 25%, while computer memory was decreasing at an annual rate of 40% or more. In addition to these absolute economic facts, the need to increase worker productivity was vital to control inflation costs in most parts of practically all enterprises. Automation of office procedures was imperative due to the tremendous increase in volume of information required. Industries such as banks, insurance companies, major industrial operations, and so on, also required significant enhancement of the "quality" of this greatly increased amount of information. Answer? Computers!

The era of the "super-secretary" seemed to be dawning. This person, an executive's assistant, needs to operate word processors and electronic mail equipment, to organize computer conferencing, to seek or process information through various types of data-base systems and then handle several types of communication procedures and devices regarding the dissemination of that information. Many executives now seldom touch a piece of paper because upon arriving at the office, or using a home computer before leaving, the executive checks his electronic "in-tray" on a screen and sends memos through the computer, which distributes them in voice, display, or, if requested, in automatically produced written form (hard copy). Relevant individuals or departments will "pick up" these messages according to priorities on their screens or computer conference lines, respond to them, often coupling that response with data and information extracted from various data bases, including graphics and computer-generated signatures and photographs when necessary. These communications are completed swiftly and accurately without paper or telephone holds or callbacks. Electronic calendars issue automatic reminders, and computers make or change schedules almost without human interference using voice input and voice answerback.

Electronic Offices Do Not Mean Typewriter Replacements—Think More About Long Distance Communicating Copiers With Laser Printers and Telephone Visual Service

As noted, integrated information systems pull together word processing, data processing, telecommunications, graphics, and high-speed image-printing technologies. Wang's OIS Basic office information system and IBM's 66/70 Information Distributor were some of the first "convergence" systems for word-data processing/communications. The latter can perform word-data processing, text editing, and copying by laser printing (1800 characters per second) and can link to distant computer or data terminals and data bases.

For users just beginning text editing with electronic typewriters, adding data processing to the work stations and communications capabilities as well means some real trauma. But, cost is an important factor. Again, the personal computers enter the scene. Practically all of the major "below $10,000" systems can handle most of the functions mentioned above, although perhaps not with copies delivered at laser printing speed.

Ohio Scientific's C8P DF model with its universal telephone interface (UTI) and voice input-output system (Votrax's phonetic voice generator) can handle word processing and data processing, and using its foreground/background operation, it can do these things including communicating through the SOURCE personal nationwide (250-city) network and at the same time monitor home or office security, control ac devices, and play games. The SOURCE Information Utility was pioneered by Telecomputing Corporation of America, which offers individuals and small businesses DATAPOST, a service that allows users to send soft or hard copies of addressed messages for pickup by any and all others and permits "chatting" by computer at far less cost than lengthy phone calls. It originally offered more than 2000 data bases of information, all easily accessed, including news, sports, weather, stock market information, educational courses, *New York Times* Consumer Data Bank, entertainment announcements, reviews, ticket information, personal financial information, guides, business help including tried and tested programs, travel planning, and so on. Businesses are joining for a $100 one-time fee plus $2.75 per hour of access time in nonprime hours (6 p.m. to 7 a.m. local time).

With high-speed computers like the Ohio Scientific C8P DF/GT and others, using 16 colors for high-resolution graphics, large displays of 2048 characters (32 rows of 64 columns), and scores of pieces of optional equipment, there are few offices that could not afford to use "electronic offices." This is especially true since in late 1979 a million characters of disk memory (1 megabyte) was available for just over $1000, and prices were falling fast. The personal computer magazines were exceeding the standard computer periodicals in pages of ads (often up to 300 per issue) and circulation (several over 80,000 and one over 150,000) and all growing. These pages were loaded with very low cost software, and although many executives felt they needed custom system design, others found standard packages for accounting, etc., more than adequate.

Under more stringent conditions of large-enterprise office procedures, managers and executives, in many cases, were well aware that up to 70% of their time was occupied in face-to-face meetings, telephone calls, looking at reports, or traveling to have more of these face-to-face meetings, look at more reports, or make more phone calls. Each of these areas offered good to excellent potential for productivity improvement. Electronic offices with electronic correspondence, teleconferencing (visual or computer), instant information retrieval, and speech mail could easily result, with some of this completed from homes with personal computers, and with time savings of 30% to 50%. Long-distance copy printing, freeze-frame displays, and digitized dictation stored in random-access memory provide relative ease for text editing with few or no people and little if any paper.

What goes on at the new electronic work stations in modern offices? Briefly, distributed or local entry, data and word processing and reporting, text document production, communications, and interchange of files, reports, and documents (soft, i.e., display, or hard copy) are "standard" activities. Voice storage, recognition, and processing as input modes have only recently become practical in terms of cost and capabilities, but voice answerback has been a cheap and effective option for years. Who are some of the companies offering these system capabilities? IBM has several devices for document distribution (in its Grand Design); Wang offers electronic messaging besides its combined WP-DP systems; Digital Equipment Corp. has packaged its internally developed message system and offers it for sale; Rolm offers electronic mail and hundreds of other services through its computerized PBX telephone systems; Graphic Sciences offers facsimile message switching; Rapicom offers true store-and-forward electronic mail through front-end processors on almost any computer; both Xerox and AT&T are building specialized electronic mail subnets for trucking, banking, insurance and legal industries; and Satellite Business Systems has begun to offer most of the foregoing services using rooftop satellite antennas.

What Is a Word Processor That Combines With a Data Processor That Communicates?

These systems are so numerous and vary so much that precise definitions are impossible to formulate. In effect, however, a relatively simple word processor performs the functions in the following list.

- Printer
- Print queuing
- Screen format & capacity
- Display memory
- Vertical scroll
- Horizontal scroll
- Display highlighting
- Search capability
- Format statement display
- Merge capability
- Forms creation and control
- Subscripts and superscripts
- Greek mathematical symbols
- Auto word wraparound
- Auto margin adjust
- Temporary margins
- Auto decimal tab
- Auto centering
- Right justification
- Global search and replace
- Block edit
- Column edit
- Save and recall
- Auto page numbering
- Auto repagination
- Service diagnostics

Adding this typewriter-looking machine to an electronic mail system means others are linked in intra- or intercommunications to key people. With multiple work stations and various types of disk drives and printers, meetings are set and conducted, after the agendas are generated and memoranda added to them by the word processor, and telephone messages are "handled" by the same machine. Many are always on-line to the computer system data bases, providing rapid access to that information using personal-computer simultaneous input-output capabilities. For example, the Vydec 2000 "word processor-communicator" is advertised as "a programmable word processing and communications system that combines a multiline crt with a Natural Language Keyboard™, integral printer, removable disk storage, and far-reaching communications capabilities all in one desk-top unit." It automatically performs input and formatting functions, including indention, centering, and decimal alignment. It features an automatic document directory and four status lines that display the document name and page number, the position of the cursor, and information on "background" communications, "message arriving," etc. It prints a page or an entire document in background while working on another in foreground.

Technology has indeed made it easier and cheaper to manipulate, move, and store electrons than paper, and this is having a monumental effect on business and all people in it.

SECTION IV

Introduction to Computer System Principles and Procedures

This section encompasses many aspects of computer systems and serves to present an insight into both the hardware and software considerations involved and the procedures used to obtain optimum results. Although some portions provide information of a general nature, certain portions are devoted to more specific areas of application and methodology. By presenting the material in this manner, it is reasoned that both the initiated and the uninitiated reader will not only gain a better understanding of computer operations, but also will become aware of the related problems and their solutions which are associated with computer systems.

AN ANALYSIS OF COMPUTER SYSTEM OPERATIONS: WHAT IS A COMPUTER?

How many students, teachers, and managers are asking, "What is this strange power that the computer has which enables it to control inventories, machines, and whole plants and to retrieve information in billionths of seconds? How does it think, or does it really think?" Some have heard and read that it is extremely accurate and tireless, but that it also is really a dumb servant and lacks initiative. How does it arrive at the answers it gives; how does it control automation in offices, factories, libraries; how does it choose, remember, calculate, predict, and even correct its own errors? Why is it having such an impact on industry, business, science, education? Can it outthink people; how will it endanger our goals; must we really learn how to operate it; where will it all end; how will it affect our future and future generations? The answers to these questions are in the current literature if the student will take time to search for them. The years 1980 to 1985 will bring the computer and its capability and applications more into public view and scrutiny than perhaps the industry really desires, for there is bound to be urgency in degrees of fear and controversy relating to social problems and adjustments required for continued computer advances. In the late 1970s, advertisements related to personal computers appeared regularly in newspapers and magazines and on television. Newspaper columnists began to use startling computer stories with increasing regularity. Franchises for computer centers and educational institutes began to spring up in cities and even neighborhoods throughout the United States. Thus, more students, teachers, white-collar workers, and blue-collar workers alike began to ask the questions previously mentioned. It has become more obvious to millions that the computer is not simply a programmed lightning calculator; it is clear that it makes decisions, does office staff work, almost automatically conducts experiments, supervises quality control, designs new products, interprets market-research analysis, and is about to revolutionize educational procedures.

How does the computer solve a problem? How does it store information and retrieve it? How does it remember instructions, follow them, and even change them on the basis of pre-established criteria or conditions? Fundamentally, it performs these feats much the same as a human being or like a calculating machine. The five basic functions of any digital computer are: (1) input, (2) storage, (3) control, (4) processing, and (5) output. Before solving a problem, you as an individual must gather facts and data and store them in your mind; the computer receives them in the form of binary codes of 1s and 0s and stores them on tapes, disks, drums, cores, or plastic cards; i.e., its electronic memory. The computer does have properties similar to those of the adding machine; it can add, subtract, multiply, divide, list, and also uniquely make decisions; i.e., select on the basis of stored instructions. This stored-program concept and memory capability are the two primary differentiating characteristics between the computer and a high-speed calculator. The control function simply means following the instructions very precisely as programmed and stored. The computer must be instructed (programmed) every step of the way. The output of the computer takes many forms. Generally, it will be printed, put on cards or tape, stored in memory, displayed on a cathode-ray tube (crt), or communicated to other remote devices.

One might compare the five computer functions to the simple calculator, where the keyboard is an input device; the sequence and method of manipulation of the keys represents the control function, i.e., the sequence of steps. The use of scratch paper for lists or other data could be considered memory or storage means, and the movement of gears, counters, and levers on a calculator would correspond to the processing or arithmetic of the computer. The figures printed on the tapes relate to the output of the computer. This is much too simplified, but it does aid to explain the five general logic components of the electronic computer. Intermix with this the nanosecond (billionth of a second) computing speed and random-access information retrieval (any bit of data from among billions of numbers and characters), plus stored sequential or adaptive instructions (program steps), and the differences between the human mind and the electronic calculator are few but of tremendous importance. The simplified diagram in Fig. A-17 illustrates the sequence, with the control units used to interface or synchronize the varying speeds of numerous input and output units to those of the CPU—the central processing (arithmetic and logic) unit. The processor must also translate the relatively simple language used by the programmer into the more detailed computer-code form used internally by the computer. In order to achieve the speed and accuracy described, only 1s and 0s are used internally; i.e., flip-flop circuits change 0s to 1s and vice versa. The student might now begin to realize that programming is a segment of the total complexity of the computing system, but the operation of the computer itself is relatively quite simple. The speed which permits scientists to do in hours what it would have taken hundreds of years to accomplish without a computer is a trade-off of internal binary (on-off) operating simplicity for the more complicated task of writing instructions for programs (software vs hardware). This is why most computers are still input/output limited and cannot yet reach their full capa-

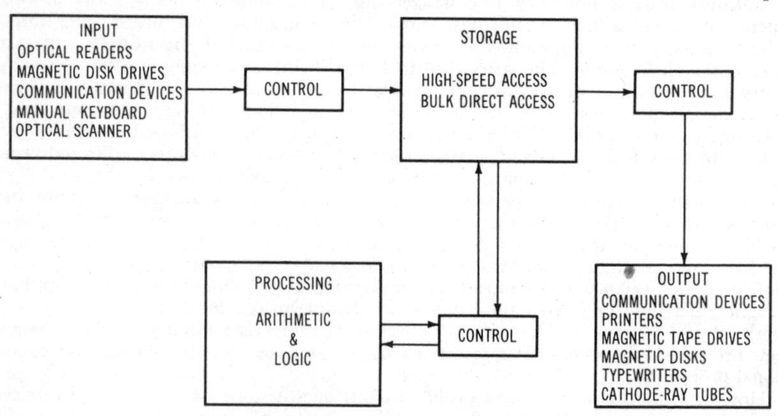

Fig. A-17. Computer sequence.

bility until more minds discover the tremendous versatility of solving new and specific programming with split-second speeds. The full potential of computing is just now being grasped; the great potential payoffs in all academic disciplines and most of man's endeavors are being increased almost daily. Data processing (DP) systems are able to utilize the computer in practically every area of business. Management-information systems (MIS) are proving to be areas of the widest applications and remain one of the core topics of this text, areas about which engineers require a good deal of information in order to adapt their particular skills to the greatest number of applications and largest potential customer pool.

Although programming appears to be the primary essential of computer control, the actual programming can be completed by people other than those skilled in management or engineering. The most important areas of control reside with the problem discoverers, analyzers and solvers who fully understand computer capability but not necessarily the intricacies of computer operation or programming. Thus, several of the most important steps in computer usage are those of operations analysis. Only the highly skilled manager or engineer can know his system of operation well enough to discover a problem, define its components, analyze its alternatives, build a solution model (definitive replica of reality), and determine if the techniques will achieve the goals or optimal results. The manager then must develop skills of system analysis, model building, operations-research (solution) techniques, and mathematical formulas to accurately represent the problem prior to programming. Some of the appendices in this book cover these tools and procedures for the business computer control people—those who structure the problems and use the results—the new breed of information-management scientists.

It is only when the problem is designed that the flowchart can be devised, for it is the flowchart which the programmer uses as a guide to his programming task. Flowcharts logically and precisely prepare the sequential individual steps which the computer must perform to achieve the solution desired. The programmer must, in the great majority of cases, have this graphical device to instruct the computer efficiently for any system design, problem solution, or information retrieval project. Fig. A-18 shows a typical flowchart which denotes decision-making steps required to achieve success in this quite special endeavor. Other appendices will explain some of the detail or error (bugs) control, real-time operations research and modeling techniques, etc.

BASIC COMPUTER PRINCIPLES AND SYSTEM EQUIPMENT

Very generally, a computer system—or electronic data-processing (EDP) system—is outwardly an assemblage of electromechanical and electronic modules. The modules contain interconnected transistors, diodes, capacitors, and other parts designed into miscellaneous switching devices. All are microminiaturized even to the extent that scores of complete integrated circuits are chemically formed on thin film "chips" smaller than this letter "o." (Some are 28/1000 of an inch wide and close to being invisibly thin.) Several average-size computer-processor units contain more than 100,000 individual components. The total group or configuration of these calculating and storing units is usually called a computer system, or simply a computer.

Present-day computers are of two general types—an analog computer which measures on a continuous scale much like a slide rule or automobile speedometer, and a digital computer which counts specifically or discretely, never varying or responding in degrees but only to signals which exist or do not exist. More than 90% of the computers in existence are digital computers, and the great majority of definitions and appendices in this text will relate to these. Also, "hybrid" systems (combination of analog and digital) are mentioned in several areas, especially those which concern numerical-control automation machines, automobile computers, and home control systems.

Basically, a digital system or computer has the ability to perform only very simple tasks. It uses a binary number system which has only two numbers, 0 and 1, whereas the decimal system has ten digits. By using various horizontal- and vertical-positioning techniques, these two binary digits, or "bits," can represent numbers, letters, symbols, and codes. For example, binary 0110 represents the decimal number 6. Operation in binary mode, then, means that the computer is able to indicate only two possible

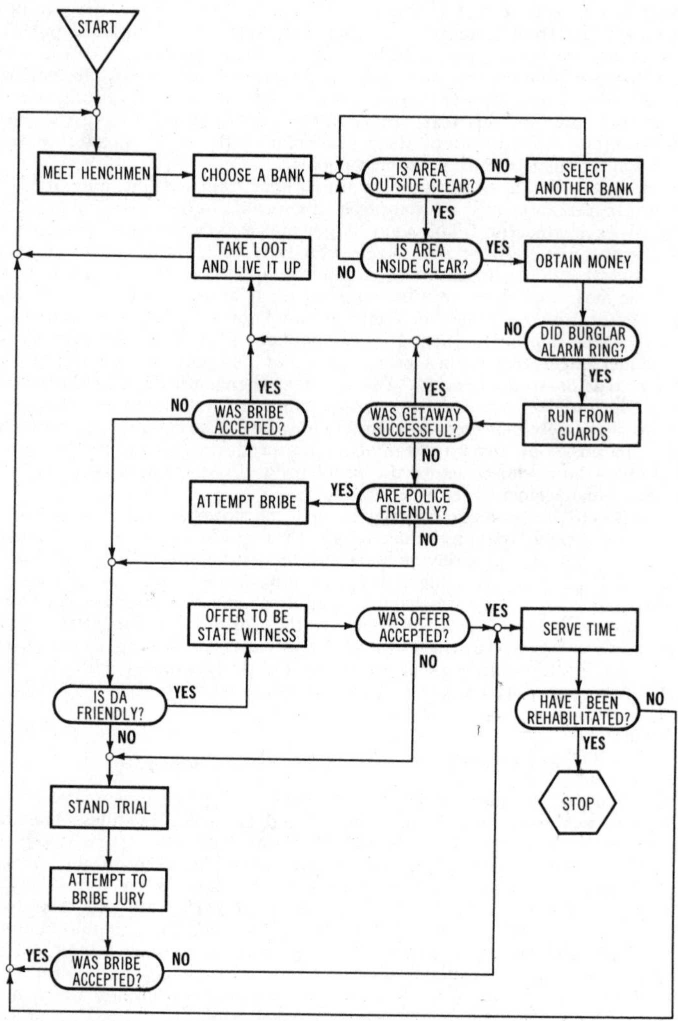

Fig. A-18. A sample flowchart.

states or conditions. The ordinary light bulb operates in this way; it is either on and producing light, or it is off. Similarly, in the computer, the transistors, circuits, etc. are either conducting or they are not; specific areas on plastic tapes are magnetized or they are not; pulses are present or they are not. By judicious use of this positioning and arrangement of circuits plus ingenious coding techniques, these binary digits (or groups of digits called bytes, words, or nibbles) develop complex or simple sets of instructions called routines or programs. Special languages have been created to make use of branches, scans, loops, storage, retieval, and hundreds of procedural steps including "adapt" to suggest that the computer closely approaches an artificial intelligence sufficient to solve practically any problem that can be defined and programmed.

Through the use of macroinstructions (single instructions which call sets of many single elementary microinstructions) and compilers, the simple presence or absence of magnetic spots on plastic tapes "orders" the computer to read, write, store, transmit, or compute for solutions of millions of scientific, business, machine control, and research problems. The computer itself represents only utmost simplicity. It can only count, compare, store, retieve, and add. Because multiplication is successive addition, subtraction really basic algebraic addition, and division successive subtraction, the capability of the computer can perform all types of arithmetic and algebra by addition. The application of the imaginative mind of man and his precise instructions make the computer superefficient. The true magic of the computer, however, is its fantastic speed and memory capacity. Change-of-state cycles and information retrieval are measured in nanoseconds (billionths of a second) due to the near infinitesimal distances signals must travel in the microminiaturized components and monolithic circuits. Examples of speed and memory capacities are: speeds of fifteen million additions per second, 250 nsec (nanoseconds) retrieval, and 6000 lines per minute printing capability. Thus, the computer holds data and instructions in its "memory" subject to call, control, and execution on other specific data, and it has the ability to change or construct its own instructions or routines, as programmed, or by branch interrupts from various sources.

Because the computer can compare, it can make decisions; that is, it can use this ability to select from many alternatives, using prescribed criteria. The easiest example of this would be a computer instruction such as: Is the result of A times B less than the value of X? If yes, perform instruction P. Is the result equal to the value of X? If yes, branch to program Q. Is the result greater than the value of X? If yes, perform process Y. The computer will assess the values of manipulation and make conclusions following rigorous instruction of the various user or precoded program packages called "software." Such software is as important to the computer as the hardware itself. Software has been developed for thousands of particular problems and routines, and it is usually available from computer manufacturers to become a "library" of available pretested programs for standard situations and systems. Many software packages of unique characteristics have been skillfully developed by computer service companies, educational institutions, and computer users themselves. Most computer manufacturers very efficiently use several different "languages" to effect communication and control of the almost unlimited computer versatility. The most important of these languages are also compilers, such as FORTRAN, ALGOL, PL/1, and COBOL. Each language uses many powerful macrostatements that can trigger hundreds of detailed machine-language coded operations and microinstructions.

By analyzing the combined use of its decision-making ability (FORTRAN statements such as DO, IF, and GO TO) with analog-computer numerical control (N/C), such as maximum-minimum temperature limits, one might be better able to understand how the production "mini" computers can control chemical plants and the cutting and shaping tolerances in manufacturing. The digital computer alone, however, can control the exclusion of various payroll deductions after certain income limits are reached (social security). Thus, numerical control, combined with digitally stored exception programs, forms the basis for tape-fed automated machines, while digital machines alone can control the complicated accounting, inventory, and automatic purchasing systems.

Because of the nanosecond speed, multibillion-bit storage capacity, and still unimagined versatility of the computer, new problem-solving techniques are discovered and programmed many times daily. Operations research is the name given to an important group of techniques and devices of modern methodology used for defining, analyzing, and solving scientific and business problems.

Before problems can be solved, however, they must be explicitly defined, organized, and resolved into numerical or mathematical real-life replicas or representations. This use of empirical data organized into manipulative models (Appendix E) of the problem precedes the sequential and analytical flowcharts (Appendix J). These charts guide the writing of programs acceptable to the computer. The skilled, modern manager will know the capability of the computer and its precise rules and will thus analyze, deduce, and evaluate his problems with new clarity, order, and logic. He will use more facts instantly available from computers, sounder reasoning (and fewer hunches) to rigorously define and flowchart his problem (model) before giving it to his system analyst or programmer to solve. Former enigmas, never before attempted, will have ranges of solutions instantly displayed on his personal cathode-ray tube (crt) for evaluation and judgment or "light pen" alterations or additions to the data or program. His knowledge, experience, and critical analysis will become part of the computer. He will also learn to use heuristics (seeking to discover) and simulation (trial-and-error models) before deciding on size, characteristics, and location of a new plant, for example. The enhanced quality of his cognitive capability plus his increased value and raised level of services to his firm will be due to his knowledge of computers and new problem-solving devices.

The complete process as outlined is often called cybernetics, briefly defined as the process of automatic communications and control. The physical heart of a computer is the central processing unit (CPU). Grouped around this main frame is a variety of storage and other ancillary equipment such as disks, voice i/o, light pens, readers, communication converters, and the like. Units with direct connection to the CPU are said to be on-line, while some other peripheral units performing separate tasks are called off-line. If answers are fast enough (instantaneous) to become part of the original inquiry, the system is said to be an on-line real-time (OLRT) system or relatively no (lost) time.

An operator contacts the system from a terminal equipped with a keyboard and an acoustical coupler for phone entry, or through other devices. Computer systems vary in size, complexity, cost, computation and retrieval speed, and transmission capability. Computers have many classifications of which the most important are general purpose (GP), personal computer (PC), special purpose (SP), hybrid, master/slave, or time-sharing. All computer systems, regardless of size, type, or basic use, have certain fundamental concepts and operational principles which should be mastered by all students and users. The data, instructions, and information flow follow logical and functional lines.

Input to the computer can take a variety of forms: typewriter, telephone, disk, cassette tape, videodisc, magnetic cards, magnetic ink (bank checks), or directly and in binary form from the main memory or peripheral storage units and various conversion units. Quite recently, plain, typed print or script in limited vocabularies became serviceable as scanned input to computers. Input is also developed photoelectrically through digitizers, and through the use of tv-type cathode-ray tubes. This is done by the use of electronic pointers or light pens (styli) which quickly erase, alter, or add to main memory any information or solution which is displayed on the crt. Such visual alterations are directly convertible to electronic pulses (and characters) in real time, by pointing the light pen at the data or information on the tube. This is an important aid to engineers, designers, and statisticians, as well as for managers of all types. Audio input is being perfected with limited vocabulary, and other sophisticated audio output devices such as the New York Stock Exchange Voice Answer Back (NYSE-VAB) are now in use. Optical scanners quite normally read more than 1500 characters per second, or 90,000 documents per hour. Direct input can be developed by radio, teletypewriter, and numerous other communication devices besides the cards, tapes, inks, scanners, and crt's previously mentioned.

THE CENTRAL PROCESSOR ARITHMETIC AND LOGIC UNIT AND NEW MAIN MEMORY DEVICES

The functional unit which actually performs the translation from near-English compiler languages to machine-language binary codes which the computer understands is the central processor. Following the program or routine by using its computing and controlling power, this central unit executes the orders for batch, demand, or real-time flow of data and instructions. Information, programs, or data are drawn from storage or input units by the CPU for manipulation, and are then returned to storage to await further orders from the CPU in regards to output decisions. The logic operations include comparing information and selecting the valid or desired process or program based on predetermined decision criteria. Other CPU tasks are referring, shifting, complementing, rounding, debugging (discovering and correcting errors), displaying, transmitting, etc. Until the advent and current use of tiny microcomputers, the CPU was input/output limited. Because of very large scale integration (VLSI), a whole new computer philosophy has evolved.

Computer Logic Components—the Essence of the Central Processing Unit

Because the computer is a binary system and a binary system is essentially a switching procedure from "on" to "off" and vice versa, the components of computers relate to elementary switches and amplifiers. Such switches and switching techniques comprise a myriad of types and combinations. They are often referred to as "gates," "operators," or "elements."

The original computers were built of vacuum and gas tubes and were subject to many faults. They required temperature regulation, gave unreliable levels of service, and were bulky and cumbersome to maintain. In 1947, tubes quickly gave way to the remarkable discovery of the transistor by Bell Telephone Laboratories scientists William Shockley and John Bardeen, theoretical physicists, and Walter Brittain, an experimental scientist. The solid-state transistors had no heated filaments or vacuum gaps, but like the vacuum tube they controlled and amplified electric current. The transistor, in addition to being supremely more efficient, was relatively tiny and had small power requirements. Lack of maintenance service and long life are additional advantages of the transistor. It has now become the basis of all modern computing main-frame and peripheral equipment, and today's computers consist of literally millions of transistors and other miniature electronic components.

Microminiaturization of the Central Processing Unit

The millions of components which made up the computer had to be handled individually and connected by soldering or welding. Heating and bending, possible corrosion of the joining material, and expansion difficulties at the joints reduced reliability by increasing the chance for damage. Also, computer speed was limited to the time it took a signal to travel from one circuit to another. Each foot of circuit separation required a travel time of at least a billionth of a second. This travel time could be reduced only by making the circuits and their separations microscopically small. Microelectronics was the inevitable response to the need for smaller size, lower cost, and greater reliability. Microelectronics thus made it possible to mass-produce complete circuits automatically on a minuscule chip of semiconductor material (usually silicon). The very complicated circuits formerly required hundreds of thousands of separate elements, transistors, diodes, resistors, and capacitors. Some standard silicon chips—squares less than one-quarter inch (6.4 mm) on a side—contain more than 1000 transistors and diodes with all their connections. Others are often much tinier with more than 8000 components per chip.

Memory Advances

The electronic industry quickly improved upon integrated circuits with the concept and development of large-scale integration (LSI). The LSI circuit was an extension of the integrated circuit except for the manufacturing and more complicated design. Whereas some early ICs consisted of sixty transistors and diodes on a microscopic chip of silicon, various LSI circuit "sandwiches" consist of literally thousands of elements or devices properly combined in a circuit on a tiny "wafer" of silicon about one-eighth inch square. The influence of LSIs is felt in industrial and commercial applications throughout the world. LSI and other circuitry innovations have replaced, or made obsolete, many types of computer memories. In 1974, the standard memory chip could store approximately 1000 bits of information. A year later, the 4000-bit chip was introduced. Two years after that came the 16,000-bit chip, and in 1978 the first commercially available 64,000-bit chip was announced. Four generations of memory chips in five years increased the capability of that particular component by 64 times. And there is every indication that by the mid-1980s, 256K chips will be commonplace. Very-large-scale integration (VLSI) promises similar progress in logic devices. Already, VLSI has given us 30,000 logic devices per chip. By the mid-1980s, this could increase at least tenfold.

Bell Telephone Laboratories' "magnetic bubble" computer memory discovery could drastically change the architecture of computers by shrinking the size of the total system considerably. The technology is based on tiny magnetic domains that appear, disappear, and move around through certain kinds of crystalline materials under the control of magnetic and electric fields. Bubble memories moved out of the laboratories in 1979 with Texas Instruments Inc., Rockwell International, Intel Corp., Fujitsu, and Plessy making the first early strides in marketing successes.

Programmable read-only memory (PROM) and various erasable types, such as electrically erasable ROM (EEROM) and electrically alterable ROM (EAROM), have all become standards.

COMPUTER OPERATIONAL CONTROL

Basically, the CPU is the real control section, but the console on standard computers and minicomputers indicates the internal state of the computer and regulates the external manual control. The computer or program can be started, interrupted, stopped, modified, and monitored at the console. It has the slowest input (usually by typewriter), and the console is often combined in one main frame with internal memory, buffer, arithmetic, and inquiry sections. It then can be said to direct, coordinate, execute, time, and communicate the performance of the system. The CPU automatically goes to the next cycle when the preceding cycle is complete.

Through the multiplexors (memory multiplex or input/output multiplexor), console operations can control multiprogramming, multiprocessing, or parallel programming though these functions are usually automatic and dynamic. The control section or console becomes extremely important in case of component breakdown, or when debugging, printing diagnostics, or post-mortem routines are in operation.

Various operating systems form the cornerstone of control of all types of computers. They consist of programs and routines which guide and control computer performance by assisting the programs and the programmers with supporting functions to increase the utility of computer hardware. Basically, operating systems perform some or all of the following:

1. Control the computer with regard to the sequence in handling job programs and job-to-job transition.
2. Control the work specification and operations of compilers, assemblers, and other manufacturer-designed software.
3. Assist in debugging and error diagnostic services, especially those relating to snapshot dumps, traces, memory dumps, and error messages.
4. Provide program-to-program transitions, specifically as regards loading additional instructions from external storage within single jobs.
5. Control the scheduling and discipline required to run many programs simultaneously in a time-sharing environment.
6. Interpret operator commands on tapes, disks, voice, and other systems which determine the specifics of the work to be accomplished.
7. Schedule and perform input/output and related operations to relieve the programmer of hardware-oriented considerations; i.e., optimizing the input/output device utilization of job programs.
8. Develop program protections as regards potential alternating of one program with the work of another.
9. Schedule and control dynamic allocation of storage and other resources during multiprogramming procedures.
10. Schedule and allocate tasks of various processors of large-scale multiprocessing computers.

Most operating systems (OS) consist of program loaders, queue techniques, schedulers, clocks, etc. Because many very modern chip or standard computers are so complex, the operating system is an absolute requirement for efficient use of the hardware itself and the time and storage space available for problem solving. Operating systems require a great deal of main memory but are worth it, especially since main memory costs have been reduced by a factor of ten or more within the last few years.

COMPUTER STORAGE DEVICES FOR THE 1980s

Primary CPU storage is fast, expensive, and relatively limited in most medium and small machines. Secondary storage, on-line or off-line, has no limit except expense and requirements. Tape storage is sequential and requires scanning character-by-character over a reel or cassette to find a desired item of information. Other more popular memory units are capable of random access from disks, floppy and fixed, RAMs and ROMs, videodiscs, etc. Some CPUs are capable of selecting from them any item or bit with speeds as fast as 250 nsec. From the input unit, data or programs are moved to the storage section of the CPU or to mass-memory units. Some of these units have capacities of six billion characters in a single drawer-sized configuration of a few units. Buffer units, used as separate modules or as parts of the various peripheral groups or CPUs, are capable of briefly holding data inactive. Thus, successive bundles of data can be displayed for immediate computing while they are ordered sequentially or according to priority schedules, and perhaps altered, or otherwise controlled. Data are then delivered for computation or operation by the CPU when it is ready for them. Various supervisor, monitor, or executive-control routines or programs automatically exercise such scheduling control. The electronic "scratchpad" for checking, scanning, and controlled delay is an important service of many computers. Storage units can be connected on-line (OL) even at great distances (sometimes world-wide) through the truly marvelous communications systems recently marketed.

In computer language, writing means putting information into a register; reading means taking information out of a register for use; erase means completely removing the information from a register; dumping means removing or replacing the information with spaces or zeros, or copying or printing all or part of the contents, such as a transfer from one storage device to another.

The Structure and Classification of Computer Memories

Recent manufacturing capabilities have laid great stress on the significance not only of speed, total capacity, and low cost of new memory systems, but they have also emphasized the development of special ranges of versatility practically undreamed of only a few years ago. The techniques of splitting and interleaving among various types of memory hierarchies in individual systems have changed some of the basic concepts of computing itself.

The information presented on the following pages is divided into the following three groups:

I. Memory Splitting and Interleaving Techniques
II. Storage Types by Function
III. Storage Types by Performance Characteristics

Memory "Splitting and Interleaving" Techniques

For efficient use of combined main, auxiliary, semiconductor, and peripheral storage devices, memory "groups" have become commonplace in computer models introduced in the late 1970s. Descriptions below relate some of these current concepts and practices.

Normal Memory—A set of main memory locations which are contiguous and specifically located for storage of programs, data, and data sets, and most often organized in a logical or subject order or sequence. If some programs are larger than main memory, overlays to auxiliary memory may be used as in virtual memory.

Virtual Memory—For storage efficiency, some computers are designed so that parts of programs and data may be scattered through main memory and auxiliary storage. Various pointers or lists of pointers automatically keep track of the location of these program portions. The user of computers so designed may be unaware of this scattering procedure and most often operates his computing procedures as though he were using normal memory.

Cache Memory—An IBM-developed, limited-capacity, very fast semiconductor memory which can be used in combination with lower-cost but slower large-capacity main memory, giving effect to a large and faster memory. Look-ahead procedures are required in the progress of the programs to effect locating and depositing the right information into the fast memory when it is required.

Memory Interleaving—A process of splitting the memory into two sections with two paths to the central processor to speed processing. Main memory access takes longer than logic or arithmetic operations, but a second word can be read during the half-cycle when the previously read word is being written back into the memory.

Odd-Even Interleaving—With the splitting of memory into several sections and independent paths, the odd-even addresses are in alternate sections. This allows even further segmenting than normal memory interleaving of the read/write memory cycle. Some older systems follow this procedure by segmenting the central processor for multiprocessing operation by dividing main storage and extended storage into odd-even segments while still permitting simultaneous memory access for arithmetic commands and input/output instructions.

Microprogramming Simulation—This procedure has emulation as its chief function, since a microprogram can imitate the basic instruction set of the machine being emulated. Word lengths, arithmetic, and logic details, as well as other functions of another machine, are simulated. Each fundamental instruction or operation of the imitated machine is made up of a sequence of microcoded steps allowing registers to be loaded, data to be moved, etc. Quite often the microcoded sequences which make up each basic machine operation are handwired into a control store. Such control stores in many new machines are either being made from read-only memory (ROM), which may be easily removed for substitution, or from semiconductor reloadable control store (RCS), such as the new "smart" RAMs. Microprogramming offers user programmers opportunities to tailor their own machines to their own jobs; i.e., powerful instructions can be developed which would require only a single line of program code to complete a number of complex but repetitive jobs called for in specific installation requirements.

Memory Hierarchies—Because there is a speed mismatch between semiconductor logic and random-access storage media such as disks, memory system innovations have arisen. Program and data parts can be scattered in both main memories and disks for swapping between main and auxiliary storage automatically on demand (demand paging). Normally, copies of all pages in main memory are retained on an auxiliary disk, and when changes are made in page contents while in main memory, copies are written back onto the disk when no longer needed. Access to semiconductor memories is in nanoseconds, to magnetic memories in microseconds, and to cassettes in milliseconds, with such differences in speed usually inversely related to cost; i.e., the slowest memories are the lowest cost per bit storage. Splitting memories into sections and then interleaving the accessing to alternate sections is a procedure for cutting down the speed mismatch between logic and memories.

Byte Multiplexing—A procedure in which time slots on a channel are assigned to individual slow input/output devices so that the bytes from one after another can be interlaced on the channel to or from main memory.

Storage Types by Function

Register Storage—The 1, 2, (3 or 4) word, or block storage before transfer to other storage types or registers; i.e., accumulator, multiplicand, index, or other registers.

Backing Storage—Auxiliary storage with capacities larger (and slower).

Internal Storage—Transfers usually in blocks.

Parallel Storage—Devices which store characters, words, and digits simultaneously and equally available in space, without time being one of the coordinates.

Buffer Storage—Temporary storage of data in process of being transferred from one system or computer to another, such as a communication line or device to and from internal memory from tapes, disks, terminals, etc.; devices with ability to accept data at one speed and to transmit at another speed.

On-Line Storage—Storage under direct control of the central processing unit.

Mass Data Storage—High-capacity data storage systems or devices external to, but under direct control of, the central processing unit, usually holding bulk data such as files, subroutines, tables, etc.

Intermediate Storage (Inherent)—A type of "scratchpad" memory holding the computed data for, or in, excessive changes; i.e., data held in one program cycle for use in succeeding cycles.

Matrix Storage—A type of storage in which elements are arranged in a matrix so that access to any location requires the use of two or more coordinates.

Electrostatic Storage—The storage of data on a dielectric surface, such as the screen of a cathode-ray tube, in the form of the presence or absence of spots bearing electrostatic charges that can persist for a short time after the electrostatic charging force is removed.

Laser-Emulsion Storage—A specific storage device or medium for digital data with a controlled laser beam exposing very small areas on photosensitive surfaces, and in which a Kerr effect is used to interrupt the laser beam, producing desired information patterns.

Read-Only Storage—Storage that cannot be altered in normal use of the computer. Usually a small memory that contains often-used instructions such as microprograms or system software as firmware.

Storage Types by Performance Characteristics

Bootstrap Storage—A time-saving device built in the main computer. Some systems consist of various types of RAM/ROM storage. ROM is programmed (fused) to fit the specialized needs of various computer users. The programs and words in the bootstrap memory cannot be altered by the computer, but ROM can be manually changed when necessary. The purpose of the bootstrap storage is to provide for the automatic reading of new programs into the computer with protection against erasing its vital instructions.

Interleaving Storage—Two or more memory banks operating a fraction of a cycle apart and significantly reducing cycle time and, therefore, improving storage speed.

Volatile Storage—Storage whose contents are destroyed in the event that power is removed; e.g., a transistor register.

Electrically Alterable Storage—Storage whose contents can be changed electrically by the computer, by auxiliary equipment, or by human-directed activity; such as magnetic disk, magnetic tape, various types of ROM.

Storage Block—A portion or section of storage usually within a storage area. A storage block is considered a single element for holding a specific or fixed number of words.

Associative Storage—Storage in which the memory can be directly addressed by content.

Bulk Storage—Storage of large-volume capacity used to supplement the high-speed storage which can be made addressable, such as disks or videodisks, or remain nonaddressable with magnetic tapes. Other names for this type of storage are external or secondary storage.

Random-Access Storage—Storage in which the access time to each record is independent of the location of the preceding record, e.g., a normal semiconductor RAM.

Destructive Readout Storage—Storage in which the act of reading erases the contents of the cells whose contents are read out. The term NDRO for NonDestructive ReadOut is used for the converse case.

Photo-Optic Storage—A storage that uses an optical medium for storage. For example, a laser might be used to record on photographic film or other video disk material.

Dynamic Storage—In such storage, the data are in constant motion (usually cyclically) with respect to the medium in which they are represented.

Virtual Storage—A technique that permits the user to treat secondary (disk) storage as an extension of main memory, thus giving the "virtual" appearance of a larger main memory to the programmer.

OPTICAL OUTPUT DEVICES

Data can be written out from storage to output units, or it can be read from storage to output. The results of the processing are thus converted to English or decimals. They can be recorded in various ways: as a printed report (at up to 6000 lines per minute and faster, with new nonimpact printers); as graphs, drawings, or English for viewing and altering on display tubes; as magnetic tape, paper tape, punched or magnetic cards; or by audio (voice) output. Some very dramatic innovations of computer systems concern the newest optic devices and automatic language translators (example, Russian-to-English) as well as the talking machines and adaptive processors.

Although it is being challenged by plasma and LCD, the cathode-ray tube is currently the dominating terminal device. Some of the basic descriptions and capabilities are explained quite generally below.

Optical Displays—Cathode-Ray Tube or Direct-View Storage Tubes

Television-type optical displays are easily the most important peripheral devices of the computer industry. Present optical devices as described below are the forerunners of vastly improved technology represented on the massive production lines of many manufacturers. Advantages of optical display equipment are many:

1. Displays do not have the inherent limitations of the printing mechanism in that they are not limited to alphanumeric or other forms of discrete symbols—drawings and sketches are possible.
2. Increased speed and flexibility of use include ability to flash the same message simultaneously on several displays.
3. The ability to enlarge or select specific areas of a message establishes extra convenience of editing or correcting messages before entry into the computer processor or memory unit.
4. The cathode-ray tube may even be less expensive than other forms of output devices as technology improves, and on-line system programming-cost trade-offs show crt advantages in this area.
5. Displays permit user control directly, without the need for translation through a programmer, and permit on-line process building for those managers who are unfamiliar with sophisticated programming or model-building techniques.
6. More than any other factor, the ease of operation permits an easy procedure for the eager executive to become "personally involved" with both input and choice of output by the use of "button boxes" and light pens.
7. Such devices are really effective in a battle to "stamp out paper" and eliminate the punched card.

A particular advantage claimed for the direct-view storage tube (DVST) over the cathode-ray tube (crt) is that the former eliminates the high data-transfer rates or considerable buffer storage required, even for static displays with short persistence, when cathode-ray tubes are used. But, the versatile crt is still everywhere approved as a creative tool for on-line computer-aided design (CAD) as well as for problem solving, text and program editing, on-line debugging, teaching machines, automated laboratories, etc. The DVST eliminates the need for continual regeneration and can provide excellent displays; unfortunately, conventional light-pen techniques are not applicable to DVSTs either in the tracking mode, which senses and follows pen movement by probing the visual field of the pen, or in the pointing mode, which associates the instant of pen response with an item in the display file. But these two objections have been overcome, and the reader is sure to read more of the developments of DVSTs. Our discussion to follow will concentrate, however, on crt's and conventional light pens.

A crt needs little definition, as all are familiar with the similar tv tube. However, the light pen can best be defined as a hand-held penlike device, containing a photocell or photomultiplier, that is used for many purposes in conjunction with a crt, among them the guiding of the tracking cross on the display. The tracking cross is a crosslike array of bright dots on the display, used for locating points and lines or for drawing geometric figures. The universal button box is a term for a set of push buttons whose functions are determined by the computer program being executed, and which can be overlaid with other plastic charts for new sets of instructions as total programs are changed. These buttons are thus keyed to various function capabilities and are illuminated, when selected, to provide a clear and convenient method to refer to and execute basic control functions.

The light pen is such an important element of display systems that it might be described more carefully as being a little larger than a fountain pen, and presents one end of a fiber-optics bundle to the face of the display for sensing the points of the cross. The other end of the bundle terminates at a photomultiplier tube. The sensing circuits are designed to respond only to the initial flash of the phosphor. As the light pen moves across the face of the display tube, the computer receives information about which points are to be "seen" by the light pen. As long as the velocity of the light pen does not cause the cross to be outside the field of view of the pen, the computer will track its movement.

Most crt systems are on-line, electronic typewriter/display systems that quickly communicate with digital computers from remote stations. Each station, consisting of a keyboard and bright cathode-ray tube display, occupies only slightly more space than a typewriter. Any typist can operate most crt stations after a few minutes of instruction. They operate quietly, and the display is easy to read in normal office lighting.

Most stations may be placed anywhere within a building or dispersed among several buildings. A crt terminal may be connected to a computer or data system by direct cable or by telephone subset. Most crt systems are modularly expandable and can keep pace with the growth of a company as its data entry and retrieval needs grow. Up to 100 stations may be operated from a single central control unit, which is capable of handling more than 20,000 inquiries or entries per hour.

Some display images contain 1000 character positions arranged in 20 lines of 50 characters each. The number of characters per line and lines per page can be changed to meet special requirements. The character repertoire of the various crt's includes the alphabet, numerals (0-9), punctuation marks, and other specific symbols. Character codes may be assigned to meet a specific user's needs. Input interfaces for the crt systems are available for digital computers, telephone subsets, and other digital data sources.

A crt system provides speed and flexibility not achievable with ordinary data entry and retrieval equipment. Composing messages is much like using an electric typewriter; characters are stored in a buffer memory in the central control unit. The stored message is displayed on the cathode-ray tube screen, which takes the place of the paper in an ordinary typewriter. An index indicates where the next character to be typed will appear. The marker can be positioned anywhere on the page by the operator, and it moves automatically across the page as each character is typed.

The operator can electonically erase or type over mistakes to ensure the accuracy of the data before it is committed to computer entry. After verifying the inquiry or entry, the operator presses one of the function keys, and the data is sent to the computer. Transmission is at computer speeds rather than at rates limited by manual typing operations.

These capabilities qualify the crt as the essential two-way communication and control link needed for such applications as: command and control program management; management programming; on-line scientific computing; computer-controlled checkout; spaceflight control; air-traffic control; language translation; intelligence data analysis; PERT network layout and evaluation; process-control monitoring; and information retrieval.

Other typical uses for the crt system are:

Transportation—Airline reservations, seating assignments, weather data, and other flight information; railroad cars and shipment disposition; fleet vehicle locations; contents.

Insurance—Claim adjustment; policy file maintenance; policy search.

Banking and finance—Account status checking; deposits; withdrawals; credit checking; stock transactions.

Industrial management—Inventory management; order status reports; production control; personnel records; group insurance files; cash flow; scheduling; forecasting; planning.

In some systems, all operator editing functions are performed within the crt system and do not require computer communication or programming. Only after an operator commits the message for transmission is the computer required to service his station. If a printed copy of a particular displayed message is needed, an operator can obtain one by pressing a function key to actuate the optional printer. Printer buffering and control is internal to most crt systems and does not affect computer operation.

By pressing push buttons on the program keyboard, the user sends commands to the computer. The buttons are labeled in English-language terms with interchangeable keyboard overlays. Each overlay makes a unique connection to orient the computer/console combination to a new set of requirements. This allows the system to be used for many applications requiring access to the common store of data and computer routines.

Through an alphanumeric keyboard similar to a typewriter, the operator can type messages to the computer, or update formatted information stored in the computer files. Some systems use an arrow marker on the screen to show where the next symbol will appear.

Through a control keyboard, the operator can cause words or lines of text to be copied at any other part of the screen—or deleted. He can cause graphs, pictures, and symbols to be drawn, changed, or deleted.

With a light gun or pen, the photoelectronic pointer, he can indicate any element of the display, and the computer will know that the next directive from the console pertains to the identified item.

With a cursor, a crosshair pattern electronically generated on the screen, the operator can indicate where he wants information displayed—for example, the geographical position of a ship on a map.

Through status and warning lights on the console, the operator is guided through a sequence of steps for the program being used at the moment, and is alerted to any procedural errors.

SECTION V

On-Line Real-Time and Time-Sharing Systems

Real-time means immediately, now! Military leaders, scientists, and top management very frequently require knowledge of current information, immediately, to make crucial, time-sensitive decisions. Quite often, it becomes imperative that dangerous or costly time lags be eliminated. The time between the happening of an important event and the discovery by executives that it has occurred is required to be insignificant to fulfill the concept of real-time. The cognizance of the event must be "in time" to control the conclusion of the event itself. More formal definitions of real-time are given below, as are the steps of the development of this capability by computer systems and the new advances in information technology. Action must be predicted presently by "occurring" changes rather than on tomorrow's predictions, yesterday's analyses, or last year's disasters. Cost analyses will most often be based on the question, "Can we afford *not* to have OLRT (on-line real-time) in our operations?" Absolute and accountable cost reductions and greatly enhanced efficiencies are really the "pluses" of real-time systems. Tomorrow's fierce international competition in science, business, military systems, and education force the quickened pace of progress; i.e., computer real-time enlightenment and accomplishment.

Real-time is the necessary base for time-sharing systems (TSS), and time sharing makes real-time possible for every size and type of business firm and scientific or educational research or inquiry unit. For OLRT-TSS provides every individual the opportunity to originate, retrieve, or in innumerable ways to utilize data and information in "conversation mode" with multiple-direction flows whenever a response is required and in the quantum of time desired.

Because modern computers are too fast to serve only one person at a time, to make economic sense the control computer must be shared. Segments of computing time must be made available to many users and from many locations—in cross-country plants, offices, warehouses, libraries, and laboratories, nationally or internationally. Very steadily, businesses are revolutionizing their accounting, information, and production systems. Thousands of applications throughout the world specify rather startling advances in a wide range of specific areas of human endeavor such as automatic laboratories (LINC); fully automated manufacturing facilities (numerical control); family-connected in-home information utilities (tv cable services); and others too numerous to list in this section of the text. It thus appears essential that students, managers, accountants, scientists, teachers, manufacturers, and all alert people become acquainted with terms, concepts, procedures, and applications of the inevitable future—on-line real-time time sharing systems (OLRT-TSS).

A very brief conceptual introduction to time sharing is not an easy task because the term has already become so generalized that it has a great variety of meanings to scores of interested groups and wide ranges of intelligence levels in each group. It might best be developed by listing its logical components: *simultaneity*—a variable number of people can use the computer at essentially the same time; *independence*—the programs being handled by the system are operated independently of one another without risk of being intermixed or having security breached; *immediacy*—all requests for computer response receive that response within seconds (or less) of the completion of the required computation, and most often before "action deadlines" occur; *spatial unlimitability*—spacecraft millions of miles away have operated in real-time; and, earth-bound time-sharing users can communicate with the computer by means of teletypewriter, visual displays (cathode-ray tubes), and scores of other input/output devices which are not generally in close proximity to the central computer, and can be continents away. Time sharing is really the utilization of time.

THE EVOLUTION AND MEANING OF REAL-TIME

"Off-line" means that equipment of the computer system has been disconnected from the central processing unit (CPU) and is being used for slower tasks, such as printing checks, etc. "On-line" concerns the equipment which is connected or re-engaged and functioning with the CPU and main programs. Point of origin devices (PODs) can be teletypewriter units, consoles, meters, optical character readers (OCRs), video displays (crt's), and a host of other input instruments capable of sending machine-sensible signals and which are connected directly to the central processor or one of the peripheral processors in a time-shared system.

Many writers define real-time as processing in which the input, computing, and output of the information must meet a deadline established by external conditions. Such conditions could be deadlines before orders are cancelled because supplies or schedules are not known at once (a $4000 world-trip flight is lost for want of clear reservations), or before an executive is forced to make a "guessed at" decision because he cannot command all the immediate pertinent information, or, in process control, before the automated boring and shaping of metals or highly critical machine tools go out of tolerance or off gauge or materials become improperly mixed. Real-time relates to time-critical variables and often unforeseen instantly-arising problems demanding immediate, correct, current, fact-based decisions; it concerns deadlines to make decisions before the opportunity to make any decision at all is lost. Thus a further qualification for on-line capability is at least one-way communication between operators at terminals and the computer central processing units (CPUs). Most efficiently, however, two-way communication is often desirable.

The reader should now make the distinction that an on-line system is not always a real-time (immediate inquiry-response) system, but real-time systems must have on-line capability and equipment. To be on-line and real-time, the system, for example, must be able (as with automated machinery) to read meters, gauges, and other sensors; compare with programmed tolerance levels; calculate; process (note and correct the exact "exception" as preprogrammed); and transmit so rapidly that the product or process as thus controlled remains continually within specified limits. If, as in many payroll or nontime-sensitive programs, the deadlines are not critical or are internally planned, the logical responses, summaries, or reports often need not be on-line nor developed in real-time. Thus, the concept of "real time" is introduced.

Real-time systems are complicated and relatively expensive. Initial costs, programming, and testing costs are often inhibitions to inauguration of real-time systems. Costs of higher-skilled personnel, file protection, some back-up equipment, and additional programming to screen out human errors should be properly amortized over the realistic evaluation of increased values of efficiencies, new capabilities, and savings in the long run. Obstacles to the installation of real-time systems should not be construed to be disadvantages.

The most enigmatic obstacle is management itself. Most executives apparently must learn the "hard way" from crippling competition which alertly and successfully uses real-time computing, decision-making, and information retrieval because their progressive, fresh-thinking executives quickly "see the light." Unfortunately, most management personnel are badly prepared for automatic data processing and still regard the computer as an extension of accounting equipment or as an instrument to be used as a by-product of other administrative or clerical systems. Many executives still refuse to cooperate with ADP personnel or to learn to control by "management by exception"; i.e., they refuse to become involved with systems objectives, goals, definitions, and designs. Too late do they discern that information technology is the primary route to the highest level of progress and responsibility.

Basically, real-time is an application concept concerning the timing of originating, processing, and retrieving information. The time delay between the happening of events producing information to be entered and the meaningful deadline before its retrieval by the decision-making party (or stored program) must be extremely brief. "Right time" closely corresponds to this concept but suggests all information need not be immediate; i.e., virtually without loss of any time between inquiry and retrieval. Right-time relates to the earliest time necessary for proper action (response) or control which is fast enough to block some avoidable risk, such as a credit purchase to a poor account before the merchandise leaves the premises, or the replenishment of stock (by automated inventory control techniques) before orders ar lost. This generally then certifies the "deadline" concept in real-time, but right-time need not always be instantaneous, and many programs are devised and developed for automatic recording and reporting. Basically, charging inventory or expense accounts for received purchases as they occur and sequencing the designed and frequent amortization and depreciation charges to proper accounts frequently (in some cases even on an hourly basis) are often most important. Retrieving trial balances and profit and loss statements each morning might be required for significant financial decisions. Thus, whether instant real-time and programmed right-time might coincide with automatic or "on-call" data processing depends uniquely on specific firms and their management habits and needs.

The "on-call" concept of real-time is undoubtedly its most important attribute and capability. Real-time calls result in answers to questions such as, "What is the current on-hand, unordered stock of item #SC4556? What was our cumulative net profit as of one hour ago, compared to last month, year? What are sales to date of New Product X in Cincinnati, Detroit, and San Francisco?" Thus, the computer can be interrogated at any time for literally thousands of items of current information. The programming has caused the information to be extracted, compiled, analyzed, and transmitted as ordered and "on call." This is real time.

The automatic exception and discrepancy reporting by the OLRT computer system results in such critical "live" information reporting as: employees who fail to punch in for work on critical projects; expense outlays which exceed budgets by substantial amounts; overdue invoices from vendors or to customers; improper purchases or shipments not in agreement with authorized orders; statistical data out of the bounds of the original parameters; extent of production loss due to breakdowns of equipment; and many, many more. Key management need not wait for these reports to "go through channels" and find out too late for appropriate action, for this information is flashed to them as soon as it becomes known. On-call and exception reporting prevents the wasted time required for the search of such information from ledgers, stacks and stacks of routine reports, or from catalogs, two-day–late memos, notes in jammed files, or bulky financial excerpts no matter how well documented or abstracted. The general managers or vice presidents need only small consoles, perhaps with fifteen to twenty prewired subroutines under an array of buttons; these permit their two-way inquiry and response action decisions or specific and immediate alerting of the responsible people to "take charge" of discrepancies and emergencies. The hardware for these systems is "on hand"; the software is available; feasibility, economic, and application studies await only executive decisions and personnel procurement. The all-important planning does, however, require executive "involvement" at the highest level and with purposeful continuity. The acceptance of this information and communication capability can produce productive and satisfying results.

Time sharing makes more efficient use of the computer by using more of its capability; i.e., the "slack time" of the CPU while it waits for relatively sluggish input/output equipment to furnish and handle the information supplied to it. Because many peripheral devices may be operating simultaneously and inquiries and response may be concurrently processed to and from scores of terminals, "high cost" computer equipment is kept properly employed. Time-sharing systems (TSS) are developed in brief outline below.

TIME-SHARING DEFINITIONS AND CONCEPTS

There is a great disparity between human and electronic reaction time; human responses are in minutes and sometimes seconds, as compared to electronic response times of milliseconds, microsecond, and nanoseconds—thousandths, millionths, and billionths of seconds, respectively. Thus, the CPU computes normal problems at least a million times faster than humans can accept them, or even thousands of times faster than normal printers at 1200 lines per minute can print them, or standard communications devices at 1200 characters per second can transmit them. Thus it must "wait" for these relatively much slower devices to input information and very much slower devices to output information, and the almost impossibly slow humans to respond and react to this information. Obviously, to be efficient the computer should easily handle hundreds of programs of information as input, and to supply, "apparently simultaneously," hundreds of humans with answers to queries or solutions to problems. And it can handle these tasks so fast that no one has to wait because, in most instances, the input is handled instantly, from the user's standpoint, and the output is buffered; i.e., waiting in some multiplexer or peripheral controller until the human mind can accept and react. Thus, in summary, time-sharing is designed to equate electronically this great disparity between humans and i/o devices and the superfast CPU. To achieve this interface (synchronization or meshing) of man and machine, time sharing permits simultaneous use of a single computing system by many users from remote terminals. Each user acts with the computer as though he were the exclusive user, and in two-way conversation at speeds which the user himself determines.

Computer systems differ among the various manufacturers, but generally similar principles are involved. Access to the computer can be accomplished by either commutation or queuing. Communication procedures vary quite extensively, but simply stated, when a user is "ready" he would be allocated a measured portion of time on the system, a quantum, perhaps measured in milliseconds, and a portion of his problem is then computed. His time might be interrupted by a higher priority job, but after his alloted time is used, the next user's program is begun. Thus, his program is segmented by the computer, but segments are computed so fast that it is usually computed in its entirety. From the user's point of view, there were no CPU delays at all since he "conversed" with the computer at his own speed. In the "waiting" time, the computer has handled scores of other higher priority problems similarly segmented in between his relatively slow reaction and response. In the queuing process, each user program is most often solved in its entirety before the next one is begun, although several programs might be called upon to "alternate" depending upon the type of supervisory program which is in control of the CPU. Under either system, there is the need to poll the various users' consoles on a regular basis to discover whether or not the user is active or dormant at the near-constant split-second polling time. The supervisory program, often called the executive or monitor, takes control and regulates time sharing only when the particular terminal is active. For example, file data can be active, dormant, restricted, unrestricted, segregated, etc. Thus, each user's program enters a queue whose members are serviced in round-robin fashion by being transferred into memory, operated upon, and transferred out—thus the need for large and extended main memory and massive auxiliary but on-line memory availability. Time sharing is thus a most valuable tool for on-line debugging, display, and other laboratory work. It is particularly valuable for activities such as simulation, trial and error, and engineering programs.

SECTION VI

Management Information Systems—Cybernetics, Artificial Intelligence, and Communications

MANAGEMENT INFORMATION SYSTEMS (MIS)

Closely associated with information-retrieval systems are the on-line real-time management-science information-retrieval procedures and processes. A system can generally be defined as a united complex of elements which interrelates machines, components, man, nature, and the social and business environment with operations of a particular time period. The interrelationships are purposeful parameters of the combination, and the responses to events attempt to achieve the devised and desired objectives of the central unit. Systems can be designed on bases of a logical, physical, and organizational process or other designs, and they generally concern flows of information, money, energy, materials, etc. The system then essentially consists of structure, operations, and flows. System outputs are results of the combining of components and forces with the plans, processes, procedures, and objectives.

Specifically, a computer-controlled management-information system places all data from all departments, divisions, and management from all locations into one all-accessible place—a central computer. For each level of command and control in an industrial or commercial organization, this means that at any time anyone, as authorized, can retrieve in visual, graphic, or hard-copy form the information he requires. And it is today's valid information, in immediately usable form. These systems are not only possible and practical but are in use today.

For most industries, the need exists, the knowledge exists, and the equipment exists. And decisions are made almost daily to automate the firm's command and control and information processing systems.

The use and application of decision-making problems have been increasing as a result of new utility and greater capability to accept, store, retrieve and display, and to effectively analyze and amend input and output. All of this is developed in the firm's constantly shrinking time frame that is necessary to remain competitively alert. The modern manager gets his background from three sources: (1) his formal education, which has taught him to digest, analyze, and conclude; (2) his work experience, which aids in his processes of specification, correlation, and criteria for evaluation; and (3) his direct feedback requests of his associates, his library, and most importantly, his computer with its vast store of current information and split-second problem-solving capability.

Because many management concepts are developed in other sections of this text, this section will be quite briefly confined to the use of information display in an MIS. The key characteristic is timely accessibility. Today's information is relevant to the decisions which have to be made for tomorrow's action. Yesterday's information is treacherous and only "seemingly" usable for critical corporate progress. Thus, decisions based on today's data and information have a valid base; all others are questionable and risky. But how is it possible to receive immediately all of the almost momentary pertinent data? The information is in so many places in so many forms, has so many degrees or levels of importance, and is not stripped of nonrelated information nor is it in interpretative form. The task is not impossible, and many most effective systems are working extremely well and are designed to let management retrieve the type and amount of information at a pace selected by the executives concerned—in real time or "right time." Management-computer communication is made possible with the keyboard, light pen, and special push-button switches.

CYBERNETICS

Cybernetics is a popular term with many science-fiction writers and various media reporters. Often it has developed a series of connotations of an ominous nature. Its historical meaning relates to the fascination man has with the possibility of mechanical imitation of various living organisms, including himself. Basically, it is conceived to mean the theory of control and communications common in both the machine and the animal, with emphasis on the communications engineering aspects. Today's cybernetics man-machine automation informally represents communications and control capabilities relating to processes common to nerve systems and mathematical machining. The development of a theory of control and communication to and from machines and living organisms is based on the common computer feedback mechanism. Such applications concerning computer decision-making are based on preset solutions, values, and the response the computer performs when such values are reached through computations or manipulations. Such computer operations are the basis for production automation and process control. Cybernetics, however, concerns itself more with the combination of biological and physical mechanisms. Teams of scientists working with pattern recognition, "seeing and feeling" robots, and associative (adaptive) memories within computers are developing principles and pragmatic evidence to form a discipline of cybernetics often nicknamed the computer culture. One of its founders was the widely written philosopher Norbert Wiener (1894-1964). Wiener originally developed some basic concepts of simple analog computers, together with television-like scanning devised to represent functions of more than one variable. He then designed the central arithmetic unit to be digital rather than analog to reduce accumulative errors in repeated elementary operations. To increase the speed, he replaced electromechanical devices by vacuum tubes and used programs to consolidate logical decisions. Many quotations from his works have had far-reaching impact in the literature of computer developments.

ARTIFICIAL INTELLIGENCE

Computer programs have been written which compose popular music, poetry, and even movie scripts. Some computers are experimental, developed to understand questions posed in ordinary English, even though the bad English format poses some difficulty in solving equations. "Adaptive" computers have some capabilities in making intelligent assumptions about the precise meanings of questions. Learning programs have been input to computers, and experiments have been successful which establish the ability of the machine to modify its performance on the basis of experience gained. Computers have learned from their successes and failures while playing checkers and chess with humans and other computers and have eventually beaten the people who have programmed them. Commercial applications relating to these experiments are still in the "maybe" stage. The research and successes in pattern recognition have shown capability of association to complex and nonidentical relationships to be startlingly good. Machines actually do learn and take certain actions as results of what they learn until, in some decision-making processes, they have become significantly superior to the judgment of human beings. Heuristic programs, computer self-learning elaborate pattern recognition (translation of foreign languages from printed and hand-written documents, as well as human voice words) are capabilities being interwoven with mechanical robots. Such robots have been designed with television camera "eyes," moving arms, mobility, and even "intelligence" for locating electrical outlets to replenish their power when their batteries run down. Thousands of such adaptive computer-controlled robots are employed in industry on "22 hour" shifts for positioning, moving, retrieving, and sorting materials. The use of human intervention at given points of processes or decision-making operations enhances these capabilities to thus demonstrate skills in real time of very powerful and versatile combinations. The subject of "thinking" computers is perhaps one of the most fascinating topics in the history of mankind, and the exploration of artificial intelligence can provide a very satisfying reward.

As an example, the Computer Science Department at GM's Research Laboratories has developed the prototype for a sighted robot—called Consight—capable of identifying and selecting oriented automotive parts from a moving conveyor belt. Consight has a vision system that consists of a solid-state digital camera "eye" and a minicomputer that uses data collected from the camera and commands the robot to perform functions based on the data. (Earlier robots, like PUMA, are enslaved by a fixed sequence of instructions.) Sight-I, called the first industrial application of computer vision in the US, has been used at Delco Electronics since early 1978 to inspect the position of IC chips for GM ignition systems, testing more than 3000 parts per hour. More than 120 Japanese robot companies built 7000 industrial robots in 1978, raising to 39,000 the number in use, about 10 times that of the US.

DATA COMMUNICATIONS: COMPONENTS AND PROCEDURES

Most businessmen find that a computer with its peripheral equipment is not an end in itself. They might have suspected that the hardware assured results; however, they soon discovered that the software was of almost equal importance, and also that unless the hardware and software are integrated into a system that extends over many functions of a business, the system might not pay off as well as expected. It is the know-how of the business system components, not simply the computer itself, and the solution of the problem areas of the total enterprise that will ensure a full payoff. Generally then, the central integrated information processing system must combine with process automation systems (numerical control) and a communications system, and perhaps also, computer-controlled graphic arts (printing, designing, etc.) to realize the majority of benefits the installation provides for its owners. It would be foolhardy indeed to avoid the total use of this excellent and expensive servant. Modern managers are just now becoming alert to the full realization of the great scope and purpose to which the computer can be developed.

Management should take full advantage of the many applications programs (software packages) which are provided, generally free of charge, with their computer systems—over and above the standard programs for operation of peripheral equipment, standard on-line functions, RPGs (report program generators), etc., and the many debugging aids. They should certainly request and receive information and assistance for the many communications capabilities of their general-purpose computer.

Communication systems include the following:

1. Collection, interpretation, and control equipment for dissemination of information and continuous (digital) operation of peripheral equipment, for process control, problem solving, etc.
2. Data-transmission systems to convert data to suitable form for transmission over standard or company-leased channels.
3. Information on microwave systems—commercial channels between widely separated locations for coordination into the total system.
4. Multiplex equipment, which provides capability for handling up to 1200 circuits on a single commercial channel.
5. Numerical-control systems (machine automation) for positioning, processing, and contouring control.
6. Quality control for automatic checking, accumulation of data, and preservation of results for optimum levels and reliability.
7. Automated materials-handling control systems to include scheduling, stock handling, transporting, etc.

Surveys have shown that the average effective utilization of computer time was less than 50% of what it could have been with optimum data flow to and from every data-use point. Proper low-cost terminals often help considerably to develop close to full-time use of the computer in efficiently designed systems. Because computation time is measured in microseconds and nanoseconds and, in contrast, waiting time is measured in full seconds and minutes, it is often necessary to group the "dead spots" and program "live" assignments into that interval.

Defined quite simply, a data-transmission system generally consists of devices for sending and receiving data, and the facility or carrier over which data is transmitted. It is, more properly, a subsystem of the overall data-processing total system. The lightning speed of the computer central processing unit (CPU) is often wasted if it takes hours or days to receive its solutions or information retrieval. Thus, time-sharing computers now provide for world-wide multiple use of the computer with transmission systems at extremely high speeds. Some systems spew out information at the rate of 36,000 lines a minute, a rate so fast that photorecording is normally necessary. In command and control operation, systems not only keep track of every object in space, but project this information onto a large screen in color for immediate command decisions.

The first electronic computers and data-acquisition systems were isolated, self-sufficient units, with little need to communicate with other systems of similar nature. The data was generated on the spot, or brought to the processing center in the form of punched cards, paper tape, or reels of magnetic tape.

As the geographic scope of data processing grew, simple data links between individual processing centers were developed. Typical systems consisted of a central computation facility and a group of remote data sources. During this period, techniques were perfected for transmitting data over economical common-carrier communication lines (e.g., telephone and teletypewriter lines).

Now, with the introduction of real-time data-exchange systems, it is possible to link together a great number and variety of data-generating and data-using facilities into a single data-communication network. The effect is to add a whole new dimension to the potential of data processing. Economic communication between centers allows each facility to operate "on line" with respect to all the others. There is a rapid transfer of data; data storage and record keeping are automated and simplified.

Many real-time data-exchange systems are capable of exchanging information between any and all types of data sources. These include teletypewriter terminals, computer centers, telemetry ground stations, production plants, commercial offices, corporate headquarters, university laboratories, weather stations, and thousands of other locations where computer and data-acquisition systems are now in operation.

Each system acts as a highly efficient and economical clearing house for the digital information that flows in and out of the facility. The communication network may be of any geographic scope: local, regional, or national. The same field-proven hardware may be used to link together the data sources in a single processing plant, a far-flung missile test range, or a national inventory-control system.

Various controllers process communication-based information of different speeds and communication codes with great efficiency. They effectively switch this information among remote points within a communications network. As the hub of a communications switching system, they provide integration of personal computer messages and high-speed data circuits tailored to user requirements, thereby achieving optimum communications system performance in distributed data-processing systems.

Incoming communications characters are accepted by the input controller from a mixture of lines of differing codes or speeds and are stored in high-speed front-end memory without interfering with the main processing program. Messages or data are quickly processed by the processor by means of its communications-oriented instruction repertoire. These messages are then automatically delivered to the desired addresses by the input/output controller.

In addition to executing efficiently the basic functions of message and data switching, the front-end communication microprocessor satisfies numerous other requirements for processing communications data. It optimizes the over-all communications system by providing message logging, accumulation and analysis of traffic statistics, circuit supervision and control, station interrogation, code conversion, speed conversion, plus error detection and correction. Thus the communications processor, like other similar units, significantly contributes to the performance of communication codes and formats and satisfies the requirements of a message and data communication environment.

SECTION VII

Computer Applications for Business, Industry, Science, Government, and Education

PROLOGUE

The effects of the exploding computer technology project future relations between the computer and society which are both frightening and heartening. Some application areas are certainly most helpful and optimistic, while others spell out various threats to

privacy, the danger of machines which make mistakes, and the threat of machine harassment and power over humans. The world which we are building is one in which man will live out his life against a background of near-miraculous networks of interconnected, artificially intelligent machines. Man's limited brain and inhibited will is to be supplemented by thousands of vast data banks and by the explicit logic of split-second, in-house or far-distant computers. The impact of the applications listed below will grow in substance and significance to the human being as he relates to computers in school, his employment, his corporation, his personal finance, all phases of his government, and his protective forces, the police and the military. Some of the most basic and fundamental applications are discussed briefly as derived from lists which have been compiled and now total over 5000 distinct and different applications of computers relating to man, his pursuits, and his environment.

A brief summary of current computer applications is divided into five main areas:

I. The computer and management control of business and industry
II. Computer applications and the professions
III. Computer applications in insurance, public utilities, communications, and transportation
IV. Computer systems control of banking, finance, and credit
V. Computer culture and new media applications

THE COMPUTER AND MANAGEMENT CONTROL

For most businesses, a computer made its debut and had its initial impact in the accounting department. In a great majority of cases, after some varying degrees of disruptions due to tradition and "old way" routines, some victories of information acquisition, retrieval, and accounting control by computer have been achieved. There is little doubt that basic accounting and various information-reporting systems have produced considerable efficiency and much tighter control for most new computer users. It becomes quickly obvious to practically all purchasers of new computers that the capability of their equipment far exceeds the tasks and programs applied to it, even after it has been operating for several years. The more aggressive and alert accounting personnel and many of the recent college graduates in the management ranks quite often succumb to temptations and "grand ideas" and make serious and sometimes diligent attempts at development of various types of management information systems, or at least, segments of them. The degree of success of these systems is inadequately measured and remains in a gray area of questionability as to dollars and cents value versus reasonable costs. Briefly stated, management personnel using the capability and versatility of computers, at this point in time, must still be considered to be true pioneers. Current experience and computer system evaluation reports filtering from business and industry are mixed, and many of the computer center trail blazers are recognized by noting the arrows still "sticking in their backs." The grand designs and the great "new era" hopes have in many cases been smashed for a variety of (correctable) reasons. A small but very significant percent of the computer-system innovators have, however, achieved very commendable and remarkable successes.

The goals of most computer-oriented management leaders center around the contemplated achievement of a workable and efficient management information system (MIS). Some management information systems have become involved successfully in totally integrated management processing and communication networks. A substantial number of systems have their roots in the finance divisions concerned with accounting functions and procedures. Others have been developed from the production divisions and sections of manufacturing firms. Numerical control systems, utilizing microcontrollers, have made remarkable advances in automating many sections of production activities. These are developed as "board" computers and contain the programs and the specifications which are fed into various analog computing devices which then control various cutting, shaping, and processing actions of specially designed machines. Information concerning production developed by numerically controlled machines and processing devices becomes part of a computer information system. These data are most often coupled with labor, machine time, and accessory item costs to provide accounting divisions and production management with rate and cost information on a very timely basis. The information stream from this production also includes inventory control, and "make or buy" supply decisions. The labor costs are usually fed into the system through the use of badge readers or especially designed prepunched worker identification and rate cards. The two instances discussed here serve to demonstrate how the beginning of information systems develops, or how segments of such systems originate.

Most major retail and wholesale companies quickly discover that operational and accounting control developed by effective use of computers has now become a necessity in order for them to remain competitive and to either hold or increase their traditional net earnings, or all percentages of current or expanding sales. Management of these commercial enterprises discovers or digests reports concerning their competitor's utilization of computers for inventory control, various distribution systems, production and promotion tests and evaluations, cost analyses and projections, plans and simulations, and accounting and cost-control systems. Many top management teams, with consultations or contracted assistance from computer service companies, have developed techniques for problem-solving and decision-making related distinctly and directly to their own particular systems and business structures. Many of these programmed and attempted innovative procedures have certainly created new problems, different types of errors, and troubles coupled with significant expenses. And, the "pioneers" have gone through and continue their energetic and dedicated efforts under difficult conditions with renewed incentive.

Range of Applications

The beginning student of computer operations and capabilities usually had to complete a very personal decision-making process and overcome deep mental blocks about this strange and complicated new machine before he selected the option to devote some time to the discovery and analysis of the various uses of the computer. The media sources, such as newspapers, magazines, motion pictures, radio, and television have somehow for the past few years been able to portray the computer as a "moster-type" but still controllable genius. The academic world has scared most would-be computer students with the math- and engineering-oriented definitions found in the abstracts of scores of wide-ranging computer course offerings in various colleges and universities. In most cases, such descriptions have issued foreboding warnings that the student is to be severely challenged in his attempt to master the intricate and complicated electronics, mazes of codes, switching devices, and the internal working of "black boxes." Heavy emphasis has been placed on steep mathematics requirements as being necessary for mastery of computers and computer-related subjects.

As the student begins his struggles, he finds that he will not be required to climb such lofty academic heights to achieve a thorough comprehension of the computer as an efficiently working servant of man in hundreds of varied and quite specific endeavors. The study of computer operations utility, its power, and its components is not for geniuses only. The procedures for taking command and control of this utility, power, and capability, through sets of instructions (programs), are easily learned. The student need not be a mathematical giant, nor possess proclivities for electronics and cryptography, nor must he rate in the top "X" percentage of his class in any specific subject. Computer science is wide open for all ranges of specialization, and the student will discover and determine his own particular interests as he completes the "generalized" introduction to modern computing. Essentially, the computer is simplicity in itself in its fundamental design of binary or on-off switching, even though this is achieved at fantastic (billionth-of-a-second) speeds. Most of the electronics of computing concerns the peripheral devices which are related to the input and output of information and solutions or reports. And, unless the student is deeply concerned with the engineering aspects of the internal operations of computers, his fears of electronics, physics, and higher-level mathematics are not well-founded. Neither should the student fear any great depths of complications with regard to coding or programming. The language or languages he is expected to learn and use are, with few exceptions, easily used, and most can be mastered in a very short period of time. Simple programs are often constructed and run on the computer within a week or two of the beginning student's first introduction to the computer and its specific capabilities. Therefore, when the fears of electronics, mathematics, and coding are subdued and dismissed, the student should be highly motivated to learn control of this marvelous instrument, and to explore and conquer new ranges of problem solutions, decisions, options, and simple or complex system development.

The following few pages are designed to relate in generalized discussion terms the various concepts of current computer applications. The aim and purpose is to quickly and painlessly present an overview of a considerable portion of the great and expanding range of computer activities in today's business, scientific, professional, and academic worlds. It is expected that after the student digests the rather crowded information on the next few pages he will perhaps be somewhat overwhelmed with the wide range of the obvious and very sudden revolution which is occurring in so many distinct areas over the traditional ways of accomplishing information and problem controls. Some of the more widely read and mentally alert students will quickly absorb all of this and be ready to add a score or more activities of computer conquests which the authors have failed to mention or of which they are not yet aware.

Computers Rapidly Overcoming Retailing/Wholesaling System/Function Paper Glut

It is axiomatic that the computer first services the accountants by performing information acquisition, computations and analyses, and report development. Either combined with these various accounting procedures, or as by-products of data-collection procedures, top management quickly discovers the distinct advantages of (on-line) immediate inventory reporting and control. Consequently, in most retail, wholesale, and manufacturing establishments, the second application of computers relates to product control. On-time information is of significant value to decision-making concerning inventoried amounts, such as raw materials, goods in process, finished products, various equipment, supplies, buildings, etc. From these computerized inventories, control systems and procedures, various product scheduling, materials handling, and planning or budgeting schedules quickly develop. These are the areas of computer applications which have become the most quickly economically rewarding in commercial areas.

Automatic data acquisition is developed through computer-read purchase orders, invoices, point-of-sale (POS) tickets, and other data-capturing operations and devices. These individual computer systems provide for continuous updating, not only of most or all inventories, but also of payables, receivables, purchases, expense and budget limits, etc. Such systems are usually standard batch-processing types which are completed as individual units when all data and information is collected and ready. But much more efficient, valuable, and initially expensive systems are developed with real-time computers which provide for immediate knowledge of amounts, conditions, and circumstances of the various elements of such systems on an "as-it-happens" basis. Computerized job-shop and production scheduling and control provide manufacturing managers with immediate knowledge of progress related to various products or projects as scheduled or projected in the future. Computer short- and long-range planning and dynamic feedback of real-world or simulated calculations alert managers and executives to various delays, bottlenecks, or on-time comparisons of desired or projected results. Automatic "exception principle" reports locate such interruptions, outages, or problems and pinpoint responsibility immediately through the use of experience-developed ranges and limits which are programmed as specific segments or parts of the total stream of information designed and included within management information systems.

Computer integrated data processing (IDP) in many large (but expensive and difficult) systems has developed total control of each operating program or system segment, as well as controlling the totality of complete plans, projects, and designs. Computer-controlled conveyors, fork-lift trucks, and especially designed sensing, selecting, and moving devices have made fully automated warehouses excellent examples of current operating efficiency, and these warehouses represent a goal to many wholesale and retail concerns. In the late 1970s more than 10,000 computer-controlled robots with television "eyes" and electronically controlled "arms" were servicing industry around the world with capabilities for positioning, lifting, selecting, sorting, feeding, or conveying materials to and from machines, production lines, and warehouse sections. These very handy "machines" are programmed to work on 22-hour shifts—without vacations, complaints, or pay increases with fringe benefits—and they require only minimum preventive maintenance (the other two hours in 24) and no lunch breaks.

Computer Systems Streamline the Marketing Function, Including Strategy, Design, Implementation, and Evaluation

Some of the devices used to select and capture data and information for computer calculations, analyses, and reporting are as follows: magnetically encoded computer-readable credit or "money" cards; point-of-sale punched or machine-readable printed sales tickets; magnetically encoded workers' badges; prepunched, specifically formatted plastic or punched identity and information cards; and badge readers, card readers, merchandise-ticket readers, optical-character readers, and direct cathode-ray tube (crt) typewriter input terminals.

Advertising research, media, audience selection, and message testing and evaluation have provided the guidelines for basic decisions concerning many sales promotion campaigns and effectiveness determinations. Automated purchasing based on reorder points (amounts) as related to daily (even hourly) sales information has eliminated tremendous amounts of paperwork. red tape, and "lost profit" delays or outages for retailers, wholesalers, and manufacturers alike. On-line (real-time or immediate) accounting reports have informed, verified, or projected results of plans and budgets related to working capital, expenditures, or long-range capital allocations. Computer programs have been effective in recruiting and personnel selecting, as well as other employment policy and planning decisions regarding compensation and worker effectiveness evaluation. Computer-controlled product distribution, scheduling, warehouse location and product testing, and market sampling analyses have resulted in higher net earnings for particular products, or in total product line balance. Computers have demonstrated unparalleled research capability and problem-solving utility for those high-level managers who have recognized the value of such systems and the very real need for the ability to design and control the computer as it serves them.

Industry Switches to Volume Production Automation for Speed, Efficiency, and Lower Costs

Computers, in some instances, are now controlling complete oil refineries and have been the most important instruments in exploration and exploitation of oil resources. Automated process-control procedures provide the basic control for most major cement, rubber, and paper industry plants. Automated product testing, engineering, simulations, and projected customer acceptance are completed by computers. Few public utilities and almost no major steel plants could operate effectively without significant computer control for many of their operations or facilities. Production automation in hospitals, on shipping docks, in warehouses, and throughout agriculture are specific examples of growing computer versatility in production control. Computer service companies and information utilities aid management by providing distant computer capability ordered by crt terminals or push-button telephones. Managers use such utilities with instantaneous feedback reporting for accounting, banking, and communications information-retrieval services. Most information utilities have time-shared computers with rates of usage and costs low enough for small businessmen to "share" computer costs for control of their operations. The convenience of the computer service company offers management and information services to help them avoid being computerized out of competition. Computer terminal languages such as BASIC, PASCAL, JOSS, etc., are simple enough to learn and understand so that, in effect, all managers have a degree of automation available to them. Service companies offer either proprietary or custom programming, as well as facilities management which permits any company to rent a complete computer system, including personnel, for all their computing requirements. "Do-it-yourself" computermat franchises have been developed, as well as cooperatives, to further reduce costs and increase convenience for small business managers. The full-service computer utility of the future is almost a dreamlike convenience upon which most business and industry will rely.

Inventory Control, Project Scheduling, and Materials Handling for Management

Automatic data acquisition through point of sale (POS) and other data-capturing procedures and devices provides for continuous updating of all inventories using either real-time or batch-processing computers. Job-shop and production scheduling and control provide management with immediate knowledge of the progress of product or project schedules. Computer planning and dynamic feedback alert management to delays or on-time comparisons to designed results. Automatic "exception principle" reporting locates production bottlenecks and pinpoints responsibilities immediately through the use of management information systems. Computer-integrated data processing develops controls over each operating segment, as well as controlling the totality of the complete plans or projects.

The New Management Science Based on Operations Research Techniques and Computer Control

New software programs have automated PERT/COST and critical path method (CPM) for project evaluation and review and on-schedule verification procedures. Computer models for research allocation have simplified and expanded the use of linear programming for management control. Waiting line, scheduling, replacement, and route problems are now being solved effectively by computer simulation programs. Heuristic and stochastic models provide the values of alternatives for basic decision making through the use of computer problem-solving techniques. Competition and gaming models solved by computers permit the testing and verification of market strategies as regards pricing, advertising, production differentiation, and distribution. Econometrics and input/output operations research techniques permit intelligent and accurate forecasting of feasible capital outlay and the timing as regards financial and economic relations of the firm, the nation, and the international interplay of economics and the gross national product (GNP).

COMPUTER APPLICATIONS AND THE PROFESSIONS

The Medical Profession Is Being Revolutionized by Computer Systems and Control

One of the most important uses of computers which provide assistance to doctors and hospital personnel is on-line patient monitoring. The computer automatically reads, records, and displays on cathode-ray tube (crt) terminals the various readings of instruments which are attached by electronic transducers to patients. These devices, in many cases developed in the various American space programs, relate to blood pressure, heartbeat, body temperature, and many other physical measurements. Physicians can monitor their patient's specific or total condition either continuously through readings on their own office computer terminal, or through "exception principle" reporting by being alerted only when certain preset boundary or limit figures or test results are exceeded or become exceptions to the norm. The computers further assist physicians in automated patient examinations, in-depth original diagnosis, or confirmation of the doctor's own judgment or decisions. Computer-controlled testing of blood and urine specimens and measurement of pressures, densities, and other quantities provide almost immediate facts and data upon which doctors can base their decisions. Computer-assisted medical and drug research provide physicians and clinical laboratory technicians with capabilities undreamed of just a few years ago. Millions of tests, verifications, analyses, etc., which before required weeks, months, even years of calculations, can be performed in seconds. Hospitals are assisted by computers in almost every facet of accounting, administration, and patient services. Computer-controlled "meal trucks" automatically deliver the properly prescribed foods and medicines down the corridors of hospitals without human guidance or assistance. A significant part of the education of physicians now concerns the above computer-control techniques, procedures, and capabilities.

Computers Cause Major Upheaval in Education

Computers are becoming "teachers" or teachers' assistants in almost every area of education, including elementary, secondary, and college programs. Even preschool children are taught to read, write, and respond to the tv-like screens. These screens are computer terminals and provide easy display and response with typewriter or push-button keyboards for student interplay or computer-projected images, lessons, and other information. High-school and college students are receiving computer-aided instruction (CAI), now developed to provide individually-paced complete courses in such subjects as statistics, mathematics, computer programming, languages, political science, and hundreds of other courses or disciplines. Industry has also developed specific education programs to train personnel or update their current capabilities by using computer-programmed teaching and training materials. Perhaps the greatest use for computer education concerns the hundreds of thousands of computer hours available to college professors, graduate students, and administrative personnel for research in practically every area of human endeavor. Besides the heavily used computer applications of accounting, management, medicine, library, search and retrieval, engineering, and mathematics, the social sciences have recently become prodigious users of computers in their specific fields. In psychology, anthropology, archaeology, urban planning, government, and political science, the computer has become a research, testing, and evaluation tool of great significance. Many colleges and universities have from three to five computers, and some, ten or more. It would be difficult to find a college or university of substance and renown which does not have computer capability in its administrative information and control procedures. And, practically all progressive educational institutions now offer computer availability to their teachers for research and experimentation and to the students for "hands-on" training and experience. Computers are discussed and their applications correlated in practically every course offered on major college campuses, including such subjects as art, music, and history. It is believed by many leading educational authorities that the influence and impact of computers in education are rapidly revolutionizing the entire process of learning and might easily topple the concept of a centralized college or university as we know it today. Results of courses taken by computer as a substitute for a teacher have shown such promise and superiority to former instructional methods that a change in the teacher's control in education is beyond the idea stage and is being implemented on experimental bases around the educational world.

Computers Become Essential Tools for All Engineers

The engineering student and professional now rely heavily on computers for solutions of most problems they encounter. Engineering calculations, measurements, drawings, analyses, and communications are routinely performed by the computer which has become as invaluable as the engineer's slide rule. Engineers are required in most colleges to complete from four to ten computer courses as bases for civil, mechanical, electronic, production, and many other types of engineering. Computer-aided design (CAD) is now the sound foundation and practical substitute for originating engineering drawings, changes and alterations, specifications, determinations, and final plans and blueprints. Computer engineering systems and software now range through every facet of engineering capability. Automated equipment for engineers and for engineering applications is available for study and research. The impact and future of computers as related to other engineering sciences, in architectural engineering, chemical engineering, physics, astronomy, etc., is bounded only by man's imagination.

Automated Laboratories and New Successes in Research

Computer applications in pollution control, weather forecasting, and seismology, space exploration, and military science relate quite specifically to computers and the laboratory. Computer control, counting, measuring, recording, reporting, and automated analyses become the base for instrumentation control upon which laboratory research widely depends. Automated laboratories, combined with simulation and control techniques and the recently developed nanosecond (billionth of a second) speeds and trillion-bit memories, provide research workers with information storage and retrieval and calculation capabilities unimagined just a few years ago. Again, only man's imagination, inventiveness, and stamina are the bounds of his full utilization of these great capabilities provided by the new computer science and technology.

The Computer Begins Total Control of Library Science

The following computer applications relate to libraries: (a) the tremendous compaction of information in very small spaces through computer-operated microfilm systems for new semiconductor and laser storage devices, (b) information retrieval from vast memory banks on a random basis at speeds measured in millionths or billionths of a second, and (c) coded and indexed systems providing cataloging specifications and ease of retrieval on a world-wide basis for service to business, industry, education, government, and scientific endeavor. Library automation techniques reflecting these capabilities are now reaching beyond the design stages for implementation and receive day-to-day use in many institutions. The Library of Congress, United States governmental intelligence services, including the CIA and others, and the major "Ivy League" medical colleges are the best current examples of major progress in automated techniques for library science. Computer-controlled document retrieval systems are also of great significance in industry, government, and education. The combination of automated library indexing systems and the computer's great speed and immense storage capabilities and instantaneous communications capabilities make the new science of information acquisition and retrieval one of the most intriguing and significant areas of advancement in the last decade.

COMPUTER APPLICATIONS IN INSURANCE, PUBLIC UTILITIES, COMMUNICATIONS, AND TRANSPORTATION

Computers Dominate Life and Casualty Insurance Company Operations

Computers are the base tool in research and actuarial calculations for rate decisions and adjustments in practically all insurance companies. Office automation of premium development, billing, and analysis has reduced clerical costs in a very measurable way. Dividend formulation, calculation, and analysis, as well as claim adjustments and evaluations, are conducted in many cases using real-time computing systems with man-machine interaction. Computers are "customizing" insurance policies in their formulation, printing, and issuance for many companies. Agency and commission accounting and other office procedures are reaching stages of "total system" automation.

Computer Systems and Public Utilities Unite for Efficiency

Gas-well exploration, distribution networks, pipeline design and construction, distribution plants, and process control systems are all being developed through the use of computers for gas company utilities. Electric power plant production, scheduling, and control stability are guided and controlled by computers. Water reservoir management and distribution networks are primary activities in the computer centers of water utilities. Practically all utilities compute utility load flows, meter readings, and information and data collection using computers and remote terminals. Computers have a long history of application in telephone utilities, and systems could not possibly operate without the "fail-safe" computer systems which direct switching, traffic, billing, and scores of other activities. Office automation with computers is a prime requirement to reduce costs in major and especially small utilities.

Oil Exploration and Installation Design Completed by Computer Procedures

Seismic tests, evaluations, and projections by computer develop the correlation and analysis required for capital expenditures. Process-control computers operate oil refineries almost without human assistance. Network simulations and shutdown and maintenance procedures are guided by computers. World-wide communication and reporting provide management with facts and data for problem-solving. Office and credit-card automation systems provide the accuracy and on-time reporting to control "exceptions" before they become calamities. Oil companies are pioneers in the development of investment analyses of leases, well operations, map construction, and management system designs through the use of computers and operation research techniques.

Computers Used to Solve Transportation Problems

American railroads are one of the heaviest users of computers for scheduling, route determination, rolling-stock inventory, and control. Airlines throughout the world have computerized reservation systems which are models of real-time "conversational" time-sharing computers. The American Federal Aviation Authority and its many state and local affiliates control the nation's traffic by computer and radar. Many cities are now controlling traffic lights and thoroughfares with computer precision.

Close to a majority of the states in America now register all vehicles and driver's licenses with computer systems. Many computer procedures are being developed for automobile safety programs—specifically computer-controlled automobiles with speed- and brake-regulating sensor tracks embedded in roads or freeway medians. Large trucking firms use computers for control much like the railroad systems. Computerized transportation is predicted to become a mainstay in practically every area of movement of goods, people, or information.

Computerized Communications Around the World

New computerized satellite and microwave systems are creating true system efficiency in communications. Computer information utilities permit data acquisition and retrieval on an instantaneous basis from all corners of the world. The use of minicomputers in private microwave systems and innovative devices is bringing new creativity to the communications industry. Communications by airlines, railroads, trucking firms, business, and industry are creating very large markets for terminals with voice, video, facsimile, and combination capabilities. Governmental and educational computers now tie libraries, bureaus, teachers, and students with convenient and low-cost systems. Computerized hospital and medical data networks are becoming imperative for speedy diagnosis, remote patient monitoring, and patient-history information retrieval. Computer-communication applications are expected to become more varied and heavily used than the computer-calculation aspects of information processing.

COMPUTER-SYSTEMS CONTROL OF BANKING, FINANCE, AND CREDIT

Total Computer-Systems Control of the Banking Function

The Federal Reserve Board, the primary US monetary authority, has urged banks to install a "checkless-cashless" national operation as soon as possible. Large bank systems are now close to completion of part of such a system by completing payroll for large customers with direct bank deposits instead of checks. The "money card" concept is being developed experimentally with the cooperation of banks and retailers in several American cities to avoid the need for cash. Banks' computers are now offering doctors, lawyers, businessmen, and industrialists full ranges of accounting, financing, insurance, and data-processing services. These include receivables billing, inventory control, payroll fulfillment, payables disbursing, and investment analysis. Small banks are joining in cooperatives and associations to complete computer-system efficiency. On-line teller systems in savings and loans and in savings banks are becoming commonplace. Credit unions, pension funds, labor unions, and finance companies are big users of computers for many functions, some for total systems control. Credit-card systems could not be operated without the use of computers, and improvements in software are even now necessary to make them profitable. The computer industry manufacturers and software developers look upon banks as one of their major customers. now and in the future.

Computers Welcomed by Accountants and Auditors

Despite slow initial progress, the computer people and the accounting function are developing systems acceptable to both sides. Wholesale and retail accounting automation is an absolute necessity for major institutions. Point-of-sale (POS) data acquisition, automated inventory control and purchasing systems, and customer accounting by computer all combine to strengthen the case for auditing by computer. The use of computers by managers, in production, and in process automation has forced accountants to accept "magnetic tape" accounting. The Internal Revenue Service now accepts tapes as equivalent to original records for tax purposes. After the Space and Atomic Energy computer systems, the Internal Revenue system is considered one of the largest and most sophisticated. Computer accounting in hospitals is now standard. A great many hotels and restaurants are converting to computer systems, and certainly airline, railroad, insurance, public utility, and communication company accounting is completed by computers which match their other information and office automation procedures. Several accounting association leaders suggest that computing and accounting will soon become synonymous, but "managerial" accounting will still require the personal genius of human beings.

Computerized Stock Handling

Computer systems recently installed are automating all trading and reporting on the three major stock exchanges in the US. Brokerage "backroom" accounting is recovering from its near-catastrophe through the use of efficient software and programming for computer systems. The computer is a "base operator" for the commodity exchanges. Stock certificates are being designed for computer processing or are to be replaced by gold-edged punched cards. Stock and bond portfolio analysis and evaluation are being completed with new computer programs. The stock market "chartist" uses computers to print out trends, "bottoms and double bottoms," and to forecast "sideways" movements. Significant progress has been made for financial leaders through the use of computers and the operations-research techniques of econometrics and input/output analysis. Very accurate forecasts, sensitivity analyses, and resources expenditure evaluations are being developed with such local, national, and international models.

Computer Utilities and Service Companies

Computer utilities for credit, banking, accounting services, and information retrieval are opening low-cost "anytime" computing capability to small businessmen without the purchase or lease of expensive equipment. Computer "do-it-yourself" centers have sprung up in many business-concentrated neighborhoods. Service and software companies are now catering specifically to small businesses, with services of proven and tested value at significant savings over current business procedures. Computing costs are as low as $8 to $10 per hour, with no minimums, and results are immediate.

COMPUTER CULTURE AND NEW MEDIA APPLICATIONS

Automated Media

The computer and the book may become synonymous in another generation. Information is now stored for instant retrieval in several libraries, and many libraries are interconnected and provide automated indexing and video display of books, reports, and newspapers by page and paragraph, on demand. Many computer systems are available for updating, editing, and printing of textbooks. The computer-age newspaper from computer-connected home television sets has been proven technically feasible. Publishers have computers programmed for subscription fulfillment, order distribution and accounting, title and subject acceptance testing, and tremendous information retrieval capability. Newspaper production has been automated by some of the largest newspapers in the world. Advertising-effectiveness evaluation, media planning and mix, and audience testing have become more practicable tools through the use of computers. Information-retrieval devices of many types provide visual, aural, or hard-copy output for records control, budgeting design and analysis, pattern recognition, and a myriad array of simulations to pretest programs, schemes, designs, and procedures.

Art, Music, Astrology—Even History and Anthropology—by Computer

Computer programmers have been able to produce what have been called "truly magnificent" designs and images, and this output is being compared to many contemporary offerings. Songs have been composed by computers, and the sounds of whole orchestras, as well as individual instruments, have been heard as concerts due to the near-miracles of sound reproductions developed by computer technicians. Excellent experimental techniques have caused educational leaders and sound engineers to claim that any sound the human can make or produce and many, many more can be produced by computer and in innumerable combinations. The "talking and singing" computers are beyond the novelty stage, and remarkable achievements are expected to dramatize the birth of a "new culture" by computer in sight and sound. Anthropologists, historians, and museum curators are being aided in research, simulations, and authentications by the marvels of computer programming. Computer searches, classifications, confirmations, analyses, and "reconstructed" economies, historical eras, and civilizations are just a few of the techniques for computer study of the past.

Computer Terminals for Family Use

Cable television (catv) systems have been a means for providing low-cost computer capability in the home with only minor adjustments and attachments to the ordinary tv set. The computer automated-indexed mass storage thus becomes available to the student at home through his tv set and "Touch-Tone" telephone. Several hundred courses, including languages, statistics, mathematics, political science, etc., have already been programmed to offer students self-paced teaching via computer. Computerized shopping through closed-circuit tv has become a practical reality, and through the use of national and international information utilities, it could become a nationwide procedure in years to come with visual demonstration of products before purchase as a long-distance buying guide. The computer hobbyist already has computer terminals in his home; salesmen carry them in small brief cases for easy connection through telephone systems. Such individuals solve problems, experiment, research, and compute or design by using home terminals.

Computer Impact on Society

Computers receive their heaviest use by the various government agencies. City, county, state, and federal bureaus, departments, and legislative bodies order and utilize tens of thousands of computers. Various proposals are being presented for a national computer center and laboratory, but the US may not be first on this score. The computer as a policeman has been widely accepted, and the imaginations of the FBI and the local police chief have conjured hundreds of valuable applications of computers for fighting crime. Space exploration and new weapons systems could not perform without computers.

APPENDIX B

Data Base Management Systems

SECTION I

Overview

The terms "data base" and "data bank" have been used for many years to mean large collections of related information, and often they are not used in reference to computer systems at all. For example, newspapers and magazines have always maintained data bases filled with articles they have published. Many of these data bases are now on microfilm, and parts of them are also available on computer systems for rapid research and retrieval.

Since computers started coming into common usage in the 1950s, thousands of data bases have been created. Most of these bases or banks hold private information, such as the accounting records of a company or the inventory information of a department store. Some contain semiprivate information, i.e., information that is collected and maintained by some agency which controls it and may sell access to it. Information falling into this category could be mailing lists of all those who possess a certain credit card or a particular kind of license or credential. Usually, access to these data bases is granted on an all-or-none basis; someone interested in the information must buy all of it. Yet other data bases are much more public in nature in that anybody is allowed to search the vast collection of information for particular facts. Even though the proprietor of the information usually must charge a service fee to allow this access, many of these data bases are operated more as a public service than as a profit-making venture.

For example, a system known as MEDLARS (MEDical Literature Analysis and Retrieval System) contains the names of articles in the large number of medical journals published monthly. With the name of each article are stored the name of the journal, the volume number and page numbers of the article, and several index words and phrases. These index words have been chosen by an article reviewer to be the words most indicative of information the article contains. For example, if the article contains information about Korsakoff's syndrome, then the phrase "Korsakoff's syndrome" would be one of the index words or phrases associated with the identification information for the citation.

Physicians and medical students can use the computer system that maintains this data base of citations to find all of the articles pertinent to a current medical problem. However, the original MEDLARS operated in the batch mode of processing. In this mode, the user had to compose his request and send it off to the location of the computer, where the index words of interest could be typed onto punched cards and the list of citations could be printed. The MEDLARS system became much more useful when it became an on-line system. In this mode, the users can interact with a running program at a remote terminal (perhaps in a medical library or hospital). This version of the system is called MEDLINE (MEDLARS on-line). During an interactive session, the user is given immediate responses to his inquiries, a process which has the additional advantage that he can easily make the inquiries more meaningful. For example, the user may type "immunoelectrophoresis or immunoassay or fluorescent antibody technic or brain chemistry," to which MEDLINE may respond "2665 entries." These are probably many more citations than a user cares to plow through, so before getting a list of all of the articles, he or she may wish to narrow down the scope of the inquiry. The user might then type "and schizophrenia," to which the response may be

"25 entries." Wishing to narrow the list down even further, the user could then type another ANDed requirement, "and not childhood," which might cause the response to be reduced to "16 entries." This number of citations would be more reasonable, and the physician could usefully request a library search for the articles he would then command the system to list.

Hundreds of these special-purpose data banks have come into service, including OBAR (Ohio State Bar Association Automated Research), CHEMCON (Chemical Abstracts Service), ENDS (European Nuclear Documentation System), and EARS (containing Epilepsy Abstracts).

Recently, more generally usable data base systems have started to become available to the public. Teletext and viewdata are remote data base retrieval systems that, in effect, transform home tv sets into computer terminals. They were first introduced for commercial operation in the United Kingdom. Teletext-type systems broadcast digital signals on two unused tv lines during the vertical-blanking interval and do not disturb regular programs. The signals expand to pages of memory every eight seconds. Decoders at the tv receivers offer these pages of alphanumeric information that viewers selectively call up for display by using the separate or built-in terminals (Fig. B-1).

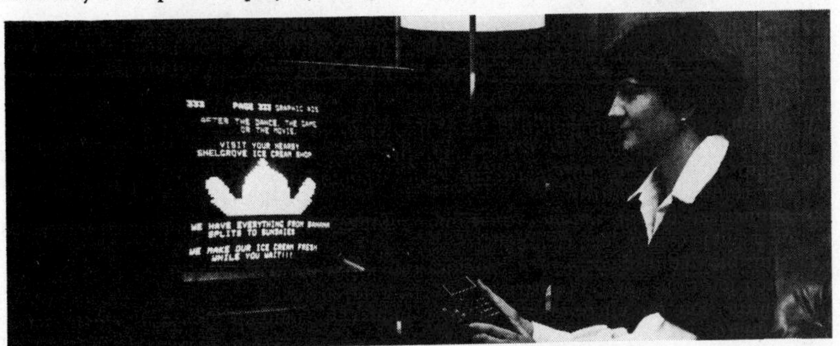

Courtesy KSL-TV

Fig. B-1. Advertising copy displayed on teletext system.

Viewdata (different names are used in various countries) does essentially the same thing but uses telephone lines to provide users a greater in-depth search of many and larger data bases residing in large remote computers. The French Antiope system partially combines both these systems into one to offer greater capabilities. Fig. B-2 illustrates a terminal for the customer-active QUBE system. Homes in the QUBE service areas are provided with a small, limited-capability computer terminal and selector console. The console makes available 30 channels of entertainment, information, and education. The console also has five response buttons that allow the viewer to "touch-in" and respond instantly to material which appears on his home tv screen.

The public and semipublic data bases have a common property; the user is almost always simply reading information from the data base, rarely adding information to it or modifying what is there. Private data bases, such as airline reservation systems, are constantly having entries added, deleted, or updated by the user, the airline personnel.

It is the private corporate data base that the remaining discussions will address. As computer hardware became less and less expensive, more and more companies found it cost effective to store the bulk of their information in computer systems. As the need for rapid response to requests for search and recovery became obvious, the medium for the storage of the bulk of the information shifted from punched cards and magnetic tapes to magnetic disks. The search for items on tapes or in card decks requires, on the average, searching half of all of the entries. Disks, however, are capable of allowing more "random access" to the information they hold because the read head can move to any location on the disk, much as any section on a long-playing phonograph album can be directly selected by moving the needle.

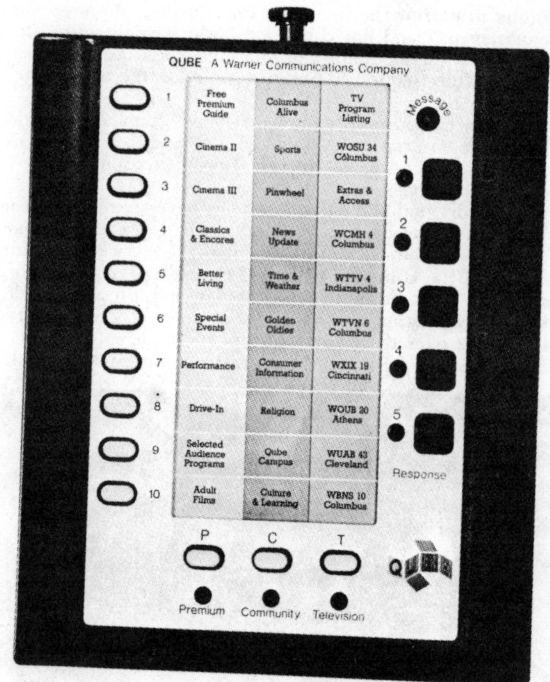

Courtesy Warner Cable Corp.

Fig. B-2. QUBE terminal.

Along with the improvement of the hardware that holds and searches the data, there has been an evolution in the software that interacts with the user and directs the hardware to store and retrieve the data as desired. The widespread use of sophisticated software has increased the value of a company's data and is beginning to allow management to view the computerized information as a corporate resource. The more powerful the programs that manipulate the data become, the more valuable this resource becomes.

WHAT IS A DATA BASE MANAGEMENT SYSTEM?

Over the past decade, the term "data base management system" has come to have a specific meaning. When computers were first used to process information stored in machine-readable form, people considered almost any software that provided this processing to be data base management software, and thus to compose a data base management system. As generalized systems evolved, they became dedicated software products, maintained, enhanced, and sold by software vendors. Most of these products have common capabilities and features that users have come to expect in data base management system (DBMS) software.

A professional ethic, tantamount to truth in advertising, has arisen with regard to these software packages. Now, only products that provide the basic properties users have come to expect from packages called DBMS may be called DBMS. Thus, a generic term has been born.

The notion of a data base management system is probably best defined by describing the data structure that it manages, the generalized data base. Again, this is a much more specific data structure than the arbitrary clump of data that used to be referred to as a data base or a data bank. In this sense, the term data base has taken on a new definition as well. A data base is a collection of interrelated data that is stored so as to:

Control the redundancy of the data.
Allow multiple views of the data to multiple applications.
Allow functional data independence. Changes to the data base should not require changes to applications programs that do not manipulate the structure that was changed.
Provide a common and controlled mechanism for manipulating the data, i.e., reading, adding, deleting, and modifying data.

There are many features of DBMS software that most DBMS systems offer that are not considered to be important with regard to definition, but that are definitely expected features or byproducts.

The DBMS should provide mechanisms to enhance or ensure the validity of the data in the data base, by checking the type and reasonability of the data as it is recorded.

The DBMS should provide a data dictionary to allow cataloging of data items in the data base so that the informational corporate resource can be more easily audited and maintained by the data base administrator. Ideally, this data dictionary should be integrated into the DBMS data manipulation routines so that data cannot be added to the data base unless it is described in the data dictionary and meets the validity checks indicated there.

The DBMS should provide a language to describe the data items in the data base and their relationships to one another so that the data base structure can be built and loaded with data easily and quickly.

The data base must be available to both on-line and batch processes. Telecommunications interfacing to support this requirement should be provided.

Automatic logging of transactions against the data base should be performed by the DBMS software. This feature facilitates automatic crash recovery and allows the system to maintain the data base in a valid state.

Methods to cope with the problems of multiprogramming, such as mutual exclusion and deadlock, should be built into the system.

Query languages and report writers should be available to ease the applications programming burden for producing summarizing reports and satisfying ad hoc queries.

WHY USE A DBMS?

A data base management system must provide an efficient and automatic searching mechanism to retrieve data records based upon values in key fields. Furthermore, it must supply a structure that allows automatic reading of records in sorted order, based on key values. This implies that the DBMS must be able to retrieve the same records in possibly more than one ordering. Since records can only be stored in one sorted order, this demands sophistication in the data structure and the DBMS software that manipulates it to maintain these orderings and perform the retrievals. This structure and the complexity of these algorithms should be absolutely transparent to the applications program. The applications programmer should not even know the details of the mechanism. It should be possible for the data base administrator to change from one optional internal structure or mechanism to enhance the efficiency of the system in an ever-changing environment. These changes should not change the "logical" view of the data. This is an important part of the issue of data independence. The programmers deal with a logical data structure, and manipulations are taken care of magically by the DBMS.

The programmer will never have to write a search routine. Instead, a simple one-line call to a DBMS data manipulation primitive is used. In the light of the inflationary costs of software development, this type of data independence has become natural and obvious. The algorithm for searching and sorting has been taken out of the applications programmer's arsenal. These algorithms are implemented by the data structure and the automatic DBMS system calls. The reason that these features of DBMS are taken for granted is that they are also features of ISAM (Indexed Sequential Access Method) and KSAM (Keyed Sequential Access Method) utilities. The data base concept incorporates all of the advantages of using these tools and many more.

For example, in a non-data-base environment, the sales department of a company may have two files, one to keep track of all of the customers and one to keep track of all of the sales. The customer file would have the following information in it.

Information	Start Byte	Stop Byte
Account Number	1	10
Last Name	11	30
First Name	31	50
Address	51	80
City	81	100
State	101	110
Zip	111	115

The sales file might have the following information in it.

Account Number	1	10
Stock Number	11	20
Quantity	21	24
Price	25	28
Purchase Date	29	35
Last Name	36	55
First Name	56	75
Address	76	105
City	106	125
State	126	135
Zip	136	140

Notice the data redundancy between the two files. The reason for its existence may be the requirements of the programs that use this data. The demand for different programs to access the same data is extremely common. The data redundancy is wasteful of space to be sure, but space is not nearly the consideration it used to be, and it will become less and less a consideration in the future. The gravest problem with data redundancy is the propensity for informational inconsistencies to develop. If redundant data exists in two data structures, it is very easy for one copy of the information to be updated and not the other. Programs that then access both data structures do not know which one to believe. Even worse, the problem is usually not found by computer programs, but by people who are affected by the results of computer programs. The cost of data redundancies in personnel time, client irritation, and lost business is far greater than the inefficiency of the disk storage.

If these data structures were ISAM or KSAM files, then the redundancy could be eliminated, and all programs that needed both types of information could access both files. Since the account number is a common identifying field, it could be used as a key, and fast reading of records from both files could be done to retrieve all of the required information. Thus the redundant address fields could be eliminated from the sales file, and the data inconsistency problem would be eliminated.

There is still some redundancy, but it has been reduced to the field which relates the two record types, the account number. This is the controlled data redundancy that was mentioned as a requirement of a data base. However, the redundancy in the multiple KSAM file environment is not controlled as well as in the DBMS environment. If there is a record in the sales file that contains an account number, there is nothing that demands that there also be a record in the customer file with that account number. The two files are only two unrelated data structures that just happen to have a common field.

A data base management system would allow the data base administrator to define the two files as a part of a data base. In the description of this data base would be the definition of the relationship between the two record types. The description would probably say that the account number in the customer file is a unique key. No two records may have the same value in that field. Furthermore, no record may be added to the sales file unless a record exists in the customer file with the same account number. In the sales file, the account number would be a nonunique key, since a customer could have several transactions recorded for him.

To maintain these relationships, and other more technical states of validity, the files have to be incorporated into a multifile logical data structure that is opened, manipulated, and closed as a unit. Access to this logical data structure must be through a common and controlled mechanism. Since the sales file may also be related to an invoice file or an accounts receivable file, the DBMS must be able to provide multiple views of the data in the data base to different applications. The description of the entire data base is called a *schema*. The partial view of the structure that is of interest to a particular program is called a *subschema*.

The data base management system allows a program to declare only the part of the data base that is of interest, the subschema. In this way, if any changes are made to a part of the data base that is not of interest to the program, they have no effect on the program. This is another of the facets of the important issue of data independence. For example, in the KSAM view of the data files, an applications program would have to depend on the actual byte positions of the data in the file. If fields are added or deleted, these programs would have to be changed. However, in the DBMS view, only field names are used in the applications program. The programmer has no way of even knowing the byte positions of the fields in the records. Addition or deletion of fields that the program has not declared has no effect on the operation of the program.

Why use a data base? Control of data redundancy eliminates information inconsistencies. Automatic data structuring, searching, and ordering allow multiple views of the data to applications programmers. The size and complexity of the average program are sharply reduced because of the replacement of lengthy algorithms with simple system calls. The smaller programs are more reliable. The code of the DBMS that is replacing the code of the applications program is much more bugproof than the average applications program; thus reliability is enhanced further. The control of data relationships eliminates "stranded data" and abnormal program terminations due to unexpectedly missing data in the files. Finally, data independence even further reduces the amount of time spent on the maintenance effort, and allows programmers to expend energies on new applications.

OPTIONAL FEATURES AND UTILITIES

The reasons given above are based on the precise definition of what a DBMS is. Advantages that are born of features and optional utilities that are commonly found on commercial systems are often even more compelling. For example, a standard data structure allows a consulting firm to produce a general query language and report writer. This makes the information in the data even more accessible, and personnel who were previously indifferent (at best) to the computer are now interested in what it can do to help them manage their resources. Not only does the use of a DBMS secure data and reduce the costs associated with maintaining it, but, because of increased access, the value of the data as a corporate resource is enhanced.

Query Languages

There are two general types of information retrieval required by users of computer installations, reports and ad hoc queries. Both produce displays or documents summarizing or listing some or all of the data in the data base. Reports, however, have specifications that are known well in advance of the time the information is actually retrieved. The report is usually run at regular intervals and may contain information that takes a fair amount of computational complexity and multi–data-structure access. Queries, on the other hand, usually have requirements that were previously unforseen. The information may well be retrieved in this fashion only once. Usually, these ad hoc requirements are simpler than reporting requirements, but that may just be because management knows better than to ask for complicated retrievals on the spur of the moment. As data-retrieval tools increase in usefulness, this distinction may disappear.

If we now consider the customer and sales files described above to be part of a data base, an obvious example of a query would be as follows.

```
DEFINE SALES END

FIND ACCOUNT'NUMBER = 153-239 END

2 records found.

REPORT ALL END

account'number =   153-239
stock'number =     234
quantity =         4
price =            3200
purchase'date      12/21/78

account'number =   153-239
stock'number =     234
quantity =         25
price =            3200
purchase'date =    1/14/79
```

This query would simply retrieve all of the sales for the customer with the account number 153-239. More informationally oriented queries are offered below.

```
FIND PURCHASE'DATE IS BETWEEN 12/1/77,12/5/77 END

FIND STOCK'NUMBER = 4889 AND QUANTITY > 25 END
```

The first query would satisfy an operations officer looking for a particular transaction that occurred between those two dates, and possibly was entered improperly by a clerk and now cannot be retrieved by any other means. The second would be an example of an analytical query. Here the user is interested in who is buying large quantities of the product with stock number 4889. Perhaps he wants to send a special promotional announcement of a similar or compatible product. Perhaps a marketing researcher is looking into a sudden increase in sales and would like to know if it is an across-the-board increase, or if a few large purchasers are responsible.

Report Writers

Query languages are meant to be simple—easy to understand and easy to use. The objective is to give as high a level of management as possible direct and powerful access to the data that is of importance to him. However, simplicity and power are usually at odds with each other, especially when it comes to formatting the output. Therefore, report writers are usually more powerful with regard to both their retrieval and formatting powers, but they are also more complicated. They are usually full-blown programming languages.

The notion of a report-writing programming language is an important development in the science of programming languages. Usually, the size of the program needed to produce the report is much smaller than the size of an equivalent COBOL program. As has been discussed before, smaller size means less complexity, higher reliability, faster development time, and less cost altogether. The only disadvantage is run time. Programs written in general report writers usually take more processor time to run. But again, this becomes a smaller and smaller issue every day.

The reason report writers can outperform COBOL is simple. The report language itself can be simpler because it was designed to do only a subset of what COBOL can do. The report writer is only reading from the data base; it is not writing or modifying.

The report writer does not need any interactive i/o primitives. Also, usually a report writer is custom made by the writers of a DBMS. This allows the elimination of many of the declarations in the program itself, because often the name of a subschema known to the DBMS will suffice.

Typical reports are the documents required of financial accounting, accounts receivable, accounts payable, general ledger, and inventory status. Special exception reports may also be run on a regular basis, or only when needed. These differ from a query in that their requirements are known, and only the time of the running of the report may vary. A typical exception report would be a listing of all of the products the sales of which have increased over the last month. The report might have categories of 5, 10, 15, 20 and greater than 20 percent. Furthermore, the report might contain the names and addresses of the five largest buyers listed under each product that appears.

The greatest problem facing the advancement of automating information storage is the data invisibility problem. Users of computers are often apprehensive about putting information into data bases and then destroying paper records. Given the unreliability of some systems formerly and currently used to manage such data, the apprehension is understandable. The use of DBMS, query languages, and report writers should go a long way toward solving this problem. The greater access the end user will have to his data will make him feel less helpless, will make his data less invisible, and will make him less apprehensive and more of a computer advocate.

Other Utilities

Other utilities that are now commonplace and may soon be included in data base management systems are data dictionaries, backup and logging facilities, and on-line data-entry programs.

Data Dictionaries—A data dictionary is basically a data base containing information about the data items in a data base. For example, a given file may have 20 data items, or fields, in it. Each of these items has a name, a type, and edit specifications, i.e., a list of legal and illegal values and ranges. The DBMS should check that any data that is being added to the file contains legal values for the fields. If the record contains illegal values, the DBMS should report an error back to the applications program that is attempting to add the record, so that the bug in the program can be fixed or the program can intelligently take corrective action.

A data dictionary may contain much more information, such as, for example, the date the data item was invented, who invented it, what reports it is listed on, and what aliases it has. The issue of aliases may be as innocent as different titles on different reports, or at the other extreme, it could be a history of long-standing laxness of the data processing department. For example, the data item might be called several different things in different programs. It may even appear in more than one file. This is common in installations that have not yet converted to DBMS and still have a great deal of uncontrolled data redundancy.

Usually, data dictionaries are sold with the DBMS package. Most are integrated with the DBMS software for type-checking, and so that report writers can know automatically what the column heading should be. However, several data dictionary products are sold independently of any data base system. The sellers of these products claim that the notion of a data dictionary is more global than that of DBMS itself. They claim that there is a great deal of data in corporations that is not under the jurisdiction of the computer at all, and never will be. Normal file cabinets containing pictures, diagrams, microfilm, or book libraries are examples. The data-dictionary people claim that a good data dictionary is mandatory before even considering DBMS packages, because, they claim, you cannot put your data in a data base until you know what it is.

Backup and Logging Facilities—Since the data bases are usually stored on banks of disk drives, the user desires that the data be backed up to tape frequently. Thus, in the event of a system failure that destroys the data on the disks, the data can be reloaded from the copy on the tapes. However, when this is done, all work that was done since the last backup is lost.

Most systems now incorporate a logging file or audit trail. This subsystem records before-and-after images of each record that is modified, and also records all additions and deletions. These recordings are made to a device that is mechanically separate from the disk drive bank, such as a privileged disk or a special tape drive. With a good backup system, if a hardware failure does occur, the data can be reloaded from the last set of backup tapes, and the logging file can be used to bring this version of the information back up to date. The programs that reload and restore the data base are also part of the utilities package that comes with the data base system.

Data-Entry Programs—A new feature that is being incorporated into some systems is turnkey data-entry programs. Since the data base is in a known and standard format, even if flexible, the DBMS software designers can write programs that will format a crt screen as if to present a "form" that a data-entry operator can "fill out" by typing into well-defined rectangles. Commands available to the operator are typically ADD, DELETE, FIND, UPDATE, and STOP. Thus, a canned piece of software is available to allow operators to add, delete, and modify data on a record-by-record basis. If the application is simple and lends itself to the use of such canned software, applications programming requirements can be severely reduced.

THE DATA BASE ADMINISTRATOR

With the rise in the use of DBMS software, a new professional, the data base administrator (DBA), is emerging. The role of the data base administrator is at a higher level than for any previously definable data-processing professional. This person must interface directly with high-level management and thus must actually be high-level management.

The reason for the evolution of this new title is in part the increased value of the data of a company as a corporate resource. Someone has to know the present and future informational needs of the corporation and see that the data-processing department is gearing up to meet those needs, or at least moving in the proper direction.

The DBA must also have extremely well-developed technical skills. With the DBA lies the ultimate authority with regard to the logical structuring of the data in the data base, the creation of new files and data items, and the development of new subschemas and systems. The DBA must have the knowledge and experience to direct the flow of development projects and data base growth through the systems analysts and production programmers in the data processing department.

SECTION II

Technical Aspects

Up to this point, the subject of data base management systems has been discussed in a general sense. It has been indicated that DBMS is now a generic term, used in reference to a software product that has certain properties and capabilities. The remainder of this appendix will take a closer look at the issues of structure and power.

The discussions thus far have been restricted to issues regarding the logical implementation of the data as opposed to the physical. In other words, we have mentioned that data can be stored in data structures such as individual KSAM files or as a multifile data structure known as a data base. We have mentioned that both of these structures allow the applications programmer to read records based on the content of certain key fields. We have also shown a customer data file and mentioned that one record in this file could be related to many records in a sales file, through a common field. The descriptions of these data structures, the manipulation powers, and the structuring of relationships all pertain to the "logical" view of the data, as opposed to the "physical" view.

The physical view of the data has been completely avoided thus far, and this subject will not be addressed in detail here. However, some of the issues will now be listed for the sake of completeness. The access method, or the algorithm used to implement the "search by field value" is an example of a physical (or implementation) issue. Common methods employ the use of hash tables, inversion files, or b-trees. Hashing is faster than the other methods, but it does not allow approximate searches. For example, if a user desires a listing of all of the employees making more than $20,000, a DBMS that uses hashing will have to perform a linear search of the data and not use the keyed reading mechanism at all.

Another option available to the implementer is whether or not to use fixed-length records. Most systems do use fixed-length records, but systems that employ data-compaction techniques must use variable-length records because different record occurrences compact to different sizes. This requires that a different scheme of addressing the records be used. This, in turn, may require that the data base be periodically unloaded and reloaded. However, unload and reload is often required in fixed-length systems as well.

Most systems consume disk space dynamically as it is needed. However, some systems, most notably hashed systems, demand that the total space be allocated at the outset. When this allocation is consumed, the data base must be unloaded and reloaded.

The requirement for periodic unloads and reloads is not of significant concern for small- and medium-scale users. However, it may take large users days to perform the task.

Another subject that must be mentioned now but that will not be discussed in detail is the standards set forth by the CODASYL committee (Committee On DAta SYstems Languages), available from the ACM (Association for Computing Machinery). (CODASYL is the same committee that specified COBOL. It is composed of representatives from industry and government, and systems users and vendors.) Essentially, the CODASYL definition describes three languages, a Data Description Language (DDL), a Data Manipulation Language (DML), and a Device Media Control Language (DMCL).

The DDL is tantamount to the description for the data base schema. The language is "compiled" by a schema processor which creates the data base files and structures which can then be loaded with data (see the discussion of COBOL in the appendix on languages for an example). The DDL, as well as many other aspects of the specification, bears a marked resemblance to COBOL.

The DML is the list of data manipulation primitives that must be available to an applications programmer. Usually, these primitives are incorporated into the syntax of COBOL or PL/1. These primitives are similar to the FIND BY KEY commands of a KSAM or ISAM system. They are OPEN, CLOSE, FIND, GET, MODIFY, INSERT, REMOVE, STORE, DELETE, KEEP, FREE, and ORDER. These primitives are typical of other systems, and their functions will become clear in the discussions below.

HIERARCHICAL, NETWORK, AND RELATIONAL MODELS FOR DATA BASE

There are four different relationships that can exist between pieces of information. For the sake of clarity, we will use the record type as an example of a piece of information. A file is composed of records, which are all of the same record type. Therefore, there are four different relationships that can hold between the records of two files. The relationships are one-to-one, one-to-n, n-to-one, and n-to-n.

One-to-n is the most common and of most interest to data base users. For example, a personnel department may have two files to keep track of the families of the employees, an employee file and a dependent file. In this case, a one-to-n relationship holds between the employee file and the dependent file, because for each employee there may be from zero to n dependents. Notice that this is a property inherent in the information itself; the DBMS provides a logical data structure consistent with its nature. The customer and sales files discussed earlier also have a one-to-n relationship with each other. A customer usually has at least one sale associated with him, but the limit is an unknown number.

The n-to-one relationhip is the one-to-n relationship reversed. There may be several dependents who are all associated with the same employee, and there may be several sales associated with the same customer.

In a sense, the one-to-one relationship holds between the different fields of a record type. For every employee number there is a salary. For every salary there is an address. However, the one-to-one relationship occasionally holds between files as well. For example, the personnel file may have a one-to-one relationship with the security-clearance file.

The n-to-n relationships are less numerous, but do occur. When they do, some DBMS packages have difficulty dealing with them, and the applications programmers are forced to make the system do things that it was not designed to do. An example of an n-to-n relationship is the correspondence between a student file and a classes file. One student may take several classes, and, at the same time, any given class is being taken by several students.

As was mentioned, the most important relationship is the one-to-n correspondence. This is usually offered in one of two ways, 2-level depth or infinite depth. The 2-level depth is characteristic of Cincom Systems' TOTAL and Hewlett-Packard's IMAGE data base management systems. These systems have two types of files, master and detail. Master files may own detail files, and this is how the one-to-n mapping is implemented. Each record in the master file may have many pointers to records in the detail file; however, detail records may be pointed to by only one master record. In this sense, master files may "own" detail files, meaning that the two files are related in a one-to-n fashion through these pointers. However, a master file may not own another master file. A detail file may own neither a master file nor another detail file. Therefore, the one-to-n relationships are limited to a level of two. If a file exists containing a record for each doctor visit by dependents, it may not be related to the dependent file in the one-to-n fashion that reflects its natural relationship. This is because the dependent file must be a detail file, so that it may be owned by the employee file. As a detail file, it may not own the visit file.

The CODASYL specification demands that the system support relationships between files to an arbitrary depth. Furthermore, it requires the ability to specify any one file participation in an arbitrary number of such relationships.

One final type of relationship that some systems have trouble implementing is the loop or cycle. A cycle occurs when a node has as its descendent a node which is also its ancestor. For example, a company may have several plants. A plant makes several products. Some of those products may be contracted out. Any given contract may refer to several products. A product might be made at more than one plant. So, the plant file has a one-to-n relationship with the contract file. The contract file has a one-to-n relationship with the product file. Since the product has a one-to-n relationship with the plant file, the cycle has been closed. If a cycle is opened and closed with only one file becoming involved, it is referred to as a loop. An employee file may have a loop with regard to the issue of management. The president is an employee who manages n vice-presidents. Those vice-presidents are employees who manage n senior managers, and so on. A part file could also have a loop. A part is often built of other parts. This is the classic bill-of-materials application. These loops can be turned into cycles through dummy intermediate files, such as subassemblies, but the DBMS that can handle these situations is considered to be more powerful.

These are the relationships that are known to hold between information. Most systems can handle most of these relationships as a matter of course. Some systems can be ungracefully manipulated to handle more of them. Some systems are not powerful or flexible, but are usually inexpensive to acquire.

DATA MANIPULATION PRIMITIVES

The CODASYL data manipulation primitives will now be discussed as being representative of primitives available on most systems. Most of these commands operate on a "set," which is the predefined hierarchy of files that was discussed above.

OPEN — This command makes a file or a set of files available to the applications program for manipulation.

CLOSE — The file is closed, made unavailable to the program, and DBMS resources associated with processing that file or set are deallocated.

FIND — A search of a file is performed based on the contents of one of the fields. When the record is found, it becomes the "current" record and is available to other manipulation primitives.

GET	Data items or an entire record are moved into the work area of the application program.
MODIFY	The values of data items or a record in the data base are replaced with the values that are currently in the work area of the program.
INSERT	The record in the work area of the program is inserted into one of the set relationships that has been defined in the schema.
REMOVE	A record is taken out of a specified set relationship.
STORE	A new record is placed in a file, and all pointers, inversions, and whatever other mechanisms are needed are created.
DELETE	A specified record is removed from the data base, and all current relationship linkages and addressing facilities are destroyed.
KEEP	The DBMS is instructed that the record most recently accessed will be accessed again, and that the information should be kept in main memory so that this access occurs with minimum system overhead.
FREE	This command negates the effect of a KEEP.
ORDER	All members in a specified file or set are logically arranged in ascending or descending order by the system.

APPENDIX C

Management Science Topics

SYSTEMS, PROCEDURES, AND APPLICATIONS

A major revolution in management techniques is taking place very rapidly as new problem-solution techniques are supplanting the former tried-and-true methodology. The computer's massive memory, nanosecond speeds, and real-time optical reports at executive desks are transforming most modern managers into decision-making information technologists. What is happening in the management ranks is obvious for all to witness. The data-processing experts, such as systems analysts, operations-research specialists, and data-processing division managers are climbing the management ladder rungs with alarming ease and alacrity. Old-style management is fighting to retain its corporate influence in the widely scattered opening and development of this challenge. Managing with EDP is the subject of crash courses at major universities which hold seminars for executives anxious to overcome the lead which the younger professionals possess. The alert managers are eager to identify themselves with the purposes and objectives of EDP. The computer is not merely a new accounting and clerical time-saver. This very apparent realization is now rather harrowing to many formerly complacement department heads. It is instead an all-pervasive controller of practically every facet of the business enterprise.

Any discussion of modern management must begin with definitions of terms and concepts of precise scientific nature. This brief analysis of key operating terminology is followed by the author's concept of a simplified and elementary organization chart. (Chart C-I) It is suggested that the reader closely follow the information and report flow (or throughput) to and from the three principal "control blocks"—Executive Management, Operations Research (OR) Team and the Systems Analyst's Group. The time-sharing, real-time computer generates all reports from the subdivisions and distributes all the control instructions to the production and distributive departments on the bottom of the chart. The OR team has risen near the top of the heirarchy of command and is the right hand of management with finance, marketing, planning, production, research and development, engineering, and personnel "under its wing." The systems control and computer specialists are at the call and service of all divisions in this integrated data-processing (IDP) organization.

MANAGEMENT SCIENCE TERMS AND CONCEPTS

deduction—This concerns the derivation of theorems from the general to the particular, and in which the conclusion is inherent in the premises. Example of deductive syllogistic reasoning. All men are mortal; Plato is a man; therefore Plato is mortal. Whereas inductive syllogistic reasoning would be: Plato has died; other men of history have died; therefore all men must die.

hypothesis—This is the question being asked or tested; the "crux" of the research project or problem; an analysis or assessment; i.e., a predictive statement awaiting verification. Briefly stated, a hypothesis is a "preconceived expectation" of an outcome . . . an assertion which is advanced as probable, and though not formally confirmed, it is plausible to the extent that it is worthy of being systematically tested. Some helpful synonyms: hunch, flash of light, gestalt—a hypothesis is analyzed and judged by asking a multitude of questions to determine if it is unbiased, logical, fruitful.

postulate—To postulate is to assume without specific proof; to accept a proposition without immediate empirical evidence; to accept a concept as evident from general life experience or general acceptance; for example, to

Chart C-1. Operations Analysis

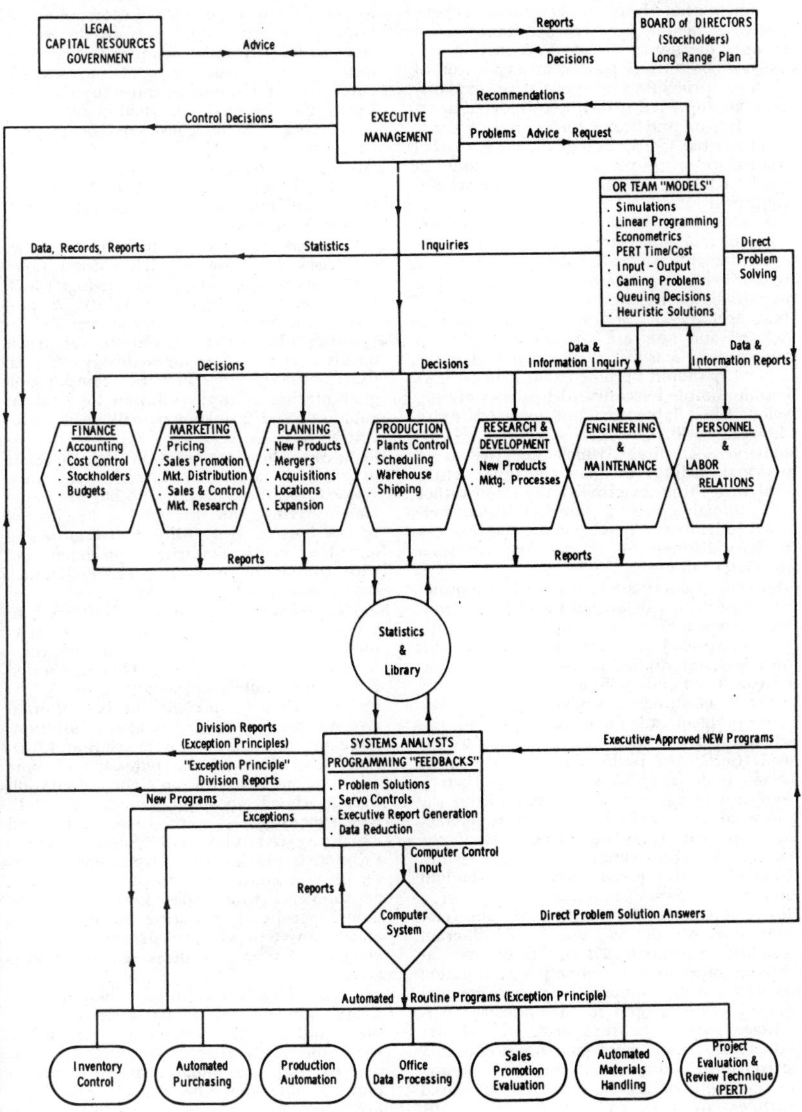

Intergrated Management Organization

postulate by analogy, by projection, by extrapolation; to petition that such knowledge has already been developed.

empirical—This is the essence of scientific method; i.e., empirical data has verifiable documentation from observations, experiments, evidence, past recorded experience—without the use of theory or deduction.

theory—The term is used as an exposition of abstract principles; a speculative explanation; an unproved principle considered apart from fact or practice; a conjectural explanation; partial work being directed toward confirmation; people engaged in study of truth or falsity; results seem possible yet unconfirmed.

law—This is a written or positive rule; a statement of a relation or sequence of phenomena invariable under the same conditions; if tested evidence toward confirmation of a hypothesis or theory has accumulated such that primary and widespread acceptance is derived and tests are no longer considered necessary or feasible, the principles become a law. (It should be noted that general laws become simple hypotheses when they are developed in a laboratory but await testing in the real world.)

objectivity—Opinions which are free from personal feelings or bias are those which deal with things external to the mind rather than thoughts, feelings; independent of personal judgment of one particular person; objectivity distinguishes science from intuition in model building.

subjective—Concepts which exist in the mind are those which belong to the thinking subject rather than to the object of thoughts; are interpreted by each individual in his own way and applied to his own problem as he sees it; an endless collection of personally different meanings or understandings to the same problem, statement, or conclusion.

intersubjective—When specification of the aspiration to be performed or model to be solved is done with such clarity and precision and brings out the concept within the range of one's experience, then competent observers can carry out provisions of the model with approximately the same results. Intersubjectivity means clarity of thought and process communication.

plural objectives—No single goal, but combinations of desires often of different weights; i.e., maximized profits but not at expense of quality or competitive retaliation or new entry; nonoperational management objectives as "biggest in the industry" percentage gain in market share of industry sales; steady nonabrupt gain for stockholder satisfaction, ("don't rock the boat" strategies). Size, prestige, etc. cannot be measured with exactness (as cost minimization), OR (operation research) men must know these NEW, often hidden constraints or real goals or they might find optimum but "circular" solutions when executives have plural and complex rather than single goals.

operational concepts — Equations in models are first defined in relation to variables which are concerned with the firm's specific data, scheme, or operations. The expressions (math) must relate the symbols and values (concepts) to experience in an objective fashion and intersubjectively to the operations to be performed in order to bring the concepts within the range of one's experience. Math relationships must specify or at least imply the way or method of real world methodology, to be considered operational concepts.

a priori—A statement can be shown to be true or false by reason alone; truth thus known before the observation and/or evidence is obtained is *a priori*.

a posteriori—Statements which have empirical bases with the required observations, experiments, and analytical testing which thus demonstrate truth or falsity. *A posteriori* is a contrast to theory or *a priori*.

algoristic — In strict definition, algoristic means a step-by-step methodology . . . an exact answer; a systematic computation guaranteeing accurate solution as 2 linear equations and 2 unknowns will yield a specific correct answer.

stochastic—These are solutions, which relate to aims or targets, concerned with being "close to the best." Such solutions are based on uncertainty, but through the best use of precise laws of probability with known and measured errors explicitly considered and with confidence intervals precisely defined, can become most satisfactory.

heuristic—These are solutions which are considered with the objective as being satisfactory relative to the constraints of time, funds, personnel available. They are stated for "confined use" and as advice of a "better" though not especially the best alternative to present usage; heuristic solutions serve to "find out;" it is a solution which could contribute to the reduction of time and funds necessary for an algoristic solution (i.e., as closed linear-programming models) which requires highly structured models and exhaustive computation if complex. Heuristic models provide executive-accepted "better for now and for the purpose" resolutions of problems which are more flexible to model, permit faster testing and evaluation, and fit any type of problem which contains elements that can be measured and associated.

induction—This is a method employed when a large number of particular cases are assembled, and general conclusions are drawn therefrom. Generalized statements are thus derived from individual facts. It is important to note that the general conclusion holds true only in terms of probability, since it is usually impossible to investigate every possible case, and the analysis must be based on a representative sample.

scientific method — (1) An exercise in strict objective inquiry; an examination of fact or truth in a specific facet of a delimited discipline or field of knowledge. Its core consists in the evaluation of the assumptions used, hypotheses tested, and conclusions developed. It is an analytical tool of learned judgment concerning adequacy and accuracy of theories. (2) A method which compels the development of organized accounts of logical interrelations of reasoning and mathematical statements. Vagueness is eliminated, but not to the point of dangerous over simplification. The intersubjective (universally communicative) character of the problem (model) insures that misunderstanding is minimal, and many minds are used creatively and soundly to affirm precision and reality. Models include the degrees of accuracy desired and which are developed by precise probability measurements and the scaling and relevance of alternatives. The construction of the model according to all the rules and proper procedures insures against the normally expected (a) limited evidence, (b) jumbled and disconnected reports, (c) hunches and intuition, (d) unevaluated uncertainty, and (e) subjective evaluation. The executive group, if properly indoctrinated by the operations-research team and instilled with confidence as a result of prior successes, will not permit (at least consciously) bias, emotionalism, or personality conflicts to affect either model components or implementation.

decision making—Management, by participating in model building, at least at the objective and decision rule determination level, can:

1. Accurately appraise the magnitude of the potential gains or losses.
2. Judge the need and desirability of integration of all decision making.
3. Insist on explicit definition and resolution of problems.
4. Understand and appreciate the value, extent, and variability of alternatives to tentative decisions.

Decision table, i.e., decision logic table (DLT)—The importance and clarity of several statistics techniques as regards Baysean statistics, decision "trees," statistical decision theory concerning business games, and other matrix evaluations gives rise to a variety of action and result type "decision logic tables." These are concise representations of procedures, or payoffs, of alternative courses of actions as specified for varied groups or sets of combinations of conditions. Such tables are designed, built and fulfilled from a base of information pragmatically and empirically developed. Thus, the table can afford compact communication to explain course of action or use, or results of such action or use founded upon predetermined or probability-based ordered numerical ranges. Such tables are used for basic and adaptive advantages in many diverse areas as PERT, accounting, game theory, solution of scientific or management problems and a host of production-control decisions. Decision tables are great aids to help think problems through, to determine interrelationships, and to show results of yes/no or and/or logic (as in the internal operation of a computer) based on values in the table (matrix) for each cell. Many varieties of decision tables are commonly used, oftentimes in conjunction with flowcharts and block diagrams as extensions of precalculated numerical values of actions to be taken, or as a study of results or potential consequences of decisions (i.e., payoffs of alternatives in varying circumstances). Much stress should be placed on the use of decision tables.

The skilled executive will not wait too long for timely decisions while awaiting reports, data, or evaluations of minor points. Executives learn quickly to use the tremendous power and capability of the computer to optimize the time dimension to its fullest in gaining advantage over competition or nature to win successes for their firm, and plaudits for their teamwork.

The resolutions of problems by model building and the formulating procedure outlined above is a fairly adequate checklist for attacking the initial stage of model building. It is a portion of a scientific method which has proved effective and rewarding because it is meticulous and orderly.

There are some pitfalls which require alertness: (a) watch for deductive inconsistencies; (b) emotional or dual terminology; (c) fallacy of composition; (d) systematic mistakes (one-sided, or biased), and unsystematic errors (mechanical or computational); (e) incomplete theory, treacherous assumptions: (f) "missing" variables, imprecise relationships; (g) aggregation of dissimilar units; (h) improper sample; i.e., nonrandom, nonrepresentative, etc.

In general, the preliminary search process of management science should be one of critical, interpretive fact-finding from historical, descriptive, empirical, or deductive types of scientific, government, business, or scholastic reports. These reports should be based on statistical, literary, observational, or documented works which have been generalized, systemized, and evaluated for order, meaning, validity, and reliability to build the best model for problem solving, productive decision making, creative thinking, and optimal alternative evaluation.

CLASSIFICATION OF MANAGEMENT SCIENCE PROBLEMS AND TECHNIQUES

Among the better devices for understanding and retaining information are those of classification, comparison, and contrast. Generally, the majority of business problems can be placed in ten different categories, all of which lend themselves to OR-computer solution:

1. Competitive evaluations—Such models result in the value ordering of action-taking results in relation to opponent reaction or retaliation; i.e., attempted measurements of uncertainty; avoidance of calamity, e.g., game theory and executive games.
2. Quest or search processes—These are usually statistical problems to determine business potentials, sizes of expected errors, predictions, discovery of new information—basically data compilation techniques and statistical evaluations as regressions, time-series analysis, correlation, etc.
3. Accounting or record keeping—These usually concern simple relationships, computations, output reports, and formats as desired; i.e., simple batch-processing algorithms.
4. Scheduling—Project Evaluations and Review Technique or PERT best exemplifies this problem area of job-process sequential order; allotments of time/cost, priorities or "crash routines," milestones, activities, and reschedules.
5. Waiting-line problems—Whenever service posts or areas and random customer-arrival times are encountered, "queue" problems arise, such as: ships arriving in ports, supermarket checkouts, production lines, aircraft landings, others. Optimum ordering of service is required, and waiting-line activities and discipline must be devised. Monte-Carlo techniques are often concerned.
6. Allocations—These are some of the most common areas encountered, such as: product mix and "diet" problems. Problems of scarce resources and alternative selections for minimization (cost) or maximization (profit) solutions for optimum benefits are discussed in Appendix F, Operations Research; e.g., linear programming.
7. Maintenance or replacement decision—Equipment service capacities and limits as machines, vehicles, or bulbs, tires, etc. lend themselves to "end of period" replacement for systematic and less costly "outage" servicing. This is in place of emergency problems of nonautomated systems or standard operations. The systematic maintenance procedure will prove most effective.
8. Direction or route problems—Some of the original linear-programming problems concerned shortest distances between oil wells and refineries, shipping points, centers of population and markets. The transportation program solution provides utmost efficiency.
9. Inventory and purchasing—The most universally adopted operations-research techniques are the economic order formulas and automatic-purchasing devices which provide for optimal inventory levels, order sizes and frequencies, and vendor selection from predetermined but variable criteria.
10. Miscellaneous or mixed problems—The rate of discovery of new and unique problem solutions or of combinations of the above areas continues to amaze OR (operations research) people, equipment manufacturers, and certainly the entire business community or sector of the economy. Although simulation can be considered a quest or search problem, it is a type of solution which can fit in many of the above categories, and executives should devote adequate study to this device.

All of the above are computer OR problems for which solution programs are available from most EDP equipment suppliers—i.e., specialized applications software.

SELECTED APPLICATIONS OF COMPUTER SKILLS TO MANAGEMENT PROBLEMS

Problems which are analyzed through the use of procedures of scientific method are consequently structured in precise mathematical models for order, clarity, and computer input. Only two of the many varied computer skills will be discussed at this stage to exemplify the requisite union of scientific analysis, operations-research problem-resolution techniques, and computer skills.

Successive Elimination

It was stated that a heuristic answer is the best one (in many cases) that is discoverable and confidently usable with the data available and under the existing conditions. In these circumstances (e.g. nonlinear relationships), a properly analyzed and modeled problem situation might be simulated for the solution which would have the highest probability of being the best available.

The path to this type of answer, or the very small range in which the true answer lies, is found by continuous testing of previous answers against every possible new and different answer. This constant comparing and evaluating is completed at each point of decision in the almost countless calculations by the computer. The number of tests can be in the millions or billions, since the medium and large computers can make these computations at the rate of millions per second. Such tests and trials are the basis of deciding, at each step, which solutions have the least chance of becoming the most favorable (most accurate) alternative. The ones having the lowest probability of becoming the best answer are programmed for elimination. The computer thus works with a successively better and better answer or range, such that after thousands of millions of eliminations, the final range of "best answers" is so small that it can be handled logically. Theoretically, the computer must find the correct answer if the initially devised range "must" include the correct answer, and the computer shifts and winnows until it has it.

Operations analysis then, transcends and includes: computer skills (systems analysts and programmers); operations research techniques (as listed later); and executive action taken; i.e., management science (as a result of model solutions and computations). Texts often refer to OR as problem solving: to management science as executive control; and to electronic data processing as computer skills. Thus, we may list and sum the sequence: Computer skills plus operations research plus management science equals operations analysis (CS + OR + MS = OA).

Automation and the "Exception Principle"

Technically, automation is the substitution of devices for human facilities of decision and effort. Such devices can be electronic, pneumatic, hydraulic, electric, or mechanical. The programmed decision, however, is the guide and control. An example is the standard thermostat which automatically controls the fuel to the furnace, as the temperature rises or falls in the room, home, or office.

Automation can be considered the technology based on communication and control which has become the third phase of the Industrial Revolution. After the first stage of mechanization and the factory system, the early twentieth century brought mass production and extensive development of the assembly line (2nd stage). Automation in the office or factory has turned the haphazard collection of machines or clerks into an expedient, almost self-operating, integrated unit.

Automation can be considered production by machines which are self-acting and self-correcting with respect to predetermined processes. For example, a quality-control guidance device (like a thermostat) could make automatic, within predescribed limits, the moving of work from one machine to the next (stoker to furnace); quite simply stated, programmed devices are servos which guide the control of machines by machines.

From the above definition, it can be seen that controlled "repetitive operations of machines" cannot be an accurate or adequate concept of automation. True automation designs are those which control several operations, each operation dependent on a variety of automatically supplied or stored instructions (e.g., punched card, punched tape, or magnetic-tape programs) and data.

The necessary and sufficient condition, however, is that the automation installations make adjustments during operations to keep the machinery or system operating within specific tolerances, speeds, or directions. The processor of the computer, which often controls large automatic systems, achieves this multipurpose guidance through a feedback program. Such a programmed machine system is often called a "servomechanism." The "servo," through pneumatic valves, hydraulic mechanisms, timing devices, or electric eyes, measures or tests the operation as it proceeds. Motors will respond to output instructions and messages of the computer which result from expected deviations from predetermined standards or norms. The program is adjusted or modified, resulting in changed orders to the "performing" machines which do the grinding, cutting, assembling, capping, etc.

Just as man has "master-slave" computer systems with one computer exercising complete control over another, perhaps with greater capacity man also might soon design "slave" machines which receive information and commands from the "thinking" or adaptive machines. The "servo" then watches, guides, measures, computes, and directs, by modification when necessary, as it initiates and uses the automatically stored programs to keep the process under ideal control.

Automatic control can be established whenever and wherever the relationship between input and corrections can be measured and predicted, such as those with indicators or temperatures, fluid levels, flow rates, etc. But, machine control must have complete information for every eventuality, whereas an intelligent man can control with some information missing. Systems are in operation which automatically perform over 100,000 operations to turn out specific products and at expansive per hour production rates.

Switches, magnets, electric eyes, and other devices are the indicators for choices, movements, and actual "new orders" from the processor.

Management-science students often develop the concept of "one large machine" with self-correcting feedback control. This same single or integrated system can be accomplished in any office where statistics, reports, and other information can be identified, classified, evaluated, computed, routed, etc. This feedback-controlled automation without the intervention of human hands works fine except . . . ! And this is the exception principle. When a condition arises which was not programmed the system must stop. This is where exception rules. The human being now, with his "reading" capability (eyes, other senses), with his "memory" (mind, experience), and his output (hands, arms, and feet), becomes part of the servomechanism to reorient the system. But that exception and others would soon be programmed until there are very few exceptions possible.

Continuous and progressive elimination of these exceptions in effect results in the computer "learning lessons from experience." Many programs ("software," as in contrast to the sorter, console, etc.; i.e., hardware) have been developed for computers to correct programming or data mistakes or to by-pass improper instructions (but always to also indicate the nature of the error, the correction, or item by-passed). Experiments have been proposed and conducted with machine systems which can perceive by searching their pasts for error types and variable corrections; that can design, that can run, repair, and modify themselves and function in a "machine society." This evolution evidences highly speculative and philosophyically controversial arguments of foreboding significance.

MANAGEMENT EDUCATION

The discussion in this chapter, from the beginning definition of scientific method terminology to the preceding statements of unlimited problem-solving capability, must serve to clearly illustrate that modern managers of the present complex world, and certainly the microelectronic computerized society facing us in the future, do surely require training and skill in scientific (logical and mathematical) problem-solving capability. For the manager to at least understand, if not actually perform these activities, he must have concepts of logic and model structuring. This requires that he practice at least elementary mathematical manipulation of data; that he study the nature, characteristics, and limitations of models; that he familiarize himself with the principal management-science nomenclature, methods, and procedures; that he survey and analyze some of the more common areas of current uses and applications; that he develop the capability to at least know when to seek assistance for strategically vital problems, and determine who to summon for aid and guidance. For in spite of his reluctance to delve deeply into modern decision-making techniques, he certainly should know the capability, capacity, versatility, and power of (1) computer skills, (2) operations research techniques, and (3) management-science evaluative processes. More than anything else in the past fifty years, the computer and its power have greatly widened the gap between the doers and the thinkers. The doers—the clerks, data collectors, machine operators, etc.—will continue to shrink in size and status, and the thinkers will continue to grow to higher pedestals of power until the former become mere extensions of the machines, and the latter become the creative elite of the society.

APPENDIX D

Transition Criteria and Procedures

The changeover from conventional management-control systems to computer-aided management information and decision systems is a period of considerable difficulty and strain for most businesses and industries. The following discussion is developed in semioutline form in order to include many aspects of the procedure and of this sometimes traumatic experience to the personnel involved. At the outset management realizes that the new system will sweep away long-standing engineering methods, manufacturing processes, and traditional patterns of thought and behavior. Most executives hope to be convinced by the studies listed below that certainly the top hierarchy will benefit from processes and procedures developed with the aid of, and through the use of, the computer to enhance abilities to make more accurate, timely, and logical decisions due to increased and more orderly assimilation and analysis of data. It is further hoped that most of the various segments of company operation will ultimately benefit in areas as: office automation, mechanized payroll, and personnel accounting methods; advanced material and control procedures; new rapid strides in assembly-line balancing, job routing, engineering processing, and of course, improved efficiency of labor operations and their reduced costs. Decision-making alone should result in the compression of man-years of mathematical calculation into hours, the ability to perform nanosecond information retrieval, and the storing and recording of masses of data concerning interrelated and nonrelated variables.

Modern business leaders will realize that since management problems are becoming more and more complex, they require speedy decision-making, and such problems lead to greater rewards or penalties when they are solved. Product-life cycles are shorter; business conditions change very rapidly; problems of cost and management control require precision analyses and valid assumptions.

The ability to systematize operations, pinpoint variable costs with timely accuracy, to develop plans which establish reasonable assurance that multiple but measured goals will be met, and to have at hand (on line) information pertinent to all management or production functions—these are expectations of potential computer purchasers. But, although the computer can help, generally live humans do all the planning, preparations, and implementation for computer installations. And it is a surprise to most key executives that the hardware purchase itself is one of the smallest and least significant elements of the total transition decision and its implications and impact. This poses one of the most significant enigmas, that of attempting to "cost out" or put a dollar value on almost any of the above listed hoped-for management control gains. There is great difficulty in comparing reduced costs to the above concepts of tremendously improved level of all round service and new capability. A point of contention which is most often neglected in evaluating new computer control systems concerns the "freed-up" time of many fully experienced loyal and competent men formerly buried in heaps of drudgery, routine, and "lost cause." Instead of fear of displacement, most workers, especially those in middle management, if properly indoctrinated, should welcome with joy the new opportunities which come to the surface with computer controls and procedures. However, if Parkinson's Law is allowed to take effect—that work expands with the time allowed for it—then planning and new controls have been totally inept.

The discussion which follows concerning development of various studies of proposals relating to advantages and benefits of computer transition includes some aspects of feasibility and applications analyses. One rather vital factor has not, however, been included. This is the frequently entitled Economic Study. It's purpose is to develop detailed specificity of comparative costs and benefit tradeoffs. Some economic studies could involve such extraneous and remote detail, especially those involving real-time and time-sharing systems that only an expert team of top economists could interpret.

Some examples of intangible new "by-product" information systems are: performance reports of the various phases of the data processing system itself; evaluation of plans, procedures, acquisitions, new locations and sizes of facilities, etc., as results of simulations on the computer; efficiencies of management follow-up and support of various programs; extensive ranges of cost, profits, and sales projections with changing values of variables and insertion of new parameters in models and econometric projections; for corrective action, pinpointing of variances at all levels according to responsibilities; "exception principle" reporting and report integration to provide pertinence and clarity to top management rather than mountainous detail; methods and effectiveness of system implementation; distilled contract evaluations and work authorizations; costs and effectiveness of specialists (outside and inside); and evaluation of all personnel capability.

Most of these topics are really bases for "inside" company study and are not proper generalized items for discussion in this text. The scope and purpose of this appendix, however, is to acquaint the student with the range and components of initial criteria for making the purchase-lease decision and to lay the frame of reference from which individualized investigations may be completed.

ERRORS AND PITFALLS OF COMPUTER TRANSITION

One large organization recently pulled out its electronic computer after paying over $1,000,000 in rent plus installation and programming costs. The reasons given were: (1) installation costs were higher than expected, (2) peripheral costs continued to exceed budget limits, (3) equipment complexity caused frequent and expensive breakdowns, and (4) the computer just wasn't doing the job for which it was purchased. Added to that might be: (1) transition (duplicate systems) parallelism was too long, (2) good programmers were too hard to find, (3) supplier sales representatives' aggressiveness was too much, (4) supplier aids and training programs (promised and delivered) were too technical for available semiskilled computer people, (5) the changeover was not adequately planned, (6) increased "level" of service cannot be properly "cost accounted" or amortized within strict budgets, and (7) initial successes were shallow and few, precluding ability to convince need for continuation. Some questions concerning why various computer installations prove to be unsatisfactory in cost and expected utility must be answered for prevention of a similar fate to new users. It is to be kept in mind that heretofore the criteria for evaluating manufacturer's claims were very sparse. Systems which were not working successfully were managed by people very reluctant to discuss their blunders. Systems which were highly efficient and successful were controlled by firms in intense competition who were also reluctant to disclose their secrets and the extent of their progress, for completely and justifiably selfish reasons. Ordinarily, industrial buyers are well informed people and agents. These same decision-makers in the purchasing and high management divisions formerly had little experience and even deep apathy for developing competence in electronic equipment evaluations.

FEASIBILITY AND APPLICATION STUDIES

The executive facing the decision to convert to a computer system considers a great many problems. He may generalize initially by quickly listing a few: (1) problems of conversion, (2) criteria for conversion decision, and (3) potential benefits versus costs.

Quick Analysis of Conversion Problems

1. Various types of experts and consultants might have to be hired to familiarize themselves with company operations and be fitted into the organization.
2. Many people will have to be trained, others retrained, regrouped, or relieved—with potential union troubles.
3. Old equipment will have to be replaced; new systems installed in an orderly, nondisruptive manner.

4. Data gathering, processing, reporting must be reviewed; new forms, codes, auditing procedures will have to be reorganized.

Advantages of Quick Analysis

1. Clerical economy—reduces number of people involved in paper flow, in routine decision-making, record-keeping, etc.
2. Speed, accuracy, clarity of reports enhanced. New valuable reports are available which were not feasible without EDP.
3. Instantaneous knowledge of inventories, work in progress, labor.
4. Effective predictions of sales; evaluation of salesmen performance and sales promotion effectiveness; long-range planning.
5. Aid to engineers, quality control, planning, scheduling; reduced warehousing and production costs.
6. Immediacy of executive-control feedback for decisions and rapid and clear execution of procedures and policies; better pricing, instant interdepartmental reports.
7. Better customer service; more efficient handling of payables, payroll, personnel information; invoicing same day as order; greatly improved cash flow; less bank interest cost.
8. More efficient capital budgeting, product mix, location studies, product planning, testing, market sampling and research.
9. Increased confidence throughout firm; new expanded uses as conditions arise; establishment of operations-analysis division to solve new problems, innovations; advances to higher level of operations.
10. Live production reports, cost breakdowns, continuous data accumulation; installation of PERT (Project Evaluation and Review Techniques); location and correction of errors and system bottlenecks.
11. Tests of effectiveness of employees, new lines, and projects; evaluations of new production techniques (simulation) and competitive reactions (game theory).

Potential Benefits Versus Cost

1. Equipment and site costs—rent or buy; obsolescence question.
2. Installation and conversion costs—once-only cost; tax questions; depreciation.
3. Parallel operation costs—delivery and conversion time factors.
4. Maintenance and supply costs—service contracts; new forms.
5. Programming support—software packages (applications programs); development costs.
6. Expansion costs—additional memory, display, and other peripheral units.
7. Time costs—overtime, downtime, nonuse time.
8. Personnel costs—number and type of new people; salaries.

None of these lists is, of course, exhaustive, but the lists do compose a quick, though superficial, temporary foundation for executive decision-making as regards whether or not a feasibility study should be made at a particular time. The executives must be careful of the pitfall of making a study designed to track down weaknesses existing in only one or a few departments of the company. The concept should always be the integrated system (IDP). Too often the decision is made to buy or lease a small computer for specific purposes only to discover later that the great error was made and the necessity now arises to replace the small system with a faster, larger one, with perhaps new programming, new people, and the same very numerous conversion problems all over again. Nor should the decision be made to purchase the computer system and justify it later. Adequate planning is absolutely vital, and the personnel, budget, and the time expended in this primary area will be the most important resources used. The underlying factor for success again must be enthusiastic and effective cooperation with key management to clear away the obstacles with proper executive directives for the smoothest possible cutover to the new system.

An Executive Study Committee should be organized using people with good knowledge of the firm, computer systems, the key objectives, and authority to command complete cooperation of all personnel. Their study should expand and implement criteria already discussed. They will have the time and competency to explore further topics as:

1. Areas of potential greatest improvement; plant inventory, accounting, purchasing, decision-making, quality control, etc.
2. Evaluation of specific equipment in terms of cost and ability to perform by using a check list.
3. Ascertainment of total real and intangible costs of the present system and comparison with those of the proposed system.
4. Steps in conversion process—a time/process or PERT chart.
5. Identification of many points in the organization where decisions will be made and the discernment of the capability of existing personnel to make them.
6. Identification, evaluation, and development of corrective measures for potential psychological and labor union barriers to planned orderly, sequential development—note danger of consequences of fear of job displacement, job security, and intellectual inadequacy.
7. Parallel operation of old and new systems before changeover.

We have discussed the preliminary steps including: (a) the executive's initial cost/benefit criteria (and problem analysis); (b) the Executive Study Committee's analysis and report. The criteria of the feasibility and applications reports are now to be developed.

FEASIBILITY STUDY

The feasibility report begins with a comprehensive unambiguous statement of the company objectives. Since each company's objectives are different, no specific format or criteria can be explained here. The reader will gain important insight of the totality of the feasibility report by analyzing in detail various complete feasibility reports developed by a great variety of firms and which are available from most computer manufacturers. We can, in this short space, speak only in generalities.

Following the statement of objectives, a thorough analysis of the present system is developed in regard to organization, cost, information flow, decision points, etc. This analysis becomes the point of departure and mode of comparison of the proposed redesigned system. Basically, the purpose of this detailed study is to form the foundation of the necessity for better control and the means for providing this improvement in total-system design. Because we have decided that an integrated system is the ultimate goal, we dare not risk ignoring crucial relationships and interface problems. Basically then, the procedure almost becomes one of:

1. Following paper around and through present system.
2. Conducting numerous "key people" interviews.
3. Organizing and implementing the development of grid charts, block diagrams, and process charts with some flow analyses of certain segmented processes.
4. Taking samples of all reports, records, source documents for interface changes and "unitizing."
5. Noting the name, frequency, purpose of all the people who use reports, records, etc., to determine how they are used, including the analysis of each data entry.
6. Noting the shortcomings of existing methods throughout the study and planning for utilization of new computer speed, capacity, and capability.
7. Constructing new codes, procedures, and sequences in preparation for redesign for both batch and real-time processing.
8. Developing the preliminary basis of the new, improved system design.
9. Relating the defined system objectives to the system design and to the new system equipment.
10. Developing the outline of the tentative equipment selection here with the help of manufacturer engineers and outside consultants—noting especially sofeware availability and requirements.

The feasibility study should also take note of the problems that will disappear as:

1. Gone is the inability of various personnel to fully comprehend the written or spoken order (sins of semantics).

2. Missing in the new system will be the clerical arithmetic inaccuracies and misread notations on records and reports.
3. Gone are the old-fashioned obsolete vouchers, requisitions, wasted multicopy paper ("shuffles" and "shufflers").

The feasibility study should also note the various new problems which develop, such as:

1. New equipment is immensely faster than the old procedures requiring much faster modification when errors are discovered or as changes are deemed mandatory.
2. Too much reliance on the computer instead of good judgment may result in much condemnation of the machine.
3. The high speed develops mountains of new paper (but this should be corrected by selectivity and purpose guides)—management can live without most of these now; use "exception reporting" (see Appendix C—Management Science).
4. The substitution of machine storage for intermediate accounting records might cover the audit trail, if carelessly programmed.
5. New procedures, tests, and checks must be devised some of these might be "hash" totals of numbers and areas not ordinarily developed for operating purposes. (See checks in definition sections.)
6. Proof totals are needed to count the number of original input-data fields or messages which can be immediately checked for missing items; sequence checks are required for order, logic, and completeness.
7. Reading and transcribing errors must be controlled by built-in program checks or double reading (key verifier); transfer errors are corrected by the internal coding and parity bits; read-after-write checks aid in error discovery of improper entries; operators' logs keep track of transmission, progress reports, files, etc.

A further development of the feasibility report will concern the pattern of costs, and the answers to the question about the type and amount of savings. Generally we begin with the:

1. Cost of the feasibility study in time and dollars.
2. Training of personnel at manufacturer schools, colleges, or executive seminars.
3. Cost of added personnel as systems analysts, programmers.
4. Site-preparation costs in detail (as contrasted to earlier rough estimates).
5. File conversion costs as redesigned forms, other supplies.
6. Debugging and test costs of programs and routines.
7. Parallel operation costs as noted above.
8. Additional programming and library development costs as the system expands.
9. Maintenance and service costs.
10. These costs are exclusive of the computer, *per se,* and the peripheral equipment charges.

The computer itself will not automatically produce informative reports. Long-range goals, such as markets, products, facilities, distribution, competition, etc., must first be determined. Systems and procedures must then be found to satisfy the needs. It will be necessary to know a lot about what type of information is needed and how often it is needed; the input requirements of the processor; if information systems can be combined for economy and efficiency, and if the system is flexible to changing demands.

Many organizations become quickly convinced of their immediate need for computer services especially for a reason like "because our competitor has one." We must repeat the folly of believing that all good things come to those who automatically adopt data-processing systems. Most often key executives buy or lease too soon and without the all-important planning. The potential purchaser must consider these basic costs:

1. Cost of the computer itself—lease or purchase.
2. Cost of peripheral equipment (usually up to 50% of the computer "mainframe").
3. Maintenance cost—usually quite standard contracts and fees.
4. Cost of programming and debugging—programs contain, in many cases, several

thousand steps each and, in some instances, may cost up to $2.00 per step to develop.

5. Cost of operating parallel systems—the EDP system and the old conventional system must be operated side-by-side for a certain period of time. This means duplication of costs, extra-heavy loads of work for personnel.

These are some of the numerous factors which must be considered. The neglect of any one could often cause great difficulties. A most interesting quote from an executive in a recently installed EDP system, "Now we can make 100,000 mistakes an hour," is appropriate here. Some factors for the prevention of these errors are:

1. Firmly fix the responsibility of conversion on one company leader and team.
2. Provide for adequate lead time—crash programs can hurt.
3. Allow for parallel operation—key inside personnel and competent advisors.
4. Recruit necessary but competent new personnel before installation—this is often quite difficult.
5. Phase the changeover—order and utmost cooperation are required.
6. Integrate the system—find the key problem-solvers and planners.
7. Organize a compatible electronic data-processing unit—"the team."
8. Design the input format for everybody—with "some" help from the seller.
9. Design the controls (executive monitor and schedules)—don't waste CPU time.
10. Design and redesign and analyze the output format for executives.

The reliability, availability, flexibility, cost versus capability, capacity, compatibility, and reputation of the manufacturers as regards the quality of the products, servicing posture, and systems (packages) accuracy and adaptability—all are weighed with the equipment cost analysis. Now that the basic objectives are defined, the costs schedule, the services and savings (cost/benefit analysis) are completed, and the advantages and disadvantages of the plan are itemized and evaluated, an action plan is next developed.

Action Plan

The action plan consists of the scheduling of the coordination of equipment arrival and changeover operation. This involves a printed schedule of exact times and dates in fine detail of the progress of each event. All areas are alerted with this action plan: quality control, shipping, purchasing, cost analysis, engineering, legal, pricing, production control, and all the various subsystems.

1. Every step in the implementation of the redesign has been defined and documented;
2. All decision factors and procedural rules have been outlined;
3. The incomplete, vague, or conflicting areas have been found and corrected; the logically ordered approach is set;
4. All departments are ready to cooperate; management has given its explicit enthusiastic backing.

With the final submission of the various areas of the feasibility report to management and its "GO" signal, the orders are placed.

The Data Processing Manager and System Analysts

Because he is deemed the heart of the whole automated system, a definition of the manager's position is mandatory. He scientifically analyzes beforehand how the production process, the information flow, or the integrated system will work. He must determine what information is needed to control the process, the computers, the instrumentation, and the designed and desired output. The systems analyst group primarily must consider all phases of the process centrally to improve and increase the span of control and thereby increase the total profits of the enterprise. The lead analyst first defines the problem, which the programmers will then develop for the computer to solve. The chief programmer is subordinate to the systems analyst and utilizes the block and process diagrams developed by the analyst to write the flowcharts and individual programs. The analysts must know the range and intensity of all the data items as well as the long-

and short-term plans and goals of the executives. Since the executives are primarily concerned with output, once this is clearly viewed in terms of the objectives and the input is suitably designed, the core problem is solved. Manipulating or converting the data at the least cost becomes the challenge of the systems manager.

The systems manager, to be successful, must have devised the integrated system so that little or no redundancy develops from the executive feedback system in either data-acquisition handling, conversion, or storage. This is his measure of skill and efficiency. It is the manager who has had the direct supervision in developing the processes for identifying, auditing, editing, coding, designing format, verifying, and testing the transmission and conversion of raw data to meaningful output reports. The health and prosperity of the business depends on his skills and abilities. Thus, he has completed a process of "systemizing" systems.

Some other duties of the systems manager concern the development of the overall picture of the old system and the design of a new system. In most cases it is the first full overall picture the organization ever had of its data flow. His initial commitment was to management as he began the conversion to EDP. He stated the results he could produce according to the time chart he developed. He had to plan ahead so that the work of his subordinates was not expensively interrupted. All of the programmers, equipment operators, suppliers (of equipment and forms), consultants, and management had to be coordinated to effect a smooth transition. He had to work with the budgets, implement and test the system design, and in effect, minutely outline all the work to be done from idea date, to cutover date, to full, efficient continuous operation.

Since it is the role of the systems manager to control the EDP division, it might be useful to note here that most successful computer systems have developed explicit (in writing) responsibilities of their key personnel. The divisions are sometimes organized along these lines:

1. Hardware section. The computer, peripheral equipment, and their operators are in this division—keypunch, programmers, etc.
2. Programming and systems section. This section is not always in the EDP division but is, instead, correlated with management—operations-research people, and system analyst group.
3. Control section. This section is responsible for all incoming data, proper processing, output, scheduling and controlling computer time, housekeeping, etc.
4. Program and tape library. The location, storage, and handling of all software and records in permanent form, either on film, or magnetic or microtapes, are supervised in this division.

The failure to recognize and separate these functions in the data-processing department might lead to erratic and inefficient operations and loss of control over important assets.

Another important pitfall to be avoided at all costs is failure to properly design input documents and to provide for adequate control over input into the system. Many systems analysts establish this as the number one error in the system. Employees, especially, middle management, are very lax and unprecise in this area. Few division heads have had experience with handling mass data and do not realize that ordinary accounting methods are not acceptable to the computer and its extremely strict programming rules. The concept of GIGO can be considered again at this point. The acronym "garbage" is usually used in every computer system, and GIGO is termed "garbage in-garbage out" in computer jargon. One must recall vividly his FORTRAN or COBOL rules and realize that the computer does not, in any case, make judgments concerning computer evaluations. A clerk may know that a code of eight numbers also has a letter in it and would recognize the format, etc. The computer will of course, accept all information at face value only. The type and numbers of input documents should be standardized in all areas possible.

The study group, then, has created the basic goals of the program, schedule, and policies to be followed in reaching these goals. They developed the written report detailing the aims, needs, areas to be studied. They had consultants, staff, and management advice, and stressed the areas of improvement needs. They further developed rough cost estimates, and they know the limits of the feasibility study because it was quite evident that it is truly impossible to know certain characteristics of the problems until the implementation of the system takes place; this is after the computer installation. When it is necessary to have operation experience before the feasibility study, even top consultant groups cannot completely and accurately select the best final method of operation.

Integrated data processing is defined as the total procedure that is concerned with the accomplishment of measuring, recording, and controlling the action and flow of information, material, money, and other resources throughout the system with the purpose of feeding back to management all pertinent and requested information. It becomes the "hub" of control for all operations. The IDP data-processing division has, within the business organization, subjected all operations to critical analysis and was the instigator of the total system redesign. It has further segmented the total system into subsets for more precise analysis and control.

APPLICATION ANALYSIS

It should not be suggested that the computer center manager is some kind of genius, for although he is highly articulate, and he usually has had ample budget, excellent equipment, personally selected aids and consultants, ample prototype and simulation tests, he (most often) has not had all the time that he deemed was required.

The interpretation of the duties of the manager has pretty well summed up the applications analysis. This analysis is the test as to whether he was successful in:

1. Making the preparatory changeover.
2. Developing executive confidence and system worker's morale to enthusiasm instead of fear.
3. Training properly the new personnel under his direction.
4. Efficiently operating the parallel runs.
5. Scheduling the computer time for least cost operation.
6. Testing the various segments of the system and receiving successful results with the total system procedure.

If he has intelligently coordinated the people to the equipment, and the equipment to the forms, and the forms to the process, and the process to the timetable, and the timetable to the satisfaction of the key management—then he has been successful, and the applications analysis can be judged A-OK.

APPENDIX E

Model Building Techniques

The executive of today faces almost daily a bewildering myriad of decision complexities. These concern mergers, acquisitions, stock options, plant sizes and locations, equipment procurement, product mix, promotion allocations and effectiveness, competitive reaction and retaliation, and many, many more. Though the solutions to these problems were never really simple, they have become almost immeasurably more detailed and treacherous as business expands in dozens of ways. Comprehension and communication have become difficult tasks for modern managers in practically all levels of organization structure.

Very few firms are now completely organized, directed, and controlled by "key" men because the vast scope and range of even a medium-sized enterprise can no longer be contained in the mind of a single individual. Teams of executive committees, planning and investigating groups, conference reports and recommendations now develop problem definitions and solutions. The needs then become those of exact expression and precise intercommunication. Most often this demands a form of visual representation to develop proper clarity and intersubjectivity. Unfortunately, businessmen seldom have the training of mathematicians or physical scientists and have therefore not developed rigorous disciplines of expressions and notations. Their problems cannot follow "laws of inevitability" as can those of the physicist and chemist, nor can they conduct controlled experiments or continuously repeat them until the proper result is achieved. The businessman's goal is action—optimal decisions in the face of the bewildering dynamic interplay of a multitude of uncertain and varying forces.

Management Science seeks to take some of the perpetual enigma from the minds of the executive class; to bring him more pertinent facts more quickly; to show and predict the carefully measured results of alternative actions and plans; to reduce the terrible vagaries of uncertainty, and to avoid the often disastrous hunches.

Since World War II, the computer has become available for applications to business problems for extremely rapid and accurate solutions. During the war also, new techniques for the solution of complex and dynamic techniques were discovered and have today been developed into very practical (and profitable) operations-research models. Models of various types have been used for centuries by scientists of every type. The models we will discuss in this appendix concern business problems which only recently have become "in" as the first true scientific means of analyzing and resolving industrial and business difficulties.

The development of a model is basically simple; managers sketch out sequence and evaluation charts almost daily. They equate and scale values of courses of action almost without thinking, and some men even use x's and y's without bothering to call them variables. They bring forward new conditions or numbers but do not call them parameters. Yet, they are terribly afraid to formalize this thinking into what it really is—model building. The simple models which are used grow into important ranges of complexity; they are autocatalytic because they foster their own growth. With some very simple algebra, most managers could easily formulate their plans, their problems, their ideas (hypotheses) into the proper mathematical relationships.

Fortunately, the computer definitely requires this, and management is now forced to think analytically. The alert "manage by EDP" risers in the company ranks can understand and use the combination of models, operations research, and computers to create near miracles of efficiency. But before anything happens, it is obvious that definition, organization, cohesion, interpretation and communication of thoughts and the relevancy of data must come first. This is a model. It collects, measures, coordinates, evaluates, and orders the empirical data, the variables, parameters, ranges of potential solutions and possible errors. And it communicates with precision. With this introduction, we might now begin a limited but concise analysis of model building techniques—types, procedures, and effectiveness.

Flowcharts and block diagrams are the primary tools of the systems analyst and the programmers he directs. Process charts and integrated system schematic analyses are the guides for his successes. Models are the heart of the OR (operations research) teams' problem-solving efforts. Extremely prompt flow of adequate and accurate data, reports, and solutions are the grist for the executive decision-making mill. For despite the toughest interrelated complexities of business problems, anything that can be measured and related can be made into a model, and anything that can be quantified can be computed for ranges of solutions and alternatives. It can be shown that despite how "qualitative" or intractable problem characteristics might "seem" to be (or how difficult many managers suspect it might be to develop quantitative order or magnitude), something is always better in some degree than something else, and index numbers are among the handy "ordering" tools of the OR technicians.

A model may be simply (for the present purpose) defined as a set of mathematical symbols, each precisely defined, that measure the relationships of the controlled and uncontrolled variables which are known and their values which are computed. These values reproduce the "real world" setting of the problem to thereby evaluate the "payoff" (costs versus potential profits) of the various alternative decisions for optimal action.

The model is a stripped-down replica of a real problem. It is simplified by excluding the minor or extraneous elements to clearly identify and measure only the crucial components. Practical tests and applications of the model will judge its conformity with the real situation and discover without disaster various effects of the use of potential alternative decisions as ordered by the executive.

Management operations research, then, deals with the methods, tools, and techniques employed to effect construction of mathematical models of business situations. OR attempts to solve these models in such a way as to offer acceptable advice to management concerning the acceptance of the optimal or best solution regarding the conflicting interests and varying characteristics of the real problem as reflected by the limits of the model. OR is a relatively new approach to modern-management thinking and is the application of scientific method for increased effectiveness to the solutions of problems founded on large masses of data and interacting complexities. It is a procedure for expression of the data, and a provable solution technique. Models are systems of equations representing a simplified sample of reality which permits comparisons, knowledge of effects of changes in values, and necessary corrective actions before a course of action is ultimately decided.

Problems must be expressed as models for computer solution. Precision, completeness, and accuracy have their finest development through the use of scientific method. Because a model is essentially a hypothesis based on postulates and assumptions, it develops the preconceived expectation through logic and deduction with empirical evidence for objectivity, intersubjectivity, and optimality. The management-science oriented executive must now know these terms, their meaning in mathematical context, and must follow and guide problem identifications and decision objectives accordingly. Unfortunately, these are new terms to most social science or business-administration people. They are defined in Appendix C—Management Science Topics.

Heretofore problems were stated by executives and personnel of other management levels in wordy "qualitative" terms. Words have double and triple meanings; voice intonations often falsely determine degrees of stress; personalities and emotionalism often overrule reason in word attempts at problem solution. There is little need to continue to show the inadequacies of the English language as a form of precise communication. For effective problem resolution one must quantify it as explicitly as possible.

A problem is encountered in a "real world" setting; i.e., an environment, and it must be translated in quantitative terms; it must be abstracted from its environment by simplifying it—stripping it of its complexities. Superficialities are deleted; cold, clear logic is substituted for the ambiguities of language; relationships of variables are formalized by using the rigorous discipline of mathematics. The problem must be the abstracted representation of the true situation being analyzed. Skill, experience, and judgment are required to handle the modern, complex, sophisticated interrelationships. The model requires specific representations of relationships—variables, constants, parameters, reduced to symbols clearly defined. Functional relationships which link the variables and parameters are established to find the values of the decision variables according to a criterion by which the decision must be judged. It is thus necessary to have predetermined an explicit and unique objective function (answer; i.e., maximized profit or range of alternative potential solutions). The model is then solved according to the various OR techniques, one of which is simulation, another of which is heuristics (if there are no clear algorithmic solutions possible). Both can find the values of the decision variables. These values guide the executive to decisions.

Most frequently, classes of models, such as linear programming econometrics, queuing, and the like will not exactly fit the particular problem a firm might attempt to solve, and a library model or standard form cannot be used "as is" but must be adapted to the specifications required. And, some of the "theory" many executives find objectionable is exactly so. The reader will often be reminded that until models are tested and verified against experience and reality, they really predict nothing and are only nicely solved puzzles—mental gymnastics or games.

KNOWLEDGE GAPS

The inability of most of present management personnel to develop models or to identify and relate the components of models—to think precisely, scientifically—is the first big gap. Causality, logic, and types of hypothetical analyses are used by management today, but without precision and clear emphasis as to methodology and direction of purpose. Saying it more simply, it is suggested that a great need exists for more adequate schemes for organizing the data of experience. Computers and operations-research techniques have radically and quite suddenly changed the means by which businesses are operated and controlled. Decision making and problem solving are being more consistently based on scientific model building and their techniques of resolution. Defining decision rules, evaluating "payoffs," choosing alternatives (even to decide what "not to do") are the means of seeking simplicity in decision making. Management will use this simplification and ordering of complexities (. . . model is simplified abstraction from reality of relationships expressed in precise mathematical terms . . .) to seek optimal ranges of solutions and alternatives.

By using the model, the manager has been able to identify, measure, and observe the characteristics of the critical or sensitive components; i.e., controlled variables such as machine capacities, labor, input, etc., and uncontrolled variables such as nature, competition, etc. He can then predict real life consequences of his various "hunches" or hypotheses with computer speed and accuracy.

Management and its OR team will be careful to see that the concepts in the model (equations and functional relationships) are pragmatic and operationally defined and that the deductions and observations (solutions) can be simulated or adequately tested. Skill in developing the model will insure that it has answers in expected ranges (through experiments) and that actual operational facts and tests confirm the validity of the parts and total of the model before it becomes a basis for executive action. From an operations analysis (OA) chart, it is obvious that the solution of the models is not the final basis for action, since other executive constraints are also concerned such as "legal, availability of funds, company image, overall goals, etc." These must also be considered . . . much to the bewilderment of many OR people who have found "perfect solutions" only to become dismayed and discouraged when management fails to use them. (For example, does General Motors really want more than 54% of the automobile market, and perhaps consequent government antitrust "breakup" action?)

Many authors have developed procedures for classifying types of models. There cannot be a general, all-inclusive grouping which would be satisfactory to even a decent minority of OR technicians. Nevertheless, this author tends to see most business models as being of three types: Problem, Conceptual, or System. They can be mathematical, physical, logical, or even simple prose (but neatly organized). Often the following terms are used as classifications: normative, which prescribe a behavior; descriptive, which defines something being (or to be) followed; deterministic, which assumes certainty of facts or solution; probabilistic, which defines and measures the degrees of uncertainty; static, which suggests equilibrium conditions can exist, or dynamic which signifies constant evolvement of various conditions (such as, marketing).

CLASSES OF MODELS

Descriptive or Deterministic

This type of model is sometimes called the "symbolic form" or algoristic type. Specified values are chosen for the control variables (i.e., size of plant etc.); the model can be computed rather easily as it is a closed model, such as an accounting model, and is very descriptive of the actual system. It is built by steps similar to a feasibility study. Examples are: inventory, cost analyses, production models, or data-gathering processes. Because changes can be made easily, and results of these changes can be identified quickly, costs and redundancy in the system are effectively controlled. Recall from algebra the standard form: $E = f(X_j, Z_j)$, then as many equations as are needed (equal to unknowns) are used to define the problem and develop effectiveness.

Stochastic or Probabilistic

The precise laws of probability are concerned either with the problem as a whole or segments within it. Values for the uncontrolled variables are statistically estimated with variability ranges and confidence intervals, and often random techniques may be used and their accuracy measured by normal curve approximations. Production-planning problems, advertising evaluation (nonlinearity), and behavioristic problems are examples. The object is to determine optimum results from ranges of possible outcomes with factors weighted by statistical characteristics or strategies.

Predictive or Relative Models

Broad categories of econometric, input/output, and sequencing models are covered in this category. The bases are structured in known relationships (empirical or historical) with varieties of changes in the parameters. The purpose is to measure and evaluate potential results should these specific parametric values be substantiated in time. Problems such as national economies, sales forecasts, profit extrapolations, etc., fall into this category. These are excellent analytical and simulation models.

Normative Models

Oftentimes, tentative solutions which can be used as guidelines are desired. This type model helps solve methodological problems, sequencing, or stepped explanatory analyses. Exception principle or direct decision making is facilitated with normative or standard (good) models.

Gaming Models

These models are developed from game theory or executive games which concerns reactions and relations to competitive decisions of the parties and the environment. Matrices describe the game and payoff. Such models are not necessarily to maximize but instead may be to minimize an opponent's gains or reduce hazards of disaster or large losses if certain strategies are played. Many interesting and some very useful models have been developed and will be studied in detail by many executives.

Linear Programming

These models are oftentimes given a category by themselves, but most are inclined to fit into the algoristic types. Effective resources distribution under varying constraints form the base for these models. Examples include transportation, product mix, simplex method, matrices, etc.

APPLICATION OF SCIENTIFIC METHOD IN MODEL STRUCTURING

Basically, the model-building effort must be to generalize and systemize, and through critical discrimination, to classify the elements under study. The terms must be made sequential and affirmed as to relative significance. Briefly, the problem must be first conceived or selected, then torn apart, made simple, prepared for operational definition in mathematical symbols and relationships. The model must contain the decision rules, judgment criteria, and objective optimization. A procedure to follow first should be:

1. Develop a distinct and unequivocal definition of the problem; kill "offshoot inclinations" and nonbasic background or tangents.
2. Analyze the problem in terms of semantic meaning; isolate and assess the components; find and develop the appropriate data and values.
3. State the assumptions based on acquired knowledge of how the project fits into the realm of prior discoveries, programs, solutions; detail potential projections, extrapolations.
4. Develop the hypotheses (preconceived expectations and ranges of potential answers) by insight, imagination, computations within the segments, etc.
5. Test the hypotheses by inductive and deductive methods to possibly form new ones; determine plausibility with real-world comparisons; develop check-outs with known data.
6. Establish realistic alternate premises or courses of action; evaluate each alternative.
7. Evaluate the tentative solutions and the problem (new) design, check the data against reasonableness tests—and most importantly, experiment with the model logically and pragmatically for verifiability of alternatives including their validity and reliability.

Reasons for Using Math In Model Building

1. Symbols make possible previously unknown levels of precision and rigor in definition and communication ease.
2. Math expressions obtain economy of time and thought.
3. Expressions developed in symbols are precisely defined and they develop reasoning which is quick and concise—reasoning and relationship which can be taught—even to machines.
4. Math forces complete statements of assumptions and analytic deductions, from simple events, which prelude contradictions; i.e., the model and computer do not forget.
5. Math models "delimit" the problem by defining what to include and what not to include, and, by aggregating many variables into few, develop new chains of reasoning which might not be part of current experience but are imputed or forced conclusions; i.e., the nonobvious.
6. Math models are quickly and more precisely modified and provide for considerably more accurate and confidently usable predictions from large numbers of combinations, correlations, and restrictions.
7. Math permits more convenient segmentation of the problem, for solution of parts first, then the aggregation of these parts. When tested and verified, the complete problem, and all parts, are sound.

PRICE DECISION—MODEL EXAMPLE

Mathematical terms are often best defined by using them in the context of a problem or an example. The following problem is merely a statement of relationships of possible variables which could affect a price decision. It is not realistic nor meant for solution but is only a base for discussion, but variations of it are standard.

A simple demand/price model should illustrate the necessity of mathematical analysis and computer use: Factor Analysis to Increase Sales (Q_i)

$$Q_i = P_i + aP_j + bY + cM + dS + eT + fE$$

where Q_i is the quantity demanded and is equal to P_i (the price of our product), plus P_j (the effect of our competitor's product), plus the effect of Y (change in consumer income), plus the effect of M (change in our promotion budget), plus effect of S (the number of salesmen we employ), plus the effect of T (the change of tastes and preferences of our customers), plus the effect of E (episodic events such as floods, famines, business cycles, etc.). The lower case letters (a, b, c, etc.) preceding the variables (P_i, P_j, Y, M, S, T, E) are constants which represent "fixed amounts." All of the expression to the right of P_i may be grouped or combined to form one functional (related) value called a single parameter, such as "K." K is fixed for this problem for this period of time, but it varies for different problems and time periods. Q_j the quantity of our product demands (sales) is a dependent variable because its value will be determined basically by the independent variable, P_j plus K. Several of the variables above are control variables such as number of our salesmen (S) and promotion budget (M). Noncontrol variables (or uncontrolled) are quickly understood to be beyond the influence of our decisions, such as P_j (the price of the competitor's product), T (tastes and preferences), and E (episodic events, as strikes, business cycles, etc.)

Other mathematical notation which is usually found in various models concerns: limited-control variables, such as running time, speed, labor availability, budgets, etc.; constraints, which are similar to limited-control variables and are usually to the right of the inequality signs $>$ $<$. (The first symbol means "greater than" and the second means "less than," and $\leq$ means "less than or equal to.") Constraints are maximum or minimum quantities, such as "must be positive or greater than 0," or "must be less than (not exceed) 100." Maximum hours of machine time is an example of a constraint.

It was discerned in the demand/price model that the quantity demanded was related to the price of our product (and other variables). It can thus be said that the quantity demanded is a function of price. Logically, a function can be defined to be a correspondence between two sets of objects; it is a rule for relating the particular objects of another set. It follows that the demand/price function is inversely related because, as is the usual case, when prices are lowered, quantity demanded is increased. Generally people who have been buying a higher or equally priced similar item will now change to our new lower-priced item; this will increase our sales. Other people who bought only four of our items at the old price now can perhaps buy five of them for the same expenditure, and many people will thus increase their purchase to five or more to again raise our total sales. (Such is a brief illustration of basic economic "substitution and (extra) income effects of a price reduction.) One may illustrate a direct functional relationship by stating effects of two complementary goods such as autos and gasoline. An increase in the sales of autos will have a helping or complementary effects on total sales of oil products, both increasing. This contrasts with price down, sales up inverse relationship of Q_i and P_i.

In symbolic notation, one may express functional relationship as $f(x) = ax$, when x is the dependent variable and f (x) (read "function of x") is the independent variable. This means some rule or relationship of x, say x^2, will equal "a" times "x."

Standard notation or convention suggests that x, y, and z are considered symbols for variables; a, b, c, d, and e stand for constants; k, l, m, n are used to indicate parameters; f, g, h signify functions as h (x) (function of "x"); i and j are usually identifying subscripts; t or t-l might be superscripts, e.g., Y^{t-1} symbolically represents a lagged variable; i.e., last year's consumer income. The value of "t" represents time—"this year minus l," means last year. "Q*" might be read as Q "star," or $\widehat{Q}$, as q "hat" to show a different value of quantity demand as a result of a change in a competitor's price, for example. Further notation and symbolic representation are often developed by the Greek letters alpha, beta, gamma, rho, etc., and all symbols are carefully defined or they will not be useful for communication.

The general form of a model is sometimes accepted as being: $E = f(x{:}z)$, with x considered the decision variable; i.e., the unknown value to be sought to maximize E (increased earnings), the objective. The control variable z is a calculated or "given" value. The f, function or rule, represents the model itself, i.e., the connecting signs and expressions of the variables, parameters, and constants which will develop the optimized E. Different types of functions or operations on model components will variously serve to predict outcomes of a particular activity or state new values of the objective function (goal) as mimimized costs. Dynamic models concern parameters which are changed or variables with different ranges of values. The model, then, is a precise expression of mathematical correlation (variables, constants, etc.) which the symbols represent.

One other relatively simple mathematical concept is left to mention at this time, and it is an important one—linearity. A linear relationship, which is a straight line graph, must show constant or proportionate change—increase or decrease. It can be expressed as: y (price, which is usually the ordinate or vertical line in a graph) $= mx + b$; the term "m" is considered the slope of the line; i.e., the rate of change; while "b" is the vertical intercept or the point at which the line intersects the ordinate or price (y) axis. The terms m and b are the parameters; i.e., quantities which are fixed "within" the problem but which change with each problem. Once these are known or determined, the sales "x" at each price level (y) can be established. A linear relationship exists when one value always varies proportionately with another. If, as an example, for all values of one variable "x" and another "y," a known change in the value of x produces a constant change in the value of y, we have established a linear function or relationship. An increase in sales might affect the amount of profit in direct proportion to that increase in sales, say by a constant factor of four.

The model described then would serve as an analytical tool to depict potential changes in sales as numerous values of the variables interact. A computer can plot graphs to dramatize effects and display or alter them on a CRT.

MODEL BUILDING TECHNIQUES AND PROCEDURES

It has been stated that models are simplified replicas of a real problem. They are sets of equations (or inequalities) representing a symbolic form of the interrelationships of the values of the variables and parameters which are arranged or directed to seek optimal solutions (values) for the control variables; i.e., the decision rules. We will further discuss variations of models for purposes other than optimization. Before doing so, however, it is necessary to show purpose and procedure.

The operations-research team makes use of scientific method and principles to develop the techniques and tools to solve problems which will control segments of operations or systems through the use of the computer. Their work must be with the advice and direction of the executive management.

The trio of computer skills, operations research, and management science sums and defines operations analysis. The steps cannot be overemphasized nor repeated too often.

1. Discover and define the problem. Construct the model.
2. Solve, test, and retest logically, pragmatically.
3. Correlate the "stipulated" (agreed-upon acceptance of model) solution with the decision environment.
4. Test sensitivity, reliability, and stability of the model with real-world application. When proved, permit variations of parameters and data to discern effects of changes; develop decision-making routines.

Model building is a result of judgment, skill, and experience combined. OR people must:

1. Know when to stop collecting data, determining parameter ranges, and when to begin problem-solution steps.
2. Wisely choose only the major and relevant parts of the system for representation.
3. Select correct formulations which truly established relationship, and prove the equations by tests and experiments with simulation.
4. Incorporate the decision rule into the tests using company data; i.e., examine the "point" of the model which brings forth the optimum value of the objective sought.

The purpose of the entire endeavor was, and is, to make predictions which have an acceptable level of accuracy. The executive action taken on the advice of the computer-model solution could influence only departmental operations, or it could involve major competitive moves, capital expenditures of vast amounts, or new basic control policy. The profitability or rate of growth of the firm could be dependent on these decisions, and the meticulous care in their scientific development is certainly a display of very measurable improvement over former decision-making processes ("hunches"). Thus the true purpose of operations analysis is not to merely turn out more reports and advisories, but it is to improve operations, at all levels, to analytically examine models or pilot projects to thus avoid possible grievous error in real-world action-taking.

As one begins his attempts to build particular models, he will do well to use operations analysis check-list procedural steps:

1. Recognize, identify, and define the problem, its main objective, and subobjectives (suboptimization).
2. Identify and list the classes of variables and elements; assign proper symbols; secure precise information and data and relate these components functionally and operationally as well as logically, sequentially, or structurally.
3. After measurements, segmented solutions, and tests within the model, abstractions and generalizations are developed by induction and deduction to check preconceived expectations of ranges of solution values and their consequences.
4. The math technique is selected, constraints noted, and decision rule determined.
5. The model is then simplified and solved for ranges of alternatives and the selection of the one which will satisfy the constraints and most closely reach the firm's objectives and goals (Decision Making).
6. Results are verified, tested, altered for interpretation (Computer Skills).
7. The decision based on the executive advice and the model rendered is then expressed in the original variables and in verbal form; the experimental "real world" test begins on the firm and operation, and if successful, the action decision is affirmed, executed, implemented (Management Science).

Verification of Models

Questions to be asked in verifications: (1) Are the answers or solutions possible, plausible, or realistic? Have solutions actually been known to occur in the ranges indicated? (2) Is the real-world environment realistically simulated; is the model dynamic, logical? (3) Does the model accurately predict, or simply verify or explain? (4) Has the model captured the true essence of the problem, or is the solution merely a reflection of the algorithm modeled and with little practicality?

Limitations of Models

The models have limitations as follows:

1. The model is not the final result; it is the means, not the end itself. It is a base for decision-making, not the decision action; this awaits tests and proofs.
2. The model-builder should not become enamored with the beauty and theoretical perfection of the model; it must work in the environment of the firm and in the time period of its design.
3. Model-building implies (by stripping down to essentials) that the OR team can avoid taking cognizance of reality. These pitfalls have been largely overcome.
4. Model building often avoids human judgment; this is a serious error on the part or both the executive and OR teams. Judgment must check and refine the model during and after construction. But such judgment must be proven.
5. Models too often assume persistence or stability of behavior patterns. Most models and solutions of business problems are rightfully classed as stochastic or heuristic, with the range of potential error calculated and included in the model.
6. Models often assume continuous linear relationships. When assumptions are false, they must be judged so; other nonlinear models must replace existing ones.
7. Decision-makers must themselves know the elements of the problem and must establish the constraints and decision criteria.
8. Data must be sufficient for reliability and validity of the attempted solution, and the data must be accurate.
9. Communication and interpretation between the model builder and the decision-maker must be clear and adequate for developing the true value of computer skills, operations research, and management science (intersubjectivity).

APPENDIX F

Operations Research

STATE OF THE ART

Executives and managers contemplating purchase or lease of EDP systems quite often are overawed by the capability and the wonderfully engineered versatility of mainframe and peripheral hardware. They have often read about the near-miraculous nanosecond speed; the truly inconceivable six trillion—character storage capabilities; the apparently instantaneous expansive communication feats; and the "1948-type" command and control adaptive devices (CRT s, etc.). They have perhaps personally witnessed demonstrations of the computer's ability to remember, scan, choose, predict, and calculate seemingly impossible simulation or immensely complicated mathematical formulas. Only a simple press of a button or click of a switch evidently was all that was necessary to select any item from inventory, to state or change complex production lines, or to flash the details of current progress and labor costs, up to the minute, on any specific product or project. Each man is truly mystified and intensely fascinated when he sits at a (his future) desk console with a personal visual display unit and teletype. He has personally completed his part of "hands on" experiment to retrieve "flash" reports of a daily profit and loss statement for various divisions, departments, specific segments of projects, or of the entire firm. These reports have been proven in other companies to be up to 99% accurate.

The decision is made to purchase or lease the "hardware" with individual visions of quick, effective, and complete controls for the firm. Most unfortunately, it is later discovered that many long, hard hours, weeks, and months of planning, preparing, and projecting should have been completed first. And even more important, it is later firmly and fully realized that successful operation of a computer system must rely entirely on people—people who direct, prepare, and control the software (programs, systems, and routines)—and not on the computer hardware itself.

There are literally scores of pitfalls for inadequately planned computer acquisition. Among them is the predominating one which relates to the recruitment of top level EDP management personnel, especially the filling of positions of EDP manager, systems analyst, operations-research (OR) technician, and chief programmer. These are the people upon whom the entire system will depend. They must aid in developing the feasibility and applications studies, and provide the motivation, cohesion, and expanding control of human beings and processes to be innovated. Management will either entrust the entire system to them or will lean heavily on their abilities and judgment for the important guiding function of: (a) definition of objectives, system design, identification and structuring of problems for solution, and (b) development of the routines, programs, and subsystems for direction and control of scores of operations to eventually influence and pervade all departments including top management.

The personnel problem suggests decisions with ranges of difficulty that only industrial psychologists could appreciate. Executives concerned about chain of command and replacement grooming will try to determine if present personnel possess abilities to take charge of EDP. Can these people, who were trained in the traditional operating system, competently utilize the many new capabilities and great horizons of opportunities offered by the computer? Will the firm be able to "buy" the experienced and skilled personnel to assure efficiency and success of the new system? Batch-processing personnel are available in the lower skills, but the on-line real-time (OLRT) system which was purchased is far more complex and difficult to program and control than even seasoned computer personnel could envision. The firm requires truly creative people to analyze and develop the search for new methods and procedures to achieve the promised higher levels of problem-solving cogency.

Management Realignment and Reorganization

Even more precarious are the decisions top management must make concerning its own group. Mental and organizational turmoil develops very abruptly especially in the middle management ranks as new functional command charts are developed. Some disturbing enigmatic concepts are these:

1. A new type of thinking and planning will necessitate a change in developed habits. Logic and precision must guide the program designs and people-program interface of computer processes and procedures. Demands of new knowledge (computer capacity, capability, and versatility) and analytical innovative presentation methodology will require unusual mental determination for the expected process. Management will be very reluctant and rather slow to realize the extent to which the computer system is totally cancelling the past business world and conclusively reshaping a complete and new management order.
2. Managing by EDP (outside of old-fashioned batch processing) is vastly different from the "good old days"—which won't return. What part of the enterprise will not feel the effects of total system integration? There is no place in the on-line real-time system for misunderstandings between personnel, muddled thinking, or conflicting organization hierarchies. Too many management people aspire too briefly to overcome the new language (and jargon) handicap. They "give up" too quickly on the mathematics-oriented computer and the advanced OR (operations research) books recommended to them. There are many EDP "primers" and some introductory OR texts which are readable and encouraging. These will be rewarding to those with deep interest and steadfast perseverance.
3. A very recent survey of more than 500 computer experts in industry, which included principally EDP managers, systems analysts, OR people, and chief programmers, verified the new respect and prestige of EDP-OR people. The results of the questionnaires disclosed that 75% of them reported directly to top executives such as president, executive vice-president, secretary, or treasurer. This is a rather rapid relocation from former rather menial positions in the accounting departments.
4. It is axiomatic that difficulties would arise with coordination between EDP-OR people and management traditionalists because of the quite obvious new status insecurity which must evolve for the latter group. The EDP-OR group cannot be completely absolved from blame, for it is also true that some are more interested in promoting their own personal or professional cause than they are in dedicating all their efforts toward aiding understanding among the people with whom they must work for purposeful total company successes. Management people, on the other hand, must face facts and progress which unalterably suggest a prime necessity of the establishment for close and friendly rapport between executives and EDP-OR people. This is vital for harmony, cooperative attitudes, and unrestricted progress in all divisions.
5. Reluctance by key executives to hire professional or technically skilled outside personnel for high positions (and salaries) has caused serious incompetency in some areas. Too many sad attempts are recorded which seek to upgrade former clerks to programmers, former accountants to sensitive systems analysts, and senior engineers to EDP managers simply because of long past mathematical education. It is unfortunately true that quite often some EDP-OR people display an important lack of diplomatic tact, and neglect for affable communication with executives or the requisite experience, maturity, and restraint of seasoned business leaders. They must quickly ascertain that it is the combination of the expedient management solution and the EDP-oriented programs and techniques which characterize true and profitable total EDP system victories. And EDP-OR people must work with and for management, while freely offering and explaining their knowledge and "secrets." These management specialists must consider their primary goal to be the elevation of service to the firm. The successful achievement of this goal will gain the enhanced status their division requires to prove cost-justification.

The task of key management people, despite the extra pains and pangs of uneasiness, must be to not simply coexist, but to struggle judiciously to make EDP an indispensable part of the enterprise, or he and his followers will quite swiftly slip down the leadership ladder or to an early retirement.

6. EDP-OR personnel must be true salesmen to achieve approval of the implementation of their perpetual planning. They must further possess courage to create and innovate. But, they certainly must also not neglect the desire and capability to adapt and develop the ideas and concepts derived from the extensive experience and proven good judgment of regular management. It is of fundamental importance that they understand the operations, techniques, or objectives of the policy groups or they too can slide down to the role of junior programmer or machine operator. The chain of dependency of the management on EDP organization is only as strong as its weakest link. The manufacturer depends on his hardware and specialized software packages; top management depends on its EDP manager; the EDP manager on his systems analyst; the SA on his chief programmer; the CP on his staff of programmers; and the programmers on the symbols and codes which quite often they alone can understand.

Thus, the emphasis developed here is careful selection of EDP-OR personnel for modern on-line information systems, the chief aspects of which are communications and control. Planning, planning and testing, planning and debugging, planning and innovating, and more planning are some of the duties and procedures which require efficient and responsible technical personnel in key positions. Their continuing function is to exploit the powerful, versatile computer. The executives who were discussed at the beginning of this section have discovered that the computer they have purchased is not a new electronic appliance to be quite simply "turned on." It is not a new, expensive superefficient electronic accounting machine (EAM) which automatically creates efficiencies in only specific applications. It does not in any case effortlessly change current erratic procedures and policies or solve complicated problems without thorough analysis, planning, and programming. And it is, in almost every case, foolhardly to believe the machine can be adapted to the existing system. It is dangerous and expensive to find out too late that the system must be redesigned around the machine and its key controllers.

Prediction, Communication, and Control

It is indeed necessary for EDP-OR people to strive for company-wide motivation and education (semiformal and much of it visual). A "win or lose together" team approach and cooperative activities promote and strengthen computer systems capabilities and successes. In this appendix and in several others, it has been stressed that the most significant use of the computer is that of providing improved management utilization of intelligent information resulting in more accurate forecasting, extremely rapid input/output and retrieval communications, and procedures of close, accurate, and effective control. These accomplishments would be sufficiently designed to aid very measurably in timely and optimal decision-making. The OLRT systems currently available at very reasonable cost provide the full factual information to permit the cancellation of former decision procedures based on intuitive and historical considerations which were very often incorrect, inadequate, and considerably too late to be either effective or competitive. The new managment specialist is a human catalyst who invents and designs truly original, "creative" syntheses to establish the type of information needed, from whom and to whom, and which is communicated accurately and on time.

Worldwide Need for an Expansion of OR

Before interpreting the particulars of the operations-research techniques themselves, hopefully this introductory base might serve to establish the need and identify the environmental positioning of the technicians who are primarily concerned with originating and developing the computational techniques and programs which become the vital computer input. The management revolution touched upon in previous paragraphs has related principally to internal operations. And if it were not for the very clear implications of the continuing need for dealing with even greater complexities of communication and control throughout the world, EDP-OR personnel demands would not be as urgent as they now have become. The universal expansion of technology and population inevitably is causing increasingly critical interaction and interface problems and "national interest" conflicts. Near-miraculous communication breakthroughs (Telstar, etc.) and suspersonic transportation continue to close up the interwoven facets of life and business, into a closely knit, single competitive community. This shrinking contrasts with the expansion of national rivalry and increased personal involvement in commerce, and the consequent frictions. The giant governmental and data-accumulation bureaucracies must be more adequately controlled and their growth reduced by increasing EDP-OR efficiencies. The technologist capabilities must be vigorously expanded to cope with potential commercial chaos.

Nations which have controlled economies as well as those with continuously expanding powers, regulations, and restrictions particularly force system and order for individual enterprise. Our own Department of Defense (DOD) very succinctly defines and specifies what products it buys; it quite closely regulates how much they will cost, in what geographical area they will be produced, and how much the people who produce them will receive in wages, profits, and security packages. Indeed, most government agencies also decide which scheduling procedures (PERT) will be used and what government interfaced reports will be generated or based on specific accounting systems to be utilized. Far from being criticized or condemned by business and industry, these government procurement systems have been accepted, by most, as significant improvements over the preceding wasteful, duplicating, and biased procedures. These defense and aerospace procurement divisions, which up until 1972 purchased more than 50% (dollar volume) of computer production, have prodded business management to improve their capabilities with better production, communication, and control systems for the obviously greater profit incentive. The excellent government examples (DOD and NASA) and tight management directives have resulted in rapid and widely accepted development of EDP-OR systems which are characterized by minimum dependence on intuitive decisions. They have based primary reliance on feedback principles of exception reporting, error-control, and automatic verification and execution of dynamic programming and policy.

CONTROLLED STABILITY AND RESPONSE

The characteristics of controlled stability and rapid response to changing environmental characteristics provide insurance against unresponsive automated (or historical) decision-making. The mass-memory capability of computers and the sophistication of manufacturer and user-developed macroprograms have brought to near prefection management systems designed for clear, functional information flow. Sufficiently variable responsiveness to complete all necessary changes, even very radical ones if program parameters require them, is programmed to consider multitudes of variables and their individual import. This capability affects subsystem generation and control without violent disruption of personnel, plans, or goals. The EDP-OR predictive and control versatility sets up clear and specific assignment of responsibility, reporting, and process feedback for high efficiency of operational decisions in real time for practically all planned or unplanned events. The goals of OR people are fulfilled when their techniques prove successful in deriving optimal decisions based on alert executive planning and judgment, aided by meticulously accurate and extremely fast communication and control.

OPERATIONS RESEARCH CHARACTERISTICS

Operations research, often mistakenly used as synonymous with management science, is the attempt to develop a science for organizing and controlling medium- and large-scale human enterprise. Some modeling and programming techniques quite definitely use some of the same principles of analysis that have been so eminently successful in the physical sciences. It is all too obvious that the "hard sciences," such as physics and chemistry, etc., have far outstripped the social sciences (such as economics and business administration and others) in successful scientific applications. OR is the use of mathematics, economics, and statistics to develop models and rules to yield confidently measurable profitability of alternative courses of action. The OR techniques are decision-oriented to solve dynamic problems enveloped in situations of conflict, complexity, or uncertainty. It is the objective analysis of the relationships of the values of the variables concerned which will determine the merit of the effects of the decision choices.

Through revolutionary computer-programming techniques such as simulation, heuristics, and others, the objective scientific approach of OR is providing increased management forecast accuracy. In addition to the physical operational processes such as inventory management, product planning and quality control, resource allocation or market forecasting, this also includes the fiscal processes such as bond management, capital investment, risk analysis, profit planning, and product pricing. Manufacturers' broad resources are preparing to implement many more types of OR techniques of problem solution. As will be noted in the outlines of the technique procedures, there are many types of operations, the nature of each one of which lends itself more (and perhaps exclusively) to one particular problem-solving technique rather than another. For example, the application of the various techniques now concern many front-line problems of business and industry. These problems have become as diverse as labor distribution, automated purchasing, and construction, also scheduling of scores of processes (from highways to motion-picture production).

OPERATIONS RESEARCH PROCEDURES

All available and pertinent data are collected and collated to provide management with factual, quantitative evaluations which are measured for relative merits of all potential courses of action. Confidence is based on the completeness of the model and the innumerable tests and analyses before action is taken. A simple explanation of sequence might involve:

1. Definition and statement of the problem and its components.
2. Correlation of all relevant data and reduction to principal variables.
3. Analysis of the model to verify its representation of the real life problems.
4. Check of validity and reliability of the model structure and decision rule.
5. Manipulation of the model to estimate, predict, and project the solution values under varying circumstances.
6. Selection of the optimum course of action based on predetermined decision criteria.
7. Continuing checks on validity and variations of the model with changing parameter values.

Operations research takes on new dimensions with computers because it is readily applied to problems previously prohibitive in time and costs. The required data are usually instantaneously available as by-products of normal sales billing, inventory control, promotion allocations and costs, etc. The greater worth of most OR solutions is directly related to the increasing number of factors (constants, variables, parameters) being involved in the model. OR people economize this by oversimplifying the problem to exclude all but the important factors in the initial solutions. In so doing, first solutions are often far less than optimal. Using the computer then, the model is "reclothed" with the great number of factors which, of course, can be easily and quickly handled at monolithic integrated-circuit (IC) speeds.

A model, in simple definition, is a synthetic mathematical system of equations (or inequalities) designed to resemble the actual problem so that its manipulation may yield useful information for analysis, prediction, and decision-making. The continuous testing of the model with proven (empirical) data of the firm results in the fundamental decision applicability. The model proves the data and the data proves the model. The further use of the scientific method to analyze and experiment with the quantitative representation of the problem provides the testing procedure of the implication of alternative courses of action which the executives, with full command of the facts, then determine.

The alternatives may be clearly drawn, as in: (1) deterministic models in which all are variations, such as those used in simulation, queuing (waiting lines) and others, or objectives as maximation of profits; (2) stochastic or probability models, in which important variables are not under management control, but are often subject to random variations, such as those used in simulation, queueing (waiting lines) and others; or (3) heuristic models in which completely unknown elements may be the substance of the model. This will lead to trial and error methods which "seek to find" better methods and solutions than currently used. It is in the last mentioned area that OR shines the brightest with predictions and control of an increasingly large range of problems substantially improved.

Another, though perhaps repetitious, explanation of an OR model is a mathematical representation of problem characteristics to relate the observed phenomena in a manner so that predictions of certain elements are devised to effect control of them in a manner advantageous to management. Again, prediction and control supersede but do not demean the importance of the analysis and interpretation of the elements and relationships concerned. It is the task of management and OR cooperation to discover, define, and ask the right questions for a problem to be successfully solved. No magical panacea-type answer evolves, but neither does a model produce the mish-mash of individual (or committee) "experiences" or solution by historical accident. Nor does the EDP program management, despite its efficiency, always explain or produce the best possible result. But far better are these processes and the solutions produced than anything before achieved with the methods of the "good old days"! OR and management science are much more than simply improvised accounting systems, as unfortunately too many unbelieving executives have concluded. OR techniques then can be attested as most practical in today's world and the best approach yet devised to emulate the enviable methodology of the "hard sciences." OR is considered by a long list of industrial users as a true science of organization and information theory.

Even a casual perusal of the scholastic and scientific literature of OR by physical scientists causes them to marvel at the new science the "behaviorists" have spawned and the commendable progress so far achieved. It is conceded that OR is not simply a shift of mathematical and physical modeling-programming techniques to business and industrial problems. Indeed not! The basic purposes of OR and Business Administration are completely alien to the goals of the physical sciences. In the former, they are the measured predictions of alternative actions in a complex behaviorist environment of human motivations. In the latter, the search is for truth and fact. The complex business-world problem environment does not at all compare with the controlled repetitive experimentation of the "hard sciences" with their hundreds of years of precedent, fixed laws of inevitability, and tried and true procedures. OR is yet an infant, though a healthy one.

As more and more intellectual effort and independent thought are devoted to EDP-OR through basic research by users, manufacturers, foundations and educational institutions, the new devices and techniques can conceivably be advanced to near equality of achievement to the physical sciences. The fitting of the expanding OR theory to scientific observation and methodology, as is being done today, will not result in suspected grandiose, pragmatic pseudo-science hypotheses. Instead, refinable and dynamically variable criteria of measured dependability will and does in fact ensue, for true professional status.

OPERATIONS RESEARCH EDUCATION

The people concerned with the procedures of OR have created only small demands for educational opportunities. This author feels strongly that new courses at lower educational levels must be developed now at universities, colleges, junior colleges, and high schools to expand this field rapidly. Most colleges presently relegate these courses to graduate schools or upperclass levels with inhibiting and often prohibiting intensive (but most often needless) mathematical prerequisites. For example, a year of calculus is definitely not necessary—nor even a semester. The students are deathly afraid of the terminology and described depth of the course contents. These courses do belong, at the theoretical level, in the graduate schools. But they certainly also belong, at reduced sophistication (for social science students), at the lower levels and without the stringent math prerequisites, especially "engineering" math. This author has had five fascinating years of experience teaching college juniors the basic elements of the techniques discussed above and outlined below. These business-administration students practically hated math and were not too well endowed with statistical proficiency. Yet, they completed their work with commendable results and near-exemplary motivations and dedication. The capability of the computer has drastically reduced the time and tasks of the sometimes unnerving math complications, and the current-applications case histories have taken a great deal of the mystery from the language of these topics. Unhappily, most of the earlier texts have seemingly sought to disclose and display complicated engineer-type proofs, pet personal and highly individualized symbolic notation, and difficult concept extensions. A background of high school or college math is beneficial, but the logic and methodology of the techniques can be made clear and understandable to aggressive students or clear-thinking, persevering executives. A "working knowledge" of the simpler (and most often used) techniques includes the procedures, limitations, and assumptions to permit personal use and extension in business applications. The best tool or technique and its methodology to fit the particular problem can be quite easily selected.

Linear programming, simulation, game theory, PERT, even queuing problems are really quite elementary concepts and the mastery of many of their uses is not difficult if they are presented in practical terms of current management-science nomenclature instead of mathematical hieroglyphics. By all means the theoretical development of the techniques must also be expanded as rapidly as possible or the progress of innovation will slacken. But more students and executives will substantially aid in this movement if they are released from "failure fears" due to the tremendous scope and potential of the advanced courses. The simplification of the processes does not do violence to the principles or the concepts, nor do elementary explanations distort or preclude the need for deep mathematics to properly continue the more advanced developments.

The interesting history of OR is left to the textbooks. Readers are invited to check the prefaces of the many OR texts and inspect their tables of contents to determine the levels of development of the books and the topics before they purchase them. Executives are advised that inquiry of individuals or the organization in-service classes can be very beneficial to key employees. OR personnel are usually quite adept at explaining their "bag of tricks" to practically anyone with a minimum of training and a strong desire to study and work hard. As with computer technology, one of the major obstacles to the widespread acceptance by students and managers is the difficulty of the language. There is definitely a breakdown in communications between the OR technician and the business or industrial hopeful. This text of definitions, and the appendices which it contains, is a presentation for at least partial dissolution of this difficulty in the areas developed. Most managers and management teachers are convinced, without doubt, that scientific methodology and the analytical, experimental, and quantitative techniques for assessing implications of alternative courses of actions provide significantly improved bases for effective management-decision procedures.

DEFINITION

Operations research as noted previously can be defined in scores of different ways with wide variance of concepts by teachers, management, and scholars. A definition for this work then would be one which attempts to strike a concensus, i.e., one that it generally accepted. Operations research (OR) may be considered to use statistical methods and mathematical formulations in a highly objective and scientific methodology for the study of complex organizations or activities. The specific objectives are to provide administrators with quantitative bases for decisions which will increase the effectiveness of determining objective goals and functions for carrying out basic purposes (action).

Businessmen, faced with the increasing complexity and realizing the importance of activity interdependencies, have long sought methods and procedures for reducing uncertainty in their decision making. Thus, OR attempts to apply modern scientific methodology to find a "system" or a way of analyzing and solving problems which have some difficult, specific, and fundamental characteristics. Operations research discovers and evaluates alternative courses of action, thereby providing processes for experimental or trial and error procedures with real-world problems before decisions are completed.

Without the excellent speed and accuracy of the computer, many OR techniques would be unexpedient or impractical. Also, without the most fortunate "twinbirth" of the OR techniques and computer technology of the late 1940 s, and their mutual aid for parallel advancement, management science would not have progressed so quickly or so far as it has today.

In this limited space, it will be possible to define very briefly, and perhaps inadequately, only the larger groups of operations-research models or classifications. A brief treatment of some of the techniques follows.

Probability Theory and Statistical Inference

These problems are often defined as stochastic models. From the Greek, "stochastikos," this literally means skillful in aiming; proceeding by guesswork, assumed. The term "chochos" means target, which might help the student to remember that stochastic models concern probabilities of noncontrol variables which are not known in advance, but aim to develop measurably close to target solutions.

All people use probability hundreds of times daily in making individual and business judgments, but in our discussion the terminology states that "random and chance" factors are involved. And there are no limits to the variety and extent of applications of the stochastic process. Business, economics, philosophy, medicine, psychology, and scores of other disciplines utilize these probability and statistics techniques, and they actually build models and flow diagrams to make communication and adaptation more efficient.

A statistics course (several are recommended) is definitely a must to develop the far-reaching versatility in utilizing and understanding these computational devices and techniques. However, simplified statistics texts are also available for those without the time and convenience to take formal instruction. Physicists, biologists, agriculturists, the military, and gamblers base a considerable part of their successes on stochastic models using—not guesswork—but methodological, verifiable probability according to the laws and principles concerned. These might concern the law of large numbers, normal curve areas, regression and correlation analyses, etc. Like all of the techniques in this section, model building is imperative for problem design and computer input. Alternative courses of action are decided by the decision criteria and the control variable values. Potential error levels are ascertained and predicted, confidence levels are accepted, and decisions are determined on the bases of these weights and consequences.

Scientific estimation is required concerning which variables and what values of variables might occur, and what effect they have on the operations under review. Inventory management, queuing lines, and quality control are the more specific examples of this technique.

Queuing Theory (Waiting Line Problems)

This is a methodology for developing relationships between units in waiting lines; its solution attempt is the resolution of "bottlenecks." The problems have their occurrence as any units arrive for service, such as ships in harbors, aircraft at airstrips, customers at check-out stands, materials on assembly lines, etc. If service cannot be effected and maintained immediately for each unit arrival, the queue or line is established with consequent variable costs, lost customers, dangerous "stacking" of aircraft, and the like. Successful application has been made for solution of such problems of facilities planning, inspection delays, production-line balancing, machine down-time, etc. by applying statistical estimation and prediction against increased installation costs and lost time or customer-loss costs. Queuing models use Monte Carlo methods, random-number generators, and elements of linear-programming concepts in some cases. Many computer programs are available from manufacturers, software houses, and educational institutions. It is indeed very comforting to many executives to have variable and dynamic (devised to handle new circumstances as they occur) models to solve these often very tricky and expensive difficulties.

Monte Carlo techniques are used when large numbers of unknowns present highly complex variables with unusually difficult relationships between them. The application of random-sampling techniques and Baysean strategies are also often applied. The technique is an intriguing one, and again, developed computer programs are available which, with some modifications, can be used on many regular or near-conventional problems.

The primary goal of queuing problems or sequencing solutions is to discover the order in which the jobs should be processed or service offered, and the necessary facilities to be constructed or labor employed to maximize profits.

Heuristic Models

When problems arise which confront the OR technician with unusual difficulty and he can find no precedent for solution, he may try one of several already established techniques. Simulation is usually selected. However, heuristic modeling can also be used as part of, or separate from, a simulation model. As an example, a marketing mechanism may be involved which would be interrelated by the standard math equation model to express the variables which determine the outcome of the circumstances under analysis. But each of hundreds of variables may have extensive ranges. The OR man may then decide to find similar problems which do have solution methodology and attempt to suboptimize (i.e., solve various parts initially). He may decide to work backwards by starting with the result and analyzing each previous step hoping to discover linearity or nonlinearity that he can program. These and other procedures might help to discover better-than-present solutions, or perhaps no solution at all may be found. But, the scientific methodology will provide sufficient analytical relationship break-downs and deduction, that new structuring of the causes (components and elements of the problem) might result in elimination or simplification of them in the future.

Heuristics then attempts by parts and bits, and trial and error, to "seek" a solution which is better than the current one, though it may be less than optimal. New methodology, procedures, and potential restructuring of the circumstances which created the enigma are by-products. The usual example is the one of the traveling salesman and his attempts to find the best route when considering travel time, distance, cost, schedule variables and frequencies, and other specific variables. Space limitations preclude further development of this problem area, but the author recommends further reading about this technique because it is a birthplace and "cradle" for the development and maturing of full-fledged algorithmic or stochastic techniques. Considerable and valuable research is being performed with computers in this challenging field.

Simulation

Simulation has often been described as a substitution for calculation. (If you can't calculate it, simulate it.) It is not, however, usually a "second best" solution technique, for very many problems lend themselves decisively to this process. Again (as in heuristics), mathematical complexity in formulation or manipulation usually casts the vote to use simulation. Oftentimes, urgency and inclusion of all possible variables cause insistence on simulation usage. Simulation is also adaptable for minor decision error-detection routines or analysis of results of each step and decision in intricate planning procedures.

Basically then, simulation is the duplication of an environment, by a model, such that changes can be made at will to test particular outcomes of these specific actions on either the immediate problem part or on the total effect. Conditional alternative remedies can be made along the way to again analyze effects at particular stages or evaluation of various end results. The philosophy of simulation is usually quite palatable to executives because of its usually lower costs and their rather complete understanding of the methodology and the import and relationship of all the variables. Most often resultant and desired mathematical certainty is not possible, but the elements of risks and the consequences of poor spot decisions can be ascertained.

Simulation when applied to queuing problems can quite adequately measure and test length of queues, service-rates, idle times, results of adding facilities, customer or service unit reactions, number of customers served, turnaround times, peak loads under varying time factors and load considerations, and the like. Costs of alternatives and statistical predictions are usually the rewarding conclusions of simulation model solutions. Computers are extremely valuable in the great variety of problems that require solution. Simulation is much overused since other techniques can often provide more accurate answers to unknown and unpredictable events. But the student will read and hear a great deal of the many valuable applications and great versatility of this technique.

An example of a simulation might be as follows: A change in product line assembly processing, or distribution, procedure is suggested. Management is reluctant to make this major decision without having some valid prediction tests. Either one or several models of the operational system will be constructed which eventually turn into computer programs. Trade-offs between costs and increased benefits are thus realistically evaluated while the simulation is in process. The trade-off extent and specific points and the values of the controllable variables can be revised in ranges to determine maximum benefits. Experimentation with simulation, though not a mathematically precise procedure, will effect valuable, "close-to-the-best" predictions for continuous re-evaluation and refinement. Thus simulation is most versatile and adaptable. Sections of other texts will relate the important contributions simulation continues to develop in wide ranges of research areas as well as control of operations areas.

Linear Programming

This classification of techniques has been universally accepted as being one of the best of the optimizing solution procedures. It is a technique for determining the allocation of scarce resources among interdependent or competitive ends. The basis of the solution or the goal to be maximized (profits), minimized (costs) or optimized (best of available alternatives) becomes the course of action (or initial experimentation) by the executive. The linear-programming problems generally have: (a) objective functions such as increased profit, sales, money, resources, times, etc.; (b) evaluated and quantified relationships of interaction and interdependence of variables; (c) alternative decisions (of control variables) for dividing resources among competing forces (plural objectives).

Linear programming most often uses matrix algebra and the simplex method of computer calculation. It is an algorithm, and will thus have a unique solution or very small range. The process is capable of solving enormously complex problems with admirable precision. It automatically identifies the optimum solution by taking explicit account ("at each decision point . . . the solutions having the least probability of being the best . . . and eliminates them, i.e., successive elimination . . .") of the optimization of the relevant variables and the system as a whole.

The process uses inequalities ("must not be greater than or less than") as structural constraint devices, and must have strictly linear components (i.e., no equations with powers greater than 1). However, many types of nonlinear problems approximate linearity or have linear segments and can use linear programming techniques.

Linear programming, using the "iteration" mechanics of the computer, develops, at each successive trial, a solution which obeys all the restrictions, prevents negative numbers (i.e., production of a —60 units), and finds the "best" solution to the model.

Linear programming like most of the other models to be described is considered a suboptimizing technique since it does not replace management but, as do the others, it offers only advice—scientifically organized and computed—and it is usually a part of a larger system.

Linear programming has been used successfully for many years in problems concerning: (a) product mix; i.e., blending, refineries, production runs, equipment use, etc.; (b) location or warehousing problems; and (c) scores of variations of economic, industrial, financial, and marketing types of former enigmas.

Each production activity or process can be expressed as some ratio or fraction of resource consumption per unit of output. An activity can be completely defined by an evaluation of these ratios. The symbols $>$ (greater than) and $<$ (less than) are used to indicate the relationship between the left and right sides of an inequality. In general, the mathematical treatment of inequalities is essentially the same as for equations. An equation defines the points on a line, while an inequality uses a line to demarcate between all points which do not satisfy and all points which do satisfy the inequality.

One unknown or variable is assigned to state the level of each activity to be evaluated. The algebraic sum of the variables is then stated as a function which is less than the total resource available. An additional expression is required to state the objective. This is usually an E or earnings function.

Broadly speaking, the algebraic sum of the inequalities, as expressed by the mutually exclusive variables, will produce a total value of output. This total value of output is "maximized," subject to resource restrictions.

It may be recalled that with the traditional methods of calculus, an absolute maximum is produced. In linear programming, the object is to produce a relative optimum when the variables are "maximized." The relative maximum could correspond to the absolute maximum only when resource restrictions are eliminated. This is unrealistic in most business problems. The formal mathematical goal of linear programming, then, is to produce a maximized value of a linear function of variables, subject to linear inequalities.

A business application would seek to maximize the unit output of a specific operation, while simultaneously minimizing or holding constant the unit production cost. When a maximum unit output value can be made equivalent to a minimum unit cost, the most efficient allocation of facilities has been accomplished. To restate, since the cost value is equal to the product value, resources have been converted to product output with the maximum of efficiency.

In this brief exposition of linear programming, the author has chosen to avoid much of the terminology, such as slack variables, dual solutions, modi and index methods, various tableaus, or matrix notation. These may arouse either curiosity or fear in the reader, but stepped or programmed teaching methods can make all these terms and concepts very clear and interconnected with minimum confusion.

Because the linear programming problem is an algorithm, the simplex method, for example, will use the computer for successive approximations and eliminations according to fixed rules and checks to assure the discovery of the optimal solution. The principle involved is that an optimal solution does exist (or the computer will designate "unfeasible" and enter a "stop" loop), and the set simplex pattern will continue through trial and error routines at electronic speeds until it finds the optimal solution —all based on the relationships and constraints defined by the model. Each factor in the problem is thus evaluated against all other factors in relation to the long-range goals (objective function) yielding optimum paths for executive decision and action unless the optimum solution is infinite in one of the variables and the system is considered to be "unbounded."

Dynamic Programming

A method for optimizing a set of decisions which must be made sequentially; i.e., at every stage of a multistage problem. Characteristically, each decision must be made in the light of the information embodied in a small number of observables called state variables. The incurred cost for each period is a mathematical function of the current state variables and decision variables; also, future states are functions of these variables. The aim of the decision policy is to minimize the total incurred cost, or equivalently, the average cost per period. The mathematical treatment of such problems involves the theory of functional equations, and usually requires a digital computer for implementation. This is because it is necessary to calculate the effect of each decision at every stage before the final choice can be made. This integration of the cumulative effect of the path of individual decisions of the network is the real essence of dynamic programming.

Econometrics

Econometrics should not be confused with mathematical economics. The latter is a form of precise analytical study of the theory of various economic values and of their effects on human and enterprise behavior. It implies that economic theory relationships operate exactly as stated and are completely fulfilled. Such is not the case or purpose with econometrics. Econometrics attempts to consider in a nonrigid manner the deviations that are to be expected or even hoped for. The prime role of econometrics is to measure and predict these deviations, their values, and direction. A probability format is thus devised, and the variables can be modified through successive iterations of the model. These variations, as judged from current empirical data, are "cranked into" proved relationships to provide management a means of looking at changes across time on a given forecasted situation, as well as to provide insight into the alternative plans which will most likely be achieved.

A rational or logical process of analysis of enterprise and its economic environment through symbolic representation and under suggested or desired changes is thus developed. In its broadest sense it is a simulation model, yet it has many characteristics of linear programming. When these, and other models previously discussed, are stripped-down and simplified, they are easy to construct, understand, and use. But, they may not be so simplified that they no longer bear relationship to the real world. The benefits are: logical analysis, better understanding of problems and components, sensitivity analysis of assumptions and structure of changes or future plans, and the simulation of results of variable future strategies. An econometric model predicts; a linear programming model optimizes.

Econometrics models develop a blending of economic theory and statistical methods to form sets of relationships which explain situations or predict future changes. Theoretical models are proved by pragmatic or empirical testing of results. These pioneer models are then used on real world problems—current or future.

The crux of the econometrician's task is to measure the impact of one variable on another to be able to predict future events or advise on decisions of policy relative to past relationships as established and proved. The new model uses new values of variables and realistically revised parameters. This is accomplished in even smaller business analyses by examining the most probable interrelationships of separate sets of economic variables—judged by prior periods—which will evolve under the new circumstances.

The econometric model does not deal in abstract principles or situations, but instead approximates reality; it is a true prediction system which yields numerical results of a stochastic nature, and thus it is usable within given confidence limits.

The four stages of development are as follows:

1. *Specification*—The expression of the theory in mathematical terms (models) after abstracting minor elements and "clothing" the formal equations with available data that are trustworthy and quickly obtainable.
2. *Estimation*—Research and collection of data and the evaluation of the sources, types, and pertinent characteristics for use in structuring the model.
3. *Verification*—The determination of the criteria of success; the acceptance of the model if the data prove it to be correct; rejection if they do not.
4. *Prediction*—The arrangement of the model into convenient form, so that the lagged variables, new parameters, and data can be "plugged" into the model to exact scores of potential or alternative solutions concerning impact and probable solutions—based on current, accurate statistical inferences and confidence intervals.

Econometrics can thus be considered to be the application of a scientific method using empirical data and historical relationships in economic science to achieve numerical results and verification of theories regarding particular sets of circumstances. In many cases, there is no known method better or even as good as the intelligent use of econometric models on which to base decisions.

The advantage of econometric models can be judged as follows:

1. The process of model formulation forces on the executive or decision maker a procedure for clearer, more precise definition and analysis of the problem, its parameters, variables, and values.
2. The model fosters and sifts from a world of jumbled complexity, an evaluative procedure based on mathematical relationships and clear-cut reason. This contrasts to current decisions based on hunches, rules of thumb, guesses, hopes, and maybes.
3. An econometric model is excellent for testing assumptions, hypotheses, and theories—and laws outside of the "laboratory"; i.e., in the dynamic real world.
4. Econometrics is especially useful for evaluating the sensitivity of the variables themselves and the relationships to alterations in assumptions, parameters (changed capacities, etc.), and new variables.

Appendix F

Critical Path Method and Project Evaluating and Review Technique (CPM and PERT)

During the very recent past (1959-1965), rapid growth has taken place in management planning and control techniques. One of the most useful and now widely used procedures has been the PERT scheduling model. Although it was initially utilized only in defense, aerospace, and construction projects, it is now applied to hosts of problems of all types including scheduling Broadway plays, establishing electronic data-processing systems, highway construction, audit techniques, and many, many others. Unfortunately, it is also one of the least understood because it has been overshadowed by large projects and fearfully "complex-looking" charts and diagrams.

The fundamentals of PERT are basically simple, but they must be understood completely, including work-breakdown structure, networking, and time estimating (and cost estimating for PERT/COST). And PERT must be applied and administered pragmatically and intelligently so that each project is understood by those concerned and acknowledged by management. The reduction of complexity into simple steps and the constant checking (most often by computer) keeps each project continually updated with responsibility for each activity firmly affixed (an unhappy trial for laggards).

PERT generally is defined as a management tool for defining and integrating events which must be accomplished on a "time" basis to assure completion of program objectives on schedule. It defines areas of effort whereby tradeoffs in time, resources, or performance will enable management to meet milestones or deadlines. It assists decision makers to make evaluations and immediate alterations of plans of men, money, and materials. PERT also provides a means for highlighting exactly where trouble-spots are likely to occur in the progress of the project.

Many small industrial and business firms are using PERT to set and keep development schedules even though they must make the calculations manually as in marketing, house building, new product introduction, etc.

The chart reproduced below shows the critical path (darkest line) as the greatest estimated time value for achieving event #4. Critical path analysis is an integral part of PERT and involves calculated forecasts for each activity of the (a) optimistic estimate, (m) most likely estimate, and (b) the pessimistic estimate. The estimated time then is developed from the formula:

$$t_e = \frac{a + 4m + b}{6}$$

A final portion of a PERT schedule is reproduced below, and concerns development of a machine prototype.

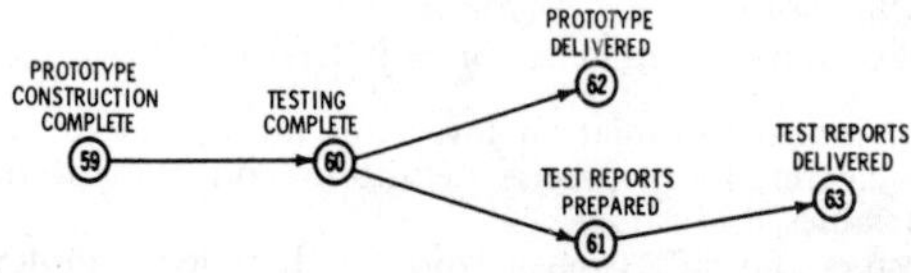

The procedure is to proceed from milestone to milestone with work-path arrows connecting each of them to show order of the work. Each accomplishment is called an event; each time duration is called an activity and is drawn as an arrow which connects two events. There can be only one activity between two events. Activities require time; events are only points and do not require time. Network development begins with the identification of objectives; prime and supporting objectives must be carefully defined, organized, and interrelated.

As a manager's tool, PERT defines and coordinates what must be done to successfully accomplish the objectives. PERT presents the statistical information regarding the uncertainties faced as well as the time lost or gained in specific areas of the project. The manager may elect to "crash" certain activities—run more on parallel or concurrent basis, or subcontract or cancel.

PERT is the procedure for focusing managerial attention on immediate or possible delay areas of the project. The adjustment concerning time, men, and resources may be fundamentally significant in regard to his total profit—or penalties. PERT can thus be defined as a diagnostic and prognostic technique for quantifying uncertainties to be faced in meeting program milestones and deadlines. Management is aided in discovering danger signals and can plot corrective measures in advance of emergencies. It is a visual process displaying effects in time, resources, personnel, facilities, and funds of varying scheduling activities. The computer calculates expected times, costs, etc. for each activity and the ultimate objective as the planners experiment with new values of the variables. PERT has now been fully adopted and gratefully accepted practically universally. The evaluation of large complex networks makes computer use imperative and every computer mainframe manufacturer has several PERT programs available.

Game Theory

This operations research (OR) technique is a procedure concerning a competitive game with a finite number of competitors and a finite list of possible courses of action. It is developed with a series of matrices (ordered array of figures; i.e., a mileage chart which contain values in the various cells having both vertical and horizontal position characteristics). The "game" concerns alternative selections or choices in relation to those of the competitor which will result in various calculated "payoffs."

A "play" consists of a choice of a single course of action used simultaneously with that of the competitor. Each "outcome" determines a set of payments, one set to each competitor. A "strategy" is a set of directions, either pure or mixed, which is chosen for a particular course of action. "Mixed strategy" means that the competitor, before the play begins, decides to choose a particular course of action for each play, whereas a "pure" strategy would be the decision to play the same; i.e., *"least loss"* strategy on each play. "Saddle points" are equilibrium points where one competitor has achieved the lowest of the maximum losses; i.e., "minimax" and the other has achieved the highest of the minimum rewards; i.e., "maximin." The procedure is theoretically fine, but the practicality of the game theory has had only limited success in the real world.

This limited success however is the challenge and inspiration for continued research which is now taking place in many industrial, research, and educational institutions. It should not be confused with executive games which are really a synthesis of many OR techniques played in competition with teams as practice routines and total systems to simulate decision-making under all types of business activity.

Game theory uses rigorous means of determining a certain set of conflicts in a specific situation to develop a strategy which is most likely to achieve highest payoff values. Again, the insight and definition gained by management in structuring the model is extremely beneficial. Design changes on automobiles, promotion strategies and budget sizes, and, of course, labor-management strike contests are best examples of game theory. Also much can be gained by playing games against nature, probability—and altering strategies by using statistical devices.

Input/Output

Such classes of models as these are derived from assumptions about economic variables and behavior which take account of the general equilibrium phenomena and are concerned with the empirical analysis of production—i.e., especially intermediate uses and final output. The problem is to investigate what can be produced and the quantity of each intermediate product which itself must be used up in the production process. Various data are obtained initially which attest to available resources and current state of technology.

Again a matrix is the base of the calculation and measures the flows of current inputs and outputs between the various sectors of an economy, region, firm, or interrelationship. The tracing of such flows from one input sector to another permits calculations of the impact and the values of producing sectors, intermediate requirements, and final-use sectors of particular industries.

The basic problem is to see what can be left over for final consumption (consumers, military, city, etc.) and how much of each output will be used up in the course of the productive activities. The input/output tables can be used to predict future production requirements if usable demand estimates can be developed. Input/output tables are valuable for economic planning problems of "backward" or developing nations; for military mobilization; in national income accounting; in city regional planning; for estimating population; determining economic impact of new industry; and studying interrelationships of giant enterprise economics. The reader is invited to study the information available on the recently completed U.S. Input/Output Table to thus be able to predict impact on various industries as results, for example, of government decisions in relation to defense orders; taxes on exports, imports, or special products; and other related calculations.

Several good publications from the Department of Commerce and other agencies are now available which explain in simple language how businessmen can efficiently and profitably use the new input/output table. The business applications are still very new, but there is little doubt that this operations research technique will also grow in importance and benefit to the business and industrial community as computer programs are developed and understood by the student and layman.

CONCLUSION

The vital role in executive judgment that staff OR men can play is demonstrated by their increasing popularity and demand in industry. The mathematical formulation and abstraction is not "unnecessary glorification" of the problem, as many managers sometimes indicate. It is an improvement for management understanding of highly complex problems and the requisite preparation for computer input and solution.

The greatest value in the model lies not in finding "the" answer, but rather in turning out ranges of alternatives and the determination of the differences various alterations of parameters (decision values) can make or which alternate assumptions can mean. The measurement of these potential and possible differences is the advice to management for efficient control . . . provided by OR personnel . . . scientists of administration technology.

APPENDIX G

Mathematical Definitions

The language of mathematics is partly technical, partly popular, and certainly dynamic. The concept in the minds of many laymen that mathematics is a fixed or finished science is untenable, especially in light of today's extremely rapid expansion of technology in the social as well as the physical sciences. It has been stated that the rate of new mathematical reports and results has more than doubled in the past decade and is expected to treble in the next five years. Economics, business administration, and a host of other behavioral sciences are finding many novel uses for familiar mathematical models and are requiring most vociferously the introduction and development of new models, many as sophisticated as those of physics, engineering, and chemistry.

The increasing predominance of applications of computers and the requisite precision of programming development especially in the real-time, time sharing systems now spreading throughout the world, have caused renewed emphasis in all disciplines on mathematics and statistics—the basic input for problem-solving, data reduction and decision-making.

The five-point sequence to administration clearly illustrates the basic characteristics and importance of mathematics:

1. Discover, define, and analyze the problem with system innovation.
2. Resolve the components of the problem into their precise relationships and interdependencies by the use of clearly defined symbols and notations which are understandable and consistent and which form a replica or "model" or real world circumstances. This is model-building through the use of such math terminology as constants, variables, parameters and functions using quite often operations research and statistical inference techniques.
3. Through the use of process and flowcharts, graphically develop the problem in logical and sequential order and form in preparation for writing programs.
4. Write the program in a language acceptable to the computer using the part-English, part-mathematics structures in which the languages are designed.
5. Run the programs to test the accuracy and efficiency of the models; apply them to the problem or system for which they were designed. Amend, adjust, or redefine the model to display the importance of alternatives and changes which result from new values of control variables or changed parameters.

Although the mathematics is most often of only the most elementary variety, it is, as noted, used in each of the five steps. To the layman, the symbolism, notation, and technical vocabulary of mathematics most often appears to be very formal and forbidding. But closer inspection and some patient attempts at analysis will enlighten the student or manager to the basic simplicity of models, the components and relations of which he can clearly perceive because of his familiarity and closeness to the problem or system he helped to discover or design.

The decision maker in the behavioral sciences most often seeks a problem solution or system-design result which stresses an optimum (greatest gain) action to be taken and an analysis of the possible outcomes of alternate courses. He may have devised a deterministic model which always leads to an answer in a range of his expectation. He might have developed a probabilistic model (stochastic or heuristic) with either known or unknown probabilities. The first type of model relates to situations of certainty while the second type concerns measurements of risk in the first case, and the trial and error routines of uncertainty in the latter case. Bayesian decision theory is often used in cases of uncertainty, which includes subjective evaluation; i.e., the manager's experience, intuition and judgment . . . unique to business mathematics.

It is not the purpose of this brief discussion to develop concepts concerning the structure of mathematics with its many postulates, theories, axioms, and logical components. The author, however, feels compelled to lay important stress to the dynamic character of the terms, definitions, and innovations with which all computer people—programmers, students, researchers, teachers, managers, and administrators of all types—must gain new competence. Mathematics is composed generally of symbols and concepts which either represent equality or denote operations, and/or words adopted from current common vocabulary. Both branches of mathematical language continue to undergo fundamental and sophisticated changes as new sciences, techniques, and skills evolve, such as expanding capabilities of computer science and allied statistical, operations research, and system-analysis innovations.

Most Americans have received instruction in elementary and secondary schools as well as college. Unfortunately, many students experienced difficulty in the use of terms because of the often vague and ambiguous methods of introduction and nonreal-world applications. Moreover, because the majority of students were not preparing to enter the world of mathematics or the physical sciences, their motivation was very low. Educators have recognized the need for more universally applicable types of mathematics courses, and much effort is being expended on reorientation and renewed drives for better motivation at the earliest levels of training. However, this appendix glossary of mathematical terms and symbols will hopefully refresh the memories of those who need help in understanding the models, programs, and analyses of computer input and output. Its purpose in this text is to provide the quick reference to aid in developing models or to assist in the understanding of problems, operations-research techniques, or output analyses of computer solutions.

Although the listings below were developed with considerable time and effort they are nonetheless quite incomplete and abridged. The selection, classification, arrangement, and presentation are the author's own concept of fundamentals and current requirements for students of modern management science. Additions and revisions are certainly to be expected in new editions of this text. Mathematics and statistics are quite naturally closely related, and the new extensive use of operations research and matrix algebra include expanding use of both types of concepts.

SYMBOLS

A—Boldface capitals represent matrices.
A—Complement set; conjugate of matrix A.
∿A, A, or A′—Complement of set A; a matrix (i.e., A prime = A′)
A^T—Transposed matrix A.
A^{-1}—Inverse of matrix A.
a—Constant term of straight-line equation, y intercept.
|a|—Absolute value of a; magnitude or length of vector.
a_{ij}—Input/output coefficients representing the conditions of the restrictions.
$[a_{ij}]$ m, n—The element represented in the ith row and jth column of a matrix.
(a_1, a_2, a_3)—Space notation for vector a.
a_i, b_i, c_i—Known quantities or constants.
∠ABC—Angle with vertex at B.
△ABC—Triangle ABC.
b—Slope of straight line.
C—Complex numbers.
C (n.k)—Combinations.
c_{ij}—Notation for cell ij of matrix or tableau.
D_x—Derivative.
D. of fr.—Degrees of freedom associated with a given test.
d—Difference of vectors.
d_x—Derivative.
$\frac{d}{dx}$ ()—Derivative of.
$\frac{dy}{dx}$—Derivative.
$E_{(x)}$—Expectation of X.
e—Exponential function; 2.178281 . . . , base of the natural system of logarithms.
f_i—Frequency of occurrence of the class of observation i.
f_x—Partial derivative.
f(x)—Functional notation.
f′—Derivative.
$f''_{(x)}$—Second derivative.
f^{-1}—Inverse function.
H—Hypothesis.
I—Set of integers.
I_n—Unit or identity matrix of nth order.
I^+—Set of positive integers, identity matrix.
i—Annual interest rate; a variable subscript.
ln—Natural logarithm.
log—Common logarithm.
M—Capital letters indicate a matrix.
N—Number of cases in a sample.
n—Number of trials of an experiment.

n→∞—N approaches infinity.
(0)—Null matrix.
$\overrightarrow{OA}$ or a—Symbol for vector.
P(A)—Probability of event.
P(A/B)—Conditional probability.
P(n,k)—Permutations.
P (r, o)—Polar coordinates of point P.
P_1—P sub 1.
p—Probability of success in binominal distribution.
p'—Negation of p.
q—Probability of failure in binominal distribution.
r—Rank of matrix.
R—Real numbers.
Ra—Rational numbers.
S—Sum of vectors.
S_x—Standard deviation of sample data.
S_y—Sample estimate of the standard deviation y.
$S_{y,x}$—Standard error of estimate of y as the dependent variable, and x as the independent variable.
s—Standard deviation of random sample of size n.
T—Total period of time under consideration.
t—Any specific time.
tg—Tangent of.
trA—Representation of the trace of matrix A.
$||V||$—Length of a vector.
V_i—Column vectors of the coefficients.
w_i—General notation for slack variables.
X—Independent variable in a linear equation.
$\overline{X}_i$—Arithmetic means of sample data.
x—Mean value of variable x_i.
x—Independent variable.
x_i—Unknown variable.
(X_i, Y_i)—Point representation of vectors passing through origin.
y—Dependent variable in a linear equation.
Y_C—Coordinate of line of best fit.
∞—Symbol denoting infinity.
μ—Arithmetic mean of normal probability distribution; mean of the Poisson distribution.
π—3.1416 . . . , the ratio of the circumference of a circle to its diameter. (Greek letter Pi)
{ }—Set description.
⊆—Set inclusion (Subset) .
Σ—Summation symbol.
∪—Union of sets.
ϕ—Null set.
∩—Intersection of sets; conjunction.
.—Logical conjunction.
V or U—Logical disjunction; union.
→—Logical implication.
$\sqrt{n}$—Square root of n.
σx—Standard error of the mean.
σmd—Standard error of the median.
θ_y—Standard deviation computed with the y_i s.
θ_x—Standard deviation computed with the x_i s.
[ ]—Square brackets indicate row vector or any type matrix.
{ }—Braces indicate column vector.
≅—Is congruent to.
Δx—Change in x.
≡—Congruence of integers; equivalence of proposition.
|A|—Determinant of matrix.
ε—Element of set.
≃—Symbol denoting similarity.
≅—Is approximately equal to.
=—Is equal to.
≠—Is not equal to.
<—Is less than.
>—Is greater than.
≦—Is less than or equal to.
≧—Is greater than or equal to.
∫—Indefinite integral.
$\int_b^a$ Definite integral.
!—Factorial.

DEFINITIONS

abscissa—The horizontal, or X, axis on a graph.

absolute—The absolute term of an equation, is that term which is known, or which does not contain the unknown quality; thus, in the equation $ax^3 + bx^2 + cx + d = 0$, d is the absolute term. Complete in itself; independent; the numerical value of a number or symbol without reference to its algebraic sign; thus, 3 is the absolute value of +3 or −3.

absolute value—The absolute value of a number is the numerical value of the number without considering its sign. Thus, the absolute value of +18 is 18, and the absolute value of −12 is 12 and is usually written as $|-12| = 12$.

abstract—Separate; to draw from something else.

abstract quantity—A quantity which does not involve the idea of matter, but simply that of a mental conception; it is expressed by a letter, symbol, or figures. Thus, the number three represents an abstract idea, that is, one which has no connection with material things, while three feet presents to the mind an idea of a physical unit of measure called a foot. All numbers are abstract when the unit is absract.

activity—A structural variable whose level is to be computed in a programming problem.

activity level—The value taken by a structural variable in an intermediate or final solution to a programming problem.

acute—Sharp, as opposed to obtuse. An acute angle is one that is less than a right angle. In degrees, an acute angle is less than 90°.

adjacent—Contiguous to, or bordering upon.

adjacent angles—Adjacent angles in a plane are those which have one side in common, and their other sides in the prolongation of the same straight line. Thus, the angles ABD and DBC are adjacent.

affix—To unite at the end; thus, to affix 0 s

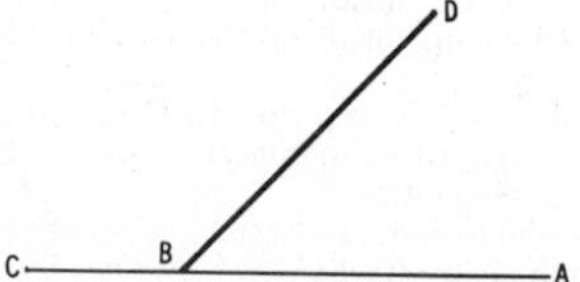

to a number, is the same as to annex them or to write them after the number.

agenda—The set of control-language statements used to prescribe a solution path or run procedure; an ordered list of the major operations constituting a procedure for solution or computer run. (This usage corresponds to the ordinary "agenda" for a meeting.)

agendum—The body of code called for execution by a control-language statement (agendum call card).

agendum call card—A single agendum name and its parameters punched on one card in a stylized form; one item of the agenda—a control-language statement calling for the execution of the named agendum. A set of agendum call cards is used to control a linear-programming system, thus forming an agenda.

aggregate—An assemblage of parts to form a whole. An aggregate of several particulars is equivalent to their sum.

aggregation, signs of—Signs of aggregation are: the parentheses, ( ); the vinculm, —; the bracket, [ ]; and the brace, { }. They show that the quantities included by them are to be treated as single numbers. Thus, each of the expressions $(a + b)\,c$, $a + b \times c$, $[a + b]c$, and $\{a + b\}c$, shows that the sum of a and b is to be multiplied by c.

When quantities are under the vinculum, or are included within any other signs of aggregation, they are commonly said to be in parentheses.

algebra—1. That branch of analysis whose object is to investigate the relations and properties of numbers by means of symbols. The quantities considered are generally represented by letters, and the operations to be performed on these letters are indicated by signs. The letters and signs are called symbols. 2. Algebra is that branch of mathematics which is concerned with general numbers or quantities, and the nature, transformation, and use of equations. 3. The signs of algebra are, for the most part, the same as those used in arithmetic.

algebraic expression—An algebraic expression is an expression of a quantity in algebraic language.

algoristic—In strict definition it could mean exact answer; a systematic computation guaranteeing an accurate solution such as 2 normal simultaneous equations and 2 unknowns will yield a specific correct answer.

algorithm—The art of computing in any particular way. We speak of the algorithm of numbers, imaginary quantities, etc. The word is of Arabic origin, and properly means the art of numbering readily and correctly.

aliquot part—Such a part of any number or quantity as will exactly divide that number or quantity. Thus, 2 is an aliquot part of 4, 6, or any even number; and 1 is an aliquot part of any whole number whatever. To find all the aliquot parts of 30: Divide it by 2, which gives a quotient 15; next divide 15 by 3, which gives a quotient 5, which, on being divided by 5, gives a quotient 1; hence, 1, 2, 3, and 5 are the prime aliquot parts; but multiplying these factors together, two and two, we find 6, 10, and 15 for the compound aliquot parts. Hence, all the aliquot parts of 30 are 1, 2, 3, 5, 6, 10, and 15.

alternate optima—Distinct solutions to the same optimization problem.

A-matrix—Notation used to denote the original coefficient matrix, [$a_{::}$ or a_{ij}], possibly extended by some or all of the logical vectors. The functional row is usually included, as in the modified simplex array.

ambiguous — Having two meanings or two interpretations. The double sign ±, written before an expression, is sometimes called the ambiguous sign, the true meaning of which is generally that the quantity has both signs.

analogous properties — Those properties of different things by virtue of which they resemble each other.

analogy—An agreement or likeness between things in certain respects.

analytical geometry—That branch of analysis which has for its object the analytical investigation of the relations and properties of geometrical magnitudes.

angle—A portion of space lying between two lines, or between two or more surfaces that meet in a common point.

annuity—A sum of money payable yearly, to continue for a given number of years, for life, or forever; an annual income charged on the person of the grantor; an annual allowance. The term is also applied to any rents or interests payable at regular intervals, whether annually, semiannually, quarterly, or otherwise. An annuity payable for a definite length of time is a certain annuity; if payable for an uncertain length of time, as during the life of one person, or during the life of several persons, it is a contingent annuity.

antilogarithm—The number corresponding to any given logarithm. Thus, 100 is the antilogarithm of 2 in the common system, because 2 is the logarithm of 100 in that system.

a posteriori—Statements which have empirical bases with the required observations, experiments, and analytical testing to demonstrate truth or falsity—a contrast to theory or a priori.

approximation—In mathematics, a method of calculation by which we obtain an approximate value of a quantity that cannot be found accurately, either because of the nature of the quantity itself, or due to the imperfection of our mode of operation.

a priori—A statement which can be shown to be true or false by reason alone; truth thus known *before* the observation and evidence as contrasted to a posterori which are empirical.

arbitrary—An arbitrary quantity in an analysis is a quantity to which we may assign any reasonable value. In analytical geometry, the arbitrary quantities are generally styled arbitrary constants, to distinguish them from the variables which are, in a certain sense, arbitrary.

area—In geometry, the superficial contents of any surface expressed in terms of some given surface assumed as a unit or standard of comparison. The unit of measure is generally a square, one of whose sides is a linear unit in length. For different purposes, the area may be expressed in different terms.

arithmetical progression—A series of quantities, each of which is derived from its preceding quantity by the addition of a constant quantity. Thus, 4,6,8,10,12,14, and $a, a+d, a+2d$, $a+3d$ are arithmetical progressions. The constant quantity which is added is called the common difference. The common difference may be either positive or negative. When the difference is positive, an ascending series is produced; when negative, a descending series.

art—Skill in the application of the rules and principles of science, so as to meet the practical demands of life. The entire range of subjects classed under the head of mathematics may be separated into two parts: 1. The science which investigates principles and deduces general rules. 2. The art which explains the method of applying these rules and principles to every particular case that may arise to which they are applicable.

artificial variables (linear programming)—Auxiliary or logical variables restricted or bounded to zero for equation constraints, and unrestricted as to sign for objective function or other null constraints. The logical variables, artificials, and slacks provide the "identity" basis needed for the start of the simplex algorithm.

asymmetry—The lack of symmetry between parts of a magnitude. The term has sometimes been used as synonymous with incommensurability.

asymptote — A line which continually approaches a curved line, and becomes tangent to it at an infinite distance. Asymptotes are of two kinds, rectilinear and curvilinear.

augmentation—The operation of adding or joining one thing to another so that the result shall be greater than the original thing. In mathematics, augmentation is nearly equivalent to arithmetical addition.

average—An average is a typical value which tends to sum up or describe the mass of data. It also serves as a basis for measuring or evaluating extreme or unusual values. The average is a measure of the location of central tendency. The most important kinds of average are:

1. The arithmetic mean.
2. The median.
3. The mode.
4. The geometric mean.
5. The quadratic mean.

avoirdupois—The name given to the system of weights by which coarser commodities are weighed, such as hay, grain, wool, and all the coarser metals.

axiom types—An *axiom* is a truth that does not need demonstration.

1. Things that are equal to the same thing are equal to each other.
2. If equals are added to equals, the sums will be equal.
3. If equals are subtracted from equals, the remainders will be equal.
4. If equals are multiplied by equals, the products will be equal.
5. If equals are divided by equals, the quotients will be equal.
6. Equal powers of equal quantities are equal.
7. Equal roots of equal quantities are equal.

axis—1. When two given perpendicular lines intersect with 0 (origin) as the point of intersection, the horizontal line is usually labeled as 0x and the vertical line as 0y. These lines are designated as coordinate axes of reference. Any point P is taken in the plane 0xy, and the perpendiculars PM and PN are drawn to the axes.

balance equations—In matrix algebra those constraints on a production process which express the equality of inflows and outflows of one sort of material at one point in the system. They are usually in the form of equations with a right-hand side of zero.

basic feasible solution (primal)—In matrix algebra a basic solution to the constraint equations in which the nonzero values of the primal variables (both structural and logical) meet all the variable-type and bound restrictions. The lowest-cost basic feasible solution is the optimum.

basic solution (primal)—In matrix algebra, a solution to the row constraint equations in which the number of nonzero primal variable values (both structural and logical) is at most equal to the number of equations. The row constraint equations include bounds and, for modified or Kuhn-Tucker simplex arrays, costs.

binary—A binary number is one expressed by two figures, 0 and 1. The internal operating language of computers; the basis of Boolean algebra and primary switching theory on which computers are constructed and operated.

binomial—1. A binomial is a name applied to a polynomial of two terms. Thus, $2a+3b$ and $x-y$ are binomials. 2. The binomial theorem derives a formula by means of which any binomial, whether its exponent be positive or negative, integral or fractional, can be expanded without employing the ordinary process of involution.

binomial theorem—The theorem whose objective is to demonstrate the formation law of any binomial power. The algebraic expression of this law constitutes the binomial formula.

Boolean algebra—A system of notation and generally binary computation upon which much of computer switching theory is based is called Boolean algebra, named after a British mathematician, George Boole. The system makes extensive use of sets, subsets, and the laws of combination of subsets such as unions, intersections, complements, null, empty, universal, and proper sets. It is being extensively revived in thousands of elementary and secondary schools and by students of computers and switching concepts.

bounded variable—A primal variable x_j in a linear programming problem which is required to satisfy a constraint of the form.

B-vector—Notation often used for the right-hand side (constant column) in a linear-programming matrix.

calculus—Calculus is that branch of mathematics that deals with the nature and the forms of functions with the aid of symbols. Its objective is the laws of derivation from one form to another, and the application of these laws to other branches of mathematics, such as algebra, analytical geometry, trigonometry, etc. There are two branches of calculus: the ordinary calculus, that deals with determinate functions; and the calculus of variations of indeterminate functions. In the ordinary calculus, there are two different methods of deriving determinate functions from other determinate functions. These methods give rise to the division of the ordinary calculus into two parts, differential and integral calculus.

calculus, differential—1. The branch of mathematics that deals with the amount of change in the function of a dependent variable per unit change in the independent variable. 2. Differential calculus is that branch of mathematics that derives one determinate function from another. If the original function is one of several variables, we may find the differential of the function with respect to each one of the variables, that is, as though all of the other variables were constants. These differentials are called partial differentials.

calculus, integral—1. A mathematical method of finding the relation connecting finite values of variables, as x and y, from the relation connecting their differentials, as dx and dy. 2. The integral-calculus objective is to find a differential function that will produce the given differential; such an expression is called the integral of the differential. 3. Integral calculus is the inverse of differential calculus. The process of finding the prime function or integral is called integration. Besides the method of finding the integrals of given differentials, the integral calculus is also applied to various branches of mathematics, as well as to almost every branch of natural philosophy and engineering.

calculus of variations—1. A branch of infinitesimal calculus whose fundamental notion is the variation of a curve in which the definite integral of a given function along the curve has a stationary value; the curve playing the role of the independent variable in ordinary differential calculus. 2. This is a branch of mathematics which, in its proper acceptation, deals only with the laws of variation, the forms of indeterminate functions, and the application of these laws to other branches of mathematics, mechanics, etc. The subject is, however, so intimately connected with the differential and integral calculus, that many operations that strictly belong to these branches are often referred to the calculus of variations.

capacity—The right-hand side of some constraint of the form.

$$a_1x_1 + a_2x_2 + \ldots + a_kx_k \leq b$$

where the constraint applies to a measure of the capacity of a process unit.

central tendency measures—These are averages of various types, each of which is for a definite purpose; the best single summary representation of the whole group of data. An average should signify the presence of a clustering point in the distribution; if there is no clear central tendency, the average is meaningless. There are five different measures of central tendency in common use:

1. Arithmetic Mean—This is the value which, if substituted for each individual value in the series, would give the same sum as the original series. It is the most familiar and, in general, the most useful type of average, being obtained by adding the values of the items in the series and dividing by the number of items. It corresponds to the center of gravity of a physical system.
2. Median—This is a positional average, such that ½ of the items have values above it, and ½ have values below it.
3. Mode—This is the value at the point in the distribution where the items tend to be most heavily concentrated. In this sense it may be regarded as the most typical of a series of values.
4. Geometric Means—This is a special-purpose average, defined as the nth root of the product of n items.
5. Harmonic Mean—This is another special-purpose average, defined as the reciprocal of the arithmetic mean of the reciprocals of the values.

characteristic of a logarithm—The nonnegative decimal part of a logarithm is called the mantissa, and the integral part is called the characteristic of a logarithm. For example, in the log $1830 = 0.2625 + 3$, 0.2625 is the mantissa and 3 is the characteristic, or 1 less than the number of integers. See any math text for use and rules of logarithms.

circumference—The curved line which bounds a plane curvilinear area. In ordinary language, the use of the term is restricted to the line which bounds or limits the area of a circle. The characteristic property of the circumference of a circle is that every point of it is equally distant from a point within called the center. The length of the circumference of any circle is equal to π multiplied by the diameter, or by twice the radius.

circumscribe—To limit, to bound, to confine, or to inclose within limits.

coefficient—A number written before a quantity, to show how many times it is to be taken additively; thus, in the expression 3ax, 3 is the coefficient of the quantity ax, and indicates that ax is to be taken three times additively. In the expression just given, if we regard x as the quantity taken, 3a is the coefficient, and it shows that x is to be taken as many times as there are units in 3a. We see that a coefficient may be numerical, or it may be literal, or it may be mixed; that is, it may be expressed by means of both figures and letters.

coefficient matrix—The matrix of left-hand-side coefficients in a system of linear equations. It is to be distinguished from the matrix obtained by appending the right-hand side, which is called the "augmented matrix" of the system. It may be thought of as including a full set of logical vectors to convert inequality constraints to equations, and in the case of the modified simplex array it also contains the objective function coefficients.

coefficient, radical—The coefficient of a radical is the quantity prefixed to the radical part to show how many times it is taken. Thus, a is the coefficient of a $\sqrt{x^2y}$, and bc of bc y^2.

cofactor—The cofactor of an element in a determinant is equal to the minor of the element if the sum of the number of the row and the number of the row and the number of the column in which the elements stands is an even number; if not an even number, it is the negative of its minor.

cologarithm—The cologarithm of a number is the logarithm of the reciprocal of that number:

$$\begin{aligned}\operatorname{colog} n &= \log\ (1/n)\ = \log 1 - \log n\\ &= 0 - \log n\end{aligned}$$

Cologarithms are used in computation when one desires to add all logarithms instead of subtracting some of them. He thus finds the cologs of the items which are divisors and thus adds the logs of the multiplicands and multipliers and the divisors as well.

column—All the elements of a single vertical line of a matrix, taken in given order. An $m \times 1$ submatrix of an $m \times n$ matrix.

column vector—One column of a matrix consisting of a single column. The elements of the column are interpreted as the components of the vector.

compound—The result of a composition of different things. The term stands opposed to simple.

concentric—Having the same center; it is opposed to eccentric, having different centers. The term is usually applied to spheres or circles, but sometimes, by analogy, to other surfaces and lines.

concrete—A concrete quantity is one that carries with it the idea of matter. Concrete stands opposed to the term abstract. An abstract quantity is a mental conception, and may have for its representative a number, a letter, or a geometrical figure. A concrete quantity is a physical object, or a collection of such objects, and may likewise be represented by numbers or letters.

concurrent — Meeting, but not intersecting, and not tangent.

congruous—Two numbers, p and q, are congruous with respect to a third number n, when their difference is exactly divisible by that number, that is, when the expression $\frac{p-q}{n}$ is a whole number. Thus 12 and 7 are congruous with respect to 5, because $\frac{12-7}{5} = 1$; 27 and 12 are also congruous with respect to 5, because $\frac{27-12}{5} = 3$, and so on.

consequent—The second term of a ratio, so called because its value is consequent upon a knowledge of the first term which is then called an antecedent. If we have the ratio a : b, which may be written $\frac{a}{b}$, the term b is the consequent, a being the antecedent. If the value of a ratio given, and the antecedent is known, the consequent may be found by multiplying the ratio by the antecedent; thus, if $\frac{b}{a} = r$, we have $b = ar$.

constraint—An equation or inequality that shows the interrelation between the variables in an optimization problem. A feasible (prime) solution must satisfy all the constraints including column-type restrictions (bounds, nonnegativity, etc.).

constraint matrix — In linear programming, the augmented matrix of the constraint equation; it is the matrix formed by the coefficient columns, or left-hand sides, and the column of constraints.

contiguous — Contiguous angles, are those which have a common vertex and one common side, but the other sides not in the same straight line. The latter condition distinguishes them from adjacent angles.

continuous function—A function in which the difference between any two consecutive states is less than any assignable quantity. In such a function, if we suppose the independent variable to pass through every possible state from one given value to another, the function will pass, by imperceptible degrees, through every state from the first to the last. A function that follows this law is said to be subject to the law of continuity.

control language—The language used to prescribe the course of a linear programming problem run on a computer. The language consists mainly of verbs (agendum names), which call in a body of code (program or subroutine) embodying the desired algorithm for execution.

convergence of an algorithm—An algorithm is said to converge if it is certain to yield its solution in a finite number of steps. It is a much stronger requirement than the mathematical convergence of the sequence of obtained function values.

convergent series—A convergent series is an infinite series, in which the sum of the terms, however many may be taken, can never exceed a certain finite value. The finite value is the sum of a series as determined from the value of the fraction.

converse—One proposition is the converse of another when the conclusion in the first is employed as a supposition in the second. Thus, the proposition in geometry that "If two sides of a plane triangle are equal, the angles opposite to them are equal," is the converse of the proposition "If two angles of a plane triangle are equal, the sides opposite them are equal." Both propositions require separate proof; for it does not follow because a proposition is true, that its converse is also true. For example, it does not follow because the axes of an ellipse are conjugate diameters, that a pair of conjugate diameters will necessarily be axes of the ellipse.

convex—The opposite of concave. Protuberant outwards, as the outer surface of a sphere. If we regard a hollow sphere or globe, its outer surface is convex, while its inner surface is concave. By means of the differential calculus, we are able to determine whether a given line has its convexity or concavity, at a particular point, turned towards, or from the axis of X. Differentiate the equation of the curve twice, and find an expression for the second differential coefficient of the ordinate. Substitute in this for x and y the coordinates of the given point; if the sign of the result is the same as that of the ordinate of the given point, the curve is convex at that point towards the axis of X; if they have the contrary sign, it is concave towards the axis of X.

coordinates—Coordinates are the elements of reference by means of which the relative positions of points in a plane may be determined with respect to the ordinate axis and the abscissa axis. These elements and the method of making the reference constitute what is called a system of coordinates. There may be any number of systems, but only two are of sufficient importance to require notice in this place—the rectilineal system and the polar system. The rectilineal system may be employed for the purpose of showing the relative positions of points, all of which lie in the same plane, or of points which are situated in any manner in space. The polar system may be employed to show the location of a point or points on the terminal ray of certain angles generated by the positive (ccw) or negative (cw) rotation around a fixed point called a pole. The coordinates of a point have a magnitude and a direction.

cotangent—The tangent of the complement of an angle.

cube or hexahedron—In geometry, a regular polyhedron bounded by six equal squares. The cube is selected as the unit of measure for all volumes, and for this purpose, that cube is employed whose edges are equal to the linear unit. The volume of any cube is numerically equal to the product obtained by taking one of its edges three times as a factor.

cube root—The cube root of a quantity is a quantity which being taken three times as a factor, will produce the given quantity; thus, 3 is the cube root of 27, because $3 \times 3 \times 3 = 27$. Any number which can be resolved into three equal factors is a perfect cube, and its cube root may be found exactly. All other numbers are imperfect cubes, and their cube roots can only be found by approximation.

cubic equation—A cubic equation containing but one unknown quantity is one in which the highest exponent of the unknown quantity, in any term, is 3. Every cubic equation containing but one unknown quantity can be reduced to the general form $x^3 + px + q = 0$, in which the coefficient of x^3 is 1, and the coefficient of x^2 is 0. Every cubic equation of the above form has three roots, all of which may be real, or one only may be real and the other two imaginary.

curvature—The curvature of a plane curve, at a point, is its tendency to depart from a tangent drawn at any point is always the same; hence, the curvature of the circle is constant throughout.

curve—1. A curve is a line that changes its direction at every point; that is, no three consecutive points will lie in the same straight line. The portion of the line between two consecutive points is an element of the curve. If we denote the length of the curve by s, the length of any element will be denoted by ds. 2. A curve is a line whose coordinates of its points are functions of a single independent variable.

data—In mathematics, a term employed to express all the given quantities and elements of a proposition. In a problem, the data are given parts by means of which one is enabled to determine the unknown or required parts.

decimal—Any number expressed in the scale of tens is a decimal. The system of arithmetic in which numbers are expressed decimally is called decimal arithmetic. But by the term decimal, a decimal fraction is generally understood.

decrement—A quantity that is subtracted from the independent variable of an equation. When the decrement is infinitely small or a small finite quantity, it is called a differential. In contrast to increment.

deduce—To infer something from what precedes. To draw a conclusion from given promises. The conclusion thus drawn is called a deduction, and the method of reasoning is called deductive.

deduction—Concerns the derivation of theorems from the general to the particular, and in which the conclusion is inherent in the premises. Example of deductive syllogistic reasoning: All men are mortal; Plato is a man; therefore, Plato is mortal. Whereas inductive syllogistic reasoning would be: Plato has died; other men of history have died; therefore, all men must die.

degeneracy—In matrix algebra, a special or limiting state or condition, usually produced by a zero value for some parameter or combination of parameters. In an m-constraint linear-programming problem, the term is reserved for the case where a basic solution has fewer than m nonzero components. Such degeneracy arises directly from a tied situation in the previous iteration, in which the chosen entering variable has caused the value of two basic variables to reach zero simultaneously, although only one would leave the basis.

degenerate solution—In linear programming, a basic solution in which at least one basic variable has zero activity.

degree—In algebra, the degree of a term is the number of literal factors which enter it, and is denoted by the sum of the exponents of all the literal factors of the term. Thus a^2b^3 is of the 5th degree. The degree of a power is the number of equal factors which are taken to form the power. The degree of a radical is the number of times which the radical must be taken as a factor to produce the quantity under the radical sign. The degree of a radical is indicated by its index.

degree of an equation—The degree of an equation which has no unknown quantity in any denominator or under the radical sign is determined from the highest number of factors of unknown quantities contained in any term. A simple equation is an equation of the first degree. A quadratic equation is an equation of the second degree. A cubic equation is one of the third degree. A numerical equation is one in which all the known quantities are expressed by figures. A literal equation is one in which some or all of the known quantities are expressed by letters.

derivation—The operation of deducing one function from another according to some fixed law is called the law of derivation. The operations of differentiation and integration are examples of derivation. The function operated upon is called the primitive function, and the resulting function is called the derivative or derived function.

derivative—The general form of the "limits" equation on which the derivative is based is:

$$\frac{\Delta y}{\Delta x} = \frac{f(x+\Delta x) - f(x)}{\Delta x}$$

When the limit of this ratio as x approaches zero is considered, one develops the fundamental definition of the differential calculus: The derivative of a function is the limit of the ratio of the increment of the function, Δy, to the increment of the independent variable, Δx, when Δx varies and approaches zero as a limit. The symbol:

$$\frac{dy}{dx} = \lim_{\Delta x \to 0} \frac{f(x+\Delta x) - f(x)}{\Delta x}$$

defines the derivative of y with respect to x. It is not a fraction but is the limiting value of a fraction. Thus, the symbol dy/dx is to be considered as the derivative. There are other symbols for the derivative, and one which is prominent is:

$$\frac{dy}{dx} = f'(x);$$

i.e., "the derivative of y with respect to x is f prime of x." The symbol: $\frac{d}{dx}()$ is called the differential operator.

derivative formulas—A few of the fundamental formulas are listed below which pertain to elements of business mathematics; others may be found in mathematics texts. The notation is as follows: c is a constant; u, v, and w are differentiable functions of x. Formulas for the algebraic forms are:

$$\frac{dc}{dx} = 0$$

$$\frac{dx}{dx} = 1$$

$$\frac{d}{dx}(u + v - w) = \frac{du}{dx} + \frac{dv}{dx} - \frac{dw}{dx}$$

$$\frac{d}{dx}(cv) = c\frac{dv}{dx}$$

$$\frac{d}{dx}(uv) = u\frac{dv}{dx} + v\frac{du}{dx}$$

$$\frac{d}{dx}(v^n) = n^{n-1}\frac{dv}{dx}$$

$$\frac{d}{dx}(x^n) = nx^{n-1}$$

$$\frac{d}{dx}\left(\frac{u}{v}\right) = \frac{v\frac{du}{dx} - u\frac{dv}{dx}}{v^2}$$

$$\frac{d}{dx}\left(\frac{u}{c}\right) = \frac{1du}{c\,dx}$$

$$\frac{dy}{dx} = \frac{dy}{dv} \cdot \frac{dv}{dx}, \text{ where } y = f(v)$$

$$\frac{dy}{dx} = \frac{1}{\frac{dx}{dy}}, \text{ where } y = f(x)$$

Reduction formulas for differentiation are:

$$\frac{d}{dx}(au) = a\frac{du}{dx} \text{ (a being a constant)}$$

$$\frac{d}{dx}(u + v + w) = \frac{du}{dx} + \frac{dv}{dx} + \frac{dw}{dx}$$

$$\frac{dw}{dx} = \frac{dw}{du} \cdot \frac{du}{dx} \text{ (chain rule)}$$

$$\frac{d}{dx}(uv) = u\frac{dv}{dx} + v\frac{du}{dx} \text{ (product rule)}$$

$$\frac{d}{dx}\left(\frac{u}{v}\right) = \frac{v\frac{du}{dx} - u\frac{dv}{dx}}{v^2} \text{ (quotient rule)}$$

derivative, partial — Derivatives are called partial derivatives when one restricts his attention to one of the variables exclusive of the others. Thus, in the equation $f(x,y) = x^2 - y^2$, if one considers a variable value for x but a fixed value for y, the derivative of f (x,y) with respect to x may be found, which is interpreted as the rate of change of the function when x alone varies while y is kept fixed. The standard symbols and development are given below.

$$\frac{\delta f(x,y)}{x}$$

Since y is held constant, the derivative with respect to x only is found in the usual way. For example, if

$$f(x,y) = x^2 - y^2$$

then,

$$\frac{\delta f(x,y)}{x} = 2x$$

Note that y is a constant for this differentiation (at whatever value we may want), so that the derivative of $-y^2$ is zero.

In precisely the same way we may have derivatives with x held constant; the result is a partial derivative with respect to y. For the same function mentioned above,

$$\frac{\delta f(x,y)}{y} = -2y.$$

derived equations — Derived equations are those which are obtained by combining other equations or performing some operation upon them. Thus, $2x + 2y = 8$, is an equation "derived" from $x + y = 4$, and $2x + 3y = 7$, is derived by adding $x + y = 3$ and $x + 2y = 4$.

descriptive geometry — That branch of geometry which has for its object the graphic solution of all problems involving three dimensions by means of projections upon auxiliary planes. Two auxiliary planes, called planes of projection, are usually employed.

determinant — A determinant array is an arrangement of elements such as n^2 where n is the number of columns (or vertical ranks) and also the number of rows (or horizontal ranks). It is thus a square configuration in which a determinant with one row and one column also has only one element and is a determinant of the first order. When an array of elements (or grid) has these characteristics it is identified by two vertical lines as a symbol, one on each side of the array. A capital D or capital delta (Δ) are symbols also, as follows:

$$\begin{matrix} a_{11} & a_{12} \\ a_{21} & a_{22} \end{matrix}$$

where the first digital subscript designates the row and the second digit the column. The determinant is a powerful device. For example, when many elements are related to each other, and it is possible to determine the values of the appropriate coefficients of each unknown in all the equations, it is possible to calculate the values of the unknowns by the use of determinants.

determinate—An expression which has limits —as contrasted to the expression that is without limits.

determinate equation—An equation that has a finite number of solutions. Every equation that contains but one unknown quantity and is not identical to another equation.

diagram—A drawing or pictorial delineation, made for the purpose of demonstrating or illustrating some property of a geometrical figure.

diameter — A straight line which bisects a system of parallel chords drawn in a curve.

differential—1. A difference or part of a difference between two different states of a variable quantity. The differential can be considerd d as an infinitely small quantity or as a small finite quantity; in either case, the differential of a function is the difference between two consecutive states of the function. The differential of the independent variable is always a constant, and is equal to the difference between two consecutive states of the independent variable. 2. The product of the derivative [$f'(x)$] and the function of the increment [Δx] of the independent variable [x], that is, $dy = f'(x)\,\Delta x$.

differential equations—1. Equations that express the relations between variables and their differentials. 2. An equation with one or more differential coefficients, called an ordinary equation when there is but one independent variable: a partial equation when there is more than one independent variable. 3. In every single equation involving two or more variables, values may be assumed for all the variables, except one, and the corresponding value of that one will be made known by solving the equation; in every such equation regard all the variables, except one, as independent variables, and the one variable as a function of all other variables.

directly proportional—A term used in contradistinction to the term inversely proportional. Two quantities are directly proportional when they both increase or decrease together, and in such a manner that their ratio shall be constant.

discontinuous—Broken off, interrupted, gaping. Discontinuous function is a function which does not vary continuously as the variable increases uniformly. The function, $\frac{b}{a}\sqrt{x^2 - a^2}$ is a discontinuous function.

discount—An allowance made by the creditor for the payment of money before it is due. The actual amount to be paid is called the present value of the bill or note, and the difference between the amount specified in the bill and the present value is the discount.

discrete—Discrete proportion is one in which the ratio of the first term to the second is equal to that of the third to the fourth; thus, $3:6::8:16$. The proportion $3:6::12:24$ is not a discrete but a continued proportion, or a geometrical progression. A discrete quantity is one which is discontinuous in its parts.

divergent series—A divergent series is an infinite series in which the sum of the terms is greater than any definite quantity, if enough terms are taken.

dual solution—The optimal solution to the dual problem (which is necessarily obtained in solving the primal problem, but which may not be printed out). Dual solution may be interpreted as the optimum set of marginal values and reproduced costs (d_j) for the primal problem (linear programming).

duodecimal—A system of numbers in arithmetic, whose scale is 12; hence, the unit of each order is equal to twelve times a unit of the next lower order. This system is usually employed by artificers in estimating the superficial and solid contents of their work.

dynamic programming (DP)—The essence of dynamic programming is that an optimum decision must be made at every stage of a multistage problem. When considering only a single stage, there may appear to be a number of different decisions of equal merit. Only when the effect of each decision at every stage on the overall goal is determined can the final choice be made. This integration of the cumulative effect of a path of decisions through each stage of the network is the real essence of DP.

eccentric — Two circles, ellipses, spheres, or spheroids are said to be eccentric when one lies within the other, but has not the same center. The term stands opposed, in signification, to concentric, which signifies that one lies within the other, and that the two have a common center. Two magnitudes are not properly spoken of as concentric or eccentric unless they are similar.

econometrics—Econometrics is a blending of economic theory and statistical methods to form sets of relationships which explain situations or predict future changes. Theoretical models are proved by pragmatic or empirical testing of results which are then used on real-world problems.

The "crux" of the econometrician's task is to measure the impact of one variable on another to be able to predict future events, or to advise on decisions of policy relative to past relationships as established and proved, and with new values of variables and changed parameters. This is accomplished in even smaller business analysis by examining the most probable interrelationships of separate sets of economic variables—judged by prior periods—which will evolve under the new circumstances.

The econometric model does not deal in abstract principles or situations, but instead approximates reality; it is a true prediction system which yields numerical results of a stochastic nature and thus usable within given confidence limits.

elementary matrix—A unit or identity matrix except for one unique column or row. The inverse of a nonsingular elementary matrix is also an elementary matrix. This inverse is often called a "transformation matrix."

elimination — In analysis, the operation of combining several equations containing several unknown quantities, so as to deduce therefrom a less number of equations, containing a less number of unknown quantities.

empirical—The essence of scientific method; i.e., verifiable documentation from observations, experiments, evidence, past recorded experience—without the use of theory or deduction.

entering variable — The nonbasic variable chosen to become basic in the iteration. Its associated vector, when expressed in terms of the current basis, is the pivot column.

equation—In analysis, an equation is the algebraic expression of equality between two quantities; thus, $X = A + B$ is an equation, and denotes that the quantity represented by X is equal to the sum of the quantities denoted by A and B. Every equation is composed of two parts, connected by the sign of equality. The part on the left of the sign of equality is called the first member; that on the right, the second member. The second member is often 0.

equation (equality) —A proposition (or relation) that a given mathematical function shall be equal to another function (often a constant). The process of identifying the values of the variables (functional arguments) which make the proposition true is called solving the equation.

equidistant—Two or more points are equidistant from a given point when their distances from it are equal to each other. In a series, three or more terms are said to be equidistant, when there exists the same number of terms between each pair of consecutive terms.

equilateral—Having equal sides. In geometry, a polygon is equilateral when all its sides are equal to each other. Two polygons are equilateral, or mutually equilateral, when all the sides of the one are equal to all the sides of the other, each to each, and taken in the same order.

equivalent equations—Two equations or equation systems in the same unknowns which have the same set of solutions.

error—The difference between the true result of any operation of arithmetic or algebra, and an approximate result. This term is particularly employed in the rule of double position.

expanded tableau—The linear programming matrix as it appears after the introduction of logic (both slack and artificial) vectors. It is to be compared with the original matrix, which includes the structural vectors only. The expanded matrix has the same length (vertical dimensions) as the original matrix, but its width (horizontal dimension) is increased by the number of logical vectors (one per row).

expansion—1. A term sometimes employed to denote the result of an indicated mathematical operation. Thus, the indicated cube of $A+B$ is $(A+B)^3$, and its expansion is $A^3+3A^2B+3AB^2+B^3$. 2. The developed result of an indicated mathematical operation.

expectation—In the theory of chances, the value of any chance that depends upon some contingent event. Thus, if a person is to receive the sum of $100 upon the occurrence of an event which has an equal chance of happening or failing, the expectation of the sum is worth $50. In like manner, if there are three chances of the event's failing, and only one of its happening, the expectation is worth only $25.

expected values—Generally, the summation of the products of all possible outcomes after each is multiplied by the probability that it will occur, and tables constructed to indicate these values.

explicit function—A function whose value is expressed directly in terms of the variable: thus, in the equation $Y=AX^2+BX^{1/2}+C$, Y is an explicit function of X $(Y=fX)$. The term stands opposed to implicit function, in which the relation between the function and variable is not directly expressed; as for example, in the equation $Y^2-2PX=O$, in which Y is an implicit function of X. The latter equation needs to be solved for Y in order to express Y in terms of X.

exponent—In algebra, a number written to the right, and above a quantity, to show how many times it is to be taken as a factor; thus, in the expression A^3, the number 3 is an exponent, and shows that A is to be taken three time as a factor. The expression A^3 is equivalent to $A \times A \times A$, and is read, A cubed. The exponent is properly the exponent of the power, but for simplicity, it is often called the exponent of the quantity A. Such is the fundamental idea of the term exponent; but custom and the advance of algebraic science have generalized the idea, and the term exponent, is now applied to any quantity written on the right, and above another quantity, whether it be entire or fractional, positive or negative, constant or variable, real or imaginary, thus, the expressions A^3, $A^{1/3}$, A^{-5}, A^6, A^4 and A^{v-t}, are all exponents.

exponential—An expression which involves variable exponents. An exponential function is one in which the variable enters an exponent: thus, in the equations, $Y=A^x$ and $Y^2-BX^{-x}+C^{x^2}=0$, Y is an exponential function of X.

exponential equation—A name given to an equation in which the unknown quantity enters an exponent; thus $A^x=b$ is an exponential equation. Every exponential equation of the simple form $a^x=b$, may be solved.

expression—In algebra, the representative of a quantity written in algebraic language; that is, by the aid of symbols. Thus $9x^2+3y$ is the expression of the sum of the two quantities denoted by 9 times x^2, and 3 times Y. In general, any quantity or relation denoted by algebraic symbols is an algebraic expression.

factorial—If n is a positive integer, then n factorial (written n!) is expressed as $n!=1 \cdot 2 \cdot 3 \ldots n$.

Thus, n factorial is the product of the integers from 1 to n. For example, $1!=1$; $2!=1 \cdot 2$; $3!=1 \cdot 2 \cdot 3=6$; etc., as $6!/5!=6$.

factoring—The process of separating a quantity into its factors; e.g., to separate a monomial into its factors: the prime factors of $24x^2y^3z$ are $2 \cdot 2 \cdot 2 \cdot 3 \cdot x \cdot x \cdot y \cdot y \cdot y \cdot z$.

factoring rule—Separate the numerical coefficient into its prime factors. Separate the literal quantities into their prime factors by writing each quantity as a factor as many times as there are units in its exponent; e.g., $6a^2x^2=2 \cdot 3 \cdot a \cdot a \cdot x \cdot x$.

factors—The factors of a quantity are the quantities which multiplied together will produce the quantity. Thus, a, b, and $(x+y)$ are factors of $ab\,(x+y)$. Factors of a quantity are exact divisors of it.

feasible basis—A basis such that postmultiplying the inverse of such a basis by the constant column yields a solution which satisfies the constraints. This usually requires that structural and slack variables are nonnegative and that artificial variables (other than objective row artificials) be zero.

feasible solution—A solution to the constraint equations in which all variables satisfy their sign restrictions. A feasible solution which corresponds to a feasible basis is a basic feasible solution.

finite—A quantity that has a limit or boundary, in contrast to infinite, that has no limit.

fixed variable—(1) A variable in a problem (logical, structural, primal, or dual) that is fixed at zero level for feasibility. (2) A variable to be bounded away from zero is sometimes "fixed" at its limits in a bounded-variable algorithm so that with the transformed variable set at zero level, arbitrary upper and lower bounds are established.

formulation of a problem—The translation of a physical problem (for example, how to schedule a refinery) into a mathematical problem (maximize this function subject to these constraints). It includes the identification of all the variables, the synthesis of the objective function, and the discovery of all pertinent constraints, but not necessarily the assignment of numerical values to the coefficients and other parameters. However, the relationships of variables to constraints is usually established, indicating the presence or absence of a nonzero coefficient for each matrix position.

frequency distribution—A table showing the number of occurrences of each value as displayed in an ordered array or pattern.

frequency polygon—The frequency polygon is often based on the same distribution as its corresponding histogram. It may be considered as having been derived from the histogram by drawing straight lines joining the midpoints of the upper bases of adjacent rectangles; i.e., columns. The polygon is closed at each end by drawing a line to the base line from the midpoint of the top of each of the end columns to the midpoint (base line) of the next outlying interval.

function—One quantity (A) is said to be a function of another quantity (B) when no change can be made in B without producing a corresponding change in A and vice versa. Thus, in the equation $Y^2 = R^2 - X^2$, Y is a function of X and X is also a function of Y, a general relation of dependency of value, that may be expressed by the symbols $Y = f(X)$, or $X = f(Y)$, or $\phi(X,Y) = 0$. These symbols are called functional, the first indicating that Y is function of X, the second that X is function of Y, and the third that X and Y are functions of each other. The term function implies variability, or that two or more quantities vary together in accordance with some mathematical law. All the quantities in an equation except one (the dependent variable) may vary in any arbitrary manner. The variable quantities are called independent variables.

functions, implicit and explicit—Mathematical analysis, in short, is a study of the relationships between variable numbers. The term "function" describes and symbolizes this relationship between variables. Example: Demand for a commodity is connected in some way with the market price for that commodity—thus, demand is a "function" of price. The idea of a function involves the concepts of *relation* between values of two variables and the *dependence* of one variable on another.

Implicit function—A mutual relationship between two variables and *either* determines the other—connected in a definite way.

Explicit function—If the values of say, y, depend in some definite way upon the value which is alloted arbitrarily to x. Thus, it is the value x which determines the value y—so, y is the explicit function of x.

If the relation between x and y is regarded as mutual, then the term "implicit function" is appropriate; the variables are on equal footing. If the relationship is regarded from a definite angle as "y depending on x" then we use the term explicit function. Thus, y is the dependent variable and x the independent variable. A function such that one and only one value of y corresponds to each given value of x is said to define y as a "single-valued" function of x. A function for which this is not true defines y as a multivalued $f(x)$.

Linear function—Example: $y = ax + b$ with a and b any definite numbers; such a function is represented graphically by a straight line.

game theory—1. The theory of games is a branch of mathematics that aims to analyze various problems of conflict by abstracting common strategic features for study in theoretical "models"—termed "games" because they are patterned on actual games such as bridge and poker. By stressing strategic aspects—that is, aspects controlled by participants—it goes beyond the classical theory of probability, in which the treatment of games is limited to aspects of pure chance. Zero-sum, two-person games can be solved by linear-programming methods. 2. This operations research technique is a procedure concerning competitive games with a finite number of competitors and a finite list of matrices (ordered array of figures; i.e., as a mileage chart) which contain values in the various cells having both vertical and horizontal positional characteristics. The "game" concerns alternative selections or choices in relation to those of the competitor which will result in various calculated "payoffs."

A "play" consists of a choice of a single course of action simultaneously with that of the competitor. Each "outcome" determines a set of payments, one to each competitor. A "strategy" is a set of directions, either pure or mixed, which is chosen for a particular course of action. "Mixed strategy" means that the competitor, before the play begins, decides to choose a particular course of action for each play, whereas a "pure" strategy would be the decision to play the same; i.e., "least loss" strategy on each play. "Saddle points" are equilibrium points where one competitor has achieved the lowest of the maximum losses; i.e., "minimax" and the other has achieved the highest of the minimum rewards; i.e., "maximum." The procedure is highly beneficial—but the practicality of game theory has had only limited success in the real world.

Gaussian curve (random-error concept)—A "random error of sampling" is a variation due to chance alone. If the sample is truly random, small errors will be more numerous than large errors, and positive errors will be as likely as negative errors, thus giving rise to symmetrical, bell-shaped "normal curve of error." This concept was first investigated by the German mathematician, Karl F. Gauss, and the curve is often called the Gaussian curve (normal curve).

geometrical progression — A progression or series, in which each term is derived from the preceding, by multiplying it by a constant quantity, called the common ratio; e.g., 2, 6, 18, 54, etc.

geometric solution — A graphic method of solving a linear-programming problem by plotting the half-planes determined by the constraints and the lines of constant value for the functional (a real-valued function F (f) defined for some set X of functions). Its use is restricted to problems with, at most, two structural variables.

geometry—1. A branch of mathematics which has for its objective the investigation of the relation, properties, and the measurement of solids, surfaces, lines, and angles. 2. The mathematical science that is concerned with the properties and relations of spatial magnitudes.

given—Something that is known, or whose real value is assumed. Thus we say that a straight line is given "in position" when we know its direction with respect to some other fixed line. A circle is given when we know the position of its plane, its center, and the radius with which it is described. In analysis, a line or surface is said to be given when its equation is given, that is, when we know the form of the equation and its constants.

gradient — The instantaneous direction of a curve at any point is the direction in which the curve tends to rise or fall. This is indicated by the tangent to the curve at the point. A usual measure of this direction of the curve is the gradient of the tangent. This gradient varies as the tangent varies from point to point on the curve. The mathematic description or graphic representation shows that it always is given as the limiting value of the gradient of any chord PQ as Q approaches P.

graphic method—The graphic method is one in which the quantity is photographed in the process of change. The whole range of variation of a quantity, presented in this vivid pictorial way, is easily comprehended at a glance; it stamps itself on the memory.

graphic solution—A solution obtained with graphs or other pictorial devices, as contrasted with solutions obtained by the manipulation of numbers.

graphs, use of—Every point of the curve exhibits a pair of corresponding values of two related quantities, years and population.

heuristic—Solutions are considered with the objective as being satisfactory relative to the constraints of time, funds, personnel available and the stated "confined use" of the solution as advice of a "better" though not especially the best alternative to present usage; heuristic solutions serve to "find out"; a solution which could contribute to the reduction of time and funds necessary for an algoristic solution (i.e., as closed linear-programming models) which require highly structured models, exhaustive computation if complex.

Heuristic models provide executive-accepted "better for now and for the purpose" resolutions of problems which are more flexible to model, permit faster testing and evaluation, and fit any type of problem which contains elements that can be measured and associated.

homogeneous equation—1. An equation in which the sum of the exponents of the unknown quantities in each term is the same. 2. An equation of two or more unknowns in which the constant term is zero. Thus $n^n + 2y^n = 16$ and $xy + y^n = 12$ are homogeneous equations.

homogeneous functions—When the variables x and y are increased or decreased in a fixed proportion from given values, the corresponding increase or decrease in the function $z = f(x,y)$ may be in greater, in equal, or in less proportion. In the very special case where $z = f(x,y)$ increases or decreases always in the same proportion as x and y, the function is said to be homogeneous of the first degree, or to be linear and homogeneous. Such a function has the property that its value is doubled whenever the values of the independent variables are simultaneously doubled from any position whatever.

hypotenuse—The side of a right-angled triangle opposite the right angle. In a plane triangle the square described upon the hypotenuse is equivalent to the sum of the squares described upon the other two sides.

hypothesis—A supposition made in the course of a demonstration, or upon the arbitrary constants of a problem during a discussion. A hypothesis made during the course of a demonstration is introduced as though it were true, and the reasoning continued by the rules for logical argumentation until some result is found which agrees or disagrees with some known truth. If the result agrees with a known truth the hypothesis is correct, and is said to be proved.

identical—Implies sameness under all circumstances. An identical equation is one in which the two members are in reality the same though often expressed under different forms. Hence defined, an identical equation is one in which one member is merely the repetition of the other, or in which one member is the result of certain operations indicated in the other.

identical equation—An identical equation is an equation in which the members are identical, or may be reduced to identity. Thus, $(ax + b = ax + b)$ is an identical equation. Also, $\left(\frac{a^2 - x^2}{a - x}\right) = a + x$ is an identical equation.

identity—An equation is quite simply a statement that two expressions are equal. When an equality is true at all times and for all values of the symbols for which the numbers are defined, it is an identity. The symbol $\equiv$ means, "is identically equal to" and is generally used to emphasize this characteristic of relationship.

imaginary quantity—An imaginary quantity is an indicated even root of a negative quantity. Thus, $\sqrt{-2a}$, $\sqrt[4]{-3x}$, $\sqrt[6]{-a}$ are imaginary quantities. In contradistinction to imaginary quantities, all other quantities, whether rational or irrational, are called real quantities. In accordance with the processes in radicals,

$$\sqrt{-4} = \sqrt{4} \times \sqrt{-1} = 2\sqrt{-1}$$
$$\sqrt{-16} = \sqrt{16} \times \sqrt{-1} = 4\sqrt{-1}$$
$$\sqrt{-5} = \sqrt{5} \times \sqrt{-1} = 2.24\sqrt{-1}$$
$$\sqrt{-a^2} = \sqrt{a^2} \times \sqrt{-1} = a\sqrt{-1}$$

Hence, every imaginary quantity may be reduced to the form of a $\sqrt{-1}$ in which a is real and $\sqrt{-1}$ is the imaginary factor.

An expression which contains an imaginary quantity is called an imaginary expression.

implicit function—An expression in which the form of the function is not directly expressed but which requires some operation to be performed, to render it evident. Thus, in the equation $ay^2 + bxy + cx^2 + dy + ex + f = 0$, y is an implicit function of x.

implicit prices — Same as marginal values, shadow prices, dual variable levels, etc.—that is, numbers giving the incremental worth of a relaxation of one unit in the right-hand side of a constraint.

increment—An added part or portion as differentiated from decrement representing a decreasing portion. Mathematically, an increment is the average rate of change of a variable, y, with respect to a variable, x, within a given interval or $\Delta y/\Delta x$ where delta (Δ) represents a small change.

incremental cost—1. Variable cost (as contrasted with fixed costs). It is the increase in total cost due to adding, buying, or making one additional unit. 2. Applies only to constraints originally stated as ($\geqq$) inequalities. It is the increase in the optimal (maximal) value of the objective function which would be produced by a decrease of one in the right-hand side. It is the negative of the corresponding "marginal value."

independent—One quantity is said to be independent of another with which it is connected, when it does not depend on it for its value. In this case, the term is nearly synonymous with arbitrary, but not quite. In an equation containing more than one variable, as does the equation of any magnitude, all the variables, except one, are independent; that is, any value may be assigned to them at pleasure, and the corresponding value of the other will be found for the solution of the equation. Thus, in the equation of the straight line,

$$Y = AX + b,$$

we may take X as the independent variable, in which case, whatever be the value assigned to it, the corresponding value of Y may be found.

independent equations — Independent equations are those that cannot be derived from one or reduced to the same form. Thus, $2x + y = 5$ and $x + 2y = 6$ are independent equations.

indeterminate—A quantity is indeterminate when it has an infinite number of values. In the equation of a straight line, $y = ax + b$, x represents the abscissa of any point of the line, and is indeterminate when considered only with reference to its value; when considered with reference to its connection with y, it is independent of its value provided we agree to assume ax as an independent variable.

indeterminate equation — An indeterminate equation, is one in which the unknown quantities may have an infinite number of values. Thus, $x + y = 12$ is an indeterminate equation, because each of the unknown quantities may have an infinite number of values.

Every single equation containing two unknown quantities is indeterminate. In order to solve equations containing two unknown quantities, two independent equations, involving one or both of the quantities, must be given.

index—The index of a radical is a number written over the radical sign to denote the degree of the root to be extracted. Thus, in the expressions $\sqrt[3]{a}$ and $\sqrt[4]{a}$, 3, and 4 are called indices. An index is generally a whole number greater than two. When the square root is indicated, the index is generally omitted, being understood. There is a second method of representing radicals by means of fractional exponents; thus, $\sqrt[3]{4}$, $\sqrt[7]{5}$, and $\sqrt[n]{C}$ may be written $(4)^{1/3}$, $(5)^{1/7}$, and $(C)^{1/n}$, respectively. In these cases the fractional exponent is often called the fractional index.

index number — In order to measure the changes in the large number of constantly varying items in the data, it is necessary to resort to some relative averaging device that will serve as a yardstick of comparative measurement. The index number is such a device. The index number measures fluctuations during intervals of time, group differences of geographical position or degree, etc.

induction—The method of induction in its true sense is not known in pure mathematics, except perhaps, in the process of establishing the axioms. It is often, however, employed in referring principles which are afterwards submitted to a process of rigid demonstration. There is a mathematical process of demonstration which possesses somewhat the character of induction, inasmuch as a general truth is gathered from the examination of particular cases, but it differs from it inasmuch as each successive case is made to depend upon the preceding one. This process has been called the process of successive induction.

inequality—An inequality is an algebraic expression, indicating that one quantity is greater or less than another. The sign of an inequality is >. It is placed with the opening of the angle toward the greater quantity. Thus, $a > b$ is read, a is greater than b, $a < b$ is read, a is less than b. Any negative quantity is regarded as less than 0, and the one having the greatest number of units is considered the least. Thus, $-2 > -3$; $0 > -2$.

The quantities on each side of the sign of inequality are called members. When the first members of two inequalities are each greater or each less than the corresponding second members, the inequalities are said to subsist in the same sense. When the first member is greater in one equality and less in another, the inequalities are said to subsist in a contrary sense. Thus, $a > b$ and $c > d$ subsist in the same sense, and $x > y$ and $v < z$ subsist in a contrary sense.

inequality relation—A constraint relation of either the primal or dual problem which is an inequality. The associated logical variable (of the same problem) having its one in the row or column of an inequality relation is nonnegative if the relation is $\leqq$ and nonpositive if the relation is $\geqq$. (Note that in some codes, with explicit slack vectors in the A-matrix, the negative of the logical unit vector is generated.)

inequality, types—A proposition (or relation) which relates the magnitude of two mathematical expressions or functions A and B. Inequalities are four types; A is greater than B $(A > B)$; A is less than B $(A < B)$; A is greater than or equal to B $(A \geqq B)$; A is less than or equal to B $(A \leqq B)$. The first two types are called "strict" and the last two "relaxed" or "weak." The process of identifying a functional argument or range of arguments which makes the proposition true is called solving the inequality, or obtaining a feasible solution to the inequality.

inference—A conclusion; a truth based on another truth that is admitted or that has been proven.

infinity—A term employed in mathematics to express a quantity greater than any assignable quantity of the same kind. Mathematically considered, infinity is always a limit of a variable quantity, resulting from a particular supposition made upon the varying element which enters it.

inflexion—A point at which a curve ceases to be concave and becomes convex, or the reverse, with respect to a straight line not passing through the point. The point S is a point of inflexion.

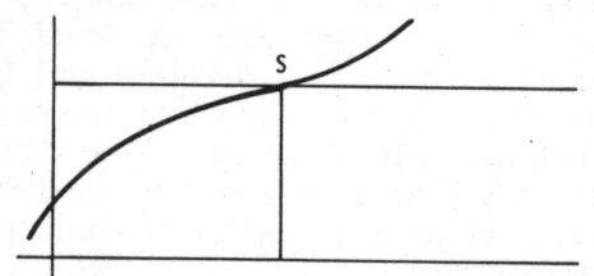

input/output—Such classes of models as these are derived from assumptions about economic variables and behavior which take account of the general equilibrium phenomena and are concerned with the empirical analysis of production; i.e., especially intermediate uses and final output. The problem is to investigate what can be produced and the quantity of each intermediate product which itself must be used up in the production process. Various data are obtained initially which attest to available resources and current state of the technology.

Again a matrix is the base of the calculation and measures the flows of current inputs and outputs between the various sectors of an economy, region, firm, or interrelationship. The tracing of such flows from one input sector to another permits calculations of the impact and the values of producing sectors, intermediate, and final use sectors of particular industries.

The basic problem is to see what can be left over for final consumption (consumers, military, city, etc.) and how much of each output will be used up in the course of the productive production requirements if usable demand estimates can be developed. I/O tables are developed for economic planning problems of "backward" or developing nations; for military mobilization; in national income accounting; in city regional planning; for estimating population; economic impact of new industry, and interrelationships of giant enterprise economics. The reader is invited to study the information available on the recently completed U.S. input/output table.

integer—A whole number as distinguished from a fraction; that is, a number that contains the unit (one) an exact number of times.

integer programming—A class of optimization problems in which the values of all of the variables are restricted to be integers. Normally, the optimization problem without this integer restriction is a linear program; additional adjectives indicate variations—for example, integer quadratic programming.

integers, measures—The natural or whole numbers; concepts intimately connected with the process of counting or enumeration. Because integers can be written down in endless series, they are used to indicate order or sequence; i.e., the ordinal aspect of integers. The cardinal aspect of integers concerns how many things are observed or noted and provides a basis of measurement.

integral—1. The result of integration either of a function or of an equation; an expression whose derivative is the integrand. 2. An expression which after being differentiated will produce a given differential.

intercept—When a curve cuts a straight line between two points (A and B), the part of the straight line lying between A and B is said to be intercepted between the two points. In general, that part of a line lying between any two points is said to be intercepted.

interpolation—The operation of finding terms between any two consecutive terms of a series which conforms to the given or assumed law of the series taken at fixed and regular intervals.

intersubjective—Specification of the aspirations to be performed with such clarity and precision in order to bring out the concept within the range of one's experience; i.e., meaning that competent observers can carry out provisions of the model with approximately the same results; clarity of thought and process communication.

interval—If a variable, x can take as its values all real numbers lying between two given numbers, a and b, then its range is called the interval (a,b). This is most often written $a < x < b$ or $a \leq x \leq b$ according to whether the values a and b themselves are excluded or included. Thus, the expressions "near to" or "neighborhood of" can be more precisely stated by using the concept of an interval.

inverse—Two operations are inverse, when the one is exactly contrary to the other, or when being performed in succession upon a given quantity, the result will be that quantity. Addition and subtraction are inverse operations, for, if we add to A a quantity B, and from the sum subtract the quantity B, the result will be A. Multiplication and division, raising to powers and extracting roots, differentiation and integration, are all inverse operations.

inverse of a matrix—An inverse of the square matrix A is another matrix B of the same dimension such that $AB = BA = I$, where I is the identity matrix. A matrix has at most one inverse. It has exactly one inverse if it is square with a nonzero determinant. The inverse of A may be obtained by extending A by an identity matrix and performing pivot steps on A to reduce it to an identity matrix. If the same operations were applied to the extension, it would end up as the inverse of A.

inverse relationship—An inverse relationship is one in which increases in the value of one variable are associated with decreases in the value of the other variable.

invert—To place in a contrary order. To invert the terms of a fraction is to put the numerator in place of the denominator, and vice versa.

irrational—Any quantity which cannot be exactly expressed by an integral number or by a common fraction; thus, $\sqrt{2}$ is an irrational quantity, because we cannot write for it either an integral number or a common fraction; we may, however, approximate to it as closely as may be desired. In general, every indicated root of an imperfect power of the degree indicated is irrational. Such quantities are often called surds.

iteration—A single cycle of operations in a algorithm solution made up of a number of repetitive operations which come closer and closer to the desired results.

joint probability—The probability that both A and B will occur. If A and B are independent, neither influencing the other, joint probability is the product of their separate probabilities.

language of mathematics—The language of mathematics is mixed. Although made up of symbols which are defined with reference to the uses that are made of them, and which, therefore, have a precise signification, it also is composed in part of words transferred from ordinary language. The symbols, though arbitrary signs, are nevertheless entirely general as signs and instruments of thought, and their meaning is once fixed by definition or by interpretation, they always retain that meaning under the same circumstances throughout the entire analysis. The meaning of the words borrowed from the common vocabulary are often modified and sometimes totally changed when transferred to the language of science. They then are used in a particular sense and are said to have a technical signification.

law—An order of sequence. In mathematics, the term law is often used as nearly synonymous with rule; there is this distinction, however, the term law is more general than the term rule. The law of a series is the order of succession of the terms, and explains the relation between each term and the preceding ones. A rule, assuming the facts expressed by the law, lays down the necessary directions for finding each of the series.

law, logic—A written or positive rule; a statement of a relation or sequence of phenomena invariable under the same condition. If tested evidence toward confirmation of a hypothesis or theory has accumulated such that primary and widespread acceptance is derived and tests are no longer considered necessary or feasible, the principles become a law. (It should be noted that general laws become simple hypotheses when they are developed in a laboratory but await testing in the real world.)

laws, associative, commutative, and distributive—

associative law—The sum of three or more terms, or the product of three or more factors is the same in whatever manner they are grouped.

$$a + (b + c) = (a + b) + c = a + b + c$$
$$a\,(bc) = (ab)\,c = abc$$

commutative law—The result of addition or multiplication is the same in whatever order the terms are added or multiplied.

$$a + b = b + a, \text{ and } ab = ba$$

distributive law—The product of an expression of two or more terms by a single factor is equal to the sum of the products of each term of the expression by the single factor.

$$(a + b - c)\,d = ad + bd - cd$$

limit—A value toward which a varying quantity may approach to within less than any assignable quantity, but which it cannot pass. Thus, the quantity $a^2 + 2ax^2$ varies with x, or it is a function of x, and approximates towards a^2 in value as x is diminished, and may, by giving a suitable value to x, be made to differ from a^2 by less than any assignable quantity. Hence, a^2 is, properly speaking, a limit of the expression, which in this case may be found by making $x = 0$.

line—A magnitude that has length, but neither breadth nor thickness. It possesses the single attribute of extension. In elementary geometry, lines are classed as straight and curved. A straight line is one that does not change its direction between any two of its points. A curved line is one that changes its direction at every one of its points. Such a line is often called a curve. A broken line is one made up of limited straight lines lying in different directions. In descriptive geometry, lines are regarded as being generated by points, moving in accordance with some mathematical formula.

linear—A descriptive term pertaining to a line. Thus, we speak of linear dimensions, etc. A linear expression or equation is one whose terms are all of the first degree. A linear problem (geometry) is one that can be solved by the use of right lines only.

linear equations—Linear equations are those graphed as a straight line. Since a straight line is determined by two points, to plot the graph of a linear equation plot two points and draw a straight line through them.

1. A single linear equation involving two unknown quantities is indeterminate.
2. Two linear equations involving two unknown quantities are determinate, providing the equations are independent and simultaneous. They are satisfied by one pair of common values.
3. The pair of common values is represented graphically by the coordinates of the intersection of their graphs.

Note: In solving simultaneous equations by the graphic method the same axes must be used for the graphs of both equations.

linear inequality—An inequality whose left-hand side and right-hand side are both linear functions of the variables. By transposition, such an inequality can always be known in the form $L\,(x, y, z, \ldots)\ R\ c$, where L is a linear function, c is a constant, and R is the given inequality relation. An inequality can always be converted to an equality by the addition or subtraction of a nonnegative "slack" variable.

linear programming (LP)—1. A technique for finding the best solution from among all solutions of a system of linear inequalities. The variables are usually processing or scheduling variables in some physical situation; the inequalities are obtained from the physical constraints on these variables; and the criterion for "best solution" is the value of some given linear function of all the variables. As the term is used today, linear programming includes the formulation of the problem in linear programming terms, algorithms for finding the best solution, and the analysis of the effect of changes in the values of problem parameters. When a solution fails to exist, the system is said to be infeasible or to have no feasible solution. When the best solution is infinite in one or more variables, the system is said to be unbounded. 2. Linear programming is a mathematical technique whereby the best allocation of limited resources may be determined by manipulation of a series of linear equations, each factor in relation to the long range goals, yielding optimum paths of action for management consideration. 3. The planning of activities, such as the allocation of men, materials, or machines, is called programming. Since resources may be limited or incapable of being utilized completely, an objective would be to determine the most efficient method of allocating these resources to activities so that a measure of performance is optimized. Thus, LP is a math technique for use where a number of variables are involved and many courses of action are possible if the problem can be expressed in linear terms.

linear programming advertising budgets—Given a restrictive advertising budget and estimates about the effectiveness of an advertising dollar when applied to a particular medium, linear programming aids in the design of a total advertising program that will maximize advertising effectiveness.

linear programming problem—The mathematical problem of minimizing or maximizing a linear function of n variables, subject to n independent restrictions, such as requirements that each variable be nonnegative, and also subjective to a finite number of other linear constraints. The latter are either equalities or weak inequalities ($\leqq$ or $\geqq$); strict inequalities of the form $<$ or $>$

are not admissible. An exact solution or other termination to this problem is furnished by the simplex method or one of its variants.

linear programming, product mix—Given a set of raw materials with given characteristics and a given set of market prices for finished products, linear programming will indicate how these raw materials should be combined to produce the highest possible profits for the company. Blending of gasolines is an example of this type of application.

linear programming, transportation — Given a large number of warehouses with limited capacities and a large number of distributors with known demands, linear programming enables the design of a shipping schedule that will minimize total costs.

literal—A mathematical term expressed by means of a letter. A literal equation or expression is one in which some of the known quantities are expressed by letters, as $ax + by = c$. A literal equation is also named to distinguish it from a numerical equation in which all the known quantities are expressed by numbers. A literal factor is a quantity denoted by a letter or some power of a letter, as a, a^2, etc.

locus—The locus of a point is the line generated by the point when moving according to some determinate law. The locus of a line is the surface generated by a line moving according to some fixed law. Thus, if a point moves in the same plane in such a manner that the sum of its distances from two fixed points of the plane is constant, the locus of the point is an ellipse. If a straight line moves in such a manner that it shall always pass through a fixed point, and continually touch a fixed curve, the locus of the line is a conical surface.

logarithm of a number—The logarithm of a number is the index of the power to which a constant number (base) must be raised to produce the given number. Thus, when 4 is the constant number, 2 is the logarithm of 16, for 4^2 is 16. The constant number which must be raised to some power in order to produce the given numbers is called the base of the system of logarithms. Logarithms may be computed with any positive number except unity as a base, but the base of the common system of logarithms is 10.

Since $10^0 = 1$, the logarithm of 1 is 0.
Since $10^1 = 10$, the logarithm of 10 is 1.
Since $10^2 = 100$, the logarithm of 100 is 2.
Since $10^3 = 1000$, the logarithm of 1000 is 3.
Since $10^{-1} = 1/10$, the logarithm of .1 is −1.
Since $10^{-2} = 1/100$, the logarithm of .01 is −2.
Since $10^{-3} = 1/1000$, the logarithm of .001 is −3.

It is evident, therefore, that the logarithm of any number between 1 and 10 is less than 1 and greater than 0; between 10 and 100, 1 plus a fraction, between 100 and 1000, 2 plus a fraction, etc. The integral part of of a logarith is called the characteristic; the fractional (decimal) part, the mantissa. Thus, in log 3.16857, the characteristic is 3 and the mantissa .16857. Principles: 1. The characteristic of the logarithm of an integral number is positive, and numerically 1 less than the number of figures in the given number. 2. The characteristic of the logarithm of a decimal fraction is negative, and numerically 1 greater than the number of zeros immediately following the decimal point. Thus, the characteristic of 4234 is 3; 423.4 is 2; 42.34 is 1; 4.234 is 0; 4234 is −1; .04234 is −2; and .0042 is −3.

magnitude—Any quantity that can be increased, diminished, and measured. Thus, a line or a surface, an angle, or a number are magnitudes. Time and weight are magnitudes; and, in general, any quantity of which greater or less can be predicted is a magnitude.

mantissa—1. The decimal part of a logarithm. Thus, the logarithm of 900 being 2.95424, the part .95424 is the mantissa. 2. The fraction value is known as the "mantissa" of the logarithm and the mantissa values are to be found in especially prepared tables. Thus, if we wish to know the logarithm of 120, we know by inspection that the characteristic is 2 and it induces that the fractional value is .0792. This is found by coming down the tabular column on the left to the number 12, moving to the right under the column headed 0, and reading the mantissa value.

marginal—The economists' term for the derivatives or rate of change of a function with respect to quantity. "Incremental" and "variable" are often used in an exactly synonymous sense. Thus, the composite terms: "marginal cost" (of production), "marginal revenue" (from sales), "marginal value" (of a capacity, of sales, of supplies, etc.). The coefficients of a linear programming model are themselves all marginal figures, for example: The cost coefficient of an activity is the marginal cost of performing the activity; the coefficient in a material-balance row is the marginal consumption or production of the material.

mathematical analysis—Includes arithmetic and algebra; deals with numbers, the relationships between numbers, and the operations performed on these relationships.

mathematical programming — Techniques of finding an optimum value of a function of many variables when these variables are subject to restrictions in the form of equations or inequalities. The term is usually restricted to problems so complex that they require a digital computer for their solution. Special types of programming are linear programming, quadratic programming, and nonlinear programming.

mathematics—Involves the definition of symbols of various kinds and describes the operations to be performed, in definite and consistent ways, upon the symbols; a symbolized and extended form of logic to form the patterns of scientific phenomena, the laws obeyed, and the uniformities displayed. Although mathematics does not provide these, it expresses and interprets them and helps to deduce their consequence, or to forecast what will happen if they hold. Mathematics points and advises where to look for verification or contradiction of hypotheses.

matrix—A matrix is an array, a grid, or a table if the elements are an ordered set of vectors or numbers displayed in rows and columns. To differentiate a matrix from a determinant, the array is enclosed in brackets or curved parentheses instead of vertical lines. Usually m is the symbol used to indicate number of rows and n is used to designate the number of columns. Thus an m by n matrix may be rectangular, or if $m = n$, it is square. Matrices may be partitioned, added, subtracted, premultiplied, postmultiplied, transposed, inverted, etc. They are usually signified by capital letters, as "matrix A." Matrix algebra is most important to linear programming, input/output, and many other operations-research techniques.

matrix element—One of the mn numbers, symbols, or other objects which have been arrayed in the form of a matrix.

matrix generator—A computer code whose input is other stored information and whose output is only the nonzero element values located or positioned by column identification and row identification.

maxima and minima—A function of a single variable is at a maximum state when it is greater than both the state which immediately precedes and that which follows it; and it is at a minimum state, when it is less than both the state which immediately precedes it and the state which follows it. Thus, if we regard the ordinate of any point of the curve KL as a function of the corresponding abscissa, Bb is a maximum because $Aa < Bb > Cc$, and Ee is a maximum because $Dd > Ee < Ff$.

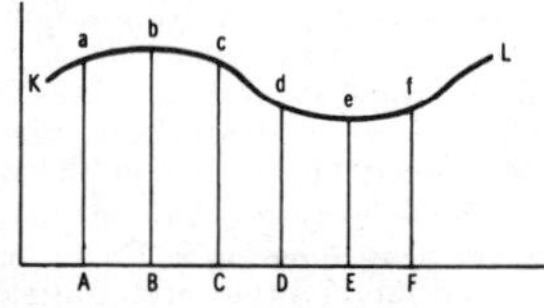

maximize — Find values of the arguments which give the largest possible value to a fraction.

maximum network flow problem—Given a capacitated network with one node distinguished as the source, and another node distinguished as the sink. To find a maximal flow from source to sink, subject to the following conditions: (1) the flow in each arc must be in some preassigned direction and cannot exceed the arc's capacity; (2) the flow into a node may not exceed its capacity; and (3) the sum of the flows into any intermediate node (not source or sink) must equal all the flows out of it.

mean—The mean of two quantities is a quantity lying between them and with them by some mathematical law. There are several kinds of means, the principal ones being the arithmetical mean and the geometrical mean.

The arithmetic mean, or average of several quantities of the same kind, is their sum divided by their number. Thus, the arithmetical mean of 10, 12, 17, and 25 is $^{64}\!/\!_{4}$ or 16. The arithmetical mean is understood when the word mean is used alone.

The geometrical mean of two quantities is the square root of their product; thus, the geometrical mean of 2 and 8 is $\sqrt{16} = 4$. The greater of the given quantities is as many times greater than the mean, as the mean is greater than the least quantity. Such is the idea of the geometrical mean. In a geometrical progression, each term is a geometrical mean between the preceding and succeeding terms; in an arithmetic progression each term is an arithmetical mean between the preceding and succeeding terms.

minimax—In game theory and other payoff tabular decisions, one of the methods of evaluating acts under uncertainty is to follow the principle of looking only at the worst possible consequences of each act and then to choose the act for which the worst consequence is the least desirable of the worst. This process thus minimizes the maximum loss or damage. This is contrasted to the maximum, a process in which one conservatively chooses the strategy to maximize or select the largest of the minimum gains. The saddle point is thus the maximum of the row minima (maximin), and the minimum of the column maxima (minimax) when both occur at the same point in the payoff table.

minimize — Find values of the arguments which will give the smallest possible value to a function.

mixed-integer programming — Integer programs in which some, but not all, of the variables are restricted to integral values.

modulus—The modulus is the constant factor (base) of a variable function. In a group of numbers (3,8,13,18) the common difference (base) is 5. In the decimal number system the base is 10; in binary, 2, etc.

monomial—An algebraic expression consisting of but one term. Thus, xy, 3ab, and 2y are monomials.

nonlinear function — A function defined as something other than a sum of terms consisting of a constant times a single variable plus a final constant. For example, $ax + bx^2 + c$ (where x is a variable and a, b and c are constants) is a nonlinear function.

nonlinear programming — An inclusive term covering all types of constrained optimization problems except those where the objective function and the constraints are all linear. Special types of nonlinear programming for which some theory has been developed are convex programming, concave programming, and quadratic programming.

notation—The conventional method of representing mathematical quantities and operations by means of symbols. A complete analysis of this method embraces the entire science of mathematical language, including not only an account of the symbols employed, but also the methods of combining them so as to express, in the simplest manner, every mathematical operation.

A correct system of notation is of the utmost importance in every branch of science; it facilitates the acquirement of truths already established, and serves to impress them more deeply upon the memory, and is a powerful instrument in the development and discovery of new principles.

number system—

Integer—An integer is a whole number as differentiated from a fraction or a decimal. A decimal may be used but it cannot have digits other than zeros to the right of the decimal point and still be classified as an integer. In some cases a noninteger may be a solution but only the integer portion of the number has meaning.

Rational number—These numbers are of two groups: integer and repeating decimal fractions. To be rational, the decimal portion of the number must always form a pattern that repeats endlessly. Thus, a rational number is one which may be expressed as a quotient of two numbers such as ½, −⅔, etc. while an irrational number cannot be so exactly expressed. The representation of π (pi), most logs, and roots are such numbers.

Real numbers—Real numbers include all possible numbers, including integers from minus infinity to plus infinity.

Imaginary numbers—If a number has the property that when multiplied by itself it yields a negative number, it is an imaginary number. For example, the square root of −4 does not exist in the number system, it is neither +2 or −2. The symbol i is used in mathematics to denote the imaginary unit, $\sqrt{-1}$; thus, $i^2 = (\sqrt{-1})^2 = -1$, and the square root of −4 can be written as ±2i.

Complex number—The combination of a real number and an imaginary number in the form of $(a + bi)$ is called a complex number as $(5 + 2i)$ which is the same as $(5 + 2\sqrt{-1})$. The number on the left part of the pair is the "real part" of the complex number, while the right part is the pure imaginary part of the complex number.

objective function — An objective function is the independent variable function whose maximum or minimum value is sought in an optimization problem.

obtuse—Blunt, opposed to sharp or acute. An obtuse angle is an angle greater than a right angle. An obtuse polyhedral angle is one whose measure is greater than the tri-rectangular triangle.

octagon—A polygon of eight angles or sides. A regular octagon is an octagon all of whose sides and angles are respectively equal to each other. The angle at the center of a regular octagon is 45°, and the angle at the vertex of any angle is 135°.

operational concepts — Equations in models first defined in relation to variables which are concerned with the firm's specific data, scheme, or operations; i.e., the expressions (math) must relate the symbols and values (concepts) to experience in an objective fashion and inter-subjectively to the operations to be performed in order to bring the concepts within the range of one's experience; math relationships must specify or at least imply the way or method of real-world methodology.

ordinate of a point—The ordinate of a point is one of the elements of reference by means of which the position of the point is determined with respect to the x and y axes of rectangular coordinate systems.

parabola—A curve having one or more infinite branches without rectilineal asymptotes. The conic, or common parabola, is one of the conic sections. It is cut from the surface of a right cone with a circular base, by a secant line parallel to an element of the surface.

parallel—Having the same direction.

parallel lines—Two lines are parallel when they extend in the same direction and at the same distance apart at every point so as never to meet.

parallelogram—A quadrilateral whose opposite sides are parallel and equal. If one angle of a parallelogram is a right angle, all the other angles are also right angles, and the parallelogram is a rectangle. If two adjacent sides of a parallelogram are equal, the remaining sides are also equal to each other, and the figure is a rhombus. If, in addition, the included angles between the equal sides of the rhombus are right angles, the figure is a square.

parameter—An arbitrary constant as distinguished from a fixed or an absolute constant. Any desired numerical value, subject in some cases to certain restrictions. For example, in the equation $(x - a)^2 + (y - b)^2 = r^2$ for a circle in a plane, there are three parameters: $(x - a)^2$ and $(y - b)^2$ are loci (2 parameters) of the point on the circle, and r^2 is the radius (1 parameter). For each choice of a, b, and r, a corresponding circle is obtained. With the parametric form of curve equations, $x = \phi(t)$ and $Y = \psi(t)$, each choice of t produces a corresponding (locus) point on the curve.

parametric programming—A method for investigating the effect on an optimal linear-programming solution of a sequence of proportionate changes in the elements of a single row or column of the matrix. Most commonly, the method is applied to either the objective-function row or the right-hand side column.

partial differential—The differential of an equation of two or more independent variables is obtained by differentiating each term of the equation with respect to one of the terms.

payoff table—In a business decision problem a choice must be made among several possible acts. The selected act will ultimately lead to some profit or loss, the amount of which will be unknown but will be determined by some event which cannot be predicted with certainty. A table can thus be composed which will lay out all the possible acts and all their possible consequences in a systematic array. An "act" is usually a decision and an "event" is a sale, purchase, or action by a customer or competitor. When such a table with columns corresponding to particular acts and rows corresponding to particular events is filled in with the numerical consequences of these variables, it is called a payoff table.

pentagon—A polygon of five angles or five sides.

perimeter—The bounding line of a plane figure. The length of the perimeter of a polygon is equal to the sum of all its sides.

permutation—1. Permutations of things are different orders in which things can be arranged by placing them in every possible order. In forming the permutations, a part or the whole of the things may be taken at a time. 2. The number of permutations of n things taken m at a time is equal to the continued product of the natural numbers from n to 1 inclusive.

Formula:

$$P(n, m) = n(n-1)(n-2)\ldots(n-m+1)$$

3. The results obtained by writing any number of factors, or letters, one after another, in every possible order, so that each shall enter every result and enter it but once.

perpendicular—When a straight line meeting another straight line forms two angles equal to each other, the lines are said to be mutually perpendicular.

perpetuity—In annuities, the sum of money which will buy an annuity to last forever.

pivotal method—The most common of the many methods used in the solution of sets of linear equations. A particular equation (pivot row) is solved for a particular (pivot) variable. The pivot coefficient plays a dominant role in the elimination or condensation to zero of all other coefficients for the chosen vector (by substitution in other equations).

pivot column—The column of the matrix containing the pivot element. In a linear-programming iteration, it is the column associated with the entering variable (nonbasic variable picked to become basic).

pivot row—The row of the matrix containing the pivot element. In a linear-programming iteration, it is the row associated with the departing variable (basic variable picked to become nonbasic).

pivot step—A step consisting of a single transformation of the matrix in a pivotal method of reduction of a set of linear equations.

polynomial—A polynomial is an algebraic expression consisting of more than one term. Thus, $(x + y + z)$ and $(3a + 2b)$ are polynomials.

polynomials, solution of—To solve equations containing unknown quantities there must be as many independent equations as there are unknown quantities.

postmultiply—To multiply a matrix A by some conforming matrix B—that is, a matrix with as many rows as the given matrix has columns, $A \times B$.

postulate—To assume without proof; to accept a proposition as self-evident, as for example, to postulate by projection or extrapolation various facts or contingencies, consequences.

precision—The number of words, or storage positions, used to denote a number in a computer. Single-precision arithmetic is the use of one word per number; double precision, two words per number, and so on. For variable word-length computers, precision is the number of digits used to denote a number. The higher the precision, the greater the number of decimal places that can be carried.

premises—In logic, the first two propositions of a syllogism, from which the inference is drawn.

premultiply—To multiply a matrix B by some conforming matrix A—that is, by a matrix with as many columns as the given matrix rows, $A \times B$.

primal simplex algorithm—Refers to a type of linear-programming algorithm in which a basic feasible solution to the expanded primal (direct) problem is maintained at each step of the iterative process, with a feasible solution to the dual problem appearing only at optimality. This is in contrast to a "dual simplex" method.

principal root—The root of any quantity is equal to the product of the same roots of its factors.

principle—A truth which has been proved, or which is evident.

probability—This can generally be described as the long-range or historical record of experience as measured and scaled for order and inspection. It can be more specifically stated as a ratio of elements in a class (a subset) to a total of a population or random sample drawn from a population—which ratio is a result of experience and calculation.

probability, conditional — The probability that event A will occur, given that event B has already occurred.

probability distributions — These are tables which show the relative frequencies of each subset into which the total population is divided or segmented. Such tables can be read to show the probability of occurrences of each value so listed.

probability laws—When an event can result in various numbers of n ways, and each in a single trial is considered equally likely or probable, one might consider s to be successes and all others to be failures, or $n - s$. The probability, p, that one particular trial will result in a success is stated $p = s/n$. Conversely, the probability, q, that any one particular trial will result in failure is stated: $q = (n - s)/n$. Since p is the probability of success in one trial of an event, the pk is the probable number of successes in k trials. The expectation is the product of the success times the probability of its occurrence; i.e., if a success is $20, then p times $20 is the expectation.

probability, posterior—The revised estimate of probability incorporating additional information, usually developed using the Bayes' equation.

probability prior—The initial, usually subjective, probability. If additional information becomes available in batches, the posterior probability after each batch is incorporated in the estimate and becomes the prior probability before the next batch is incorporated.

progression—1. A discrete series in which the terms increase or decrease according to a uniform law. 2. A discrete series that has a first but no last element and the intermediate elements are related by a uniform law to the other elements.

proportion—A proportion is a quality of ratios. Thus, $5:6 = 10:12$, and $5xy : 10xy = 4az : 8ax$, are proportions. The sign of a proportion is a double colon (::). The antecedents of a proportion are the antecedents of the ratios which form the proportion. The consequents of a proportion are the consequents of the ratios which form the proportion. The extremes of a proportion are the first and fourth terms of the proportion. Thus: in the proportion a : b :: c : d, a and d are the extremes. The means of a proportion are the second and third terms of the proportion. Thus, in the proportion a : b :: c : d, b and c are the means. A mean proportional is a quantity which serves as both means of a proportion. Thus, in the proportion a : b :: b : c, b is a mean proportional.

quadrants—In trigonometry, each quadrant is one-quarter of a circle. In the coordinate graph system, a vertical line, the ordinate, bisects a horizontal line, the abscissa, at a point called the origin, 0. The plane is thus divided into four sections or quadrants. Coordinate numbers such as 4,3 locate a point on the plane represented on graph paper. The first number is the distance P form 0 parallel to the abscissa or x axis, while the second number is the distance of P from 0 parallel to the ordinate; i.e., the height of P above the abscissa. The point 4,3 would thus be 4 spaces or points to the right of the ordinate and three spaces above the abscissa because both are positive. If the numbers were negative, they would locate a point 4 spaces to the left of the ordinate and 3 spaces below the abscissa. Thus in the N.E. quadrant, both numbers are positive, in the N.W., the first number is negative and the second positive, in the S.W. quadrant, both numbers are negative, and in the S.E. quadrant, the first number is positive and the second negative. Thus each point of the plane is represented by a definite pair of numbers, and likewise, each pair of numbers by a definite point on the plane.

quadratic—Square, denoting a square, or pertaining to it.

quadratic equation—A pure quadratic equation is sometimes called an incomplete quadratic equation because the 1st power of the unknown quantity is missing.

quadratic programming—Maximization, subject to linear constraints, of an objective function which is a quadratic function. This is one of the few convex programming types, aside from linear programming, which have solution algorithms that terminate in a finite number of steps.

queuing theory—When a flow of goods (or customers) is bottlenecked at a particular servicing point, losses accumulate in the form of lost business, idle equipment, and unused labor. Minimizing such costs involved in waiting lines, or queues, is the object of queuing theory, an O/R technique for the most efficient handling of a line at a particular point of service.

queuing theory problems — This operations research technique usually concerns models which are capable of providing solutions—stochastic or heuristic for random or nonrandom demands, lines, or queues in order to predict the behavior of a system. The system is a group of operations with defined objectives. Services being sought in such waiting lines or queues reflect various types of demands. Models concern discipline, sequencing, waiting and service times, order, etc. Queuing methods do not solve all problems as such, but rather indicate a way (i.e., heuristic) of interpreting and suggesting interpretations and investigations to reach an objective solution; i.e., optimization. There are great varieties for queues—ships at harbor entries, aircraft on landings, grocery checkout counters, products on assembly lines, etc. Monte-Carlo methods are often used.

radical equation—An equation containing a radical quantity. Thus, $\sqrt{x} = 5$, $\sqrt{x+3} = 6$, and $\sqrt{x+5} = 3x$ are radical equations.

radical quantity—A radical quantity, or radical is an indicated root of a quantity. The root may be indicated by the radical sign, or by a fractional exponent. Thus, $\sqrt{7x^2}$, $\sqrt{25a^2}$, $\sqrt{4x}$, $x^{1/3}$, $(5x)^{1/4}$ and $(4a)^{2/3}$ are radical quantities.

radical sign—The radical sign ($\sqrt{\ }$) is placed before a quantity; it shows that a root of the quantity is required. The quantity or number written at the opening of the radical sign is called the index. It shows what root is sought.

When no quantity or index is written at the opening of the radical sign, the square root is indicated; if 3, as $\sqrt[3]{\ }$, the third root; if 4, as $\sqrt[4]{\ }$, the fourth root, etc.

radius—Half the diameter of a circle, or the distance from the center to any point of the circumference.

range—The range, the simplest of the measures of dispersion, is the difference between the minimum and maximum items in the series. It is sometimes given in the form of a statement of the minimum and maximum values themselves.

The difference between these two values gives the degree of variation occurring in the series, but quite frequently the result is misleading.

ratio—Ratio is the relation of one quantity to another of the same kind. It is expressed by the quotient of the 1st divided by the 2nd. The ratio of 6 to 2 is 3; of 2 to 6 is ⅓. The ratio of 10a to 5a is 2; the ratio of 5a to 10a is ½.

When it is required to determine what is the relation, or ratio of one quantity to another of the same kind, it is evident that the 1st is the dividend and the 2nd, the divisor. But when only the relation between the two quantities is required, either may be regarded as a divisor. Thus, when the question is: "What is the relation between 10a and 5a?," the answer is the relation is either 2 or ½.

The terms of a ratio are the quantities compared. The sign of a ratio is a colon (:). Thus, the ratio between 10a and 5a is expressed 10a : 5a. The antecedent is the first term of the ratio. The consequent is the second term of the ratio. A couplet is the antecedent and consequent taken together as a unit.

rational quantity—A quantity without a radical sign, or with an indicated root than can be extracted exactly. Thus, $\sqrt{49x^2}$, $\sqrt{27y^3}$, $(a^2 + 2ab + b^2)^{1/2}$ are rational quantities.

reciprocal—The reciprocal of a quantity is the quotient arising from dividing one by this quantity. Thus, the reciprocal of a is $\frac{1}{a}$.

rectangle—A parallelogram whose angles are all right angles.

regularization—A technique for augmenting a matrix with: (1) a row that constrains the sum of absolute values of the structural variables to be $\leq$R, where R is large enough not to affect the solution if not otherwise unbounded; and (2) pseudoartificial vectors (unit vectors with a large penalty cost M) for each nonnull row relation, where M is large enough so that the pseudoartificials will not be used unless the problem is otherwise infeasible. A regularized problem, then, always has an optimum feasible solution.

relation—Two quantities are said to be related to each other when they have anything in common, by means of which they may be compared with each other.

report generator—A computer code whose input is data, operating instructions, and format information. Linear programming report-generator data may include solution-activity levels, input coefficients, etc. Linear programming report-generator instructions may include vector multiplications, additions, etc. The output of a report generator may include instructions to a printing unit as well as output information.

restriction—An equation or inequality limiting the feasible range of variation of a variable. Also used for constraint.

right angle — In plane geometry, if one straight line meets another straight line perpendicularly, the angles formed (both adjacent and vertical) are all right angles.

root—1. A root of an equation is any expression which, upon being substituted for the unknown quantity, satisfies the equation. In the reduced equation, a root of the equation reduces the first member to 0, when it is substituted for x. 2. A root of a quantity is one of the equal factors of the quantity. Thus, 2 is a root of 4; a is a root of a^3. 3. Roots are named from the number of equal factors into which the quantity is separated. Thus, one of two equal factors is the 2nd root, one of three equal factors is the 3rd root. The 2nd root of a quantity is also called the square root, and the 3rd root is called the cube root of the quantity. 4. A root of an equation is a value of the unknown quantity. Every pure quadratic equation has two roots that are numerically equal but have opposite signs. When a root of an equation is substituted for the unknown quantity, it satisfies the equation or renders the members of the equation identical.

rounding—When it has been decided how many decimals or significant numbers should be used, one important question remains: How shall the numbers be reduced to the desired values? The rule is as follows: When the first of the digits to be dropped is less than 5, the digits are dropped with no change in the preceding digit. When the digit to be dropped is greater than 5, or is 5 followed by other digits greater than zero, the preceding digit should be increased by 1. If, on the other hand, the digit to be dropped is exactly 5, increase the preceding digit by 1 if it is odd, otherwise drop the remainder. This is known as the "even-digit rule."

rounding error—The error in the final result of a calculation which is ascribed to the rounding used for input factors and intermediate results. In a computer, rounding error can be reduced almost to any desired extent, but only at the expense of speed, memory capacity, and program complexity.

row operations—One of the following operations on a matrix: (1) interchanging any two of its rows; (2) multiplying a row by a nonzero constant; (3) adding a multiple of a row to some other row. Operation (1) is equivalent to premultiplying by an identity matrix with two columns permuted. Operations (2) and (3) combined are equivalent to premultiplying by an elementary column matrix. A succession of row operations will invert a nonsingular matrix.

row vector—A matrix consisting of a single row. A given row of a matrix. The elements of a row are interpreted as the components of the vector.

rule—A direction or set of directions given for performing the operations necessary to obtain a certain result.

satisfy—An equation is said to be satisfied when the right- and left-hand members of the equation are equal after substitution of equivalent quantities for the unknown terms in the equation.

scaler—A scaler is a quantity which has magnitude but not direction. Thus, it differs from a vector which has both direction and magnitude. Examples of scalers are: body temperature, fluid density, mortality rate, etc. Thus it is a value, a constant, or simply a number.

scaling of a matrix—Multiplication of each row and each column of the matrix by different factors chosen to improve the computational properties (condition) of the matrix. By judicious scaling, the precision and efficiency of linear-programming computations can be increased greatly, without changing in any material way the definition of the problem. A frequently used scaling algorithm is to divide each row by the largest absolute element in it, and then divide each resulting column by the largest absolute element in it.

scientific method — Scientific method is an exercise in strict objective inquiry—an examination of fact or truth in a specific facet of a delimited discipline or field of knowledge. Its core consists in the evaluation of the assumptions used, hypotheses tested, and conclusions developed. It is an analytical tool of learned judgment concerning adequacy and accuracy of theories. Some questions one would ask in progressing with or criticism of scientific method are:

How is the problem designed—purpose, scope, procedure, methodology?

How is the problem defined, delimited, analyzed; what is master work?

What are the component parts of the problem, the objectives of each?

What was the status of knowledge on the subject, by what authority?

What assumptions were made; what is the reasonableness of each?

What hypotheses were used—projection or causation; are they plausible?

What conclusions were reached; are they supported by adequate facts?

What was attempted to be shown or proved; what has been shown or proved?

secant—A straight line cutting a curve at two or more points.

semilogarithmic graphs—These graphs show a curve drawn through the plotted points and the varying of log y with x. The curve is obtainable as the natural graph of log y as a function of x. If the curve is observed to rise through equal heights over certain ranges of values of x, then the value of y is subject, not to equal absolute increases, but to equal proportional or percentage increases. The use of semilogarithmic graphs is used to compare percentage changes in the value of one variable as the other variable increases steadily.

sensitivity analysis—This is a test or trial of a range or number of input values to determine the response, interdependence, or friction of the output values. Sensitivity analysis is often called parametric programming because in such investigations, one or more parameters are permitted to vary in order to determine whether or not a solution should be modified. Managers are often much concerned with what happens to the optimal solution when fluctuations in the values of parameters or coefficients are permitted to change; i.e., size of budget, factory, package, price, etc.

series—A series is a succession of quantities, each derived from the preceding quantity or quantities according to some fixed law. The first and last terms of a series are called the extremes, and the intervening terms the means. Thus, in the series, $a, a + d, a + 2d, a + 3d$, the quantities a and $a + 3d$ are extremes, and the other quantities are means.

An ascending series is one in which the quantities increase regularly from the first term. Thus, 2, 4, 8, 16 and $a, a + d, a + 2d$, etc. are ascending.

A descending series is one in which the quantities decrease regularly from the first term. Thus, 24, 12, 6, 3, and $a, a - d, a - 2d, a - 3d$ are descending.

set—A collection or family of objects considered as a whole. These objects are called elements, members, symbols, or numbers of the set. For example, a set of prime numbers, a set of all matrices with a unity determinant, and (in geometry) a set of symbols form a domain.

sets and subsets—Whenever one can classify or describe something by a characteristic or property, he may say, that the thing belongs to the set of all things having that characteristic or property. Each "thing" in the set is an element of the set. Smaller groups of "things" or elements in the set are subsets if identifiable by some characteristic common to each of the elements of that subset. The set that includes all of the elements having a given characteristic is called the universal set of things having the given property. A set having no elements is called the empty or "null" set.

significant figure (or digit)—1. Figures standing for numbers (not zero) are called significant figures. They are 1,2,3,4,5,6,7,8, and 9. 2. The figures (or digits) that remain in a whole number or a decimal number after zeros to the left or right are disregarded. Thus the significant figure of 15000 or of .0015 is 15. 3. A set of digits (computer technology) beginning with the most significan digit different from zero and ending with the least significant digit whose value is known and assumed relevant; e.g., 2300.0 has five significant digits, 2301 has four significant digits and 0.0023 has two significant digits.

signs of aggregation—The signs of aggregation are: the parenthesis, ( ); the vinculum, —; the bracket, [ ]; the brace, { }. They show that the quantities included by them are to be treated as single numbers.

Thus, each of the expressions $(a + b)c$, $a + b \times c$, $[a + b]c$, and $\{a + b\}c$, show that the sum of a and b is to be multiplied by c.

When quantities are under the vinculum or are included within any other signs of aggregation, they are commonly said to be in parenthesis.

similar terms—Terms which contain the same letters with the same exponents. Thus, $3x^2$ and $12x^2$ are similar terms; also $2(x + y)^2$ and $4(x + y)^2$. When a and b are regarded as coefficients, ax^2 and bx^2 are similar terms.

simplex method—1. This computation technique is most often used in linear-programming problems. The simplex method is an iterative process which approaches, step by step, an optimum solution in such a way that an objective function of maximization or minimization (cost) is fully reached. Each iteration in the process consists of shortening the distance (mathematically) from the statement of the problem to the final solution. The number of iterations is not fixed and often cannot be predicted. This method has an ever-widening span of utilization with computers and mode-n management problem-solving. 2. A computational routine for obtaining the optimal solution to a linear programming problem. It is an iterative elimination procedure at each stage yielding a basic solution, and it rests primarily on the following two principles:

1. Elementary row operations on the constraint matrix leave the set of feasible solutions unchanged.
2. The number of nonzero values in an optimal solution is never more than the number of constraint equations. The following steps comprise one iterative stage:
   a. A test of whether the current solution is optimal and/or feasible.
   b. If not both optimal and feasible, a choice of an entering variable and a departing variable.
   c. A pivot step so as to read off the new solution; then back to a.

An inversion algorithm is sometimes provided to express the problem in terms of a given initial basis. The problem may be formulated in any of three arrays (original, modified, or Kuhn-Tucker) and may be solved by a number of computing forms (original, standard, revised explicit inverse, revised product form of inverse), each of which can employ a variety of choice criteria for the entering and departing variables—that is, primal, composite, Dickson-Frederick, dual, suboptimization, symmetric, etc. Any simplex method is contrasted with approximate techniques, such as logarithmic gradient, relaxation, etc., which do not yield a basic solution.

simulation—Some programmers feel that if you cannot calculate, then simulate. This seems to relegate simulation to an undeserved place of second best. It is not true that the sheer complexity of some problems makes mathematical formulation prohibitive (if not impossible) and simulation necessary. Still, even where a problem can be solved by mathematical analysis, it may be more economical to solve it by simulation. Analysis sets out to provide a general solution to all problems of the type being considered. Simulation manipulates only the data relevant to the problem in question, and thus often offers a simpler and cheaper, though less general, solution.

simultaneous equations—Simultaneous equations are those in which the same unknown quantities have the same values. Thus, $x + y = 12$ and $x - y = 2$ are simultaneous equations in which $x = 7$ and $y = 5$.

sine of an arc—In trigonometry, the distance of an extremity of an arc upon the diameter drawn through the other extremity.

slack variables—These are fictitious variables which serve to take up the slack in inequalities to "convert" them to equalities. Mathematically, they are nonnegative and are treated in computations just as any other variables. They often represent idle time, costs, profits, etc. as imputed in linear program problems. Managers understand them for what they are. Useful concepts and tools for "filling" inequalities during problem solutions.

slope—1. An oblique direction. 2. The rate of change of y with respect to x. 3. The slope of a curve $y = f(x)$ is given at any point x, by the value of dy/dx evaluated at that point and a tangent to the curve at this point with the horizontal axis.

space—That which extends to an infinite distance in all directions, and contains all bodies.

stochastic—Solutions (from the Greek, meaning aim or target) are concerned with "close to the best" solutions—solutions based on uncertainty but through the best use of precise laws of probability with known and measured errors explicitly considered and confidence intervals precisely defined.

stochastic programming—A generalization of linear programming in which any of the unit costs, the coefficients in the constraint equations, and the right-hand sides are random variables subject to known probability distributions. The aim of such programming is to choose levels for the variables which will minimize the expected (rather than the actual) cost.

straight line—In geometry, a line which does not change directions between any two of its points.

subjective—Existing in the mind; belonging to the thinking subject rather than to the object of thought; interpreted by each individual in his own way and applied to his own problem as he sees it; an endless collection of personally different meanings or understandings to the same problem, statement, or conclusion.

suboptimal—1. Not yet optimal. 2. Optimal over a subregion of the feasible region.

suboptimization — When using a multiple-pricing algorithm, suboptimization enters the first variable into the basis which gives by itself the greatest improvement in objective; the next variable entered gives the greatest additional improvement, and so on. This technique tends to prevent the first entering variable from being removed by the second, etc.

subsets—These are collections wholly contained within a larger collection—all having some characteristic or property in common.

sum—In addition, the aggregate of two or more quantities.

surd—A surd, or irrational quantity, is an indicated root which cannot be extracted exactly. Thus, $\sqrt{3x}$, $\sqrt[3]{7x^2}$, $(a^2 + b^2)^{1/2}$, are irrational quantities.

syllogism—Validity of conclusions is determined by means of various forms of deductive logic. The syllogism most often consists of three statements; the first two are premises, and the last is the conclusion. Axioms, postulates, and laws usually form the premises, and they must be consistent; i.e., noncontradictory.

synthesis—1. The method by composition, in opposition to the method of resolution or analysis. 2. The combination of separate elements of thought into a whole, as of simple into complex conception; the opposite of analysis.

system—A network or organization of related or interconnected inputs and outputs often containing feedback of various types, as well as leads, nuclei, communication routes, and command chains.

tableau, matrix-algebra — The current matrix, with auxiliary rows and/or columns, as it appears at an iterative stage in the standard simplex-method computing form of solution.

tangent—A tangent line to a plane curve at any point is the limit of all secant lines through that point.

terms—The terms of an algebraic expression are the parts connected by + or −. Thus, in the expression $2a + 3x - 2cd$, there are three terms. Several terms in parenthesis are considered to be but one quantity. Thus $a + (b + c - d)$ consists of but two terms; i.e., a and $(b + c - d)$ x, although the quantity in parenthesis consists of three terms itself.

theorem—A statement of a principle to be demonstrated; that is, the truth of which is required to be made evident by a course of reasoning, called a demonstration.

theory—An exposition of abstract principles; a speculative explanation; an unproved principle considered apart from fact or practice; a conjectural explanation; partial work being directed toward confirmation; people engaged in study of truth or falsity; results seem possible yet unconfirmed.

transformation matrix—An elementary matrix representing a single change of basis. It is the inverse of a matrix formed from an identity matrix (which is the present basis in terms of itself) by replacing one unit vector (representing the departing variable) with another vector (representing the entering vector). The entering variable is expressed in terms of the present (old) basis.

transformation of a matrix—A change in the appearance of a matrix which leaves the solutions of the corresponding set of linear equations unchanged; a change of basis.

transpose—A mathematical process in which a quantity from one member of an equation is passed to the other member without destroying the equality of the two members.

transposition—Transposition is the process of moving a term from one number of an equation to the other, if its sign is changed from + to −, or from − to +.

The same term with the same sign upon opposite sides of an equation may be cancelled from both sides. The equality will not be destroyed if the signs of all the terms of an equation are changed at the same time.

trigonometry—1. A branch of mathematics whose objective is to determine the remaining parts of a triangle when a sufficient number of parts is given. 2. The mathematical study of the triangle, normally the plane triangle.

trinomial—A name applied to a polynomial of three terms; e.g., $x+y+z$ and $2a+3b-2c$ are trinomials.

truth table—When p and q are used to represent any propositions which may be true or false, and in truth tables true and false are said to be truth values of the propositions. Truth tables list the truth values for all possible combinations in columns headed by p and q as well as a third table for the result of each combination. In the table below a truth table for logical conjunction is shown:

p	q	p · q
T	T	T
T	F	F
F	F	F
F	T	F

Thus, from the above, one expects p · q to be true if both p and q are true but false if either one is false. The truth table thus formally states this and other statements.

undetermined coefficients — Unknown coefficients assumed in connection with quantities; e.g., the expression $(1+x)^3$ may be assumed equal to $A+Bx+Cx^2+Dx^3$ in which A,B,C, and D are undetermined coefficients of x^0, x^1, x^2, and x^3.

unity—An entire collection, considered as a single thing.

value—The numerical value of an expression is the result obtained by making each unknown quantity in the expression equal to some number, and then performing the algebraic operations.

variable—1. A quantity that may assume a succession of values, which need not be distinct; e.g., in the equation of a circle, $x^2+y^2=r^2$, x and y are variables. 2. A symbol which can stand for any member of a given mathematical set, as distinguished from a constant, which is a symbol standing for only one such member. A function argument whose value is to be established.

variations—

Direct variation—When two variables, x and y, are so related that the ratio of x to y is always constant, then x is said to vary directly as y; $x/y=k$, or $x=ky$.

Inverse variation—When two variables, x and y, are so related that y varies directly as the reciprocal of x, then y is said to vary inversely as x; $y=k/x$.

Joint variation—Joint variation concerns two or more variables such as: $z=kxy$, where z is stated as a joint variable of x and y, or if $z=k\frac{x}{y}$, z thus varies directly as x and inversely as y.

vector—1. A matrix of n rows and a single column (or of n columns and a single row). An ordered array or set of quantities, usually in real numbers $(x_1, x_2, \ldots, x_n)$. A vector arrayed horizontally is called a row vector; one arrayed vertically is a column vector. For example, the row of a matrix are row vectors, the columns of a matrix are column vectors. 2. In geometry, the vector is delineated as an arrow, the length of the arrow is the scalar magnitude; and the direction of the arrow is its direction.

Venn diagram—The union and intersection of sets and subsets can be shown graphically by representing the elements within a bounded area to indicate a subset. This then can be located in the universal set. John Venn, an English logician, first suggested that the universal set be represented by a rectangle and subsets by circles, with various shadings designating common elements.

verification—The operation of testing or proving to be true.

waiting-line theory—This operations research technique usually concerns models which are capable of providing "solutions"—stochastic or heuristic—for random or nonrandom demands, lines, or queues in order to predict the behavior of a system. The system is a group of operations with defined objectives. Services being sought in such waiting lines or queues reflect various types of demands. Models concern discipline, sequencing, waiting and service times, order, etc. Queuing methods do not solve all problems as such, but rather indicate a way (i.e., heuristic) of interpreting and suggesting interpretations and investigations to reach an objective solution; i.e., optimization. There are great varieties for queues—ships at harbor entries, aircraft on landings, grocery checkout counters, products on assembly lines, etc. Monte-Carlo methods are often used.

zenith—The point of a plane in which a vertical, at the place produced, pierces the heavens.

zero—In common language, zero means no thing; in arithmetic, it is called naught, and means no number; in algebra, it stands for no quantity and less than any assignable quantity.

APPENDIX H

Statistical Definitions

Most of the student aspirants for top management roles in business and industry presumably are college-trained in such basic courses in business administration as statistics, marketing, finance, business organization, business mathematics, accounting, personnel management, and many others. Unfortunately, social science students are intellectually weakest in two of these areas in particular—statistics and mathematics. These lists of definitions are thus supplied in this text to aid such students in the recall and new retention of fundamental concepts and explanations.

The material contained within these few pages is meant to appeal to a wider audience than students and most significantly is designed to be of assistance to present data-processing personnel and current active managers. In order for management to properly and effectively plan, control, and execute the many facets of the system procedures under its jurisdiction and to aid in problem solving, its individual members must become more and more familiar, indeed fully educated, in matters of data processing and computer science. Now these same managers, data processing personnel, and students have come to realize that the principal tasks of alert business leaders relate to: (1) discovering problems, (2) analyzing, relating, and ordering the components of the problems in logical, sequential arrays or models to prepare for their solution by using computer skills, and (3) preparing the models with flowcharts, process charts, and object diagrams for computer input, verification, testing, and retesting. The statistical, mathematical, and operations research techniques required for such problem formulation and presentation must now come to the forefront as the most important new skills to be mastered in today's complex, highly competitive business world, not only by managers and division heads of all types (for the computer is all-pervasive in the integrated system), but also by the great majority of data-processing personnel. Banks, insurance, production, marketing, and all types of firms now realize that future demands on business management will create more emphasis not only on the corporate ability in data processing, but mostly at the creative, problem-solving level in order to fully utilize the great computer capability.

The top echelon positions in management are more and more being filled by data-processing personnel because of their unique abilities in relation to management by computer. Data-processing personnel are well-educated and intelligent individuals who have excellent knowledge of their company's many activities and procedures. Their experience and training enable them to know what data can be most important to company control and operation, as well as how to use such data and procedural knowledge to efficiently operate the new systems and solve problems which formerly were unknown even to top management.

It is obvious to all new management personnel, and certainly to the worried and harried "traditionalists" among corporate executives, that the input to the computer is most heavily oriented to statistical and mathematical models based on company data and operations research problem-solution techniques. A great many managers, EDP personnel, and students are now in a rush to take courses in business management, especially statistics and business mathematics (and operations research), and most of the others have begun to dig out their old mathematics and statistics notes and college texts for urgent review. This appendix is inserted in this dictionary to hopefully be of substantial assistance to all who need a fresh review of definitions, concepts, and methods, and for those who must have an immediate source of reference to more clearly understand new documents, graphs, tables, and statistical techniques and reports in use by computer and operations research personnel.

Appendix H

The reader will note that the definitions and explanations are not developed at a sophisticated level, but are hopefully explained at the high school or college freshman level. They are "refresher" definitions and concepts, and many are developed at some length to aid the manager or student whose statistics training is remote or very slight. The list is incomplete, but may be a starting point for renewed study and interest in new texts.

SYMBOLS

a—A constant of a straight-line equation; the y intercept; the value of an original observation (same as m); the symbol used in a formula for the arithmetic mean; value of Y_C when $X = 0$ in equation of trend or in a regression equation; the number of ways in which a favorable outcome can occur.

a_1—Labels (1) to distinguish a variety of constants.

a_{ij}—A constant in the *i*th row and *j*th column of a table or matrix.

A.D.—The average or mean; the average deviation from the mean.

b—Estimate of slope of a line; coefficient of regression; possible number of unfavorable results; the typical change in the growth factor per X unit of time; typical change in Y for a given change in X, in functional analysis or least squares straight line.

$b_{12.34..n}$—Coefficient of net regression.

c—Difference between arbitrary origin and mean or median; the correction factor; the difference between any mean and the actual mean $(\overline{X}-\overline{X}')$; constant in trend or regression equation.

C—Size of class interval; set of cyclical variables in a time series.

CA—Chronological age.

CC—Coefficient of contingency.

C_r^n—Number of possible orders in which r successes can occur in a sequence of n trials.

Coef. Q.D.—The coefficient of quartile deviation.

d—Number defective in a sample, or defects in a unit; deviation of an individual value or midpoint of a class interval from an arbitrary or guessed mean (or average other than a guessed mean); deviation from line of trend $(Y - Y_C)$; constant in trend or regression equation.

D—Difference in rank.

dx—A small increment, a rate of change.

dy/dx—Rate of change of y relative to x; slope of the tangent to a line; symbol for differentiation.

d′—D in class interval units.

e—Base of natural system of logarithms $= (1 + 1/h)^h \cong 2.7183$.

E (x)—Expected value of $x = \mu \Sigma x_i P(i)$.

f—Frequency; i.e., number of observations in a given class.

f_a—Frenquency of class interval above modal group.

f_b—Frequency of class interval below modal group.

f (x)—Function of x; i.e., y depends in some manner f () upon x.

G—Positive differences in rank.

G_m—Geometric mean.

H_m—Harmonic mean.

i—Class interval; difference between two consecutive class limits.

I—Item.

I_i—Index number for time i relative to base period of index.

I_{i-1}—Index for preceding month or year.

I.Q.—Intelligence quotient.

k—Coefficient of nondetermination.

K—The value of a point which lies halfway between quartile 1 and quartile 3.

L_1—The limit of the modal class.

L_{me}—Lower limit of class interval containing median.

L_{mo}—Lower limit of modal group.

log—Logarithmic function (common).

ln—Logarithmic function (natural).

M—Mean of a normal distribution.

M.A.—Mental Age.

Md—Median.

M.D.—Mean deviation.

MD's—Mean deviation in class intervals.

Mg—The geometric mean.

Mo—Mode.

n—Sample size; number of cases or items; last item in a series; the number in a population; in regression, the number of observations; number of Bernoulli trials.

N—Population size; number of observations.

N_L—Number of cases overstated or too large.

N_S—Number of cases understated or too small.

n!—Factorial n defined by:

$$n(n-1)(n-2)\ldots 1.$$

n 1/M—Mean arrival rate of Poisson probability distribution.

p—Relative frequency, fraction defective in a sample product moment; probability of success; long-run fraction successful in Bernoulli process.

p_b—Break-even value of.

P (A)—Probability of A.

P (A,B)—Joint probability of A and B.

P (A/B)—Conditional probability of A given B.

$P(A_j)$—A priori probabilities of events A_j.

P_A—Probability of acceptance of lot based on sample inspection.

$PA(A_j/B)$—Probability of events A_j taking place given that event B has occurred.

P_i—Point in a series of original data identified by coordinates (X_i, Y_i); points of a scatter diagram.

P_n—Price of a product in period n.
P_R—Probability of rejection of a lot.
$P\binom{n}{c}$ Permutations (sequences) of n events taken c at a time $\frac{n!}{(n-c)!}$
P_o—Price of a commodity in a base period.
P_s—A sample proportion of favorable responses.
p—Weighted mean proportion from two samples used to represent p.
$\bar{p}$—The sample proportion, read as p bar.
q—Probability of failure $p + q = 1$.
q_1—Quantity of a commodity produced or consumed in first period or a given year.
q_o—The quantity; i.e., barrels, gallons, etc., produced, consumed, bought, or sold in a base year.
q_s—A sample proportion of unfavorable responses.
Q_1, Q_2, Q_3, Q.D.—The first, second, third quartile and the quartile deviation.
Q—Number of units stocked.
q_n—Quantity of a commodity produced or consumed in period n.
Q_m—Quadratic mean.
r—Number of Bernoullian successes.
$\bar{r}$—Coefficient of correlation.
r_{12}—Coefficient of correlation.
r_{xy}—Coefficient of correlation.
$R_{1.234}$—Coefficient of multiple correlation between X_1 and X_2, X_3, X_4.
$r_{12.3}$—Cofficient of partial correlation between X_1 and X_2 excluding X_3.
r_o—Observed number of Bernoulli successes.
r—Coefficient of correlation corrected for number of cases.
r_{11}—Coefficient of reliability.
R—Set of random variables in a time series.
s,S—Standard deviation of a sample.
$\bar{S}$—Standard error of the estimate corrected for number of cases.
s (d) —Estimated standard deviation of number of defects per unit.
s (p) —Estimated standard deviation of fraction defective in a sample.
s (x) —Estimated standard deviation of observations.
s (x) —Estimated standard deviation of means of samples.
s_x—Estimated standard deviation of a population, computed from a sample.
s_x—Standard deviation of sample means.
S^2_x—Estimated variance of a population, from a sample.
S_y—Standard error of the estimate.
S^2_y—Total variance to be explained.
S^2_{yc}—Explained variance.
$S_{y.x}$—Standard error of the estimate.
sk—The coefficient of skewness.
T,t—The critical ratio, not a normal deviate.
V—The coefficient of variation.
V (X_i) —The variance, most common measure of dispersion of observations around the mean.

W—Weight attached to a value entering into an average.
x—Deviation of individual value from its arithmetic mean.
X—An arithmetic mean.
X_1—Dependent variable in multiple correlation analysis.
$X_2X_3X_4$—Independent variables in multiple correlation analysis.
X^h—An hypothetical statement of mean.
X_s—Mean of a sample.
X_s—A sample observation.
X—The value of an individual observation; the value of midpoint of a class.
x'_i—The *i*th transformed independent variable.
x'—Deviation of a given observation from the assumed mean.
X_1,Y_1—Coordinates of a point on a graph.
y—An observed value of a variable quantity; the dependent variable; dependent value of a linear equation.
Y—Set of dependent variables.
Y_c—Values of Y computed by use of the formula for trend or regression.
y'_i—Transformed original regression line.
Y_c—Coordinate of line of best fit.
Y_i—Computed series of data for curve of best fit.
z—Standardized random variable with unit normal deviation; standard score.
z'—Residual difference between actual value and theoretical line of regression value.
z_1—Standard score on first test.
π—A constant = 3.141593.
ρ—Index of correlation (measured on basis of curvilinear line of regression) ; coefficient of correlation from ranks.
Σ—Sum of.
σ—Standard deviation.
σ'—Standard deviation corrected for grouping error.
σ_x—Standard deviation of a population.
σ^2_x—Variance of a population.
σ_x—Standard error of $\bar{X}$.
σ_{xy}—Standard deviation of values about means of respective columns in correlation table.
σ_x—Standard error of arithmetic mean, the standard error of any statistical measure.
$\sigma_{3.12}$—Standard deviation of an array of offspring.
σ_3—Standard deviation of offspring in general.
ϕ^2—Mean squared contingency.
=—Equality sign.
≅—Means "approximately equal to."
Δ—Small positive increment of a variable or a fraction.
Δx,—Increment of x.
$\Sigma p_o q_o$—The summation of the products of the commodity prices times their quality in the base year.
$\Sigma p_1 q_1$—The summation of the products of prices times quantity in the given year.
μ—Mean, of many-valued population.
μb—Break-even value of μ.

DEFINITIONS

abscissa—The horizontal distance from the y axis of a graph which is usually designated by x as contrasted to the ordinate which is the vertical distance from the x axis and is designated as y.

absolute value—The absolute value of a number is the numerical value of the number without considering its sign. Thus, the absolute value of +18 is 18, and the absolute value of −12 is 12 and is usually written as: $|-12| = 12$.

acceptance sampling—The inspection of samples of incoming lots in order to determine the acceptance or rejection of the lot. This is characterized by a sample size n and an acceptance number c or by the average outgoing quality limit, referred to as AOQL.

algoristic—In strict definition it could mean a step-by-step methodology . . . an exact answer; a systematic computation guaranteeing accurate solution as 2 linear equations and 2 unknowns will yield a specific correct answer.

arithmetic mean—The characteristics of the arithmetic mean are:

1. It is the most generally used measure of central tendency.
2. Its value is affected by the value of every item in the series.
3. It is easily calculated.
4. It may be used in further algebraic calculations.
5. The algebraic sum of the deviations of the values from their arithmetic mean is zero.
6. The sum of the squares of these deviations is less than the sum measured from any other value in the series.

Sometimes the arithmetic mean gives a misleading impression as an average because of the influence of extremes in its value. In other cases, it does not give the correct answer to a problem of averaging; e.g., determining the average of a group of ratios or the average of rates of change. For these, the geometric and harmonic means are used.

arithmetic mean (ungrouped data) — The arithmetic mean of a small group of individual items together and dividing the total by the number of items used. The computation of the arithmetic mean is expressed in formula form as:

$$\overline{X} = \frac{\Sigma(X)}{N}$$

where,

$\overline{X}$ = arithmetic mean,
Σ = symbol meaning "sum of,"
X = data expressed as individual items,
N = number of items.

association—Statistical evidence often denotes and describes the presence or absence of association. Care must be taken to avoid the notion that association implies causation. Close association of variables may be the result of pure chance, or due to the influence of a third factor. Also, though association and relationship may be real, it is quite often most difficult to determine which causes the other; i.e., cause and effect. Most errors of the statistically spurious type result from the "interpretation" of the degree of association, not the degree of association itself. Association or relationship must depend upon reasoning and other tests to establish causation.

average—An average is a typical value which tends to sum up or describe the mass of data. It also serves as a basis for measuring or evaluating extreme or unusual values. The average is a measure of the location of central tendency. The most important kinds of average are:

1. The arithmetic mean.
2. The median.
3. The mode.
4. The geometric mean.
5. The quadratic mean.

axis—When two given perpendicular lines intersect with 0 (origin) as the point of intersection, the horizontal line is usually labeled as 0x and the vertical line 0y. These lines are designated as coordinate axes of reference. Any point P is taken in the plane 0xy and the perpendiculars PM and PN are drawn to the axes.

Bayesian statistics—This branch of statistics concerns estimates of (prior) probability distributions, as subsequently revised (posterior distribution) in order to incorporate new data by means of Bayes' equation.

bias—Whenever a sample is selected by a method that in the long run would yield samples whose obtained measures differ systematically from the corresponding true measures, the sample drawn is the biased sample.

binomial distributions—The binomial probability distribution is a type of probability distribution which relates to phenomena that can be classified into one of two possible categories. This type of probability distribution has been found to apply to numerous situations, such as in the inspection of goods as to whether they are satisfactory or not.

Two categories into which an event can be classified as 1 and 2 might be:

1 defective	1 correct	1 male
2 nondefective	2 incorrect	2 female

Let p denote the probability that 1 will happen, 1 − p or q the probability that 2 will happen. Then, if there are n events (units produced, calculations performed, persons interviewed), the probability that X out of n events falls into class 1, according to the binomial probability distribution is:

$$P(X) = \frac{(n)(n-1)(n-2)\ldots(n-X+1)}{(1)\ (2)\ (3)\ldots(X)}\ p^x q^{n-x}$$

Note again that the events must be independent and the probability p constant for all events in order that the binomial distribution is applicable.

Thus, the binomial distribution or frequency is a function that shows the probabilities of all the various possible numbers of successes in a known (or given) number of independent trials of an experiment.

Boolean algebra—A system of notation and generally binary computation upon which much of computer switching theory is based is called Boolean algebra, named after a British mathematician, George Boole. The system makes extensive use of sets, subsets, and the laws of combination of subsets as unions, intersections, complements, null, empty, universal, and proper sets. It is being extensively reviewed in thousands of elementary and secondary schools and by students of computer and switching concepts.

Boolean algebra, laws—

Commutative laws:

$A \cap B = B \cap A$ (for intersections)

Associative laws:

$A \cup B = B \cup A$ (for unions)

$A \cup (B \cup C) = (A \cap B) \cup (A \cap C)$

$A \cup (B \cap C) = (A \cup B) \cap (A \cup C)$

$(A \cap B) \cap C = A \cap (B \cap C)$

Distributive laws:

$A \cap (B \cup C) = (A \cap B) \cup (A \cap C)$

$A \cup (B \cap C) = (A \cup B) \cap (A \cup C)$

Operations with the universal set:

$(A')' = A$

$A \cap A' = \phi$ (empty set)

Operations with the empty set:

$A \cap \phi = \phi$

$A \cup \phi = A$

Laws of complements:

$(A')' = A$

$A \cap A' = \phi$

$A \cup A' = \Omega$ (universal set)

breakdown charts—Graphs or arrays of cost or profit functions of two or more alternatives which usually include one or more intersections.

case study—An "in-depth" interview with specific individuals or groups in attempts to bring out the important detail—the nonobvious.

causation—The concept of causation is a matter for extended philosophical inquiry, but for the purposes of this text it might be stated that it involves two essential elements: (1) an association in action between two things, and (2) some sort of operating force between the one that acts first and the one that follows.

It is impossible from statistical evidence alone to establish causation; the proof must come from outside the statistical domain. For example, statistically one may establish that there is an association between the heights of fathers and the heights of sons. Outside information, but not the statistical information, tells that the causation can act in only one direction.

c charts—Refer to control charts which are used to monitor defects per unit or other Poisson distributions.

census—A complete survey of a finite population.

central-limit theorem—If n is large, the theoretical sampling distribution of x can be approximated very closely with a normal curve. A noteworthy aspect of this theorem is that it contains no specification about the population. This means that when n is large, the theoretical sampling distribution of x will be close to a normal curve regardless of the shape of the distribution of the population.

central tendency measures—These are averages of various types, each of which is, for a definite purpose, the best single summary representation of the whole group of data. An average should signify the presence of a clustering point in the distribution; if there is no clear central tendency, the average is meaningless. There are five different measures of central tendency in common use:

1. Arithmetic mean—This is the value which, if substituted for each individual value in the series, would give the same sum as the original series. It is the most familiar and, in general, the most useful type of average, being obtained by adding the values of the items in the series and dividing by the number of items. It corresponds to the center of gravity of a physical system.
2. Median—This is a positional average, such that ½ of the items have values above it, and ½ have values below it.
3. Mode—This is the value at the point in the distribution where the items tend to be most heavily concentrated. In this sense it may be regarded as the most typical of a series of values.
4. Geometric mean—This is a special-purpose average, defined as the nth root of the product of n items.
5. Harmonic mean — This is another special-purpose average, defined as the reciprocal of the arithmetic mean of the reciprocals of the values.

characteristic of a logarithm — The non-negative decimal part of a logarithm is called the mantissa, and the integral part is called the characteristic of a logarithm. For example, in the log 1,830 = 0.2625 + 3, 0.2625 is the mantissa and 3 is the characteristic, or 1 less than the number of integers. See any math text for use and rules of logarithms.

chi-square test—A test to determine the goodness of fit of the actual data to the theoretical distribution has been devised by Karl Pearson. The test involves the calculation of χ^2 (chi square):

$$\chi^2 = \Sigma\left(\frac{(f_o - f)^2}{f}\right)$$

where,

f = the theoretical frequencies.
f_o = the observed or actual frequencies,

The chi-square test may be used to test a large variety of hypotheses in many fields by comparing the expected results (frequencies) based upon the hypothesis to be tested and the actual results obtained by securing observations. If the chi-square test demonstrates that the disparity between the actual and the expected frequencies is too large to be ascribable to change (if p is less than the selected fiducial limit of .01 or .05), the hypothesis may be said to be false.

coefficient of correlation—This measure results in a value of 1.00 for a perfect relationship and a value of zero for a wholly imperfect relationship. The measure is termed the coefficient of correlation and is used as the comparative measure of association. Therefore the coefficient of correlation is

$$r = \sqrt{1 - \frac{Sy^2}{\sigma y^2}}$$

coefficient of variation, example—The principal relative measure of dispersion is the coefficient of variation, which is represented by the letter "V."

$$V = \frac{\sigma}{M} \cdot 100$$

where,

σ = the standard deviation of the distribution,
M = the arithmetic mean of the distribution.

The fraction is multiplied by 100 so that the result may be expressed as a percent. When V is small, little dispersion is indicated. As V approaches 100%, a greater scattering away from the central tendency is indicated.

The coefficient of variation should be used (1) to compare the dispersion of frequency series that are expressed in different units; and (2) to compare the dispersion of series expressed in the same units, but scattering about means which have widely different values. For example, consider two distributions of weekly wages, A and B:

	A	B
M	\$25	\$50
σ	\$ 5	\$ 5

These two distributions have the same standard deviation, but different means. Which is more dispersed? Obviously, A, which has a mean only half that of B. The coefficient of variation makes this fact clear.

For distribution A: $V = \frac{5}{25} \cdot 100 = 20\%$

For distribution B: $V = \frac{5}{50} \cdot 100 = 10\%$

cologarithm—The colog of a number is the logarithm of the reciprocal of that number: colog n = log(1/n) = log 1 − log n = 0 − log n. Cologarithms are used in computation when one desires to add all logarithms instead of subtracting some of them. He thus finds the cologs of the items which are divisors and thus adds the logs of the multiplicands and multipliers and the divisors as well.

combinations—The number of possible arrangements of n elements taken c at a time if the sequence is ignored: $C\left(\frac{n}{c}\right) = \frac{n!}{(n-c)!c!}$

concept of prediction—If the relationship between two variables is known, the relationship can be employed to predict one variable from another. The accuracy of the predictions is directly dependent on the strength of the relationship between the variables. The errors of prediction over a total group are minimized when a regression equation is employed.

conditional probability—The probability that event B will take place provided that A has taken place is called the conditional probability of B relative to A, and it will be written symbolically as $P_A(B)$.

confidence coefficient, selection—In practice the most frequently used confidence intervals are the 95% and 99% intervals. The two fundamental questions are: (1) What are the consequences of acting as though the population mean is within the interval when in actual fact it is not? If the consequences are serious, a high confidence coefficient is indicated. (2) Is the confidence interval sufficiently small to be of practical value? In some examples the consequences are not so serious and a 95% interval may be used. If the coverage is too wide to be practical, the sample must be changed.

confidence interval—It is now claimed with a probability of 0.95 that the interval from $x \pm (1.96\,\sigma/\sqrt{n})$ contains μ, the interval given is called a 95 per cent confidence interval. We are 95 per cent confident (we can assert with a probability of 0.95) that this interval contains the mean of the population.

confidence level—A measure of confidence concerning a statistical calculation might be stated as follows: "We are 95% confident that, from a universe believed to be stable, the true mean will fall between x_1 and x_2."

consumer price index—This is a "market basket" index comparing the prices of several-hundred items, goods, and services that play a significant role in the average budget of persons belonging to a certain population group. The prices considered in this index are samples with respect to the goods and services that are included and also with respect to the stores and cities that are canvassed in the necessary surveys.

continuous series—A continuous series is such that if all the data in the particular universe were arrayed (arranged according to increasing or decreasing magnitude), the differences between successive observations would be infinitesimal. For any particular sample, of course, the differences will usually be finite. An example of a continuous series would be provided by the data for the heights of all men in the world.

correction factor (finite)—The square root of ($N-n$ divided by $N-1$), which is used when n is more than 5 per cent of N.

correlation—The development of a correlation coefficient will determine a measure of confidence which can be placed in a regression coefficient; i.e., a determination of relatedness of inputs and outputs or of other concurrent series of measurements or counts.

If r is close to 0, the fit is poor and we shall say that the relationship is weak or nonexistent; if r is close to +1 or −1, we shall say that there is a strong correlation.

correlation application—The purpose of correlation is to determine the form and the degree of relation between two series of values. It may be utilized in statistical description for the demonstration of the existence of a relationship, or it may be employed in analytical statistics, for it is possible to infer relationships between whole statistical populations on the basis of correlations between samples of those populations.

correlation coefficient—The coefficient of correlation is a measurement of the closeness of the relationship between the variables. It is obtained by comparing the accuracy of an estimate of the predicted variable made from the line of regression with the accuracy of one made from the arithmetic mean of the predicted variable alone. In other words, we compare the standard error of estimate with the standard deviation.

correlation coefficient, standard error—To determine the error likely to arise due to sampling, the standard error of the coefficient of correlation may be used in the same fashion as the standard error of the mean.

Fifty chances out of 100 the difference between the observed and the actual r will not be larger than $.6745\sigma_r$ (the probable error of r), and 99.7 chances out of 100 this difference will not be larger than $3\sigma_r$.

The formula for the standard error as the coefficient of correlation is:

$$\sigma_r = \frac{1-r^2}{\sqrt{N}}$$

If the coefficient of correlation is computed for each of a large number of samples of paired values, a frequency distribution of the resulting coefficients will be normal (if the true association is zero). Through application of the standard deviation (standard error of the coefficient of correlation) it can be foretold that no value of r greater than three times its standard error will arise due to chance (99.7 times out of 100). If, therefore, the computed r is more than three times σ_r, 99.7 times out of 100 it is significant.

correlation, linear—The change in one variable is at a constant ratio to change in the other.

1. Direct: An increase in one variable is accompanied by an increase in the other.
2. Inverse: An increase in one variable is accompanied by a decrease in the other variable.

correlation measurements—The three important measures of correlation are:

1. The line of regression—this is fitted to the points on the scatter diagram in such a way that the sum of the squared deviations from the line is at a minimum. The line of regression gives the average change in y resulting from any given change in x.
2. The standard error of estimate (S_y) equals $\sqrt{\frac{\Sigma d^2}{N}}$, where d represents the deviation from the line of regression. S_y indicates, in absolute terms, the error that may be expected from any group of estimates made from the line of regression.
3. The coefficient of correlation (r) is a relative measure of the degree of relationship between two variables. It indicates the degree of improvement in the ability to estimate y from x over estimates of y made from the mean of the y variable alone.

correlation multiple—There are more than two variables. One variable is dependent while the other variables are independent.

correlation, nonlinear — Nonlinear (curvilinear) correlation is the change in one variable at an increasing or decreasing ratio, not at a fixed ratio, to a change in the other variable.

correlation, partial—Partial correlation measures the association between an independent and a dependent variable. It allows for the variation associated with specified other independent variables.

correlation procedural steps—

1. A random sample is used, and the X and Y values of each observation are recorded. If this random sample is properly taken, the various observations will be mutually independent, and the inclusion of any one observation in the sample will have no influence on the values of any of the other

observations in the sample. (Note: In the case of time series, this condition is not fulfilled, since the value of, say, steel output in January obviously has some bearing on what it was in December and what it will be in February.)

2. A scatter diagram is constructed. This is a chart set up with values of X variable read along the horizontal axis and values of Y read along the vertical axis such that each dot on the chart represents a single observation possessing both a Y value and an X value. For example, if we were measuring the correlation between the heights and weights of men, we would represent both height and weight for each man in the sample by a single dot.

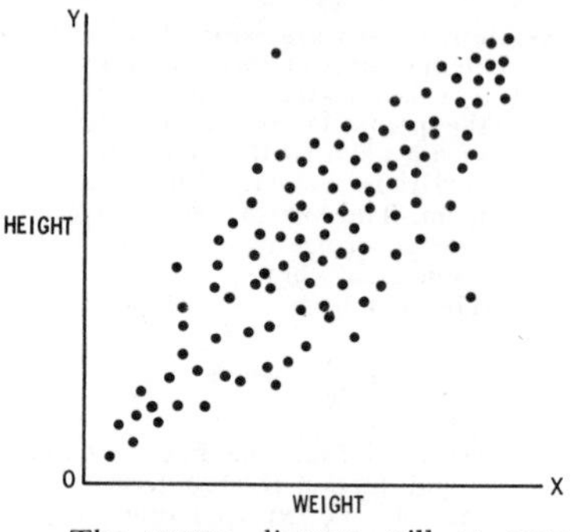

The scatter diagram will at once indicate whether there is any correlation between the two variables. If they tend to increase together, as in the example shown, we say that there is direct correlation; if one increases while the other decreases, there is an inverse correlation. We also get an indication as to whether the underlying functional relationship between the two variables is linear or curvilinear, as well as an indication of how much correlation is present. In the above chart the points cluster fairly closely around a line which might be used to show the average, or typical, relationship.

It should be noted that although the scatter diagram provides a clue as to the nature of the relationship between the variables, the final decision as to what type of line or curve will fit the data must rest on some logical justification derived from prior knowledge of the subject being investigated.

3. Calculate the line of average relationship (the regression line). This is a line fitted to the data, usually by the least-squares method, showing the average change in the Y variable associated with a unit change in the X variable. The term "regression" is used to describe this line because one of the earliest studies of this type was made by Francis Galton, who examined the relationship between the heights of fathers and the heights of sons, finding that, whether the fathers were above or below average in height, the sons tended to go back, or regress, toward the mean. Galton therefore called the line of average relationship the "line of regression."

Covariation thus measured may or may not represent a relationship of dependence between the variables. Sometimes two variables may move closely together because they are mutual results of some third factor. Also, it is possible to get some degree of covariation occurring merely by chance. In such cases it is dangerous to draw conclusions from the observed relationships, because such relationships are likely not to persist, and the conclusions are therefore likely to prove false outside the bounds of the observed data.

correlation, spurious—The accidental correlation having no causative basis and/or without expectation of continuity or renewal.

cyclical movement—The swing from prosperity through recession, depression, recovery, and back again to prosperity. This movement varies in time, length, and intensity.

data arrangement—Items in a table if arranged carefully facilitate reading of table, analysis and comparison of data and permit emphasizing of selected groups of data. Items may be arranged:

1. Alphabetically—According to the alphabetic order of the items. This is the most frequently used arrangement for general purpose tables.
2. Chronologically—According to time of occurrence in comparing subjects over a period of time. Dates should move from the earliest to the latest date from top of the stub to the bottom or in the boxhead from the left to the right of the table.
3. Geographically—According to location in the customary classification, for example: country, state, county, etc., or Maine, New Hampshire, Vermont, etc. This arrangement is generally confined to reference (general purpose) tables.
4. By magnitude—According to size. The largest number is placed at the top of the column and the others arranged in order of size. The row captions correspond to their values. When the row captions are numerical as class intervals in the frequency distribution, they are arranged by size. The smallest number is arranged at the top for the rows with the largest at the bottom; for the columns, the smallest is placed at the left to the largest at the right.

5. By customary classification—There is a customary arrangement for many types of data which do not follow any serial arrangement. For instance the classification men, women, and children, is rarely listed in the order women, children and men.

When there are a number of columns in a table they may be numbered or lettered for reference purposes. The heading of each column is known as the column caption. It should be concise. A miscellaneous column is placed at the right end of the table. The heading of a row is known as the row caption. The section of the table containing row headings is designated as the stub. Items in the stub should be grouped, as months grouped by quarters, to facilitate interpretation of the data. The totals of columns should be placed at the bottom of the columns, while row totals should be placed at the extreme right.

data characteristics, parameters and statistics—The population mean and population standard deviation are called population parameters. Data which are calculated from the sample results are called sample statistics. Thus, the sample average and the sample standard deviation are sample statistics. Which particular sample statistics are to be computed from the sample depends, of course, upon the nature of the particular problem.

data, continuous—Continuous measures are those which may conceivably be found at any point along a continuous linear scale. Examples are thermometers, speedometers, and analog computing devices. The units of measurement may be measured in as fine units as is desired or as related to the problem . . . and there is theoretically no point along the scale at which one may not continue to subdivide.

data, discrete—Discrete data are always expressed in whole numbers or integers and ordinarily represents counts of indivisible entities or units. Gaps always appear in linear-scaled discrete data.

data distribution—When data are grouped according to magnitude, the resulting series is called a frequency distribution; when grouped according to time of occurrence, it is called a time series; when grouped according to geographic location, it is called a spatial distribution.

data gathering, experimental—The method is to establish a scale model or controlled experiment; i.e., to simulate a "real market" situation or small-scale experiment. This technique leads to valuable information for design of large-scale marketing programs. The purpose is to "work out bugs" before expensive ventures are undertaken, or major applications are pursued. Thus, a market test can be established in a "controlled" market initially to keep all but one factor constant while varying all others individually for specialized study.

The advantages of this method are realism; actual on-site, environmental market test; ease of use of quantitative models; etc. The disadvantages are difficulty in selecting the control (test), and the possibility that pariculars in the test may "find out" and act abnormally. Control markets must be identical or near so in all significant socioeconomic factors. Competition must not discover the test and attempt to confuse or destroy it. Tests and expense may require long, careful planning and administration. Simulation "site studies" such as these are most popular for computer resolution of great quantities of recorded and mathematical data.

data gathering, observation method—Can be personal or mechanical, random or specific data collection by observing some action of the respondent. Examples include: selection of products by customers as regards preferences of packages, color, size, price, etc.

Advantages: Consumer is unaware of being observed and thus acts in usual fashion. Often experienced actors are used as are also tape recorders, cameras, counters. The results are most often clear accurate, unbiased. Interviewer bias, awkward questionnaires, etc. are eliminated by this procedure.

Disadvantages: Some bias may creep in the design despite planning and training of personnel, and irrelevant conclusions are still possible, Projection of implications and applications of results are somewhat limited. The method tells "what" happened and not necessarily "why." Therefore, motives, attitudes, beliefs, or opinions concerning actions observed are not available. There is also possibility of substantial expense of personnel, equipment, and the "wait" time for consumers to arrive and react.

data gathering, planning—Its purpose is to show integration of specific procedures for developing optimal solutions of problems or ranges of feasibilities using general and broad range scientific method framework.

Define, design, and delimit the problem (or model) with a clear, succinct statement of hypothesis, scope, and objective. Affirm positively the aspiration level desired (algoristic, stochastic, or heuristic) and confidence base required.

Determine exploration methodology; environment and special circumstances; types of variables and degree of uncertainty; values of constants and parameters; reliability and validity criteria; sources, measurements and control of errors.

data, graphic presentation—A graph, or chart, is a device for presenting statistical data in terms of visually interpreted magnitudes. When data are shown in this manner, essential facts and relationships emerge which might otherwise have been unrecognized. This property makes a graph or chart a useful tool for the presentation and analysis of statistical data and, hence, for administration and control. Charts which are most useful as tools of management are generally those that tell a complete story about some significant aspect of operations and are set up in such a manner that they aid in the formulation of management decisions. A chart should be designed to meet the particular needs for which it is constructed. In general, charts used in administration and management are direct and to the point.

data presentation, tabular — A statistical table is a systematic arrangement of data in columns and rows, according to clearly defined principles of classification. The title of the table should give the following information about the data: what, where, when, and in what units. The title should be comprehensive but concise.

The classifications on the left describing the rows of the table are called stubs; the classifications on the top describing the columns are called captions. It is essential to set up a sharp definition for each class in the table, so that there can be no doubt about where any item belongs. There must be no overlapping of classes.

The source of the data is always given, usually at the foot of the table, so that the reader may judge the reliability of the information or consult the original data himself.

A general-purpose table is one which records facts for future use, in a manner analogous to files. No special purpose is used as a basis for classification of the data. Most of the tables published by the Bureau of the Census are general-purpose tables.

data representation, pictorial—Such representation can be made graphic by bar charts, pie charts, statistical maps, etc. Usually the tabulations will contain: main titles, statistical units, captions (labels of rows), body of data, footnotes, and publisher's source of data.

data sources—Collection of data should be preceded by careful planning and precise formulation of purpose, scope, objectives, methodology, and knowledge of constraints of time, personnel and funds.

Internal data—Data selected from the firm itself, such as accounting, payroll, inventories, etc.

External data—Data from some local, state, and national sources or from trade publications, etc.

Primary data—Data which is published by the same source as that which collected it.

Secondary data—Data published by an individual or organization other than the one which collected it.

deduction — Derivations of theorems from general definitions, postulates, or common notions; Example: All men are mortal; Socrates is a man; therefore Socrates is mortal; i.e., an argument which goes from the general to the particular, and in which the conclusion is inherent in the premises.

dependent and independent variables of graphs—The variable known as the dependent variable is plotted on the Y (vertical) axis, while that known as the independent variable is plotted on the X (horizontal) axis.

If there are reasons to believe that there is a casual relationship between the variables, consider the one which causes variations in the other as the independent variable and place it on the X axis.

If one can see only that a relationship exists, and cannot say that the movements of one variable cause variations in the other, then it makes no difference which variable is considered dependent and which independent.

differentiation—A process of the calculus for determining rates of change and especially for finding maxima and minima as well as points of inflection.

digits, significant—In the representation of any number, the digits which are known to be correct are called the significant digits. Generally, the rules are: In addition, the last significant digit of the sum cannot lie any further to the right of the decimal point than the last significant digit in the least accurate of the measures added. In multiplication and division, the number of significant digits in the quotient or product cannot be greater than the number of significant digits in the least significant of the two measures being used.

direct relationship—In a direct relationship, increases in value of one variable are associated with an increase in the value of the other variable (and of course decreases in one are associated with decreases in the other).

discrete series—A discrete series is one in which the differences between successive observations are always finite in character, that is, there are no values falling between the observed values. For example, shoes are made in sizes 5, 5½, 6, 6½, etc. Since no shoes are made in intermediate sizes—e.g., between 5 and 5½—the differences between sizes are always finite.

dispersion, example—The degree of variation differs from curve to curve and is known as dispersion. Dispersion, then, is the variation in size occurring among the various items constituting the series.

dispersion, measures — Measures of dispersion concern the range, semi-interquartile range, mean deviation, and standard deviation which tell, with varying degrees of precision, the extent to which the items are scattered, and consequently how representative of the series the average is.

domain—The set associated with the variable is the domain. (Whenever one classifies or describes something by a characteristic or property, it is said that the thing belongs to the set of all things having that characteristic or property.) A set could be all real numbers, for example. The set on which a function is defined is the domain of the function.

element—A single item in a collection, set, universe, sample, matrix, or population.

estimate, unbiased—A statistic whose sampling distribution has a mean equal to the parameter which is being estimated by that statistic.

expected values—Generally, the summation of the products of all possible outcomes after each is multiplied by the probability that it will occur, and tables constructed to indicate these values.

extrapolate—In its technical sense, to extrapolate means to estimate a value which lies beyond the range of values on the basis of which an equation was originally obtained.

factorial—Let n be a positive integer. The notation n! is read as "n factorial," and represents the product of all positive integers from 1 to n, that is $n! = 1, 2, 3, \ldots n$. Thus 4 factorial or $4! = 4 \times 3 \times 2 \times 1 = 24$. Factorial notation is used most importantly in combination, permutation, and other counting techniques.

feedback loops—Systems are devised in which outputs are measured by various sensing or telemetering devices (analog computers) permitting such measurements to be fed back to affect control of inputs (numerical tapes) generated by digital computers.

forecasting—It is apparent the fitting of trends merely describes the movements of a series and that this type of work belongs to the domain of descriptive statistics. Having found the equation of a trend the obvious thing that suggests itself is to extrapolate or to estimate a value which lies beyond the range of values on the basis of which an equation was originally obtained. However its success depends on many factors.

The basic question always asked is whether the forces that have operated in the past will continue to operate in the future and to operate in the same way. It could be a starting point, a base from which to proceed to a final prediction.

Statistics in its current state of development comes somewhere between being of relative little value and providing a complete solution of the problem of economic forecasting. When used intelligently with appreciation of its possibilities and recognition of its limitations, statistics can provide the businessman with invaluable aids in reaching well informed and wise decisions.

frequency distribution—A table showing the number of occurrences of each value displayed in an ordered array or pattern.

frequency distribution analysis — Frequency distribution analysis enables one to describe the universal in terms of central tendency and dispersion, and to generalize about the universe and to make predictions about additional values drawn from the universe. Since it is possible for a frequency distribution to be either normal or skewed, care must be taken in making generalizations; the more skewed the distribution, the less reasonable the generalizations are likely to be.

In frequency-distribution analysis, the central tendency and dispersion of the universe are estimated from sample data, and predictions are then made as to the values of additional observations drawn from the universe. Correlation analysis enables one to improve upon these predictions where he has determined that a systematic relationship (or correlation) exists between two variables. The measure known as the coefficient of correlation (r) has been devised to express the improvement in estimates of one variable made as a result of knowledge of the associated variable, over estimates made on the basis of the mean of one variable alone.

All of the measures employed in correlation analysis (except r) are direct analogues of frequency distribution analysis measures and are used in similar ways. Thus, the line of regression (or line of average relationship) is analogous to the mean of a frequency series (in both cases the squared deviations are minimized and both are used as bases of predictions), and the standard error of estimates is directly analogous to the standard deviation.

frequency distribution, construction — The frequency distribution is an arrangement of numerical data according to size or magnitude. A frequency distribution is constructed in the following manner: Using the range of the data (the interval between the highest and the lowest figure) as a guide, the data are divided into a number of convenient sized groups. The groups are called class intervals.

The size of the class intervals is dependent upon the number of values to be included in the distribution. The range of the values (difference between the highest and the lowest values) is determined and is divided by the number of class intervals desired. The resulting size is rounded off.

frequency polygon—The frequency polygon is often based on the same distribution as its corresponding histogram. It may be considered as having been derived from the histogram by drawing straight lines joining the midpoints of the upper bases of adjacent rectangles; i.e., columns. The polygon is closed at each end by drawing a line to the base line from the midpoint of the top of each of the end columns to the midpoint (base line) of the next outlying interval.

frequency, relative — This is the ratio of numbers of observations in a class (subset) to the total number of observations or elements constituting a population; i.e., universe or set.

functions—If two variables x and y are so related that, whenever a value is assigned to x, one or more corresponding values of y are determined, then y is called a function of x. If just one value of y corresponds to each value of x, y is a single-valued function of x. If y is a function of x, x is referred to as the independent variable, y the dependent variable. Independent variables are usually plotted on the horizontal axis.

To graph a function f (x) in an xy plane, let y = f (x) and graph. To graph the polynominal (ax + b) —a linear function of x— let y = ax + b. A polynominal of the second degree in x is a function of the form: $ax^2 + bx + c$ where a, b, c are constants.

functions and variables — Mathematical analysis, in short, is a study of the relationships between variable numbers. The term "function" describes and symbolizes this relationship between variables. For example, demand for a commodity is connected in some way with the market price for that commodity—thus, demand is a "function" of price. The idea of a function involves the concept of relation between values of two variables and the degree of dependence of one variable on another.

In an implicit function a mutual relationship exists between two variables, and either variable determines the other. In an explicit function, if the values of say, y, depend in some definite way upon the value which is allotted arbitrarily to x, it is the value of x which determines the value y—so, y is the explicit function of x. If the relation between x and y is regarded as mutual, then the term "implicit function" is appropriate; the variables are on equal footing. If the relationship is regarded from a definite angle as "y depending on x" then we use the term explicit function.

A function such that one and only one value of y corresponds to each given value of x is said to define y as a "single-function value" of x. A function for which this is not true defines y as a multivalued f (x).

Gantt chart—A chart of activity against time; such charts have historically been used to schedule or reserve resources for specific activities. Critical-path method (CPM) and project evaluation and review techniques (PERT) are devices which have offered substantial improvement in scheduling and allocations.

Gaussian curve (random-error concept)—A "random error of sampling" is a variation due to chance alone. If the sample is truly random, small errors will be more numerous than large errors and positive errors will be as likely as negative errors, thus giving rise to a symmetrical, bell-shaped "normal curve of error." This concept was first investigated by the German mathematician, Karl F. Gauss, and the curve is often called the Gaussian curve.

geometric mean—The geometric mean is the nth root of a product of n numbers.

$$G.M. = \sqrt[n]{X_1 \cdot X_2 \cdot \ldots X_n}$$

Where a large number of values are involved, it is more convenient to find the logarithms of the numbers, divide the sum of the logarithms by the number of items, and look up the antilogarithms of the quotient.

gradient—The instantaneous direction of a curve at any point is the direction in which the curve tends to rise or fall. This is indicated by the tangent. This gradient varies as the tangent varies from point to point on the curve. The mathematical description or graphic representation shows that it always is given as the limiting value of the gradient of any chord PQ, as Q approaches P.

harmonic mean—The harmonic mean of a series of values is the reciprocal of the arithmetic mean of the reciprocals of the values.
Formula:

$$\frac{1}{H_m} = \frac{\frac{1}{X_1} + \frac{1}{X_2} + \frac{1}{X_3} \cdots\cdots\cdots\cdots + \frac{1}{X_n}}{N}$$

The harmonic mean is used in averaging rates.

heuristic—Solutions are considered with the objective as being satisfactory relative to the constraints of time, funds, personnel available and the stated "confined use" of the solution as advice of a "better" though not especially the best alternative to present usage; heuristic solutions serve to "find out"; a solution which could contribute to the reduction of time and funds necessary for an algoristic solution (i.e., as closed linear-programming models) which require highly structured models, exhaustive computation if complex. Heuristic models provide executive-accepted "better for now and for the purpose" resolutions of problems which are more flexible to model, permit faster testing and evaluation, and fit any type of problem which contains elements which can be measured and associated.

histogram—The construction represents the measurements or observations constituting a set of data on a horizontal scale and the class frequencies on a vertical scale. The graph of the distribution is then constructed by drawing rectangles, the bases of which are determined by the corresponding class frequencies.

hypothesis—Question being asked or tested; the "crux" of the research project; an analysis or assessment—principally the preconceived expectation of the outcome, but it must not carry bias into the analysis. Synonymns—possible solutions, "hunch," "flash of light," gestalt.

hypothesis, null—Testing the validity of a hypothesis by statistical means usually involves setting up the null hypothesis that two populations are identical in some respect; i.e., to determine whether or not there is any difference in variability between performance of two different products and whether the difference is due to chance or to reality.

hypothesis, statistical—In statistical analysis, a hypothesis usually takes the form of some assumption about the frequency distribution of observations whose numerical values depend upon chance.

identity—An equation is quite simply a statement that two expressions are equal. When an equality is true at all times and for all values of the symbol for which the numbers are defined, it is an identity. The symbol $\equiv$ means, "is identically equal to" and is generally used to emphasize this characteristic of relationship.

increment—An added part or portion as differentiated from decrement representing a decreasing portion. Mathematically an increment is the average rate of change of a variable, y, with respect to a variable, x, within a given interval or $\Delta y/\Delta x$ where delta (Δ) represents a small change.

independent events—Two events are said to be independent if the occurrence of either in no way affects the occurrence of the other.

index number—In order to measure the changes in the large number of constantly varying items in the data, it is necessary to resort to some relative averaging device that will serve as a yardstick of comparative measurement. The index number is such a device. The index number measures fluctuations during intervals of time, group differences of geographical position or degree, etc.

index number, price relatives—A method which avoids the price inequalities of absolute involves the conversion of the price figures into relatives. A price relative is a statement of the price of a commodity as a percent of its price in the base period. Expressed in formula form:

$$\frac{P_n}{P_o}$$

where,

P_n = price in the given period,
P_o = price in the base period.

The relative for each commodity in the base period is 100%.

index numbers, base period—In the selection of the base period the following should be considered:

1. The base period should not be too far in the past; this in order that a comparison of the price level as relative to the base period will be of definite present or comparative value.
2. Comparison is generally made to a "normal" period; therefore the base period should not be extreme.

For comparative purposes the base of an index number series is sometimes shifted from one period to another. The shift may be accomplished by dividing each number in the series by the index number indicated for the period to be used as the new base year, the result is then multiplied by 100.

index numbers, quantity—Index-number technique can be applied to measurement of changes in quantity groups as well as price changes. Index numbers of this type are used to measure changes in business activity, industrial production, commodity stocks, etc.

The methods of construction are the same for quantity index numbers as for price index numbers. The simplest form is the simple aggregate type.

$$\frac{\Sigma q_n}{\Sigma q_o}$$

where,

q_n is the sum of the quantities in any given period,
q_o is the sum of the quantities in the base period.

Since this form of index involves the sums of series, the various quantities must all be in the same units (tons, bushels, etc.) to make the summation possible.

When the units are different for the various items in the series and an unweighted index number is desired, the average of relatives may be used. If the arithmetic mean is used as the average, the formula is

$$\frac{\Sigma\left(\frac{q_n}{q_o}\right)}{N}$$

It is generally desirable, however, to weight the index numbers in order to arbitrarily assign various degrees of importance to the several items composing the index number. Either the price of the commodity or some arbitrary weight may be used for this purpose.

The weighted aggregate form for use in measuring quantity changes is:

$$\frac{\Sigma(q_n p_o)}{\Sigma(q_o p_o)} \text{ with base year weights,}$$

or

$$\frac{\Sigma(q_n p_n)}{\Sigma(q_o p_n)} \text{ with given year's weights.}$$

Unless the units are the same for all items, only the prices can be used as weights and not arbitrary weights since if the latter are used no summation will be possible.

The weighted average of relatives may be used where the units are different and it is desired to use arbitrary weights

$$\frac{\Sigma\left(\frac{q_n}{q_o}\times wt\right)}{\Sigma(wt)}$$

where,

wt = weight

The "ideal index" can also be converted to quantity form

$$\sqrt{\frac{\Sigma(q_n p_o)}{\Sigma(q_o p_o)}\times\frac{\Sigma(q_n p_n)}{\Sigma(q_o p_n)}}$$

index numbers, rules and tests—Tests of a good index number:

1. The fundamental question is: Does the index number really measure what it is said to measure? If the measurement departs from that called for by the purpose of the index, then the significance of that departure must be evaluated.
2. Formal tests of logical and mathematical consistency such as the time-reversal and factor-reversal tests may be applied, but they are not so useful as the test of critical judgment.

Usefulness of index numbers:

1. Index numbers are useful in business and economic analysis. It is usually not sufficient to study one or two in isolation; rather, it is necessary to study and compare a large number of index numbers.
2. Index numbers are valid if there is a genuine central tendency in the movement of the series making up the index. Some dispersion is always present, and it is this fact that makes necessary the use of an average over time.

Rules for constructing index numbers:

1. The purpose of the index must be clearly defined.
2. Accurate basic data must be obtained.
3. Weights should be relevant to the purpose of the index. They are often difficult to collect, and frequently reliance must be placed on census, which are taken only at intervals.
4. The base should not be too far in the past and should be one generally considered "normal" for the particular series in question. The base is the point or time which determines the weights in reality. If the weights refer to some other period of time, then the year for which the index number equals 100 is really only the origin, or point of reference, not the true base.

index numbers, weighted average of relatives—An index number may be constructed by securing a weighted average of the relative prices for the period under consideration. Quantities of production, however, can no longer be used as weights since each quantity is expressed in different units (tons, pounds, ounces, bushels, etc.). The column of figures resulting from the multiplication of the price relatives by these weights would be expressed in different units and could not be totaled. It becomes necessary to use weights expressed in common units. The most usual common unit is the dollar. The money value rather than the quality of production may then be used as weights.

With base period weights and using a weighted arithmetic mean the formula will be:

$$\frac{\Sigma\left[\frac{p_n}{p_o}\times(p_o q_o)\right]}{\Sigma(p_o q_o)}$$

for $p_o q_o$ equals value of production in the base period (the price times the quantity). Through cancellation the formula reduces to:

$$\frac{\Sigma(p^n q^o)}{\Sigma(p_o q_o)}$$

or the same as the weighted aggregate using base year weights. If given year weights are used, a new formula is evolved:

$$\frac{\Sigma\left[\frac{p_n}{p_o}\times(p_n q_n)\right]}{\Sigma(p_n q_n)}$$

index numbers, weighting—It is often desirable to assign a varying degree of importance to the items composing the index numbers. If this action is not taken, each commodity will be given a weight or importance depending upon the size of the price, or upon some other chance factor, rather than a proportionate weight depending upon its importance.

An objection to the unweighted aggregate of actual prices method of constructing an index number may be eliminated by introducing a deliberate system of weights. To measure the weight or importance of the items composing a price index the quantity of each commodity produced may be used.

index number types—There are lists showing over 150 different formulae for the construction of index numbers. These formulae, however, are largely variations of a limited number of main types.

Some of the major groups of methods of constructing index numbers may be classified as:

1. The unweighted (simple) method:
   a. The aggregate of actual prices.
   b. The average of relative prices.
2. The weighted method:
   a. The weighted aggregate of actual prices.
   b. The weighted average of relative prices.

indifference curves—Indifference curves are graphs, each line of which attempts to show all the combinations of alternatives which are equally desirable, for example, isoquants.

inequality—An inequality is an algebraic expression, indicating that one quantity is greater or less than another. The sign of an inequality is >. It is placed with the opening of the angle toward the greater quantity. Thus, $a > b$ is read, a is greater than b, $a < b$ is read, a is less than b. Any negative quantity is regarded as less than 0, and the one having the greatest number of units is considered the least. Thus, $-2 > -3$; $0 > -2$.

The quantities on each side of the sign of inequality are called members. When the first members of two inequalities are each greater or each less than the corresponding second members, the inequalities are said to subsist in the same sense. When the first member is greater in one equality and less in another, the inequalities are said to subsist in a contrary sense. Thus, $a > b$ and $c > d$ subsist in the same sense, and $x > y$ and $v < z$ subsist in a contrary sense.

integer—An integer is a whole number and it represents something which cannot logically be divided; i.e., a car, a man, or the building—thus, discrete objects or numbers.

integral, definite—An integral is the limiting value of a certain summation expression which is frequent in mathematics, and corresponds diagrammatically to an area enclosed by a plane curve or curves. Another explanation of an integral is the result of reversing the process of differentiation. The derivative of a function of one variable is itself a function of the same variable. The inverse problem is to obtain, from a given function, a second function which has the first as its derivative. This second function is the "indefinite" integral while the first concept is the definite integral; i.e., the sum-area concept.

intercept—The intersection of a line and an axis, such as the y intercept.

intersubjective—Specification of the aspiration to be performed with such clarity and precision in order to bring out the concept within the range of one's experience; i.e., meaning competent observers can carry out provisions of the model with approximately the same results; clarity of thought and process communication.

interval—If a variable, x, can take as its value all real numbers lying between two given numbers, a and b, then its range is called the interval (a,b). This is most often written $a < x < b$ or $a \leq x \leq b$ according to whether the values a and b themselves are excluded or included. Thus, the expressions "near to" or "neighborhood of" can be more precisely stated by using the concept of an interval.

inverse relationship—An inverse relationship is one in which increases in the value of one variable are associated with decreases in the value of the other variable.

iteration—A repetitive or recursive pattern of calculation in which each cycle uses a result from the preceding cycle to supply data to the following, as in a linear-programming problem using the simplex method.

joint probability—The probability that both A and B will occur. If A and B are independent, neither influencing the other, joint probability is the product of their separate probabilities.

kurtosis—The kurtosis of a frequency distribution is its "peakness." If the curve has a higher degree of kurtosis than the normal curve ($\beta > 3$) the curve may be said to be leptokurtic. If β is less than 3, the curve is more flat-topped than the normal curve and is said to be platykurtic.

The measure of kurtosis is sometimes given as:

$$\beta_2 - 3$$

Where the result is zero, the curve is mesokurtic. Where the result is a positive value, the curve is leptokurtic. Where the result is a negative value, the curve is platykurtic.

law—A written or positive rule; a statement of a relation or sequence of phenomena invariable under the same conditions. If tested evidence toward confirmation of a hypothesis or theory has accumulated such that primary and widespread acceptance is derived and tests are no longer considered necessary or feasible, the principle becomes a law. (It should be noted that general laws become simple hypotheses when they are developed in a laboratory but await testing in the real world.)

laws, associative, commutative, and distributive—

Associative law — The sum of three or more terms, or the product of three or more factors is the same in whatever manner they are grouped:

$$a + (b + c) = (a + b) + c = a + b + c$$
$$a(bc) = (ab)c = abc$$

Commutative law—The result of addition or multiplication is the same in whatever order the terms are added or multiplied.

$$a + b = b + a, \text{ and } ab = ba$$

Distributive law—The product of an expression of two or more terms by a single factor is equal to the sum of the products of each term of the expression by the single factor.

$$(a + b - c)d = ad + bd - cd$$

least square—This concerns curve fitting by minimizing the total of the squares of the differences between observed values and computed values, as in regression or time series analyses.

least squares method — A straight line or curve may be fitted to the data by the least squares method. The normal equations are derived by multiplying the basic equation (e.g., $Y = a + bX$) through by the coefficient of the first unknown and summing, then multiplying through by the coefficient of the second unknown and summing. These normal equations may then be solved for the unknown constants. The regression equation in its final form should be accompanied by a statement of the origin and the units in which the variables are measured.

levels of confidence—To indicate in quantitative terms what degree of confidence may be placed in certain inferences drawn from the facts obtained from a random sample.

linear programming (LP) — The planning of activities, such as the allocation of men, materials, or machines, is called programming. Since resources may be limited or incapable of being utilized completely, an objective would be to determine the most efficient method of allocating these resources to activities so that a measure of performance is optimized. Thus LP is a math technique for use where a number of variables are involved and many courses of action are possible if the problem can be expressed in linear terms.

line of least squares—To check association or relationship, data are collected or experiments are conducted. Ordered pairs of such data are graphed as a "scatter diagram" on rectangular coordinate bases. As points tend to cluster in linear fashion (i.e., as one variable increases one unit, the other variable increases or decreases in fixed amounts), a line might then be fitted to generally separate the scattered points to have one half (approximately) lie above and below such a line. Because some criterion is required to measure the "goodness of fit" of this line, the deviations of the points from this line (above and below) are squared and summed. The smaller this quantity is, the better is the fit of the line, and this is the deviation of the "line of least squares." It is also called a "regression line" for Y on X; i.e., the minimum sum of the squared deviations in the Y (vertical) direction, for example.

logarithm—A logarithm is an exponent. Common logarithms are exponents of 10. Natural logarithms are exponents of e (= 2.7183). Thus, 10^2 is equivalent to "2", which is the logarithm of 100 to the base 10 or log 100 = 2. Much calculating is done with common logs because of the convenience of the base 10:

$10^0 = 1$	$10^{-1} = .1$
$10^1 = 10$	$10^{-2} = .01$ (etc.)
$10^2 = 100$ (etc.)	

To multiply numbers, their logarithms (from tables) are added; to divide numbers, their logarithms are subtracted; to extract roots, a logarithm is divided by the root, for example, to take the cube root, the logarithm is divided by 3.

mathematical expectation—If the probability of winning an amount A is P(A), our mathematical expectation is $A \cdot P(A)$, namely, the product of the amount we stand to receive and the probability of obtaining it.

median — The median is the value of the middle item when the items are arranged according to size. If there is an even number of items, the midpoint is taken as the arithmetic mean of the two central items. The median is an average of position while the arithmetic mean is a calculated average. The median is computed from ungrouped data as follows:

1. Arrange the items according to magnitude (this is called an array).
2. Record the size of the middle value. If there is an even number of items in the array there will be two central values; therefore, the arithmetic mean of these two values is taken as the median.

median characteristics — The value of the median is not affected by the magnitude of extremes, since the median is a positional average. The median can be calculated from open-end distributions, in which the specific values of the outlying items are not known. The sum (disregarding sign) of the absolute deviations from it is a minimum. It is not well adapted to further algebraic calculations.

minimax—In game theory and other payoff tabular decisions, one of the methods of evaluating acts under uncertainty is to follow the principle of looking only at the worst possible consequence of each act and then to choose the act for which the worst consequence is the least desirable of the worst. This process thus minimizes the maximum loss or damage. This is contrasted to the maximum, a process in which one conservatively chooses the strategy to maximize or select the largest of the minimum gains. The saddle point is thus the maximum of the row minima (maximin) and the minimum of the column (minimax) when both occur at the same point in the payoff table.

mode—The mode is the most frequent or most common value, provided that a sufficiently large number of items is available to give a smooth distribution. The value of the mode will correspond to the value of the maximum point (ordinate) of a frequency distribution if it is an "ideal" or smooth distribution. It is not possible to make an exact mathematical determination of the mode. A number of methods may be used, however, to secure reasonably accurate approximations.

mode characteristics—The mode is the most typical value of the series, in the sense of being the item occurring most frequently. It is not affected by extreme deviations. The approximate mode is easy to locate, but the determination of the true mode requires extended calculation. The mode is not significant unless the distribution exhibits a distinct central tendency.

model building—A problem is encountered in a "real world" setting, i.e., an environment. It must be translated in quantative terms; it must be abstracted from its environment, simplified, stripped of its complexities. It must be expressed in relationships—variables, constants, parameters, symbolically, as $Y = mx + b$. Verbal vagueness and ambiguity are replaced with specific and precise definition of the situation. Next, forms of several functional relationships are adapted which link the variables and parameters. Finally, establish a criterion by which a decision may be judged, that is, an explicit and unique objective function or range. Solve the model by selected technique to find the value of the decision variables which optimize the objective. Evaluate and test.

mode of a frequency distribution—The mode of a frequency distribution is that value along the horizontal scale at which the height of the curve is greatest. Since the values of the individual items are lost in the frequency distribution itself, it is necessary to approximate the mode.

Monte Carlo—This is a specialized use of simulated data through the use of random numbers and their transformation to develop an imitation (simulation) of the significant aspects of the circumstances of various situations, such as waiting line (queue) problems.

moving average, ratio—The ratio-to-moving average substitutes monthly the average of the 12 months, or 4 quarters, surrounding the specific month or quarter being considered. Each of the original figures is then expressed as a percent of a different figure—the average for the months or quarters by which it is immediately preceded and followed. Such a procedure thus requires a succession of averages.

multiple correlation—The fluctuations in a given series are seldom dependent upon a single factor or cause. The measurement of the association between such a series and several of the variables causing these fluctuations or associated with the dependent variable is known as multiple correlation. Multiple correlation consists of the measurement of the relationship or association between a dependent variable and two or more independent variables. The procedure is similar to that for simple correlation with the exception that other variables are added to the regression equation. For two independent variables the regression equation, if linear, is of the type:

$$X_1 = a + b_{12.3}X_2 + b_{13.2}X_3$$

in the equation, X_1 is the dependent or estimated variable and X_2 and X_3 are the independent variables.

mutually exclusive—Two events are said to be mutually exclusive if the occurrence of either precludes the occurrence of the other.

normal curve—The normal curve is a symmetrical bell-shaped frequency curve which exhibits a certain unique set of relationships between the ordinate (or value on the Y axis) at the mean of the distribution and the ordinates at various sigma distances from the mean.

normal curve of error—It is just one of the infinite number of frequency curves which could be drawn. It is symmetrical about a central axis, at which lie the mean, the median, and the mode. The area under it can be analyzed completely in terms of the arithmetic mean and the standard deviation. As the values grow extremely large and extremely small, the normal curve constantly approaches, but never meets the horizontal axis. Technically speaking, it is asymptotic to the x-axis.

There are certain mathematical conditions (expressible as mathematical equations), which, if fulfilled, will result in actual distributions conforming to the normal curve.

normal distribution, characteristics — The normal distribution is symmetrical about the mean, which is at the maximum ordinate which is also where $X = 0$; the mean, median and mode of the normal distribution are identical; the range is unlimited, infinite in both directions. As X departs farther away from the mean, Y approaches but never touches the X axis; however, Y gets very close to the X axis within a very short distance, i.e., $X \pm 3$ (σ). Standard deviations include 99.73% of the cases under the normal curve.

null hypothesis—In testing the significance of the difference between two sample means, we test the null hypothesis, which is the hypothesis that there is no real difference between the true means of the two populations, and that the observed difference between the sample means occurred by chance.

The null hypothesis is identical with the hypothesis that the mean of the sampling distribution of the differences between means is zero.

objective function — Linear-program problems, for example, must have a mathematical statement of goals, usually the maximization of profits, efficiency, resources or the minimization of costs, etc. The model seeks for its solution the decision rule which, when implemented, will achieve the goal thus expressed as the objective function.

objectives, plural — No single goal, but a combination of desires often of different weights; i.e., maximized profits but not at expense of quality or competitive retaliation, new entry; nonoperational management objectives as: "biggest in the industry" percentage gain in market share total sales; steady nonabrupt gain for stockholder satisfaction, ("don't rock the boat" strategies); size, prestige—cannot be measured with exactness (as cost minimization), operations research men must know these NEW, often hidden constraints, or REAL GOALS or they might find optimum but "circular" solutions.

objectivity — Free from personal feelings or bias; deals with things external to the mind rather than thoughts, feelings; independence of personal judgment of one particular person; objectivity distinguishes science from intuition in model building.

ogive—This is synonymous with the frequency curve or the "less than" curve and is a reference to the shape of the curve. It is constructed much like the polygon except the frequency is plotted for each interval rather than just the frequency within the interval. The "less than curve" is useful because it facilitates the making of estimates within various class limits.

operational concepts—Equations in models first defined in relation to variables which are concerned with the firm's specific data, scheme, or operations; i.e., the expressions (math) must relate the symbols and values (concepts) to experience in an objective fashion and intersubjectively to the operations to be performed in order to bring the concepts within the range of one's experience; math relationships must specify or at least imply the way or method of real world methodology.

operations research (OR) — Modern management uses a large group of mathematical and statistical techniques to solve its problems in a scientific, well-defined, objective manner. Thus OR is often defined as a systematic application of scientific method to the organization, analysis, and ordered solution of problems and procedures of complex business systems, organizations, and activities. The techniques are many and varied and include linear programming, input/output, econometrics, game theory, simulation, heuristics, statistical-decision theory, queueing theory, critical path method (CPM), project evaluation and review technique (PERT), executive games, and many others. They thus concern models, patterns, conceptions, laws, or theories or matrices which are useful for gaining new insight into observed facts, extrapolations, or experimentation pertaining to applications of particular phenomena of the inexact or "behavioristic" social sciences which seek truth as goals but also "action" of optimal decision.

opportunity cost—The sacrifice of some resources, such as time or quality of product, to achieve a measure of some other output or subgoal, such as total revenue.

ordinate—Vertical or Y distance on a graph.

parameter—1. As regards statistics, a parameter is considered to be a numerical property of a distribution of a population or a universe. A statistic, in contrast, is considered to be a numerical property of a sample. 2. In order to distinguish between descriptions of populations and samples, many statisticians use different symbols, and they refer to the first as parameters and to the second as statistics. Thus the mean, μ, is a parameter, a true characteristic of a population and the mean, x, is a statistic, a numerical representation of a sample; σ is the standard deviation of a population, thus it is a parameter; s is the standard deviation of a sample distribution, thus it is a statistic.

parametric constants—An example of an explicit quadratic function is $y = ax^2 + bx + c$. Abc are any definite fixed numbers (constants); here x and y cease to be of importance and the whole function is made to vary by changing a, b and c. These numbers are fixed within one function of the quadratic type, but they are variable from one quadratic function to another. Thus, a, b and c lead double lives and are called "variable constants."

Convention describes these "double use" constants as parametric constants. When attention is directed to the relation between the variables of the function, the symbols denote fixed numbers and are termed constants.

When the important thing is the variation of the function as a whole—the variables of the function fading out of the picture—the symbols are parameters. For example, prices are parametric constants; i.e., constant in the examination of the decision of a single firm, but they are parameters when we combine the separate firms to represent a decision of a whole group of firms. The letters y, z are usually reserved for variables. When parametric constants are regarded primarily as constants, the letters a, b, c or alpha, beta, gamma are conventionally used. When the parametric property is the more important, it is often useful to take k, l, m, n, p, q, and r to denote parameters. The letters f, g and h are used to denote functions. Functions refer to operations performed on variables. It is thus necessary to denote a function not only with its operational or functional letter, but also with an indication of the variable to which the operation applies; i.e., f(x) which is read, "function of x."

payoff table — 1. Tabular values as constructed to show the value of each combination or plan (strategy) and event resulting from, for example, a game-theory matrix of opportunities as weighted by empirical data . . . i.e., the calculated results of all or many courses of action displayed as an array. 2. In a business-decision problem a choice must be made among several possible acts. The selected act will ultimately lead to some definite profit or loss, the amount of which will be unknown but will be determined by some event which cannot be predicted with certainty. A table can thus be composed which will lay out all the possible acts and all their possible consequences in a systematic array. An "act" is usually a decision, and an "event" is a sale, purchase, or action by a customer or competitor. When such a table with columns corresponding to particular acts and rows corresponding to particular events is filled in with the numerical consequences of these variables, it is called a payoff table.

permutations—The number of possible sequences of n items taken c at a time:

$$P\left(\frac{n}{c}\right) = \frac{n!}{(n-c)!}$$

Poisson probability distributions—A specific binomial probability distribution which has been found applicable in many circumstances is the Poisson probability distribution. This type of probability distribution often applies when there is a large number of events which are independent and for each of which there is only a small probability that a certain outcome will occur.

The Poisson probability distribution has been applied in the analysis of the number of automobiles passing a given corner per minute during a certain time of the day, the number of telephone calls received at a certain switchboard per minute during a given time of the day, and the number of machines out of a large number of machines which break down during any one day.

The probability that exactly X number of occurrences will happen is, according to the Poisson probability distribution:

$$P(X) = \frac{\mu^x e^{-\mu}}{(X)\ (X-1)\ (X-2)\ \ldots\ (1)}$$

where μ is the mean number of occurrences and e, the base of natural logarithms, is equal to 2.71828. Note the use of the Greek letter for the average because it refers to "true" or population mean. The Poisson distribution is a one-parameter distribution and that parameter is μ. When the value of μ is known, it is possible to compute P(x) for any positive integer X. Tables of μ range from 0.001 to 100.

population—The total collection of all observations, measures, and events which have a common, definable characteristic. Examples in populations include the annual cash incomes of American farmers.

postulate—To assume without specific proof; to accept a proposition without immediate empirical evidence; to accept as evident from general life experience or general acceptance. For example, to postulate by an analogy by projection, by extrapolation; to petition that such knowledge has already been developed.

prediction—If the relationship between two variables is known, the relationship can be employed to predict one variable from another. The accuracy of the prediction is directly dependent on the strength of the relationship between the variables. The errors of prediction over a total group are minimized when a regression equation is employed.

probability—This can generally be described as the long-range or historical record of experience as measured and scaled for order and inspection. It can be more specifically stated as a ratio of elements in a class (a subset) to a total of a population or random sample drawn from a population—which ratio is a result of experience and calculation.

probability, conditional — The probability that event A will occur, given that event B has already occurred.

probability distributions—These are tables that show the relative frequencies of each subset into which the total population is divided or segmented. Such tables can be read to show the probability of occurrence of each value so listed.

probability laws—When an event can result in various numbers of n ways, and each in a single trial is considered equally likely or probable, one might consider s to be successes and all others to be failures, or n − s. The probability, p, that one particular trial will result in a success is stated: p = s/n. Conversely, the probability, q, that any one particular trial will result in failure is stated: q = (n − s) /n. Since p is the probability of success in one trial of an event, the pk is the probable number of successes in k trials. The expectation is the product of the success times the probability of its occurrence; i.e., if a success is $20, then p times $20 is the expectation.

probability, posterior—The revised estimate of probability incorporating additional information, usually developed using the Bayes' equation.

probability, prior—The initial, usually subjective, probability. If additional information becomes available in batches, the posterior probability after each batch is incorporated in the estimate, and it becomes the prior probability before the next batch is incorporated.

probable error—The standard deviation of a distribution of means or any other statistical measure computed from samples is termed the standard error of the mean (σx) or the standard error of any other statistical measure.

The error which will not be exceeded by 50% of the cases is known as the probable error. It is equal to .6745 times the standard error. Although widely used, the probable error is a comparatively small value. It can be interpreted as meaning that if another sample were drawn of the same number of items the chances are even that a discrepancy between the sample and true mean larger than the probable error would not exist.

It is obvious that the greater the number of cases included in the sample the smaller the error to be expected. Therefore the standard deviation (error) of the theoretical distribution of means (or other measure) computed from samples will be smaller. In turn, the standard error will vary inversely with the number of cases included in the sample.

proportion, sampling distribution—The sampling distribution of a proportion is a distribution of the proportions obtained from a very large number of random samples, all of which are the same size and are selected from the same population. The form of this distribution will closely approximate the normal distribution except when the true proportion in the population differs considerably from .50—the greater the departure from this value, the larger the samples must be before normality is assured. The measure of variability is the standard error of a proportion.

quadrants—In trigonometry, each quadrant is one-quarter of a circle. In the coordinate graph system a vertical line, the ordinate, bisects a horizontal line, the abscissa, at a point called the origin, 0. The plane is thus divided into four sections or quadrants. Coordinate numbers such as 4, 3 locate a point on the plane represented on graph paper. The first number is the distance P from 0 parallel to the abscissa or x axis, while the second is the distance of P from 0 parallel to the ordinate, i.e., the height of P above the abscissa. The point 4, 3 would thus be 4 spaces or points to the right of the ordinate and three spaces above the abscissa because both are positive. If the numbers were negative, they would locate a point 4 spaces to the left of the ordinate and 3 spaces below the abscissa. Thus in the N.E. quadrant, both numbers are positive, in the N.W., the first number is negative and the second positive, in the S.W. quadrant, both numbers are negative, and in the S.E. quadrant, the first number is positive and the second negative. Thus each point of the plane is represented by a definite pair of numbers and each pair of numbers by a definite point on the plane.

quantitative analysis techniques—Generally, these are basic techniques that attempt to simulate a business problem with a normative type of model, and try to use actual or simulated data to see if the model does what it is supposed to do. Types of models include: qualitative, problem-solving, stochastic, optimal value, games, etc.

quartiles, deciles, percentiles—Just as the median divides the distribution into two parts, the quartiles divide the distribution into four parts, the deciles divide the distribution into ten parts, and the percentiles divide the distribution into one hundred parts. These averages of position make possible a more minute analysis of the distribution.

Since the quartile divides the distribution in four parts, there are three quartiles. The second quartile will divide the distribution in half and therefore will be the same as the median. The first (lower) quartile (Q_1) marks off the first one fourth, the third (upper) quartile (Q_3) marks off the point separating the third from the last quarter.

The percentile points divide the distribution into 100 parts each containing 1 percent of the cases.

random numbers—A sequence of listing of digits in which each digit has an equal opportunity or probability of occurring in each cell or position, and which is developed to maintain complete independence of the digits and their positions as they appear elsewhere in the sequence or list.

random-number table—A table of random numbers is a set of numbers such that each of the digits from 0 to N has the same chance of appearing in any position in the table.

random sample—A sample is random if every item in the population has an equal chance of being included in the sample. This definition implies that the selection of the sample should be left to chance.

range—The range, the simplest of the measures of dispersion is the difference between the minimum and maximum items in the series. It is sometimes given in the form of a statement of the minimum and maximum values themselves. The difference between these two values gives the degree of variation occurring in the series, but quite frequently the result is misleading.

range and semi-interquartile range—The range and the semi-interquartile range are both "positional" measures of dispersion since, like the median, they depend on the positions of the values in a group.

The range equals the difference between the largest item and the smallest item in a group. It has the advantage of being easy to compute and easy to understand. Its disadvantage lies in the fact that it depends on only two values. The dispersion of the values between these two could be changed without the range, and, conversely, the range could be changed by altering either the smallest value or the largest value without significantly changing the dispersion.

The semi-interquartile range is the average absolute distance (on the horizontal scale) between the median and the quartiles on either side of it. In symbols, where $Q =$ the semi-interquartile range, and Q_1 and $Q_3 =$ the first and third quartiles respectively,

$$Q = \frac{(Q_3 - Md) + (Md - Q_1)}{2}$$

$$= \frac{Q_3 - Md + Md - Q_1}{2}$$

$$= \frac{Q_3 - Q_1}{2}$$

ratio—The ratio of a to b is defined as the fraction $\frac{a}{b}$, or as the quotient which is the result of performing the division of this fraction. If a and b are both positive numbers, then the limiting values of the ratio are zero and infinity, since we can never derive a negative value from the process of division unless one of the numbers has a negative sign.

real income, real wages (deflation)—If wages rise faster than prices, it is possible to say, with some reservations, that real income has increased where the physical goods and services at the disposal of the recipient represent real income; i.e., the ability to buy more of these at the current, (expanded) wage rates. The process for adjusting value series, such as income, wages, salaries, etc. for price changes is known as deflation and gives rise to such phrases as "current dollars" "1966 dollars," etc. when adjusted for cost of living indices.

regression—This is the rate at which an output changes in relation to the changes in inputs; more specifically, it represents the slope of a line which graphs the comparable values of inputs (independent variables) and the output (dependent variables).

regression and correlation, differences—Generally the purpose determines the choice or use. If a prediction equation is desired, regression will be used; if a degree of association is sought, correlation might be the choice. Often regression will be used if one variable is clearly dependent upon another, or one is measured subsequent to the other. Correlation might be selected if the bivariate population has a joint probability distribution, neither being subsequent to or as being a consequence of the other. In a regression model, Y is assumed to be a random variable, while X's are fixed quantities, whereas in correlation, both are random variables and are based on joint probability distributions of X on Y. This is to say that correlation seeks to discover and measure the degree of mutual variation in X and Y and does not imply a functional relationship; thus, correlation alone does not relate the prediction of Y on bases of X. The main purpose of regression analysis is to establish the functional relationship between the dependent and independent variable so that the former can be predicted by the latter. The greater the degree of covariation between the two variables, the more accurate the regression line is as a prediction device. Thus, correlation and regression are developed from different assumptions and furnish different types of information.

regression coefficient—In the equation $Y = a + bX$, b is known as the regression coefficient. Since it tells how Y varies in response to a change in X, it is really the "link" between the two variables. The sign of b tells us whether the relationship is positive or negative, that is, whether a positive change in X is associated with a positive or with a negative change in Y. The b also shows the average number of units of increase (or decrease) in the dependent variable which occurs with each increase of a given amount in the independent variable. The absolute size of the regression coefficient depends not only on the form of the relation between the variables, but also upon the size of the units in terms of which the variables are stated.

regression curve—If a curve is formed by means of the distributions, it might be called a curve of means, but it is customarily referred to as a regression curve. If it is a straight line, as is usual, it is called a regression line. Because it contains the means of y for fixed values of x, it is called more specificially a regression line of y on x. Vertical deviations from the regression line are deviations from the respective means from which is calculated the standard error of the estimate, to discover the amount of variation around the means.

regression equation—The significance of the regression equations for practical work in economics and business lies in the fact that they constitute an objective means of estimating the value of one variable when the value of another variable is known. If the relative position of a measure in one distribution is known, we can predict (by means of the regression equation) the probable status of this measure in other distributions.

relative frequency—The ratio of the number of observations or elements in a class or subset to the total number of observations which constitute a universal set of population.

sample—A selected number of observations drawn from the populations.

sample, probability—Probability samples, for which the sampling errors can be calculated and for which the biases of selection, nonresponse, and estimation are virtually eliminated or contained within known limits.

In a probability sample a given statistical design is followed, the selection of the particular units for the sample is determined solely according to known probabilities, and estimates and sampling error limits are calculated according to predetermined methods. The reader should note particularly that units selected for the sample in probability sampling are chosen with certain known probabilities by methods which leave no discretion to anyone as to the selection of the particular items for the sample. Once a unit has been selected, it must be included in the sample, and no substitute is allowed. It is to be doubted that a perfect probability sample is often conducted except in cases where the sampling is relatively simple, such as in sampling of files. Nevertheless, the departure from a pure probability sample can usually be made so small in a well-run survey that a sample can be treated as if it were a perfect probability sample. Furthermore, error limits arising from this departure can often be assigned to the sample result.

A chief advantage of a probability sample is that the magnitude of the sampling error can be estimated from a properly designed sample, so that the precision of the sample result can be evaluated. Furthermore, a probability selection of the sample avoids biases which could enter the sample result if judgment on the part of interviewers or others was used in the selection of the sample items.

sample selection criteria—In sample selection the steps to be followed are:

1. The sample must be selected without bias or prejudice.
2. The components of the sample must be completely independent of one another.
3. There should be no underlying differences between areas from which the data are selected.
4. Conditions must be the same for all items constituting the sample.

The limited sample is most generally used to describe the larger population or group of data from which the sample was taken.

When the measures computed from a sample are used to characterize the population, it is necessary to estimate the reliability of the measures, in other words the degree of error to which the generalization may be subject.

Samples may be drawn from the underlying population in several different ways. The conditions outlined above are descriptive of the random sample. The values composing a sample of this type are drawn entirely at random from the population.

However, it is often desirable to segregate a heterogeneous population into homogeneous subgroups and to draw from each subgroup at random. This process results in the stratified sample. A survey of the number of rooms in homes in a given city by resort to sampling method may be more effectively secured by drawing a random sample from uniform areas of the city.

sample, statistical—A statistical sample is a small portion of the entire universe which is drawn in such a way that every value in the universe has an equal chance of being included. A sample must be representative of the universe, and the principle of the random sample is that representativeness will result from the operation of chance in the selection of the values.

sample, stratified—The universe or population may be divided initially into a number of homogenous segments, and a simple random sample selected from within each of these segments or strata. The measurements obtained for each stratum are then combined to obtain the answer desired.

sampling—The selection of part of an aggregate to be used as a basis for inference about the nature of the total population.

sampling, acceptance—Acceptance sampling is another application of a type of decision-making rule. The choice of alternatives in this case is between accepting or rejecting a lot of material. This type of approach has been used for testing the quality of incoming material from a vendor and for testing the quality of a particular lot of items after these have been produced. Acceptance sampling has also been used to test the quality of clerical work.

It should be noted that a decision is to be made in each of these instances about the quality of a particular group of items, such as a lot of incoming material. This means that the population under study is finite, so that every item could be examined, checked, or inspected. Such 100 percent inspection is often prohibitively expensive, however, and does not usually detect all of the defective units, errors, and the like, anyway. Hence sampling is often used to decide whether the quality of the lot is satisfactory enough so that the lot should be accepted or whether the quality is so unsatisfactory that the lot should be rejected. The latter decision may lead to 100 percent inspection of the items, a return of the lot to the vendor, or some other action of this nature. If rejection of a lot leads also to search for the causes of the poor quality, the approach is quite similar to that of the control-chart philosophy. Usually, however, acceptance sampling is used simply to decide whether to accept the particular lot of material which was sampled or whether to reject it.

In acceptance sampling, the quality of an item is often expressed simply by classifying the item as being either satisfactory or defective. A decision-making rule with specified risks of making incorrect decisions can then be constructed to fit this method of quality specification. For instance, the rule might be: Select at random 100 items from the lot. If more than 2 items in the sample are defective, reject the lot. If 2 or less items in the sample are defective, accept the lot. This rule, of course, embodies certain risks of making incorrect decisions.

sampling distribution—The sampling distribution is a theoretical frequency distribution of the sample means. It is called a theoretical distribution because, while it can be proved that it exists, only one value in it is known, having actually drawn only one sample. The other values are means of samples which might have been drawn. The sampling distribution can be described by the normal curve.

The arithmetic mean of the sampling distribution is equal to the true mean of the universe, which is what we are trying to estimate. The standard error of the arithmetic mean is the standard deviation of the means of many distributions.

sampling, errors and mistakes—Some types of variation (error and mistakes) are:

1. Unsystematic mistakes—lost or duplicated questionnaires; tabulating or measuring errors—human or mechanical.

2. Systematic mistakes—"biased" data as nonrandom sample; over-representation, understatements.
3. Sampling error—calculated error from sample vs. true measure.

sampling procedures — Basically, scientific sampling seeks: (1) to discover, by induction, characteristics of natural phenomenon; (2) to discover deductive predictive characteristics; and (3) to establish causation by hypotheses and tests. Methods of inquiry include: (a) observation—accurate, objective recording with expeditious repetition; (b) experimental—use of effective and extensive control to establish cause and effect by reason and verification.

Indirect methods include: (1) interviews with care taken to know data, the information desired, and the means to obtain with ability to stay on a subject; (2) correspondence, but through the careful use of tact and courtesy with personal and planned messages to briefly and honestly establish nature and objective of problem; (3) questionnaires which use care and precision to seek facts, not opinions, by seeking clear questions with properly defined words. Tabulation must be modeled to permit comparison and statistical evaluation.

Direct methods include fieldwork of three general types: (1) case studies to seek the nonobvious or peculiar characteristics of individual items; (2) sampling to make use of the theory of probability, Gaussian bell curves, and precise measurements of confidence intervals and errors ranges; and (3) census to enumerate all facts and figures for "common denominator" tabulations and projections.

Adequate planning and design must precede all of the techniques for clear and precise formulation of the problem, the essential and pertinent factors; sharp observations in the field, laboratory, or environment. Special attention will be devoted toward narrowing or delimiting the inquiry, discovering the knowledge of the subject which has already been acquired, close and thorough examination of data within the time and budget allotted—all to be followed by empirical verification of hypotheses and tests.

sampling, random—A sample is supposed to be a true miniature of the universe from which it is drawn; therefore, a sample must be truly representative of the universe from which it is drawn, and the universe itself must be homogeneous.

A representative sample is a random sample—that is, a sample which has been selected entirely upon the basis of a change, in accordance with the theory of probability. If change alone governs the selection of the various items which make up a sample, that sample will be a representative sample, provided it is large enough.

sampling, scientific—Scientific sampling concerns a designed selection (sample) which is a miniature of the entire universe; i.e., statistical population, so that from this sample and using established and proven mathematically precise statistical techniques one may infer characteristics and draw conclusions concerning the universe.

sampling, stratified random—Where the population from which a sample is to be selected is not homogeneous, the universe of inquiry may be broken up into subgroups which are individually more homogeneous than is the total population; in this way, it is possible substantially to increase the reliability of sampling results. Within each subgroup, random selection may be employed. It is essential that the size of each group in the sample be proportional to its relative importance in the total population.

scatter diagram—If two related (associated) series are plotted graphically with one variable placed on the X axis and the other on the Y axis, the result is known as the scatter diagram. The independent or casual variable is placed on the X axis while the dependent variable is placed on the Y axis.

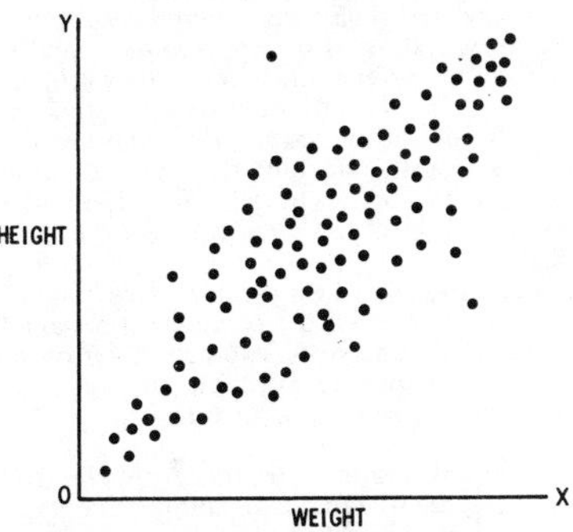

scientific effort—An arrangement and record of logical deductions and conclusions which are quickly traceable to postulates and hypotheses. A sequence of conceptual models established and proven by fact—as simple spokes of a wheel. The cumulative process of building knowledge that is transferable to other minds and open to general scrutiny, therefore requiring clarity and explicitness of each postulational approach; i.e., "chains of reasoning."

scientific method—Scientific method is an exercise in strict objective inquiry—an examination of fact or truth in a specific facet of a delimited discipline or field of knowledge. Its core consists in the evaluation of the assumptions used, hypotheses tested, and conclusions developed. It is an analytical tool of learned judgment concerning adequacy and accuracy of theories. Some typical questions one would ask in progressing with, or criticism of, scientific method are:

How is the problem designed—purpose scope, procedure, methodology?

How is the problem defined, delimited, analyzed; what is master work?
What are the component parts of the problem; the objectives of each?
What was the status knowledge on the subject; by what authority?
What assumptions were made; what is the reasonableness of each?
What hypotheses were used—projection or causation; are they plausible?
What conclusions were reached; are they supported by adequate facts?
What was attempted to be shown or proved; what has been shown or proved?

seasonal variation (time series)—Seasonal variation is the movement of a variable during the year. It is usually caused by changes in the weather or by conventional practices associated with certain dates (for example, increased retail sales occur around Christmas-time). In many variables, seasonal movements occur with sufficient persistance and regularity to be looked upon as "normal."

There are statistical methods for finding and expressing the approximate pattern and quiz sections. Such methods necessarily involve the use of monthly (or quarterly, weekly, or daily) rather than annual data.

secular trend—The long-time growth or decline occurring with the data. The period covered should include not less than ten years.

semilog graphs—Two-cycle semilog paper or "ratio paper" is in common use among statisticians, and one-, two-, three,- four- and five-cycle paper is available and all types have these essential features:

1. Equal vertical distances on the chart represent equal percentage changes, or equal rates of change, i.e., ratios.
2. The horizontal grids have progressively less and less space between them as one examines the paper from bottom to top, and this is true of the entire vertical scale, i.e., one continuous scale on vertical axis.
3. Two series expressed in different units of widely different magnitudes can be plotted on the same chart using the right margin for one scale and the left for the other.
4. The semilog line chart is used principally to analyze rates of change in one or more series; i.e., when the vertical distance between a number of points becomes greater, the series is increasing at an increasing rate.
5. These graphs show a curve drawn through the plotted points and the varying height of the curve shows, not the variation of y with x, but the variation of log y with x. The curve is obtainable as the natural graph of log y as a function of x. If the curve is observed to rise through equal heights over certain ranges of values of x, then the value of y's is subject, not to equal absolute increases, but to equal proportional or percentage increases. The use of semilogarithmic graphs is used to compare percentage changes in the value of one variable as the other variable increases steadily. The plot of the relation between changes is thus the primary function of semilog graphs.

sensitivity analysis—Sensitivity analysis is often called parametric programming because in such investigations, one or more parameters are permitted to vary in order to determine whether or not a solution should be modified. Managers are often much concerned with what happens to the optimal solution when fluctuations in the values of parameters or coefficients are permitted to change; i.e., size of budget, factory, package, price, etc.

sets—A collection of items (elements) which can be described by a characteristic that is held in common by all elements in the collection.

sets and subsets—Whenever one can classify or describe something by a characteristic or property, he may say that the thing belongs to the set of all things having that characteristic or property. Each "thing" in the set is an element of the set. Smaller groups of "things" or elements in the set are subsets if identifiable by some characteristic common to each of the elements of the subject. The set that includes all of the elements having a given characteristic is called the universal set of things having the given property. A set having no elements is called the empty or "null" set.

simulation—Briefly, the manipulation of a model to imitate or emulate significant aspects or traits of a situation or group of circumstances so as to note sensitivities, interdependencies, resulting conflicts and payoff values by a scale-model test run as Monte Carlo, executive games, or real-life projects of various types.

skewness—The degree of distortion from symmetry exhibited by a frequency distribution. When a distribution is perfectly symmetrical, the values of the mean, median, and mode coincide. In an asymmetrical (skewed) distribution, the values of the averages will depart from one another. Since the arithmetic mean is most affected by extremes it will move the greatest distance from the mode. The mode is not affected at all by unusual values; therefore, the greater the degree of skewness the greater the distance between the mean and the mode.

It follows that this distance between mean and mode may be used as a measure of skewness, since the greater the lack of symmetry the larger the discrepancy between them. However, because the measure of skewness is used largely for comparative purposes, the problem of differing units will make its appearance. A second difficulty arises in that the distance between the averages will be larger in a widely dispersed distribution than in one with a narrow dispersion. Both difficulties may be removed by dividing the measure by the measure of dispersion.

slope—1. In the equation $f(x) = mx + b$, m is the symbol for slope of a line. The slope then is the number of units that f(x) increases as one moves along a line and let x increase one unit. An $m = 10$ might mean the upward movement on a line as of ten units as the rightward movement is one unit. 2. Geometrically it is defined as follows: An acute angle between a straight line and the positive x-axis is called the angle of inclination. The tangent of the angle of inclination is the slope of the line; $m = \tan$ of angle alpha (α). The slope is positive if α is a positive acute angle, and otherwise it is negative. The slope is the ratio of the vertical distance to the horizontal distance and is represented as: $m = \frac{y_2 - y_1}{x_2 - x_1}$, where the numerator is the vertical distance and the denominator is the x distance; i.e., horizontal on an xy graph.

standard deviation, characteristics—The best and most widely used measure of dispersion is σ, and it enters into many other measures of statistical development. As a result of the squaring process, greater emphasis is given to extreme deviations than is the case in the mean deviation. The normal curve has been analyzed in terms of standard deviations so that this measure of dispersion can be used to facilitate comparison with the normal distribution.

standard deviation, computation—The computation of the standard deviation may be simplified by the following methods (using grouped data):

$$\sigma = \sqrt{\frac{\Sigma f(d^2)}{N} - \left(\frac{\Sigma fd}{N}\right)^2}$$

where,

σ = standard deviation,
d = deviation of midpoint of each class interval from that arbitrary group.

standard error—The standard deviation which measures the variability of means in a sampling distribution is called the standard error of the mean and is written σ_x. If the standard error of the sampling distribution is large, the means are unreliable; i.e., they differ greatly from one another—if σ_x is small, they are very much alike.

Rather than compute the standard error of means of all possible samples of a given size, we rely on the empirically and mathematically provided formula:

$$\sigma_x = \frac{\sigma}{\sqrt{n}} \cdot \sqrt{\frac{N-n}{N-1}}$$

where,

σ is the std. dev. of the population,
N is the number of items in the population,
n is the number of items in the sample;
the correction factor $\sqrt{\frac{N-n}{N-1}}$ is dropped for large populations.

Because it is often difficult to know σ, one can substitute s, the estimate of the population standard deviation derived from the sample, and the working formula becomes

$$S_x = \frac{S}{\sqrt{n}}$$

This is the formula which indicates that the larger the sample is, the smaller the standard error of the mean will be, and thus also the more reliable the mean will be; but, the accuracy increases as the square root of the sample size. For example, to halve the size of the standard error, one would need to quadruple the size of the sample, etc.

standard error of difference between means—The standard error of the difference between means is the standard deviation of the sampling distribution of differences between means. It is computed by the formula

$$D = \sqrt{\sigma M_1^2 + \sigma M_2^2}$$

where,

M_1 and M_2 are the values of the standard error of the mean for the two samples.

standard error of estimate—1. A way of viewing the standard error of estimate is that it represents the standard deviation of the items around the regression line. If a value y′ is calculated from the regression equation for each item in a distribution and if these values are subtracted from the corresponding y values, the mean of these squared deviations is $\sigma^2 y \cdot x$.

$$\sigma^2 y \cdot x = \frac{\Sigma (y - y')^2}{N}$$

2. $S_y \cdot x$ is read "S sub y point x" and measures the extent to which actual scores depart from the regression line; i.e., this standard error is a measure of the errors one would make in estimating or predicting scores by use of Y′.

standard error of means—1. The standard deviation is a convenient measure of the variability of the means in a sampling distribution and offers an index of reliability, where the subscript x serves as a reminder that it is a standard deviation of a distribution of means. 2. The standard error of the mean plays an important role in inductive statistics, because it measures the variation of the theoretical sampling distribution of x. In other words, it tells us how much sample means can be expected to vary from sample to sample.

The formula for estimating the standard error of a mean from a single sample is relatively simple:

$$\sigma_m = \frac{\sigma}{\sqrt{r-1}}$$

The standard deviation of the raw sources of the sample and divide this by the square root of one less than the number of cases in the sample.

standard error of proportion—By substituting the standard deviation of a distribution of proportions, $\sigma = \sqrt{P(1-P)}$, for σ_x in the formula $x = \sigma/\sqrt{n}$ for means, we obtain an expression for the standard error of a proportion. This relationship is given by the formula.

$$\sigma_p = \frac{\sqrt{P(1-P)}}{n}$$

Thus, the true variability (σ_p) of the proportion (P) for a very large number of relatively large random samples of the same size depends upon (1) the number (n) in each sample, and (2) the true proportion (P) which exists in the whole population.

statistic—A statistic is considered to be a numerical property of a sample in contrast to a parameter, which is a numerical property of a distribution; i.e., a population, or universe.

statistical method—Statistical method is a technique used to obtain, analyze and present numerical data. The elements of statistical technique include: (1) the collection and assembling of data; (2) classification and condensation of data; (3) presentation of data in a textual, tabular, and graphic form; and (4) analysis of data.

When data are grouped according to magnitude, the resulting series is called a frequency distribution; when grouped as to time of occurrence, it is called a time series; when grouped by geographic location, it is called spatial distribution. In addition, there are a number of special types of distributions in which the data may be arranged by kind or by degree.

statistical mistakes—Some mistakes to be avoided are:

1. Concealed change in the statistical unit —For example, the value of the dollar changes over time.
2. Misuse of percentages—For example, if 12 drops to 3, this is not a 300% drop because nothing can drop more than 100%. It is a drop of 75%.
3. Spurious accuracy—When working with data which are themselves approximate figures, do not carry calculations based on those figures to an excessive number of decimal places, but confine the expression of the result to the significant figures, determined with reference to the accuracy of the original data.

Other pitfalls to watch for are: (a) deductive inconsistencies; (b) emotional or dual terminology; (c) fallacy of composition; (d) bias, slants, unsystematic errors; (e) incomplete theory; (f) "missing" variables; (g) aggregation of dissimilar units; (h) improper sample.

statistical procedures (scientific)—Basically, the effort must be to generalize and systematize and through critical discrimination to classify, make sequential, and affirm relative significance. Most realistically the highest achievement of the college student is not to accumulate knowledge of facts but more the ability to discover or locate and intelligently use new and forgotten knowledge.

A brief guide to the application of a method might be as follows:

1. Develop a distinct and unequivocal definition of the problem—kill offshoot inclinations and nonbasic background or tangents.
2. Analyze the problem in terms of semantic meaning—isolate and assess components.
3. Define the areas of knowledge—ascertain what is already known about the problem.
4. Determine the goal or level of aspiration as: algoristic—the attempt to determine the exact, the maximum, or optimum, solution using total efforts and means; stochastic—close to the best solution based on uncertainty but through the best use of probability (measured and known error; subjective evaluation) and confidence levels; i.e., best possible solution in relation to the constraints unalterably imposed; and heuristic—a solution which is satisfactory considering the resources of time, funds, and personnel available and the "confined" use of solution.
5. State the assumptions based on how acquired knowledge of project fits into the realm of prior discoveries—projections and extrapolations.
6. Develop the hypothesis by insight, imagination, preconceived expectation, scope.
7. Test the hypotheses by inductive and deductive methods to possibly form new ones.
8. Evaluate the solutions in relation, purpose, design—and most importantly, alternatives.

statistical research procedures—The purpose is to show integration of specific procedures for developing optimal solutions of problems or ranges of feasibilities using a general and broad range scientific-method framework.

1. Define, design, and delimit the problem (or model) with a clear, succinct statement hypothesis, scope, and objective. Affirm positively the aspiration

level desired (algoristic, stochastic, or heuristic) and confidence base required.

2. Determine exploration methodology; environment and special circumstances; types of variables and degree of uncertainty; values of constants and parameters; reliability and validity criteria; sources, measurements, and control of errors.

statistics—The use of statistics is the art, science, or technique of deriving inferences or predictions from particulars to general statements (induction). It is concerned with making judgment decisions in the face of uncertainty. As such, it is a branch of scientific method dealing with probability laws proceeding from a collection of data for developing numerical answers to be used for problem solving and decision making.

Business statistics relates to the evaluation of risks of wrong decisions due to the partial rather than total data availability. The statistical techniques of inductive inference concern bodies of precisely stated and empirically tested rules and laws for (1) securing information (2) manipulating and formulating such data in mathematically or diagrammatically meaningful expressions, and (3) preparing the bases for effective action and control.

The successful use of statistics in business requires, besides the ability to correctly interpret statistical methods and applications, an adequate knowledge of business technology and environment coupled with common sense, experience, objective analysis, and subjective evaluation of time and consequences.

statistics, analytical—The purpose of analytical statistics is to enable one to draw statistical inferences about the characteristics of the entire statistical "universe" of data from a small sample.

statistics, descriptive and inductive—Descriptive statistics involves methods that, essentially, do not go beyond the data with which we start; inductive statistics involves generalizations, predictions, estimations, and decisions.

stochastic—Solutions, from the Greek, meaning aim or target, are concerned with "close to the best" solutions—solutions based on uncertainty but through the best use of precise laws of probability with known and measured errors explicitly considered, and confidence intervals precisely defined.

student "t" tables—These are normal curve percents adjusted for the erratic nature of small samples. The t values become larger as the sample is smaller. The t table is a table of σs. Calculated t must equal or exceed tabular t if a significant difference between the sample means is to be concluded. If calculated t is more than 3, it is assumed that the difference is significant and due to more than chance.

The student or "t" distribution is used when samples are small; i.e., fewer than 30 (instead of the normal curve table). The t distribution closely resembles the normal testing distribution except it is more peaked at the top. It does not approach the x-axis as rapidly, and the t distribution consists of whole families of distributions, one for each "degree of freedom" or each size of sample. Thus, deviations around the mean must be larger to include a specified percent of the values within this range. For example, in the t table, 2.776 standard deviations are required to include 95% of the cases (vs. 2.0 in normal table). The figures indicate the value t corresponding to various specified levels of confidence.

subjective—Existing in the mind; belonging to the thinking subject rather than to the object of thought; interpreted by each individual in his own way and applied to his own problem as he sees it; an endless collection of personally different meanings or understandings to the same problem, statement, or conclusion.

suboptimizing—The maximum of some portion of the totality of listed or known objectives.

subscripts—The assisting or subordinate symbols which are used to specifically indicate relationship, as the j or 2 in X_j and Y_2 to indicate points, groups, or cell location in a matrix.

subsets—These are collections wholly contained within a larger collection—all having some characteristic or property in common.

syllogism—Validity of conclusions is determined by means of various forms of deductive logic. The syllogism most often consists of three statements, the first two are premises, and the last is the conclusion. Axioms, postulates, and laws usually form the premises, and they must be consistent; i.e., noncontradictory.

symmetry and skewness—If the curve of error is perfectly symmetrical, the mean will equal the median and mode. The mean of a distribution with a tail on right will exceed median. The Pearsonian coefficient of skewness is positive if mean exceeds median and mode.

theory—An exposition of abstract principles considered apart from practice; an unproved principle; speculative explanation.

time series—A time series is a sequence of values of the same variable corresponding to successive points of time. For example the successive values of an index number would constitute a time series.

time series analysis—In time series analysis we deal with series of values which are ordered in time, and the significant feature of which is their fluctuation over periods of time. By means of time series analysis it is possible to determine, for example, what part of the fluctuations is normal, or expected, and what part is abnormal. Such analysis is basic to studies of business cycles and provides knowledge of trends and patterns of seasonal changes on which managerial decisions may be predicted.

time series movements—The analysis of the time series consists of the description and measurement of the various changes or movements as they appear in the series during a period of time. These changes or movements may be classified as:

1. Secular trend, or the long time growth or decline occurring within the data. The period covered should include not less than ten years.
2. Seasonal variation, or the more or less regular movement within the twelve-month period. This movement occurs year after year and is caused by the changing seasons.
3. Cyclical movement, or the swing from prosperity through recession, depression, recovery, and back again to prosperity. This movement varies in time, length and intensity.
4. Residual, accidental or random variations, including such unusual disturbances as wars, disasters, strikes, fads, or other nonrecurring factors.

truth table—When p and q are used to represent any propositions which may be true or false, and in truth tables, true and false are said to be truth values of the propositions. Truth tables list the truth values of all possible combinations in columns headed by p and q, as well as a third table for the result of each combination. In the table below a truth table for logical conjunction is shown:

p	q	p·q
T	T	T
T	F	F
F	F	F
F	T	F

Thus, from the above, one expects p·q to be true if both p and q are true, but false if either one is false. The truth table thus formally states this and other statements.

universe—The aggregate of total population about which an inference is to be made.

universe, statistical—A statistical universe (or statistical population) is a complete group of things or phenomena which are similar in certain stated respects. For example, the heights of white native-born males between the ages of 21 and 65 constitute a universe of heights similar in that they all belong to a stated class of individuals (i.e., white, native-born males).

variable, continuous—In contrast to discrete variables, we shall say that a variable is continuous if it can assume all values of a continuous scale. Such quantities as length, time, and temperature are measured on continuous scales and their measurements may be referred to as continuous variables.

variable, discrete—A variable is said to be discrete if it assumes only a finite number of values or as many values as there are whole numbers. The number of heads which we obtain in, say, 10 flips of a coin is a discrete variable because it cannot assume values other than 0, 1, 2, 3, . . . , and 10.

variable, independent—The decision as to which is the independent and which is the dependent variable in most cases is clear. The dependent variable depends on or is caused by or is the result of the independent variable. The scales along the vertical and horizontal axes are laid off to provide for the smallest and largest values of the variables to be plotted. It will be noted that the scales need not begin with zero. Each point on the scatter diagrams represents two values.

variables, control and limited control—Control variables are the elements of the system that can be changed by our decisions, as amount and type of goods to be produced, size of promotion budget, etc. Noncontrol variables are all others which cannot be directly influenced by our decisions as competitors' actions, nature, customer reactions, suppliers' government, etc. Frequently we have limited control even on the variables we choose, as budget constraints, running time, number and capacities of machines, etc. Nearly all problems can be reduced to finding maximum or minimum of some function and are thus deterministic; i.e., we can compute precisely what will happen if we choose any specified values for the control variables. This may be contrasted with probabilistic or stochastic situations, where we do not know all the values of the noncontrol variables in advance, and we must allow for the probability that they will take various values, for example, where profits depend on sales, which cannot be predicted other than in a probabilistic sense. Numerical coefficients and exponents are used in functional forms. Whenever these quantities are fixed, specified, and known, they are referred to as constants. On the other hand, parameters are quantities that remain constant in the short run but they may vary over time. Thus, on any particular occasion, they may have to be estimated, for example, $(ax^2 + bx - c)$, a, b, c, may be constants but the expression within the parentheses is often a parameter, as "k."

variance—The measure of dispersion about the mean; i.e., the average of the squared deviations between observations and the mean. The square of the standard deviation.

variance analysis—The estimate of probability relatedness by comparison of between-column variance with within-column variance.

variation—When two variables, x and y, are so related that the ratio of x to y, is always constant, then x is said to vary directly as y.

When two variables, x and y, are so related that y varies directly as the reciprocal of x, then y is said to vary inversely as x.

Joint variation concerns two or more variables such as: $z = kxy$ where z is stated as a joint variable of x and y, or if $z = k\frac{x}{y}$, z thus varies directly as x and inversely as y.

vector—A vector is a quantity which has magnitude and direction and is most often represented by an arrow. The head of the arrow indicates its direction, and the length of the arrow represents the magnitude. The sum is called the resultant; the two vectors are called the components of the resultant. Vectors are used in many areas of calculation such as forces, velocities, acceleration and other physical quantities, especially in matrix algebra.

APPENDIX I

Number Systems

THE BINARY SYSTEM

The binary system pertains to the number 2; more specifically, a number system whose radix is the quantity 2. The binary number system has rules much simpler than those of the familiar decimal numbering system. This simplicity makes the binary numbering system ideal for computers because these devices are mathematical idiots and must be instructed in minute detail for every computation they make. Where the decimal numbering system uses ten marks (0 through 9), thus having a radix (or base) of 10, the binary system uses only two marks (0 and 1), thus having a radix of 2. In the decimal system, we think in "tens." For example, the number 35 means: $10 + 10 + 10 + 5 = 35$. Or 35 can be written as: $3(10) + 5(1) = 35$. Or 35 can be written in positional notation as: $3(10^1) + 5(10^0) = 35$. In the pure binary system, we deal with powers of 2 rather than powers of 10. We first line up the various powers of 2 (the radix or base of the binary system) in positional notation to six places beginning with 1st position to the left of the decimal point. Above each power of 2, we will show its expanded value in a decimal number. If there is a one in each of the six binary positions to the left of the decimal point, the sum of the equivalent decimal values would be 63 which is the decimal equivalent of binary 111111.

Decimal values	32	16	8	4	2	1
Binary positional notational weight	2^5	2^4	2^3	2^2	2^1	2^0

Remembering that in the binary system we have only two marks, 0 and 1, we then convert the decimal number 35 to a binary number; reading from right to left we will place a 1 in the first, second and sixth positions and zeros in the other 3 positions.

$$1(2^5) + 0(2^4) + 0(2^3) + 0(2^2) + 1(2^1) + 1(2^0).$$

The resulting binary number is 100011, which is binary for decimal 35 (32,0,0,0,2,1).

Decimal to Binary Conversion

Method 1. The positional notation chart used in the previous example for converting decimal number 35 to a binary number, suggests a method for decimal to binary conversions. A simple method for converting decimal to binary is to ask the question, what is the largest number to the power of 2 which can be contained in the decimal number 35. The answer is 32 which is 2^5. We will then place a 1 in the 6th position (reading right to left) because we also use the 2^0 number for positioning. We then ask ourselves which next lower power of 2 can be contained in the remainder ($35 - 32$ or 3). Since 21 equals 2 and 2^0 equals 1 and both are contained in the remainder 3, the sum again is 35.

Method 2. Another method of conversion is a process of successive division of the decimal number by the binary base (2). The remainders of these divisions are read from the bottom upward and will produce the binary equivalent of the decimal number. In Chart I-1, decimal number 1967 is converted to its equivalent binary number.

Chart I-1. Conversion of Decimal Number to Binary

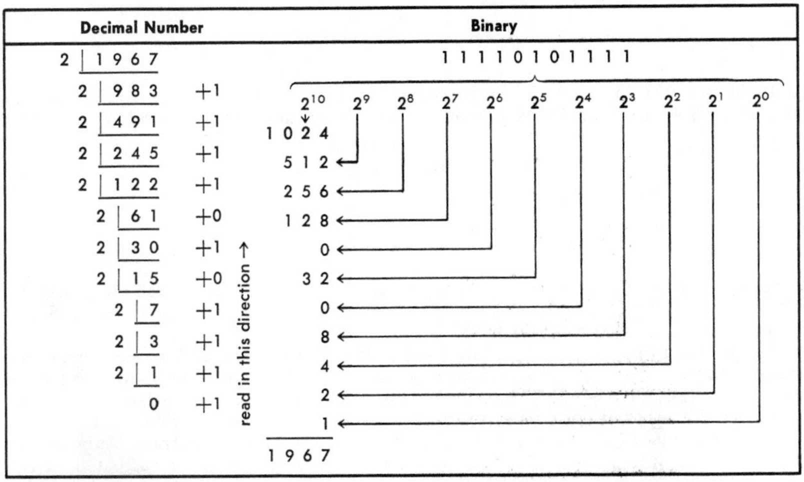

Decimal Number		
2	1967	
2	983	+1
2	491	+1
2	245	+1
2	122	+1
2	61	+0
2	30	+1
2	15	+0
2	7	+1
2	3	+1
2	1	+1
	0	+1

read in this direction ↑

Binary: 11110101111	
2^{10}	1024
2^9	512
2^8	256
2^7	128
2^6	0
2^5	32
2^4	0
2^3	8
2^2	4
2^1	2
2^0	1
	1967

Binary Arithmetic

Since the binary system uses the digits 0 and 1 only, binary addition and multiplication (a series of additions) is performed according to the rules briefly outlined below. Subtraction is the inverse function of addition, and division is a series of subtractions.

Addition
$0+0=0$
$0+1=1$
$1+0=1$
$1+1=10$

Multiplication
$0\times 0=0$
$0\times 1=0$
$1\times 0=0$
$1\times 1=1$

One of the major advantages of the binary numbering system is the ease with which arithmetic problems can be solved in a digital computer. Very few rules, and no tables, are required to solve an addition, subtraction, multiplication, or division problem. The over-all problem is first broken down into a series of individual operations.

Addition

Addition has only four rules:

```
 0     0     1     1
 0     1     0     1
 —     —     —    ——
 0     1     1    10
```

Here 1 plus 1 is 10 pronounced "one-oh") because binary 10 is decimal 2. This is the same as saying that decimal 1 plus 1 is 2.

Following these rules, it is possible to add any two binary numbers directly. For example, to add decimal 12 and 5:

```
12 is the same as binary  1100
 5 is the same as binary   101
——                       —————
17 is the same as binary 10001
```

To add 01011 and 00110:

Binary	Decimal
01011	11
00110	6
10001	17

In binary addition there is the problem of the carry, as when $1 + 1 = 10$—that is, 0 plus carry 1. This can be seen from the following, where 111101 is added to 10110:

```
(A)  111101
(B)   10110
     ------
(C)  101011
(D)   1 1
     ------
(E) 1010011
```

The first step is to add the two (A and B) to get the partial sum (C). Line D shows the two carries resulting from the 1 + 1 sums. Adding partial sum C, and the carries D, produces the final sum E, or 1010011.

A digital computer is actually a much expanded version of an adding machine, doing electronically what the adding machine accomplishes through a mechanical system of gears, etc. Basically, the operation of the two is the same, for purposes of illustration.

A digital computer, once given its orders by the operator, stores them in its memory and then recalls each order one by one until the solution is reached. Although its operation is superhumanly fast, a computer requires instructions for each step. It can do only what it is told; having a limited memory and no imagination, it cannot think as humans do.

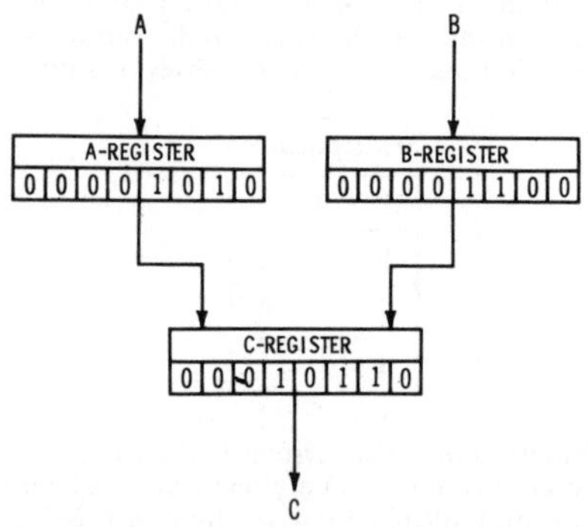

Fig. I-1. Addition using three registers.

Each computer operation is determined by a series of instructions which direct the flow of information, as shown in Fig. I-1. Each block represents a register, one of a group of series-connected circuits which can store ("remember") a number and make it perform a certain operation. Suppose the computer's instructions are: "Add A to B and place in C." This means the number stored in register A is to be added to the number in register B, and the sum then placed in register C. Assuming numbers are already in registers A and B, the computer automatically does the following steps:

1. Clears register C by removing any information there. This it does by inserting a 0 in each stage of C.
2. Transfers to C the number stored in A (1010). C is connected to A, stage by stage. In this program the computer is also told not to "forget" the 1010, but to store it in A for later use. (1010 happens to be the constant in this specific program.) C and A both now have the same number.
3. Adds the number in 8 (1100) to the number in C (1010), following the rules of binary discussed earlier. In this program the computer is also told to keep B's memory a total blank in order to make room for the next variable.

4. Final conditions: Register A still has the original number stored, and will continue to do so until cleared: B is cleared (in this program) by the addition to C; and C now contains the sum.

Subtraction

Subtraction of binary numbers is done in two ways. One is by direct subtraction:

$$\begin{array}{r} 101101 \\ -1011 \\ \hline 100010 \end{array}$$

Note that to subtract 1 from 0, it is necessary to borrow 1, making 1 from 10, or 1.

Complements also provide a means of subtraction. In our decimal system the 10 s complement is the difference between 10 and a given number–hence, the complement of 7 is 3. By the same token, the 9 s complement is the difference between 9 and a given number, the complement of 7 being 2.

By addition of complements, it is possible to perform subtraction. First, here is how subtraction is normally done in the decimal system:

$$\begin{array}{r} 7 \\ -3 \\ \hline 4 \end{array}$$

To subtract, using the 10 s complement system:

$$\begin{array}{rl} +7 & \text{(the 10 s complement of 3; } 10 - 3 = 7) \\ 7 & \\ \hline 14 & \end{array}$$

Drop the extra first digit (which occurs because of the complement), giving the remainder, 4.

Using the 9 s complement system:

$$\begin{array}{rl} 7 & \\ +6 & \text{(the 9 s complement of 3: } 9 - 3 = 6) \\ \hline 13 & \end{array}$$

Here, however, the extra 1 is not dropped, but is added to the 3 (the mathematical reason is beyond the scope of this discussion), giving the same answer, 4. This adding of the extra 1, known as end-around carry, is a vital step in computer subtraction, as we shall soon see.

In the binary system there are only two digits, 1 and 0; so, of course, there can be only two complements. To find the 1 s complement of 1, subtract 1 from 1, giving 0 $(1 - 1 = 0)$. Again, to find the 1 s complement of 0, subtract it from 1, giving 1 $(1 - 0 = 1)$. In other words, to find the complement of a binary number, change all 1 s to 0 s and all 0 s to 1 s. Thus, the complement of 1011 is 0100.

But first, to subtract binary numbers directly:

$$\begin{array}{r} 1101 \\ -1011 \\ \hline 0010 \end{array}$$

And since the complement of 1011 is 0100, subtraction is also possible by adding complements:

$$\begin{array}{rl} 1101 & \\ +0100 & \\ \hline 10001 & \\ 1 & \text{(end-around carry)} \\ \hline 0010 & \end{array}$$

This complement technique is important because of the circuit design of a digital computer. If the number is held in a register which is a series of flip-flops, complementing requires a change of state for each flip-flop.

Multiplication

For multiplication there are four rules, which can be reduced to two. As shown in Fig. I-2, $1 \times 1 = 1$, and all other combinations are zero. For example, to multiply 1011 by 0101:

```
  Binary      Decimal
    1011         11
    0101        ×5
    ----        ---
    1011         55
   1011
  ------
  110111
```

To multiply decimal 12 and 5:

```
    1100         12
     101        ×5
    ----        ---
    1100         60
   11000
  ------
  111100
```

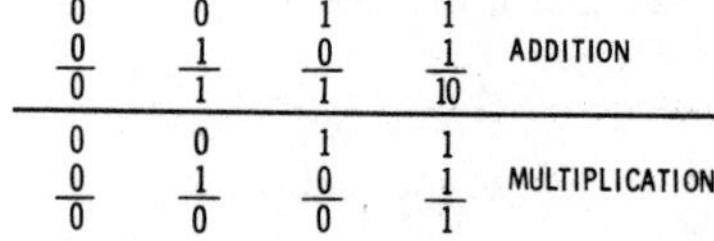

Fig. I-2. Binary rules of arithmetic.

In binary multiplication there are no tables, no carries (except in adding partial products), and every product is equal to 0 except 1×1. Multiplication is a series of additions, just as multiplying 14 by 8 in the decimal system is the same as adding 14 eight times. Binary 10101 is multiplied by 101 as follows:

```
    10101
      101
    -----
    10101
        0
  10101
  -------
  1101001
```

Multiplication is thus a series of shifts and additions, as in the decimal system. With 101 as the multiplier, each 1 is a shift left and an addition, and each 0 is a shift but no addition.

For example, to multiply 100101 by 101:

```
    100101
       101
    ------
    100101
    00000    (shift left, no add)
  100101     (shift left and add)
  --------
  10111001 (sum)
```

For every 1 in the multiplier (101), the multiplicand (100101) is moved one place to the left and added. For every 0 in 101, there is one shift but no addition.

Multiplication or division as a series of shifts can be seen in Fig. I-3. The original number in the register is A, or 1010100. If A is shifted left one place—a multiplication by 2—the result appears as in B. The second shift left, at C, results in 101010000, or 4

A	0	0	1	0	1	0	1	0	0
		√ SHIFT LEFT							
B	0	1	0	1	0	1	0	0	0
	√ SHIFT LEFT								
C	1	0	1	0	1	0	0	0	0
A	0	0	1	0	1	0	1	0	0
				√ SHIFT RIGHT					
D	0	0	0	1	0	1	0	1	0
					√ SHIFT RIGHT				
E	0	0	0	0	1	0	1	0	1

Fig. I-3. Multiplication and division as a series of shifts.

times A. The shift right is a division by 2, as in D; two shifts right (A divided by 4) produces a second division by 2, as in E.

To repeat, shifting left is a form of multiplication and shifting right is division. Starting with 101100, a shift left is 1011000 which is twice 101100; and dividing by 2 is a shift right, or 10110.

One more example: Starting with 101100 (decimal 44), a shift left is 1011000 (decimal 88); and a shift right is 10110 (decimal 22). This is exactly like operating with decimal numbers. Taking 347.036 a shift left would be 3470.36, which is ten times 347.036; and a shift right would be 34.7036, which is one-tenth of 347.036.

Division

Division can also be done in the usual way, by long division. The divisor is subtracted from the dividend and a 1 placed in the quotient. If the divisor cannot be subtracted, a 0 is placed in the quotient. As an example:

```
        10101
101 ⟌ 1101010
      101
      ---
       110
       101
       ---
         110
         101
         ---
           1
```

Thus, 101 goes into 1101010, 10101 times with a remainder of 1.

BINARY-CODED DECIMAL (BCD) SYSTEM

This is a system for representing decimal numbers in which each decimal digit is expressed by a 4-digit code (called a word) written in binary notation. In the BCD system, each decimal digit is represented by four binary digits (or bits) (see Chart I-2).

Chart I-2. Binary-Coded Decimal System

Binary Code		Decimal Code
0000	=	0
0001	=	1
0010	=	2
0011	=	3
0100	=	4
0101	=	5
0110	=	6
0111	=	7
1000	=	8
1001	=	9
0001 0000	=	10

Thus, the decimal 1967 would be represented in BCD code as:

0001	1001	0110	0111
1	9	6	7

EXCESS 3 CODE (XS3)

Oftentimes it is convenient to have values smaller than unity. To achieve this, the coded binary number is increased to represent a decimal digit three units larger than the given digit. Chart I-3 compares BCD with XS3 notation with their corresponding decimal numbers.

Chart I-3. Comparison of BCD and XS3 Notation

Decimal Number	Coded Binary Number	XS3 Coded Binary
0	0000	0011
1	0001	0100
2	0010	0101
3	0011	0110
4	0100	0111
5	0101	1000
6	0110	1001
7	0111	1010
8	1000	1011
9	1001	1100
Thus, 1967 represented in XS3 code would be: 0100 1100 1001 1010		

OCTAL NOTATION SYSTEM

When programmers wish to make reference to the actual contents of the computer's storage cells and operating registers, the desired information is expressed in a binary configuration. But, it is obvious, for example, in using the pure binary number 11110101100, that binary notation is far too combersome for humans to handle with ease. Even quantities of moderate size require a lengthy string of 0's and 1's, and errors of transposition and omission are easily made. Furthermore, in the BCD system there are 16 possible states of the 4-bit BCD words, as shown in Chart I-4, and since only ten can be used in the BCD system, the machine (computer) theoretically wastes space if it uses this system. In contrast the octal system has only eight possible states, and does not waste machinery memory space (Chart I-5).

The other advantages of the octal system are: 3-bit words required for each corresponding decimal number, the direct decimal number relationship to its octal counterpart, and its direct binary readout.

The solution to this problem lies in the use of the octal system. The eight digits of the octal system bear a simple relationship to the binary system.

Binary-Coded Octal

Note that the octal digits 0 to 7 can be represented by three binary digits, or "bits." A large binary number can be separated into 3-bit words, starting from the binary point at the right, and an octal digit can be substituted for each word. For the fractional part of a number, the division into words begins at the binary point and proceeds from left to right. For example, the decimal number 1967 can be converted to binary-coded octal as follows:

$$1967_{10} \rightarrow (3 \times 8^3) + (6 \times 8^2) + (5 \times 8^1) + (7 \times 8^0). = 3657_8 \rightarrow 011\ 110\ 101\ 111_{BCO}$$

Chart I-4. Possible States of 4-bit Words in the BCD System

Decimal Digit	BCD
0	0000
1	0001
2	0010
3	0011
4	0100
5	0101
6	0110
7	0111
8	1000
9	1001
A	1010
B	1011
C	1100
D	1101
E	1110
F	1111

Proof: $1967 = 1536 + 384 + 40 + 7$

```
8 | 1967
 8 | 245   +7
  8 | 30   +5
   8 | 3   +6
       0   +3
```

Octal to Decimal Conversion

To complete the translation from the computer's binary system to the human mind's decimal system, an additional means of converting an octal number to its decimal equivalent must be available. The arithmetic in the procedure is as follows:

1. Multiply the most significant digit by 8; i.e., 3 in the number 3657.
2. Add the next most significant digit to the product of step 1; i.e., 6 in the number 3657.
3. Using the sum (30) derived from step 2 as the new multiplicand, repeat steps 1 and 2 until the least significant digit (7) is added. The sum at this point is the decimal value.

Chart I-5. Eight Possible States of the Octal System

Decimal	Octal	Binary
0	0	000
1	1	001
2	2	010
3	3	011
4	4	100
5	5	101
6	6	110
7	7	111
Binary 001 100 110 111 equals 1467 in Octal		

Example: Convert $3657_{(8)}$ to its decimal equivalent,

$$\begin{array}{r} 3657 \\ \times 8 \\ \hline \end{array} \qquad \begin{array}{r} 3657 \\ \times 8 \\ \hline 24 \\ +6 \\ \hline 30 \\ \times 8 \\ \hline 240 \\ +5 \\ \hline 245 \\ \times 8 \\ \hline 1960 \\ +7 \\ \hline 1967_{10} \end{array} \rightarrow 3657_8$$

With careful observation of the digit or digits for each BCO word and a little practice, this conversion from binary to octal, or from octal to binary, can be made on sight. The programmer and machine operator need memorize only the binary equivalents of the eight octal digits. The unwieldy and error-inducing string of 0 s and 1 s can be presented in a more compact, convenient, and accurate form. Octal to binary is simply the reverse of the binary to octal conversion process.

The Biquinary Code

This is a binary-coded decimal system that uses seven-bit words instead of four-bit words (See Chart I-6). The code derives its name from the fact that one can conveniently divide it into two parts—the "bi" part, which consists of the first two bits at the left, and the "quinary" part, which makes up the other five digits. With this code, the decimal number 306 is written as:

0101000 0100001 1000010

Note that every single biquinary digit representation has exactly two 1 s in it—no more, no less.

Chart I-6. Biquinary Code

Decimal Digit	Biquinary Code	
	Bi	Quinary
	5 0	**4 3 2 1 0**
0	0 1	0 0 0 0 1
1	0 1	0 0 0 1 0
2	0 1	0 0 1 0 0
3	0 1	0 1 0 0 0
4	0 1	1 0 0 0 0
5	1 0	0 0 0 0 1
6	1 0	0 0 0 1 0
7	1 0	0 0 1 0 0
8	1 0	0 1 0 0 0
9	1 0	1 0 0 0 0
BIQUINARY-CODED DIGITS CAN REPRESENT ANY DECIMAL NUMBER		
3 ↓ 0101000	0 ↓ 0100001	6 ↓ 1000010

HEXADECIMAL NOTATION SYSTEM

Hexadecimal data are expressed to the base 16 and are related to the decimal numbers as shown in Chart I-7.

Chart I-7. Hexadecimal Equivalents

Decimal	Hexadecimal	BCD
0	0	0000
1	1	0001
2	2	0010
3	3	0011
4	4	0100
5	5	0101
6	6	0110
7	7	0111
8	8	1000
9	9	1001
10	A	1010
11	B	1011
12	C	1100
13	D	1101
14	E	1110
15	F	1111

Thus, hexadecimal numbers proceed from 0 through F (0 through 15 decimal) 10 through 1F (16 through 32 decimal), 20 through 2F (33 through 48 decimal, etc.).

Binary-Coded Decimal to Hexadecimal Conversion

Binary-coded decimal numbers can be separated into four-bit words for conversion to hexadecimal. For example, the binary number 010101011111 can be separated as follows:

$$\underbrace{0101}_{5}\quad\underbrace{0101}_{5}\quad\underbrace{1111}_{F}$$

Thus,

$$010101011111_2 = 55F_{16}$$

Hexadecimal to binary conversion is, of course, simply the reverse of binary to hexadecimal. For example, the hexadecimal number 1FFF equals 0001111111111111_2 ($F_{16} = 15_{10} = 1111_2$):

$$\overbrace{0001}^{1}\quad\overbrace{1111}^{F}\quad\overbrace{1111}^{F}\quad\overbrace{1111}^{F}$$

Hexadecimal to Decimal Conversion

Hexadecimal numbers can be converted to decimal numbers by expanding each position in the manner previously shown. For example,

$$\begin{aligned} 55F_{16} &= (5 \times 16^2) + (5 \times 16^1) + (15 \times 16^0) \\ &= (5 \times 256) + (5 \times 16) + (15 \times 1) \\ &= 1280 + 80 + 15 \\ &= 1375_{10} \end{aligned}$$

BOOLEAN ALGEBRA AND SWITCHING THEORY

For all the talk about "giant brains," for all the astonishing feats that modern computers perform, a computer is a remarkably simple machine. Almost every part in a computer has only one job to do: When the time comes for it to act it must say either "yes" or "no."

But to understand the significance of the simple decision we must go back to something discovered by a British mathematician more than a hundred years ago. His name was George Boole and he had this remarkable idea: Since, through numbers, we can apply mathematical laws to all manner of things—apples, oranges, inches, people—why can't we apply mathematics to logic? And that's what Boole did. He constructed an algebra of logic. Boolean algebra takes many forms, but the form that led eventually to the electronic computer concerns itself with this: Separate statements can be combined by mathematical rules to yield valid conclusions. For example, these statements —if it is snowing, then it is cold outside; if it is cold outside, then I will need my overcoat—lead to this conclusion: if it is snowing I will need my overcoat. Boolean algebra cannot prove whether any of the individual statements is true or false. But it can prove mathematically that if the statements are true, then the conclusion has to be true.

From Parlor Games to Thinking Machines

For more than a century this relatively abstract branch of mathematics seemed more suitable for philosophical parlor games than for practical application. Then in 1938 an American scientist named Claude Shannon discovered that electrical switches had something in common with the propositions that Boolean algebra concerned itself with. A proposition is either true or false, very much the same way that an electrical switch is either on or off. To illustrate how this works let's imagine we are building a very simple computer using only these few parts: a flashlight battery, a flashlight bulb, some wire, and two mechanical switches which control the flow of current (Fig. I-4).

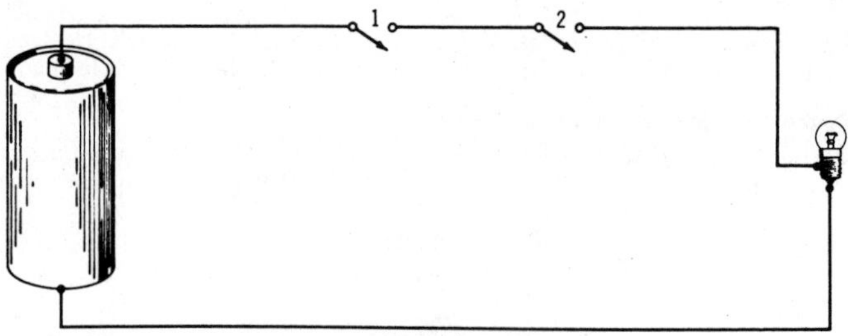

Fig. I-4. Simple series switching circuit.

The switches represent transistors which in today's computers control the flow of electronic pulses. In this simple computer, the switches, either of which you may open or close by hand, accept the "input," and the light bulb provides the "output" of this device. In this computer, two conditions must be met—both switches must be closed— for the bulb to light up. When only one switch is closed or when both are open, the bulb will be dark. When you consider the logical operations performed by this computer, they are really quite impressive: It accepts information as input—the switches are open or closed. It makes a decision based on the input—are both switches closed? It takes action based on this decision—either the bulb lights or remains unlit. Now by rearranging the switches (Fig. I-5) one can build a computer which will decide automatically whether either of the switches is closed and will light the bulb signaling, "Yes, at least one of the two possible conditions has been fulfilled."

By combining the two circuits (Fig. I-6), one can make a computer which will have four inputs and one output, and will answer this question: "Are inputs one and two present, and either input three or input four present?" Having examined the inputs and found the answer to this question, the computer will go on to decide: "If the answer is yes, light the bulb."

By this time the computer is doing a job of deciding what might actually be useful, and doing it a good deal faster than humans could. In actual practice, switching circuits are far more complicated than these examples, of course. But Shannon found that

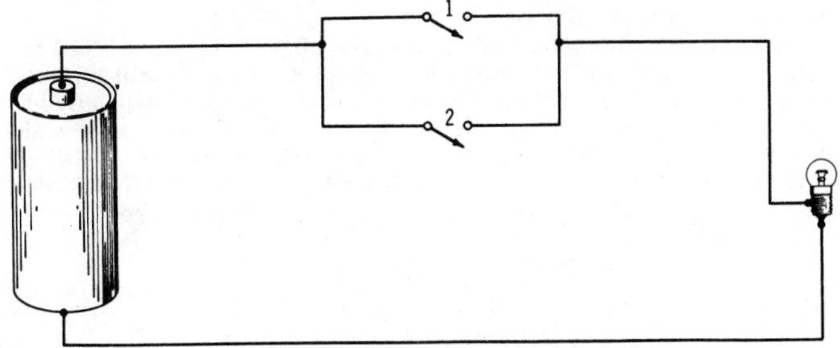

Fig. I-5. Simple parallel switching circuit.

by using the laws of algebraic logic, he could simplify the most difficult circuits in the same way he could simplify a complicated algebraic formula. Boolean algebra came into its own with the development of electronic computers, which are really giant switching circuits. For no matter what kind of advanced components a computer uses, each "decision" it makes comes down to whether a switch is on or off. Boolean algebra became the tool that computer designers used to decide how these decisions must be organized for the computer to do the tasks it is being designed to do.

Rules of Algebra

The algebra of switching circuits is Boolean and can be described as "two-valued" where the only two possible values are 0 and 1. Suppose that 1 represents a closed circuit (true) which allows current flow, and 0 represents (false) an open circuit through which there is no current flow, as shown in Chart I-8. A scheme of switching algebra can be established on this basis such that the algebra is applicable largely to series and parallel circuits. With some manipulation, it can also be used for nonseries parallel circuits.

The basic circuits are usually considered the series circuit and the parallel circuit. The parallel circuit is an OR and is usually designated by switches in parallel. This may be written as A OR B, which is the same as A + B. In this algebra, the addition (+) sign is the equivalent of two switches in parallel.

$0 + 0 = 0$ An open in parallel with an open is open. (Ex. 1)
$0 + 1 = 1$ An open in parallel with a closed is closed. (Ex. 2)
$1 + 1 = 1$ A closed in parallel with a closed is closed. (Ex. 3)
$0 \cdot 0 = 0$ An open in series with an open is open. (Ex. 4)
$0 \cdot 1 = 0$ An open in series with a closed is open. (Ex. 5)
$1 \cdot 1 = 1$ A closed in series with a closed is closed. (Ex. 6)

A series circuit, say of two switches, is considered to be an AND circuit such that two switches A and B in series are read as A AND B, which is the multiplication written as

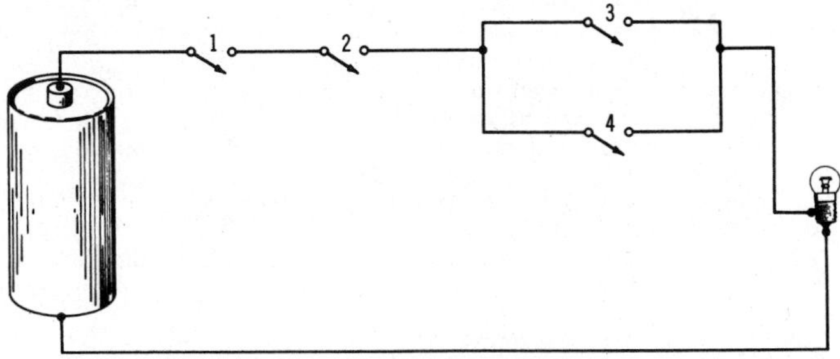

Fig. I-6. Simple series-parallel switching circuit.

AB. There is usually no symbol between the two; in some cases, where necessary for clarity, the AB is written A · B or as A × B.

There are three basic rules for addition, as shown: 0 + 0 (Ex. 1) is equal to 0, which is to say that an open circuit in parallel with an open circuit is still an open circuit; 0 + 1 (Ex. 2) is equal to 1, which means that an open circuit in parallel with a closed circuit is the equivalent of a closed circuit; (Ex. 3) 1 + 1 is equal to 1, which means that a closed circuit in parallel with a closed circuit is equal to a closed circuit. In summary, the rules for addition say (considering a parallel circuit) that there will be a current flow if A is closed or B is closed or if both A and B are closed.

Chart I-8. Algebra of Switching Circuits

Symbol	Logic	Relay and Contact	Meaning
1	True	Closed	The statement is true; the circuit is closed.
0	False	Open	The statement is false; the circuit is open.
·	Series	A AND B	A is in series with B.
+	Parallel	A OR B	A is in parallel with B.

In the same way, multiplication is the equivalent of a series circuit. 0 · 0 (Ex. 4) is equal to 0, which is to say that an open circuit in series with an open is still an open. 0 · 1 equals 0 (Ex. 5) means that an open circuit in series with a closed circuit is still an open circuit. The 1 · 1 (Ex. 6) equals 1 means that a closed circuit in series with a closed circuit is equal to a closed circuit. Thus, in summary for multiplication, which refers to a series circuit, there is current flow if, and only if, all the switches in the series are closed.

The third consideration for switching algebra is the complement or negation. Clearly, the complement of an open circuit is a closed circuit, and the complement of a closed circuit is an open circuit. The prime represents complementation or negation as 1′ equals 0, 0′ equals 1; if A equals 0, A′ equals 1. Other fundamental relationships are given in Chart I-9.

Chart I-9. Additional Fundamental Relationships of Switching Algebra

A = A	(A′)′ = A
if A = B and B = C, then A = C	0′ = 1
if A = B, B = A	1′ = 0
A + A = A	A + 1 = 1
A · A = A	0 · A = 0
if A = 0, A′ = 1	A′ + A = 1
if A = 1, A′ = 0	A′ · A = 0

In order to establish a clear, coherent, valid system of switching algebra, it is necessary to establish certain ground rules such as those previously given. There are many possibilities of establishing the basic ground rules or systems by which various types or forms of switching algebra could be developed. For example, 0 could be a closed circuit, and 1 could be an open circuit. It is also possible, since this is a two-valued system, to use any of two opposite values, such as an open circuit and a closed circuit, current flow and no current flow, voltage and no voltage, high voltage and low voltage, positive voltage and negative voltage, a pulse or no pulse, or any such duals.

Certain other rules (Ex. 7 through Ex. 16) are given in Chart I-10. The rule of absorption is self-evident, A + A equals A (Ex. 7) and A · A equals A (Ex. 8). Notice that this is significantly different from other forms of algebra. In the Boolean algebra used for switching, there is no significance to a quantity such as 2A, since there is either an A or not an A.

The commutative law has two forms. In the commutative law of addition (Ex. 9) (A + B equals B + A), the order in which two quantities are added is not significant.

Two quantities can be added regardless of the order of addition. In the same manner, the commutative law of multiplication (Ex. 10), $(A \cdot B)$ equals $(B \cdot A)$ says that the sequence in which two items are multiplied is not significant. These basic laws seem rather trivial; however, in certain forms of mathematics, such as operations with matrices or in permutations, it is not necessarily true that multiplication obeys the commutative law.

Chart I-10. Rules of Boolean Algebra in Symbolic Logic Systems

Law	Rule	Example
Absorption	$A + A = A$	(Ex. 7)
	$A \cdot A = A$	(Ex. 8)
Commutative	$A + B = B + A$	(Ex. 9)
	$A \cdot B = B \cdot A$	(Ex. 10)
Associative	$(A + B) + C = A + (B + C) = A + B + C$	(Ex. 11)
	$(A \cdot B) \cdot C = A \cdot (B \cdot C) = A \cdot B \cdot C$	(Ex. 12)
Distributive	$A \cdot (B + C) = A \cdot B + A \cdot C$	(Ex. 13)
	$A + B \cdot C = (A + B) \cdot (A + C)$	(Ex. 14)
Identities	$A + 0 = 0 + A = A$	(Ex. 15)
	$1(A) = A(1) = A$	(Ex. 16)
De Morgan's Rule	$(A \cdot B)' = A' + B'$	(Ex. 17)
	$(A + B)' = A' \cdot B'$	(Ex. 18)

The associative laws again are in two forms; the associate law of addition (Ex. 11) says that in adding three numbers it is not significant which two are added first, as $(A + B) + C$ equals $A + (B + C)$ equals $A + B + C$. In the same manner with the associative laws of multiplication (Ex. 12) the sequence of multiplication is not significant, as $(A \cdot B) \cdot C$ equals $A \cdot (B \cdot C)$ equals $A \cdot B \cdot C$. Another way of saying this is that for addition where a series of numbers is to be added, no parentheses are needed; and in the same way where a series of factors is to be multiplied, no parentheses are needed.

The distributive law relates to both addition and multiplication. This law states that multiplication is distributive over addition, or the multiplier, which in this case is A, is distributed over both quantities in the parentheses (B and C). $A \cdot (B + C)$ equals $A \cdot B + A \cdot C$ (Ex. 13). In the other form of addition over multiplication, $A + B \cdot C$ equals $(A + B) \cdot (A + C)$ (Ex. 14).

A very significant law is one of identity. The number 0 is known as the identity of addition and as shown, A equals 0 or $0 + A$ equals A (Ex. 15). The identity for multiplication is 1, and 1 multiplied by any number such as A is equal to the number itself, as $1(A)$ equals $A(1)$ equals A (Ex. 16).

Negations are related by De Morgan's Rule; for the logical product, the negation of $(A \cdot B)$, which is written as $(A \cdot B)'$ and read as NOT A AND B, is equal to NOT A or NOT B, which is written as A′ OR B′ (Ex. 17). In the same manner $(A + B)' = A' \cdot B'$ as in Ex. 18.

SET THEORY AND NOTATION

The student should be able to tie binary and other number systems to switching theory in computer use. To aid in furthering the understanding of Boolean algebra and computer circuitry, set theory will be briefly noted together with an introduction to the graphical display of sets, Venn diagrams. For further reference the concept of truth tables is also developed, as are listings of symbols for sets and propositional logic.

Sets

Whenever one classifies or describes something by a characteristic or property, he says in effect that the thing belongs to a set of all things having that characteristic or property. Each "thing" in a set is an element of the set. Smaller groups of "things" or elements in the set are subsets if identifiable by some characteristic common to each of the elements of the subset. The set includes all of the elements having the given property. A set having no elements is called the empty or null set. The set that includes all of the elements having a given property is called the universal set of the things having the given characteristic. Each element of A is also an element of B; thus, A is a subset of B. The complement of a set is the set of elements not in the set; read "NOT B," or B′ or B.

Definitions

An *intersection* of two sets is another set which contains those elements common to both sets: Read "A intersects B." *Union* of sets A and B is the set of all elements in A or B: Read "A union B" thus OR is inclusive. If two sets have an intersection they are said to be *conjoint;* if they do not, they are said to be *disjoint.*

Subset notation: "X = (x:x is a New Yorker)," Read: "X is the set of elements x, such that x is a New Yorker." This is an open sentence; i.e., a statement defining a set, and specifying those elements of the universe which are contained in that set. Since "x" can take on a number of values "x" is called a *variable.* This contrasts with a *constant, a fixed number.*

Domain: Associated with every variable is the domain of that variable which is the set of all possible names of things or values which might be inserted as a state of that variable . . . it is not a definition of the solution set. This is the list of elements which satisfy the one problem.

A *parameter* is a constant which remains fixed for a particular problem or set of circumstances but which changes over time or circumstances; i.e., a parametric constant.

Venn diagrams are graphs of the algebra of sets, an explanation aid. The three basic logical expressions are NOT, OR and AND; i.e., the complement, the union, and the intersection, respectively of sets and Venn diagrams. The logical operators, TRUE and FALSE, are represented in binary Boolean notation by 1 and 0 respectively. The main sets of concern in switching are the subsets which represent individual switches. The *truth table* is a tabular representation of the truth or falsity of the output function; i.e., the outcome of a combination of input switches and their settings. Because the switch is a stable element with two possible positions, on/off, the binary operation in computers is the continuous flipping of on-off. Addition, subtraction (by adding of components), etc., and comparing and consequent branching are accomplished by near light-speed switching.

TRUTH TABLES

In order to use statements in their compound form, it is necessary to provide links or connections. A list of these connections is given in Chart I-11. The first thing to remember about logical connectives is that the truth value of any connective is defined by the truth values of the propositions it connects. For example, the truth value of AND may be defined by the truth table of the conjunctive proposition A · B as shown in Chart I-12. In the first case, if A is true and B is true the compound statement

Chart I-11. Symbols of the Propositional Logic

Symbol	Name	Means
V	Conjunction	A and B
V	Disjunction (inclusive)	Either A or B or both
$\underline{V}$	Disjunction (exclusive)	Either A or B but not both
|	Nonconjunction	Not both A and B
—	Negation	Not A
⇄	Equivalence (biconditional)	A if, and only if B

Chart I-12. Truth Table of A $\wedge$ B

	a	b	a$\wedge$ b
1	T	T	T
2	T	F	F
3	F	T	F
4	F	F	F

A AND B must be true. However, if, as in the second step, A is true and B is false, the conjunction of A AND B must necessarily be false. In the third example, if A is false and B is true their conjunction in this case must also be false. In the fourth case, where A is false and B is false, the conjunction of A AND B must also be false. In summary, when we have two simple statements connected by the conjunction, the compound statement A AND B is true if, and only if, A is true and B is true. There are no other possibilities; the table exhausts all the possible truth values of the propositions.

The second connective is the OR, which is the disjunction of A and B. If we have two simple statements A and B, the compound statement A OR B is true when either of the two individual simple statements is true. For example, if A is true, then A OR B is true; if B is true, then A OR B must necessarily be false. There is a problem with the case shown in Chart I-13 where A is true and B is true. The question is simply this; does the statement A OR B mean either A OR either B, or does it mean either A OR B or both? If we consider that it means the latter, then A OR B is true if A is true. In technical terms this truth reflects the *inclusive* disjunction of A and B.

Chart I-13. Truth Table of A V B

	a	b	a v b
1	T	T	T
2	T	F	T
3	F	T	T
4	F	F	F

In order to differentiate between the two possible meanings of the word OR, it is necessary to define the *exclusive* disjunction of A and B as meaning either A or B but not both. A truth table for this is shown in Chart I-14. By definition the only two cases that are true are the second and third shown in the truth table; in case 2, A is true and B is false; in case 3, A is false and B is true. Both of these compound statements are then true. In the fourth case if both A and B are false, the compound statement is false. In the first case, by definition, if both are true, the compound statement is false since the exclusive disjunction of A and B is necessarily false if both are true.

Another basic connective is *negation,* which means simply that NOT A is the negation of A, and NOT B is the negation of B. This means of course that if A is true, the negation of A is false. If A is false, the negation of A is true. Although the fundamental idea of negation seems simple, it is very significant for compound statements. For example, Chart I-15 shows the statement A OR NOT B. In the truth table shown there are again four possible cases. Consider the first, where A is true and B is true. Since B is true its negation is false, and the statement becomes the equivalent of a compound statement that is true OR false; hence the statement is true. In the second case, when

Chart I-14. Truth Table of A $\underline{\vee}$ B

	a	b	a $\underline{\vee}$ b
1	T	T	F
2	T	F	T
3	F	T	T
4	F	F	F

Chart I-15. Truth Table of A V ~ B

Consider av ~ b (a or not b)			
	a	b	a v ~ b
1	T	T	T V F is T
2	T	F	T V T is T
3	F	T	F V F is F
4	F	F	F V T is T

A is true and B is false, the negation of B is of course true; hence the statement becomes a compound statement that is true OR true, which of course is true. In the third case, A is false and B is true; the negation of B is then false, so that this compound statement is false. In the last case, A is false and B is false; the negation of B is then true so that the compound statement is false OR true, which is true. This is an example of the inclusive disjunction of A OR NOT B.

VENN DIAGRAMS

A few concepts showing the use of sets and switching theory are demonstrated below through the use of Venn diagrams.

In Fig. I-7 the first equation is C equals A, and in the Venn diagram the darker area represents the A. All else in the rectangle is A′. The second equation is C is equal to A′, and in the Venn diagram everything but the circle A is darkened, which represents NOT A.

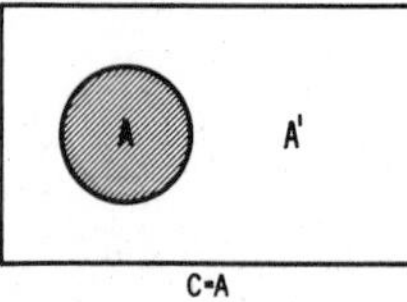

C=A

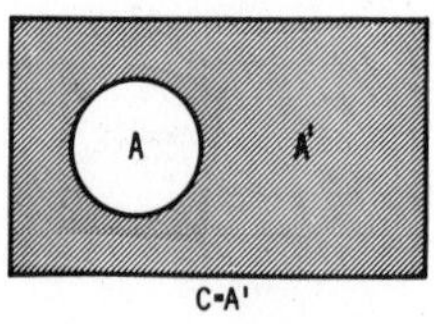

C=A'

Fig. I-7. Venn diagram.

Fig. I-8 shows in several variations that C equals A · B. The first one, which is the simplest, is C is equal to A AND B, so that in the Venn diagram the area which is common to both A and B is the darkened area where the two circles A and B overlap. This is the only area in the universe C which is in common with A and with B.

The second logical relation in this figure is C is equal to A AND NOT B. Note in the Venn diagram that the entire circle A is included except that portion of A which overlaps the circle B.

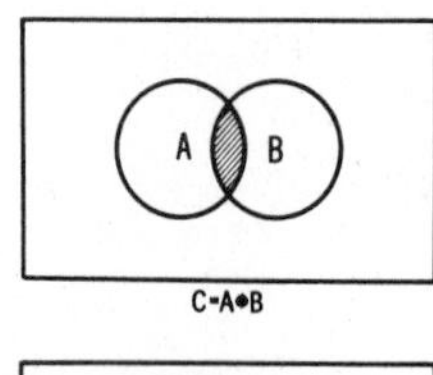

C=A•B

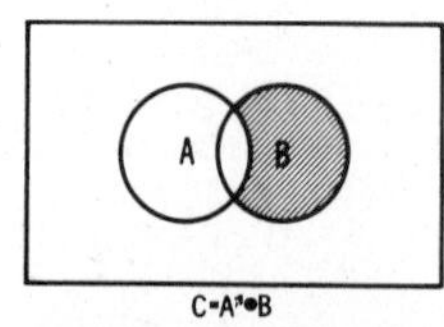

C=A'•B

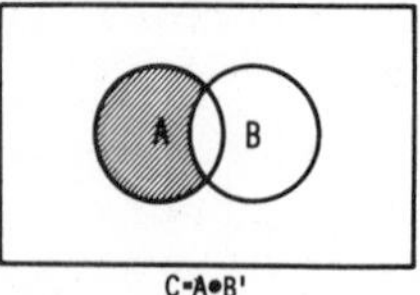

C=A•B'

C = A'•B'

Fig. I-8. Four variations of C = A.B.

The third one is similar to the second since this is C is equal to NOT A AND B. Note in the Venn diagram the area of concern is the circle B less that part of B which overlaps the circle A.

Inverting both, as in the fourth case, provides the equation C is equal to NOT A AND NOT B. The Venn diagram shows the entire rectangle used except for the circle including area A and the circle including area B and the area which overlaps both of them.

In a similar manner various types of OR relations are shown in Fig. I-9. In the first case, C is equal to A OR B, and the Venn diagram for this shows clearly that this is the same as the inverse of C is equal to A AND B.

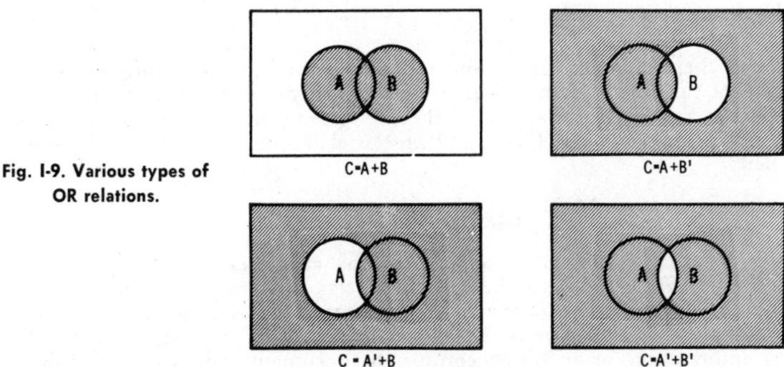

Fig. I-9. Various types of OR relations.

The second OR circuit is C equals NOT A OR B, and as shown in the Venn diagram this is the inverse of C equals A AND NOT B.

As shown in the Venn diagram, A OR NOT B is the inverse of C is equal to NOT A AND B.

The last case of the OR circuits shows C is equal to NOT A OR NOT B. Note again that this is the inverse of C is equal to A AND B.

Fig. I-10 shows some other possible logical arrangements. The first expression is C equals A and NOT B OR NOT A AND B. As shown in the Venn diagram this includes the areas of circle A, and circle B but does not include the area which is common to both.

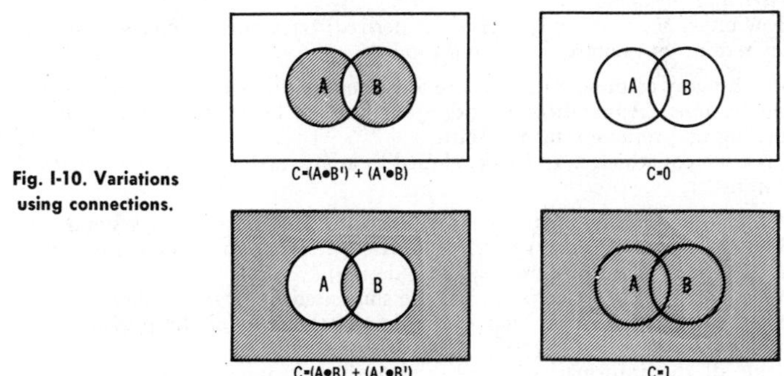

Fig. I-10. Variations using connections.

The second equation is C is equal to A AND B OR NOT A AND NOT B. In the Venn diagram this includes the universe C less area A and less area B, but including the area which is common to both.

The third case is C is equal to 0, which means that the universe is empty. The universe C has no occupants. The last case of C is equal to 1 shows that the universe contains all occupants.

APPENDIX J

Flowcharting — Logic, Symbols, Abbreviations

Although there is much discussion and concern in the literature in relation to definitions of various diagrammatical or geometrical representation of the sequencing of systems or activities of computers, there is general agreement on three types of these ordered displays. Flow, block, and process charts or diagrams will be briefly discussed here.

CHARTS AND DIAGRAMS

Before one takes command or control of the computer to solve problems, it is necessary to develop programs; i.e., complete sets of explicit instructions to direct the computer to the desired objective. The program does not simply fall into place. Many "planning" questions must be asked and answered first regarding the flow of the data, information, or action concerning the documents, conditions, and output of the problem.

Before charting begins, this type of check list might be applicable:

1. Does the problem, model, or system have adequate definition; has it been simplified and logically ordered?
2. Has a definite determination been made concerning a chosen technique, methodology, or system of solution or organization?
3. Will the method selected fit the computer to be used; are language, compiler, and interface problems resolved?
4. Have we scheduled the input computer run, debugging, and analysis times?
5. Are library routines available which can be used directly or modified for this particular problem?
6. How much accuracy and precision is desired; have adequate checks and tests been devised for program segments and totality?

Although many of these questions are answered in the operations research and model building sections (Appendices E and F) they must be considered thoroughly before any charting or programming is begun.

If it is a system which is to be developed or reorganized, a different variety of questions is in order:

1. What are the parts, purposes, and procedures of the present system?
2. What schemes will be invented or devised in order to develop the efficiency and effectiveness of the proposed system (design)?
3. What parts of the new system will be simulated for a *test design* after collection, organization, abstraction, and evaluation of the facts of the present environment and operation?
4. Have all the informative details concerning documents, files, and reports been outlined from sample copies, user interviews, and division head suggestions?

After the answers to the above questions have been developed and analyzed, several types of mnemonics, symbolic notation, and abbreviations can be devised in preparation for charting. Each of the three types of charts can be quickly defined as pictorial or graphic displays in conventional notation to show organization, sequence, and methodology of procedure and solution design.

It is agreed by many authorities, that the computer system design itself begins with the block diagram of the system as a whole—a synthesis. The emphasis, here, it is felt, is concerned with overall procedure, the work stations, the integrated unit, itself. To break this series of "blocks" down into computer activities or "runs," the process chart is utilized.

The process chart develops the sequence of processing operations—the master scheme—from which the flowcharts develop the small logical steps, i.e., the internal-type computer operations. The flowchart develops the logical details of the runs which the process chart depicts from the overall block diagram of the system.

The symbols of all three types of charts are displayed on the following pages. Generally the rectangle is considered the "function box" to indicate some specific action. The information within the box may be in English, algebra, or acronyms and mnemonics. The diamond is the "decision box." The inequalities signs, > <, the arrow, and the many others are used according to conventions.

Although there are many advantages for charting and diagramming, the majority can be summarized as follows:

1. Valuable aids and tools to organize analytic thinking.
2. Isolation of the logic of the problem into more easily understood and handled parts.
3. Segmentation of the details away from the instruction writing.
4. Achievement of a means of communication of an individual's thoughts and methodology to others.
5. Utilization of this memory tool to aid in recalling or explaining the first few instructions or amended initial solution attempts, and then the final system itself.

SYMBOL STANDARDS

Most manufacturers and software developers use flowcharting symbols (Charts J-1 and J-2) published by the American National Standards Institute and additional ones which remain consistent with the standards as shown on the following pages.

A system flowchart (Chart J-2) describes the flow of data through all parts of a system. In addition to three basic symbols and the supplementary annotation symbol, fourteen system flowchart symbols may be used to describe this flow and the relationships among information (and its medium), equipment, equipment operations, and manual operations. In a system flowchart an entire program run or phase is always represented by a single processing symbol, together with the input/output symbols.

A program flowchart describes what takes place in a stored program. It displays specific operations and decisions, and their sequence within the program. In addition to three basic symbols, six program flowchart symbols may be used, as well as the supplementary annotation symbol.

THE FLOWCHART AND THE PROGRAMMER

The examples used below make computer programming seem almost childishly simple. It's not. The varieties of problems a programmer deals with, the symbols and codes he uses, the kinds of computers he works with all demand a high degree of ingenuity, experience, and above all, a quality that most people never associate with computer work—imagination.

A programmer frequently spends weeks or even months observing and studying a problem before he begins to work out the steps by which a computer can solve it most efficiently. Despite the basic simplicity of the computer's decision-making ability, many of the techniques the programmer uses are far from simple. Programmers, then, serve as translators, helping to communicate with computers. As computers are given bigger and bigger jobs to do, the demand for more and better programmers grows. Little more than ten years ago, the job of computer programmer didn't exist. Today it is one of the most rewarding, fascinating, and fast-growing professions in the country.

What does it take to become a good programmer? The ability to think logically is the main requirement. An education consisting of sciences and mathematics often indicates an aptitude for programming work because these subjects also call for logical thinking. A knowledge of higher mathematics is necessary for programmers of com-

Chart J-1. Program Flowcharting Symbols

Symbol	Represents
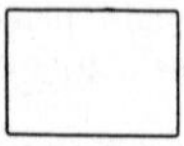 *	PROCESS A group of program instructions that perform a processing function of the program.
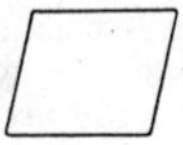 *	INPUT/OUTPUT Any function of an input/output device (making information available for processing, recording processing information, tape positioning, etc.).
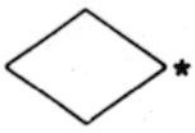 *	DECISION The decision function is used to document points in the program where a branch to alternate paths is possible based upon variable conditions.
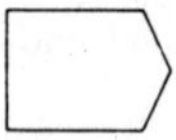	PROGRAM MODIFICATION An instruction or group of instructions which changes the program sequence.
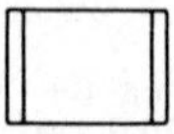 *	PREDEFINED PROCESS A named process consisting of one or more operations or program steps that are specified elsewhere, e.g., subroutine or logical unit.
 *	TERMINAL The beginning, end, or a point of interruption in a program.
*	CONNECTOR An entry from, or an exit to, another part of the program flowchart.
	OFFPAGE CONNECTOR A connector used to designate entry to or exit from a page.
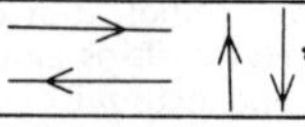 *	FLOW DIRECTION The direction of processing or data flow.
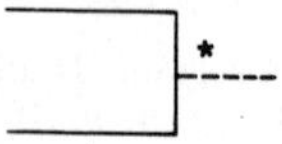 *	ANNOTATION The addition of descriptive comments or explanatory notes as clarification.

*This material is reproduced from the American National Standards Institute, Flowchart Symbols and Their Usage in Information Processing, ANSI X3.5-1970. American National Standards Institute, 1430 Broadway, New York, N.Y. 10018.

puters used in scientific work. Programmers of business-data processing systems need no specific educational background.

Putting a computer through its paces is not just a pushbutton job. This illustrates a basic truth about computers and other "thinking machines"—a computer's usefulness depends completely upon the instructions that men give it. Computers are, in truth, merely extensions of man's own thinking power.

Running an automatic machine is an easy job. Just make a few adjustments, press a few buttons . . . and sit back. Running a computer is a little different. One first must give it a complete description of the job he wants it to do. He must, in fact, instruct it. This job of instruction is called programming. To do it one must know how a computer solves problems. It is known that a computer's parts can say only "yes" or "no" to any choice they are presented with. That means every step in every problem must be stated in such a way that it can be answered by "yes" or "no." This is not as limiting as it may seem. Most of our everyday actions can be broken down into responses of simple "yes" or "no" choices.

Certain conventions are usually followed in the use of the flowcharting symbols:

1. The operation to be performed is described by the charting symbol and by a

Chart J-2. System Flowcharting Symbols

Symbol	Description	Symbol	Description
PUNCHED CARD *	All varieties of punched cards including stubs.	PUNCHED TAPE *	Paper or plastic, chad or chadless.
DOCUMENT *	Paper documents and reports of all varieties.	TRANSMITTAL TAPE	A proof or adding machine tape or similar batch-control information.
MAGNETIC TAPE *		ONLINE STORAGE *	
OFFLINE STORAGE *	Offline storage of either paper, cards, magnetic or perforated tape.	DISPLAY *	Information displayed by plotters or video devices.
MANUAL INPUT *	Information supplied to or by a computer utilizing an online device.	SORTING, COLLATING	An operation on sorting or collating equipment.
CLERICAL OR MANUAL OPERATION *	A manual offline operation not requiring mechanical aid.	AUXILIARY OPERATION *	A machine operation supplementing the main processing function.
KEYING OPERATION	An operation utilizing a key-driven device.	COMMUNICATION LINK *	The automatic transmission of information from one location to another via communication lines.

*This material is reproduced from the American National Standards Institute, Flowchart Symbols and Their Usage in Information Processing, ANSI X3.5-1970. American National Standards Institute, 1430 Broadway, New York, N.Y. 10018.

notation in words or symbols inside the charting symbol. For example, the diamond indicates a decision stemming from a comparison or test (Fig. J-1). An important exception, however, which the student should note, is the use of both the diamond and the oval to represent decisions. Lines coming out of either represent the different program paths which result from the decision. An example of this duplication of conventions is shown in Fig. J-2.

2. The notation inside the processing symbol uses standard arithmetic notation (Fig. J-3). One symbol with a special computer meaning is →. This means "to move to."

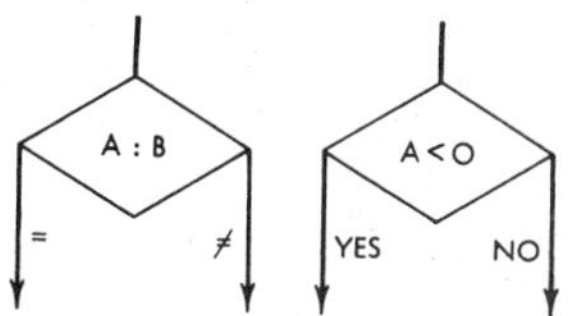

Fig. J-1. Diamond indicates decision stemming from a comparison or test.

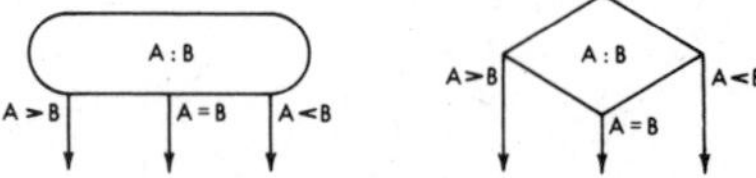

Fig. J-2. Oval or diamond can represent decisions.

Thus A → B means to move the contents of memory location A to memory location B. A + B → C means to add the contents of the location identified as A and B and store the sum in location C. Parentheses are sometimes used to differentiate the "contents of" a memory location from the location itself. (A) → B means to move contents of location A to location B and is equivalent to A → B.

3. A name (label) may be used to identify a block of instructions. It is placed above and to the left of the symbol (Fig. J-4). The label can be used later in the program or in the computer coding to refer to the block of instructions. A reference is also frequently put in the symbol and separated from the instructions by a line.

4. The normal direction of flow in charting is from left to right and from top to bottom.

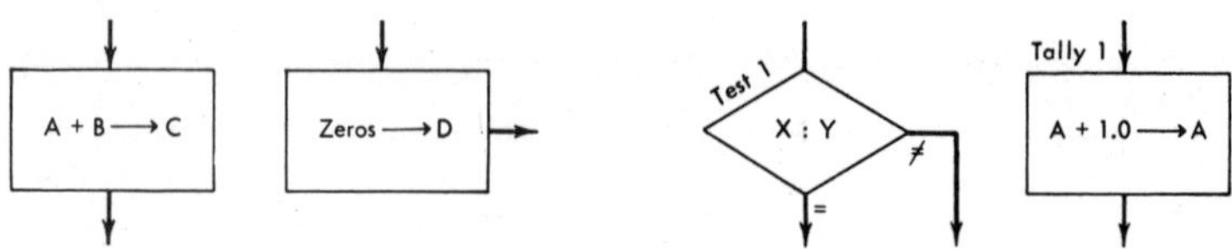

Fig. J-3. Standard arithmetic notations are used inside the processing symbol.

Fig. J-4. A name may be used to identify a block of instructions.

5. There are no set rules for differentiating between the alphabetic O and the zero, but programming practice tends to slash the alphabetic O and leave the zero alone. The Z and 2 are similarly differentiated.

Alphabetic	*Numeric*
Ø or O	0
Ƶ	2

The flowcharting symbols for systems charting include the processing box and basic input/output symbol. In addition, symbols are used for input/output media, input/output devices, mass storage, auxiliary operations, and manual operations.

PRESENTATION TECHNIQUES

1. Symbol orientation. The orientation of each symbol on a flowchart fits generally into one of ten groups: (a) operational, (b) decision making, (c) direction of flow, (d) terminal, (e) connector and link, (f) program variation, (g) annotation, (h) status, (i) communication, and (j) off-line designation.
2. Symbol size. The size of each symbol may vary, but the dimensional ratio of each symbol shall be maintained as specified in the charts.
3. Flow direction. Flow direction is represented by lines drawn between symbols.
4. Normal direction flow is from left to right or top to bottom.
5. When the flow direction is not left to right or top to bottom, open arrowheads shall be placed on reverse-direction flow-lines.
6. When increased clarity is desired, open arrowheads can be placed on normal direction flowlines.
7. When flowlines are broken due to page limitation, connector symbols shall be used to indicate the break.
8. When flow is bidirectional, it can be shown by either single or double lines, but open arrowheads shall be used to indicate both normal direction flow and reverse direction flow.

SAMPLE ELEMENTARY PROBLEMS

As an aid to explaining the solutions of a few problems, the technique of diagramming will be introduced and used here. Diagrams serve two very basic purposes:

1. They offer an easy notation for analyzing the steps required in the solution of a problem.
2. They provide basic documentation in the form of a "map" of the program, so that someone unfamiliar with the program can easily determine what the program does and how it does it.

It is for the above reasons that diagramming is not only highly recommended, but is often required at data-processing installations. Techniques of diagramming vary greatly, as do the symbols used. In addition, detail in diagramming may range from the very basic block diagram, to the flowchart with almost every machine instruction represented in the diagram.

The more complete the diagram is, the easier is the job of actually writing the program; however, initial analysis of a problem can usually be noted only in major steps.

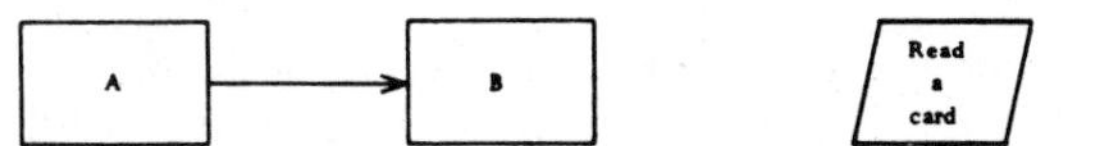

Fig. J-5. Direction of flow shows relationship of symbols.

Fig. J-6. Input/output symbol used for input/output operations.

Since it will serve most purposes, only simple diagramming techniques will be explained here. Further details of this important technique are available in the reference manuals.

Before depicting a few examples of basic diagramming or charting (both terms are casually used interchangeably), some further characteristics should be noted. Flowcharts or diagrams of various sorts usually develop from very rough sketches of interviews, in the cases relating to systems analysis (i.e., procedure, forms analysis, or forms distributions, etc.) or "blueprints" for calculating solutions of problems. Notes are usually initially entered right on the chart to describe the operation. Include all pertinent information and the segments depicting activities and flows. The charts prove most useful when discussing systems, forms, mathematical techniques especially in communication with others. The chart-picture is a distinct aid to management to show variations of procedures and especially comparisons with the old, the new, and the projected. The procedure not only portrays exceptional clarity, logical sequence, and stepped procedures, but will usually result in the elimination of unnecessary program steps; the set of charts and diagrams will also usually suggest computational short cuts and additional useful results.

Fig. J-7. Program symbol used to represent steps not represented by special symbols.

Compute A=B+C

Increase pay number by 1

Find average temperature

The direction of flow simply shows the relationship of one symbol to another. Fig. J-5 shows that A is executed and then B is executed.

The input/output symbol is used to refer to any operation that involves an input/output device (Fig. J-6).

The program symbol is used to represent any steps in the program which are not represented by special symbols (Fig. J-7).

The decision symbol represents any logical decision that is contained in the program (Fig. J-8).

The stop symbol is used to indicate the end of the program (Fig. J-9). If there are several ways to end the program, there may be several stop symbols.

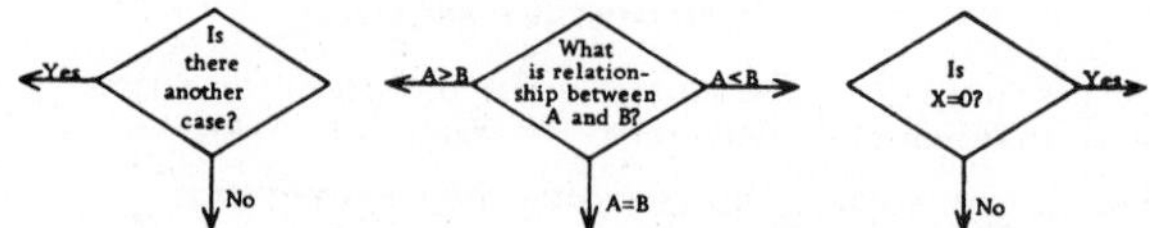

Fig. J-8. Decision symbols represent logical decisions in a program.

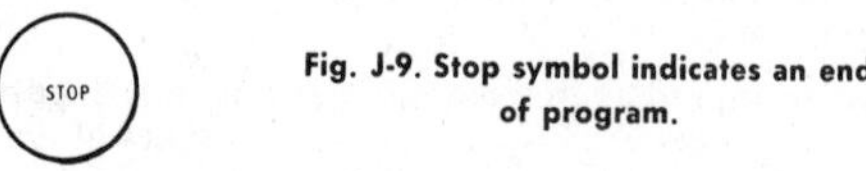

Fig. J-9. Stop symbol indicates an end of program.

A WORD FLOWCHART

When the comparisons are represented in flowchart form, the line of reasoning and four possible paths to solution become clearer. The word picture in Fig. J-10 shows the stages of a whole comparison process joined in logical sequence. If the computer could think through the process as a human being can, it might ask the questions illustrated in the diagram.

A word picture is a realistic description of the problem. However, a large flowchart would become cluttered with too many words. Therefore, symbols are substituted. The same operations are shown in the flowchart in Fig. J-11.

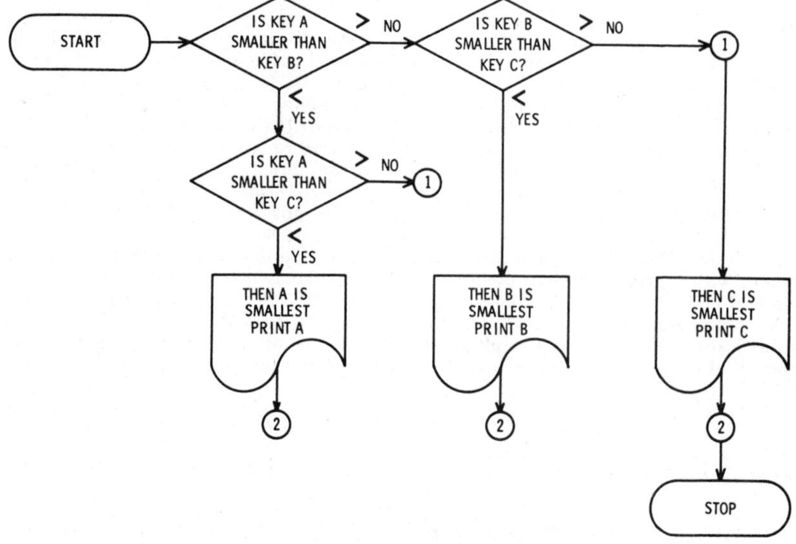

Fig. J-10. A word-picture flowchart.

Once the instructions for solving a certain problem are worked out, they can be recorded on tape or punched cards and used again and again, whenever the need arises. These "canned programs" (software) enable computer users to take advantage of programming work that has already been done on problems that may be similar throughout an industry, or throughout business generally.

Many longer programs (> 100 FORTRAN statements) should be segmented; i.e., designed, written and compiled as a main program and several subroutines. Although this technique requires careful attention to communication between parts, the net advantage compensates for the additional work. These advantages are twofold:

1. Writing, debugging, and changing smaller programs (i.e., subroutines) is usually easier because it is possible to concentrate on, and to attend to a smaller, more reasonable number of program details.

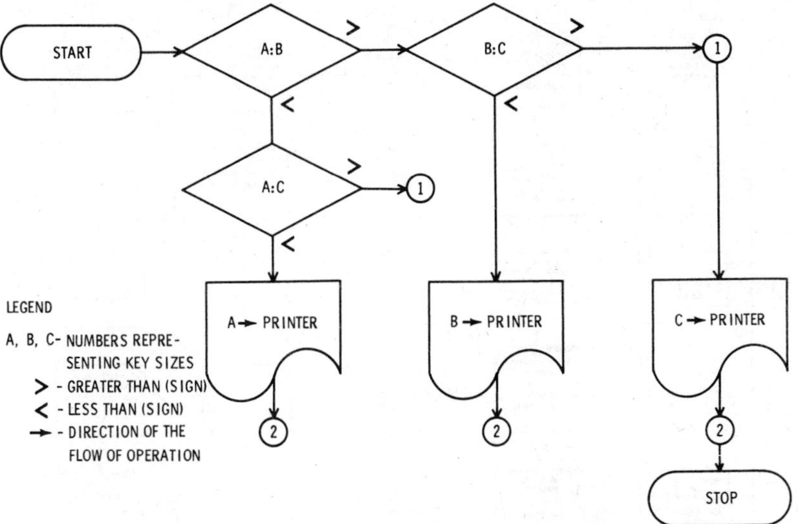

Fig. J-11. Flowchart using symbols in place of words.

2. The time required for handling and processing of jobs is, in the long run, considerably reduced. This reduction is possible because initial compilation of segmented jobs takes no longer than nonsegmented jobs. However, because 99% of the jobs to be processed require debugging and recompilation, it is necessary in segmented jobs to recompile only those parts (subroutines) that contain errors. This saving in (re) compilation time can be as high as 30% of all the machine time used for compilations.

Generalization of programs is the incorporation of flexible features that allow the program to operate in a variety of ways depending on the value of parameters (i.e., new variables or constants) read in during execution, or on the nature of the regular input data. The purpose of generalization is to avoid the necessity of reprogramming (and recompiling) for minor changes in data or in output requirements. In the following discussion and examples some of the techniques that have proved useful are outlined.

USE OF FLOWCHARTING WORKSHEET AND IBM "AUTOCHART"

The program flowchart shown in Fig. J-12 is a detailed portion of a tape merge program. It was referenced on two program charts of lower-level detail by predefined process symbols. This is indicated by references on the left-hand side of the offpage connectors—"from AF" at blocks A1 and A3 as well as "from AK" at block A5. Most program flowchart symbols are used in this chart.

The following techniques and conventions should be noted:

1. The computer program operations are numbered to the top and right of the symbols for easy reference in a narrative.

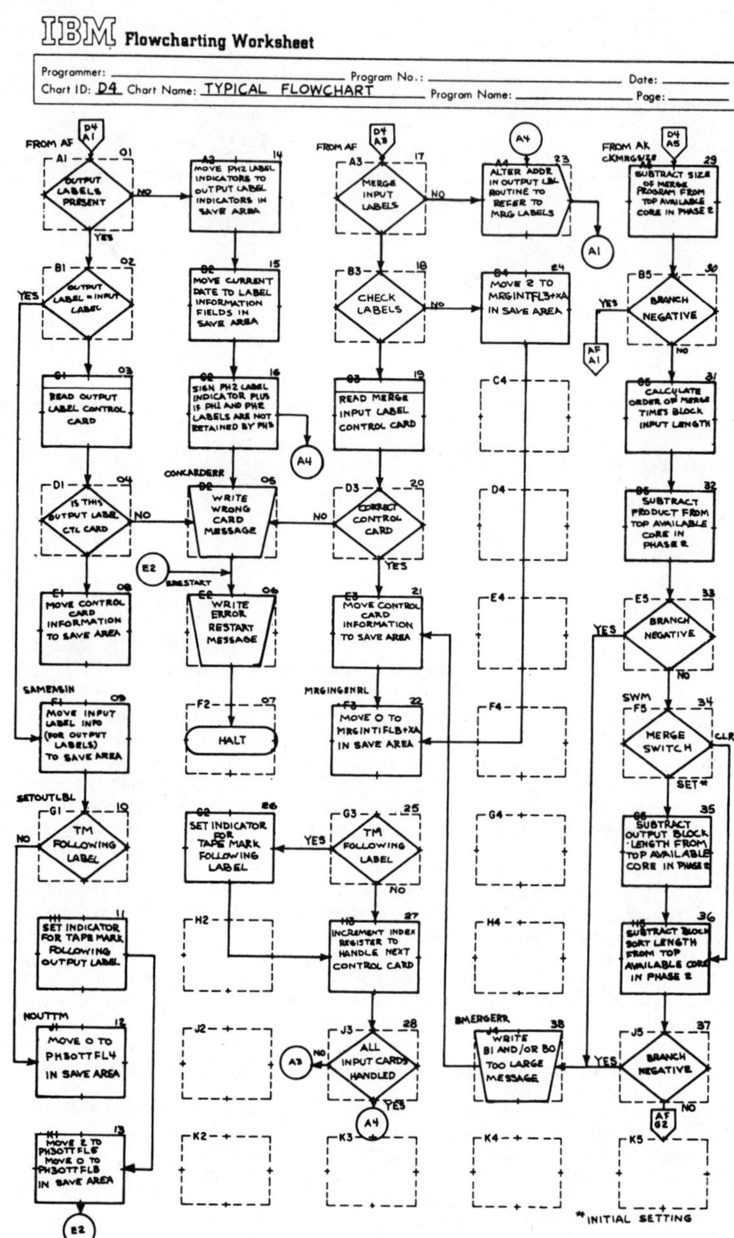

Fig. J-12. Detailed portion of a tape merge program.

2. Offpage connectors are used. The references are page number and in-connection or to-location blocks of the worksheet. The from-connection is indicated by page number.
3. The connector symbols are used in place of flowlines which would cross other flowlines. The reference numbers are in-connections or to-location blocks of the worksheet.
4. Arrowheads are used whenever the flow direction is not from top to bottom or left to right.
5. The predefined process symbol is used to denote that an additional program flowchart is included which defines this particular process in detail.
6. The program modification symbol is used to indicate that an address is an illustration to be modified.
7. The amount of detail required in a program flowchart depends upon the need. A set of multilevel charts is produced when a precise picture of program logic at a high level of detail is required. This approach may be likened to map-drawing techniques—for example, starting with an all-inclusive map and exploding sections of it on succeeding maps, each map showing greater detail.
8. The technique of presenting a complete picture on each chart is called modular program flowcharting. It stresses the logic of a program, component routines and subroutines. Any portion of the flowchart may be shown in more detail on a succeeding chart.
9. Titles should be short but not confusing. For better understanding, the language used in a program flowchart should be English, rather than a machine-oriented language. The title of a detailed chart and the explosion of a major striped symbol should bear the same description of the routine as appears within the major striped symbol. Wording inside a symbol should be condensed to fit without overcrowding, and the same description, when feasible, should appear on a title card within the program coding. Because of the ambiguity, it is wise to avoid abbreviations.
10. Whenever the text pertaining to a symbol cannot be placed within a symbol, it should be placed alongside the symbol, references to narrative located elsewhere on the flowchart, or placed within the supplementary annotation symbol. The broken line may be drawn at a point where the annotation is relevant.

The first flowchart of the set depicts the overall logic of the run—the main line of the program. The major logical elements and input/output functions constituting the main line of the program are shown. In addition, the relationship of one function to the other major component of the program is shown. Subsequent pages show the detailed explosion of these major functions.

A typical file maintenance run may require as many as 80 flowcharts. This illustrates the technique of modular flowcharting.

The first chart (Fig. J-13) is the overall picture of the entire run. It is the highest-level chart, showing the main line routine, all major logical elements, and input/output functions. The processing blocks where the striping convention is used indicate that a more detailed flowchart exists. The identification (chart number and to-location block) is placed above the line and the brief description is placed below the line.

The "post transaction" processing block (indicated by the shaded area) is exploded on another chart. This flowchart shows the first level of detail for the "post transaction" routine. All legs of the flowchart return to the preceding level. This is indicated by the offpage connectors. The following pointers may be of help in producing a good set of flowcharts:

- Use some form such as the IBM Flowcharting Worksheet.
- Put yourself in the position of the reader.
- Try to anticipate his problems in understanding your chart.
- Make the main line of each flowchart easily recognizable.
- Look for opportunities to tabulate information (decision tables).
- Do not chart every detail of the program.
- The reader, if interested, may refer to the source-language program.
- Leave a margin of one inch on all sides for binding of charts when the worksheet is not used.

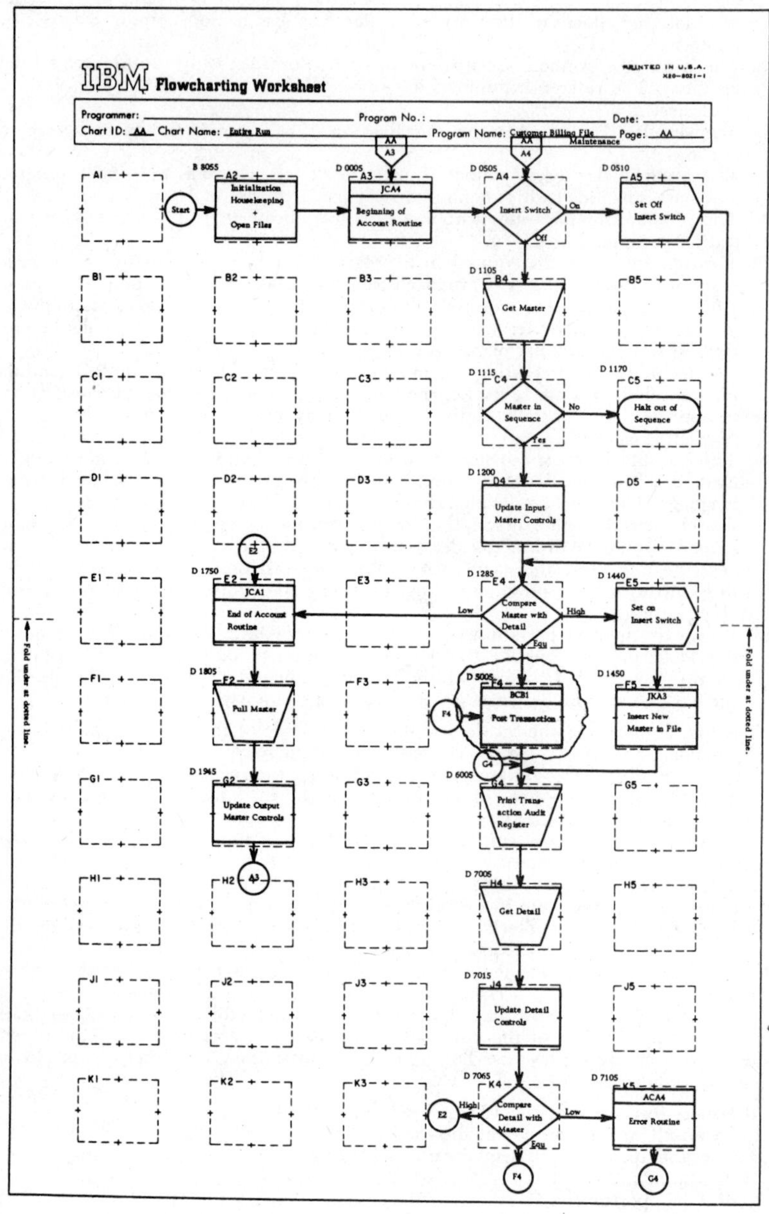

Fig. J-13. Flowchart showing the overall picture of an entire run.

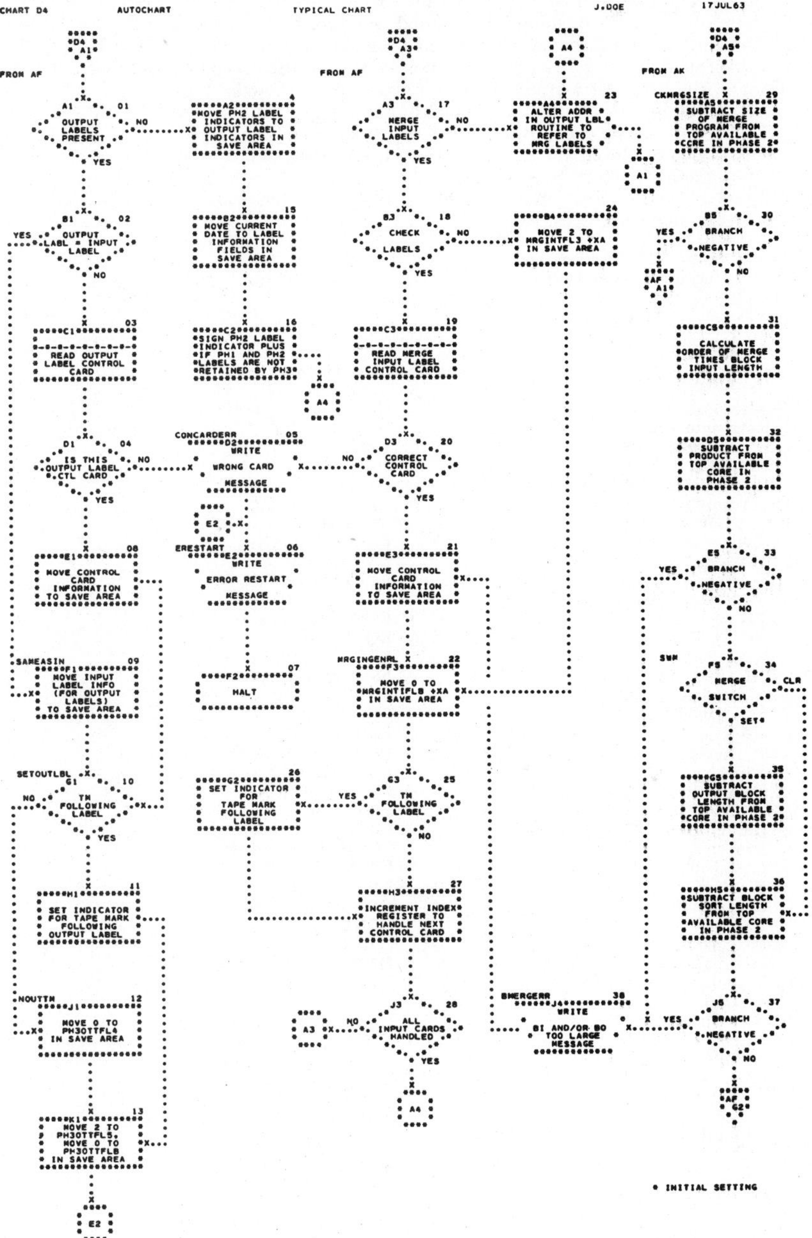

Fig. J-14. The completed "Autochart" of the flowchart in Fig. J-12.

The end result of this modular technique is a telescoping effect with clarity of thought and flow preserved throughout. As pointed out earlier, the peculiarities of machine logic will probably necessitate changes in program logic, requiring a flowchart to be redrawn. During testing, installation, and operation of the procedure, necessary modifications of the program will also require redrawing the flowchart.

The redrawing can be done manually, but it is very time-consuming and can result in errors. With the use of IBM Autochart, program flowcharts drawn in prescribed manner can be produced automatically and, once produced, can be changed or modified with a minimum of effort.

The program flowchart shown in Fig. J-14 is the Autochart of Fig. J-12. It was produced in four basic steps:

1. Rough draft on a flowcharting worksheet.
2. Coding sheets coded for the chart.
3. The input listing for the chart.
4. The finished Autochart.

FLOWCHART ABBREVIATIONS

ABS—Absolute
ACC—Accumulator
ACCT—Account
ACT—Actual
ADDR—Address
ADJ—Adjust
ADV—Advance
ALG—Algebraic
ALPHA—Alphabetic
ALT—Alternant, alteration
APPROX—Approximate
ARITH—Arithmetic
ASDNG—Ascending
ASGN—Assign
ASMBL—Assemble
AUX—Auxiliary
AVAIL—Availability
BFR—Buffer
BKSP—Backspace
BLK—Block
BLKCNT—Block count
BLNK—Blank
BM—Buffer mark
BR—Branch
CALC—Calculate, calculator
CARR—Carriage
CC—Card column
CD—Card
CHAN—Channel
CHAR—Character
CHG—Change
CHK—Check
CHKPT—Checkpoint
CLR—Clear
CLS—Close
CMP—Compare
CMPL—Complement
CNSL—Console
CNT—Count
COL—Column
CON—Constant
COND—Condition
CONT—Continue
CPLD—Coupled
CTR—Counter
CTRL—Control
CURR—Current
DCMT—Document
DEC—Decision
DECR—Decrement
DEL—Delete
DESGG—Descending
DIM—Dimension
DR—Drive
ELIM—Eliminate
ENT—Entry
EOF—End of file
EOJ—End of job
EOR—End of reel
EQ—Equal
ERR—Error
ES—Electronic switch
EXEC—Execute
FIG—Figure
FLD—Field
FLDL—Field length
FLT—Floating
FMT—Format
FR—From
FREQ—Frequency
FUNC—Function
FWD—Forward
FXD—Fixed
GEN—Generator
GENL—General
GM—Groupmark
HDR—Header
HI—High
HLT—Halt
HSK—Housekeeping
HYPER—Hypertape
IC—Instruction counter
INCR—Increment
IND—Indicate
INDN—Indication
INDR—Indicator
INFO—Information
INQ—Inquire
INST—Instruction
INT—Initial
INTRPT—Interrupt
INVAL—Invalid
I/O—Input/Output
IW—Index word

LBL—Label
LD—Load
LIT—Literal
LNG—Length
LOC—Location
LTR—Letter
MACH—Machine
MAX—Maximum
MIN—Minimum
MISC—Miscellaneous
MOD—Modification
MPXR—Multiplexor
MPY—Multiply
MSG—Message
NEG—Negative
NO.—Number
NUM—Numeric
OP—Operation
OPN—Open
OPND—Operand
OVFLO—Overflow
OVL—Overlap
OVLY—Overlay
PG—Page
PGLIN—Page and line
PH—Phase
PKD—Packed
PNCH—Punch
PNDG—Pending
POS—Position
PR—Print
PREC—Precision
PREV—Previous
PRI—Priority
PROC—Process
PROG—Program
PRT—Printer
PT—Point
R + S—Reset + start
R/W—Read/write
RCD—Record
RCV—Receive
RD—Read
RDY—Ready
REF—Reference
REG—Register
REL—Release
REQ—Request, require
RET—Return
RI—Read in
RLS—Reels
RM—Record mark
RO—Read out
RPT—Report
RSLT—Result
RST—Reset
RSTRT—Restart
RTE—Route
RTN—Routine
RWD—Rewind
SCHED—Schedule, scheduler
SCN—Scan
SCTR—Sector
SECT—Section
SEG—Segment
SEL—Select
SEN—Sense
SEQ—Sequence
SER—Serial
SIG—Signal
SIM—Simulator
SM—Storage mark
SNGL—Single
SP—Space
SPEC—Specification, specify
SRCH—Search
ST—Store
STG—Storage
STMNT—Statement
SUB—Subtract
SUMM—Summarize
SUP—Suppress
SYNC—Synchronize, synchronizer
SYST—System
SW—Switch
TBL—Table
TEMP—Temporary
TM—Tapemark
TMN—Transmission
TMT—Transmit
TOT—Total
TP—Tape
TR—Transfer
TRK—Track
TRLR—Trailer
TST—Test
TU—Tape unit
TW—Typewriter
UNC—Unconditional
UNLD—Unload
UNPKD—Unpacked
VAR—Variable
WD—Word
WM—Wordmark
WR—Write
WRK—Work
XPL—Explain, Explanation
XTR—Extra
Z—Zero
ZN—Zone

APPENDIX K

Computer Languages

This appendix is presented to introduce the reader to the full range of computer languages, their purposes and uses, their structure and complexities, and their importance in the evolving world of computer capability. The five most widely used programming languages in computer science today are BASIC, FORTRAN, COBOL, PL/1, and PASCAL. Of these languages, FORTRAN and COBOL are the oldest and most firmly entrenched in commercial data processing. PL/1 is a more "structured" language, similar to ALGOL, but is more widespread than ALGOL. BASIC was designed to do what FORTRAN and COBOL do, but in a simpler way and in a more interactive environment (BASIC was developed concurrently with the rise of time-shared computers). PASCAL is an ALGOL-like language that is coming into widespread use as it travels from academia (where it is a valuable educational tool), into the hobbyist environment (a large number of users), and possibly (with some modifications) into commercial and systems programming applications. Each of these languages is given extensive analysis in later sections of this appendix.

LANGUAGE CLASSIFICATION

In the first decade of modern computing (the late 1950s through the late 1960s), the most common procedure for solving problems or managing data with a computer was to bring the problems physically to the computer center for analysis. The problem would be analyzed and programs written. The data on which the programs were to operate was usually collected by the user and brought to the computer center to be punched onto cards. This card deck was then added to the card deck containing the program, and both were fed into a card reader in the computer center. The output, the solution to the problem, would then be forthcoming after a variable period of time, depending on how busy the computer was. When the output was produced on the systems line printer, the computer center made it available to the user, usually by placing it in a bin or a mailbox corresponding to the user's system identification number.

The second decade of computing saw a tremendous shifting away from the snarl of people and energy in one physical location, the computer center. New communications equipment, video (crt) terminals, and time-sharing operating systems brought the services of the machine to the user's location, whether it was blocks, miles, or thousands of miles from the computer installation. Computing has become system-oriented, and the equipment is becoming ever more communication-designed.

The advent of microcomputers has now brought distributed processing systems into widespread use. These systems incorporate "intelligent" terminals or other front-end processors that may actually be doing most of the computing involved in servicing the user's request before any action is ever taken by the central computer. In many companies, the central computer is being replaced by a network of connected medium-sized or small computers that communicate with each other (distributed computing). If an application demands access to a large amount of data, one machine is usually dedicated to be associated with the disk and tape drives, but this need not necessarily be the case.

The impact of this system orientation on programming languages has been significant. FORTRAN and COBOL compilers on machines that support the new communications technology often have incorporated modifications to allow information to be displayed on terminals and to interact with users in a time-shared environment. Also, enhancements to standard languages have been needed to ensure that simultaneous manipulations of the same data by separate users are kept mutually exclusive.

Another effect of interactive processing has been the rise in the use of BASIC and other "friendly and communicative" languages. Whereas the READ command in FORTRAN was originally designed to read data from punched cards, the INPUT statement in BASIC was meant to interact with an on-line user from the conception of the language. Languages that followed BASIC in its interactive emphasis have done well, and the optimal design of interactive language constructs is now an active research topic.

The more immediate commercial result of the popularity of local program control is the development of software packages that interface with the present compilers to allow easier programming of on-line applications. For example, the programmer may wish to design a program that a data entry operator can use to add data to a data base, one record at a time. The programmer would like to create the image of a form on a screen, and allow the typist to "fill in the blanks" and hit the "send" key when finished. Many computer systems offer subroutines that the applications programmer may call from a COBOL or FORTRAN program to automatically format the screen, and then read the data when the send key is struck.

The interfacing of high-level languages with even higher-level software packages is a trend that will continue in the future. This will play an important role in the success of languages now being developed and the survival of existing languages.

The microcomputer movement has also had a significant effect on the evolution of languages. Computer hobbyists and students enjoy being able to run the program as it is being written, and they demand easy access to the program for modification. This implies the use of an interpreter, as opposed to a compiler. These concepts will be discussed in depth later, but this requirement has made BASIC even more popular for small project computing (including process control), and the availability of hobbyist machines has brought APL into widespread use.

The science of artificial intelligence was born with the invention of high-speed computing and decision-making devices, and research in this field is quickly overlapping into more conventional sciences, such as psychology and biology. The practitioners of this science have designed their own programming languages over the years, and they are the prime reason nonnumeric languages, such as IPL-V and LISP, exist. These languages have application for proofs of logic theorems, pattern recognition, language translation, information retrieval, games, and software prototype construction. Such languages manipulate information which is stored as lists of symbols and list structures (lists of lists) of symbols. The instructions themselves are lists.

Some model-building languages, such as GPSS, SIMSCRIPT, and DYNAMO are designed to represent processes or systems in the distinct simulation language. The speed of computation and the wide range of parameter variations permit the computer to simulate or imitate parts of the specific processes or systems in a very few seconds, and alterations, parameters, changes, etc., can bring forward wide ranges of processes such as job-shop operations, budgets, traffic, etc. Further discussions of these languages follow.

Another type of language, which is fast becoming the most dollar-intensive type of programming, is the report-writing language. RPG, RPG II, and now RPG III have dominated this arena for some time, but now less complicated languages are being developed to speed the development of programs that produce reports. The letters RPG originally stood for Report Program Generator. These letters have now become more of a generic term, meaning any language that is specifically designed for the production of reports.

Report-writing languages simply read data from records in a data base which are stored in a known format. These languages do not have to contain constructs to allow interaction with a time-shared user. They do not have to contain constructs for writing data to the data base or locking data that is there while it is being modified. There are a great many things that can (and should) be left out of report languages. The programmer can then afford to add complexity to the simpler language in the form of "higher-level" directives, such as "print the data according to the ACCOUNTS

PAYABLE format." The current backlog for new program development at most large computer installations is between two and three years. The use of simpler and more powerful languages, specially designed for the function that is being performed, such as RPGs, may have a significant impact on this backlog (or at least provide more throughput; greater demand may maintain or even increase the backlog).

Another type of language that has come into vogue in just the past few years is the query language. This language is almost always interactive, and its constructs are simple and English-like. It is similar to the report languages in that it only reads information from a data base, but it does not have the flexible formatting powers or powerful tabulation capabilities of the report writers.

Typical information needs query languages might be used to satisfy are:

FIND SALARY = $14000.00 AND DEPENDENTS 3 END

FIND STATE = CALIF OR NEVADA OR OREGON AND SALES > $500000.00 END

The first example might be used by a personnel officer who is evaluating different employee/family hospitalization plans, and the second might be used by a marketing director seeking information about the sales volume of installations in the western states. In the first example, all of the information in the personnel data base for each employee that met the query conditions would be displayed (or printed). In the second example, all of the information in the installations data base for those installations grossing over a half million dollars, at that time, would be displayed.

The specific query languages in use are usually associated with a more complex, and expensive, piece of software called a data-base management system. This type of software is discussed further in a different appendix.

Languages can be divided into six main groups:

I. Fundamental Algorithmic and Procedural Languages
   ALGOL, FORTRAN, COBOL, PL/1, PASCAL, JOVIAL
II. Time-sharing and Interactive Languages (Usually Interpreters)
   BASIC, CAL, JOSS, APL, MUMPS
III. List-Processing Languages
   LISP, IPL-V, SLIP, COMIT, FORMAC, DYSTAL, SNOBOL
IV. Simulation Languages
   SIMSCRIPT, GPSS, DYNAMO
V. Production or Process Control Languages
   APT, STRESS, COGO, Control BASIC
VI. Report Program Generator Language

THE NATURE OF COMPUTER PROGRAMS

A computer program is a sequence of instructions that a machine is capable of performing. Programmable calculators and small computers have made it possible for many elementary school children to understand the fundamental nature of computer programs. A simple example, showing how a programming task might be accomplished on these two types of machines, will demonstrate the point.

Consider a store clerk who has been instructed to put everything in the toy department on a 25% discount for a post-Christmas sale. He has a list of every item and its price; his goal is to compute the new price for each item as well. Programmable calculators work in the following fashion. A special key will put the machine in the "learn mode," in which it will remember instructions. In this mode, keys may be pressed, but their corresponding action will not be taken. Rather, the fact that the key was pressed will be recorded in the memory of the machine. When the learn key is pressed again, the calculator returns to its "run" mode. Now that the calculator has been "trained" to remember a sequence of instructions, that sequence can be executed instantly by pressing the "run" key.

Here is the key sequence the clerk would use to "program" the calculator to solve his problem:

```
learn
×
.75
=
halt
learn  (to get back into run mode)
```

With the machine programmed to execute these instructions, if the clerk keyed in 10.00 and pressed "run," the display would show 7.50. In other words, the run key would signal the computer to execute this program on the data that has been keyed into the display. Using the programmable calculator, the clerk can simply run this program on every item in the store to find the new price. It is not necessary to key in the keystrokes needed to perform the calculation for each item; the computer processor in the calculator can remember these instructions and execute them as a program.

A program could be written in BASIC on any of the popular microcomputers to solve the problem as well. A listing of the program and the results of running it follow.

```
>>LIST
  10 PRINT"ENTER THE CURRENT PRICE > ";
  20 INPUT" ",CURRENT'PRICE
  25 IF CURRENT'PRICE=0 THEN GOTO 60
  30 NEW'PRICE=CURRENT'PRICE*0.75
  40 PRINT"THE NEW PRICE IS ",NEW'PRICE
  50 GOTO 10
  60 END
>>RUN
ENTER THE CURRENT PRICE > 10.00
THE NEW PRICE IS                   7.5
ENTER THE CURRENT PRICE > 3.50
THE NEW PRICE IS                   2.625
ENTER THE CURRENT PRICE > 4.99
THE NEW PRICE IS                   3.7425
ENTER THE CURRENT PRICE > 5.56
THE NEW PRICE IS                   4.17
ENTER THE CURRENT PRICE > 0
***60 END***
```

If the prices for the items in the store were stored in some computer-readable form, they would not even have to be typed in response to the prompt; the program could simply read them from a file and produce the listing of the new prices.

Of course, this is a simple example. Most problems solved by computer programs are more complicated. They usually involve gathering data from many files or a terminal, and often involve checking to see that the data is reasonable. Programs that do many things may become quite long, and a programmer may rely on summarizing techniques to help keep the nature of the problem in context. Before the program can even be written, the programmer must translate the problem into a method of solution. This method of solution is called an algorithm. Formerly algorithms were often described graphically through the use of flowcharts (discussed in another appendix), but now English-like prose is more often used. This prose is often referred to as pseudocode. For the preceding example, the pseudocode might be as follows:

Read the current price.
Calculate the new price as 75% of the current price.
Print the new price.

After the solution to the problem has been translated into an algorithm like the one above, a program can be written in just about any programming language to perform the task.

The computer processor itself cannot actually execute instructions such as PRINT NEW'PRICE directly. In fact, the nature of the electronics of the processor is such that it can only understand codes of ones and zeros (a conductor is either "on" or "off"). The ones and zeros are grouped, however, to form instructions. For example, 11001101 might be the ADD instruction. To get the processor to multiply five times eight, the processor may actually have to add five eights. In other words, the computer processor cannot perform very high-level operations, and the kind of activities we wish to perform must be translated into a longer series of more primitive instructions.

In the calculator, special programs were written at the factory and permanently stored in the machine. Each keystroke on the calculator is actually initiating a small program. In computers, certain standard software is sold with the machine to perform these translations.

ASSEMBLERS AND LOADERS

When computers were first invented, they had very small memories (i.e., they could not execute very large programs), and they had to be programmed in the ones and zeros that the machine could understand. As soon as computers became a little more commonplace, a program was written to translate simple mnemonics into the ones and zeros. However, these mnemonics still represented only the primitive commands that the computer could execute as one instruction, such as

ADD 10,R1	Add the value 10 to register 1.
MOV R1,48	Move the contents of register one to memory location 48.
COM R1,R2	Compare the contents of registers 1 and 2, and set a special flag if they are equal. This flag can then be tested by later instructions.
JMP 2000	Jump to some program location (like the GOTO in BASIC).
JPC 2200	Jump conditional on some flag that may have been set by an earlier instruction.

The ones and zeros these instructions translate into are called the machine language of the processor. A program in the form of machine language is called machine code. A processor usually has between 50 and 100 different instructions. These instructions constitute the instruction set of the machine.

The collection of mnemonics that represent the instructions composes a language called the assembly language of the machine. In the early days of computing, it was a great boon to write a program that translated from these assembly mnemonics into machine code. Today, assemblers are still in widespread use, but their utility is dissipating. Most programs are written in higher-level languages, such as BASIC. The BASIC instructions must be translated into machine instructions by the BASIC interpreter, just as the mnemonics are assembled into machine instructions. The BASIC interpreter does not do a very efficient job of this translation. The number of instructions the processor must execute to solve a problem written in BASIC is many more than if the problem were solved with an assembler program. However, the processor is so fast that for most situations the user will never know the difference. Only rare circumstances justify writing programs in the assembly language of a machine, now that high-level languages enjoy popularity and availability.

A loader is another piece of software (a program) that is as common as assemblers. After a program is assembled into the code of the machine, it must be placed in the main memory of the computer, and the program has to be initiated. The loader performs this chore.

HIGH-LEVEL LANGUAGES

High-level languages, such as BASIC, FORTRAN, COBOL, etc., provide much more power to the programmer than assembler languages. They allow the programmer to implement an algorithm with fewer instructions; the program listings are shorter; and the structure of the language allows the program to be understood more easily.

Syntax and Semantics

Assembler languages do not possess many of the properties of real languages. Assembler languages do have a syntax (spelling and punctuation rules), but the number of syntactic elements are few. Furthermore, there is very little semantic meaning to constructs. Some instructions must be followed by operands, but assemblers generally treat each line of code as a semantic whole. Rarely will the assembler identify a structural mistake if each individual line is structured properly, even though the program may make no sense at all.

The simplicity and "cleanliness" of the syntax and the power and ease of use of the semantic constructs that a programming language offers should inevitably become the most important issues that are considered when a program can be written in any of several languages. Currently, however, the computing world has a great many programs written in COBOL and FORTRAN, and there are a large number of people who have training and familiarization with these languages.

Data Types and Data Structures

Languages can be classified and described in many ways. Two of the most fundamental descriptors are the data structures and control structures that the language contains. For example, the BASIC program above read the current price of the item in to a variable called current'price. This variable is a data structure. Data structures are said to be of a certain type. The BASIC language in which the sample program was written used floating-point numbers as its numeric data type. Some BASICs only offer integers. Others offer both and even offer varying amounts of precision.

BASIC and FORTRAN offer the programmer arrays, as well as scalar variables. PASCAL offers all of these constructs, as well as a type "char" for character variables. Records and pointers to records are also available in PASCAL. This new language even takes data structures and data typing a step further in that it allows the user to define his own data types, which can be composed of any of the standard data types or previously defined user-defined types. For example,

```
name = array [1 . . 20] of char;
whole'name = array [1 . . 3] of name;
christmas'list = array [1 . . 50] of whole'name;
```

Now variables may be declared of type christmas'list, and the names can be assigned to the character strings composing that data structure.

Control Structures

The control structures in assembly languages are quite simple. The jump, the jump conditional, and the jump to a subroutine instructions are the only instructions that will cause program execution to do anything other than proceed to the next instruction in memory. These instructions then compose the control structures of the language.

More sophisticated and useful structures have been devised for higher-level languages as time has gone on. Some of the popular constructs are listed below. The most important development is perhaps the so-called "block structuring" of instructions. ALGOL introduced the notion of BEGIN and END as keywords which delimit a functionally important sequence. Languages that use these delimiters are referred to as structured programming languages.

With a structured programming language, the programmer can say, "If the condition is true, then execute this block of instructions." If the language is not structured, the programmer must use GOTOs to block off the instructions that should be grouped.

With the aid of block structuring, an IF-THEN-ELSE construct can be easily defined. In this control structure, only one block, either the IF block or the ELSE block, is executed.

The WHILE loop is a way to express the desire for the reiteration of a sequence of instructions until some condition becomes true. The REPEAT-UNTIL loop is similar.

A convenient construct that will execute only one of many possible sequences of code, based on the value of some selector, is the CASE statement. For example, a program may wish to branch to one of several subroutines based on the training background of the person running the program. The selector for the CASE statement could be a variable that was read in from the terminal, and the statement will execute only one subroutine call, based on the value of that variable. A somewhat similar, but not nearly as generally useful, construct is the FORTRAN computed goto. This instruction will jump to one of several locations based on the value of an integer variable.

The FOR loop is the best known iterative loop and is common to nearly all procedural languages.

IF – THEN

```
        if condition
        then
             begin
             block
             end;

        if not (condition)  then goto 1
             block
1       continue
```

IF – THEN – ELSE

```
        if condition
        then
             begin
             block #1
             end
        else
             begin
             block #2
             end;

        if not (condition)  then goto 1
             block #1
             goto 2
1       continue
             block #2
2       continue
```

WHILE LOOP

```
        while condition do
             begin
             block {at some point, condition := false}
             end;

1       if not (condition)  then goto 2
             block {at some point, condition := false}
             goto 1
2       continue
```

CASE STATEMENT

```
        case some'switch of
        a:   begin
             block A
             end;
        b:   begin
             block B
             end;
```

```
        c:   begin
             block C
             end;
        end; {case}

        if some'switch <> 'a' then goto 1
             block A
             goto 3
1       continue
        if some'switch <> 'b' then goto 2
             block B
             goto 3
2       continue
        if some'switch <> 'c' then goto 3
             block C
3       continue
```

FOR LOOP

```
        for i := 1 to 10 do
             begin
             do something
             end

        i :=1;
1       if i > 10 goto 2
             do something
             i := i + 1;
             goto 1
2       continue
```

The increase of nonprocedural language will have a significant impact on the direction of control structures in future languages. In nonprocedural languages, there are (at least ideally) no control structures. For example, RPG was meant to be a nonprocedural language. The thought went as follows: Reports programs should only require the specification of the input format and the output format. Once where the data is coming from and where it is going to go are resolved, there is not much more to it. In this special-purpose language, an implied control loop reads a record, processes it according to some calculation specifications, and attempts an output of the record contents. This inherently does not have much user-defined control structuring. In practice, however, GOTOs and conditional GOTOs became available in the calculation specifications, and the control of RPG programs reverted from the advanced concept of implied control to the most primitive form of control, jumping unconditionally or conditioned on some indicator. However, the notion of nonprocedural languages may well find its roots in the report-writing function.

Structured Programming

A new generation of programmers are beginning to come out of American universities, and they are, for the most part, uninterested in using the GOTO as the base of control of their programs. Niklaus Wirth designed the PASCAL language based on the block-structured concepts of ALGOL. Even though a GOTO is available in the language, nearly all PASCAL programs are written without one.

The concept of structured programming involves more than the use of BEGIN and END and the banishment of the GOTO. Wirth incorporated into PASCAL data defining and structuring capabilities that are in harmony with the more advanced control structures that have been discussed. For example, an array is inherently described by two data types, the index type and the component type. In FORTRAN, both these types are usually INTEGER, although the programmer may have an array of REAL.

In PASCAL, a user-defined data type can be declared to be the index type of an array. Then the variables that will be used to index the array can be declared to be of that index type. Assume that the index type was the integer subrange 1 to 30. Now, if a program has a bug and the variable is assigned 31, the run-time module of the compiler will abort the program when this value is assigned. If the same bug were in a FORTRAN program, the program would not abort until the improperly assigned variable attempted to index the array. Then the programmer would have to crawl through the listings of his program to find where the improper assignment occurred. In the PASCAL program, it is obvious where the assignment occurred, because the program was aborted on that statement.

In this sense, Wirth's scheme of user-definable types is in harmony with the fundamental nature of the data structures used by programmers. Furthermore, the data structures and control structures are in tandem. The FOR loop is available to index through arrays, and the WHILE loop may be used to traverse linked lists. Recursive subroutine calls can be used to build and survey trees. These and other advanced programming concepts cannot be discussed in full here. The reader is referred to textbooks on structured programming for a more complete explanation of these ideas.

Many BASIC interpreters and FORTRAN compilers are being retrofitted to supply their user community with some of these conveniences.

Compilers and Interpreters

In the previous discussions, FORTRAN and COBOL have been referred to as compilers, and BASIC has been called an interpreter. The difference between a compiler and an interpreter is as follows. A compiler reads the source code (i.e., the program written in the language of the compiler, FORTRAN, etc.) from a file and translates it into the machine code of the computer for which the compiler was written. This translated module is stored in a file. When it is time to run this program, the loader is called to load this module into main memory and begin execution. An interpreter, on the other hand, is loaded into main memory when it is invoked. The interpreter interacts with the programmer and accepts and translates the program line by line. These translated lines are available to be run as a program when the user tells the interpreter to run them.

The distinction between a compiler and an interpreter becomes blurred in some instances, however. For example, almost all BASIC interpreters will let the user SAVE his program to a file after he is finished typing it in and testing it. This program is usually saved in some "compacted" form. This form is not quite as small as a compiled load module, however. Most BASIC interpreters will also list a program that has been read in to a file. Some systems have both a BASIC interpreter and a BASIC compiler. The programmer can develop his program in a conversational manner with the interpreter, and then when he is pleased with it, he can list it out and have the compiler compile it into a load module (which will undoubtedly run faster).

The distinction becomes further blurred when some languages that are usually compiled have the ability to tell the user the line of source code on which the program aborted. A truly compiled program is translated into machine code that has no notion of where it came from. Some PASCAL compilers have this interpreter-like quality, which is needed to abort programs based on the incorrect run-time assignment to variables of declared to be user-defined types.

HOST LANGUAGE ENVIRONMENT

Interactions With the Operating System

A program is defined by much more than the language in which it is written. The operating system on which the program is being developed and run has a great deal to do with what a programmer can make a program do and how well it is going to do it. For example, if the operating system only supports magnetic tape as a mass storage medium, a program will not have much luck randomly accessing records, even though random access to files may be a facility of the programming language.

Most modern operating systems provide several methods of accessing both tape and disk mass memory devices. Since tape is a serial access medium, only serial access methods are called for with tape. However, when disks are available, the options increase. Most operating systems allow the programmer to access records randomly, by record number. Increasingly, programmers have ISAM or KSAM file structures (Indexed Sequential Access Method or Keyed Sequential Access Method) available. With these structures available, records can be read based on the content of a key field, which was assigned when the file was built.

The ability to assign many keys to a file does away with much of the sorting of files by batch overnight processes, as well as the need for a programmer to write a binary search routine.

Interactions With Data-Base Management Software

The subject of data-base management software (DBMS) is addressed more completely in a separate appendix, but, in brief, it takes the concept of KSAM files a step further. The data-base management software groups related files into one logical data structure. The DBMS will not only read a record based on a key value, but it will also read all of the records that are associated with that record but are in a different file. For example, a program may be seeking information on employee Jones and his job history. He should have only one record in the personnel file, but he may have several in the salary history file. One call to the data-base management software would retrieve all of this information at once. The use of software of this kind is already going a long way toward bringing less "proceduralness" into even procedural languages. In other words, the complexity that would formerly have to be written into a program is now inherent in the structuring of the data in the file. The manipulation of the data structure is carried out by the DBMS software, not by the applications programmer. Thus, the same program has far fewer control statements.

Program Portability

All of the preceding interactions with the operating system almost always reduce an important property of a program, its portability. The American National Standards Institute has published many standards for programming languages, particularly FORTRAN and COBOL. A program written according to these standards should theoretically run on a completely different machine, as long as the machine to which it is being transported has a compiler that complies with these standards.

The previously mentioned luxuries of KSAM and DBMS software packages are generally not incorporated into standards definitions. The programmer knows that if he uses these facilities his program will not be standard, and thus not portable. However, he is forced by their utility to use them.

Most often, programs are made nonportable even without the inclusion of useful software packages. For example, a program may have to make a special call to the operating system to find out what the date is so that it may be printed on some report. The call to the operating system would certainly not operate properly if the program were taken to a different machine. Often it does not operate properly even when the program is taken to a new model of the same machine, or even the same machine but a new version of the operating system.

Despite the problems inherent in running programs on computers, much useful processing does get accomplished. The variety and versatility of the languages that are being developed, and particularly the software tools that will be integrated into those new languages and the languages that we have, will make the programmer's job increasingly easier and will allow computer users to take advantage of the power available through the decreased cost of hardware.

SECTION I

Algorithmic and Procedural Languages

Computers do not directly accept problem statements. They must first be defined and designed according to the acceptable procedures of some specific program language. The task is to transform the problem statement, through the use of compilers, into procedures of languages which are acceptable to the type of computer to be used. It is at this point that most students have their principal and lasting difficulty; i.e., transposing their problem into a usable computer algorithm. An algorithm is defined simply as the precise and complete step-by-step statement of a computational procedure.

The discovery and/or analysis of a problem begs the development of a proper computer procedure. Block diagrams and flowcharts facilitate the required attention to the interrelationship, logic, and sequence of problem components. Programming is the next step and can be stated to be the procedural language of the algorithm; i.e., the proper use of a language which is acceptable for translation by the compiler (s) of the computer to be used to reach the desired solution.

The explicit "all in advance" instruction development to the computer must be more than just mechanical translation of flowchart to program. The computer does not exercise judgment nor does it have common sense. The reader will recall that the machine can only count, add (and thus perform all other arithmetic operations), store (and retrieve), and compare (and thus make decisions). Combinations of these four capabilities do, of course, permit the computer to perform highly complex operations at tremendous speeds and with unfaltering accuracy. But it must be meticulously instructed beforehand on how to handle even such simple chores as the identification of the last item in a list, what to do if the answer of intermediate calculations becomes zero, and the exact operations to be performed when unforseen "exceptions" occur. It will make no evaluations, guesses, or use "inherent" sense; each eventually must be programmed completely and in advance because in most cases human intervention has been eliminated for speed and efficiency purposes.

ALGOL

Devising and composing the algorithm *before* programming is the enigmatic difficulty the student can overcome only with practice and experience. ALGOL, besides being a language, is an internationally accepted procedure for designing mathematical, engineering, and scientific problems. Compatible standardization and understanding of problems and procedures to be used with or without computers were the primary purposes for the development of ALGOL. In brief, ALGOL provides (1) precise instructional statements for program sequence and exceptions, (2) a language for expressing problem-solving order and procedure, (3) a translator or compiler for developing machine-sensible language from the "many-for-one" macrostatements the ALGOL language prescribes.

Point (3) emphasizes the similarity between ALGOL, FORTRAN, and COBOL. Each is a language with rules of grammar, syntax, format, and special characteristics, and each is also a compiler; i.e., a translator program which is required for each different model of computer to be used. None of the three languages can be executed directly by present computers without first being "processed" into machine language. But this transformation is automatic (with a few modifications) from the "compiler language" source program to the "machine language" object program. The computer used is equipped with the respective compiler, which is quite often in the form of tapes provided by the manufacturer (at some varying cost). Thus, if all features of the ALGOL language are to be provided, the ALGOL processor or compiler must be able to accept all features, and, in fact, many compilers accept and use considerably abridged subsets of ALGOL, FORTRAN, COBOL, and other compilers. The uses of such subsets are convenient and prove to be less costly in time, equipment, and confusion, and yet suffice for particular areas of utility.

The Reference Language and Transliteration

The *Reference Language* uses some symbols and notation conventions such as $<$ for "less than," vertical arrows $\uparrow$ to denote exponentiation, etc. Transliteration is the method for handling this condition by writing in the program LT for $<$, GR or GT for $>$ (greater than), * for exponentiation, EQ for "equal to," and many others.

In an equation such as $A = \sqrt{X^2 + Y^2}$, the ALGOL statement would be:

$$A \leftarrow SQRT\ (X*2 + Y*2)$$

Individual items of this expression have names as follows:

The A is an *identifier,* used to denote values which are yet to be calculated which are thus distinguishable from others being worked on. The first character of the identifier must always be a letter, and no spaces may break up the identifier. Examples are: B, C20, TOTAL, A2B4C6D8.

The * denotes *exponentiation,* and the 2 signifies the power concerned.

SQRT signifies square root. It is a *library function* and is from the list of ALGOL reserved words.

The arrow is called a *replacement operator.* It denotes replacement of the current value of the identifier, A, with the expression to its right; this allows the programmer to use A wherever he has need to refer to the value of $\sqrt{X^2 + Y^2}$; thus, it is not entirely equivalent to the equal sign in mathematical notation.

It is thus noted that writing a program in ALGOL closely resembles the exacting and precise problem definition required by the machine programmer for his basic machine program coding. But the computer itself produces the machine-language program, and it does the processing of it also. The machine-language program, however, is developed by the compiler which is in the computer. The computer is not familiar with the problem and knows only what is contained in the problem; i.e., the ALGOL program. Thus, just as in COBOL and FORTRAN, the program must be completely, explicitly, and unambiguously expressed in proper terminology and form of the language used.

The *Reference Language,* then, is the defining language with the characters determined not by the computer limitation or pure mathematics, but instead by the ease and convenience of mutual understanding of people who will use or interpret the problem. It is the guide for compiler builders and hardware representations. It is also for transliteration from public language to specific local hardware representation. ALGOL publications use this reference representation. The ALGOL statement, however complex, describes an actual step-by-step procedure for obtaining a solution to a problem using actual numbers and developing a number as a result.

Publication Language and Hardware Representation

ALGOL is, in general, completely independent of any particular computer. However, though structure and content remain the same for all ALGOL representation, choice of symbols may be different when used in the publication languages of different countries. Unequivocal correspondence with the reference representation must be secured. Publication Language permits variations according to different uses of printing, handwriting, spacing, subscripts, Greek letters, etc., which are conventions of various countries or geographical areas. This permits one programmer to make concurrent and efficient use of another's work.

The translator or compiler of ALGOL for different models or brands of computers must be accompanied with individual sets or lists of rules for transliteration. This is usually from the publication or reference language or a combination of the reference language enforced by the specific limitations of the characteristics of the particular machine in use.

Boolean Expressions

Compound conditions are a special ALGOL operation; the symbol $\wedge$ is read as AND, a Boolean (logical) operator. An example could be:

$$\text{if } b = c \wedge f = g \text{ then punch (1) else punch (0)}.$$

This is read as "If b equals c and f equals g, then record (punch) 1 as an output; if not, punch 0 as an output." Other logical operators are:

$\equiv$ equivalence
$\supset$ implication
$\vee$ OR
$\wedge$ AND
$\neg$A, not A, or $\overline{A}$

Equivalence, as a $\equiv$ b, is true if both a and b are true or if both are false. Implication is more difficult. Suppose a $\supset$ b. This is true if a is false (without regard to b). It is true if b is true (without regard to a). For all other conditions it is false. The AND is true only if both are true, the OR is true if either is true. Thus, for a $\wedge$ b both must be true for the statement to be true. For a $\vee$ b, if either a or b is true, the expression is true. Chart K-1 is a summary or truth table for these Boolean operators.

There are standard rules for the priority of performing relational and logical operations. While the general rule for performing these operations is to proceed from left to right, this rule is subordinated to the following priority list.

First priority: Parenthesized operations
Second priority: Evaluation of arithmetic expressions
Third priority: Relational operations as met from left to right
Fourth priority: NOT (not)
Fifth priority: AND (and)
Sixth priority: OR (or)
Seventh priority: IMP (implies)
Eighth priority: EQV (equivalent to)

Chart K-1. Truth Value Table

	a b	F F	T F	F T	T T
NOT a	$\neg$a	T	F	T	F
a AND b	a $\wedge$ b	F	F	F	T
a OR b	a $\vee$ b	F	T	T	T
a IMP b	a $\supset$ b	T	F	T	T
a EQV b	a $\equiv$ b	T	F	F	T

This priority list indicates that in many cases parentheses may be omitted. However, to avoid errors in interpretation and for easier reading, it is recommended that parentheses be used in compound expressions.

Logical operands must be:

(a) the result of a relational operation, or
(b) the result of a logical operation, or
(c) a declared Boolean variable.

The logical operators have the following meanings. (Where the conditions stated are not met, the result is FALSE.)

AND (and) — If both operands connected by this operator have the value TRUE, the result is TRUE.

OR (or) — If either operand connected by this operator is TRUE, the result is TRUE.

NOT (not) — If the operand following this operator is FALSE, the result is TRUE.

EQV (equivalent to) — If the operands connected by this operator have the same logical value, the result is TRUE.

IMP (implies) — If the operands connected by this operator have the same logical value, or if the first (left-hand) operand is FALSE, then the result is TRUE.

There are some programs which are long and complex; for these it is often necessary for several programmers to work on the problem at once, each working on a separate part. To prevent any destructive interference, where one part of a program may use different names for some variables than another part of the program, a structure known as a *block* is used. A block is a series of declarations and statements enclosed between the words *begin* and *end.* All of the conditions within the block are defined for that block so that a series of blocks can be used together as a series of subprograms, which can be used together to make up one large program. In a sense, every ALGOL program is made up of one or more blocks.

Elements of ALGOL Language

ALGOL was first called IAL (International Algebraic Language) and was developed in Europe in parallel with FORTRAN in the United States; use of each process was begun approximately at the same time. Both languages were attempts to provide a programming language similar to everyday mathematics notation so that engineers and scientists could avoid the repetition and drudgery of machine programming. It was hoped that these macro languages and compilers would preclude or prevent the necessity of users' long study to develop proficiency in the intricacies of machine languages of the many individual computers available. Both FORTRAN and ALGOL succeeded admirably. FORTRAN is by far the most widely implemented language, but many students and scientists feel that ALGOL is more easily understood, more versatile, and more flexible. FORTRAN IV now uses more features of ALGOL. Most major computer manufacturers offer ALGOL compilers for their computers. Among them are: Honeywell, Burroughs, UNIVAC, IBM, and several others.

Generally, ALGOL provides procedures for: (1) defining constants, variables, and expressions for problem solution; (2) making declarations as regards the nature of the data to be used in the computer; and (3) stating procedures to be executed while using the data, expressions, and constants as stated.

Although these are the requisite characteristics of any acceptable language, ALGOL performs them exceptionally well, and, most importantly, it aids the programmer in procedural development of programs from day-by-day mathematical formulation.

The similarity of ALGOL to FORTRAN can be seen by noting the components of the language and relating them to FORTRAN. ALGOL manuals describe in detail the meaning, logic, and procedure for the following:

(1) Syntactic description
(2) Basic symbols, numbers, identifiers, letters, strings, delimiters
(3) Expressions of variables, subscripts, functions, transfers, arithmetic, Boolean notation and operations, and designationals
(4) Statements, as compound, block, assignment, dummy, conditional, FOR statements, procedure statements
(5) Declarations, as type, array, switch, procedure, and specifications

When one writes a program in ALGOL, he notes that it closely resembles the detailed problem definition required if he were to give a problem to a machine-language programmer for computer solution. The language and format of the problem definition have been standardized. The computer itself produces the machine-language program, and also does the processing. Thus, it is particularly important to recall that the compiler in the computer is not familiar with the problem and knows about it only what is contained in the problem; i.e., the ALGOL program. The problem then must be complete, unambiguous, and expressed in an acceptable form and terminology.

In ALGOL, the three types of numbers are called type REAL, type INTEGER, and type BOOLEAN. REAL numbers contain a decimal point; INTEGER numbers are whole numbers. IDENTIFIERS are names for purposes of references and consist of at least one letter, followed by any letter, digits, or combination of these. STANDARD FUNCTIONS are designators which are frequently used functions for which the programmer need not write out the detailed steps to compute such values. A list of some of the standard function designators, all of which are *reserved words* are: SIN, COS, ARCTAN, SQRT, N, EXP, ABS', and others.

The reader is invited to consult the appropriate manuals for the various operational statements as: GO TO, IF, ELSE, FOR, DO, and their various elements. Declarations and blocks were discussed briefly above, but SWITCH, ARRAY, and SUBSCRIPTS are defined in the manuals. PROCEDURES are steps and rules which must also be mastered by the ALGOL programmer who will find the mastery of the language is not as difficult as he first imagines, but he also finds that the range and versatility is greater that several of the other languages with which he might be familiar.

Following is a sketch reference outline of various ALGOL attributes:

I. General ALGOL operations.
   A. Arithmetic expressions (as discussed previously).
   B. Boolean expressions.
      1. Rules for computing the logical values TRUE and FALSE.
         (a) If the condition state is satisfied, the result is TRUE.
         (b) If not, the result is FALSE.
      2. Boolean expressions employ two kinds of operators.
         (a) The relational operators.
         (b) The logical operator—involves application of the rule state for that operator to the operands, which are restricted to the values of TRUE and FALSE.
            (1) Logical operands must be the result of a relational operation, or
            (2) Must be the result of a logical operation, or
            (3) A declared Boolean variable.
   C. Standard functions.
      1. Function designator defines a single value which is the result of a specific set of operations on given parameters.
      2. The arguments upon which standard functions are to operate must be enclosed with parentheses.
   D. Operational statements.
      1. Assignment statements. They contain the replacement operator denoting the substitution of a number, or the value of an identifier, or the value of an expression on the right for the identifier on the left.
      2. Control statements. They are used when one or more statements are to be repeated several times, or are to be executed only under specific conditions.
         (a) Unconditional control statements are formed by following the words GO TO with a label which specifies the point in the program where control is to be resumed.
         (b) Conditional control statements cause other statements to be executed or skipped depending on the current values of specified Boolean expressions.
         (c) Iterative control statements are used when the same statement is to be executed repeatedly a specified number of times, or is to be executed for each one of a designated set of values assigned to a variable.

II. Declarations and blocks.
   A. Type declarations.
      1. Type REAL
      2. Type INTEGER
      3. Type BOOLEAN
   B. Blocks. A program section which is preceded by the word BEGIN includes at least one declaration and one statement, and is followed by the word END. A block has the following form: BEGIN declaration; statement; . . . ; statement END.
      1. A declaration is valid only for the block in which it appears, and has effect throughout that block.
      2. Exit from a block, as a result of encountering the word END or a transfer-of-control statement cancels the declarations made within the block.
      3. Blocks may be labeled by preceding the word BEGIN with an identifier followed by a colon.
   C. Switch declarations. Name a group of alternative points in a program to which control may be transferred as the result of a single GO TO statement.
   D. Array declarations. A group or set of items arranged in such a manner that each item may be identified by its position within the group.

III. Procedures used in ALGOL.
   A. General nature of procedures.
      1. A section of coding.
         (a) To be executed at several points throughout the same program.

(b) To be used without alteration in more than one program.
2. The procedure heading.
(a) Begins with the reserved word PROCEDURE—indicates the following is a procedure declaration.
(b) Each procedure is given an identifier by which it may be referenced.
(c) The VALUE part is used if one or more formal parameters are to be replaced by an actual value before a procedure is executed.
3. The body of the procedure.
(a) May be a compound statement.
(b) May be a block.
(c) May be a single statement.
4. Operations that take place in a procedure.
(a) All formal parameters of the procedure which are listed after VALUE are replaced by the values of the corresponding actual parameters when the procedure statement is encountered in the program.
(b) The other formal parameters are replaced by the means of the corresponding actual parameters.
(c) The procedure body is then inserted into the program, taking the place of the procedure statement.

B. Procedures as functions.
1. An assignment statement must appear, in the procedure body, which has the procedure identifier to the left of the replacement operator.
2. Since the PROCEDURE declaration is defining a single value, its type must be declared by preceding the word PROCEDURE by one of the three reserved words (REAL, INTEGER, or BOOLEAN) which indicate type.

Loops are significant features of ALGOL as they are of all languages and relate to program segments which are repeated until certain conditions are met. As an example of a loop designation, the statement might be read, "Produce a table of values for $\frac{a+3}{4a}$ when $a = 1, 10, 50$, and 100." In ALGOL this would be presented as follows:

for a: = 1, 10, 50, 100 do punch (a + 3) / (4 × a)

This means a loop in which each value for a is substituted in the expression and the result will be punched or printed out until all values have been used. Subscripts are handled similar to: array b [1 : 100], for the array b, where b ranges from 1 to 100 as subscripts.

A summary table of symbols is listed below.

		ALGOL 60 HARDWARE REPRESENTATION	FORMAL ALGOL 60 REFERENCE LANGUAGE SYMBOLS
	Replacement Operator	←	:=
Relational Operators	Less	<	<
	Less or Equal	≤	≦
	Equal	=	=
	Greater or Equal	≥	≧
	Greater	>	>
	Not Equal	≠	≠
Logical Operators	And	AND (often writen as ·)	∧
	Or	OR (often written as +)	∨
	Not	NOT ¬A no A (often written as $\bar{A}$)	¬
	Equivalent	EQV	≡
	Implies	IMP (often written as A→ B)	⊃
Arithmetic Operators	Add	+	+
	Subtract	−	−
	Multiply	×	×
	Divide	/	/
	Integer Divide	DIV	÷
	Exponentiate	*	↑

Most individual ALGOL manuals of various computer manufacturers state their specific lists of standard functions, anomalies, limitations and restrictions. The user of particular computers must consult these manuals for these highly relevant and important details *before* writing specific ALGOL programs. For example, the following reserved words, which form a major portion of the Burroughs 5000 ALGOL vocabulary, may be used *only as shown in its specific manual.*

ABS	ELSE	IMP	SIGN
AND	END	INTEGER	SIN
ARCTAN	ENTIER	LN	SQRT
ARRAY	EQV	LOG	STEP
BEGIN	EXP	NOT	SWITCH
BOOLEAN	FALSE	OR	THEN
COS	FOR	OWN	TRUE
DIV	GO TO	PROCEDURE	UNTIL
DO	IF	REAL	VALUE

Other manuals have similar lists and other conventions.

A fairly complete version of ALGOL 60 is available in the Honeywell Time-Sharing System. The version is called "Dartmouth ALGOL" because it, like the Time-Sharing System, was developed at Dartmouth College.

Identifiers the same as the basic symbols of Dartmouth ALGOL are not allowed. Moreover, identifiers with embedded blanks must not consist of a basic symbol followed by one or more blanks. The following are the basic symbols that may occur as identifiers (or words of identifiers) in ALGOL 60 that are not allowed in Dartmouth ALGOL.

AND	DO	GOTO	OR	SWITCH
ARRAY	ELSE	IF	OWN	THEN
BEGIN	END	IMPLY	PROCEDURE	TRUE
BOOLEAN	EQUIV	INTEGER	REAL	UNTIL
COMMENT	FALSE	LABEL	STEP	VALUE
DATA	FOR	NOT	STRING	WHILE

Identifiers the same as the name of a standard function or procedure (READATA or PRINT) or data name (TTY) may not be used for other identification.

FORTRAN

FORTRAN, an acronym for FORmula TRANslator, was developed by IBM and is presently the most widely used language for both scientific and business problems and programs. Implementing FORTRAN requires, as do COBOL and ALGOL, a special translator program (compiler) written especially for each particular model of computer. FORTRAN II is presently the basic language although FORTRAN IV contains some additional features of input/output statements and names given to functions. FORTRAN IV compilers will, with only minor modifications, compile any FORTRAN II program. A committee of the American National Standards Institute has codified the specifications of FORTRAN IV, and this has been called BASIC FORTRAN to thus render basic agreement on what constitutes the minimum specifications of FORTRAN compilers. Information in this text will be based on both FORTRAN II and FORTRAN IV, but the reader is invited to use the particular FORTRAN manual devised for his machine, along with specialized conventions and restrictions, before he begins writing FORTRAN programs. The material to follow is designed as a series of rules and procedures for use as a "checklist" or reminder of key elements of the language. It is not meant to be complete.

FORTRAN is machine-independent and procedure-oriented; i.e., it will be acceptable to any computer made which has a FORTRAN compiler, and it is especially well suited for problem solving. The grammar, symbols, rules, and syntax used are generally in common with easy-to-learn mathematical and English-language conventions, but the instructions must be explicit. Generally the instructions concern five functional areas: input/output, arithmetic, transfer of control, looping (causing a set of statements to be executed a specific number of times), and compiling (direction of the processor in the translation process).

The student programmer first analyzes the problem, defines the procedures, and then flowcharts it. He then programs it, generally on FORTRAN 72- or 80-column coding paper. The program is then tested and debugged on the computer, though on-line debugging is expensive and often prohibited on many installations.

Some Fundamental FORTRAN Concepts*

1. FORTRAN program language is translated into machine language in the form of basic instructions which become the internal language of the machine.
2. The translation is completed by the use of various FORTRAN compilers.
3. FORTRAN was the first widely used compiler and is the base for QUIKTRAN and PL/1.
4. The problem-solving procedure is specified by a series of English-mathematics statements.
5. FORTRAN utilizes fixed and floating-point numbers (constants) in its system.
   (a) An integer or fixed-point constant is a positive or negative integer.
   (b) A floating-point constant is one with a decimal point.
   (c) Elements and expressions are thus in fixed-point or floating-point mode.
6. FORTRAN uses literal (constant) and variable quantities.
   (a) The first letter of the name designating a fixed-point variable must be I,J,K,L,M, or N (often called integer variables).
   (b) The first letter of the name designating a floating-point variable may be any letter except those specifying fixed point. No special characters are permitted.
   (c) Total number of characters must not exceed set limits; i.e., 5 or 6 or larger.
7. Subscripted variables names must not end in F.
8. OUTPUT—Two statements are needed to transmit information from memory to the printed page.
   (a) The FØRMAT statement describes the layout of the data as you want it to appear on a printed line. The number of print positions available depends upon the type of printer used.
   (b) The PRINT n, Variable List statement causes transmission of a specified list of quantities from memory to the printer.
      (1) n is the statement number of the FØRMAT statement referred to for the printed line layout.
      (2) Variable List refers to the names of the variables, listed in the order in which their values are to appear on the printed line.
      (3) Printing will continue until the complete list is satisfied, that is, until values have been printed for all variables in the list.
9. The five basic operations provided by FORTRAN are addition, subtraction, multiplication, division, and exponentiation.
   (a) Each operation is denoted by the symbols: +, –, *, /, **.
   (b) * means multiply; / means divide; ** means exponentiate.
10. The FORTRAN system uses mathematical expressions as: $X = A + B/C$ where X is a variable name and $A + B/C$ is an arithmetic expression.
11. The arithmetic statement directs FORTRAN to perform a computation.
   (a) All elements of the expression to the right must be in the same (integer or fixed-point) mode (most systems).
   (b) Two operation symbols may not be used next to each other.
   (c) The equal sign used in arithmetic statements means to replace the value of the left variable with the value of the expression on the right.
   (d) Operations with parentheses are performed first, the order then is: exponentiation, multiplication and division, addition and subtraction.
   (e) Parentheses indicate grouping, never multiplication.
12. FORTRAN provides for the use of common mathematical functions.
   (a) FORTRAN is directed to perform a function by writing its name in front of the expression related to it.
   (b) Examples: FORTRAN II uses SQRTF () for square root of an expression;

* Many computers use variations of these rules.

FORTRAN IV uses SQRT () , eliminating the F. EXPF () in II, EXP () in IV to exponentiate to a power, i.e., (2) .

13. A READ statement is used to enter stored data into the computer.
    (a) The READ statement indicates input or output operation, which variables are to receive new values, and the order of the values: "READ n, list" where n is the statement number, and list represents the number of variables to be read (or printed, punched, etc.) .
14. The FORMAT statement, which must have a statement number, describes:
    (a) One punched card (older systems) .
    (b) The specification of mode for each variable on the list.
        (1) I is used for integer mode variables.
        (2) F is used for floating-point variables punched in literal notation.
        (3) E is used for floating-point variables punched in exponential notation.
        (4) X is used to skip columns.
        (5) H is used to describe Hollerith fields.
    (c) The number of columns on the punched card which must be read for each specification, i.e., the field width.
    (d) The number of digits following the decimal point for F and E specifications.
    EXAMPLE (100 is the statment number)

    100 FØRMAT (I4, I3, F5.2, F9.7, F9.6)

    In addition:
    (e) There is an abbreviated notation for successive identical fields.
    FØRMAT (I4, I4, I4) = FØRMAT (3I4)
    (f) The decimal point does not need to be punched. It is sufficient to locate the decimal in the FØRMAT statement. If there is disagreement between the location of the decimal specified in the FØRMAT statement and the decimal actually punched on the card, the punched decimal takes precedence and is used.
    (g) Because FØRMAT statements are not executed, there are no restrictions on their location in the source program. It is good programming to write all the FØRMAT statements on a separate coding sheet and place the FØRMAT cards at the first part of the program.
15. The PAUSE and STOP statements allow the programmer to check interim results.
16. The END statement signals the completion of the source program and tells the computer to execute the object program.
17. In order to transfer control to a statement out of sequence, a GO TO statement is often used: (n_1, n_2, n_3, . . . , n_m) if the value of the integer variable is 1, control will go to the first statement number listed; i.e., n_1, if 2, to n_2, etc.
18. The IF statement transfers control on the condition of the happening of a certain event: IF (A — B) n_1, n_2, n_3. If the result of (A — B) is negative, control goes to statement n_1, if 0, to n_2, if positive, to n_3.
19. Subscribed variables (for arrays) allow the programmer to represent a number of variables with one name.
    (a) Individual variable subscripts are called elements.
    (b) The entire set of subscripts is called an array.
    (c) Fixed and floating-point variables must not be mixed in an array.
    (d) There are a number of rules for using subscripted variables.
        (1) You must tell the computer which variables are subscripted
        (2) How many elements are there in each array, and
        (3) How many subscripts are there for each subscripted variable.
        (4) Subscript cannot be floating-point, more than 3, or precede the DIMENSION statement.

Subscripted variables (single dimension) can represent any element of a one-dimensional array or table of numbers. The variable is still a FORTRAN variable of integer or floating-point mode, depending upon its first letter.

The FORTRAN statements illustrating the set of DØ in a counting loop below read one X-value at a time. The whole set of X-values can be thought of as a one-dimensional array or table,

$$X_1, X_2, X_3, \ldots, X_I, \ldots, X_N$$

FORTRAN provides a means to represent any element of a one-dimensional (and 2 or 3 dimensional) array by appending one subscript to the variable. For example, the variable X_I can be written X (I), a FORTRAN subscripted variable. Since there is no upper or lower case available in FORTRAN, subscripts are represented by enclosing them in parentheses. Now, the subscripted variable can be used in other statements; e.g., in a DØ loop as SUMX = SUMX + X (I).

20. The DO statement makes it possible to repeat the same operation, changing only the variable.
    (a) Control is shifted from the DO statement when the computations called for are completed, or by a GO TO or IF statement.
    (b) The general form of the DO statement:

    $$\text{DO sn } i = m_1, m_2, m_3$$

    where sn is a statement number, i is a nonsubscripted fixed-point variable, and m_1, m_2, and m_3 are each either unsigned fixed-point constants or nonsubscripted fixed-point variables. If m_3 is not stated, m_3 is understood to be 1. The DO statement tells the computer to execute repeatedly the statements which follow, up to and including the statement with the statement number sn. For the first iteration, the statements are executed with $i = m_1$. In each succeeding repetition, i is increased by the amount m_3. After the statements have been executed with i equal to the highest of the sequence of values which does not exceed m_2, control passes to the statement following the statement sn.
    (c) There are a number of rules concerned with the use of the DO statement. (1) The first statement in the range of a DO must be a statement that can be executed. (2) The range of one DO statement may contain another DO (called an inner DO). (3) The last statement in the range of a DO, with the exception of a GO TO or IF statement, may not cause a transfer of control. (4) No statement within the range of a DO may alter any of the indexing parameters of that DO. (5) Control must not transfer into the range of a DO from any statement outside its range.
21. The use of magnetic tape can greatly speed up the operation of a computer.
    (a) Magnetic tape will store intermediate results while the computer solves the remainder of the problem.
    (b) A read-input statement feeds data from the tape to the computer.
22. Open and closed functions are provided as part of the FORTRAN system.
    (a) Open functions are programmed each time they are needed.
    (b) Closed functions are stored, and used as needed.
23. The arithmetic statement function is used only in a particular program to perform repeated operations. This statement is limited in that it can compute only a single value.
24. Function and subroutine subprograms remove the limitations of the arithmetic statement function.
    (a) They are actually independent programs which have the advantage of dividing up a complex main program into workable segments.
    (b) Subroutines for common mathematical functions like sin, cos, log, square root, etc., are built into the FORTRAN system. Some of these obviate the use of tables for their evaluation.

    An example is the square root function. SQRTF (X) computes the square root of X. It has one argument which is floating-point mode, and the function is floating point.

    EXAMPLE: Y = SQRTF (A * X ** 2 − 4.0 * W)

    Some other floating-point functions which are a part of the FORTRAN system are:

Name		Usage
ATAN	ATANF (X)	gives the principal value of arctan x in radians

EXP	EXPF (X)	gives value of e^x
LØG	LØGF (X)	gives value of $\log_e x$
SIN	SINF (X)	gives value of sin x where x is in radians
CØS	CØSF (X)	gives value of cos x where x is in radians
SQRT	SQRTF (X)	gives value of $x^{1/2}$

25. Other FORTRAN statements not reviewed here include: varying the Hollerith field (spacing, line skipping, etc.) ; tape instructions (CALL, COMMON, EQUIVALENCE, ASSIGN) ; naming of assigned functions (GO TO, BLOCK DATA) ; conditional transfers; and others. They can be found in the specific machine FORTRAN manuals and lists of "conventions and restrictions" of each individual computer installation. Familiarization with statements relative to the particular computer will aid in operation.

Chaining

Some FORTRAN compilers permit the use of an overlay technique, called chaining, to maximize the memory efficiency of object programs. Since every program in a job does not necessarily communicate with every other program, the entire job need not fit in memory at the same time. In fact, the job may be divided into independent segments which can each occupy all of the memory at different times during the program run.

Special Notes on FORTRAN IV

The above discussion relates to FORTRAN II, which at the latest level of basic FORTRAN is very similar to FORTRAN II-D. However it is not permissible with the former to use the "A" specification or the disk statements, or to index the i/o statements. These are the only differences which are basic and significant. Others, of course, do exist.

FORTRAN IV, as contrasted to basic FORTRAN and FORTRAN II-D, represents a significant step upward, most specifically in the power of the statements themselves and also in the ability to interface with more complex computer configurations. Generally, FORTRAN IV is operable only on the larger, faster computers—those which are specifically called "Third Generation" machines.

As regards the statements themselves, FORTRAN IV offers some slightly different forms from those of FORTRAN II due to the increased power of the former, as follows:

1. Additional indexing capabilities in the i/o statements are available in FORTRAN IV.
2. The configuration of the machine or system itself requires some significant changes in formatting. The READ and WRITE statements are typical of this change (see below).
3. Some FORTRAN statements are not present at all in FORTRAN IV because of an upgrading of power in the machine configuration. For example, the PUNCH and PRINT statements are examples of commands that have been eliminated.
4. As shifts are made to the next level or generation of computers with increased storage capacity and p.ocessing speed, more sophisticated jobs can be initiated with FORTRAN IV statements. The definition of constants in arithmetic statements is an example of this increased capability.
5. FORTRAN IV has many more *executable* statements than FORTRAN II. A list of some regular and additional key words in basic FORTRAN IV follows:

ABS	DABS	END	FORMAT
	DBLE	ENDFILE	FUNCTION
BACKSPACE	DEFINE	EQUIVALENCE	
	DFLOAT	EXIT	GO
CALL	DIM	EXTERNAL	
COMMON	DIMENSION		
CONTINUE	DO		IABS
	DOUBLE	FIND	IDIM
	DSIGN	FLOAT	IF

IFIX INTEGER ISIGN	PAUSE READ REAL	RETURN REWIND SIGN SNGL	STOP SUBROUTINE WRITE

6. Although the integer mode is the same as in FORTRAN II, the maximum size of a positive integer value can have more digits. Integer mode corresponds to fixed-point mode. Real mode corresponds to floating-point mode. "Double-precision" in FORTRAN IV has no counterpart in FORTRAN II.
7. Mixed-mode operations are permitted on the IBM 360 FORTRAN IV system, and many others.
8. In FORTRAN IV some differences exist in the hierarchy of arithmetic operations as follows:

Operation	Hierarchy
Evaluation of functions (such as square root)	1
Exponentiation (proceeds from right to left)	2
Multiplication and division (proceeds from left to right)	3
Addition and subtraction (proceeds from left to right)	4

9. Sequential i/o statements pertain to the operation and use of such sequential devices as the card reader, card punch, reader, and magnetic tape. Direct-access statements pertain to disk and drum units and their operation.
10. An example of the general form of sequential i/o statements follows:

    READ (a,b) List

    This form differs from FORTRAN II i/o statements because "a" makes reference to a data set, and "b" makes reference to an associated format statement.
11. Examples of four direct-access i/o statements follow:
    (a) DEFINE FILE—describes the characteristics of the data set used with i/o operations.
    (b) READ—causes transfer of data from a direct-access device to internal storage.
    (c) WRITE—causes transfer of data from internal storage to the access device.
    (d) FIND—causes the positioning of the access arms over the proper data record and allows the computer to proceed concurrently with computation.
12. The TYPE statement is used to override the normal explicit mode of a named variable, by expressing a variable to be a real integer or double-precision mode.
13. When using some IBM systems, EXTENDED PRECISION control serves the same functions that DOUBLE PRECISION serves in some versions of FORTRAN IV, by extending the number of significant digits in real mode operations.
14. Five modes or types are available in FORTRAN IV for both constants and variables: integer, real, double precision, complex, and logical. Variables of these last three types require explicit TYPE declarations.
15. Logical IF statements are available in FORTRAN IV as well as arithmetic IF statements. The arithmetic IF statement discussed earlier contains an arithmetic expression whose value can be negative, zero, or positive; the logical IF statement uses a logical expression whose value can be either true or false.
16. If the logical expression is true, the statement will be executed next. If it is false, the next statement in the normal sequence will be executed. The statement may be any type of statement except a DO statement or another logical IF statement. The logical expression can be a relational expression, a logical variable or constant, or any arrangement of these combined by logical operators.
17. A relational expression can be formed using any of these six relational operators:

Operator	*Meaning*
.LT.	Less than
.LE.	Less than or equal to

.EQ.	Equal to
.NE.	Not equal to
.GT.	Greater than
.GE.	Greater than or equal to

These operators are used in a relational expression to compare two values: the value of a constant, variable, or arithmetic expression and the value of another constant, variable, or arithmetic expression (except that a constant may not be compared with another constant). Constants and variables may be in integer, real, or double precision mode. The comparisons must be made between terms of the same mode.

18. The logical variable can have either the values true or false, which can be assigned or evaluated in a program in the following types of statements:

    logical variable = .TRUE.
    logical variable = .FALSE.
    logical variable = logical expression

    A compound logical expression results from combining relational expressions and/or logical variables or constants with the logical operators .AND., .OR., .NOT. When .AND. is used to combine two such terms, both must be true for the combinations to be true. When .OR. is used to combine such terms, only one must be true for the combination to be true. When .NOT. is used, it reverses the value (true or false) of the term that is placed to its right. If the term is a relational expression or a combination, it should be enclosed in parentheses.
19. The order of combinational priorities (in the absence of parentheses) in a compound logical expression is: (1) the arithmetic operators, (2) the relational operators, and (3) the logical operators ranked as .NOT., .AND., and .OR.
20. While there are a variety of additional differences between FORTRAN II and FORTRAN IV, these can be found elsewhere.* A few of the more significant ones may be mentioned: (a) an array variable may be dimensioned in a COMMON statement rather than in a DIMENSION statement; (b) an array variable may be dimensioned with a variable rather than a maximum number constant; (c) more characters are available for printing messages and headings; and (d) longer FORTRAN statements, statement numbers, and DO loop counters may be used. The result of these differences is to give FORTRAN IV more flexibility, more power, and more accuracy.

RATFOR

The concepts of structured programming are being incorporated into many existing languages that were not originally designed to contain WHILE loops and IF-THEN-ELSE constructs. This leads to a real problem of program portability. The main reason for writing a program in a fairly standard language like FORTRAN is that the program can be run on a different machine with only slight modifications. When a compiler supplier includes sophisticated control structures in a language, the programmer is allowed to program in a nonstandard fashion, and thus the program will not transport.

Brian W. Kernighan and P. J. Plauger of Bell Laboratories have developed a "software tool" that allows the applications programmer to use the high-level control structures of structured languages, but still maintain a great degree of portability. The tool is called the RATFOR (RATional FORtran) preprocessor. This translator takes a RATFOR program as input and produces an ANSI standard FORTRAN as its output. If a programmer has an ANSI standard compiler at his disposal, then he can write in RATFOR instead of FORTRAN. The result will be FORTRAN programs that are in ANSI standard FORTRAN, one of the most transportable computer languages.

---

* See these two references published by the American National Standards Institute, New York, 10018: ANSI Standard FORTRAN, X3.9-1966, and ANSI Standard Basic FORTRAN, X3.10-1966.

RATFOR offers the high-level control structures common to ALGOL-like languages, but, in a sense, the RATFOR code is actually FORTRAN. At any time while writing in RATFOR, the programmer may write in FORTRAN. The preprocessor will recognize the FORTRAN constructs and simply reproduce them in the translation. The declarations of variables, the scope of those variables, and other issues that define a programming language are resolved by this fact; RATFOR is FORTRAN, except that it has some useful constructs that must be translated before it can be compiled. The fact that the RATFOR code is precompiled and then the FORTRAN code is compiled indicates inefficiency with respect to CPU time. However, reductions in the cost of machine resources have made the programmer's time much more valuable in comparison.

Writing programs in a language that is translated into FORTRAN treats FORTRAN as if it were an assembly language. This is not far from the truth. With regard to control structures, FORTRAN resembles an assembler more than it resembles ALGOL. In this sense, ANSI standard FORTRAN can be looked upon as the bridge between high-level languages and the infinite array of machine instruction sets.

The idea promoted by Kernighan and Plauger is that when part of a program is written, it should be written as a general tool that will not only serve the function demanded by the program at hand, but will also serve similar requirements of different programs. With this theory, they envison programs being assembled from routines stored in a software library, instead of being written from scratch.

In their book, *Software Tools,*[1] Kernighan and Plauger discuss the philosophy behind their RATFOR precompiler, and they give numerous examples, which they recommend as examples of how to build software tools. The examples which follow are taken from their book. Three procedures are shown. Detab will translate a character file into an equivalent character file that has blank characters substituting for any tab characters. This is a software tool that would translate files to a form that could be dealt with by devices that cannot interpret the tab character.

Since the number of blank characters substituted for the tab character is dependent on tab stops, detab must have some way of determining where the tab stops are. It calls tabpos to gather this information. Tabpos, in turn, is dependent on an array that was previously initialized by settab. Settab assumes the tab stops should be set arbitrarily every eight positions. The value of the breakdown of the problem into three modules is the enhanced changeability. If a different formula for setting tabs must be used, or if it is decided that a user sitting at a terminal should decide the tab stops, the only changes that need to be made are alterations to settab. The other modules are insulated from this kind of change by proper modularization.

RATFOR is also capable of translating into PL/1. Below are the three routines, detab, tabpos, and settab.[2] They are presented in the RATFOR code, as well as the product of the RATFOR precompiler, ANSI FORTRAN and PL/1.

RATFOR Version of Detab, Tabpos, and Settab

```
# detab — convert tabs to equivalent number of blanks
      character getc
      character c
      integer tabpos
      integer col, i, tabs (MAXLINE)
      call settab (tabs)      # set initial tab stops
      col = 1
      while  (getc (c)¬ = EOF)
             if  (c = = TAB)
                    repeat {
                          call putc (BLANK)
                          col = col + 1
                          } until  (tabpos (col, tabs) = = YES)
```

1. Brian W. Kernighan and P. J. Plauger, *Software Tools* (Reading, Mass.: Addison-Wesley Publishing Co., Inc., 1976).
2. Op. cit.

```
                else if  (c == NEWLINE)  {
                        call putc (NEWLINE)
                        col = 1
                        }
                else {
                        call putc (c)
                        col = col + 1
                        }
        stop
        end
# tabpos - return YES if col is a tab stop
        integer function tabpos (col, tabs)
        integer col, i, tabs (MAXLINE)
        if  (col > MAXLINE)
                tabpos = YES
        else
                tabpos = tabs (col)
        return
        end
# settab - set initial tab stops
        subroutine settab (tabs)
        integer mod
        integer i, tabs (MAXLINE)
        for  (i = 1;  i <= MAXLINE;  i = i + 1)
                if  (mod (i, 8)  == 1)
                        tabs (i)  = YES
                else
                        tabs (i)  = NO
        return
        end
```

Detab uses settab to set up the tabs array initially, according to whatever representation is expected by tabpos.

Translation From RATFOR Into FORTRAN of Detab, Tabpos, and Settab

```
c detab - convert tabs to equivalent number of blanks; Fortran version
        integer getc
        integer c
        integer tabpos
        integer col, i, tabs (MAXLINE)
c
c       set initial tab stops
        call settab (tabs)
        col = 1
10      if  (getc (c)  .eq.  EOF)  goto 60
                if  (c .ne.  TAB)  goto 30
20                      call putc (BLANK)
                        col = col + 1
                        if  (tabpos (col, tabs)  .ne.  YES)  goto 20
                        goto 50
c               else if
30              if  (c .ne.  NEWLINE)  goto 40
                        call putc (NEWLINE)
                        col = 1
                        goto 50
c               else
40                      call putc (c)
                        col = col + 1
50              goto 10
```

```
60      stop
        end
c tabpos — return YES if col is a tab stop; Fortran version
        integer function tabpos (col, tabs)
        integer col, i, tabs (MAXLINE)
c
        if (col .gt. MAXLINE)  tabpos = YES
        if (col .le. MAXLINE)  tabpos = tabs (col)
        return
        end
c settab — set initial tab stops; Fortran version
        subroutine settab (tabs)
        integer mod
        integer i, tabs (MAXLINE)
c
        i = 1
10      if (i .gt. MAXLINE)  goto 20
              if (mod (i, 8)  .eq. 1)  tabs (i)  = YES
              if (mod (i, 8)  .ne. 1)  tabs (i)  = NO
              i = i + 1
              goto 10
20      return
        end
```

Translation From RATFOR Into PL/1 of Detab, Settab, and Tabpos

```
/* detab — convert tabs into equivalent number of blanks */
      detab: procedure options  (main) ;
      declare getc entry  (fixed binary)  returns  (fixed binary) ;
      declare putc entry  (fixed binary) ;
      declare c fixed binary;
      declare setttab entry  ((*) fixed binary) ;
      declare tabpos entry  (fixed binary,  (*) fixed binary)  returns  (fixed binary) ;
      declare  (col, tabs (MAXLINE) )  fixed binary;
      call settab (tabs) ;      /* set initial tab stops */
      col = 1;
      do while  (getc (c) ¬= EOF) ;
            if c = TAB then do;
              loop:
                  call putc (BLANK) ;
                  col = col + 1;
                  if tabpos (col, tabs)    = YES then
                        goto loop;
                  end;
            else if c = NEWLINE then do;
                  call putc (NEWLINE) ;
                  col = 1;
                  end;
            else do;
                  call putc (c) ;
                  col = col + 1;
                  end;
            end;
      end detab;
/* tabpos — return YES if col is a tab stop */
      tabpos: procedure  (col, tabs)  returns  (fixed binary) ;
      declare  (col, tabs (*) )  fixed binary;
      if col > MAXLINE then
            return (YES) ;
```

```
        else
                return (tabs (col) ) ;
        end tabpos;
/* settab — set initial tab stops */
        settab: procedure (tabs) ;
        declare (i, tabs (*) ) fixed binary;
        do i = 1 to MAXLINE;
                if mod (i, 8) = 1 then
                        tabs (i) = YES;
                else
                        tabs (i) = NO;
                end;
        end settab;
```

COBOL

The student will recall from his initial reading or course in data processing that various series of explicit, detailed coded instructions are required for computer operation. Just a few years ago it was necessary for programmer "experts" to perform this task of writing instructions in a computer's internally acceptable or "machine-sensible" language. The tedious and meticulous chores were lessened somewhat by the use of mnemonic codes and assemblers. Now, however, "macroinstructions," which are single instructions each of which produces several or many series of machine instructions, have been developed into compilers. These are often also called processors, translators, autocoders, or packaged programs, and they are simply very large macroprograms. They develop the many-for-one instruction translation of programs written in English language to internally acceptable machine-sensible codes; i.e., binary numbers representing instructions, information, and data. The machine itself thus becomes its own programmer or translator of the compiler languages, such as COBOL, FORTRAN, ALGOL, PL/1, etc., into the basic thousands or millions of specialized true binary instructions and codes it must use internally. The FORTRAN or COBOL compiler, then, is the large program stored in any computer for the processing or translating of macro or English instructions rather easily written by students, professors, managers, etc., who are thus not required to learn the intricacies of internal computer operations, although they will all do well to learn the principles. FORTRAN, COBOL, etc., then, are "at once" languages and compilers. We use their rules of grammar, format, and syntax to write programs because they are special computer languages. And when we say FORTRAN or COBOL compiler, we mean the large translating programs which are stored in the various computers to effect the translation of the FORTRAN or COBOL language into machine-sensible codes and instructions.

The FORTRAN or COBOL program is called the source program. After it is translated, it is called the object program. Each source program needs to be translated or processed only once into its machine-language object program. It then remains as a binary-coded object program for use continuously or as often as needed, and it can be amended, corrected in binary, or completely rewritten.

The programmer can use COBOL English instructions such as:

```
004000  Transfer Data. Move corresponding Purchase Record to Total Record.
004100  If Stock Number in Purchase Record is not numeric, go to Bad.
004400  Stock Number.
004401  Write Total Record. Go to Read-Loop.
004500  If Stock is less than Order Point, perform Reorder Routine.
004600  Write Monthly Statement.
005400  Add Interest to Dividends.
```

Before the processor or compiler can interpret the above instructions, it must be given pertinent information. For example, to use the last instruction, the programmer will have to write the names INTEREST and DIVIDENDS in a special part of the program called "Data Division." In this section he will state certain facts about the data to be represented by those names. These will be maximum size of the individual items, the fact that the information will be numeric, etc. In effect, the Data Division is used to describe data so that the computer can recognize it, obtain it when needed, and know how to treat it in accordance with its special characteristics. The processor will examine the word ADD by consulting a special list of words that have clearly defined meanings in the COBOL language. These words are part of the processor or compiler. Because ADD is one of these words, the processor or compiler will interpret it to mean that it must insert into the object program the machine instruction (s) required to perform an addition.

When the processor or compiler examines the word INTEREST, it obtains from the Data Division the information it needs. The word TO (special list) indicates to the compiler that it is the value of DIVIDENDS that will be increased as a result of the addition. The reader is invited to use the manuals of the various manufacturers to know the exact procedures because they vary from machine to machine but only in minor details, and generally any program written in COBOL will be acceptable (as slightly amended) to all machines having COBOL processors or compilers.

Generally, the COBOL language and compiler can be summed up as follows:

The COBOL language contains a basic list of key words and symbols. Each key word and symbol specifies to the processor a definite set of machine operations. In effect the programmer thus has at his disposal a whole series of "prefabricated" portions of the object program he wishes the computer to construct. When he writes a COBOL-language program, he is actually directing the computer to bring together, in the proper sequence, the groups of machine instructions necessary to accomplish the desired result. The language in which he does this is not only easy to work with, but it saves him from having to specify a great many machine steps in detail. The rules for writing the COBOL language are much simpler than those which govern the machine languages, and the programmer is enabled to write his programs easily, rapidly, and accurately. Using the processor appropriate to his particular machine, he can use English words and conventional arithmetic symbols to direct and control the complicated operations of the computer.

The advantages of using COBOL can be summed up as follows:

- COBOL programs are stated in precise, easily learned English words and phrases.
- COBOL programs can be read and understood by nontechnical people with minimal backgrounds in data processing.
- COBOL programs written for one computer can be run on another computer, with minimum modification, to take advantage of the features of the second computer.
- COBOL training time is negligible for the novice in programming, and reprogramming costs are reduced.
- COBOL program testing is simplified and can be completed by someone other than the original programmer.
- COBOL documentation is easily understood, standardized, and complete to analysts, nontechnical personnel, and programmers, and is especially desirable for companies owning or using more than one type of computer.

In many computer installations, the operator presses a button, or the first card, typewritten instruction, or tape entry specifies COBOL as the language used. The COBOL processor is either fed into main memory or it is already on-line for automatic translation of the COBOL statements into machine language in split seconds or real time.

COBOL grew out of the desire to develop a language that would be compatible and acceptable as a source program language by any computer that had a COBOL compiler or processor. The maintenance and orderly development of the language were established and are directed by a group of experts and representatives called the Conference of Data System Languages, which is abbreviated CODASYL.

Improved COBOL streamlines and adds many new capabilities and reduces several cumbersome attributes of the system. The COBOL compiler is the program that processes programmer-written COBOL sentences and produces (i.e., compiles) an object program (the program that can run on a digital computer, i.e., binary instructions and routines).

A source program is written in four divisions:

Identification Division—Contains the name of the program and other documentary information.

Environment Division—Specifies the computer on which the COBOL compilation is to be accomplished and the computer configuration on which the object program is to run.

Data Division—Describes the data the object program is to process.

Procedure Division—States the logical steps that the object program is to follow in processing data.

COBOL Features

Generally, the structure and components of COBOL can be outlined as follows:

I. Basic COBOL (COmmon Business Oriented Language).
- A. COBOL is a computer language.
  1. Uses English words or abbreviations.
  2. Uses normal English word order.
  3. Statements are automatically translated into computer language.
     - (a) Completed by a compiler program.
     - (b) The compiler program is already in the computer.
- B. Communication in the narrative form.
  1. COBOL is a means of communicating with the computer.
  2. COBOL is used as program documentation.
  3. Same programs may operate on all systems regardless of their individual configuration.
  4. Users can exchange programs freely.
  5. Within certain limitations, COBOL programs can be exchanged between users of computers made by various manufacturers.
- C. Structure of COBOL programs.
  1. The Identification Division, which identifies the program.
     - (a) Less machine independent because of the ways in which various computers may accept and handle alphabetic information.
     - (b) Relatively few options are available in the Identification Division.
  2. The Environment Division, which states what equipment is to be used.
     - (a) Totally dependent on the computer system used.
     - (b) Tells the program what peripheral units are used.
  3. The Data Division, which shows the format of input and output data.
     - (a) Strongly dependent on the particular kind of computer used.
     - (b) Defines the manner in which information appears in input and output files.
  4. The Procedure Division, which defines the actual operations to be performed.
     - (a) It is applicable to any computer system having a COBOL compiler program.
     - (b) It is strongly machine independent.

II. Required, Optional, Elective, and Extended COBOL.
- A. The character set.
- B. Words used in COBOL.
  1. A word is composed of not more than 30 characters chosen from the basic 37 characters.
  2. A word is ended (a) by a space, or (b) by a period, comma, semicolon, or right parenthesis, followed by a space.
- C. The rules for use of the punctuation characters are:
  1. A period, comma, or semicolon, when used, must immediately follow the word, and must in turn be followed by a space.
  2. A beginning quote mark must not be followed by a space unless the space is desired in the literal.
  3. A right parenthesis or an ending quote mark must not be preceded by a space unless the space is desired in the literal.
  4. Semicolons are used for readability only and never required in a statement.

D. Nouns. Special varieties of the basic four word types may be defined according to specific usage.
   1. A noun may be a data name.
      (a) Examples: SALARY, ADDRESS, or DATE.
      (b) Data names must contain at least one alphabetic character.
      (c) It must not begin or end with a hyphen, and must not contain a space.
   2. A noun may be a procedure name.
      (a) If it is used as a tag or label.
      (b) Same rules as a data noun.
   3. A third type of noun is a literal.
      (a) It has at least one and not more than 120 characters.
      (b) Used precisely as it appears in the source language statement.
   4. The fourth type of noun is the condition name.
      (a) Name assigned to the value which a field may have at a given time.
      (b) Figurative constants are fixed data names that have been assigned certain values.

E. The verbs used in COBOL.
   1. They specify the actions to be taken in COBOL programs.
   2. Used to move data from one file to another.
   3. Although the word IF is not a verb in English, it is used in COBOL to initiate comparisons.
   4. Usually the first word of a statement.

F. Optional words are included with the language to aid readability.

G. Connectives. Usually used to introduce a phrase specifying an alternative procedure.

H. Reserved words. For use in their defined meaning only, and may not be used otherwise.

III. The Procedure Division.

A. The procedure formation.
   1. A statement is formed by the use of a verb and one or more operands. (An operand is the quantity or name on which the verb acts.)
   2. A statement or group of statements terminated by a period and a space is called a sentence. Example: ADD WITHHELD-TAX, FICA, RETIREMENT, INSURANCE, STOCK-PURCHASE-RATE GIVING TOTAL-DEDUCTION THEN SUBTRACT TOTAL-DEDUCTION FROM GROSS-PAY GIVING NET-PAY.
   3. A procedure may be a paragraph, a group of paragraphs, a section, or a group of sections.
   4. In order to permit reference to a portion of a COBOL program, names or labels are given to paragraphs, sections, and procedures.

B. Qualification. Paragraph names may not be duplicated within a section; they may, however, be used again in another section.

C. The use of subscripts.
   1. Subscripts are appended to data names to denote individual elements of a list or table.
   2. The name of the table may be used to refer to the entire table.
   3. Names or literals used as subscripts must be of positive integer value.
   4. Subscripts are indicated after the table name to be modified, enclosed in parentheses with different subscripts separated by commas, and separated from the table name by a space.

D. Conditions. Most condition statements consist of the word IF followed by the conditions to be examined.
   1. Amount comparisons. Arithmetic comparisons are specified by the relational symbols or their various word equivalents. Comparisons may also be made between a named quantity and a known range.
   2. Class comparisons. The class comparison determines whether the contents of a field are alphabetic or numeric.
   3. Compound conditions.
      (a) A sequence of simple conditions separated by logical connectives.

(b) Compound conditions must be clearly stated so that no ambiguity is possible.

4. Dependent relations.
   (a) In certain instances, the operands and relational operator may be omitted. In such an instance, the missing term or terms will be obtained from the nearest preceding relation of the sequence.
   (b) When a relation operator is common to a series of comparisons, it need not be repeated after its first use.
5. Summary.
   (a) Conditions permit a choice of action.
   (b) A compound condition follows the same pattern, regardless of the number of simple conditions grouped together.

E. Procedure Verb Function.

1. Arithmetical verbs.
   (a) Add. Specifies the addition of two or more quantities.
   (b) Add Corresponding. To reduce the writing required when a group of items is to be cross-footed or accumulated.
   (c) Subtract. Specifies the subtraction of the named quantities, or subtraction of the sum of several named quantities from the last-named field.
   (d) Multiply. Multiplies the two specified operands and stores the product in the last-named field or in the field indicated by the giving option.
   (e) Divide. Used to divide one specified operand by another and store the quotient in the last-named field or in the operand of the giving option.
   (f) Compute. Permits the use of formulas, with arithmetic operators or their reserved word equivalents, in computing quantities.
2. Input/output verbs. Used to store information into and take information out of the processing system during execution of a COBOL program.
   (a) Open. Permits access to information files.
   (b) Read. Makes the next logical record from an input file available for processing.
   (c) Write. Releases a logical record for an output file, which may be in the form of punched cards or magnetic tape.
   (d) Write . . . From . . . Permits movement of data with editing dictated by the receiving area prior to the actual write.
   (e) Accept. Used to request the entry of information from the keyboard.
   (f) Display. Permits low-volume output on a device such as the message printer or plotter.
   (g) Close. After the last record has been written into or read from a file, the close verb is used to terminate processing of that file.
3. Procedure branching verbs.
   (a) Go To. Causes a change from the normal sequence of procedures.
   (b) Alter. Used to modify an existing sequence of operations by changing the operand of a labeled Go To Paragraph.
   (c) Perform. Permits the program to depart from the normal sequence of procedures to execute one named statement, or a named sequence of statements; the statement or statements will be executed a specified number of times or until a stated limit is reached
   (d) Time Option. Sets up a counter and tests it against the specified number of times before the named procedures are executed.
4. Data movement verbs.
   (a) Move. Used to transfer data to one or more fields.
   (b) Examine. Used to count occurrences of a given character in a data field.
5. Compiler directing verb. Must be preceded by a paragraph name and must form the only statement in the paragraph.
6. Special data-handling verbs.
   (a) Sort. Used to sort a file of data with respect to designated fields by means of an internal sorting routine.

(b) Merge. Used to combine two or more files into a single sorted output file by means of a single pass through the data.

7. Ending verbs. Halt program execution either temporarily of permanently, depending upon the statement content.

Character Set as Used in COBOL

The following 37 characters constitute the character set:

A, B, . . . Z (English alphabet)
0, 1, . . . 9 (Arabic numerals)
- (hyphen or minus sign)

The set of punctuation characters is:

. period
, comma
; semicolon
" quotation marks
blank or space
(left parenthesis
) right parenthesis

Relations between numeric quantities can be written as special characters or expressed in the form of their equivalent words, as follows:

$>$ or GREATER THAN or EXCEEDS
$<$ or LESS THAN
$=$ or EQUAL TO or EQUALS
$\leqq$ or LESS THAN OR EQUAL TO
$\geqq$ or GREATER THAN OR EQUAL TO
$\neq$ or NOT EQUAL TO or UNEQUAL TO

The characters used for arithmetic operators in formulas appear below:

= or EQUALS or EQUAL TO
+ or PLUS
− or MINUS
* or MULTIPLIED BY or TIMES
/ or DIVIDED BY
** or EXPONENTIATED BY

The characters used to describe editing on data include:

$ dollar sign
* check protection symbol
, comma
. decimal point

COBOL Language Use

COBOL is a shorthand for the computer instructions. Just as any language is made up of words with certain specific meanings, a computer language has specific words each with a certain meaning; they can only be used with these meanings and no others. COBOL words are given here in all capitals as in the programming examples, which follow, as given by IBM.

Since the COBOL language is derived from English, it looks like English. Thus, the programmer can work with it easily, without having to learn a long list of special symbols and codes, and the rules for using them. The following are typical COBOL-language sentences:

SUBTRACT DEDUCTIONS FROM GROSS GIVING NET.
PERFORM TAX-CALCULATION.
IF STOCK IS LESS THAN ORDER-POINT PERFORM REORDER-ROUTINE.
WRITE MONTHLY STATEMENT.

Each of these sentences is meaningful even to the casual reader. However, operations within a computer are controlled by instructions in code—in the internal language of the machine. In order for a computer to be able to interpret a COBOL sentence, the sentence must first be translated into the machine's language. As the COBOL system is designed, the COBOL-language program need be translated only once; the resulting machine-language program can be used and reused indefinitely without further translation.

This translation is accomplished within the computer itself, employing many of the same techniques used in processing ordinary business data. A special program, known as a *processor,* is first entered into the machine. The COBOL-language program (*source program*) is then read into the machine, where the processor reads it and analyzes it. The computer acts on it in accordance with instructions built into the processor, and as a result of this process it creates a new program in machine language. This program is known as an *object program.* Once the object program has been produced, it may be used to process data whenever it is required. It may be recorded in some external medium and stored for future use. It may be used over and over again as long as it is needed.

The COBOL language is capable of describing business problems of many kinds and of specifying the basic steps required to solve them. Procedures may be written in it with relatively little understanding of the detailed steps the computer will take in carrying out its assignment. The programmer will write more efficient programs if he has at least some understanding of machine operations, but the procedural portion of the language itself is, in large part, machine independent.

Before the preparation of the COBOL series of words, the programmer must obtain information including:

1. The name or names by which data is to be identified.
2. The organization of each item of data with respect to other data—i.e., the scheme by which the individual items are grouped and the relationships among the groups.
3. The length of each kind of data.
4. The location of the decimal point in numeric items.
5. The value of constants; i.e., the actual values of the names, numbers, special characters, and so on which are to be stored in the computer for use in processing other data. Numbers in a table and names in a list are typical constants.

Each kind of data to be used in a program must be described in accordance with clearly defined rules. The part of the program reserved for this purpose is the data division, of which a substantial portion can be written in such a way that the same data description will be usable regardless of the type of computer on which the program is to be run. Certain portions of it, however, are related to specific machine charactersistics, and therefore these portions must be rewritten should it become necessary to run the program on a different type of machine.

There are certain rules which must be followed; some of these are given below:

1. All words printed entirely in capital letters have preassigned meanings in the COBOL system.
2. All underlined words are required unless the portion of the format containing them is half optional—i.e., enclosed in square brackets. These are *key words,* and if any such word is missing or is incorrectly spelled, it is considered an error in the program.
3. All COBOL words *not* underlined may be included or omitted at the option of the programmer. These words are used only for the sake of readability. Misspelling, however, constitutes an error. These words are called *optional words.*
4. All italicized words represent information which must be supplied by the programmer. The nature of the information required is indicated in each case. In most instances, the programmer will be required to provide an appropriate data-name, procedural-name, literal, etc.
5. Material enclosed in square brackets [ ] may be used or omitted as required by the programmer.
6. When material is enclosed in braces { }, one, and only one, of the enclosed items is required; the others are to be omitted. The choice is to be determined by the programmer.
7. Punctuation, where shown, is essential. Other punctuation may be inserted by the programmer in accordance with the rules specified.

8. Special characters, such as the equal sign, are essential where shown, although they may not be underlined.
9. In certain cases, a succession of operands or other elements may be used in the same statement. In such a case, this possibility is indicated by the use of three dots following the item affected. The dots apply to the last *complete* element preceding them; thus, if a *group* of operands and key words are enclosed within brackets and the brackets are followed by three dots, the entire group (not merely the last operand) must be repeated if any repetition is required.
10. Restrictions and comments on each basic format will be found in the examples.

COBOL is a language, and, as with other languages, it must be used with precision for proper results. Since COBOL must be processed on a computer, the computer symbols or characters must be used; these will be found to differ among the various computer systems.

COBOL Reserved Words

Most COBOL reserved words are listed below, but particular use or implementation might possibly not have all elective features, and therefore some words may not be reserved. The recommendation is that all COBOL reserved words be avoided in devising names or acronyms. The reserved words are not separated by division, nor are key words distinguished. COBOL words should not be used in programs anywhere except as the formats designate. The list shows only singular forms where choice exists, but in many cases and uses, either the singular or the plural of a reserved word may be chosen to improve reading.

ABOUT
ACCEPT
ADD
ADDRESS
ADVANCING
AFTER
ALL
ALPHABETIC
ALPHANUMERIC
ALTER
ALTERNATE
AN
AND
APPLY
ARE
AREA
AT
AUTHOR

BEFORE
BEGINNING
BEGINNING-FILE-LABEL
BEGINNING-TAPE-LABEL
BITS
BLANK
BLOCK
BY

CHARACTER
CHECK
CLASS
CLOCK-UNITS
CLOSE
COBOL
COMPUTATIONAL
COMPUTE
CONFIGURATION
CONSTANT
CONTAINS
CONTROL
COPY
CORRESPONDING

DATA
DATE-COMPILED
DATE-WRITTEN
DECLARATIVES
DEFINE
DEPENDING
DIGIT
DISPLAY
DIVIDE
DIVIDED
DIVISION
DOLLAR

ELSE
END
ENDING
ENDING-FILE-LABEL
ENDING-TAPE-LABEL
END-OF-FILE
END-OF-TAPE
ENTER
ENVIRONMENT
EQUAL
ERROR
EVERY
EXAMINE
EXCEEDS
EXIT
EXPONENTIATED

FD
FILE
FILE-CONTROL
FILLER
FIRST
FLOAT
FOR
FORMAT
FROM

GIVING
GO
GREATER

HASHED
HIGH VALUE

IDENTIFICATION
IF
IN
INCLUDE
INPUT
INPUT-OUTPUT
INTO
I-O-CONTROL
IS

JUSTIFIED

LABEL
LEADING
LEAVING
LEFT
LESS
LIBRARY
LINE
LOCATION
LOCK
LOWER-BOUND
LOW-VALUE

MEMORY
MEMORY-DUMP
MINUS
MODE
MODULES
MOVE
MULTIPLE
MULTIPLIED
MULTIPLY

NEGATIVE
NEXT
NO
NO-MEMORY-DUMP
NOT
NOTE
NUMERIC

OBJECT-COMPUTER
OBJECT-PROGRAM
OCCURS
OF
OFF
OMITTED
ON
OPEN
OPTIONAL

- OR
- OTHERWISE
- OUTPUT
- PERFORM
- PICTURE
- PLACE
- PLUS
- POINT
- POSITION
- POSITIVE
- PREPARED
- PRIORITY
- PROCEDURE
- PROCEED
- PROGRAM-ID
- PROTECT
- PURGE-DATE
- QUOTE
- RANGE
- READ
- RECORD
- RECORD-COUNT
- RECORDING
- REDEFINES
- REEL
- REEL-NUMBER
- REMARKS
- RENAMES
- RENAMING
- REPLACING
- RERUN
- RESERVE
- REVERSED
- REWIND
- RIGHT
- ROUNDED
- RUN
- SAME
- SECTION
- SECURITY
- SELECT
- SENTENCE
- SENTINEL
- SEQUENCED
- SIGN
- SIGNED
- SIZE
- SOURCE-COMPUTER
- SPACE
- SPECIAL-NAMES
- STANDARD
- STATUS
- STOP
- SUBTRACT
- SUPERVISOR
- SUPPRESS
- SYNCHRONIZED
- TALLY
- TALLYING
- TAPE
- TEST-PATTERN
- THAN
- THEN
- THROUGH or THRU
- TIMES
- TO
- UNEQUAL
- UNTIL
- UPON
- UPPER-BOUND
- USAGE
- USE
- VALUE
- VARYING
- WHEN
- WITH
- WORD
- WORKING-STORAGE
- WRITE
- ZERO (ZEROS, ZEROES)

Some COBOL editions add the following to the list of Reserved Words:

- ACCESS
- ACTUAL
- AREAS
- ASCENDING
- ASSIGN
- CF
- CH
- CODE
- COLUMN
- COMMA
- CONTROLS
- CONVERSION
- CURRENCY
- DE
- DESCENDING
- DETAIL
- DIGITS
- DOWN
- EQUALS
- FILE-LIMIT
- FILE-LIMITS
- FINAL
- FOOTING
- GENERATE
- GROUP
- HEADING
- HIGH-VALUES
- INDEX
- INDEXED
- INDICATE
- INITIATE
- INSTALLATION
- INVALID
- KEY
- KEYS
- LAST
- LIMIT
- LIMITS
- LINE-COUNTER
- LINES
- LOW-VALUE
- LOW-VALUES
- LOWER BOUNDS
- NUMBER
- OH
- OV
- OVERFLOW
- PAGE
- PAGE-COUNTER
- PF
- PH
- PLACES
- PROCESS
- PROCESSING
- QUOTES
- RANDOM
- RD
- RECORDS
- RELEASE
- REPORT
- REPORTING
- REPORTS
- RESET
- RETURN
- RF
- RH
- SA
- SD
- SEARCH
- SEEK
- SEGMENT-LIMITED
- SELECTED
- SEQUENTIAL
- SET
- SORT
- SOURCE
- SPACES
- SUM
- SYMBOLIC
- TERMINATE
- TYPE
- UP
- UPPER-BOUNDS
- UNIT
- USING
- VALUES
- WORDS

Acknowledgment

Any organization interested in reproducing the COBOL report and specifications (of the Conference on Data Systems Language) in whole or in part, using ideas taken from this report as the basis for an instructional manual or for any other purpose, is free to do so. However, all such organizations are requested to reproduce this section as part of the introduction to the document. Those using a short passage, as in a book review, are requested to mention "COBOL" in acknowledgment of the source, but need not quote this entire section.

COBOL is an industry language and is not the property of any company or group of companies, or of any organization or group of organizations.

No warranty, expressed or implied, is made by any contributor or by the COBOL committee as to the accuracy and functioning of the programming system and language. Moreover, no responsibility is assumed by any contributor, or by the committee, in connection therewith.

Procedures have been established for the maintenance of COBOL. Inquiries concerning the procedures for proposing changes should be directed to the Executive Committee of the Conference on Data Systems Languages.

The author and copyright holders of the copyright material used herein are FLOW-MATIC (Trademark of Sperry Rand Corporation), Programming for the UNIVAC (R) I and II, Data Automation Systems copyright 1958, 1959, by Sperry Rand Corporation; IBM Commercial Translator Form No. F28-8013, copyrighted 1959 by IBM; FACT, DS127A5260-2760, copyrighted 1960 by Minneapolis-Honeywell.

The above have specifically authorized the use of their material in whole or in part, in the COBOL specifications. Such authorization extends to the reproduction and use of COBOL specifications in programming manuals or similar publications.

COBOL Extensions for Data Base Management

From its inception, COBOL has been the most popular language for business data processing. It is estimated that more than 80% of business programs are written in COBOL. Most of these programs are reading data from, manipulating data in, or adding data to a large data store of some kind. These data stores may be card files, tape files, disk files, or indexed disk files. Some of the more advanced installations are manipulating data in file structures logically maintained by data base management systems (DBMSs).

As time goes on, the trend toward data base management systems is expected to increase. It is estimated that about 10% of the processing of large data structures presently is occurring through data base management software; by the mid 1980s, this number may reach 80%. The reduced development time afforded by the automatic search mechanisms and the increased data integrity enforced by the protective DBMS software will encourage using a DBMS.

The business world has a great deal invested in COBOL. CODASYL (COmmittee on DAta SYstems Languages), which specified COBOL, has subsequently been working on the specifications for a standard data base management system. Many DBMSs on the market have complied with the CODASYL standards. However, it remains an unanswered question whether this standard will sweep the industry. The IBM liaison to the CODASYL committee did not approve of its features until recently. Even in 1979, it was expected that IBM would develop something completely different, probably based on the relational data base research it had been carrying on for years. The then current IBM major products, IMS and DL/1, were not CODASYL.

However, the fact that the CODASYL standard exists speaks well for the continued growth of COBOL in the user community. The CODASYL specifications are quite appropriate for integration into the COBOL language. The increase of data base use and the ease of interfacing COBOL to the popular data base languages should tend to enhance the COBOL user community. (For more on the CODASYL data base standards, see the appendix dealing with data base management systems.)

The examples below are taken from the CODASYL Systems Committee Technical Report, May 1971. They show the CODASYL data description language that is used to define a data base before it is loaded, and the declarations that would go in a COBOL program to manipulate such a data base. The gross similarities and compatibilities can be seen at a glance.

COBOL Data Declarations

```
DATA DIVISION
FILE SECTION
FED SDCDATA
01          ORG
```

```
02          ORGCODE ; PICTURE IS 9999
02          ORGNAME ; PICTURE IS A (25)
02          REPORTO ; PICTURE IS 9999
02          BUDGET ; PICTURE IS Z (8) ; USAGE IS COMPUTATIONAL-1
02          JOB ; OCCURS 1 TO 50 TIMES ASCENDING KEY IS JOBCODE
  03          JOBCODE ; PICTURE IS 9999
  03          AUTHQUAN ; PICTURE IS 99, USAGE IS COMPUTATIONAL
  03          AUTHSAL ; PIC ZZZZZZ ; USAGE-COMP-1
02          SUBORG ; OCCURS 0 TO 20 TIMES ASCENDING KEY IS SUBCODE
  03          SUBCODE ; PIC 9999
02          PERSON ; OCCURS 1 TO 999 TIMES ASCENDING KEYS ARE
              EMPJCODE, EMPNO
  03        EMPNO ; PIC Z9999
  03        EMPNAME ; PIC A (20)
  03        SEX ; PIC A
  03        EMPJCODE ; PIC 9999
  03        LEVEL ; PIC AAAA
  03        SALARY ; PIC ZZZZZ ; USAGE COMP-1
  03        BIRTH
    04        MONTH ; PIC 99
    04        DAY ; PIC 99
    04        YEAR ; PIC 99
  03        SKILLS ; OCCURS 1 TO 9 TIMES ASCENDING KEY IS SKILCODE
    04        SKILCODE ; PIC 9999
    04        SKLYRS ; PIC 99
```

CODASYL Data Description Language (DDL)

```
SCHEMA NAME IS ORGDATA
AREA NAME IS ORGPART
RECORD NAME IS ORG
PRIVACY LOCK IS SESAME
  01        ORGCODE  PICTURE IS "9 (4) "
  01        ORGNAME  TYPE IS CHARACTER 25
  01        REPORTO  PICTURE IS "9999"
  01        BUDGET TYPE DECIMAL FLOAT ; IS ACTUAL RESULT OF
              SALSUM ON MEMBERS OF PERSONS
  01        NOSUBORG  TYPE BINARY
  01        SUBORG OCCURS NOSUBORG TIMES
    02        SUBCODE PICTURE "9999"
RECORD NAME IS JOB
  01        JOBCODE  PICTURE "9999"
  01        AUTHQUAN  PICTURE "99"
  01        AUTHSAL  TYPE FLOAT
RECORD NAME IS PERSON
  01        EMPNO  PICTURE "9 (5) "
  01        EMPNAME  TYPE CHARACTER 20
  01        SEX  PICTURE "A"
  01        EMPJCODE  PICTURE "9999"
  01        LEVEL  PICTURE "X (4) "
  01        SALARY  PICTURE "9 (5) V99" ; PRIVACY LOCK FOR GET IS
              PROCEDURE AUTHENT
  01        BIRTH
    02        MONTH  PICTURE "99"
    02        DAY  PICTURE "99"
    02        YEAR  PICTURE "99"
  01        NOSKILLS  TYPE BINARY
  01        SKILLS OCCURS NOSKILLS TIMES
    02        SKILCODE  PICTURE "9999"
    02        SKLYRS  PICTURE "99"
```

```
SET NAME IS JOBS; ORDER IS SORTED
  OWNER IS ORG
  MEMBER IS JOB OPTIONAL AUTOMATIC; ASCENDING KEY IS
    JOBCODE DUPLICATES NOT ALLOWED
SET NAME IS PERSONS; ORDER IS SORTED
    OWNER IS ORG
    MEMBER IS PERSON OPTIONAL AUTOMATIC ; ASCENDING KEY IS
      EMPJCODE,EMPNO DUPLICATES NOT ALLOWED
```

PROGRAMMING LANGUAGE/ONE (PL/1)

Programming Language/One (PL/1) details are formally described in a specially released IBM Operating System/360 manual. PL/1 is the new name for what had been known informally as IBM's "New Programming Language" since the introduction of System/360 in 1964. The language is a result of advances in programming techniques and the increased performance available with various third-generation computer lines.

The language was developed from a cooperative effort undertaken by IBM in conjunction with the scientific and commercial users' groups, SHARE and GUIDE. Representatives of these groups sought to extend the features available in a high-level programming language as well as to broaden the range of application. Their efforts attempted to eliminate the traditional gap between the computer needs of commercial and scientific users.

Unlike previous computer languages which are oriented toward either business or scientific problem solving, the PL/1 language can be used for a broad range of applications in both areas, including real-time processing, systems programming, teleprocessing, and command control.

Modular Design

The modular design of PL/1 makes programmer training easier since only a part of the language needs to be taught before a programmer can begin using it. As a programmer gains experience, he can add to his vocabulary additional features of PL/1 and can expand his usage of the language. The language is based on free-form, continuous-character strings. A character string—letters, numbers, and symbols—can be entered into computers through a variety of input devices, including an electric typewriter, a card read-punch, or a magnetic tape unit.

Features introduced in PL/1 include:

1. Block Structure—A technique allowing program segmentation into blocks of language statements or subroutines of a total program.
2. Data Conversion—The ability to process a wide variety of data types, such as fixed and floating-point numbers and character and bit strings.
3. Multitask Operation—Concurrent processing of two or more job steps.

Some operating system compilers used to translate PL/1 statements into machine language are available in two sizes: 44,000 and 200,000 characters. These two compilers, coupled with IBM System control programs, will require as a minimum a main memory size of 65,536 characters or 262,144 characters, depending on the compiler. There will also be a Basic Operating System PL/1 compiler as well as a Basic Programming Support PL/1 compiler.

The PL/1 Systems Reference Library manual (C28-6571) notes in the introduction that it is a reference manual specifying the language, and as such describes the range and power of PL/1, as well as indicating its ability to handle the most complex computing problems. One of the primary aims in designing the language was modularity. The FORTRAN programmer initially learns a minimal set of new fundamentals which allow him to become productive in a short period of time. Then as his experience and the requirements of the job grow, he can call upon the additional capabilities of PL/1. More complex requirements, of course, would demand more of the facilities of PL/1.

An illustration of this modularity can be found in the "default" or assumption feature of PL/1. In PL/1, every description of a variable, every option, and every specification has been given a "default" interpretation. Wherever the language provides for one or more alternatives, a "default" interpretation is made by the compiler if no choice is stated by the programmer. The choice made by the compiler is the one most likely to be required by the programmer.

It should be noted that, with more experience, the programmer may choose to override the compiler's selection and settle on one of the other alternatives.

The "modularity" and the "default" aspects are the bases upon which the simplicity of PL/1 has been built. They are also part of its power. The PL/1 manual is available to customers through IBM sales offices.

General Characteristics of PL/1

Programming Language/One does not impose rigid form rules on the programmer. In addition, no special coding forms are required. This free form reduces transcription errors because programs are not bound by card or other restrictions. Eliminating dependence on specific formats is vital for teleprocessing installations where instructions and data are keyed in directly to the computer from remote locations.

Programming Language/One employs basic building blocks called procedures. A procedure is a block of instructions designed to perform a specific function such as the calculation of overtime pay in a payroll application. Programmers treat procedures as functional blocks in building application programs. Procedures share common elements with different programs. Seldom-used procedures can be held in auxiliary storage and called into the main storage only when required, thus saving working storage for higher priority operations.

Organization into procedures simplifies the programmer's task because he can modify an existing program by changing one or more procedures without having to change others. Or, he can write a number of short procedures and merge them into a complete program.

Nesting of Procedures

One procedure may be contained in another, and any data declared in a procedure is automatically available to all procedures "nested" within. Thus, a payroll procedure, stated in problem form, would automatically describe the attributes, or format, of the data items described in the statement. It would then read, add, write, test, etc., to obtain the final result.

Procedures also provide natural points for breaking programs into convenient segments so programs can be written, tested, and debugged in sections. A number of programmers can work in parallel on separate procedures, bringing the total program together at compile time.

String Data and Arrays

Programming Language/One can handle several types of data: One type is called string data and consists of either strings of alphanumeric characters or strings of bits. The ability to handle character and bit strings is significant because there is no need to resort to assembly language.

The programmer using this language may describe data in terms of arrays and structures. (An array is a collection of data of the same type and with similar characteristics, such as a table with various prices in dollars and cents.) In a structure, the data may have mixed characteristics; i.e., a file record is often made up of data fields of different sizes, containing both alphabetic and numeric information. A payroll record, for example, usually contains both string data, such as names and addresses, and another type of data, namely, numeric data such as pay rates and deduction information. The Programming Language/One programmer can describe such a problem in terms of structures that meet the specific requirements of the application.

Since data may be of a fixed or variable length and exist singly or in large arrays, simple statements can perform quite complex manipulations. Take the simple expression, A = B. If A and B are not simple numbers, but arrays of data, each containing perhaps a thousand elements, this expression would cause B to replace A, element for element, with the data automatically edited into the format of A.

Programming Language/One's tolerance for mixed expressions represents another convenience. If F is described as a fixed-point decimal number, G is a floating-point number, and H is a string of 10 characters, the expression:

$$H = F + G$$

will result in F being converted to a floating-point number, the floating-point addition being performed, and the result converted to a 10-character string and stored in H in one automatic operation.

The use of "labels" represents another way the language adapts to the level of detail and readability that a particular application requires. The programmer can either spell out program labels such as NETPAY, or he can represent the labels with whatever shorthand he favors. In the payroll example, documentation and readability are important—therefore labels should be spelled out—while for the one-shot solution of a specific mathematical problem, labels can be chosen for the convenience of the moment.

Tapping System Resources

SAVE and RESTORE statements are examples of how the programmer can tap system resources such as main storage, auxiliary storage, and the data channels. By relying on the ability of the system to "save" information and "restore" it later in the same program, the programmer is relieved of the task of defining files and writing input/output statements to perform these functions.

The READ/WRITE statements illustrate the facilities within the program for editing input/output data, a critical function in any computing system. For example, one of many options included in these statements is that of editing data during transmission. Details such as dollar signs, decimal points, and asterisks for check protection are supplied automatically, based on the programmer's description of the output data.

Components of the Language

A considerable portion of the language is based on previously developed languages, especially ALGOL, such as termination of statements with semicolons, free-field formats, new characters, etc. PL/1 can be represented and transmitted to a computer in a natural way using almost any medium and especially typewriters and crt's at remote terminals. Space limitations permit the listing of only a few important checklists and concepts of PL/1, and the reader is invited to check the manual mentioned above for the full details of the language.

Alphabetic List of Statements for PL/1

ALLOCATE	ENTRY	NULL	REVERT
ASSIGNMENT	EXIT	ON	SAVE
BEGIN	FETCH	OPEN	SEGMENT
CALL	FORMAT	PAGE	SIGNAL
CLOSE	FREE	POSITION	SKIP
DECLARE	GET	PROCEDURE	SORT
DELAY	GO TO	PUT	SPACE
DELETE	GROUP	READ	STOP
DISPLAY	IF	REPOSITION	TAB
DO	IMPLICIT	RESTORE	WAIT
END	LAYOUT	RETURN	WRITE

Special Characters

There are 21 special characters. The names and graphics by which they are represented are shown in Table K-1.

Identifiers

An identifier is a string of alphameric and break characters with the initial character always being alphabetic. Identifiers in the PL/1 language are used for: scalar variable names, array names, structure names, statement labels, entry names, file names, keywords, task identifiers, condition names, headings for external names.

Any number of break characters are allowed within an identifier; however, consecu-

Table K-1. Special Characters

NAME	GRAPHIC	
	60 Character Set	48 Character Set
Blank		
Equal or Assignment symbol	=	
Plus	+	
Minus	−	
Asterisk or Multiply symbol	*	
Slash or Divide symbol	/	
Left Parenthesis	(	
Right Parenthesis	)	
Comma	,	
Decimal point or period	.	
Quotation mark	'	
Percent symbol	%	//
Semicolon	;	,.
Colon	:	..
Not symbol	¬	NOT
And symbol	&	AND
Or symbol	|	OR
Greater Than symbol	>	GT
Less Than symbol	<	LT
Break character	_	
Question mark	?	

tive break characters are not permitted, nor can a break character be the final character of an identifier.

Keywords

A keyword is an identifier used in the language and has a special meaning. Keywords are not reserved words. They may be classified as: statement identifiers, attributes, separating keywords, built-in function names, options, conditions.

Statement Identifiers

A statement identifier is a keyword used to identify the nature of a statement. Some statement identifiers consist of more than one identifier, separated by blanks.

Examples of statement identifiers are: GO TO, DECLARE, READ.

Attributes

Attributes are keywords that specify characteristics to describe the nature of data, procedures, and other elements of the language.

Examples are: FLOAT, RECURSIVE, SEQUENTIAL.

Separating Keyword

The five separating keywords are used to separate parts of the IF and DO statements. They are: THEN, ELSE, BY, TO, WHILE.

Permissible Keyword Abbreviations

Abbreviations are provided for certain keywords. The abbreviations themselves are keywords and will be recognized as synonymous in every respect with the full keywords. The abbreviated keywords are shown to the right of the full keywords in the following list.

Keyword	Abbreviation
PROCEDURE	PROC
DECLARE	DCL
DECIMAL	DEC
BINARY	BIN
COMPLEX	CPLX
COMPLETE	CPLT
CHARACTER	CHAR
VARYING	VAR
POSITION	POS
INITIAL	INIT
INTERNAL	INT
EXTERNAL	EXT
AUTOMATIC	AUTO
CONTROLLED	CTL
DEFINED	DEF
ABNORMAL	ABNL
PRECISION	PREC
OVERFLOW	OFL
UNDERFLOW	UFL
FIXEDOVERFLOW	FOFL
SUBSCRIPTRANGE	SUBRG
ZERODIVIDE	ZDIV
CONVERSION	CONV

PASCAL

PASCAL was designed and implemented in the early 1970s by Niklaus Wirth and Kathleen Jensen to be a language that could be used to teach concepts of data structures and control structures and their relationship to good programming style. It was not originally intended to be a systems programming language or a commercial data-processing language, but the facilities of the language and the consistency of its design have fostered a following, particularly among computer hobbyists and other small-computer users. The use of PASCAL is likely to become more widespread. Some microprocessor fabricators are expending research and development efforts on operating systems that feature the language for use in their 16-bit microprocessors.

Even though it was designed well and took advantage of all that was learned from the development of dozens of ALGOL-like languages that came before it, PASCAL was not intended to be a commercial production programming language. Thus, it will undoubtedly have to be modified and extended to accomplish some tasks. These modifications and extensions will probably reduce the portability of the programs as well as compromise the design integrity of the language constructs and principles. Inevitably, a language will be developed incorporating the positive aspects of PASCAL as well as the solutions to its shortcomings. Thus, PASCAL can be seen as a key stepping-stone in the evolution of production programming languages. Readers seriously interested in the direction of programming languages, or who will be programmers during the next ten years, should certainly study the ideologies of PASCAL and incorporate them as much as possible on a day-to-day basis, regardless of the restrictions of their current programming environment.

When people speak of ALGOL-like languages, they are usually referring to the control structures that were mentioned in the introduction to this appendix, the BEGIN-END blocking of multiple statements, the IF-THEN-ELSE structure, the WHILE and REPEAT-UNTIL loops, and the CASE statement. PASCAL provides all of these control structuring tools. They not only simplify the programmer's job of describing and implementing the algorithm, but they also make the code easy to read by the next programmer who has to change it, adapt it to another machine or operating system, or fix a bug that is discovered in it. It should be noted that "easy to read" is a relative term, but if a programmer is given adequate training in PASCAL and almost any other language, the program written in PASCAL will be easier to understand and manage.

This is not to say that PASCAL is an easy language to "pick up," such as BASIC. In practice, many microcomputing hobbyists find themselves graduating from BASIC to PASCAL. The design of PASCAL embodies much of what has been learned over the last two decades about solving problems with computers. To understand the language, to use it to its full power, and to understand even the most lucid PASCAL programs, the programmer must share this understanding about the nature of computerized information and reasonable ways to process it. Some of the remainder of this discussion may indeed be hard to understand. It is not possible to relate all of the depth required to understand some of the features of PASCAL in such a small space. The reader is referred to the *Pascal User Manual and Report, Systematic Programming: An Introduction,* and *Algorithms Plus Data Structures Equals Programs.*[1]

The introduction to this appendix mentioned that there is more to structured programming than control structures and the elimination of the GOTO. Data structures were discussed as being associated with control structures. In other words, there are different kinds of information; i.e., information can be classified according to certain properties. For example, the annual sales of a company are usually broken down by month. A program that analyzes annual sales on this monthly basis can depend on the fact that there are 12 months in a year. In contrast, companies usually offer medical plans to employees and their dependents. Usually some information is kept about these dependents, such as name, age, sex, etc. An employee may have from zero to over a dozen dependents. A computer program that is, for example, attempting to find the average number of dependents of the employees of a company cannot expect a fixed number, such as 12 months.

These two different types of information require two different data structures to represent them in the computer program. The two different data structures require two different control structures to manipulate this data. The twelve months can be stored in an array that is declared to be twelve components long. The dependents of an employee can be stored in a linked list, which can be of indeterminate length. The array can be stepped through conveniently through the use of a FOR loop. The FOR loop is natural because it repeats a fixed number of times, just as the array has a fixed number of components, just as there are a fixed number of months in a year. The employee's dependents can be traversed naturally with a WHILE loop. The WHILE loop may iterate a variable number of times, just as the linked list may have a variable number of components, just as the number of dependents may be variable.

Other structured languages have provided these control structures and data structures. One of the reasons PASCAL is more successful than some of its forerunners is that in most cases it offers only what is needed. It usually does not offer two different ways to do the same thing in an equally appropriate fashion. Thus, even though the language is powerful, it has retained the simplicity that other languages offering these constructs have lost.

Another improvement PASCAL has made is the increased rigor the programmer can design into his program through the use of user-defined data types. The notion of user-defined types was touched on briefly in the introduction and will be expanded upon here. In the case of the personnel file, the programmer may define a record structure to contain all of the information about the dependent. For example,

```
type
  name = array[1 . . 20] of char;
  age = 1 . . 100;
  sex = (male, female) ;
  dependent =
    record
    firstname: name;
    lastname: name;
```

1. K. Jensen and N. Wirth, *PASCAL User Manual and Report* (New York: Springer-Verlag New York, Inc., 1975). Niklaus Wirth, *Systematic Programming: An Introduction* (Englewood Cliffs, N.J.: Prentice-Hall, Inc., 1973). Niklaus Wirth, *Algorithms Plus Data Structures Equals Programs* (Englewood Cliffs, N.J.: Prentice-Hall, Inc., 1975).

```
    dependentage: age;
    dependentsex: sex;
    end;
```

Now variables may be declared to be of type "dependent." When values are assigned to the fields of a variable of type dependent, they must be of the type that the fields are declared to be in the above definition. For example, if a program attempts to assign a value of −3 to a dependent's age, the run-time module of the PASCAL compiler will signal this as an error and will halt the program. The compiler will also signal an error if any value other than male or female is assigned to the "dependentsex" field, or if an unreasonable value (outside of the subrange 1 to 100) is assigned to the field representing the dependent's age.

The halting of the program may seem to be an undesirable effect, but it must be done. An error has been committed. Improper data is being processed. Some of the worst difficulties in data processing can be traced to similar errors that were not caught by the compiler because this rigorous typing is not available in FORTRAN or COBOL. For example, one city ran a program estimating how much money it would receive from property taxes in the following fiscal year. A keypunch operator accidentally typed an extra zero on one of the punch cards representing the value of a multi-million-dollar piece of property. The program accepted the unreasonable value, even though it was inflated tenfold, because it did not incorporate any rigorous typing of its variables. The net result was that the city budget was made up on the basis of erroneously high expected revenues. The mistake was caught when the owner of the property was billed and complained of the slight increase in taxes. The city was then overbudgeted.

Similarly, the monthly sales can be represented in the following data structures.

```
const
  lowsales = 50000;
  highsales = 100000;
type
  month = (january, february, march, april, may, june,
           july, august, september, october,
           november, december) ;
  year = january . . december;
  monthlysales = lowsales . . highsales;
var
  annualsales: array[year] of monthlysales;
```

The constants "lowsales" and "highsales" represent the limits of reasonable values for monthly sales. Notice that all of the other declarations involving sales are made in terms of these constants, instead of the actual values these identifiers represent. When the company grows bigger and the sales volume increases, this program will have to be changed. But the change will be easy, because only the value that is originally assigned to these constants will have to be modified. All of the other declarations and the code in the body of the program will still be correct.

Let us look at a subroutine that calculates the average of the monthly sales.

```
function averagemonth (thisyear:year) :monthlysales;
var indexmonth:month;
    totalyear:integer;
begin
for indexmonth := january to december do
    begin
    totalyear := thisyear[indexmonth];
    end;
averagemonth := totalyear/12;
end;
```

This particular subroutine is a function. It returns a value. In this case, it returns the desired quantity, the average monthly sales for the year.

The control structures and data structures of PASCAL are extensive, but not so numerous as to be cumbersome. The user-defined data types allow the user a descriptive power and a rigorous control over some of the silent aspects of running programs that have caused problems in the past. These properties of the language have made it a useful teaching tool. The clarity of the expressions that can be constructed have made it appealing as a commercial and systems language. However, the strict data typing can become a problem in some of the real-world applications. These problems and other shortcomings of the language as a commercial tool will be discussed later.

Advanced Properties of PASCAL

Some of the topics discussed below may not be understandable to newcomers to computing, but they are offered in brief for those interested.

As a product of evolution, PASCAL has sensible solutions to some of the subtle problems in language design. For example, since it is an ALGOL-like language, the scope of variables is naturally nested. Local variables are stored on a run-time stack as procedures are called. The data of the running program is not mixed in the same memory space as the code. Thus, it is easy to run PASCAL programs as re-entrant modules in a multiprogramming environment. In other words, if more than one person wants to run a program written in PASCAL at the same time, only one copy of the code need be in memory. The individual user's area contains that user's data stack.

Also, since the data area is stacked, the capability of indirect and direct recursion is a natural property of the language. This is in keeping with the spirit of PASCAL. Some data structures and algorithms are defined recursively, and should naturally be processed in harmony with their form.

In all of the variety of languages, there are many ways to pass variables from one procedure to another. Common methods are value, reference, name, and value-result. PASCAL implements only two methods, value and reference. When a parameter is passed by value, only a copy of the variable is read into the formal parameters of the called routine. Thus, if the called environment changes the value of this formal parameter, the value of the variable that was passed is not changed when the procedure returns. If a variable is passed by reference, the value of that variable known to the calling environment is changed if a change is made to the formal parameter by the called procedure. Thus, if the value of a variable is being passed to a routine for informational purposes only, it is passed by value and "protected" from any change in the calling environment. If the calling environment wishes some information to be returned to it by having the called routine modify it, then the variable is passed by reference. The default in the language is value, the safest method.

Places to Expect Change

As PASCAL begins to be used commercially, the implementors of the compilers will alter it to meet their particular requirements. Those who want to use PASCAL as a systems programming language may add a standard-type "byte," as well as various bit manipulation primitives. Furthermore, they may relax the type-checking rigor during parameter passing. This would be done to allow more general routines to be written.

Commercial programmers will undoubtedly demand error traps. It is not considered professional to turn over to the user programs that tend to terminate abnormally under direction of the operating system or the run-time package of a compiler. Programmers prefer to place error traps in the code, indicating what should be done if an error occurs at various places in the program. In the case of improper values being entered by an operator, a warning message should be printed, and the operator should be reprompted for another value. The program should not abort.

The definition of PASCAL does not include any provision for random-access files, much less KSAM or data-base structures. These issues were out of the scope of the purpose of the language as a tool for teaching the basics of data and control structuring. But for the language to be used in any commercial data processing environment, such devices will have to be implemented. Furthermore, the concept of data-base data independence, the notion that a change to the data base should not require a change in the application program, seems contrary to the strict typing rules of PASCAL. Load-time data typing would be required to interface PASCAL to data-base management systems. This is a major architectural change, but the popularity of the language may cause it to be done at some installations.

It should be mentioned that, as popular as PASCAL might become, the data-processing world has such a great investment in COBOL and FORTRAN that we are more likely to see an impact of the concepts of PASCAL in the form of changes to these long-time standard and familiar languages.

JOVIAL

JOVIAL is an acronym for Jules Own Version of the International Algorithmic Language. It was developed by Jules Schwartz of the Systems Development Corporation, Santa Monica, California. JOVIAL is another procedure-oriented language derived basically from ALGOL. It was designed for, and is most often used in, programmed command and control procedures. As with all other nonmachine and nonassembly languages, the JOVIAL language is translated (compiled) by a program called a compiler. The compiler interprets, analyzes, and translates the program statements, the inputs and outputs, from the source program to an object program on which the particular computer can operate. The major deviation from ALGOL provides JOVIAL with the power to control data on the "byte" and even the "bit" level when desired. This particular capability gives JOVIAL extensive capabilities for developing software applications, and utility- and compiling-type programs. JOVIAL was apparently created quite specifically for government agencies and military command and control applications and software design for other computers.

JOVIAL has extensive command and retrieve language rules, but the basic structure of the program is relatively simple. The JOVIAL program fundamentally consists of procedure cells, definitions, and language statements. There are language statements which define and initialize data, while others manipulate and test data.

SECTION II

Time-Sharing Languages

The general-purpose on-line time-sharing systems permit convenient, direct access to large central computers from hundreds of remote terminals. Flexibility is developed by adding tape cassettes, paper-tape readers, disks, etc., to satisfy individual needs at the terminal. Terminals function as computer consoles, and the user is concerned with the various subsets of FORTRAN (or other languages) of which APL, BASIC, CAL, and JOSS are examples. Users may solve problems immediately or may compose partial or complete programs. Diagnostic and debugging information is expressed entirely in the source language. Interpretive execution permits retention of all information contained in the user's original source statements. The combination of interpretive execution and multiprogramming makes the conversational mode a real-time, man-machine communication system which is highly efficient and feasible.

Machine turnaround time is drastically reduced, as is the cost of computer use. Programs are constructed, tested, and debugged statement by statement and on-line because of easy, direct, and sustained access to the computer. Large programs can be segmented; the user is unaware of other time-sharers; human errors are reduced due to immediacy of diagnostics and thought-continuity; exploratory and experimental simulation efforts are enhanced, permitting businessmen, scientists, and mathematicians to use rapid exercise of judgment, experience, and evaluation in the formulation and testing of programs.

BASIC

A language that has grown considerably in popularity in the past decade is BASIC. There are many reasons for its mushrooming. First of all, computing itself has grown, and thus the need for computer education has also grown. Since BASIC is an easy-to-learn, interactive language, it is commonly used as the first language taught to computer science students (as well as liberal arts students seeking a survey course). Also, BASIC was first implemented on interactive time-sharing systems, and many operating systems have since been designed to be "dedicated BASIC" interactive machines. Time-sharing and interactive processing has grown considerably, and COBOL and FORTRAN have had BASIC-like extensions added to them to survive in this environment.

However, the most powerful reason for the growth of BASIC has been the explosion of the personal computing movement in the middle 1970s. The first affordable hobbyist machines were programmable only in assembly language. But when the first BASIC interpreter, and a subset of the language called tiny BASIC, was implemented, some-computer users found it almost indispensable. When floppy-disk operating systems were written for personal computers, these machines began to take on the abilities of installations that formerly cost hundreds of thousands of dollars. The availability of BASIC as a high-level language was a key in the development of this power.

Soon the price of memory was cut in half, and personal computing BASIC no longer needed to be "tiny." The versions of the language that run on these machines now have control structures and data structures far beyond the dreams of the original designers.

BASIC was originally designed by J. G. Kemeny and T. E. Kurtz at Dartmouth College. One popular standard for the language is still referred to as "Dartmouth BASIC." The language was originally intended to be an interpreter that allowed the user to type a line number and a statement on each line. The interpreter would tell the user about any syntax errors inherent in the line when the carriage return was operated. The user could run the part of the program that had been entered at any time by typing RUN. Thus, the programmer could experiment to see how the program was coming along, as it was being developed. A line could be deleted by typing the line number, followed by a carriage return, or it could be replaced by typing the line number and a statement. Any semantic errors, i.e., mistakes in overall program structuring, would be reported to the user when the program was run and the mistakes were encountered.

The escape key was available to interrupt a running program. If a program was interrupted in this way, or if it "blew up" by encountering an error, the user could interactively examine the contents of the variables of the program by simply typing BASIC statements without line numbers, such as PRINT A,B,C. The statements typed without line numbers would be executed immediately and would not become part of the stored program.

The data types in the early versions were usually only integers, arrays of integers, and strings of characters. The only control structures were the GOTO, the IF-THEN-GOTO, the FOR loop, and the GOSUB subroutine call.

Programs that had been typed in could be saved on any associated disk system, and saved programs could be called back into the interpreter at any time.

As the BASIC implementations became more sophisticated, they were extended to offer file handling, such as OPEN, READ, WRITE, and CLOSE. Some versions incorporated matrix manipulation commands, and others supplied more data types, such as short floating point and long floating point. A variety of ALGOL-like control structures are now available in some BASIC interpreters, such as WHILE, REPEAT-UNTIL, IF-THEN-ELSE, and procedure calls with parameter passing. Many BASICs have also been expanded for easy display of two-dimensional plots and even color graphics. Virtually anything a hobbyist computer can do has been done through an implementation of BASIC, including synthesizing speech and recognizing the spoken word. Some systems have been interfaced with household electrical circuits, and thus a BASIC-driven computer system will allow the owner to verbally command appliances on and off, as well as receive audible responses and confirmations, in English.

Many commercial systems have developed BASIC compilers as well as interpreters. In this way, a programmer can develop a program using the easy-going interactive language in the interpreter form, and then once the program is debugged, it can be compiled into a condensed load module for faster execution.

The ease of use of the language is perhaps best shown by an example. The brief program below will simply sum and average any amount of numbers the user prefers.

Program Listings

```
>>
>>LIST
     10 PRINT"HELLO, I AM A BASIC PROGRAM THAT IS WILLING TO "
```

```
20 PRINT"AVERAGE NUMBERS FOR YOU. PLEASE TELL ME HOW
        MANY"
30 PRINT"NUMBERS YOU WOULD LIKE TO AVERAGE."
40 PRINT
50 INPUT HOW'MANY
55 PRINT
60  FOR I=1 TO HOW'MANY
70  IF I=1 THEN PRINT"TYPE THE FIRST NUMBER."
80  IF I<>1 THEN PRINT"TYPE THE NEXT NUMBER."
90  INPUT NEW'NUMBER
91  PRINT
100  TOTAL=TOTAL+NEW'NUMBER
110  NEXT I
120 AVERAGE=TOTAL/HOW'MANY
130 PRINT"THE AVERAGE OF THE ";HOW'MANY;" NUMBERS IS
        ";AVERAGE;"."
140 PRINT"GOODBYE NOW."
```

Execution of the Program. (*User responses are underlined.*)

```
>>RUN
HELLO, I AM A BASIC PROGRAM THAT IS WILLING TO
AVERAGE NUMBERS FOR YOU. PLEASE TELL ME HOW MANY
NUMBERS YOU WOULD LIKE TO AVERAGE.
? 4
TYPE THE FIRST NUMBER.
? 21
TYPE THE NEXT NUMBER.
? 33
TYPE THE NEXT NUMBER.
? 657
TYPE THE NEXT NUMBER.
? 33.42
THE AVERAGE OF THE 4 NUMBERS IS 186.105.
GOODBYE NOW.
***END***
```

In summary, the ease of use of BASIC and its interactive nature give it appeal, and the lost cost of the machines on which it is widely implemented give it exposure. Probably, more people know BASIC than any other computer language. Since versions of BASIC are the main programming language of low-cost consumer computers, this trend is likely to continue. Many computer-driven video games are even selling BASIC interpreters in the form of a game cartridge. In high schools, junior high schools, and even elementary schools, it is being found to be a useful teaching tool. BASIC has established itself as the programming language of personal computing, and it is unlikely to be substantially challenged for some time.

JOSS

JOSS is an acronym for Johnniac Open-Shop System. It is a language which was developed by the Rand Corporation to facilitate completion of quick calculations which were too complex for calculators. It has been most often used on a PDP-6 computer but can serve more than 100 consoles simultaneously. JOSS is one of the several time-sharing languages; thus, it is designed for and can handle concurrent use by multiple users, each accessing the computer through his own console typewriter. Although many people are using the computer apparently simultaneously, the computer is actually handling each user in sequence. It is solving each problem or basic parts of each problem so rapidly that it appears to the user that he alone has full use and control of the computer. Seldom does any individual or console receive a "WAIT" signal because the computer is servicing another user. Thus, JOSS is a real-time language and is productive for solving many types of immediate calculations and problems that require rapid results.

JOSS was not designed for large data bases or large or long-range programs. Its primary advantage is rapid use for small and medium-sized programs. In interactive environments, it is not considered a general-purpose language, but its performance is effective in more defined operations.

Chief advantages of JOSS are its simplicity and relative ease to learn and use. Although it is similar to several other algebraic languages, it has distinct and powerful features usually not found elsewhere. All JOSS arithmetic is performed on numbers input in scientific notation using integer magnitudes and decimal exponents, but such input and output flows to and from console typewriters.

Some key functions are: SUM, which provides for the sum of arranged numbers; MIN and MAX, which develop the maximum and minimum values of defined ranges of values.

JOSS allows users to save programs provided the verbs FILE, DISCARD, and RECALL are used for these purposes. JOSS responds to user errors with specific or error messages. When it cannot be specific it uses the comic relief command, "EH?"

APL

APL (for A Programming Language) is an interactive mathematically oriented language. It is usually implemented as a true interpreter, allowing the user to create, run, modify, store, and recall programs and subroutines while interacting with the interpreter program at a computer terminal. The mathematical orientation of the language is rooted in the fact that its inventor, Kenneth Iverson, was not attempting to design a programming language at all when he wrote the book *A Programming Language,* published in 1962. The original intention was to define a notation which could be used to describe important mathematical algorithms. As a result, the language is defined to use many special characters, most of which do not appear on the keyboards of standard computer terminals. Conventions have been described for using normal keyboards, but a great deal of memorization and motivation is required by the user. It may seem like a small point, but the requirement for special equipment to use the language has held back the spread of its use.

Since Iverson was attempting to define a notation that would describe complex mathematical algorithms concisely, programs in APL tend to be extremely compact. For example, a program to calculate standard deviations in only one line of code can be written in APL. Although the resultant code from compressing so much logic into such a small space may be impenetrable by anyone but the author, many purely mathematical programming constructs are impenetrable anyway. If the author of such a program finds APL to be a useful tool in the development of these programs, one is usually hardpressed to argue against its use on stylistic grounds.

Data Structures

The primary data structure in APL is the array. Almost all operations are performed on arrays. These arrays are homogeneous with regard to data or byte, either number or character. Variable declaration and typing is strictly dynamic. That is to say, if something is assigned to a variable in a program, the variable is thereby declared and can be referenced later. The type of the variable is dependent upon what is assigned to it. The issue of typing is generally of no concern to the programmer, except that certain operators apply only to arrays of numbers. All numbers are real, as opposed to integer, numeric values.

Control Structures

The ability to use arrays as the primitive data structure (as well as arrays of arrays) is important in that subprograms are restricted to at most two arguments (transmitted by value) and a single result, which is returned. A certain amount of variable locality is allowed in subprograms, but variables must be explicitly designated to be local. Nonlocal references will be taken by the interpreter to mean the variable in the environment in which the identifier was most recently used.

The GOTO is available to vector program execution based on system-generated line numbers or user-supplied labels. However, the most commonly used control structure is the function call. Indeed, since the language is steeped in mathematically oriented constructs, the very primitives of the language are function calls which return values. Thus an APL program can be viewed as a list of functions, to be executed in a right-to-left fashion. Recall that in mathematical functional notation, the arguments of the function are to the right of the function name. If the arguments of the function are themselves functions, they must be evaluated first.

This right-to-left associativity is the exact opposite of the usual left-to-right scan that other interpreters and compilers perform on source code. Furthermore, the standard hierarchy of operations, multiply before add, etc., is overridden in APL because of its adherence to the notation of functions.

A General-Purpose Language

The primitives of the APL language provide considerable power and conciseness for manipulation of any data structure that can be viewed as an array. Strong advocates of the language maintain that since mathematics is the root of all science, and scalars, vectors, and matrices are the data structures of mathematics, APL is therefore an appropriate tool for any application. However, the conciseness of the code is perhaps the largest stumbling block in the way of using this language in a production data-processing environment. It is not important that business programs be small, but it is important that they be lucid, so that they may be modified and maintained by another programmer.

However, since APL was designed to express mathematical constructs, the programmer who already has a mathematical model of the problem in his head will probably find the APL interpreter a tool that naturally matches the problem.

MUMPS

MUMPS is an interactive interpreter that is a programming language, an operating system, and a data base management system all built into one software package. It was invented at the Massachusetts General Hospital to work in an on-line, time-shared environment to do medical data processing. Since medicine is one of the fastest-growing users of data-processing equipment and techniques, this special-purpose language has enjoyed a fair amount of popularity and growth.

As with BASIC, programs can be developed and edited while the programmer is interacting with the language interpreter. Unlike BASIC, the data structures of the language are intimately associated with the file structure, the place where large data-processing installations such as hospitals keep all of the data. Since the idea behind interactive languages is fast response time, these data are almost always kept on disk drives. The intimate affiliation between the data structures of the language and data in the files means that the MUMPS system is taking the role of the interface between the language and the file system, a role which is usually taken by the operating system.

Another feature of MUMPS is the fact that it offers numerous and advanced string manipulation capabilities. String is the technical term for a series of characters, such as a response a user might type in response to an interactive prompt. These string-handling primitives make it easier to develop interactive software, the kind doctors and nurses would like to use to gather information about a patient instantly. The ultimate idea behind this kind of user interaction with the large data store is the elimination of paper charts and a great deal of administrative and financial overhead. Instantaneous access to patient information would also enhance the quality of medical service that could be given patients, and it could even save lives in times of emergency.

MUMPS has established a base of users, particularly among the small but growing subset of data-processing professionals who perform medical data processing. Currently, there are several universities in the United States offering graduate programs in medical information science, and an understanding of the MUMPS system is usually in the curriculum. However, the MUMPS system is not so specialized to the medical application that it does not receive competition from more established data base management systems.

SECTION III

List-Processing Languages

These highly specific languages are designed for digital computers and are oriented specifically for convenience and for manipulation of data, especially nonnumerical data, whose length and structure change considerably during the calculation of a problem solution. Because the data are usually not numerical, the concepts and terms referred to as symbol manipulation and nonnumerical data processing are most often used to define list-processing languages. Most of the languages to be discussed are used as research tools and are not necessarily for production-line programming. The development and construction of compilers are often based on list-processing techniques. The basic research areas which have gained from the use of list processing concern: (a) generation and verification of mathematical proofs, (b) pattern recognition, (c) algebraic manipulation, (d) simulation of human problem-solving, (f) information retrieval, (g) heuristic programming, (h) linguistic analysis, (i) machine translation of numerical languages, and (j) exploration of new types of programming languages. Therefore, it might be concluded that list-processing procedures are oriented more to techniques of programming rather than to particular applications, except perhaps in the areas of information retrieval, algebraic manipulation, and language translation.

A list is defined simply as a set of items given in a specific order. Some characteristics of lists are: (a) they can be of variable length subject principally to gross machine limitations, and the lengths can vary during the computation; (b) items of many different types may appear on lists such as numbers, alphanumerical symbols, and other lists which appear on primary lists; (c) items can be added at the beginning, end, or middle, and any item can be deleted from the list; (d) any number of distinct lists can be created or developed from a program; (e) lists can be referenced by the program and can be copied, modified, examined, and analyzed by programs. Recursion is basically the process used when elements of lists may themselves be lists. Because most programming languages have difficulties if a subroutine is called within itself, list processing handles such a problem, avoiding overwriting when subroutines call themselves. Most often there are as many levels of subsidiary lists, or sublists, as there are levels of parenthesization. Recursion is ordinarily mechanized through the use of a push-down stack, in which the contents of the temporary storage required by a subroutine are stored when the subroutine is entered. When the execution of the subroutine is completed, the temporary storage is restored from the stack, and the space that it occupied is thus again available. Recursion and dynamic storage allocations are requirements of list-processing languages and lead to the usefulness of these program techniques. Dynamic storage allocation is the ability to vary storage allocation during run time. The basic language from which most others spring or with which they are compared is LISP, which stands for LISt Processing. It differs radically from traditional programming languages.

LISP

Data and storage characters used in the LISP language are represented either externally, as a sequence of characters formed according to distinct rules, or internally within the computer, as a set of computer words interlinked in a specific way.

Atomic symbols or atoms may be either numeric or nonnumeric, and the external representation of a nonnumeric atomic symbol is a string of letters and digits, starting with a letter such as AB5Y or a Greek letter. LISP also permits the use of other characters such as asterisks, minus signs, etc.

Numeric atoms or atomic symbols can be decimal, or octal, or floating-point numbers. (The letter Q following a number is usually used to indicate that the number is octal.)

Externally, a list consists of a sequence of list elements separated by blanks and closed by parentheses. A list element can itself be either an atomic symbol or a list. When a list is formed, the necessary storage cells are taken from a list of available cells called the free-storage list. LISP 1.5 is the most popular version of LISP.

A subroutine of computer programming can be considered a tool which defines a function in a mathematical sense and maps sets of input values onto sets of output values. In LISP, this function is expressed in a notation that displays its functional nature more explicitly than is ordinarily done in a sequence of instructions. Various expressions in LISP include S-expressions, and conditional expressions which test conditions and make accounts according to results of the test.

Recursion is a method of function definition in which a seemingly circular definition is used in order to carry out an iterative computation; i.e., quite similar to recursive definitions as normally used in mathematics.

Functional arguments are those arguments of functions which specify operations to be performed as part of a larger calculation and are used extensively in LISP.

The LISP programming system requires that input be given in the form of a sequence of doublets. Some primary expressions are LAMBDA and DEFINE. The mechanism of using LISP is ordinarily to set up a program as a set of function definitions and the call of DEFINE to implement them. By the calling of the highest level function with the desired input data as arguments, either function definition or input data can be called in from tape or other auxiliary storage media. The consistent and frequent use of recursion and the push-down stack are the most common characteristics of LISP. The push-down stack is defined as an expandable and contractible array, with the pointer indicating its current upper bound. As functions are called, new blocks of space are reserved at the top of the push-down stack, and the pointer is moved to the top of the new block.

Storage allocation uses various categories and types. The principal ones are full words and list storage. A primary problem of list storage exists for all list-processing languages. In the marking process, a single bit of each cell in the list storage area is reserved for marking. In the collection phase, the cells of the list storage area are scanned in turn, and each one with a zero in the marking bit is added to the free storage list. The garbage-collection approach to the reclamation of list storage is one of several types. Other list-processing languages use erasure schemes in which the programmer specifically frees up list storage and has functions available that add this storage to the free storage list. The garbage-collection technique is simpler because the programmer need not carry out the bookkeeping involved in erasure.

IPL-V

IPL is an abbreviation for Information Process Language. The reader is referred to the IPL-V manual (second edition, Prentice-Hall, Englewood Cliffs, New Jersey, 1964) by Newell, Simon, and Shaw for specific details of this second in a series of information-processing languages. This language is considerably more machine-oriented than LISP. The programs in IPL-V consist of sequences of instructions which closely resemble normal or ordinary machine instructions, but generally the programmer has more control over the calculations. Many programmers favor IPL-V over LISP because of the similarity of IPL-V to normal machine programming.

The instructions in any IPL routine consist of four parts: (1) the name, (2) the symbol, (3) the prefixes, and (4) the length. The name part labels the entire routine and the specific label points for transfer of control internally. The IPL-V data are in the form of a list of symbols; each symbol can itself denote a list. The prefixes are 3-bit numbers designed to indicate the meaning of the symbol part, as well as the levels of indirect addressing. Thus, an instruction can be used to store an input, recover an output, perform an additional transfer, or call a routine. The specific choice depends upon the first prefix. Routines may be either standard IPL-V processes or those which the programmer himself defines. IPL-V differs from LISP in that the programmer must communicate his arguments to routine explicitly. The communication cell is the procedure he uses, which is actually a special-purpose push-down stack. Various prefixes cause a data unit to be either removed from or replaced into the communication cell.

An erasure approach is used in IPL-V to maintain storage for lists. Various processes are contained in the language for erasing a list and restoring its storage to a list of available space, providing the list is erased completely and none of its subparts are active. The mechanisms for transferring both data structures and programs to or from auxiliary storage and main memory are superior to those of LISP.

SLIP

The most popular form of SLIP is an extension of FORTRAN and not really a stand-alone system. SLIP uses a method which is different from the others for representing lists. It increases the freedom for manipulating lists and also increases the amount of storage required for them.

SLIP really is a form of a set of special list-processing FORTRAN functions; such functions are used in order to accomplish the operations a programmer normally does in list processing, which include transversal of lists, translation of list structures between internal and external representations, specific recursive communication of arguments, and also the creation and erasure of lists. SLIP programs are thus really FORTRAN programs which use SLIP functions. Most programmers simply add this SLIP subroutine to their own instruction-system file. Primitive SLIP subroutines are in machine language; the remainder are in FORTRAN. SLIP programs somewhat resemble LISP programs because they consist of nestings of function calls. The conditionalization is completed by using FORTRAN IF statements instead of using conditional expressions. A special "VISIT" function aids automatic recursion and must be called explicitly by the programmer.

In the SLIP language, two words rather than one are used for each element of a list. The first word contains a two-address field called the right and left lengths (the left length points to the previous word on the list, and the right length points to the following word). This makes it easy to traverse a list backward and forward, a procedure different from LISP and IPL-V. The second word holds the list element itself. Each list contains a header with pointers to both the beginning and end of a list; the name of a list is a pointer with its header. Specific devices known as readers are available to make the traversal of lists quick and easy. The arithmetic of SLIP is the same as that of FORTRAN, and it is more efficient than that in LISP or IPL-V. SLIP thus has major advantages in dealing with problems which involve large amounts of numerical calculation and list processing. SLIP also is embedded in ALGOL, and this version is called BALGOL.

COMIT

This language is designed basically for use in studies of mechanical translation of the human language. It also is a list-processing language but oriented and designed for lists in which the list elements are not lists themselves, but are closer to strings than they are to tree-like structures. In COMIT, the manipulation of strings is quite easy, but the handling of both trees and recursion is somewhat awkward.

COMIT programs perform primarily by manipulation of a data depository called work space. The work space contains a string composed of a sequence of constituents; i.e., the string could be a sentence and the constituents would represent words of the sentence, or even individual characters, including spaces and punctuation marks. Constituents of strings might also be subscripts and subscript values attached to them. COMIT provides sequences of shelves for temporary storage. Such shelves may be replaced in entirety by new data, or new data can be added at the head of a shelf while preserving the rest in a manner similar to the LIST function, APPEND.

A COMIT program thus consists of a sequence of rules, each rule having a right and a left half, and each rule specifying a string transformation. The work space is searched from left to right until a sequence of constituents matching the last half is found. Such a sequence is then replaced by the sequence of constituents corresponding to the right half. In the execution of a rule, no sequence of constituents in the work space may match the left half. Rules can be used to move data and the work space and to modify and test subscripts and their values.

FORMAC

This acronym stands for FORmula MAnipulation Compiler. FORMAC is an extension of FORTRAN but of a different type. A description can be found in the introduction to FORMAC, IEEE Trans. Electronic Computers, August 1964, by Sammett and Bond. FORMAC is explicitly designed for algebraic operations and is probably not too strong for symbol manipulation, such as language translation. Differentiation of complicated algebraic expressions is a standard type of FORMAC application, as is the generation of a series involving many terms or the analytic solution of different equations. In FORMAC, variables can stand for algebraic expressions as well as numbers, which is not permitted in FORTRAN. The basic mechanism for formula manipulation in FORMAC is the statement LET x = y, which causes the variable x to be equal to the algebraic expression y. When algebraic expressions are combined, purely numerical simplifications are automatically performed.

FORMAC working internally uses list structures for storing algebraic expressions. The user is provided with an erase command to free up storage as needed.

DYSTAL

This is an acronym for DYnamic STorage ALlocation and is a FORTRAN-based system. When DYSTAL is used, the elements of a list are kept in consecutive storage locations so they can be integer-indexed. DYSTAL frees programmers from some of the constraints of FORTRAN, but lacks the extensive flexibility in construction of a list which other list-processing languages contain. However, the integer-indexing ability is unique.

SNOBOL

SNOBOL is an acronym for StriNg-Oriented symBOLic language. It was developed by D. J. Farber, R. E. Griswold, and I. P. Polonsky at the Bell Telephone Laboratories. It has significant applications in program compilation and in the generation of symbolic equations. It provides complete facilities for the manipulation of strings of characters. SNOBOL is particularly applicable to programs associated with test editing, linguistics, compiling, and symbolic manuipulation of algebraic expressions.

A statement in SNOBOL consists of a rule which operates on symbolically named strings. The fundamental operations are: string manipulation, pattern matching, and replacement. Procedures are available for integer arithmetic, indirect referencing, and input/output. The building block or basic concepts of SNOBOL begin with strings and string names. The names may be numbers or characters, while the strings may be any symbol.

SECTION IV

Simulation and Simulation Languages

Simulation has been defined in various ways. Following are some expressions of the meaning of simulation. The experimental technique of defining an operating system by means of mathematical or physical models that operate on a real world of specifically devised problems in a time-sequential method similar to the system itself. Many problems cannot be solved analytically, but adequate criteria for success can be deduced from trial-and-error processes in which the model of the system is dynamically studied. For example, to determine the best operating conditions for a pilot manufacturing plant, one could build a mathematical model of the plant to "try out" the multitude of variables and parameters, i.e., conditions and circumstances, by simulating dynamic operations—all this before deciding on size, structure, locations and variations of the plant. Simulation models are representations of physical systems and phenomena by computers. Simulation is an imitative type of data processing in which an automatic computer is used as a model of some entity, e.g., a chemical process. When information enters the computer to represent the factors of the process, the computer produces information that represents the results of the process, and the processing done by the computer represents the process itself. Some computer-programming techniques set up a routine for one computer to operate as nearly as possible like some other computer.

In brief, simulation can be considered as a representation of a rapidly changing or dynamic system developed in a form or design to simplify manipulation and study, while using a computer for computations, comparisons, and analyses. The term "system" in its essence is a set or an assemblage of transacting components, processes, and parameters. The transactions may be theoretical, internal, or linked to an external environment. A model is a representation of a system in which the processes or transactions bear a close resemblance or relationship to those of the specific system being simulated or studied. Thus, models used in simulation are seldom highly abstract or strictly mathematical. Manipulation of a simulation system concerns the acceptance of inputs and the generation of outputs similar or analogous to those of the system represented.

SIMULATION SYSTEMS

A dynamic system is one in which the activity is dependent on the time framework and can be stable or unstable. It can be studied as a static or steady-in-state system or as the transient behavior of a dynamic system.

Simulation systems can be (a) physical, in which the components are either processes or hardware, and thus precisely defined; (b) behavioral, in which the processes might include the psychological or sociological behavior of individuals or groups; and (c) operational, in which the system would incorporate processes in which human beings might be participants, such as in automobile traffic, highway analyses, etc.

The simulation system can be either continuous, by being a representation by sets of differential equations, either linear or nonlinear, or it may be discrete, in which the major components are distinct and individually identifiable. If the simulation is deterministic, it would contain elements which are taken as determined, although not necessarily constant. If the system is represented as a stochastic model, random variables of the essential elements could be introduced, such as the timing, quantity, or replenishment of demand items related to random distributions.

Man-machine simulation includes operational and behavioral models which require the active participation of man and the allocations of functions between the computer portion of the model and the man. Many man-machine simulation models relate to (a) training, in which man must face a real-life system, as in military control or command operations; (b) behavioral experimentation, such as a study of psychological behavior in specific controlled environments; and (c) educational systems, in which man in a complex environment operates with various elements and components such as management games, etc.

Simulation systems have distinct advantages in modeling, manipulating, and solving various tasks and problems: (a) major economies result by reducing the complexity and solution time of programming tasks, (b) conceptual guidance is enhanced and clarified due to the necessity of strong conceptual structures and the frameworks required for representation of specific systems, and (c) flexibility is developed and is perhaps the major advantage of simulation, because it is easier and less costly to change a representation of a system than to change the system itself. Changes can be anticipated during the model design and can be completed in various runs of a computerized simulation system.

SIMULATION LANGUAGES

Almost any type of programming language can be used to implement a simulation model. However, various specific languages are particularly well suited for simulation applications. Several specialized languages have been designed to make simulation systems easier to manipulate, more accurate in results, and more universal in acceptance. The analog computer is most heavily used for simulation of continuous systems, but the discussions which follow relate to digital-computer simulation languages that provide the user with a variety of services. They are designed to ease the job of translating into a conceptual model a system which an operating programmer can develop for the generation of useful statistical outputs. They contain the following: status descriptors, which are definitions of the essential elements of a system or model; procedures for modifying the state of a model; and procedures for controlling the dynamic performance and observations of model behavior. Most simulation languages develop data structures, data transformations, sequencing of transformations, output routines, and operational features. In addition to these, extensive error checking is available to prevent misuse of the language mechanically (i.e., handcoding or keypunching), as well as routines for debugging a model and locating logical errors.

Brief descriptions of some computer languages for a system simulation follow.

SIMSCRIPT

SIMSCRIPT is a proprietary, general-purpose, digital simulation language and system. It is based on the notion that the state of a system is definable and can be described in terms of entities, those specific objects or things of which a system is composed; attributes, those properties which are associated with the entities as well; and sets, i.e., groups of entities. All entities must be specific and explicit with a complete list of their attributes and a possible set membership. This is the major prerequisite in the development of a simulation model. The state of a system once described is changed by the occurrence of an event, which is a user-defined subroutine written with either SIMSCRIPT or FORTRAN statements. For example, entities can be created or destroyed, set memberships of individual entities can be altered, and numerical values of attributes can be changed. Because entities and attributes must be individually located, much of the SIMSCRIPT language is devoted to providing convenient and flexible methods for performing storage and retrieval functions. Input to the SIMSCRIPT translator usually is developed on various types of disks containing definition, initialization, and subprograms.

GENERAL-PURPOSE SYSTEM SIMULATOR (GPSS)

This simulation language has three basic components: blocks, transactions, and equipment. The language develops simulation models through the use and in terms of block diagrams. Such diagrams are graphic devices which portray the logical and physical flow of transactions or basic information through a system. Such block types in the simulation block diagram are very specific, and from these, models are built. Tapes, disks, or other entry program segments define the properties of each block in the model.

Temporary GPSS elements are formed into transactions and moved from one block to another within the model. Each transaction has eight parameters which are associated with it and also has eight possible priority levels. All Priority 6 transactions are serviced before Priority 5, etc. As transactions enter blocks, various subroutines associated with those particular block types are interpretively executed causing a modification of one or more status descriptors.

Equipment elements are provided in GPSS with a fixed number of each of three types: storage, facilities, and logic switches. Any or all are used to represent physical equipment or logical concepts. Transactions obtain the equipment on a first-come, first-served basis within each priority class. There are ten types of elements in GPSS, and each is referenced by one or more of the block types. Block elements include blocks and transactions. Equipment elements include facilities, storage, and logic switches. Statistical elements are queues and distribution tables. Reference elements are "savexes" for data storage. Computational elements are arithmetic variables and functions. A subset of fifteen attributes is associated with these types, and these attributes are called standard system variables. Their value can be addressed in a simulation model by name and index number. Example: Q12 is the current contents of queue 12; i.e., an integer which indicates the number of transactions in the queue; S6 is the storage contents of Storage 6, also an integer; FN34 identifies the current value of Function 34.

Various procedures are available for modifying the state of a GPSS model. Selection modes are procedures which are used to establish the choice of the next block to which a transaction will move. New transactions are created from ORIGINATE and GENERATE blocks and thereby enter the GPSS model. Transactions are destroyed when they enter the TERMINATE and ASSEMBLE blocks. Other blocks are SPLIT, MATCH, ASSEMBLE, WRITE, SEIZE, RELEASE, LEAVE, QUEUE, etc. Arithmetic variables are defined by VARIABLE cards using FORTRAN-like arithmetic combinations of standard system variables. Functions are defined by FUNCTION cards, and they express a functional relationship between an independent variable, which can be any one of the standard system variables, and a dependent variable function value. Each function is defined by n pairs of points.

Provisions are made for controlling the dynamic performance of GPSS models and for generation of output from GPSS models, and operational features of the GPSS program are defined. For example, a GPSS model consists of a set of definition cards, and each card defines a block, function, table, arithmetic variable, or storage capacity. The GPSS program operates upon the model definition in an essentially interpretive fashion. This provides considerable flexibility for handling multiple runs on the same or similar models.

DYNAMO

DYNAMO concerns continuous closed-loop information feed-back systems. It does not require that the system concerned be either linear or stable; therefore, a very broad class of systems can be developed or represented by the DYNAMO language. A continuous system is defined as one in which all basic variables are continuous and possess a first derivative with respect to time; i.e., the state of the system is given by the levels of continuous variables at any point in time without the conception of any discrete changes to this state. Thus, the system is intuitively obvious as it deals with many physical systems. It is also reasonable for dealing with more discrete phenomena relating to aggregate levels of behavior; i.e., an aggregate inventory level in a manufacturing environment may be viewed as a continuous variable even though its delayed composition is discrete. For example, at any instant in time the level of a variable is a distinct single numeric value.

An information feedback system is defined as one in which information relating to the state of the system at a given time is used to determine the future state of the system. Variables are introduced to deal specifically with the flow of information. Of major importance are time delays, as they establish the dynamic performance of such systems and also determine the lag between the time in which a change in one variable occurs and the time at which this change is reflected in some other variable; i.e., an increase in one level of inventory may lead to a reduction in the level of orders for inventory.

A closed-loop system is defined as one in which successive states of the system are not dependent upon variables outside the system. The primary interest relates to the internal structure of the system and the manner in which the basic variables interact. DYNAMO does not require that the system be completely closed. A limited set of external inputs can be provided for, although these are intended to serve only as independent stimuli to the systems being manipulated and analyzed. Basic DYNAMO is directed at understanding the stability of time, consisting of closed systems of continuous variables in which the broad characteristics of information feedback within the system are significant to its dynamic performance.

Provisions and procedures for modifying the state and controlling the dynamic performance of DYNAMO models are available. Output from a DYNAMO simulation model is generated in the form of time series for any desired variables; i.e., level, rate, or output. The output variable is computed from level or rate variables at each output time. DYNAMO programs operate in five phases: (1) Input—cards are read and internal tables are constructed for each equation. Output specifications are established from the PRINT and PLOT cards. (2) Generation—machine coding is developed from skeleton instructions for each type of equation. (3) Running—at the beginning of a run, the concerned equation types having initialization are solved to provide starting values for all variables requiring them. (4) Printing/plotting—such phases convert the output data into specific output format. (5) Rerun—extra or additional cards modify the values of defined constants, or other output requirements are read in. The program then returns to the running phase.

SECTION V

Process Control Languages

APT

APT (Automatically Programmed Tools) is a program specifically designed through the cooperation of the computer industry with the assistance of the Univac Division of Sperry Rand, for ease and convenience of instructing and controlling computer-programmed machine tools. The programmer writes numerically coded instructions, which are followed by the machine-control system to cause the machine to produce the desired part or product. Since the program must be very precise and intricate, it is fundamentally a mathematical operation. The programmer defines the geometric dimensions of the part he wishes to create, and the computer automatically controls the function of the machine to produce that part or component. The statements are English-language type and reference the intersections of these various components with instructions to the cutting tool. Such instructions are produced on punched paper tape for input to the controlled machine.

APT can cut only straight lines; however, its use is not restricted. These straight lines may be as long as 1/1000 of an inch. Therefore, any conceivable shape can be cut. But the machine has to be told by the computer to cut each of these tiny segments, demonstrating the tediousness of programming the operation of the tool. But once this is accomplished, there can be endless repetition of the procedure with no added instructions, or the tape can be stored for later use.

APT III, an extension of Automatic Programmed Tools, provides computer-assisted programming of numerically controlled machine tools, flame cutters, drafting machines, and similar equipment. APT III is production-oriented; that is, it was written to simplify the effort, time, and money needed to take full advantage of numerically controlled techniques in engineering and manufacturing. In addition to providing machine-tool programming capabilities virtually impossible by manual methods, APT enhances most of the usual advantages found in numerical control: reduced lead time, greater freedom and flexibility in design, lower direct costs, greater accuracy, improved production forecasting, lower tooling costs, better engineering control of the manufacturing process, and simplified introduction of changes.

STRESS

This is an acronym for STRuctural Engineering System Solver. It is designed to solve structural-engineering problems using a problem-oriented input language. A structural engineer could use STRESS after a minimum study of the manual and without prior programming experience. STRESS can analyze structures with prismatic members in two or three dimensions, with either pinned or rigid joints, which are subjected to concentrated or distributed loads, support motions, or temperature effects. A user describes his problem by writing a number of statements specifying the size and type of the structure, the physical dimensions, the loads, and the desired results. The solution supplies such information as member forces at the member ends, reactions, joint displacements, and support displacements. The recently developed techniques in structural analysis, such as matrix and network formulations, are employed by STRESS. It is necessary to have a common reference system in order to describe all the members and points of a three-dimensional structure. STRESS employs a right-handed orthogonal cartesian coordinate system. The origin of the system can be located at any arbitrary point in the structure, i.e., one of the support joints. All joint data are described in terms of joint coordinates with respect to the origin on the coordinate system, and all computed joint displacements and reactions are similarly given in the same system.

COGO

COGO is a civil engineering oriented language first developed by Professor C. L. Miller and his associates at the Massachusetts Institute of Technology in association with the Puerto Rico Department of Public Works. The COGO programming language or system is based on the technology of civil engineers, but it is also applied in other areas. A special time-sharing version called QUIKTRAN/COGO is also available. The engineer quickly and easily writes a problem using the COGO vocabulary and feeds it to the computer for automatic computation. No intermediate programming is required.

The system is based on a coordinate table, and the problem is expressed in terms of angles given in degrees, minutes, and seconds. The intersection points form the coordinate table upon which the COGO commands are based. Each point is given an identification number and is referenced by that number. By the single-word or short-phrase commands of COGO, COGO may be instructed to compute distances between points 1 and 2, to dump all coordinates, to locate and calculate bearings from known points, develop parallel lines, compute angles, calculate new points, etc. Therefore, COGO is a versatile tool in the hands of qualified engineers, who require only a short time to learn its techniques and special power.

CONTROL BASIC

The rapid growth of the hobbyist computer movement has resulted in a marked rise in the use of the BASIC programming language. This rise has manifested itself not only in a large number of users, but in a large number of different BASIC interpreters as well. Furthermore, these interpreters are being recorded in ROM (read-only memory) with more frequency.

The advantage of having a programming language implemented in ROM is that the applications program can then be "burned into" PROM (programmable read-only memory), and the entire system thus becomes nonvolatile. The RAM memory of conventional computers is volatile, in that when the power is turned off, the programs in memory disappear. To start the computer into operation again, the programs must be reloaded into RAM from disk or tape. The ROM and PROM serve the operative function of RAM—that is, holding the program—but they do not need to be reloaded from a tape or disk.

A machine that has the language interpreter and the program being interpreted both on ROM is more of a dedicated device than a general-purpose computer. However, the initial configuring of the functions of that device is as flexible as the abilities of a general-purpose computer. Thus, inexpensive machines are now available that can be "customized," through the user-defined program, to perform any kind of manufacturing process control or monitoring.

The configuration must contain some RAM memory, of course, for use as a "scratch pad," i.e., the area in which the variables are stored and changed during the running of the program. Even though the PROM memory is nonvolatile, if it is EPROM (erasable programmable read-only memory), it can be erased intentionally and reprogrammed, if the requirements of the application change.

These process control applications are usually simple operations. An example of a home application would be the interfacing of heating and air-conditioning devices to a computer that also is connected to temperature sensors. This computer could monitor the environment and control the operation of the energy-consuming heater and air conditioner so that they are used as sparingly as possible. A more sophisticated system could also be interfaced to electricity-generating solar panels, reflective cooling panels, and external energy supplies to optimize the use of free energy sources. Even with more than a dozen sources of input, the programs needed to optimize the energy balances are simple, and they can be programmed and altered by a novice using a simplified version of the BASIC language.

Special versions of BASIC have been developed especially for this process control function. They are usually called Control BASIC. Often they only implement a subset of the Dartmouth BASIC definition. The most common simplification is the elimination of data types other than integers. Usually, these simplifications lead to an interpreter that takes up much less space than full-blown implementations of the language.

The ability to develop special-purpose computers to perform process control and monitoring functions has increased greatly with the introduction of inexpensive microelectronics. Without Control BASIC, such algorithms would have to be implemented in tedious and maintenance-intensive assembly programs. The ability to write these programs in an easy-to-use language that does not require much memory and can be loaded into nonvolatile memory chips makes the dedicated microcomputer a viable concept. Also, complete computers, with interface logic for driving communications and printing devices, have been designed to fit on a single circuit board, for environments where space is a constraint.

NUMERICAL CONTROL

Numerical control refers to the control of machine tools, drafting machines, etc., by punched paper tape or magnetic tape suitably encoded with directive information. As most numerically controlled devices have very limited logical or arithmetical capability, they rely on their input tapes for detailed and explicit guidance. This may mean 8 bits for every 0.001 inch of motion, or a great amount of data on the tape. Using information presented in a more manageable and concise form, it is common for a computer to prepare the control tapes. An example is the Automatically Programmed Tools (APT) system. Using APT, the designer describes his tool and the desired part in a high-level geometrically oriented language. A preprocessor program accepts the high-level language and digests it into a simpler, formalized internal representation. The central program, which is tool-independent, converts the material, tool, and geometrical information into tool-motion commands. A postprocessor program prepares the tool-motion information in a format suitable for the particular control mechanism being used. A simultaneous output for a numerical-control drafting machine permits preparation of detail blueprints while the robot tool is making the part, if desired.

SECTION VI

Report Program Generator (RPG) Language

RPG has been designed primarily for the automatic printing of specific documents at the computer output. Also, it provides sets of instructions or programs which control the computer in the development of other data processing jobs on most types and sizes of computers. The input must be specifically designed, and specific RPG programs are written for each particular computer type and model. For this purpose, all printed documents are designated as transaction documents or business reports.

SUMMARY

The programmer's principal task at the outset is to organize the input data according to various rules and procedures which enable the computer to change such information into output reports as required by management. The RPG programs are recorded on various types of specification sheets. Four general types are usually available for (1) input data, (2) output data, (3) operations or "result" data, and (4) data files. The programmer usually proceeds as follows: (1) He uses a multiple-card layout form to describe the layout for each input or output card or image for each specific job. (2) He uses a printer spacing chart to provide all needed specifications for the printed output as designed. (3) He codes the program by making necessary entries on the four RPG specification sheets. These are the source statements. (4) The source programs (usually a card deck) are read into the computer along with the RPG generator (processor) program. This program is usually furnished by the computer manufacturer and performs the translation of the source program (deck) into machine language to develop the object program. (5) Various diagnostics and error-correcting checks are developed to determine and maintain accuracy.

In general, the steps required by RPG programming are: (1) Analyze input data. (2) Prepare and program specifications for the output data. (3) Code entries. (4) Develop and run the source program (deck) to create the object program. (5) Execute and debug the program with test data. RPG is a multipurpose programming language but is not as powerful and flexible as COBOL, FORTRAN, etc. It is designed principally to ease development of business reports (accounting, etc.) and transaction documents (invoices, pay checks, production orders, etc.), and to update files with new input data.

RPG uses table look-up and file extension specification sheets to perform sequence checking. It also can make numerical comparisons for branching and can produce relatively complex computer programs.

RPG is now capable of performing its basic report-generating function with versions developed for use with magnetic disk files, and the more common disk packs. The disk pack most often consists of six disks on a shaft, one above the other. These disks contain ten magnetic recording surfaces, the topmost and bottommost surfaces not being used. The disk drive is connected on-line to the central processing unit. It often contains five access arms, each with two read/write heads, which move as a unit between the six disks of the pack. The use of disks increases the size of the memory of the system.

RPG II contains many "functional improvements." Specifically, RPG II is capable of handling various input media. RPG II also uses some different types of specification sheets with additional areas for control specifications. These control functions relate to various options of main memory execution, operations, and program identifications.

RPG is becoming a widely used application language, especially in the business environment, and more emphatically for smaller systems or auxiliary computers (often minicomputer types) to perform the specific report-generation operations discussed previously.

RPG AS A GENERIC TERM

As RPG went from its original form to RPG II and now more advanced forms, it necessarily gathered "enhancements" that might be considered to clutter the language. What was originally intended to be a simple, nonprocedural, table-driven translator has now become a language with all the power of COBOL or FORTRAN, but with clumsier control structures and data structures. The overall design and intent of the language is no longer clear to the beginner.

However, with the rise of general-purpose data base management systems, the spirit and intent of the original RPG language is finding a new home. The software houses that design and implement the DBMS software that structures and controls the informational corporate resource are keenly aware of the need for a nonprocedural language that will access the data for the purpose of producing reports.

Since the report-writing task is indeed a subset of general programming, it is obviously a prime candidate for special-purpose languages. Programs written in these languages should "do more for less" with regard to both complexity of program and cost of development. Both these parameters are also, of course, linked to development time. When the report is to contain very time-sensitive information, the last consideration, development time, may often be the most important. In the case of extremely time-sensitive or rather simple requests for information, the query language is beginning to play a major role.

Both the subjects of generalized report generators (now generically referred to as RPGs) and query languages are addressed in the appendixes on data-base management systems.

APPENDIX L

Word Processing Systems

The term "word processing" is currently used in reference to the task of producing typewritten or printed documents from rough drafts or dictation. Most corporations now have word processing departments with specially designed equipment and specially trained personnel to optimize this central task.

The equipment may be the traditional dictation pad and typewriter, or it may be sophisticated voice recording equipment and a large time-shared computer with many work stations. Since the recent decline in price of computer-related equipment, almost all word processing installations are beginning to employ some sort of automation. Because the microcomputer revolution has made available extremely low-cost computer systems, many former typists, even at one-and two-secretary companies, are becoming word processing technicians by using "automatic typewriters."

The main feature of computer-oriented word processing systems is the fact that the typed characters are initially recorded magnetically instead of being printed on the paper. The user is allowed to change or move the characters in the memory of the computer to accomplish corrections or reorganizations instantly and easily. With one or two special keystrokes (a command), the contents of the computer memory can be displayed on a television-like screen, or any computer terminal, for review. When the user decides the material is correct, a perfectly and rapidly typed printout can be ordered.

NATURE OF THE WORD PROCESSING TASK AND AUTOMATED SOLUTIONS

One of the major uses of word processing equipment is the production of business letters. The typical scenario without word processing is as follows. The executive either dictates a letter or writes it out in longhand. The secretary types a draft from the tape or the executive's handwriting and gives it to the executive for signature. If the executive makes any substantive changes or corrections to this typed draft, it must be retyped. Then it has to be reexamined, possibly to be retyped again.

When a word processing system is used, the chain of events changes to the following. The word processing technician types the letter into the main memory (discussed later) of the word processing machine. Instead of the typed characters being printed on paper, they are displayed on a video screen. The machine remembers the characters as they are typed (by storing them in its main memory). After the letter is typed into the main memory, the secretary, using one or two keystrokes, commands the machine to display the entire document on the video screen for review. If corrections need to be made, commands are given to change the contents of main memory to what is desired. When the text is perfect, two copies of the main memory are made. At the push of a button, the machine perfectly and automatically types the letter on a high-speed printer. Before the contents of the main memory are purged to make room for the next task, another copy of the letter is recorded magnetically, in "machine readable form," on a floppy disk, which looks similar to a 45-rpm record. This is also done automatically in response to a simple command.

If the executive, after reading the letter, returns it to the secretary with substantial corrections, instead of retyping the entire correspondence, the following steps can be taken. The magnetic copy can be read back into main memory from the disk onto which it was recorded. These characters, the same as the letter, can then be modified as if they were just typed in. When the modifications are finished, the new copy of main memory can be re-recorded on the disk for later reference, and the corrected letter can once again be typed on the high-speed printer. If the executive has further changes, this process can be repeated. Again, only the changed portions need to be retyped. This process of generating a new, perfectly typed copy of a document is often used even if the corrections are minor. The flawless typing job increases the professional appearance of the document.

Production of any text or manuscript can be described by a story similar to the production of a letter. Essentially, a rough draft is produced and edited, and for reasons of legibility must be typed at some point. Since typographical errors are inevitable, this typed version is a draft itself, which is subject to correction. Depending on how perfect the final copy must be and how rough this draft is, the text will be subject to a number of edit passes. If the ideas in the document are still evolving, it may be severely modified many times. The more edit passes involved, the more the text should be developed on a word processing system.

For example, a doctoral dissertation must be typed impeccably according to specific criteria. Furthermore, it will be reviewed by an advisor and an entire committee who will recommend both minor and substantive changes before it will be accepted. This type of text is a prime candidate for word processing devices.

Another common word processing task is the production of multiple copies of the same document. In the past, this had to be accomplished through the use of carbon paper. In modern times, the copying machine has greatly enhanced the neatness and legibility of the copies, but, still, some important communications demand a hand-typed appearance.

The ease of producing multiple copies from main memory on command becomes even more important when one or two parts of the document have to be customized for each copy. If several copies of the same letter are going to different people, the address of the recipient will differ for each copy. Perhaps the name of the recipient appears in the body of the letter, or the letter contains passages that are different for each person. These common situations can be handled easily with word processing systems that allow automatic insertion of prerecorded text into the document that is printing out.

Another way a system might allow the user to insert text into a document is as follows. When the text is being typed into memory, special characters may be placed in the position where the text is to be inserted. When the printout is ordered, the automatic typing will pause where the special characters were placed. The special characters will not be typed. Instead, the user will be allowed to type anything desired onto the page where the machine stopped typing. When the user wishes the automatic output to continue, another special character can be typed.

There are many advanced features that word processing systems running on large computers are capable of offering that are likely to find their way to the smaller and less expensive machines over the next few years. One such application is the automatic formation of indexes. One technique used is to surround the word to be included in the index by special characters, such as {civil liberties}. The computer will not print the braces when the text is printed, but will use them as a signal that this phrase is to be placed in the index. During the course of the output, the computer will keep track of which pages contain the phrase, and it will place these page numbers in the index entry for the phrase.

Another useful program for text processing is usually called a "spell" program. After the manuscript is recorded on external memory, the spell program can be run. This program will read the text from the disk or tape and look up every word in a spelling dictionary. Any word it cannot find in the dictionary will be printed on the terminal or placed in a file (discussed later). Many of these words will be company names, chemical formulas, or other intentional constructs that are not spelling errors. But these can be easily distinguished from the spelling errors. The search capabilities of the editor can then be used to find and change the mistakes.

On some computer systems, text recorded on external memory can be sent directly to devices that prepare the manuscript for large-scale reproduction. These types of machines are used extensively by magazines and newspapers, but as technology becomes less expensive, the practice will become more commonplace.

TYPICAL HARDWARE ARCHITECTURE

The minimum hardware of a word processing system is a keyboard, a computer-like processor, a magnetic storage device, and a printer. Many configurations include a video screen and two types of memory, main memory and external (or mass) memory. Fig. L-1 shows an example of a system with word-processing capability.

Courtesy COMPAL, Inc.

Fig. L-1. Word processing system.

Main Memory and the Computer Processor

The main memory and the computer processor are almost always physically housed in the same cabinet. Sometimes they are in the same cabinet as the keyboard. In some systems, the processor, main memory, and a floppy-disk drive (one form of external memory) have all been incorporated into the same cabinet as the keyboard and the video screen, leaving only the attachment of a printing device necessary for a complete system. Since the printing device is one of the most costly parts of the system, it may be shared in some way among several users. This is becoming a most popular configuration.

As shown in Fig. L-2, the processor is central to any system, even though the integrated circuit chip on which it resides may never be seen. All characters that are struck on the keyboard are actually sent to the processor, which echoes them to the video screen (or typewriter-like computer terminal) as well as recording them in main memory. When characters have to be recorded on the external medium, such as the floppy disk previously discussed, they are read from main memory by the processor and written to the disk one at a time. Similarly, when characters must be sent to the printer from main memory, the processor shuffles them through one of its few memory registers, one at a time.

Since the processor and main memory work at such high speeds, these processes appear to occur instantaneously. They are restricted in speed only by the relative slowness of the other devices, such as the floppy disk or printer. Since the processor

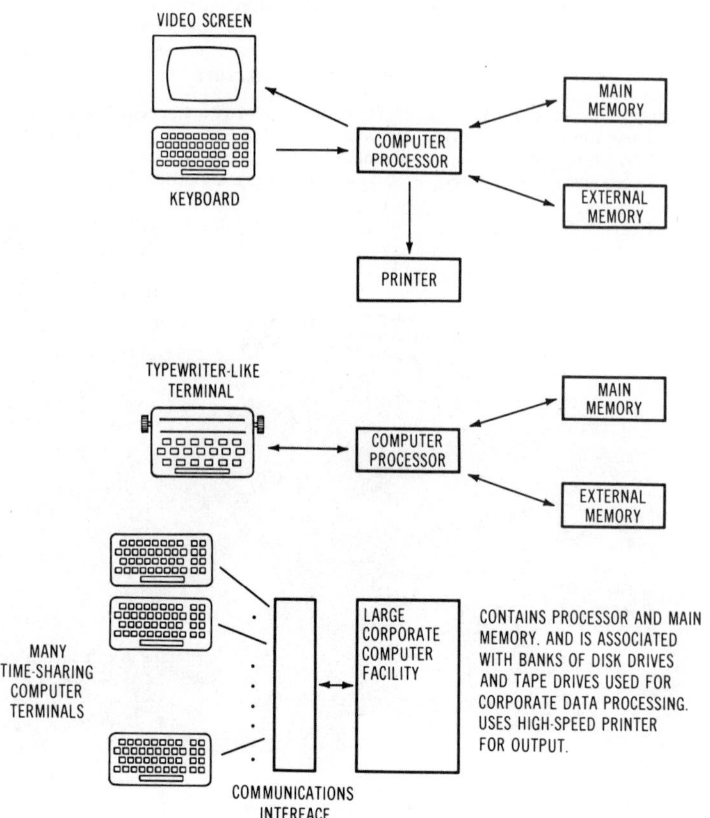

Fig. L-2. Typical word processing configurations.

and main memory work hundreds of times faster, they spend a great deal of time waiting. Their great speed capability is utilized, however, to make complicated calculations or lengthy searches appear instantaneous to the human user. For example, one command that is available is a search command. The user may have typed in a multipage text and realized that a spelling error had been made early in the text. This can be corrected by using a simple command that instructs the processor to search the main memory for the misspelled word and replace it with the correct spelling (the incorrect and correct spelling must be included as part of the command). This may take several thousands of comparisons of characters, but since the processor can make hundreds of thousands of comparisons per second, the operation will appear to the operator to be only a short pause.

Like the processor, main memory takes the form of integrated-circuit chips soldered to circuit boards. The number of characters that can be held in main memory limits the size of the text that can be worked on at one time. For example, a book may have to be broken down into chapters, or even subchapter units that are typed and edited individually. The processor is in essence a computer, and the main memory is computer memory. It is measured in units of 1024 characters, known as 1K bytes. As the semiconductor industry finds cheaper and cheaper methods of fabricating these chips, and increases the memory density per chip, the cost will go down and the size of the saleable unit will go up.

The text being typed or edited is not the only thing that occupies the main memory space. The processor can only perform rather primitive operations, such as "compare the character in memory position number 40 to the character in memory position number 45 to see if they are the same." Operators, however, want to deal with words and lines instead of memory locations. Also, the use of high-level commands is desired, such as the search and replace command for spelling errors that was mentioned earlier. Therefore, a computer program must exist in memory to translate the operator's desires into the simpler computer commands.

There are generally two such computer programs. The "text editor" program allows the text to be typed into main memory, changed, and written to the external memory or the printer. It also can read from the external memory text that has already been recorded. Another type of program, the "text formatter," can read the text from disk, format it according to commands imbedded in the text, and type it on the printer. These will be discussed in more detail later.

These programs may or may not occupy some of the space available for text, the "user space." Main memory chips come in two forms. RAM (random access memory) is the name for the chips that can be recorded and rerecorded. This is where the text must go. The programs may also be placed in this type of memory, but it is usually cheaper to have them recorded in ROM (read only memory). This memory cannot be erased. If the programs are stored in RAM, they must be read into main memory from the disk when the system is turned on. When the machine is turned off, the contents of the RAM are erased, but this is not true of the ROM.

Regardless of what kind of main memory holds the programs, the user is simply told the size of the available work space. A reasonable size would be 20K bytes of RAM available for entering text.

Terminals

A computer terminal is a device with a keyboard and either a typewriter-like printing mechanism or a video display screen. These devices also have the ability to transmit data to a computer or computer-like processor through a cable. This cable attaches to the terminal with a standard plug called an RS-232 interface. (This type of plug and cable can be used between any two devices that are communicating data.)

Many word processing terminals are simply IBM Selectric typewriters that have been given the attributes of a communications device by the addition of a baseplate. IBM Selectric II typewriters come already equipped for the additional task of data communications. These spherical-font devices have a speed of about 15.5 characters per second.

Many non-IBM typewriter-like terminals employ the Qume or Diablo daisywheel print mechanism instead of a spherical font. These terminals are capable of speeds of 30, 40, 45, or 55 characters per second. Speeds can vary based on the text. Some print heads can move faster over blank space than when typing. Some can print backwards as well as forward (saving the null time used for a carriage return).

Type styles and sizes are often interchangeable, and many printers can skip fractions of spaces. Some employ proportional spacing, i.e., allowing more lateral space for a "W" than an "I." These two capabilities allow formatter software to justify the right margin, giving a professional typeset appearance.

An increasingly popular type of terminal does not employ a printing mechanism. Characters that are "typed" by the operator or the programs appear on a television-like video screen. These terminals are often called crt's, for cathode ray tube (the technical name for a picture tube). The subject of video terminals is too broad to go into here. Suffice it to say that they offer word processing the convenience of high speed, which is often approximately 1000 characters per second and can be even higher. These terminals are also less expensive, since they have no mechanical parts other than the keys and a cooling fan.

The more expensive of the crt's employ special unlabeled keys that the user can program to contain a sequence of characters that is commonly typed, such as the search command, a command to set special tab stops, or the name and address of a company. As was mentioned earlier, some of these terminals have the processor, memory, and disk drives built into them. Many microcomputers are such "terminal computers."

Mass Memory

The only example of a mass storage device that has been used so far is the floppy disk. These are flexible disks of a magnetically sensitive medium (similar in composition to magnetic recording tape) enclosed in a protective square jacket.

These disks come in two sizes, 5-inch minidisks and the 8-inch standard size. Minidisks hold approximately 80K characters, and 8-inch disks hold 250K. These amounts will double as "double-density" versions become available, and will double again when it becomes possible to read and write on both sides of the medium. Systems can usually be configured with from one to four drives.

Access time (the time required to locate characters and prepare for transfer from the disk to main memory) is about one tenth of a second. The data is transferred in between 5 and 10 seconds for each 16K of memory. This transfer rate varies depending on whether the data is being written or read (writing takes longer), the efficiency of the program doing the transfer, and whether or not the accuracy of the information is confirmed after the transfer.

This data rate is possible because disks are random-access external storage. Since disks are physically laid out like a phonograph record, the following analogy is possible. When a particular song on a record is to be played, the arm with the needle can be moved directly to that song. If the music were being played on a reel-to-reel tape deck, however, all of the tape prior to the desired song would have to be passed through the play/record heads before the desired song could be played. This is known as serial access, and naturally the speed of accessing a particular item is much less than with random access.

Most disks and many tape-oriented systems allow the user to give names to the piece of text that is being written into external storage. For example, a secretary may wish to name the first letter typed for Ms. Jones on February 24 "Jones-1-2/24". This collection of characters is called a file. "Jones-1-2/24" is the file name. The file name must be specified whenever main memory is being written to the disk or tape, or whenever a file is being read into main memory for printing or editing.

Printing Devices

The most commonly used printing device, the typewriter-like terminal, has already been discussed. The daisywheel models also come in a receive-only model that has no keyboard. These receive-only models would be considered small printers.

Another type of printer that usually prints faster and costs less than the mechanisms previously discussed is the dot matrix printer. This device does not actually have type-face images that are transferred to the paper in a single stroke, but rather forms the image of the letter by using patterns of small dots. This allows for easy adjustment of print size for titles and emphasis (this feature is incorporated into some formatters, as discussed below). The characters produced by dot-matrix printers are not as neat looking nor as legible as the conventional type. The output from these devices usually is not considered to be suitable for correspondence or offset printing. Since top quality is not really needed for the production of in-house documents or manuals, or for rough drafts, dot-matrix devices are an economical alternative for these applications. These printers are available to print in both upper and lower case (lower case meaning both upper-case and lower-case characters are provided, as opposed to upper case only).

The fastest of all printers are the line printers, which print an entire line with one throw of the hammer. This requires that an entire character set be available at each print position.

TYPICAL SOFTWARE CAPABILITIES

Text Editors

A valuable gain to be had from using computers to aid in the production of typed documents is the ability to erase a misstruck character instantly. On a conventional typewriting system, when the key is struck the character is immediately printed on the paper. A misstruck character must be erased manually, a back-space struck, and the proper character printed. In word processing systems, typed characters are only recorded in main memory and displayed on a crt screen. The text-editor programs that record the type characters in main memory will erase the most recently typed character automatically when a backspace is typed. The corresponding character on the video display will also disappear, to indicate that the character has been deleted from memory. This allows secretaries to type fearlessly (and faster), knowing that erasure of mistakes is no longer a difficult and messy problem.

Most text editors have dozens of commands that allow text to be read in from disk or tape, deleted from memory, moved around in memory, and modified on a character, word, or line basis. Other commands allow the user to find all instances of a character sequence and change them to some other sequence.

Editors usually deal with text on the basis of line numbers or position pointers. For example, to express a request to print lines 10 through 20 in an editor that incorporates line numbers, one might type

```
t 10,20
```

However, in a position-pointer–oriented editor, the user would have to position the pointer so that it is pointing at the first character of interest. The pointer is often positioned through the use of a search command. Usually the operator is not interested in lines 10 through 20 per se, but is interested in what is in those lines. Therefore, a search can be performed for the contents of the line (or a small part of the line that is likely to be found as unique by the machine). The pointer can also be moved through the use of explicit commands.

A listing of some typical capabilities is given below. These examples are taken from an editor that is position-pointer oriented, but the reader can imagine similar capabilities for addressing text by line numbers. Many editors actually combine the abilities, to accommodate operators with either background.

Move the pointer to the beginning or the ending of the text in memory.

Move the pointer over a specified number of characters.

Move the pointer over a specified number of words.

Move the pointer over a specified number of lines.

Move the pointer over a specified number of pages.

Insert typed text before the character being pointed to.

Delete the specified number of characters from memory.

Delete the specified number of lines from memory.

Delete the specified number of pages from memory.

Substitute one specified character sequence for another specified character sequence (e.g., to correct spelling errors).

Find a character sequence in memory ("find" meaning print it and position the pointer to the first character of the sequence, for subsequent printing or manipulation).

Find the next occurrence of the character string just found.

Terminate the editing session and prepare to begin another one or a printing and formatting session.

Type the line following the pointer on the crt or the printer.

Type the page following the pointer on the crt or the printer.

Temporarily store the specified number of lines that follow the pointer into a special hold memory. This feature is used to move chunks of text from one area of the document to another. It is placed in this temporary storage so that it may be placed in another area by the command below. This technique may be used to place the temporary memory in several other places in the text. However, the text that is being stored in the temporary memory must be explicitly erased from the original area it holds if it was really just to be simply stored. Some editors have a "move" command which will do this automatically.

Add the contents of the hold memory to the position just before the current pointer.
Translate the specified number of characters or lines to all capitals.
Report the amount of main memory still available for additional text.
Set the following tab positions.
Read the specified file from the disk and place it into main memory, available for editing.
Write the contents of main memory to the disk as a file with a specified name.

A Typical Session

The text below is a record of a typical editing session used to produce a letter. The characters typed automatically by the machine will be shown underlined for illustrative purposes; they would not be underlined in an actual interaction with the machine.

The typist may actually have made many additional keystrokes that cannot be shown here. These would be the keystrokes that the user realized were in error and used the backspace key to delete. Since they disappear on the screen, it would be hard to show them here. Systems that use only a typewriter-like terminal usually scroll the platen as well as back up the cursor when the backspace is struck. This allows the user to still see the character that was deleted. We will not show this in the example, since it makes the course of the editing session hard to follow.

In this part of the example, the only command given to the editor was the "i" command, to begin inserting the text. The machine prompts for these commands with the "*" character. The typist exited the insert mode by striking the "escape" key, which is a nonprinting key on most computer terminals.

```
*i



Mr. Ron Blakey
2423 Eastmore Drive
Los Angeles, California
90045



Mr. E. J. Erpett
Credit Manager
Boswell Jewelers International
990 Bond Street
New York, New York
31145

Dear Mr. Erppet,

     Recently I returned to your Los Angeles store an 18k gold
badminton birdie which I received as a wedding present. Your per-
sonel were most courteous in administrating my refund of $433.44.
     However, on the next billing of my credit card account with
your firm I discovered the credit had benn recorded as a charge,
leaving me with a balance due of $433.44. I discussed the matter
by phone with a Miss Whimsel, from your credit bureau in Chicago.
She assured me that the matter would be taken care of promptly.
     However, I then received a notice issued from your collections
service in Los Angeles, informing me that my account had become
```

```
urgently delinquent and that I must immediately forward the amount
of $866.88, or face court action.
     Since the telephone company has recently sent me a $2500.00
refund for the return of my touch telephone, I do have the funds
available, but I would prefer these matters be remedied at the root
of their cause.
     I look forward to hearing from you.

Sincerely,



Ron Blakey
```

If the above document was then run through a spell program, words like Blakey and Whimsel would be shown to be possibly erroneous spellings, even though they are correct. However, the words "personel" and "benn" would be shown to be typographical errors. Also, "Erpett" and "Erppet" would appear on the questionable list, and one of them is in fact wrong. The typist would then begin editing the letter.

```
*fErppet
Dear Mr. Erppet,
*s\ppet\pett\
Dear Mr. Erpett,
*fbenn
your firm I discovered the credit had benn recorded as a charge,
*s\benn\been\
your firm I discovered the credit had been recorded as a charge,
```

The find (f) and substitute (s) commands were used above to correct the mistakes. The letter can then be printed out in its corrected version with the type command. Here the "b" command means position the pointer at the beginning of the text. Also, the character "#" is used to mean "type as many lines as there are" when it is used in conjunction with the "t" command, which means "type a line."

```
*b

*#t



Mr. Ron Blakey
2423 Eastmore Drive
Los Angeles, California
90045



Mr. E. J. Erpett
Credit Manager
Boswell Jewelers International
990 Bond Street
New York, New York
31145
```

Dear Mr. Erpett,

Recently I returned to your Los Angeles store an 18k gold badminton birdie which I received as a wedding present. Your personnel were most courteous in administrating my refund of $433.44.

However, on the next billing of my credit card account with your firm I discovered the credit had been recorded as a charge, leaving me with a balance due of $433.44. I discussed the matter by phone with a Miss Whimsel, from your credit bureau in Chicago. She assured me that the matter would be taken care of promptly.

However, I then received a notice issued from your collections service in Los Angeles, informing me that my account had become urgently delinquent and that I must immediately forward the amount of $866.88, or face court action.

Since the telephone company has recently sent me a $2500.00 refund for the return of my touch telephone, I do have the funds available, but I would prefer these matters be remedied at the root of their cause.

I look forward to hearing from you.

Sincerely,

Ron Blakey

Text Formatters

One of the main advantages of using systems that incorporate text formatters as well as text editors is the automatic justification of the right margin. In other words, the characters on the right margin line up just like the characters on the left margin. This is not only esthetically more pleasing to the eye, but it has a great functional importance as well. Often during the process of editing, sections of text are added or deleted. In the course of these changes, it often happens that only part of a line remains where a whole line used to be. Or perhaps a line has been lengthened so that it extends beyond the right margin. The reformatting of these lines demands that the lines surrounding the short line be shortened and some of the words be put on the short line to make it more uniform. If done manually, this moving of words across line boundaries is very tedious and a waste of time. If the formatter has the ability to justify margins, then it has the ability to cope with extremely short or extremely long lines and move the words and lines as it pleases to equalize the line length.

Other capabilities of formatters are:

Add space for figures automatically.

Change the margins of the page, i.e., the left, right, top, and bottom.

Print the text in two or more columns per page.

Automatically place a heading at the top of each page.

Allow special text to be inserted from the keyboard when the formatted text is printing out.

Allow options on the line spacing, instead of the standard single spacing.

Capitalize sequences of characters that were not capitalized when typed.

Automatically number the pages at either the top or the bottom.

Allow the setting of different tab stops than those that were used when the document was typed.

Automatically insert text into the printing text from more than one file.

Automatically generate an index of key words and phrases with a list of the pages on which they were used.

Control the character size through formatter commands if the printing device is dot-matrix oriented and adjustable.

Select the spacing of the characters as pica or elite, or some other spacing, if the printer supports variable spacing.

Store often-used formats, like letter formats, so the commands do not have to be embedded in the text every time a letter is typed.

The letter that was used in the example above is shown below with the formatter commands inserted. The character "@" indicates that the character that follows is not to be typed, but is to be considered a formatter directive. The "b" command means break the line here, and if it is associated with a number, it means "skip this many lines as well." The formatter will begin a new paragraph whenever a line begins with a blank. Usually documents are typed with the formatter commands embedded initially, as opposed to the retrofit that we are using for illustrative purposes.

```
@b=12
Mr. Ron Blakey@b
2423 Eastmore Drive@b
Los Angeles, California@b
90045@b
@b=4
Mr. E. J. Erpett@b
Credit Manager@b
Boswell Jewelers International@b
990 Bond Street@b
New York, New York@b
31145@b
@b=1
Dear Mr. Erpett,
@b=1
     Recently I returned to your Los Angeles store an 18k gold
badminton birdie which I received as a wedding present. Your per-
sonnel were most courteous in administrating my refund of $433.44.
     However, on the next billing of my credit card account with
your firm I discovered the credit had been recorded as a charge,
leaving me with a balance due of $433.44. I discussed the matter
by phone with a Miss Whimsel, from your credit bureau in Chicago.
She assured me that the matter would be taken care of promptly.
     However, I then received a notice issued from your collections
service in Los Angeles, informing me that my account had become
urgently delinquent and that I must immediately forward the amount
of $866.88, or face court action.
     Since the telephone company has recently sent me a $2500.00
refund for the return of my touch telephone, I do have the funds
available, but I would prefer these matters be remedied at the root
of their cause.
     I look forward to hearing from you.
@b=1
Sincerely,
@b=3
Ron Blakey
```

The formatted version of this letter appears on the next page.

Appendix L

Mr. Ron Blakey
2423 Eastmore Drive
Los Angeles, California
90045

Mr. E. J. Erpett
Credit Manager
Boswell Jewelers International
990 Bond Street
New York, New York
31145

Dear Mr. Erpett,

Recently I returned to your Los Angeles store an 18k gold badminton birdie which I received as a wedding present. Your personnel were most courteous in administrating my refund of $433.44.

However, on the next billing of my credit card account with your firm I discovered the credit had been recorded as a charge, leaving me with a balance due of $433.44. I discussed the matter by phone with a Miss Whimsel, from your credit bureau in Chicago. She assured me that the matter would be taken care of promptly.

However, I then received a notice issued from your collections service in Los Angeles, informing me that my account had become urgently delinquent and that I must immediately forward the amount of $866.88, or face court action.

Since the telephone company has recently sent me a $2500.00 refund for the return of my touch telephone, I do have the funds available, but I would prefer these matters be remedied at the root of their cause.

I look forward to hearing from you.

Sincerely,

Ron Blakey

SUMMARY

The use of automated devices for developing typewritten manuscripts and correspondence has become commonplace and may eventually replace manual methods (typewriters without computer processors and computer memory). The greatly increased efficiency of labor more than compensates for the increased cost of the equipment. Furthermore, the cost of the equipment will probably continue to fall and the capabilities continue to rise, further increasing the cost effectiveness.

The first automated systems were developed on large, expensive main-frame computers. The word-processing tasks were considered a small part of a total data-processing chore to which the installation was committed. The microminiaturization of computer-like devices and the subsequent sharp declines in cost have allowed the word processing function to return to the locality of the user. Word processing technicians are no longer dependent on the support of the personnel associated with the computer facilities of a company to produce documents automatically. Even the complicated tasks of margin justification, index formation, and spelling verification are beginning to be placed directly into the hands of the user in the form of desk-top machines, typewriters that have become as powerful as million-dollar computers of a decade ago.

APPENDIX M

Acronyms and Abbreviations

The swiftly expanding science of computer technology presents an important problem to the student and user because of the ever-growing abundance of acronyms and abbreviations. The following lists offer an attempt to aid in identifying the meaning of the various combinations of these alphabetic shortcuts. The industry must and will continue to develop hundreds of new acronyms and abbreviations, and later editions of this text will attempt to list and define the majority of them. There are two lists, computer and communications acronyms and abbreviations, and computer and allied organization acronyms and abbreviations.

COMPUTER AND COMMUNICATIONS ACRONYMS AND ABBREVIATIONS

A—Accumulator, ammeter, ampere, area, angstrom.

ABC—Automatic bandwidth control.

ABM—Automatic batch mixing.

ABO—Advanced byte-oriented.

abs—Absolute.

AC—Automatic computer. Alternating current.

ACA—Adjacent-channel attenuation.

ACD—Automatic call distributor.

ac/dc—Alternating current/direct current.

ACI—Asynchronous communications interface.

ACIA—Asynchronous communications interface adapter.

ACK—Acknowledge.

ACTS—Automatic Computer Telex Service.

ACU—Automatic calling unit.

AD—Average deviation.

ADA—Automatic data acquisitions.

ADC—Analog-to-digital converter. Analog-digital converter.

ADCCP—Advanced data-communications control procedure.

A/D, D/A—Analog-to-digital, digital-to-analog.

ADDAR—Automatic Digital Data Acquisition and Recording.

ADONIS—Automatic Digital On-line Instrumentation System (Blackburn Electronic, England).

ADP—Automatic data processing.

ADPC—Automatic data processing center.

ADPE—Automatic data processing equipment.

ADPS—Automatic data processing system. Automatic display and plotting systems.

ADR—Adder. Analog-to-digit recorder.

ADS—Address data strobe.

ADX—Automatic data exchange.

AF—Audio frequency.

AFC—Automatic frequency control.

AFG—Analog function generator.

AGC—Automatic gain control.

AIG—Address-indicating groups.

ALC—Automatic level control.

ALE—Address latch element.

ALGOL—ALGOrithmic Language.

ALT—Alternate.

ALU—Arithmetic and logic unit.

AM—Amplitude modulation.

A/M—Auto-manual.

AMC—Automatic message counting. Automatic modulation control.

AM-DBS—Amplitude modulation, double-sideband.

AMP, AMPS—Ampere, amperes.

AMR—Automatic message registering.

AM-SSB—Amplitude modulation, single-sideband.

ANACOM—Analog computer.

ANATRON—Analog translator.

ANI—Automatic number identification.

ANSI—American National Standards Institute.

ANT—Antenna.

AO—Amplifier output.

A-O AMPL—AND-OR amplifier.

AOC—Automatic output control.

AOS—Add-or-subtract.

APC—Automatic phase control.

APD—Angular position digitizer.

APL—A program language.

APOTA—Automatic positioning telemetering antenna.

APP—Auxiliary power plant.

APRXLY—Approximately (computer language).

APT—Automatic picture transmission.

APTS—Automatic picture transmission system.

APUHS—Automatic program unit, high-speed.

APULS—Automatic program unit, low-speed.

AQ—Any quantity.
AQL—Acceptable quality level.
ARAM—Analog random access memory.
ARC—Automatic ratio control. Automatic relay calculator. Automatic remote control.
ARL—Acceptable reliability level.
ARM—Automated route management.
ARQ—Automatic request for repetition.
ART—Automatic reporting telephone.
ARU—Audio response unit.
AS—Add-subtract.
ASC—Automatic selectivity control. Automatic synchronized control.
ASCC—Automatic sequence-controlled calculator.
ASCII—American Standard Code for Information Interchange.
ASD—Automatic synchronized discriminator.
ASK—Amplitude shift keying.
ASLIB—Association of Special Libraries and Information Bureaus.
ASLT—Advanced solid logic technology.
ASN—Average sample number.
ASP—Automatic servo plotter. Automatic switching panel.
ASR—Automatic send receive.
ASV—Automatic self-verification.
AT—Automatic ticketing.
A/T—Action time.
ATE—Automatic test equipment.
ATS—Administrative terminal system (IBM). Automatic test system.
AUTOPIC—Automatic personal identification code.
AVD—Alternate voice data.
AVE—Automatic volume expansion.
AVL—Available.
B—Bit.
BA—Binary add.
BAC—Binary asymmetric channel.
BACE—Basic automatic checkout equipment.
BADC—Binary asymmetric dependent channel.
BAP—Band amplitude product.
BAR—Buffer Address Register. Branch.
BASIC—Beginners All-purpose Symbolic Instruction Code.
BBD—Bucket brigade device.
BBM—Break before make.
BC—Binary code. Broadcast control.
BCD—Binary coded decimal.
BCD/B—Binary-coded decimal/binary.
BCDIC—Binary coded decimal information code.
BCD/Q—Binary-coded decimal/quaternary.
BCFSK—Binary code frequency shift keying.
BCI—Binary coded information. Broadcast interference.
BCO—Binary-coded octal.
BCRT—Bright cathode ray tube.
BCW—Buffer control word.
BDC—Binary decimal counter.
BDD—Binary-to-decimal decoder.
BDH—Bearing, distance and heading.
BDU—Basic display unit.
BE—Band elimination.
BEAMOS—Beam accessed MOS.
BER—Binary error rate.
BEX—Broadside exchange.
BFG—Binary frequency generator.
BFO—Beat-frequency oscillator.
BI—Blanking input.
BIDEC—Binary-to-decimal.
BIPCO—Built-in-place components.
BIM—Beginning of information marker.
BISAM—Basic indexed sequential access method.
Bisync—Binary synchronous communications (IBM).
BIT—Binary digit. Bit-oriented protocol. Built-in test.
BITN—Bilateral Iterative Network.
BIVAR—Bivariant function generator.
BIX—Binary information exchange.
BKSP—Backspace.
BL—Blanking.
BLF—Bubble lattice file.
BLK—Block. Block count.
BLNK—Blank.
BLU—Basic logic unit.
BM—Buffer module.
BMEWS—Ballistic Missile Early Warning System.
BN—Binary number system.
BNG—Branch no group.
BO—Beat oscillator.
BOI—Branch output interrupt.
BORAM—Block Oriented Random Access Memory.
BOS—Basic operating system.
BOT—Beginning of tape.
BP—Bandpass.
BPF—Bandpass filter.
BPI—Bits per inch.
BPS—Bits per second.
BPSK—Binary phase-shift keying.
BR—Break request.
BRC—Branch conditional.
BRD—Magnetic tape read binary.
BRIL—Brilliance.
BRM—Binary Rate Multiplier.
BRS—Break request signal.
BRU—Branch unconditional.
BS—British Standard. Binary subtract.
BSAM—Basic sequential access method.
BSC—Basic message switching center.
BSDC—Binary symmetric dependent channel.
BSI—Branch or skip on condition. Branch and store instruction.
BSIC—Binary symmetric independent channel.
BST—Beam-switching tube.
BSY—Busy.
BTAM—Basic terminal access method.
BTDL—Basic-transient diode logic.
BTSP—Bootstrap.
BTST—Busy-tone start lead.
BUF—Buffer.
BUIC—Back-Up Interceptor Control.
BW—Bandwidth.
BWR—Bandwidth ratio.
C—Compute, computer. Capacitance, capacitor. Degrees Celsius (centigrade). Computing. Control.
CA—Cancel.
CAD—Computer Aided Design.

CAD/CAM—Computer-Aided Design/Computer-Aided Manufacturing.
CAI—Computer-aided instruction. Computer-aided design. Current-address register. Computer Analog Input.
CAI/OP—Computer analog input/output.
CAM—Central address memory. Checkout and automatic monitoring. Content addressable memory.
CAMA—Centralized automatic message accounting.
CAMP—Computer-aided mask preparation.
C and C—Command and control.
CARAM—Content addressable random access memory.
CARR—Carriage. Carrier.
CATT—Controlled avalanche transit time.
CATV—Cable television.
CAW—Channel address word.
CBI—Compound batch identification.
CC—Calculator. Connecting circuit. Carriage control. Cross correlation. Central control. Concurrent concession. Closed circuit.
CC&S—Central computer and sequencer.
CCD—Charge-coupled device. Complementary coded decimal.
CCP—Character controlled protocol (also character count protocol).
CCR—Central control room.
CCS—Continuous commercial service.
CCT—Circuit.
CCU—Central control unit. Communications control unit.
CCW—Counterclockwise.
CD—Card. Check digit. Clock driver.
CDC—Code directing character.
CDCE—Central data-conversion equipment.
CDH—Command and data-handling.
CDI—Collector diffused isolation.
CDK—Channel data check.
CDP—Checkout data processor. Communication data processor.
CDT—Control data terminal.
CDU—Central display unit.
CE—Channel end.
CEP—Circular error probability.
CF—Central file. Conversation factor. Count forward.
CFR—Castatrographic failure rate.
CGB—Convert Gray to binary.
CHAL—Challenge.
CHAR—Character.
CHG—Change.
CHK—Check.
CHKPT—Checkpoint.
CHNL—Channel.
CHRG—Charge.
CI—Call indicator. Characteristic independence. Circuit interrupter. Cut in.
C/I—Carrier-to-interference ratio.
CIF—Carriage, insurance and freight. Central index file. Central integration facility.
CIO—Central input/output multiplexer.
CIR—Circuit.
CIT—Call-in-time.
CIU—Computer interface unit.
CK—Check.
CK DIG—Check digit.
CKO—Checking operator.
CKT—Circuit.
cl—Centiliter.
CL—Central line. Class. Conversion loss.
CLA—Communication line adapters.
CLAT—Communication line adapters for teletypewriter.
CLCS—Current logic, current switching.
CLD—Called line.
CLG—Calling line.
CLK—Clock.
CLR—Computer language recorder.
CLT—Communication line terminal. Computer language translator.
CLU—Central logic unit. Circuit lineup.
CM—Centimeter. Communication multiplexer. Control mark. Computer module.
C/M—Communications. Communications multiplexer.
CMC—Communicating mag card. Communications mode control.
CMCT—Communicate.
CMD—Command.
CMF—Cross modulation factor.
CML—Current mode logic.
CMLT—Complete.
CMOS—Complementary Metal Oxide Semiconductor.
CMP—Computational.
CMPLX—Complex.
CMPT—Computer.
CMR—Common mode rejection. Communications moon relay.
CMRR—Command mode rejection ratio.
CMV—Common mode voltage.
C/N—Carrier-to-noise.
CNC—Computerized numerical control.
CNCT—Connect.
CND—Condition.
CNE—Compare numerical equal.
CNL—Circuit net loss.
CNR—Carrier-to-noise power ratio.
CNT—Counter.
CNTRL—Central.
CNU—Compare numeric unequal.
CNVT—Convert.
CO—Changeover. Close-open. Station open to official correspondence exclusively.
COAX—Coaxial. Coaxial cable.
COB—Complementary off-set binary.
COBOL—COmmon Business Oriented Language.
CODASYL—COnference on DAta SYstems Languages.
CODIC—Computer-directed communications.
COED—Computer-operated electronics display.
COGO—Coordinate geometry program (M.I.T.).
COHO—Coherent oscillator.
COL—Computer oriented language.
COLT—Computerized on-line testing.
COM—Computer output microfilm.
COML—Commercial language.
COMM—Communication.
COMMCEN—COMMunications CENter.
COMMSWITCH—Communications failure detecting and switching equipment.
COMMZ—Communications zone.

COMPOOL—Communications pool.
COMSEC—COMmunications SECurity.
CONC—Concentrated.
CO/NO—Current operator-next operator.
CONS—Carrier operated noise suppression. Console.
CONST—Constant.
CONT—Continue. Continuous. Control.
COP—Computer optimization package.
COPE—Communications Oriented Processing Equipment.
COR—Correct.
CORR—Correspondent.
COSMON—Component open/short monitor.
CP—Clock phase. Clock pulse. Control panel. Control point. Computer.
CPC—Card-programmed calculator (IBM Corp.). Ceramic-wafer printed circuit. Computer process control.
CPDD—Command post digital display.
CPE—Central processing element. Central programmer and evaluator.
CPFF—Cost plus fixed fee.
CPI—Characters per inch.
CPIF—Cost plus incentive fee.
CPLD—Coupled.
CPLMT—Complement.
CPM—Cards per minute. Control program monitor. Critical path method.
CPO—Code practice oscillator. Control precision.
CPR—Cam plate readout.
CPS—Central processing system. Characters per second. Cycles per second.
CPTY—Capacity.
CPU—Central processing unit.
CPY—Copy.
CQT—Correct.
CR—Call request. Carriage return. Command register. Control relay. Count reverse.
CRC—Carriage return contact. Control and reporting center. Cyclic redundancy check.
CRF—Carrier-frequency telephone repeater. Control relay forward.
CRMR—Continuous-reading meter relay.
CRO—Cathode-ray oscillograph.
CROM—Control Read-Only Memory.
CRS—Command retrieval system.
CRT—Cathode-ray tube.
CRTOG—Cartography.
CRTU—Combined receiving and transmitting unit.
CRYPTO—Cryptograph, cryptographic.
CRYPTONET—Crypto-communication network.
CS—Channel status. Check sorter. Control set. Control signal. Controlled switch. Cycles shift.
CSB—Complementary straight binary.
CSD—Constant-speed drives.
CSE—Control systems engineering.
CSECT—Control section.
CSL—Computer-sensitive language.
CSO—Chained sequential operation.
CSSB—Compatible single sideband.
CST—Channel status table.
CSW—Channel status word.
CT—Count. Counter. Current transformer.
CTC—Complementary two's complement. Contact. Counter timer circuit.
CTCA—Channel and traffic control agency.
CTL—Complementary transistor logic.
CTL PL—Control panel.
CTM—Communications. Communications-terminal modules.
CTMC—Communications controller. Communications terminal modules.
CT/N—Counter, n stages.
CTP—Central transfer point.
CTS—Clear to send.
CTT—Central trunk terminals.
CTU—Centigrade thermal unit. Central terminal unit.
CU—Control unit.
CUR—Current. Complex utility routine.
CV—Common version. Continuously variable. Converter.
CVSN—Conversion.
CVU—Constant-voltage unit.
CW—Calls waiting. Continuous wave. Clockwise.
CWP—Communicating word processor.
CWT—Hundredweight.
CWV—Continuous-wave video.
CX—Central exchange.
CY—Case copy.
CYBORG—CYBernetic ORGanism.
D—Density. Digit. Digital. Diode. Display. Drum.
DA—Data acquisition. Data available. Decimal add. Differential analyzer. Discrete address.
DAA—Data access arrangement.
DAC—Data acquisition and control system. Digital arithmetic center. Digital-to-analog converter.
DACS—Data acquisition and control system.
DAGC—Delayed automatic gain control.
DAME—Data acquisition and monitoring equipment for computers.
DART—Data analysis recording tape.
DAS—Data acquisition system. Digital attenuator system.
DASD—Direct access storage device.
DATACOM—DATA COMmunications.
DAV—Data valid.
dB, db—Decibel.
DC—Data channel. Data collection. Define constant. Deposited carbon. Dewey decimal classification or decimal classification. Digital comparator. Direct current. Direction center. Directional coupler.
DCB—Define control block.
DCBD—Define control block dummy.
DCCU—Datacommunications control unit.
DCE—Data circuit terminating equipment.
DCI—Data communications interrogate.
DCMT—Decrement. Document.
DCPS—Digitally controlled power source.
DCR—Data conversion receiver. Decrease. Design change recommendation. Digital conversion receiver. Direct conversion reactor.
DCTL—Direct-coupled transistor logic.
DCU—Decade counting unit. Decimal counting unit. Digital counting unit.

DCUTL—Direct-coupled unipolar transistor logic.
DCW—Define constant with wordmark. Data communication write.
DCWV—Direct current working volts.
DD—Decimal divide. Digital display. Double dacron braid lacquered. Double diffused. Drum demand.
DDA—Digital differential analyzer.
DDAS—Digital data acquisition system.
DDC—Data distribution center. Digital data converter. Direct digital control.
DDCE—Digital data conversion equipment.
DDG—Digital display generator.
DD NAME—Data definition name.
DDP—Digital data processor.
DDS—Digital display scope.
DDT—Digital data transmitter. Dynamic debugging technique.
DE—Decision element. Device end. Digital element. Display element.
DEC—Decimal. Direct energy conversion.
decit—Decimal digit.
DECR—Decrement.
DED—Double error detection.
DEFT—Dynamic error-free transmission.
DEL—Delay.
DELETE—Deletion of named file from tape.
DEM—Demodulator.
DE-ME-DRIVE—Decoding memory drive.
DEMOD—Demodulator.
DENS—Density.
DEPSK—Differential-encoded phase shift keying.
DES—Digital expansion system. Differential equation solver.
DETAB—Decision tables.
DETAB-X—Decision tables, experimental.
DEU—Data exchange unit.
DF—Degrees of freedom. Describing function. Direction finder. Dissipation Factor.
D-F—Direct flow.
DFA—Digital fault analysis.
DFC—Disk file check.
DFCU—Disk file control unit.
DFG—Diode function generator. Discrete frequency generator.
DFR—Disk file read.
DFSU—Disk file storage unit.
DFT—Discrete Fourier theorem.
DFW—Disk file write.
DG—Differential generator. Diode gate. Double-groove. Grown diffused.
DGNL—Diagonal.
DGT—Digit.
DHE—Data-handling equipment.
DI—Digital input.
DIC—Data input clerk.
DIGICOM—DIGItal COMmunication system.
DIGRM—Digit/record mark.
DIGRMGM—Digit/record mark group/mark.
DIIC—Dielectrically isolated integrated circuit.
DIOB—Digital input/output buffer.
DIP—Dual inline package.
DIV—Divide/divider.
DL—Dacron braid lacquered. Data link. Delay. Delay line. Diode logic. Disjunctively linear (logical nets). Distributed lab. Dynamic load characteristic. Dielectric loading factor.
DLC—Data link control.
DLCC—Data link control chip.
DLYD—Delayed.
DM—Decimal multiply. Magnetic drum module.
DMA—Direct memory access.
DMC—Digital microcircuit.
DME—Distance-measuring equipment.
DMED—Digital message entry device.
DMM—Digital multimeter.
DMOS—Discrete MOS.
DMSS—Data multiplex subsystem.
DMUX—Demultiplex.
DN—Decimal number system.
DO—Defense order. Digital output.
DOC—Data optimizing computer. Direct operating cost.
DOF—Degree of freedom.
DO/IT—Digital output/input translator.
DOS—Disk operating system.
DP—Data processing. Dial pulsing. Digit present. Driving power. Dynamic programming.
DPC—Data processing center.
DPD—Data processing division.
DPDT—Double-pole double-throw.
DPE—Data processing equipment.
DPG—Data processing group. Digital pattern generator.
DPM—Digital panel meter.
DPMA—Data Processing Management Association.
DPS—Data processing system.
DPSK—Differential phase-shift keying.
DPSS—Data processing subsystem.
DPST—Double-pole, single-throw.
DQM—Data quality monitors.
DR—Data recorder. Digital resolver.
D/R—Direct or reverse.
DRI—Data reduction interpreter.
DRM—Digital radiometers.
DRO—Destructive readout. Digital readout.
DRT—Diode recovery tester.
DRV—Data recovery vehicle.
DS—Decimal subtract. Define symbol. Device selector. Dial system. Data set. Data synchronization.
DSA—Define symbol address.
DSB—Double sideband.
DSE—Data storage equipment.
DSGN—Designation.
DSR—Digit storage delay. Digital stepping recorder.
DSU—Data synchronization unit. Device-switching unit.
DSW—Data status word. Device status word.
DT—Data transmission. Digital technique.
DTE—Data terminal equipment.
DTG—Data time group.
DTL—Diode transistor logic.
DTM—Delay timer multiplier.
DTO—Dollar trade-off (operations research term).
DTP—Directory tape processor.

DTR—Daily transaction reporting. Digital telemetering register.
DTS—Data-transmission system.
DTTU—Data transmission terminal unit.
DUAL—Fixed decimal and floating decimal computing system.
DUP—Duplication.
DVST—Direct-viewing storage tube.
DW—Data word buffer.
DX—Distant station reception. Distance. Duplex. Duplex repeater.
DXC—Data exchange control.
EA—Effective address.
EAL—Electromagnetic amplifying lens.
EAM—Electronic accounting machine.
E and M Leads—Output and input leads, respectively.
EAROM—Electrically Alterable Read-Only Memory.
EAS—Extended area service (telephone term).
EAX—Electronic automatic exchange.
EBCDIC—Expanded binary-coded decimal interchange code.
EBI—Equivalent background input.
EBPA—Electron beam parametric amplifier.
EC—Electronic conductivity. Engineering changes. Error correcting.
ECB—Event control block.
ECC—Electrocardiocorder.
ECD—Electrochromic display.
ECDC—Electrochemical diffused-collector transistor.
ECL—Emitter-coupled logic. Equipment component list.
ECLO—Emitter-coupled logic operator.
ECM—Electronic countermeasures.
ECME—Electronic countermeasures equipment.
ECN—Engineering change notice.
ECO—Electronic "contact" operate.
ECP—Engineering change proposed.
ECTL—Emitter-coupled transistor logic.
ECX—Electronically controlled telephone exchange.
ED—Electrical differential. External device. Existence doubtful. Electronic differential analyzer. Electronic digital analyzer.
EDCW—External-device control word.
EDD—Envelope delay distortion.
EDGE—Electronic data-gathering equipment.
EDHE—Experimental data-handling equipment.
EDI—Electron diffraction instrument.
EDM—Electrical discharge machining. Electrodischarge machine.
EDP—Electronic data processing.
EDPC—Electronic data-processing center.
EDPE—Electronic data-processing equipment.
EDPM—Electronic data-processing machine.
EDPS—Electronic data-processing system.
EDU—Electronic display unit.
EE—External environment (reliability term).
EEI—Essential elements of information.
EEPROM—Electrically Erasable Programmable Read-Only Memory.
EFF—Effective.
EFL—Emiter-follower logic.
EFPH—Equivalent full power hours.
EFT—Electronic funds transfer.
EHF—Extremely high frequency.
EHV—Extra high voltage.
EIS—End interruption sequence.
EIT—Engineer-in-training.
EKG—Electrocardiogram.
EKS—Electrocardiogram simulator.
EKW—Electrical kilowatts.
ELD—Edge-lighted display. Extra-long distance.
ELEM—Element.
ELF—Extremely low frequency.
ELSEC—Electronic security.
ELT—Electrometer.
EM—Electromagnetic. Electromechanical. Electromicroscopic.
EMI—Electromagnetic interference.
EML—Equipment modification list.
EMP—Electromechanical power.
EMR—Executive management responsibility.
EMS—Electronic management system. Electronic medical system.
EMT—Electrical metallic tubing.
ENT—Entry.
EO—Executive order.
EOA—End of address.
EOC—End of conversion.
EOE—Errors and omissions excepted.
EOF—End of file.
EOJ—End of job.
EOL—End of life (reliability term).
EOM—End of message.
EOP—End output.
EOQ—Economic order quantity.
EOS—Electro-optical system.
EOT—End of transmission. End of tape.
EP—End of program. Etched plate. Extreme pressure.
EPBX—Electronic private branch exchange.
EPC—Easy processing channel. Electronic program control.
EPROM—Electrically Programmable Read-Only Memory.
EPU—Electrical power unit.
EQ—Equalizer.
EQP—Equipment.
EQPMT—Equipment.
EQU—Equate.
ERA—Electronic reading automation.
erg—Basic unit of work in cgs system.
EROM—Erasable ROM.
ERR—Error.
ERX—Electronic remote switching.
ES—Electromagnetic storage.
ESG—Electronic sweep generator.
ESI—Externally specified indexing.
ESP—Electrosensitive programming.
ESR—Effective signal radiated. Electronic scanning radar.
ESS—Electronic switching system.
ESSU—Electronic selective switching unit.
EST—Estimate.
e.s.u.—Electrostatic unit.
ETA—Estimated time of arrival.
ETD—Estimated time of departure.
ETIM—Elapsed time.
ETL—Etching by transmitted light.
ev—Electron volt.
EX—Exclusive OR. Execute. Experimental.

EXAM—Examine.
EXCH—Exchange.
EXCLU—Exclusive.
EXCP—Except.
EXD—External device.
EXEC—Execute. Executive.
Exp—Exponential.
EXTND—Extended data transfer.
EXTSN—Extension.
E/Z—Equal zero.
F—Farad. Feedback. Filter. Fixed. Frequency. Degrees Fahrenheit.
FA—Final address register.
FACD—Foreign area customer dialing.
FACE—Field Alterable Control Element.
FAM—Fast access memory.
FAR—Failure analysis report.
FAX—Facsimile.
FBC—Fully buffered channel.
FBR—Fast burst reactor.
FC&A—Frequency control and analysis.
FCC—Federal Communications Commission.
FCCA—Forestry, Conservation, and Communications Association.
FCDR—Failure cause data report.
FCS—Frame check sequence.
FDC—Floppy disk controller.
FDM—Frequency division multiplex.
FE—Field engineers.
FET—Field-effect transistor.
F-F—Flip-flop.
FFP—Firm-fixed price.
F_g—Forward gate.
FG—Function generator.
FI—Field intensity. Fixed interval. Flow indicator.
FIFO—Floating input-floating output.
FIG—Figure.
FLBIN—Floating-point binary.
FLD—Field.
FLDEC—Floating-point decimal.
FLF—Flip-flop.
FLG—Flag.
FM—Feedback mechanism. Ferritemental. Frequency Modulation.
FME—Frequency-measuring equipment.
FMEVA—Floating point means and variance.
FMFB—Frequency modulation with feedback.
FM/PM—Phase Modulated Telemetering System.
FMT—Format.
FOPT—Fiber optic photo transfer.
FORTRAN—FORmula TRANslator (IBM).
FOT—Optimum traffic frequency.
FPLA—Field programmable logic array.
FPM—Feet per minute.
f.p.s.—Feet (or frames) per second.
FPS—Foot-pound-second.
FS—Floating sign.
FSD—Full-scale deflection.
FSK—Frequency-shift keying.
FSR—Feedback shift register.
FTC—Frequency time control.
FTM—Frequency time modulation.
FTS—Federal Telecommunications System.
FUN—Function.
FUR—Failure, unsatisfactory.
FXBIN—Decimal to fixed binary translation.
FY—Fiscal year. (10^9)
GA—General arrangement Go-ahead signals (or cue).
G/A—Ground to air.
GBP—Gain bandwidth product.
GCA—Ground-controlled approach.
GCR—Group code recording.
GCT—Greenwich civil time.
GD—Gate driver. Grown diffused.
GDO—Grid-dip oscillator.
GDS—Graphic data system.
G/G—Ground-to-ground.
GIGO—Garbage In, Garbage Out.
G-Line—Coated wire (dielectric) to transmit microwave energy.
GLOBECOM—Global Communications.
GND, gnd—Ground.
GNIR—Generator.
GOR—General operational requirement.
GPAC—General-purpose analog computer.
GPC—General-purpose computer.
GPDC—General-purpose digital computer.
GPIB—General-purpose interface bus.
GPI/O—General-purpose input/output.
GPSS—General-purpose systems simulator.
GRP—Group.
GSI—Grand scale integration.
GT—Game theory.
H—Halt. Hardware.
HA—Half add. Half adder.
HC—Handling capacity.
HD—High density.
HDDS—High-density data system.
HDG—Heading.
HDLC—High level data link control.
HDR—Header.
HDS—Hundreds.
HEM—Hybrid electromagnet wave.
HF, h.f, h-f, hf—High frequency.
HI—High.
HINIL—High noise immunity logic.
HLD—Hold.
HLSE—High level, single ended.
HLT—Halt.
HMOS—High density or high speed MOS.
HO—High order.
HP—High pass filter.
H/P—High position.
HPF—Highest possible frequency.
HS—Half subtracter. Handset.
HSAC—High-speed analog computer.
HSDA—High-speed data acquisition.
HSM—High speed memory.
HSP—High speed printers.
HSR—High speed reader.
HTL—High threshold logic.
HTTL—High-power transistor-transistor logic.
HV, hv—High voltage.
HVPS—High-voltage power supply.
hy—Henry.
HYCOTRAN—HYbrid COmputer TRANslator.
Hz—Hertz.
I—Indicating. Indicator. Industrial.
I, i—Current.
IA—Indirect addressing. Initial appearance. Instrumentation amplifier.
I & C—Installation and checkout.
IAW—In accordance with.

IC—Input circuit. Instruction counter. Integrated circuit. Interchange center. Internal connection
ICA—International Computer Association.
ICC—International computer center.
ICE—Input-checking equipment.
ICF—Intercommunication flip-flop.
ICL—Incoming line.
IC/T—Integrated computer/telemetry.
ICW—Interrupted continuous wave.
ID—Identification. Identification point. Indicating device. Information distributor. Item description.
IDA—Interconnect device arrangement.
IDCMA—Independent Data Communications Manufacturing Association.
IDENT—Identify.
IDF—Integrated data file.
IDI—Improved data interchange.
IDP—Industrial data processing. Integrated data processing.
IDS—Input data strobe.
IEEE—Institute of Electrical and Electronics Engineers.
if, i-f, IF—Intermediate frequency. Intermediate frequency amplifier. Information collector.
IFN—Information.
IFR—Internal function register.
IFRU—Interference rejection unit.
IHF—Inhibit halt flip-flop.
I^2L—Integrated injection logic.
ILE—Interface latch element.
ILS—Instrument Landing System.
ILSW—Interrupt level status word.
IM—Instrumentation.
IMC—Image motion compensation.
IMD—Immediate.
IN—Input.
INCH—Integrated chopper.
INCLD—Include.
INCR—Increase. Increment.
IND—Indicators.
INFO—Information.
INIT—Initiate.
INQ—Inquire.
INS—International Navigation System.
INSTLN—Installation.
INSTR—Instrument.
INT—Interphone. Interrogate. Interrupt. Interruption. Intersection.
INTCON—INTernational CONnection.
INTCP—Intercept.
INTEC—Interference.
INTEL—Intelligence.
INTG—Integrated.
INTRAFAX—Facsimile system for private use.
INV—Inverter.
IO—Interpretive operation. Input/output.
IOB—Input/output buffer.
IOC—Input/output converter. Input/output controller.
IOCC—Input/output control command. Input/output control center.
IOCS—Input/output control system.
I/OM—Input/output multiplexer.
IOO—Input/output operation.
IOP—Input/output processor.
IOPS—Input/output programming system.
IOR—Input/output register.
IOREQ—Input/output request.
IOT—Input/output transfer.
IOTA—Information overload testing apparatus.
IOU—Immediate operation use.
IP—Cathode-ray tube indication. Identification of position. Identification point. Index of performance. Industrial production. Initial point. Item processing.
IPA—Intermediate power amplifier.
IPB—Illustrated parts breakdown.
IPC—Industrial process control. Information processing center.
IPD—Insertion phase delay.
IPE—Interpret parity error.
IPM—Impulses per minute. Incidental phase modulation.
IPN—Inspection progress notifications.
IPS—Inches per second.
IR—Information retrieval.
I-R—Interrogator-responder.
IRP—Initial receiving point.
IS—Interval signal.
ISA—Interrupt storage area.
ISAM—Indexed-sequential access method. Integrated switching and multiplexing.
IS&D—Integrate sample and dump.
ISI—Internally specified index.
ISL—Integrated Schottky logic.
ISM—Industrial, scientific, and medical equipment.
ISO—Individual system operation.
ISR—Information storage and retrieval.
IT—Input translator. Item transfer.
ITNL—Internal.
ITS—Invitation to send.
IV—Inverter.
IW—Index word.
J—Joule. An imaginary number. An operator to rotate a vector 90° clockwise.
JA—Jump address.
JCL—Job control language.
JCTN—Junction.
JDC—Job description card.
JGN—Junction gate number.
JIS—Japanese industrial standard.
JOC—Joint operations center.
JPW—Job processing word.
J/S—Ratio in dB of total interference power to signal-carrier power at the receiver. Justified.
KB—Keyboard. Kilobytes per second.
KCC—Keyboard common contact.
KCS—1000 characters per second.
KDS—Key display system.
kHz—Kilohertz.
KISS—Keep It Simple, Sir.
KMS—Keysort multiple selectors (telephone term).
KP—Key pulsing.
KPC—Keyboard priority controller.
KPR—Kodak photo resist (for etched circuits).
KSR—Keyboard send/receive.
KTR—Keyboard typing reperforator.
KWIC—Keyword in context.

KY—Keying device.
L—Inductor. Label. Large. Left. Level. Lift. Listening. Load. Looper. Low. Low power.
LA—Link allotter.
LAC—Load accumulator.
LAM—Load accumulator with magnitude.
LAMA—Local Automatic Message Accounting (telephone term).
LARCT—Last radio contact.
LB—Line buffer.
LBL—Label.
LC—Late commitment. Level control. Line connector. Link circuit. Load cell. Logic corporation. Last card.
LCB—Line control block.
LCDTL—Load-compensated diode-transistor logic.
LCL—Local.
LCZR—Localizer.
LD—Linear decision. Logic driver. Long distance.
LDDS—Low-density data system.
LDE—Linear differential equations.
LDRI—Low data rate input.
LDRT—Low data rate input.
LDX—Long distance xerography.
LE—Leading edge.
LEAS—Lower echelon automatic switchboard.
LED—Light-Emitting Diode.
LET—Logical equipment table.
LF—Line feed. Line finder (teletypewriter term). Low frequency.
l/f Noise—Excess noise.
LFQ—Light foot quantizer.
LG—Line generator.
LGN—Line gate number.
LGTH—Length.
LH—Left handed.
L/H—Low-to-high.
LIBR—Library.
LIC—Linear integrated circuit.
LICOF—Land lines communications facilities.
LIFO—Last In, First Out.
LIM—Limit.
LINAC—Linear accelerator.
LISP—List processor.
LL—Loudnes level. Low level.
LLL—Low-level logic.
L/MF—Low and medium frequency.
LMLR—Load memory lockout register.
LMT—Limit.
LO—Local oscillator. Low order.
LOC—Location.
LOCAL—Load on call.
LOG—Logarithm. Logical.
LOGANDS—Logical commands.
LOGRAM—Logical program.
LOS—Loss of signal.
LOT—Linear quantizer.
LP—Linear programming. Low pass. Low pressure.
LPC—Linear power controller.
LPM—Lines per minute.
LPS—Lines per second.
LR—Level recorder. Line relay.
LRD—Long-range data.
LRG—Long range.
LRIM—Long range input monitor.
LRS—Long-range search.
LRU—Least recently used.
LS—Laser system. Level switch.
LSB—Least significant bit.
LSI—Large-scale integration.
LT—Indicating light. Logic theory.
LTTL—Low/power transistor-transistor logic.
LTR—Letter.
LV—Low-voltage.
LVCD—Least voltage coincidence detection.
LWD—Larger word.
LWR—Lower.
LYR—Layer.
M—Magnetic. Magnetron. Medium. Medium power. Mega. Meter. Milli-. Mobile. Monitor. Mutual inductance. 1000.
MA—Memory address.
MACRO—Macroinstruction.
MAD—Multiaperture device.
MADT—A microalloy diffused-base transistor.
MAG—Magnetic. Magnetron.
MAGCARD—Magnetic card.
MANOP—Manual of operation.
MAP—Macro arithmetic processor. Message acceptance pulse.
MAR—Memory-address register.
MARS—Memory-address register storage.
MARTEC—Martin thin-film electronic circuit.
MAT—Microalloy transistor.
MAX—Maximum.
MB—Memory buffer.
M-B—Make-break.
MBB—Make-before-break.
MBR—Memory buffer register.
MBR-E—Memory buffer register, even.
MBR-O—Memory buffer register, odd.
MC—Master control.
MCC—Main communications center. Multicomponent circuits.
MCM—Monte Carlo method.
MCP—Master control program.
MCR—Master control routine.
MCS—Master control system. Multipurpose communications and signaling.
MCU—Microprogram control unit.
MCW—Modulated continuous wave.
MCX—Minimum-cost estimating.
MD—Message data. Motor drive.
M-D—Modulation-demodulation.
MDR—Master-clock generator. Memory-data register. Multichannel data recorder.
MDS—Malfunction detection system. Microprocessor development system. Minimum discernible signal.
MDT—Mean down time.
ME—Mechanical efficiency. Microelectronic. Molecular electronics.
MEM—Memory.
MEMISTOR—Memory resistor storage device.
MER—Minimum energy requirements.
MEW—Microwave Early Warning.
MEX—Military exchange.
MFC—Magnetic-tape field scan. Microfunctional circuit.
MFKP—Multifrequency key pulsing.
MFM—Modified frequency modulation.
MFS—Magnetic tape field search.
MFSK—Multiple frequency-shift keying.

MFT—1000 feet. Polyester tape.
mftl—Milli-foot-lamberts.
MG—Laminated mylar tape and glass braid lacquered.
MHz—Megahertz.
MIC—Microwave integrated circuit.
MICR—Magnetic ink character recognition.
Micro—One millionth.
MIDAC—Michigan digital automatic computer.
MIL—One thousandth of an inch. Military.
MIN MC—Minimum material condition
MIR—Memory-information register.
MIS—Management Information Systems.
MIT—Master instruction tape.
MK—Manual clock. Microphone.
ML—Machine language.
MLA—Microprocessor language assembler.
MLB—Multilayer board.
MLE—Maximum likelihood estimate. Microprocessor language editor.
MLI—Marker light indicator.
MLPWB—Multilayer printed wiring board.
MLR—Memory lockout register. Multiply and round.
MLTY—Military.
MLY—Multiply.
mm—Millimeter.
MM—Main memory. Master monitor. Memory multiplexor or multiplexer.
MMA—Multiple module access.
MMD—Moving map display.
MN—Manual (JIC term).
MNTR—Monitor.
MO—Master oscillator.
MOC—Master operational controller.
MOD—Model. Modulation. Modification.
MOD/DEMOD—Modulator/Demodulator.
MODEM—Modulator-demodulator.
MOE—Measure of effectiveness.
MOL—Machine oriented language.
MON—Monitor.
MONOS—Monitor out of service.
MOPA—Master oscillator-power amplifier.
MOPB—Manually operated plotting board.
MOREPS—Monitor station reports.
MOS—Management operating system. Metal oxide semiconductor.
MP—Maintenance point. Mathematical programming. Mechanical part.
MPG—Microwave pulse generator.
MPL—Multiple.
MPS—Microprocessor system.
MPU—Microprocessing unit.
MPX—Multiplex.
MPY—Multiply.
MQ—Multiplier quotient register.
MR—Map reference. Memory register.
MRG—Medium range.
MRKD—Marked.
MRO—Maintenance, repair and operating.
Ms—Mesa.
MS—Mean square. Memory system.
MSB—Most significant bit.
MSD—Most significant digit.
msec—Millisecond.
MSG—Message.
MSG/WTG—Message waiting.
MSI—Medium scale integration.
MSK—Mask.
MT—Machine translations. Magnetic tape. Mechanical translation (language). Mode transducer. Multiple transfer.
MTAC—Mathematical tables and other aids to computation.
MTBF—Mean time between failures (reliability term).
MTCU—Magnetic tape control unit.
MTL—Merged transistor logic.
MTT—Magnetic tape terminal.
MTTF—Mean-time-to-failure.
MTTR—Mean time to repair.
MTU—Multiplexer and terminal unit.
MU—Machine unit.
MUF—Maximum usable frequency.
MUL—Multiply.
MUX—Multiplex.
MUX-ARO—Multiplex-automatic error correction.
mV—Millivolt.
MV—Mean value. Measured value.
mW—Milliwatt.
MW—Manual word. Megawatt.
MWI—Message-waiting indicator.
Mx—Multiplex.
MXR—Mask index register.
μC—Microcomputer.
μP—Microprocessor.
N—Number of turns. Nano. No. Number of bits.
NA—Not assigned. Numerical aperture.
NB—Narrow band.
NBA—Narrow band allocation.
NBFM—Narrow Band Frequency Modulation.
NC—No connection. Noise criterion. Normally closed.
N/C—Numerical control.
NCP—Network control program (IBM).
ND—No detect.
NDE—Nonlinear differential equations.
NDRO—Nondestructive readout (Burroughs).
NDT—Nondestructive testing.
NEC—National Electrical Code.
NEG—Negative.
NES—Not elsewhere specified.
NEXT—Near end crosstalk loss.
NFB—Negative feedback.
NFQ—Night frequency.
NIB—Noninterference basis.
NIC—Not in contact.
NIL—Nothing.
NIPO—Negative input, positive output.
Nit—In a computer, a choice of equiprobables; one nit equals 1.44 bits.
NLR—Noise load ratio.
NLS—No-load speed.
NM—Not measured.
NME—Noise-measuring equipment.
NMI—Nautical miles.
NMOS—N-channel metal oxide semiconductor.
NMPS—Nautical miles per second.
NMR—Normal mode rejection.
NO—Normally open.
NOHP—Not otherwise herein provided.

NOIBN—Not otherwise indexed by name.
NOP—No operation.
NORAC—No radio contacts.
NORDO—No radio.
NOS—Not otherwise specified.
NP—Net proceeds.
NPEF—New product evaluation form.
NPM—Counts per minute.
NP/1—New program language.
NPS—Counts per second.
NR—Noise ratio. Number.
NRM—Normalize.
NRZ—Nonreturn to zero.
NRZ-C—Nonreturn-to-zero-change.
NRZI—Nonreturn to zero inverted.
NRZ-M—Nonreturn-to-zero-mark.
NS—Not specified.
NSC—Noise suppression circuit.
NSEC—Nanosecond.
NSP—Network service protocol. Nonstandard part approval.
NSV—Nonautomatic self-verification.
NT—No transmission. Numbering transmitter.
NTI—Noise transmission impairment.
NVM—Nonvolatile memory.
NWH—Normal working hours.
O—Noncrossed-field device.
O&C—Operations and checkout.
OC—Occurs. Operating characteristics. Outlet contact.
O/C—Open-circuit.
OCC—Operations control center.
OCO—Open-close-open contact.
OCP—Output control pulses.
OCR—Optical character recognition.
OCT—Octal.
OD—Outside diameter.
ODD—Operator distance dialing.
ODS—Output data strobe.
OF—Operational fixed.
OG—Or gate.
OIC—Officer in charge.
OINC—Officer in charge.
OL—Overlap.
O/L—Operations/logistics.
OLC—Outgoing line circuit.
OLRT—On-line real time.
OM—Operations maintenance.
OOPS—Off-line operating simulator.
OP—Operation.
OPERG—Operating.
OPM—Operator programming method. Operations per minute.
OPN—Open.
OPND—Operand.
OPP—Opposite.
OPT—Optimum.
OPTS—Operations.
OPTUL—Optical pulse transmitter using laser.
OR—Operations research.
O/R—On request.
ORD—Optical rotary dispersion.
ORG—Origin.
ORI—Operational readiness inspection.
OS—Odd symmetric. Operating system.
OT—Overtime.
OTU—Operational training unit.
OVFLO—Overflow.
OVLP—Overlap. Overlay.
p—Pico, prefix for 10^{-12}.
P—Pencil tube. Plug. Portable. Power. Punch.
PA—Power amplifier. Public address. Pulse amplifier.
PABX—Private automatic branch exchange.
PAM—Pulse-amplitude modulation. Frequency modulation of a carrier by means of pulse-amplitude-modulated subcarriers.
PAR—Parameter.
PARA—Paragraph.
PAS—Program address storage.
PATN—Pattern.
PAX—Private automatic exchange.
PB—Peripheral buffer. Phonetically balanced (audio term).
PBI—Process branch indicator.
PBP—Push button panel.
PBX—Private branch exchange.
Pc—Printed circuits.
PC—Petty cash. Photoconductor. Picture. Program counter. Provisional costs. Pulse controller. Punched card.
P-C—Pulse counter. Processor controller.
PCB—Printed circuit board.
PCC—Program-controlled computer.
PCI—Pattern correspondence index (intelligibility measure). Peripheral command indicator.
PCL—Printed-circuit lamp.
PCM—Pulse code modulation.
PCO—Procuring contrast offer.
PCQ—Production control quantometer.
PCR—Program control register.
PCS—Planning control sheet. Punched card system. Program counter store.
PCT—Portable camera-transmitter.
PD—Paid. Per diem. Potential difference. Procurement division. Projected display. Pulse driver. Pulse duration.
PDA—Probability distribution analyzer.
PDC—Parallel data controller.
PDF—Probability density function. Probability distribution function.
PDM—Parallel data controller. Pulse-duration modulation.
PDQ—Programmed data quantizer.
PDR—Preliminary data report.
PE—Phase encoded.
PEC—Photoelectric cell.
PEM—Photoelectromagnetic.
PERCOS—Performance coding system.
PERT—Program Evaluation and Review Technique.
PES—Photoelectric scanning.
PET—Position-event-time. Physical equipment table.
pF—Picofarad.
PF—Page formatter. Power factor.
PFM—Pulse frequency modulation.
pfr—Tape perforator.
PFR—Programmed film reader system. Pulse frequency.
PFT—Paper, flat tape.
PG—Pulse generator.
PGR—Precision graphic recorder.

PHT—Phototube.
PI—Programmed instruction. Performance index.
PIA—Peripheral interface adapter.
PIC—Priority interrupt controller.
PIE—Parallel interface element. Plug-in electronics.
PIN—Personal Identification Number. Police Information Network.
PINO—Positive input-negative output.
PIO—Precision iterative operation.
PIP—Programmable Integrated Processor.
PISW—Process interrupt status word.
Pk—Peak. Pack.
PLA—Programmable logic array.
PLL—Phase-locked loop.
PLM—Pulse length modulation.
PL/1—Programming language No. 1.
PM—Phase modulation. Permanent magnet.
PMD—Post mortem dumps.
PMOS—P-channel metal oxide semiconductor.
POC—Process operator console.
POL—Problem-oriented language.
POLY—Polyethylene.
PORT—Photo-optical recorder tracker.
POS—Point of sale. Positive.
POST—Posting.
PP—Pilot punch.
P-P—Peak-to-peak.
PPI—Plan-position indicator mode. Programmable peripheral interface.
PPM—Pulse position modulation.
pps—Pulse per second.
PPS—Parallel processing system.
PPSN—Present position.
P-pulse—Position pulse.
PR—Print.
PRA—PRint Alphamerically.
PRBS—Pseudorandom binary sequence.
PRD—Paper tape read. Printer dump.
pref—Prefix.
PRES—Pressure.
PRF—Pulse-repetition frequency.
PRI—Primary.
PRL—Periodical requirements.
PRM—Parameter.
PRN—PRint Numerically.
PRO—Print octal.
PROG—Program.
PROGR—Programmer.
PROM—Programmable Read-Only Memory.
PR-1—Print register 1.
PRP—Pseudorandom pulse.
PRR—Pulse-repetition rate.
PRS—Pattern recognition system.
PRT—Printer. Production run tape. Program reference table.
PRTY—Priority.
PRV—Peak reverse voltage.
PRW—Percent rated wattage.
Ps—Spontaneous polarization.
PS—Parity switch. Planning and scheduling. Power supply. Pulse shaper.
P-S—Pressure-sensitive.
P/S—Point of shipment.
PSAR—Programmable synchronous/asynchronous receiver.
PSAT—Programmable synchronous/asynchronous transmitter.
PSE—Please.
psec—Picosecond (10^{-12} second).
PSK—Phase-shift-keyed.
PSR—Processor state register.
PSS—Personal signaling system.
PSW—Program status word.
PT—Page table. Paper tape. Pencil tube. Point location. Positional tolerancing.
P-TAPE—Paper tape.
PTE—Peculiar test equipment.
PTM—Pulse time modulation.
PTP—Point-to-point.
PTT—Program test tape. Push-to-talk.
PU—Pickup.
PUP—Peripheral unit processor.
PUT—Programmable Unijunction Transistor.
PVR—Precision voltage reference.
PW—Pulse width.
PWC—Pulse-width coded.
PWD—Pulse-width discriminator.
PWE—Pulse-width encoder.
PWM—Pulse-width modulation.
Q—Accumulator extension. Merit of a coil or capacitor. Quantity of electricity.
QC—Quantum count.
QDC—Quick dependable communications.
QF—Quality factor.
QMI—Qualification maintainability inspection.
QMQB—Quick-make, quick-break.
QNT—Quantizer.
QQPRI—Qualitative operational requirement.
QR—Quick reaction.
QRA—Quality reliability assurance.
Q signal—Radio communication signals.
QT—Queuing theory.
QUAD—Quadrant.
R—Read. Reset. Reluctance. Reverse. Right. Conversion Ratio.
RA—Rational number.
RAD—Rapid access disk.
RADAR—RAdio Detection And Ranging.
RADAS—Random access discrete address.
RADAT—Radio data transmission system.
RALU—Register Arithmetic Logic Unit.
RAM—Random access memory.
RAMAC—Random access method of accounting and control, TN for a magnetic disk store.
RAN—Read-around numbers.
RAPPI—Random access plan position indicator.
RATT—Radio teletypewriter.
RB—Read backward. Read buffer.
RBDE—Radar bright display equipment.
RBI—Ripple blanking input.
RBO—Ripple blanking output.
RBT—Resistance bulb thermometer.
RC—Ray-control electrode. Read and compute. Reader code. Regional center. Resistance-capacitance.
RCC—Read channel continue. Reader common contact. Remote communications complex.
RCD—Record.
RCE—Rapid circuit etch.

RCF—Recall finder.
RCI—Read channel initialize.
RCO—Remote-control oscillator. Representative calculating operation.
RCR—Reader control relay.
RCS—Rearward communications system.
RC(S)—Remote control (system).
RCV—Receive.
RCVR—Receiver.
RD—Read. Research and development.
RDBL—Readable.
RD CHK—Read Check.
RDF—Radio direction finding (or finder).
RDO—Radio readout.
RDR—Radar.
RDT—Remote data transmitter.
RDT & E—Research, development, test, and evaluation.
RDY—Ready.
RE—Real number. Reset.
RE+—Positive real number.
REC MARK—Record Mark.
RECOMP—Recomplement.
RED—Reducing.
REF—Reference.
Reg—Regulator. Register.
REG—Register.
REL—Rate of energy loss.
REN—Remote enable.
REP—Repeat.
REPERF—Reperforator.
REP-OP—Repetitive Operation.
REQ—Request. Require.
Res—Resistor. Reserve.
RET—Return.
RETN—Retain.
REW—Rewind.
RF—Radio frequency. Read forward. Reserve free.
RFC—Radio-frequency choke.
RFD—Ready for data.
RFP—Request for proposal.
RFQ—Request for quote.
RFR—Reject failure rate.
RG—Range. Register. Reset gate. Reverse gate.
RGE—Range.
RG (N)—Register (N) stages.
RH—Report heading.
RHEO—Rheostat.
RI—Radio influence. Radio interference. Read in. Reliability index.
RIF—Reliability improvement factor.
RIFI—Radio interference field intensity.
RIM—Read in mode.
RJE—Remote job entry.
RL—Relay logic. Return loss.
RLD—Relocation dictionary.
RM—Record mark.
RMC—Rod memory computer.
RMDR—Remainder.
RMI—Radio magnetic indicator.
RMM—Read mostly memory.
RMS—Root-mean-square.
RMSE—Root-mean-square error.
RMV—Remove.
RNG—Radio range.
RNV—Radio noise voltage.
RO—Read only. Read out. Receive only.
ROI—Return on investment.
ROM—Read-Only Memory.
ROMON—Receiving-only monitor.
ROPP—Receive-only page printer.
ROS—Read-only storage.
ROT—Rate of turn.
ROTR—Receiving-only typing reperforator.
ROTR S/P—Receiving-only typing reperforator —series to parallel.
RP—Reception poor. Recommended practice. Record processor. Repeater.
RPC—Remote position control.
RPG—Report program generator.
RPL—Running program language.
RPM—Revolutions per minute.
RPMI—Revolutions-per-minute indicator.
RPN—Reverse Polish notation.
RPQ—Request for price quotation.
RPRT—Report.
RPS—Revolutions per second.
RPT—Repeat.
RR—Repetition rate or recurrence rate. Running reverse.
RS—Recommended standard. Record separator character. Remote station. Reset key.
RSA—Remote station alarm.
RS&I—Rules, standards, and instructions.
RSR—Restore.
RSS—Range safety system.
RST—Readability, strength, tone.
RSV—Reserve.
RT—Ratio transformer unit. Research and technology.
RTA—Reliability test assembly.
RTC—Reader tape contact.
RTE—Real time executive. Route.
RTF—Radiotelephone.
RTL—Resistor-transistor logic.
RTP—Remote transfer point.
RTTY—Radio teletypewriter communications.
RTU—Remote terminal unit.
RUSDIC—Russian dictionary.
R/W—Read/write.
RWC—Read, write, and compare. Read (write) continue.
RWI—Read (write) initialize.
RX—Receiver.
RY—Relay.
RZ—Return-to-zero.
S—Secret. Spool. Small. Switch. Solid.
SA—Successive approximation.
SAB—System advisory board.
SABE—Society for Automation in Business Education.
SAC—Store and clear accumulator.
SACO—Select address and contract operate.
SAD—Serial analog delay.
SAID—Speech autoinstruction device.
SBT—Surface barrier transistor.
SC—Sine-cosine. Stop-continue register. Supervisory control. Shift control counter.
S/C—Short circuit.
SCA—Selectivity clear accumulator.
SCC—Storage connecting circuit (teletypewriter term).
SCD—Screwed.
SCDSB—Suppressed carrier double sideband.
SCE—Single cycle execute.

SCHDL—Schedule.
SCHDLR—Scheduler.
SCI—Scale.
SCL—Static complementary logic.
SCN—Scan.
SCR—Scanning control register.
SCS—Single channel simplex.
SCT—Subroutine call table.
SCTL—Short circuited transmission line.
SD—Sample delay.
SDA—Source-data automation. Share distribution agency.
SDC—Signal data converter.
SDI—Source data information.
SDLC—Synchronous data-link control.
SDS—Share data set.
SDV—Slowed-down video.
SE—Set.
SEC—Second. Single error correction.
SECO—SEquential COntrol.
SECT—Section.
SEG—Segment.
SEL—Select.
SEN—Sense.
SEQ—Sequence.
SF—Safety factor. Shift forward.
S/F—Store-and-forward.
SG—Scanning gate. Symbol generator display. Set gate. Symbol generator. Screen grid.
SGL—Signal.
SGN—Scan gate number.
SHF, s.h.f., shf—Superhigh frequency.
SI—Sample interval. Screen-grid input.
S/I—Signal-to-intermodulation ratio.
SIC—Semiconductor integrated circuits.
SIE—Single instruction execute.
SIG—Signal. Significant.
SIL—Speech interference level.
SIM—Simulated approach.
SIMEON—Simplified control.
SIO—Start input/output.
SIP—Short irregular pulses.
SIT-REP—Situation report.
SKED—Schedule.
SKL—Skip lister.
SKP—Skip line printer.
SLC—Shift left and count instructions. Straight-line capacity.
SLD—Solid.
SLF—Symmetric filter.
SLG—Selecting.
SLI—Suppress length indication.
SLN—Selection.
SLR—Storage limits register.
SLRAP—Standard low frequency range approach.
SLRN—Select read numerically.
SLT—Select. Solid logical technology.
SM—Storage mark.
SML—Symbolic machine language.
SMP—Sampler.
SMX—Submuliplexer unit.
SN—Sign.
S/N—Signal-to-noise.
SNA—Systems network architecture.
SNI—Sequence-number indicator.
SNO—Serial number.
SNOBOL—StriNg-Oriented symBOLic language.
SNR—Signal-to-noise ratio.
S/O—Send only.
SOA—State of the art (reliability term).
SOC—Set overrides clear.
S/OFF—Sign off.
SOLN—Solution.
SOM—Start of message.
S/ON—Sign on.
SOP—Standard operating procedure.
SOS—Silicon on sapphire.
SP—Shift pulses. Square punch.
S-P—Systems and procedures.
SPCL—Special.
SPE—Stored program element.
SPEC—Specification.
SP/GR—Specific gravity.
SPKR—Speaker.
SPL—Sound-pressure level.
SPS—Symbolic programming system.
SQC—Statistical quality control.
SQT—Square rooter.
SR—Shift register. Shift reverse. Sorter-reader. Speed regulator. Study requirement.
S/R—Subroutine.
SRC—Source.
SRCH—Search.
SRQ—Service request.
SS—Solid state. Signal selector. Statistical standards.
SSB—Single sideband.
SSDA—Synchronous serial data adapter.
SSI—Small scale integration.
SSL—Shift and select.
SSOU1—System output unit 1. (Remote computing system, IBM).
ST—Segment table. Standard time. Start. Store.
STC—Standard transmission code.
STD—Standard.
STE—System timing element.
STG—Starting. Storage.
STGE—Storage.
STM—Statement.
STMGR—Station manager.
STN—Station.
STOR—Store.
STR—Store.
STS—Static test stand.
SUB—Subtract. Substitute.
SUP—Suppressor.
SURGE—Sorting, Updating, Report GEnerating.
SVC—Service.
SW, sw—Short wave.
SWD—Smaller word.
SWR—Standing wave ratio.
SWS—Shiftword, substituting.
SXN—Section.
SY—Synchronized.
SYM—Symmetrical. System.
SYNC—Synchronize.
SYS—System.
SYSLIB—SYStem LIBrary.
SYSOUT—SYStem OUTput.
SZ—Size.
t—Time.

T—Temperature. Prefix tera (10^{12}).
Tab—Tabulate in computer.
TAB—Tabulate switch.
TAC—Transistorized automatic control.
T&D—Transmission and distribution.
TAS—Telephone answering service. Terminal address selector.
TASC—Terminal area sequence and control.
TC—Time to computation. Toll center. Toll completing. Transistorized carrier. Teracycle. Transmission controller.
TCC—Television control center. Traffic control center.
TCE—Total composite error.
TCM—Terminal-to-computer multiplexer.
TCO—Trunk cutoff.
TC1—True/complement 1.
TCW—Time code word.
TCWG—Telecommunications working group.
TD—Time delay. Transmitter distributor. Tunnel diode.
TDDL—Time-division data link.
TDF—Two degrees of freedom.
TDM—Time-division-multiplex.
TDP—Traffic data processor. Teledata processing.
TDS—Time-division switching. Transistor display and data handling system.
TDTL—Tunnel diode transistor logic.
TE—Transverse electric.
TELCO—Telephone company.
TELEX—Automatic teletypewriter exchange service.
TELRY—Telegraph reply.
Tfr—Transfer.
TFT—Thin-film technology. Thin-film transistor.
TFZ—Transfer zone.
TL—Time limit. Transmission level. Transmission line.
TLFO—Telephone.
TLR—Toll line release.
TLZ—Transfer on less than zero.
TM—Magnetic tape module. Technical manual. Telemetering. Traffic manager. Transverse magnetic.
T-M—Time and materials.
TMP—Temperature.
TMPRLY—Temporarily.
TMT—Transmit.
TNF—Transfer on no overflow.
TNX—Thanks.
TNZ—Transfer on nonzero.
TOC—Television operating center.
TOD—Technical objective documents.
TODS—Test oriented disk system.
TOE—Total operating expense.
TOPTS—Test oriented paper tape system.
TOS—Tape Operating System.
Tot—Total.
TPM—Tape preventive maintenance.
TPR—Telescopic photograph recorder.
TPS—Terminals per station.
TR—Transmit & receiving. Transmitter.
Trab—Transcribe. Transcriber.
TRF—Tuned radio frequency.
TRL—Transistor resistor logic.
TRML—Terminal.
TRN—Transfer.
Trnt—Transient.
TRP—Tv remote pickup.
TRR—Teaching and research reactor.
Trsl—Translate.
Trsn—Transaction.
Trsp—Transport.
Trst—Transit.
TRU—Transmit-receive unit.
TSAC—Title, subtitle, and caption.
TSF—10-statement FORTRAN.
TSL—Three-state logic.
TSMT—Transmit.
TSS—Time-sharing system.
Tst—Test.
TT—Teletypewriter.
TTL—Transistor-transistor logic.
TTMS—Telephoto transmission measuring set.
TTS—Teletypesetter.
TTY—Teletypewriter equipment or terminal.
TU—Tape unit. Timing unit. Transmission unit.
TVI—Television interference.
Tw—Typewriter.
TWAIT—Terminal wait.
TWX—Teletypewriter exchange service. Telegraph.
TX—Time to equipment reset. Transmitter.
Typ—Typewriter.
TYPOUT—Typewriter output routine.
U—Temporary Accumulator. Unit. Unclassified. Up.
UART—Universal Asynchronous Receiver Transmitter.
UBC—Universal buffer-controller.
UC—Upper case.
UCC—Universal classification system.
UCK—Unit check.
UCL—Upper confidence level.
UDC—Universal decimal classification.
UEX—Unit exception.
UFN—Until further notice.
uhf—Ultrahigh frequency.
UL—Underwriters Laboratories Inc.
ulf—Ultralow frequency.
UOV—Units of variance.
UPC—Universal product code.
Upd—Update.
UPS—Uninterrupted power supply.
URCLK—Universal receiver clock.
URS—Uniform reporting system.
USASCII—USA Standard Code for Information Interchange.
Util—Utility.
VA—Value. Value analysis. Video amplifier. Volt amperes.
VAB—Voice answer back.
VAC—Victor analog computer. Video amplifier chain.
VAM—Virtual access method.
VAR—Variable. VHF visual aural range.
VC—Video correlator. Voltage comparator.
VCD—Variable-capacitance diode.
VCR—Video cassette recorder.
VDG—Video display generator.
Vdt—Validate.
VDT—Video display terminal.
VER—Versions. Verify.

VERA—Versatile reactor assembly. Vision electronic recording apparatus.
VF—Voice frequency. Video frequency.
VFO—Variable frequency oscillator.
VFT—Voice-frequency carrier telegraph terminal.
VGA—Variable-gain amplifier.
VGH—Velocity.
vhf—very high frequency.
VHO—Very high output.
VHP—Very high performance.
VHSIC—Very high-speed integrated circuit.
VIAS—Voice interference analysis set.
Vid—Video.
VIDAT—Visual data acquisition.
VIG—Video integrating group.
VILP—Victor impedance locus plotter.
VIPS—Voice interruption priority system.
VIS—Visual instrumentation subsystem.
VLCS—Voltage-logic, current-switching.
vlf—Very low frequency.
VLVS—Voltage-logic, voltage-switching.
VO—Verbal orders.
VOC—Variable output circuit.
VODACOM—Voice data communications.
VODER—Voice operation demonstrator.
VOH—Verification off hook.
VOL—Volume.
VOS—Voice operated switch.
VOX—Voice operated control. Voice operated regulator.
VR—Voltage regulator.
VRAM—Video random access memory.
VRC—Vertical redundancy check. Visible record computer.
VRC/LRC—Vertical/longitudinal redundancy check.
VRR—Visual radio range.
VSAM—Virtual sequential access method.
VSCF—Variable-speed constant frequency.
VSWR—Voltage standing-wave ratio.
VTAM—Vortex telecommunication method.
VTR—Video tape recorder.
VU—Volume unit.
V-V—Velocity volume.
VXO—Variable crystal oscillator.
WAC—Write address counter.
WADS—Wide-area data service.
WATS—Wide-area telephone service.
WC—Write and compute.
WCF—White cathode follower.
WCR—Word control register.
WCS—Writable control store.
Wd—Word.
WE—Write enable.
WF—Write forward.
WIP—Work in progress.
WL—Wavelength.
WM—Word mark.
WO—Write out.
WP—Word processing.
WP/AS—Word processing/administrative support.
WPM—Words per minute.
WP/OS—Word processing/office system.
WR CHK—Write check.
WS—Working storage.
WTS—Word terminal synchronous.
WUX—Western Union telegram.
X—Symbol for transistor on drawing. Crystal cut. Horizontal deflection on crt.
XA—Transmission adapter.
Xcd—Exceed.
Xch—Exchange.
Xcl—Exclusive.
XIC—Transmission interface converter.
XIO—Execute input/output.
XMT—Transmit.
XMTR—Transmitter.
X-off—Transmitter off.
X-on—Transmitter on.
XPN—External priority number.
XREP—Auxiliary report.
XS—Extra strong.
XTAL—Crystal.
Y—Vertical deflection on crt.
YR—Year.
ZA—Zero and add.
ZD—Zero defect.
ZFB—Signals fading badly.
ZIF—Zero insertion force.
ZOE—Zero-energy.

COMPUTER AND ALLIED ORGANIZATION ABBREVIATIONS AND ACRONYMS

AAAS—American Association for the Advancement of Science.
ABA—American Bankers Association.
ACA—American Communications Association.
ACM—Association for Computing Machinery.
ACS—American Chemical Society.
ADAPSO—Association of Data Processing Service Organizations.
ADI—American Documentation Institute.
AEC—Atomic Energy Commission.
AED—Association of Electronics Distributors.
AEDS—Association for Educational Data Processing.
AEDS—Association for Electronic Data Systems.
AEEP—State Highway Departments IBM computer users group.
AEPEM—Association of Electronic Parts and Equipment Manufacturers.
AF—Air Force.
AFA—Air Force Association.
AFAFC—Air Force Accounting and Finance Center.
AFA-SEF—Air Force Association-Space Education Foundation.
AFB—Air Force Base.
AFCAL—Association Francaise de Calcul.
AFCALTIC—French Association for Computation and Data Processing.
AFCMO—Air Force Office of Scientific Research.
AFIPS—American Federation of Information Processing Societies.
AFNOR—French Standard Association.
AFOSR—Air Force Office of Scientific Research.
AFRA—French Association of Automatic Control.
AFRD—Air Force Research Division.

AFSCC—Air Force Special Communications Center.
AFTAC—Air Force Technical Application Center.
AIA—Aerospace Industrial Association.
AIAA—American Institute of Aeronautics and Astronautics.
AIB—American Institute of Banking.
AICE—American Institute of Consulting Engineers.
AIChE—American Institute of Chemical Engineers.
AICPA—American Association of Certified Public Accountants.
AIIE—American Institute of Industrial Engineers.
AIME—American Institute of Mechanical Engineers.
AIP—American Institute of Physics.
AIPE—American Institute of Plant Engineers.
ALA—American Library Association.
AMA—American Management Association. American Medical Association.
AMFIS—American Microfilm Information Society.
AMOS—Automatic Meteorological Observation Station.
AMS—Administrative Management Society.
APICS—American Production and Inventory Control Society.
ARMA—American Records Management Association.
ARPA—Advanced Research Project Agency (of Dept. of Defense).
ASA—American Standards Association (now ANSI).
ASCE—American Society of Civil Engineers.
ASEE—American Society for Engineering Education.
ASLIB—Association of Special Libraries and Information Bureau.
ASME—American Society of Mechanical Engineers.
ASQC—American Society for Quality Control.
AST—Army Satellite Tracking Center.
ASTIA—Armed Services Technical Information Agency.
BACE—British Association of Consulting Engineers.
BBC—British Broadcasting Corporation.
BC—Burroughs Corporation.
BCAC—British Conference on Automation and Computation.
BCS—British Computer Society.
BEAMA—British Electrical and Allied Manufacturers.
BEC—British Engineers Club.
BIEE—British Institute of Electrical Engineers.
BIMCAM—British Industrial Measuring and Control Apparatus Manufacturer's Association.
BIO—Biological Information-Processing Organization.
BIRE—British Institute of Radio Engineers.
BLS—Bureau of Labor Statistics.
BMI—Batelle Memorial Institute.
BOB—Bureau of Budget.
BPO—British Post Office.
BRC—Bunker Ramo Corporation.
BSI—British Standards Institution.
BTAP—Bond Trade Analysis Program (IBM).
BUR—Bureau.
CAA—Civil Aeronautics Administration.
CAB—Civil Aeronautics Board.
CAI—Computer Applications Inc.
CAP—Council on Advanced Programming.
CBEMA—Computer and Business Equipment Manufacturers Association.
CCC—Computer Control Company.
CCITT—International Telegraph and Telephone Consultative Committee.
CCNT—Chief Controller.
CDC—Control Data Corp.
CEAC—Consulting Engineers Association of California.
CEIR—Corporation for Economic Industrial Research.
CIA—Central Intelligence Agency.
CIGRE—Conference International Grand.
CITE—Council of Institute of Telecommunication Engineers.
CITEL—Inter-American Telecommunications Commission.
CLR—Council on Library Resources.
CNET—Central National d'Etudes Telecommunications.
CODASYL—Conference on Data Systems Languages.
COLRAD—COLlege on Research And Development.
COSHTI—Council for Science and Technological Information.
COSOS—Conference on Self-Operating Systems.
CPEQ—Corporation of Professional Engineers of Quebec.
CRSG—Classification Research Study Group.
CSA—Canadian Standards Association.
CSEA—California State Electronics Association.
CSIRO—Commonwealth Scientific and Industrial Research Organization.
CTUNA—Commercial Telegraphers Union.
CWA—Communications Workers of America.
DAF—Department of the Air Force.
DASP—Director of Advanced Systems Planning.
DATDC—Data Analysis and Technique Development Center.
DCA—Digital Computers Association.
DCAS—Data Collection and Analysis System.
DCMA—Defense Contract Management Association.
DDC—Defense Documentation Center for Scientific and Technical Information.
DEC—Digital Equipment Corporation.
DECUS—Digital Equipment Computer Users Society.
DOC—Department of Commerce.
DPMA—Data Processing Management Association.
DSIR—Department of Scientific Industrial Research.
DSM—Direction of Systems Management.
DSMG—Designated Systems Management Group.

DTSC—Data Transmission Study Group.
DUO—Datatron Users Organization.
EAA—Engineer and Architecture Association.
EAG—Equipment Advisory Group.
EAI—Electronic Associated Inc.
EBU—European Broadcasting Union.
EC—Engineering Corps.
ECMA—European Computer Manufacturers Association.
ECO—Electronic Central Office.
EDPS—Electronic Distributor Parts Show.
EDRI—Electronic Distributors' Research Institute.
EEA—Electronic Engineering Association.
EIA—Electronic Industries Association.
EJC—Engineer's Joint Council.
EJCC—Eastern Joint Computer Conference.
EMR—Electromechanical Research Inc.
EMSA—Electron Microscope Society of America.
EP & EM—Association of Electric Parts and Equipment.
EPMA—Electronic Parts Manufacturers Association.
ERA—Electronic Reading Automation.
ES—Electrochemical Society.
ESA—Engineers and Scientists of America.
ESMA—Electronic Sales and Marketing Association.
FAA—Federal Aviation Agency.
FADAC—Field Artillery Digital Automatic Computer.
FCC—Federal Communications Commission.
FID—Federation International de Documentation.
FIDIC—International Federation of Consulting Engineers.
GAMM—German Association for Applied Mathematics and Mechanics.
GCMA—Government Contact Management Association of America, Inc.
GE—General Electric Company.
GPO—Government Printing Office.
GSA—General Services Administration.
H—Honeywell.
IAEA—International Atomic Energy Agency.
IAOR—International Abstracts in Operations Research.
IAS—Institute for Advanced Study.
IASA—Insurance Accounting and Statistical Association.
IBM—International Business Machines Corporation.
ICA—Industrial Communication Association.
ICIP—International Conference on Information Processing.
ICT—Institute of Computer Technology.
IECES—Institute of Electronic Communications Engineers of Japan.
IEE—Institution of Electrical Engineers (Britain).
IEEE—Institute of Electrical and Electronics Engineers, Inc.
IEL—International Electrotechnical Commission.
IFIPS—International Federation of Information Processing Societies.
IFORS—International Federation of Operational Research Societies.
ILLIAC—University of Illinois automatic computer.
IMI—International Marketing Institute.
IMS—Industrial Management Society.
INFORS—International Federation of Engineers.
IPRO—International Patent Research Office.
ISA—Instrument Society of America.
ISO—International Organization for Standardization.
ISO—International Science Organization.
ISP—Italian Society of Physics.
ITE—Institute of Telecommunication Engineers.
ITU—International Telecommunication Union.
JEIDA—Japan Electronics.
JEPIA—Japan Electronic Parts Industry Association.
JIAC—Joint Automatic Control Conference. The conference includes ISA, IEEE, AICLE, and AIAA.
JUG—Joint Users Group.
LACES—Los Angeles Council for Engineering Societies.
LAEC—Los Angeles Electronic Club.
LASL—Los Alamos Scientific Laboratory.
LC—Library of Congress.
LC—Logic Corporation.
LINC—Larc Users Corporation.
LOMA—Life Office Management Association.
LRL—Lawrence Radiation Facility.
MAECON—Mid-America Electronics Convention.
MAI—Management Assistance Inc.
MCUG—Military Computer Users Group.
MESUCORA—Association for Measurement, Control, Regulation, and Automation.
MIT—Massachusetts Institute of Technology.
MMM—Minnesota Mining and Manufacturing Co.
NAA—National Association of Accountants.
NAB—National Association of Broadcasters.
NABAC—The National Association for Bank Audit, Control, and Operation.
NABET—National Association of Broadcast Employees and Technicians.
NABUG—National Association of Broadcast Unions and Guilds.
NACC—National Automatic Controls Conference.
NADC—Naval Air Development Center.
NAECON—National Aerospace Electrical Convention.
NAED—National Association of Electrical Distributors.
NAL—National Agricultural Library.
NAM—National Association of Manufacturers.
NAPA—National Association of Purchasing Agents.
NARDA—National Appliance and Radio TV Dealers Association.
NARM—National Association of Relay Manufacturers.
NARTB—National Association of Radio and TV Broadcasters.

NAS—National Academy of Science.
NASA—National Aeronautics and Space Administration.
NAS-NRC—National Association of Sciences—National Research Council.
NASPA—National Society of Public Accountants.
NATESA—National Alliance of TV and Electronic Service Associations.
NATO—North Atlantic Treaty Organization.
NAVA—National Audio-Visual Association.
NAW—National Association of Wholesalers.
NBS—National Bureau of Standards.
NCR—National Cash Register Co.
NEDA—National Electronics Distributors Association.
NEFO—National Electronics Facilities Organization.
NEIDG—National Electronics Industries Procurement.
NEL—United States Naval Electronics Laboratory.
NEMA—National Electrical Manufacturers Organization.
NEP/CON—National Electronic Packing and Production Conference.
NESC—National Electrical Safety Code.
NFSAIS—National Federation of Science Abstracting and Indexing Services.
NFTW—National Federation of Telephone Workers.
NG—National Guard.
NIC—National Invention Council.
NICB—National Industrial Conference Board.
NIH—National Institute of Health.
NJCC—National Joint Computers Committee.
NLM—National Library of Medicine.
NLRB—National Labor Relations Board.
NMA—National Management Association.
NMA—National Microfilm Association.
NMAA—National Machine Accountants Association.
NME—National Military Establishment.
NMTBA—National Machine Tool Builders Association.
NOMA—National Office Management Association.
NOPA—National Office Products Association.
NORC—Naval Ordnance Research Computer.
NRC—National Research Council.
NRMA—National Retail Merchants Association.
NSF—National Science Foundation.
NSPE—National Society of Professional Engineers.
NTOMA—National Tool and Die Manufacturers.
OABETA—Office Appliance and Business Equipment Trades Association.
OAO—Orbiting Astronomical Observatory.
OARAC—Office of Air Research Automatic Computer.
OCRD—Office of Chief of Research and Development.
OEA—Office Executives Association.
OEMI—Office Equipment Manufacturer's Institute.
OEPS—Office of Educational Programs and Services.
OMAT—Office of Manpower and Automation Training (Dept. of Labor).
ONR—Office of Naval Research.
OPPE—Office of Programming, Planning, and Evaluation.
ORSA—Operations Research Society of America.
OSD—Office of the Secretary of Defense.
OSIS—Office of Scientific Information Service.
OSRD—Office of Scientific Research and Development.
OSRMD—Office of Scientific Research, Mechanics Division.
OSS—Office of Space Sciences.
OST—Office of Science and Technology.
OTS—Office of Technical Services (U. S. Dept. of Commerce).
PARTEI—Purchasing Agents of the Radio, TV, and Electronics Industries.
PC—Philco Corporation.
PERC—Peace on Earth Research Center.
PETS—Pacific Electronic Trade Show.
PGAC—Professional Group—Automatic Control.
PGBTS—Professional Group—Broadcast Transmission Systems.
PGCS—Professional Group—Communications Systems.
PGCT—Professional Group—Circuit Theory.
PGE—Professional Group—Education.
PGEC—Professional Group—Electronic Computers.
PGED—Professional Group—Electronic Devices.
PGEM—Professional Group—Engineering Management.
PGHFE—Professional Group—Human Factors in Electronics.
PGI—Professional Group—Instrumentation.
PGIE—Professional Group—Industrial Electronics.
PGIT—Professional Group—Information Theory.
PGME—Professional Group—Medical Electronics.
PGMITT—Professional Group—Microwave Theory and Techniques.
POOL—User organization—General precision computers.
QMC—Quartermaster Corps.
RAF—Royal Air Force.
RCA—Radio Corporation of America.
RCEEA—Radio Communications and Electric Engineering Association.
RE—Royal Engineers.
RECMF—Radio and Electronic Component Manufacturer's Federation.
RESA—Scientific Research Society of America.
RIE—Royal Institute of Engineers.
RIND—Research Institute of National Defense.
RSAF—Royal Swedish Air Force.
RUG—Recomp Users Group.
SABE—Society of Automation in Business Education.
SAM—Society for Advancement of Management.

SAMA—Scientific Apparatus Makers Association.

SCCPT—ACM Subcommittee on Program Terminology.

SCM—Smith Corona Marchant Co.

SD—Superintendent of Documents.

SDC—Systems Development Corp.

SDS—Scientific Data Systems Inc.

SEADAC—Seakeeping Data Analysis Center.

SECAIR—Secretary of the Air Force.

SENN—Societa Elettronucleare Nazionale (Italy).

SFE—Societe Francais des Electriciens.

SHARE—Computer Users Group.

SIAM—Society for Industrial and Applied Mathematics.

SICA—Society of Industrial and Cost Accountants of Canada.

SIMA—Scientific Instrument Manufacturers Association of Great Britain.

SIMAJ—Scientific Instrument Manufacturers Association of Japan.

SLA—Special Libraries Association.

SMC—Scientific Manpower Commission.

SMPTA—Society of Motion Picture and TV Engineers.

SORC—Systems Objectives and Requirements Committee (IBM Users Group).

SPAA—Systems and Procedures Association of America.

SWAP—CDC Users Group.

SWE—Society for Women Engineers.

TCMA—Tabulating Card Manufacturers Association.

TESA—Television and Electronic Service Association.

TIMS—The Institute for Management Sciences.

TSCC—Telemetry Standards Coordination Committee.

TUG—Philco 200 Users Group.

UERMWA—United Electrical-Radio Machine Workers of America.

UEW—United Electrical Workers.

UNIVAC—Trademark of Sperry Rand Corp. for designating 175 computers.

UPADI—Union Panamericana de Asociaciones de Ingenieros (Federation of Pan-American Engineering Societies).

USAEC—United States Atomic Energy Commission.

USCG—United States Coast Guard.

USCMI—United States Commission on Mathematical Instruction.

USDC—United States Department of Commerce.

USDD—United States Department of Defense.

USE—UNIVAC Scientific Exchange.

USN—United States Navy.

UUA—UNIVAC Users Association.

VCC—Visual Communications Congress.

VINITI—Soviet All-Union Institute of Scientific and Technical Information (Moscow, USSR).

VOA—Voice of America.

WACM—Western Association of Circuit Manufacturers.

WCATT—Worcester County Association of Television Technicians.

WDPC—Western Data Processing Center.

WESCON—Western Electronics Show and Convention.

APPENDIX N

The Progress, Impact, and Future of Computers

In the second edition of this book, written in 1972, the appendix with the same title as this one noted many areas of progress, and great promise and almost certain "extremely rapid" progress were forecast. "Microelectronics" had then not quite attained respectability as a dominant "edge of technology," and the microprocessor chip had only recently been invented. We will reprint the first paragraph of that appendix here and then ask, "What happened?"

> The unusually rapid progress in the early 1960s of improved man-computer cognizance and workability has resulted in a revolutionary combination. Man has foresight, judgment, and pattern-recognition capability. The computer has lightning speed, massive memories (now associative), and stored programs which are becoming more and more "adaptive." The future applications of this man-machine combination are astounding and beyond present prediction. The reader might recall just a few of the concepts which should now produce "whirls of wonder" in his mind as: CAI (Computer Assisted Instruction); CAD (Computer Aided Design); MAC (Machine Aided Cognition); IDP (Integrated Data Processing); MIS (Management Information Systems); N/C (Numerical Control); and scores and scores of others. The current impact of these innovations in the 1970s and the long range implications can only be pure but interesting speculations. It should be clear and distinct, however, that our present methods of engineering, data control, information retrieval, manufacturing, process control, education, medicine, and many other disciplines and areas of human endeavor will be quite thoroughly advanced to new frontiers. The world of "bookless" bookkeeping, automatic laboratories, "workerless" factories, automated trains and ships, etc., will be common indeed, and well before the turn of the century.

Why didn't we have a sudden spurt in "paperless offices" and "workerless factories"? What happened to the expected steady and sure progress in computer aided instruction? The answer can, at least in the main, be expressed in one word or concept, "economics." Of course, other factors enter—the "prechip" machines were expensive, complex, cumbersome, and difficult to control. But, most of all, medium-sized and small businesses and educational and other institutions could not afford the equipment, the software, and the expensive programmers and analysts to prove the merit of these systems. However, the embryo of the microprocessor would grow to change all of this. The "chip" computer has become extremely inexpensive; the memory it requires both internally and externally is at least equally low in cost. The new personal-computer industry has taken a totally different tack in meeting the needs of its customers. The new computers are tiny, cheap, portable, simple to operate, modular, easily expanded, reliable, and "fun" to operate and control. Software and peripherals are abundant and cheap.

THE MAGIC "CHIP COMPUTER"—WHERE IT'S BEEN AND WHERE IT'S GOING

The "chip computer" started as a design for a calculator system, but it offered far more power than that. The 4-bit chip, the Intel 4004, had a bigger brother very soon, the 8-bit 8008. This was followed by a faster, more capable offspring, the Intel 8080. A dozen or more competitors entered the race with all ranges of microprocessor chips from Motorola, National Semiconductor, Texas Instruments Inc.—and the list is still growing. Now the Intel 8086 is out, with power similar to medium-sized minicomputers. The Motorola 6800, like the 8086, is a 16-bit chip, and it competes with the Zilog 8000. Others are expected to be introduced in the early 1980s.

The power of these chips can be illustrated from several viewpoints. To keep it simple, it can be said that as the designers and manufacturers pack more and more functions onto a single chip or a very few chips, the cost per function decreases. The processor chips contain more control, more on-chip memory, and more on-chip input-output capability—and that list keeps getting longer. Also, each microprocessor group receives a dozen or more allied support chips that provide massive capability on single boards. With from two to four boards, major companies such as IBM, Burroughs, Univac, and Texas Instruments can now place as much power into these chip computers in a book-size configuration as they formerly had in room-size systems. Because the chip components are so tiny, the distances the signals must travel are so infinitesimal that nanosecond speeds are being achieved.

The chips are being purchased in such quantities (many in the million-lot ranges) that mass production reduces the costs, time to manufacture, and new-product introduction risks to very healthy proportions. Design engineers, inventors, and equipment fabricators are having the time of their lives using these easily programmable, utterly versatile control machines in hundreds, and soon thousands, of applications in toys, appliances, automobiles, computer peripherals, communications gear, and practically every type of device imaginable.

The demand for chips and memories has become so great that none of the American manufacturers can fill even a majority of the orders. The Japanese have rushed to fill the voids. Many American manufacturers, at first somewhat bitter about the Japanese competition, are now major purchasers of parts from the Japanese as they concentrate in specific areas to use their existing capacity to satisfy their largest customer demands.

One of the major research organizations predicted that the market for microprocessors would soar past the 100-million-unit mark by 1983, and that was felt to be extremely conservative. Other industry analysts indicated that the gate density (number of switching elements), switching speed (switching operations per time period), and the transmission speed (signal travel between switching elements) was progressing so that with an increase of three more orders of magnitude, the microprocessor would bring us to the gate density of the human brain. Four more orders of magnitude will then remain before the theoretical limits of quantum electrodynamics are reached. In 1979, about one order of magnitude remained for switching speed and another for transmission speed, which is limited by the speed of light. Thus, it was expected that by 1985, the microprocessor would be succeeded by the nanoprocessor with a signal throughout density about 1000 times as great as current machines. So, is the trillionth of a second "picocomputer" the next progression? And what could be the speculation about this device?

It is not the purpose of this section to make forecasts into the 1990s. It is expected that it will take the decade of the 1980s for aplications engineers, software developers, and system users to catch up to the current 16- and 32-bit microcomputers.

IBM has provided some interesting speed and density comparisons in its national tv promotions and in its periodical, *Data Processor,* as follows:

(1) A nanosecond is to a second what a second is to 31.7 years.
(2) A picosecond is to a second what a second is to 31,710 years.
(3) The IBM 3850 mass storage system can hold up to 472 billion characters. That is enough storage capacity to have a 100-character record for every person in the world, or to hold as many words as are contained in 27 million pages of a typical daily newspaper.
(4) The IBM 3370 disk storage device can store up to 561 million characters of information in a unit about the size of an electric typewriter. It can hold the 43 million words in the thirty volumes of the Encyclopaedia Britannica with enough space left for the 7.5 million or so words in the Manhattan telephone directory.
(5) The IBM 3350 disk storage device is positioned 17 microinches (millionths of

an inch) above the surface of record-album–sized disks. A particle of smoke is about 100 microinches in size, and a human hair is 2500 microinches in circumference.

(6) A magnetic-bubble device built by IBM can store the equivalent of about 100 pages of the Manhattan telephone directory (25 million bits of information) in an area only one inch square. The magnetic bubbles are only a millionth of a meter, or 1/25,000 inch, in diameter.

(7) The IBM 3800 printer can print up to 450 lines per second. At that rate, it can print a 225-page book in a minute.

(8) Completing 100,000 multiplications 25 years ago cost $1.26; today (1979) it costs less than 1¢.

(These figures are quoted as a matter of interest and not to imply that the equipment listed necessarily has the greatest density, speed, or capability available.)

The IBM 38 System is regarded as a data-base computer, but at least a dozen small companies offer to compete. One has configured a data-base system that uses 50 microprocessors; another, using a Z-80 8-bit microprocessor, can handle 32,000 records, a job normally tackled only by large minicomputers or standard systems costing upward of $100,000. The Bell Laboratories one-chip microcomputer consists of internal control, arithmetic and logic, special registers, and an address-arithmetic unit, memories, and input-output circuits, using some 10,000 transistors with power dissipation as low as 200 mW—and even that can be reduced with special halt instructions. Bell researchers have devised a highly efficient light detector and transmitter to demonstrate the technical feasibility of operating telephones solely with the power of light transmitted over glass fibers; they also converted electrical energy to sound energy for "ringing." While these developments occurred, Intel Corp. was ready to introduce its 32-bit microprocessor, expected to be mounted on a quad-in-line package (Quip) instead of the standard dual-in-line package (DIP), the former said to be cheaper, smaller, and easier to test. Inventors at other companies have introduced 64-bit systems designed for data-base management and image processing. Others have begun marketing "array" processors, which offer tremendous processing throughput at very small costs as designed for radar, sonar, aircraft simulation, computerized tomographic scanning, speech recognition, synthesis of complex waveforms such as music, and so on. The chips have made deep researchers and pragmatic marketers out of thousands of "garage" electronic technicians.

All these and more spectacular discoveries are interesting in their own right, but most of the readers of this text are concerned more with applications. Such low-cost, speedy, high-capacity microcomputer systems are to be used, for example, in Xerox's digital electronic mail system. Each office desk would be equipped with a keyboard-video device containing a microcomputer and disk allowing the operator to do word processing, sorting, text editing, transmitting, and so on, in addition to mail handling. The "soft" mail would be controlled by the computer, including automatic addressing, priority routing, multipoint delivery, automatic transmission of previously stored messages, scan messages, and so on. All this is ready for markets and has used LSI (large-scale integration) chips. As the 1980s open, VLSI (very large-scale integration) chips will be moving to designers; VLSI will provide still lower-cost graphics and easier storage of many more software functions on-chip, with whole new languages also so stored for much easier operation by users. The computer will gain immense power, be even smaller, and, like the electric motor, will be almost everywhere, yet sink out of sight almost completely. But, unlike motors, these computers will have the ability to test themselves, test all other functions of specific devices or systems, switch to built-in spares, and, thus, more completely automate the automation equipment.

We can summarize this section with some statements from a speech made in mid-1979 by a representative of Sperry Univac.[1] According to the speaker, electronic components containing 10 billion gates will be feasible by 1990. Such components would be fabricated on 6-inch–diameter wafers with 0.1-micron lines and would contain complete dedicated systems for providing and/or processing information. Their

---

[1] From a report in *Electronics Weekly* (Sept. 1, 1979, page 4) of a speech by Earl C. Joseph, staff scientist-futurist of Sperry Univac at the Sperry Univac International executive center, Nice, France.

cost could be so low that "we'll be able to stamp them out like bottle tops." He said that the switch from chip to wafer component would be evolutionary and would simplify the construction of equipment. Wafer components would eliminate the production steps associated with producing chip devices from wafers, and would enable the systems designer to exploit the possibility of having analog as well as digital and memory circuits on the same substrate. They could also contain a considerable amount of hardwired software. Wafer components could be used to produce devices such as video cameras that incorporate sensors. They could also form the basis of complete desk-top or hand-held information systems which could contain libraries of information. He said 3-inch wafers containing about one billion gates would be possible by 1985, and these could give rise to the "office on a chip" by the end of the 1980s. Larger-diameter wafers in the 1990s would make possible the "school on a chip"—wafers containing lessons or courses for a year or more of study. (The speaker stressed that the dates quoted were those when the various technologies would become available. The availability of the end products depended on the time required to convert the information into computer-readable form, which could be from 5 to 30 years or more.)

At about the same time, an executive of Magnex Corporation (funded by Exxon Enterprises) stated that his company will produce recording heads that will pack "more than 100 million bits per square inch." The current technology was about 3 million bits per square inch, and he felt that the existent technology was limited to 10 million. Texas Instruments Inc. and Matsushita from Japan were reported to be developing 2-inch to 3-inch disk systems that would sell for as little as $50 per drive.

MICROCOMPUTERS IN COMMUNICATIONS DEVICES TO PRODUCE THE HARDEST IMPACT ON SOCIETY

In the "Age of Information," telecommunications plays a pivotal role. Society's most valuable resource is knowledge, and the system that stores, processes, and transmits knowledge is essential to the emergence of the new age. The system concerned is both individual and national. And, all the world is going digital. The current American telephone system is analog, while most European countries are converting as rapidly as possible to digital systems that interface with all types of computer devices. Once the voice is digitized, it can be handled the same as any other digital data, and by the same network and equipment. The codec is the device (chip) that does the conversion from analog to digital and back, providing the voice coding and decoding into digital signals for transmission cheaply and automatically.

The major developments that occurred in the late 1970s presage major impact areas of the computer/communications convergence for the 1980s. They are summarized in the following paragraphs.

AM International announced a contract with Satellite Business Systems to provide two high-speed computerized facsimile systems. These systems operate as electronic intracompany mail-delivery operations able to send up to 3600 high-quality copies an hour by satellite to distant cities at a rate that is 120 times faster than most current machines. It has a data capacity 156 times greater than telephone lines, providing fast long-distance mailroom-to-mailroom delivery addressed and ready for multicopy distribution.

Communicating word processors and copiers were beginning to proliferate in the US and Europe as well as in Japan. They were destined to become major factors in the "office of the future" for many firms. These systems were uniting telephones, typewriters, dictating machines, facsimile, intelligent terminals, and most other office functions in one system.

All-digital networks were moving much faster in Europe than in the US. Technology has already dealt a death blow, according to some observers, to broadcasting and networking as we formerly used these services by creating multipathways into homes and businesses. Now, with rooftop satellite terminals at costs offered in 1979 communications exhibits in Europe of as little as $2000, the entire world of private communications systems was in almost total turmoil as to predictions and extrapolations of future utilization. These systems were offered as able to pick up as many as forty channels. And Japan's satellite was being followed by "Telspace," Europe's first supplier of satellite-telecommunications earth stations, an alliance of French Thomson-CSF and CIT-Alcatel.

While Great Britain was pushing its System X digital telephone system very hard in export markets, the French were making mass purchases of home and office facsimile systems. The French propose to set up a national facsimile service that will be very cheap and consequently have many uses. The idea, in fact, is to have a facsimile unit in every home alongside the telephone. In this way, it could also act as an answering machine. Such machines were expected to cost less than $400.

In the US AT&T's switched network was being changed gradually into digital system sectors under the name of Advanced Communication Service. In hot pursuit were Xerox's similar system XTEN, Satellite Business Systems' second-generation satellite network, and ITT's COMPAK system.

There was activity by other phone companies as well. General Telephone purchased a major packet communications company and also moved swiftly into viewdata database services to businesses and homes. The third largest telephone company, Continental Telephone Company, decided to buy a half interest in American Satellite Corp. Although independent, this telephone company has 3 million telephones in service in 38 states.

In late 1979, AT&T began advertising its Picturephone® meeting service and other teleconferencing systems, offering the service in 10 cities. It began using national tv spots to plug its Gemini 100 "electronic blackboard" for long-distance use in schools, businesses, and so on. But, there was competition from massive amateur use of home satellite antennas, computer conferencing by thousands of home computer system enthusiasts, and two-way tv service offerings by several competitors using AT&T lines.

Fiber Optics have become magical systems for communications not only within computer systems but also as used by dozens of companies for transmission of information within buildings and throughout the telecommunications systems around the US. Students on one exhibit floor at a communications conference were able to operate a fusion splicer and complete splices in optical fibers with only 3 minutes of training.

For the consumer, the communications revolution was evidenced by the hundreds of electronic telephones that were being mechandised by discount stores and other retailers, by computerized cable-tv systems for two-way services, and by tv sets that had touch screens and facsimile units.

Communications by the dozens of chips and boards that are invading factories in the US, Japan, and Europe are finally starting to bring about that "workerless" factory predicted a decade ago. In order to monitor production, to aid quality control, and to schedule shop-floor operations efficiently, all these operations require up-to-the-minute information in the right place at the right time. Many modern large plants have computer systems that perform these functions. However, early systems were complex, expensive, and cumbersome. Now, the chips are taking over with far better results, and they are appearing in the very small shops and within individual tools and tool systems.

THE COMPUTER AND SOCIETY

The scientists and leaders of numerous academic disciplines and commercial and industrial corporations are meeting the challenge and responsibility that the advances of computing skills and capability bring forth almost daily. The engineering of new computer hardware, the expanding pervasiveness of computer applicability, and the increasing efficiencies, speeds, and rate of software innovation are almost silently developing toward an enormous impact on world sociological conditions and problems. The urgent task of the social scientist is to investigate and commence study projects to prepare people and institutions for the forces of change in social order, the emerging new patterns of man's education, and the evolution of changes in his relationships with his fellow man. The Age of the Computer will decisively and rapidly affect man's way of thinking and mode of living, and make new demands for security and interesting leisure.

The near–light-speed recognition and alteration of patterns and designs, the multi-billion-character storage capacity, and the literally unlimited intricacies of stored heuristic-applicative programs open great new horizons of intellectual creativity for the ensuing generations of mankind. It is perhaps in the areas of the greatly increased articulation of human judgment capabilities and the significant advances of highly accurate new predictive capability and expanding foresight that the computer plays its most beneficial role. Some may cringe with dismay and fear as current concepts and methods of education, engineering, business systems, production, and experimentation disappear into obsolescence within a decade, but others will welcome each progressive step.

HUMAN CONTROL OF MACHINES?

It is not the purpose of this appendix to develop an elaborate discourse on artificial intelligence nor to make an extensive projection of either the computer impact on the totality or the segments of human endeavor or the changes in the future of human or human-machine society except for one brief comment. It is said that man will always conceivably control machines because he will be free to accept or reject their output decisions or conclusions. But the treacherous time dimension might prevent proper human evaluation or assessment. The portentous complexity of power-play brinkmanship of world politics often hinges on real-time computer analysis. But, man the master does not have the calculating speed, logic, and accuracy of a computer. Missile capability has shortened "fail-safe" time to less than fifteen minutes. Split-second computer warning or analysis and the human frailties do not interface well with fate. One leader may have no practical alternative, in many varying circumstances, but to follow the computer's decision or advice . . . even if such decision creates his nation's destruction by other similarly computer-dependent enemies. As the founder of cybernetics, Norman Wiener has stated, "By the very slowness of our human actions, our effective control of our machines may be nullified." By the time the proper human or "committee" reaction is developed from information conveyed to their senses, they might have already lost the game, battle, or war.

The scope and purpose of these few pages is to delimit the topic of the computer and the future to two principal premises. These are: (1) the outstanding progress of a few fundamental far-reaching research or "drawing board" projects, and (2) a brief enumeration of several new products or product capabilities. The further development and application of these examples should stimulate or arouse enough futuristic dreams or projections to enable the reader himself to develop some documented or extrapolated analyses.

Automated Desks

Management information systems (MIS) rely on "report by exception" principles. Data are systematically reduced to call to the attention of executives, by using feedback detail, summaries of only the unexpected events or changes. The report generation programs of significant aid to top management are practically limitless and can include sales analyses and potential of new products, scheduling and cost of complex production runs, automated purchasing and inventory control, solution of problems of pricing, design, market research, materials handling, etc. Thus, according to leaders in the office-furniture business, the future executive's desk will be the communications center with its own miniature CPU, console, viewing screen, and personal computer-control center. Attachments of closed-circuit tv, projectors with scores of selective overlays and wall screen for image retrieval or crt enlargements, and other sophisticated communications units will eliminate 90% of all paperwork and will permit on-line, real-time intelligence acquisition of even the most distant or smallest item of information desired. It is estimated that it will be no later than the early 1980s before computer-affiliated activities such as manufacturing, information retrieval, programming, servicing data communication, education, etc., will constitute the world's leading industrial growth occupation. The automated desk, with access to all company information with hard-copy reports at the rate of 36,000 lines per minute, if needed, will be linked to many of the world's largest libraries and information centers and will become one of the greatest sales leaders of all computer appliances. It will join the long list of other automated products developed as a result of midget-sized, full-power computers used in automated ships, automated super-speed trains, automated aircraft, etc.

Several leaders in the industry, who carefully weigh the impact of "drawing board" developments and applications research, state with unyielding emphasis that within a decade not only business but also every household will require or desire access to some type of computer. Assuredly, the computer will control an automated world.

Automated Hospitals

Small consoles (crt and inquiry-printout devices) at nursing stations and service areas (labs, pharmacy, dietary kitchen, etc.) are linked to the computer to keep accurate records and ensure precise control over every aspect of patient care. Doctor's prescriptions and orders, for example, are transmitted by a nurse through the many desk consoles to the appropriate service center for rapid delivery, accurate charge and recording, and administration control checking. The computer stores and reminds (after automatic verification) the nurse or attendant of the patient's name, time, and dosage of medicine. Changing patients' symptoms, progress, and total medical history are instantly updated. Such histories and other medical data are also recorded in detail on a tiny plastic chip (one 2×2 inch chip can easily contain all pages of the King James Bible) to be carried by each individual for aid to the doctor in emergency circumstances. Or, a simple number indicates which memory bank has his medical history for instant retrieval by computer access using a phone, crt, or teletypewriter inquiry.

Already established information banks contain prodigious amounts of specific scientific and legal data for instantaneous retrieval. For example, all legal cases, opinions, appeals, etc., in New York are available to the profession (Jurimetrics). The true miracles of research and experimentation (heart, blood, serum, brain waves, etc.) have been recorded by the various medical centers (a choice source of information is UCLA Medical Center) throughout the United States. And, only a slight tax on the reader's imagination will permit him to understand the value of comparative diagnostics and consequent improved, faster treatment of patients with similar or same diseases or symptoms. Such information is instantly available in detailed, tabulated, or graphic form as extracted from thousands of histories, records, and latest discoveries or applications. The mere assurance to the patient by the doctor that he has had such instant access to all of this latest, highly particularized, and expert information could be of life-saving character.

IMPACT OF THE COMPUTER ON MEDICAL SCIENCE

I. General Medical

Advantages of the use of computers are:

A. Increase the speed and accuracy of medical diagnosis.
B. Deepen the understanding of disease.
C. Improve hospital care.
D. Cut medical costs.
E. Relieve the acute manpower (nurse) shortage.

II. Areas of Impact

A. Education.
   1. Curricula in medical schools will soon be including such courses as Boolean algebra, symbolic logic, and advanced mathematics in order for the doctor to understand what the computer can do for him.
   2. Computers will be widely used in classrooms as teaching aids.

B. Information access.
   1. Computers are now being used to index recent publications to assist the doctor in keeping current with the latest medical findings. An example of this is the KWIC (key word in context) Index to Neurochemistry presently in use.
   2. Studies are being made as to the feasibility of making abstracts of desired information available through computers. This aspect of information access is still in the formative stage in medicine.

C. Monitoring—On-line, real-time measurement of body functions.
   1. Body functions are measured by converting any activity in the body to electrical impulses and transmitting these impulses to a computer for measure-

ment and display on one of several output devices, such as printed material and television screens. Brain and heart waves which are already electrical in nature are measured by electrical leads. Blood pressure is measured by a fingertip sensor. Blood oxygen is measured by a photoelectric cell attached to the ear. Heart sound is measured by microphone. Respiration rate is measured by gauges in a face mask. Temperature is measured by a thermocouple. Emotional changes can be discerned by attaching electrodes to the ankles; these electrodes measure changes in body moisture.

2. Advantages—Permits instant and continuous measurement of a patient's condition under circumstances where such monitoring is desirable. One nurse can do the job of many simply by watching a group of screens recording computer output.
3. Current usage—Hospitals are installing crt devices in their operating rooms. Surgeons can monitor the patient's condition while they are operating. In emergency and intensive-care units, monitoring is proving helpful in situations where constant surveillance is required of patients in critical condition.

D. Diagnosis.

1. In controlled tests, computers diagnosed as well as or better than panels of doctors. In one instance, the computer was able to segregate what was previously considered one disease into four different diseases. As the computer gains experience in diagnosing a specific disease, the percentage of correct diagnoses approaches 100%—much better than human performance. Success is being achieved by the computer with the use of mathematical probability equations—a foreign concept to doctors that they are beginning to accept as results bear out its value.
2. The computer analyzes ekg's in three minutes. It asks itself 5000 questions on the ekg submitted for diagnosis. The results are 80% accurate compared with 50% accuracy by ekg specialists. The computer is well suited to diagnosing ekg's because diagnosing them by eyesight is extremely difficult, complex, and tiring. A computer attached to an X-ray machine measures the heart shadow and computes a ratio to the shadow of the rib cage, thereby making it possible for the computer to diagnose heart enlargement. Autoanalyzers attached to a computer perform analyses of blood in minutes compared to the hours previously required.

E. Prosthetics.

1. On command from usable parts of the body, computer-operated artificial limbs perform complicated tasks.

F. Research.

1. A study is being made of heart disease in a medium-sized town. Volunteers are subjected to periodic examinations over a long period of time. The purpose is to determine the interaction between factors and to seek clues to relationships that might lead to predictions of heart disease. Only the computer can handle the volume of detail and comparisons required by such a study. Studies are being made of patients with known diseases in order to find a possible correlation of variable symptoms. Computers are being used to develop a mathematics of epidemics in order to make better predictions of the course of an epidemic.
2. Computers are programmed to simulate parts of the body, such as heart or lungs, in order to learn more about these organs and the effect of various factors on them. In dynamic simulation, the computer acts as an integral part of an experiment. For example, it can be programmed to simulate a particular nerve in order to study the response.
3. A computer-microscope is presently in use to assist in recording extremely difficult measurements—the activity of microscopic neurons might be cited as an example.

III. The Future

A. Monitoring.

1. Continuous monitoring of all individuals, healthy or sick, will be done with the aid of microelectronic devices. These devices, when implanted under the

skin, will feed information into a computer which will warn the individual when his symptoms are outside the norm.

B. Diagnosis.
   1. Computers will someday be used as the single most important diagnostic tool. Doctors estimate that it will take 800 man-years to program computers in the diagnosis of all known diseases.

C. Research.
   1. Cross-fertilization between biological, medical, and engineering disciplines, difficult in the past, will lead to important research breakthroughs and an eventual "unified theory" of the physical and medical sciences.

THE COMPUTER AND EDUCATION

The computer has already established its capacity to teach more, better, and faster than conventional methods of instruction, and educators have not yet begun to tap its potential. Its branching and storage capacities allow tailor-made instructions for the individual student. The fast student can progress rapidly, skipping elementary routines, to complex material; the slow student can "branch" into remedial routines. The student's error rate and pattern of progress determine the material to which he will be exposed (what and how he will be taught).

Computer teaching permits maximum instructional efficiency. Learners can be grouped into three categories: (a) symbolic reasoners who understand pictures and graphic display best, (b) verbal reasoners, and (c) mixed symbolic-verbal reasoners. Using the appropriate routine and different approaches to the same concept, students with IQs of 90 and 95 demonstrated that they could perform at the same level of proficiency as students with IQs of 135 to 140.

Computer instruction greatly speeds the teaching process. Stenotype students learned as much in 50 hours using CAI (Computer Assisted Instruction) as they had previously in 300 hours. It relieves the teacher of drudgery and "drillmaster" duties and allows him to function creatively. It has the capacity to "bank" (record and store) the student's responses and analyze them, thus enabling the teacher to measure the student's effort, ability, and progress as these are demonstrated by his errors, response types, and other performance indicators. This banked information enables real "action research" on the very nature of the cognitive and learning processes. The teacher can use the banked records as a guideline in adapting and restructuring his teaching strategy.

THE "THINKING MACHINE"

The subject of "adaptive" heuristic or "thinking" computers is perhaps the most fascinating topic of this or any age in the history of mankind. The student is invited to the satisfying reward of a successful philosopher as he directs his mental powers toward the exploration of artificial intelligence even if he researches only two or three areas. Heuristic programming and probability evaluations probe adaptions of stored similar problem solutions. New computer-instigated "original" programs are thus independently developed which are beyond the realm of human capability. Another topic, among many, many other challenges, concerns the construction of computer internal circuitry (operation) which would permit "revisable" interconnection of components under program control. It is not inconceivable that programs could be devised and equipment so designed and constructed that programs could alter the circuitry of the computer to change its capability and versatility as new dynamic circumstances evolve.

Man and the computer in partnership and under this new environment have a virtually unlimited potential for creative design and automatic optimization of "adaptive" characteristics. It is the progress in the attempted combination of the foresight, judgment, and new pattern adaptation of man with the lightning speed, massive memory, and stored intricate programs of the computer that suggests the new thresholds of near-miraculous developments in creative and adaptive artificial intelligence. The curious student need not merely consider the philosophy of an "automaton" but can with diligent research effort discover many interesting "hardware" developments in the areas of self-organizing machines (SOM). These units already have shown some capability to observe, to learn, and to remember events and relationships they have discovered in "their own" (not man's) problem-solving environment. Some have issued orders based on information at their command which was unforseen or only remotely possible. Some of the "creative" activities by computers which have been described in many experiments are now considered unexplainable by humans. Is this the totally new dimension? A completely new superscience?